About the author

Respected wine critic and vigneron James Halliday has a career that spans over forty years, but he is most widely known for his witty and informative writing about wine. As one of the founders of Brokenwood in the Lower Hunter Valley, New South Wales, and thereafter of Coldstream Hills in the Yarra Valley, Victoria, James is an unmatched authority on every aspect of the wine industry, from the planting and pruning of vines through to the creation and marketing of the finished product. His winemaking has led him to sojourns in Bordeaux and Burgundy, and he has had a long career as a wine judge in Australia and overseas.

James has contributed to more than 60 books on wine since he began writing in 1979. His books have been translated into Japanese, French, German, Danish, Icelandic and Polish, and have been published in the UK and the US, as well as in Australia. He is also the author of *James Halliday's Wine Atlas of Australia* and *The Australian Wine Encyclopedia*. In June 2010 James was made a Member of the Order of Australia.

Wine zones and regions of Australia

NEW SOUTH WALES			
WINE ZONE		**WINE REGION**	
Big Rivers	(A)	Murray Darling	1
		Perricoota	2
		Riverina	3
		Swan Hill	4
Central Ranges	(B)	Cowra	5
		Mudgee	6
		Orange	7
Hunter Valley	(C)	Hunter	8
		Upper Hunter	9
Northern Rivers	(D)	Hastings River	10
Northern Slopes	(E)	New England	11
South Coast	(F)	Shoalhaven Coast	12
		Southern Highlands	13
Southern New South Wales	(G)	Canberra District	14
		Gundagai	15
		Hilltops	16
		Tumbarumba	17
Western Plains	(H)		

SOUTH AUSTRALIA			
WINE ZONE		**WINE REGION**	
Adelaide Super Zone includes Mount Lofty Ranges, Fleurieu and Barossa wine regions			
Barossa		Barossa Valley	18
		Eden Valley	19
Fleurieu	(J)	Currency Creek	20
		Kangaroo Island	21
		Langhorne Creek	22
		McLaren Vale	23
		Southern Fleurieu	24
Mount Lofty Ranges		Adelaide Hills	25
		Adelaide Plains	26
		Clare Valley	27
Far North	(K)	Southern Flinders Ranges	28
Limestone Coast	(L)	Coonawarra	29
		Mount Benson	30
		Mount Gambier*	31
		Padthaway	32
		Robe	33
		Wrattonbully	34
Lower Murray	(M)	Riverland	35
The Peninsulas	(N)	Southern Eyre Peninsula*	36

VICTORIA			
WINE ZONE		**WINE REGION**	
Central Victoria	(P)	Bendigo	37
		Goulburn Valley	38
		Heathcote	39
		Strathbogie Ranges	40
Gippsland	(Q)	Upper Goulburn	41
		Alpine Valleys	42
North East Victoria	(R)	Beechworth	43
		Glenrowan	44
		King Valley	45
		Rutherglen	46
North West Victoria	(S)	Murray Darling	47
		Swan Hill	48
Port Phillip	(T)	Geelong	49
		Macedon Ranges	50
		Mornington Peninsula	51
		Sunbury	52
		Yarra Valley	53
Western Victoria	(U)	Ballarat*	54
		Grampians	55
		Henty	56
		Pyrenees	57

* Regions that have taken, or are likely to take, steps to secure registration.

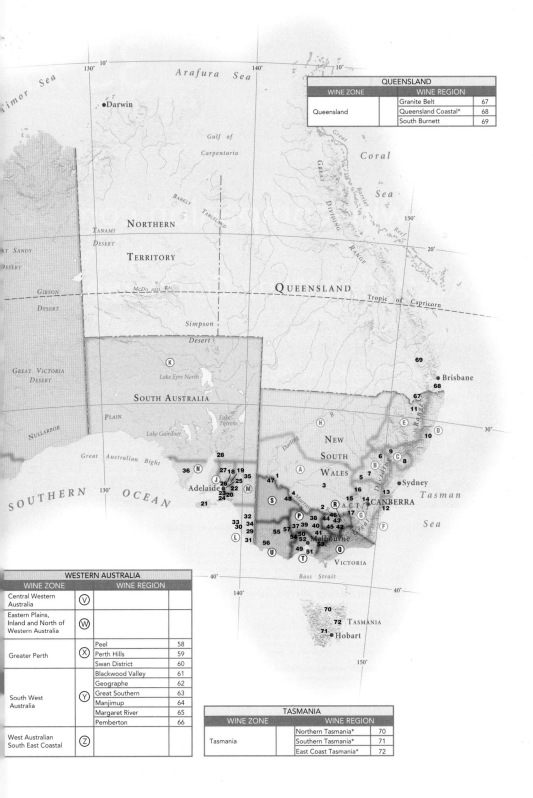

QUEENSLAND

WINE ZONE	WINE REGION	
Queensland	Granite Belt	67
	Queensland Coastal*	68
	South Burnett	69

WESTERN AUSTRALIA

WINE ZONE		WINE REGION	
Central Western Australia	Ⓥ		
Eastern Plains, Inland and North of Western Australia	Ⓦ		
Greater Perth	Ⓧ	Peel	58
		Perth Hills	59
		Swan District	60
South West Australia	Ⓨ	Blackwood Valley	61
		Geographe	62
		Great Southern	63
		Manjimup	64
		Margaret River	65
		Pemberton	66
West Australian South East Coastal	Ⓩ		

TASMANIA

WINE ZONE	WINE REGION	
Tasmania	Northern Tasmania*	70
	Southern Tasmania*	71
	East Coast Tasmania*	72

THE BESTSELLING AND DEFINITIVE GUIDE
TO AUSTRALIAN WINES

James Halliday
Australian
Wine Companion

2011 Edition

hardie grant books
MELBOURNE · LONDON

www.winecompanion.com.au

Published in 2010 by
Hardie Grant Books
85 High Street
Prahran, Victoria 3181, Australia
www.hardiegrant.com.au

The *Australian Wine Companion* is a joint venture between
James Halliday and Explore Australia Publishing Pty Ltd.

The map in this publication incorporates data copyright
© Commonwealth of Australia (Geoscience Australia) 2004.
Geoscience Australia has not evaluated the data as altered and incorporated within this publication and therefore gives no warranty regarding accuracy, completeness, currency or suitability for any particular purpose.

Australian wine zones and wine regions data copyright
© Australian Wine and Brandy Corporation, April 2005

ISBN 978 1 74066 895 8

Typeset by Megan Ellis
Printed and bound in Australia by Ligare Book Printers

10 9 8 7 6 5 4 3 2 1

Front cover: Lincoln Seligman, *Wrapped Wine Bottles, Number 1*, 1995 (acrylic on paper)

Contents

Introduction

It's an ill wind that blows no one any good: the Australian wine industry escaped from a Federal budget super profits tax equivalent simply because there are precious few making even modest profits, many haemorrhaging in the aftermath of the global financial crisis, a strong though volatile dollar, a wine press in the UK either hostile or indifferent to Australia's export offerings, and – most of all – the environmental and financial calamities eviscerating grape growers in the Murray Darling Basin.

So the Henry Review recommendation that all forms of alcohol should be taxed on the same volumetric basis (determined by the alcohol content) has not been accepted by the Federal Government. The grape and wine surplus has been cited by the government as the prime reason why the existing tax structure should not be changed 'at this time', an ominous signal for the future.

The one certainty is that the Federal Government will be hell bent on increasing the amount of tax revenue it derives from the sale of all forms of alcohol, wine included. Doubtless the increase will be justified by health and social concerns about alcohol abuse, and Australia will continue to be the highest-taxed major wine producer in the world. (In this context, New Zealand is not a major wine producer.)

In a macabre way, it may significantly reduce the pressure on the water-use from the Murray Darling Basin, simply by institutionalising prices for wine grapes at or below the cost of production. The prospects of other agricultural industries stepping in to fill the void are not great. Even less likely is a return to 'normal' rainfall, an elastic term if ever there was one. The Australian Bureau of Meteorology has joined the CSIRO in forecasting large decreases in annual rainfall for the southern half of the continent, and increases in the northern half – changes that will have a broader impact than just the Murray Darling.

It is a grim outlook, throwing a shadow over the generally agreed way forward for an industry that is under pressure on all fronts: move the focus of its winegrowing and marketing onto regional wines that are linked to specific varieties. Warming isn't the greatest concern, for there are both micro and macro changes in viticulture and winemaking practices that can moderate the impact of warming. But vines, whether dry grown or irrigated, old or young, have basic water requirements to produce commercial quantities of grapes. (They are technically a drought-resistant plant, and keep a measure of function for several years without water, but do not produce grapes.)

It is true that some adaptive measures will have benefits for both warmer and drier conditions alike, and it will be many years before there are permanent, large-scale changes in the varietal make-up of the 62 Australian wine regions. But grapegrowing and winemaking have long lead times, and reputations are not won overnight – although loss can be disconcertingly rapid.

New features of this edition

Selection and arrangement of tasting notes

The continued growth in the number of Australian wineries (111 new wineries this year) and the consequent rise in the number of tasting notes (8116 wines were tasted for this edition) has forced a major change in the way the information in the *Australian Wine Companion* is presented.

The extra wineries and wines resulted in the near-to-final draft being 120 pages over length, bordering on 900 pages. It is simply not possible to produce a soft-cover book of this length that will stand up to a year's wear and tear. Various options were considered, and the most logical of these was to move some of the tasting notes that in prior years would have been in the book to www.winecompanion.com.au.

There is already a substantial body of current information put onto the website each year that doesn't appear in the book, notably tasting notes for wines rated between 84 and 86 points, and scores (and prices) for wines rated between 80 and 83 points. Henceforth the highest rated wines for each winery will appear in full in this book, as will notes for wines that represent particularly good value for money. Here there is no pre-set pattern: it may be a 93-point wine costing (say) $20, or an 87-point wine priced at $7. Wines that fall into this category carry the special symbol ✪. All other tasting notes will appear only on the website, but the name, points, price and drink-to date for wines scoring 87 or more will still be shown in the book.

This transfer of information has been forced on us, and is not a deliberate ploy to create additional website traffic. That said, it is clear that the website will increasingly be the major repository of new content, and we will continue to look at ways of providing the maximum amount of information in a seamless fashion across this book and the website.

Below is a summary of the arrangement of this year's tasting notes.

- 2112 tasting notes for every winery's best wines (be they in a 5-glass, 4½-glass, 4-glass bracket, etc.) are in this book and on the website.

- 1785 tasting notes for wines offering special value for money (in addition to above) are in this book and on the website.

- 2612 wines not in either of the above categories but scoring 87 or more points are listed in this book with their points, drink to date and price recorded; the tasting notes are on the website.

- 312 wines in the 4-glass (87–89 points) bracket of wineries with many higher pointed wines are not listed in this book, but tasting notes appear on the website.

- 1006 wines in the 3½-glass bracket (84–86 points) have tasting notes on the website.

- 298 wines were also tasted and scored in the 3-glass bracket (80–83 points) and under are listed without tasting notes on the website.

The consequence of this change (apart from significant space savings) is a book that is easier to read in terms of layout and puts more focus on wines you may wish to buy or drink.

Other new features

As well as the changes in the selection and arrangement of tasting notes, the following features have been added to the 2011 edition of the *Wine Companion*.

- For the first time, **Ben Edward**'s initials appear after the notes of the wines he tasted.

- A new introductory section, **Varietal wine styles and regions** (pages 54–57), discusses how the relationship between wine varieties and regions gives rise to successful wine styles.

- The **Best wineries of the regions** continues to list five black- or red-star wineries, but introduces red print for the names of the wineries that are generally recognised as the greatest, their reputation usually built over decades rather than years.

How to use the *Wine Companion*

The *Australian Wine Companion* is arranged with wineries in alphabetical order. Wineries beginning with 'The' such as 'The Blok Estate' are listed under 'T' and winery names including numbers are treated as if the number is spelt out (for example, 2 Mates is listed under 'T'). The index lists the wineries by region, which adds another search facility.

   The entries should be self-explanatory, but here I will briefly take you through the information provided for each entry, using Larry Cherubino Wines as an example.

Wineries

Larry Cherubino Wines ★★★★★

15 York Street, Subiaco, WA 6000 **Region** Western Australia
T (08) 9382 2379 **F** (08) 9382 2397 **www**.larrycherubino.com **Open** Not
Winemaker Larry Cherubino **Est.** 2005 **Cases** 6000 **Vyds** 20 ha
Larry Cherubino has had a particularly distinguished winemaking career, first at Hardys Tintara, then Houghton, and thereafter as consultant/Flying Winemaker in Australia, NZ, South Africa, the US and Italy. In 2005 he started Larry Cherubino Wines and has developed three ranges: at the top is Cherubino (Riesling, Sauvignon Blanc, Shiraz and Cabernet Sauvignon); next The Yard, five single-vineyard wines from WA; and at the bottom another five wines under the Ad Hoc label, all single-region wines. The range and quality of his wines is extraordinary, the prices irresistible. Exports to the UK, the US, Canada, The Netherlands and Switzerland. Winery of the year 2011 *Wine Companion*.

Winery name Larry Cherubino Wines

Although it might seem that stating the winery name is straightforward, this is not necessarily so. To avoid confusion, wherever possible I use the name that appears most prominently on the front label of the wine. When the winery name appears in red, the winery is generally acknowledged to have a long track record of excellence.

Winery rating ★★★★★

The effort to come up with a fair winery rating system continues. As last year, I looked at the ratings for this and the previous two years; if the wines tasted this year justified a higher rating than last year, that higher rating has been given. If, on the other hand, the wines are of lesser quality, I took into account the track record over the past two years (or longer where the winery is well known) and made a judgement call on whether it should retain its ranking, or be given a lesser one. Where no wines were submitted by a well-rated winery with a track record of providing samples, I used my discretion to roll over last year's rating.

While there are (only) 1465 wineries profiled in this edition, there are more than 2600 wineries to be found on www.winecompanion.com.au.

The precise meanings attached to the winery star rating is as follows; the percentages at the end of each rating is that of the total number of wineries in the *Wine Companion* database at the time of going to print. Two caveats: first, I retain a discretionary right to depart from the normal criteria. Second, the basis of the rating will best be understood on the website, where all wine ratings appear.

★★★★★ Outstanding winery regularly producing wines of exemplary quality and typicity. Will have at least two wines rated at 94 points or above, and had a five-star rating for the previous two years. 3.3%
Where the winery name is itself is printed in red, it is a winery generally acknowledged to have a long track record of excellence – truly the best of the best. 4.5%

★★★★★ Outstanding winery capable of producing wines of very high quality, and did so this year. Also will usually have at least two wines rated at 94 points or above. 9.7%

★★★★☆ Excellent winery able to produce wines of high to very high quality, knocking on the door of a 5-star rating. Will normally have one wine rated at 94 points or above, and two (or more) at 90 and above, others 87–89. 12%

★★★★ Very good producer of wines with class and character. Will have two (or more) wines rated at 90 points and above (or possibly one at 94 and above). 12.2%

★★★☆ A solid, usually reliable, maker of good, sometimes very good wines. Will have one wine at 90 points and above, others 87–89. 7.3%

★★★ A typically good winery, but often has a few lesser wines. Will have wines at 87–89 points. 6%

★★☆/NR The ★★☆ and NR ratings appear in this book and www.wine companion.com.au. The ratings are given in a range of circumstances: where there have been no tastings in the 12-month period; where there have been tastings, but with no wines scoring more than 86 points (NR); and where the tastings have, for one reason or another, proved not to fairly reflect the reputation of a winery with a track record of success. 45%

Contact Details 15 York Street, Subiaco, WA 6000 **T** (08) 9382 2379 **F** (08) 9382 2397

The details are usually those of the winery and cellar door, but in a few instances may simply be a postal address; this occurs when the wine is made at another winery or wineries, and is sold only through the website and/or retail.

Region Western Australia

A full list of zones, regions and subregions appears on pages 50–53. Occasionally you will see 'Various' as the region. This means the wine is made from purchased grapes, in someone else's winery. In other words, it may not have a vineyard or winery in the ordinary way.

www.larrycherubino.com

An increasingly important reference point, often containing material not found (for space reasons) in this book.

Open Not

Although a winery might be listed as not open or only open on weekends, some may in fact be prepared to open by appointment. Many will, some won't; a telephone call will establish whether it is possible or not.

Winemaker Larry Cherubino

In all but the smallest producers, the winemaker is simply the head of a team; there may be many executive winemakers actually responsible for specific wines in the medium to large companies (80 000 cases and upwards).

Est. 2005

Keep in mind that some makers consider the year in which they purchased the land to be the year of establishment, others the year in which they first planted grapes, others the year they first made wine, and so on. There may also be minor complications where there has been a change of ownership or break in production.

Vyds 20 ha

Shows the hectares of vineyard/s owned by the winery.

Cases 6000

This figure (representing the number of cases produced each year) is merely an indication of the size of the operation. Some winery entries do not feature a production figure: this is either because the winery (principally, but not exclusively, the large companies) regards this information as confidential.

Summary Larry Cherubino has had a particularly distinguished winemaking career, first at Hardys Tintara, then Houghton, and thereafter as consultant/Flying Winemaker in Australia, NZ, South Africa, the US and Italy.

My summary of the winery. Little needs be said, except that I have tried to vary the subjects I discuss in this part of the winery entry.

New wineries

 The vine leaf symbol indicates the 111 wineries that are new entries in this year's *Wine Companion*.

Tasting notes

While the points and glass symbols given below remain unchanged, the ever-increasing number of wineries (there are still more births than deaths) and increased total number of tasting notes has necessitated the move to www.winecompanion.com.au of some tasting notes that in prior years would have appeared in the book as well as the website.

Full tasting notes for the highest rated wines for each winery appear in the book, as do notes for wines that represent particularly good value for money. However, only the name, points, price and drink-to date for wines scoring 87 or more will be shown in the book, with the full notes for these wines appearing on www.winecompanion.com.au.

A summary of the criteria used to determine the ratings follows.

Ratings

94–100 ♥♥♥♥♥ **Outstanding.** Wines of the highest quality, often with a distinguished pedigree. Tasting notes will always appear in the *Wine Companion*.

90–93 ♥♥♥♥♀ **Highly recommended.** Wines of great quality, style and character, worthy of a place in any cellar. If the highest-pointed wines fall into this group, the tasting notes appear in full, otherwise the wines will be listed with rating, price and drink-to details, with the full entry on www.winecompanion.com.au.

87–89 ♥♥♥♥ **Recommended.** Wines of above-average quality, fault-free, and with clear varietal expression. If the highest-pointed wines fall into this group, the tasting notes appear in full, otherwise the wines will be listed with rating, price and drink-to details, with the full entry on www.winecompanion.com.au.

87–100 ✪ **Special value.** Wines considered to offer special value for money; tasting notes will always appear in the *Wine Companion*.

84–86 ♥♥♥♀ **Acceptable.** Wines of good commercial quality, free of any significant fault. Tasting notes will only appear on www.winecompanion.com.au.

80–83 ♥♥♥ **Over to you.** Everyday wines, usually cheap and with little or no future, lacking character and flavour. No tasting notes are published, but points and price are shown on www.winecompanion.com.au.

75–79 ♥♥♀ **Not recommended.** Wines with one or more significant winemaking faults. No tasting notes are published, but points and price are shown on www.winecompanion.com.au.

♥♥♥♥♥ Cherubino Porongurup Riesling 2009 An exercise in restraint on the bouquet, which hides the quite remarkable intensity and drive of the palate, with lime and lemon juice on the mid-palate framed by lingering minerally acidity. Gold-plated 20-year development potential. Screwcap. 12.2% alc. **Rating** 97 **To** 2030 $35

The tasting note opens with the vintage of the wine tasted. This tasting note will have been made within the 12 months prior to publication. Even that is a long time, and during the life of this book the wine will almost certainly change. More than this, remember the tasting is a highly subjective and imperfect art. The price of the wine is listed where information is available. Tasting notes for wines 94 points and over, for wines offering particularly good value, and for unusual wines, are printed in red.

Screwcap

This is the closure used for this particular wine. The closures in use for the wines tasted are (in descending order): screwcap 84% (last year 79%), one-piece natural cork 9% (last year 14%), Diam 6% (last year 5%). The remaining 1% (in approximate order of importance) are ProCork, Twin Top, Crown Seal, Zork, Vino-Lok and Synthetic. I believe the percentage of screwcap will continue to rise.

12.2% alc.

As with closures, I have endeavoured always to include this piece of information, which is in one sense self-explanatory. What is less obvious is the increasing concern of many of Australian winemakers about the rise in levels of alcohol, and much research and practical experiment (picking earlier, higher fermentation temperatures in open fermenters, etc.) is occurring. Reverse osmosis and yeast selection are two of the options available to decrease higher than desirable alcohol levels. Recent changes to domestic and export labelling mean the stated alcohol will be within a maximum of 0.5% of that obtained by analysis.

To 2030

Rather than give a span of drinking years, I have simply provided a (conservative) 'best by' date. Modern winemaking is such that, even if a wine has 10 or 20 years' future during which it will gain greater complexity, it can be enjoyed at any time over the intervening months and years, and quite possibly for yet another 10 or more years past the best by date.

Australian vintage 2010: a snapshot

If winemakers and grapegrowers were praying for a smaller vintage (on the nimby principle, unlikely) it appears they got what they were looking for. At the time of going to press, a national crush of 1.4 million tonnes was the guesstimate. The actual figure will be largely dependent on the irrigation/inland rivers regions spread along the Murrumbidgee and Murray–Darling rivers, but the other regions are almost entirely looking at below-average crops, mainly due to a heat spike affecting the eastern states in late November, which badly interrupted flowering and fruit-set, but also unsettled weather through much of the growing season. Easter was a critical time in Western Australia and Victoria: if you picked before Easter, the outcome was very good, picking after Easter full of problems. Most of the harvest came in before Easter except for cabernet sauvignon. That said, only New South Wales is hedging its bets on quality; in Victoria and South Australia the overall quality is expected to be the best since 2006, while Western Australia (particularly Margaret River) had yet another excellent vintage.

SOUTH AUSTRALIA

Barossa Valley set the scene that is remarkably consistent throughout the state. Good winter and spring rainfall (best for five years) was unambiguously welcome, with an early budburst prompted by warm spring weather. An unusual burst of heat in mid-November was not (welcome), causing major disruptions to flowering, grenache badly hit, chardonnay likewise. From this point on it was a mild and dry vintage, the low yields prompting early ripening of below-average size crops. Varietal expression was particularly good, and the outlook is for some superb red wines, the best since '06. The **Eden Valley** did not escape the problems with fruit-set, and veraison was early. Stand-out shiraz, riesling and chardonnay look certain to follow. **McLaren Vale** and **Southern Fleurieu** suffered the same fruit-set problems (grenache half a tonne per acre) but are ecstatic about the quality of the reds, described as shining by one maker; shiraz superb, cabernet not far behind. A near-identical vintage in **Langhorne Creek**, with great winter and spring rain that led to the Bremer River flowing, and indeed flooding in parts. Verdelho, shiraz and petit verdot paid no attention to the November heat, but the other varieties did; the outcome is an excellent year for wine quality, not so good for bank balances. **Coonawarra** danced to the same tune, the only cloud on the horizon for a very good to excellent vintage was the necessity of precisely timing the picking schedule, avoiding the astringency of picking too early, and avoiding the late season rain and botrytis. **Wrattonbully** and **Mount Benson/ Robe** did not disrupt the pattern, the most important red varieties (cabernet sauvignon, shiraz and merlot) and whites (chardonnay and sauvignon blanc) all of very good quality – cabernet outstanding – with the proviso that low to moderate crops came off at the right time, but high-cropping vineyards ran into the rain after Easter with predictable low-quality results.

VICTORIA

Pyrenees, **Bendigo** and **Heathcote** all enjoyed winter and spring rainfalls that were close to long-term average, and far better than any of the past five years. The November heat impacted more on some regions than others, but was in no way comparable to the effect in South Australia. Heathcote was the star, the absolutely perfect weather between January and March making up for the tickle of heat in November. In Bendigo and the Pyrenees on-and-off rainfall through the growing season and into harvest meant split-second timing was essential, and led to the vintage extending well into April. **Strathbogie Ranges**, Heathcote and the Pyrenees shared one important thing in common: sugar and flavour accumulation proceeding at exactly the same time, resulting in wines with great balance, intense flavour yet lower than the alcohol levels of recent years. The **Goulburn Valley/Nagambie Lakes** shared a dry winter and early spring with more southerly Victorian regions, notably the Yarra Valley. Here the similarity ended: good rains in the Eildon catchment meant that Goulburn Valley vineyards had ample access to irrigation water for the first time in a number of years, but the same could not be said for those vineyards in the Yarra Valley that do not have access to the Yarra River. But in both regions, and elsewhere around the Port Phillip Zone, periodic rainfall in modest quantities through the summer and early autumn significantly reduced vine stress. The **Yarra Valley** had a vintage unrecognisable from that of a year before, and one of the best, if not the best, since 2006. Pinot noir, shiraz, merlot and cabernet sauvignon (the latter particularly) are all very good to excellent, the chardonnay perhaps a little fuller-bodied than perfect. **Mornington Peninsula** had an outstanding vintage, chardonnay especially, pinot noir deeply coloured and flavoured. **Geelong** picked its way through the rain periods without too much difficulty for the better vineyards. Yield was down 10% to 15%, but the excellent quality more than compensated. **Henty** in the far west had an ideal year, altogether missing the November heat, but for the rest of the regions it was a mixed bag. The **Alpine Valleys** picked excellent grapes before the Easter rain, average after; **Beechworth** started the season with frost in October, January heat, and February rain, not very different from **Gippsland**. **Macedon Ranges** had issues with rain during flowering, rain that came and went through the growing season, although generally to the advantage of the vines.

NEW SOUTH WALES

Hunter Valley returned to earth after the great 2009 vintage. Winter rainfall was good, and a very warm to hot spring failed to affect budburst and flowering. Late November saw 46°C temperatures followed by hail, then alternating hot weather and periods of rain, the latter largely welcome. Natural fruit thinning courtesy of the weather, followed by sorting boards in the winery, paid big dividends for those who took the trouble with semillon and chardonnay. Rain came at precisely the wrong time for shiraz, but, once again, bunch thinning and sorting tables helped. Over the hills to **Mudgee**, crop levels were down between 25% and 50% of normal, and, coupled with continuing drought and high temperatures, led to a record early start to vintage. Nonetheless, this came after heavy rain over the new year period saved heavily stressed vines, the white wines coming off satisfactorily. More rain in late February will result in very uneven red wines, covering the full spectrum from good to poor. **Orange** had way below-average rainfall up to the new year, and warmer than average conditions. There was a total reversal from January onwards, with white grapes down 35% and reds down 45%. If you wanted botrytis, it was easy to find; if you didn't, strict thinning and picking protocols were essential. **Canberra District** began the 2010 growing season with weather that grapegrowers dream about: good rains, warm weather and no frosts. Rain throughout January, February and March saw the dams full for the first time in 12 years, but as the weeks went by, life became more difficult. Riesling cruised through with minimal problems, chardonnay and the few plots of gruner veltliner likewise. The best growers and makers will have good shiraz. The same swings affected the **Southern Highlands**, the dry spring and warm start to the new year, then January and February cool and wet, March much the same. The early ripening white varieties performed best. **Hilltops** was not immune to the problem of rain (normally welcome) coming at the wrong time, with heavy rain at the end of February before the whites were picked, and more heavy rain at the beginning of March before shiraz was picked. The saving grace came with dry and sunny weather for three weeks after the early March rainfall, allowing shiraz and cabernet sauvignon to fully ripen; the outstanding variety is cabernet sauvignon. Those who take grapes from **Tumbarumba** were very pleased. The **Shoalhaven Coast** made heavy weather of things, with sustained humidity in January and very heavy rain in February reducing yields to 50% of normal in some instances, hand-picking and sorting offset at least some of the problems. **Riverina** had ideal weather until mid-February, by which time the white wines had largely been harvested, but not all the red wines. Intermittent rain for the next month, together with unusually high humidity, provided a challenge for winemakers, but resulted in the earliest ever harvest of the grapes for De Bortoli's Noble One. Overall, the crop was down 15%.

WESTERN AUSTRALIA
Margaret River continues to be the envy of all other Australian regions, notching its fourth great vintage in a row. Good winter and spring rains were followed by a very warm and dry harvest, cooler weather in March allowing flavour to catch up with sugar development in the reds. Chardonnay, sauvignon blanc and cabernet sauvignon, the three mainstays of the region, are all considered to be outstanding by all the reporting wineries. **Great Southern** had a cold, wet spring, and cool to mild weather leading into summer, giving expectations of a late vintage. However, warm days and mild nights from February through to the end of March brought the picking calendar forward, with riesling, chardonnay and sauvignon blanc all being harvested in great condition with good varietal definition, very good natural acidity and high-quality potential. That's where the good news finished, with 80 mm of rain falling between the end of March and the first week of April, causing real problems for higher-yielding shiraz vineyards in particular. The rain-resistant cabernet has fared quite well, and the overall style will see finer structure and lower alcohol than normal. **Manjimup** saw serious rain through to December 2009, reaching 950 mm in some parts. January to March then turned around to be the driest on record, with temperatures 1°C to 2°C above the average. Warm nights added to this go-stop sequence, and while there was no heavy rainfall through to the end of the first week of April (when the white harvest

finished) there were a lot of unsettled heat troughs in later April with thunderstorms, hail and humidity affecting the ripening of the red grapes. There was great variation between vineyards, but overall chardonnay, verdelho, shiraz and cabernet sauvignon did best. **Pemberton**, next door to Manjimup, experienced similar conditions; sauvignon blanc and chardonnay will be very good, and, in a pattern repeated in the majority of West Australian regions, merlot could well be the flagbearer for the reds. **Geographe** had a smooth run throughout vintage, copying much from nearby Margaret River. Here, too, merlot is the standout red variety, all the whites with very good varietal definition. **Swan Valley** had a season not unlike that of the southern parts of Western Australia. Good winter and spring rain finished in October, except for heavy rain during the third week of November, followed by three months of no rain. The usual hot and dry temperatures followed through January, February and the first three weeks of March, interspersed with periods of extreme heat. It is little short of extraordinary that the progression of picking was not very different from that of many parts of Victoria. While some had completed the vintage by the end of February, others still had fruit to be picked as late as March 23, when rain put an end to the matter. Shiraz and verdelho are standouts. **Perth Hills** provided more of the same, with good winter rainfall, then the driest spring on record, hot and dry on the lead up to harvest, then mild and dry weather during harvest. Viognier, shiraz and petit verdot the best of a very good bunch.

TASMANIA

Always difficult to pigeonhole because of the diversity of sites in northern, southern and eastern Tasmania. Overall, a wet winter with above-average rainfall extending into spring was welcome after years of below-average rainfall. Mild ripening conditions followed, producing outstanding sparkling wine base, but slightly more variable conditions thereafter, with warm periods followed by some rain in northern Tasmania; the south and east were less affected, the outlook very good indeed.

QUEENSLAND

The Granite Belt had good winter and early spring rain, but frosts in October caused losses of up to 80% of the crop. The warm weather that followed helped the frost-affected vines' recovery (for next year) but a rain depression arrived just before vintage started and lasted for 14 days. Although the southern part was less affected, rot necessitated very careful selection. The red wines (Shiraz, Merlot, Cabernet Sauvignon) fared best; some indeed were excellent.

Winery of the year

Larry Cherubino Wines

One of the many reasons why I ended up selecting Larry Cherubino Wines as my Winery of the Year (there were over 30 others with a plausible claim) was its focus on single-vineyard and single-region wines. It is a path that more and more Australian wine producers must follow if we are to fundamentally change the negative perceptions of domestic and (most significantly) export markets about the diversity, the quality and the style of our wines, and of our aspirations for the future.

Larry is careful not to criticise Houghton, Western Australia's leading winery (and part of Constellation Wines Australia), where he worked until 2005, but accurately observes that many exceptionally good but small batches of grapes (and potentially wine) get lost in the maw of the management and financial protocols of the big wineries.

Since founding his eponymous wine business in 2005 (after leaving Houghton), Larry's day job (as he calls it) has been that of a consultant in the broader sense, and winemaker (for others) in the narrower sense. This, he says, allows him the luxury of making small batches of exquisite (my word, not his) wines under the Larry Cherubino label.

From 2007 onwards he has made these wines at Wise Wine in Margaret River where he is consultant winemaker, variously bringing to the Wise winery juice (for riesling, semillon and sauvignon blanc), grapes (for chardonnay) and grapes or must (for shiraz, merlot and cabernet sauvignon) using his own fermenters and barrels.

Part of his intake comes from 12 ha under long-term lease, part from 8 ha of family vineyards, both in the Margaret River. He is adamant that he is not interested in growth; quality is the paramount objective. His strike-rate is 11 wines at 94 to 97 points (five special value) and another 11 at 90 to 93 points (six special value) and a solitary wine at 89 points.

No other winery had such a percentage success rate. Is there a reason? Yes, for whether the wines are Riesling, Chardonnay, Sauvignon Blanc, Semillon Sauvignon Blanc, Shiraz, Cabernet Sauvignon or Cabernet Merlot, all have balance, line, length and, above all else, elegance. If this were not enough, every one of those varietal styles has at least one wine at 94 points or above.

Best of the best wines

I make my usual disclaimer: while there are two periods of intense tasting activity in the 12 months during which the tasting notes for this edition were made, and while some wines are tasted more than once, an over-arching comparative tasting of all the best wines is simply not possible, however desirable it might be.

So the points for the individual wines scoring 94 or above stand uncorrected by the wisdom of hindsight. Nonetheless, the link between variety and region (or, if you prefer, between variety and terroir) is in most instances strikingly evident. It is for this reason that I have shown the region for each of the best wines. Medium and longer term prosperity will depend on a sense of place, of regional identity. It is also the reason for the new overview of the varietal/regional mosaic.

Brand Australia has been the foundation upon which the success of the past 20 years has been built, but all recognise the need to move on. While some naysayers may regard this as marketing rhetoric, the truth is that Australia is blessed with an unmatched range of terroir (including climate in that deceptively simple term) enabling it to make wines ranging from the uniquely complex fortified wines of Rutherglen (fashioned from frontignac and muscadelle, known locally as muscat and tokay), to the 100-year-old Para Liqueur of Seppeltsfield in the Barossa Valley, all the way through to the exceptional sparkling wines of Tasmania, grown in a climate every bit as cool as that of Champagne.

This is one of the principal reasons for the wines with the same points to be arranged by region, even though the main text is alpha-ordered. I should also point out that the cut-off for listing the wines of each variety differs considerably, depending on the strength of the class concerned.

Best of the best by variety

Riesling

These wines, with one exception, give a remarkably accurate picture of the present state of play with riesling; the exception is Tasmania, which has a number of wines at 95 points. The Clare and Eden valleys remain the leaders, but Western Australia is closing the gap.

RATING	WINE	REGION
97	2009 Larry Cherubino Cherubino Riesling	Porongurup
96	2009 Larry Cherubino The Yard Kalgan River	Albany
96	2007 Jacob's Creek Steingarten	Barossa Valley
96	2009 Annie's Lane Copper Trail	Clare Valley
96	2003 Cardinham Estate	Clare Valley
96	2009 Crabtree Watervale	Clare Valley
96	2009 Grosset Springvale Watervale	Clare Valley
96	2009 Knappstein Ackland Vineyard Watervale	Clare Valley
96	2009 Knappstein 8:8:18	Clare Valley
96	2009 KT & The Falcon Melva Watervale	Clare Valley
96	2009 KT & The Falcon Peglidis Vineyard Watervale	Clare Valley
96	2008 O'Leary Walker Drs' Cut Polish Hill River	Clare Valley
96	2009 Paulett Antonina Polish Hill River	Clare Valley
96	2005 Paulett Polish Hill River Aged Release	Clare Valley
96	2009 Pikes The Merle Reserve	Clare Valley
96	2007 Taylors St Andrews	Clare Valley
96	2009 Ducketts Mill	Denmark
96	2003 Rickety Gate	Denmark
96	2009 Cascabel	Eden Valley
96	2009 Henschke Julius	Eden Valley
96	2009 Penfolds Bin 51	Eden Valley
96	2004 Pewsey Vale The Contours Museum Reserve	Eden Valley
96	2009 Seppelt Drumborg	Grampians
96	2009 Howard Park	Great Southern
96	2004 Crawford River	Henty
96	2009 Lethbridge Dr Nadeson Portland	Henty
96	2009 Word of Mouth	Orange
96	2005 Abbey Creek Vineyard	Porongurup
96	2009 Larry Cherubino The Yard	Porongurup
96	2008 Delatite	Upper Goulburn

Chardonnay

This list underlines the flexibility of chardonnay, whether as a fighting varietal or as a flagship of the modern industry. These wines come from 14 regions (more if you dissect Eileen Hardy), but all have cool to temperate climates, most with a maritime influence.

RATING	WINE	REGION
97	2007 Penfolds Yattarna	Adelaide Hills
97	2008 Bindi Quartz	Macedon Ranges
97	2009 Brookland Valley	Margaret River
97	2007 Cullen Kevin John	Margaret River
97	2007 Hardys Eileen Hardy	Cool-climate blend
97	2008 Hardys Eileen Hardy	Cool-climate blend
97	2008 Moorooduc Estate The Moorooduc	Mornington Peninsula
96	2008 Ashton Hills	Adelaide Hills
96	2008 Grosset Piccadilly	Adelaide Hills
96	2008 Michael Hall Piccadilly Valley	Adelaide Hills
96	2008 Ngeringa	Adelaide Hills
96	2008 Tapanappa Tiers Vineyard Piccadilly Valley	Adelaide Hills
96	2009 Wignalls	Albany
96	2008 Giaconda	Beechworth
96	2008 by Farr	Geelong
96	2008 Shadowfax	Gippsland
96	2008 Seppelt Drumborg Vineyard	Grampians
96	2009 Lake's Folly	Hunter Valley
96	2009 Bindi Composition	Macedon Ranges
96	2008 Curly Flat	Macedon Ranges
96	2009 Brookland Valley Reserve	Margaret River
96	2009 Evoi Reserve	Margaret River
96	2008 Hay Shed Hill Block 6	Margaret River
96	2007 Leeuwin Estate Art Series	Margaret River
96	2007 Peccavi	Margaret River
96	2008 Pierro	Margaret River
96	2008 Stella Bella	Margaret River
96	2008 Vasse Felix Heytesbury	Margaret River
96	2008 Woodlands Chloe Reserve	Margaret River
96	2008 Woodside Valley Estate Le Bas	Margaret River
96	2008 Xanadu Reserve	Margaret River
96	2008 Kooyong Single Vineyard Selection Faultline	Mornington Peninsula
96	2008 Moorooduc Estate McIntyre Vineyard	Mornington Peninsula
96	2008 Prancing Horse Estate	Mornington Peninsula
96	2008 Ten Minutes by Tractor Wallis Vineyard	Mornington Peninsula
96	2008 Tuck's Ridge Buckle	Mornington Peninsula
96	2008 Yabby Lake Block 6	Mornington Peninsula
96	2008 Yabby Lake	Mornington Peninsula
96	2009 Bellwether Tamar Valley	Northern Tasmania

96	2008 Velo Wooded	Northern Tasmania
96	2007 Brokenwood Forest Edge Vineyard	Orange
96	2008 Fonty's Pool Vineyards Single Vineyard	Pemberton
96	2007 Derwent Estate	Southern Tasmania
96	2008 Cassegrain Fromenteau Reserve	Tumbarumba
96	2009 Penfolds Bin 311	Tumbarumba
96	2008 Domaine Chandon Barrel Selection	Yarra Valley
96	2008 Giant Steps Tarraford Vineyard	Yarra Valley
96	2009 Oakridge 864 Van der Meulen Vineyard	Yarra Valley
96	2008 Seville Estate Reserve	Yarra Valley
96	2008 YarraLoch Stephanie's Dream	Yarra Valley
96	2007 Yering Station Single Vineyard Coombe Farm Vineyard	Yarra Valley

Semillon

Little needs to be said, except to repeat Bruce Tyrrell's comment on the impact of screwcaps: 'Hunter Valley semillon is entering a golden age.' Every vintage between 2002 and '09 is represented; as the years roll by that range may increase.

RATING	WINE	REGION
96	2009 Briar Ridge Signature Release Karl Stockhausen	Hunter Valley
96	2005 Brokenwood Brycefield Belford Vineyards	Hunter Valley
96	2009 McLeish Estate	Hunter Valley
96	2005 Meerea Park Terracotta	Hunter Valley
96	2009 Pepper Tree Alluvius	Hunter Valley
96	2009 Pepper Tree Limited Release	Hunter Valley
96	2009 Pokolbin Estate Ken Bray	Hunter Valley
96	2009 Poole's Rock	Hunter Valley
96	2005 Thomas Braemore Individual Vineyard	Hunter Valley
96	2004 Thomas Braemore Individual Vineyard	Hunter Valley
96	2005 Tyrrell's Belford Reserve	Hunter Valley
96	2009 Tyrrell's Johnno's Hand Pressed	Hunter Valley
95	2009 Cirillo 1850s Old Vine	Barossa Valley
95	2004 Kaesler Reid's Rasp	Barossa Valley
95	2009 Brokenwood	Hunter Valley
95	2005 Brokenwood Maxwell Vineyard	Hunter Valley
95	2009 David Hook Pothana Vineyard Belford	Hunter Valley
95	2005 De Bortoli Murphy's Vineyard	Hunter Valley
95	2009 De Iuliis	Hunter Valley
95	2009 De Iuliis Sunshine Vineyard	Hunter Valley
95	2006 Drayton's Susanne	Hunter Valley
95	2006 Drayton's Vineyard Reserve Pokolbin	Hunter Valley
95	2007 Hungerford Hill	Hunter Valley
95	2009 Keith Tulloch Field of Mars	Hunter Valley
95	2004 Keith Tulloch Museum Release	Hunter Valley
95	2009 Marsh Estate Holly's Block	Hunter Valley

95	2002 McWilliam's Mount Pleasant Elizabeth	Hunter Valley
95	2005 McWilliam's Mount Pleasant Lovedale Limited Release	Hunter Valley
95	2009 Mistletoe Home Vineyard	Hunter Valley
95	2009 Mistletoe Reserve	Hunter Valley
95	2008 Mistletoe Reserve	Hunter Valley
95	2004 Mistletoe Reserve	Hunter Valley
95	2009 Mount View Estate Reserve	Hunter Valley
95	2008 Pokolbin Estate Ken Bray	Hunter Valley
95	2009 Pokolbin Estate Phil Swannell	Hunter Valley
95	2005 Saddlers Creek Classic Hunter	Hunter Valley
95	2009 Thomas Braemore Individual Vineyard	Hunter Valley
95	2003 Tower Estate Museum Release	Hunter Valley
95	2005 Tyrrell's Single Vineyard HVD	Hunter Valley
95	2009 Vasse Felix	Margaret River
95	2009 Xanadu	Margaret River

Sauvignon blanc

Sauvignon blanc is facing its moment of destiny as the woes of Marlborough gather force. Australia has stuck to its knitting, producing wines that have structure, and do not seek to emulate the Marlborough style. This variety is not going to go away any time soon.

RATING	WINE	REGION
96	2009 Dandelion Vineyards Wishing Clock	Adelaide Hills
96	2009 Geoff Weaver Lenswood	Adelaide Hills
96	2009 Shaw & Smith	Adelaide Hills
96	2009 Leeuwin Estate Art Series	Margaret River
96	2009 Larry Cherubino Cherubino	Pemberton
96	2009 Terre à Terre	Wrattonbully
95	2009 Bird in Hand	Adelaide Hills
95	2009 Wirra Wirra Hiding Champion	Adelaide Hills
95	2009 Aramis Vineyards White Label	McLaren Vale
95	2009 Willow Creek Vineyard Tulum	Mornington Peninsula
95	2009 Yabby Lake Vineyard Red Claw	Mornington Peninsula
95	2009 Paul Nelson Fume Blanc	Mount Barker
95	2009 Hillbrook	Pemberton
95	2009 Oakridge Limited Release Fume	Yarra Valley
95	2009 Shelmerdine Vineyards	Yarra Valley
94	2009 Barratt Piccadilly Valley	Adelaide Hills
94	2009 Deviation Road	Adelaide Hills
94	2009 Fox Gordon Sassy	Adelaide Hills
94	2009 Hahndorf Hill	Adelaide Hills
94	2009 Henschke Coralinga	Adelaide Hills
94	2009 Hewitson LuLu	Adelaide Hills
94	2009 Mayhem & Co	Adelaide Hills

94	2009 Somerled Steeplechase	Adelaide Hills
94	2008 The Pawn Jeu de Fin Reserve Release	Adelaide Hills
94	2009 Tower Estate	Adelaide Hills
94	2009 Verdun Park Lyla	Adelaide Hills
94	2009 Montgomery's Hill	Albany
94	2009 Watson Wine Group Rex Watson	Coonawarra
94	2008 Bannockburn	Geelong
94	2009 Leura Park Estate Bellarine Peninsula	Geelong
94	2008 Scotchmans Hill Cornelius Bellarine Peninsula	Geelong
94	2008 Metcalfe Valley	Macedon Ranges
94	2009 Ashbrook Estate	Margaret River
94	2009 Clairault	Margaret River
94	2009 Evans & Tate	Margaret River
94	2009 Hamelin Bay	Margaret River
94	2009 Saracen Estates	Margaret River
94	2009 Stella Bella	Margaret River
94	2008 Watershed Awakening	Margaret River
94	2009 Howard Park	Margaret River/ Pemberton
94	2009 Port Phillip Estate	Mornington Peninsula
94	2009 West Cape Howe	Mount Barker
94	2009 Brokenwood Forest Edge Vineyard	Orange
94	2008 Patina	Orange
94	2009 Printhie	Orange
94	2009 Ross Hill Vineyard	Orange
94	2009 Larry Cherubino The Yard	Pemberton
94	2009 Limbic	Port Phillip Zone
94	2008 Blue Metal Vineyard Signature Fume Blanc	Southern Highlands
94	2009 Stefano Lubiana	Southern Tasmania
94	2009 Balgownie Estate Black Label	Yarra Valley
94	2008 De Bortoli Reserve Release	Yarra Valley
94	2008 Gembrook Hill	Yarra Valley
94	2007 Helen's Hill Estate Evolution	Yarra Valley

Sauvignon semillon blends

If there is to be a challenge to the extent of the monopoly the Hunter Valley has on semillon, it is Margaret River's vice-like grip on sauvignon semillon blends. The maritime climate replicates that of Bordeaux, the Old World home of the blend (the percentage of muscadelle is rapidly decreasing in Bordeaux).

RATING	WINE	REGION
96	2009 Cullen Vineyard Sauvignon Blanc Semillon	Margaret River
96	2007 Stella Bella Suckfizzle Sauvignon Blanc Semillon	Margaret River
95	2009 Grosset Semillon Sauvignon Blanc	Clare Valley/ Adelaide Hills
95	2009 Cullen Mangan Vineyard Sauvignon Blanc Semillon	Margaret River

95	2009 Hamelin Bay Semillon Sauvignon Blanc	Margaret River
95	2009 Moss Wood Ribbon Vale Semillon Sauvignon Blanc	Margaret River
95	2009 Pedestal Vineyard Sauvignon Blanc Semillon	Margaret River
95	2009 Vasse Felix Sauvignon Blanc Semillon	Margaret River
95	2008 Fonty's Pool Lucia Limited Release Sauvignon Blanc Semillon	Pemberton
94	2009 Sorrenberg Sauvignon Blanc Semillon	Beechworth
94	2009 A. Retief Sauvignon Blanc Semillon	Canberra District
94	2009 Pikes Valley's End Sauvignon Blanc Semillon	Clare Valley
94	2009 Harewood Estate Reserve Semillon Sauvignon Blanc	Great Southern
94	2009 Henschke Eleanor's Cottage Sauvignon Blanc Semillon	Eden Valley/ Adelaide Hills
94	2009 Alkoomi White Label Semillon Sauvignon Blanc	Frankland River
94	2009 Pepperilly Estate Sauvignon Blanc Semillon	Geographe
94	2009 Tatler Over the Ditch Semillon Sauvignon Blanc	Hunter Valley/ Marlborough
94	2009 Tulloch Semillon Sauvignon Blanc	Hunter Valley
94	2009 Cape Mentelle Sauvignon Blanc Semillon	Margaret River
94	2009 Eagle Vale Estate Semillon Sauvignon Blanc	Margaret River
94	2009 Evans & Tate Semillon Sauvignon Blanc	Margaret River
94	2009 Fire Gully Sauvignon Blanc Semillon	Margaret River
94	2009 Flametree Sauvignon Blanc Semillon	Margaret River
94	2009 Hay Shed Hill Block 1 Semillon Sauvignon Blanc	Margaret River
94	2009 Leeuwin Estate Siblings Sauvignon Blanc Semillon	Margaret River
94	2009 Lenton Brae Semillon Sauvignon Blanc	Margaret River
94	2008 Lenton Brae Wilyabrup Semillon Sauvignon Blanc	Margaret River
94	2009 Lenton Brae Wilyabrup Semillon Sauvignon Blanc	Margaret River
94	2009 Mainbreak Sauvignon Blanc Semillon	Margaret River
94	2009 Pierro Semillon Sauvignon Blanc LTC	Margaret River
94	2009 Rockfield Estate Semillon Sauvignon Blanc	Margaret River
94	2009 Rosily Vineyard Semillon Sauvignon Blanc	Margaret River
94	2009 Wills Domain Semillon Sauvignon Blanc	Margaret River
94	2009 Xanadu Sauvignon Blanc Semillon	Margaret River
94	2009 Goundrey G Sauvignon Blanc Semillon	Pemberton
94	2005 Yarra Yarra Sauvignon Blanc Semillon	Yarra Valley

Other white wines

This group of wines shows that the 'alternative' varieties' Charge of the Light Brigade is yet to inflict many casualties on viognier, pinot gris, verdelho and gewurztraminer. The cause of the newer alternatives was not helped by the embarrassing discovery that the CSIRO-supplied albarino is in fact savagnin, a gewurztraminer clone grown in the Jura region of France.

RATING	WINE	REGION
96	2008 Yalumba The Virgilius Viognier	Eden Valley
95	2009 Paracombe Pinot Gris	Adelaide Hills
95	2008 Yalumba Viognier	Eden Valley

95	2009 Borrodell on the Mount Wine Maker's Daughter Gewurztraminer	Orange
94	2009 Leabrook Estate Pinot Gris	Adelaide Hills
94	2009 Nova Vita Firebird Pinot Gris	Adelaide Hills
94	2009 Pike & Joyce Pinot Gris	Adelaide Hills
94	2009 Fox Gordon Abby Viognier	Adelaide Hills
94	2009 Tower Estate Pinot Gris	Adelaide Hills
94	2009 Clonakilla Viognier	Canberra District
94	2009 Lark Hill Gruner Veltliner	Canberra District
94	2009 Skillogalee Gewurztraminer	Clare Valley
94	2008 Scotchmans Hill Cornelius Bellarine Peninsula Pinot Gris	Geelong
94	2009 Galli Estate Artigiano Viognier	Heathcote
94	2009 Wanted Man Single Vineyard Marsanne Viognier	Heathcote
94	2009 Oakvale Reserve Block 37 Verdelho	Hunter Valley
94	2009 Two Rivers Hidden Hive Verdelho	Hunter Valley
94	2009 Ashbrook Estate Verdelho	Margaret River
94	2008 Wood Park Home Block Viognier	King Valley
94	2009 Devil's Lair Fifth Leg White	Margaret River
94	2009 Sandalford Estate Reserve Verdelho	Margaret River
94	2009 Gemtree Moonstone	McLaren Vale
94	2008 Kooyong Beurrot Pinot Gris	Mornington Peninsula
94	2008 Moorooduc Estate Garden Vineyard Pinot Gris	Mornington Peninsula
94	2009 Paradigm Hill Pinot Gris	Mornington Peninsula
94	2009 Willow Creek Vineyard Tulum Pinot Gris	Mornington Peninsula
94	2009 di Lusso Estate Pinot Grigio	Mudgee
94	2007 Mitchelton Marsanne	Nagambie Lakes
94	2009 Belgravia Pinot Gris	Orange
94	2008 Vincognita Nangkita Madeleines Viognier	Southern Fleurieu
94	2008 Mount Mary Triolet	Yarra Valley
94	2007 Yarra Yering Carrodus Viognier	Yarra Valley
94	2008 Yeringberg Marsanne Roussanne	Yarra Valley
94	2008 Yeringberg Viognier	Yarra Valley

Sparkling

The best sparkling wines are now solely sourced either from Tasmania or from the coolest sites in the southern parts of the mainland, with altitude playing a major role. They are all fermented in the bottle, and the best have had extended lees contact prior to disgorgement, giving them great complexity.

RATING	WINE	REGION
97	1998 Mount William Winery Special Late Disgorged 10 Years on Lees Blanc de Blancs	Macedon Ranges
97	1998 Bay of Fires Arras EJ Carr Late Disgorged	Northern Tasmania
96	2003 Bindi Extended Lees Aged Chardonnay Pinot Noir	Macedon Ranges
96	2003 Mount William	Macedon Ranges

96	2003 Bay of Fires Arras Pinot Noir Chardonnay	Northern Tasmania
96	2002 Domaine Chandon Prestige Cuvee	Yarra Valley
95	2001 Granite Hills Knight Vintage	Macedon Ranges
95	2005 Clover Hill Blanc de Blancs	Northern Tasmania
95	2006 Domaine Chandon Tasmanian Cuvee	Tasmania
95	2005 Yarrabank Cuvee	Yarra Valley
95	2001 Yarrabank Late Disgorged	Yarra Valley
94	NV Petaluma Bridgewater Mill Pinot Noir Chardonnay	Adelaide Hills
94	1999 Petaluma Croser Late Disgorged Piccadilly Valley Pinot Noir Chardonnay	Adelaide Hills
94	NV Petaluma Croser Pinot Noir Chardonnay	Adelaide Hills
94	2006 Petaluma Croser Piccadilly Valley Pinot Noir Chardonnay	Adelaide Hills
94	2004 Romney Park Blanc de Blancs	Adelaide Hills
94	2004 Starvedog Lane Chardonnay Pinot Noir Pinot Meunier	Adelaide Hills
94	2000 Freycinet Radenti Chardonnay Pinot Noir	East Coast Tasmania
94	2005 Brown Brothers Patricia Pinot Noir Chardonnay Brut	King Valley
94	NV Brown Brothers Pinot Noir Chardonnay Pinot Meunier	King Valley
94	2003 Mount William Jorja-Alexis Pinot Rose	Macedon Ranges
94	1998 Beckingham Pas de Deux Pinot Noir Chardonnay	Mornington Peninsula
94	NV Jansz Premium Non Vintage Cuvee	Northern Tasmania
94	2006 Jansz Premium Vintage Rose	Northern Tasmania
94	2003 Pipers Brook Vineyard Kreglinger Vintage Brut	Northern Tasmania
94	2004 Winstead Ensnared Sparkling Pinot Noir	Southern Tasmania
94	2006 Houghton Wisdom Chardonnay Pinot Noir	Pemberton
94	2006 Coldstream Hills Chardonnay Pinot Noir	Yarra Valley
94	NV Domaine Chandon Brut Rose Non Vintage	Yarra Valley
94	2006 Domaine Chandon Z*D Blanc de Blancs	Yarra Valley
94	2001 Punch Easdown Vineyard Kinglake Pinot Noir Chardonnay	Yarra Valley
94	2004 Yarra Burn Blanc de Blancs	Yarra Valley
94	2005 Yarra Burn Blanc de Blancs	Yarra Valley

A tiny group of wines, sparkling reds are eagerly sought by the small percentage of wine drinkers who understand the peculiarities of the style and who, better still, are prepared to cellar them for a year or more, the longer the better.

RATING	WINE	REGION
95	NV Rockford Black Shiraz	Barossa Valley
95	2002 Ashton Hills Sparkling Shiraz	Clare Valley
95	NV Primo Estate Joseph Sparkling Red	McLaren Vale
94	2005 Peter Lehmann Black Queen Sparkling Shiraz	Barossa Valley
94	NV Turkey Flat Sparkling Shiraz	Barossa Valley
94	2004 Leasingham Classic Clare Sparkling Shiraz	Clare Valley
94	2006 Grampians Estate Black Sunday Friends Sparkling Shiraz	Grampians
94	2006 Grampians Estate Rutherford Sparkling Shiraz	Grampians

94	2003 Mount William Jorja-Alexis Pinot Rose	Macedon Ranges
94	NV Domaine Chandon Brut Rose Non Vintage	Yarra Valley
94	NV Domaine Chandon Sparkling Pinot Shiraz	Yarra Valley

Sweet

Tasmania may have been under-represented in the dry riesling group, but it comes into its own here: from gently sweet Kabinett styles through to Auslese-equivalent or above, its truly cool climate gives the wines tremendous zest and length to the piercing lime-accented flavours of riesling.

RATING	WINE	REGION
96	2007 Heggies Reserve 242 Botrytis Riesling	Eden Valley
96	2008 Delatite Late Harvest Riesling	Upper Goulburn
95	2007 Tamar Ridge Kayena Vineyard Limited Release Botrytis Riesling	Northern Tasmania
95	2009 Bloodwood Silk Purse	Orange
95	2009 Centennial Vineyards Reserve Single Vineyard Riesling [836]	Southern Highlands
95	2006 Craigow Dessert Gewurztraminer	Southern Tasmania
95	2008 Pressing Matters R69 Riesling	Southern Tasmania
94	2009 Mount Horrocks Cordon Cut	Clare Valley
94	2008 Craigow Dessert Riesling	Southern Tasmania
94	2008 Frogmore Creek Iced Riesling	Southern Tasmania
94	2008 Pooley Coal River Late Harvest Riesling	Southern Tasmania
94	2009 Pressing Matters R69 Riesling	Southern Tasmania
94	2009 Delatite Late Harvest Riesling	Upper Goulburn

It makes no sense to put the semillons and the rieslings into the same group. Altogether different dynamics are in play with the semillon, which largely comes from the Riverland; these are barrel-fermented, highly botrytised wines with vanilla bean, peaches and cream, crème brulee, apricot or cumquat flavours – take your pick.

95	2007 De Bortoli Noble One	Riverina
95	2008 De Bortoli Noble One	Riverina
94	2007 Hobbs of Barossa Ranges Viognier	Barossa Valley
94	2009 Scarborough Wine Co Late Harvest Semillon	Hunter Valley
94	2006 di Lusso Estate Passito	Mudgee
94	2009 Robert Stein Harvest Gold	Mudgee
94	2002 Lillypilly Estate Family Reserve Noble Blend	Riverina
94	2007 McWilliam's Morning Light Botrytis Semillon	Riverina
94	2007 Nugan Estate Cookoothama Darlington Point Botrytis Semillon	Riverina
94	2007 Westend Estate 3 Bridges Reserve Botrytis	Riverina
94	2009 Oakridge Limited Release Viognier	Yarra Valley

Rose

The number of roses on the market continues to grow, seemingly unabated and unstoppable. There are no rules: they can be bone-dry, slightly sweet or very sweet. They can be and are made from almost any red variety, red blends or red and white blends. They may be a convenient way of concentrating the red wine left after the rose is run off (bleeding or saignee) from the fermenter shortly after the grapes are crushed, or made from the ground up using grapes and techniques specifically chosen for the purpose. The vast majority fall in the former camp; those listed mainly come from the latter.

RATING	WINE	REGION
96	2009 Charles Melton Rose of Virginia	Barossa Valley
96	2009 Spinifex Luxe	Barossa Valley
96	2009 Turkey Flat Rose	Barossa Valley
95	2009 Michael Hall Sang de Pigeon Shiraz Saignee	Barossa Valley
95	2009 SC Pannell Arido Rose	McLaren Vale
94	2009 Bird in Hand Pinot Rose	Adelaide Hills
94	NV BK Wines Collage	Adelaide Hills
94	2009 Head Rose	Barossa Valley
94	2009 Jacob's Creek Three Vines Shiraz Grenache Sangiovese	Barossa Valley
94	2009 Kalleske Rosina	Barossa Valley
94	2009 Spinifex Rose	Barossa Valley
94	2009 Torbreck Saignee	Barossa Valley
94	2009 Yelland & Papps Delight Grenache Rose	Barossa Valley
94	2009 Farr Rising Saignee	Geelong
94	2009 Taminick Cellars 1919 Series Alicante Rose	Glenrowan
94	2008 Brookland Valley Verse 1 Rose	Margaret River
94	2009 Hardys Chronicle No. 1 Twice Lost Shiraz Cabernet Rose	McLaren Vale
94	2009 Wirra Wirra Mrs Wigley Grenache Rose	McLaren Vale
94	2009 Zonte's Footstep Scarlet Ladybird Single Site Rose	Fleurieu Peninsula
94	2009 Port Phillip Estate Salasso	Mornington Peninsula
94	2009 Brook Eden Vineyard Pinot Rose	Northern Tasmania
94	2009 Terra Felix La Vie En Rose	Upper Goulburn

Pinot noir

Only one wine falls outside the key areas for pinot noir, Abbey Creek from Porongurup, made by Rob Diletti, a winemaker of great talent and rapidly growing reputation. Older vines, except for plantings of new French clones, themselves a plus, and more sophisticated winemaking, are the drivers behind many excellent wines.

RATING	WINE	REGION
97	2008 Bindi Block 5	Macedon Ranges
97	2008 Tuck's Ridge Buckle	Mornington Peninsula
97	2008 Yabby Lake Vineyard Block 5	Mornington Peninsula

97	2008 Serrat	Yarra Valley
96	2008 Ashton Hills Piccadilly Valley	Adelaide Hills
96	2008 Ashton Hills Reserve	Adelaide Hills
96	2008 Romney Park	Adelaide Hills
96	2007 Freycinet	East Coast Tasmania
96	2006 Bannockburn Vineyards Serre	Geelong
96	2008 by Farr Sangreal	Geelong
96	2008 by Farr Tout Pres	Geelong
96	2008 Provenance	Geelong
96	2008 Bass Phillip Premium	Gippsland
96	2008 Bindi Original Vineyard	Macedon Ranges
96	2008 Kooyong Single Vineyard Selection Ferrous	Mornington Peninsula
96	2007 Main Ridge Half Acre	Mornington Peninsula
96	2007 Merricks Creek Close Planted	Mornington Peninsula
96	2008 Montalto Lake Block	Mornington Peninsula
96	2008 Montalto	Mornington Peninsula
96	2008 Moorooduc Estate The Moorooduc	Mornington Peninsula
96	2007 Ocean Eight Aylward	Mornington Peninsula
96	2008 Paringa The Paringa Single Vineyard	Mornington Peninsula
96	2008 Port Phillip Estate	Mornington Peninsula
96	2008 Quealy Seventeen Rows	Mornington Peninsula
96	2008 Willow Creek Vineyard Tulum	Mornington Peninsula
96	2008 Yabby Lake Block 2	Mornington Peninsula
96	2007 Yabby Lake	Mornington Peninsula
96	2008 Stoney Rise Holyman	Northern Tasmania
96	2007 Tamar Ridge Kayena Reserve Limited Release	Northern Tasmania
96	2008 Abbey Creek Vineyard	Porongurup
96	2008 Massoni	Mornington Peninsula
96	2008 Stefano Lubiana Estate	Southern Tasmania
96	2008 Hillcrest Premium	Yarra Valley
96	2006 Mount Mary	Yarra Valley
96	2008 Punch Lance's Close Planted	Yarra Valley
96	2008 Punch Lance's	Yarra Valley

Shiraz

Here patterns within patterns emerge, driven by vintage. 2007 was a good vintage in the Hunter Valley and Western Australia, but not South Australia; 2006 was poor for red wines in Western Australia, but very good (along with '08) in South Australia. And so it goes on, demonstrating that vintage variation is every bit as much a factor as it is in Bordeaux or Burgundy.

RATING	WINE	REGION
97	2008 Kaesler Alte Reben	Barossa Valley
97	2009 Collector Marked Tree Red	Canberra District
97	2006 Henschke Hill Of Grace	Eden Valley
97	2006 Best's Thomson Family	Grampians

97	2007 Mistletoe Grand Reserve	Hunter Valley
97	2007 Pokolbin Estate Reserve	Hunter Valley
97	2004 Tahbilk 1860 Vines	Nagambie Lakes
96	2008 Bird in Hand Nest Egg	Adelaide Hills
96	2008 Romney Park	Adelaide Hills
96	2007 Charles Melton Voices of Angels	Barossa Valley
96	2008 Chateau Tanunda The Chateau 100 Year Old Vines	Barossa Valley
96	2006 Craneford Fire Station	Barossa Valley
96	2006 Gibson Reserve	Barossa Valley
96	2008 Glaetzer Amon-Ra Unfiltered	Barossa Valley
96	2008 Glaetzer Bishop	Barossa Valley
96	2005 Grant Burge Meshach	Barossa Valley
96	2006 Haan Prestige	Barossa Valley
96	2008 Head The Brunette Single Vineyard Syrah	Barossa Valley
96	2008 Hentley Farm The Beast	Barossa Valley
96	2008 John Duval Entity	Barossa Valley
96	2006 Kurtz Lunar Block Individual Vineyard	Barossa Valley
96	2005 Penfolds Grange	Barossa Valley
96	2006 Penfolds St Henri	Barossa Valley
96	2005 Saltram The Journal	Barossa Valley
96	2008 Turkey Flat	Barossa Valley
96	2008 Tollana Brian and Julie Hurse Vineyard Bin TR568	Bendigo
96	2007 Turner's Crossing Vineyard The Cut	Bendigo
96	2008 Clonakilla O'Riada	Canberra District
96	2009 Collector Reserve	Canberra District
96	2007 Kilikanoon Alliance Hermitage	Clare Valley
96	2006 O'Leary Walker Claire Reserve	Clare Valley
96	2006 Sons of Eden Remus Old Vine	Eden Valley
96	2007 Alkoomi Jarrah	Frankland River
96	2008 Larry Cherubino Cherubino	Frankland River
96	2008 by Farr	Geelong
96	2008 Lethbridge	Geelong
96	2008 Paradise IV Dardel	Geelong
96	2006 Best's Bin No. 0	Grampians
96	2007 Mount Langi Ghiran Langi	Grampians
96	2008 The Story Rice's Vineyard	Grampians
96	2008 The Story Westgate Vineyard	Grampians
96	2007 Forest Hill Vineyard Block 9 Mount Barker	Great Southern
96	2007 Domaine Chandon	Heathcote
96	2007 Heathcote Estate	Heathcote
96	2007 Red Edge	Heathcote
96	2006 YarraLoch The Collection	Heathcote
96	2007 Brokenwood Graveyard Vineyard	Hunter Valley
96	2007 Glenguin Estate Aristea	Hunter Valley
96	2007 McWilliam's Mount Pleasant Maurice O'Shea	Hunter Valley
96	2007 Meerea Park Alexander Munro Individual Vineyard	Hunter Valley
96	2007 Tintilla Patriarch Syrah	Hunter Valley

96	2007 Tyrrell's Single Vineyard Stevens	Hunter Valley
96	2008 Marchand & Burch	Margaret River
96	2008 Sandalford Prendiville Reserve	Margaret River
96	2007 Cape Barren Blewitt Springs Vineyard Reserve Release Old Vine	McLaren Vale
96	2008 Chalk Hill Reserve	McLaren Vale
96	2005 DogRidge Most Valuable Player	McLaren Vale
96	2005 Hardys Eileen Hardy	McLaren Vale
96	2008 Paxton Quandong Farm	McLaren Vale
96	2008 Richard Hamilton Gumprs'	McLaren Vale
96	2008 Richard Hamilton Hamilton Centurion Old Vine	McLaren Vale
96	2008 Wirra Wirra RSW	McLaren Vale
96	2007 Woodstock The Stocks Single Vineyard	McLaren Vale
96	2007 Paringa Estate Reserve Special Barrel Selection	Mornington Peninsula
96	2008 Red Hill Estate	Mornington Peninsula
96	2004 Tahbilk Eric Stevens Purbrick	Nagambie Lakes
96	2008 Bellarmine	Pemberton
96	2007 Castle Rock	Porongurup
96	2008 Dalwhinnie Southwest Rocks	Pyrenees
96	2008 M. Chapoutier Australia Domaine Terlato & Chapoutier lieu-dit Malakoff	Pyrenees
96	2007 Mt Billy Willie John	Southern Fleurieu
96	2008 Goona Warra	Sunbury
96	2008 Oakridge 864 Syrah	Yarra Valley
96	2008 Toolangi Reserve	Yarra Valley

Shiraz viognier

In best Australian tall-poppy syndrome fashion it has already become fashionable in some quarters to challenge the remarkable synergy obtained by co-fermenting around 5% of viognier with shiraz. When used in cool to temperate regions, the enhancement of colour, aroma and flavour is remarkable, as is the softening and smoothing of texture. It is not a panacea for lesser quality grapes, and yes, it is and should remain a subtext to the thrust of shiraz's flavour. Nonetheless, the wines in this group offer pleasure second to none.

RATING	WINE	REGION
97	2009 Clonakilla	Canberra District
96	2008 Head The Blonde	Barossa Valley
96	2008 Boireann Maggie's	Granite Belt
96	2008 Pepper Tree The Gravels Single Vineyard Reserve	Wrattonbully
96	2008 De Bortoli Estate Grown	Yarra Valley
96	2008 Serrat	Yarra Valley
96	2006 Yering Station Single Vineyard Smedley Lane Vineyard	Yarra Valley
95	2007 Mount Torrens Vineyards Solstice	Adelaide Hills
95	2008 Head Red	Barossa Valley
95	2008 Turner's Crossing Vineyard	Bendigo

95	2008 Kalgan River	Great Southern
95	2009 Grove Estate The Cellar Block	Hilltops
95	2008 Mistletoe Hilltops	Hunter Valley
95	2008 Pepper Tree The Pebbles Limited Release Single Vineyard	Wrattonbully
95	2007 Yarra Yering Dry Red No. 2	Yarra Valley
95	2006 Yering Station Carr C Block Vineyard	Yarra Valley

Cabernet sauvignon

The affinity of cabernet sauvignon with a maritime climate is put beyond doubt by its home in Bordeaux's Medoc region. So it comes as no surprise to find that most (but not all) of Australia's top-quality cabernets come from regions with climates similar to Bordeaux (conspicuously Coonawarra and Margaret River) and/or which are within 50 km of the sea, with no intervening mountain.

RATING	WINE	REGION
97	2008 Balnaves of Coonawarra The Tally Reserve	Coonawarra
97	2004 Hardys Thomas Hardy	McLaren Vale
96	2008 Setanta Black Sanglain	Adelaide Hills
96	2008 Penfolds Cellar Reserve	Barossa Valley
96	2008 Crabtree Windmill Vineyard	Clare Valley
96	2006 Lindemans St George	Coonawarra
96	2007 Majella	Coonawarra
96	2008 Pepper Tree Calcare Single Vineyard Reserve	Coonawarra
96	2007 Wynns	Coonawarra
96	2006 Wynns John Riddoch	Coonawarra
96	2008 Tallavera Grove Vineyard Jokers Peak The Volcanics Single Vineyard	Orange
96	2007 Fire Gully Reserve	Margaret River
96	2007 Forester Estate Yelverton Reserve Cabernet	Margaret River
96	2007 Hay Shed Hill Block 2	Margaret River
96	2008 Sandalford Estate Reserve	Margaret River
96	2004 Houghton Gladstones	Margaret River
96	2007 Houghton Wisdom	Margaret River
96	2008 Houghton Wisdom	Margaret River
96	2007 Howard Park Abercrombie	Margaret River
96	2008 Howard Park Abercrombie	Margaret River
96	2004 Tahbilk Eric Stevens Purbrick	Nagambie Lakes
96	2008 Pepper Tree Elderslee Road Single Vineyard Reserve	Wrattonbully
96	2008 Hillcrest Premium	Yarra Valley
96	2008 Seville Estate Old Vine Reserve	Yarra Valley
95	2008 Murray Street Vineyard	Barossa Valley
95	2007 Barwick The Collectables	Blackwood Valley
95	2005 Leasingham Classic Clare Cabernet	Clare Valley
95	2006 Taylors 40th Anniversary	Clare Valley
95	2008 Balnaves	Coonawarra
95	2006 Brand's Laira The Patron	Coonawarra

95	2004 Patrick T Limited Release	Coonawarra
95	2006 Punters Corner	Coonawarra
95	2006 Wynns Alex 88 Single Vineyard	Coonawarra
95	2007 Wynns Glengyle Single Vineyard	Coonawarra
95	2008 Frankland Estate Isolation Ridge Vineyard	Frankland River
95	2005 Mount Langi Ghiran Langi	Grampians
95	2008 Kalgan River	Great Southern
95	2007 West Cape Howe Book Ends	Great Southern
95	2006 John's Blend Individual Selection	Langhorne Creek
95	2007 Clairault Estate	Margaret River
95	2007 Evans & Tate Redbrook	Margaret River
95	2008 Hay Shed Hill Block 2	Margaret River
95	2007 Vasse Felix	Margaret River
95	2008 Vasse Felix	Margaret River
95	2008 Wise Eagle Bay	Margaret River
95	2008 Chapel Hill	McLaren Vale
95	2006 Hardys Thomas Hardy	McLaren Vale
95	2007 Wirra Wirra The Angelus	McLaren Vale
95	2006 Huntington Estate Signature	Mudgee
95	2006 Tahbilk	Nagambie Lakes
95	2008 Summerfield Jo Cabernet	Pyrenees
95	2007 Sirromet St Jude's Road Grand Reserve	Queensland Coastal
95	2008 Centennial Vineyards Single Vineyard Reserve	Southern Highlands
95	2004 Domaine A	Southern Tasmania
95	2006 Taylor Ferguson Fernando The First Coonawarra/	Wrattonbully/ Barossa
95	2006 Oakridge 864	Yarra Valley
95	2008 St Huberts	Yarra Valley
95	2005 Whispering Hills Appassimento	Yarra Valley
95	2006 Yering Station Single Vineyard Yarra Edge Vineyard	Yarra Valley

Cabernet and family

This group revolves around the grapes of Bordeaux, and primarily blends thereof, but with some single varieties most notably merlot, the majority from moderately cool regions, Margaret River once again the leader of the band. Also included are the classic Australian cabernet and shiraz (or vice versa) blends.

RATING	WINE	REGION
97	2007 Cullen Diana Madeline	Margaret River
96	2006 Wolf Blass Black Label Cabernet Sauvignon Shiraz Malbec	Barossa Valley
96	2007 Mountadam The Red	Eden Valley
96	2006 Bannockburn Vineyards Bruce	Geelong
96	2008 Moss Wood Amy's	Margaret River
96	2007 Stella Bella Cabernet Sauvignon Merlot	Margaret River
96	2007 Vasse Felix Heytesbury	Margaret River

96	2008 DogRock Degraves Road	Pyrenees
96	2004 McWilliam's 1877 Cabernet Sauvignon Shiraz	Riverina
96	2004 Houghton Jack Mann	Swan Valley
96	2007 De Bortoli Melba Reserve	Yarra Valley
96	2007 Yarra Yering Carrodus Cabernet Merlot	Yarra Valley
95	2008 Elderton Ode to Lorraine Cabernet Sauvignon Shiraz Merlot	Barossa Valley
95	2006 Pondalowie Vineyards Special Release Malbec	Bendigo
95	2007 Grosset Gaia	Clare Valley
95	2006 Neagles Rock Vineyards One Black Dog Reserve Cabernet Shiraz	Clare Valley
95	2006 Jamiesons Run Mildara Cabernet Shiraz	Coonawarra
95	2006 Zema Estate Saluti Cabernet Shiraz	Coonawarra
95	2008 Irvine The Baroness	Eden Valley
95	2007 Alkoomi Blackbutt	Frankland River
95	2008 Frankland Estate Olmo's Reward	Frankland River
95	2006 Lake Breeze Arthur's Reserve Cabernet Sauvignon Petit Verdot Malbec	Langhorne Creek
95	2008 Brookland Valley Cabernet Sauvignon Merlot	Margaret River
95	2008 Carpe Diem Vineyards Platinum Selection Merlot	Margaret River
95	2007 Chalice Bridge Estate Merlot	Margaret River
95	2008 Flametree Cabernet Merlot	Margaret River
95	2007 McHenry Hohnen Rolling Stone	Margaret River
95	2007 Umamu Estate Cabernet Merlot	Margaret River
95	2008 Woodlands Emily Special Reserve	Margaret River
95	2008 Woodlands Margaret	Margaret River
95	2006 Pirramimma Petit Verdot	McLaren Vale
95	2008 Doherty The Doherty Signature Collection Cabernet Merlot	Margaret River
95	2007 De Bortoli Melba Lucia	Yarra Valley
95	2008 Wedgetail Estate The North Face	Yarra Valley

Shiraz and family

A class utterly dominated by Rhône Valley blends of some or all of shiraz, grenache and mourvedre, the Italians making a small mark with sangiovese and nebbiolo.

RATING	WINE	REGION
96	2008 Flaxman The Stranger Shiraz Cabernet	Barossa Valley
96	2007 Hewitson Private Cellar Shiraz Mourvedre	Barossa Valley
96	2006 Murray Street Vineyard Benno	Barossa Valley
96	2007 Sons of Eden Kennedy Grenache Shiraz Mourvedre	Barossa Valley
96	2008 Spinifex Indigene	Barossa Valley
96	2008 Turkey Flat Mourvedre	Barossa Valley
96	2006 Wendouree Shiraz Malbec	Clare Valley
96	2008 Lindemans Limestone Ridge Vineyard Shiraz Cabernet	Coonawarra
96	2007 Greenstone Vineyard Sangiovese	Heathcote

96	2008 Jasper Hill Emily's Paddock Shiraz Cabernet Franc	Heathcote
96	2008 Brown Hill Estate Bill Bailey Shiraz Cabernet	Margaret River
95	2007 The Lane Single Vineyard John Crighton Shiraz Cabernet Sauvignon	Adelaide Hills
95	2008 Chateau Tanunda The Everest Old Bushvine Grenache	Barossa Valley
95	2008 John Duval Plexus Shiraz Grenache Mourvedre	Barossa Valley
95	2005 Murray Street Vineyard Shiraz Cabernet	Barossa Valley
95	2008 The Colonial Estate John Speke Single Vineyard Grenache Shiraz Mourvedre	Barossa Valley
95	2007 Ferngrove The Stirlings Shiraz Cabernet Sauvignon	Frankland River
95	2006 The Islander Estate Vineyards Old Rowley Grenache Shiraz Viognier	Kangaroo Island
95	2008 Grove Estate Sommita Nebbiolo	Hilltops
95	2007 Chalice Bridge Estate Shiraz Cabernet Sauvignon	Margaret River
95	2008 Boat O'Craigo Dundee Shiraz Grenache Viognier	Yarra Valley
94	2007 Wicks Estate Eminence Shiraz Cabernet	Adelaide Hills
94	2005 Tenafeate Creek Shiraz Cabernet Sauvignon	Adelaide Zone
94	2005 Burge Family Limited Production Shiraz Souzao	Barossa Valley
94	2008 Glaetzer Wallace Shiraz Grenache	Barossa Valley
94	2008 Landhaus Estate Shiraz Mourvedre	Barossa Valley
94	2007 Magpie Estate The Schnell Shiraz Grenache	Barossa Valley
94	2008 Penfolds Bin 138 Shiraz Mourvedre Grenache	Barossa Valley
94	2008 Penfolds Koonunga Hill Seventy Six Shiraz Cabernet	Barossa Valley
94	2006 Rockford Rod & Spur Cabernet Shiraz	Barossa Valley
94	2006 The Colonial Estate Emigre	Barossa Valley
94	2008 Turkey Flat Butchers Block Shiraz Grenache Mourvedre	Barossa Valley
94	2008 Surveyor's Hill Hills of Hall Shiraz Cabernet	Canberra District
94	2006 Wendouree Shiraz	Clare Valley
94	2006 Lindemans Limestone Ridge Vineyard Shiraz Cabernet	Coonawarra
94	2008 Henschke Henry's Seven	Eden Valley
94	2008 Frankland Estate Smith Cullam Shiraz Cabernet	Frankland River
94	2007 Wyndham Estate George Wyndham Founder's Reserve Shiraz Grenache	Hunter Valley
94	2007 Bleasdale Petrel Reserve Shiraz Cabernet Malbec	Langhorne Creek
94	2007 Bremerton B.O.V.	Langhorne Creek
94	2007 Paramoor The Fraser Shiraz Cabernet Sauvignon	Macedon Ranges
94	2008 Aramis White Label Shiraz Cabernet	McLaren Vale
94	2008 Cape Barren Native Goose GSM	McLaren Vale
95	2008 Chapel Hill Bush Vine Grenache	McLaren Vale
94	2008 d'Arenberg The Cadenzia Grenache Shiraz Mourvedre	McLaren Vale
94	2008 Paxton AAA Shiraz Grenache	McLaren Vale
94	2008 Primo Estate Il Briccone Shiraz Sangiovese	McLaren Vale
94	2006 Richard Hamilton Burton's Vineyard Old Bush Vine Grenache Shiraz	McLaren Vale

94	2007 SC Pannell Shiraz Grenache	McLaren Vale
94	2008 McPherson Basilisk Shiraz Mourvedre	Nagambie Lakes
94	2007 Stanton & Killeen Shiraz Durif	Rutherglen

Fortified wines

A relatively small but absolutely sensational group of wines, as quintessentially Australian as a Drizabone, and of unique style.

RATING	WINE	REGION
100	1909 Seppeltsfield 100 Year Old Para Liqueur 100 ml	Barossa Valley
98	1959 Saltram Vintage Rare Tawny	Barossa Valley
98	NV Chambers Rosewood Rare Muscat	Rutherglen
97	NV Seppeltsfield Paramount Tokay 500 ml	Rutherglen
97	NV All Saints Rare Muscat	Rutherglen
97	NV All Saints Rare Muscat Museum Release	Rutherglen
97	NV All Saints Rare Tokay (375 ml)	Rutherglen
97	NV Campbells Isabella Rare Tokay	Rutherglen
97	NV Chambers Rosewood Rare Muscadelle	Rutherglen
97	NV Morris Old Premium Liqueur Muscat	Rutherglen
97	NV Seppeltsfield Rare Muscat	Rutherglen
97	NV Seppeltsfield Rare Tokay	Rutherglen
97	NV Stanton & Killeen Rare Muscat	Rutherglen
96	NV Penfolds Great Grandfather Rare Old Liqueur Tawny	Barossa Valley
96	NV Seppeltsfield Paramount Muscat 500 ml	Rutherglen
96	NV Seppeltsfield Paramount Tawny 500 ml	Barossa Valley
96	NV Seppeltsfield Rare Tawny DP90	Barossa Valley
96	NV Campbells Merchant Prince Rare Muscat	Rutherglen
96	NV Chambers Rosewood Special Tokay	Rutherglen
96	NV Morris Old Premium Liqueur Tokay	Rutherglen
96	NV Pfeiffer Rare Muscat	Rutherglen
96	NV Seppeltsfield Grand Tokay	Rutherglen
96	NV Stanton & Killeen Grand Muscat	Rutherglen

Best wineries of the regions

The nomination of the best wineries of the regions has evolved into a three-level classification. At the very top are the wineries with their names and stars printed in red; these have been generally recognised for having a long track record of excellence – truly the best of the best. Next are wineries with their stars (but not their names) printed in red, and which have had a consistent record of excellence for at least the last three years. Those wineries with black stars have been consistently at or near the top for this period.

ADELAIDE HILLS

Anvers ★★★★★
Ashton Hills ★★★★★
Barratt ★★★★★
Bird in Hand ★★★★★
Chain of Ponds ★★★★★
Deviation Road ★★★★★
Geoff Weaver ★★★★★
Hahndorf Hill Winery ★★★★★
Howard Vineyard ★★★★★
K1 by Geoff Hardy ★★★★★
La Linea ★★★★★
Leabrook Estate ★★★★★
Mike Press Wines ★★★★★
Mount Torrens Vineyards ★★★★★
Murdoch Hill ★★★★★
Nepenthe ★★★★★
Ngeringa ★★★★★
Nova Vita Wines ★★★★★
Paracombe Wines ★★★★★
Petaluma ★★★★★
Pike & Joyce ★★★★★
Romney Park Wines ★★★★★
Setanta Wines ★★★★★
Shaw & Smith ★★★★★
Starvedog Lane ★★★★★

ADELAIDE ZONE

Hewitson ★★★★★
Penfolds Magill Estate ★★★★★
Tenafeate Creek Wines ★★★★★

ALBANY

Kalgan River Wines ★★★★★

BALLARAT

Tomboy Hill ★★★★★

BAROSSA VALLEY

Barossa Valley Estate ★★★★★
Charles Melton ★★★★★
Chateau Tanunda ★★★★★
David Franz ★★★★★
Deisen ★★★★★
Dorrien Estate ★★★★★
Dutschke Wines ★★★★★
Elderton ★★★★★
Epsilon ★★★★★
Gibson Barossavale/Loose End
    ★★★★★
Glaetzer Wines ★★★★★
Glaymond/Tscharke Wines ★★★★★
Grant Burge ★★★★★
Haan Wines ★★★★★
Hare's Chase ★★★★★
Head Wines ★★★★★
Hentley Farm Wines ★★★★★
Heritage Wines ★★★★★
Jacob's Creek ★★★★★
John Duval Wines ★★★★★
Kaesler Wines ★★★★★
Kalleske ★★★★★
Kurtz Family Vineyards ★★★★★

Landhaus Estate ★★★★★
Langmeil Winery ★★★★★
Laughing Jack ★★★★★
Magpie Estate ★★★★★
Massena Vineyards ★★★★★
Maverick Wines ★★★★★
Murray Street Vineyard ★★★★★
Penfolds ★★★★★
Peter Lehmann ★★★★★
Rockford ★★★★★
Rohrlach Family Wines ★★★★★
Saltram ★★★★★
Seabrook Wines ★★★★★
Seppeltsfield ★★★★★
Sheep's Back ★★★★★
Smallfry Wines ★★★★★
Sons of Eden ★★★★★
Spinifex ★★★★★
St Hallett ★★★★★
Teusner ★★★★★
The Colonial Estate ★★★★★
Thorn-Clarke Wines ★★★★★
Torbreck Vintners ★★★★★
Trevor Jones/Kellermeister ★★★★★
Turkey Flat ★★★★★
Two Hands Wines ★★★★★
Westlake Vineyards ★★★★★
Wolf Blass ★★★★★
Yelland & Papps ★★★★★

BAROSSA VALLEY/ADELAIDE HILLS
Fox Gordon ★★★★★

BEECHWORTH
Giaconda ★★★★★
Smiths Vineyard ★★★★★
Sorrenberg ★★★★★

BENDIGO
Balgownie Estate ★★★★★
BlackJack Vineyards ★★★★★
Bress ★★★★★
Harcourt Valley Vineyards ★★★★★
Killiecrankie Wines ★★★★★
Newbridge Wines ★★★★★

Pondalowie Vineyards ★★★★★
Turner's Crossing Vineyard ★★★★★

CANBERRA DISTRICT
Capital Wines ★★★★★
Clonakilla ★★★★★
Collector Wines ★★★★★
Eden Road Wines ★★★★★
Lark Hill ★★★★★
Lerida Estate ★★★★★
Mount Majura Vineyard ★★★★★
Ravensworth ★★★★★
Shaw Vineyard Estate ★★★★★

CENTRAL VICTORIA ZONE
Mt Terrible ★★★★★

CENTRAL WESTERN AUSTRALIA ZONE
Across the Lake ★★★★★

CLARE VALLEY
Annie's Lane ★★★★★
Crabtree Watervale Wines ★★★★★
Gaelic Cemetery Wines ★★★★★
Greg Cooley Wines ★★★★★
Grosset ★★★★★
Jim Barry Wines ★★★★★
Kilikanoon ★★★★★
Kirrihill Wines ★★★★★
Knappstein ★★★★★
KT & The Falcon ★★★★★
Leasingham ★★★★★
Mitchell ★★★★★
Mount Horrocks ★★★★★
Neagles Rock Vineyards ★★★★★
O'Leary Walker Wines ★★★★★
Paulett ★★★★★
Pikes ★★★★★
Skillogalee ★★★★★
Taylors ★★★★★
Wendouree ★★★★★
Wilson Vineyard ★★★★★

COONAWARRA
Balnaves of Coonawarra ★★★★★

Brand's Laira Coonawarra ★★★★★
Jamiesons Run ★★★★★
Lindemans ★★★★★
Majella ★★★★★
Murdock ★★★★★
Parker Coonawarra Estate ★★★★★
Punters Corner ★★★★★
Wynns Coonawarra Estate ★★★★★
Zema Estate ★★★★★

EDEN VALLEY
Eden Hall ★★★★★
Eden Springs ★★★★★
Flaxman Wines ★★★★★
Heggies Vineyard ★★★★★
Henschke ★★★★★
Irvine ★★★★★
Mountadam ★★★★★
Pewsey Vale ★★★★★
Poonawatta Estate ★★★★★
Radford Wines ★★★★★
Springton Hills Wines ★★★★★
Yalumba ★★★★★

EDEN VALLEY/CLARE VALLEY
Leo Buring ★★★★★

GEELONG
Austin's Wines ★★★★★
Bannockburn Vineyards ★★★★★
Bellarine Estate ★★★★★
Clyde Park Vineyard ★★★★★
Curlewis Winery ★★★★★
Farr Rising/by Farr ★★★★★
Lethbridge Wines ★★★★★
Leura Park Estate ★★★★★
Oakdene Vineyards ★★★★★
Paradise IV ★★★★★
Provenance Wines ★★★★★
Scotchmans Hill ★★★★★
Shadowfax ★★★★★

GEOGRAPHE
Capel Vale ★★★★★

GIPPSLAND
Bass Phillip ★★★★★
Bellvale Wines ★★★★★
Caledonia Australis ★★★★★
Phillip Island Vineyard ★★★★★

GLENROWAN
Baileys of Glenrowan ★★★★★
Taminick Cellars ★★★★★

GRAMPIANS
Best's Wines ★★★★★
Clayfield Wines ★★★★★
Grampians Estate ★★★★★
Hyde Park Wines ★★★★★
Kimbarra Wines ★★★★★
Mount Langi Ghiran Vineyards
   ★★★★★
Seppelt ★★★★★
The Story Wines ★★★★★
Westgate Vineyard ★★★★★

GRANITE BELT
Boireann ★★★★★
Summit Estate ★★★★★

GREAT SOUTHERN
Abbey Creek Vineyard ★★★★★
Alkoomi ★★★★★
Bobtail Ridge Wines ★★★★★
Castelli Estate ★★★★★
Castle Rock Estate ★★★★★
Duke's Vineyard ★★★★★
Ferngrove ★★★★★
Forest Hill Vineyard ★★★★★
Frankland Estate ★★★★★
Harewood Estate ★★★★★
Marchand & Burch ★★★★★
Moombaki Wines ★★★★★

HEATHCOTE
Domaine Asmara ★★★★★
Greenstone Vineyard ★★★★★
Heathcote Estate ★★★★★
Jasper Hill ★★★★★
La Pleiade ★★★★★

Shelmerdine Vineyards ★★★★★
Stefani Estate ★★★★★

HENTY
Crawford River Wines ★★★★★

HILLTOPS
Barwang ★★★★★
Chalkers Crossing ★★★★★
Grove Estate Wines ★★★★★

HUNTER VALLEY
Allandale ★★★★★
Audrey Wilkinson Vineyard ★★★★★
Bimbadgen Estate ★★★★★
Briar Ridge Vineyard ★★★★★
Brokenwood ★★★★★
Capercaillie ★★★★★
Chateau Francois ★★★★★
Chateau Pâto ★★★★★
Chatto Wines ★★★★★
David Hook Wines ★★★★★
De Iuliis ★★★★★
Drayton's Family Wines ★★★★★
First Creek Wines ★★★★★
Glenguin Estate ★★★★★
Hungerford Hill ★★★★★
Keith Tulloch Wine ★★★★★
Lake's Folly ★★★★★
Margan Family ★★★★★
McLeish Estate ★★★★★
McWilliam's Mount Pleasant
    ★★★★★
Meerea Park ★★★★★
Mistletoe Wines ★★★★★
Mount View Estate ★★★★★
Noonji Estate ★★★★★
Oakvale ★★★★★
Pepper Tree Wines ★★★★★
Pokolbin Estate ★★★★★
Poole's Rock/Cockfighter's Ghost
    ★★★★★
Saddlers Creek ★★★★★
Scarborough Wine Co ★★★★★
Tamburlaine ★★★★★
Thomas Wines ★★★★★

Tintilla Wines ★★★★★
Tower Estate ★★★★★
Tulloch ★★★★★
Two Rivers ★★★★★
Tyrrell's ★★★★★
Wandin Valley Estate ★★★★★

KANGAROO ISLAND
The Islander Estate Vineyards
    ★★★★★

KING VALLEY
Brown Brothers ★★★★★

LANGHORNE CREEK
Angas Plains Estate ★★★★★
Bleasdale Vineyards ★★★★★
Bremerton Wines ★★★★★
John's Blend ★★★★★
Lake Breeze Wines ★★★★★

LANGHORNE CREEK/MCLAREN VALE
Beach Road ★★★★★

MACEDON RANGES
Bindi Wine Growers ★★★★★
Curly Flat ★★★★★
Granite Hills ★★★★★
Mount William Winery ★★★★★

MARGARET RIVER
Ashbrook Estate ★★★★★
Brookland Valley ★★★★★
Brown Hill Estate ★★★★★
Cape Mentelle ★★★★★
Celestial Bay ★★★★★
Chalice Bridge Estate ★★★★★
Chapman Grove Wines ★★★★★
Clairault ★★★★★
Cullen Wines ★★★★★
Devil's Lair ★★★★★
Driftwood Estate ★★★★★
Edwards Wines ★★★★★
Evans & Tate ★★★★★
Evoi Wines ★★★★★
Fermoy Estate ★★★★★

Fire Gully ★★★★★
Flametree ★★★★★
Forester Estate ★★★★★
Fraser Gallop Estate ★★★★★
Hamelin Bay ★★★★★
Happs ★★★★★
Hay Shed Hill Wines ★★★★★
Hutton Wines ★★★★★
Juniper Estate ★★★★★
Leeuwin Estate ★★★★★
Lenton Brae Wines ★★★★★
Merops Wines ★★★★★
Moss Wood ★★★★★
Peccavi Wines ★★★★★
Pedestal Vineyard Wines ★★★★★
Pierro ★★★★★
Rockfield Estate ★★★★★
Rosily Vineyard ★★★★★
Sandalford ★★★★★
Stella Bella Wines ★★★★★
Streicker ★★★★★
Thompson Estate ★★★★★
Vasse Felix ★★★★★
Voyager Estate ★★★★★
Watershed Wines ★★★★★
Were Estate ★★★★★
Wills Domain ★★★★★
Wise Wine ★★★★★
Woodlands ★★★★★
Woodside Valley Estate ★★★★★
Xanadu Wines ★★★★★

MARGARET RIVER/DENMARK
Howard Park/MadFish ★★★★★

MCLAREN VALE
Aramis Vineyards ★★★★★
Cape Barren Wines ★★★★★
Chalk Hill ★★★★★
Chapel Hill ★★★★★
Clarendon Hills ★★★★★
Coriole ★★★★★
d'Arenberg ★★★★★
DogRidge Wine Company ★★★★★
Gemtree Vineyards ★★★★★
Hardys ★★★★★

Kangarilla Road Vineyard ★★★★★
Kay Brothers Amery Vineyards
    ★★★★★
Marius Wines ★★★★★
McLaren Vale III Associates ★★★★★
Mitolo Wines ★★★★★
Mr Riggs Wine Company ★★★★★
Paxton ★★★★★
Penny's Hill ★★★★★
Pirramimma ★★★★★
Primo Estate ★★★★★
Richard Hamilton ★★★★★
SC Pannell ★★★★★
Scarpantoni Estate ★★★★★
The Old Faithful Estate ★★★★★
Tintara ★★★★★
Wirra Wirra ★★★★★

MCLAREN VALE/BAROSSA VALLEY
Dandelion Vineyards ★★★★★

MCLAREN VALE/FLEURIEU PENINSULA
Reynella ★★★★★

MORNINGTON PENINSULA
Allies Wines ★★★★★
Darling Park ★★★★★
Eldridge Estate of Red Hill ★★★★★
Hurley Vineyard ★★★★★
Kooyong ★★★★★
Main Ridge Estate ★★★★★
Merricks Creek Wines ★★★★★
Merricks Estate ★★★★★
Montalto Vineyards ★★★★★
Moorooduc Estate ★★★★★
Ocean Eight Vineyard & Winery
    ★★★★★
Paradigm Hill ★★★★★
Paringa Estate ★★★★★
Port Phillip Estate ★★★★★
Prancing Horse Estate ★★★★★
Quealy ★★★★★
Red Hill Estate ★★★★★
Scorpo Wines ★★★★★
Stonier Wines ★★★★★
Ten Minutes by Tractor ★★★★★

Tuck's Ridge ★★★★★
Willow Creek Vineyard ★★★★★
Yabby Lake Vineyard ★★★★★

MOUNT BARKER
3 Drops ★★★★★
Gilberts ★★★★★
Paul Nelson Wines ★★★★★
Plantagenet ★★★★★
Poacher's Ridge Vineyard ★★★★★
West Cape Howe Wines ★★★★★

MOUNT BENSON
M. Chapoutier Australia ★★★★★

MOUNT LOFTY RANGES ZONE
Michael Hall Wines ★★★★★

MUDGEE
di Lusso Estate ★★★★★
Robert Oatley Vineyards ★★★★★
Robert Stein Vineyard ★★★★★

NAGAMBIE LAKES
Tahbilk ★★★★★

NEW ENGLAND
Richfield Estate ★★★★★

ORANGE
Belgravia Vineyards ★★★★★
Bloodwood ★★★★★
Cumulus Wines ★★★★★
Philip Shaw Wines ★★★★★
Printhie Wines ★★★★★

PEMBERTON
Bellarmine Wines ★★★★★
Fonty's Pool Vineyards ★★★★★
Truffle Hill Wines ★★★★★

PORT PHILLIP ZONE
Onannon ★★★★★

PYRENEES
Amherst Winery ★★★★★
Dalwhinnie ★★★★★
Mitchell Harris Wines ★★★★★
Summerfield ★★★★★

PYRENEES/MORNINGTON PENINSULA
Massoni ★★★★★

RIVERINA
De Bortoli ★★★★★
McWilliam's ★★★★★
Nugan Estate ★★★★★

RUTHERGLEN
All Saints Estate ★★★★★
Buller ★★★★★
Campbells ★★★★★
Chambers Rosewood ★★★★★
Morris ★★★★★
Pfeiffer Wines ★★★★★
Stanton & Killeen Wines ★★★★★
Warrabilla ★★★★★

SHOALHAVEN COAST
Coolangatta Estate ★★★★★

SOUTH AUSTRALIA
Tapanappa ★★★★★
Tollana ★★★★★

SOUTHERN FLEURIEU
Madeleines Wines ★★★★★
Mt Billy ★★★★★

SOUTHERN HIGHLANDS
Centennial Vineyards ★★★★★
Pulpit Rock ★★★★★

STRATHBOGIE RANGES
Maygars Hill Winery ★★★★★
Plunkett Fowles ★★★★★

SUNBURY
Craiglee ★★★★★
Galli Estate ★★★★★

SWAN VALLEY

Faber Vineyard ★★★★★
Houghton ★★★★★
John Kosovich Wines ★★★★★

TASMANIA

Bay of Fires ★★★★★
Bream Creek ★★★★★
Craigow ★★★★★
Derwent Estate ★★★★★
Domaine A ★★★★★
`ese Vineyards ★★★★★
Freycinet ★★★★★
Frogmore Creek ★★★★★
Jansz Tasmania ★★★★★
Kate Hill Wines ★★★★★
Meadowbank Estate ★★★★★
Morningside Vineyard ★★★★★
Pipers Brook Vineyard ★★★★★
Pirie Tasmania ★★★★★
Pooley Wines ★★★★★
Pressing Matters ★★★★★
Stefano Lubiana ★★★★★
Stoney Rise ★★★★★
Tamar Ridge ★★★★★

UPPER GOULBURN

Delatite ★★★★★

VARIOUS

Ainsworth & Snelson ★★★★★
Hesketh Wine Company ★★★★★
Postcode Wines ★★★★★

WESTERN AUSTRALIA

Larry Cherubino Wines ★★★★★

WRATTONBULLY

Terre à Terre ★★★★★

YARRA VALLEY

Carlei Estate & Carlei Green Vineyards
★★★★★
Coldstream Hills ★★★★★
De Bortoli ★★★★★
Domaine Chandon ★★★★★
Dominique Portet ★★★★★
Gembrook Hill ★★★★★
Giant Steps/Innocent Bystander
★★★★★
Helen's Hill Estate ★★★★★
Hillcrest Vineyard ★★★★★
Hoddles Creek Estate ★★★★★
Jamsheed ★★★★★
Lillydale Estate ★★★★★
Mandala ★★★★★
Mayer ★★★★★
Mount Mary ★★★★★
Oakridge ★★★★★
PHI ★★★★★
Punch ★★★★★
Serrat ★★★★★
Seville Estate ★★★★★
St Huberts ★★★★★
Stuart Wines ★★★★★
Tarrawarra Estate ★★★★★
The Wanderer ★★★★★
Toolangi Vineyards ★★★★★
Wantirna Estate ★★★★★
Warramate ★★★★★
Wedgetail Estate ★★★★★
William Downie ★★★★★
Yarra Burn ★★★★★
Yarra Yarra ★★★★★
Yarra Yering ★★★★★
Yarrabank ★★★★★
YarraLoch ★★★★★
Yering Station ★★★★★
Yeringberg ★★★★★

Ten of the best new wineries

Each one of these wineries making its debut in the *Wine Companion* has earnt a five-star rating. They (and two other unlucky wineries) are thus the pick of the 111 new wineries in this edition. Margaret River hogs the limelight with three wineries, partly reflecting the golden run of vintages over '07 to '10 inclusive, partly the economic health of Western Australia, and partly the inherent quality of the grapes grown and the wines made in the region. South Australia provided Langhorne Creek, McLaren Vale, Barossa Valley, Eden Valley and the Adelaide Zone, leaving Heathcote in Victoria and Hunter Valley in New South Wales with one winery each.

BEACH ROAD Langhorne Creek/McLaren Vale, SA / PAGE 98
Winemaker Briony and viticulturist Tony Hoare met while undertaking the wine science degree at the Roseworthy campus of Adelaide University. This led to their marriage and, after 15 years, working for producers here and in Europe, they set up their own wine consulting business and established Beach Road, with a focus on alternative varieties. This stemmed from Briony's vintage experience in Piedmont, working with barbera, nebbiolo, gavi and moscato, and from the substantial exposure both had to grenache, shiraz and mourvedre, but it was their Fiano and Greco di Tufo that had outstanding success at the Australian Alternative Wines Show 2009.

DANDELION VINEYARDS McLaren Vale/Barossa Valley, SA / PAGE 199
Dandelion Vineyards is a partnership between Peggy and Carl Lindner, Elena and Zar Brooks, and Fiona and Brad Rey. The Lindner and Rey families are viticulturists, the Brooks winemaker (Elena) and marketing supremo (Zar). The packaging is striking, the individual wine names pure Zar Brooks. The wines range from conventional to unconventional. In the former category, the trophy-winning 2009 Wonderland of the Eden Valley Riesling. Unconventional is the 2007 Lion's Tooth of McLaren Vale Shiraz, which is co-fermented with riesling. Everyone involved in the venture has a (real) day job that allows them the luxury of making small quantities of genuinely exciting wines.

DOMAINE ASMARA Heathcote, Vic / PAGE 218
Andreas Greiving was raised on the family farm in northwestern Germany, where in his childhood he successfully made fruit wines. This planted the seed in his mind of owning a vineyard, but he became a chemical engineer, working for large companies in both Europe and Asia. When the GFC struck, he was offered a substantial redundancy payment that enabled him to buy the 12-ha vineyard, which had been planted in 2001. Andreas and dentist wife Hennijati finished building their house on the property in May 2010, and opened the cellar door and bistro a few months later. Aged 47, Andreas has no desire to get back into the corporate world, happily doing all the work in the vineyard, with help from his wife.

NOONJI ESTATE Hunter Valley, NSW / **PAGE 468**
This is a great example of how to satisfy an urge to become vignerons. Buy a small, 40-year-old vineyard planted to the right varieties that needs a lot of TLC but doesn't cost too much; spend weekends and holidays rehabilitating it; and, having done so, get one of the best contract winemakers in the Hunter able to handle small volumes of grapes. Owners Peter and Barbara Jensen have done all that, and are now enjoying the sweet taste of success.

PAUL NELSON WINES Great Southern, WA / **PAGE 490**
How to cram a lifetime into eight years. A 2001 BSc in viticulture and oenology from Curtin University, plus two vintages in Western Australia by '02, then late '02 a vintage in Santa Ynez (California) with organic zinfandel and viognier, next to South Africa with Distell ('03–'06 vintages), Rheinhessen, Germany, (November '03), Cyprus ('04–'06) with maratheftiko, xynesteri and lefkada, then to Indage in India ('07), back to Western Australia's Houghton ('08), and finally chief winemaker with Galafrey ('09). He drew breath once in South Africa, and made Bianca Swart his partner.

PECCAVI WINES Margaret River, WA / **PAGE 492**
In these uncertain times no start-up winemaking venture is guaranteed success. However, Jeremy Muller, owner of Peccavi Wines, has made all the right moves. He has appointed a highly qualified and experienced viticulturist in the form of Colin Bell, and his contract winemaking team is headed by Brian Fletcher, one of Margaret River's most experienced winemakers, supported by Amanda Kraemer, who was winner of the Young Australian Winemaker of the Year Award 2005, and Bruce Dukes, another Margaret River veteran. The result has been wines of exceptional quality.

PEDESTAL VINEYARD WINES Margaret River, WA / **PAGE 493**
Some might say this is a marriage made in heaven. It is based on a 13-year-old vineyard owned by wine retailer Greg Brindle and wife Kerilee, with winemaker Larry Cherubino and wife Edwina as partners in the business. Yes, I know Cherubino has already taken pride of place in this edition of the *Wine Companion*, but that shouldn't disqualify what is a separate business producing such outstanding wines, and the near certainty of continuing to do so in the years ahead.

SPRINGTON HILLS WINES Eden Valley, SA / **PAGE 603**
The Ciccocioppo family migrated from central Italy in the 1950s with wine in their veins. Second generation John Ciccocioppo and wife Connie purchased a grazing property at Springton, and in 2001 began planting shiraz and riesling. Each year they increased the shiraz and riesling blocks, but also added smaller amounts of cabernet sauvignon, grenache and a little montepulciano. John and brother Remo under-took TAFE studies in winemaking, and prior to the '05 vintage a small winery was erected onsite. The '06 Eden Valley Shiraz won a double gold medal at the Sydney International Wine Show '09.

STREICKER Margaret River, WA / **PAGE 613**

Life in the fast lane for New York resident John Streicker evidently comes naturally. In 2002 he purchased the Yallingup Protea Farm and vineyards, followed by the acquisition of the long-established Ironstone Vineyard in 2003, and finally the Bridgeland Vineyard, planted in 1998/99 by the previous owner, and boasting an 18-ha dam. With just under 150 ha of mature vineyards to pick the eyes out of, and Bruce Dukes as winemaker, it is no surprise the wines are exceptional.

TENAFEATE CREEK WINES Adelaide Zone, SA / **PAGE 635**

The Tenafeate Creek Wines property is only 1 ha, and when long-term friends Larry Costa, a former hairdresser, and Dominic Rimaldi decided to make a small amount of red wine in 2002, it was a hobby. Then the winemaking bug took hold, and although Larry had macular degeneration that had ended his career as a hairdresser, he took on responsibility for the red wines, fermented in open milk vats and basket pressed. The wines have had remarkable success, and are modestly priced, with several back vintages available at cellar door.

Ten dark horses

The principal requirement for inclusion in this group was a first-time five-star rating. This year outposts such as Queensland's Granite Belt and New South Wales' Southern Highlands and Hilltops stand shoulder to shoulder with the Hunter and Barossa valleys, Rutherglen, Langhorne Creek and the Mornington Peninsula.

CENTENNIAL VINEYARDS Southern Highlands, NSW / PAGE 159
The Southern Highlands is centred around the towns of Moss Vale (where I spent my childhood during the Second World War), Bowral and Mittagong. It is a beautiful region, and Centennial Vineyards is one of its showpieces. The climate is unpredictable, so Centennial does not hesitate to source grapes from Orange. Winemaker Tony Cosgriff is especially talented, providing high-quality, cool-climate wines with a common core of finesse and elegance. Another feature is value for money.

CHATEAU FRANCOIS Hunter Valley, NSW / PAGE 168
The annual production of this off-the-beaten track winery is very small, but Don Francois sells limited quantities of several back-vintages of beautiful estate-grown Semillon at ludicrously low prices. A few days before writing this I had a glorious bottle of the 2003 Semillon ($14) that was unbelievably fresh and long. Forty-year-old vines are part of the package, as is Don's skill making the wine for almost as long.

CHATEAU TANUNDA Barossa Valley, SA / PAGE 169
Owner John Geber (a former South African) is every bit as much a cricket tragic as a wine tragic, weaving the strands together in tireless promotion, first with Cowra Estate but since 1998 with the historic Chateau Tanunda winery. He was among the early movers in understanding the benefits of making single-vineyard Shirazs that reflected the 'Terroirs of the Barossa Valley' (adopting that phrase as an integral part of the branding process), and producing a series of exceptional wines from the '08 vintage.

DAVID FRANZ Barossa Valley, SA / PAGE 200
David Franz is one of Margaret and Peter Lehmann's sons. He has dabbled with tertiary courses in graphic design, architecture and hospitality business management before backpacking with wife Nicki in various parts of the world. Impending fatherhood forced him back to Australia and, almost incidentally, into small-scale winemaking. The genes are strong, it seems, for the wines are excellent.

DRAYTON'S FAMILY WINES Hunter Valley, NSW / PAGE 223
The death of quietly spoken Trevor Drayton in 2007 caused by an explosion at the winery was a horrific event, following as it did the deaths of Reg and Pam Drayton in the 1994 Seaview air disaster and the '79 death of Barrie Drayton, overcome by chlorine fumes at his winery. Winemaker William (Will) Rikard-Bell was working with Trevor at the time, and suffered terrible burns that very nearly took his life. However, in '09 he was married, and made the brilliant gold-medal and trophy-winning Reserve Chardonnay instrumental in the winery's five-star rating.

GROVE ESTATE WINES Hilltops, NSW / PAGE 288

I have visited the Grove Estate vineyard on a number of occasions in the last 20 years, and have always been impressed by every aspect of the site. The founding partners' intention was to simply sell the grapes from the 55 ha of vines (10 varieties, including four Italian), but in 1997 they decided to hold back some grapes for Grove Estate Wines. The quality has always been very good, but it has been the Nebbiolos made in '06, '07 and '08 that have propelled Grove Estate into the front line, none more so that the gold-medal and trophy-winning '07 Sommita Nebbiolo.

LAKE BREEZE WINES Langhorne Creek, SA / PAGE 368

Successive generations of the Follett family have lived at Langhorne Creek since 1880. Up to the 1930s, they were broad-acre farmers; they then diversified by establishing vineyards and selling the grapes until '87 (a time of grape surplus), when they decided to have part of the grape production vinified. The wines have always been good, especially at the modest prices most are sold for. A high percentage of the portfolio are medium-bodied, supple and elegant red wines attesting to the quite cool, maritime-moderated climate.

OCEAN EIGHT VINEYARD & WINERY Mornington Peninsula, Vic / PAGE 476

This is the second venture of the Aylward family (Chris, Gail and son Michael) who established Kooyong in 1996, and quickly gained a high reputation for the wines made for them by Sandro Mosele. In 2003 they sold Kooyong to Giorgio and Dianne Gjergja, retaining a 3.6-ha planting of pinot gris at Shoreham, where the winery is situated. They also purchased land at Tuerong, planting 7 ha of pinot noir and 3 ha of chardonnay, providing high-quality grapes, pinot noir to the fore.

SUMMIT ESTATE Granite Belt, Qld / PAGE 617

Owned by a syndicate of 10 professionals who live and work in Brisbane, this is another face of the thriving Granite Belt region. With the talented Paola Cabezas Rhymer as winemaker, you find the QC Cabernet Sauvignon Merlot Petit Verdot Malbec and the Alto Spanish Collection Monastell Garnacha Shyra Tempranillo Cabernet Tannat (both from 2008) as flagships, the labels not only suggesting a food match but providing detailed recipes. Wine education courses, contract winemaking and wines from other wineries being sold make this a must-visit destination.

TAMINICK CELLARS Glenrowan, Vic / PAGE 626

The address of 339 Booth Road, Taminick via Glenrowan puts you on notice: James Booth may have obtained his wine science degree from Charles Sturt University as recently as 2008, but his great grandfather Esca Booth established Taminick Cellars in 1904, and planted 9 ha of shiraz (and other varieties) in '19. This blend of old and new is a potent one, with a fresh and lively '08 barrel-fermented Chardonnay ($12), an '08 co-fermented Shiraz and Trebbiano ($18) called Ianus, an alternative spelling of Janus, representing the new, fortified wines the old.

Special value wines

As always, these are lists of 10 of the best value wines, not the 10 best wines in each price category. There are literally dozens of wines with similar points and prices, and the choice is necessarily an arbitrary one. I have, however, attempted to give as much varietal and style choice as the limited numbers allow.

TEN OF THE BEST VALUE Whites $10 and under

89	2009 Angove Butterfly Ridge Riesling Traminer	$7.25
87	2009 McWilliam's Inheritance Riesling	$7.50
88	2009 De Bortoli Montage Semillon Sauvignon Blanc	$9.50
90	2006 Kopparossa Hoggies Estate Chardonnay	$9.95
88	2008 Littore Family Littore Family Wines Pinot Grigio	$9.95
93	2009 Angove Long Row Riesling	$10
91	2009 Light's View Wines/Pure Vision Organic Nature's Step Wild Ferment Chardonnay	$10
90	2009 Light's View/Pure Vision Organic Nature's Step Wild Ferment Sauvignon Blanc	$10
88	2009 Deakin Estate Sauvignon Blanc	$10
87	2009 Casella yellow tail Sauvignon Blanc Semillon	$10

TEN OF THE BEST VALUE Reds $10 and under

89	2008 Quarisa 30 Mile Shiraz	$9
90	2009 Kopparossa Hoggies Estate Cabernet Sauvignon	$9.95
88	2008 Littore Family Wines Tempranillo	$9.95
92	2006 Heaslip Philly's Block Dry Grown Hand Picked Clare Valley Cabernet Sauvignon	$10
90	2009 Deakin Estate Rose	$10
90	2008 Henry's Drive Vignerons Morse Code Padthaway Shiraz	$10
90	2007 Wombat Lodge Margaret River Cabernet Sauvignon Merlot Petit Verdot Malbec Cabernet Franc	$10
89	2006 Heaslip Dayspring Dry Grown Hand Picked Clare Valley Shiraz	$10
89	2006 Stuart Huma Yarra Valley Shiraz	$10
88	2008 De Bortoli Sacred Hill Cabernet Merlot	$10

Unexpectedly, there were more red than white wines to choose from, the reverse of the situation a year ago.

TEN OF THE BEST VALUE Whites $10–$15

94	2009 Mike Press Adelaide Hills Chardonnay	$11
92	2008 Broken Gate Side Gate Clare Valley Riesling	$12
95	2008 BackVintage Margaret River Chardonnay	$13
94	2007 Juul Hollydene Estate Semillon	$14
94	2009 Two Rivers Hidden Hive Hunter Valley Verdelho	$14
93	2009 Charles Sturt University Chardonnay	$14.30
93	2009 Chateau Dorrien San Fernando Estate Cloud Catcher Sauvignon Blanc	$15
93	2009 Barwick Sauvignon Blanc Semillon	$15
92	2009 Helen's Hill Estate Ingram Rd Yarra Valley Sauvignon Blanc	$15
92	2009 Madeleines Nangkita Single Vineyard Gewurztraminer	$15

TEN OF THE BEST VALUE Reds $10–$15

93	2006 BackVintage Barossa Shiraz	$13
93	2008 Bidgeebong Triangle Shiraz	$13
94	2008 Mike Press Adelaide Hills Cabernet Sauvignon	$14
93	2008 Evans & Tate Gnangara Cabernet Merlot	$14
92	2008 Dalfarras Cabernet Sangiovese	$14.95
94	2008 Arundel Shiraz	$15
94	2009 Jacob's Creek Three Vines Shiraz Grenache Sangiovese	$15
94	2008 Kirrihill Clare Valley Shiraz	$15
94	2008 Old Plains Longhop Mount Lofty Ranges Shiraz	$15
94	2009 Taminick Cellars 1919 Series Alicante Rose	$15

Australia's geographical indications

The process of formally mapping Australia's wine regions is all but complete, although will never come to a halt – for one thing, climate change is lurking in the wings. The division into states, zones, regions and subregions follows; those regions or subregions marked with an asterisk are not yet registered, and may never be, but are in common usage. I have given up any attempt to make sense of the Hunter Valley Zone. Thus you will find no mention of the Lower Hunter Valley, in its place simply Hunter Valley.

I am still in front of the game with Tasmania, dividing it into Northern, Southern and East Coast, and, to a lesser degree, have anticipated that the Darling Downs and coastal hinterland region of Queensland will seek recognition under this or some similar name. In similar vein, I have included Ballarat (with 16 wineries); the promising Mount Gambier district, which has already produced a trophy-winning Pinot Noir and excellent Sauvignon Blanc (four wineries); and the equally promising Southern Eyre Peninsula (three wineries).

An intriguing addition is the proposed Mountain Foothills GI, not as a subregion of Orange, but a region in its own right (its original application was as a subregion to be called Orange Foothills).

State/Zone	Region	Subregion
AUSTRALIA		
South Eastern Australia	* The South Eastern Australia Zone incorporates the whole of the states of NSW, Vic and Tasmania and only part of Qld and SA.	
NEW SOUTH WALES		
Big Rivers	Murray Darling Perricoota Riverina Swan Hill	
Central Ranges	Cowra Mudgee Orange Mountain Foothills*	

State/Zone	Region	Subregion
Hunter Valley	Hunter	Broke Fordwich Mount View★ Pokolbin★ Upper Hunter Valley★
Northern Rivers	Hastings River	
Northern Slopes	New England Australia	
South Coast	Shoalhaven Coast Southern Highlands	
Southern New South Wales	Canberra District Gundagai Hilltops Tumbarumba	
Western Plains		

SOUTH AUSTRALIA

Adelaide (Super Zone, includes Mount Lofty Ranges, Fleurieu and Barossa)		
Barossa	Barossa Valley Eden Valley	 High Eden
Far North	Southern Flinders Ranges	
Fleurieu	Currency Creek Kangaroo Island Langhorne Creek McLaren Vale Southern Fleurieu	
Limestone Coast	Coonawarra Mount Benson Mount Gambier★ Padthaway Robe Wrattonbully	
Lower Murray	Riverland	

State/Zone	Region	Subregion
Mount Lofty Ranges	Adelaide Hills	Lenswood
		Piccadilly Valley
	Adelaide Plains	Polish Hill River★
	Clare Valley	Watervale★
The Peninsulas	Southern Eyre Peninsula★	

VICTORIA

Central Victoria	Bendigo	
	Goulburn Valley	Nagambie Lakes
	Heathcote	
	Strathbogie Ranges	
	Upper Goulburn	
Gippsland		
North East Victoria	Alpine Valleys	
	Beechworth	
	Glenrowan	
	King Valley	
	Rutherglen	
North West Victoria	Murray Darling	
	Swan Hill	
Port Phillip	Geelong	
	Macedon Ranges	
	Mornington Peninsula	
	Sunbury	
	Yarra Valley	
Western Victoria	Ballarat★	
	Grampians	Great Western
	Henty	
	Pyrenees	

WESTERN AUSTRALIA

Central Western Australia		
Eastern Plains, Inland and North of Western Australia		

State/Zone	Region	Subregion
Greater Perth	Peel	
	Perth Hills	
	Swan District	Swan Valley
South West Australia	Blackwood Valley	
	Geographe	
	Great Southern	Albany
		Denmark
		Frankland River
		Mount Barker
		Porongurup
	Manjimup	
	Margaret River	
	Pemberton	
West Australian South East Coastal		

QUEENSLAND

Queensland	Granite Belt	
	Queensland Coastal★	
	South Burnett	
	Darling Downs★	

TASMANIA

Tasmania	Northern Tasmania★	
	Southern Tasmania★	
	East Coast Tasmania★	

AUSTRALIAN CAPITAL TERRITORY

NORTHERN TERRITORY

Varietal wine styles and regions

For better or worse, there simply has to be concerted action to highlight the link between regions, varieties and wine styles. It's not a question of creating the links: they are already there, and have been in existence for periods as short as 20 years or as long as 150 years. So here is an abbreviated summary of those regional styles (in turn reflected in the Best of the Best lists commencing on page 17).

Riesling

The link between riesling and the **Eden Valley** dates back to 1847, when Joseph Gilbert planted his Pewsey Vale vineyard, and quickly made its way to the nearby **Clare Valley**. These two regions stood above all others for well over 100 years, producing rieslings that shared many flavour and texture characteristics: lime (a little more obvious in the Eden Valley), apple, talc and mineral, lightly browned toasty notes emerging with 5–10 years bottle age. Within the last 20 or so years, the subregions of the **Great Southern** of Western Australia have established a deserved reputation for finely structured, elegant wines with wonderful length, sometimes shy when young, bursting into song after five years. The subregions are (in alpha order) **Albany, Denmark, Frankland River, Mount Barker** and **Porongurup**. **Tasmania**, too, produces high-class rieslings, notable for their purity and intensity courtesy of their high natural acidity. Finally, there is the small and very cool region of **Henty** in Western Victoria (once referred to as Drumborg), with exceptional riesling sharing many things in common with Tasmania.

Semillon

There is a Siamese-twin relationship between semillon and the **Hunter Valley**, producing a wine style like no other in the world for well over 100 years. The humid and very warm climate (best coupled with sandy soils not common in the region) results in wines that have a median alcohol level of 10.5% and no residual sugar when they are cold-fermented in stainless steel and bottled within three months of vintage. They are devoid of colour and have only the barest hints of grass, herb and mineral wrapped around a core of acidity. Over the next 5–10 years they develop a glowing green-gold colour, a suite of grass and citrus fruit surrounded by buttered toast and honey notes. Like rieslings, screwcaps have added decades to their cellaring life. The **Adelaide Hills** and **Margaret River** produce entirely different semillon, more structured and weighty, its alcohol 13% to 14%, and as often as not blended with sauvignon blanc, barrel fermentation of part or all common. Finally, there is a cuckoo in the nest: Peter Lehmann in the **Barossa/Eden Valley** has adapted Hunter Valley practices, picking early, fermenting in steel, bottling early, and holding the top wine for five years before release – and succeeding brilliantly.

Chardonnay

This infinitely flexible grape is grown and vinified in all 62 regions, and accounts for half of Australia's white wine grapes and wine. Incredibly, before 1970 it was all but unknown, hiding its promise here and there (**Mudgee** was one such place) under a cloak of anonymity. It was there and in the **Hunter Valley** that the first wines labelled chardonnay were made in 1971 (by Craigmoor and Tyrrell's). Its bold yellow colour, peaches and cream flavour and vanillan oak were unlike anything that had gone before and it was accepted by domestic and export markets with equal enthusiasm. When exports took off into the stratosphere between 1985 and '95, one half of Brand Australia was cheerful and cheap oak-chipped chardonnay grown in the **Riverina** and **Riverland**. By coincidence, over the same period chardonnay from the emerging cool-climate regions was starting to appear in limited quantities, its flavour and structure radically different from the warm-grown, high-cropped wine. Another 10 years on, and by 2005/06 the wine surplus was starting to build rapidly, with demand for chardonnay much less than its production. As attention swung from chardonnay to sauvignon blanc, the situation became dire. Lost in the heat of battle were (and to a degree still are) supremely elegant wines from most cool regions, **Margaret River** and **Yarra Valley** the leaders of the large band. Constant refinement of the style, and the adoption of the screwcap, puts these wines at the forefront of the battle to re-engage consumers here and abroad with what are world-class wines.

Sauvignon Blanc

Two regions, the **Adelaide Hills** and **Margaret River** stood in front of all others until they were recently joined by **Orange**; these three produce Australia's best sauvignon blanc, wines with real structure and authority. It is a matter of record that Marlborough sauvignon blanc accounts for one-third of Australia's white wine sales; all one can say (accurately) is that the basic Marlborough style is very different, and look back at what happened with Australian chardonnay. Margaret River also offers complex blends of sauvignon blanc and semillon in widely varying proportions.

Shiraz

Shiraz, like chardonnay, is by far the most important red variety and, again like chardonnay, is tremendously flexible in its ability to adapt to virtually any combination of climate and soil/terroir. Unlike chardonnay, a recent arrival, shiraz was the most important red variety throughout the 19th and 20th centuries. Its ancestral homes were the **Barossa Valley**, the **Clare Valley**, **McLaren Vale** and the **Hunter Valley**, and it still leads in those regions. With the exception of the Hunter Valley, it was as important in making fortified wine as table wine over the period 1850–1950, aided and abetted by grenache and mourvedre (mataro). In New South Wales the **Hilltops** and **Canberra District** are producing elegant, cool-grown wines that usually conceal their power (especially when co-fermented with viognier), but not their silky length. Further north, but at a higher altitude, **Orange** is also producing fine, fragrant and spicy wines. All the other New South Wales regions are capable of producing good shiraz of seriously good character and quality; shiraz ripens comfortably, but quite late in the season. Polished, sophisticated wines are the result. Victoria has a cornucopia of regions at the cooler end of the spectrum; the coolest (though not too cool for comfort) are the **Yarra Valley**, **Mornington Peninsula**, **Sunbury** and **Geelong**, all producing fragrant, spicy, medium-bodied wines. **Bendigo**, **Heathcote**, **Grampians** and **Pyrenees**, more or less running east–west across the centre of Victoria, are producing some of the most exciting medium-bodied shirazs in Australia, each with its own terroir stamp, but all combining generosity and elegance. In Western Australia, **Great Southern** and three of its five subregions, **Frankland River**, **Mount Barker** and **Porongurup**, are making magical shirazs, fragrant and spicy, fleshy yet strongly structured. **Margaret River** has been a relatively late mover, but it, too, is producing wines with exemplary varietal definition and finesse.

Cabernet Sauvignon

The tough-skinned cabernet sauvignon can be, and is, grown in all regions, but it struggles in the coolest (notably Tasmania) and loses desirable varietal definition in the warmer regions, especially in warmer vintages. Shiraz can cope with alcohol levels in excess of 14.5%; cabernet can't. In South Australia, **Coonawarra** stands supreme, its climate (although not its soil) strikingly similar to that of Bordeaux, the main difference being lower rainfall. Perfectly detailed cabernets are the result, with no need of shiraz or merlot to fill in the mid-palate, although some excellent blends are made. **Langhorne Creek** (a little warmer) and **McLaren Vale** (warmer still) have similar maritime climates, doubtless the reason why McLaren Vale manages to deal with the warmth of its summer/autumn weather. The **Eden Valley** is the most reliable of the inner regions, the other principal regions dependent on a cool summer. In Western Australia, **Margaret River**, with its extreme maritime climate shaped by the warm Indian Ocean, stands tall. It is also Australia's foremost producer of cabernet merlot et al. in the Bordeaux mix. The texture and structure of both the straight varietal and the blend is regal, often to the point of austerity when the wines are young, but the sheer power of this underlying fruit provides the balance and guarantees the future development of the wines over a conservative 20 years, especially if screwcapped. The **Great Southern** subregions of **Frankland River** and **Mount Barker** share a continental climate that is somewhat cooler than Margaret River, and has a greater diurnal temperature range. Here cabernet has an incisive, dark berry character and firm but usually fine tannins – not demanding merlot, though a touch of it and/or malbec can be beneficial. It is grown successfully through the centre and south of Victoria, but is often overshadowed by shiraz. In the last 20 years it has ceased to be a problem child and become a favourite son of the **Yarra Valley**; the forward move of vintage dates has been the key to the change.

Pinot Noir

The promiscuity of shiraz (particularly) and cabernet sauvignon is in sharp contrast to the puritanical rectitude of pinot noir. One sin of omission or commission, and the door slams shut, leaving you on the outside. Tasmania is the El Dorado for the variety, and the best is still to come, with better clones, older vines and greater exploration of the multitude of mesoclimates that Tasmania has to offer. While it is north of Central Otago (New Zealand), its vineyards are all air conditioned by the Southern Ocean and Tasman Sea, and it stands toe-to-toe with Central Otago in its ability to make deeply coloured, profound pinot with all the length one could ask for. Once on the mainland, Victoria's Port Phillip Zone, encompassing Geelong, Macedon Ranges, Sunbury, Mornington Peninsula and Yarra Valley is the epicentre of Australian pinot noir, Henty a small outpost. The sheer number of high-quality, elegant wines produced by dozens of makers put the Adelaide Hills and Porongurup (also capable of producing quality pinot) into the shade.

Sparkling Wines

The patter is eerily similar to that of pinot noir, Tasmania now and in the future the keeper of the Holy Grail, the Port Phillip Zone the centre of activity on the mainland.

Fortified Wines

Rutherglen and Glenrowan are the two (and only) regions that produce immensely complex, long-barrel-aged muscat and muscadelle, the latter called tokay for over a century, now renamed topaque. These wines have no equal in the world, Spain's Malaga nearest in terms of lusciousness, but nowhere near as complex. The other producer of a wine without parallel is Seppeltsfield in the Barossa Valley, which each year releases an explosively rich and intense tawny liqueur style that is 100% 100 years old.

Australian vintage charts

Each number represents a mark out of 10 for the quality of vintages in each region.

red wine   white wine

2006	2007	2008	2009

NSW

Hunter Valley

2006	2007	2008	2009
6	8	2	7
7	10	7	10

Upper Hunter Valley

6	7	2	7
7	8	6	9

Mudgee

8	5	8	8
7	7	7	9

Cowra

6	7	9	7
6	6	7	8

Orange

9	6	8	8
8	7	7	9

Riverina

6	7	7	7
7	7	8	6

Canberra District

8	8	8	9
9	8	9	9

Southern Highlands

8	3	9	6
8	5	8	9

Hilltops

10	6	9	8
9	6	8	8

Tumbarumba

7	7	7	8
9	9	9	8

Shoalhaven

2006	2007	2008	2009
9	7	4	7
8	8	4	7

VIC

Yarra Valley

2006	2007	2008	2009
9	7	7	**
9	8	7	7

Mornington Peninsula

9	9	9	9
8	8	8	9

Geelong

8	7	7	9
8	7	7	9

Macedon Ranges

9	8	7	7
8	8	7	8

Sunbury

8	8	8	9
7	7	7	8

Grampians

8	8	7	8
8	7	7	9

Pyrenees

9	8	8	7
8	7	8	7

Henty

8	4	9	8
9	8	8	8

Bendigo

8	6	8	4
8	7	8	7

Heathcote

2006	2007	2008	2009
9	7	9	7
7	6	7	6

Goulburn Valley

9	8	8	7
8	7	9	8

Upper Goulburn

8	**	7	6
8	4	8	8

Strathbogie Ranges

7	**	8	6
8	7	7	7

Glenrowan & Rutherglen

7	**	7	N/A
7	**	6	N/A

King Valley

8	**	7	8
7	**	9	7

Alpine Valleys

8	**	7	8
7	**	7	8

Beechworth

8	**	7	2
7	**	6	7

Gippsland

9	9	8	6
8	8	7	8

Murray Darling

8	8	8	8
9	8	8	8

SA

	2006	2007	2008	2009
Barossa Valley	10	7	8	7
	7	6	7	7
Eden Valley	7	8	7	9
	8	7	8	8
Clare Valley	8	7	6	9
	7	6	8	8
Adelaide Hills	7	8	7	9
	9	6	7	9
Coonawarra	7	7	9	7
	6	7	7	8
Padthaway	8	8	6	6
	7	7	6	8
Mount Benson & Robe	7	7	8	7
	7	7	8	8
Wrattonbully	9	6	7	6
	7	6	8	7
McLaren Vale	8	7	7	8
	7	6	7	7
Southern Fleurieu	8	8	8	7
	8	8	7	7

	2006	2007	2008	2009
Langhorne Creek	8	8	8	N/A
	9	8	8	N/A
Kangaroo Island	8	7	8	9
	7	8	8	10
Riverland	9	8	6	6
	8	9	8	7

WA

	2006	2007	2008	2009
Margaret River	7	8	9	9
	9	8	9	9
Great Southern	6	8	8	8
	8	9	8	9
Manjimup	6	8	8	7
	8	9	9	8
Pemberton	6	9	8	8
	8	9	9	9
Geographe	6	8	8	8
	8	9	7	8
Swan District	7	8	8	10
	8	7	8	10
Peel	9	9	8	8
	9	9	5	7

	2006	2007	2008	2009
Perth Hills	8	8	7	10
	7	7	8	8

QLD

	2006	2007	2008	2009
Granite Belt	8	8	6	6
	7	7	8	8
South Burnett	7	8	6	7
	8	8	7	8

TAS

	2006	2007	2008	2009
Northern Tasmania	8	7	8	8
	7	8	7	8
Southern Tasmania	9	7	7	8
	8	8	7	8

** Frost or bushfire smoke taint precludes ratings.

Plantings and production

The Australian Bureau of Statistics changed its methodology in collating production figures for the 2009 vintage, and warns against comparison with prior years' figures. The reality is that there is no other yardstick, and the end result of a harvest of 1.68 million tonnes has been adopted by all sectors of the industry.

The decrease in the plantings of and tonnes produced by chardonnay and semillon seems very much in line with all the anecdotal pointers in the surplus discussion. These varieties dominate the plantings of white wine grapes along the Murray; 55% of the Australian chardonnay crush was grown on the Murray, a further 19% from the Riverina/Murrumbidgee region. The Riverina has infinitely better water resources than the Murray, although this advantage may not last forever.

The picture with semillon is slightly different: 25% came from the Murray, 44% from the Riverina. (Yes, the Hunter Valley had a great vintage, which gave it a 6.7% share of the total.) Riesling and sauvignon blanc held their own (just), as did the tonnage of the 'other white' category, with a mysterious drop similar to '06.

In the wash up, the white tonnage decreased by 6.7% (no surprise), but the red crush fell by 9.8% (which was a surprise, at least in comparative terms). Pinot noir was impacted by bushfires and smoke taint in parts of southern Victoria, but the continuing increase in pinot plantings might have been expected to offset that loss.

Given that merlot held its own (who is drinking it?) and that the cabernet sauvignon decline was marginal, the obvious question is whether shiraz has finally ended its long march. But here, too, we see a significant increase in plantings since 2006 (and prior), yet a fall in production. It's going to be a while before the fat lady sings on this issue.

Finally, unless money can be found to keep track of the myriad of other varietal plantings (including both alternative and traditional varieties) the industry will be blindfolded as it seeks to respond to warmer summers and lower rainfall.

	2006	2007	2008	2009
CHARDONNAY				
hectares	31,219	32,151	31,564	29,832
tonnes	397,322	366,936	428,082	384,185
RIESLING				
hectares	4,400	4,432	4,400	4,516
tonnes	38,380	31,002	39,305	39,620
SAUVIGNON BLANC				
hectares	4,661	5,545	6,404	6,135
tonnes	40,513	36,515	62,420	63,638
SEMILLON				
hectares	6,236	6,752	6,716	6,479
tonnes	96,934	75,170	100,031	81,851
OTHER WHITE				
hectares	17,683	24,303	23,109	14,300
tonnes	228,311	192,026	223,075	226,320
TOTAL WHITE				
hectares	64,199	73,183	72,193	61,262
tonnes	801,460	701,649	852,913	795,614
CABERNET SAUVIGNON				
hectares	28,103	27,909	27,553	27,537
tonnes	274,350	183,052	258,066	248,451
GRENACHE				
hectares	2,025	2,011	2,011	N/A
tonnes	22,697	15,602	19,755	N/A
MOURVEDRE				
hectares	875	794	785	N/A
tonnes	10,882	6,596	8,401	N/A
MERLOT				
hectares	10,593	10,790	10,764	10,990
tonnes	123,084	90,461	125,285	126,915
PINOT NOIR				
hectares	4,254	4,393	4,490	4,771
tonnes	33,921	26,251	43,923	31,310
SHIRAZ				
hectares	41,115	43,417	43,977	44,082
tonnes	422,430	283,741	441,950	394,070
OTHER RED				
hectares	7,002	11,309	10,902	8,649
tonnes	92,845	63,639	86,741	87,281
TOTAL RED				
hectares	93,967	100,623	100,482	96,029
tonnes	980,209	669,042	984,121	888,027
TOTAL GRAPES				
hectares	168,791	173,776	172,675	157,291
tonnes	1,781,668	1,370,690	1,837,034	1,683,641
PERCENTAGE (TONNES)				
White	44.98%	51.18%	46.43%	47.26%
Red	55.02%	48.82%	53.57%	52.74%
YIELD PER HECTARE (TONNES/HECTARE)				
	10.55	7.88	10.63	10.70

Acknowledgements

It is, I suppose, inevitable that the production of a book such as this should involve many people in a long chain of events, some seemingly trivial, others of fundamental importance.

The starting point is the making of the thousands of bottles of wine Ben Edwards and I taste each year, and the end point is the appearance of the book on retailers' shelves across Australia in August 2010. Well prior to that date, many hundreds of tasting notes for the 2012 edition will have already been made, and details of yet more new wineries will have been entered.

My foremost thanks must go to the winemakers for sending the wines to me at their cost, and in particular those who treat submission dates as serious deadlines rather than an approximate wish-list on my part. Those who ignored the deadlines are increasingly likely to fall on their own sword as the competition for space in the book intensifies.

Next are those responsible for getting the wine to me, whether by the excellent parcel delivery service of Australia Post, by courier or by hand delivery. I am reliant on the goodwill and tolerance of many people involved in what may seem as a warped version of trivial pursuits as the wines arrive, are placed in bins, in due course fork-lifted up one storey and removed from those bins, unpacked, listed, entered into the database, with precise names cross-checked, alcohol, price and closure type recorded, tasting sheets printed for the day's tasting of 120 wines, initially arranged by producer, but then re-sorted by variety, moved onto a long tasting bench, opened, poured at the same pace I taste, the Riedel glasses returned to washing racks, washed, rinsed and dried (my task each day), the tasting notes typed, the database now returning the notes to a winery-by-winery sequence, proof-checked by me (and at least three others at subsequent stages before going to print).

In the meantime, my office team of Paula Grey and Beth Anthony has been busy chasing up new, missing or inconsistent details regarding the winery and the wines. To those who remember to provide the price (and if a lab label, the alcohol) my special thanks. I only wish I could extend those thanks more often.

Then there is the ever-patient, and deadline-conscious, team at Hardie Grant, working on cover design (surely brilliant), page design, paper type and two-colour printing, which give rise to the galley pages for proofreading again and again.

To my team of Ben Edwards, Paula Grey, Beth Anthony; Coldstream Post Office (Barry, Trevor and Val); Pam Holmes (and others at Coldstream Hills); John Cook (programmer); and the Hardie Grant team led by believer-in-chief Sandy Grant, Jane Winning (editor), Megan Ellis (typesetter) and Gayna Murphy (cover designer). This is as much their book as it is mine.

Australian wineries and wines

A note on alphabetical order
Wineries beginning with 'The' are listed under 'T'; for example,
'The Blok Estate'. Winery names that include a numeral are treated
as if the numeral is spelt out; for example, '2 Mates'
is listed under 'T'.

🍇 A. Retief   ★★★★☆

PO Box 1268, Strawberry Hills, NSW 2012 (postal) **Region** Southern NSW Zone
T 0400 650 530 **F** (02) 8569 2048 **www**.awrwines.com.au **Open** Not
Winemaker Alex Retief **Est.** 2008 **Cases** 1000

Owner and winemaker Alex Retief's wine career was prompted by his parents planting a vineyard near Ladysmith, in the Gundagai region, in 1997. The following year he enrolled in the wine science course at CSU, and in 2001 was accepted as the trainee winemaker at the university's winery under Greg Gallagher. When his traineeship finished in mid '02 he went to California's Sonoma Valley for four months, working at Fetzer Vineyards, returning to the Hunter Valley for the '03 vintage with Andrew Margan. He was winemaker there for two and a half years, punctuated with a harvest in Languedoc in '04, before heading back to France in '05 for a two-year appointment as winemaker at Chateau de Lagarde in Bordeaux. Since then he has worked for Peter Lehmann Wines in Sydney as a sales representative, thereafter starting his own boutique wine distribution company. Its portfolio includes A. Retief, imported wines from Chateau de Lagarde, and local wines Eden Road, Cape Bernier, Capanno and Lawsons. The A. Retief wines are made by him from contract-grown grapes in the Canberra District/ Hilltops/Gundagai regions

ŸŸŸŸŸ **Sauvignon Blanc Semillon 2009** Given the full White Bordeaux treatment, barrel fermentation and then nine months in barrel with lees stirring (battonage); has worked very well indeed, the fruit quality high, the oak (surely) not new; tangy citrus flavours with just a hint of toast make an impressive wine. Screwcap. 12.5% alc. **Rating** 94 **To** 2013 $25

ŸŸŸŸŸ **Cabernet Sauvignon Petit Verdot Malbec 2008 Rating** 93 **To** 2025 $28
        Shiraz 2008 Rating 90 **To** 2018 $28

ŸŸŸŸ **Shiraz Sangiovese Malbec 2008 Rating** 88 **To** 2020 $28

Abbey Creek Vineyard   ★★★★★

2388 Porongurup Road, Porongurup, WA 6324 **Region** Porongurup
T (08) 9853 1044 **F** (08) 9454 5501 **Open** By appt
Winemaker Castle Rock Estate (Robert Diletti) **Est.** 1990 **Cases** 800 **Vyds** 1.6 ha

This is the family business of Mike and Mary Dilworth, the name coming from a winter creek that runs alongside the vineyard and a view of The Abbey in the Stirling Range. The vineyard is equally split between riesling, pinot noir, sauvignon blanc and cabernet sauvignon planted in 1990 and '93. The Rieslings have had significant show success for a number of years, now joined by the Pinot Noir at the top of the tree.

ŸŸŸŸŸ **Porongurup Riesling 2005** Glorious pale-green; an incredibly youthful palate,
✪   with most of its characters almost identical to those of the '09, although a little
        more formed and intense. Screwcap. 12.5% alc. **Rating** 96 **To** 2020 $25
        Porongurup Pinot Noir 2008 A wonderfully elegant pinot, with all the
        style and finesse one could hope for, built around bright cherry fruit and a
        long, expanding finish. Trophy Best Pinot Noir WA Wine Show '09. Screwcap.
        13.2% alc. **Rating** 96 **To** 2015 $28
✪   **Porongurup Riesling 2009** Very light straw-green; flowery apple blossom with
        a dusting of talc; the palate is pure, precise and perfectly balanced, apple, lime and
        minerally acidity all combining. Screwcap. 12.5% alc. **Rating** 95 **To** 2024 $25

ŸŸŸŸŸ **Porongurup Sauvignon Blanc 2009 Rating** 90 **To** 2011 $22

Ada River   ★★★★

2330 Main Road, Neerim South, Vic 3831 **Region** Gippsland
T (03) 5628 1661 **F** (03) 5628 1661 **Open** W'ends & public hols 10–6
Winemaker Peter Kelliher **Est.** 1983 **Cases** 1200 **Vyds** 10 ha

The Kelliher family first planted vines on their dairy farm at Neerim South in 1983, extending the vineyard in '89 and increasing plantings further by establishing the nearby Manilla Vineyard in '94. Until 2000, Ada River leased a Yarra Valley vineyard; it has relinquished that lease and in its place established a vineyard at Heathcote in conjunction with a local grower.

ΥΥΥΥΥ **Reserve Heathcote Shiraz 2007** Dense, inky colour; intense black fruits, licorice and bitter chocolate aromas are replicated on the full-bodied palate, the tannins almost absent until the aftertaste. A drought wine, but a good one. Screwcap. **Rating** 94 **To** 2022 $45

ΥΥΥΥ **Gippsland Chardonnay 2008 Rating** 89 **To** 2013 $20
Gippsland Pinot Gris 2008 Rating 88 **To** 2012 $29
Heathcote Shiraz 2008 Rating 88 **To** 2016 $25

Alkoomi   ★★★★★

Wingebellup Road, Frankland River, WA 6396 **Region** Frankland River
T (08) 9855 2229 **F** (08) 9855 2284 **www**.alkoomiwines.com.au **Open** 7 days 10–5
Winemaker Stephen Craig, Merv Lange, Andrew Cherry **Est.** 1971 **Cases** 90 000
Vyds 103.5 ha
For those who see the wineries of WA as suffering from the tyranny of distance, this most remote of all wineries shows there is no tyranny after all. It is a story of unqualified success due to sheer hard work, and no doubt to founders Merv and Judy Lange's aversion to borrowing a single dollar from the bank. The substantial production is entirely drawn from the estate vineyards – now over 100 ha. Wine quality across the range is impeccable, always with precisely defined varietal character. Winemaker Stephen Craig (appointed 2009) brings experience from three years at Tyrrell's, seven years at Goundrey, and vintages in Spain, France and California. In April '10 Merv and Judy announced that from July '10 their daughter Sandy Hallett would assume full ownership and control of Alkoomi, having been an integral part of the business for many years. She and husband Rod, together with daughters Laura, Emily and Molly, represent the second and third generations to be involved in this remarkably successful family business.

ΥΥΥΥΥ **Jarrah Frankland River Shiraz 2007** Holding crimson-purple hue; scented, spicy red and black berry fruit on the bouquet, followed by a near-perfect medium-bodied palate with outstanding texture and structure. Diam. 13.7% alc. **Rating** 96 **To** 2022 $44.70
Blackbutt 2007 The estate plantings, now up to 40 years old, provide effortless power to the array of red and black fruits that drive the bouquet and palate alike; cedary oak and slippery/silky tannins add lustre to a quality wine. Cabernet Sauvignon (48%)/Malbec (28%)/Cabernet Franc (16%)/Merlot (8%). Screwcap. 13.6% alc. **Rating** 95 **To** 2027 $63.50

✪ **Black Label Frankland River Riesling 2009** A pure and fine bouquet, then a super-elegant palate with some citrus and green apple fruit interwoven with crystalline acidity. A long life ahead. Screwcap. 12.5% alc. **Rating** 94 **To** 2029 $20.30

✪ **White Label Frankland River Semillon Sauvignon Blanc 2009** Lively, zesty, tangy fruit flavours come through the length of an impressive palate, oak irrelevant; does offer some cellaring scope. Screwcap. 12.7% alc. **Rating** 94 **To** 2013 $20.30

ΥΥΥΥΥ
✪ **Black Label Frankland River Shiraz Viognier 2008** Typical vivid colour for this blend; the bouquet is full of red fruit aromas coupled with spice, the fresh palate with a juicy lift on the finish. Screwcap. 13.8% alc. **Rating** 93 **To** 2015 $20.30
Wandoo Frankland River Semillon 2006 Rating 92 **To** 2016 $34.75
Frankland River Semillon Sauvignon Blanc 2009 Rating 92 **To** 2011 $20.30
Black Label Frankland River Cabernet Sauvignon 2007 Rating 92 **To** 2020 $22.35

✪ **White Label Frankland River Shiraz 2008** Deep colour; classic cool-grown, medium-bodied shiraz, the black cherry and plum fruit flavours with good length; could not ask any more at this price. Screwcap. 13.5% alc. **Rating** 91 **To** 2017 $15.90

ỸỸỸỸ **White Label Frankland River Sauvignon Blanc 2009** Rating 89
To 2011 $15.90

All Saints Estate ★★★★★

All Saints Road, Wahgunyah, Vic 3687 **Region** Rutherglen
T (02) 6035 2222 **F** (02) 6035 2200 **www**.allsaintswine.com.au **Open** Mon–Sat 9–5.30,
Sun 10–5.30
Winemaker Dan Crane **Est.** 1864 **Cases** 25 000 **Vyds** 39.77 ha
The winery rating reflects the fortified wines, but the table wines are more than adequate.
The Terrace restaurant makes this a most enjoyable stop for any visitor to the northeast. The
faux castle, modelled on a Scottish castle beloved of the founder, is classified by the Historic
Buildings Council. All Saints and St Leonards are owned and managed by fourth-generation
Brown family members, Eliza, Angela and Nicholas. Eliza is an energetic and highly intelligent
leader, wise beyond her years, and highly regarded by the wine industry. Exports to the US.

ỸỸỸỸỸ **Rare Rutherglen Tokay NV** Dark olive mahogany; a sumptuous palate based
on a 50-year-old solera; another level of complexity altogether, again with a rich
tapestry of rancio followed by a drying finish. Vino-Lok. 18% alc. **Rating** 97
To 2011 $110
Rare Rutherglen Muscat NV Mid-brown; deliciously fresh and lively with a
surge of fruit at once very complex yet vibrant; Christmas pudding with spice and
a long, cleansing finish. Vino-Lok. 18% alc. **Rating** 97 To 2011 $110
Rare Rutherglen Muscat Museum Release NV The ultimate in complexity
and concentration; from a solera started in 1920, and only 250 litres are released
in 500 square bottles of 500 ml each year, the presentation doing full justice
to a remarkable wine. Its raisin flavour explodes with Christmas pudding (and
accompanying hard sauce) as it enters the mouth, yet the finish has the fine
balance and length of all very great wines, whether fortified or not. Cork. 18% alc.
Rating 97 To 2011 $1000
Grand Rutherglen Tokay NV The next step in a clear flavour progression, much
darker and headed towards olive-brown; great concentration of tea leaf, some
burnt toffee and cake; material up to 25 years old. Vino-Lok. 18% alc. **Rating** 95
To 2011 $65
Grand Rutherglen Muscat NV Brown hues now dominant; extremely rich,
luscious and viscous burnt toffee and spice; mouthfilling; long finish. Vino-Lok.
18% alc. **Rating** 94 To 2011 $65

ỸỸỸỸỸ **Family Cellar Marsanne 2007** Rating 93 To 2015 $30
✪ **Rutherglen Tokay NV** Typical golden colour, with hints of brown; the palate
has good varietal expression courtesy of tea leaf, honey, malt and cake; the spirit is
especially good, soft and clean. Vino-Lok. 17% alc. **Rating** 93 To 2011 $20
Rutherglen Muscat NV Rating 93 To 2011 $20
Alias II 2008 Rating 92 To 2017 $50
Limited Release Pierre 2008 Rating 92 To 2018 $30
Family Cellar Chardonnay 2008 Rating 90 To 2015 $30

ỸỸỸỸ **Family Cellar Marsanne 2008** Rating 89 To 2013 $30
Family Cellar Durif 2007 Rating 89 To 2027 $50

Allandale ★★★★★

132 Lovedale Road, Lovedale, NSW 2321 **Region** Hunter Valley
T (02) 4990 4526 **F** (02) 4990 1714 **www**.allandalewinery.com.au **Open** Mon–Sat 9–5,
Sun 10–5
Winemaker Bill Sneddon **Est.** 1978 **Cases** 20 000 **Vyds** 6.47 ha
Owners Wally and Judith Atallah have overseen the growth of Allandale from a small cellar
door operation to a sound business. Allandale has developed a reputation for its Chardonnay,
but offers a broad range of wines of consistently good quality, including red wines variously

sourced from the Hilltops, Orange and Mudgee. Exports to the UK, Norway, Fiji, Singapore and Malaysia.

ŸŸŸŸŸ **Hunter Valley Semillon 2004** Glowing, almost iridescent green-gold; the screwcap has done its job to perfection, allowing the wine to develop just a touch of honey to join the citrus flavours, without a hint of tiredness. Now or in another 10 years. Screwcap. 11.5% alc. **Rating** 94 **To** 2020 $30

✪ **Hunter Valley Semillon 2003** Bright green-yellow; a wine that has won awards from the outset, getting better as it develops; while at the upper end of the alcohol scale for Hunter semillon, has the requisite acidity for yet further development, although its mouthfeel cannot be better than it is now. Trophy Best Mature White NSW Wine Awards '09. Screwcap. 12% alc. **Rating** 94 **To** 2012 $50

ŸŸŸŸŸ **Hunter Valley Chardonnay 2008** Very well made; has a mix of nectarine, white
✪ peach and citrus fruit given further complexity by the barrel fermentation of one of six different components that were ultimately blended to make this wine. Screwcap. 13.5% alc. **Rating** 92 **To** 2013 $19

ŸŸŸŸ **Orange Sauvignon Blanc 2009** **Rating** 89 **To** 2011 $20
Hunter Valley Verdelho 2009 **Rating** 89 **To** 2014 $18

Allies Wines   ★★★★★
15 Hume Road, Somers, Vic 3927 (postal) **Region** Mornington Peninsula
T 0439 370 530 **F** (03) 5983 1523 **www**.allies.com.au **Open** Not
Winemaker Barney Flanders, David Chapman **Est.** 2003 **Cases** 1400
Barney Flanders and David Chapman call Allies a collaboration; both come from a restaurant background dating back many years, Barney on the floor and David in the kitchen. In 1997 they turned their sights to wine; Barney graduated from CSU with a wine science degree in '99, and has since worked on the Mornington Peninsula and in the Yarra Valley, Trentino, Sonoma and Côte Rôtie. David left the restaurant scene in 2004 and is studying wine science at CSU. They own no vineyards and have made wine from various vineyard sources in various regions, have a long-term lease over a 2.5 ha block of pinot noir within the Merricks Grove vineyard. At the top end of those releases come the limited-production Garagiste wines.

ŸŸŸŸŸ **Garagiste Chardonnay 2008** Pale gold, bright hue; the bouquet is understated, showing ripe lemon, cinnamon and a suggestion of steely minerality; the palate follows this line with tightly wound lemon fruit, enveloping a core of fine French oak, cashews and clove; racy acidity provides a long, even and precise finish, promising a graceful evolution over time. Screwcap. 13% alc. **Rating** 95 $42 BE

✪ **Stone Axe Vineyard Heathcote Shiraz 2008** Deep crimson; a luscious wine, with perfectly ripened fruit aromas and flavours; blackberry, plum and a touch of licorice; exemplary tannin and oak handling. Screwcap. 13.8% alc. **Rating** 95 **To** 2023 $25

Garagiste Pinot Noir 2008 A restrained and tightly wound bouquet, showing elements of red fruits, delving into a touch of black; the red fruit and fine spices open up on the palate, with quite firm, yet almost plush silky tannins and bright acid, drawing the palate out to a fine, long and expansive conclusion. Screwcap. 13% alc. **Rating** 94 $42 BE

ŸŸŸŸŸ **Saone Mornington Peninsula Viognier 2009** **Rating** 92 $25 BE
Saone Mornington Peninsula Viognier 2008 **Rating** 90 **To** 2013 $25
Mornington Peninsula Pinot Noir 2008 **Rating** 90 **To** 2014 $27

Allinda   ★★★☆
119 Lorimers Lane, Dixons Creek, Vic 3775 **Region** Yarra Valley
T (03) 5965 2450 **F** (03) 5965 2467 **Open** W'ends & public hols 11–5
Winemaker Al Fencaros **Est.** 1991 **Cases** NA
Winemaker Al Fencaros has a Bachelor of Wine Science (CSU) and was formerly employed by De Bortoli in the Yarra Valley. All of the Allinda wines are produced onsite; all except the

Shiraz (from Heathcote) are estate-grown from a little over 3 ha of vineyards. Limited retail distribution in Melbourne and Sydney.

🍷🍷🍷🍷♀ **Riesling 2008** A surprise packet from the Yarra Valley; has strong herb, nettle and spice, plus a touch of minerality; almost sauvignon blanc-like. Screwcap. 12.5% alc. **Rating** 92 **To** 2014 $17.50

Alta Wines   ★★★★

102 Main Street, Hahndorf, SA 5245 **Region** Adelaide Hills
T (08) 8388 7155 **F** (08) 8388 7522 **www**.altavineyards.com.au **Open** Not
Winemaker Sarah Fletcher **Est.** 2003 **Cases** 16 000 **Vyds** 23 ha
Sarah Fletcher came to Alta with an impressive winemaking background: a degree from Roseworthy, and thereafter seven years working for Orlando Wyndham. There she came face to face with grapes from all over Australia, and developed a particular regard for those coming from the Adelaide Hills. So she joined Alta, which had already established a reputation for its Sauvignon Blanc. The portfolio has been progressively extended with varieties suited to the cool climate of the Adelaide Hills. Exports to the UK, Canada and Hong Kong.

🍷🍷🍷🍷♀ **Adelaide Hills Sauvignon Blanc 2009** A well balanced blend of fresh cut grass and a touch of tropical fruits; the palate is generous, with fine, cleansing acidity providing real harmony to the finish. Screwcap. 12.5% alc. **Rating** 90 **To** 2012 $19.95 BE

🍷🍷🍷🍷 **for Elsie Pinot Noir Rose 2009** **Rating** 89 **To** 2011 $17.95 BE

Amadio Wines   ★★★★☆

461 Payneham Road, Felixstow, SA 5070 **Region** Adelaide Hills
T (08) 8337 5144 **F** (08) 8336 2462 **www**.amadiowines.com.au **Open** Mon–Fri 9–6, Sat 9–5.30
Winemaker Danniel Amadio **Est.** 2004 **Cases** 80 000 **Vyds** 150 ha
Danniel Amadio says he has followed in the footsteps of his Italian grandfather, selling wine from his cellar (cantina) direct to the consumer, cutting out wholesale and distribution. He also draws upon the business of his parents, built not in Italy, but in Australia. Amadio Wines has substantial vineyards, primarily in the Adelaide Hills, and also small parcels of contract-grown grapes from Clare Valley, McLaren Vale and Langhorne Creek, covering just about every variety imaginable, and – naturally – with a very strong representation of Italian varieties. Exports to the UK, the US, Canada, Russia, South Korea, Singapore, Hong Kong and China.

🍷🍷🍷🍷🍷 **Reserve Block 2A Adelaide Hills Barossa Valley Shiraz 2006** Has retained excellent hue; the bouquet and palate of this 70/30 blend live up to the promise of the colour, the Adelaide Hills component providing the bright fruit flavours, the Barossa Valley dark berry and chocolate nuances. Quality cork, properly inserted. 14.8% **Rating** 94 **To** 2021 $35

🍷🍷🍷🍷♀ **Adelaide Hills Pinot Grigio 2009** **Rating** 93 **To** 2011 $18
Reserve D3/V14 Adelaide Hills Merlot 2006 **Rating** 92 **To** 2016 $35
✪ **Adelaide Hills Sangiovese 2008** Has a considerable volume of aroma and flavour, with cherry stone, multi-spice and sour cherry all intermingling and strongly expressive of the variety. Screwcap. 14% alc. **Rating** 91 **To** 2013 $18
Grande Reserve Pinot Chardonnay Brut NV **Rating** 90 **To** 2012 $28

🍷🍷🍷🍷 **Adelaide Hills Merlot Rose 2009** **Rating** 88 **To** 2011 $15

Amberley   ★★★★

Cnr Thornton Road/Wildwood Road, Yallingup, WA 6282 **Region** Margaret River
T (08) 9750 1113 **F** (08) 9750 1155 **www**.amberley-estate.com.au **Open** 7 days 10–4.30
Winemaker Lance Parkin **Est.** 1986 **Cases** NFP

Initial growth was based on its ultra-commercial, fairly sweet Chenin Blanc, which continues to provide the volume for the brand. However, the quality of all the other wines has risen markedly over recent years as the 31 ha of estate plantings have become fully mature. Now part of CWA following Constellation Wines' acquisition of Canadian winemaker Vincor, which had in turn acquired Amberley Estate in early 2004. Exports to the UK and the US.

ΨΨΨΨΩ **Secret Lane Margaret River Semillon Sauvignon Blanc 2009** Bright, clean and fresh, with more or less equal contributions of gooseberry, citrus and tropical aromas and flavours. Gold medal Perth Wine Show '09. Screwcap. 13% alc. **Rating** 91 **To** 2012 $19.95
Secret Lane Margaret River Sauvignon Blanc 2009 Light straw-green; fresh, crisp and clean, with a mix of tropical passionfruit (dominant) and citrus (subordinate) on a lively, light palate. Screwcap. 13% alc. **Rating** 90 **To** 2011 $19.95

ΨΨΨΨ **Secret Lane Margaret River Cabernet Merlot 2008** **Rating** 88 **To** 2014 $19.95

Amherst Winery ★★★★★

Talbot-Avoca Road, Amherst, Vic 3371 **Region** Pyrenees
T (03) 5463 2105 **www**.amherstwinery.com **Open** W'ends & public hols 10–5
Winemaker Adam Koerner **Est.** 1989 **Cases** 3000 **Vyds** 4.5 ha
Norman and Elizabeth Jones have planted vines on a property with an extraordinarily rich history, which is commemorated in the name Dunn's Paddock Shiraz. Samuel Knowles was a convict who arrived in Van Diemen's Land in 1838. He endured continuous punishment before fleeing to SA in 1846 and changing his name to Dunn. When, at the end of 1851, he married 18-year-old Mary Therese Taaffe in Adelaide, they walked from Adelaide to Amherst pushing a wheelbarrow carrying their belongings, arriving just before gold was discovered. The lease title of the property shows that Amherst Winery is sited on land once owned by Samuel Dunn. Exports to China.

ΨΨΨΨΨ **Dunn's Paddock Pyrenees Shiraz 2008** Dense crimson; a rich, plush, full-bodied shiraz; dark plum, blackberry, licorice and tar flavours are perfectly matched by French oak (15 months' maturation) and ripe tannins. Screwcap. 14.5% alc. **Rating** 95 **To** 2028 $28
Reserve Pyrenees Shiraz 2008 Similar top colour to the Dunn's Paddock, perhaps a touch deeper; for some reason the French oak is more obvious on the bouquet, along with a touch of spice; the full-bodied palate is very powerful and concentrated with savoury notes to the black fruits; 100 cases made. I prefer its junior brother. Screwcap. 14.5% alc. **Rating** 94 **To** 2023 $48
Chinese Gardens Pyrenees Cabernet Sauvignon 2008 Red-purple; ripe blackcurrant and cassis aromas are also the driving force on the palate, albeit complexed by 15 months' maturation in French oak; the tannins are spot on. Given the drought, a mighty effort. Screwcap. 14.5% alc. **Rating** 94 **To** 2023 $28

ΨΨΨΨΩ **Lachlan's Pyrenees Chardonnay 2008** **Rating** 91 **To** 2013 $25
✪ **Daisy Creek Pyrenees Shiraz Cabernet 2008** Bright colour; an attractive display of blackberry and redcurrant on the bouquet, with more of the same on the palate plus a touch of regional mint; the extract is controlled, especially the tannins, making this a now or later proposition. Garish label. Screwcap. 13% alc. **Rating** 90 **To** 2018 $16

ΨΨΨΨ **Daisy Creek Pyrenees Chardonnay 2008** **Rating** 88 **To** 2012 $16

Amietta Vineyard ★★★★

30 Steddy Road, Lethbridge, Vic 3332 **Region** Geelong
T (03) 5281 7407 **F** (03) 5281 7427 **www**.amietta.com.au **Open** 1st Sun each month 10–4, or by appt
Winemaker Nicholas Clark, Janet Cockbill **Est.** 1995 **Cases** 450 **Vyds** 2.7 ha

Janet Cockbill and Nicholas Clark are multi-talented. Both are archaeologists, but Janet is a multi-tasking genius, combining archaeology, radiography, organic viticulture and wrangling their two small sons. Nicholas studied viticulture at CSU, and both he and Janet worked vintage at Michel Chapoutier's biodynamic Domaine des Béates in Provence in 2001. Plantings include lagrein and carmenere. Amietta is producing cameo wines of some beauty.

ＹＹＹＹＹ **The Angels' Geelong Rose 2009** Pale vibrant pink; strawberry with a touch of sea salt complexity; fresh, crisp and slightly savoury, harmoniously assembled; good fun drinking. Screwcap. 12.8% alc. **Rating** 90 **To** 2012 $24 BE

Anderson   ★★★★

Lot 13 Chiltern Road, Rutherglen, Vic 3685 **Region** Rutherglen
T (02) 6032 8111 **F** (02) 6032 7151 **www.**andersonwinery.com.au **Open** 7 days 10–5
Winemaker Howard and Christobelle Anderson **Est.** 1992 **Cases** 1500 **Vyds** 8.8 ha
Having notched up a winemaking career spanning over 30 years, including a stint at Seppelt (Great Western), Howard Anderson and family started their own winery, initially with a particular focus on sparkling wine but now extending across all table wine styles. The original estate plantings of shiraz, durif and petit verdot (6 ha) were expanded in 2007–08 with tempranillo, saperavi, brown muscat, chenin blanc and viognier.

ＹＹＹＹＹ **Basket Press Reserve Shiraz 2004** Deep, dark crimson–purple colour after five years! Unashamedly full-bodied in every way, with licorice, plum, prune and blackberry fruit, yet not overly tannic. French oak also helps, the cork most unlikely to outlive the wine. 15.3% alc. **Rating** 92 **To** 2015 $25
Cellar Block Black Gold 2005 Powerful but well balanced and structured vintage style fortified shiraz; the low baumé heightens the spicy black fruit and shiraz; will grow in bottle if the cork lasts. 18% alc. **Rating** 91 **To** 2014 $30
Pinot Gris 2008 The elevation of the Whitlands high plateau invests the wine with above-average intensity and length, very much in true gris style, tangy and flavoursome. Screwcap. 12% alc. **Rating** 90 **To** 2011 $18.50
Methode Champenoise Pinot Noir Chardonnay 2000 Yellow-gold, some green tints; strong bready, toasty characters have developed, how much from lees and how much from subsequent bottle maturation not clear. Cork. 12.5% alc. **Rating** 90 **To** 2011 $25
Reserve Cuvee Methode Champenoise Pinot Noir Chardonnay 1996 Deeper gold than the '00; a very powerful bouquet and palate, with the toasty characters joined by some marmalade on the palate. Drink asap. Cork. 11.4% alc. **Rating** 90 **To** 2011 $27
Classic Muscat NV In the middle of the Classic range, still with a degree of spicy primary fruit, but also some rancio richness developing. Cork. 17.5% alc. **Rating** 90 **To** 2011 $30

ＹＹＹＹ **Rutherglen Shiraz Rose 2009 Rating** 88 **To** 2010 $18.50

Angas Plains Estate   ★★★★★

Lot 52 Angas Plains Road, Langhorne Creek, SA 5255 **Region** Langhorne Creek
T (08) 8537 3159 **F** (08) 8537 3353 **www.**angasplainswines.com.au **Open** 7 days 11–5
Winemaker Peter Douglas (Contract) **Est.** 1994 **Cases** 3000 **Vyds** 27 ha
In 1994 Phillip and Judy Cross began planting a vineyard on their 40-ha property, situated on the old flood plains of the Angas River, which only flows after heavy rains in its catchment of the Adelaide Hills. With the assistance of son Jason they manage the property to minimise water use and maximise the accumulation of organic matter. Skilled contract winemaking has resulted in some excellent wines from the estate-grown shiraz (14 ha), cabernet sauvignon (12 ha) and chardonnay (1 ha). Exports to China.

♟♟♟♟♟ PJ's Langhorne Creek Shiraz 2008 Strong, deep red-purple; a complex, rich wine from start to finish; plum and blackberry fruit is cradled by ripe tannins and positive oak on the medium- to full-bodied palate, all the components in balance. Gold medal Sydney Wine Show '10. Screwcap. 14.5% alc. **Rating** 95 **To** 2020 $39.95

PJ's Langhorne Creek Cabernet Sauvignon 2008 Good red-purple; shows the ability of Langhorne Creek to produce cabernet with exemplary varietal character centred around ripe but not the least jammy blackcurrant fruit and balanced tannins; 16 months in 95% French oak; the gurgling, gushing back label is, well, unfortunate. Screwcap. 14% alc. **Rating** 94 **To** 2023 $25

♟♟♟♟♀ Special Reserve Shiraz 2007 **Rating** 92 **To** 2016 $39.95 BE

Special Reserve Langhorne Creek Cabernet Sauvignon 2008 **Rating** 92 **To** 2015 $25 BE

Emily Cross Langhorne Creek Shiraz 2008 **Rating** 91 **To** 2020 $50 BE

♟♟♟♟ PJ's Sauvignon Blanc 2009 **Rating** 87 **To** 2012 $14.95 BE

Angelicus   ★★★☆

Lot 9 Catalano Road, Burekup, WA 6227 **Region** Geographe
T 0429 481 425 **www**.angelicus.com.au **Open** W'ends & public hols, or by appt
Winemaker John and Sue Ward **Est.** 1997 **Cases** 500 **Vyds** 2 ha
Dr John and Sue Ward moved from Sydney to WA with the aim of establishing a vineyard and winery, settling first on a property in the Middlesex Valley of Pemberton. Despite the success of that venture, they have decided to move to the Geographe region, where they have purchased a 51-ha block of granite-strewn rocky hillside facing north and west at Burekup, 200 m above sea level, looking towards the Indian Ocean. They have retained the Angelicus label and the stock from their previous vineyard. In 2009 they planted 0.5 ha of grenache (bush vines, managed biodynamically), 1 ha of tempranillo and 0.5 verdelho in '10.

♟♟♟♟♀ Pinot Noir 2008 Light, bright and clear colour; an energetic pinot, light-bodied but complex, with a display of aromas and flavours ranging from red berry to gently savoury/foresty nuances. Screwcap. 13.6% alc. **Rating** 90 **To** 2014 $24

Angove Family Winemakers   ★★★★

Bookmark Avenue, Renmark, SA 5341 **Region** Riverland
T (08) 8580 3100 **F** (08) 8580 3155 **www**.angove.com.au **Open** Mon–Fri 9–5, w'ends 10–4
Winemaker Tony Ingle, Paul Kernich, Ben Horley, Alex Russell **Est.** 1886
Cases 1.5 million **Vyds** 480 ha
Exemplifies the economies of scale achievable in the Riverland without compromising potential quality. Very good technology provides wines that are never poor and sometimes exceed their theoretical station in life. The vineyard is currently being redeveloped with changes in the varietal mix. Angove's expansion into Padthaway, the Clare Valley, McLaren Vale and Coonawarra (these latter three via contract-grown fruit) has resulted in premium wines to back up its Riverland wines. Exports to all major markets.

♟♟♟♟♀ Long Row Riesling 2009 Has a voluminous and striking bouquet, the aromas
✪ with tropical notes verging on traminer; the wine backs off a little on the palate, which is no bad thing, but has continuity and length to the citrus flavours and crisp finish. Screwcap. 12.5% alc. **Rating** 93 **To** 2012 $10

✪ Nine Vines Grenache Shiraz Rose 2009 Bright light fuschia; grenache perfume to the fore on the bouquet; has plenty of flavour without reliance on residual sugar; needs a touch more acidity? Screwcap. 12.5% alc. **Rating** 92 **To** 2010 $15

✪ Vineyard Select McLaren Vale Shiraz 2008 Dark crimson-purple; has a potent bouquet of black fruits and licorice, then a rich full-bodied palate adding a dash of dark chocolate to the blackberry base. A lot of wine for the price. Screwcap. 14.5% alc. **Rating** 91 **To** 2018 $18

✪   **Organic Shiraz Cabernet 2008** Bright hue; a lively and juicy wine with abundant plum and black cherry fruit supported by good acidity and tannins, oak a minor support role. Screwcap. 13.5% alc. **Rating** 90 **To** 2014 $14.95

�♥ **Butterfly Ridge Riesling Traminer 2009** I fully expected some sweetness, but
✪   lo and behold, although the wine is juicy, it is dry; this in turn makes it a great bargain to buy today and drink tonight at your favourite Chinese restaurant. Screwcap. 12% alc. **Rating** 89 **To** 2012 $7.25
     Vineyard Select Clare Valley Riesling 2009 Rating 88 **To** 2014 $16.40

✪   **Long Row Sauvignon Blanc 2009** Skilled winemaking, including the use of a selected yeast, gives the wine clear varietal character in a gently tropical spectrum to start with, finishing with cleansing, grassy acidity. Screwcap. 11.5% alc. **Rating** 88 **To** 2010 $9.75

✪   **Long Row Shiraz 2008** Bright colour; ripe red and blue fruit bouquet, complemented by attractive spice notes; the palate is vibrant and fresh, showing a slight tarry note to the dark finish. Screwcap. 14.5% alc. **Rating** 88 **To** 2014 $9.75 BE

✪   **Long Row Chardonnay 2008** Over a year in bottle hasn't hurt it, but don't delay, as it's at the peak of development of secondary flavours, screwcap notwithstanding. 13.5% alc. **Rating** 87 **To** 2010 $9.75

✪   **Sparkling Zibibbo NV** Incredibly floral and heady muscat (aka zibbibo); will doubtless gain some yardage from name (and aroma). Cork. 8% alc. **Rating** 87 **To** 2010 $10

Angullong Wines   ★★★★

Victoria Street, Millthorpe, NSW 2798 **Region** Orange
T (02) 6366 4300 **F** (02) 6466 4399 **www**.angullong.com.au **Open** W'ends & public hols 11–5
Winemaker Jon Reynolds **Est.** 1998 **Cases** 8000 **Vyds** 216.7 ha
The Crossing family (Bill and Hatty, and third generation James and Ben) have owned a 2000-ha sheep and cattle station for over half a century. Located 40 km south of Orange, overlooking the Belubula Valley, more than 200 ha of vines have been planted since 1998. In all, there are 15 varieties, with shiraz, cabernet sauvignon and merlot leading the way. Most of the production is sold to Hunter Valley wineries. Exports to Denmark.

♥♥♥♥♡ **Orange Sauvignon Blanc 2009** Pale straw-green; delicate and crisp aromas
✪   and flavours predominantly in a grassy/citrus range, with just a hint of passionfruit; leaves the mouth fresh and clean. Screwcap. 13% alc. **Rating** 90 **To** 2010 $15

✪   **Orange Cabernet Merlot 2008** Clear colour; a most attractive light- to medium-bodied blend, with fresh cassis and blackcurrant fruit on the supple palate, the tannins superfine but enough to provide structure. No need to wait. Screwcap. 14% alc. **Rating** 90 **To** 2012 $15
     Fossil Hill Orange Sangiovese 2008 Strongly varietal sour cherry/savoury aromas and flavours, the medium-bodied palate with considerable length, the tannins fine. Screwcap. 14% alc. **Rating** 90 **To** 2014 $20

♥♥♥♥ **Orange Verdelho 2009** Straw-green; a potent bouquet of orange blossom leads
✪   into a palate where pineapple and other tropical fruits coalesce; lots of flavour. Screwcap. 13.5% alc. **Rating** 89 **To** 2011 $15

✪   **Orange Shiraz 2008** Good crimson hue although not deep; has an abundance of soft, plush fruit on the bouquet and palate in a red flavour spectrum, the cool climate showing only on the very finish. Screwcap. 14% alc. **Rating** 89 **To** 2013 $15
     Fossil Hill Orange Shiraz Viognier 2008 Rating 89 **To** 2017 $20
     Fossil Hill Orange Barbera 2008 Rating 89 **To** 2014 $20

Angus the Bull   ★★★

PO Box 611, Manly, NSW 1655 **Region** South Eastern Australia
T (02) 8966 9020 **F** (02) 8966 9021 www.angusthebull.com **Open** Not
Winemaker Hamish MacGowan **Est.** 2002 **Cases** 22 000
Hamish MacGowan has taken the virtual winery idea to its ultimate conclusion, with a single wine (Cabernet Sauvignon) designed to be drunk with premium red meat, or, more particularly, a perfectly cooked steak. Parcels of grapes are selected from regions across Victoria and SA each year, the multi regional–blend approach designed to minimise vintage variation. Exports to the UK and other major markets.

♀♀♀♀ **Cabernet Sauvignon 2008** Good hue and clarity; a complex bouquet with some undefinable aromas, then a palate with good varietal character before a slightly edgy finish. Plenty of overall flavour. Screwcap. 14.5% alc. **Rating** 89 **To** 2015 $19.95

Angus Wines   ★★★★

PO Box 383, Goolwa, SA 5214 **Region** Southern Fleurieu
T (08) 8555 2320 **F** (08) 8555 2323 www.anguswines.com.au **Open** Not
Winemaker Adam Hooper, Angas Buchanan **Est.** 1995 **Cases** 600 **Vyds** 1.25 ha
Susan and Alistair Angus were pioneer viticulturists on Hindmarsh Island, and established 3.75 ha of shiraz and 1.25 ha of semillon. The wines were of consistently very good quality, but the dramatic reduction in water availability has meant they have had to remove all except 1.25 ha of shiraz. Part is bottled under the Angus Wines label; some is sold in bulk to other wineries. Every aspect of packaging and marketing the wine has a sophisticated touch. Exports to the UK.

♀♀♀♀♀ **A3 Shiraz 2008** Dense, deep crimson-purple; intense black fruits, licorice and tar drive the full-bodied palate; not as tannic as some prior vintages, but will benefit from cellaring. Screwcap. 15% alc. **Rating** 92 **To** 2018 $40

 ## Anna's Vineyard   ★★★

PO Box 158, Port Lincoln, SA 5606 **Region** Southern Eyre Peninsula
T (08) 8621 2900 **F** (08) 8621 2990 www.annasvineyard.com **Open** Not
Winemaker David O'Leary, Simon Greenleaf **Est.** 1997 **Cases** 250 **Vyds** 0.6 ha
Anna and Hagen Stehr have established a micro-vineyard on the southernmost tip of the Eyre Peninsula, overlooking Prosper Bay near Port Lincoln. Viticulture has been carried out on a no-holds-barred organic basis, with no sprays of any type. They hark back to the foundation days of Botobolar in Mudgee, with a camomile, powdered milk and nettle brew to apply to the vines, backed up by planting garlic, basil and marigolds around the vineyard to protect from disease. Exports to the UK.

♀♀♀♀♀ **Limited Release Liqueur Shiraz 2005** Dense colour; immensely rich black fruits, mocha and dark chocolate; decades to go. Screwcap. 18.5% alc. **Rating** 90 **To** 2025 $27

Annapurna Estate   ★★★☆

Simmonds Creek Road, Mt Beauty, Vic 3698 **Region** Alpine Valleys
T (03) 5754 1356 **F** (03) 5754 4517 www.annapurnaestate.com.au **Open** Wed–Sun, public & school hols 10–5
Winemaker Ezio Minutello **Est.** 1989 **Cases** 4000 **Vyds** 21 ha
Wendy and Ezio Minutello began the establishment of the vineyard at 550 m on Mt Beauty in 1989, planted to pinot noir, chardonnay, pinot gris and merlot. Finally, in 1999, the first wines were released. Annapurna, the second-highest mountain after Mt Everest, is Nepalese for 'goddess of bountiful harvest and fertility'. Ironically, it did not save the 2007 vintage, entirely lost to smoke taint.

ŶŶŶŶŶ **Sparkling White 2005** Cleaner and fresher than the Blanc de Noir; bottle-fermented and aged on lees (period undefined); fresh and lively; slightly green fruit balanced by dosage. Chardonnay/Pinot Noir. Diam. 12.8% alc. **Rating** 90 To 2012 $34

ŶŶŶŶ **Mt Beauty Vineyards Chardonnay 2005** Pale but bright green; a delicate but
✪   well-balanced chardonnay, with touches of barrel ferment and mlf well controlled; the flavours are in a citrus and stone fruit spectrum, the acidity still brisk. Screwcap. 13.8% alc. **Rating** 89 To 2013 $20

✪   **Mt Beauty Vineyards Pinot Noir Reserve 2005** Light, developed (not excessively so) colour; strong savoury, spicy elements have developed in both bouquet and palate balanced by sweet plum and cherry fruit. Nice wine, ready now. Screwcap. 14.5% alc. **Rating** 89 To 2011 $20
Sparkling Red 2005 Rating 89 To 2011 $38
Mt Beauty Pinot Gris 2008 Rating 88 To 2012 $20
Mt Beauty Vineyards Methode Classique 2004 Rating 88 To 2011 $48

Annie's Lane   ★★★★★

Quelltaler Road, Watervale, SA 5452 **Region** Clare Valley
T (08) 8843 0003 **F** (08) 8843 0096 **www**.annieslane.com.au **Open** Mon–Fri 8.30–5, w'ends 11–4
Winemaker Alex MacKenzie **Est.** 1851 **Cases** NFP
The Clare Valley portfolio of Foster's, the name coming from Annie Weyman, a turn-of-the-century local identity. The brand consistently offers wines that over-deliver against their price points, with both wine show success and critical acclaim. Copper Trail is the flagship release, and there are some very worthy cellar door and on-premise wines. Exports to the UK, the US and Europe.

ŶŶŶŶŶ **Copper Trail Clare Valley Riesling 2009** Pale bright green; an evocative bouquet of lime, lemon and apple blossom together with a touch of zest is followed by an immaculately proportioned and balanced palate with a lingering crisp finish. All class, with a long future. Screwcap. 12% alc. **Rating** 96 To 2024 $37
✪   **Clare Valley Riesling 2009** Bright straw-green; flowery lime and lemon blossom and a touch of lime zest; a generous palate filled with juicy citrus fruit; good acidity on the long finish; now or in a decade. Screwcap. 12% alc. **Rating** 94 To 2019 $20

ŶŶŶŶŶ **Clare Valley Riesling 2008** Light straw-green; classic lime, straw and toast
✪   aromas starting to develop; opens quietly in the mouth, then builds impressively through to the finish, given additional focus and elegance by the low alcohol. Screwcap. 11.5% alc. **Rating** 93 To 2014 $20
✪   **Clare Valley Rose 2009** Vivid fuchsia/magenta; as bright and lively as the colour suggests, with an interplay of strawberry, cherry and raspberry before an almost imperiously dry finish. Screwcap. 12% alc. **Rating** 93 To 2011 $20
✪   **Clare Valley Shiraz 2008** Opaque crimson-purple; a trenchantly full-bodied wine, with layers of blackberry, plum and prune; however, surprises with the restrained, indeed slightly short, finish. Screwcap. 14.5% alc. **Rating** 93 To 2020 $20

ŶŶŶŶ **Clare Valley Chardonnay 2009 Rating** 89 To 2014 $20
Clare Valley Cabernet Merlot 2008 Rating 89 To 2015 $20

Anniebrook   ★★★

247 Wildwood Road, Carbunup River, WA 6280 **Region** Margaret River
T (08) 9755 1155 **F** (08) 9755 1138 **Open** Sat–Thurs 9.30–4.30
Winemaker Flying Fish Cove (Simon Ding) **Est.** 1986 **Cases** 3000 **Vyds** 6.84 ha
A long time ago Wally Lewis (no relation to the celebrated rugby league player) and wife Dawn were third-generation graziers and sheep farmers. In 1985 they decided they had to find a much larger property further inland for their sheep farming, or radically change their

existing business. They opted for the latter, simultaneously planting vines and flowers; they have planted shiraz, semillon, cabernet franc, chardonnay and sauvignon blanc, and 2 ha of flowers. For almost 20 years they sold the grapes to a nearby winemaker, but in 2006 took the plunge and established their own brand. Ambience and the Anniebrook River, which flows through the centre of the property, are ready attractions for cellar door visitors.

🍷🍷🍷🍷 **Wildwood Margaret River Rose 2009** Pale magenta; an extremely fragrant and aromatic red berry, spice and herb bouquet, the palate fruity and ever so slightly sweet; would have been great if dry. Screwcap. 13% alc. **Rating** 89 **To** 2011 $14

Anvers ★★★★★

Cnr Chalk Hill Road/Foggo Road, McLaren Vale, SA 5171 **Region** Adelaide Hills
T (08) 8323 9603 **F** (08) 8323 9502 **www**.anvers.com.au **Open** Not
Winemaker Kym Milne MW **Est.** 1998 **Cases** 10 000 **Vyds** 24.5 ha

Myriam and Wayne Keoghan established Anvers with the emphasis on quality rather than quantity. The principal vineyard is in the Adelaide Hills at Kangarilla (16 ha of cabernet sauvignon, shiraz, chardonnay, sauvignon blanc and viognier), the second (94-year-old) vineyard at McLaren Vale (shiraz, grenache and cabernet sauvignon). Winemaker Kym Milne has experience gained across many of the wine-producing countries in both northern and southern hemispheres. Exports to the UK and other major markets.

🍷🍷🍷🍷🍷 ✪ **Adelaide Hills Chardonnay 2008** Pale green-straw; a highly fragrant nectarine and grapefruit bouquet leads into an equally attractive palate; barrel-fermented and matured, but the oak plays no more than a support role. Screwcap. 13.5% alc. **Rating** 94 **To** 2013 $24

McLaren Vale Shiraz 2006 A lively, energetic and very attractive wine, with fragrant spice and black fruit aromas leading into a medium-bodied palate with a similar suite of flavours, tannins and oak in perfect harmony. Cork. 15% alc. **Rating** 94 **To** 2018 $28

🍷🍷🍷🍷½ **The Warrior Shiraz 2006 Rating** 93 **To** 2016 $47

✪ **Adelaide Hills Sauvignon Blanc 2009** A crisp, herbal style, with grass, asparagus and stony elements; no Marlborough here! Has good structure and length. Screwcap. 12.5% alc. **Rating** 90 **To** 2011 $20

✪ **Razorback Road Adelaide Hills Shiraz Cabernet Sauvignon 2006** A 70/30 blend, the spicy shiraz fruit providing the flavour, the cabernet contributing the structure; only light- to medium-bodied, but an enjoyable wine. Screwcap. 14.5% alc. **Rating** 90 **To** 2013 $20

🍷🍷🍷🍷 **McLaren Vale Shiraz 2007 Rating** 89 **To** 2014 $28
Langhorne Creek Cabernet Sauvignon 2007 Rating 89 **To** 2015 $28

Arakoon ★★★★☆

7/229 Main Road, McLaren Vale, SA 5171 **Region** McLaren Vale
T (08) 8323 7339 **www**.arakoonwines.com.au **Open** By appt
Winemaker Raymond Jones **Est.** 1999 **Cases** 3500

Ray and Patrik Jones' first venture into wine came to nothing: a 1990 proposal for a film about the Australian wine industry with myself as anchorman. Five years too early, say the Joneses. In 1999 they took the plunge into making their own wine, and exporting it along with the wines of others. As the quality of the wines has increased, so has the originally zany labelling been replaced with simple, but elegant, labels. No new releases; these wines still available. Exports to Sweden, Denmark, Germany, Singapore and Malaysia.

🍷🍷🍷🍷🍷 **Doyen Willunga Shiraz 2007** Bright colour; a focused black fruit bouquet, with some charry oak and a slight floral edge to the fruit; the palate is full-bodied, with a savoury mineral edge to the fruit; good acid drive provides lightness and length on the finish. Screwcap. 14.5% alc. **Rating** 94 **To** 2018 $45 BE

🍷🍷🍷🍷½ **Clarendon Shiraz 2007 Rating** 90 **To** 2016 $32 BE
Sellicks Beach Shiraz 2007 Rating 90 **To** 2014 $20 BE

Aramis Vineyards ★★★★★

Spoon, 19 Gouger Street, Adelaide, SA 5000 **Region** McLaren Vale
T (08) 8238 0000 **F** (08) 8234 0485 **www**.aramisvineyards.com **Open** Mon–Tues 8–6,
Wed–Sat 8–late
Winemaker Scott Rawlinson **Est.** 1998 **Cases** NFP **Vyds** 25.6 ha

The estate vineyards have been planted to just two varieties: shiraz and cabernet sauvignon.
Viticulturist David Mills is a third-generation McLaren Vale resident and has been involved in
the establishment of the vineyards from the beginning. Winemaker Scott Rawlinson was with
Mildara Blass for eight years before joining the Aramis team under the direction of owner
Lee Flourentzou. He has established what must be one of the most exclusive cellar doors
in Australia at the upmarket Adelaide restaurant Spoon in the CBD. While all the Aramis
wines are available by the bottle or by the glass, Spoon does also carry a wine list featuring
outstanding Champagnes and icon white and red wines from around the world, and of course
Australian wines. Exports to the UK, the US, Canada, Germany, Denmark, Singapore and
Hong Kong.

♀♀♀♀♀ **White Label Adelaide Hills Sauvignon Blanc 2009** Light straw-green;
✪   a deliciously fragrant bouquet with passionfruit, gooseberry and citrus, the
        palate – if anything – picking up the pace even further. A bold and very successful
        extension of the portfolio. Screwcap. 13.5% alc. **Rating** 95 **To** 2011 $19
        The Governor McLaren Vale Syrah 2008 Rich and full-bodied, but with
        more facets than the Black Label; oak plays an obvious role and the tannins are
        finer; blackberry fruit does have some chocolate, but not to the extent of the Black
        Label. Excellent achievement for the vintage. Screwcap. 14.5% alc. **Rating** 95
        To 2023 $56
✪   **White Label McLaren Vale Shiraz Cabernet 2008** Dense purple-red; that
        regional dark chocolate fires the opening salvo on the bouquet and medium- to
        full-bodied palate; however, there is a more than ample offer of blackcurrant and
        blackberry fruit to provide flavour balance, fine tannins and oak filling out the
        finish. Screwcap. 14.5% alc. **Rating** 94 **To** 2020 $19

♀♀♀♀♀ **Black Label McLaren Vale Shiraz 2008** **Rating** 93 **To** 2028 $25
        O'Aristocratis McLaren Vale Sparkling Syrah 2005 **Rating** 92 **To** 2015 $68
        Sparkling Shiraz 2005 **Rating** 90 **To** 2013

Arete Wines ★★★★

1 Banyan Court, Greenwith, SA 5125 (postal) **Region** Barossa Valley
T 0418 296 969 **F** (08) 8289 8470 **www**.aretewines.com.au **Open** Not
Winemaker Richard Bate **Est.** 2008 **Cases** 500

The name chosen by owner Richard Bate comes from Greek mythology, describing the
aggregate of all the qualities of valour, virtue and excellence that make up good character.
Having graduated with a Bachelor of Science (wine science major) degree from CSU, Richard
worked at Barossa Valley Estate, then Saltram, Wolf Blass and Penfolds. His next move was to
work for the Burgundian cooper François Frères distributing barrels within Australia, before
venturing into the challenging world of the small winemaker. His intention is to make single-
vineyard wines wherever possible, with small quantities of each wine part of the strategy.

♀♀♀♀♀ **The Road Less Travelled Adelaide Hills Sauvignon Blanc 2009** If you
✪   don't like Marlborough sauvignon blanc, this may be the wine for you. Oxidatively
        handled juice through a basket press, then barrel fermented with wild yeast on
        unclear juice, and weekly battonage. Despite (or because of this) has very good
        line, length and mouthfeel. Screwcap. 12.5% alc. **Rating** 93 **To** 2013 $20

Arlewood Estate ★★★★

Cnr Bussell Highway/Calgardup Road, Forest Grove, WA 6286 **Region** Margaret River
T (08) 9755 6267 **F** (08) 9755 6267 **www**.arlewood.com.au **Open** Sat 11–5, or by appt
Winemaker Bill Crappsley **Est.** 1988 **Cases** 6000 **Vyds** 9.7 ha

A series of events in 2007 have led to major changes in the Arlewood Estate structure. The Gosatti family sold the Harmans Road vineyard to Vasse Felix, but retained ownership of the brand and all stock. It will continue to have access to the cabernet sauvignon and merlot up to and including the 2009 vintage. In mid '08 Arlewood acquired the former Hesperos Estate vineyard, 10 km south of Margaret River, and Bill Crappsley, already a partner with the Gosattis in Plan B (see separate entry), became full-time winemaker for Arlewood and Plan B. Exports to the UK, the US, Switzerland, Singapore, Malaysia, Hong Kong, Philippines, South Korea and China.

ΨΨΨΨΨ **Reserve Margaret River Semillon Sauvignon Blanc 2007** A 50/50 blend, barrel ferment used to invest the wine with texture and flavour complexity; here the higher percentage of sauvignon blanc has given the wine some juicy fruit flavours alongside herbal notes. Screwcap. 14% alc. **Rating** 93 **To** 2012 $35
Reserve Margaret River Semillon Sauvignon Blanc 2008 A 65/35 blend with both flavour and texture complexity from partial barrel fermentation (20% of the semillon was fermented in new French oak), grassy/herbal characters to the fore, but with some riper notes from the sauvignon blanc; good length. Screwcap. 13.5% alc. **Rating** 92 **To** 2013 $35

✪ **Margaret River Cabernet Merlot 2008** A 60/40 blend that has some cedar and earth overtones to its quite powerful blackcurrant, cassis and plum flavours; good length and balance. Screwcap. 14% alc. **Rating** 92 **To** 2018 $20
La Bratta 2007 La Bratta is the village in Italy where Gary Gosatti's mother was born, and grandfather made wine. The Merlot/Malbec/Cabernet Sauvignon that went to make this wine come from the original Arlewood Vineyard, and have produced a wine of considerable stature, its black and redcurrant fruit supported by Italianate tannins and French oak; 250 cases made. Screwcap. 15% alc. **Rating** 92 **To** 2020 $58
Margaret River Chardonnay 2007 Straw-green; an elegant style, with nectarine and white peach fruit subtly supported by barrel ferment French oak; perhaps lacks some intensity on the finish; 200 dozen made. Screwcap. 14% alc. **Rating** 90 **To** 2015 $35

ΨΨΨΨ **Margaret River Sauvignon Blanc Semillon 2009** Rating 89 **To** 2011 $20
Margaret River Marsanne Roussanne 2009 Rating 89 **To** 2014 $20
Margaret River Shiraz 2007 Rating 89 **To** 2017 $20

Arrowfield Estate   ★★★☆

Golden Highway, Jerrys Plains, NSW 2330 **Region** Upper Hunter Valley
T (02) 6576 4041 **F** (02) 6576 4144 **www.**arrowfieldestate.com.au **Open** 7 days 10–5
Winemaker Barry Kooij, Adrianna Mansueto **Est.** 1968 **Cases** 80 000 **Vyds** 27.1 ha
Arrowfield continues in the ownership of the Inagaki family, which has been involved in the Japanese liquor industry for over a century. It has low-yielding, old vines in the Upper Hunter Valley, and also buys grapes from other parts of Australia, making varietal wines appropriate to those regions. In 2007 it merged with Mornington Peninsula winery Red Hill Estate, the merged group trading as InWine Group Australia, with Brenton Martin installed as CEO. Exports to the US, Canada, Ireland, Thailand, Japan, Hong Kong and Singapore.

ΨΨΨΨΨ **Show Reserve Hunter Valley Chardonnay 2008** Good green-gold; a moderately complex fusion of melon and stone fruit with barrel ferment oak inputs; the balance is also good. Screwcap. 13.5% alc. **Rating** 90 **To** 2014 $30

ΨΨΨΨ **Show Reserve Hunter Valley Semillon 2009** Rating 89 **To** 2010 $30
Shiraz 2006 Rating 89 **To** 2014 $20
Show Reserve Hunter Valley Shiraz 2007 Rating 88 **To** 2013 $30

Arundel   ★★★★☆

Arundel Farm Estate, PO Box 136, Keilor, Vic 3036 **Region** Sunbury
T 0408 576 467 **F** (03) 9335 4912 **www**.arundelwinery.com.au **Open** Not
Winemaker Mark Hayes **Est.** 1995 **Cases** 2300 **Vyds** 6.2 ha
Arundel was built around an acre of cabernet and shiraz planted in the 1970s but abandoned.
When the Conwell family purchased the property in the early 1990s, the vineyard was
resurrected and the first vintage was made by Rick Kinzbrunner in '95. Thereafter the cabernet
was grafted over to shiraz, the block slowly increased to 1.6 ha, and an additional 4 ha of shiraz
and 1.6 ha of viognier and marsanne planted.

ƤƤƤƤƤ Shiraz 2008 Dense, inky purple-crimson; a full-bodied wine laden with luscious
✪   black fruits yet is neither extractive nor jammy; spice and licorice add flavour
       perspective, fine-grained tannins give the needed structure. Thoroughly stained
       cork. 14% alc. **Rating** 94 **To** 2023 $15

ƤƤƤƤ   Viognier 2008 **Rating** 89 **To** 2012 $13.50

Ashbrook Estate   ★★★★★

379 Harmans Road, Wilyabrup via Cowaramup, WA 6284 **Region** Margaret River
T (08) 9755 6262 **F** (08) 9755 6290 **www**.ashbrookwines.com.au **Open** 7 days 10–5
Winemaker Tony and Brian Devitt **Est.** 1975 **Cases** 14 000 **Vyds** 17.4 ha
This fastidious producer of consistently excellent estate-grown table wines shuns publicity and
the wine show system alike, and is less well known than is deserved, selling much of its wine
through the cellar door and by an understandably very loyal mailing list clientele. All the white
wines are of the highest quality, year in, year out. Exports to the UK, Canada, Germany, India,
Japan, Singapore, Hong Kong, Taiwan and China.

ƤƤƤƤƤ Margaret River Sauvignon Blanc 2009 Distinctly grassy characters on the
✪   bouquet suggest there may be some oak (there is none), the firm palate offering
       some gooseberry and kiwi fruit, backed by firm acidity and a long finish.
       Screwcap. 14% alc. **Rating** 94 **To** 2011 $22
       Margaret River Chardonnay 2008 Glowing yellow-green; in the mainstream
       of Margaret River chardonnay, with a depth of flavour seldom found in other
       regions; luscious stone fruit with toasty/creamy notes from barrel ferment in
       new oak, and 6 months' maturation in oak. Screwcap. 14.5% alc. **Rating** 94
       To 2014 $28
✪   Margaret River Verdelho 2009 Tangy and juicy, citrus woven through the
       tropical fruit inherent in the variety; cleansing acidity on the finish increases the
       length of a very good verdelho. Screwcap. 14% alc. **Rating** 94 **To** 2016 $22
✪   Margaret River Shiraz 2005 Expected colour development; the fragrant red
       fruit bouquet leads into a vibrant, medium-bodied palate with more of those red
       fruits, finishing with superfine tannins and a blessing of French oak. Screwcap.
       15% alc. **Rating** 94 **To** 2019 $29
       Margaret River Cabernet Merlot Cabernet Franc 2004 An elegant,
       light- to medium-bodied wine speaking equally of its varietal base and regional
       origin, with redcurrant and blackcurrant fruit on both bouquet and palate; has a
       deliciously fresh finish. Screwcap. 14% alc. **Rating** 94 **To** 2020 $29

ƤƤƤƤƤ Margaret River Semillon 2009 **Rating** 93 **To** 2015 $22
       Margaret River Riesling 2009 **Rating** 91 **To** 2014 $22

Ashton Hills   ★★★★★

Tregarthen Road, Ashton, SA 5137 **Region** Adelaide Hills
T (08) 8390 1243 **F** (08) 8390 1243 **Open** W'ends & most public hols 11–5.30
Winemaker Stephen George **Est.** 1982 **Cases** 1500 **Vyds** 3 ha
Stephen George wears three winemaker hats: one for Ashton Hills, drawing upon an estate
vineyard high in the Adelaide Hills; one for Galah Wines; and one for Wendouree. It would
be hard to imagine three wineries with more diverse styles, from the elegance and finesse of

Ashton Hills to the awesome power of Wendouree. The Riesling, Chardonnay and Pinot Noir have moved into the highest echelon. Exports to Hong Kong.

♟♟♟♟♟ **Adelaide Hills Chardonnay 2008** Superb green-straw; an immaculately crafted wine, with flavours of white peach, melon and fig; it is the texture that is quite outstanding, the creamy mouthfeel tied by a bow of acidity on the finish; you know French oak plays an integral part, but it's never obvious. Screwcap. 13.5% alc. **Rating** 96 **To** 2018 $38

Piccadilly Valley Pinot Noir 2008 Shows some colour development; as always, has an extremely expressive and complex bouquet, with forest undergrowth and spicy red fruits; the palate is a precise replay of the bouquet, with great length and immaculate balance. Screwcap. 14% alc. **Rating** 96 **To** 2016 $33

Reserve Adelaide Hills Pinot Noir 2008 Relatively light, but bright, hue; fractionally more purple than the Estate; very stylish, and in the mainstream of the Ashton Hills style, with spices and savoury notes surrounding the plum and black cherry fruit. Trophy Adelaide Hills Wine Show '09. Screwcap. 14.5% alc. **Rating** 96 **To** 2015 $67

Adelaide Hills Riesling 2009 Bright pale green-straw; charged with delicious lime juice flavours, the palate perfectly balanced and long. Drink now or in 15 years. Trophy Adelaide Hills Wine Show '09. Screwcap. 13% alc. **Rating** 95 **To** 2024 $33

Adelaide Hills Chardonnay 2007 Brilliant green-yellow; the bright bouquet does not fully prepare you for the energy and drive of the long palate, built around grapefruit, nectarine and crunchy acidity. Screwcap. 13.5% alc. **Rating** 95 **To** 2015 $45

Estate Adelaide Hills Pinot Noir 2008 Clear colour with the first traces of development; a fragrant bouquet of spiced berries leads into a long, intense palate, red fruits, spice and forest neatly offsetting each other. Trophy Cold Climate Wine Show '09. Screwcap. 14.5% alc. **Rating** 95 **To** 2015 $45

Reserve Adelaide Hills Pinot Noir 2007 More texture and complexity than the varietal; no hint of mint, but spicy/foresty/bramble characters run alongside the predominantly dark fruits; in the mainstream of the Ashton Hills style. Screwcap. 14% alc. **Rating** 95 **To** 2013 $67

Clare Valley Sparkling Shiraz 2002 Spent four years in barrel before tiraging, followed by bottle fermentation for unspecified time. While the dosage is said to be high, in fact it is not obvious due to the tannins in the base wine; has great length. Cork. 13% alc. **Rating** 95 **To** 2020 $47

♟♟♟♟♟ **Three Pinot Gris Gewurztraminer Riesling 2009** **Rating** 90 **To** 2017 $31
Salmon Brut 2008 **Rating** 90 **To** 2013 $38

🍇 Atze's Corner Wines ★★★★☆

Box 81, Nuriootpa, SA 5355 **Region** Barossa Valley
T 0407 621 989 **F** (08) 8562 1989 **www**.atzescornerwines.com.au **Open** Not
Winemaker Andrew Kalleske (Contract) **Est.** 2005 **Cases** 400 **Vyds** 30 ha
The seemingly numerous members of the Kalleske family have widespread involvement in grape growing and winemaking in the Barossa Valley. This particular venture is that of Andrew Kalleske, son of John and Barb Kalleske. In 1975 they purchased the Atze Vineyard, which included a small block of shiraz planted in 1912, but with additional plantings along the way, including more shiraz in '51. Andrew Kalleske purchases a small amount of grapes from the family vineyard; it has 20 ha of shiraz, with small amounts of mataro, petit verdot, grenache, cabernet sauvignon, tempranillo, viognier, petite sirah, graciano, montepulciano, vermentino and aglianico. Local boutique winemakers provide the physical facilities for the winemaking, with Andrew involved.

♟♟♟♟♟ **Eddies Old Vine Barossa Valley Shiraz 2006** From vines planted in 1912 for the Atze family and 57-year-old vines that have been tended by Andrew Kalleske's parents for the last 35 years. Top-quality shiraz, a great vintage and good winemaking have produced a wine of distinction. High-quality cork. 15.5% alc. **Rating** 94 **To** 2021 $52

ŸŸŸŸ♀ Eddies Old Vine Barossa Valley Shiraz 2005 Rating 91 To 2020 $52
        The Bachelor 2006 Rating 91 To 2016 $26

ŸŸŸŸ The Bachelor 2007 Rating 88 To 2015 $26

Audrey Wilkinson Vineyard   ★★★★★

Oakdale, De Beyers Road, Pokolbin, NSW 2320 **Region** Hunter Valley
T (02) 4998 7411 **F** (02) 4998 7824 **www**.audreywilkinson.com.au **Open** Mon–Fri 9–5,
w'ends & public hols 9.30–5
Winemaker Jeff Byrne **Est.** 1999 **Cases** 15 000 **Vyds** 42.27 ha
One of the most historic properties in the Hunter Valley, set in a particularly beautiful location
and with a very attractive cellar door. In 2004 it was acquired by Brian Agnew and family,
and is no longer part of the Pepper Tree/James Fairfax wine group. The wines are made from
estate-grown grapes, the lion's share to shiraz, the remainder (in descending order) to semillon,
malbec, verdelho, tempranillo, merlot, cabernet sauvignon, muscat and traminer; the vines
were planted between the 1970s and '90s. More recently, a small McLaren Vale vineyard of
3.45 ha, planted to merlot and shiraz, was acquired. Exports to NZ.

ŸŸŸŸŸ The Ridge Reserve Semillon 2009 Bright straw-green; typically expressive
        bouquet of the vintage, with grass and a hint of citrus intermingling; abundant
        fruit on entry into the mouth, then tightens up nicely on the long and crisp finish.
        Screwcap. 11.5% alc. **Rating** 94 To 2018 $35
        The Ridge Reserve Semillon 2008 Bright straw-green; a very focused and
        powerful semillon, flavours spanning citrus at one end, herb and grass at the other;
        lots to build on. Screwcap. 11.2% alc. **Rating** 94 To 2020 $35

ŸŸŸŸ♀ The Lake Reserve Shiraz 2006 Rating 92 To 2016 $50
✪   McLaren Vale Merlot 2008 Fresh black plum and olive bouquet, complemented
        by a touch of clove; medium-bodied, vibrant and juicy, with just enough tannins to
        signify serious intent. Screwcap. 14% alc. **Rating** 90 To 2015 $20 BE

ŸŸŸŸ Winemakers Selection Traminer 2009 Rating 89 To 2012 $20
        Winemakers Selection Semillon 2009 Rating 89 To 2014 $20
        McLaren Vale Shiraz 2008 Rating 89 To 2014 $20 BE
        Barossa Valley Tempranillo 2008 Rating 88 To 2013 $20

Auldstone   ★★★

296 Booths Road, Taminick via Glenrowan, Vic 3675 **Region** Glenrowan
T (03) 5766 2237 **F** (03) 5766 2131 **www**.auldstone.com.au **Open** Thurs–Sat & school
hols 9–5, Sun 10–5
Winemaker Michael Reid **Est.** 1987 **Cases** 2000 **Vyds** 14.4 ha
Michael and Nancy Reid have restored a century-old stone winery and have replanted the
largely abandoned vineyard around it (shiraz, cabernet sauvignon, merlot, chardonnay, riesling
and muscat). All the Auldstone varietal and fortified wines have won medals (usually bronze)
in Australian wine shows. Exports to Singapore and China.

ŸŸŸŸ Liqueur Muscat NV Fragrant raisin and toffee bouquet; the toasty palate, rich
        fruit and clean spirit combine well to produce a rich, almost savoury expression of
        the style. Cork. 18% alc. **Rating** 89 To 2020 $30 BE

Austin's Wines   ★★★★★

870 Steiglitz Road, Sutherlands Creek, Vic 3331 **Region** Geelong
T (03) 5281 1799 **F** (03) 5281 1673 **www**.austinswines.com.au **Open** By appt
Winemaker Scott Ireland, Richard Austin **Est.** 1982 **Cases** 20 000 **Vyds** 61.5 ha
Pamela and Richard Austin have quietly built their business from a tiny base, and it has
flourished. The vineyard has been progressively extended to over 60 ha, and production has
soared from 700 cases in 1998. Scott Ireland is full-time resident winemaker in the capacious
onsite winery, and the quality of the wines is admirable. Exports to the UK, the US, Canada,
Taiwan, Singapore, Hong Kong, Japan and China.

ΨΨΨΨ Chardonnay 2008 Bright green-tinged hue; a vibrant and elegant style not
common in Geelong; has impressive thrust and length, oak little more than a
vehicle. Gold medal Geelong Wine Show '09. Screwcap. 13.5% alc. **Rating** 94
To 2016 $27.50
Shiraz 2006 Strong crimson-purple, great for a four-year-old wine; emphasises
the synergy between shiraz and the cool Geelong climate; an array of black fruits,
licorice and spice flavours drive the long palate. Screwcap. 14% alc. **Rating** 94
To 2021 $27.50

ΨΨΨΨΨ Sauvignon Blanc 2009 **Rating** 91 To 2011 $20

ΨΨΨΨ Pinot Noir 2008 **Rating** 88 To 2013 $29.50

Bacchus Hill   ★★★☆
100 O'Connell Road, Bacchus Marsh, Vic 3340 **Region** Sunbury
T (03) 5367 8176 **F** (03) 5367 2058 **www**.bacchushill.com.au **Open** Fri–Sun &
public hols 10–3, Mon–Thurs by appt
Winemaker Bruno Tassone **Est.** 2000 **Cases** 2600 **Vyds** 15.5 ha
Bruno Tassone migrated from Italy when he was eight, and grew up watching his father carry
on the Italian tradition of making wine for home consumption. Tassone, a lawyer, followed the
same path before purchasing a 35-ha property with wife Jennifer. Here they have planted 2 ha
each of riesling, semillon, sauvignon blanc, chardonnay, pinot noir, shiraz, cabernet sauvignon,
1 ha of chenin blanc and 0.5 ha of nebbiolo. Exports to Canada.

ΨΨΨΨΨ Riesling 2009 Bright straw-green; bone-dry, with a strong, minerally texture and
structure; should mature very nicely. Diam. 11% alc. **Rating** 90 To 2017 $25

ΨΨΨΨ Le Repaire de Bacchus Sauvignon Blanc 2009 **Rating** 88 To 2011 $22
Premium Shiraz 2007 **Rating** 88 To 2015 $35
Le Repaire de Bacchus Cabernet Sauvignon 2008 **Rating** 88 To 2025 $30

Back Pocket   ★★★★
90 Savina Lane, Severnlea, Qld 4380 **Region** Granite Belt
T 0418 196 035 **F** (07) 4683 5184 **www**.backpocket.com.au **Open** Not
Winemaker Peter Scudamore-Smith MW (Contract) **Est.** 1997 **Cases** 400 **Vyds** 2 ha
Mal Baisden and Lel Doon purchased the 20-ha Back Pocket property in 1997, which had
long been used for fruit growing, with a small patch of shiraz planted in the early '80s. It
was progressively expanded to its present level: shiraz (0.7 ha), tempranillo (0.5 ha), fiano and
graciano (0.4 ha each). The Old Savina Shiraz recognises the efforts of the Savina family,
who planted the shiraz; Arabia, a budget-priced shiraz; Castanets, 100% tempranillo; and
Pickpocket, a rose produced from the juice run-off to concentrate the shiraz.

ΨΨΨΨΨ Castanets 2009 Bright purple-crimson; has a fragrant bouquet, more red
fruits than black, and a pure palate with fine tannins; nicely left field. Tempranillo.
Screwcap. 13.5% alc. **Rating** 93 To 2014 $23

BackVintage Wines   ★★★★☆
2/177 Sailors Bay Road, Northbridge, NSW 2063 **Region** Various
T (02) 9967 9880 **F** (02) 9967 9882 **www**.backvintage.com.au **Open** Mon–Fri 9–5
Winemaker Michael Dijrstra, Nick Bulleid MW, Rob Moody (Contract) **Est.** 2003
Cases 10 000
BackVintage Wines is a virtual winery with a difference; not only does it not own vineyards,
nor a winery, it sells only through its website, or by fax or phone. The team of Michael
Dijrstra, Nick Bulleid and Rob Moody source parcels of bulk wines they consider to represent
excellent quality and value for money. They are then responsible for the final steps before the
wine goes to bottle. In times of surplus they are able to pick and choose, and it looks as if the
days of surplus will extend well into the current decade.

ŶŶŶŶŶ **Margaret River Chardonnay 2008** Imagine this: estate-grown, whole bunch-
✪ pressed, 100% barrel fermented in French oak, matured on lees for nine months;
the nectarine and grapefruit thrive on the oak, and the wine has great line and
length, the finish excellent. The price is as sad as it is ludicrous, a fantastic bargain.
Screwcap. 13% alc. **Rating** 95 **To** 2014 $13

ŶŶŶŶŶ **Barossa Shiraz 2006** Good hue and depth; a complex, well-balanced wine from
✪ a very good vintage makes a mockery of its price; it has excellent line and length,
bringing cedar, cigar box and blackberry fruit and a savoury twist on the finish
into a coherent whole. Screwcap. 14.5% alc. **Rating** 93 **To** 2019 $13

✪ **Margaret River Sauvignon Blanc Semillon 2008** Although the sauvignon
blanc component is greater than the semillon, grassy, citrussy characters are the
dominant play on a clean and crisp palate that finishes very well. Great bargain.
Screwcap. 12.5% alc. **Rating** 91 **To** 2012 $13

✪ **Coonawarra Cabernet Sauvignon 2006** Good colour, still crimson; the
aromatic bouquet offers a mix of ripe blackcurrant, earth and cedar/mocha oak,
the long palate providing a replay, but adding fine-grained tannins; 15 months in
American and French oak. Screwcap. 13.8% alc. **Rating** 91 **To** 2016 $13

ŶŶŶŶ **Eden Valley Riesling 2008** Bright, light greenish hue; has lime and lemon
✪ aromas and flavours; the only criticism is a lack of drive on the palate, but it's hard
to quibble at this price, for it is true to region and variety. Screwcap. 13.1% alc.
Rating 88 **To** 2013 $11
Chardonnay Pinot Cuvee Brut NV Rating 88 **To** 2011 $13
Barossa Cabernet Sauvignon 2005 Rating 87 **To** 2011 $13

Baddaginnie Run   ★★★★☆

PO Box 579, North Melbourne, Vic 3051 **Region** Strathbogie Ranges
T (03) 9348 9310 **F** (03) 9348 9370 **www**.baddaginnierun.net.au **Open** Not
Winemaker Toby Barlow **Est.** 1996 **Cases** 2000 **Vyds** 24 ha
Winsome McCaughey and Professor Snow Barlow (Professor of Horticulture and Viticulture
at the University of Melbourne) spend part of their week in the Strathbogie Ranges, and part
in Melbourne. The business name, Seven Sisters Vineyard, reflects the seven generations of the
McCaughey family associated with the land since 1870; Baddaginnie is the nearby township.
The vineyard is one element in a restored valley landscape, 100 000 indigenous trees having
been replanted. The wines are made at Plunkett Fowles under the direction of son Toby
Barlow, former Mitchelton winemaker. Exports to Canada and China.

ŶŶŶŶŶ **Strathbogie Ranges Shiraz 2008** Light, clear red; a truly delicious wine,
sandwiched in at the last minute between some five-red-star wineries; I thought
the comparison would be fatal, but it certainly isn't. This medium-bodied shiraz
has vibrant and fresh red cherry, black cherry and blackberry fruit, the tannins fine,
the French and American oak in its due place. Screwcap. 13.5% alc. **Rating** 94
To 2018 $24

Badger's Brook   ★★★☆

874 Maroondah Highway, Coldstream, Vic 3770 **Region** Yarra Valley
T (03) 5962 4130 **F** (03) 5962 4130 **www**.badgersbrook.com.au **Open** Wed–Sun 11–5
Winemaker Contract **Est.** 1993 **Cases** 3000 **Vyds** 5.1 ha
Situated next door to the well-known Rochford, the vineyard is planted to chardonnay,
sauvignon blanc, pinot noir, shiraz (1 ha each), cabernet sauvignon (0.5 ha), merlot, viognier
(0.2 ha each), with a few rows each of viognier, roussanne, marsanne and tempranillo. All of
the grapes are Yarra Valley sourced, including for the second Storm Ridge label. Now houses
the smart brasserie restaurant Bella Vedere Cucina with well-known chef Gary Cooper in
charge. Exports to Asia.

ＹＹＹＹ♀   Yarra Valley Rose 2009 Light pink; fragrant, flowery red berry/strawberry
✪   aromas; fresh, long, well-balanced palate; good Rose. Screwcap. 12.5% alc.
            Rating 90 To 2011 $18

ＹＹＹＹ   Yarra Valley Pinot Noir 2008 Rating 89 To 2014 $27
            Yarra Valley Chardonnay 2008 Rating 87 To 2012 $22
            Yarra Valley Shiraz 2006 Rating 87 To 2015 $25

Baileys of Glenrowan   ★★★★★

Cnr Taminick Gap Road/Upper Taminick Road, Glenrowan, Vic 3675 **Region** Glenrowan
T (03) 5766 2392 **F** (03) 5766 2596 **www.**baileysofglenrowan.com.au **Open** 7 days 10–5
Winemaker Paul Dahlenburg **Est.** 1870 **Cases** 15 000 **Vyds** 143 ha
Just when it seemed that Baileys would remain one of the forgotten outposts of the Foster's
group, the reverse has occurred. Since 1998, Paul Dahlenburg has been in charge of Baileys
and has overseen an expansion in the vineyard and the construction of a 2000-tonne winery.
The cellar door has a heritage museum, winery-viewing deck, contemporary art gallery and
landscaped grounds, preserving much of the heritage value. Baileys has also picked up the
pace with its Muscat and Tokay, reintroducing the Winemaker's Selection at the top of the
tree, while continuing the larger-volume Founder series. In April 2009 Foster's announced the
winery, vineyards and brand would be listed for sale as a going concern basis; until sold, the
winery will continue to operate as usual, and every effort made to protect the value of what
is an iconic brand. Exports to the UK and NZ.

ＹＹＹＹＹ   Winemaker's Selection Old Tokay NV Obvious age showing from its
            mahogany/olive-green colour; classic tea-leaf, butterscotch and malt flavours;
            great harmony with the spirit; a long finish, at once sweet yet dry and spicy. Cork.
            16.5% alc. Rating 95 To 2011 $75
            Winemaker's Selection Old Muscat NV Gloriously rich, luscious and
            powerful; retains the essence of raisin muscat, but complexed by rancio and
            oriental spices; again, perfect harmony with the fortifying spirit. Cork. 17% alc.
            Rating 95 To 2011 $75
            Founder Liqueur Muscat NV Intense, lively, grapey varietal character of raisins
            and plum pudding; acidity gives more lift and intensifies the flavour, yet does not
            bite; the volatile component of the acidity appears low. Cork. 17% alc. Rating 94
            To 2011 $24

ＹＹＹＹ♀   Founder Liqueur Tokay NV Rating 93 To 2011 $24
            Founder Tawny Port NV Rating 92 To 2011 $24

Baillieu Vineyard   ★★★★

Merricks Wine General Store, 3460 Frankston-Flinders Road, Merricks, Vic 3916
Region Mornington Peninsula
T (03) 5989 8088 **F** (03) 5989 7199 **www.**baillieuvineyard.com.au **Open** 7 days 9–5
Winemaker Balnarring Estate (Kathleen Quealy) **Est.** 1999 **Cases** 3000 **Vyds** 10 ha
Charlie and Samantha Baillieu have re-established the former Foxwood Vineyard, growing
chardonnay, viognier, pinot gris, pinot noir and shiraz. The north-facing vineyard is part of the
64-ha Bulldog Run property owned by the Baillieus.

ＹＹＹＹ♀   Mornington Peninsula Shiraz 2007 Holding crimson-purple hue well; a
            classy cool-grown style, with enough pepper and spice – but not too much – for
            the cherry and plum fruit of the palate that finishes with fine tannins. Screwcap.
            13.5% alc. Rating 93 To 2017 $27
            Mornington Peninsula Chardonnay 2008 Bright green-straw; an elegant
            chardonnay from start to finish, stone fruit–driven despite mlf; has good length and
            balance, the oak very subtle. Screwcap. 13% alc. Rating 92 To 2014 $22
            Mornington Peninsula Pinot Gris 2009 The aromas of brown pear and
            honeysuckle leap from the glass and continue on to the expressive palate with
            touches of spice and incipient honey. Screwcap. 13.5% alc. Rating 92 To 2011 $25

Mornington Peninsula Shiraz 2006 A very lively, light- to medium-bodied wine, with a strong dusting of spice and pepper to its juicy red and black fruit aromas and flavours. No need for patience. Screwcap. 13.5% alc. **Rating** 91 **To** 2014 $27

Mornington Peninsula Rose 2009 Pale magenta; has a fragrant mix of strawberry and warm spices, the latter a textural as well as flavour component; good acidity to close. Screwcap. 13% alc. **Rating** 90 **To** 2011 $20

Balgownie Estate   ★★★★★

Hermitage Road, Maiden Gully, Vic 3551 **Region** Bendigo
T (03) 5449 6222 **F** (03) 5449 6506 **www**.balgownieestate.com.au **Open** 7 days 11–5
Winemaker Mark Lane **Est.** 1969 **Cases** 8500 **Vyds** 29.45 ha
Balgownie Estate continues to grow in the wake of its acquisition by the Forrester family. A $3 million winery upgrade coincided with a doubling of the size of the vineyard, and in 2004 Balgownie Estate opened a cellar door in the Yarra Valley (see separate entry). Mark Lane, Winestate Winemaker of the Year '08, has moved from Swings & Roundabouts to take up his position at Balgownie Estate. Exports to the UK, the US and other major markets.

♟♟♟♟♟ Black Label Bendigo Grampians Shiraz 2008 Crimson-purple; everything is correct, the bouquet of lifted dark fruits, the medium-bodied palate with very good texture and structure to the abundant black fruits. Screwcap. 14.5% alc. Rating 94 To 2020 $24

Black Label Bendigo Yarra Valley Cabernet Merlot 2008 Strong crimson; clever winemaking has blended Bendigo (51%)/Yarra Valley (41%) Cabernet with Grampians (8%) Merlot; this is a distinguished wine, medium- to full-bodied yet elegant, with a nod to Bordeaux thanks to its slightly savoury twist on the finish. Screwcap. 14% alc. Rating 94 To 2023 $24

♟♟♟♟♟ Bendigo Viognier 2008 Rating 91 To 2013 $40

♟♟♟♟ Bendigo Merlot 2008 Rating 88 To 2017 $60

Balgownie Estate (Yarra Valley)   ★★★★☆

Cnr Melba Highway/Gulf Road, Yarra Glen, Vic 3775 **Region** Yarra Valley
T (03) 9730 0700 **F** (03) 9730 0750 **www**.balgownieestate.com.au **Open** 7 days 10–5
Winemaker Mark Lane **Est.** 2004 **Cases** 5000 **Vyds** 6.84 ha
The Yarra Valley operation of Balgownie Estate neatly fits in with the Bendigo wines, each supporting the other. Winemaking to one side, Balgownie has the largest vineyard-based resort in the Yarra Valley, with 65 rooms and a limited number of spa suites. It specialises in catering for conferences and functions, and Rae's Restaurant is open seven days for breakfast and lunch.

♟♟♟♟♟ Black Label Sauvignon Blanc 2009 An intense and highly fragrant bouquet, with pristine varietal aromas and flavours ranging through passionfruit to citrus to herbs, although predominantly at the tropical end of the spectrum. Screwcap. 13% alc. Rating 94 To 2011 $24

♟♟♟♟♟ Pinot Noir 2008 Rating 93 To 2014 $29

Black Label Pinot Gris 2009 Rating 90 To 2011 $24

♟♟♟♟ Premium Cuvee Brut NV Rating 88 To 2013 $19

Ballabourneen Wines   ★★★★☆

Broke Road, Rothbury, NSW 2320 **Region** Hunter Valley
T (02) 4930 7027 **F** (02) 4930 9180 **www**.ballabourneenwines.com.au
Open Thurs–Sun 10–5, or by appt
Winemaker Daniel Binet **Est.** 1994 **Cases** NA **Vyds** 4.5 ha
In December 2008, young gun Daniel Binet, until that time winemaker at Capercaillie, formed a partnership with Alex and Di Stuart, who between 1994 and '98 had established 2 ha of

chardonnay, 1.5 ha of verdelho and 1 ha of shiraz, using organic principles. The formerly low profile of Ballabourneen will lift, the cellar door having been established in what was previously the Evans Family Wines cellar door on what is known locally as 'The Golden Mile' of the Broke Road. The 2009 vintage provided semillon, chardonnay, shiraz and chambourcin, with a first-up release of Tempranillo Rose and Sparkling Moscato (what else?)

ŢŢŢŢŢ **Hunter Valley Semillon 2009** Has those unusual but very attractive citrus zest aromas and flavours of '09 semillons, which could easily be confused as rieslings; has excellent drive. Screwcap. 10.5% alc. **Rating** 94 **To** 2019 $22

Ballandean Estate Wines ★★★★☆

Sundown Road, Ballandean, Qld 4382 **Region** Granite Belt
T (07) 4684 1226 **F** (07) 4684 1288 **www.**ballandeanestate.com **Open** 7 days 9–5
Winemaker Dylan Rhymer, Angelo Puglisi **Est.** 1970 **Cases** 15 000 **Vyds** 35.25 ha
The senior winery of the Granite Belt is owned by the ever-cheerful and charming Angelo Puglisi and wife Mary. Mary has introduced a gourmet food gallery at the winery, featuring foods produced in the Granite Belt by local food artisans as well as Greedy Me gourmet products made by Mary herself. 2009 saw Ballandean wines appearing on the wine lists of Vue de Monde in Melbourne and Aria in Brisbane. One of the specialities of the winery has always been Sylvaner, the 2006 vintage released mid-'10. A winery on the ascendant. Exports to Canada and Taiwan.

ŢŢŢŢŢ **Generation 3 2005** Impressive red-purple; the wine lives up to the promise of the colour, with a harmonious bouquet and a classy medium-bodied palate; good texture, structure, balance and length, the black fruits neatly caressed by a touch of oak and supported by tannins. A screwcap would have guaranteed the survival of the wine for several generations to come, the base of the ProCork deeply and evenly stained, showing failure of the membrane. Cabernet Sauvignon/Shiraz. 14.5% alc. **Rating** 94 **To** 2020 $45

ŢŢŢŢŢ **Late Harvest Sylvaner 2002 Rating** 93 **To** 2014 $32
Family Reserve Granite Belt Cabernet Merlot 2007 Rating 90 **To** 2017 $25

ŢŢŢŢ **Family Reserve Viognier 2008 Rating** 89 **To** 2013 $22
Family Reserve Shiraz 2008 Rating 89 **To** 2020 $25
Family Reserve Shiraz 2007 Rating 89 **To** 2014 $25
Family Reserve Shiraz 2006 Rating 89 **To** 2015 $25

Ballast Stone Estate Wines ★★★★☆

Myrtle Grove Road, Currency Creek, SA 5214 **Region** Currency Creek
T (08) 8555 4215 **F** (08) 8555 4216 **www.**ballaststonewines.com **Open** 7 days 10.30–5
Winemaker John Loxton **Est.** 2001 **Cases** 80 000 **Vyds** 410 ha
The Shaw family have been vintners for over 35 years, commencing plantings in McLaren Vale in the early 1970s. Extensive vineyards are now held in McLaren Vale (60 ha) and Currency Creek (350 ha), with a modern winery in Currency Creek. The family produces around 80 000 cases under the Ballast Stone Estate label as well as supplying others. The wine portfolio impressively over-delivers on value. Exports to the UK, the US and other major markets.

ŢŢŢŢŢ **RMS McLaren Vale Cabernet Sauvignon 2005** Unashamedly full-bodied, made from 65-year-old vines (uncommon) and spent 32 months in French oak hogsheads; the palate is long and intensely focused, the blackcurrant fruit, tannins and oak all having their say. Cork. 15% alc. **Rating** 94 **To** 2022 $50

ŢŢŢŢŢ **Currency Creek Rose 2009** Very aromatic strawberry and raspberry aromas
❍ carry through to a crisp, zesty minerally palate with a pleasingly dry finish. Truly lovely rose. Sangiovese. Screwcap. 12.5% alc. **Rating** 93 **To** 2010 $17
❍ **McLaren Vale Shiraz 2008** Dense colour; an unequivocally full-bodied shiraz typical of its region, with a rich display of dark chocolate, licorice and blackberry; solid tannins are in balance. Screwcap. 14.5% alc. **Rating** 91 **To** 2028 $17

Currency Creek Sauvignon Blanc 2009 Rating 90 To 2011 $17

⊘ Stonemason Currency Creek Shiraz 2008 Good colour and clarity; a supple, light- to medium-bodied red, with no frills, but does have good black fruit flavours and adequate tannins. Astonishing gold medal Sydney Wine Show '10. Screwcap. 14.5% alc. Rating 90 To 2012 $12

🍷🍷🍷🍷 Stonemason Currency Creek Semillon Sauvignon Blanc 2009 This isn't a
⊘ great, or even very good, wine, but it's hard to imagine what more you would seek at this price point; it is varietally correct, with a mix of passionfruit, lemon and grass, the finish clean. Screwcap. 11.5% alc. Rating 88 To 2011 $12

⊘ Stonemason Currency Creek Cabernet Sauvignon 2008 Very good colour; light- to medium-bodied with blackcurrant fruit needing a little more density and structure – but then it's only $12, and good value. Screwcap. 14.5% alc. Rating 87 To 2011 $12

Balnaves of Coonawarra   ★★★★★

Main Road, Coonawarra, SA 5263 **Region** Coonawarra
T (08) 8737 2946 **F** (08) 8737 2945 **www.**balnaves.com.au **Open** Mon–Fri 9–5, w'ends 12–5
Winemaker Pete Bissell **Est.** 1975 **Cases** 9000 **Vyds** 55 ha
Grapegrower, viticultural consultant and vigneron, Doug Balnaves has over 50 ha of high-quality estate vineyards. The wines are invariably excellent, often outstanding, notable for their supple mouthfeel, varietal integrity, balance and length; the tannins are always fine and ripe, the oak subtle and perfectly integrated. Coonawarra at its best. Winery of the Year 2008 Wine Companion. Exports to the UK, The Netherlands, Germany, Denmark, Canada, Vietnam, Japan, Malaysia, Indonesia and Hong Kong.

🍷🍷🍷🍷🍷 The Tally Reserve Cabernet Sauvignon 2008 Vivid crimson-purple; like a rich little boy, has everything he wishes; a fragrant dark berry bouquet with notes of French oak, leather and spice, then a full-bodied palate with a dazzling array of flavours; however, it is in the supple texture, perfect balance and line that the greatness of the wine finally takes shape. ProCork. 14.5% alc. Rating 97 To 2038 $90

Shiraz 2008 Dense, deep purple-crimson; has more structure and depth than the usual silky medium-bodied Balnaves style; the difference lies in style, not quality, for this medium- to full-bodied shiraz has layers of black berry fruits, pepper and spice, French oak from top rank barrel makers adding a further dimension, as do firm tannins. Screwcap. 14.5% alc. Rating 95 To 2028 $24

Cabernet Sauvignon 2008 Bright purple-crimson; a more classic Balnaves style, although very intense and long; cassis and blackcurrant fruit has an intriguing web of spice, briar and leather underlying the primary fruit; it has literally devoured the French oak in which it spent 16 months, and has excellent tannins. ProCork. 14.5% alc. Rating 95 To 2033 $35

Cabernet Merlot 2008 Dense purple; another powerful wine from Balnaves, with intense blackcurrant, plum and cassis fruit; the density of the fruit is matched by the tannins and oak; will be very long lived. Screwcap. 14.5% alc. Rating 94 To 2030 $24

The Blend 2008 A blend of Cabernet Sauvignon (75%)/Merlot (25%) and an irrelevant 1% of other varieties; has excellent colour, and a racy character to the cassis, blackcurrant and spice fruit obscured by the sheer power of the other Balnave reds. Screwcap. 14.5% alc. Rating 94 To 2020 $19

🍷🍷🍷🍷⌣ Sparkling Cabernet NV Rating 90 To 2015 $28

Balthazar of the Barossa   ★★★★☆

PO Box 675, Nuriootpa, SA 5355 **Region** Barossa Valley
T (08) 8562 2949 **F** (08) 8562 2949 **www.**balthazarbarossa.com **Open** At the Small Winemakers Centre, Chateau Tanunda
Winemaker Anita Bowen **Est.** 1999 **Cases** 6000

Anita Bowen announced her occupation as 'a 40-something sex therapist with a 17-year involvement in the wine industry'. Anita undertook her first vintage at Mudgee, then McLaren Vale, and ultimately the Barossa; she worked at St Hallet while studying at Roseworthy College. A versatile lady, indeed. As to her wine, she says, 'Anyway, prepare a feast, pour yourself a glass (no chalices, please) of Balthazar and share it with your concubines. Who knows? It may help to lubricate thoughts, firm up ideas and get the creative juices flowing!' Exports to Canada, Malaysia, China and Singapore.

ŸŸŸŸŸ **Shiraz 2007** Crimson-purple; the decision to pick in mid-February paid big dividends with this Shiraz, ditto the 21 months in French oak hogsheads, mainly seasoned; it has juicy plum and black cherry fruit, and none of the toughness that marred many '07s. Screwcap. 14.3% alc. **Rating** 94 **To** 2027 $49.95

ŸŸŸŸŸ **Ishtar Adelaide Hills Pinot Grigio 2009** Rating 93 To 2011 $19.50
Ishtar Grenache Shiraz Mourvedre 2008 Rating 91 To 2012 $19.50
Ishtar Goddess White Viognier 2009 Rating 90 To 2013 $19.50

Banks Road   ★★★★☆
600 Banks Road, Marcus Hill, Vic 3222 **Region** Geelong
T (03) 5258 3777 **F** (03) 5258 2797 **www**.banksroadwine.com.au **Open** W'ends 11–5
Winemaker Peter Kimber, William Derham **Est.** 2001 **Cases** 2000 **Vyds** 6 ha
Banks Road, owned and operated by William Derham, has two vineyards: the first, 2.5 ha, is on the Bellarine Peninsula at Marcus Hill, planted to pinot noir, chardonnay, pinot gris, shiraz and sauvignon blanc; the second is at Harcourt in the Bendigo region, planted to shiraz and cabernet sauvignon, the vines ranging from 8 to 12 years of age.

ŸŸŸŸŸ **Geelong Shiraz 2007** Strong colour; a most attractive medium-bodied wine, with a honeycomb of spice running through the blackberry and plum fruit; has very good balance and mouthfeel, the fruit perfectly ripened. Screwcap. 14% alc. Rating 94 To 2017 $30

ŸŸŸŸŸ **Geelong Pinot Noir 2008** Rating 92 To 2014 $30
Geelong Chardonnay 2008 Rating 91 To 2013 $25

Banksia Grove   ★★★☆
215 Heathcote-Redesdale Road, Heathcote, Vic 3523 **Region** Heathcote
T (03) 9948 0311 **F** (03) 9948 0322 **www**.banksiagrovewine.com.au **Open** By appt
Winemaker Ian Leamon (Contract) **Est.** 2002 **Cases** 1250
When Kim and Bernadette Chambers purchased the Banksia Grove vineyard in early 2002, they inherited some of the oldest vines in Heathcote, planted in the late 1970s. The prior owners had sold the grapes each year, and made no wine. The Chambers have worked hard to restore the somewhat dilapidated vineyard they inherited, and have extended the plantings by 2 ha, so that there are now 5 ha of shiraz, and 0.6 ha each of cabernet sauvignon and chardonnay. The wines are released with some bottle age.

ŸŸŸŸŸ **Heathcote Shiraz 2005** Excellent colour; an ultra-powerful full-bodied shiraz that has many good characters, but can't escape the tentacles of the alcohol; a true blue curate's egg, the points a compromise. Cork. 15.6% alc. **Rating** 90 To 2018 $26

ŸŸŸŸ **Heathcote Chardonnay 2008** Rating 89 To 2013 $20

Bannockburn Vineyards   ★★★★★
Midland Highway, Bannockburn, Vic 3331 (postal) **Region** Geelong
T (03) 5281 1363 **F** (03) 5281 1349 **www**.bannockburnvineyards.com **Open** By appt
Winemaker Michael Glover **Est.** 1974 **Cases** 10 000
With the qualified exception of the Cabernet Merlot, which can be a little leafy and gamey, Bannockburn produces outstanding wines across the range, all with individuality, style, great

complexity and depth of flavour. The low-yielding estate vineyards play their role. Winemaker Michael Glover is determined to enhance the reputation of Bannockburn. Exports to Canada, Dubai, Korea, China, Singapore and Hong Kong.

ŦŦŦŦŦ **Serre 2006** Bright, clear hue; a very sophisticated Pinot Noir, with red and black cherry, spice, cedar and a little forest floor all seamlessly interwoven on both bouquet and palate; the texture and mouthfeel are admirable. Cork. 12.5% alc. **Rating** 96 **To** 2016 $95

✪ **Bruce 2006** A distinctly elegant wine, with fine tannins supporting a mouthwatering array of predominantly red fruits. Very clever winemaking has produced an excellent result. Cabernet Sauvignon/Merlot/Shiraz. Cork. 14% alc. **Rating** 96 **To** 2016 $25

Geelong Chardonnay 2007 A clever feat of winemaking to cut back the normally very opulent Bannockburn style in the face of a very warm vintage: preventing mlf, reducing the percentage of new oak to one-third and reducing the time in barrel to 12 months. The end result is a vibrantly juicy and long palate. Cork. 13.5% alc. **Rating** 95 **To** 2014 $55

S.R.H. 2006 Bright green-straw; marries layered complexity with finesse; a potentially great Chardonnay playing dice with the cork gods; the points are a compromise – buy the wine if you are happy to run the gauntlet. 13.5% alc. **Rating** 95 **To** 2015 $75

Geelong Shiraz 2006 Some colour shift towards maturity; an exceptionally complex bouquet with a full array of Asian spices including cinnamon and garam marsala; the palate retains these characters woven through the blackberry and black cherry fruit, the tannins fine and soft. Cork. 15% alc. **Rating** 95 **To** 2021 $52

✪ **Geelong Sauvignon Blanc 2008** Bright green-straw; a complex wine from go to whoa; there are layers of ripe gooseberry and passionfruit supported by well-judged barrel ferment in older oak; its own master, neither in a Loire or White Bordeaux mould. Oh, why a cork? 13% alc. **Rating** 94 **To** 2013 $28

Geelong Pinot Noir 2007 The class of the wine is immediately apparent, with great mouthfeel, balance and length; perhaps there is a touch of mint (possibly reflecting low alcohol), but it is a minor part of a delicious Pinot made in a difficult year. Cork. 12% alc. **Rating** 94 **To** 2014 $57

ŦŦŦŦŦ **Geelong Riesling 2008 Rating** 90 **To** 2016 $26

Banrock Station   ★★★

Holmes Road (off Sturt Highway), Kingston-on-Murray, SA 5331 **Region** Riverland
T (08) 8583 0299 **F** (08) 8583 0288 **www**.banrockstation.com.au **Open** Mon–Fri 9–4, w'ends & public hols 9–5
Winemaker Paul Burnett **Est.** 1994 **Cases** NFP **Vyds** 240 ha
The eco-friendly $1 million visitor centre at Banrock Station is a major tourist destination. Owned by Constellation, the Banrock Station property covers over 1700 ha, with 240 ha of vineyard and the remainder being a major wildlife and wetland preservation area. Recycling of all waste water and use of solar energy add to the preservation image. Each bottle of Banrock Station wine sold generates funds for wildlife preservation, with $5 million already contributed. The wines have consistently offered good value, even the more expensive alternative variety releases that have recently come onto the market. Exports to the UK, the US and Canada.

ŦŦŦŦ ✪ **Mediterranean Collection Pinot Grigio 2009** Early picking and highly protective winemaking has given the wine unexpected zest and length. Drink asap. Screwcap. 12% alc. **Rating** 88 **To** 2011 $15

✪ **Mediterranean Collection Savagnin 2009** Here the new-style label is positively terse: 'fresh and lively white peach and pear complemented by subtle oak and spice'. It also has good vibrancy and length into the bargain. Screwcap. 13% alc. **Rating** 88 **To** 2011 $15

Mediterranean Collection Fiano 2009 Given its growing conditions and young vines, has good flavour, encompassing (according to the spiffy new labels) 'fresh lime, grapefruit, stone fruit and tropical fruit', which doesn't leave anything of consequence out. Screwcap. 13.5% alc. **Rating** 87 **To** 2011 $15

Mediterranean Collection Montepulciano 2008 Fresh cherry and bramble bouquet; light bodied, with good acidity and a slight savoury, briny conclusion; interesting and well constructed. Screwcap. 14% alc. **Rating** 87 **To** 2012 $15 BE

Bantry Grove   ★★★★

519 Three Brothers Road, Newbridge, NSW 2795 **Region** Orange
T (02) 6368 1036 **F** (02) 6368 1002 www.bantrygrove.com.au **Open** By appt
Winemaker Richard Parker **Est.** 1990 **Cases** 265 **Vyds** 12.3 ha
Terrey and Barbie Johnson (and family) grow beef cattle on a property at the southern end of Orange. Seeking to diversify, and to lessen the impact of drought through the establishment of an irrigated perennial crop, the Johnsons have planted a vineyard at an elevation of 960 m, making it one of the coolest in the region. The plantings began in 1990 with chardonnay and cabernet sauvignon, the latter now grafted or removed because the climate is simply too cool. Most of the 80–85-tonne production from the chardonnay, merlot, sauvignon blanc, pinot noir and pinot gris is sold to McWilliam's and Centennial Vineyards, leaving enough to make 265 cases for the Bantry Grove label. The wines are sold through membership of Bantry Grove's Inner Circle Wine Club and local outlets, with some Sydney distribution.

♟♟♟♟♟ **Orange Sauvignon Blanc 2008** More in a citrus and grass spectrum than the tropical end; clean and well balanced, with good acidity on the long finish. Screwcap. 13.4% alc. **Rating** 91 **To** 2011 $17

Orange Chardonnay 2007 A tight, cool-climate style with nectarine, citrus and racy acidity driving the palate; still very fresh and may never be particularly complex, but is nonetheless commendable. Screwcap. 13.8% alc. **Rating** 90 **To** 2014 $17.50

Orange Pinot Noir 2008 Bright hue; has a slightly curious high-toned edge to the bouquet, but the red-fruited palate flavours and texture are clearly varietal; light-bodied, but quite long. Very promising. Screwcap. 14.5% alc. **Rating** 90 **To** 2013 $21

♟♟♟♟ **Orange Chardonnay 2008** Rating 89 **To** 2013 $19
Orange Merlot 2007 Rating 89 **To** 2013 $19

Barambah   ★★★☆

79 Goshnicks Road, off Redgate Road, Murgon, Qld 4605 **Region** South Burnett
T 1300 781 815 **F** 1300 138 949 www.barambah.com.au **Open** Thurs–Sun 10–5
Winemaker Peter Scudamore-Smith MW (Contract) **Est.** 1995 **Cases** 1000 **Vyds** 12 ha
Barambah has been purchased by Brisbane couple Jane and Steve Wilson. They live in a historic 19th-century West End home, but have owned a 1600-ha cattle property, Barambah Station, for the past seven years. This made them near-neighbours of Barambah, and they had ample opportunity to watch the development of the estate vineyard and the quality of its wines. When the opportunity came to purchase the winery and vineyard, they obtained consultancy advice from Peter Scudamore-Smith MW. His response was so positive they did not hesitate to buy the property.

♟♟♟♟♟ **Rack Dried Semillon 2009** Bright green; a mix of rack-dried and cane-cut semillon refermented in French barriques with dry semillon using the Italian passito method; bright acidity finishes an impressive wine. Screwcap. 9.5% alc. **Rating** 92 **To** 2013 $24

♟♟♟♟ **First Grid Shiraz 2008** Rating 89 **To** 2018 $32
First Grid Shiraz 2007 Rating 88 **To** 2015 $32

Barnadown Run ★★★★

390 Cornella Road, Toolleen, Vic 3551 **Region** Heathcote
T (03) 5433 6376 **F** (03) 5433 6386 **www**.barnadownrun.com.au **Open** 7 days 10–5
Winemaker Andrew Millis **Est.** 1995 **Cases** 1200 **Vyds** 5 ha
Named after the original pastoral lease of which the vineyard forms part, established on
the rich terra rossa soil for which Heathcote vineyards are famous. Owner Andrew Millis
carries out both the viticulture and winemaking at the vineyard, which is planted to cabernet
sauvignon, merlot, shiraz and viognier. Exports to Canada, Norway, Hong Kong, Singapore
and China.

ΨΨΨΨ **Henry Bennett's Voluptuary 2005** A blend of Shiraz (60%)/Cabernet
Sauvignon (25%)/Malbec (7.5%)/Merlot (7.5%), all stated to be approximate!
Henry Bennett founded the Barnadown lease, and enjoyed, so it is said, luxury
and sensual pleasure, the inspiration for this wine; is certainly rich and ripe, and has
structure from the pressings. Diam. 14.5% alc. **Rating** 92 **To** 2015 $44

Barokes Wines ★★★

Suite 402, 111 Cecil Street, South Melbourne, Vic 3205 (postal) **Region** Various
T (03) 9675 4349 **F** (03) 9675 4594 **www**.wineinacan.com **Open** Not
Winemaker Steve Barics **Est.** 2003 **Cases** 250 000
Barokes Wines packages its wines in aluminium cans. The filling process is patented, and the
wine has been in commercial production since 2003. The wines show normal maturation
and none of the cans used since start-up show signs of corrosion. Wines are supplied in bulk
by large wineries in South Eastern Australia, with Peter Scudamore-Smith acting as blending
consultant. The wines are perfectly adequate for the market they serve, with remarkably even
quality, and are prolific winners of bronze and silver medals at international wine shows. In
2009 Barokes took the final step at the Berlin Wine Trophy Competition, where its Cabernet
Shiraz Merlot received a gold medal. Exports to all major markets with increasing success,
with production rising from 60 000 to 250 000 cases (24 cans per case).

ΨΨΨΨ **Bin 241 Chardonnay Semillon NV** We don't know when the 250 ml
✪   aluminium can was filled, but the wine is fresh and not the least bit reductive; a
faint touch of sweetness does no harm. 13% alc. **Rating** 87 **To** 2010 $4.50

Barossa Valley Estate ★★★★★

Seppeltsfield Road, Marananga, SA 5352 **Region** Barossa Valley
T (08) 8568 6900 **F** (08) 8562 4255 **www**.bve.com.au **Open** 7 days 10–4.30
Winemaker Stuart Bourne **Est.** 1985 **Cases** 50 000 **Vyds** 40.12 ha
Barossa Valley Estate is jointly owned by Constellation Wines Australia and Barossa Growers
Holdings Limited, the latter representing the grower shareholders of the original co-operative.
The 40 ha of vines directly owned by Barossa Valley Estate (shiraz, cabernet sauvignon, merlot,
grenache, chardonnay and marsanne) contribute only a small part of the production; most of
the grapes come from the grower shareholders. Across the board, the wines are full flavoured
and honest. E&E Black Pepper Shiraz is an upmarket label with a strong reputation and
following; the Ebenezer range likewise. Exports to the UK, the US and other major markets.

ΨΨΨΨΨ **Ebenezer Shiraz 2006** Solid colour, still in the red spectrum (no browning);
rich black fruit and licorice aromas, then a powerful full-bodied palate with
intense black fruits, licorice and ripe tannins. Will live for decades. Screwcap.
14.8% alc. **Rating** 95 **To** 2036 $32
✪   **E Bass Barossa Valley Shiraz 2006** Excellent colour; a prime example of a
very good vintage in the Barossa Valley, and also control of alcohol; blackberry and
plum fruit is supported by fine-grained tannins and a touch of oak. Gold medal
Sydney Wine Show '10. Screwcap. 14.5% alc. **Rating** 94 **To** 2020 $20

Ebenezer Cabernet Sauvignon 2006 From one of the relatively rare vintages in the Barossa Valley that was perfect for cabernet sauvignon; the wine has the slight savoury olive twist to its pure blackcurrant fruit one finds in cooler climates; the tannins are persistent and long, and in balance. Screwcap. 15.3% alc. **Rating** 94 To 2026 $32

ŶŶŶŶŶ **E Bass Eden Valley Riesling 2009** Floral citrus aromas lead into a bright and
✪ crisp palate that gains momentum on the long back-palate and finish; here lime juice and mineral notes prevail. Screwcap. 11% alc. **Rating** 93 **To** 2019 $18
E Bass Shiraz Tempranillo 2005 Rating 90 **To** 2015 $20

ŶŶŶŶ **E Minor Shiraz 2008** Strong purple; the bouquet offers plum, prune and
✪ blackberry fruit, the full-bodied palate quickly falling into step; bold flavours, not over-much finesse. Screwcap. 14% alc. **Rating** 89 **To** 2015 $15
E Minor Cabernet Merlot 2007 Rating 88 **To** 2013 $15

Barratt ★★★★★
Uley Vineyard, Cornish Road, Summertown, SA 5141 **Region** Adelaide Hills
T (08) 8390 1788 **F** (08) 8390 1788 **www**.barrattwines.com.au **Open** Fri–Sun & most public hols 11.30–5 (closed Jun–Jul)
Winemaker Lindsay Barratt **Est.** 1993 **Cases** 2000 **Vyds** 8.4 ha
This is the venture of former physician Lindsay Barratt and wife Carolyn. Lindsay has always been responsible for viticulture and, following his retirement in 2001, has taken full, hands-on responsibility for winemaking. In '02 he received his graduate diploma in oenology from the University of Adelaide, and the quality of the wines is beyond reproach. Limited quantities are exported to the UK, Malaysia, Taiwan and Singapore.

ŶŶŶŶŶ **Piccadilly Valley Sauvignon Blanc 2009** Spotlessly clean and fresh; the wine is
✪ more slanted to citrus and herbal characters than tropical, but both are present in a harmonious mode; zesty food style. Screwcap. 14% alc. **Rating** 94 **To** 2011 $23
The Reserve Piccadilly Valley Pinot Noir 2008 Similar colour to the Bonython, sharing the spicy notes and the complexity, but with greater fruit intensity on both bouquet and palate; the length and persistence of the palate is also superior. ProCork. 14% alc. **Rating** 94 **To** 2016 $49

ŶŶŶŶŶ **The Bonython Piccadilly Valley Pinot Noir 2008 Rating** 93 **To** 2015 $29
The Ambrose Piccadilly Valley Merlot 2006 Rating 93 **To** 2014 $29
Piccadilly Sunrise Rose 2009 Rating 90 **To** 2011 $21

Barrgowan Vineyard ★★★★☆
30 Pax Parade, Curlewis, Vic 3222 **Region** Geelong
T (03) 5250 3861 **F** (03) 5250 3840 **www**.barrgowanvineyard.com.au **Open** By appt
Winemaker Dick Simonsen **Est.** 1998 **Cases** 150 **Vyds** 0.5 ha
Dick and Dib (Elizabeth) Simonsen began the planting of their shiraz (with five clones) in 1994, intending to simply make wine for their own consumption. With all five clones in full production, the Simonsens expect a maximum production of 200 cases, and accordingly release small quantities of Shiraz, which sell out quickly. The vines are hand-pruned, the grapes hand-picked, the must basket-pressed, and all wine movements are by gravity.

ŶŶŶŶŶ **Simonsens Bellarine Peninsula Shiraz 2008** Deep purple-crimson; blood
✪ plum, licorice, blackberry and spice aromas on the bouquet flow through seamlessly onto the medium-bodied palate; good line, length and balance. Screwcap. 13.4% alc. **Rating** 94 **To** 2023 $25

Barringwood Park ★★★★☆

60 Gillams Road, Lower Barrington, Tas 7306 **Region** Northern Tasmania
T (03) 6492 3140 **F** (03) 6492 3360 **www.**barringwoodpark.com.au **Open** Wed–Sun &
public hols 10–5 (closed Aug)
Winemaker Tom Ravich (Contract) **Est.** 1993 **Cases** 1800 **Vyds** 5.2 ha
Judy and Ian Robinson operate a sawmill at Lower Barrington, 15 minutes south of Devonport
on the main tourist trail to Cradle Mountain, and when they planted 500 vines in 1993 the
aim was to do a bit of home winemaking. In a thoroughly familiar story, the urge to expand
the vineyard and make wine on a commercial scale soon occurred, and they embarked on a
six-year plan, planting 1 ha per year in the first four years and building the cellar and tasting
rooms during the following two years. Another 1.2 ha have recently been planted, and I think
I must acknowledge some responsibility for urging the Robinsons to do so.

♗♗♗♗♗ **Forest Raven Pinot Noir 2008** Vibrant colour; attractive perfume redolent
of raspberry, blueberry, plum, orange rind and clove; a bright and varietal palate,
with elegant and layered red fruits and spice, held together with lively acidity,
fine tannins and a savoury core of ironstone to conclude. Screwcap. 13.2% alc.
Rating 92 **To** 2016 $29.50 BE
Northbank Chardonnay 2008 Pale colour, vibrant hue; a restrained style
relying on fine lemon fruit, a touch of anise and delicate oak for personality;
the palate is light, almost ethereal, exhibiting grace with an underlying energy
provided by fine acidity; certainly in the elegant end of the spectrum. Screwcap.
13.2% alc. **Rating** 90 **To** 2016 $28 BE
Schonburger 2009 Highly perfumed, with musk and candied orange at the
core; the palate is thoroughly seductive and enchanting, with perfume being offset
by generosity without heaviness; long and even to conclude. Screwcap. 12.6% alc.
Rating 90 **To** 2014 $25 BE
Meunier Rose 2009 Pale, bright pink; fresh, bright strawberry fruit; a long
palate that is neither green nor sweet, simply nicely balanced. Screwcap. 13.5% alc.
Rating 90 **To** 2012 $21.50
Pinot Meunier 2008 Pale, bright pink; bright fresh strawberry fruit; not green;
long, not sweet. Silver medal Tas Wine Show '10. Screwcap. 12.8% alc. **Rating** 90
To 2013 $23

♗♗♗♗ **Pinot Gris 2009** Rating 89 **To** 2012 $28
Mill Block Pinot Noir 2008 Rating 89 **To** 2015 $35 BE
IJ Blanc de Blancs 2007 Rating 87 **To** 2013 $36

Barristers Block ★★★★

141 Onkaparinga Valley Road, Woodside, SA 5244 **Region** Adelaide Hills
T 0427 076 237 **F** (08) 8364 2930 **www.**barristersblock.com.au **Open** 7 days 10–5
Winemaker Simon Greenleaf, Shaw & Smith, Tim Knappstein (Contract) **Est.** 2004
Cases 3000 **Vyds** 18 ha
Owner Jan Siemelink-Allen has over 20 years in the industry, and five years in SA's Supreme
Court in a successful battle to reclaim ownership of 10 ha of cabernet sauvignon and shiraz in
Wrattonbully after a joint venture collapsed; it is not hard to imagine the origin of the name.
In 2006 she and her family purchased an 8-ha vineyard planted to sauvignon blanc and pinot
noir near Woodside in the Adelaide Hills, adjoining Shaw & Smith's vineyard. As well as having
senior management positions, Jan is a member of the SA Premier's Wine Industry Advisory
Council; no rose-tinted spectacles here. Exports to the UK, Germany, Vietnam, Malaysia,
Hong Kong and Singapore.

♗♗♗♗♗ **Bully Barossa Wrattonbully Shiraz 2008** Good hue; a well-made, medium- to
full-bodied wine that achieves synergies from the regional blend with its spice and
licorice edge to the rich blackberry fruit at its heart; French oak is balanced and
integrated. Screwcap. 14.5% alc. **Rating** 93 **To** 2019 $27

Adelaide Hills Sauvignon Blanc 2009 A restrained and pure varietal wine, the aromas and flavours clear, although not especially intense, ranging through citrus, apple and passionfruit. Screwcap. 13% alc. **Rating** 90 **To** 2011 $19

 # Barton Creek   NR
154 Peabody Road, Molong, NSW 2866 **Region** Orange
T (02) 6364 2160 **F** (02) 6364 2063 **www**.nyranghomestead.com.au **Open** By appt
Winemaker Madrez Wine Services **Est.** 1998 **Cases** 400 **Vyds** 5.5 ha
The eight-variety vineyard of Barton Creek has been established on the Nyrang Homestead property. The bluestone home was built in the first few years of the 20th century, and contains 36 rooms including seven bathrooms, seven guest rooms, a grand dining room, butler's pantry and wine cellar. It is surrounded by 2 ha of gardens, the plants direct descendants of those first planted. Then there is a school house (available as studio-style accommodation), a coach house, stables, shearing shed, groom's cottage, milking bale and a modern machinery shed. Since 1996 it has been owned by Stephen Sykes and Greg Urbansky, who have undertaken extensive conservation work on the property.

Barton Estate   ★★★
2307 Barton Highway, Murrumbateman, NSW 2582 **Region** Canberra District
T (02) 6230 9553 **F** (02) 6230 9565 **www**.bartonestate.com.au **Open** Not
Winemaker Capital Wines, Canberra Winemakers **Est.** 1997 **Cases** 500 **Vyds** 8 ha
Bob Furbank and wife Julie Chitty are both CSIRO plant biologists: he is a biochemist (physiologist) and she is a specialist in plant tissue culture. In 1997 they acquired the 120-ha property forming part of historic Jeir Station, and have since planted 15 grape varieties. The most significant plantings are to cabernet sauvignon, shiraz, merlot, riesling and chardonnay, the Joseph's coat completed with micro quantities of other varieties.

ΨΨΨΨΨ Blue Rose 2009 Bright, light magenta; an unusual blend of Cabernet Franc/
❂   Malbec works well, giving abundant small red fruits on both bouquet and palate; crisp acidity lengthens the palate and dries the finish. Well above average. Screwcap. 12% alc. **Rating** 91 **To** 2011 $18

Barton Jones/Blackboy Ridge   ★★★☆
39 Upper Capel Road, Donnybrook, WA 6239 **Region** Geographe
T (08) 9731 2233 **F** (08) 9731 2232 **www**.bartonjoneswines.com.au **Open** Fri–Mon 10–4
Winemaker David Crawford **Est.** 1978 **Cases** 2000 **Vyds** 3 ha
The 22-ha property on which Blackboy Ridge Estate is established was partly cleared and planted to 2.5 ha of semillon, chenin blanc, shiraz and cabernet sauvignon in 1978. When current owners Adrian Jones and Jackie Barton purchased the property in 2000 the vines were already some of the oldest in the region. The vineyard and the owners' house are on gentle north-facing slopes, with extensive views over the Donnybrook area. A straw-bale cellar door was completed in July 2010.

ΨΨΨΨΨ Barton Jones The Box Seat Semillon 2007 The hue is still bright and light;
❂   the wine spent eight months in new French oak, but the intensity of the fruit carries the oak without demur; should continue to develop well, braced by its modest alcohol. Screwcap. 12% alc. **Rating** 92 **To** 2015 $21

ΨΨΨΨ Blackboy Ridge Geographe Semillon Sauvignon Blanc 2009 Rating 88
       To 2013 $16
       Blackboy Ridge Geographe Cabernet Shiraz 2008 Rating 88 To 2012 $16

Barton Vineyard

2464 Macquarie Road, Campbell Town, Tas 7210 **Region** Northern Tasmania
T (03) 6398 5114 **F** (03) 6398 5170 **www**.bartonvineyards.com **Open** Last Sunday each
month, or by appt
Winemaker Rebecca Wilson, Winemaking Tasmania **Est.** 2001 **Cases** 300 **Vyds** 2 ha
This is the venture of Milly and Frank Youl. Frank is a sixth-generation Tasmanian with a
farming background on a merino sheep stud; the property, long known as Barton, is adjacent
to the Macquarie River. After planting a few trial vines in 1987, the Youls finally took the
plunge (ignoring most advice) and planted pinot noir and riesling on a north-facing slope
in 2001. They have a small cottage for fly fishers near the Macquarie River, and I believe
I stayed in that cottage one year with fellow judges from the Tasmanian Wines Show. The
cottage brings the Youl family history full circle, as forebear James Youl introduced trout
into Australia.

♟♟♟♟   **Pinot Noir 2008** From the high altitude midlands of Tasmania, the label design
reflecting the more normally fine-wool sheep farming; this is unmistakably pinot,
the bouquet quite aromatic, the palate with plenty of flavour, but a somewhat
sweet finish. Screwcap. 13.5% alc. **Rating** 88 **To** 2014 $22

Barwang ★★★★★

Barwang Road, Young, NSW 2594 (postal) **Region** Hilltops
T (02) 9722 1299 **F** (02) 9722 1260 **www**.mcwilliamswinesgroup.com **Open** Not
Winemaker Andrew Higgins **Est.** 1969 **Cases** NFP **Vyds** 100 ha
Peter Robertson pioneered viticulture in the Young region when he planted his first vines in
1969 as part of a diversification program for his 400-ha grazing property. When McWilliam's
acquired Barwang in 1989, the vineyard amounted to 13 ha; today the plantings are 100 ha.
Wine quality has been exemplary from the word go, value for money no less so. The Barwang
label also takes in 100% Tumbarumba wines, as well as Hilltops/Tumbarumba blends.

♟♟♟♟♟   **Tumbarumba Chardonnay 2008** A restrained bouquet speaking of a high
altitude birth; lemon lies at the heart, with an enticing array of savoury mineral
elements and spice, not least of all a touch of anise; the palate is linear and tightly
wound, with tangy acid setting the light-bodied finish off harmoniously. Screwcap.
13% alc. **Rating** 94 **To** 2016 $20 BE
✪   **Tumbarumba Chardonnay 2007** Glowing yellow-green; delicious cool-grown
style, with an intense interplay between grapefruit on the one hand, and stone fruit
on the other; has drive and energy, and is in no way oak-dependent. Screwcap.
13% alc. **Rating** 94 **To** 2017 $20
✪   **Hilltops Cabernet Sauvignon 2008** Deep crimson; an excellent cabernet from
the first whiff through to the finish and aftertaste, blackcurrant fruit the vehicle
for the adornment of oak and gentle extract of tannins. Seriously underpriced.
Screwcap. 14% alc. **Rating** 94 **To** 2024 $20

♟♟♟♟♟   **Hilltops Shiraz 2008 Rating** 93 **To** 2020 $20

♟♟♟♟   **Hilltops Cabernet Sauvignon 2007 Rating** 87 **To** 2014 $20

Barwick Wines

Yelverton North Road, Dunsborough, WA 6281 **Region** Margaret River
T (08) 9755 7100 **F** (08) 9755 7133 **www**.barwickwines.com **Open** 7 days 11–4
Winemaker Nigel Ludlow **Est.** 1997 **Cases** 120 000 **Vyds** 194 ha
The production gives some guide to the size of the three estate vineyards. The first is the
Dwalganup Vineyard in the Blackwood Valley region; the second is St John's Brook Vineyard
in Margaret River; and the third is the Treenbrook Vineyard in Pemberton. Taken together,
the three vineyard holdings place Barwick in the top 10 wine producers in WA. The wines
are released under four labels, The Collectables at the top from small parcels of estate-grown
grapes. Exports to the UK, the US and other major markets.

♙♙♙♙♙ **The Collectables Blackwood Valley Cabernet Sauvignon 2007** Very good colour; a fragrant bouquet of blackcurrant and cassis leads into a very focused and intense palate with notes of olive and herb, but primarily driven by the pure cabernet black fruit flavours and accompanying cedary French oak. Screwcap. 14% alc. **Rating** 95 **To** 2022 $35

♙♙♙♙♀ **Sauvignon Blanc Semillon 2009** Very well put together; the bouquet has both
✪ tropical and grassy components that mesh well, the palate taking the process a step further, adding gooseberry and passionfruit; structure enhanced by a small barrel ferment component. Screwcap. 13% alc. **Rating** 93 **To** 2011 $15
✪ **O-V Pemberton Viognier 2009** A major surprise; this dessert style seldom works with viognier; luscious stone fruit flavours are balanced and lengthened by citrussy acidity. 375 ml. Screwcap. 9.5% alc. **Rating** 93 **To** 2011 $20
Pemberton Sauvignon Blanc 2009 **Rating** 90 **To** 2011 $20

♙♙♙♙ **Margaret River Chardonnay 2008** **Rating** 89 **To** 2013 $20
The Collectables Pemberton Pinot Noir 2008 **Rating** 89 **To** 2013 $30
✪ **Shiraz 2007** Some colour development; spice, pepper, blackberry and a wisp of dark chocolate on the bouquet are repeated on the medium-bodied palate. Obvious value. Screwcap. 14% alc. **Rating** 89 **To** 2015 $15

Basedow ★★★

PO Box 6612, Silverwater, NSW 1811 (postal) **Region** Barossa Valley
T 1300 887 966 **F** (02) 6574 5164 **www.**basedow.com.au **Open** Not
Winemaker Graeme Scott, Daniela Neumann **Est.** 1896 **Cases** 10 000
An old and proud label, once particularly well known for its oak-matured Semillon, but which has changed hands on a number of occasions before passing into the ownership of James Estate in 2003. Continues making traditional styles, big in flavour, but not so much in finesse, the alcohol remaining relatively high.

♙♙♙♙♀ **Johannes Barossa Valley Shiraz 2007** Good colour; has rich plum and blackberry fruit on both bouquet and palate, vanillan oak making its presence felt on the palate; the tannins are ripe, the balance good. Screwcap. 14% alc. **Rating** 90 **To** 2020 $39

Bass Fine Wines ★★★★

16 Goodman Court, Invermay, Launceston, Tas 7250 **Region** Northern Tasmania
T (03) 6331 0136 **F** (03) 6331 0136 **Open** Mon–Fri 9–5, w'ends 9–4
Winemaker Guy Wagner **Est.** 1999 **Cases** 3000
Owner/winemaker Guy Wagner has built the scope of his business over a period of 10 years, the greater expansion starting in 2007–08. He now makes wines for 17 small vineyards in Northern Tasmania in addition to his own wines; the 2008 crush was over 220 tonnes, with just one cellar hand to assist him. At the end of that year his partnership in the Rosevears winery ended, and a new winery was constructed prior to the 2009 vintage at Invermay, well inside the city of Launceston. The cellar door at this location has glass walls, allowing visitors to observe the workings of a small winery. Retail distribution in Tas, Vic, NSW and ACT. Exports to the US.

Bass Phillip

Tosch's Road, Leongatha South, Vic 3953 **Region** Gippsland
T (03) 5664 3341 **F** (03) 5664 3209 **Open** By appt
Winemaker Phillip Jones **Est.** 1979 **Cases** 1500
Phillip Jones retired from the Melbourne rat-race to handcraft tiny quantities of superlative Pinot Noir which, at its best, has no equal in Australia. Painstaking site selection, ultra-close vine spacing and the very, very cool climate of South Gippsland are the keys to the magic of Bass Phillip and its eerily Burgundian Pinots. Tastings are sporadic and the rating is very much that of the best, not the lesser, wines.

♟♟♟♟♟ **Premium Pinot Noir 2008** Again, very good colour; small wonder the price is where it is; this has exceptional structure and intensity, the dark plum fruit lancing in its purity and extreme length. ProCork. 13.8% alc. **Rating** 96 **To** 2025 $150
The Estate Pinot Noir 2008 Similar colour to Premium; the family plum and spice fruit core is here on the bouquet and entry to the palate, but it is at this stage that the surge and thrust through to the finish puts it in a class above the Crown Prince, the finish and aftertaste wonderfully long. ProCork. 13.5% alc. **Rating** 95 **To** 2023 $85
Crown Prince Pinot Noir 2008 From the 12-year-old vines on Bass Phillip's Village Vineyard; excellent depth and hue to the colour; fragrant plum and spice aromas flow on to the palate, which has great length and intensity with a savoury flourish. ProCork. 13.8% alc. **Rating** 94 **To** 2018 $65

battely wines   ★★★★
1375 Beechworth-Wangaratta Road, Beechworth, Vic 3747 **Region** Beechworth
T (03) 5727 0505 **F** (03) 5727 0506 **www**.battelywines.com.au **Open** By appt
Winemaker Russell Bourne **Est.** 1998 **Cases** 500 **Vyds** 5 ha
Dr Russell Bourne is an anaesthetist and former GP at Mt Beauty who has always loved the food, wine and skiing of North East Victoria. He completed his oenology degree at CSU in 2002 following his 1998 acquisition of the former Brown Brothers Everton Hills vineyard. He has since planted 1.6 ha of shiraz and viognier, more recently adding counoise, the first planting of this variety in Australia. Since 2001 all wines have come from the estate vineyards. Exports to the UK, the US and Hong Kong.

♟♟♟♟♀ **Beechworth Durif 2008** Deep crimson; a strongly accented bouquet of dark berry fruits leads into a full-bodied palate where succulent fruit and truculent tannins wage war on each other – best stand back for five or so years and let the victor emerge. A heavily stained cork may crash the party, however. 15.5% alc. **Rating** 90 **To** 2018 $40

♟♟♟♟ **Beechworth Syrah 2006 Rating** 89 **To** 2016 $56

Battle of Bosworth   ★★★★
Binney Road, Willunga, SA 5172 **Region** McLaren Vale
T (08) 8556 2441 **F** (08) 8556 4881 **www**.battleofbosworth.com.au **Open** Fri–Mon
Winemaker Joch Bosworth **Est.** 1996 **Cases** 5000 **Vyds** 80 ha
Battle of Bosworth is owned and run by Joch Bosworth (viticulture and winemaking) and partner Louise Hemsley-Smith (sales and marketing). The wines take their name from the Battle of Bosworth (which ended the War of the Roses), fought on Bosworth Field, Leicestershire in 1485. The vineyards were established in the early 1970s by parents Peter and Anthea Bosworth, in the foothills of the Mount Lofty Ranges in McLaren Vale. Conversion to organic viticulture began in 1995, with vines now 20 years and older fully certified A-grade organic by ACO. The label depicts the yellow soursob (*Oxalis pes caprae*), hated by gardeners everywhere, but whose growth habits make it an ideal weapon with which to battle weeds in organic viticulture. Shiraz, cabernet sauvignon and chardonnay account for three-quarters of the plantings, with an additional nine varieties making up the numbers. Exports to the UK, the US and other major markets.

♟♟♟♟♀ **McLaren Vale Shiraz 2008** Deep, dark and concentrated black fruit and mulled spices bouquet; the palate is thick with mocha, bitter chocolate and a slight tarry edge to the fruit; chewy and ample to conclude. Screwcap. 14.5% alc. **Rating** 92 **To** 2015 $25 BE
McLaren Vale Cabernet Sauvignon 2008 Deep blackcurrant fruit is framed by anise and olive; full-bodied and rich, with generous levels of dark fruit, and just a little savoury complexity thrown in for good measure. Screwcap. 14% alc. **Rating** 91 **To** 2015 $25 BE

♟♟♟♟ **White Boar 2007 Rating** 89 **To** 2014 $45 BE

Bawley Vale Estate ★★★

226 Bawley Point Road, Bawley Point, NSW 2539 **Region** Shoalhaven Coast
T (02) 4457 2555 **F** (02) 4457 2649 **www**.bawleyvaleestate.com.au **Open** W'ends &
public hols 11–4.30
Winemaker Crooked River Winery (Michelle Crockett) **Est.** 2003 **Cases** 2500 **Vyds** 2.4 ha
Bawley Vale Estate sits on 40 ha of prime south coast land acquired by Raymond and Loris
McLoughlin in 2003. They have planted 0.7 ha of cabernet sauvignon, 0.4 ha each of verdelho,
chardonnay and shiraz, 0.3 ha of chambourcin, 0.2 ha of arneis, plus small plantings of merlot,
along with citrus and olive groves. The wines are sold through local restaurants and bottle
shops and (of course) via the cellar door and website.

♀♀♀♀ Murramarang Vineyard Gantry Chardonnay 2007 Utterly belies its low
  alcohol/early picking for there are quite sweet stone fruit flavours, although the
  finish fades away somewhat. Screwcap. 12% alc. **Rating** 87 **To** 2011 $22

Bay of Fires ★★★★★

40 Baxters Road, Pipers River, Tas 7252 **Region** Northern Tasmania
T (03) 6382 7622 **F** (03) 6382 7225 **www**.bayoffireswines.com.au **Open** 7 days 10–5
Winemaker Fran Austin **Est.** 2001 **Cases** NFP
In 1994 Hardys purchased its first grapes from Tasmania with the aim of further developing
and refining its sparkling wines, a process that quickly gave birth to Arras. The next stage was
the inclusion of various parcels of chardonnay from Tasmania in the 1998 Eileen Hardy, then
the development in 2001 of the Bay of Fires brand, offering wines sourced from various parts
of Tasmania. The winery was originally that of Rochecombe, then Ninth Island, and now, of
course, Bay of Fires. Its potential has now been fully realised in the most impressive imaginable
fashion. Exports to all major markets.

♀♀♀♀♀ Arras EJ Carr Late Disgorged 1998 Shows what can be achieved in more
  ways than one; smooth but complex mid-palate, then a long, lingering finish; has
  real Champagne characteristics; nothing exaggerated; the dosage (low) spot on;
  still remarkably fresh. Trophy Tas Wine Show '10. Cork. 12.5% alc. **Rating** 97
  To 2015 $190
  Arras Brut Elite Chardonnay Pinot Noir NV Good mousse, bright colour;
  toasty brioche aromas, the fruit of the palate also evident; a beautiful wine in
  the mouth; very pure, with white fruit to the fore, but pinot also adding to the
  complexity and length of a perfectly balanced wine. Cork. 12.8% alc. **Rating** 96
  To 2015 $50
  Arras Pinot Noir Chardonnay 2003 Glowing yellow-green; it has exceptional
  intensity on the bouquet and palate alike; stone fruit, citrus and creamy brioche
  flavours flow seamlessly along the palate, the finish lingering for minutes. Trophy
  Tas Wine Show '10. Cork. 13.1% alc. **Rating** 96 **To** 2015 $75
  Riesling 2008 Sourced from a number of small vineyards; touches of nettle and
  herb on the bouquet, with contrasting spicy notes running through the fine lime/
  citrus fruit core; has excellent balance and glorious length. Trophy Tas Wine Show
  '10. Screwcap. 11.7% alc. **Rating** 95 **To** 2014 $31.50
  Chardonnay 2008 The fragrant bouquet is driven by citrus and white peach, as
  is the vibrant and lively palate, complexed by a touch of toasty oak and Tasmanian
  acidity. Gold medal Tas and Sydney Wine Shows '10. Screwcap. 13% alc. **Rating** 94
  To 2016 $38.50

♀♀♀♀♀ Tasmanian Cuvee Brut NV Rating 93 **To** 2012 $33
  Riesling 2009 Rating 92 **To** 2025 $31 BE
  Pinot Gris 2009 Rating 92 **To** 2014 $31 BE
  Tasmanian Cuvee Rose NV Rating 92 **To** 2012 $38.50 BE
  Sauvignon Blanc 2009 Rating 91 **To** 2012 $31

Bay of Shoals   ★★★☆

Cordes Road, Kingscote, Kangaroo Island, SA 5223 **Region** Kangaroo Island
T (08) 8553 0289 **F** (08) 8553 2081 **www**.bayofshoalswines.com.au **Open** 7 days 11–5
Winemaker Anne Trautwein **Est.** 1994 **Cases** NA **Vyds** 10 ha
John Willoughby's vineyard overlooks the Bay of Shoals, which is the northern boundary of
Kingscote, Kangaroo Island's main town. Planting of the vineyard began in 1994 and it now
comprises riesling, chardonnay, sauvignon blanc, cabernet sauvignon and shiraz. In addition,
460 olive trees have been planted to produce table olives.

ŸŸŸŸ **Kangaroo Island Riesling 2009** Light straw-green; an aromatic bouquet
of wild herbs, lime and apple, the palate with gentle citrus flavours. Screwcap.
12.5% alc. **Rating** 89 **To** 2019 $18
Kangaroo Island Chardonnay 2009 One of the cross-dressing chardonnay–
sauvignon blanc brigade unadorned by oak; in fact works well here, with attractive
white flesh stone fruit flavours. Screwcap. 13.5% alc. **Rating** 89 **To** 2012 $18

🍂 Beach Road   ★★★★★

PO Box 1106, McLaren Flat, SA 5171 **Region** Langhorne Creek/McLaren Vale
T (08) 8327 4547 **F** (08) 8327 4547 **www**.beachroadwines.com.au **Open** Not
Winemaker Briony Hoare **Est.** 2007 **Cases** 1000
This is the thoroughly impressive venture of winemaker Briony Hoare and viticulturist Tony
Hoare, who began their life partnership after meeting while studying wine science at the
Roseworthy campus of Adelaide University. Their involvement in the industry dates back to
the early 1990s, Briony working around Australia with many of the flagship wines of (then)
Southcorp, Tony gaining extensive experience in Mildura, the Hunter Valley and McLaren
Vale (it was in McLaren Vale that he spent five years as viticulturist for Wirra Wirra). In 2005
the pair decided to go it alone, setting up a wine consultancy, and in '07 launching Beach
Road. An early focus on Italian varieties stemmed from Briony's vintage in Piedmont where
she worked with barbera, nebbiolo, gavi and moscato. Along the way, however, they both had
a lot of exposure to grenache, shiraz and mourvedre; it is not surprising that one of the first
wines to be released was a Shiraz Grenache, joined by Petit Verdot in '05, Fiano, Greco di Tufo
and Primitivo (the Italian name for zinfandel). The '09 Fiano was awarded the trophy for Best
White Wine at the Australian Alternative Varieties Wine Show '09, while the '09 Greco di
Tufo secured the Chairman's Selection Trophy from Max Allen.

ŸŸŸŸŸ **Petit Verdot 2006** Still deep crimson-purple; dark fruits and bitter chocolate
aromas flow into a rich, concentrated and deep, yet supple, palate; the tannins are
ripe and soft, the oak buried under the avalanche of fruit. Screwcap. 15.5% alc.
Rating 94 **To** 2026 $38
Primitivo 2008 Bright hue; a scented and spicy bouquet and a delicious follow-
on with the palate, the red cherry and spice fruits reminiscent of Californian
zinfandel from cooler regions; very good length and balance, even if oak is
obvious. Screwcap. 14.5% alc. **Rating** 94 **To** 2016 $25

ŸŸŸŸŸ **Shiraz Grenache 2006 Rating** 91 **To** 2016 $25
Fiano 2009 Rating 90 **To** 2012 $22
Greco di Tufo 2009 Rating 90 **To** 2012 $22

ŸŸŸŸ **Petit Verdot 2005 Rating** 89 **To** 2013 $38

Beckett's Flat   ★★★☆

49 Beckett Road, Metricup, WA 6280 **Region** Margaret River
T (08) 9755 7402 **F** (08) 9755 7344 **www**.beckettsflat.com.au **Open** 7 days 10–6
Winemaker Belizar Ilic **Est.** 1992 **Cases** 8000 **Vyds** 13.6 ha
Belizar (Bill) and Noni Ilic opened Beckett's Flat in 1997. Situated just off the Bussell
Highway, midway between Busselton and the Margaret River, it draws upon estate vineyards,
first planted in 1992 (cabernet sauvignon, shiraz, sauvignon blanc, chardonnay, verdelho,

semillon and merlot). The wines, which are made onsite, include a range of kosher wines under the Five Stones label. Exports to Canada.

ŸŸŸŸ   **Single Vineyard Estate Margaret River Sauvignon Blanc 2009** Quite pungent green nettle bouquet; fresh, crisp and fine with good varietal intensity. Screwcap. 13% alc. **Rating** 89 $19.50 BE

Beckingham Wines   ★★★★

6-7/477 Warrigal Road, Moorabbin, Vic 3189 **Region** Mornington Peninsula
T 0400 192 264 **www**.beckinghamwines.com.au **Open** W'ends 10–5
Winemaker Peter Beckingham **Est.** 1998 **Cases** 4000
Peter Beckingham is a chemical engineer who has turned a hobby into a business, moving operations from the driveway of his house to a warehouse in Moorabbin. The situation of the winery may not be romantic, but it is eminently practical, and more than a few winemakers in California have adopted the same solution. His friends grow the grapes, and he makes the wine, both for himself and as a contract maker for others.

ŸŸŸŸŸ   **Pas de Deux Pinot Noir Chardonnay 1998** Good mousse, and a bright, light yellow-gold colour; with over 10 years on lees, continues to show remarkable elegance and finesse; the bouquet has toast and brioche complexity, the palate creamy and long, finishing with crisp acidity. Trophy Winewise '09. Cork. 11.5% alc. **Rating** 94 To 2013 $60

ŸŸŸŸ♀   **Reserve Sunbury Shiraz 2003 Rating** 90 To 2011 $25

ŸŸŸŸ   **Cornelia Creek Shiraz 2003 Rating** 89 To 2011 $28
Cornelia Creek Shiraz 2002 Rating 88 To 2011 $18
Cornelia Creek Cabernet Sauvignon 2004 Rating 88 To 2013 $20

Beelgara   ★★★★

Farm 576 Rossetto Road, Beelbangera, NSW 2680 **Region** Riverina
T (02) 6966 0200 **F** (02) 6966 0298 **www**.beelgara.com.au **Open** Mon–Sat 10–5, Sun 10–4
Winemaker Rod Hooper, Danny Toaldo, Sean Hampel **Est.** 1930 **Cases** 510 000
Beelgara Estate was formed in 2001 after the purchase of the 60-year-old Rossetto family winery by a group of growers, distributors and investors. The emphasis has changed significantly, with a concerted effort to go to the right region for each variety (in the Regional Reserve range), while still maintaining very good value for money. Exports to the US and other major markets.

ŸŸŸŸ♀   **Black Label Mount Lofty Grenache Rose 2009** Pale puce; fragrant small red
✪   fruits; cherry, raspberry; a vibrantly crisp and clean palate, with a long, dry finish. Top-end rose. Screwcap. 11.5% alc. **Rating** 92 To 2011 $18
✪   **Black Label Adelaide Hills Sauvignon Blanc 2009** Has clear varietal character on both bouquet and palate, with clean passionfruit/tropical aromas and more grassy flavours in the mouth. Screwcap. 11.5% alc. **Rating** 90 To 2011 $18
✪   **Regional Reserve Yarra Valley Chardonnay 2008** Still very fresh, crisp and lively, and will hasten slowly in its development; has the regional hallmark length and juicy white peach and nectarine flavours; needless to say, good acidity. Screwcap. 12% alc. **Rating** 90 To 2014 $19.95

ŸŸŸŸ   **Rascals Prayer Sauvignon Blanc 2009** The aromatic bouquet is clearly
✪   varietal, and there are some gooseberry fruit flavours on the palate. A regional blend (unstated) gives the wine good presence. Screwcap. 11.5% alc. **Rating** 88 To 2010 $13.95
Black Label Clare Valley Shiraz 2008 Rating 88 To 2012 $18
Rascals Prayer Shiraz 2008 Rating 88 To 2012 $15
Regional Reserve Clare Valley Shiraz 2007 Rating 88 To 2013 $19.95
Black Label Clare Valley Cabernet Sauvignon 2008 Rating 88 To 2013 $18
Black Label Adelaide Hills Pinot Grigio 2009 Rating 87 To 2011 $18

✪   **Estate Range Rose 2009** Bright colour, with a light red fruit bouquet; clean fruited palate, with sweetness evident, but in balance with the fruit. Screwcap. 10.5% alc. **Rating** 87 **To** 2012 $9
Rascals Prayer Cabernet Sauvignon 2008 Rating 87 **To** 2012 $15
Moscato Frizzante 2009 Rating 87 **To** 2010 $14.95

Belgravia Vineyards   ★★★★★
84 Byng Street, Orange, NSW 2800 **Region** Orange
T (02) 6360 0495 **F** (02) 9475 5109 **www**.belgravia.com.au **Open** 7 days 10–4
Winemaker Phil Kerney (Contract) **Est.** 2001 **Cases** 10 000 **Vyds** 193 ha
Belgravia is an 1800-ha mixed farming property (sheep, cattle and vines) 20 km north of Orange. There are now over 190 ha of vineyard, with 10 ha devoted to the Belgravia brand. In 2006 Belgravia opened its cellar door at the heritage-listed former Union Bank building in Orange, which also operates as a wine bar and restaurant. Exports to the UK, Denmark, Germany and Hong Kong.

♟♟♟♟♟ **Orange Riesling 2009** A particularly intense riesling, with great thrust through
✪   the palate and onto the finish and aftertaste; lime, mineral and a touch of green apple; very good balance and length. Screwcap. 11.4% alc. **Rating** 94 **To** 2018 $22
✪   **Orange Pinot Gris 2009** Orange continues to impress; this wine has seriously intense flavours and an extremely long finish. Positively demands seafood. Screwcap. 12.5% alc. **Rating** 94 **To** 2012 $22
♟♟♟♟♡ **Orange Syrah 2008** Medium red-purple; an elegant, medium-bodied wine
✪   with an interplay of red fruits, spice and pepper, the palate long and fine. Screwcap. 14.2% alc. **Rating** 92 **To** 2017 $22
✪   **Orange Gewurztraminer 2009** Well made, and draws out some lychee, musk and spice flavours on the palate in particular; on retasting, ginger joins the fray. Great for Chinese food. Screwcap. 13.1% alc. **Rating** 91 **To** 2014 $22
Orange Sauvignon Blanc 2009 Rating 90 **To** 2011 $22
The Apex Orange Chardonnay 2009 Rating 90 **To** 2013 $30
The Apex Orange Chardonnay 2008 Rating 90 **To** 2015 $30
Orange Roussanne 2009 Rating 90 **To** 2014 $22
Orange Sangiovese 2008 Rating 90 **To** 2012 $22
♟♟♟♟ **Orange Shiraz Viognier 2008 Rating** 89 **To** 2014 $22
Orange Merlot 2008 Rating 89 **To** 2015 $22

Bellarine Estate   ★★★★★
2270 Portarlington Road, Bellarine, Vic 3222 **Region** Geelong
T (03) 5259 3310 **F** (03) 5259 3393 **www**.bellarineestate.com.au **Open** 7 days 11–4
Winemaker Anthony Brain **Est.** 1995 **Cases** 6000 **Vyds** 12 ha
Important changes were made at Bellarine Estate prior to the 2007 vintage, with an onsite winery commissioned, and Anthony Brain (with extensive cool-climate winemaking experience) installed as winemaker. The vineyard is planted to chardonnay, pinot noir, shiraz, merlot, viognier and sauvignon blanc. The winery was opened in time for the 2007 vintage and offers small-run bottling services for others. Julian's Restaurant is open seven days for lunch and Fri/Sat evenings for dinner. Exports to the US.

♟♟♟♟♟ **James' Paddock Geelong Chardonnay 2008** Bright straw-green; vibrant cool-grown chardonnay; intense white peach and grapefruit flavours have absorbed the French oak in which the wine was fermented and matured for 10 months; delicate, lingering finish. Screwcap. 14% alc. **Rating** 94 **To** 2015 $28
Two Wives Geelong Shiraz 2008 Good crimson-purple hue; a fragrant bouquet with spice and black fruits intermingling, then a lively, medium-bodied palate that has abundant energy and drive, oak neatly married to the fruit. Screwcap. 14.5% alc. **Rating** 94 **To** 2020 $32

ŸŸŸŸŸ Phil's Fetish Geelong Pinot Noir 2008 **Rating** 93 **To** 2014 $30
✪   Portarlington Ridge Sauvignon Blanc 2009 Pale straw; has a slightly sweaty
      bouquet that would pass unnoticed by many consumers; in the mouth the wine is
      fresh and crisp, with no hangover from the bouquet, the flavours an appealing mix
      of citrus and tropical. Screwcap. 12% alc. **Rating** 92 **To** 2012 $18.50
      Cellar Reserve Geelong Shiraz Viognier 2008 Rating 92 **To** 2018 $36
      Sharon's Vineyard Geelong Riesling 2008 Rating 91 **To** 2015 $24
✪   Portarlington Ridge Geelong Pinot Noir 2009 Crimson-purple; the bouquet
      offers plum and (less) cherry fruit, the palate with the same faintly citrussy acidity as
      the '08; left-of-centre food style. Screwcap. 13.2 % alc. **Rating** 90 **To** 2016 $18.50

ŸŸŸŸ   Portarlington Ridge Geelong Pinot Gris 2009 **Rating** 89 **To** 2011 $18.50

Bellarmine Wines   ★★★★★
56 Lawler Street, North Perth, WA 6006 (postal) **Region** Pemberton
T 0422 802 240 **F** (08) 9242 3807 **www.**bellarmine.com.au **Open** Not
Winemaker Dr Diane Miller **Est.** 2000 **Cases** 6000 **Vyds** 20 ha
This vineyard is owned by German residents Dr Willi and Gudrun Schumacher. Long-term
wine lovers, the Schumachers decided to establish a vineyard and winery of their own, using
Australia partly because of its stable political climate. The vineyard is planted to merlot, pinot
noir, chardonnay, shiraz, riesling, sauvignon blanc and petit verdot. Following the departure of
long-term winemaker Mike Bewsher, Diane Miller, previously head of the Vintage Wineworx
contract winemaking facility, was appointed winemaker and operations manager. Exports
to Germany.

ŸŸŸŸŸ Pemberton Shiraz 2008 Deeply coloured; intensely fragrant black cherry, plum,
✪   licorice and spice aromas are precisely repeated on the rich and supple medium-
      to full-bodied palate; the tannins are round and ripe, oak a background whisper.
      Screwcap. 15% alc. **Rating** 96 **To** 2018 $22
✪   Pemberton Riesling 2009 A clean, delicate bouquet of citrus blossom and spice
      is followed by a beautifully balanced palate in Mosel Kabinett style, the essence of
      lime juice offset by crisp acidity. Screwcap. 11% alc. **Rating** 95 **To** 2019 $18
✪   Pemberton Riesling Dry 2009 The bouquet is clean and fresh, the palate
      vibrant and long; here intense lime flavours have a steely core prolonging the length
      and drive through to the finish. Screwcap. 12.5% alc. **Rating** 94 **To** 2021 $18

ŸŸŸŸŸ Pemberton Chardonnay 2009 Pale, bright crystal; a delicate but complex
✪   chardonnay with nectarine and a touch of French oak on the bouquet, the palate
      adding grapefruit to the equation; long finish, crisp acidity promising well for the
      future. Screwcap. 13.5% alc. **Rating** 93 **To** 2019 $19
      Pemberton Pinot Noir 2008 Rating 93 **To** 2015 $25
✪   Pemberton Sauvignon Blanc 2009 Opens surreptitiously on the bouquet and
      fore-palate, then jumps out at you on the back-palate and finish, with a blast of
      herb, grass, asparagus and citrus. Screwcap. 12% alc. **Rating** 91 **To** 2011 $18

Bellbrae Estate   ★★★★☆
520 Great Ocean Road, Bellbrae, Vic 3228 **Region** Geelong
T (03) 5264 8480 **F** (03) 5222 6182 **www.**bellbraeestate.com.au **Open** W'ends 11–5,
7 days (Jan)
Winemaker Matthew di Sciascio, Peter Flewellyn **Est.** 1999 **Cases** 2000 **Vyds** 4.1 ha
Bellbrae Estate (and the Longboard Wines brand) is the venture of friends Richard Macdougall
and Matthew di Sciascio. Sharing a common love of wine, surf and coastal life, they decided
to establish a vineyard and produce their own wine. In 1998 Richard purchased a small sheep
grazing property with 8 ha of fertile, sheltered north-facing slopes on the Great Ocean Road
near Bellbrae, and with Matthew's help as business associate, Bellbrae Estate was born. Since
2003 all the wines have been Geelong-sourced.

ＹＹＹＹＹ Gundrys Geelong Shiraz 2008 Deep crimson-purple; a rich black fruit and licorice bouquet, the medium- to full-bodied palate with plush dark plum and cherry fruit, and no hint of the herb of the Longboard; finishes with ripe tannins. Screwcap. 13.5% alc. **Rating** 94 **To** 2023 $32

ＹＹＹＹＹ **Wally's Fortified Cabernet Sauvignon Shiraz 2008** Rating 92 To 2018 $20
Southside Geelong Sauvignon Blanc 2009 Rating 90 To 2011 $22
Addiscott Geelong Pinot Noir 2008 Rating 90 To 2015 $34
Longboard Geelong Shiraz 2008 Rating 90 To 2017 $22

ＹＹＹＹ   Longboard Geelong Pinot Noir 2008 Rating 89 To 2014 $24

Bellvale Wines   ★★★★★

95 Forresters Lane, Berrys Creek, Vic 3953 **Region** Gippsland
T (03) 5668 8230 **F** (03) 5668 8230 **www**.bellvalewine.com.au **Open** By appt
Winemaker John Ellis **Est.** 1998 **Cases** 3000 **Vyds** 20 ha
John Ellis is the third under this name to be actively involved in the wine industry. His background as a former 747 pilot, and the knowledge he gained of Burgundy over many visits, sets him apart from the others. He has established pinot noir (10 ha), chardonnay (8 ha) and pinot gris (2 ha) on the red soils of a north-facing slope. He chose a density of 7150 vines per ha, following as far as possible the precepts of Burgundy, but limited by tractor size, which precludes narrower row spacing and even higher plant density. Exports to the UK, the US, Denmark, Singapore and Japan.

ＹＹＹＹＹ The Quercus Vineyard Gippsland Pinot Noir 2008 Bright crimson; it has black cherry fruit on the bouquet and a long, layered palate, its mouthfeel slippery one moment, textured (by fine tannins) the next. Diam. 13% alc. **Rating** 94 To 2016 $35

🍇 Bellwether   ★★★★☆

PO Box 344, Coonawarra, SA 5263 **Region** Coonawarra
T 0417 080 945 **www**.bellwetherwines.com.au **Open** Not
Winemaker Sue Bell **Est.** 2009 **Cases** 1000
Sometimes good things come from bad. When Constellation decided to sell (or mothball) its large Padthaway winery, built by Hardys little more than 10 years previously at a cost of $20 million, chief winemaker Sue Bell was summarily retrenched. In quick succession she received a $46,000 wine industry scholarship from the Grape and Wine Research Development Council to study the wine industry in relation to other rural industries in Australia and overseas, and its interaction with community and society. She also became Dux of the Len Evans Tutorial, her prize an extended trip through Bordeaux and Burgundy. She had decided to stay and live in Coonawarra, and the next stroke of good fortune was that a beautiful old shearing shed at Glenroy in Coonawarra came on the market, and will be her winery and cellar door, the latter opening in the first half of 2011. She is making two wines: a Coonawarra Cabernet and a Tasmanian Chardonnay, having had the opportunity to work with chardonnay from Tasmania, the Yarra Valley and South Australia while at Stonehaven, the Chardonnay from Tasmania a stand out.

ＹＹＹＹＹ Tamar Valley Chardonnay 2009 A variety of fermenting and maturing vessels ranging from puncheons and barriques to tanks were used, with only 30% new French oak; wild fermented and part spontaneous mlf. The bouquet is very complex, with cashew nut and flint nuances, the palate an excitement machine with its tremendous drive and layered flavours of grapefruit and nectarine powered by Tasmanian acidity; stupendous length. Screwcap. 12.5% alc. **Rating** 96 **To** 2017 $50

ＹＹＹＹＹ Coonawarra Cabernet Sauvignon 2006 Rating 93 To 2021 $50

🍇 Beltana Springs ★★★

RMB 501 Corberding Road, Brookton, WA 6306 **Region** Perth Hills
T (08) 9642 1125 **F** (08) 9642 1022 **www**.beltanasprings.com **Open** By appt
Winemaker Mark Standish **Est.** 2000 **Cases** 750 **Vyds** 6 ha
When Blair and Jolyon Montague became interested in starting a vineyard in the Perth Hills, they sought the advice of the famed viticultural researcher Dr John Gladstones. He studied the climate of what became Beltana Springs, describing it as very similar to the Douro Valley in Portugal, suggesting a focus on grape varieties suited to warmer climates. Thus shiraz and grenache collectively lead the plantings, together with cabernet sauvignon. Exports to the UK, the US and other major markets.

🍷🍷🍷🍷 **Dale River Grenache Rose 2006** If ever there was proof of the effectiveness of
✪ the screwcap, it comes with the two Dale River Roses, both fresh and crisp, this particular wine rising four years old, with a touch more red fruits than the '07, and slightly greater acidity. Screwcap. 13.5% alc. **Rating** 88 **To** 2010 $15
Dale River Grenache Rose 2007 Pale salmon-pink; a spicy bouquet leads into a crisp palate, with red fruits and crisp acidity on a dry finish. Screwcap. 13.5% alc. **Rating** 87 **To** 2010 $15
Dale River Shiraz 2007 Light colour; a distinctly spicy, savoury shiraz that has more drive and persistence than the colour would suggest, likewise balance. Screwcap. 13.5% alc. **Rating** 87 **To** 2014 $22.50

Belvoir Park Estate ★★★☆

39 Belvoir Park Road, Big Hill, Vic 3453 **Region** Bendigo
T (03) 5435 3075 **F** (03) 5435 3076 **www**.belvoirparkwines.com.au **Open** W'ends & public hols 11–5
Winemaker Ian Hall, Achilles Kalanis **Est.** 1997 **Cases** 1000 **Vyds** 3 ha
Ian and Julie Hall have established a boutique winery and vineyard on deep, granite-based soils 13 km south of Bendigo. Wines are crafted onsite using traditional techniques: hand-pruned and hand-picked grapes, followed by small batch processing via open fermenters and a basket press.

🍷🍷🍷🍷🍷 **Bendigo Riesling 2009** Light straw-green; an aromatic, flowery bouquet leads into a firm, crisp and bone-dry palate. Bred to stay. Screwcap. 11.5% alc. **Rating** 90 **To** 2020 $22

🍷🍷🍷🍷 **Bendigo Cabernet Sauvignon 2007** **Rating** 88 **To** 2014 $25

Ben Potts Wines ★★★★☆

Wellington Road, Langhorne Creek, SA 5255 **Region** Langhorne Creek
T (08) 8537 3029 **F** (08) 8537 3284 **www**.benpottswines.com.au **Open** 7 days 10–5
Winemaker Ben Potts **Est.** 2002 **Cases** 800
Ben Potts is the sixth generation to be involved in grapegrowing and winemaking in Langhorne Creek, the first being Frank Potts, founder of Bleasdale Vineyards. Ben completed the oenology degree at CSU, and ventured into winemaking on a commercial scale in 2002 (aged 25). Fiddle's Block Shiraz is named after great-grandfather Fiddle; Lenny's Block Cabernet Sauvignon Malbec after grandfather Len; and Bill's Block Malbec after father Bill. Exports to Switzerland, Hong Kong and Singapore.

🍷🍷🍷🍷🍷 **Fiddle's Block Langhorne Creek Shiraz 2006** The colour is partially developed; a complex bouquet has black fruits, abundant spice, some chocolate and plenty of quality oak; the palate picks up all these characters and rolls them into a coherent whole; excellent length. Cork. 15% alc. **Rating** 94 **To** 2021 $32

🍷🍷🍷🍷🍷 **Lenny's Block Langhorne Creek Cabernet Sauvignon 2006** **Rating** 90 **To** 2016 $32

Bended Knee Vineyard   ★★★★☆

PO Box 334, Buninyong, Vic 3357 **Region** Ballarat
T (03) 5341 8437 **F** (03) 5341 8437 **www.**bendedknee.com.au **Open** Not
Winemaker Peter Roche **Est.** 1999 **Cases** 250 **Vyds** 1.2 ha
Peter and Pauline Roche have 0.5 ha each of chardonnay and pinot noir planted at moderately
high density, and 0.2 ha of ultra-close-planted pinot noir at the equivalent of 9000 vines per
ha. Here four clones have been used: 114, 115, G5V15 and 777. The Roches say, 'We are
committed to sustainable viticulture and aim to leave the planet in better shape than we found
it.' Ducks, guinea fowl and chooks are vineyard custodians, and all vine canopy management
is done by hand, including pruning and picking. Although production is tiny, Bended Knee
wines can be found at some of Melbourne's best restaurants.

♟♟♟♟♟ Wild Thing Chardonnay 2008 Wild yeast-fermented with 50 cases made; an
        intense and tangy bouquet and palate, with fresher acidity than Bowen Hill, giving
        it more length and definition. Screwcap. 12.5% alc. **Rating** 94 **To** 2016 $35

♟♟♟♟♟ Bowen Hill Chardonnay 2008 **Rating** 93 **To** 2015 $28
        Pinot Noir 2008 **Rating** 90 **To** 2014 $28

Bent Creek Vineyards   ★★★★

1 Blewitt Springs Road, McLaren Flat, SA 5171 **Region** McLaren Vale
T (08) 8383 0414 **F** (08) 8344 7703 **www.**bentcreekvineyards.com.au **Open** Sat &
public hols 11–5
Winemaker Peter Polson, Tim Geddes **Est.** 2001 **Cases** 7500
Peter Polson is now the sole owner of Bent Creek, which has acquired a second 5-ha
vineyard at McLaren Vale. As a parallel development, Tim Geddes is now assisting Peter in
the winemaking. In 2009 it opened a new cellar door and barrel storage facility (just across
the road from the prior facility). On the other side of the coin, heat and drought have made
inroads, and no chardonnay was picked in '09; even the 50-year-old vines have suffered
greatly.

♟♟♟♟♟ Black Dog McLaren Vale Shiraz 2008 Strong purple-crimson; ultra-typical
        McLaren Vale; medium- to full-bodied, with voluminous black fruits wrapped in
        dark chocolate and a slice of vanillan oak. Amusing but true back label. Screwcap.
        14.5% alc. **Rating** 92 **To** 2012 $22
        Reserve McLaren Vale Shiraz 2008 Very good colour; there is a lot of good
        regional fruit here, but I cannot help but wonder why reverse osmosis was
        (apparently) not used to reduce the spike of heat on the finish. Cork. 15.2% alc.
        Rating 90 **To** 2018 $39

♟♟♟♟ Adelaide Hills Sauvignon Blanc 2009 **Rating** 89 **To** 2010 $19
  ✪   Nero McLaren Vale Sparkling Shiraz NV The recommendation on the front
        label to 'drink now to five years' is utterly Delphic, since there is no clue about the
        timing of 'now'. Nonetheless, not bad advice if you treat now as being the time
        you read the label, for the wine has good regional chocolatey flavour that sits well
        with the style. Cork. 13% alc. **Rating** 89 **To** 2014 $14
        McLaren Vale Cabernet Merlot 2008 **Rating** 88 **To** 2013 $20

Berrys Bridge   ★★★★

633 Carapooee Road, Carapooee, Vic 3478 **Region** Pyrenees
T (03) 5496 3220 **F** (03) 8610 1621 **www.**berrysbridge.com.au **Open** By appt
Winemaker Jane Holt **Est.** 1990 **Cases** 1000 **Vyds** 7 ha
While the date of establishment is 1990, Roger Milner purchased the property in '75. In the
mid-'80s, with Jane Holt, he began the construction of the stone house-cum-winery. Planting
of the existing vineyard commenced in '90, and has been managed on what is described
as an 'ecologically friendly option when selecting vineyard inputs. Many species of insect-
eating birds love this habitat contributing to a healthy and diverse environment'. Jane has a

Bachelor of Wine Science from CSU, while Roger worked at Chateau Reynella in the '70s. They moved to the vineyard full-time in '98, helped by Ian McDonald, who moved from a corporate background to the more friendly ambience of Berrys Bridge. Exports to the US and Switzerland.

🍷🍷🍷🍷 **Pyrenees Cabernet Sauvignon 2006** Dense, deep colour; dark black fruits with a strongly savoury backdrop; licorice, too, makes its mark on the full-bodied palate. ProCork. 14.6% alc. **Rating** 93 **To** 2016 $28

Pyrenees Shiraz 2006 Dense, inky colour foretells the full-bodied palate; masses of black fruits run through the palate, alcohol fractionally stripping the fruit on the back-palate. ProCork. 15.5% alc. **Rating** 92 **To** 2016 $35

Berton Vineyard ★★★

55 Mirroci Avenue, Yenda, NSW 2681 **Region** Riverina
T (02) 6968 1600 **F** (02) 6968 1620 **www.**bertonvineyards.com.au **Open** Mon–Fri 10–4, Sat 11–4
Winemaker James Ceccato **Est.** 2001 **Cases** 15 000 **Vyds** 11 ha
The Berton Vineyard partners – Bob and Cherie Berton, Paul Bartholomaeus, James Ceccato and Jamie Bennett – have almost 100 years combined experience in winemaking, viticulture, finance, production and marketing. 1996 saw the acquisition of a 30-ha property in the Eden Valley and the planting of the first vines. It took two years for the dam to fill, and the vines struggled on the white rock soil. Exports to the UK, the US and other major markets.

🍷🍷🍷 ✪ **FoundStone Unoaked Chardonnay 2009** Clearly defined varietal nectarine fruit, unadorned by oak; the palate is fresh and zesty, with good weight and a vibrant citrus finish. Screwcap. 14% alc. **Rating** 88 **To** 2013 $10 BE

✪ **FoundStone Shiraz 2009** Bright colour; juicy red and black fruits, showing a touch of fruitcake and spice; clean, clearly defined and well constructed; very good value and ready for early consumption. Screwcap. 14.5% alc. **Rating** 88 **To** 2012 $10 BE

✪ **FoundStone Pinot Grigio 2009** Fresh and crisp pear bouquet and palate; vibrant and varietal to conclude. Screwcap. 13% alc. **Rating** 87 **To** 2012 $10 BE

The White Viognier 2009 Yellow-green; while not overly expressive of the variety, does have the correct mouthfeel, with some apricot and peach flavours; is ready. Screwcap. 14.5% alc. **Rating** 87 **To** 2010 $12

Reserve Coonawarra Cabernet Sauvignon 2007 A distinctly earthy, savoury manifestation of Coonawarra cabernet in a medium-weight frame; some black fruits are evident, interesting given that cork has only been in the bottle for a short time (as at August '09). 14.5% alc. **Rating** 87 **To** 2013 $18

Reserve Riverina Botrytis Semillon 2007 From what appears to be significantly botrytised grapes, but nonetheless thins out on the mid- to back-palate. Reasonable price is a plus. Screwcap. 11.5% alc. **Rating** 87 **To** 2013 $18

Best's Wines ★★★★★

111 Best's Road, Great Western, Vic 3377 **Region** Grampians
T (03) 5356 2250 **F** (03) 5356 2430 **www.**bestswines.com **Open** Mon–Sat 10–5, Sun 11–4
Winemaker Adam Wadewitz **Est.** 1866 **Cases** 24 000 **Vyds** 60 ha
Best's winery and vineyards are among Australia's best-kept secrets. Indeed the vineyards, with vines dating back to 1867, have secrets that may never be revealed: for example, one of the vines planted in the Nursery Block has defied identification and is thought to exist nowhere else in the world. Part of the cellars, too, go back to the same era, constructed by butcher-turned-winemaker Henry Best and his family. Since 1920, the Thomson family has owned the property, with Ben, the fifth-generation, having taken over management from father Viv. Best's consistently produces elegant, supple wines; the Bin No. 0 is a classic, the Thomson Family Shiraz (from vines planted in 1868) magnificent. Very occasionally a Pinot Noir (with 15% Pinot Meunier) is made solely from the 1868 plantings of those two varieties; there is no other pinot of this vine age made anywhere else in the world; the 2008 vintage will be released in March '11. Exports to the UK and other major markets.

♥♥♥♥♥ **Thomson Family Great Western Shiraz 2006** Superb crimson hue; a
fragrant bouquet with spice, pepper and black cherry fruit, then a glorious silken,
supple palate, with red and black cherry and plum foremost, the tannin and oak
contribution perfectly judged. The quality of the cork is good, but ... 14% alc.
Rating 97 To 2026 $150

Bin No. 0 Great Western Shiraz 2006 Crimson-purple; a fragrant bouquet
of black cherry, plum and spice, unfolding onto a medium-bodied palate
with excellent texture built around fine, ripe tannins; the spicy black fruits are
positively elegant. Trophy Sydney Wine Show '10. Screwcap. 14.1% alc. Rating 96
To 2031 $60

Great Western Old Clone Pinot Noir 2008 Slightly lighter, brighter colour
than the standard wine; a very different style, with elegance and precision to the
fragrant bouquet and vibrant palate; has lovely red fruit and spice flavours and
perfect texture. Screwcap. 13.2% alc. Rating 95 To 2017 $65

Great Western Chardonnay 2007 Glowing yellow-green; a harmonious wine
from start to finish, barrel ferment in unison with the white peach fruit; overall
freshness to a lively, juicy palate. Screwcap. 13% alc. Rating 94 To 2014 $25

✪ **Bin No. 1 Great Western Shiraz 2008** Good colour; abundant pepper and
spice notes run through both bouquet and the medium-bodied palate; the fruit
flavours are of plum and black cherry, the tannins soft and fine, oak merely a bit
player. Screwcap. 14.5% alc. Rating 94 To 2018 $25

♥♥♥♥♡ **Great Western Riesling 2009** Marries generosity of fruit flavour with a tight,
✪ focused finish; the flavours are of ripe citrus, verging on tropical, and the wine
will develop smoothly over the next few years. Screwcap. 12% alc. Rating 93
To 2018 $22

Great Western Chardonnay 2008 Rating 93 To 2014 $25

✪ **Concongella Vineyard Great Western Pinot Noir 2009** Excellent deep,
bright crimson; overall, full-bodied, but not to the point of becoming dry red; will
greatly benefit from five or so years in bottle to allow more texture to the plum
and black cherry fruit to develop. Screwcap. 13.5% alc. Rating 93 To 2018 $22

Bin No. 1 Great Western Shiraz 2007 Rating 93 To 2020 $60

Great Western Riesling 2008 Rating 92 To 2014 $22

Concongella Vineyard Great Western Chardonnay 2006 Rating 92
To 2014 $25

Bin No. 0 Great Western Shiraz 2007 Rating 92 To 2025 $65

Great Western Cabernet Sauvignon 2008 Rating 92 To 2018 $25

Concongella Vineyard Great Western Dolcetto 2009 Rating 90
To 2013 $22

Great Western Pinot Meunier 2008 Rating 90 To 2028 $65

♥♥♥♥ **Great Western Sparkling Shiraz 2006** Rating 87 To 2012 $25

Bethany Wines   ★★★★☆

Bethany Road, Bethany via Tanunda, SA 5352 **Region** Barossa Valley
T (08) 8563 2086 **F** (08) 8563 0046 **www**.bethany.com.au **Open** Mon–Sat 10–5, Sun 1–5
Winemaker Geoff and Robert Schrapel **Est.** 1977 **Cases** 25 000 **Vyds** 36 ha
The Schrapel family has been growing grapes in the Barossa Valley for over 140 years, but the
winery has only been in operation since 1977. Nestled high on a hillside on the site of an
old bluestone quarry, Geoff and Rob Schrapel produce a range of consistently well-made and
attractively packaged wines. They have vineyards in the Barossa and Eden valleys. Exports to
the UK, the US and other major markets.

♥♥♥♥♥ **GR11 Reserve Barossa Shiraz 2006** Has retained good purple-red hue; a rich,
opulent, yet well-balanced shiraz full of blackberry, plum and black cherry fruit,
vanillan oak well suited and matched, the tannins ripe. Top-quality cork. 15% alc.
Rating 94 To 2016 $85

ŶŶŶŶŶ Eden Valley Riesling 2009 Rating 93 To 2016 $32
LE Reserve Shiraz 2006 Rating 92 To 2020 $48

ŶŶŶŶ Cordon Pruned Select Late Harvest Riesling 2009 Rating 89 To 2012 $22
Barossa Semillon 2008 Rating 88 To 2013 $18

Bettenay's ★★★★

Cnr Harmans South Road/Miamup Road, Wilyabrup, WA 6284 **Region** Margaret River
T (08) 9755 5539 **F** (08) 9755 5539 **www**.bettenaywines.com.au **Open** 7 days 11–5
Winemaker Greg and Bryce Bettenay **Est.** 1989 **Cases** 5000 **Vyds** 11 ha
Relying upon advice from his soil scientist father in selecting the property, Greg Bettenay
began planting the vineyards in 1989, and now has cabernet sauvignon (4.5 ha), chardonnay,
sauvignon blanc, shiraz (1.5 ha each), semillon and merlot (1 ha each). The development also
extends to two cottages and a luxury treetop spa apartment known as The Lakeside Loft.
The third generation has joined the business in the form of son Bryce, bringing yet another
perspective to the winemaking.

ŶŶŶŶŶ Margaret River Sauvignon Blanc 2009 An austere yet complex wine with a
range of aromas and flavours at the grassy/herbaceous end of the spectrum (not
tropical); gives the impression of some oak, but there is none. Screwcap. 12.5% alc.
Rating 90 To 2012 $24
Margaret River Semillon Sauvignon Blanc 2009 Predominantly semillon
in the blend, and the wine shows it with its firm structure and length; while the
herbaceous characters ex semillon are present, the sauvignon blanc contributes
some tropical elements; will build. Screwcap. 12.5% alc. Rating 90 To 2013 $24

Bidgeebong Wines ★★★★

352 Byrnes Road, Wagga Wagga, NSW 2650 **Region** Gundagai
T (02) 6931 9955 **F** (02) 6931 9966 **www**.bidgeebong.com.au **Open** Mon–Fri 9–4
Winemaker Andrew Birks **Est.** 2000 **Cases** 5000
Encompasses what the founders refer to as the Bidgeebong triangle – between Young, Wagga
Wagga, Tumbarumba and Gundagai – which provides grapes for the Bidgeebong brand.
A winery was completed in 2002, and will eventually handle 2000 tonnes of grapes for
Bidgeebong's own needs, and those of other local growers and larger producers who purchase
grapes from the region. Exports to Canada, Singapore and China.

ŶŶŶŶŶ Triangle Shiraz 2008 Strong, deep colour; the medium- to full-bodied blend
✪ of Gundagai/Tumbarumba fruit is wholly synergistic and carries the alcohol
remarkably well; ripe blackberry and plum fruit has a spicy, lively backdrop.
Screwcap. 15.5% alc. Rating 93 To 2020 $13
Tempranillo by Birks 2008 A highly expressive and fragrant wine, the palate
light- to medium-bodied, but full of fresh red fruits and a dab of spice; well made.
Screwcap. 12.8% alc. Rating 91 To 2014 $22

ŶŶŶŶ Verdelho 2006 Rating 89 To 2012 $22
Regional Selection Tumbarumba Merlot 2008 Rating 88 To 2014 $22

Big Brook Wines ★★★★

PO Box 3024, Adelaide Terrace, Perth, WA 6832 **Region** Pemberton
T (08) 9776 1166 **F** (08) 9221 2990 **www**.bigbrookwines.com.au **Open** Not
Winemaker The Vintage Wineworx (Sandra Claning) **Est.** 2008 **Cases** 3000 **Vyds** 9.6 ha
This is a family-owned winery established by the O'Toole family of Perth; while the
establishment date is 2008, the vineyard was then already 10 years old. Planted to chardonnay,
cabernet sauvignon, merlot and sauvignon blanc, it is adjacent to the Big Brook Forest from
which it takes its name. Throughout the year a brook runs through the vineyard and feeds the
dam, which has a population of the much-prized marron. It is seldom called on to provide
water for the vines, which are predominantly dry-grown. Exports to the US.

♀♀♀♀♀ Reserve Pemberton Chardonnay 2009 Pale colour, bright hue; a restrained and cool bouquet of grapefruit and spice; the acidity features prominently and drives the crunchy citrus fruit to a long and even finish. Screwcap. 12.4% alc. **Rating** 91 **To** 2015 $23 BE

♀♀♀♀ Pemberton Sauvignon Blanc Semillon 2009 Rating 88 **To** 2012 $19 BE

big shed wines   ★★★☆
1289 Malmsbury Road, Glenlyon, Vic 3461 **Region** Macedon Ranges
T (03) 5348 7825 **F** (03) 5348 7825 **www**.bigshedwines.com.au **Open** 7 days, winter 10–6, summer 10–7
Winemaker Ken and Miranda Jones **Est.** 1999 **Cases** 1200 **Vyds** 2 ha
Founder and winemaker Ken Jones was formerly a geneticist and molecular biologist at Edinburgh University, so the chemistry of winemaking comes easily. The estate-based wine comes from 2 ha of pinot noir (clones MV6 and D5V12); the other wines are made from purchased grapes grown in various parts of Central Victoria.

♀♀♀♀♀ Macedon Ranges Chardonnay 2006 Bright and full yellow-gold; has held together remarkably well; attractive stone fruit is balanced by citrussy acidity; good line and length. Go the screwcap. 13.2% alc. **Rating** 90 **To** 2014 $30

Billanook Estate   ★★★
280 Edward Road, Chirnside Park, Vic 3116 **Region** Yarra Valley
T (03) 9735 4484 **F** (03) 9735 1919 **www**.billanookestate.com.au **Open** W'ends & public hols 10–6, or by appt
Winemaker Domenic Bucci, John D'Aloisio **Est.** 1994 **Cases** 1200 **Vyds** 15.5 ha
The D'Aloisio family has been involved in the agricultural heritage of the Yarra Valley since the late 1960s, and in '94 planted the first vines on their 36-ha property. The vineyard is planted to cabernet sauvignon (4.4 ha), shiraz (3.3 ha), chardonnay (3.2 ha), sauvignon blanc (1.7 ha), pinot noir (1.4 ha) and merlot (1.1 ha). Most of the grapes are sold to various wineries in the Valley, leaving a small percentage for the Billanook Estate label.

♀♀♀♀ Methode Champenoise Yarra Valley Chardonnay Pinot Noir 2005 A 60/40 blend; how long it spent on lees isn't specified; chardonnay is the flavour driver with strong citrus components; low dosage. Diam. 12.5% alc. **Rating** 88 **To** 2013 $30

Billy Pye Vineyard   ★★★
PO Box 229, Ashton, SA 5137 **Region** Adelaide Hills
T (08) 8390 1332 **F** (08) 8390 3435 **Open** Not
Winemaker Colin Best, John Bowley **Est.** 1997 **Cases** 80 **Vyds** 2.1 ha
The history of Billy Pye Vineyard is fascinating, dating back to 1858 when William Grasby began establishing an apple orchard on a property near Balhannah on the upper reaches of the Onkaparinga River. The neighbouring property on the southern side had been owned since 1868 by colourful local character WH (Billy) Pye, a surveyor and engineer. His property contained the largest hill in the area, known locally as Billy Pye Hill, where he built his house. In 1997 Sandra Schubert, a fifth-generation Grasby, began to plant a vineyard on the northern slopes of Billy Pye Hill in partnership with John Bowley, leaving the top of the hill with the native vegetation Billy had loved. John Bowley and Colin Best, the latter Leabrook winemaker, both studied civil engineering at Adelaide University, and worked together many years ago.

♀♀♀♀ Pinot Noir 2008 Light colour with some development; a fragrant and spicy bouquet and light-bodied palate, with a foresty, savoury finish. Needs more red fruit, but has good texture and balance. Screwcap. 14% alc. **Rating** 88 **To** 2013 $25
Merlot 2007 Purple-crimson; the aromas and flavours run the full gamut from ripe plum to savoury black olive, although lacking cohesion for the time being. Screwcap. 14.8% alc. **Rating** 88 **To** 2014 $25

Bimbadgen Estate ★★★★★

790 McDonalds Road, Pokolbin, NSW 2320 **Region** Hunter Valley
T (02) 4998 7585 **F** (02) 4998 7732 www.bimbadgen.com.au **Open** 7 days 10–5
Winemaker Simon Thistlewood, Jane Hoppe **Est.** 1968 **Cases** 50 000
Established as McPherson Wines, then successively Tamalee, Sobels, Parker Wines and now
Bimbadgen Estate, this substantial winery has had what might be politely termed a turbulent
history. It has over 50 ha of estate plantings, mostly with relatively old vines, supplemented by
a separate estate vineyard at Yenda (19 ha) for the lower-priced Ridge series, and purchased
grapes from various premium regions. Exports to all major markets.

ΨΨΨΨΨ Signature Palmers Lane Vineyard Semillon 2009 Very pale straw; slashing
freshness and vibrancy, citrus, mineral and acidity all woven together; long finish.
Screwcap. 11% alc. **Rating** 94 **To** 2020 $65
Signature Palmers Lane Vineyard Semillon 2008 If there has been a
(conventional) Hunter semillon with lower alcohol, I haven't seen it. Piercingly
fresh and only just started its journey, it has positive herb and citrus flavours on a
long palate; will live for decades. Screwcap. 9% alc. **Rating** 94 **To** 2028 $65

ΨΨΨΨΨ Art Series Shiraz Cabernet Sauvignon 2008 **Rating** 93 **To** 2020 $25
Estate Hunter Valley Shiraz 2007 **Rating** 92 **To** 2020 $23
Art Series Shiraz Viognier 2007 **Rating** 92 **To** 2020 $25
Members Collection Shiraz Cabernet 2006 **Rating** 92 **To** 2021 $35
Family Selection Megan's Mischief Shiraz 2006 **Rating** 91 **To** 2016 $75
Estate Limited Release Orange Barbera 2008 **Rating** 90 **To** 2014 $25

ΨΨΨΨ Art Series Roussanne Marsanne Viognier 2009 **Rating** 89 **To** 2014 $25
Estate Orange Merlot 2008 **Rating** 89 **To** 2014 $23

binbilla ★★★★

Good Friday Gully Road, Maimuru, NSW 2594 (postal) **Region** Hilltops
T (02) 6383 3305 **F** (02) 6383 3237 www.binbillawines.com **Open** Not
Winemaker Nick O'Leary (Contract) **Est.** 2001 **Cases** 1000 **Vyds** 6 ha
Gerard and Berenice Hines planted their vineyard in 2001, with 4 ha of cabernet sauvignon
(since grafted over to viognier), 2 ha of shiraz and 1 ha of riesling, which produced the first
wines in '04. The more recent grafting of some vines to viognier has seen the release of a
Shiraz Viognier. The only wine that is not estate-grown is the Chardonnay, which is grown
on a nearby Hilltops vineyard. The quantity made will increase as the vines come into full
bearing, but is unlikely to exceed 1000 cases a year, with limited retail and restaurant listings
in Melbourne, Sydney and Brisbane.

ΨΨΨΨΨ Hilltops Riesling 2009 Pale brilliant green; fragrant apple and lime blossom
✪ aromas, then a very well-balanced palate following the track of the bouquet. Gold
medal National Cool Climate Wine Show '09. Screwcap. 12% alc. **Rating** 93
To 2019 $18
✪ Good Friday Hilltops Shiraz 2007 Good depth and hue; a gently spicy
bouquet leads into a light- to medium-bodied palate, fine tannins and mocha oak
adding to the red and black fruits evident throughout; good balance and length.
Screwcap. 14.2% alc. **Rating** 90 **To** 2016 $19
✪ Hilltops Shiraz Viognier 2008 Bright, light crimson; like the Shiraz, no
more than light- to medium-bodied, the red fruit aromas and flavours lifted and
sweetened by the co-fermented viognier; very fine tannins to conclude. Screwcap.
13.1% alc. **Rating** 90 **To** 2015 $19

Bindi Wine Growers ★★★★★

343 Melton Road, Gisborne, Vic 3437 (postal) **Region** Macedon Ranges
T (03) 5428 2564 **F** (03) 5428 2564 **Open** Not
Winemaker Michael Dhillon, Stuart Anderson (Consultant) **Est.** 1988 **Cases** 2000

One of the icons of Macedon. The Chardonnay is top-shelf, the Pinot Noir as remarkable (albeit in a very different idiom) as Bass Phillip, Giaconda or any of the other tiny-production, icon wines. The addition of Heathcote-sourced Shiraz under the Pyrette label confirms Bindi as one of the greatest small producers in Australia. Notwithstanding the tiny production, the wines are exported (in small quantities, of course) to the UK, the US and other major markets.

ŤŤŤŤŤ **Quartz Chardonnay 2008** Pale straw-green; improbably though it may seem, this takes the purity and intensity of '09 Composition to another level; the flavours persist in the mouth for an astonishingly long time after the wine is swallowed, fruit, acid, oak and mineral so seamlessly intertwined it is impossible to separate them. Diam. 14% alc. **Rating** 97 **To** 2022 $75

Block 5 Pinot Noir 2008 Bright, clear colour; the bouquet is, by some margin, the most fragrant and aromatic, bringing both red and black fruits into play, the intense, silky palate coursing majestically to a long, lingering finish, red and black fruits echoing throughout. Diam. 14% alc. **Rating** 97 **To** 2020 $100

Composition Chardonnay 2009 Pale but bright quartz-green; in some ways this is an exercise in minimalism, but not when the wine spears through to the finish and aftertaste, white peach and mineral in a dervish dance. Think of Grand Cru Chablis. Diam. 13.5% alc. **Rating** 96 **To** 2019 $45

Original Vineyard Pinot Noir 2008 Similar colour and clarity to Block 5; plum, dark cherry and spice aromas cascade into a powerful palate with its continuously moving interplay between dark fruits and savoury/foresty notes. Diam. 14% alc. **Rating** 96 **To** 2019 $75

Macedon Extended Lees Aged Chardonnay Pinot Noir 2003 Glowing gold-green; at the very top end of Australian sparkling wine, albeit with its own very special character; a three-way marriage of brioche and toast, luscious citrus fruit, then lingering, piercing but balancing acidity. Disgorged Jan '10. Diam. 12% alc. **Rating** 96 **To** 2016 $55

Pyrette Heathcote Shiraz 2009 Bright red-crimson; only a skilled pinot maker could induce Heathcote to provide such an elegant shiraz; vibrantly fresh; spice, pepper, damson plum and fine-grained tannins chase each other around through the very long and perfectly balanced palate. Diam. 13.5% alc. **Rating** 95 **To** 2021 $40

Composition Pinot Noir 2009 Bright, clear crimson-purple, best of the three pinots; opens with dark berry fruit aromas, then a palate with great drive and energy; the texture is complex, as are the flavours, mixing black cherry, plum, spice and forest. Diam. 13% alc. **Rating** 94 **To** 2018 $50

Bird in Hand ★★★★★

Bird in Hand Road, Woodside, SA 5244 **Region** Adelaide Hills
T (08) 8389 9488 **F** (08) 8389 9511 **www**.birdinhand.com.au **Open** 7 days 11–5
Winemaker Andrew Nugent, Kym Milne, Sarah Siddons **Est.** 1997 **Cases** 60 000
Vyds 29 ha
This very successful business took its name from a 19th-century gold mine. It is the venture of the Nugent family, headed by Dr Michael Nugent; son Andrew is a Roseworthy graduate. The family also has a vineyard in the Clare Valley, the latter providing both riesling and shiraz (and olives from 100-year-old wild trees). In 2007 a state-of-the-art winery and a straw and mud barrel cellar were completed. The estate plantings (merlot, pinot noir, cabernet sauvignon, sauvignon blanc, riesling and shiraz) provide only part of the annual crush, the remainder coming from contract growers. Exports to the UK, the US and other major markets.

ŤŤŤŤŤ **Nest Egg Adelaide Hills Shiraz 2008** The deepest crimson-purple of the three Bird in Hand Shirazs, and takes the flavour dimensions to another level; blackberry, plum, spice, licorice and French oak all intermingle; an intense and very long palate has great finesse. Screwcap. 14.5% alc. **Rating** 96 **To** 2020 $75

Honeysuckle Clare Valley Riesling 2009 Flowery apple blossom aromas, then a crisp palate that reveals its residual sweetness later than one might expect, as it is so well balanced by acidity. Long future. Strange to go to Clare, but it succeeds. Screwcap. 9% alc. **Rating** 95 **To** 2019 $25

○ **Adelaide Hills Sauvignon Blanc 2009** An elegant and quite juicy wine, with pleasing tropical fruit flavours on the palate, the finish lengthened and enlivened further by lemony acidity. Screwcap. 13.5% alc. **Rating** 95 **To** 2011 $25
Nest Egg Adelaide Hills Chardonnay 2009 Bright, light green-straw; a very elegant and fine wine with immaculate balance of fruit and oak; nectarine and white peach fruit is woven through quality French oak, fruit very much in the ascendant. Screwcap. 13.5% alc. **Rating** 95 **To** 2017 $60

○ **Adelaide Hills Pinot Rose 2009** Bright pink; perfumed aromas of spiced strawberries, the palate flirting with intense fruit and balancing acidity; has character and length. Screwcap. 12.5% alc. **Rating** 94 **To** 2012 $20

♀♀♀♀♀ **Adelaide Hills Chardonnay 2009** Rating 93 To 2014 $25
Mt Lofty Ranges Shiraz 2008 Rating 93 To 2018 $30
Clare Valley Riesling 2009 Rating 92 To 2019 $25
Mt Lofty Ranges Cabernet Sauvignon 2008 Rating 92 To 2016 $30
Adelaide Hills Sparkling Pinot Noir 2009 Rating 92 To 2014 $25
Two in the Bush Mt Lofty Ranges Shiraz 2008 Rating 90 To 2016 $20
Adelaide Hills Tempranillo 2007 Rating 90 To 2012 $30

♀♀♀♀ **Two in the Bush Adelaide Hills Semillon Sauvignon Blanc 2009** Rating 89 To 2011 $20
Two in the Bush Adelaide Hills Chardonnay 2009 Rating 89 To 2012 $20
Joy 2007 Rating 89 To 2013 $60

Birthday Villa Vineyard ★★★

Lot 2 Campbell Street, Malmsbury, Vic 3446 **Region** Macedon Ranges
T (03) 5423 2789 **F** (03) 5423 2789 **www.**birthdayvilla.com.au **Open** W'ends by appt 10–5
Winemaker Greg Dedman (Contract) **Est.** 1968 **Cases** 300 **Vyds** 2 ha
The Birthday Villa name comes from the 19th-century Birthday Mine at nearby Drummond discovered on Queen Victoria's birthday. Gewurztraminer (1.5 ha) was planted in 1962; cabernet sauvignon (0.5 ha) followed later. The quality of the Gewurztraminer comes as no surprise; the very cool climate is suited to the variety. On the other hand, the Cabernet Sauvignon comes as a major surprise, although there are likely to be vintages where the variety will provide a major challenge as it struggles for ripeness.

♀♀♀♀ **Malmsbury Cabernet Sauvignon 2007** This is a very difficult environment for cabernet, and the wine struggles for ripe fruit flavours; it is fragrant and does have some red fruits (along with greener notes); well made given the challenges. Screwcap. 12.5% alc. **Rating** 87 **To** 2013 $25

Biscay Wines ★★★★

Lot 567 Barossa Valley Highway, Tanunda, SA 5352 **Region** Barossa Valley
T (08) 8563 0297 **F** (08) 8563 0187 **Open** By appt
Winemaker John and Trevor Hongell **Est.** 1998 **Cases** 800 **Vyds** 11 ha
John and Carolyn Hongell, along with youngest son Trevor as vineyard manager and budding winemaker, have been producing small parcels of wine under the John Hongell label since 1998, the grapes sourced solely from the family-owned Biscay Vineyard. The vineyard was first planted in 1943 to grenache, with further plantings of shiraz in '92, on Biscay clay soils in the southern Barossa Valley using single-wire trellis and minimal irrigation. Yields are kept low giving the resultant fruit intense colour and great varietal character. In his various previous lives, John was a brewer, production director for Dalgety Wines and then manager of Saltram. Long industry experience taught him that sales were far better pulled by demand than pushed by supply, and despite growing interest from the UK, the US and Canada, production has been deliberately restricted during the establishment phase.

♀♀♀♀♀ **John Hongell Old Vine Barossa Valley Grenache Shiraz 2008** Light red; a 68/32 blend of estate-grown fruit, the grenache planted in 1942; the flavours are in the red berry/Turkish delight/raspberry spectrum of grenache, structure from the shiraz. Screwcap. 15% alc. **Rating** 90 **To** 2016 $20

BK Wines   ★★★★☆

23 Onkaparinga Valley Road, Charleston, SA 5244 **Region** Adelaide Hills
T 0410 124 674 **F** (08) 8 8389 6984 **www**.bkwines.com.au **Open** Fri–Sun 11–5, or by appt
Winemaker Brendon Keys **Est.** 2007 **Cases** 850
BK Wines is owned by the Keys and Scott families. Brendon Keys came from NZ, and has
worked in the US, Argentina, NZ and SA. BK Wines is an out-of-hours occupation; his main
job is winemaker for Adelaide Hills Winery, which opened in November 2008. BK is thus a
virtual winery, as it relies on leased vineyard blocks, and the wine is not made onsite. Exports
to Singapore.

🍷🍷🍷🍷🍷 Collage NV Pale salmon; four months in barrel with battonage pays big
✪   dividends; strawberry and spice aromas and flavours in abundance, the palate fresh
         and dry. Saignee Pinot Noir Rose. Screwcap. 12.8% alc. **Rating** 94 **To** 2012 $19

🍷🍷🍷🍷🍷 Le Levrier Adelaide Hills Pinot Gris 2009 **Rating** 93 **To** 2012 $23.50
         La Bombe de Belle Piccadilly Valley Pinot Noir 2008 **Rating** 91
         To 2014 $35
         Jean Bernard Adelaide Hills Syrah 2008 **Rating** 91 **To** 2020 $35
         Ma Fleur Piccadilly Valley Chardonnay 2008 **Rating** 90 **To** 2014 $35

Black Estate Vineyard   ★★★

Patons Road, Axe Creek, Vic 3551 **Region** Bendigo
T (03) 5442 8048 **F** (03) 5442 8048 **www**.blackestate.com.au **Open** By appt
Winemaker Greg Dedman (Contract) **Est.** 1999 **Cases** 250 **Vyds** 1.5 ha
Robert and Leanne Black purchased their 8-ha property in 1997; it was part of a larger block
that in the latter part of the 19th century was home to the then-renowned 14-ha Hercynia
Vineyard. After a trial planting of 100 shiraz cuttings in 1998, they completed planting of their
vineyard in the spring of '99. Future plantings of cabernet sauvignon and possibly riesling or
verdelho will depend on water availability.

🍷🍷🍷🍷 Shiraz 2006 Good colour for age; generous black fruits are swathed in even more
        generous American and French oak; soft tannins. Screwcap. 14.5% alc. **Rating** 88
        To 2016 $20

Blackbilly Wines   ★★★★

Kangarilla Road, McLaren Vale, SA 5171 **Region** McLaren Vale
T 0419 383 907 **F** (08) 8323 9747 **www**.blackbilly.com **Open** By appt
Winemaker Nick Haselgrove, Warren Randall **Est.** 2003 **Cases** 6500
Blackbilly has emerged from the numerous changes in the various Haselgrove wine interests.
These days the people behind Blackbilly are Nick Haselgrove, Warren Randall, Warren Ward
and Andrew Fletcher. Blackbilly is able to access the 400 ha of vines owned by Tinlins,
along with smaller suppliers in McLaren Vale. Exports to the UK, the US, Canada, Ireland,
Philippines and China.

🍷🍷🍷🍷 Adelaide Hills Pinot Gris 2009 A zesty pinot gris with attitude, citrus, green
✪   apple and brown pear all interwoven; a long, fruit-filled, but dry, finish. Screwcap.
         13.5% alc. **Rating** 93 **To** 2011 $22
✪   McLaren Vale Tempranillo 2008 Good colour; a richly fruited tempranillo,
         with red cherry and a slash of citrus-like acidity; good mouthfeel and texture.
         Screwcap. 14.5% alc. **Rating** 92 **To** 2014 $22
         McLaren Vale Shiraz 2008 Dense inky purple; very ripe yet not unduly
         extractive or hot; full-bodied plum, prune and dark chocolate fruit is balanced by
         some fresh acidity on the finish. Screwcap. 14.5% alc. **Rating** 90 **To** 2020 $22

🍷🍷🍷🍷 Adelaide Hills Sauvignon Blanc 2009 **Rating** 89 **To** 2011 $22
        NV4 Pinot Chardonnay Cuvee Brut NV **Rating** 87 **To** 2012 $20

Blackford Stable Wines ★★★

PO Box 162, Charleston, SA 5244 **Region** Adelaide Hills
T (08) 8389 5312 **F** (08) 8389 5313 **www**.blackfordstable.com.au **Open** Not
Winemaker Nicky Cowper **Est.** 1998 **Cases** 200 **Vyds** 28.7 ha
Two odysseys lie entwined in the history of Blackford Stable. The first was that of Charles
Newman, who left his home in Blackford, Somerset, UK, in 1837, aged 16, to (successfully)
seek fame and fortune in Australia, and whose great-great-granddaughter and family live in
the Blackford homestead. The second odyssey was that of the Cowper family, whose 18-year-
old daughter Nicky moved from the beauty of NZ's southern Hawke's Bay region to begin
studies in oenology at the University of Adelaide's Waite Institute, convincing her parents,
Stephen and Angela, to follow her and relocate permanently to Australia. A property they
purchased is part of the original Blackford estate; the stone stables are the embryonic home
of Blackford Stable Wines. They have progressively planted 28 ha of chardonnay, sauvignon
blanc, semillon, riesling, pinot gris, merlot and cabernet sauvignon since 1998, selling most of
the grapes while Nicky completed her studies and then worked vintages in the Barossa Valley,
Adelaide Hills, McLaren Vale, Vic, France, the US and South Africa.

ΥΥΥΥ **Adelaide Hills Cabernet Sauvignon 2007** Light colour, although the hue
is good; light- to medium-bodied, with a range of varietal flavours ranging
across cassis, blackcurrant, leaf and mint; just needed a bit more push. Screwcap.
13.5% alc. **Rating** 89 **To** 2015 $22
Adelaide Hills Merlot 2007 Minty, leafy red berry aromas are followed by a
palate with similar, slightly hard-edged flavours; should have more ripe fruit given
the alcohol. Screwcap. 13.5% alc. **Rating** 87 **To** 2014 $22

BlackJack Vineyards ★★★★★

Cnr Blackjack Road/Calder Highway, Harcourt, Vic 3453 **Region** Bendigo
T (03) 5474 2355 **F** (03) 5474 2355 **www**.blackjackwines.com.au **Open** W'ends &
public hols 11–5
Winemaker Ian McKenzie, Ken Pollock **Est.** 1987 **Cases** 5000 **Vyds** 6.7 ha
Established by the McKenzie and Pollock families on the site of an old apple and pear orchard
in the Harcourt Valley, Blackjack is best known for some very good shirazs. Ian McKenzie,
incidentally, is not to be confused with Ian McKenzie formerly of Seppelt (Great Western). A
welcome return to top form. Exports to NZ.

ΥΥΥΥΥ **Bendigo Shiraz 2007** Vibrant purple-crimson; rich and ripe aromas and flavours;
abundant plum and black berry fruit is backed by a twitch of dark chocolate, ripe
tannins and well-balanced oak. Screwcap. 14.5% alc. **Rating** 94 **To** 2027 $35
Block 6 Bendigo Shiraz 2007 Despite lower alcohol than the Bendigo, little
difference in hue or depth; slightly more spicy and lively, but the base fruit
characters are similar, the tannins fine and well integrated. Screwcap. 13.5% alc.
Rating 94 **To** 2022 $35

ΥΥΥΥΥ **Bendigo Cabernet Merlot 2007** **Rating** 92 **To** 2020 $25

ΥΥΥΥ **Chortle's Edge Bendigo Shiraz 2007** **Rating** 89 **To** 2015 $19

Blackwood Crest Wines ★★★☆

RMB 404A, Boyup Brook, WA 6244 **Region** Blackwood Valley
T (08) 9767 3029 **F** (08) 9767 3029 **Open** By appt 10–5
Winemaker Max Fairbrass **Est.** 1976 **Cases** 3000 **Vyds** 8 ha
Blackwood Crest has been holding a low profile while developing its vineyards (cabernet
sauvignon, shiraz, riesling, semillon, sauvignon blanc, pinot noir and merlot) and a 100-
tonne winery. It has been an ongoing project, and progresses as time allows, fitting that Max
Fairbrass's grandparents took up the property as virgin bush in 1908.

 $\Upsilon\Upsilon\Upsilon\Upsilon\Upsilon$ **Semillon Sauvignon Blanc 2009** In the crisp, lively low alcohol style that has become de rigeur; the semillon gives the wine thrust and punch on the finish that can catch you by surprise. Screwcap. 11.5% alc. **Rating** 90 **To** 2011 $15

$\Upsilon\Upsilon\Upsilon\Upsilon$ **Riesling 2009 Rating** 87 **To** 2016 $17

Blackwood Wines   ★★★

Kearney Street, Nannup, WA 6275 **Region** Blackwood Valley
T (08) 9756 0077 **F** (08) 9756 0089 **www**.blackwoodwines.com.au **Open** 7 days 10–4
Winemaker Stuart Pearce **Est.** 1996 **Cases** 20 000 **Vyds** 5 ha
Blackwood Wines draws upon estate plantings of chardonnay, merlot, chenin blanc and pinot noir, supplemented by contract-grown fruit that significantly broadens the product range. Redevelopment of the cellar door and winery has seen production increase significantly from 5000 cases a few years ago. Exports to the US, The Netherlands, United Arab Emirates, Hong Kong and Singapore.

$\Upsilon\Upsilon\Upsilon\Upsilon$ **Fishbone Margaret River Cabernet Merlot 2008** Red fruit aromas blended with a little cedar and a touch of rolled leaf; medium-bodied with fine tannins and crisp acidity; correct, lacking a little complexity. Screwcap. 13.5% alc. **Rating** 88 **To** 2015 $20 BE
Fishbone Unwooded Chardonnay 2009 Nectarine and a little struck match on the bouquet; fleshy, forward and showing good flavour development. Screwcap. 12.8% alc. **Rating** 87 **To** 2012 $15 BE
Fishbone Shiraz 2008 Good colour; quite a dark bouquet, with tar and blackberry evident; the palate is firm on entry, but softens with generous red fruit on the finish. Screwcap. 15% alc. **Rating** 87 **To** 2014 $15 BE

Bleasdale Vineyards   ★★★★★

Wellington Road, Langhorne Creek, SA 5255 **Region** Langhorne Creek
T (08) 8537 3001 **F** (08) 8537 3224 **www**.bleasdale.com.au **Open** Mon–Sun 10–5
Winemaker Michael Potts, Paul Hotker, Ben Potts **Est.** 1850 **Cases** 100 000 **Vyds** 47 ha
This is one of the most historic wineries in Australia. Not so long prior to arrival of the 21st century, its vineyards were flooded every winter by diversion of the Bremer River, which provided moisture throughout the dry, cool growing season. In the new millennium, every drop of water is counted. Bleasdale has taken the opportunity presented by the challenges of this coming decade by removing under-performing vineyard blocks and to better reflect the mix of its wine portfolio. Its overall plantings have reduced from 61 ha, retaining only the best and oldest red vines. The make-up is now 30% shiraz, 28% cabernet, 10% malbec and 2% petit verdot, the remainder made up of 15% verdelho for table wine, 10% chardonnay, and an additional 5% old verdelho and grenache for fortified winemaking. Selected areas will be replanted with coming varieties including malbec, tempranillo and petit verdot. Exports to all major markets.

$\Upsilon\Upsilon\Upsilon\Upsilon\Upsilon$ **The Powder Monkey Langhorne Creek Shiraz 2008** Oak dominates the bouquet at first, but there is an underlying power of black fruits and graphite lurking beneath; the palate is incredibly solid and the concentration and complexity of the fruit undoubted; this wine will demand time and needs a good 3–5 years to achieve harmony. Screwcap. 15% alc. **Rating** 95 **To** 2028 $75 BE
Petrel Reserve Shiraz Cabernet Malbec 2007 A seamless union of these three varieties, with lifted perfume, red fruits and a touch of cedar on the bouquet; medium-bodied, with ample fine-grained tannins and restrained sweet dark fruits, all complemented by a little touch of spice for added interest; long and fine. Screwcap. 14.5% alc. **Rating** 94 **To** 2016 $29 BE
Double Take Langhorne Creek Malbec 2008 Quite amazing colour with a strong purple hue; the bouquet is vibrant and redolent of violets, blueberry and cinnamon; the concentration of the wine is staggering, but there is not a trace of heaviness to the palate; a great example of how expressive the variety can be. Screwcap. 16% alc. **Rating** 94 **To** 2016 $80 BE

ΨΨΨΨΩ Generations Langhorne Creek Shiraz 2008 Rating 93 To 2018 $38
       Frank Potts 2006 Rating 93 To 2021 $29 BE
       T&M McLaren Vale Langhorne Creek Tempranillo Malbec 2008
       Rating 90 To 2014 $24
✪   Second Innings Langhorne Creek Malbec 2008 Crimson-purple; masses
       of plum and plum pudding flavours, the tannins soft but needed to give the wine
       structure; thoroughly enjoyable. Screwcap. 14.5% alc. Rating 90 To 2015 $15
✪   Langhorne Creek Sparkling Shiraz NV Bright colour; spiced damson plum
       bouquet, with a rich fruitcake palate; quite sweet, but the finish is fresh and the
       tannins drying; well-balanced. Diam. 13.5% alc. Rating 90 To 2014 $19 BE

ΨΨΨΨ   Bremerview Langhorne Creek Shiraz 2007 Rating 89 To 2015 $18
       Bremerview Langhorne Creek Shiraz 2008 Rating 88 To 2014 $18 BE

Blickling Estate   ★★★★☆
Green Valley Road, Bendemeer, NSW 2355 Region New England
T (02) 6769 6659 F (02) 6769 6605 www.blickling.com.au Open 7 days 9–5
Winemaker First Creek Wines Est. 1999 Cases 4000 Vyds 9.8 ha
Rolf Blickling has established his vineyard (planted to riesling, chardonnay, sauvignon blanc,
pinot noir, cabernet sauvignon and shiraz) at an elevation of 950 m. Frosts in spring and April
underline how cool the climate is, necessitating careful site selection. The cellar door also
operates a lavender and eucalyptus oil distillery. This is the leader of the pack in New England,
perhaps in part due to skilled contract winemaking in the Hunter Valley.

ΨΨΨΨΨ Cabernet Sauvignon 2008 Not for the first time, a convincing Cabernet
✪   Sauvignon from Blickling; the crimson-purple colour is excellent, the blackcurrant
       fruit has fine, persistent tannins woven throughout; the line, length and balance are
       all spot on. Screwcap. 14.5% alc. Rating 94 To 2020 $22

ΨΨΨΨΩ Riesling 2009 Light straw-green; very fragrant, with an appealing mix of lime and
✪   passionfruit, the generous palate carrying on in precisely the same direction; ready
       to roll right now, although will hold. Screwcap. 13% alc. Rating 93 To 2014 $19
       Wooded Chardonnay 2008 Rating 91 To 2013 $22
       Shiraz 2008 Rating 90 To 2014 $22

ΨΨΨΨ   Sauvignon Blanc 2009 Rating 88 To 2010 $19

Bloodwood   ★★★★★
231 Griffin Road, Orange, NSW 2800 Region Orange
T (02) 6362 5631 F (02) 6361 1173 www.bloodwood.com.au Open By appt
Winemaker Stephen Doyle Est. 1983 Cases 4000 Vyds 8.43 ha
Rhonda and Stephen Doyle are two of the pioneers of the Orange district. The estate
vineyards (chardonnay, riesling, merlot, cabernet sauvignon, shiraz, cabernet franc and malbec)
are planted at an elevation of 810–860 m, which provides a reliably cool climate; frost can
be an issue, but heat seldom is. The wines are sold mainly through the cellar door and by an
energetic, humorous and informatively run mailing list (see, for example, the tasting note for
Big Men in Tights). Has an impressive track record across the full gamut of varietal (and other)
wine styles, especially Riesling, in a variety of styles; all of the wines have a particular elegance
and grace. Very much part of the growing reputation of Orange. Exports to the UK.

ΨΨΨΨΨ Silk Purse 2009 Pale straw-green; a truly delicious wine; juicy lime flavours
✪   intensified by a touch of botrytis, but without warping varietal character; the
       balance is immaculate, the sweetness balanced by acidity. Screwcap. 10.5% alc.
       Rating 95 To 2014 $25
✪   Riesling 2009 A gloriously fragrant bouquet with a surge of lime/lemon
       blossom, then an emphatic palate full of lime and a hint of herb; finishes well.
       Screwcap. 12.5% alc. Rating 94 To 2018 $20

✪   Shiraz 2007 Good colour; an elegant medium-bodied wine, instantly attesting to its cool-grown origins, with supple mouthfeel to the medium-bodied palate; red fruits intermingle with black fruits, fine French oak and spice playing a positive role. Screwcap. 14% alc. **Rating** 94 **To** 2017 $25

♀♀♀♀♀ **Maurice 2005** **Rating** 93 **To** 2017 $30
       Chardonnay 2009 **Rating** 92 **To** 2014 $25
       Cabernet Sauvignon 2005 **Rating** 92 **To** 2015 $25
✪   **Big Men in Tights 2009** Bright puce; a rose that abounds with plum and strawberry jam fruit on a long and lingering palate; hilarious back label. Screwcap. 13.5% alc. **Rating** 90 **To** 2011 $16
       Chirac 2007 **Rating** 90 **To** 2014 $40

♀♀♀♀   **Pinot Noir 2009** **Rating** 89 **To** 2014 $35

Blue Poles Vineyard   ★★★☆

PO Box 34, Mount Lawley, WA 6929 **Region** Margaret River
T (08) 9757 4382 **F** (08) 6210 1390 **www**.bluepolesvineyard.com.au **Open** Not
Winemaker Vasse River Wines (Sharna Kowalczuk) **Est.** 2001 **Cases** 750 **Vyds** 6.7 ha
Geologists Mark Gifford and Tim Markwell formed a joint venture to locate and develop Blue Poles Vineyard. Their search was unhurried, and contact with the University of Bordeaux (supplemented by extensive reading of technical literature) showed that a portion of the property included a block that mimicked some of the best vineyards in St Emilion and Pomerol, leading to the planting of merlot and cabernet franc in 2001. Further soil mapping and topography also identified blocks best suited to shiraz and Rhône Valley white varietals, which were planted in 2003. The vineyard maintenance has proceeded with minimal irrigation, and no fertilisers.

♀♀♀♀♀ **Reserve Margaret River Merlot 2007** Good colour; vibrant and fresh, and, as befits merlot, medium-bodied; the aromas and flavours combine red and black fruits, with the barest touch of savoury olive. Screwcap. 14% alc. **Rating** 91 **To** 2017 $35

Blue Pyrenees Estate   ★★★★☆

Vinoca Road, Avoca, Vic 3467 **Region** Pyrenees
T (03) 5465 1111 **F** (03) 5465 3529 **www**.bluepyrenees.com.au **Open** Mon–Fri
10–4.30, w'ends & public hols 10–5
Winemaker Andrew Koerner, Chris Smales **Est.** 1963 **Cases** 50 000 **Vyds** 170 ha
Forty years after Remy Cointreau established Blue Pyrenees Estate (then known as Chateau Remy), the business was sold to a small group of Sydney businessmen led by John Ellis (no relation to John Ellis of Hanging Rock). Former Rosemount senior winemaker Andrew Koerner heads the winery team. The core of the business is the very large estate plantings, most decades old, but with newer arrivals including viognier, petit verdot and pinot meunier. Exports to the UK, the US and other major markets.

♀♀♀♀♀ **Cabernet Sauvignon 2008** Blackcurrant, cassis and mint combine on the
✪   bouquet, with well-handled oak; the palate has good depth, fruit, tannins and oak in exemplary balance. Trophy for Best Cabernet in Commerical Classes Sydney Wine Show '10. Screwcap. 14% alc. **Rating** 94 **To** 2016 $18 BE

♀♀♀♀♀ **Reserve Shiraz 2006** **Rating** 93 **To** 2020 $35 BE
       Estate Red 2006 **Rating** 90 **To** 2017 $35 BE

♀♀♀♀   **Shiraz 2006** **Rating** 89 **To** 2016 $18

Blue Wren   ★★★

433 Cassilis Road, Mudgee, NSW 2850 **Region** Mudgee
T (02) 6372 6202 **F** (02) 6372 6206 **www**.bluewrenwines.com.au **Open** 7 days 10.30–4.30
Winemaker Frank Newman **Est.** 1998 **Cases** 4000 **Vyds** 32.21 ha
Roy Hofmeier and Vikki Williams purchased Blue Wren from the Anderson family in 2005.
They have now combined the Bombira Vineyard with the former Augustine vineyards
purchased in 2007, with some vines up to 70 years old. The plantings consist of cabernet
sauvignon (12 ha), shiraz (11.02 ha), gewurztraminer (3.2 ha), chardonnay (2.1 ha), pinot noir
(1.6 ha), verdelho (1.39 ha) and merlot (0.9 ha).

ＹＹＹＹ **Mudgee Merlot 2007** Light but good hue; a medium-bodied wine with
appropriate red and blackcurrant fruit, and a gently savoury, and quite long, finish.
Screwcap. 13.8% alc. **Rating** 89 **To** 2012 $16
Reserve Shiraz 2007 Better hue than the varietal; chocolate, black fruits and
vanilla on the bouquet are followed by a medium- to full-bodied palate with a
similar flavour profile, and a slightly sweet sensation on the aftertaste. Screwcap.
14.5% alc. **Rating** 88 **To** 2016 $22
Mudgee Chardonnay 2009 Very pale colour; a lively, zesty unwooded wine,
headed to cross-dressing with sauvignon blanc thanks to its lively citrus and grassy
flavours. Screwcap. 12% alc. **Rating** 87 **To** 2010 $18

Bluemetal Vineyard   ★★★★☆

112 Compton Park Road, Berrima, NSW 2577 **Region** Southern Highlands
T (02) 4877 1877 **F** (02) 4877 2583 **www**.bluemetalvineyard.com **Open** Thurs–Mon
10–5, or by appt
Winemaker Jonathan Holgate, Nick Bulleid (Consultant) **Est.** 1999 **Cases** 2700
Vyds 10.8 ha
Bluemetal Vineyard is situated on part of a cattle station at 790 m; the name comes from the
rich red soil that overlies the cap of basalt rock. A wide range of grape varieties is planted,
including sauvignon blanc, cabernet sauvignon, merlot, pinot gris, sangiovese and petit verdot.
The wines have been very competently made. Exports to the UK.

ＹＹＹＹＹ Signature Southern Highlands Fume Blanc 2008 Fragrant citrus and
passionfruit aromas flow through onto the lively palate, where oak simply
provides texture without diminishing the fruit profile; the finish is long and fresh.
Exemplary winemaking. Screwcap. 13% alc. Rating 94 To 2011 $25

ＹＹＹＹＱ **Signature Southern Highlands Fume Blanc 2009** Rating 91 To 2011 $25
Signature Southern Highlands Pinot Gris 2009 Rating 90 To 2011 $25

ＹＹＹＹ **Southern Highlands Sauvignon Blanc 2009** Rating 89 To 2010 $20
Lava One Southern Highlands Botrytis Sauvignon Blanc 2008 Rating 89
To 2012 $25
Southern Highlands Sangiovese 2008 Rating 88 To 2014 $20
Signature Southern Highlands Petit Verdot 2008 Rating 87 To 2012 $25

Boat O'Craigo   ★★★★☆

458 Maroondah Highway, Healesville, Vic 3777 **Region** Yarra Valley
T (03) 5962 6899 **F** (03) 5962 5140 **www**.boatocraigo.com.au **Open** Fri–Mon 10.30–5.30
Winemaker Al Fencaros, The YarraHill (Contract) **Est.** 1998 **Cases** 3500 **Vyds** 21.63 ha
Steve Graham purchased the property, which is now known as Boat O'Craigo (a tiny place
in a Scottish valley where his ancestors lived), in 2003. It has two quite separate vineyards: a
hillside planting on one of the highest sites in the Yarra Valley, and at Kangaroo Ground on the
opposite side of the valley. Exports to Finland, China and Hong Kong.

♥♥♥♥♥ **Dundee Yarra Valley Shiraz Grenache Viognier 2008** Bright colour; dark and savoury on the bouquet, with spice, tar and licorice giving way to red and black fruits; the palate follows the theme, with roasted meat and some red fruit highlights providing contrast; savoury, intense and surprisingly long; plenty of flavour at 13.3% alc/v. Screwcap. 13.3% alc. **Rating** 95 **To** 2018 $26 BE

♥♥♥♥♡ **Rob Roy Yarra Valley Pinot Noir 2008 Rating** 92 **To** 2014 $26 BE

♥♥♥♥ **Black Spur Yarra Valley Chardonnay 2007 Rating** 88 **To** 2012 $20 BE

Bobtail Ridge Wines ★★★★★

Lot 50 Yarnup Road, Frankland River, WA 6396 **Region** Frankland River
T (08) 9856 6289 **F** (08) 9856 6287 **www**.bobtailridge.com.au **Open** 7 days 10–4
Winemaker Alkoomi Wines **Est.** 1980 **Cases** 500 **Vyds** 11.4 ha
June and Jeremy Roberts were among the early movers in Frankland River, diversifying part of their property by planting vines with the intention of having the grapes vinified. Farming and family commitments delayed that process until 2003, when a Shiraz designed for easy drinking and short-term cellaring was made. In the meantime the plantings had been increased with riesling (3.3 ha), semillon, sauvignon blanc and cabernet sauvignon (1.6 ha each), shiraz (2.5 ha) and merlot (0.8 ha). After some experimentation, they now make a Semillon, Riesling, Shiraz and Cabernet Merlot, the red wines matured in French oak. The family does all the vineyard work as part of its farming activities, using a minimal spraying program and hand-pruning the vines. The majority of the grapes are sold to Alkoomi, with only limited quantities vinified under the Bobtail Ridge label, which are consistently of excellent quality.

♥♥♥♥♥ **Frankland River Riesling 2008** Light straw-green; the bouquet is still
✪ developing, but the palate is almost aggressive in its varietal expression, hurling herb, citrus and mineral notes right through the length of the palate. Screwcap. 11.5% alc. **Rating** 95 **To** 2023 $18
✪ **Frankland River Riesling 2009** Bright straw-green; aromas of citrus and green apple are replayed on the long, crisp and lively palate, finishing with crackling dry acidity; a track record of developing beautifully, its best years are still in front of it. Screwcap. 12% alc. **Rating** 94 **To** 2024 $18
✪ **Frankland River Semillon 2007** Some colour development, although the hue is bright; follows in the footsteps of the '04, '05 and '08 in the 2010 *Wine Companion*, all outstanding, and all with the citrussy edge that this release has, adding to both flavour and length. Screwcap. 13% alc. **Rating** 94 **To** 2017 $18

Bochara Wines ★★★★

1099 Glenelg Highway, Hamilton, Vic 3300 **Region** Henty
T (03) 5571 9309 **F** (03) 5571 9309 **www**.bocharawines.com.au **Open** Fri–Sun 11–5, or by appt
Winemaker Martin Slocombe **Est.** 1998 **Cases** 1000 **Vyds** 4.2 ha
This is the small business of experienced winemaker Martin Slocombe and former Yalumba viticulturist Kylie McIntyre. They have established 1 ha each of pinot noir and sauvignon blanc and 0.2 ha of gewurztraminer, supplemented by grapes purchased from local growers. The modestly priced but well-made wines are principally sold through the cellar door on the property, a decrepit weatherboard shanty with one cold tap that has been transformed into a fully functional two-room tasting area, and through a number of local restaurants and bottle shops. The label design, incidentally, comes from a 1901 poster advertising the subdivision of the original Bochara property into smaller farms.

♥♥♥♥♡ **GT Gewurztraminer 2009** Fresh musk bouquet, with grapefruit playing a
✪ supporting role; the palate is quite fresh, with a talc-like quality, and fresh acidity providing good life and energy. Screwcap. 12.1% alc. **Rating** 90 **To** 2012 $15 BE
Pinot Noir 2009 Bright colour; lifted dark plum and black cherry bouquet, with a touch of warm spice and a suggestion of mint; juicy and fleshy on entry, with an ironstone minerality, toasty oak and fine tannin backbone to conclude. Screwcap. 14.2% alc. **Rating** 90 **To** 2014 $22 BE

Bogong Estate ★★★

Cnr Mountain Creek Road/Damms Road, Mt Beauty, Vic 3699 **Region** Alpine Valleys
T 0419 567 588 **F** (03) 5754 1320 **www**.pinotnoir.com.au **Open** 7 days 11–5
Winemaker Bill and Kate Tynan **Est.** 1997 **Cases** 1500 **Vyds** 10 ha
Bill Tynan and family began the establishment of their vineyard in 1997, having chosen to focus exclusively on pinot noir for its site suitability and versatility for red wines, sparkling and rose. Clones D5V12, MV6, Burgundian 114 and 115 are grown in separate blocks with variations in soil, altitude and micro-climate characteristics. The wines are fermented in numerous small open fermenters, mainly using wild yeasts for added complexity, and all batches are basket-pressed. The estate takes its name from Victoria's highest peak, Mt Bogong, meaning 'big fella', which provides a spectacular view framing the vineyard. Wines are released under two labels: the more complex Bogong Estate, and everyday drinking wines under pinotnoir.com.au.

ΨΨΨΨ   **Alpine Valleys Pinot Noir 2008** Distinct savoury/briary notes are threaded through the plum and black cherry fruit, the flavours prominent. Good food style for richer dishes; attractive new label. Screwcap. 14% alc. **Rating** 87 **To** 2013 $25
pinotnoir.com.au Red Pinot Noir 2008 Slightly brighter colour than the Bogong Estate; similar savoury/briary nuances, but the tannins are less extractive as befits the fresh, light cherry fruit. Wildly different label design. Screwcap. 13.5% alc. **Rating** 87 **To** 2012 $18

Boireann ★★★★★

26 Donnellys Castle Road, The Summit, Qld 4377 **Region** Granite Belt
T (07) 4683 2194 **www**.boireannwinery.com.au **Open** 7 days 10–4.30
Winemaker Peter Stark **Est.** 1998 **Cases** 800 **Vyds** 1.6 ha
Peter and Therese Stark have a 10-ha property set among the great granite boulders and trees that are so much a part of the Granite Belt. They have planted no fewer than 11 varieties, including four that go to make the Lurnea, a Bordeaux-blend; shiraz and viognier; grenache and mourvedre providing a Rhône blend, and a straight merlot. Tannat, pinot noir (French) and sangiovese, barbera and nebbiolo (Italian) make up the viticultural League of Nations. Peter is a winemaker of exceptional talent, producing cameo amounts of quite beautifully made red wines that are of a quality equal to Australia's best.

ΨΨΨΨΨ   **Maggie's Granite Belt Shiraz Viognier 2008** Outstanding deep crimson-purple; has all the synergy to be gained from the co-fermentation of these varieties, with the depth of power and flavour of Guigal's La Mouline from the Northern Rhône; this will not come into full flower for a decade. Diam. 14.5% alc. **Rating** 96 **To** 2030 $55

✪   **Granite Belt Shiraz 2008** Saturated crimson-purple; the black fruits of the bouquet are followed by a dense full-bodied palate of blackberry, plum and licorice; the most concentrated Boireann wine to date, with a long cellaring future. From Harrington Glen grapes. Diam. 14% alc. **Rating** 95 **To** 2028 $25
Vigne Juvenile Granite Belt Shiraz Viognier 2008 Excellent vibrant crimson-purple, this wine has a great deal to offer from its fragrant bouquet, its lively spicy palate, and its surprising structure. And yes, the name has echoes of Torbreck. Diam. 14% alc. **Rating** 94 **To** 2020 $28
The Lurnea 2008 Purple-crimson; an estate-grown blend of Merlot/Cabernet Sauvignon/Petit Verdot/Cabernet Franc; has the excellent colour of all the '08 Boireanns; this is yet another distinguished Bordeaux blend attesting to Peter and Therese Stark's dedication as viticulturists and to Peter's exceptional winemaking skills. Diam. 13.5% alc. **Rating** 94 **To** 2020 $28

ΨΨΨΨΨ   **Granite Belt Merlot 2008 Rating** 93 **To** 2018 $25
Granite Belt Mourvedre Tannat 2008 Rating 93 **To** 2028 $28
Granite Belt Cabernet Sauvignon 2008 Rating 92 **To** 2018 $25
Granite Belt Grenache 2008 Rating 90 **To** 2016 $18

🌿 Bonking Frog ★★★

Cnr South West Highway/Dardanup West Road, North Boyanup, WA 6237
Region Geographe
T (08) 9731 5137 **www.**bonkingfrog.com.au **Open** By appt
Winemaker Naturaliste Vintners (Bruce Dukes) **Est.** 1996 **Cases** 700 **Vyds** 3 ha
Julie and Phil Hutton put their money where their hearts are, electing to plant a merlot-only
vineyard in 1996. Presumably knowing the unpredictable habits of merlot when planted on
its own roots, they began by planting 3500 Swartzman rootstock vines, and then 12 months
later field-grafting the merlot scion material. Small wonder their backs are still aching. I don't
doubt for a millisecond the sincerity of their enthusiasm for the variety when they say, 'Fruity,
plummy, smooth and velvety. Hints of chocolate too. If you're new to wine and all things
merlot, this is a wonderful variety to explore. A classic red, known for its go-anywhere, please-
everyone style, it makes a welcome place for itself at any table.' And the frogs? Well, apparently
they bonk – loudly.

🍷🍷🍷🍷 **Summer Merlot Rose 2008** Light pink in mainstream rose style, with small
red berry fruits and crisp acidity on the finish. Screwcap. 14% alc. **Rating** 88
To 2010 $17

Borambola Wines ★★★

Sturt Highway, Wagga Wagga, NSW 2650 **Region** Gundagai
T (02) 6928 4210 **F** (02) 6928 4210 **www.**borambola.com **Open** 7 days 10–4 by appt
Winemaker Chris Derrez **Est.** 1995 **Cases** 1200 **Vyds** 9.16 ha
Borambola Homestead was built in the 1880s, and in the latter part of that century was the
centre of a pastoral empire of 1.4 million ha, ownership of which passed to the McMullen
family in 1992. It is situated in rolling foothills 25 km east of Wagga Wagga in the Gundagai
region. The vineyards surround the homestead and include shiraz, cabernet sauvignon and
chardonnay. Exports to Singapore and China.

🍷🍷🍷🍷 **Hiraji's Spell Shiraz 2007** A dark fruit and bitter chocolate bouquet, seasoned
with a touch of mint; the palate is rich, bordering on hefty, and the warmth from
the alcohol is prominent; good flavour though, and well put together. Screwcap.
14.8% alc. **Rating** 87 To 2015 $20 BE
The Quarrel Cabernet Sauvignon Shiraz Merlot 2008 Lively and juicy
red fruit bouquet and palate; clean and showing a little savoury anise character;
reasonable length. Screwcap. 14% alc. **Rating** 87 To 2014 $20 BE

Borrodell on the Mount ★★★★☆

Lake Canobolas Road, Orange, NSW 2800 **Region** Orange
T (02) 6365 3425 **F** (02) 6365 3588 **www.**borrodell.com.au **Open** 7 days 10–5
Winemaker Chris Derrez, Lucy Maddox, Peter Logan, Phil Kerney **Est.** 1995
Cases 3000 **Vyds** 6 ha
Borry Gartrell and Gaye Stuart-Nairne have planted pinot noir, sauvignon blanc, pinot
meunier, traminer and chardonnay adjacent to a cherry, plum and heritage apple orchard
and truffiere. It is a 10-min drive from Orange, and adjacent to Lake Canobolas, at an
altitude of 1000 m. The wines have been consistent medal winners at regional and small
winemaker shows.

🍷🍷🍷🍷🍷 **Wine Maker's Daughter Orange Gewurztraminer 2009** Light straw-green;
✪ has a track record of producing traminer with clear varietal expression, and this
is no exception; a fragrant display of rose petal, spice and musk on the bouquet is
followed by a perfectly balanced and crisp palate without a hint of phenolics on its
long, dry finish. Screwcap. 12.1% alc. **Rating** 95 To 2014 $25

🍷🍷🍷🍷🍷 **Orange Pinot Noir 2007 Rating** 91 To 2013 $30
Sister's Rock Orange Sparkling Pink Pinot Noir 2006 Rating 91
To 2014 $32

ＹＹＹＹ   **Orange Chardonnay 2008** Rating 89 To 2013 $20
Ruby 2006 Rating 89 To 2014 $25

Boston Bay Wines   ★★★★

Lincoln Highway, Port Lincoln, SA 5606 **Region** Southern Eyre Peninsula
T (08) 8684 3600 **F** (08) 8684 3637 **www**.bostonbaywines.com.au **Open** 7 days 12–4
Winemaker David O'Leary, Nick Walker **Est.** 1984 **Cases** 4500 **Vyds** 6.95 ha
A strongly tourist-oriented operation that has extended the viticultural map in SA. It is situated on the same latitude as Adelaide, overlooking the Spencer Gulf at the southern tip of the Eyre Peninsula. Say proprietors Graham and Mary Ford, 'it is the only vineyard in the world to offer frequent sightings of whales at play in the waters at its foot'.

ＹＹＹＹＹ   **Shiraz 2006** Retains good hue; smart new labelling introduces an attractive medium-bodied shiraz, with spice/pepper, cherry and plum fruit, and oak in good balance. Screwcap. 14.5% alc. **Rating** 90 To 2018 $20

Botobolar   ★★★

89 Botobolar Road, Mudgee, NSW 2850 **Region** Mudgee
T (02) 6373 3840 **F** (02) 6373 3789 **www**.botobolar.com **Open** Mon–Sat 10–5, Sun 10–3
Winemaker Kevin Karstrom **Est.** 1971 **Cases** 3000 **Vyds** 19.4 ha
One of the first (possibly the first) fully organic vineyards in Australia, with present owner Kevin Karstrom continuing the practices established by founder Gil Wahlquist. Preservative-free reds and low-preservative dry whites extend the organic practice of the vineyard to the winery. Dry Red is consistently the best wine to appear under the Botobolar label, with gold-medal success at the Mudgee Wine Show. Its preservative-free red wines are in the top echelon of this class. Since 2008 the vineyard has been undergoing progressive retrellising, which will lead to a temporary reduction of production. Exports to Denmark and Japan.

ＹＹＹＹ   **Low Preservative Mudgee Semillon 2009** Has ample flavour and depth; ripe lemon rind/lemon cake, although not a lot of finesse. Contains less than 100 ppm SO$_2$; with screwcap can be cellared for some years. 12.5% alc. **Rating** 88 To 2012 $19.95
✪   **Preservative Free Mudgee Shiraz 2009** So far, good purple hue; a rich, slightly rustic, full-bodied wine with abundant fruit, the strong tannins providing a de facto anti-oxidation defence. Screwcap. 13% alc. **Rating** 88 To 2012 $19.95
The King Mudgee Cabernet Sauvignon Shiraz 2006/07 A 50/50 blend, but we are not told what the vintage split is; the colour is very good, suggesting an '07 bias; while the flavours are fresh, the tannins are more so – again pointing to youth. Approach with caution for the time being. Screwcap. 14% alc. **Rating** 88 To 2016 $22.95

Bou-saada   ★★★★

Kells Creek Road, Mittagong, NSW 2575 **Region** Southern Highlands
T (02) 4878 5399 **F** (02) 4878 5397 **www**.bousaada.com **Open** By appt
Winemaker High Range Vintners (Jonathan Holgate) **Est.** 1997 **Cases** 500 **Vyds** 6.2 ha
Alastair and Michele Graham purchased the 40-ha property in 1996, planting the vineyard the following year with sauvignon blanc, followed by merlot, chardonnay and riesling. There are a little over 6 ha of vines, and the wines are estate grown. The name, incidentally, is a pilgrimage town in Algeria built around an oasis, with 'Bou' meaning father and 'saada' peace and happiness. The cellar door is made from Sydney blue gum and stringybark grown in the locality.

ＹＹＹＹＹ   **Southern Highlands Riesling 2008** Pale straw-green; a clean, gently floral
✪   bouquet leads into a finely tempered palate with an appealing array of lime, apple and passionfruit flavours. Screwcap. 12% alc. **Rating** 91 To 2018 $20

✪   **Southern Highlands Sauvignon Blanc 2008** Very interesting wine; the label correctly suggests there are overtones of the Loire Valley, for it has an angular complexity to its herb/grass/oak/gooseberry/asparagus flavours. Screwcap. 13% alc. **Rating** 90 **To** 2011 $18

🍷🍷🍷🍷   **First Fruits Fume Blanc 2007 Rating** 88 **To** 2011 $18

Bowen Estate   ★★★☆

Riddoch Highway, Coonawarra, SA 5263 **Region** Coonawarra
T (08) 8737 2229 **F** (08) 8737 2173 **www**.bowenestate.com.au **Open** 7 days 10–5
Winemaker Emma Bowen **Est.** 1972 **Cases** 12 000 **Vyds** 16.9 ha
Bluff-faced regional veteran Doug Bowen, now with daughter Emma at his side in the winery, presides over one of Coonawarra's landmarks. Doug has now handed over full winemaking responsibility to Emma, 'retiring' to the position of viticulturist. Exports to the UK, the US, the Maldives, Singapore, China, Japan and NZ.

🍷🍷🍷🍷   **Coonawarra Shiraz 2007** The one-piece cork is a defiant stand emphasising the conservative traditional values of Bowen Estate; the colour is still a bright crimson, but the flavours can't escape the clutches of the high alcohol that cuts short the finish. 15% alc. **Rating** 88 **To** 2013 $29.80

Bowman's Run   ★★★

1305 Beechworth-Wodonga Road, Wooragee, Vic 3747 **Region** Beechworth
T (03) 5728 7318 **Open** Most w'ends & by appt
Winemaker Daniel Balzer **Est.** 1989 **Cases** 150 **Vyds** 1 ha
Struan and Fran Robertson have cabernet sauvignon, riesling and small plots of shiraz and traminer dating back to 1989. The tiny winery came on-stream in 2000, and is part of a larger general agricultural holding.

🍷🍷🍷🍷   **Seven Springs Beechworth Riesling 2009** Pale quartz-green; fresh and crisp, with a touch of apple blossom on the bouquet, then a minerally palate; still tightly furled, needing time. Screwcap. 11.5% alc. **Rating** 87 **To** 2014 $25

Box Stallion   ★★★★☆

64 Turrarubba Road, Merricks North, Vic 3926 **Region** Mornington Peninsula
T (03) 5989 7444 **F** (03) 5989 7688 **www**.boxstallion.com.au **Open** 7 days 11–5
Winemaker Alex White **Est.** 2001 **Cases** 9000 **Vyds** 16 ha
Box Stallion is the joint venture of Stephen Wharton, John Gillies and Garry Zerbe, who have linked two vineyards at Bittern and Merricks North, with 16 ha of vines planted between 1997 and 2003. What was once a thoroughbred stud has now become a vineyard, with the Red Barn (in their words) 'now home to a stable of fine wines'. Exports to the US, Canada, Japan and China.

🍷🍷🍷🍷🍷   **Mornington Peninsula Shiraz 2006** Bright colour; black cherries, smoky paprika and cinnamon all merge together on the bouquet; the palate is still fresh, fleshy and showing a complex fresh herb character across the palate; generous and a little chewy on the finish. Diam. 14.6% alc. **Rating** 94 **To** 2016 $30 BE

🍷🍷🍷🍷🍷   **Mornington Peninsula Sauvignon Blanc 2009 Rating** 90 **To** 2012 $20 BE

🍷🍷🍷🍷   **The Enclosure Mornington Peninsula Chardonnay 2008 Rating** 88 **To** 2014 $25 BE
The Enclosure Mornington Peninsula Pinot Noir 2008 Rating 87 **To** 2013 $30 BE
Mornington Peninsula Tempranillo 2007 Rating 87 **To** 2013 $40 BE

Boynton's Feathertop   ★★★★☆

Great Alpine Road, Porepunkah, Vic 3741 **Region** Alpine Valleys
T (03) 5756 2356 **F** (03) 5756 2610 **www**.boynton.com.au **Open** 7 days 10–5
Winemaker Kel Boynton **Est.** 1987 **Cases** 10 000 **Vyds** 18 ha

Kel Boynton has a beautiful vineyard, framed by Mt Feathertop rising above it. Overall, the red wines have always outshone the whites. The initial very strong American oak input has been softened in more recent vintages to give a better fruit/oak balance. The wines are released under the Boynton Reserve and Feathertop labels. The smoke and bushfires of the 2007 and '09 vintages have not stopped Kel from planting a spectacular array of varieties, headed by sauvignon blanc (2.5 ha), shiraz and pinot gris (2 ha each), merlot, savagnin and nebbiolo (1.5 ha each), cabernet sauvignon and sangiovese (1 ha each), then half a hectare each of tempranillo, pinot noir, pinot meunier, vermentino, chardonnay, riesling, friulano and semillon, culminating with a combined half-hectare of malbec, dornfelder and petit verdot. Exports to Austria.

ⵗⵗⵗⵗⵗ **Alpine Valleys Shiraz 2006** Still has crimson hues; a medium-bodied shiraz
✪   showing very cool climate characteristics, with a distinctive lift from the viognier component; the tannins are superfine, the oak restrained. Screwcap. 13.5% alc. **Rating** 93 **To** 2015 $25

✪   **Alpine Valleys Riesling 2008** Light green-straw; an unusual wine with a quiet bouquet and entry to the mouth, then accelerates hard through to a lime sherbet finish with lingering acidity; draws you back again to the wine. Screwcap. 12% alc. **Rating** 91 **To** 2015 $20

✪   **Alpine Valleys Sauvignon Blanc 2009** Crisp mineral, herb and grass aromas and flavours that run through the palate and lingering finish. Screwcap. 13% alc. **Rating** 90 **To** 2010 $20

            Alpine Valleys Shiraz 2008 Crimson-red; a complex web of black fruits, licorice and fruitcake aromas, then a medium-bodied but rich palate; does shorten slightly on the finish. Screwcap. 14% alc. **Rating** 90 **To** 2017 $25

            Alpine Valleys Merlot 2008 Light crimson; fragrant cassis/red berry fruit aromas; the light-bodied palate offers more of the same, with savoury olive notes on the finish. True to variety. Screwcap. 14% alc. **Rating** 90 **To** 2015 $25

ⵗⵗⵗⵗ **Alpine Valleys Cabernet Sauvignon 2005 Rating** 89 **To** 2014 $25

Brackenwood Vineyard   ★★★★

17 High Street, Willunga, SA 5172 **Region** Adelaide Hills
T 0400 266 121 **F** (08) 8110 9889 **www**.brackenwoodvineyard.com.au
Open Wed–Sun 11–4, Sat 10–4
Winemaker Damon Nagel, Reg Wilkingson, Adrian Kenny **Est.** 1999 **Cases** 1500
Vyds 7.6 ha

Brackenwood Vineyard is situated at the extreme southern end of the Adelaide Hills, skirted by the Old Victor Harbour Road. Damon Nagel has established shiraz (2.65 ha), riesling (1.7 ha), sauvignon blanc (1.3 ha), nebbiolo (1.2 ha) and chardonnay (0.75 ha). All wines are estate-grown.

ⵗⵗⵗⵗⵗ **Adelaide Hills Riesling 2005** Bright green-straw, excellent for age; developing at a leisurely pace, citrus and mineral notes now joined by honey and a hint of toast. Screwcap. 13% alc. **Rating** 92 **To** 2013 $24

✪   **Adelaide Hills Sauvignon Blanc 2009** Pale, bright green-straw; an interesting wine, wild yeast and lees stirring in tank (but no oak) adding both flavour and texture to the tangy mix of citrus, stone fruit and tropical fruit flavours. Screwcap. 12.3% alc. **Rating** 92 **To** 2011 $19

            MC Adelaide Hills Syrah 2009 Clear purple-crimson; a highly aromatic and perfumed bouquet reflecting the whole berry (carbonic maceration) ferment; spicy notes and some briar appear on the finish. Screwcap. 13.5% alc. **Rating** 90 **To** 2014 $21

ⵗⵗⵗⵗ **Adelaide Hills Riesling 2009 Rating** 89 **To** 2015 $19

Brand's Laira Coonawarra

Riddoch Highway, Coonawarra, SA 5263 **Region** Coonawarra
T (08) 8736 3260 **F** (08) 8736 3208 **www.**mcwilliamswines.com **Open** Mon–Fri 9–4.30,
w'ends & public hols 10–4
Winemaker Peter Weinberg **Est.** 1966 **Cases** NFP **Vyds** 278 ha
Part of a substantial investment in Coonawarra by McWilliam's, which first acquired a 50%
interest from the Brand family, increased to 100%, and followed this with the purchase of 100
ha of additional vineyard land. Significantly increased production of the smooth wines for
which Brand's is known has followed. The estate plantings include the 100-year-old Stentiford
block. Exports to India and Fiji.

ΨΨΨΨΨ The Patron 2006 The bouquet is incredibly backward and restrained, and time
is necessary to uncover the full gamut of aromas and flavours that lie therein;
cassis and olive with a touch of mint are on display; the palate is laden with dark
ripe fruits, but there is a lightness to the depth that is quite disarming; layered,
long, dark and mysterious, age will be the Patron's friend. Cabernet Sauvignon.
Screwcap. 15% alc. **Rating** 95 **To** 2025 $75 BE
Stentiford's Old Vine Shiraz 2005 Produced from the shiraz block planted in
1893, with that effortless intensity and length given by very old vines, black fruits
on the mid-palate, moving into a more savoury finish, the tannins ripe and fine.
Screwcap. 15.5% alc. **Rating** 94 **To** 2030 $75
Vintage No. 40 Cabernet Sauvignon 2005 A supple, smooth and carefully
crafted wine with classic blackcurrant and mulberry aromas and flavours; French
oak has also played an important role; shrugs off its alcohol. Screwcap. 15% alc.
Rating 94 **To** 2025 $45

ΨΨΨΨΨ Cabernet Merlot 2008 Excellent crimson-purple; offers abundant blackcurrant,
✪   blueberry and cassis fruit that has no dead fruit/overripe characters; fine, savoury
tannins and oak. Great future. Screwcap. 15% alc. **Rating** 93 **To** 2023 $22
Shiraz 2007 Rating 92 **To** 2018 $22 BE
Chardonnay 2008 Rating 90 **To** 2014 $22
Blockers Cabernet Sauvignon 2007 Rating 90 **To** 2017 $25

Brandy Creek Wines

570 Buln Buln Road, Drouin East, Vic 3818 **Region** Gippsland
T (03) 5625 4498 **www.**brandycreekwines.com.au **Open** Thurs–Sun & public hols 10–5,
Thurs–Sat nights
Winemaker Peter Beckingham (Contract) **Est.** 2005 **Cases** 2000 **Vyds** 3 ha
Marie McDonald and Rick Stockdale purchased the property on which they have since
established their vineyard, cellar door and café restaurant in 1997. Pinot gris, tempranillo and
pinot meunier have been progressively established, with other varieties purchased from local
growers. The café (and surrounding vineyard) is situated on a northeast-facing slope with
spectacular views out to the Baw Baw Ranges.

ΨΨΨΨ Shiraz 2007 A light- to medium-bodied wine with clear cool-grown
characteristics reflected by the mix of licorice, leaf, pepper and spice of the red
fruits. Screwcap. 14.1% alc. **Rating** 89 **To** 2015 $33
Longford Vineyard Shiraz 2008 Bright colour; aromatically shows a blend
of red fruits and fresh turned earth, very much in tune with Gippsland terroir;
medium-bodied, spicy and with prominent acidity the dominant character, food is
demanded with this wine. Screwcap. 15.1% alc. **Rating** 88 **To** 2015 $33 BE
Tempranillo 2008 Meaty and a little touch of mint, and the wine is certainly
fresh; a little clipped on the finish, but not bad flavour, with a varietal fragrance and
savoury note that works. Screwcap. 14.4% alc. **Rating** 87 **To** 2012 $28 BE

Brangayne of Orange   ★★★★☆

837 Pinnacle Road, Orange, NSW 2800 **Region** Orange
T (02) 6365 3229 **F** (02) 6365 3170 **www**.brangayne.com **Open** Mon–Fri 11–1, 2–4, Sat
10–5, Sun by appt
Winemaker Simon Gilbert **Est.** 1994 **Cases** 3000 **Vyds** 25.7 ha
The Hoskins family (orchardists) decided to diversify into grapegrowing in 1994 and have
progressively established high-quality vineyards. Right from the outset, Brangayne has
produced excellent wines across all mainstream varieties, remarkably ranging from Pinot Noir
to Cabernet Sauvignon. Son David has been managing the business since 2005, which sells a
substantial part of its crop to other winemakers. Exports to the UK, Canada and Spain.

♟♟♟♟♟ **Shiraz 2006** Has retained excellent crimson hue; classic cool-grown spice and
cracked pepper nuances behind black fruits and licorice on the bouquet, the finely
structured, long, medium-bodied palate providing more of the same. Screwcap.
14.9% alc. **Rating** 94 **To** 2021 $35

♟♟♟♟♀ **Sauvignon Blanc 2009 Rating** 93 **To** 2012 $24
✪ **Chardonnay 2009** Pale straw-green; a highly fragrant and floral bouquet with
citrus, pear and lemongrass, veering to grapefruit and nectarine on the palate. A la
mode unoaked wine. Screwcap. 12.5% alc. **Rating** 92 **To** 2013 $19.50
Cabernet Sauvignon 2006 Rating 92 **To** 2020 $35
Tristan Cabernet Sauvignon Shiraz Merlot 2005 Rating 90 **To** 2015 $29

Brave Goose Vineyard   ★★★★

PO Box 633, Seymour, Vic 3660 **Region** Goulburn Valley
T (03) 5799 1229 **F** (03) 5799 0636 **www**.bravegoosevineyard.com.au **Open** By appt
Winemaker John Stocker **Est.** 1988 **Cases** 400
Dr John Stocker and wife Joanne must be among the most highly qualified boutique vineyard
and winery operators in Australia. John Stocker is the former chief executive of CSIRO and
chairman of the Grape and Wine Research & Development Corporation for seven years, and
daughter Nina has completed the Roseworthy postgraduate oenology course. Moreover, they
established their first vineyard (while living in Switzerland) on the French/Swiss border in
the village of Flueh. On returning to Australia in 1987 they found a property on the inside
of the Great Dividing Range with north-facing slopes and shallow, weathered ironstone soils.
Here they have established 2.5 ha each of shiraz and cabernet sauvignon, and 0.5 ha each of
merlot and gamay, selling the majority of grapes from the 20-year-old vines, but making small
quantities of Cabernet Merlot, Merlot and Gamay. The brave goose in question was the sole
survivor of a flock put into the vineyard to repel cockatoos and foxes.

♟♟♟♟♀ **Shiraz 2008** Crimson-purple; an elegant medium-bodied shiraz, clearly picked
before the heatwave took hold; spicy blackberry and plum fruit has both precision
and length, the supporting tannins fine, the oak subtle. Screwcap. 13.5% alc.
Rating 92 **To** 2018 $25
✪ **Merlot 2008** Bright colour; an elegant merlot with sweet plum and cassis fruit;
the tannins are fine, and underwrite the finish. Screwcap. 13.2% alc. **Rating** 90
To 2016 $20

Bream Creek   ★★★★★

Marion Bay Road, Bream Creek, Tas 7175 **Region** Southern Tasmania
T (03) 6231 4646 **F** (03) 6231 4646 **www**.breamcreekvineyard.com.au **Open** At Potters
Croft, Dunalley, tel (03) 6253 5469
Winemaker Winemaking Tasmania (Julian Alcorso) **Est.** 1973 **Cases** 5500 **Vyds** 7.6 ha
Until 1990 the Bream Creek fruit was sold to Moorilla Estate, but since then the winery has
been independently owned and managed under the control of Fred Peacock, legendary for
the care he bestows on the vines under his direction. Fred's skills have seen both an increase
in production and also outstanding wine quality across the range, headed by the Pinot Noir.

The list of trophies and gold, silver and bronze medals won extends for nine neatly-typed A4 pages. The Tamar Valley vineyard has been sold, allowing Fred to concentrate on the southern vineyards, where he is still a consultant/manager of non-estate plantings. Exports to Canada, Sweden, Singapore and Indonesia.

ỸỸỸỸỸ **Riesling 2009** Bright straw-green; has considerable depth and length to its ripe lime juice flavours; good balance and a great future. Screwcap. 11.8% alc. Rating 94 To 2019 $22
Chardonnay 2008 Bright straw-green; strong grapefruit and citrus aromatics and flavours; has very good length and balance, the oak subtle. Screwcap. 13.7% alc. Rating 94 To 2014 $23

ỸỸỸỸỸ **Pinot Noir 2008** Rating 92 To 2016 $30

ỸỸỸỸ **Riesling 2008** Rating 88 To 2014 $22
Sauvignon Blanc 2009 Rating 87 To 2011 $24
Schonburger 2009 Rating 87 To 2012 $21

Bremer River Vineyards ★★★

c/- Post Office, Langhorne Creek, SA 5255 (postal) **Region** Langhorne Creek
T 0408 844 487 **F** (08) 8370 0362 **Open** Not
Winemaker Bleasdale (Michael Potts) **Est.** 1990 **Cases** 300 **Vyds** 22 ha
Brian and Pat Silcock began the establishment of their Langhorne Creek vineyard in 1970, ultimately planting 10 ha each of shiraz and cabernet sauvignon, plus 2 ha of merlot. In 2002 they decided to have a small part of the grape production vinified, selling through a mailing list and direct into selected SA restaurants and bottle shops.

ỸỸỸỸ **Langhorne Creek Shiraz 2008** Good hue; a rich blackberry and plum bouquet is supported by mocha/vanillan oak, soft, ripe tannins coming through on the medium- to full-bodied palate; no need for patience. Screwcap. 14.5% alc. Rating 89 To 2013 $15

Bremerton Wines ★★★★★

Strathalbyn Road, Langhorne Creek, SA 5255 **Region** Langhorne Creek
T (08) 8537 3093 **F** (08) 8537 3109 www.bremerton.com.au **Open** 7 days 10–5
Winemaker Rebecca Willson **Est.** 1988 **Cases** 35 000 **Vyds** 101.5 ha
The Willsons have been grapegrowers in the Langhorne Creek region for some considerable time but their dual business as grapegrowers and winemakers has expanded significantly. Their vineyards have more than doubled (predominantly cabernet sauvignon and shiraz), as has their production of wine. In 2004 sisters Rebecca and Lucy (marketing) took control of the business, marking the event with (guess what) revamped label designs. Can fairly claim to be the best producer in Langhorne Creek. Exports to all major markets.

ỸỸỸỸỸ **Old Adam Shiraz 2007** Purple-red; the bouquet is dominated by dark aromas of licorice, chocolate liqueur, blackberries and cherries; there is a noticeable red and black fruit quality to the palate, with a warm and plush quality that gives way to fine-grained tannins and toasty oak. Cork. 15% alc. Rating 94 To 2020 $45 BE
B.O.V. 2007 Bright colour; concentrated aromas of black fruits abound, with a touch of olive and cedar to complement; the palate is firm and rigidly structured, showing the nature of a drought vintage; however, there is ample generosity of fruit on the finish, and the tannins, while plentiful, are quite silky and long. Shiraz/Cabernet Sauvignon. Cork. 14.5% alc. Rating 94 To 2018 $75 BE
Reserve Cabernet 2006 Good colour; the bouquet is quite unevolved and still very fresh, showing cedar, black olives and cassis; this complexity follows through on the palate, delivering ample fruit on entry, and firming up to a full-bodied, quite dry and savoury finish, with the oak just poking through at the very end. Cork. 15% alc. Rating 94 To 2018 $45 BE

ṢṢṢṢṢ Coulthard Langhorne Creek Cabernet Sauvignon 2008 A pure red and
✪ blackcurrant bouquet with the merest suggestion of mint; the palate displays great
warmth and depth of fruit, but the key is the texture, which is silky and very fine;
this wine creeps up on your palate and does not want to let go; very long indeed.
Screwcap. 14.5% alc. **Rating** 93 **To** 2016 $22 BE

✪ **Langhorne Creek Sauvignon Blanc 2009** Bright and clear colour; a fragrant
bouquet with grass and asparagus notes that are joined on the palate by more
tropical notes, moving to citrus on the finish. Screwcap. 11% alc. **Rating** 92
To 2010 $18

Reserve Chardonnay 2008 Rating 92 **To** 2013 $32

✪ **Selkirk Langhorne Creek Shiraz 2008** Highly perfumed and loaded with juicy
and accessible red and black fruit, and combined with a light seasoning of spice;
forward and fleshy, with an attractive almost jube-like quality, the wine will deliver
easy drinking from an early age. Screwcap. 14.5% alc. **Rating** 91 **To** 2016 $22 BE

ṢṢṢṢ Langhorne Creek Verdelho 2009 **Rating** 89 **To** 2011 $18
Langhorne Creek Racy Rose 2009 **Rating** 88 **To** 2011 $16 BE
Tamblyn Langhorne Creek Cabernet Shiraz Malbec Merlot 2008
Rating 88 **To** 2015 $18 BE
Special Release Langhorne Creek Malbec 2008 **Rating** 88 **To** 2014 $24 BE

Bress   ★★★★★

3894 Calder Highway, Harcourt, Vic 3453 **Region** Bendigo
T (03) 5474 2262 **F** (03) 5474 2553 **www**.bress.com.au **Open** W'ends & public hols 11–5,
or by appt
Winemaker Adam Marks **Est.** 2001 **Cases** 5000 **Vyds** 23 ha
Adam Marks has made wine in all parts of the world since 1991, and made the brave decision
(during his honeymoon in 2000) to start his own business. Having initially scoured various
regions of Australia for the varieties best suited to those regions, the focus has switched to
three Central Victorian vineyards, in Bendigo, Macedon Ranges and Heathcote. The Harcourt
vineyard in Bendigo is planted to riesling (2 ha), shiraz (1 ha) and 3 ha of cabernet sauvignon
and cabernet franc; the Macedon vineyard to chardonnay (6 ha) and pinot noir (3 ha); and the
Heathcote vineyard to shiraz (2 ha). Exports to the Maldives.

ṢṢṢṢṢ Gold Chook Heathcote Shiraz 2008 Good hue, although faintly burred,
reflecting minimal fining and filtration; a very good shiraz that presents the full
face of Heathcote without excessive alcohol or extraction; blackberry, plum and
spice are supported by perfectly weighted ripe tannins and positive French oak.
Screwcap. 14% alc. **Rating** 95 **To** 2020 $40
Gold Chook Macedon Chardonnay 2008 Bright green-straw; marries
tightness, complexity and finesse on an extremely long palate framed by the
natural acidity of Macedon. Screwcap. 12.5% alc. **Rating** 94 **To** 2016 $35

ṢṢṢṢṢ Margaret River Semillon Sauvignon Blanc 2009 A vibrant, crisp, clean and
✪ direct blend, grass, herb and lemon driving the energetic palate while leaving
room for its gooseberry/passionfruit coating. Screwcap. 12.5% alc. **Rating** 93
To 2011 $20

✪ **Unfiltered Heathcote & Bendigo Shiraz 2008** Lighter-bodied than Gold
Chook, with the fruit aromas and flavours more in the red spectrum, just a few
darker notes; the lively, spicy palate has good line, length and balance. Screwcap.
13.5% alc. **Rating** 92 **To** 2016 $22
Gold Chook Harcourt Valley O.D. Riesling 2009 **Rating** 91 **To** 2017 $35

Brian Barry Wines   ★★★★

PO Box 128, Stepney, SA 5069 **Region** Clare Valley
T (08) 8363 6211 **F** (08) 8362 0498 **www**.brianbarrywines.com **Open** Not
Winemaker Brian Barry, Judson Barry **Est.** 1977 **Cases** 1500 **Vyds** 25.5 ha

Brian Barry is an industry veteran with a wealth of winemaking and show-judging experience. His is a vineyard-only operation (16 ha of riesling, 4 ha of cabernet sauvignon, 2 ha of shiraz, and lesser amounts of merlot and cabernet franc), with a significant part of the output sold as grapes to other wineries. The wines are made under contract at various wineries under Brian's supervision. As one would expect, the quality is reliably good. Exports to the UK and the US.

🍷🍷🍷🍷🍷 **Juds Hill Clare Valley Riesling 2009** Light straw-green; lime, herb and mineral
✪ aromas lead into a taught palate, with green lime and apple flavours, and a finish that needs to soften a bit. Smart new label design. Screwcap. 12% alc. **Rating** 91 To 2019 $22

🍷🍷🍷🍷 **Juds Hill Vineyard Clare Valley Shiraz 2006** **Rating** 89 To 2026 $30

Briar Ridge Vineyard ★★★★★
Mount View Road, Mount View, NSW 2325 **Region** Hunter Valley
T (02) 4990 3670 **F** (02) 4990 7802 **www**.briarridge.com.au **Open** 7 days 10–5
Winemaker Karl Stockhausen, Mark Woods **Est.** 1972 **Cases** 18 000 **Vyds** 39 ha
Semillon and Shiraz have been the most consistent performers, underlying the suitability of these varieties to the Hunter Valley. The Semillon, in particular, invariably shows intense fruit and cellars well. Briar Ridge has been a model of stability, and has the comfort of substantial estate vineyards from which it is able to select the best grapes. It also has not hesitated to venture into other regions, notably Orange. Exports to the US, Canada, Singapore and China.

🍷🍷🍷🍷🍷 **Signature Release Karl Stockhausen Hunter Valley Semillon 2009** Bright
✪ pale green; the unusually expressive bouquet of citrus/lemon blossom is a product of the great '09 vintage; the palate has great structure and guarantees a 20-year life under screwcap. Screwcap. 10% alc. **Rating** 96 To 2030 $26
Dairy Hill Semillon 2009 Pale straw-green; a highly aromatic bouquet with the mix of lemon, lime and mineral that is the mark of the vintage; a lively palate with a subliminal touch of CO_2 leaves the mouth fresh, the flavours repeating on the aftertaste. Screwcap. 11% alc. **Rating** 94 To 2018 $29
Cellar Reserve Orange Shiraz 2008 Deep purple-crimson; shows why so many Hunter Valley (and other regions) are turning their attention to Orange; a beguiling array of blackberry, licorice and spicy aromas and flavours, along with a nudge of cedary oak; high-quality tannins. Screwcap. 14.5% alc. **Rating** 94 To 2020 $26
Currawong Single Vineyard Orange Cabernet Sauvignon 2008 Strong purple-red; an aromatic and powerful bouquet with plum, cassis and spice all in play; these characters stream through to the palate, there joined by positive tannins and complementary oak. Screwcap. 15% alc. **Rating** 94 To 2020 $35

🍷🍷🍷🍷🍷 **Signature Release Karl Stockhausen Hunter Valley Semillon 2005**
✪ **Rating** 93 To 2020 $35
Homestead Verdelho 2009 Bright glints of green; Top 40, NSW Wine Awards '09, and it's not hard to see why, for it has the intensity and length typical of '09; moreover, will develop richness with time in bottle. Screwcap. 13.8% alc. **Rating** 92 To 2014 $21
Early Harvest Semillon Sauvignon Blanc 2009 **Rating** 91 To 2011 $21
Briar Hill Single Vineyard Hunter Valley Chardonnay 2009 **Rating** 91 To 2014 $30
Cellar Reserve Orange Chardonnay 2009 **Rating** 90 To 2012 $26

🍷🍷🍷🍷 **Botrytis Semillon 2008** **Rating** 89 To 2011 $25

Briarose Estate ★★★★
Bussell Highway, Augusta, WA 6290 **Region** Margaret River
T (08) 9758 4160 **F** (08) 9758 4161 **www**.briarose.com.au **Open** 7 days 10–4.30
Winemaker The Vintage Wineworx, Bill Crappsley (Consultant) **Est.** 1998 **Cases** 8000
Vyds 13.56 ha

Brian and Rosemary Webster began developing the estate plantings in 1998, which now comprise sauvignon blanc (2.33 ha), semillon (1.33 ha), cabernet sauvignon (6.6 ha), merlot (2.2 ha) and cabernet franc (1.1 ha). The winery is situated at the southern end of the Margaret River region, where the climate is distinctly cooler than that of northern Margaret River.

ŶŶŶŶŶ **Margaret River Sauvignon Blanc 2009** A touch of textural complexity is added by the small barrel-fermented proportion; there are some tropical notes, but overall grass, asparagus and citrus are dominant on the long, crisp palate. Screwcap. 13.5% alc. **Rating** 92 **To** 2012 $25

Blackwood Cove 2008 The colour is not convincing; a fragrant blend of Cabernet Sauvignon/Merlot/Cabernet Franc that emphatically echoes its cool-grown origins; there is a mix of contrasting small red berry fruits and more herbal notes. Screwcap. 14% alc. **Rating** 92 **To** 2020 $32

Reserve Margaret River Merlot 2008 Light red; a light-bodied but lively wine that reflects this cool corner of Margaret River; it is all about cassis and red cherry, not structure, to be enjoyed sooner than later. Screwcap. 14% alc. **Rating** 90 **To** 2013 $25

Brick Kiln   ★★★★

PO Box 56, Glen Osmond, SA 5064 **Region** McLaren Vale
T (08) 8357 2561 **F** (08) 8357 3126 **www**.brickiln.com.au **Open** Not
Winemaker Linda Domas, Phil Christiansen **Est.** 2001 **Cases** 1500 **Vyds** 8 ha
This is the venture of Malcolm and Alison Mackinnon, Garry and Nancy Watson, and Ian and Pene Davey. They purchased the Nine Gums Vineyard in 2001, which had been planted to shiraz in 1995–96. The majority of the grapes are sold, with a lesser portion contract-made for the partners under the Brick Kiln label, which takes its name from the Brick Kiln Bridge adjacent to the vineyard. Exports to the UK, Canada, China and Hong Kong.

ŶŶŶŶŶ **The Grove McLaren Vale Shiraz 2008** Here the best six French oak barrels (largely new) were selected, giving this full-bodied wine a distinct point of difference from the varietal, both in flavour and texture terms; while still rich, ripe and opulent, the black fruits have better definition. Screwcap. 14.6% alc. **Rating** 93 **To** 2023 $36

✪ **McLaren Vale Shiraz 2008** Deep colour; the first whiff on the bouquet with its dark chocolate and mocha cries McLaren Vale (and American and French oak) and nothing thereafter upsets the apple cart, the rich, ripe and opulent fruit flavours doing the hard yards. Screwcap. 14.6% alc. **Rating** 90 **To** 2018 $18

Brindabella Hills   ★★★★☆

156 Woodgrove Close, via Hall, ACT 2618 **Region** Canberra District
T (02) 6230 2583 **F** (02) 6230 2023 **www**.brindabellahills.com.au **Open** W'ends & public hols 10–5
Winemaker Dr Roger Harris, Brian Sinclair **Est.** 1986 **Cases** 2200 **Vyds** 5 ha
Distinguished research scientist Dr Roger Harris presides over Brindabella Hills, which increasingly relies on estate-produced grapes, with small plantings of riesling, shiraz, chardonnay, sauvignon blanc, merlot, sangiovese, cabernet sauvignon and cabernet franc. Wine quality has been consistently impressive.

ŶŶŶŶŶ ✪ **Reserve Canberra District Shiraz 2008** A selection of the best barrels can mean many things; whatever, this wine has greater depth to its medium- to full-bodied palate, more dark fruit flavours and more structure. Leave it alone while drinking the standard wine. Screwcap. 14.5% alc. **Rating** 95 **To** 2021 $35

ŶŶŶŶŶ **Canberra District Shiraz 2008 Rating** 93 **To** 2016 $28
✪ **Canberra District Sauvignon Blanc 2009** A pure and lively wine with a constantly changing mix of citrus and tropical fruit aromas and flavours before shortening fractionally on the finish. Screwcap. 11.9% alc. **Rating** 90 **To** 2010 $18

ŶŶŶŶ   Riesling 2009 Rating 88 To 2013 $25
Argenteus 2008 Rating 88 To 2012 $20

Brini Estate Wines   ★★★★☆

RSD 600 Blewitt Springs Road, McLaren Vale, SA 5171 (postal) **Region** McLaren Vale
T (08) 8383 0080 **F** (08) 8383 0104 **www.**briniwines.com.au **Open** Not
Winemaker Brian Light (Contract) **Est.** 2000 **Cases** 4000 **Vyds** 16.4 ha
The Brini family has been growing grapes in the Blewitt Springs area of McLaren Vale since
1953. In 2000 John and Marcello Brini established Brini Estate Wines to vinify a portion
of the grape production; up to that time it had been sold to companies such as Penfolds,
Rosemount Estate and d'Arenberg. The flagship Sebastian Shiraz is produced from dry-grown
vines planted in 1947, the other wines from dry-grown vines planted in '64. Exports to the
UK, Russia and Hong Kong.

ŶŶŶŶŶ   Limited Release Sebastian Shiraz 2008 Deep red-purple, similar to Single
Vineyard; full-bodied, dense and layered, the competition for space vigorous and
unresolved; black fruits, plum, tar, prune, dark chocolate and strong (French) oak
are all present. Screwcap. 15% alc. **Rating** 93 **To** 2028 $50
Sebastian Single Vineyard McLaren Vale Shiraz 2008 Good colour; potent
blackberry, prune and plum fruitcake aromas and flavours, dark chocolate in the
background; it hardly needs be said alcohol is the common factor in the three
Brini Shirazs. Screwcap. 15% alc. **Rating** 92 **To** 2020 $28
Estate Grown McLaren Vale Grenache 2007 Good hue; ignores its alcohol,
with its fresh, firm medium-bodied palate and its range of spicy cherry fruit plus a
touch of French oak. Screwcap. 15% alc. **Rating** 90 **To** 2015 $25

ŶŶŶŶ   Blewitt Springs Single Vineyard McLaren Vale Shiraz 2008 Rating 89
To 2017 $19
Blewitt Springs Single Vineyard McLaren Vale Shiraz 2007 Rating 88
To 2015 $19

Broke's Promise Wines   ★★★

725 Milbrodale Road, Broke, NSW 2330 **Region** Hunter Valley
T (02) 6579 1165 **F** (02) 9972 1619 **www.**brokespromise.com.au **Open** W'ends 11–5
Winemaker Margan Family, Michael McManus **Est.** 1996 **Cases** 700 **Vyds** 3.3 ha
Joe and Carol Re purchased Broke's Promise in 2005 from Jane Marquard and Dennis Karp,
and have continued the winemaking arrangements with Andrew Margan. The vineyard
(chardonnay, barbera, verdelho, shiraz and semillon) is complemented by an olive grove.

Broken Gate Wines   ★★★★

57 Rokeby Street, Collingwood, Vic 3066 **Region** South Eastern Australia
T (03) 9417 5757 **F** (03) 8415 1991 **www.**brokengate.com.au **Open** Mon–Fri 8–5
Winemaker Josef Orbach **Est.** 2001 **Cases** 20 000
Broken Gate is a Melbourne-based multi-regional producer, specialising in cool-climate
reds and whites. Founder Josef Orbach lived and worked in the Clare Valley from 1994 to
'98 at Leasingham Wines, and is currently studying wine technology and viticulture at the
University of Melbourne. His is a classic negociant business, buying grapes and/or wines from
various regions; the wines may be either purchased in bulk, blended and bottled by Orbach,
or purchased as cleanskins. The wine glut has been a great boon for his business.

ŶŶŶŶŶ   Side Gate Geelong Shiraz 2007 Strong colour; a fragrant bouquet of dark
❂   berries and spice, then a polished and supple medium-bodied palate, red fruits
emerging along with the black; fine savoury tannins on the finish. Screwcap.
13.5% alc. **Rating** 93 **To** 2017 $17
❂   Side Gate Clare Valley Riesling 2008 Has a zesty, brisk bouquet, then an
attractive, long palate with intense lime/citrus flavours; purchased in bulk, bottled
by Broken Gate – a spectacular example of the availability of high-quality wine in
these times of surplus. Screwcap. 12.5% alc. **Rating** 92 **To** 2017 $12

○ **Side Gate Strathbogie Ranges Sauvignon Blanc 2009** Light straw-green; some herb and grass aromas, the palate adding citrus and a hint of passionfruit; well-made wine. Silver medal Concours des Vins, Melbourne. Screwcap. 12.5% alc. **Rating** 90 **To** 2011 $17

○ **Clare Valley Shiraz 2008** Solid red-purple; interesting wine – the question is whether there is low-level volatile acidity, but even if there is, it only serves to lift the aromas and flavours; all up, has more vibrancy than many, and the balance is good. Screwcap. 14.2% alc. **Rating** 90 **To** 2018 $20

♟♟♟♟ **Side Gate Adelaide Hills Pinot Noir 2008 Rating** 88 **To** 2014 $15
Geelong Pinot Noir 2008 Rating 87 **To** 2013 $25

Brokenwood ★★★★★

401-427 McDonalds Road, Pokolbin, NSW 2321 **Region** Hunter Valley
T (02) 4998 7559 **F** (02) 4998 7893 **www**.brokenwood.com.au **Open** 7 days 9.30–5
Winemaker Iain Riggs, PJ Charteris **Est.** 1970 **Cases** 100 000 **Vyds** 12.49 ha
This deservedly fashionable winery, producing consistently excellent wines, has kept Graveyard Shiraz as its ultimate flagship wine, while extending its reach through many of the best eastern regions for its broad selection of varietal wine styles. Its big-selling Hunter Semillon remains alongside Graveyard, and there is then a range of wines coming from regions including Orange, Central Ranges, Beechworth, McLaren Vale, Cowra and elsewhere. The two-storey Albert Room tasting facility (named in honour of the late Tony Albert, one of the founders) was opened in 2006. Exports to all major markets.

♟♟♟♟♟ **Brycefield Belford Vineyards Hunter Valley Semillon 2005** A new wine for
○ Brokenwood, and has handsomely repaid four years cellaring prior to release. It is still as fresh as a daisy, the aromas of almond and citrus leading into a lively palate that dances on the tongue. Halfway to full maturity; a beautiful teenager. Screwcap. 11% alc. **Rating** 96 **To** 2015 $36

○ **Forest Edge Vineyard Orange Chardonnay 2007** A very complex wine with a deliberate nod in the direction of Burgundy; the thrust and energy of the back-palate and finish is remarkable. Trophy Best Wine of Show NSW Wine Awards '09. Screwcap. 13.5% alc. **Rating** 96 **To** 2017 $30

Graveyard Vineyard Hunter Valley Shiraz 2007 Deep purple-crimson, it proclaims its breed and quality from the first whiff, overflowing with black fruits, tannins and oak in support. It will slowly gain notes of earth, briar and polished leather as it develops in bottle, the screwcap giving it an indefinite life span. Screwcap. 13.5% alc. **Rating** 96 **To** 2035 $140

○ **Hunter Valley Semillon 2009** A delicate yet positive flowery bouquet hints at what is to come on the vivid mid-palate, with citrus to the fore, and background touches of stone fruits; the zesty acidity cleanses the finish and guarantees a long life if you wish to cellar it. Screwcap. 11% alc. **Rating** 95 **To** 2014 $20

Maxwell Vineyard Hunter Valley Semillon 2005 Still pale quartz-green; extraordinarily fresh and lively, with fragrant lemon and lemon zest aromas and flavours, the acidity perfectly balanced, the finish lingering for an eternity. Why this should all be drunk in the next five years (as the label suggests) I don't know – and don't agree. Screwcap. 11% alc. **Rating** 95 **To** 2020 $36

Indigo Vineyard Beechworth Chardonnay 2008 The complete package, notwithstanding the vintage; the expressive chardonnay fruit from the altogether superior Dijon clones has been enhanced, not obscured, by barrel ferment in a mix of new and older fruit; impeccable balance and length. Screwcap. 14% alc. **Rating** 95 **To** 2014 $30

Indigo Vineyard Beechworth Shiraz 2008 Bright crimson-red; a come-hither bouquet of dark cherry, plum and spice, then a particularly long and complex medium-bodied palate with dark fruits, licorice and pepper all held together by high-quality tannins. Screwcap. 14.5% alc. **Rating** 95 **To** 2023 $50

Forest Edge Vineyard Orange Sauvignon Blanc 2009 Demonstrates why Orange sauvignon blanc is enjoying such show success; fragrant and aromatic, with blossom nuances to a willowy palate, the flavours running from grapefruit to gooseberry and a touch of lime; lovely finish. Screwcap. 13.5% alc. **Rating** 94 To 2011 $25

Forest Edge Vineyard Orange Chardonnay 2008 Like its predecessors, whole-bunch-pressed and wild yeast-fermented in French barriques, all with minimum intervention; no way-out funky characters are obvious, the purity and intensity of the fruit has outwitted the winemaking team. Screwcap. 13% alc. **Rating** 94 To 2013 $30

Indigo Vineyard Beechworth Pinot Noir 2008 Bright red-crimson; distinguished wine made from clones 114, 115 and MV6; red and black cherry fruit is held in a fine web of superfine tannins; very good line, balance and length. Screwcap. 14% alc. **Rating** 94 To 2013 $35

ΨΨΨΨ **Beechworth Pinot Noir 2008 Rating** 93 To 2014 $30
Indigo Vineyard Beechworth Viognier 2008 Rating 91 To 2012 $30

ΨΨΨΨ **Cricket Pitch Red 2008 Rating** 88 To 2012 $19

Brook Eden Vineyard   ★★★★☆

Adams Road, Lebrina, Tas 7254 **Region** Northern Tasmania
T (03) 6395 6244 **F** (03) 6395 6211 **www**.brookeden.com.au **Open** Thurs–Tues 11–5 (closed Jun–Jul)
Winemaker Winemaking Tasmania **Est.** 1988 **Cases** 1400 **Vyds** 2.25 ha
Peter McIntosh and Sue Stuart purchased Brook Eden from Sheila Bezemer in 2004. At 41° south and at an altitude of 160 m it is one of the coolest sites in Tasmania, and (in the words of the new owners) 'represents viticulture on the edge'. While the plantings remain small (1 ha pinot noir, 0.75 ha chardonnay and 0.25 ha each of riesling and pinot gris), yield has been significantly reduced, resulting in earlier picking and better quality grapes.

ΨΨΨΨΨ **Pinot Rose 2009** Light magenta; fragrant red fruit aromas, then perfectly balanced strawberry fruit drives the palate; pleasing dry finish. Gold medal Australian Small Winemakers Show '09. Screwcap. 13.5% alc. **Rating** 94 To 2011 $25

ΨΨΨΨ **Pinot Noir 2008 Rating** 92 To 2015 $39
TRS Riesling 2009 Rating 91 To 2020 $25
Riesling 2009 Rating 90 To 2024 $25
Chardonnay 2008 Rating 90 To 2016 $32
Water's Edge Unwooded Pinot Noir 2008 Rating 90 To 2012 $26

Brookland Valley   ★★★★★

Caves Road, Wilyabrup, WA 6280 **Region** Margaret River
T (08) 9755 6042 **F** (08) 9755 6214 **www**.brooklandvalley.com.au **Open** 7 days 10–5
Winemaker Pete Dillon **Est.** 1984 **Cases** NFP
Brookland Valley has an idyllic setting, plus its café and Gallery of Wine Arts, which houses an eclectic collection of wine, food-related art and wine accessories. After acquiring a 50% share of Brookland Valley in 1997, Hardys moved to full ownership in 2004. The quality, and consistency, of the wines is awesome. Wine Companion Winery of the Year '09. Exports to the UK and the US.

ΨΨΨΨΨ **Margaret River Chardonnay 2009** Bright colour; an absolutely pristine, poised,
✪   complex and enthralling example of the variety and the region; grapefruit, grilled cashew, clove and cinnamon weave together tantalisingly; the palate is pure and precise, with the fruit being driven by the nervy acidity, while the mere suggestion of toasty oak is unveiled on the amazingly long finish; brilliantly constructed and super value. Gold medal Sydney Wine Show '10. Screwcap. 13.5% alc. **Rating** 97 To 2020 $38 BE

Reserve Margaret River Chardonnay 2009 The use of oak is certainly evident in this wine, but the underlying concentration of fruit almost demands it; grilled cashew, florals, grapefruit and nectarine are framed by ample, yet well-handled fine French oak; the palate is the real show stopper, as the depth of character is awesome, and the tightly wound fruit slowly unravels, revealing a generous, rich and inviting offering; a poised wine with great concentration. Screwcap. 13.4% alc. **Rating** 96 **To** 2018 $63 BE

Cabernet Sauvignon Merlot 2008 Vivid hue; pristine bouquet with cassis, cedar and suggestions of violets on display; there is a healthy dose of new oak, but the fruit swallows it with ease; full-bodied with generous levels of cassis fruit and a distinctly juicy character to the fruit; long and luscious, this will start to hit its straps in 5 years or more. Screwcap. 13.8% alc. **Rating** 95 **To** 2025 $45 BE

✪ **Verse 1 Margaret River Chardonnay 2008** Right in the mainstream of winery style, with delicious white peach, nectarine and grapefruit aromas and flavours supported by quality French oak; has very good line, length and balance. Screwcap. 13.5% alc. **Rating** 94 **To** 2015 $20

✪ **Verse 1 Margaret River Rose 2008** Light but bright crimson-pink; the palate literally dances with juicy berry fruit flavours, and a long, lingering finish. Still as fresh as a daisy, but to be drunk without delay. Merlot (95%)/Cabernet Franc (5%). Screwcap. 12.5% alc. **Rating** 94 **To** 2010 $20

Reserve Margaret River Cabernet Sauvignon 2003 Colour still deep; a fragrant bouquet with sombre black fruits and intriguing notes of herb (not green); the palate is medium- to full-bodied, with substantial tannins supporting the blackcurrant fruit on the long finish. Cork. 14% alc. **Rating** 94 **To** 2023 $63

♟♟♟♟♟ **Verse 1 Margaret River Semillon Sauvignon Blanc 2009** **Rating** 90 **To** 2012 $21 BE
Verse 1 Margaret River Chardonnay 2009 **Rating** 90 **To** 2015 $21 BE
Verse 1 Margaret River Cabernet Merlot 2008 **Rating** 90 **To** 2017 $21 BE

Brookman Wines   NR

RSD 525 Brookmans Road, Blewitt Springs, SA 5171 (postal) **Region** McLaren Vale
T (08) 8383 0161 **F** (08) 8383 0811 **www**.brookmanwines.com.au **Open** Not
Winemaker Silvestro Genovese, Linda Domas (Contract) **Est.** 2004 **Cases** 2000
Vyds 25 ha
This is the venture of Silvestro and Ida Genovese in a later-life occupation, albeit taking them back to their Italian roots. Silvestro has solely overseen the establishment of the estate vineyards planted to shiraz, grenache, merlot, cabernet sauvignon, semillon, sauvignon blanc, chenin blanc and chardonnay. Exports to the US, China, Japan and Canada.

Broomstick Estate   ★★★★☆

4 Frances Street, Mount Lawley, WA 6050 (postal) **Region** Margaret River
T (08) 9271 9594 **F** (08) 9271 9741 **www**.broomstick.com.au **Open** Not
Winemaker Mark Warren (Happs) **Est.** 1997 **Cases** 1000 **Vyds** 16.6 ha
The property that Robert Holloway and family purchased in 1993 on which the vineyard is now established was an operating dairy farm. In 1997, 5.5 ha of shiraz was planted. Over the following years 3.8 ha of merlot and then (in 2004) 5.3 ha of chardonnay and 2 ha of sauvignon blanc were added. The Holloways see themselves as grapegrowers first and foremost, but make a small amount of wine under the Broomstick Estate label. The name of the business derives from the vineyard's proximity to the town of Witchcliffe, or 'Witchy' as the locals call it. The label design reflects the association of witches with broomsticks and ravens.

♟♟♟♟♟ **Margaret River Shiraz 2008** Bright red-purple; a super-fragrant bouquet of
✪ black fruits, spice, leather and licorice, the medium- to full-bodied palate singing precisely the same song; good length and balance. Screwcap. 13.5% alc. **Rating** 94 **To** 2018 $22.50

♟♟♟♟♟ **Margaret River Chardonnay 2009** **Rating** 90 **To** 2013

Brothers in Arms ★★★☆

PO Box 840, Langhorne Creek, SA 5255 **Region** Langhorne Creek
T (08) 8537 3182 **F** (08) 8537 3383 **www**.brothersinarms.com.au **Open** Not
Winemaker Justin Lane, Jim Urlwin **Est.** 1998 **Cases** 16 000 **Vyds** 300 ha
The Adams family has been growing grapes at Langhorne Creek since 1891, when the first vines at the famed Metala vineyards were planted. Guy Adams is the fifth generation to own and work the vineyard, and over the past 20 years has both improved the viticulture and expanded the plantings. It was not until 1998 that they decided to hold back a small proportion of the production for vinification under the Brothers in Arms label, and now dedicate 50 ha to the Brothers in Arms wines (shiraz, cabernet sauvignon, malbec and petit verdot); the grapes from the remaining 250 ha are sold. Exports to the UK, the US and other major markets.

♟♟♟♟♟ **Langhorne Creek Shiraz 2006** A very concentrated and powerful wine with sombre dark fruits, chocolate, licorice and earth aromas and flavours. Built for the long haul. Screwcap. 15% alc. **Rating** 93 **To** 2026 $39

❂ **No. 6 Langhorne Creek Shiraz Cabernet 2006** Slightly diffuse colour; the bouquet has blackberry and blackcurrant fruit, the palate more of the same, but with a delicious spicy/savoury twist to the finish. Screwcap. 14.5% alc. **Rating** 93 **To** 2011 $19

❂ **No. 6 Langhorne Creek Shiraz 2007** Strong crimson-purple; a potent, full-bodied wine with blackberry and prune aromas and flavours; fills the mouth with flavour, adding a hint of licorice and surrounding warmth. Screwcap. 15.5% alc. **Rating** 90 **To** 2015 $19

♟♟♟♟ **Formby & Adams Cutting Edge Cabernet Shiraz 2007** Rating 89 **To** 2013 $16
Formby & Adams Leading Horse Cabernet Sauvignon 2007 Rating 87 **To** 2012 $16

🌿 Brothers Parade ★★★

PO Box 200, Milsons Point, NSW 1565 **Region** Adelaide Hills
T 0402 855 444 **www**.brothersparade.com.au **Open** Not
Winemaker Trent Fraser, Danniel Amadio **Est.** 2008 **Cases** 1700
Brothers Parade is a highly unusual partnership. With a friendship going back to primary school, it brings together Sydney Swans defender Jared Crouch (living in Sydney) with best friend Trent Fraser (now based in New York). The name comes from Norwood's main street, The Parade, the epicentre of their childhood world. This is thus the ultimate virtual winery, friends and family living in the Adelaide Hills involved in both sourcing the grapes and winemaking.

♟♟♟♟ **Adelaide Hills Shiraz 2007** Good hue; very typical cool-grown fruit profile; black cherry, spice, licorice and an altogether savoury caste. Needs a few years. Screwcap. 14% alc. **Rating** 87 **To** 2015 $19.95

Brown Brothers ★★★★★

Milawa-Bobinawarrah Road, Milawa, Vic 3678 **Region** King Valley
T (03) 5720 5500 **F** (03) 5720 5511 **www**.brownbrothers.com.au **Open** 7 days 9–5
Winemaker Wendy Cameron, Joel Tilbrook, Catherine Looney, Geoff Alexander,
Chloe Earl **Est.** 1885 **Cases** 1.1 million **Vyds** 750 ha
Draws upon a considerable number of vineyards spread throughout a range of site climates, ranging from very warm to very cool. A relatively recent expansion into Heathcote has added significantly to its armoury. It is known for the diversity of varieties with which it works, and the wines represent good value for money. Deservedly one of the most successful family wineries – its cellar door receives the greatest number of visitors in Australia. Exports to all major markets.

♟♟♟♟♟ **Patricia Shiraz 2006** Good depth to the colour; a complex bouquet of predominantly black fruits with splashes of spice and licorice; the palate has good tension between its many components, particularly the superfine tannins on the finish. Screwcap. 14.5% alc. **Rating** 94 **To** 2021 $55.90

Patricia Cabernet Sauvignon 2005 No clue is given about the origin of the wine other than 'cool climate'; it has retained excellent colour, and has developed a range of secondary, complex aromas and flavours in a cedary/earthy spectrum; the palate is well balanced and long. Screwcap. 14.5% alc. **Rating** 94 **To** 2020 $55.90

Patricia Pinot Noir Chardonnay Brut 2005 Produced from the Whitlands Vineyard, with four years on yeast lees; very elegant, fine and long, and no attempt to build flavour through high dosage; Brown Brothers has the style down pat. Will improve on cork. 13% alc. **Rating** 94 **To** 2014 $44.90

✪ **Pinot Noir Chardonnay Pinot Meunier NV** Bright green-gold; a seriously good wine at this price, it has a complex web of brioche and toast around delicate but persistent citrus and stone fruit flavours; excellent acidity and dosage. Cork. 12.5% alc. **Rating** 94 **To** 2010 $22.90

♟♟♟♟♟ **Limited Release Banksdale King Valley Chardonnay 2008** **Rating** 93 **To** 2014 $24.90

Limited Release King Valley Pinot Grigio 2008 **Rating** 90 **To** 2012 $29.90
Limited Release Merlot 2006 **Rating** 90 **To** 2016 $29.90

✪ **Cellar Door Release Milawa Graciano 2008** A variety Brown Brothers has grown for decades; has a particular slippery yet savoury texture, and cinnamon/nutmeg spice flavours are a backdrop to the fruit. Cork. 14.5% alc. **Rating** 90 **To** 2014 $19.90

♟♟♟♟ **Limited Release Heathcote Shiraz 2007** **Rating** 89 **To** 2017 $29.90
✪ **Victoria Tempranillo 2008** Good colour; has more texture and structure than many tempranillos, with a savoury (rather than citrus) note on the back-palate and finish extending the length of the red fruits. Screwcap. 14.5% alc. **Rating** 89 **To** 2014 $17.90

✪ **Limited Release Heathcote Durif 2007** Dark purple-black; a formidably full-bodied wine, with a savoury/dusty array of black fruits; curiously (although probably deliberately) the tannins are not particularly strong. For those with a big vinous or steak appetite. Cork. 14.5% alc. **Rating** 89 **To** 2014 $19.90

King Valley Prosecco 2009 **Rating** 89 **To** 2011 $18.90
Sparkling Shiraz 2007 **Rating** 87 **To** 2012 $25.90

Brown Hill Estate ★★★★★

Cnr Rosa Brook Road/Barrett Road, Rosa Brook, WA 6285 **Region** Margaret River
T (08) 9757 4003 **F** (08) 9757 4004 **www**.brownhillestate.com.au **Open** 7 days 10–5
Winemaker Nathan Bailey **Est.** 1995 **Cases** 3000 **Vyds** 22 ha

The Bailey family is involved in all stages of wine production, with minimum outside help. Their stated aim is to produce top-quality wines at affordable prices, via uncompromising viticultural practices emphasising low yields. They have shiraz and cabernet sauvignon (7 ha each), semillon (4 ha) and sauvignon blanc and merlot (2 ha each). By the standards of the Margaret River, the prices are indeed affordable.

♟♟♟♟♟ **Bill Bailey Margaret River Shiraz Cabernet 2008** The grapes were picked six weeks later than usual (wither global warming?), but in good balance; the palate is medium-bodied (not thick as the back label suggests) with attractive dusty/grainy tannins, and displays a range of blackberry, plum and blackcurrant fruit, oak not intrusive. Screwcap. 14.8% alc. **Rating** 96 **To** 2020 $50

Fimiston Reserve Margaret River Shiraz 2008 Deep, dark purple-crimson; the bouquet has abundant black cherry and blackberry fruit framed by vanillan oak, characters that are mirrored on the medium-bodied palate, the almost sweet tannins a feature of the finish. Screwcap. 14.5% alc. **Rating** 94 **To** 2018 $30

ŸŸŸŸ♀ **Lakeview Margaret River Sauvignon Blanc Semillon 2009** Cold
fermentation and bottling within 12 weeks of picking produces an arresting
bouquet of passionfruit and – unusually but obviously – pear, the palate incisive and
long, drawn out by citrussy acidity. Screwcap. 13.5% alc. **Rating** 93 **To** 2012 $17

Chaffers Margaret River Shiraz 2008 Deeply coloured; has an aromatic
blackberry and spice bouquet, then a medium-bodied palate with near-identical
flavours, a dash of cedary oak and savoury tannins. Screwcap. 14% alc. **Rating** 91
To 2016 $18

Charlotte Margaret River Sauvignon Blanc 2009 Rating 90 **To** 2010 $17

Block 45 Paddy's White 2009 Fragrant lime zest and a touch of passionfruit
on the bouquet leads into an extremely, almost painfully, vibrant palate with
unsweetened lemon juice flavour. Seafood special. Screwcap. 13.5% alc. **Rating** 90
To 2010 $17

Hannans Margaret River Cabernet Sauvignon 2008 A medium-bodied
wine that takes its time to express itself, finally delivering the goods on the back-
palate and finish, where blackcurrant meets with savoury tannins to establish its
varietal identity. Screwcap. 14% alc. **Rating** 90 **To** 2020 $18

ŸŸŸŸ **Croesus Reserve Margaret River Merlot 2008 Rating** 89 **To** 2016 $30

Brown Magpie Wines   ★★★★☆

125 Larcombes Road, Modewarre, Vic 3240 **Region** Geelong
T (03) 5261 3875 **F** (03) 5261 3875 **www.**brownmagpiewines.com **Open** 7 days Jan 12–3,
w'ends 12–3 Nov–June
Winemaker Loretta and Shane Breheny, Karen Coulston (Consultant) **Est.** 2000
Cases 3500 **Vyds** 9 ha
Shane and Loretta Breheny's 20-ha property is situated predominantly on a gentle, north-
facing slope, with cypress trees on the western and southern borders providing protection
against the wind. Vines were planted over 2001–02, with pinot noir (5 ha) taking the lion's
share, followed by pinot gris (2 ha), shiraz (1.5 ha) and 0.25 ha each of chardonnay and
sauvignon blanc. Viticulture is Loretta's love; winemaking (and wine) is Shane's.

ŸŸŸŸ♀ **Paraparap Geelong Pinot Noir 2008** Light crimson-red; the bouquet has
cherry, spicy and plum aromas leading into a smooth and supple red fruit palate
that has good line, length and balance. Screwcap. 14% alc. **Rating** 93 **To** 2015 $27

Modewarre Mud Geelong Shiraz 2008 Similar brilliant colour; overall, has
greater intensity than the standard wine, but the bouquet and palate of both run
along similar early-picked lines; here spice and pepper have a slightly bigger say.
Screwcap. 12.5% alc. **Rating** 93 **To** 2020 $30

Geelong Shiraz 2008 Bright, fresh crimson-red hue; an elegant light- to
medium-bodied shiraz, with a fragrant bouquet of red and black fruits and a lively
palate, oak and tannins appropriately restrained. Screwcap. 12.5% alc. **Rating** 92
To 2018 $27

Geelong Pinot Gris 2009 Aromas and flavours of brown pear and peach skin
give this Pinot Gris real character; indeed, it might have benefited from a touch
more acidity. Screwcap. 14.5% alc. **Rating** 91 **To** 2012 $22

Geelong Pinot Noir 2008 Bright light crimson; spicy plum aromas precede
a palate with considerable energy and drive, savoury/forest characters coming
through strongly on the finish and aftertaste. Screwcap. 14% alc. **Rating** 90
To 2014 $22

Browns of Padthaway   ★★★★☆

Riddoch Highway, Padthaway, SA 5271 **Region** Padthaway
T (08) 8765 6040 **F** (08) 8765 6003 **www.**browns-of-padthaway.com **Open** By appt
Winemaker O'Leary Walker Wines **Est.** 1993 **Cases** 20 000 **Vyds** 300 ha
The Brown family has for many years been the largest independent grapegrower in Padthaway,
a district in which most of the vineyards were established and owned by Wynns, Seppelt,

Lindemans and Hardys, respectively. Since 1998, after a slow start, Browns has produced excellent wines and wine production has increased accordingly. Exports to the UK, the US, Germany, Malaysia, Thailand, Japan and NZ.

🍷🍷🍷🍷 **Melba Lillian Family Reserve Chardonnay 2007** Bright, showing green-yellow colour is a portent of things to come; this is Padthaway Chardonnay at its best, with elegant grapefruit and nectarine aromas and flavours, the oak integrated and balanced. Screwcap. 12.5% alc. **Rating** 95 **To** 2014 $24

🍷🍷🍷🍷 **Myra Family Reserve Cabernet Sauvignon 2004 Rating** 92 **To** 2019 $24
✪ **Riesling 2006** Glorious green-yellow; bottle age has been a boon, allowing the depth of the lime-accented fruit to fully develop and reach the start of a long plateau of maturity. Screwcap. 12.5% alc. **Rating** 91 **To** 2016 $16
Myra Family Reserve Cabernet Sauvignon 2006 Rating 90 **To** 2026 $24

🍷🍷🍷 **Sauvignon Blanc 2008** Bright colour; an honest, full-flavoured sauvignon blanc
✪ with a blend of grassy and tropical aromas and flavours; the palate has good length and an emphatic finish. Screwcap. 12.5% alc. **Rating** 89 **To** 2010 $16
✪ **T-Trellis Shiraz 2007** Good depth to the colour; a full-bodied palate ranges through black fruits, dark chocolate and vanilla, supported by positive tannins; traditional style, both alcohol and American oak part of the scene. Screwcap. 15% alc. **Rating** 89 **To** 2017 $18

Brumby Wines

Sandyanna, 24 Cannon Lane, Wood Wood, Vic 3596 **Region** Swan Hill
T 0438 305 364 **F** (03) 5030 5366 **www**.brumbywines.com.au **Open** Mon–Fri 9–5
Winemaker Neil Robb, John Ellis, Glen Olsen (Contract) **Est.** 2001 **Cases** 2000
Vyds 7.3 ha
The derivation of the name is even more direct and simple than you might imagine: the owners are Stuart and Liz Brumby, who decided to plant grapes for supply to others before moving to having an increasing portion of their production from the shiraz (4 ha), chardonnay and durif (3 ha each) vinified under their own label.

🍷🍷🍷🍷 **Durif 2004** Even deeper than the '05; has changed little since tasted four years
✪ ago, the luscious fruits still in abundance – if anything, has improved over the intervening time. Quality cork has done its job. 14% alc. **Rating** 90 **To** 2018 $18

🍷🍷🍷 **Durif 2005 Rating** 89 **To** 2018 $18

Bruny Island Wines ★★★☆

4391 Main Road, Lunawanna, Bruny Island, Tas 7150 (postal) **Region** Southern Tasmania
T 0409 973 033 **F** (03) 6293 1088 **www**.brunyislandwine.com **Open** Most days 11–4
Winemaker Bernice Woolley **Est.** 1998 **Cases** 600 **Vyds** 2 ha
Richard and Bernice Woolley have established the only vineyard on Bruny Island, the southernmost commercial planting in Australia (1 ha each of chardonnay and pinot noir). Bernice has a degree in marketing from Curtin University, and she and Richard operate budget-style holiday accommodation on the property.

🍷🍷🍷🍷 **Chardonnay 2009** Pale, bright quartz-green; a fragrant bouquet, the aromas similar to the Unwooded, simply because the oak influence is very subtle; the palate, too, is on the same track. Silver medal Hobart Wine Show '09. Screwcap. 13.6% alc. **Rating** 90 **To** 2014 $30

🍷🍷🍷 **Unwooded Chardonnay 2009 Rating** 89 **To** 2013 $25
Unwooded Chardonnay 2008 Rating 89 **To** 2012 $23
Sauvignon Blanc 2009 Rating 87 **To** 2011 $25
Reserve Pinot Noir 2008 Rating 87 **To** 2014 $35

B3 Wines   ★★★☆

Light Pass Road, Tanunda, SA 5352 **Region** Barossa Valley
T (08) 8363 2211 **F** (08) 8363 2231 **www**.b3wines.com.au **Open** By appt
Winemaker Craig Stansborough **Est.** 2001 **Cases** NA

Peter, Michael and Richard Basedow are the three Brothers Basedow (as they call themselves), fifth-generation Barossans with distinguished forefathers. Grandfather Oscar Basedow
established the Basedow winery (no longer in family ownership) in 1896, while Martin
Basedow established the Roseworthy Agricultural College. Their father, John Oscar Basedow,
died in the 1970s, having won the 1970 Jimmy Watson Trophy for his '69 Cabernet
Sauvignon, a high point for the family. This is a virtual winery enterprise; grapes are purchased
mainly from the Barossa Valley, Coonawarra, Adelaide Hills and Eden Valley. Exports to the
US, Canada, Sweden, Denmark, India, South Korea, Taiwan, Hong Kong, Singapore, Japan
and China.

ȲȲȲȲȲ **Adelaide Hills Sauvignon Blanc 2009** Light straw-green; a fragrant bouquet
✪   with fresh-cut grass, gooseberry and lychee aromas leads into a zesty lemon-
         accented palate with good mouthfeel. Screwcap. 13% alc. **Rating** 90 **To** 2010 $18

ȲȲȲȲ   **Barossa Grenache Shiraz Mourvedre 2007 Rating** 89 **To** 2012 $20
         Eden Valley Riesling 2009 Rating 87 **To** 2012 $18

Buckshot Vineyard   ★★★★☆

PO Box 119, Coldstream, Vic 3770 **Region** Heathcote
T 0417 349 785 **www**.buckshotvineyard.com.au **Open** Not
Winemaker Rob Peebles **Est.** 1999 **Cases** 700 **Vyds** 2 ha

This is the venture of Meegan and Rob Peebles, which comes on the back of Rob's 15-plus-
year involvement in the wine industry. That involvement included six vintages in Rutherglen
starting in 1993, followed by 10 years at Domaine Chandon, squeezing in weekend work at
Coldstream Hills' cellar door in '93. It is a tribute to the soils of Heathcote, and a long-time
friendship with John and Jenny Davies, that sees the flagship Shiraz, and a smaller amount of
Zinfandel (with some shiraz) coming from a small block, part of a 40-ha vineyard owned by
the Davies just to the southwest of Colbinabbin. The wines are made by Rob at Domaine
Chandon; 25% of the wine is exported to the UK and the US, with considerable success.

ȲȲȲȲȲ **Heathcote Shiraz 2008** Good hue, although not dense; a fragrant bouquet
         with spice and pepper notes, the medium-bodied palate adding black fruits on
         entry, and an attractive twist of savoury tannins on the finish. Screwcap. 14.5% alc.
         Rating 94 **To** 2016 $30

ȲȲȲȲȲ **The Square Peg 2008 Rating** 90 **To** 2015 $25

Buller (Rutherglen)   ★★★★★

Three Chain Road, Rutherglen, Vic 3685 **Region** Rutherglen
T (02) 6032 9660 **F** (02) 6032 8005 **www**.buller.com.au **Open** Mon–Sat 9–5, Sun 10–5
Winemaker Andrew Buller **Est.** 1921 **Cases** 4000 **Vyds** 32 ha

Andrew Buller controls this division of the family company, concentrating on Rutherglen
regional wines, headed by Shiraz and Durif, and on the high-quality fortified wines that
give rise to the winery's five-star rating. He sources the grapes from the family's 90-year-old
Calliope Vineyard, and his own Inigo Vineyard. Exports to the UK and the US.

ȲȲȲȲȲ **Rare Rutherglen Liqueur Muscat NV** Deep brown with a touch of olive
         on the rim; full and deep, almost into chocolate, with intense raisined fruit;
         richly textured, with great structure to the raisined/plum pudding fruit flavours,
         and obvious rancio age. Clean finish and aftertaste. Diam. 18% alc. **Rating** 95
         To 2011 $100

Rare Rutherglen Liqueur Tokay NV Medium deep golden-brown; a mix of sweet tea leaf and Christmas cake is a highly aromatic entry point for the bouquet; the palate has a sweet core of muscadelle fruit, and rancio, tea-leaf, nutty and cake elements surrounding the core. Diam. 18% alc. **Rating** 94 **To** 2011 $100

▼▼▼▼ **Fine Old Tawny NV Rating** 89 **To** 2011 $22

Buller (Swan Hill)   ★★★☆

1374 Murray Valley Highway, Beverford, Vic 3590 **Region** Swan Hill
T (03) 5037 6305 **F** (03) 5037 6803 **www**.buller.com.au **Open** Mon–Fri 9–5, Sat 10–4, Sun 10–4 (school & public hols only)
Winemaker Richard Buller **Est.** 1951 **Cases** 120 000 **Vyds** 27.5 ha
Controlled by Richard and Susan Butler, along with their children Richard Jr, Angela and Kate, Buller offers traditional wines that in the final analysis reflect both their Riverland origin and a fairly low-key approach to style in the winery. The estate vineyard is planted to a wide variety of grapes, and additional grapes are purchased from growers in the region. Brands include the value-for-money Beverford range, Caspia, Black Dog Creek from the King Valley and Fine Old fortifieds. Exports to the UK, the US and other major markets.

▼▼▼▼▼ **Black Dog Creek King Valley Cabernet Merlot 2008** Strong colour; has
✪ good weight and substance to its blackcurrant and spice fruit, with ripe tannins in very good balance. Well-made wine. Screwcap. 14.5% alc. **Rating** 90 **To** 2014 $15

▼▼▼▼ **Beverford Durif 2007** Typical deep purple colour; equally typical density of
✪ flavour although not texture, a lack possibly attributable to its breeding (a cross of syrah and peloursin). Screwcap. 15% alc. **Rating** 89 **To** 2014 $13
Beverford Moscato 2009 Rating 87 **To** 2010 $13

Bulong Estate   ★★★★☆

70 Summerhill Road, Yarra Junction, Vic 3797 (postal) **Region** Yarra Valley
T (03) 5967 1358 **F** (03) 5967 1350 **www**.bulongestate.com **Open** 7 days 11–4
Winemaker Matt Carter **Est.** 1994 **Cases** 1000 **Vyds** 31 ha
Judy and Howard Carter's beautifully situated 45-ha property looks down into the valley below and across to the nearby ranges, with Mt Donna Buang at their peak. Most of the grapes from the immaculately tended vineyard are sold, with limited quantities made onsite for the Bulong Estate label. The wines in the current release portfolio show confident winemaking across the range.

▼▼▼▼▼ **Yarra Valley Merlot 2005** Has retained very good hue, still purple; attractive
✪ cassis and plum aromas are followed by a harmonious, supple palate with plum and redcurrant fruit, the finish soft but long. Cork. 13.5% alc. **Rating** 94 **To** 2018 $24

▼▼▼▼▽ **Yarra Valley Sauvignon Blanc 2009** Pale green-straw; a quite fragrant bouquet
✪ with a touch of passionfruit that comes through as the major component of the tropical flavours of the palate. Nice wine. Screwcap. 12.5% alc. **Rating** 90 **To** 2011 $19
Yarra Valley Pinot Noir 2008 Rating 90 **To** 2013 $24

▼▼▼▼ **Yarra Valley Chardonnay 2008 Rating** 89 **To** 2013 $24
Reserve Yarra Valley Cabernet Franc 2006 Rating 89 **To** 2016 $38

Bundaleer Wines   ★★★★

PO Box 41, Hove, SA 5048 **Region** Southern Flinders Ranges
T (08) 8296 1231 **F** (08) 8296 2484 **www**.bundaleerwines.com.au **Open** At North Star Hotel, Nott Street, Melrose Wed–Sun 11–5
Winemaker Angela Meaney **Est.** 1998 **Cases** 3500 **Vyds** 7 ha
Bundaleer is a joint venture between third-generation farmer Des Meaney and manufacturing industry executive Graham Spurling (whose family originally came from the Southern Flinders Ranges). Planting of the vineyard (shiraz and cabernet sauvignon) began in 1998,

the first vintage in 2001. It is situated in an area known as the Bundaleer Gardens, on the edge of the Bundaleer Forest, 200 km north of Adelaide. Exports to the UK, China and Hong Kong.

ŸŸŸŸŸ **Clare Valley Riesling 2009** Light straw-green; a fragrant and flowery bouquet is followed by a delicate but long and very well focused palate with a mix of lime, lemon and mineral; clean, bright finish. Screwcap. 12% alc. **Rating** 93 **To** 2019 $17

✪ **Southern Flinders Ranges Shiraz 2008** Deep, dense crimson-purple; blackberry, licorice, prune and plum coalesce on the bouquet and medium- to full-bodied palate; soft tannins and minimal oak impact. Screwcap. 13.5% alc. **Rating** 92 **To** 2018 $19

✪ **Southern Flinders Ranges Cabernet Sauvignon 2008** Bright crimson-purple; a very attractive medium-bodied, single-vineyard cabernet, presumably picked before the heatwave (or had its alcohol reduced by reverse osmosis); ripe blackcurrant fruit is augmented by balanced French oak from 18 months in barrel. Screwcap. 14% alc. **Rating** 92 **To** 2017 $19

Bundaleera Vineyard ★★★★

449 Glenwood Road, Relbia, Tas 7258 (postal) **Region** Northern Tasmania
T (03) 6343 1231 **F** (03) 6343 1250 **Open** W'ends 10–5
Winemaker Pirie Consulting (Andrew Pirie) **Est.** 1996 **Cases** 1000
David (a consultant metallurgist in the mining industry) and Jan Jenkinson have established 2.5 ha of vines on a sunny, sheltered north to northeast slope in the North Esk Valley. The 12-ha property on which their house and vineyard are established gives them some protection from the urban sprawl of Launceston. Jan is the full-time viticulturist and gardener for the immaculately tended property.

ŸŸŸŸŸ **Pinot Noir 2008** Excellent colour; very good length, drive, nervosity, and balance; plum, black cherry and fine tannins, the oak positive. Screwcap. 14.5% alc. **Rating** 92 **To** 2014 $25

ŸŸŸŸ **Riesling 2009 Rating** 87 **To** 2015 $19.50

Bunkers Wines NR

1142 Kaloorup Road, Kaloorup, WA 6280 (postal) **Region** Margaret River
T (08) 9368 4555 **F** (08) 9368 4566 **www**.bunkerswines.com.au **Open** Not
Winemaker Brian Fletcher **Est.** 1997 **Cases** 8000 **Vyds** 33 ha
Over the past 20-plus years, Mike Calneggia has had his fingers in innumerable Margaret River viticultural pies. He has watched ventures succeed, others fail, and while Bunkers Wines (owned by Mike and Sally Calneggia) is only a small part of his viticultural undertakings, it has been carefully targeted from the word go. It has the five mainstream varieties (cabernet, semillon, merlot, chardonnay and shiraz) joined by one rising star, tempranillo, in the warm and relatively fertile northern part of the Margaret River. He has secured the services of the immensely experienced Brian Fletcher as winemaker, and Murray Edmonds as viticulturist (both formerly at Evans & Tate). Mike and daughter Amy are responsible for sales and marketing, supported by direct sales specialist Cat Duncan. They say, 'The world of wine is full of serious people making serious wines for an ever-decreasing serious market … Bunkers wines have been created to put the "F" word back in to wine, "FUN" that is.'

Bunnamagoo Estate ★★★★

Henry Lawson Drive, Mudgee, NSW 2850 **Region** Central Ranges Zone
T 1300 304 707 **F** (02) 6377 5231 **www**.bunnamagoowines.com.au **Open** 7 days 10–4
Winemaker Robert Black **Est.** 1995 **Cases** 30 000 **Vyds** 128 ha
Bunnamagoo Estate (on one of the first land grants in the region) is situated near the historic town of Rockley. Here a 6-ha vineyard planted to chardonnay, merlot and cabernet sauvignon has been established by Paspaley Pearls, a famous name in the West Australian pearl industry. Increased production has led to the building of a winery and cellar door in Henry Lawson

Drive, Mudgee (with 122 ha of vines). Robert Black is now full-time winemaker. Exports to the US.

ΨΨΨΨΨ **Semillon 2009** The Hunter Valley was not alone in experiencing an outstanding semillon vintage, the same applied in Mudgee; has excellent line and length, with ripe citrus flavours that have devoured the oak the wine was exposed to. Screwcap. 12% alc. **Rating** 93 **To** 2017 $21.95

1827 Handpicked Cabernet Sauvignon 2007 An elegant cabernet, with strong secondary aromas and flavours starting to express themselves in a range of spicy, savoury, earthy and cedary spectra, the fruit with a certain degree of austerity; an instinctive look back over the shoulder to Bordeaux. Diam. 13.5% alc. **Rating** 91 **To** 2017 $49.95

Shiraz 2007 A light- to medium-bodied shiraz with mocha oak and spice characters joining the black cherry fruit; the finish of the medium-bodied palate is deceptively long, the tannins fine. Screwcap. 14.2% alc. **Rating** 90 **To** 2017 $23.95

ΨΨΨΨ **Chardonnay 2008** **Rating** 88 **To** 2013 $21.95

Burge Family Winemakers ★★★★☆
Barossa Way, Lyndoch, SA 5351 **Region** Barossa Valley
T (08) 8524 4644 **F** (08) 8524 4444 **www**.burgefamily.com.au **Open** Fri, Sat, Mon 10–5
Winemaker Rick Burge **Est.** 1928 **Cases** 3500 **Vyds** 9.5 ha
Rick Burge and Burge Family Winemakers (not to be confused with Grant Burge, although the families are related) has established itself as an icon producer of exceptionally rich, lush and concentrated Barossa red wines. 2008 marked 80 years of continuous winemaking by three generations of the family, sandwiched between the much-reduced yields from '07 and '09; in these years some of the signature wines were not made. The gap has been partly filled by the restricted release of '05 and '06 vintage wines. Exports to Canada, Germany, Belgium, The Netherlands, Hong Kong, Singapore and Japan.

ΨΨΨΨΨ **Limited Production Barossa Valley Shiraz Souzao 2005** Amazing retention of deep crimson-purple hue, which Rick Burge says is derived from the 17% Souzao; the wine is full-bodied but well balanced, with an abundance of black fruits and ripe tannins in support. Cork. 14.5% alc. **Rating** 94 **To** 2020 $28

ΨΨΨΨΨ **Barossa Valley Dry Shiraz Rose 2009** Light, bright magenta; an aromatic small
✪ red fruit bouquet leads into a crisp, dry, well-balanced palate of commendable length. Smart rose in every respect. Screwcap. 12% alc. **Rating** 91 **To** 2011 $20

Olive Hill Barossa Valley Mourvedre Shiraz Grenache 2008 **Rating** 91 **To** 2018 $25

Burk Salter Wines ★★★★
Lot 5, Paisley Road, Blanchetown, SA 5357 **Region** Riverland
T (08) 8540 5023 **F** (08) 8540 5023 **www**.burksalterwines.com.au **Open** Fri–Sun & public hols 11–4.30
Winemaker Rocland Estate (Peter Gajewski) **Est.** 2002 **Cases** 3000 **Vyds** 21.4 ha
The husband and wife team of Gregory Burk Salter and Jane Vivienne Salter is the third generation of the Salter family to grow grapes at their Blanchetown property. They have a little over 20 ha of chardonnay, semillon, colombard, ruby cabernet, shiraz, merlot, cabernet sauvignon and muscat gordo blanco; 450 tonnes are sold each year, the remaining 50 tonnes contract-made at various small Barossa Valley wineries. The cellar door and a self-contained B&B adjoin the vineyard, which has Murray River frontage.

ΨΨΨΨΨ **Moorunde Reserve Merlot 2008** An altogether superior wine to the standard; excellent colour, and the texture and structure is much tighter; indeed, a remarkable achievement for merlot from such a hot region, the dark plum fruit not baked. Trophy Best Regional Wine Inland Regions Wine Show '09. Great label. Screwcap. 14.7% alc. **Rating** 92 **To** 2014 $28

Moorunde Reserve Cabernet Sauvignon 2008 Good colour, bright and strong; an uncompromisingly full-bodied Cabernet, with lush blackcurrant fruit, tannins, alcohol and oak all intermingling on the bouquet and palate. Blue-Gold Sydney International Wine Competition '10, silver medal Inland Wine Show '09. Screwcap. 15% alc. **Rating** 90 **To** 2015 $28

ΥΥΥΥ
☼
Muscat Gordo Blanco 2009 Like all the Burk Salter wines, estate-grown; yet another intelligently made wine, with a fleshy texture and soft, balanced sweetness. The front label should give some clue about the style. Screwcap. 12.5% alc. **Rating** 88 **To** 2011 $12

☼
Semillon Chardonnay 2009 Early picking has invested this wine with some juicy citrussy nuances, while not stripping the stone fruit of the chardonnay component; cleverly made. Screwcap. 11% alc. **Rating** 87 **To** 2011 $12
Merlot 2008 Rating 87 **To** 2012 $16

Burke & Wills Winery   ★★★★

3155 Burke & Wills Track, Mia Mia, Vic 3444 **Region** Heathcote
T (03) 5425 5400 **F** (03) 5425 5401 **www**.wineandmusic.net **Open** By appt
Winemaker Andrew Pattison, Gary Baldwin (Consultant) **Est.** 2003 **Cases** 1500
Vyds 4 ha
After 18 years at Lancefield Winery in the Macedon Ranges, Andrew Pattison moved his operation a few miles north in 2004 to set up Burke & Wills Winery at the southern edge of Heathcote, continuing to produce wines from both regions. While establishing 1 ha of shiraz, 0.5 ha of gewurztraminer and 0.5 ha of merlot, malbec and petit verdot at Burke & Wills, he still retains a 19-year-old vineyard at Malmsbury at the northern end of the Macedon Ranges, with 1 ha of cabernet sauvignon, merlot, malbec, cabernet franc, and 0.5 ha each of chardonnay and pinot noir. Additional grapes come from contract growers in Heathcote. Exports to the UK.

ΥΥΥΥΥ
☼
Mia Mia Heathcote Planters' Blend 2008 Crimson-purple; only one small barrel made of this blend of Shiraz/Petit Verdot/Malbec/Merlot, shiraz (60%) and petit verdot (30%) the dominant players; the blend works very well, the flavours synergistic, the texture and structure very good. Heavily stained Diam a worry. 14% alc. **Rating** 93 **To** 2020 $25
Mia Mia Heathcote Gewurztraminer 2009 Light straw-green; just when you think there is no varietal character, a waft of rose petal on the bouquet and a touch of lychee on the crisp palate tells you all is well. Screwcap. 13% alc. **Rating** 90 **To** 2015 $22
Camp 5 Heathcote Shiraz Cabernet Merlot 2006 Retains good hue; a light-bodied wine by the normal standards of Heathcote, doubtless reflecting the moderate alcohol; while not particularly complex, does have bright red fruit flavours and good length. Screwcap. 13.5% alc. **Rating** 90 **To** 2016 $22

ΥΥΥΥ
Pattison Family Reserve Macedon Ranges Chardonnay 2006 Rating 89 **To** 2014 $22
Pattison Family Reserve Macedon Ranges Cabernet Merlot 2007 **Rating** 89 **To** 2017 $25

Burnbrae   ★★★★

548 Hill End Road, Mudgee, NSW 2850 **Region** Mudgee
T (02) 6373 3504 **F** (02) 6373 3435 **www**.burnbraewines.com.au **Open** Mon–Sat 9–5,
Sun 9–4
Winemaker Frank Newman **Est.** 1968 **Cases** 4500 **Vyds** 16 ha
Tony and Jill Bryant were broadacre farmers who had a long-held dream of having a vineyard and winery. Following the sale of the family farm in the 1990s Tony studied viticulture and marketing, and went on to manage wineries in the Mudgee area, before starting his own viticultural consultancy business. In 2004 he and Jill were able to take the final step by purchasing Burnbrae, and acquiring the services of industry veteran Frank

Newman as winemaker. Burnbrae also provides contract winemaking services for others, and Tony is currently president of the Mudgee Wine and Grape Growers Association. Exports to Singapore.

🍷🍷🍷🍷🍷 **Mudgee Riesling 2009** Light straw-green; a skilfully made riesling, with a touch of residual sugar balanced by citrussy acidity; equally suited to an aperitif or with food. Screwcap. 11% alc. **Rating** 90 **To** 2014 $22

 Mudgee Sauvignon Blanc 2009 A more than creditable wine, with good structure and texture; the faintly herbal acidity freshens and lengthens the attractively grassy palate; clean finish. Screwcap. 12% alc. **Rating** 90 **To** 2011 $18
Mudgee Botrytis Semillon NV Very well made, particularly given its multi-vintage background; butterscotch, honey and a touch of lemony acidity to give balance. Cork. 13% alc. **Rating** 90 **To** 2012 $25

🍷🍷🍷🍷 **Mudgee Shiraz 2007 Rating** 89 **To** 2014 $28
Reserve Mudgee Shiraz 2006 Rating 88 **To** 2014 $80
Clive Gale 2007 Rating 88 **To** 2017 $25

🌿 By The Palate ★★★☆
6 Northcliffe Street, Cumberland Park, SA 5041 (postal) **Region** Barossa & Adelaide Hills
T 0411 861 604 **www**.bythepalate.com.au **Open** Not
Winemaker Tom White **Est.** 2009 **Cases** 5000
Owners Tom and Bridget White established Mt Jagged Wines (see separate entry) in 1989, producing cool-climate styles. In 2008 Tom decided to move outside of his comfort zone, and focus on warmer climate shiraz, predominantly from the Barossa and Eden valleys. The other string to his bow is a single white wine, a blend of sauvignon blanc and pinot gris, coming from the Adelaide Hills. This is an entirely separate business to Mt Jagged, and is a virtual winery set-up, purchasing the grapes and making the wines in other producers' wineries around the Barossa and Adelaide Hills.

🍷🍷🍷🍷🍷 **Single Vineyard Greenock Creek Barossa Shiraz 2008** Deep, dark purple-red; brooding black fruits and licorice on the bouquet, then a thick, almost viscous, full-bodied palate with layers of prune, licorice, dark chocolate and blackberry. Stained Diam. 14.5% alc. **Rating** 93 **To** 2023 $45

🍷🍷🍷🍷 **BTP Barossa Valley Shiraz 2008 Rating** 89 **To** 2020 $19

Byrne & Smith Wines ★★★☆
PO Box 640, Unley, SA 5061 **Region** South Australia
T (08) 8272 1900 **F** (08) 8272 1944 **www**.byrneandsmith.com.au **Open** Not
Winemaker Duane Coates (Contract) **Est.** 1999 **Cases** NFP **Vyds** 500+ ha
Byrne & Smith is a family-owned wine business. The Byrne family has been involved in the SA wine industry for three generations, with vineyards spanning over 500 ha in SA's prime wine-producing regions including Clare Valley, Eden Valley, Adelaide Plains and Riverland. The vines vary from 20 to over 35 years of age. The portfolio includes Antiquarian, Thomson Estate, Devlin's Mount and Le Beau! Exports to the UK, the US, Canada, Germany, Denmark and China.

🍷🍷🍷🍷🍷 **Thomson Estate Clare Valley Shiraz 2008** Deep purple-crimson; ripe
 black fruits on the bouquet flow onto the medium- to full-bodied palate, which is supple and long, tannins and oak in balanced support. Screwcap. 13.5% alc. **Rating** 92 **To** 2018 $19

🍷🍷🍷🍷 **Devlin's Mount Shiraz 2008** Bright colour; clean and flavoursome commercial shiraz, with attractive plum and blackberry fruit; supple, light- to medium-bodied palate. Ready now. Screwcap. 14% alc. **Rating** 89 **To** 2013 $15
Antiquarian McLaren Vale Shiraz 2006 Rating 89 **To** 2016 $38
Thomson Estate Clare Valley Semillon Sauvignon Blanc 2009 Rating 88 **To** 2011 $19

Thomson Estate Limestone Coast Cabernet Sauvignon Tempranillo
2007 Rating 88 To 2013 $19

Caledonia Australis   ★★★★★

PO Box 626, North Melbourne, Vic 3051 **Region** Gippsland
T (03) 9329 5372 **F** (03) 9328 3111 **www.**caledoniaaustralis.com **Open** Not
Winemaker Martin Williams MW, Mark Matthews **Est.** 1995 **Cases** 4500 **Vyds** 16.18 ha
In November 2009 Mark and Marianna Matthews acquired Caledonia Australis, and there
has been no change in the pre-existing management arrangements, notwithstanding the
skills the Matthews bring to the table. Mark is winemaker with vintages in numerous wine
regions around the world, works as a winemaking teacher at NMIT, and also runs a contract
winemaking business specialising in small high-quality batches. Marianna has extensive
experience with major fast-moving consumer goods brands globally. Exports to the US,
Singapore, Hong Kong and Japan.

♀♀♀♀♀ Gippsland Chardonnay 2008 Pale, bright straw-green; has started to develop
some creamy/nutty characters ex barrel ferment, and also an added dimension to
its display of white peach and grapefruit flavours running through the length of
the palate. Screwcap. 14% alc. **Rating** 94 To 2016 $29.95
Gippsland Pinot Noir 2008 Light, bright crimson; the complex bouquet offers
plum and red cherry against a backdrop of spice and a veneer of toasty oak; the
palate is bright and fresh, carrying the same fruit flavours, here set against foresty/
savoury notes. Screwcap. 13.5% alc. **Rating** 94 To 2015 $31.95

🍇 Calulu Park Vineyard   ★★★★

1800 Warburton Highway, Woori Yallock, Vic 3139 **Region** Yarra Valley
T (03) 5964 7450 **Open** Nov–Mar 7 days 9–5; April–Oct by appointment
Winemaker Franco D'Anna (Hoddles Creek Estate) **Est.** 1982 **Cases** 1000 **Vyds** 7 ha
Joe and Helen Tricarico purchased a bushland lot in 1974, first establishing a berry farm,
followed in '82 by a small vineyard. The first purchaser of the grapes was Coldstream Hills in
'86, and continued to buy the grapes for some years thereafter. Since that time the vineyard
has been expanded to 7 ha, with the majority of the fruit going to Constellation Wines. The
first Calulu Park wines were made in 2002.

♀♀♀♀♀ Yarra Valley Merlot 2008 Good colour; a spicy red fruit and plum bouquet,
then a well balanced medium-bodied palate with appealing varietal fruit flavours,
finishing with fine tannins. Screwcap. 13.2% alc. **Rating** 93 To 2017 $19
Yarra Valley Pinot Noir 2008 Light, bright magenta-red; a delicious light-
bodied rose-crossover, made with an appropriately gentle hand from vines that
supplied Coldstream Hills over 20 years ago; the wine has deceptive length.
Screwcap. 13.2% alc. **Rating** 90 To 2013 $19

Campania Hills   ★★★☆

447 Native Corners Road, Campania, Tas 7026 **Region** Southern Tasmania
T (03) 6260 4387 **Open** By appt
Winemaker Winemaking Tasmania (Julian Alcorso) **Est.** 1994 **Cases** 500 **Vyds** 1.5 ha
This is the former Colmaur, purchased by Jeanette and Lindsay Kingston in 2005. They had
just sold their business, built up over 22 years, and thought they were returning to country life
and relaxation when they purchased the property, with 1.5 ha of vines equally split between
pinot noir and chardonnay (plus 700 olive trees). Says Lindsay, somewhat wryly, 'We welcome
visitors. The last lot stayed three hours.'

♀♀♀♀♀ Pinot Noir 2008 Very good colour; spicy black fruits on the bouquet; then a
smooth palate with good length. Screwcap. 13.5% alc. **Rating** 90 To 2015 $22

Campbells   ★★★★★

Murray Valley Highway, Rutherglen, Vic 3685 **Region** Rutherglen
T (02) 6033 6000 **F** (02) 6032 9870 **www**.campbellswines.com.au **Open** Mon–Sat 9–5,
Sun 10–5
Winemaker Colin Campbell **Est.** 1870 **Cases** 35 000 **Vyds** 57.82 ha
Campbells produces a wide range of table and fortified wines of ascending quality and price,
which are always honest. As so often happens in this part of the world, the fortified wines are
the best, with the extremely elegant Isabella Rare Tokay and Merchant Prince Rare Muscat at
the top of the tree; the winery rating is for the fortified wines. A feature of the Vintage Room
at the cellar door is an extensive range of back vintage releases of small parcels of wine not
available through any other outlet, other than to Cellar Club members. Exports to the UK,
the US and other major markets.

ΨΨΨΨΨ **Isabella Rare Rutherglen Tokay NV** Very deep olive-brown; broodingly
✪   complex, deep and concentrated aromas, then layer upon layer of flavour in the
        mouth, of almost syrupy consistency. Incredibly intense and complex, with the
        varietal tea-leaf/muscadelle fruit continuity. 375 ml. Cork. 18% alc. **Rating** 97
        To 2011 $110

✪   **Merchant Prince Rare Rutherglen Muscat NV** Dark brown, with olive-green
        on the rim; particularly fragrant, with essency, raisiny fruit; has an almost silky
        viscosity to the intense flavours, which flood every corner of the mouth, but yet
        retains elegance. 375 ml. Cork. 18% alc. **Rating** 96 **To** 2011 $110
        The Brothers Rutherglen Shiraz 2006 A new flagship wine featuring the
        skills of Colin (winemaker) and brother Malcolm (viticulturist). Excellent purple-
        crimson; this supple, medium-bodied wine is a cut above any previous Campbell
        red, with immaculate fruit, oak and tannin balance. Quality cork. 14.5% alc.
        Rating 94 **To** 2021 $60.70
        The Barkly Rutherglen Durif 2007 Deeper colour than the Limited Release,
        although the hue is similar; likewise, distinctly richer and riper, but is not jammy
        or over the top. Great example of full-bodied durif. Cork. 14.5% alc. **Rating** 94
        To 2020 $42.80
        Grand Rutherglen Tokay NV Olive mahogany; much, much more complex
        than the Classic, with all the key varietal characteristics enhanced by rancio; the
        palate is very long, and has no stale characters whatsoever. 375 ml. Cork. 17.5% alc.
        Rating 94 **To** 2011 $65
        Grand Rutherglen Muscat NV Full olive-brown; highly aromatic; a rich and
        complex palate is silky smooth, supple and long, the strong raisin fruit balanced
        by the clean, fresh, lingering acid (and spirit) cut on the finish. 375 ml. Cork.
        17.5% alc. **Rating** 94 **To** 2011 $65

ΨΨΨΨΨ **Bobbie Burns Rutherglen Shiraz 2008** Bright, clear red-purple; an elegant
✪   wine, a far cry from the 16% alcohol Bobbie Burns wines of bygone days; has a
        mix of supple, perfectly ripe, plum (mainly) and blackberry fruit, oak and tannins
        both balanced and integrated. Screwcap. 14.5% alc. **Rating** 93 **To** 2023 $22.95
        Liquid Gold Classic Rutherglen Tokay NV Rating 93 **To** 2011 $34.60
        The Brothers Rutherglen Shiraz 2005 Rating 92 **To** 2015 $60.70
        Classic Rutherglen Muscat NV Rating 92 **To** 2011 $34.60

✪   **Rutherglen Tokay NV** Bright, light golden-brown; classic mix of tea-leaf and
        butterscotch aromas lead into an elegant wine that dances in the mouth; has
        balance and length. 375 ml. Cork. 17.5% alc. **Rating** 92 **To** 2011 $16.90
        Limited Release Rutherglen Durif 2007 Rating 90 **To** 2015 $28

✪   **Rutherglen Muscat NV** A complex and very luscious wine, which has some
        spicy elements not unlike tokay adding interest. 375 ml. Screwcap. 17.5% alc.
        Rating 90 **To** 2011 $16.90

ΨΨΨΨ **Rutherglen Shiraz Durif 2008 Rating** 87 **To** 2013 $15.80

Cannibal Creek Vineyard ★★★★

260 Tynong North Road, Tynong North, Vic 3813 **Region** Gippsland
T (03) 5942 8380 **F** (03) 5942 8202 **www**.cannibalcreek.com.au **Open** 7 days 11–5
Winemaker Patrick Hardiker **Est.** 1997 **Cases** 3000 **Vyds** 5 ha
The Hardiker family moved to Tynong North in 1988, initially grazing beef cattle, but aware of the viticultural potential of the sandy clay loam and bleached subsurface soils weathered from the granite foothills of the Black Snake Ranges. Plantings began in 1997, using organically based cultivation methods; varieties include pinot noir, chardonnay, sauvignon blanc, merlot and cabernet sauvignon. The family decided to make their own wine, and a heritage-style shed built from locally milled timber was converted into a winery and cellar door.

♀♀♀♀♀ **Sauvignon Blanc 2009** Pale straw-green; an aromatic blend of citrus, gooseberry and cut grass that has considerable thrust and length, and a vibrant minerally finish. Screwcap. 12.5% alc. **Rating** 93 **To** 2011 $28
Chardonnay 2006 Light, bright colour, particularly given age; a restrained wine, with bright minerally overtones to the grapefruit and peach fruit, the oak balance good. Diam. 13.2% alc. **Rating** 90 **To** 2014 $24

♀♀♀♀ **Merlot 2006 Rating** 89 **To** 2012 $28
Cabernet Sauvignon 2008 Rating 87 **To** 2014 $28

Canobolas-Smith ★★★★

Boree Lane, off Cargo Road, Lidster via Orange, NSW 2800 **Region** Orange
T (02) 6365 6113 **F** (02) 6365 6113 **www**.canobolassmithwines.com.au
Open Sat & public hols 11–5
Winemaker Murray Smith **Est.** 1986 **Cases** 2000 **Vyds** 8 ha
The Smith family, led by Murray Smith, was one of the early movers in Orange. The vineyard has always been dry-grown, gaining strength from the free-draining clay loam derived from basalt soils. The wines are released under three labels, the best-known the striking blue label, which adorned all of the wines up to 2002. In that year the Strawhouse label came into being, with grapes sourced from a vineyard immediately to the north of Canobolas-Smith. The newest label is The Shine, utilising the golden mean enunciated by Pythagoras, and is reserved for very special wines.

♀♀♀♀♀ **Orange Shiraz 2006** A mulled red fruit bouquet, with spice and a touch of leather for complexity; medium-bodied, soft and approachable, with a distinct orange rind contrasting to the ripe dark fruit. Screwcap. 14% alc. **Rating** 90 **To** 2015 $28 BE

Cape Barren Wines ★★★★★

PO Box 738, North Adelaide, SA 5006 **Region** McLaren Vale
T (08) 8267 3292 **F** (08) 8361 8003 **www**.capebarrenwines.com **Open** By appt
Winemaker Rob Dundon **Est.** 1999 **Cases** 3700 **Vyds** 29 ha
Cape Barren was founded in 1999 by Peter Matthews, who worked tirelessly to create wines of distinction from some of the oldest vineyards in McLaren Vale. Peter sold the business in late '09 to Rob Dundon and Tom Adams, who together have amassed in excess of 50 years experience in winemaking, viticulture and international sales. Rob and Tom intend to build on Peter's foundations of old vine, hand-tended grape supply of the highest quality. The jewels in the viticultural crown are 5 ha of 120-year old shiraz in McLaren Flat and 4 ha of 80-year-old shiraz and grenache at Blewitt Springs. Exports to the UK, the US and other major markets.

♀♀♀♀♀ **Blewitt Springs Vineyard Reserve Release Old Vine McLaren Vale Shiraz 2007** The vines in question are 70 years old, a year or so younger than I; the colour is excellent, and the moment you smell the bouquet you know this is going to be a very classy wine, the medium-bodied palate with dark berry fruits perfectly matched by fine, ripe tannins and integrated oak. Diam. 14.5% alc. **Rating** 96 **To** 2027 $37.95

Native Goose McLaren Vale GSM 2008 Bright, light crimson; a fragrant bouquet of a posy of red fruits and flowers, then a firm medium-bodied palate sustained by silky tannins. Great result for a hot vintage. Screwcap. 15% alc. Rating 94 To 2016 $24.95

Cape Bernier Vineyard ★★★☆

230 Bream Creek Road, Bream Creek, Tas 7175 **Region** Southern Tasmania
T (03) 6253 5443 **F** (03) 6253 6087 **www**.capebernier.com.au **Open** 7 days 9–5, or by appt
Winemaker Winemaking Tasmania (Julian Alcorso) **Est.** 1999 **Cases** 1800 **Vyds** 4 ha
Alastair Christie and family have established 2 ha of pinot noir (including three Dijon clones), another 1.4 ha of chardonnay and 0.6 ha of pinot gris on a north-facing slope overlooking historic Marion Bay. The property is not far from the Bream Creek vineyard, and is one of several developments in the region changing the land use from dairy and beef cattle to wine production and tourism. Exports to Japan.

ΨΨΨΨΨ **Chardonnay 2008** The structure, and in particular the acidity, of Tasmanian
✪ white wines stands out like a beacon in mainland tastings; this is a wonderfully crisp, juicy and lively wine, with white peach and citrus flavours, oak in the background. Screwcap. 13.5% alc. **Rating** 93 To 2016 $26

ΨΨΨΨ **Pinot Gris 2009 Rating** 89 To 2011 $23
Cabernet Merlot 2008 Rating 88 To 2014 $23
Pinot Noir 2008 Rating 87 To 2017 $28

Cape Grace ★★★★

281 Fifty One Road, Cowaramup, WA 6284 **Region** Margaret River
T (08) 9755 5669 **F** (08) 9755 5668 **www**.capegracewines.com.au **Open** 7 days 10–5
Winemaker Mark Messenger (Consultant) **Est.** 1996 **Cases** 2000 **Vyds** 6.25 ha
Cape Grace can trace its history back to 1875 when timber baron MC Davies settled at Karridale, building the Leeuwin lighthouse and founding the township of Margaret River; 120 years later, Robert and Karen Karri-Davies planted the vineyard to chardonnay, shiraz and cabernet sauvignon, with smaller amounts of merlot, semillon and chenin blanc. Robert is a self-taught viticulturist; Karen has over 15 years of international sales and marketing experience in the hospitality industry. Winemaking is carried out on the property; consultant Mark Messenger is a veteran of the Margaret River region. Exports to Singapore and Hong Kong.

ΨΨΨΨΨ **Margaret River Chardonnay 2008** Bright yellow-green; has the layered depth of good Margaret River chardonnay; nectarine and white peach are set in a nutty/toasty embrace; needs a touch more energy and drive to the fruit. Screwcap. 13.5% alc. **Rating** 91 To 2014 $38

Cape Horn Vineyard ★★★☆

Stewarts Bridge Road, Echuca, Vic 3564 **Region** Goulburn Valley
T (03) 5480 6013 **F** (03) 5480 2198 **www**.capehornvineyard.com.au **Open** 7 days 11–5
Winemaker Ian Harrison, John Ellis (Contract) **Est.** 1993 **Cases** 2500 **Vyds** 11 ha
The unusual name comes from a bend in the Murray River considered by riverboat owners of the 19th century to resemble Cape Horn, which is depicted on the wine label. The property was acquired by Echuca GP Dr Sue Harrison and her schoolteacher husband Ian in 1993. Ian has progressively planted their vineyard to chardonnay (3 ha), shiraz, cabernet sauvignon (2 ha each), durif, marsanne (1.5 ha each) and zinfandel (1 ha).

ΨΨΨΨΨ **Echuca Sparkling Durif Shiraz 2007** At least you know what you will be buying – a powerful licorice and black fruit wine with a generous dosage to balance the tannins. And in fact, the balance is very good. Diam. 14% alc. **Rating** 90 To 2014 $30

ΨΨΨΨ **Echuca Goulburn Valley Cabernet Sauvignon 2006 Rating** 89 To 2013 $20

Echuca Goulburn Valley Chardonnay 2008 Rating 88 To 2012 $19
Echuca Goulburn Valley Late Picked Marsanne 2009 Rating 88
To 2014 $18
Echuca Goulburn Valley Cabernet Sauvignon 2007 Rating 87 To 2012 $20

Cape Jaffa Wines   ★★★★☆

Limestone Coast Road, Mount Benson via Robe, SA 5276 **Region** Mount Benson
T (08) 8768 5053 **F** (08) 8768 5040 **www**.capejaffawines.com.au **Open** 7 days 10–5
Winemaker Derek Hooper **Est.** 1993 **Cases** 12 000 **Vyds** 24.9 ha
Cape Jaffa was the first of the Mount Benson wineries and all of the production now comes
from the estate plantings, which include three major Bordeaux red varieties, plus shiraz,
chardonnay, sauvignon blanc, semillon and pinot gris. The winery (built of local rock) has
been designed to allow eventual expansion to 1000 tonnes, or 70 000 cases. In 2008 Cape
Jaffa became a fully certified biodynamic vineyard. Exports to the UK, Canada, Thailand,
Cambodia, Philippines, Hong Kong and Singapore.

ㅇㅇㅇㅇㅇ La Lune Mount Benson Shiraz 2007 The biodynamic viticultural background
in all the Cape Jaffa wines is emphasised by the cloth labels, the name and the
Diam cork, the heavyweight bottle out of sync. Deeply coloured, rich and intense,
this is in fact a high-quality shiraz, opulence balanced by spicy notes and good
acidity. 14% alc. **Rating** 94 To 2020 $37

ㅇㅇㅇㅇㅇ Sauvignon Blanc 2009 A well-made wine with an expressive bouquet and lively,
❂   juicy palate; citrus, passionfruit and touches of herb all add up to a positive, drink-
now style. Screwcap. 13.5% alc. **Rating** 90 To 2011 $15

ㅇㅇㅇㅇ La Lune Mount Benson Semillon Sauvignon Blanc 2008 Rating 88
To 2013 $25
Shiraz 2007 Rating 88 To 2015 $20

Cape Mentelle   ★★★★★

Wallcliffe Road, Margaret River, WA 6285 **Region** Margaret River
T (08) 9757 0888 **F** (08) 9757 3233 **www**.capementelle.com.au **Open** 7 days 10–4.30
Winemaker Robert Mann, Simon Burnell, Tim Lovett **Est.** 1970 **Cases** 90 000
Vyds 166 ha
Part of the LVMH (Louis Vuitton Möet Hennessy) group. Cape Mentelle is firing on all
cylinders with the winemaking team fully capitalising on the extensive and largely mature
vineyards, and which obviate the need for contract-grown fruit. It is hard to say which of the
wines is best; the ranking, such as it is, varies from year to year. That said, Sauvignon Blanc
Semillon, Chardonnay, Shiraz and Cabernet Sauvignon lead the portfolio. Only one wine
submitted for this edition, but there is no reason to suspect the high quality of its wines has
diminished. Exports to all major markets.

ㅇㅇㅇㅇㅇ Margaret River Sauvignon Blanc Semillon 2009 Pale straw; a classy SBS, a
lively, fresh and pure array of citrus and herbal notes, the percentage of oak ex a
portion of barrel fermentation judged to perfection. Gold medal Sydney Wine
Show '10. Screwcap. 13% alc. **Rating** 94 To 2012 $28

Cape Naturaliste Vineyard   ★★★★☆

1 Coley Road (off Caves Road), Yallingup, WA 6282 **Region** Margaret River
T (08) 9755 2538 **F** (08) 9755 2538 **www**.capenaturalistevineyard.com.au
Open 7 days 10.30–5
Winemaker Ian Bell, Bruce Dukes **Est.** 1997 **Cases** 3500 **Vyds** 9.7 ha
Cape Naturaliste Vineyard has a long and varied history going back 150 years when it was
a coach inn for travellers journeying between Perth and Margaret River. Later it became a
dairy farm, and in 1970 a mining company purchased it, intending to extract the mineral
sands. The government stepped in and declared it a national park, whereafter (in 1980) Craig
Brent-White purchased the property. The vineyard is planted to cabernet sauvignon, shiraz,

merlot, semillon and sauvignon blanc, and is run on an organic/biodynamic basis. The quality of the wines would suggest the effort is well worthwhile. Exports to Hong Kong, Singapore and Indonesia.

ＹＹＹＹＹ **Torpedo Rocks Reserve Margaret River Shiraz 2007** Curiously, fractionally more developed than the standard wine; more juicy fruit and more (although balanced) oak are the immediate differences; the medium- to full-bodied palate also has extreme length. Screwcap. 14% alc. **Rating** 94 To 2022 $40

ＹＹＹＹＹ **Torpedo Rocks Reserve Margaret River Cabernet Sauvignon 2007** **Rating** 93 To 2017 $40
Torpedo Rocks Margaret River Cabernet Shiraz 2007 Rating 92 To 2017 $32

✪ **Margaret River Shiraz 2007** Bright crimson; red and black fruit aromas, along with a sprinkling of spice, are repeated on the medium-bodied palate, underpinned by savoury tannins. Screwcap. 14% alc. **Rating** 91 To 2016 $19
The Westerly Paddock Margaret River Merlot 2007 Rating 90 To 2014 $27

ＹＹＹＹ **Margaret River Semillon Sauvignon Blanc 2009** Vibrant, piercingly crisp,
✪ herb and grass aromas and flavours lead the charge on a classic seafood and summer style. Screwcap. 13% alc. **Rating** 89 To 2011 $18.50
✪ **Margaret River Cabernet Sauvignon 2007** Good purple-red; lively and bright cabernet varietal expression on the bouquet and light- to medium-bodied palate; a mysterious tribute to 'the tropical flavours of this most enjoyable wine' on the back label. Screwcap. 14.1% alc. **Rating** 89 To 2013 $19

Capel Vale ★★★★★

118 Mallokup Road, Capel, WA 6271 **Region** Geographe
T (08) 9727 1986 **F** (08) 6364 4882 **www**.capelvale.com **Open** 7 days 10–4
Winemaker Justin Hearn **Est.** 1974 **Cases** 70 000 **Vyds** 165.27 ha
Capel Vale was established by Perth-based medical practitioner Dr Peter Pratten in 1974. The first vineyard adjacent to the winery was established on the banks of the quiet waters of Capel River. The very fertile soil gave rise to extravagant vine growth, providing 95% of the winery's intake until the mid-1980s. The viticultural empire has since been expanded, spreading across Capel (35.66 ha), Mount Barker (25.06 ha), Pemberton (76.65 ha) and Margaret River (27.9 ha), with 18 varieties planted; the most recent arrivals are petit verdot, sangiovese, tempranillo and nebbiolo. Every aspect of the business is subject to the close scrutiny of Peter Pratten. Exports to all major markets.

ＹＹＹＹＹ **Regional Series Mount Barker Shiraz 2008** Bright, deep colour; highly perfumed aromas of blackberry, violets, fresh bitumen and ironstone; medium-bodied, juicy and generous, the structure could almost be overlooked, but provides a rock-solid framework for the lavish bright fruit on offer; quite a silky and sexy fragrant style. Screwcap. 14% alc. **Rating** 95 $23.95 BE
Single Vineyard Whispering Hill Shiraz 2008 Good crimson hue; an elegant, sophisticated shiraz, bringing spicy fruit, French oak and persistent, fine-grained tannins into immediate play; has deceptive power and length. Screwcap. 14% alc. **Rating** 95 To 2023 $54.95
Regional Series Margaret River Cabernet Sauvignon 2008 Bright colour; a distinctly cedary bouquet, with cassis and a touch of black olive thrown in for good measure; the palate shows abundant black and red fruits, with the oak merely seasoning the fruit; the tannins are fine and plentiful; plenty of wine for the price. Screwcap. 13.5% alc. **Rating** 94 $23.95 BE
The Scholar Margaret River Cabernet Sauvignon 2008 Good hue, although not especially deep; the varietal character of the wine is undoubted, and while there is a question mark over the persistent tannins at this stage, they are part and parcel of high-quality cabernet with a long future. Gold medal Sydney Wine Show '10. Screwcap. 14.5% alc. **Rating** 94 To 2023 $74.95

ΨΨΨΨΩ   Regional Series Margaret River Cabernet Merlot 2008 Rating 93
To 2020 $23.95
Regional Series Pemberton Chardonnay 2009 Rating 92 To 2016 $23.95

✪   Debut Verdelho 2009 Floral aromas with some white flower and spice nuances
are followed by a juicy, lively palate with both line and length. Screwcap. 13% alc.
Rating 92 To 2011 $17.95
Whispering Hill Mount Barker Riesling 2009 Rating 90 To 2017 $28.95

ΨΨΨΨ   Debut Sauvignon Blanc Semillon 2009 Rating 89 To 2010 $17.95
Debut Unwooded Chardonnay 2009 Rating 88 To 2012 $17.95
Debut Chenin Blanc 2009 Rating 88 To 2012 $17.95
Debut Merlot 2008 Rating 88 To 2014 $17.95
Debut Cabernet Merlot 2008 Rating 88 To 2014 $17.95

Capercaillie   ★★★★★

4 Londons Road, Lovedale, NSW 2325 **Region** Hunter Valley
T (02) 4990 2904 **F** (02) 4991 1886 **www.**capercailliewine.com.au **Open** Mon–Sat 9–5,
Sun 10–5
Winemaker Various **Est.** 1995 **Cases** 3000 **Vyds** 5 ha
A highly successful winery in terms of the quality of its wines, as well as their reach outwards
from the Hunter Valley. The Capercaillie wines have always been particularly well made, with
generous flavour. Following the example of Brokenwood, its fruit sources are spread across
southeastern Australia, although the portfolio includes high-quality wines that are 100%
Hunter Valley. The business is owned by Patricia Sutherland following the sudden death of
husband Alasdair, its future direction uncertain at the time of going to press. The five-star
rating has been deliberately retained in the interim. Exports to the UK and Dubai.

ΨΨΨΨΩ   Cuillin Chardonnay 2009 Bright straw-green; interesting wine; is the funky
bouquet partly driven by reduction or not? I suppose it doesn't matter, for the
wine also has considerable vibrancy and drive to its nectarine and citrus fruit.
Screwcap. 12.5% alc. Rating 92 To 2013 $23

ΨΨΨΨ   Hunter Valley Gewurztraminer 2009 Has a little more life and energy than
✪   the Audrey Wilkinson; both wines come from old plantings and it is the fruit
weight rather than varietal character that sustains the wine. Screwcap. 12.5% alc.
Rating 89 To 2013 $19
Wrattonbully Merlot 2008 Rating 88 To 2013 $27 BE

Capital Wines   ★★★★★

2918 Barton Highway, Murrumbateman ACT 2582 **Region** Canberra District
T (02) 6236 8555 **F** (02) 6236 8557 **www.**capitalwines.com.au **Open** By appt
Winemaker Andrew McEwin **Est.** 1986 **Cases** 2000 **Vyds** 5 ha
This is a newly constituted venture between Mark and Jenny Mooney (of the Royal Hotel
at Gundaroo) and Andrew and Marion McEwin (of Kyeema Wines). They have joined forces
to found Capital Wines, which purchased Kyeema Wines and related contract winemaking in
2008. The new venture has seen the creation of a new series of wines (The Ministry Series),
with clever graphic design and generally invigorated marketing efforts. The estate vineyard
is still an important source, but grape purchases and an expanded winery are also part of the
new venture. Whether by coincidence, or not, consecutive releases of the new wines are of
impressive quality, and has led to a doubling of sales. Exports to Singapore.

ΨΨΨΨΨ   Kyeema Vineyard Reserve Canberra District Shiraz 2008 Bright crimson;
has black fruits with splashes of spice on the bouquet; the medium-bodied palate
has excellent texture and structure, throwing sidelights onto the spicy fruits, the
tannins perfectly weighted. Screwcap. 13.5% alc. Rating 95 To 2023 $52

✪   The Whip Riesling 2009 A distinctively floral and fragrant bouquet with hints
of passionfruit and spice, then an elegant, wholly satisfying palate with abundant
fruit, yet not the least bit heavy. Screwcap. 12% alc. Rating 94 To 2019 $18

✪   **The Senator Chardonnay 2009** Bright greenish hue; a particularly elegant and vibrant chardonnay with white peach and grapefruit flavours that have absorbed the 100% barrel ferment oak inputs; clever use of older oak with a touch of new French helps sustain the long finish. Screwcap. 12.8% alc. **Rating** 94 **To** 2016 $22

✪   **The Backbencher Merlot 2008** Crimson-purple; in Gilbert & Sullivan terms, the very model of a fine merlot, with juicy cassis and plum fruit supported by fine, ripe tannins. Screwcap. 13.2% alc. **Rating** 94 **To** 2016 $25

�♀   Kyeema Vineyard Reserve Canberra District Merlot 2008 **Rating** 93 **To** 2020 $46

    The Ambassador Tempranillo 2008 Rating 92 **To** 2015 $27

✪   **The Swinger Sauvignon Blanc 2009** From the hilarious Ministry series of labels; offers an appealing mix of grass, gooseberry, mineral and a touch of tropical characters; good balance and length. Screwcap. 12% alc. **Rating** 91 **To** 2011 $18

    The Frontbencher Shiraz 2008 Rating 91 **To** 2018 $25

✪   **The Fence Sitter Rose 2009** Bright cherry and raspberry flavours from early-picked cabernet franc/merlot specifically for rose, given skin contact before pressing, and cool-fermented to dryness; a nice tweak on the finish. Screwcap. 12.7% alc. **Rating** 90 **To** 2010 $18

♙♙♙♙   The Treasury Late Picked Riesling 2009 **Rating** 89 **To** 2011 $25

Cappastone Wines

PO Box 14, Red Cliffs, Vic 3496 **Region** Murray Darling
T F (03) 5024 5976 **www**.cappastonewines.com.au **Open** Not
Winemaker Contract **Est.** 2009 **Cases** 1500
This is the venture of Reg Cua and Dale Stephens. It takes its name from a mountain in Calabria that provided a refuge for those fleeing the Second World War. It is a symbol of life, fulfilment and opportunity the owners wish to bring to the business and the wines it makes. It is a virtual winery, the cornerstone being the white frontignac Moscato.

♙♙♙♙   **Moscato 2009** Very pale colour; drier than most, which is a relief; clean and crisp, with pleasant fruit on the mid-palate. Screwcap. 5.5% alc. **Rating** 87 **To** 2011 $12

Captains Creek Organic Wines ★★★☆

160 Mays Road, Blampied, Vic 3364 **Region** Ballarat
T (03) 5345 7408 **F** (03) 5345 7408 **www**.captainscreek.com **Open** W'ends & public hols 11–5, or by appt
Winemaker Kilchurn Wines (David Cowburn) **Est.** 1994 **Cases** 500 **Vyds** 2 ha
Doug and Carolyn May are the third generation of farmers at the Captains Creek property, and have been conducting the business for over 20 years without using any chemicals. When they began establishing the vineyard in 1994, with chardonnay (1.5 ha) and pinot noir (0.5 ha), they resolved to go down the same path: they use preventive spray programs of copper and sulphur, thermal flame weeding, and beneficial predatory insects to control weeds and mites.

♙♙♙♙♀   Hepburn Chardonnay Pinot Noir (Late Disgorged) 2004 Fine mousse; bright straw-green; fine and intense, the citrussy fruit complexed by five years on yeast lees; very long, crisp finish. Diam. 12% alc. **Rating** 92 **To** 2013 $45

Cardinham Estate ★★★★☆

Main North Road, Stanley Flat, SA 5453 **Region** Clare Valley
T (08) 8842 1944 **F** (08) 8842 1955 **Open** 7 days 10–5
Winemaker Scott Smith **Est.** 1981 **Cases** 5000 **Vyds** 50 ha
Cardinham Estate was founded by Fred Dinham as a single, 24-ha, vineyard in 1981. Now known as the Home Block, continuous improvement and land availability has seen the vineyards expand to 50 ha. Noel and wife Heather Smith moved to Clare to run the vineyards, eventually living on the Home Block. With falling grape prices and an oversupply of

the wrong varieties, things were very tight, but hard work prevailed and the rewards were realised when Noel was able to purchase more land and sons Scott and Shane returned to help. By the 1990s the whole family was involved in the venture, which now includes the Stradbroke, Russ' and Carters Vineyards. Their work was rewarded by winning three trophies at the Canberra International Riesling Challenge '09, including the coveted Best Riesling in the World Trophy (for the '03 Riesling), the first awarded to an Australian winery. Exports to the US, Hong Kong and China.

ŶŶŶŶŶ   **Clare Valley Riesling 2003** Aged Release. Brilliant green-straw; a very complex
✪   bouquet with a multitude of aromas, and then flavours on the lime and spice
         palate. Was a very good wine at 12 months old, and is great now. Screwcap.
         12.5% alc. **Rating** 96 **To** 2013 $20

ŶŶŶŶŶ   **Clare Valley Riesling 2009 Rating** 93 **To** 2015 $20
         The Stradbrooke Clare Valley Shiraz 2006 Rating 90 **To** 2021 $50
         The Stradbrooke Clare Valley Cabernet Sauvignon 2006 Rating 90
         To 2016 $50

ŶŶŶŶ   **Clare Valley Shiraz 2006 Rating** 89 **To** 2016 $25

🍇 Carldenn Homestead Wines   ★★★

80 Mitchell Road, Walliston, WA 6076 **Region** Perth Hills
T (08) 9291 7788 **Open** W'ends & public hols 9–5
Winemaker Bella Ridge Estate (Alon Arbel) **Est.** 1998 **Cases** 700 **Vyds** 0.5 ha
Dennis and Carline Humphrey, together with their four children, have been long term residents of the Perth Hills. In the late 1970s they had an orchard and a commercial tomato patch on a northwest-facing slope; when neither the orchard nor tomatoes paid their way, the 0.5 ha of land became vacant until (in Dennis' words) 'I needed to grow something to help with paying off the mortgage'. With encouragement from then regional doyen Peter Fimmel, he close-planted 1000 chardonnay and 1000 semillon vines, plus 500 of merlot. Looking after the vineyard and the cellar door is now a full-time job for this industrial electrician.

ŶŶŶŶ   **Sparkling Perth Hills Methode Champenoise 2007** A Chardonnay/
         Semillon base with very ripe fruit giving notes of banana and honey, but tempered
         by acidity. Cork. 12.5% alc. **Rating** 87 **To** 2011 $27

Carlei Estate & Carlei Green Vineyards ★★★★★

1 Alber Road, Upper Beaconsfield, Vic 3808 **Region** Yarra Valley
T (03) 5944 4599 **F** (03) 5944 4599 **www.carlei.com.au Open** W'ends 11–6, or by appt
Winemaker Sergio Carlei **Est.** 1994 **Cases** 10 000 **Vyds** 2.25 ha
Sergio Carlei has come a long way in a short time: graduating from home winemaking in a suburban garage to his own (commercial) winery in Upper Beaconsfield; Carlei Estate falls just within the boundaries of the Yarra Valley. Along the way Carlei acquired a Bachelor of Wine Science from CSU, and established a vineyard with organic and biodynamic accreditation adjacent to the Upper Beaconsfield winery. His contract winemaking services are now a major part of the business, and showcase his extremely impressive winemaking talents. Exports to the US, Canada, Sweden, China, Singapore and Malaysia.

ŶŶŶŶŶ   **Estate Sud Heathcote Shiraz 2007** Deeper colour, with more purple; while
         having some of the savoury elements of Nord, has a much greater well of black
         fruits and flecks of licorice; the slightly tarry tannins are held in check (just) by the
         fruit, and do lengthen the finish. Diam. 14.9% alc. **Rating** 94 **To** 2017 $59
         Estate Nebbiolo 2006 From the cool Upper Goulburn Valley; Sergio Carlei has
         thrown the full book of nebbiolo crafting at the wine: fermentation and extended
         post-fermentation maceration in a large open oak vat, then 24 months in new and
         used French oak barriques. For those with a love of Barolo, this is full of interest,
         the savoury, almost lemony, tannins providing both structure and flavour. Screwcap.
         13.5% alc. **Rating** 94 **To** 2015 $59

ΨΨΨΨΩ Green Vineyards Cardinia Ranges Pinot Gris 2009 Rating 92 To 2012 $25
Tre Bianchi Cardinia Ranges Sauvignon Semillon Chardonnay 2008
Rating 91 To 2013 $25
Estate Pinot Noir 2006 Rating 90 To 2015 $49
Estate Nord Heathcote Shiraz 2007 Rating 90 To 2014 $59

ΨΨΨΨ Green Vineyards Heathcote Shiraz 2007 Rating 88 To 2014 $29

Carpe Diem Vineyards ★★★★☆

213 Johnson Road, Wilyabrup, WA 6280 **Region** Margaret River
T (08) 9755 6118 **F** (08) 9755 6118 **www.**carpediemvineyards.com.au **Open** By appt
Winemaker Gianfranco Anderle **Est.** 2003 **Cases** 1500 **Vyds** 12 ha
The 2000 Sydney Olympics brought Luigi and Anita Anderle to Australia for the first time.
They took the opportunity to see more of Australia, and fell in love with the Margaret River.
As a result, son Gianfranco and wife Francesca flew to WA to check out the region. Events
moved quickly: they returned to Italy, sold all of their assets, and returned to the Margaret
River to purchase a 30-ha property at Wilyabrup, moving permanently to the region with
their children. Gianfranco's parents followed a couple of years later. Gianfranco is a qualified
oenologist, with an Honours degree, and already had 22 years of winemaking experience
when he arrived in Australia. The vineyard plantings are a mix of Margaret River staples
(5.5 ha of sauvignon blanc and semillon, and 3.3 ha of cabernet sauvignon and merlot) the
Italian connection cemented with 1 ha each of sangiovese and nebbiolo, and 0.5 ha each of
vermentino and pinot grigio.

ΨΨΨΨΨ Platinum Selection Margaret River Merlot 2008 Has an intensely aromatic
bouquet with spice, bracken, leaf and cassis fruit; the palate takes command pulling
these characters together and presenting them in a smooth and supple frame, cassis
and blackcurrant fruit to the fore. Screwcap. 13.8% alc. Rating 95 To 2020 $41

ΨΨΨΨΩ Platinum Selection Margaret River Malbec 2008 Rating 92 To 2015 $41
Margaret River Cabernet Sauvignon 2008 Rating 91 To 2020 $26
Margaret River Sauvignon Blanc 2009 Rating 90 To 2012 $26
Platinum Selection Margaret River Nebbiolo 2008 Rating 90 To 2015 $41
L'Attimo Riserva Speciale Nebbiolo 2007 Rating 90 To 2014 $50

ΨΨΨΨ Margaret River Sangiovese 2008 Rating 89 To 2017 $26
Passito Dolce 2008 Rating 87 To 2013 $50

Carrickalinga Creek Vineyard ★★★☆

Lot 10 Willson Drive, Normanville, SA 5204 **Region** Southern Fleurieu
T 0403 009 149 **www.**ccvineyard.com.au **Open** W'ends 11–5.30 (summer)
Winemaker Tim Geddes (Contract) **Est.** 2001 **Cases** 300 **Vyds** 3 ha
Tim Anstey and Helen Lacey acquired their north-sloping property 2 km from the St Vincent
Gulf after Tim's retirement from university teaching. The choice of region was driven by Dr
John Gladstones' enthusiasm for the mild, maritime climate of the lower Fleurieu Peninsula,
for red grapes in particular. In 2001 they planted 1 ha each of shiraz and cabernet sauvignon,
followed later by 0.7 ha of chardonnay and 0.3 ha of viognier. The purpose-built hillside cellar
door has spectacular views of both the coast and surrounding hills. Tim Geddes calls the shots
with the winemaking; Tim Anstey is 'cellar hand'.

ΨΨΨΨΩ Southern Fleurieu Shiraz 2008 Deep purple-crimson; an excellent full-bodied
✪ shiraz that has abundant black fruits, ripe tannins and good oak; good texture and
mouthfeel. Screwcap. 14.5% alc. Rating 93 To 2020 $18

Casa Freschi ★★★★

PO Box 45, Summertown, SA 5141 **Region** Langhorne Creek
T 0409 364 569 **F** (08) 8390 3232 **www.**casafreschi.com.au **Open** Not
Winemaker David Freschi **Est.** 1998 **Cases** 2000 **Vyds** 7.55 ha

David Freschi graduated with a degree in oenology from Roseworthy College in 1991 and spent most of the decade working overseas in California, Italy and NZ. In 1998 he and his wife decided to trade in the corporate world for a small family-owned winemaking business, with a core of 2.4 ha of vines established by his parents in '72; an additional 1.85 ha of nebbiolo have now been planted adjacent to the original vineyard. Says David, 'The names of the wines were chosen to best express the personality of the wines grown in our vineyard, as well as to express our heritage.' A second 3.2-ha vineyard has subsequently been established in the Adelaide Hills, planted to chardonnay, pinot gris, riesling and gewurztraminer. Exports to Canada.

ŸŸŸŸŸ **Profondo Grand 2006** Slightly opaque colour; a complex crosshatch of varietal and regional inputs, bitter chocolate, herbs and spices running through the main agenda of black fruits. Is developing slowly; high-quality cork is slightly reassuring. Cabernet Sauvignon/Shiraz/Malbec. 14% alc. **Rating** 92 **To** 2016 $60
La Signorina 2009 The original fruit salad and puppy dogs' tails wine, but is remarkably fresh and tangy, citrus characters emerging on top of a pile of other flavours. Pinot Gris/Chardonnay/Riesling/Gewurztraminer. Screwcap. 13% alc. **Rating** 90 **To** 2012 $29

Cascabel ★★★★☆

Rogers Road, Willunga, SA 5172 (postal) **Region** McLaren Vale
T (08) 8557 4434 **F** (08) 8557 4435 **www**.cascabelwinery.com.au **Open** Not
Winemaker Susana Fernandez, Duncan Ferguson **Est.** 1997 **Cases** 2500 **Vyds** 4.9 ha
Cascabel's proprietors, Duncan Ferguson and Susana Fernandez, have planted a mosaic of southern Rhône and Spanish varieties. The choice of grapes reflects the winemaking experience of the proprietors in Australia, the Rhône Valley, Bordeaux, Italy, Germany and NZ – and also Susana's birthplace, Spain. Production has moved steadily towards the style of the Rhône Valley, Rioja and other parts of Spain. Exports to the UK, the US, Canada, Switzerland, Spain, Hong Kong and Japan.

ŸŸŸŸŸ **Eden Valley Riesling 2009** Bright straw-green; lime blossom aromas, then an
✪   exceptionally vibrant and intense palate charged with juicy lime fruit; great length is a given after such a palate. Screwcap. 12% alc. **Rating** 96 **To** 2024 $21

ŸŸŸŸŸ **McLaren Vale Monastrell 2008 Rating** 90 **To** 2018 $45

ŸŸŸŸ **El Sendero McLaren Vale Tempranillo 2008 Rating** 88 **To** 2015 $34

Casella Wines ★★★

Wakely Road, Yenda, NSW 2681 **Region** Riverina
T (02) 6961 3000 **F** (02) 6961 3099 **www**.casellawines.com.au **Open** Not
Winemaker Alan Kennett, Phillip Casella **Est.** 1969 **Cases** 12 million
A modern-day fairytale success story, transformed overnight from a substantial, successful but non-charismatic business making 650 000 cases in 2000. Its opportunity came when the US distribution of Lindemans Bin 65 Chardonnay was taken away from WJ Deutsch & Sons, leaving a massive gap in its portfolio, which was filled by yellow tail. It built its US presence at a faster rate than any other brand in history. Exports to all major markets, and is now rapidly penetrating the UK market. It has been aided in all markets by making small batches (500 dozen or so) of Reserve and Limited Release wines, and by spreading its net for these across three states, gold medals at major shows the result. (None of these top-end wines were submitted this year.)

ŸŸŸŸ **yellow tail Moscato 2009** A clever take on moscato, delivering positive citrussy
✪   flavours on the fore-palate, then balancing sweetness and acidity well on the finish. Screwcap. 7.5% alc. **Rating** 89 **To** 2010 $10
✪   **yellow tail Semillon Sauvignon Blanc 2009** A well put together wine, with a mix of tropical and citrus flavours; good balance and not obviously sweet. Screwcap. 12.5% alc. **Rating** 87 **To** 2010 $10

○ **yellow tail Pinot Grigio 2009** Well made; has an unexpected but enjoyable thrust of citrus in place of residual sugar; does shorten slightly on the finish. Screwcap. 11.5% alc. **Rating** 87 **To** 2010 $10
yellow tail Rose 2009 Cleverly made; red fruits, a hint of spice and just a hint of sweetness will satisfy those who shop in this price range. Screwcap. 13.5% alc. **Rating** 87 **To** 2010 $10

○ **yellow tail Shiraz 2008** A very well made wine at the price; blackberry and red cherry fruit are the drivers rather than oak or tannins; any sweetness is not obvious. Good example of an uncomplicated drink-now style. Screwcap. 13.5% alc. **Rating** 87 **To** 2010 $10

○ **yellow tail Cabernet Sauvignon 2008** Well put together; gently sweet cassis and raspberry fruit on the mid-palate, and no obvious residual sugar on the finish, which has some length. Screwcap. 13.5% alc. **Rating** 87 **To** 2010 $10

Cassegrain   ★★★★☆

764 Fernbank Creek Road, Port Macquarie, NSW 2444 **Region** Hastings River
T (02) 6582 8377 **F** (02) 6582 8378 **www**.cassegrainwines.com.au **Open** 7 days 9–5
Winemaker John Cassegrain (Chief), Michelle Heagney (Senior) **Est.** 1980
Cases 60 000 **Vyds** 34.9 ha
Cassegrain has continued to evolve and develop. It continues to draw on the original Hastings River vineyard of 4.9 ha, the most important varieties being semillon, verdelho and chambourcin, with pinot noir and cabernet sauvignon making up the numbers. However, Cassegrain now part-owns and manages Richfield Vineyard (see separate entry) in the New England region, with 30 ha of chardonnay, verdelho, semillon, shiraz, merlot, cabernet sauvignon and ruby cabernet. These estate vineyards are supplemented by grapes purchased from Tumbarumba, Orange and the Hunter Valley. Exports to the UK, the US, and other major markets.

♀♀♀♀♀ **Fromenteau Reserve Chardonnay 2008** Light straw-green; proclaims its cool
○ climate origins from the first whiff through to the long, bell-clear, lingering finish; along the way, juicy white peach and a splash of grapefruit mark their presence, the oak subtly adding to complexity. Screwcap. 13.5% alc. **Rating** 96 **To** 2014 $32

♀♀♀♀♀ **Edition Noir New England Durif 2008** Usual strong colour; a sombre, dark
○ fruit rendition of durif, black berries backed by fine tannins that give the wine excellent texture and length. Screwcap. 14.5% alc. **Rating** 93 **To** 2015 $23.50
Semillon 2009 Rating 92 **To** 2018 $18.95
Reserve Falerne Cabernet Sauvignon and Merlot 2007 Rating 92 **To** 2022 $32
Edition Noir New England Riesling 2009 Rating 90 **To** 2014 $23.50
Reserve Shiraz 2007 Rating 90 **To** 2015 $32

♀♀♀♀ **Edition Noir New England Gewurztraminer 2009 Rating** 89 **To** 2012 $23.50
Fromenteau Reserve Chardonnay 2006 Rating 89 **To** 2013 $32
Shiraz 2008 Rating 89 **To** 2016 $18.95
○ **Stone Circle Regional Selection New England Australia Shiraz 2008**
More purple hues than the standard, the bouquet more fragrant and tending more to red fruits; the light- to medium-bodied palate has foresty notes that belie its alcohol; interesting style (rather than quality) contrast. Screwcap. 14.5% alc. **Rating** 89 **To** 2014 $16.95
Cassae NV Rating 89 **To** 2011 $21.95
Verdelho 2009 Rating 88 **To** 2010 $18.95
Edition Noir Tumbarumba Pinot Noir 2008 Rating 88 **To** 2012 $23.50

Castelli Estate   ★★★★★

380 Mt Shadforth Road, Denmark, WA 6333 **Region** Great Southern
T (08) 9364 0400 **F** (08) 9364 0444 **www**.castelliestate.com.au **Open** By appt
Winemaker Mike Garland **Est.** 2007 **Cases** 4000

Castelli Estate will cause many small winery owners to go green with envy. When Sam Castelli purchased the property in late 2004, he was intending simply to use it as a family holiday destination. But because there was a partly constructed winery he decided to complete the building work and lock the doors. However, wine was in his blood courtesy of his father, who owned a small vineyard in Italy's south. The temptation was too much, and in 2007 the winery was commissioned, with 20 tonnes of Great Southern fruit crushed under the Castelli label. In 2008 the amount increased to 30 tonnes, and '09 40 tonnes. There is room for expansion because the winery actually has a capacity of 500 tonnes, and the underground cellar is fully climate controlled. Fruit is sourced from some of the best vineyards in WA, including the Hadley Hall, Kalgan River, Whispering Hill and Omodei vineyards. These are geographically distributed across WA's southern regions including Frankland River, Mount Barker, Pemberton and Porongurup.

ΨΨΨΨΨ **Frankland River Shiraz 2008** Striking crimson-purple; the bouquet swells with spice, black cherry and satsuma plum, the palate marrying intensity with elegance in a way only cool climates can achieve, the slightly savoury finish yet another plus. Screwcap. 13.9% alc. **Rating** 95 **To** 2023 $28

Frankland River Cabernet Sauvignon 2008 Strong colour; a serious cabernet with a touch of austerity, even though it has volumes of varietal fruit; black olive is interleaved with blackcurrant, the tannins fine but firm, the finish long. Screwcap. 14.5% alc. **Rating** 94 **To** 2023 $28

ΨΨΨΨΨ
✪ **Cerca Pemberton Frankland River Sauvignon Blanc Semillon 2009** A clean, fragrant and lively bouquet opens proceedings with passionfruit, a touch of lychee and a glimpse of herb, the palate introducing citrus as the main theme, with an invigorating finish. Screwcap. 12% alc. **Rating** 93 **To** 2011 $18

✪ **Cerca Frankland River Pemberton Cabernet Sauvignon Merlot 2008** Light, bright colour; highly fragrant red and black fruit aromas and an elegant, but intense, medium-bodied palate, the tannins fine and supple. The Cabernet is Frankland, the Merlot Pemberton. Top value. Screwcap. 14.3% alc. **Rating** 93 **To** 2018 $18

✪ **Porongurup Riesling 2009** Very pale; both bouquet and palate are still closed for business, but the clarity and balance of the wine guarantees good bottle development over the next 10 years. Don't bother opening it for at least two years. Screwcap. 11.8% alc. **Rating** 90 **To** 2020 $18

Pemberton Merlot 2008 Rating 90 **To** 2015 $25

Castle Lion Vineyard   ★★★★

Mulberry on Swan, 34 Hamersley Road, Caversham, WA 6055 **Region** Peel
T (08) 9525 4097 **F** (08) 9526 2458 www.castlelion.com.au **Open** Wed–Sun 10–5
Winemaker Stuart Pierce **Est.** 2001 **Cases** 5000 **Vyds** 13.57 ha
This is the venture of the Avila family, with roots going back to the Castilla y Leon region of Spain, and the ancient city of Avila. Planting of the vineyard began in 2001 (shiraz, cabernet sauvignon and merlot) and the vines are grown organically, although not yet certified as such. The Semillon Sauvignon Blanc, with a string of medals to its credit, is made from purchased grapes, one suspects from the Margaret River or similar region. Exports to China and Hong Kong.

ΨΨΨΨΨ **Reserve Range Frankland River Cabernet Sauvignon 2007** Good hue and depth; a very pure expression of Cabernet Sauvignon from start to finish; cassis aromas and flavours are offset by more savoury notes; the texture and structure is especially good. Screwcap. 14.5% alc. **Rating** 93 **To** 2020 $22

Ring Master Viognier 2008 Full yellow-gold; very complex and rich, with apricot and peach, but it wouldn't be easy to drink much more than a glass of this, nor easy to find the right food match. Screwcap. 14.5% alc. **Rating** 90 **To** 2012 $39

ΨΨΨΨ **Sparkling Rose 2007 Rating** 88 **To** 2011 $24

Castle Rock Estate ★★★★★

2660 Porongurup Road, Porongurup, WA 6324 **Region** Porongurup
T (08) 9853 1035 **F** (08) 9853 1010 **www.**castlerockestate.com.au **Open** 7 days 10–5
Winemaker Robert Diletti **Est.** 1983 **Cases** 4000 **Vyds** 11.2 ha

An exceptionally beautifully sited vineyard (riesling, pinot noir, chardonnay, sauvignon blanc, cabernet sauvignon and merlot), winery and cellar door on a 55-ha property with sweeping vistas from the Porongurups, operated by the Diletti family. The standard of viticulture is very high, and the site itself ideally situated (quite apart from its beauty). The two-level winery, set on a natural slope, maximises gravity flow, in particular for crushed must feeding into the press. The Rieslings have always been elegant and have handsomely repaid time in bottle; the Pinot Noir is the most consistent performer in the region; the Shiraz is a great cool-climate example, and Chardonnay has joined a thoroughly impressive quartet, elegance the common link. Rob Diletti's excellent palate and sensitive winemaking mark Castle Rock as one of the superstars of the future. Exports to Japan and Singapore.

ΨΨΨΨΨ **Shiraz 2007** Excellent crimson-purple; an altogether impressive wine that has all
✪ the cool-climate indicia of spice, pepper, plum and licorice, and also the texture and supple tannins that Castle Rock lacked in bygone years. Increased vine age plays a part, along with skilled winemaking born of experience. Screwcap. 13.5% alc. **Rating** 96 **To** 2022 $27

✪ **Great Southern Riesling 2009** Classic Castle Rock style, its undoubted great future becoming apparent on the fine but very intense back-palate, finish and aftertaste where various citrus flavours intermingle with minerally acidity; a wine of great length. Screwcap. 12.5% alc. **Rating** 95 **To** 2025 $21

✪ **Diletti Chardonnay 2008** The wine combines textural and flavour complexity with a steely core of acidity; nutty characters are the background to stone fruit and grapefruit flavours; the balance is very good, and the wine will only get better. Two trophies Sydney Wine Show '10. Screwcap. 13% alc. **Rating** 94 **To** 2015 $27

✪ **Pinot Noir 2008** Bright red; spotless aromas of cherry and plum lead into a pure palate, with primary fruit characters still foremost. It is another step along the way in Rob Diletti's pinot noir journey, and bodes very well for the future – and for this wine, which won the trophy for Best Pinot Noir at the Melbourne Wine Show '09. Screwcap. 13% alc. **Rating** 94 **To** 2015 $28

Catherine Vale Vineyard ★★★★

656 Milbrodale Road, Bulga, NSW 2330 **Region** Hunter Valley
T (02) 6579 1334 **F** (02) 6579 1299 **www.**catherinevale.com.au **Open** W'ends & public hols 10–5, or by appt
Winemaker Hunter Wine Services (John Hordern) **Est.** 1994 **Cases** 1500 **Vyds** 4.45 ha

Former schoolteachers Bill and Wendy Lawson have established Catherine Vale as a not-so-idle retirement venture. The lion's share of the vineyard planting is of chardonnay and semillon, with smaller amounts of verdelho, arneis, dolcetto and barbera. The Lawsons chose to plant the latter three varieties after visiting the Piedmont region of Italy, and are very much hands-on viticulturists. Exports to Japan.

ΨΨΨΨΨ **Semillon 2008** Light straw-green; offers an array of herb, spice, grass and lanolin
✪ aromas and flavours, the palate buttressed by firm acidity. Give it four to five years for a surprise. Screwcap. 11% alc. **Rating** 90 **To** 2018 $14

✪ **Madeira NV** I ran the gauntlet of a broken bottle neck to taste this wine, partly because the light orange-brown colour looked good, and I wasn't disappointed. The name Madeira hasn't been specifically caught under the EU Wine Agreement, doubtless because no one on the European side thought about it, but the Hunter Valley has always made some of these almond biscuit and orange-peel wines. Cork. 18% alc. **Rating** 90 **To** 2011 $25

ΨΨΨΨ **Gabrielle Dolcetto Rose 2008** No shortage of colour; unusual style, firm, bone
✪ dry and with a mix of spicy and savoury components. If you want a rose with
meat dishes, this is the go. Screwcap. 10.5% alc. **Rating** 89 **To** 2011 $14
Chardonnay 2008 Rating 87 **To** 2012 $16
Verdelho 2008 Rating 87 **To** 2012 $14
Winifred Barbera 2008 Rating 87 **To** 2013 $19

Caught Redhanded   ★★★☆
1 Esplanade, Sellicks Beach, SA 5174 **Region** Adelaide Zone
T 0419 252 967 **Open** Not
Winemaker Phil Rogers, Linda Domas (Consultant) **Est.** 2009 **Cases** 500
Phil Rogers, a casualty of the 2001 Ansett Airlines collapse, enrolled at the start of '02 in the
CSU Bachelor of Wine Science program, completing his first vintage in '03 at Rosemount
in McLaren Vale. His practical training involved 12 months as the trainee winemaker under
the direction of Adrian Drumm at the Charles Sturt winery, followed by vintage at Hardys
Chateau Reynella, later in the same year making Brunello de Montalcino and Chianti Classico
in Tuscany, then back to commercial production in '07 with McLaren Vale Shiraz and Adelaide
Hills Syrah. Aromatic whites followed in '08, and in '09 the portfolio was expanded to include
very small quantities of Adelaide Hills Pinot Noir, Pinot Gris and Merlot, Langhorne Creek
Cabernet Sauvignon and continuing Shiraz. This hectic pace was easy meat for someone
who had spent the last four years of his career with Ansett in the high-stress world of airline
operations, dealing with bad weather, broken aircraft, sick flight attendants and unpaid pilots.

ΨΨΨΨΩ **McLaren Vale Shiraz 2008** Dense colour; brooding black fruit and dark
chocolate aromas are decidedly accurate portents of the dark, savoury palate
with a strong streak of bitter chocolate; doesn't show any significant alcohol heat.
Screwcap. 15% alc. **Rating** 90 **To** 2020 $20

ΨΨΨΨ **Fortified NV Rating** 89 **To** 2011 $15
Langhorne Creek Cabernet Rose 2009 Rating 87 **To** 2011 $15
Adelaide Hills Syrah 2007 Rating 87 **To** 2013 $25

Celestial Bay   ★★★★★
33 Welwyn Avenue, Manning, WA 6152 (postal) **Region** Margaret River
T (08) 9450 4191 **F** (08) 9313 1544 **www.**celestialbay.com.au **Open** Not
Winemaker Bernard Abbott **Est.** 1999 **Cases** 8000 **Vyds** 60 ha
Michael and Kim O'Brien had a background of farming in the Chittering Valley when
they purchased their 104-ha property. It is very much a family enterprise, with son Aaron
studying viticulture and oenology at Curtin University, and daughter Daneka involved in
marketing and sales. Under the direction of vineyard manager Sam Juniper, vines have been
rapidly planted. The plantings are totally logical: semillon, sauvignon blanc, chardonnay, shiraz,
cabernet sauvignon, merlot, malbec and petit verdot. Winemaker Bernard Abbott celebrated
his 25th Margaret River vintage in 2010. Exports to the UK, the US, Canada, China,
Singapore and Hong Kong.

ΨΨΨΨΨ **Margaret River Shiraz 2008** Deep purple-crimson; has a fragrant bouquet of
✪ black fruits, licorice and spice, then a vividly flavoured palate of dark berry and
spice that thrusts through to a lingering finish. Screwcap. 14% alc. **Rating** 94
To 2020 $25
Zenith 2008 Deep purple-red; a very powerful, focused and intense wine,
cabernet fruit flavours enhanced by petit verdot/shiraz, the petit verdot also
providing much of the high-quality tannin support; will be long lived. Screwcap.
14% alc. **Rating** 94 **To** 2028 $35

ΨΨΨΨΩ **Margaret River Shiraz Cabernet 2008 Rating** 93 **To** 2028 $25

ΨΨΨΨ **Margaret River Cabernet Sauvignon 2008 Rating** 89 **To** 2014 $25
Margaret River Semillon Sauvignon Blanc 2009 Rating 87 **To** 2012 $20 BE

Centennial Vineyards ★★★★★

'Woodside', Centennial Road, Bowral, NSW 2576 **Region** Southern Highlands
T (02) 4861 8700 **F** (02) 4681 8777 **www**.centennial.net.au **Open** 7 days 10–5
Winemaker Tony Cosgriff **Est.** 2002 **Cases** 10 000 **Vyds** 29 ha

CentennialVineyards, a substantial development jointly owned by wine professional John Large and investor Mark Dowling, covers 133 ha of beautiful grazing land, with the vineyard planted to pinot noir (7.6 ha), chardonnay (7 ha), sauvignon blanc (4.2 ha), tempranillo (3.5 ha), pinot gris (2.7 ha), savagnin (2 ha), riesling (1.8 ha) and pinot meunier (0.2 ha). Production from the estate vineyards is supplemented by purchases of grapes from other regions, including Orange. The consistency of the quality of the wines is wholly commendable, reflecting the skilled touch of Tony Cosgriff in a region that often throws up climatic challenges. Exports to the US, Denmark, Singapore, China and Korea.

ＹＹＹＹＹ **Reserve Single Vineyard Riesling [922] 2009** Pale, bright quartz; utterly
✪ delicious lime juice fruit, the sweetness from 22 grammes per litre residual sugar perfectly balanced by zesty acidity; eerily close to Mosel. Screwcap. 9.4% alc. **Rating** 95 **To** 2017 $25

Single Vineyard Reserve Cabernet Sauvignon 2008 Bright purple-red; a powerful, full-bodied evocation of cabernet, with intense blackcurrant and cedar, the question (if there is one) lying with the persistent, earthy tannins, the saving grace being they are not dry. Orange. Diam. 14.8% alc. **Rating** 95 **To** 2023 $30

✪ **Reserve Single Vineyard Riesling [836] 2009** An immaculately made wine, the interplay between residual sugar, acidity and alcohol constantly changing; the balance is such that the sweetness (from 36 grammes per litre of residual sugar) is not at all challenging. Screwcap. 8.4% alc. **Rating** 95 **To** 2017 $25

✪ **Woodside Single Vineyard Riesling [115] 2009** Similar colour to Reserve; all three Rieslings come from the estate vineyard; a fragrant and floral bouquet of lime blossom, then a long, crisp palate with a skein of mineral. 115 indicates 5 grammes per litre residual sugar. Screwcap. 11.1% alc. **Rating** 94 **To** 2017 $20

Reserve Single Vineyard Chardonnay 2008 Bright straw-green; typical elegant Centennial style, the grapefruit and nectarine fruit supported by fine, spicy barrel ferment oak; the palate is long and fine, the finish clean. Screwcap. 13.8% alc. **Rating** 94 **To** 2016 $30

✪ **Single Vineyard Reserve Shiraz Viognier 2007** Still brilliant crimson-red; the bouquet with that unmistakable viognier lift, the palate very juicy and fresh, denying its alcohol (seems lower); the plum fruit has drive through the finish, making oak and tannins bit players. Diam. 14.5% alc. **Rating** 94 **To** 2017 $30

Reserve Single Vineyard Sangiovese 2008 Good colour; a high-quality sangiovese from Orange, its red cherry and savoury spice components in perfect balance; very good texture. Screwcap. 14.3% alc. **Rating** 94 **To** 2013 $30

ＹＹＹＹＹ **Reserve Pinot Noir 2008 Rating** 93 **To** 2011 $30
Reserve Cabernet Merlot 2008 Rating 92 **To** 2016 $30
Bowral Extreme Brut NV Rating 92 **To** 2014 $30
Woodside Single Vineyard Sauvignon Blanc 2009 Rating 91 **To** 2011 $22
✪ **Winery Block Chardonnay 2008** Although the alcohol is slightly lower than Old Block, there are touches of white peach and nectarine absent from the Old Block. That said, the acidity is high, and both wines are relatively austere. Screwcap. 12.6% alc. **Rating** 91 **To** 2015 $20
Woodside Single Vineyard Shiraz 2008 Rating 91 **To** 2018 $23
Reserve Single Vineyard Barbera 2008 Rating 91 **To** 2015 $30
Pinot Noir Chardonnay NV Rating 91 **To** 2013 $28
Old Block Chardonnay 2008 Rating 90 **To** 2014 $20
Woodside Pinot Noir 2008 Rating 90 **To** 2013 $23
Brut Rose NV Rating 90 **To** 2013 $28

Ceravolo Wines ★★★★☆

Suite 16, 172 Glynburn Road, Tranmere, SA 5073 (postal) **Region** Adelaide Plains
T (08) 8336 4522 **F** (08) 8365 0538 **www.**ceravolo.com.au **Open** Not
Winemaker Joe Ceravolo, Colin Glaetzer, Ben Glaetzer (Contract) **Est.** 1985 **Cases** 20 000
Dentist turned vigneron and winemaker, Joe Ceravolo, and his wife, Heather, have been
producing single-vineyard wines from their estate on the Adelaide Plains since 1999. Significant
wine show success has added to the reputation of their brand, particularly with Shiraz, Petit
Verdot, Merlot and Sangiovese. Their son Antony, with wife Fiona, is now working with them
to take their family business into the next generation. The Ceravolos are also establishing new
vineyards around their home in the Adelaide Hills, focusing on cooler climate Italian varieties
such as picolit and primitivo. Wines are released under Ceravolo, St Andrews Estate and
export-only Red Earth labels. Exports to the UK, the US and other major markets.

♟♟♟♟♟ **Adelaide Plains Petit Verdot 2007** Strong, deep crimson-purple; dense plum,
prune and blackberry flavours are achieved without harsh extract, and easily
carry the alcohol. This is Ceravolo's ace in the hole. Cork. 15% alc. **Rating** 94
To 2017 $25

♟♟♟♟♀ **Adelaide Plains Sangiovese Rose 2009** Pale pink; an aromatic bouquet with
✪ red cherry and strawberry dominant; the palate moves to pure red cherry, crisp,
dry and very long, the acidity with a subliminal savoury character. Very satisfying
style. Screwcap. 13% alc. **Rating** 93 To 2012 $17

✪ **The Raconteur Australian Vintage Shiraz 2008** Dark, deep red-purple; well
made; the relatively low baume allows the spice, chocolate and black fruits to have
free play; the length is good, as is the overall balance. Screwcap. 18% alc. **Rating** 90
To 2017 $18

♟♟♟♟ **Adelaide Plains Cabernet Sauvignon 2008 Rating** 89 To 2016 $20

Chain of Ponds ★★★★★

Adelaide Road, Gumeracha, SA 5233 **Region** Adelaide Hills
T (08) 8389 1415 **F** (08) 8389 1877 **www.**chainofponds.com.au **Open** Mon–Fri 9.30–
4.30, w'ends & public hols 10.30–4.30
Winemaker Greg Clack **Est.** 1993 **Cases** 35 000
The Chain of Ponds brand has been separated from the now-sold 200 ha of vineyards, which
were among the largest in the Adelaide Hills. It is now owned by Chris Milner and has
contract growers throughout the Adelaide Hills for the Chain of Ponds label, two single-
vineyard reds from Kangaroo Island, and the Norello blends with a SA appellation. Exports to
the UK, the US, Canada, Singapore, Vietnam, China and NZ.

♟♟♟♟♟ **Corkscrew Rd Adelaide Hills Chardonnay 2006** Attractive wine from start
to finish; yellow and white peach flavours, subtle French oak in the backdrop;
good mouthfeel and length. Screwcap. 13.5% alc. **Rating** 94 To 2015 $33

The Cachet Adelaide Cabernet Sauvignon Shiraz Merlot 2004 A dark
and savoury wine, with black fruits framed by a struck match complexity; the
palate is full, rich, savoury and drying, with vibrant acidity leading the charge, and
providing length to the almost chewy and tannic structure of the wine. Cork.
13.5% alc. **Rating** 94 To 2018 $60 BE

♟♟♟♟♀ **Novello Adelaide Hills Semillon Sauvignon Blanc 2009** Interesting
✪ capsicum, grass and cucumber aromas, backing off slightly on the palate, there
yielding to some attractive tropical notes. Has character. Screwcap. 12.5% alc.
Rating 91 To 2012 $14

✪ **Grave's Gate Adelaide Shiraz 2007** Better colour hue, better freshness and
better flavours than most '07 reds at this price point (or higher, perhaps); has
supple, ripe red and black cherry fruit plus spice and a hint of licorice; tannin and
oak handling good. Screwcap. 14% alc. **Rating** 91 To 2017 $19.95

Black Thursday Adelaide Hills Sauvignon Blanc 2009 Rating 90
To 2010 $19.95

The Ledge Adelaide Hills Shiraz 2007 Rating 90 To 2016 $30 BE
The Ledge Adelaide Hills Shiraz 2006 Rating 90 To 2016 $30

ΨΨΨΨ Novello Adelaide Hills Rose 2009 Pale fuchsia-pink; a delicately fragrant
✪ bouquet of cherry and raspberry, then a well-balanced palate. Sangiovese. Screwcap.
11% alc. Rating 89 To 2011 $14
The Amadeus Adelaide Hills Cabernet Sauvignon 2006 Rating 87
To 2012 $30

Chalice Bridge Estate ★★★★★

796 Rosa Glen Road, Margaret River, WA 6285 **Region** Margaret River
T (08) 9433 5200 **F** (08) 9433 5211 **www**.chalicebridge.com.au **Open** By appt
Winemaker Bob Cartwright (Consultant) **Est.** 1998 **Cases** 20 000 **Vyds** 122 ha
Planting of the vineyard (now fully owned by the Edinger family) began in 1998; there are
now over 28 ha each of cabernet sauvignon and shiraz, 27 ha of chardonnay, 12.5 ha of
semillon, 18 ha of sauvignon blanc and 7.5 ha of merlot; it is the second-largest single vineyard
in Margaret River. The 2006 appointment of former Leeuwin Estate senior winemaker Bob
Cartwright was major news. Sensible pricing also helps, cross-subsidised by the sale of the
major part of the annual crop. Exports to Macau, Vietnam, Hong Kong and China.

ΨΨΨΨΨ The Chalice Limited Release Margaret River Chardonnay 2007 At July
'09, still unbelievably pale green, the wine having dismissed its 14 months in new
French oak with ease; it has superb finesse and balance, and a very long future
during which time it will continue to gain complexity. Screwcap. 13.5% alc.
Rating 95 To 2020 $50
✪ Margaret River Shiraz Cabernet Sauvignon 2007 The deep purple-crimson
colour accurately suggests a very good wine is to follow; there is an abundance of
black fruits that have a common core of supple vibrancy, oak merely a backdrop.
It's a wine designed to be enjoyed without effort. Screwcap. 14.5% alc. Rating 95
To 2020 $25.95
✪ Margaret River Merlot 2007 Bright crimson; an aromatic bouquet with small
berry fruit and a nice touch of olive; fine, gently savoury tannins click in on the
palate, which has excellent varietal expression and mouthfeel. Screwcap. 14.5% alc.
Rating 95 To 2020 $25.95
✪ Margaret River Cabernet Sauvignon 2007 A generous wine; cassis and
blackcurrant flavours run through the supple medium-bodied palate; tannins fine,
good oak. Screwcap. 13.5% alc. Rating 94 To 2020 $25.95

ΨΨΨΨΨ Margaret River Cabernet Sauvignon Merlot 2007 Solid red-purple; positive
✪ varietal fruit aromas come through on the medium- to full-bodied palate, where
tannins soon make themselves felt; needs a few years, but will definitely repay
patience. Screwcap. 13.5% alc. Rating 91 To 2020 $19.95

ΨΨΨΨ Margaret River Sauvignon Blanc 2009 Rating 89 To 2011 $19.95
Margaret River Wild Rose 2008 Rating 89 To 2011 $19.95
Margaret River Shiraz 2007 Rating 89 To 2017 $25.95

Chalk Hill ★★★★★

PO Box 205, McLaren Vale, SA 5171 **Region** McLaren Vale
T (08) 8556 2121 **F** (08) 8556 2221 **www**.chalkhill.com.au **Open** Not
Winemaker Emmanuelle Bekkers **Est.** 1973 **Cases** 35 000 **Vyds** 74.3 ha
The growth of Chalk Hill has accelerated after passing from parents John and Diana Harvey to
grapegrowing sons Jock and Tom. Both are heavily involved in wine industry affairs in varying
capacities (Tom was a participant in the second intake of the Wine Industry Future Leaders
Program) and the business has strong links with Greening Australia. (Chalk Hill donates 25c
for each bottle sold, the highest per-bottle donation in the Australian wine industry.) Further
acquisitions mean the vineyards now span each subregion of McLaren Vale, and have been
planted to both the exotic (savagnin, barbera and sangiovese) and the mainstream (shiraz,

cabernet sauvignon, grenache, chardonnay and cabernet franc). Exports to all major markets; exports to the US and Canada under the Wits End label.

ᵀᵀᵀᵀᵀ **Reserve McLaren Vale Shiraz 2008** Dense, opaque purple; Chalk Hill nailed the picking date, for this wine is not overripe nor extractive, just unfathomably deep on both bouquet and palate; blackberry, licorice, chocolate and plum all compete for attention, oak and tannins conceding defeat. Screwcap. 14.5% alc. **Rating** 96 **To** 2040 $50

Alpha Crucis McLaren Vale Shiraz 2008 Dense purple-crimson; a massive shiraz full of black fruits, licorice and dark chocolate; despite its concentration, is neither jammy nor unduly extractive. Screwcap. 14% alc. **Rating** 94 **To** 2030 $60

Alpha Crucis McLaren Vale Cabernet Sauvignon 2008 Red-purple; a complex medium- to full-bodied wine with strong varietal expression; blackcurrant fruit has fine-grained, savoury tannins running through it; excellent length and balance; a triumph for the vintage. Screwcap. 14.5% alc. **Rating** 94 **To** 2023 $60

ᵀᵀᵀᵀᵀ **McLaren Vale Cabernet Sauvignon 2008 Rating** 92 **To** 2028 $25
McLaren Vale Sangiovese 2008 Rating 92 **To** 2014 $25
McLaren Vale Shiraz 2007 Rating 90 **To** 2017 $25

✪ **The Procrastinator 2009** Light, bright crimson; attractive cassis and red cherry fruit aromas and flavours, structure provided by fine tannins. Cabernet Franc. Screwcap. 13% alc. **Rating** 90 **To** 2016 $20

ᵀᵀᵀᵀ **Rose 2009 Rating** 89 **To** 2011 $20
McLaren Vale Barbera 2008 Rating 89 **To** 2015 $30

Chalkers Crossing ★★★★★

285 Grenfell Road, Young, NSW 2594 **Region** Hilltops
T (02) 6382 6900 **F** (02) 6382 5068 **www**.chalkerscrossing.com.au **Open** Mon–Fri 9–5
Winemaker Celine Rousseau **Est.** 2000 **Cases** 10 000 **Vyds** 10 ha
Owned and operated by Ted and Wendy Ambler, Chalkers Crossing's Rockleigh Vineyard was planted in 1997–98. It also purchases grapes from Tumbarumba and Gundagai. Winemaker Celine Rousseau was born in France's Loire Valley, trained in Bordeaux and has worked in Bordeaux, Champagne, Languedoc, Margaret River and the Perth Hills. This Flying Winemaker (now an Australian citizen) has exceptional skills and dedication. Exports to the UK, Canada, Ireland, Germany, Denmark, Sweden, Singapore, China, Hong Kong and Japan.

ᵀᵀᵀᵀᵀ **Hilltops Shiraz 2007** Deep crimson; spicy, charry, black fruits on the bouquet, then a luscious and complex palate, fruit, oak and tannins playing chasey with each other; extreme overall complexity. The Achilles heel is the alcohol. Screwcap. 15.5% alc. **Rating** 95 **To** 2027 $30

✪ **Tumbarumba Chardonnay 2008** Displays all the usual elegance and subtlety of Chalkers Crossing Chardonnays; white peach and grapefruit sit with more creamy cashew notes; a restrained and pure wine in every way. Screwcap. 14% alc. **Rating** 94 **To** 2014 $22

Hilltops Shiraz 2008 Bright colour; the bouquet exhibits a multifaceted personality of black fruits, vanilla, spice and a little tar; the palate is warm and unctuous with ample levels of black and blue fruits; silky and fine to conclude. Gold medal Sydney Wine Show '10. Screwcap. 15% alc. **Rating** 94 **To** 2018 $30 BE

ᵀᵀᵀᵀᵀ
✪ **Hilltops Semillon 2009** Vivid green hue; restrained bouquet showing straw and lemon; the palate is tightly wound at first, opening with surprising generosity; clean, fresh and vibrant to conclude. Screwcap. 12.5% alc. **Rating** 93 **To** 2015 $18 BE

✪ **Hilltops Riesling 2009** A wine that is as much about structure as flavour; citrus, apple and green pear flavours coalesce on the strong palate and long finish; six months on lees in tank is the key. Screwcap. 12.5% alc. **Rating** 91 **To** 2018 $18

⊙   **Kingsvale Hilltops Shiraz 2009** Vibrant hue; lifted purple fruit bouquet, with a gentle underpinning of iodine and licorice; medium-bodied with a savoury edge to the quite plump fruit on offer; distinctly European in style. Screwcap. 14% alc. **Rating** 91 **To** 2015 $18 BE

♟♟♟♟   **Tumbarumba Sauvignon Blanc 2009** **Rating** 89 **To** 2012 $18 BE

Chalmers   ★★★★

PO Box 2263, Mildura, Vic 3502 **Region** Murray Darling/Heathcote
T 0400 261 932 **F** (03) 9038 4458 **www.chalmerswine.com.au Open** Not
Winemaker Sandro Mosele (Contract) **Est.** 1989 **Cases** 4000 **Vyds** 19 ha
In March 2008, founders Bruce and Jenny Chalmers sold (to Macquarie Diversified Agriculture Fund) what was the largest vine nursery propagation business in Australia, plus 650 ha of planted vines, an additional 600 ha available for planting, plus 1500 ha of protected forest along a 14-km Murray River frontage. The Chalmers have, however, kept the brands and the winemaking side of the business, with a medium-term grape-supply contract from Macquarie. The future home of Chalmers is an 80-ha property on the Mt Camel Range, 50 km north of Heathcote. The east-facing, sloped block, running to the top of the ridge, is being planted to vermentino, fiano, greco di tufo, moscato giallo, nero d'avola, lagrein, sagrantino, lambrusco maestri, aglianico, shiraz and malbec. Exports to the UK and Denmark.

♟♟♟♟♟   **Vermentino 2009** Early picking and modest alcohol underpin a delicious light-bodied white wine, with lemon, stone fruit and mineral flavours running through the palate and aftertaste. Screwcap. 11.5% alc. **Rating** 92 **To** 2013 $25
Nero d'Avola 2009 Clear, light colour; bright red fruits run through the bouquet and palate in a wine that is halfway between rose and conventional red wine; has a cleansing savoury/lemony twist on the finish. Diam. 13% alc. **Rating** 90 **To** 2014 $29

♟♟♟♟   **Negroamaro Rosato 2009** **Rating** 88 **To** 2011 $18
Sagrantino 2008 **Rating** 88 **To** 2013 $31
Fiano 2009 **Rating** 87 **To** 2011 $25
Lagrein 2006 **Rating** 87 **To** 2026 $27

Chambers Rosewood   ★★★★★

Barkly Street, Rutherglen, Vic 3685 **Region** Rutherglen
T (02) 6032 8641 **F** (02) 6032 8101 **www.chambersrosewood.com.au**
Open Mon–Sat 9–5, Sun 10–5
Winemaker Stephen Chambers **Est.** 1858 **Cases** 15 000 **Vyds** 50 ha
On the basis of these tasting notes, joyfully written after the Chambers family relented and sent samples of its greatest fortified wines, one is left with no option but to say Chambers Rare Muscat and Rare Muscadelle (or Topaque or Tokay, what's in a name?) are the greatest of all in the Rutherglen firmament. Exports to the UK, the US, Belgium, Sweden and NZ.

♟♟♟♟♟   **Rare Rutherglen Muscat NV** Beautifully fragrant, with a sense of true age, depth and power; floral on entry, the acidity is extraordinary and gives the wine amazing life and nerve; the layers of flavour are almost countless, and this wine is truly something that every wine lover must experience at least once in their lives; one sip was taken for this entire note and the flavour is still building; thanks to the Chambers for sending these in this year. Cork. 18% alc. **Rating** 98 **To** 2011 $250
Rare Rutherglen Muscadelle NV Pure power and grace, showing surprising restraint and poise; heavily toasted nuts, and the essence of old, yet fresh material; prunes, fresh oak and very clean fortifying spirit provide the springboard for an experience that stays for minutes; suggested to be enjoyed with food, but maybe best contemplated on its own. Cork. 18% alc. **Rating** 97 **To** 2020 $250 BE

Special Rutherglen Tokay NV Attractive olive-green hue; explosive toasted toffee, ground grilled nuts, a touch of cold tea and plenty of bitter chocolate; the palate is layered, long, luscious and completely delicious, and the dark chocolate character holds on for the longest time; staggering complexity. Cork. 18% alc. Rating 96 To 2011 $125 BE

Grand Rutherglen Muscat NV A very appealing balance between freshness and age, with touches of oak, bitter almonds, toffee and some lifted floral, musky notes; the palate is poised, weighty and shows a very pleasant burnt caramel character on the finish; delicious. Screwcap. 18% alc. Rating 95 To 2011 $65 BE

ΥΥΥΥΥ Rutherglen Durif 2008 Excellent hue; full of vibrant and juicy red and black
✪   fruit flavours, and amazingly gives no sign whatsoever of its alcohol; drink a little
        and be merry. Screwcap. 16.1% alc. Rating 90 To 2012 $16

✪   Sweet Amber Rutherglen Apera NV Another vibrant and fresh wine, here
        halfway between what used to be called Amontillado and Oloroso respectively; it
        has an almost juicy finish that is totally beguiling. Screwcap. 18% alc. Rating 90
        To 2011 $15

ΥΥΥΥ   Dry Flor Rutherglen Apera NV Fresh and dry; despite an age of between 5
✪   and 8 years, does not have a great deal of flor character; on the other hand, has
        length, and is very refreshing. Screwcap. 18% alc. Rating 89 To 2011 $10

✪   Rutherglen Muscat NV Pink-orange; a blend of 2–4-year-old wines, and
        still showing the spicy/grapey/raisiny flavours of young muscat – but of quality.
        Screwcap. 18.5% alc. Rating 89 To 2011 $16

✪   Rutherglen Muscadelle NV Yellow-golden bronze; intense tea and butterscotch
        flavours are just starting to move towards more biscuity/cake flavours. Screwcap.
        18.5% alc. Rating 89 To 2011 $16

Chanters Ridge   ★★★★

440 Chanters Lane, Tylden, Vic 3444 **Region** Macedon Ranges
T 0427 511 341 **F** (03) 5424 8140 **www**.chantersridge.com.au **Open** W'ends 10–4 by appt
Winemaker Hanging Rock Winery **Est.** 1995 **Cases** 450 **Vyds** 2 ha
Orthopaedic surgeon Barry Elliott, as well as running the surgery unit at Melbourne's Alfred Hospital, has became involved with the Kyneton Hospital. He and his wife acquired the 24-ha property without any clear idea of what they might do with it; later his lifelong interest in wine steered him towards the idea of establishing a vineyard. He retained John Ellis as his consultant, and this led to the planting of pinot noir, and the first tiny make in 2000.

ΥΥΥΥΥ Macedon Ranges Blanc de Noirs 2003 Deep gold; five years on yeast lees;
        very complex and rich, with an overlay of honey and brioche; astute dosage to
        keep the finish dry. Diam. 12.5% alc. Rating 93 To 2012 $30

ΥΥΥΥ   Macedon Ranges Sparkling Pinot Noir NV Disgorged Sept '09, but no
✪   information on tirage date; bright spicy red cherry fruit and a pleasing dry finish.
        Diam. 13.5% alc. Rating 89 To 2012 $19.80

        Macedon Ranges Pinot Noir Rose 2008 Rating 88 To 2010 $19.80
        Macedon Ranges Pinot Noir 2006 Rating 87 To 2014 $25
        Back Paddock Macedon Ranges Pinot Noir 2005 Rating 87 To 2013 $22

Chapel Hill   ★★★★★

Chapel Hill Road, McLaren Vale, SA 5171 **Region** McLaren Vale
T (08) 8323 8429 **F** (08) 8323 9245 **www**.chapelhillwine.com.au **Open** 7 days 12–5
Winemaker Michael Fragos, Bryn Richards **Est.** 1979 **Cases** 50 000 **Vyds** 44 ha
A leading medium-sized winery in the region. In 2000 Chapel Hill was sold to the Swiss Thomas Schmidheiny group, which owns the respected Cuvaison winery in California as well as vineyards in Switzerland and Argentina. Wine quality is as good, if not better, than ever. Winemaker Michael Fragos was named Winemaker of the Year at London's International Wine & Spirit Competition '08. The production comes from the estate plantings of shiraz,

cabernet sauvignon, chardonnay, verdelho, savagnin, sangiovese and merlot, together with purchased grapes from McLaren Vale. Exports to all major markets.

ΨΨΨΨΨ **The Vicar McLaren Vale Shiraz 2008** A massive wine with impenetrable colour; there is simply more of everything, but it never appears overly heavy; red and black fruits are evident, with dark chocolate and some toasty oak adding seasoning; the palate is surprisingly accessible, with vibrant acidity providing red fruit highlights and freshness on the finish. Screwcap. 14.5% alc. **Rating** 95 **To** 2025 $60 BE
Bush Vine McLaren Vale Grenache 2008 Vibrant hue; a generous offering of sweet red fruits, supported by a touch of Provençal herbs for complexity; very fleshy mid-palate, there is real depth to the fruit in this wine, signing off with a slight savoury finish; classic. Screwcap. 15% alc. **Rating** 95 **To** 2015 $30 BE
McLaren Vale Cabernet Sauvignon 2008 Deep, dense colour; just as with the Shiraz, the region speaks loud and clear, but does not pervert the excellent display of varietal fruit with its array of blackcurrant and mulberry (and dark chocolate) fruit; excellent tannins and good oak are further pluses. Screwcap. 14% alc. **Rating** 95 **To** 2028 $30
McLaren Vale Shiraz 2008 Dense, deep purple-crimson; one shift and bang, McLaren Vale dark chocolate and luscious blackberry, plum and blueberry fruit leap from the glass, the palate a precise replicate; oak plays a lesser role in a distinguished wine. Screwcap. 14.5% alc. **Rating** 94 **To** 2020 $30

ΨΨΨΨΨ **Parson's Nose McLaren Vale Shiraz 2008** Deep colour; the bouquet
✪ proclaims its regional origins with a generous dollop of dark chocolate along with the black fruits; the palate is a generous replay of the same flavours, and has good overall balance and structure. Screwcap. 14.5% alc. **Rating** 93 **To** 2018 $16
House Block McLaren Vale Shiraz 2008 Rating 93 **To** 2018 $50 BE
✪ **il Vescovo McLaren Vale Savagnin 2009** Bright straw-green; a fragrant orange blossom bouquet leads into a vital and vibrant palate with lots of minerality and zest; good length and clean finish. Screwcap. 12.5% alc. **Rating** 92 **To** 2014 $22
McLaren Vale Chardonnay 2008 Rating 91 **To** 2014 $25
✪ **Il Vescovo McLaren Vale Sangiovese Rose 2009** Lively fresh and crisp red cherry; good length and a zesty finish; no residual sugar to speak of. Screwcap. 12.5% alc. **Rating** 91 **To** 2010 $16
Road Block McLaren Vale Shiraz 2008 Rating 91 **To** 2018 $50 BE
Il Vescovo Adelaide Hills Pinot Grigio 2009 Rating 90 **To** 2010 $22
Il Vescovo McLaren Vale Sangiovese 2008 Rating 90 **To** 2016 $20
Il Vescovo Adelaide Hills Tempranillo 2008 Rating 90 **To** 2013 $22

ΨΨΨΨ **McLaren Vale Verdelho 2009 Rating** 89 **To** 2013 $16

Chapman Grove Wines   ★★★★★

PO Box 1460, Margaret River, WA 6285 **Region** Margaret River
T (08) 9757 7444 **F** (08) 9757 7477 **www**.chapmangrove.com.au **Open** Not
Winemaker Bruce Dukes (Contract) **Est.** 2005 **Cases** 10 000 **Vyds** 32 ha
A very successful venture under the control of managing director Ron Fraser. The contract-made wines come from the extensive estate vineyards planted to chardonnay, semillon, sauvignon blanc, shiraz, cabernet sauvignon and merlot. The wines are released in three price ranges: at the bottom end, the Dreaming Dog red varietals and blends; in the middle, the standard Chapman Grove range; and, at the top, ultra-premium wines under the Atticus label. Exports to Canada, Philippines, Indonesia, Hong Kong, Singapore and China.

ΨΨΨΨΨ **Atticus Margaret River Chardonnay 2008** Pale and bright; spiced pear and nectarine bouquet, showing plenty of toasty oak; the oak comes to the fore on the palate, while showing plenty of sweet fruit; some interesting winemaking complexity in the form of struck match aromas and flavours are evident, and the finish is generous and long. Screwcap. 13.9% alc. **Rating** 94 **To** 2014 $60 BE

Atticus Margaret River Shiraz 2008 Bright cherry red; reminiscent of spiced liqueur cherries, showing a distinct clove aroma to the bouquet; medium-bodied with plenty of red fruit supported by understated oak usage; the tannins are fine and quite silky, and complement the fruit with style. Gold medal Melbourne Wine Show '09. Screwcap. 13.6% alc. **Rating** 94 **To** 2016 $60 BE

�♀♀♀♀♀ Atticus Margaret River Cabernet Sauvignon 2008 **Rating** 93 **To** 2015 $60 BE

✪ Margaret River Semillon Sauvignon Blanc 2009 Both citrus and tropical/ passionfruit aromas on the bouquet are followed by a supple palate that tracks the bouquet precisely; two-thirds semillon promises modest ageing capacity. Screwcap. 12.9% alc. **Rating** 90 **To** 2011 $19

✪ Dreaming Dog Margaret River Chardonnay 2009 I'm not sure the label does the wine justice, for it has considerable intensity and drive, and in some ways heads into sauvignon blanc taste territory with its strong citrus core. Screwcap. 13.6% alc. **Rating** 90 **To** 2012 $15

Margaret River Cabernet Sauvignon 2008 **Rating** 90 **To** 2014 $28 BE

♀♀♀♀ Dreaming Dog Margaret River Merlot 2007 **Rating** 88 **To** 2012 $14.95
Margaret River Chardonnay 2008 **Rating** 87 **To** 2012 $28 BE

Charlatan Wines   ★★★★

Cnr Kangarilla Road/Foggo Road, McLaren Vale, SA 5171 **Region** McLaren Vale
T (08) 8386 3463 **Open** 7 days 10–4
Winemaker Chad Fenton-Smith **Est.** 2005 **Cases** 350

Chad Fenton-Smith has a particularly well developed sense of humour, something that may come in very handy in the industry's turbulent times of 2010 and beyond. His entry into winemaking just happened, the opportunity coming through contacts he had made in the water-tank industry. His first vintage in 2005 was little more than a hobby: 360 bottles of Shiraz made from two rows of vines left over after a big producer had taken its required tonnes from the grapegrower concerned. Production soared to the heady heights of 700 bottles in 2006, and while it was maturing in oak Chad and his partner went to Samuel's Gorge, to spend an hour with winemaker Justin McNamee. After a few glasses of wine Chad decided to quit his job, head to Adelaide University to begin a Bachelor of Science in viticulture and oenology and endeavour to subsist on one-quarter of his previous income. His head is buzzing with ideas, which only the brave or the innocent would contemplate. And the name? Well, it was self-bestowed on someone selling wine made on a whim, and without any winemaking experience whatsoever.

♀♀♀♀♀ The Bastard Son McLaren Vale Merlot 2009 Bright crimson-purple; an
✪   uncommonly true-to-variety wine in the context of McLaren Vale, with vibrant cassis and plum fruit; texture, structure and length are very good. Screwcap. 14.4% alc. **Rating** 91 **To** 2015 $14

♀♀♀♀ Red Mosquito McLaren Vale Cabernet Franc 2009 **Rating** 88 **To** 2013 $14

Charles Melton   ★★★★★

Krondorf Road, Tanunda, SA 5352 **Region** Barossa Valley
T (08) 8563 3606 **F** (08) 8563 3422 **www.**charlesmeltonwines.com.au **Open** 7 days 11–5
Winemaker Charlie Melton, Nicola Robbins **Est.** 1984 **Cases** 15 000 **Vyds** 17.6 ha

Charlie Melton, one of the Barossa Valley's great characters, with wife Virginia by his side, makes some of the most eagerly sought à la mode wines in Australia. Inevitably, the Melton empire has continued to grow in response to the insatiable demand. There are now 7 ha at Lyndoch, 9 ha at Krondorf and 1.6 ha at Light Pass, the lion's share to shiraz and grenache, and a small planting of cabernet sauvignon. An additional 30-ha property was purchased in High Eden, with 10 ha of shiraz planted in 2009, and a 5-ha field planting of grenache, shiraz, mataro, carignan, cinsaut, picpoul and bourboulenc planted in '10. The expanded volume has had no adverse effect on the wonderfully rich, sweet and well-made wines. The original Krondorf village church (circa 1864) has been acquired and converted to guest accommodation. Exports to all major markets.

ᵀᵀᵀᵀᵀ **Barossa Valley Rose of Virginia 2009** Vivid fuchsia, it has fragrant rose petal/
✪ raspberry/spice aromas, then a vibrant, positively flavoured palate in a continuing red fruit spectrum. It has good length and a dry, almost savoury, finish. Serious rose. Screwcap. 12.5% alc. **Rating** 96 **To** 2010 $22.50

✪ **Voices of Angels Shiraz 2007** Slightly more crimson colour is an early sign of a wine with a touch more brightness than the Grains of Paradise; spices and sweet red fruits on the perfumed bouquet lead into a vibrant palate; here the barrel ferment conclusion of the whole bunch primary fermentation in French (60%)/ American (40%) oak barriques followed by lees contact resemble a pinot noir approach. Screwcap. 14.5% alc. **Rating** 96 **To** 2022 $55

Grains of Paradise Shiraz 2007 Good red-purple; attractive spicy, earthy overtones to the black fruits of the bouquet translate into an elegant medium-bodied palate showing none of the toughness of the vintage; instead, the accent is on the length and complexity of the red and black fruit flavours, the tannins positively silky. Screwcap. 14.5% alc. **Rating** 95 **To** 2022 $55

ᵀᵀᵀᵀ **The Father In Law Shiraz 2006 Rating** 89 **To** 2014 $21

Charles Sturt University Winery ★★★★
McKeown Drive (off Coolamon Road), Wagga Wagga, NSW 2650 **Region** Big Rivers Zone
T (02) 6933 2435 **F** (02) 6933 4072 **www**.csu.edu.au/winery **Open** Mon–Fri 11–5, w'ends 11–4
Winemaker Andrew Drumm **Est.** 1977 **Cases** 15 000 **Vyds** 26.6 ha
A new $2.5 million commercial winery was opened in 2002, complementing the $1 million experimental winery opened in '01. The commercial winery was funded through the sale of wines produced under the CSU brand, which always offer exceptional value. Following the University's acquisition of the former University of Sydney campus in Orange, it now has 9.8 ha of estate plantings at Wagga Wagga and 16.8 ha of mature vineyards at Orange, the latter planted to chardonnay, sauvignon blanc, shiraz, cabernet sauvignon and merlot. Interestingly, this teaching facility is using screwcaps for all its wines, white and red, recalling its pioneering use in 1977. Moreover, since 2005 its sparkling wines have been released under crown seal.

ᵀᵀᵀᵀᵀ **Chardonnay 2009** Pale straw-green; a highly aromatic bouquet of grapefruit,
✪ white peach and white flowers leads into a finely framed, light-bodied palate, with a touch of French oak. Screwcap. 12.5% alc. **Rating** 93 **To** 2012 $14.30

Limited Release The College Muscat NV Lovely, clean, grapey muscat, with just enough aged complexity to provide a luscious, textural mouthful of Rutherglen heaven. Screwcap. 18.5% alc. **Rating** 92 **To** 2020 $18

✪ **Shiraz 2008** Made from grapes grown in Orange/Gundagai, the former framing the style; light- to medium-bodied and elegant, with cherry fruit, fine tannins and subtle oak. Delicious early drinking. Screwcap. 14.5% alc. **Rating** 91 **To** 2012 $14

✪ **Cellar Reserve Tumbarumba Rose 2009** Bright pink; a floral bouquet with distinct strawberry aromas, the palate well balanced and long, with a pleasingly dry finish. Screwcap. 12% alc. **Rating** 90 **To** 2011 $15

✪ **Limited Release Orange Pinot Noir Chardonnay 2007** Some bottle-developed characters, but primarily driven by incisive fruit in a citrus and stone fruit spectrum. Crown seal. 13% alc. **Rating** 90 **To** 2013 $20

ᵀᵀᵀᵀ **Cellar Reserve Cabernet Shiraz 2008 Rating** 89 **To** 2020 $28
Limited Release Sparkling Shiraz NV Rating 88 **To** 2010 $20

Chartley Estate ★★★★
38 Blackwood Hills Road, Rowella, Tas 7270 **Region** Northern Tasmania
T (03) 6394 7198 **F** (03) 6394 7598 **www**.chartleyestatevineyard.com.au **Open** Not
Winemaker Winemaking Tasmania (Julian Alcorso) **Est.** 2000 **Cases** 1250

The Kossman family began the establishment of 2 ha each of pinot gris, sauvignon blanc and pinot noir, and 1 ha of riesling in 2000. Although the vines are still relatively young, some attractive wines from each variety have been made. Exports to Taiwan.

ΨΨΨΨΨ **Riesling 2007** Unrecognisable from the wine when first tasted, one of several from the '07 vintage that hid their light under a bushel when tasted one or two years ago. Has floral lime blossom aromas and a wonderfully fresh palate with juicy lime flavours, and impeccable line and length. Two trophies Tas Wine Show '10. Screwcap. 12.9% alc. **Rating** 94 **To** 2016 $19.95

ΨΨΨΨ **Black Crow Pinot Noir 2008 Rating** 89 **To** 2014 $25
Pinot Gris 2009 Rating 87 **To** 2011 $22.95

Chateau Dorrien   ★★★★

Cnr Seppeltsfield Road/Barossa Valley Way, Dorrien, SA 5352 **Region** Barossa Valley
T (08) 8562 2850 **F** (08) 8562 1416 **www**.chateaudorrien.com.au **Open** 7 days 10–5
Winemaker Fernando and Ramon Martin **Est.** 1985 **Cases** 4000 **Vyds** 28 ha
The Martin family, headed by Fernando and Jeanette, purchased the old Dorrien winery from the Seppelt family in 1984; in '90 the family purchased Twin Valley Estate and moved the winemaking operations of Chateau Dorrien to the Twin Valley site. All the Chateau Dorrien group wines are sold at Chateau Dorrien; Twin Valley is simply a production facility. In 2006 the Martin family purchased a 32-ha property at Myponga, with mature vineyards that now provide the grapes for San Fernando Estate, as the new name of the vineyard.

ΨΨΨΨΩ **San Fernando Estate Cloud Catcher Sauvignon Blanc 2009** Light straw-
✪   green; a strong herb, grass and capsicum bouquet, adding citrus to the long palate. A quality wine at any price. Screwcap. 12% alc. **Rating** 93 **To** 2011 $15
Barossa Valley Shiraz 2007 Strong crimson-purple; ripe plum, prune and blackberry aromas with an overlay of vanillan oak on the bouquet; a full-bodied shiraz with more luscious, supple fruit than normally encountered from '07. Diam. 14.8% alc. **Rating** 90 **To** 2020 $25

ΨΨΨΨ **San Fernando Estate Cross Winds Merlot 2009** Good colour; from the
✪   single San Fernando vineyard; has an attractive mix of plum, cassis and chocolate, the tannins fine. Screwcap. 14.3% alc. **Rating** 89 **To** 2016 $18
✪   **Golden Harvest Riesling 2009** While not about to bring the Germans to their knees, this is a well-made wine that balances lime fruit, some sweetness and acidity so well that you notice the fruit more than the sweetness. Screwcap. 9% alc. **Rating** 89 **To** 2011 $15

Chateau Francois   ★★★★★

Broke Road, Pokolbin, NSW 2321 **Region** Hunter Valley
T (02) 4998 7548 **F** (02) 4998 7805 **Open** W'ends 9–5, or by appt
Winemaker Don Francois **Est.** 1969 **Cases** 200
I have known former NSW Director of Fisheries Dr Don Francois for almost as long as I have been involved with wine, which is a very long time indeed. I remember his early fermenta-tions of sundry substances other than grapes (none of which, I hasten to add, were the least bit illegal) in the copper bowl of an antiquated washing machine in his laundry. He established Chateau Francois one year before Brokenwood, and our winemaking and fishing paths have crossed many times since. Some years ago Don suffered a mild stroke, and no longer speaks or writes with any fluency, but this has not stopped him from producing a range of absolutely beautiful semillons that flourish marvellously with age. I should add that he is even prouder of the distinguished career of his daughter, Rachel Francois, at the NSW bar. The semillon vines are now 40 years old, producing exceptional wine that is sold for the proverbial song year after year. Five-star value.

ΨΨΨΨΨ **Pokolbin Mallee Semillon 2008** The leaping trout on the label was painted
✪   by Don Francois, recalling his tenure as Director of Fisheries NSW; the wine has vibrant lemon and mineral flavours and great length to the palate. Screwcap. 11% alc. **Rating** 94 **To** 2022 $14

✪ **Pokolbin Mallee Semillon 2007** Bright glowing green-yellow; voluminous aromas of lemon, herb and grass lead into a palate in the early stages of its development, yet still braced by zesty acidity that will sustain it through its life. Screwcap. 12% alc. **Rating** 94 **To** 2022 $14

✪ **Pokolbin Mallee Semillon 2003** Light, bright glowing green-straw; a super-lively and intense palate, lingering acidity prolonging the finish. Some bottle variation on the record, a trophy one show, low points the next. Cork. 11% alc. **Rating** 94 **To** 2013 $14

♟♟♟♟ **Sparkling Pinot Noir 2002** Interesting wine; it is not clear how long it has been
✪ in bottle, and on lees, but is certainly at the peak of its development, its gentle red fruits with a barely sweet finish. Cork. 13.3% alc. **Rating** 89 **To** 2014 $18

Chateau Leamon   ★★★★☆
5528 Calder Highway, Bendigo, Vic 3550 **Region** Bendigo
T (03) 5447 7995 **F** (03) 5447 0855 **www**.chateauleamon.com.au **Open** Wed–Mon 11–5
Winemaker Ian Leamon **Est.** 1973 **Cases** 2000 **Vyds** 8 ha
One of the longest-established wineries in the region, with estate and locally grown shiraz and cabernet family grapes providing the excellent red wines. Ian Leamon is the second generation of the family to be involved, taking responsibility for winemaking in the 1980s. The estate-grown shiraz, cabernet merlot and semillon is supplemented by riesling from the Strathbogie Ranges. Exports to Canada and Singapore.

♟♟♟♟♟ **Bendigo Shiraz 2008** Fresh red-crimson; a totally delicious medium-bodied
✪ wine, with a silky texture to its gently spicy array of cherry, plum and blackberry fruit, finishing with fine tannins. Screwcap. 14.3% alc. **Rating** 94 **To** 2018 $23

♟♟♟♟♟ **Bendigo Cabernet Sauvignon Cabernet Franc Merlot 2008** Clear
✪ crimson-purple; shares the elegance of the Shiraz, with bell-clear fruit flavours of blackcurrant, plum and raspberry; fine tannins and good oak. Screwcap. 14.5% alc. **Rating** 93 **To** 2018 $23

Chateau Pâto   ★★★★★
67 Thompsons Road, Pokolbin, NSW 2321 **Region** Hunter Valley
T (02) 4998 7634 **F** (02) 4998 7860 **Open** By appt
Winemaker Nicholas Paterson **Est.** 1980 **Cases** 500 **Vyds** 2.5 ha
Nicholas Paterson took over responsibility for this tiny winery following the death of father David during the 1993 vintage. The lion's share of plantings are to shiraz (the first plantings), with smaller blocks of chardonnay, marsanne, roussanne and viognier and mourvedre; most of the grapes are sold, with a tiny quantity of shiraz being made into a marvellous wine. David's legacy is being handsomely guarded. No wine was made in 2008 due to heavy rainfall; the '09s were due for release shortly after publication of this edition.

Chateau Tanunda   ★★★★★
9 Basedow Road, Tanunda, SA 5352 **Region** Barossa Valley
T (08) 8563 3888 **F** (08) 8563 1422 **www**.chateautanunda.com **Open** 7 days 10–5
Winemaker Tim Smith **Est.** 1890 **Cases** 50 000 **Vyds** 95 ha
This is one of the most historically significant winery buildings in the Barossa Valley, built from blue stone quarried at nearby Bethany in the late 1880s. It has been restored by the Geber family and a new basket press winery installed. Chateau Tanunda owns almost 100 ha of vineyards in Bethany, Eden Valley, Tanunda and Vine Vale, with additional fruit sourced from a group of thirty growers, including descendants of the Barossa's original settlers, covering the panoply of Barossan subregions. The wines are made from hand-picked grapes, basket-pressed, and are neither fined nor filtered. There is an emphasis on single-vineyard and single-subregion wines under the Terroirs of the Barossa label. The grand building houses the cellar door and Barossa Small Winemakers Centre, offering wines made by boutique winemakers. The Chateau hosts conferences, conventions and weddings, catering for groups of up to 500,

and there is a competition-standard croquet lawn with picturesque valley views. The acclaimed charity Masters Cricket match played biennially on the CCG (Chateau Cricket Ground) sees many of the world's greats grace its stage. Exports to the UK, Germany, Switzerland, Sweden, Denmark, Belgium and China.

ΨΨΨΨΨ **The Chateau 100 Year Old Vines Shiraz 2008** Purple-crimson; sourced from a single 0.4-ha vineyard high in the hills of the Eden Valley; the register of aromas and flavours switches decisively to a brighter, yet more savoury/spicy/earthy blackberry and licorice spectrum; outstanding length and balance. Cork. 14.5% alc. **Rating** 96 **To** 2023 $95

The Everest Old Bushvine Grenache 2008 Slightly hazy colour despite two years in French oak; the Everest refers to the Barossa Valley rather than grenache per se; these irrelevancies to one side, this is a top-quality Grenache that is seldom achieved in the Barossa (more commonly in McLaren Vale), with volumes of red berry fruit and excellent tannin structure. Cork. 15% alc. **Rating** 95 **To** 2020 $160

✪ **The Chateau Eden Valley Riesling 2009** Lemon blossom and frangipani aromas lead into a vibrant, refreshing and zesty palate, which is guided by acidity. Screwcap. 11.5% alc. **Rating** 94 **To** 2016 $20

Terroirs of the Barossa Ebenezer District Shiraz 2008 Deep red-purple; the bouquet is rich and deep, with black fruits, plum cake, chocolate and mocha aromas faithfully replayed on the full-bodied, albeit quite soft, palate. From the 80-year-old vines of the Lauke Vineyard. If you use a one-piece cork, it needs to be of better quality than those in the '08 Terroirs of the Barossa Shirazs. 14% alc. **Rating** 94 **To** 2023 $48

Terroirs of the Barossa Greenock Shiraz 2008 Good hue and depth; has more savoury nuances of earth and spice on the bouquet and palate; a medium-bodied wine, more elegant than Ebenezer despite its higher alcohol and great length, but (of course) less rich. From a single, 40-year-old vineyard. Cork. 14.5% alc. **Rating** 94 **To** 2020 $48

Terroirs of the Barossa Lyndoch Shiraz 2008 Excellent crimson-purple hue; arguably the most elegant of the '08 Terroirs of the Barossa Shirazs, with plum, dark chocolate, spice and vanillan oak aromas and flavours; the medium-bodied palate has particularly good length and mouthfeel. From the 20-year-old Semmler Vineyard. Cork. 14% alc. **Rating** 94 **To** 2020 $48

Terroirs of the Barossa Greenock Shiraz 2007 Purple-crimson; rich, ripe plum, blackberry and dark chocolate aromas are reflected on the generous medium-bodied palate that has the length missing from the Ebenezer; top outcome from '07. Poor-quality cork. 14.5% alc. **Rating** 94 **To** 2017 $45

ΨΨΨΨΩ **The Chateau Old Bush Vine Grenache Rose 2009** **Rating** 93 **To** 2012 $28

The Chateau Shiraz 2008 **Rating** 93 **To** 2020 $28

✪ **Barossa Tower Garnacha Rose 2009** Magenta; flooded with sweet strawberry and raspberry fruit; dries out significantly on the finish. Serve fully chilled. Hand-picked (expensive). Screwcap. 13% alc. **Rating** 90 **To** 2011 $15

ΨΨΨΨ **Barossa Tower Shiraz 2008** A thoroughly traditional Barossa Valley Shiraz
✪ coming from five subregions and matured in American oak; medium-bodied, its plum and black fruits are supported by ripe, soft tannins; no need for cellaring. Screwcap. 14.5% alc. **Rating** 89 **To** 2013 $18

Terroirs of the Barossa Ebenezer District Shiraz 2007 **Rating** 89 **To** 2014 $45

Grand Barossa Shiraz 2007 **Rating** 89 **To** 2015 $25

The Chateau Botrytis Semillon 2008 **Rating** 89 **To** 2013 $20

The Chateau Old Vine Semillon 2009 **Rating** 88 **To** 2012 $18

Cherry Tree Hill   ★★★☆

Hume Highway, Sutton Forest, NSW 2577 **Region** Southern Highlands
T (02) 8217 1409 **F** (02) 9362 1822 **www.cherrytreehill.com.au Open** 7 days 9–5
Winemaker Anton Balog, Eddy Rossi (Contract) **Est.** 2000 **Cases** 4000 **Vyds** 14 ha

The Lorentz family, headed by Gabi Lorentz, began the establishment of the Cherry Tree Hill vineyard in 2000 with the planting of 3 ha each of cabernet sauvignon and riesling; 3 ha each of merlot and sauvignon blanc followed in '01, and, finally, 2 ha of chardonnay in '02. The inspiration was childhood trips on a horse and cart through his grandfather's vineyard in Hungary, and Gabi's son David completes the three-generation involvement as manager of the business.

ΨΨΨΨ♀ **Sunflower Paddock Cabernet Sauvignon 2005** A pleasant surprise; has aged well, and has pure and fresh varietal aromas and flavours; the tannin extract is low, but the wine still has length and balance even if on a drink-sooner-than-later watch. Screwcap. 13.1% alc. **Rating** 90 **To** 2012 $25

ΨΨΨΨ **Riesling 2008 Rating** 89 **To** 2013 $18
Riesling 2009 Rating 88 **To** 2014 $18
Sauvignon Blanc 2008 Rating 88 **To** 2010 $18

Chestnut Grove   ★★★
Chestnut Grove Road, Manjimup, WA 2658 **Region** Manjimup
T (08) 9722 4255 **F** (08) 9772 4266 **www**.chestnutgrove.com.au **Open** Mon–Fri 9–4
Winemaker David Dowden **Est.** 1988 **Cases** 15 000 **Vyds** 40 ha
A substantial vineyard that commenced in 1987, with an onsite winery constructed in '98, Chestnut Grove has come full circle from founder Vic Kordic and sons Paul and Mark, to Australian Wine Holdings in 2002, and back to the Kordics in '09 under the umbrella of Manjimup Wine Enterprises Pty Ltd. Mark is general manager of the wine business, the cellar door has reopened and Chestnut Grove has resumed exports, currently to the US and Canada.

ΨΨΨΨ **Verdelho 2009** Extremely pale quartz; a vibrantly fresh wine with pronounced acidity that will come back into balance as the fruit depth grows in bottle over the next few years. Screwcap. 13.5% alc. **Rating** 89 **To** 2013 $17

Cheviot Bridge   ★★★☆
9th Floor, 564 St Kilda Road, Melbourne, Vic 3004 (postal) **Region** Upper Goulburn
T (03) 8656 7000 **F** (03) 9510 3277 **www**.cheviotbridge.com.au **Open** Not
Winemaker Shane Virgo, Hugh Cuthbertson **Est.** 1998 **Cases** 350 000
Cheviot Bridge has been in the wine news pages for all the wrong reasons, as it has struggled with the various challenges facing the broader Australian wine industry. Nonetheless, it produces 350 000 cases of wine sourced from the Clare, Barossa and Yarra valleys, utilising custom-make facilities in various places. In March 2010 it was delisted (permanently) from the Australian Associated Stock Exchange. The brands include Cheviot Bridge Yea Valley, Long Flat Destinations, La Vie and Kissing Bridge. Exports to all major markets

ΨΨΨΨ♀ **Long Flat Destinations Coonawarra Cabernet Sauvignon 2008** Dense
✪ purple; intense black fruits on the bouquet come as no surprise, nor does the strength of the full-bodied palate; there isn't much finesse here, but it's remarkable value for long-term cellaring. Screwcap. 14% alc. **Rating** 91 **To** 2028 $16

ΨΨΨΨ **Long Flat Chardonnay 2008** Bright green-straw; you get plenty of wine
✪ for the price; the stone fruit flavours are fresh, the acidity balanced, oak barely noticeable. Screwcap. 12.5% alc. **Rating** 87 **To** 2011 $9.90
La Vie Pinot Noir Chardonnay NV Rating 87 **To** 2010 $17

Chidlow's Well Estate   ★★★
6245 Old Northam Road, Chidlow, WA 6556 **Region** Perth Hills
T (08) 9572 3681 **F** (08) 9572 3684 **www**.chidlowswell.com.au **Open** By appt
Winemaker John Griffiths **Est.** 1995 **Cases** 1000 **Vyds** 12 ha
Chidlow is around 60 km east of Perth and was originally known as Chidlow's Well. The vineyard is now owned and managed by Peter Costa and Sandy Gray, who continue to

grow the chardonnay, chenin blanc, verdelho and shiraz planted on the vineyard by the former owners.

ŸŸŸŸ **Shiraz 2009** Good colour; has been well made, blackberry and plum fruit to the
⊙ fore, French oak in the background; good balance. Screwcap. 14% alc. **Rating** 88
To 2015 $18

Chimes Estate ★★★★
9 Bernard Street, Claremont, WA 6010 (postal) **Region** Margaret River
T 0412 550 995 **F** (08) 93846001 **www**.chimesestate.com.au **Open** Not
Winemaker Fermoy Estate (Michael Kelly, Liz Dawson) **Est.** 2001 **Cases** 700 **Vyds** 7 ha
Chimes Estate founders Philip and Margaret Thompson live in Claremont, Perth, commuting
to the vineyard, orchard and olive grove on weekends and holidays. The 30-ha property,
situated 13 km northeast of the Margaret River township, is located in a valley surrounded
by state forest and cattle farms. From 2001 to '06 they established 3 ha of cabernet sauvignon,
1.5 ha each of sauvignon blanc and semillon and 1 ha of merlot (the two white varieties
planted in '06, the reds in '01 and '02). Most of the grapes are sold, but the intention is to
increase production with a Merlot as well as Sauvignon Blanc and Semillon-based wines.

ŸŸŸŸŸ **Margaret River Semillon Sauvignon Blanc 2009** While the percentages of
the varieties are not stated, the semillon's grassy/herbal characters play a major role
in the structure of the wine, the sauvignon blanc providing a feather-light touch of
tropical/lychee fruit. Screwcap. 13% alc. **Rating** 91 **To** 2012 $12.50

 ## Chirping Bird ★★★★
1203 Stumpy Gully Road, Moorooduc, Vic 3933 (postal) **Region** Mornington Peninsula
T 0418 535 161 **F** (03) 5982 0577 **www**.chirpingbird.com.au **Open** Not
Winemaker Ewan Campbell **Est.** 1999 **Cases** 1000 **Vyds** 2 ha
When Rod and Mim Smallman began the development of Chirping Bird in 1999, it was a
foregone conclusion that shiraz would be the first variety to be planted. The decision to plant
muscat (frontignac) came from left field; the original plan was to plant pinot gris, which was
then gaining a lot of attention on the Peninsula. It was suggested that muscat gave the option
of moscato, and also a fortified style. The fortified version was made in 2005, '06, '07 and '08,
and a small make will continue for several years from '10 onwards before a solera is started.
The chardonnay is contract-grown from a 1-ha planting at Red Hill.

ŸŸŸŸŸ **Chardonnay 2008** Tangy, lively, citrussy edges to the stone fruit flavour; good
⊙ length and balance. Screwcap. 13.5% alc. **Rating** 90 **To** 2013 $20
Mornington Peninsula Shiraz 2007 Good crimson-purple; ripe black fruits,
licorice and spice on the bouquet, then a surprisingly full-bodied palate with an
abundance of savoury tannins and vanillan oak. A littler overdone, but will repay
cellaring. Screwcap. 14.4% alc. **Rating** 90 **To** 2017 $25

Chrismont ★★★★☆
251 Upper King River Road, Cheshunt, Vic 3678 **Region** King Valley
T (03) 5729 8220 **F** (03) 5729 8253 **www**.chrismont.com.au **Open** 7 days 11–5
Winemaker Warren Proft **Est.** 1980 **Cases** 15 000 **Vyds** 100 ha
Arnold (Arnie) and Jo Pizzini's substantial and still expanding vineyards in the Whitfield area
of the upper King Valley have been planted with riesling, sauvignon blanc, chardonnay, pinot
gris, cabernet sauvignon, merlot, shiraz, barbera, marzemino and arneis. The La Zona range
ties in the Italian heritage of the Pizzinis and is part of the intense interest in all things Italian.
A second cellar door also operates 7 days 10–5 at Shop 1, 1605 Glenrowan-Myrtleford Road,
Milawa. Exports to the US and Sweden.

ŸŸŸŸŸ **La Zona King Valley Pinot Grigio 2009** Lively citrus and straw bouquet, with
an underpinning of mineral complexity; light-bodied, fresh and clean, with good
persistence of flavour. Screwcap. 12.5% alc. **Rating** 90 **To** 2013 $22 BE

La Zona King Valley Sangiovese 2008 Bright colour; distinctly smoky bouquet, with red cherry and briar; the palate is fleshy and fresh, vibrant acidity providing cut to the finish. Screwcap. 14% alc. **Rating** 90 **To** 2012 $24 BE

La Zona King Valley Barbera 2008 Bright colour; showing a real feral edge often ascribed to the variety, there are also smoked meats and blue fruits, laced with earth and spice; savoury and interesting. Screwcap. 14.5% alc. **Rating** 90 **To** 2012 $24 BE

Simpatico King Valley Pinot Chardonnay 2005 Shows a fresh, focused and vibrant personality, with an attractive level of toast and leesy complexity; the palate is lively, with a fine mousse and lemony acid providing length and direction. Cork. 12% alc. **Rating** 90 **To** 2015 $45 BE

ＹＹＹＹ **Il Re' King Valley Nebbiolo 2005 Rating** 89 **To** 2016 $70 BE
King Valley Riesling 2009 Rating 88 **To** 2015 $16 BE
King Valley Chardonnay 2008 Rating 88 **To** 2014 $22 BE
King Valley Merlot 2008 Rating 88 **To** 2014 $22 BE
King Valley Prosecco NV Rating 88 **To** 2012 $22 BE
La Zona King Valley Moscato 2009 Rating 88 **To** 2012 $16 BE
La Zona King Valley Savagnin 2009 Rating 87 **To** 2012 $22 BE
La Zona King Valley Rosato Mezzanotte 2009 Rating 87 **To** 2012 $18 BE

Churchview Estate ★★★★☆

Cnr Bussell Highway/Gale Road, Metricup, WA 6280 **Region** Margaret River
T (08) 9755 7200 **F** (08) 9755 7300 **www.**churchview.com.au **Open** Mon–Sat 9.30–5.30
Winemaker Greg Garnish **Est.** 1998 **Cases** 30 000 **Vyds** 65 ha
The Fokkema family, headed by Spike Fokkema, immigrated from The Netherlands in the 1950s. Business success in the following decades led to the acquisition of the 100-ha Churchview Estate property in '97, and to the progressive establishment of substantial vineyards (65 ha planted to 15 varieties). Exports to Europe, Hong Kong and Singapore.

ＹＹＹＹＹ **The Bartondale Reserve Margaret River Shiraz 2007** Good red-purple; a distinctly finer wine than the varietal, and manages to carry the alcohol quite well; ripe but spicy plum and blackberry fruit is supported by all-important tannins that paradoxically add to the elegance of the wine, and – of course – its length. Screwcap. 15% alc. **Rating** 93 **To** 2020 $36.50

The Bartondale Reserve Margaret River Chardonnay 2008 Vivid green-yellow; a complex wine that on the one hand has developed quite quickly, on the other is sustained and lengthened by attractive citrussy acidity; in the middle is peach, fig and nectarine fruit. Screwcap. 13.5% alc. **Rating** 92 **To** 2014 $29.50

The Bartondale Reserve Margaret River Marsanne 2008 Has a very interesting bouquet, with spice, chalk, pear and honeysuckle and oak aromas all evident and flowing through to the bright and long palate. Screwcap. 14% alc. **Rating** 92 **To** 2018 $29.50

ＹＹＹＹ **Margaret River Cabernet Merlot 2007 Rating** 89 **To** 2014 $18.50
The Bartondale Reserve Margaret River Cabernet Sauvignon 2007 Rating 89 **To** 2022 $36.50
Margaret River Sauvignon Blanc Semillon 2009 Rating 88 **To** 2010 $18.50

✪ **Silverleaf Margaret River Semillon Sauvignon Blanc 2009** Here the percentages are reversed, and curiously, the tropical components are a little more obvious, the citrussy acidity likewise; very clever label design and motif. Screwcap. 12% alc. **Rating** 88 **To** 2010 $12.50

Margaret River Unwooded Chardonnay 2009 Rating 88 **To** 2012 $18.50

✪ **Silverleaf Margaret River Chenin Blanc 2009** Bright straw; this is a juicy, light-bodied wine, with citrus, honeysuckle and fruit salad aromas and flavours designed for spontaneous pleasure, not introspection. Screwcap. 12.5% alc. **Rating** 87 **To** 2012 $12.50

Ciavarella ★★★☆

Evans Lane, Oxley, Vic 3678 **Region** King Valley
T (03) 5727 3384 **F** (03) 5727 3384 **www**.oxleyestate.com.au **Open** Mon–Sat 9–6, Sun 10–6
Winemaker Cyril and Tony Ciavarella **Est.** 1978 **Cases** 2500 **Vyds** 1.6 ha
Cyril and Jan Ciavarella's vineyard was begun in 1978, with plantings being extended over
the years. One variety, aucerot, was first produced by Maurice O'Shea of McWilliam's Mount
Pleasant 60 or so years ago; the Ciavarella vines have been grown from cuttings collected from
an old Glenrowan vineyard before the parent plants were removed in the mid-1980s. Tony
Ciavarella left a career in agricultural research in mid-2003 to join his parents at Ciavarella.

♟♟♟♟♟ **Oxley Estate Late Harvest Semillon Aucerot 2005** Has flourished in bottle;
intense flavours of citrus, apricot and nougat are sustained and lengthened by good
acidity. Cork. 8.5% alc. **Rating** 90 **To** 2012 $25

♟♟♟♟ **Oxley Estate Sauvignon Blanc 2009 Rating** 89 **To** 2011 $18
Oxley Estate Shiraz Viognier 2006 Rating 88 **To** 2014 $22
Oxley Estate Merlot Shiraz Cabernet 2006 Rating 88 **To** 2014 $24

Cirillo Wines ★★★★☆

Lot 298 Nuraip Road, Nuriootpa, SA 5355 **Region** Barossa Valley
T 0408 803 447 **F** (08) 8562 1597 **Open** By appt
Winemaker Marco Cirillo **Est.** 2003 **Cases** 600 **Vyds** 6 ha
In 1973 the Cirillo family acquired one of the oldest vineyards in Australia, situated in the
Light Pass district of the Barossa Valley where the soil is deep silt sand over limestone and clay.
This combination of free-draining top soil and water-holding subsoil has sustained the 3 ha of
grenache, along with 1 ha semillon (previously incorrectly called madeira) and 0.5 ha of shiraz
planted in 1850, the latter complemented by 1 ha of shiraz and 0.5 ha of mourvedre planted in
1988. Most of the grapes are sold to Torbreck, leaving only a small portion for Cirillo. Exports
to the US and Singapore.

♟♟♟♟♟ **1850s Old Vine Barossa Valley Semillon 2009** Made from semillon vines
✪ planted in the 1850s and almost certainly the oldest in the world; is very intense
and pure, with citrus and mineral drivers not unlike top-quality Hunter Valley
semillon; early picking and bottling spot on. Screwcap. 9.5% alc. **Rating** 95
To 2020 $19

♟♟♟♟♟ **1850s Old Vine Barossa Valley Grenache 2007 Rating** 90 **To** 2014 $50

♟♟♟♟ **1850s Old Vine Barossa Valley Grenache Rose 2009 Rating** 88 **To** 2011 $19

Clair de Lune Vineyard ★★★★

8805 South Gippsland Highway, Kardella South, Vic 3951 **Region** Gippsland
T (03) 5655 1032 **www**.clairdelune.com.au **Open** 7 days 11.30–5.30
Winemaker Brian Gaffy **Est.** 1997 **Cases** 600 **Vyds** 4 ha
Brian Gaffy married a successful 20-year career in civil engineering with a long-term
involvement in the Bundaburra Wine & Food Club in Melbourne. His interest in wine grew,
leading to studies at the Dookie Agricultural College, with particular input from Martin
Williams MW and Denise Miller. He has planted a vineyard on the rolling hills of the
Strzelecki Range to sauvignon blanc, chardonnay, pinot noir and a mixed block of shiraz/
merlot/cabernet.

♟♟♟♟♟ **South Gippsland Oaked Chardonnay 2008** Bright colour; a well-composed
and balanced wine, with surprisingly abundant white peach, melon and nectarine
fruit (given its modest alcohol). Screwcap. 12.5% alc. **Rating** 93 **To** 2017 $30
Reserve South Gippsland Pinot Noir 2008 Light, slightly diffuse colour;
attractive, relatively light-bodied, wine with spicy red fruits on the bouquet,
joined on the palate by a touch of forest; good length and balance. Diam. 13% alc.
Rating 93 **To** 2015 $35

♥♥♥♥ Triolet Shiraz Merlot Cabernet 2008 Rating 89 To 2014 $30
Duo Sauvignon Chardonnay 2009 Rating 88 To 2010 $27

Clairault   ★★★★★
3277 Caves Road, Wilyabrup, WA 6280 **Region** Margaret River
T (08) 9755 6225 **F** (08) 9755 6229 **www**.clairaultwines.com.au **Open** 7 days 10–5
Winemaker Will Shields **Est.** 1976 **Cases** 20 000 **Vyds** 39.8 ha
Bill and Ena Martin, with sons Conor, Brian and Shane, acquired Clairault several years ago
and have expanded the vineyards on the 120-ha property. The 12 ha of vines established by
the former owners (most now over 30 years old) have been supplemented by another 27 or so
ha of vines, with a ratio of roughly 70% red varieties to 30% white. Deeply concerned about
the environment and consumer health, Clairault has joined with ERA (Environmentally
Responsible Agriculture) to implement the elimination of chemical use and the introduction
of biological farming. Exports to the UK, the US and other major markets.

♥♥♥♥♥ Estate Margaret River Chardonnay 2008 Bright green-gold; the complex
bouquet has 100% barrel ferment and nutty inputs without suffocating the intense
fruit that defines both bouquet and palate; partial mlf has added texture to the
palate without blurring the acidity that drives the white peach and grapefruit
flavours. Screwcap. 13% alc. **Rating** 95 **To** 2020 $35
Estate Margaret River Cabernet Sauvignon 2007 The hue, strangely, is
slightly less impressive than the standard wine; however, the varietal fruit flavours
are more intense, the tannins relegated to a still-important support role; excellent
length and balance. Screwcap. 14.5% alc. **Rating** 95 **To** 2022 $45
✪ Margaret River Sauvignon Blanc 2009 A floral blend of passionfruit and
citrus rind on the bouquet is followed by a high-powered palate that drives
through to a lingering conclusion. All about the interaction of variety and region,
not winemaker tricks. Screwcap. 12.5% alc. **Rating** 94 **To** 2012 $24

♥♥♥♥♡ Margaret River Chardonnay 2008 Bright green-gold; the focus is primarily
✪ on the fruit, only 25% of the wine being barrel-fermented; the aromas and flavours
are in the grapefruit, nectarine and white peach group, the length very good.
Screwcap. 13% alc. **Rating** 93 **To** 2018 $24
✪ Margaret River Cabernet Merlot 2007 Bright colour for age; this is all about
the texture gained from the spicy/cedary tannins that run through the palate
from start to finish, extending its length, and also providing an anchor for its
blackcurrant and plum fruit. Screwcap. 14.5% alc. **Rating** 93 **To** 2022 $23
Margaret River Cabernet Sauvignon 2007 Rating 93 To 2017 $26
Claddagh 2007 Rating 93 To 2027 $80
Margaret River Semillon Sauvignon Blanc 2009 Rating 90 To 2011 $23

Clancy Fuller   ★★★☆
PO Box 34, Tanunda, SA 5352 **Region** Barossa Valley
T (08) 8563 0080 **F** (08) 8563 1613 **www**.clancyfuller.com.au **Open** Not
Winemaker Ben Radford, Pete Schell (Contract) **Est.** 1996 **Cases** 500 **Vyds** 5.5 ha
This is the venture of industry veterans who should know better: Paul Clancy, long responsible
for the Wine Industry Directory that sits in every winery office in Australia, and Peter Fuller,
who has built up by far the largest public relations business for all sectors of the wine industry.
They own 0.5 ha of shiraz planted in the 1880s, 1 ha of 40-year-old shiraz, 2 ha of 60-year-
old grenache and 2 ha of mataro.

♥♥♥♥ Two Little Dickie Birds Barossa Rose 2009 Very pale salmon; a spicy bouquet,
✪ then a lively palate with equal proportions of Grenache/Mourvedre, with almost
lemony acidity extending the finish. Screwcap. 12.5% alc. **Rating** 89 **To** 2010 $15

Clayfield Wines ★★★★★

25 Wilde Lane, Moyston, Vic 3377 **Region** Grampians
T (03) 5354 2689 **F** (03) 5354 2679 **www**.clayfieldwines.com **Open** Mon–Sat 10–5, Sun 11–4
Winemaker Simon Clayfield **Est.** 1997 **Cases** 1000 **Vyds** 2.1 ha
Former long-serving Best's winemaker Simon Clayfield and wife Kaye are now doing their own thing. They planted 2 ha of shiraz and merlot between 1997 and '99, later adding 0.1 ha of durif. Additional grapes are purchased from local growers and, when the quality is appropriate, incorporated in the Grampians Shiraz. Production is modest, but the quality is high. Exports to the US, Canada and Maldives.

🍷🍷🍷🍷🍷 **Grampians Shiraz 2006** Has retained crimson-purple hue; in very different style to the '08; medium-bodied and quite elegant, it has bright cherry and plum fruit, the tannins fine and silky, the finish long and balanced. Screwcap. 14.9% alc. Rating 95 To 2021 $45
Massif Grampians Shiraz 2008 Deep, dark red-purple; full of luscious, ripe black fruits on bouquet and palate alike; how it can carry this alcohol without heating up on the long finish, I have no idea. Screwcap. 15.5% alc. **Rating** 94 To 2023 $25
Thomas Wills Grampians Shiraz 2008 Dark, deep purple-crimson; an even bigger version of the Massif, made in heaven for those who love full-bodied shiraz, including Robert Parker Jr; confit plum and licorice allsorts; remarkably soft tannins. Screwcap. 15.8% alc. **Rating** 94 To 2025 $35

Claymore Wines ★★★★☆

91 Main North Road, Leasingham, SA 5452 **Region** Clare Valley
T (08) 8843 0200 **F** (08) 8843 0200 **www**.claymorewines.com.au **Open** 7 days 11–4
Winemaker David Mavor **Est.** 1998 **Cases** 10 000 **Vyds** 20 ha
Claymore Wines is the venture of two medical professionals imagining that it would lead the way to early retirement (which, of course, it did not). The starting date depends on which event you take: the first 4-ha vineyard at Leasingham purchased in 1991 (with 70-year-old grenache, riesling and shiraz); '96, when a 16-ha block at Penwortham was purchased and planted to shiraz, merlot and grenache; '97, when the first wines were made; or '98, when the first releases came onto the market; the labels are inspired by U2, Pink Floyd and Lou Reed. Exports to Canada, Denmark, Sweden, Malaysia, Taiwan, Hong Kong and China.

🍷🍷🍷🍷🍷 **Nirvana Reserve Clare Valley Shiraz 2006** Full purple-crimson; some Christmas cake aromas are quickly swept aside by the power and concentration of the tightly configured, full-bodied palate; here pure blackberry fruit and firm acidity promise a long future. Screwcap. 14.5% alc. **Rating** 94 To 2021 $40

🍷🍷🍷🍷🍷 ✪ **Joshua Tree Clare Valley Riesling 2009** Is very crisp and tight; green apple and some lime zest; minerally acidity on the vigorous finish. Will repay cellaring. Screwcap. 13% alc. **Rating** 91 To 2018 $18
Dark Side of the Moon Clare Valley Shiraz 2007 Rating 90 To 2020 $25

🍷🍷🍷🍷 **Dark Side of the Moon Clare Valley Shiraz 2008** Rating 89 To 2018 $25
Walk on the Wild Side Clare Valley Shiraz Viognier 2007 Rating 89 To 2014 $18
London Calling Clare Valley Merlot 2008 Rating 89 To 2014 $20
Whole Lotta Love Clare Valley Rose 2009 Rating 88 To 2010 $18

Clearview Estate Mudgee ★★★☆

Cnr Sydney Road/Rocky Water Hole Road, Mudgee, NSW 2850 **Region** Mudgee
T (02) 6372 4546 **F** (02) 6372 7577 **www**.clearviewwines.com.au **Open** Mon & Fri 10–3 (Mar–Dec), w'ends 10–4, or by appt
Winemaker Michael Slater **Est.** 1995 **Cases** 1000 **Vyds** 11 ha

Paul and Michelle Baguley acquired the vineyard from the founding Hickey family in 2006. Paul brings 10 years' experience as a viticulturist, and Paul and Michelle have introduced additional wine styles. Plantings include shiraz, chardonnay, cabernet sauvignon and semillon.

ŦŦŦŦŦ **Church Creek Semillon 2009** Crystal clear; well made, bright and lively; grass
✪ and citrus characters intermingle on both bouquet and palate; will flourish with some years in bottle. Screwcap. 10.5% alc. **Rating** 92 **To** 2019 $17

ŦŦŦŦ **Rocky Waterhole Pink Cabernet 2009 Rating** 89 **To** 2011 $17

Clemens Hill   ★★★★☆
686 Richmond Road, Cambridge, Tas 7170 **Region** Southern Tasmania
T (03) 6248 5985 **F** (03) 6248 5985 **Open** By appt
Winemaker Winemaking Tasmania **Est.** 1994 **Cases** 1900 **Vyds** 5.3 ha
The Shepherd family acquired Clemens Hill in 2001 after selling their Rosabrook winery in the Margaret River. They also have a shareholding in Winemaking Tasmania, the contract winemaking facility run by Julian Alcorso, who makes the Clemens Hill wines. The estate vineyard includes pinot noir (3.3 ha; 1.5 ha being replanted in 2009) and sauvignon blanc (2 ha). Following the death of Joan Shepherd in 2006, John took John Schuts, an assistant winemaker at Julian Alcorso's Winemaking Tasmania, into partnership.

ŦŦŦŦŦ **Pinot Noir 2008** Strong, full crimson-purple; the bouquet has rich plum and black cherry characters, the expansive palate taking these to another level, and adding a nice savoury/earthy touch, oak evident, but balanced. Gold medal Tas Wine Show '10. Screwcap. 13.5% alc. **Rating** 94 **To** 2017 $36

ŦŦŦŦŦ **Reserve Pinot Noir 2007 Rating** 91 **To** 2014 $65
Pinot Nouveau 2008 Rating 90 **To** 2014 $22

ŦŦŦŦ **Sauvignon Blanc 2009 Rating** 89 **To** 2011 $25

Clockwork Wines   ★★★☆
8990 West Swan Road, West Swan, WA 6056 (postal) **Region** Swan Valley
T 0401 033 840 **www**.clockworkwines.com.au **Open** Not
Winemaker Rob Marshall **Est.** 2008 **Cases** 7000 **Vyds** 5 ha
This is a separate business from that of Oakover Wines, although both are owned by the Yukich family. Grapes are sourced from around WA, with the majority coming from Margaret River, and also from Geographe, Frankland River and the Clockwork Vineyard in the Swan Valley. The 2007 Clockwork Cabernet Merlot, somewhat luckily, perhaps, found itself in the line-up for the Jimmy Watson Trophy at its first show entry, part of a dominant contingent from Margaret River thanks to its great vintage.

ŦŦŦŦŦ **Margaret River Shiraz 2008** Deep colour; blackberry and spice bouquet,
✪ showing some attractive mulled fruit character; medium-bodied and fleshy, with plenty of chewy tannins providing structure; well put together, and lots of wine for the price. Screwcap. 14% alc. **Rating** 90 **To** 2016 $18 BE

ŦŦŦŦ **Margaret River Cabernet Sauvignon 2007 Rating** 89 **To** 2014 $18
Margaret River Sauvignon Blanc 2009 Rating 87 **To** 2012 $18 BE

Clonakilla   ★★★★★
Crisps Lane, Murrumbateman, NSW 2582 **Region** Canberra District
T (02) 6227 5877 **F** (02) 6227 5871 **www**.clonakilla.com.au **Open** 7 days 10–5
Winemaker Tim Kirk, Bryan Martin **Est.** 1971 **Cases** 10 000 **Vyds** 12 ha
The indefatigable Tim Kirk, with an inexhaustible thirst for knowledge, is the winemaker and manager of this family winery founded by Tim's father, scientist Dr John Kirk. It is not at all surprising that the quality of the wines is excellent, especially the Shiraz Viognier, which has paved the way for numerous others to follow, but remains the best example in Australia. Exports to all major markets.

♀♀♀♀♀ **Canberra District Shiraz Viognier 2009** Deeply coloured; the bouquet is almost backward and is slow to reveal the intricate layers of black fruits that lie therein; time reveals succulent black fruits, minerals, fine spices and a touch of fresh garden herbs; the palate delivers a wonderful mixture of opulent fruit, savoury complexity, and silky fine tannins that persist for an incredibly long time; only at the very end do you get a glimpse of the fine oak in use; certain to be long lived. Screwcap. 14% alc. **Rating** 97 **To** 2025 $100 BE

✪ **O'Riada Canberra District Shiraz 2008** Crimson-purple; a supremely elegant, medium-bodied wine with a vivid array of black cherry, blackberry, pepper and multi-spice flavours reflecting the co-fermentation with 6% viognier, the inclusion of whole bunches of shiraz, and 12 months in French oak (30% new); texture and balance are exceptional. Screwcap. 14% alc. **Rating** 96 **To** 2020 $45

✪ **Hilltops Shiraz 2009** Vibrant purple hue; dominated by savoury spicy notes, of cinnamon, clove, star anise and followed up by clearly defined blackberry fruit; the palate is lively and super fresh, showing a strong core of mineral and fresh earth; will be ample, juicy, long and generous, this is delicious as a young wine, or in ten years. Screwcap. 14% alc. **Rating** 95 **To** 2018 $30 BE

Murrumbateman Syrah 2008 Black and red fruits combine seamlessly with a strong tar-like quality running through the core; medium-bodied, dark and savoury, with firm tannins taking over the palate and wrestling the dark fruit to the mineral floor; long, chewy, intense and needing time to reveal the inner beauty. Screwcap. 14% alc. **Rating** 95 **To** 2020 $90 BE

Canberra District Viognier 2009 Pristine and pure apricot meal, gentle spices and a highly appealing, almost sensual mineral core; the palate is unctuous on entry, almost thickly textured, but follows through with cleansing, savoury texture, bordering on bitterness but not overstepping the mark; eerily similar to those made in the northern Rhone in France. Screwcap. 14.5% alc. **Rating** 94 **To** 2012 $50 BE

♀♀♀♀♀ **Ballinderry 2008** Rating 93 **To** 2020 $50 BE

Jack Reidy Canberra District Shiraz 2009 Rating 91 **To** 2015 $30 BE

Clos Clare   ★★★★

Old Road, Watervale, SA 5452 **Region** Clare Valley
T (08) 8843 0161 **F** (08) 8843 0161 **Open** W'ends & public hols 10–5
Winemaker Sam and Tom Barry **Est.** 1993 **Cases** 1200
Clos Clare was acquired by the Barry family in 2008. Riesling continues to be made from the 2-ha unirrigated section of the original Florita Vineyard (the major part of that vineyard was already in Barry ownership) and newly introduced red wines are coming from a 48-year-old vineyard beside the Armagh site.

♀♀♀♀♀ **Watervale Riesling 2009** An attractive wine, with juicy lime aromas and flavours; good length and bright acidity; each way proposition: now or later. Screwcap. 13% alc. **Rating** 92 **To** 2016 $24

Cemetery Block Shiraz 2006 An unusually elegant Clare Valley wine, medium-bodied at best, with a fragrant bouquet and lively palate; fresh red and black fruits are supported by silky tannins. Screwcap. 14.7% alc. **Rating** 92 **To** 2014 $24

The Hayes Boy Grenache 2006 Just because it's easy to drink doesn't mean it's easy to make; there is no way you would guess this fresh, lithe wine has 14.9% alcohol; it is far more lively than most from Clare. Screwcap. 14.9% alc. **Rating** 90 **To** 2012 $24

Cloudbreak Wines   ★★★☆

5A/1 Adelaide Lobethal Road, Lobethal, SA 5241 **Region** Adelaide Hills
T 0431 245 668 **www.**cloudbreakwines.com.au **Open** W'ends & public hols 11–4
Winemaker Simon Greenleaf, William Finlayson **Est.** 2001 **Cases** 300

Owners Will Finlayson and Simon Greenleaf met 16 years ago while both working at Petaluma. A long-term plan to make their own wine came after Simon had done vintages in France, Chile and Spain, and Will in Oregon. In 1998 Simon's parents bought a 7-ha property, at which time it was completely overgrown with blackberries. Will says, 'We had limited funds so we did it all ourselves, from clearing the land to growing the cuttings and eventually putting the posts in – it took months of work.' Two varieties were planted first: pinot noir, using Burgundy clones 114 and 115; and pinot gris, followed by sauvignon blanc and chardonnay.

ŸŸŸŸŸ **Adelaide Hills Pinot Noir 2008** Strong, clear red-purple; a Pinot dedicated to food with its intense, savoury/spicy make-up; clones 114, 115 and MV6 cold-soaked, then oak vat-fermented and matured in French barriques. Screwcap. 13.5% alc. **Rating** 91 **To** 2015 $32

ŸŸŸŸ **Adelaide Hills Pinot Gris 2009 Rating** 89 **To** 2012 $28

Clovely Estate   ★★★★
Steinhardts Road, Moffatdale via Murgon, Qld 4605 **Region** South Burnett
T (07) 3876 3100 **F** (07) 3876 3500 **www**.clovely.com.au **Open** 7 days 10–5
Winemaker Luke Fitzpatrick **Est.** 1998 **Cases** 30 000 **Vyds** 174 ha
Clovely Estate has the largest vineyards in Qld, having established over 170 ha of immaculately maintained vines at two locations just to the east of Murgon in the Burnett Valley. There are 120 ha of red grapes (including 60 ha of shiraz) and 54 ha of white grapes. The attractively packaged wines are sold in six tiers: Double Pruned at the top; followed by Estate Reserve; Left Field, featuring alternative varieties and styles; then the White Label and The Shed ranges for everyday drinking, distributed through the Qld retail market; and at the bottom, First Picked, primarily designed for the export market (the UK, Denmark, Finland, Singapore, Taiwan and China) at low price points. Unlike many Qld wineries, the prices across the range offer very good value. The estate also has a second cellar door at 210 Musgrave Road, Red Hill.

ŸŸŸŸŸ **Estate Reserve South Burnett Cabernet Sauvignon 2007** Good hue for age; the bouquet has cedar and cassis aromas built on by the medium- to full-bodied palate, with ripe blackcurrant fruit and fine-grained tannins; good line and length. Serious cabernet. Screwcap. 13.9% alc. **Rating** 92 **To** 2017 $28

✪ **South Burnett Chardonnay 2008** Light straw-green; some very astute winemaking has paid big dividends; early picking, part barrel, part stainless-steel fermentation and maturation has led to a harmonious wine with particularly good balance and mouthfeel to the melon and stone fruit flavours. Screwcap. 12% alc. **Rating** 91 **To** 2013 $13

✪ **Left Field South Burnett Botrytis Semillon 2009** The all-important botrytis infection was obviously low, but does give the wine the edge of complexity to the citrus and tropical fruits, and also the essential acidity. Screwcap. 12.2% alc. **Rating** 91 **To** 2013 $20

Estate Reserve South Burnett Shiraz 2007 Dense crimson-purple; an unashamedly full-bodied shiraz, with multiple layers of black fruits, spice and pepper; the slightly grippy tannins need a few more years yet, but will soften. Screwcap. 14.5% alc. **Rating** 90 **To** 2020 $28

✪ **South Burnett Shiraz Merlot Cabernet 2007** Very good hue, still some crimson; a gently fragrant bouquet of cherry and some spice, then a juicy medium-bodied palate with none of the dry tannins of the Shiraz; indeed, there is good tannin structure for the plum and blackcurrant fruit provided by the merlot and cabernet. Screwcap. 14% alc. **Rating** 90 **To** 2016 $13

Left Field South Burnett Petit Verdot 2008 Typical deep colour; this amazingly resilient variety does it again, keeping very good colour, deeply flavoured black fruits and tannins in total balance. Screwcap. 14.5% alc. **Rating** 90 **To** 2015 $20

ŸŸŸŸ **South Burnett Semillon Chardonnay 2008** Bright, green-tinged colour;
✪ another neatly made wine; very juicy, with fleshy fruits verging on the tropical; a subliminal touch of sweetness, perhaps. Screwcap. 12% alc. **Rating** 89 **To** 2013 $13

○   **South Burnett Sangiovese Rose 2009** Light fuchsia-crimson; no shortage of character; the red fruits of the bouquet are joined by spicy, savoury nuances on the palate, then a just-perceptible touch of residual sweetness. Screwcap. 13% alc. **Rating** 89 **To** 2010 $13

○   **South Burnett Cabernet Merlot 2006** Retains very good hue, although not particularly deep; winemaker Luke Fitzpatrick is on the ball, here with medium-bodied blackcurrant, cassis and plum fruit offset by gently savoury tannins. Screwcap. 14.5% alc. **Rating** 89 **To** 2016 $13

Clover Hill/Lalla Gully   ★★★★☆

60 Clover Hill Road, Lebrina, Tas 7254 **Region** Northern Tasmania
T (03) 6395 6114 **F** (03) 6395 6257 www.taltarni.com.au **Open** By appt
Winemaker Loïc Le Calvez **Est.** 1986 **Cases** 8000 **Vyds** 23.9 ha
Clover Hill was established by Taltarni in 1986 with the sole purpose of making a premium sparkling wine. It has 23.9 ha of vineyards (chardonnay, pinot noir and pinot meunier) and its sparkling wine quality is excellent, combining finesse with power and length. The Lalla Gully property is situated in a sheltered amphitheatre, with a site climate 1°–2°C warmer than Clover Hill, the fruit ripening a week or so earlier. In 2009 American owner and founder of Clos du Val (Napa Valley), Taltarni, and Clover Hill brought the management of these three businesses, together with the Lalla Gully vineyard purchased later, and Domaine de Nizas (Languedoc) under the one management roof. The group is known as Goelet Wine Estates. Exports to the UK, the US and other major markets.

�♔♔♔♔   **Clover Hill Blanc de Blancs 2005** Bright yellow-green, the bouquet is fresh and vibrant, the palate intense and long, with exceedingly crisp and zesty citrus flavours, then a dry, well-balanced finish. Cork. 13% alc. **Rating** 95 **To** 2010 $55

♔♔♔♔♕   **Clover Hill 2005 Rating** 93 **To** 2012 $44
      Clover Hill Blanc de Blancs 2001 Rating 93 **To** 2014 $50

♔♔♔♔   **Lalla Gully Riesling 2008 Rating** 88 **To** 2015 $23
      Lalla Gully Pinot Gris 2009 Rating 88 **To** 2012 $23 BE
      Lalla Gully Pinot Gris 2008 Rating 87 **To** 2011 $23
      Clover Hill Rose 2006 Rating 87 **To** 2012 $20

Clown Fish   ★★★★☆

Garstone Road, Cowaramup, WA 6284 **Region** Margaret River
T (08) 9755 5195 **F** (08) 9755 9441 www.cowaramupwines.com.au **Open** By appt
Winemaker Naturaliste Vintners (Bruce Dukes) **Est.** 1996 **Cases** 3000 **Vyds** 17 ha
Russell and Marilyn Reynolds run a biodynamic vineyard with the aid of sons Cameron (viticulturist) and Anthony (assistant winemaker). Plantings began in 1996 and have been expanded to cover merlot, cabernet sauvignon, shiraz, semillon, chardonnay and sauvignon blanc. Notwithstanding low yields and the discipline that biodynamic grapegrowing entails, wine prices are modest.

♔♔♔♔♔   **Margaret River Chardonnay 2009** Light straw-green; a slightly withdrawn bouquet, then an extroverted palate with a blaze of nectarine, white peach and citrus; any oak present is irrelevant. Screwcap. 13.5% alc. **Rating** 94 **To** 2015 $23.50

♔♔♔♔♕   **Margaret River Sauvignon Blanc Semillon 2009 Rating** 90 **To** 2010 $21.50

Clyde Park Vineyard   ★★★★★

2490 Midland Highway, Bannockburn, Vic 3331 **Region** Geelong
T (03) 5281 7274 **F** (03) 5281 7309 www.clydepark.com.au **Open** W'ends & public hols 11–5
Winemaker Simon Black, Terry Jongebloed **Est.** 1979 **Cases** 6000
Clyde Park Vineyard, established by Gary Farr but sold by him many years ago, has passed through several changes of ownership. Now owned by Terry Jongebloed and Sue

Jongebloed-Dixon, it has significant mature plantings of pinot noir (3.4 ha), chardonnay (3.1 ha), sauvignon blanc (1.5 ha), shiraz (1.2 ha) and pinot gris (0.9 ha), and the quality of its wines is exemplary. Exports to the UK.

ΨΨΨΨΨ **Reserve Pinot Noir 2008** Good depth to colour; the bouquet has ripe plum and black cherry aromas, which come through strongly on the palate; here the sweet fruit core has a crosscut of forest, stem, mint and spice; good length. Screwcap. 12.5% alc. **Rating** 94 **To** 2015 $45

ΨΨΨΨΨ **Chardonnay 2008 Rating** 91 **To** 2013 $30
✪ **Sauvignon Blanc 2008** A full-bodied, full-on, rich style with plenty of winemaker inputs on the tropical fruit flavours. Definitely a food style. Screwcap. 13.5% alc. **Rating** 90 **To** 2010 $19.95

ΨΨΨΨ **Locale Pinot Noir 2008 Rating** 88 **To** 2013 $19.95

Coal Valley Vineyard ★★★★☆

257 Richmond Road, Cambridge, Tas 7170 **Region** Southern Tasmania
T (03) 6248 5367 **www**.coalvalley.com.au **Open** Thurs–Sun 10–4
Winemaker Alain Rousseau, Todd Goebel **Est.** 1991 **Cases** 1000 **Vyds** 4.5 ha
Since acquiring Coal Valley Vineyard in 1999, Gill Christian and Todd Goebel have increased the original 1-ha hobby vineyard to pinot noir (2.3 ha), riesling, cabernet sauvignon, merlot, chardonnay and tempranillo. Todd makes the Cabernet Sauvignon onsite, and dreams of making all the wines. More remarkable was Gill and Todd's concurrent lives: one in India, the other in Tasmania (flying over six times a year), and digging 4000 holes for the new vine plantings. Exports to Canada.

ΨΨΨΨΨ **Chardonnay 2009** Bright straw-green; a vibrant and intense wine; grapefruit,
✪ nectarine and grapefruit drive the palate with clarion clarity, oak a bystander; the '08 was good, this better. Screwcap. 13.5% alc. **Rating** 94 **To** 2016 $28

ΨΨΨΨΨ **Pinot Noir 2008 Rating** 93 **To** 2014 $30
Old Block Pinot Noir 2008 Rating 90 **To** 2015 $45

ΨΨΨΨ **Riesling 2009 Rating** 89 **To** 2016 $26
Barilla Bay Pinot Noir 2008 Rating 87 **To** 2015 $25

Cobaw Ridge ★★★★

31 Perc Boyers Lane, Pastoria, Vic 3444 **Region** Macedon Ranges
T (03) 5423 5227 **F** (03) 5423 5227 **www**.cobawridge.com.au **Open** Thurs–Mon 12–5
Winemaker Alan Cooper **Est.** 1985 **Cases** 1200 **Vyds** 5 ha
The 2010 vintage marked 22 years of winemaking at Cobaw Ridge by owners Alan and Nelly Cooper. When they started planting 28 years ago there was scant knowledge of the best varieties for the region, let alone the Cobaw Ridge site. They have now settled on four varieties, chardonnay and syrah always being part of the mix. Lagrein and pinot noir are more recent arrivals to thrive, cabernet sauvignon (long ago) and vermentino (more recently) removed. Son Joshua is breezing through the wine science degree at Adelaide University with lots of Distinctions, and the odd High Distinction under his belt. Part-time work with Hewitson, in SA, and M Chapoutier at Heathcote is further grist for a distinguished mill. Exports to the UK, the US and Singapore.

ΨΨΨΨΨ **Syrah 2006** Excellent, clear crimson-purple for age; a fine, elegant and restrained shiraz that emphasises its very cool climate origins; the palate is very long, but not intense; on the cusp of ripeness. Diam. 13.5% alc. **Rating** 91 **To** 2020 $40

Cofield Wines ★★★★

Distillery Road, Wahgunyah, Vic 3687 **Region** Rutherglen
T (02) 6033 3798 **F** (02) 6033 0798 **www**.cofieldwines.com.au **Open** Mon–Sat 9–5, Sun 10–5
Winemaker Damien Cofield, David Whyte **Est.** 1990 **Cases** 13 000 **Vyds** 15.4 ha

Sons Damien (winery) and Andrew (vineyard) have taken over responsibility for the business from parents Max and Karen. Collectively, they have developed an impressively broad-based product range with a strong cellar door sales base. The Pickled Sisters Café is open for lunch Wed–Mon (tel 02 6033 2377). A 20-ha property at Rutherglen, purchased in 2007, has 5.3 ha planted to shiraz, and planting of durif and sangiovese followed. Exports to China.

Rutherglen Shiraz Durif 2007 Strong red-purple; while full-bodied and quite tannic, is a legitimate regional expression of the two varieties, and there is a sufficient reservoir of fruit to carry the wine as it ages and softens somewhat. Screwcap. 14.5% alc. **Rating** 91 **To** 2022 $21.50

Quartz Vein Malbec 2008 Highly perfumed, with a touch of violet, raspberry and cedar on offer; generous medium-bodied palate, with plenty of sweet fruit and good structure to conclude; a good example of the variety. Screwcap. 13.6% alc. **Rating** 90 **To** 2014 $28 BE

King Valley Riesling 2009 An attractive, early drinking, juicy wine with a mix of tropical and citrus flavours, and good balance. Screwcap. 11.2% alc. **Rating** 89 **To** 2013 $18

Tumbarumba Pinot Noir Chardonnay NV Rating 89 **To** 2014 $25.50
Orange King Valley Sauvignon Blanc 2009 Rating 88 **To** 2012 $18
Quartz Vein Shiraz 2007 Rating 88 **To** 2014 $28 BE

Max's Footsteps Tempranillo Sangiovese 2008 Light in colour, this is a light bodied, quite fresh and juicy wine; red fruits, with a little earthy complexity; best enjoyed young. Screwcap. 13.7% alc. **Rating** 88 **To** 2012 $16.55 BE

Rutherglen Muscat NV Rating 88 **To** 2011 $25.50

Coldstream Hills   ★★★★★

31 Maddens Lane, Coldstream, Vic 3770 **Region** Yarra Valley
T (03) 5964 9410 **F** (03) 5964 9389 **www**.coldstreamhills.com.au **Open** 7 days 10–5
Winemaker Andrew Fleming, Greg Jarratt, James Halliday (Consultant) **Est.** 1985
Cases NA **Vyds** 100 ha
Founded by the author, who continues to be involved as a consultant, but acquired by Southcorp in mid-1996, Coldstream Hills is now a small part of Foster's. Expansion plans already underway have been maintained, with 100 ha of owned or managed estate vineyards as the base. Chardonnay and Pinot Noir continue to be the principal focus; Merlot came on-stream in 1997, Sauvignon Blanc around the same time, Reserve Shiraz later still. Vintage conditions permitting, Chardonnay, Pinot Noir and Cabernet Sauvignon are made in both varietal and Reserve form, the latter in restricted quantities. In 2010 what amounted to an entirely new, multi-million dollar winery was erected around the original winery buildings and facilities; it has a capacity of 1500 tonnes. Tasting notes are written by Andrew Fleming (AF) or Ben Edwards (BE). Exports to the UK, the US and Singapore.

Yarra Valley Chardonnay 2008 Bright mid-gold; ripe nectarine, pear and a touch of mealy complexity from well-handled toasty oak; the palate shows typical line and precision, with subtle fruits and gentle spices weaving together with ease; fine and lingering to conclude. Three gold medals. Screwcap. 13.5% alc. **Rating** 94 **To** 2012 $29 BE

Yarra Valley Chardonnay Pinot Noir 2006 Fresh green apple bouquet, with pear, lemon and brioche providing support; the palate is lively and focused, a rich, creamy entry giving way to a dry, slightly chalky finish; lovely persistence to conclude. Two gold, two silver medals. Cork. 12% alc. **Rating** 94 **To** 2012 $32 BE

Reserve Yarra Valley Chardonnay 2007 Attractive stone fruit aromas of white peach and nectarine, with cool-climate citrus overtones, flow into an elegant wine with balanced acidity, texture and length; white peach, citrus and quince are complexed by cashew nut barrel ferment characters. Three trophies. Screwcap. 14% alc. **Rating** NR **To** 2017 $56 AF

Reserve Yarra Valley Shiraz 2006 Fragrant aromas of rose petal, plum, black pepper and spice lead into the medium-bodied palate, which has silky tannins and length to the dark plum and cherry flavours, the oak well-integrated and balanced. One gold medal, two silvers. Screwcap. 14.5% alc. **Rating** NR **To** 2018 $40 AF

Reserve Yarra Valley Cabernet Sauvignon 2006 A rich and powerful bouquet with dark plum, black olive and blackcurrant characters evident; the palate is fleshy and concentrated, with integrated cedary oak and fine tannins. An excellent example of Yarra Valley cabernet from the warm vintage. One gold, three silver medals. Screwcap. 14% alc. **Rating** NR To 2020 $56 AF

♀♀♀♀♀ **Yarra Valley Pinot Noir 2008** Rating 93 To 2014 $35 BE
Yarra Valley Merlot 2008 Rating 91 To 2016 $35 BE

Coliban Valley Wines   ★★★★☆

Metcalfe-Redesdale Road, Metcalfe, Vic 3448 **Region** Heathcote
T 0417 312 098 **F** (03) 9813 3895 **www**.colibanvalleywines.com.au **Open** W'ends 10–5
Winemaker Helen Miles **Est.** 1997 **Cases** 400 **Vyds** 4.4 ha
Helen Miles, who has a degree in science, and partner Greg Miles have planted 2.8 ha of shiraz, 1.2 ha of cabernet and 0.4 ha of merlot near Metcalfe, in the cooler southwest corner of Heathcote. The granitic soils and warm climate allow organic principles to be used successfully. The shiraz is dry-grown, while the cabernet sauvignon and merlot receive minimal irrigation.

♀♀♀♀♀ **Reserve Heathcote Shiraz 2006** More crimson-purple than the varietal; an equally intense wine, but with more thrust and lift to the palate; most telling are the finer tannins, which extend the finish without obscuring the fruit. Diam. 15% alc. **Rating** 94 To 2020 $30

♀♀♀♀♀ **Heathcote Shiraz 2006** Rating 90 To 2016 $25

♀♀♀♀ **Heathcote Merlot 2006** Rating 89 To 2014 $20

Collector Wines   ★★★★★

12 Bourke Street, Collector, NSW 2581 (postal) **Region** Canberra District
T (02) 6116 8722 **F** (02) 6247 7682 **www**.collectorwines.com.au **Open** Not
Winemaker Alex McKay **Est.** 2007 **Cases** 2000
Owner and winemaker Alex McKay makes two Canberra District Shirazs, the Marked Tree Red from parcels of shiraz from vineyards in and around Murrumbateman, and the Reserve from a single patch of mature shiraz grown on an elevated granite saddle near Murrumbateman. Exports to The Netherlands.

♀♀♀♀♀ **Marked Tree Red Shiraz 2009** Clear crimson-purple; the poetry starts with
✪   the delicately fragrant array of black cherry, plum and spice aromas of the bouquet, and continues with the beautifully balanced palate, oak, tannins and fruit seamlessly joined. Alex Mckay's advice to drink it on release or up to 10 years (I would suggest more than 10, but that's by the by) is bang on the money. Screwcap. 13.2% alc. **Rating** 97 To 2020 $26.95
Reserve Shiraz 2009 Clear crimson-purple; an even more profound bouquet, the palate with more depth and structure, thus answering the question, how can the Reserve be better than the Marked Tree? When you are tasting that wine, the Reserve is a great wine that has a minimum 20 years life, and probably much longer. If you are patient, this will be a greater wine. Trophy Sydney Wine Show '10. Screwcap. 13.5% alc. **Rating** 96 To 2023 $49.95

Colvin Wines   ★★★☆

19 Boyle Street, Mosman, NSW 2088 (postal) **Region** Hunter Valley
T (02) 9908 7886 **F** (02) 9908 7885 **www**.colvinwines.com.au **Open** Not
Winemaker Andrew Spinaze, Drayton's Family Wines, Phil Ryan (Contract) **Est.** 1999
Cases 500 **Vyds** 5.19 ha
In 1990 Sydney lawyer John Colvin and wife Robyn purchased the De Beyers Vineyard, which has a history going back to the second half of the 19th century. By 1967, when a syndicate headed by Douglas McGregor purchased 35 ha of the original vineyard site, no

vines remained. The syndicate planted semillon on the alluvial soil of the creek flats and shiraz on the red clay hillsides. When the Colvins acquired the property the vineyard was in need of attention. Up to 1998 all the grapes were sold to Tyrrell's, but since '99 quantities have been made for the Colvin Wines label. These include Sangiovese, from a little over 1 ha of vines planted by John Colvin in 1996 because of his love of the wines of Tuscany.

ŶŶŶŶŶ **De Beyers Vineyard Hunter Valley Semillon 2007** Brilliant pale-green; is in the first stages of moving from grassy minerally characters to lemon, honey and toast; give it another three years. Screwcap. 10.4% alc. **Rating** 92 **To** 2017 $30

ŶŶŶŶ **De Beyers Vineyard Hunter Valley Sangiovese 2007 Rating** 89 **To** 2014 $33
De Beyers Vineyard Hunter Valley Shiraz 2006 Rating 88 **To** 2014 $33

Condo Wines   ★★★
3 Ward Street, Torrensville, SA 5031 (postal) **Region** Lower Murray Zone
T (08) 8443 7551 **F** (08) 8443 6489 **www.**condowines.com.au **Open** Not
Winemaker Jo Irvine, David Norman (Contract) **Est.** 1997 **Cases** 2400 **Vyds** 36.5 ha
The Condo family, headed by Frank Condo, purchased their Allawah property at Swan Reach on the Murray River in 1981, but it was not until the mid '90s that they established their vineyard, planted predominantly to cabernet sauvignon and shiraz, with small amounts of merlot and chardonnay. The winemaking is simple, designed to keep production costs to a minimum. The major focus of the business is on exports (Canada, Hong Kong and China), price being the obvious attraction.

ŶŶŶŶ **Shiraz 2008** Estate-grown on the brow of the Murray River at Swan Reach;
✪ well made, with good structure and a pleasantly savoury twist to the fruit; the tannin and oak management is likewise good. Screwcap. 13.5% alc. **Rating** 87 **To** 2011 $12

✪ **Merlot 2008** Strong colour; a very rich and full-bodied wine by the standards of the Riverland, but it lacks varietal character. Treat it as a dry red, and the value is obvious. Screwcap. 13.5% alc. **Rating** 87 **To** 2012 $12

Constable Estate Vineyards   ★★★★
205 Gillards Road, Pokolbin, NSW 2320 **Region** Hunter Valley
T (02) 4998 7887 **F** (02) 4998 6555 **www.**constablevineyards.com.au **Open** 7 days 10–5
Winemaker Liz Jackson (Contract) **Est.** 1981 **Cases** 2000 **Vyds** 5.55 ha
The business was created by long-term friends David Constable and Michael Hershon; one of its points of attraction is its spectacular formal gardens: the Rose, Knot and Herb, Secret and Sculpture. When Michael died in 2007, David purchased his interests in the property from his estate; he has since replanted half the vineyard, and is actively engaged in a program to increase the quality of the wines and the profile of the business. The varieties planted are cabernet sauvignon, verdelho, semillon, shiraz and chardonnay.

ŶŶŶŶŶ **Cabernet Merlot 2007** Good colour; has clear varietal cassis and blackcurrant fruit, backed by black olive and earthy tannins. A particularly good wine in the Hunter context, but how it won the trophy for Best Blended Red in Cowra Wine Show '09 is anyone's guess. Screwcap. 13.7% alc. **Rating** 92 **To** 2017 $45

Conte Estate Wines   ★★★☆
Lot 51 Sand Road, McLaren Flat, SA 5171 **Region** McLaren Vale
T (08) 8383 0183 **F** (08) 8383 0125 **www.**conteestatewines.com.au **Open** By appt
Winemaker Danial Conte **Est.** 2003 **Cases** 10 000 **Vyds** 50 ha
The Conte family has a large vineyard, predominantly established since 1960 but with 2.5 ha of shiraz planted 100 years earlier in the 1860s. In all there are 18 ha of shiraz, 12 ha of grenache, 7 ha each of cabernet sauvignon and sauvignon blanc and 6 ha of chardonnay. While continuing to sell a large proportion of the production, winemaking has become a larger part of the business. Exports to Canada, China, Hong Kong and Singapore.

ΨΨΨΨ♀ **Reserve Over the Hill McLaren Vale Shiraz 2007** Good hue for the vintage;
⊘ 'Over the Hill' is inspired by the 'decrepit' look of the 140-year-old vines planted
by the Hardy family; the wine can't entirely escape the clutches of the '07 vintage,
but does have lots of black fruit and bitter chocolate on a long palate. Cork.
14.5% alc. **Rating** 93 **To** 2017 $25

ΨΨΨΨ **Mixed Up Teen McLaren Vale Rose 2009 Rating** 87 **To** 2011 $14

Coobara Wines ★★★★
PO Box 231, Birdwood, SA 5234 **Region** Adelaide Hills
T 0407 685 797 **F** (08) 8568 5069 **www**.coobarawines.com.au **Open** Wed–Sat 10–5,
Sun & public hols 12–4
Winemaker David Cook, Mark Jamieson **Est.** 1992 **Cases** 4500 **Vyds** 12 ha
David Cook has worked in the wine industry for over 19 years, principally with Orlando but
also with Jim Irvine, John Glaetzer and the late Neil Ashmead. As well as working full time
for Orlando, he undertook oenology and viticulture courses, and – with support from his
parents – planted 4 ha of cabernet sauvignon and merlot on the family property at Birdwood.
In 1993 they purchased the adjoining property, planting 2 ha each of riesling and pinot gris,
and thereafter lifting the plantings of merlot and cabernet sauvignon to 4 ha each. In 2003
David decided to commence wine production, a fortuitous decision given that the following
year their long-term grape purchase contracts were not renewed. Coobara is an Aboriginal
word meaning 'place of birds'.

ΨΨΨΨ♀ **Adelaide Hills Pinot Gris 2009** Fermented and matured in two-year-old
French oak barriques, adding a measure of depth to the colour and having a major
impact on the rich, mouth-coating palate; it would be easy to pick the wine as an
Alsace tokay (the local name for pinot gris) in a blind tasting. Screwcap. 13.5% alc.
Rating 90 **To** 2012 $20

Cooks Lot ★★★☆
Cassilis Road, Mudgee, NSW 2850 **Region** Mudgee
T (02) 9550 3228 **F** (02) 9550 4390 **www**.cookslot.com.au **Open** Not
Winemaker Duncan Cook, Ian McRae **Est.** 2002 **Cases** 4000
Since 2002 Duncan Cook has managed to run several wine lives, chiefly focusing on an
almost-completed oenology degree at CSU, and winemaking (for Cooks Lot) at Miramar. He
owns no vineyards, purchasing grapes from Mudgee and Orange. Exports to China.

ΨΨΨΨ♀ **Orange Sauvignon Blanc 2009** Pale straw-green; a very appealing sauvignon
⊘ blanc that neatly marries tropical flavours with grass, green bean and asparagus
notes; good overall mouthfeel and balance. Screwcap. 13.5% alc. **Rating** 91
To 2011 $18.95

ΨΨΨΨ **Mudgee Rose 2008 Rating** 87 **To** 2010 $18.95

Coolangatta Estate ★★★★★
1335 Bolong Road, Shoalhaven Heads, NSW 2535 **Region** Shoalhaven Coast
T (02) 4448 7131 **F** (02) 4448 7997 **www**.coolangattaestate.com.au **Open** 7 days 10–5
Winemaker Tyrrell's **Est.** 1988 **Cases** 5000 **Vyds** 10.5 ha
Coolangatta Estate is part of a 150-ha resort with accommodation, restaurants, golf course, etc.;
some of the oldest buildings were convict-built in 1822. It might be thought that the wines
are tailored purely for the tourist market, but in fact the standard of viticulture is exceptionally
high (immaculate Scott Henry trellising), and the contract winemaking is wholly professional.
It has a habit of bobbing up with gold medals at Sydney and Canberra wine shows. Its 2001
Semillon was a prolific gold-medal winner up to '08, the '02 and more recent vintages likewise shining with age.

ΨΨΨΨΨ Estate Grown Semillon 2009 Semillon is highly suited to this region, and
✪ Tyrrell's maximises the quality outcome; offers a mix of citrus and mineral on
bouquet and palate, almost a crossover into riesling territory. Will cellar well.
Screwcap. 11% alc. **Rating** 94 **To** 2019 $19
Aged Release Estate Grown Semillon 2002 Bright green-gold; classic
lightly browned toast aromas offset by crunchy, zesty acidity running through
the long, grassy, lemony palate. Don't procrastinate. Twin top. 10% alc. **Rating** 94
To 2012 $25

ΨΨΨΨΨ Individual Vineyard Wollstonecraft Semillon 2009 **Rating** 93 **To** 2017 $22
Aged Release Alexander Berry Chardonnay 2005 **Rating** 91 **To** 2011 $25

ΨΨΨΨ Estate Grown Verdelho 2009 **Rating** 89 **To** 2012 $19
Estate Grown Savagnin 2009 **Rating** 89 **To** 2012 $22

Coombe Farm Vineyard ★★★★

11 St Huberts Road, Coldstream, Vic 3770 **Region** Yarra Valley
T (03) 9739 1131 **F** (03) 9739 1154 **www**.coombefarm.com.au **Open** 7 days 10–5
Winemaker Wine Network, Chris Bolden **Est.** 1999 **Cases** 3000 **Vyds** 69 ha
Coombe Farm Vineyard is owned by Pamela, Lady Vestey (Dame Nellie Melba's granddaughter),
Lord Samuel Vestey and The Right Honourable Mark Vestey. The vineyard is planted to
chardonnay (20 ha), pinot noir (19 ha), merlot and cabernet sauvignon (7 ha each) and
viognier and pinot gris (3 ha each). The vast majority of the fruit is sold to eager winemakers
in the region, a small amount made for Coombe Farm. Exports to the UK.

ΨΨΨΨΨ Yarra Valley Arneis 2008 Light green-straw; you might not pick the variety, but
✪ you would register the impact and intensity of the wine in the mouth, akin to green
fruit with a touch of sugar; now, I know that is a classic sweet and sour description,
but it's not what I mean to say – perhaps freshly squeezed lemon juice made
drinkable with a teaspoon of sugar. Screwcap. 12.7% alc. **Rating** 90 **To** 2013 $21
Yarra Valley Rose 2009 Pale blush; a quite complex rose, both in terms of
texture and savoury/spicy flavours; has length and a pleasingly dry finish enlivened
by acidity. Screwcap. 13.5% alc. **Rating** 90 **To** 2011 $25
Yarra Valley Cabernet Merlot 2006 Developed colour; a light- to medium-
bodied wine with cedar and red berry fruits supported by fine tannins; the fruit
flavours kick again (unexpectedly) on the finish and aftertaste. Screwcap. 13.5% alc.
Rating 90 **To** 2015 $25

ΨΨΨΨ Yarra Valley Chardonnay 2008 **Rating** 89 **To** 2014 $25
Yarra Valley Pinot Gris 2009 **Rating** 89 **To** 2011 $21
Yarra Valley Pinot Noir 2008 **Rating** 88 **To** 2013 $25
Yarra Valley Merlot 2008 **Rating** 87 **To** 2013 $25

Coombend Estate ★★★★☆

Coombend via Swansea, Tas 7190 **Region** East Coast Tasmania
T (03) 6257 8881 **F** (03) 6257 8884 **Open** 7 days 10–5
Winemaker Tamar Ridge (Andrew Pirie) **Est.** 1985 **Cases** 3000
In 2005 Tamar Ridge acquired Coombend Estate, including all the assets and the business
name. Tamar Ridge has immediately commenced the establishment of a large vineyard that
will dwarf the existing 1.75 ha of cabernet sauvignon, 2.25 ha of sauvignon blanc, 0.5 ha of
pinot noir and 0.3 ha of riesling. Exports to Sweden.

ΨΨΨΨΨ Riesling 2008 Apple blossom and herb aromas, then a fine and elegant palate
✪ moving more to juicy citrus flavours; excellent balance. Screwcap. 11.5% alc.
Rating 94 **To** 2023 $22.50

ΨΨΨΨΨ Pinot Noir 2007 **Rating** 93 **To** 2015 $26

Cooper Burns ★★★★☆

1 Golden Way, Nuriootpa, SA 5353 (postal) **Region** Barossa Valley
T (08) 8563 91811 **F** (08) 8563 9181 **www.cooperburns.com.au Open** Not
Winemaker Mark Cooper, Russell Burns **Est.** 2004 **Cases** 1000
Cooper Burns is the winemaking partnership of Mark Cooper and Russell Burns. It is a virtual winery focusing on small-batch, handmade wine from the Barossa Valley (grapes are sourced from Kalimna, Koonunga Hill and Moppa at the northern end of the valley). In 2006 production was increased to add a Shiraz Viognier and Grenache to the existing single-vineyard Shiraz. Exports to the US and Hong Kong.

ΨΨΨΨΨ **Barossa Valley Shiraz 2007** Deep purple, exceptional for the vintage; the bouquet and palate take their cue from the colour; this has a generosity of blackberry fruit not often encountered from '07, the length and balance impeccable; 220 dozen made. Screwcap. 14.8% alc. **Rating** 95 **To** 2027 $35

ΨΨΨΨΨ **Barossa Valley Shiraz Viognier 2007 Rating** 92 **To** 2020 $28

Cooralook Wines ★★★★☆

Level 1, 500 Chapel Street, South Yarra, Vic 3141 (postal) **Region** Mornington Peninsula
T (03) 9667 6541 **F** (03) 9827 3970 **www.yabbylake.com Open** Not
Winemaker Tom Carson, Chris Forge **Est.** 2000 **Cases** 40 000 **Vyds** 72.1 ha
Cooralook Wines, owned by Robert and Mem Kirby, has substantial vineyards on the Mornington Peninsula and in Heathcote and the Strathbogie Ranges, each vineyard focusing on the varieties most suited to each region. The wines represent great value. Exports to the US, the UK, Canada, Sweden, Singapore, Hong Kong and China.

ΨΨΨΨΨ ✪ **Mornington Peninsula Chardonnay 2008** Has abundant presence, with lip-smacking flavours running from grapefruit through the full gamut of stone fruit; has excellent length and balance, and only minimal oak. Screwcap. 13% alc. **Rating** 93 **To** 2015 $18

✪ **Strathbogie Ranges Rose 2009** Crimson-purple; a very aromatic bouquet, the palate fresh and lively with red cherry and strawberry fruit; striking rose. Shiraz. Screwcap. 13% alc. **Rating** 93 **To** 2011 $18

✪ **Grenache Shiraz 2008** A fascinating blend of 50/50 Heathcote Grenache/Mornington Peninsula Shiraz flowing in a single, unbroken line across the lively, medium-bodied palate; red and black cherry flavours, with spicy nuances, provide a wine for all places and all seasons. Screwcap. 14.5% alc. **Rating** 93 **To** 2016 $18

✪ **Shiraz 2007** Bright hue; an elegant, medium-bodied wine with dark cherry, plum, tobacco and spice aromas and flavours; the palate is fresh and lively, the finish clean. Screwcap. 13.5% alc. **Rating** 91 **To** 2016 $18

✪ **Strathbogie Ranges Pinot Noir 2009** Abounds with black cherry, plum and spice; its excellent texture is pure pinot, and provides the foil to what might otherwise have been a stolid palate. Needs a couple of years to show its best. Screwcap. 13.5% alc. **Rating** 90 **To** 2014 $18

✪ **Shiraz 2008** Deep crimson-purple; a spicy, black fruit bouquet leads into a supple, medium-bodied palate, blackberry to the fore, but also with notes of licorice and spice. Cellar-worthy. Screwcap. 14.5% alc. **Rating** 90 **To** 2018 $18

ΨΨΨΨ **Pinot Gris 2008 Rating** 89 **To** 2011 $18
Pinot Noir 2008 Rating 89 **To** 2014 $18
Strathbogie Ranges Cabernet Sauvignon Merlot 2008 Rating 89 **To** 2015 $18
Strathbogie Ranges Chardonnay 2009 Rating 88 **To** 2011 $18
Strathbogie Ranges Sauvignon Blanc 2009 Rating 87 **To** 2011 $18

Coriole ★★★★★

Chaffeys Road, McLaren Vale, SA 5171 **Region** McLaren Vale
T (08) 8323 8305 **F** (08) 8323 9136 **www**.coriole.com **Open** Mon–Fri 10–5, w'ends &
public hols 11–5
Winemaker Simon White **Est.** 1967 **Cases** 35 000 **Vyds** 48.5 ha
While Coriole was not established until 1967, the cellar door and gardens date back to 1860,
when the original farm houses that now constitute the cellar door were built. The oldest shiraz
forming part of the estate plantings dates back to 1917, and since '85, Coriole has been an
Australian pioneer of sangiovese and – more recently – the Italian white variety fiano, plus
barbera and nero d'Avola have joined the fold. Shiraz has 65% of the plantings, and it is for
this variety that Coriole is best known, led in turn by the super-premium Lloyd Reserve, the
flagship. Exports to all major markets.

ＹＹＹＹＹ **Lloyd Reserve McLaren Vale Shiraz 2007** Impenetrable colour; deep, dark
and inky, displaying mocha and an inordinate amount of black fruit; thickly
textured and a little tarry, the tannins are plentiful and very fine; monumental but
not the least bit heavy. Cork. 14.5% alc. **Rating** 94 **To** 2020 $80 BE

✪ **McLaren Vale Sangiovese 2008** The intense sour cherry characters that drive
the bouquet and palate are 100% varietal, as are the savoury tannins. Shows the
experience gained over 23 years since Coriole pioneered the variety. Screwcap.
14% alc. **Rating** 94 **To** 2018 $22

ＹＹＹＹＹ **Estate Grown McLaren Vale Shiraz 2007** Rating 92 **To** 2020 $28
The Dancing Fig McLaren Vale Shiraz Mourvedre 2008 Rating 92
To 2020 $25
McLaren Vale Barbera 2007 Rating 90 **To** 2015 $32

ＹＹＹＹ **McLaren Vale Fiano 2009** Rating 89 **To** 2013 $25
Redstone McLaren Vale Shiraz 2007 Rating 89 **To** 2020 $18.50
✪ **McLaren Vale Sangiovese Shiraz 2007** A successful blend, particularly given
that the wine is little more than light bodied; the sangiovese tannins have been
tamed by the supple shiraz component. Good to go now. Screwcap. 14% alc.
Rating 89 **To** 2010 $15
Museum Release McLaren Vale Chenin Blanc 2004 Rating 88 **To** 2014
$25 BE

🍇 Coward & Black Vineyards ★★★☆

448 Harmans South Road, Wilyabrup, WA 6280 **Region** Margaret River
T (08) 9755 6355 **F** (08) 9755 6456 **www**.cowardandblack.com.au **Open** 7 days 9–5
Winemaker Clive Otto (Contract) **Est.** 1998 **Cases** 2900 **Vyds** 9.5 ha
Martin Black and Patrick Coward have been lifetime friends since they were five years old.
They acquired a property directly opposite Ashbrook and in the same road as Vasse Felix, and
began the slow establishment of a dry-grown vineyard. A second block was commenced five
years later, by which time water was available to both of the blocks, but is seldom used. In
all there are 2.5 ha each of cabernet sauvignon and shiraz, and 1.5 ha each of chardonnay,
semillon and sauvignon blanc. The cellar door is integrated with another of their businesses,
the Margaret River Providore. The result is an organic vegetable garden, 1000 olive trees and
an 80-seat restaurant serving food that has attracted praise from all and sundry since the word
go, incorporating vegetables and fruit straight from the organic garden.

ＹＹＹＹＹ **Margaret River Chardonnay 2007** The best of the current releases; clean,
elegant and not forced to be something it is not; light-bodied, but with good focus
to its stone fruit and citrus flavours, oak in a support role. Screwcap. 13.5% alc.
Rating 92 **To** 2014 $25.50

ＹＹＹＹ **Margaret River April Harvest Semillon 2009** Rating 89 **To** 2019 $18.50
Margaret River Semillon Sauvignon Blanc 2009 Rating 88 **To** 2010 $18.50
Show Margaret River Shiraz 2006 Rating 88 **To** 2014 $22.50
Lady Margo Margaret River Rose 2009 Rating 87 **To** 2010 $16.50

Cowra Estate ★★★

Boorowa Road, Cowra, NSW 2794 **Region** Cowra
T (02) 9907 7735 **F** (02) 9907 7734 **Open** At The Quarry Restaurant Tues–Sun 10–4
Winemaker Tim Smith **Est.** 1973 **Cases** 5000 **Vyds** 73 ha
Cowra Estate was purchased from the family of founder Tony Gray by South African–born
food and beverage entrepreneur John Geber in 1995. A vigourous promotional campaign has
gained a higher domestic profile for the once export-oriented brand. John is actively involved
in the promotional effort and rightly proud of the wines. The Quarry Wine Cellars and
Restaurant offer visitors a full range of Cowra Estate's wines, plus wines from other producers
in the region. The Geber family, incidentally, also owns Chateau Tanunda in the Barossa Valley
(see separate entry). Exports to Switzerland and Denmark.

♥♥♥♥   **Chardonnay 2008** Cleverly, no mention one way or the other of oak; fresh citrus
and melon fruit, but not much drive. Screwcap. 13% alc. **Rating** 87 **To** 2010 $18

Crabtree Watervale Wines ★★★★★

North Terrace, Watervale, SA 5452 **Region** Clare Valley
T (08) 8843 0069 **F** (08) 8843 0144 **www.**crabtreewines.com.au **Open** 7 days 10.30–4.50
Winemaker Kerri Thompson **Est.** 1979 **Cases** 5000 **Vyds** 13.2 ha
In October 2007 wine industry executives Richard Woods and Rasa Fabian purchased
Crabtree and left Sydney corporate life for the ultimate seachange. Collectively, they have
decades of sales and marketing experience, but this will be an entirely new world; both are
adamant that Crabtree remain an estate brand, and therefore limited in volume. They have
acquired a highly talented and very experienced winemaker in Kerri Thompson (see KT &
The Falcon entry), particularly given that riesling (5.5 ha) is the leading estate-varietal wine.

♥♥♥♥♥   **Riesling 2009** Like the Hilltop, estate-grown, but here there is greater intensity
✪   to the highly floral bouquet and the juicy citrus fruits of the palate. Gold medal
         Adelaide Wine Show '09 thoroughly deserved. Screwcap. 12.5% alc. **Rating** 96
         To 2024 $22
✪   **Windmill Vineyard Cabernet Sauvignon 2008** Strong purple-red; an
         object lesson in how to harness Clare Valley cabernet, even in a heatwave; fine
         blackcurrant fruit is married with perfectly ripened and balanced tannins, then
         spending 18 months in one- and two-year-old French barriques; great length,
         texture and balance. Screwcap. 14% alc. **Rating** 96 **To** 2023 $22
✪   **Hilltop Riesling 2009** Has a fragrant and complex bouquet of lime and apple
         blossom, then a perfectly articulated palate follows flavour suit, the finish long and
         crisp. Trophy Sydney Wine Show '10. Screwcap. 12% alc. **Rating** 94 **To** 2020 $20
✪   **Hilltop Shiraz 2008** Dense purple-red; an opulent shiraz, full-bodied and stacked
         with dark fruits, yet retains a lively juiciness on the back-palate and finish. Great
         finish. Screwcap. 14.5% alc. **Rating** 94 **To** 2023 $22
         Pomona Cabernet Sauvignon 2008 Full red-purple; strongly varietal fruit on
         the bouquet, then a full-bodied palate with blackcurrant fruit to the fore, plus a
         touch of plum, built-in tannins supporting the palate from start to finish. Screwcap.
         14% alc. **Rating** 94 **To** 2023 $45

♥♥♥♥♀   **Tempranillo 2009** **Rating** 90 **To** 2015 $22

♥♥♥♥   **Arriviste Chardonnay Viognier 2009** **Rating** 89 **To** 2013 $22
         Zibibbo 2009 **Rating** 89 **To** 2012 $22

Craig Avon Vineyard ★★★☆

Craig Avon Lane, Merricks North, Vic 3926 **Region** Mornington Peninsula
T (03) 5989 7465 **F** (03) 5989 7615 **Open** By appt
Winemaker Ken Lang **Est.** 1986 **Cases** 700 **Vyds** 2 ha
The estate-grown wines are produced from 1.2 ha of chardonnay, 0.4 ha of pinot noir, 0.3 ha
of cabernet sauvignon and 0.1 ha of cabernet franc. They are competently made, clean and

with pleasant fruit flavour. The wines are sold through the cellar door and by mailing list. Exports to the UK.

🍷🍷🍷🍷 **Chardonnay 2008** A slightly counter-cultural style, with abundant ripe stone fruit aromas and flavours complexed by barrel ferment oak inputs; needs a touch more acidity. ProCork. 14% alc. **Rating** 90 **To** 2013 $39

🍷🍷🍷🍷 **Cabernet Sauvignon 2006** **Rating** 88 **To** 2016 $37

Craiglee ★★★★★
Sunbury Road, Sunbury, Vic 3429 **Region** Sunbury
T (03) 9744 4489 **F** (03) 9744 4489 www.craiglee.com.au **Open** Sun, public hols 10–5, or by appt
Winemaker Patrick Carmody **Est.** 1976 **Cases** 2500 **Vyds** 9.5 ha
A winery with a proud 19th-century record, Craiglee recommenced winemaking in 1976 after a prolonged hiatus. Produces one of the finest cool-climate shirazs in Australia, redolent of cherry, licorice and spice in the better (warmer) vintages, lighter-bodied in the cooler ones. Mature vines and improved viticulture have made the wines more consistent (and even better) over the past 10 years or so. Exports to the UK, the US, Hong Kong and Italy.

🍷🍷🍷🍷🍷 **Sunbury Shiraz 2007** Relatively light but bright crimson colour; very zesty and lively, ablaze with red berry fruits and delicate spices; the tannin and oak management is exemplary in a wine of great purity. Diam. 13.5% alc. **Rating** 95 **To** 2020 $45
Sunbury Shiraz 2006 Bright red with hints of purple; totally delicious wine at the heart of Craiglee style, light- to medium-bodied, but with great length, freshness and finesse; red fruits, spice and pepper intermingle; no way you would guess the alcohol, because the wine is so fresh and vibrant. Diam. 14.5% alc. **Rating** 95 **To** 2020 $45
Sunbury Cabernet Sauvignon 2007 Good hue, although not entirely bright; an elegant cabernet, with clear-cut cassis and blackcurrant fruit, the tannins ripe and fine, French oak in the background. Diam. 13.5% alc. **Rating** 94 **To** 2017 $30

🍷🍷🍷🍷 **Sunbury Chardonnay 2008** **Rating** 93 **To** 2015 $27
Sunbury Pinot Noir 2008 **Rating** 90 **To** 2014 $30

Craigow ★★★★★
528 Richmond Road, Cambridge, Tas 7170 **Region** Southern Tasmania
T (03) 6248 5379 www.craigow.com.au **Open** 7 days Christmas to Easter (except public hols), or by appt
Winemaker Winemaking Tasmania (Julian Alcorso) **Est.** 1989 **Cases** 1500 **Vyds** 9.75 ha
Hobart surgeon Barry Edwards and wife Cathy have moved from being grapegrowers with only one wine to a portfolio of several wines, while continuing to sell most of their grapes. Craigow has an impressive museum release program; the best are outstanding, while others show the impact of sporadic bottle oxidation (a diminishing problem with each vintage now under screwcap). In 2008 Craigow won the Tasmanian Vineyard of the Award. There is a degree of poetic history: the first settler, who arrived in the 1820s, was a Scottish doctor (James Murdoch), who among other things grew opium poppies for medical use; by 1872 his descendants were making wine from grapes, gooseberries and cherries. There is some suggestion that the grapes, known then as black cluster, were in all probability, pinot noir.

🍷🍷🍷🍷🍷 **Dessert Gewurztraminer 2006** Brilliant glowing yellow-green; not particularly
✪ sweet, but has considerable intensity and marvellous balance and length. Has matured slowly but surely, and is a freakish wine by Australian standards, its future stretching out indefinitely. Screwcap. 10% alc. **Rating** 95 **To** 2020 $23
Riesling 2005 Fractionally deeper than the '06, but still crystal-green; the bouquet is a little off-putting at the moment, but the palate is explosive and very long, layers of lime and grapefruit flavour wrapped around each other through to the finish. Screwcap. 12.7% alc. **Rating** 94 **To** 2025 $28

Pinot Noir 2006 Exceptionally good hue and depth for age; has begun to break free of the bonds that encircled it when first tasted at two years old; a seriously powerful, but not extractive, wine, with sultry dark plum fruit and spice flavours supported by good tannins and oak. Still on the march. Screwcap. 12.7% alc. **Rating** 94 **To** 2018 $35

✪ **Dessert Riesling 2008** Glowing pale green-yellow; of Auslese sweetness, but perfectly balanced; the future is, like the Dessert Gewurztraminer, limitless; still has improvement in front of it. Screwcap. 9.2% alc. **Rating** 94 **To** 2018 $19

🍷🍷🍷🍷½ **Riesling 2006** **Rating** 92 **To** 2026 $28
Unwooded Chardonnay 2008 **Rating** 90 **To** 2012 $19
Easy Pinot 2008 **Rating** 90 **To** 2013 $19

🍷🍷🍷🍷 **Sauvignon Blanc 2009** **Rating** 89 **To** 2012 $25

Craneford ★★★★☆

Moorundie Street, Truro, SA 5356 **Region** Barossa Valley
T (08) 8564 0003 **F** (08) 8564 0008 **www**.cranefordwines.com **Open** 7 days 10–5
Winemaker Carol Riebke, John Glaetzer (Consultant) **Est.** 1978 **Cases** 35 000

Since Craneford was founded in 1978 it has undergone a number of changes of both location and ownership. The biggest change came in 2004 when the winery, by then housed in the old country fire station building in Truro, was expanded and upgraded. In 2006 John Glaetzer joined the team as consultant winemaker, with Carol Riebke the day-to-day winemaker. Quality grapes are sourced from contract growers. Exports to all major markets.

🍷🍷🍷🍷🍷 **Fire Station Shiraz 2006** Deep purple-red; an intense, complex shiraz with a stellar array of licorice, spice and black fruits, the texture of the supple palate is also outstanding; fine tannins and well-matched oak are the final pieces of the jigsaw. Cork. 15% alc. **Rating** 96 **To** 2026 $130

🍷🍷🍷🍷½ ✪ **Allyson Parsons Barossa Valley Cabernet Sauvignon 2007** There is no question the wine has a decided savoury caste, but there is a core of very attractive black and redcurrant fruit, and the tannins are balanced, fine and ripe. Drink any time over the next four years. Screwcap. 14.5% alc. **Rating** 91 **To** 2014 $18.65
Rose of the Valley 2009 **Rating** 90 **To** 2011 $21.35
Basket Pressed Barossa Valley Shiraz 2008 **Rating** 90 **To** 2017 $26
Barossa Valley Cabernet Sauvignon 2008 **Rating** 90 **To** 2020 $26

🍷🍷🍷🍷 **Allyson Parsons Barossa Valley Shiraz 2007** **Rating** 89 **To** 2015 $18.65
GSM 2008 **Rating** 89 **To** 2015 $22
Quartet 2008 **Rating** 89 **To** 2015 $22

✪ **Private Selection Cabernet Sauvignon 2007** This is the best of Cranford's Private Selection wines, with some herb, leaf and mint notes adding to the savoury, earthy characters, but is unmistakably cabernet; good length and balance. Screwcap. 13.5% alc. **Rating** 88 **To** 2013 $10.25

✪ **Allyson Parsons Barossa Valley Semillon Sauvignon Blanc 2009** The energy and flavour of the wine largely comes from the semillon component with its citrussy drive and acidity on the finish; 12 months' cellaring might add a little generosity. Screwcap. 12.5% alc. **Rating** 87 **To** 2012 $12.65

Crawford River Wines ★★★★★

741 Hotspur Upper Road, Condah, Vic 3303 **Region** Henty
T (03) 5578 2267 **F** (03) 5578 2240 **www**.crawfordriverwines.com **Open** By appt
Winemaker John and Belinda Thomson **Est.** 1975 **Cases** 5000 **Vyds** 11.5 ha

Time flies, and it seems incredible that Crawford River has celebrated its 35th birthday. Once a tiny outpost in a little-known wine region, Crawford River is now one of the foremost producers of riesling (and other excellent wines) thanks to the unremitting attention to detail and skill of its founder and winemaker, John Thomson. His exceptionally talented daughter Belinda has returned part-time after completing her winemaking degree and working along the way in Marlborough (NZ), Bordeaux, Ribera del Duero (Spain), Bolgheri and Tuscany, and the Nahe (Germany), with Crawford River filling in the gaps. She continues working in Spain, effectively doing two vintages each year. Exports to the UK, Ireland, Canada, Japan and Southeast Asia.

ΥΥΥΥΥ **Riesling 2004** Some deepening of colour but hue still green; terrific minerally structure and intensity to an extremely long palate just starting to hit its straps; lime, apple, spice and lemony acidity. Screwcap. 12.5% alc. **Rating** 96 **To** 2024 $64
Riesling 2009 Light straw-green; the bouquet provides a quiet start, the wine bursting into song on the palate, with intense lime juice along with ripe apple notes. Still more to come. Screwcap. 13.5% alc. **Rating** 94 **To** 2019 $34

ΥΥΥΥΥ **Rose 2009 Rating** 90 **To** 2012 $25
Cabernet Sauvignon 2005 Rating 90 **To** 2018 $40

Crittenden Estate   ★★★★
25 Harrisons Road, Dromana, Vic 3936 **Region** Mornington Peninsula
T (03) 5981 8322 **F** (03) 5981 8366 **www**.crittendenwines.com.au **Open** 7 days 11–4
Winemaker Garry and Rollo Crittenden **Est.** 2003 **Cases** 5000 **Vyds** 14 ha
The wheel of fortune has turned full circle with son Rollo Crittenden returning to the (new) family wine business established by father Garry in 2003. In so doing, both father and son have severed ties with Dromana Estate, the old family business. For good measure, the Crittendens have taken a lease on a modern winery in Patterson Lakes, approximately 20 mins north of their Dromana property. Capable of handling 200 tonnes of grapes, more than that required by Crittenden Estate, it has enabled Rollo to develop a contract-winemaking business, Latitude 38.

ΥΥΥΥΥ **The Zumma Chardonnay 2008** Plenty of effort can be seen in this wine, with toasty oak, ripe nectarine, citrus fruit and a touch of minerality all playing pivotal roles; the palate shows lemony acidity, drawing out the palate for a long and complex conclusion. Screwcap. 13% alc. **Rating** 92 **To** 2015 $49 BE
Mornington Peninsula Pinot Noir 2008 An elegant bouquet, fresh and poised, with dark cherry fruit complemented by a sappy edge to the fruit; the palate is light and lacy, and takes time to unravel, with a little spice emerging on the finish. Screwcap. 13% alc. **Rating** 91 **To** 2015 $34 BE

ΥΥΥΥ **Mornington Peninsula Chardonnay 2008** Rating 89 **To** 2014 $34 BE
Los Hermanos Tributo a Galicia 2009 Rating 89 **To** 2012 $28

Cruickshank Callatoota Estate   ★★★
5058 Golden Highway, Denman, NSW 2328 **Region** Upper Hunter Valley
T (02) 6547 1088 **F** (02) 6547 1288 **www**.cruickshank.com.au **Open** 7 days 9–5
Winemaker John Cruickshank, Laurie Nicholls **Est.** 1973 **Cases** 4000 **Vyds** 32.5 ha
The change of address marks the fact that the Cruickshanks have purchased a substantial existing vineyard near Denman, the original vineyard now a coal-mining site. The new vineyard is predominantly planted to chardonnay, verdelho, cabernet sauvignon and shiraz, with 1 ha of cabernet franc and 0.5 ha of merlot. Exports to China.

ΥΥΥΥ **Hunter Valley Unwooded Chardonnay 2009** Light straw-green; has enough
✪ crispness to carry the unwooded style over the line; this comes from the mix of citrus and nectarine on the palate, and its clean finish. Screwcap. 13% alc. **Rating** 87 **To** 2012 $14
Hunter Valley Cabernet Sauvignon 2002 Has held colour well; a light-bodied, strongly regional (earthy) manifestation of cabernet; has reached its plateau of development. Cork. 13.5% alc. **Rating** 87 **To** 2012 $16

Cullen Wines ★★★★★

Caves Road, Cowaramup, WA 6284 **Region** Margaret River
T (08) 9755 5277 **F** (08) 9755 5550 **www.**cullenwines.com.au **Open** 7 days 10–4
Winemaker Vanya Cullen, Trevor Kent **Est.** 1971 **Cases** 20 000 **Vyds** 45 ha
One of the pioneers of Margaret River, which has always produced long-lived wines of highly
individual style from the mature estate vineyards. The vineyard has progressed beyond organic
to biodynamic certification and, subsequently, has become the first vineyard and winery in
Australia to be certified carbon neutral. This requires the calculation of all of the carbon used
and carbon dioxide emitted in the winery, and the carbon is then offset by the planting of
new trees. Winemaking is now in the hands of Vanya Cullen, daughter of the founders; she is
possessed of an extraordinarily good palate. It is impossible to single out any particular wine
from the top echelon; all are superb. Exports to all major markets.

♔♔♔♔♔ Kevin John Margaret River Chardonnay 2007 An outstanding wine; there
is exceptional focus and intensity to the palate, with its mix of nectarine, white
peach and grapefruit; 100% wild yeast barrel ferment has been subsumed by the
fruit. Screwcap. 13.5% alc. **Rating** 97 **To** 2017 $70

Diana Madeline 2007 This is as close to perfection as one can imagine in
terms of structure, texture and its complex fruit flavours. Great now, greater still
in another 10 years, and who knows how long thereafter. Cabernet Sauvignon/
Merlot/Cabernet Franc/Petit Verdot. Screwcap. 14% alc. **Rating** 97 **To** 2032 $105

✪ Cullen Vineyard Margaret River Sauvignon Blanc Semillon 2009 Picked
half on fruit days and half on flower days over a three-week period at baumes
between 10–12%; a 70/30 blend, 70% fermented in new French oak; so intense
was the fruit, maturation in oak was extended by one month to four months; the
energy and drive of the exuberant citrus and mineral flavours easily carries the
oak. Screwcap. 11.5% alc. **Rating** 96 **To** 2015 $35

Mangan Vineyard Margaret River Sauvignon Blanc Semillon 2009
A 60/40 blend, 80% harvested on fruit days, 20% on flower days; 25% barrel-
fermented, all of which was sauvignon blanc; this wine shares the minerality
evident in the Cullen Vineyard, but the unsweetened lemon juice flavours
highlight the minerality; has awe-inspiring drive and length. Screwcap. 11.5% alc.
Rating 95 **To** 2019 $35

♔♔♔♔♕ Margaret River White 2009 Arguably the ultimate expression of Margaret
✪ River classic dry white; while the fruit is juicy and zesty, the wine has a restraint
and elegance apparent on its long palate, and in particular, the finish. Sauvignon
Blanc (44%)/Semillon (36%)/Chardonnay (11%)/Verdelho (4%). Screwcap.
12% alc. **Rating** 93 **To** 2013 $19

Cumulus Wines ★★★★★

PO Box 41, Cudal, NSW 2864 **Region** Orange
T (02) 6390 7900 **F** (02) 6364 2388 **www.**cumuluswines.com.au **Open** During Orange
Food Week (Apr) and Wine Week (Oct)
Winemaker Debbie Lauritz, Andrew Bilenkij **Est.** 2004 **Cases** 200 000 **Vyds** 500 ha
Cumulus Wines was established in 2004, and is now majority owned by the Berardo Group
of Portugal (which has numerous world-size wine investments in Portugal, Canada and
Madeira). Over 500 ha of vineyards, planted in the late 1990s, focus on shiraz, cabernet
sauvignon, chardonnay and merlot. The wines are released under three brands: Rolling, from
the Central Ranges Zone; Climbing, solely from Orange fruit; and the third, Cumulus, super-
premium from the best of the estate vineyard blocks. Exports to the UK, the US and other
major markets.

♔♔♔♔♔ Orange Chardonnay 2008 Glowing green-gold; a serious individual
✪ vineyard wine, with fine, delicate fruit complexed but not overwhelmed by wild
fermentation in new French oak (Dargaud & Jaegle) and partial mlf. Screwcap.
13.5% alc. **Rating** 95 **To** 2016 $30

Orange Shiraz 2008 Vivid crimson-purple; a fragrant bouquet of black cherry and multi-spice, a touch of licorice adding to the flavours of a medium- to full-bodied wine; excellent intensity, length and balance. Screwcap. 14% alc. Rating 94 To 2023 $30

ŶŶŶŶŶ Orange Shiraz 2007 Rating 92 To 2017 $30
Orange Chardonnay 2009 Rating 90 To 2013 $30

✪ Rolling Central Ranges Shiraz 2008 More purple colour than Climbing; the bouquet, too, is slightly more fragrant, the palate more juicy – all in all, a complete role reversal with Climbing. Screwcap. 14% alc. Rating 90 To 2018 $18

ŶŶŶŶ Climbing Orange Shiraz 2008 Rating 89 To 2020 $21

Cupitt's Winery   ★★★★☆

60 Washburton Road, Milton, NSW 2539 **Region** Shoalhaven Coast
T (02) 4455 7888 **F** (02) 4455 7688 **www**.cupittwines.com.au **Open** Wed–Sun 10–5
Winemaker Rosie Cupitt **Est.** 2007 **Cases** 1800 **Vyds** 4 ha
Griff and Rosie Cupitt run what is effectively a combined winery and restaurant complex, taking full advantage of the location on the south coast of NSW. Rosie studied oenology at CSU and has more than a decade of vintage experience, taking in France and Italy; she also happens to be the Shoalhaven representative for Slow Food International. The Cupitts have 4 ha of vines centred on sauvignon, cabernet franc and semillon, and also buy viognier from Beechworth and Rutherglen, chardonnay and cabernet franc from the Southern Highlands, and cabernet sauvignon from Beechworth. A visit to the website is recommended.

ŶŶŶŶŶ Syrah 2008 Red-purple; this is an extremely elegant and balanced shiraz given its NSW (South Coast) origins; Rosie Cupitt's CSU oenology degree and flying winemaker experience over 10 years explains the otherwise inexplicable. Screwcap. 13.6% alc. Rating 94 To 2018 $34

ŶŶŶŶŶ Estate Grown Semillon 2009 Rating 90 To 2017 $26
Viognier 2009 Rating 90 To 2013 $28
Rosie's Cabernet Sauvignon Cabernet Franc Rose 2009 Rating 90 To 2011 $26

Curlewis Winery   ★★★★★

55 Navarre Road, Curlewis, Vic 3222 **Region** Geelong
T (03) 5250 4567 **F** (03) 5250 4567 **www**.curlewiswinery.com.au **Open** By appt
Winemaker Rainer Breit **Est.** 1998 **Cases** 1500 **Vyds** 2.8 ha
Rainer Breit and partner Wendy Oliver purchased their property in 1996 with 1.6 ha of what were then 11-year-old pinot noir vines. Rainer, a self-taught winemaker, uses the full bag of pinot noir winemaking tricks: cold-soaking, hot-fermentation, post-ferment maceration, part inoculated and part wild yeast use, prolonged lees contact, and bottling the wine neither fined nor filtered. While Rainer and Wendy are self-confessed 'pinotphiles', they have planted a little chardonnay and buy a little locally grown shiraz and chardonnay. Exports to Canada, Sweden, Malaysia, Singapore and Hong Kong.

ŶŶŶŶŶ Reserve Geelong Pinot Noir 2008 Similar colour to the standard, but the bouquet is more complex again, introducing some forest and game notes, plus more oak; good texture, structure and line. Screwcap. 13.5% alc. Rating 95 To 2014 $67
Geelong Chardonnay 2008 A sign of the times that the senior chardonnay should have lower alcohol; the flavours are of grapefruit and white peach, but with more minerality than Bel Sel, the oak absorbed by the fruit. Screwcap. 13.5% alc. Rating 94 To 2015 $40
Geelong Pinot Noir 2008 Clear red, a fraction advanced; has deeper fruit and more complexity than Bel Sel, mixing some black cherry with the red notes; has a silky mouthfeel and pure finish. A shadow over all three Pinots is a slight lack of drive through to the finish. Screwcap. 13% alc. Rating 94 To 2013 $40

ŸŸŸŸŸ   Bel Sel Geelong Chardonnay 2008 Rating 92 To 2014 $25
Bel Sel Geelong Pinot Noir 2008 Rating 91 To 2013 $25
Geelong Syrah 2008 Rating 90 To 2015 $35

Curly Flat   ★★★★★

263 Collivers Road, Lancefield, Vic 3435 **Region** Macedon Ranges
T (03) 5429 1956 **F** (03) 5429 2256 **www**.curlyflat.com **Open** W'ends 1–5, or by appt
Winemaker Phillip Moraghan, Matt Regan **Est.** 1991 **Cases** 5000 **Vyds** 4.2 ha
Phillip and Jeni Moraghan began developing Curly Flat in 1992, drawing in part on Phillip's
working experience in Switzerland in the late 1980s, and with a passing nod to Michael
Leunig. With ceaseless help and guidance from the late Laurie Williams (and others), the
Moraghans painstakingly established 8.5 ha of pinot noir, 3.5 ha of chardonnay and 0.7 ha of
pinot gris, and a multi-level, gravity-flow winery. Exports to the UK, Japan and Hong Kong.

ŸŸŸŸŸ   Chardonnay 2008 Bright, gleaming quartz-green; a super-elegant wine that
reflects its terroir in much the same way as riesling does, even though there are
more winemaking inputs; grapefruit, apple, nectarine and mineral notes are the
leaders, oak a vehicle and no more. Immaculately crafted. Screwcap. 12.8% alc.
Rating 96 To 2020 $44
Macedon Ranges Pinot Noir 2007 Good crimson-purple hue, although not
100% bright; as ever, a complex and powerful wine, with black cherry and plum
up front, then spicy/savoury/forest notes accompany the fruit on the back-palate
and finish. No doubting the security of the screwcap in protecting freshness.
Screwcap. 13.5% alc. Rating 95 To 2020 $51

ŸŸŸŸŸ   Pinot Grigio 2009 Rating 92 To 2012 $26
Williams Crossing Pinot Noir 2008 Rating 92 To 2014 $27
❂   Williams Crossing Chardonnay 2008 Much deeper colour than its big
brother; intervention by the winemaker is more obvious, and one would never
guess the alcohol is lower in this wine. Its Achilles heel is that the palate is short,
especially by comparison. Screwcap. 12.4% alc. Rating 90 To 2014 $22

Currency Creek Estate   ★★★☆

Winery Road, Currency Creek, SA 5214 **Region** Currency Creek
T (08) 8555 4069 **F** (08) 8555 4100 **www**.currencycreekwines.com.au **Open** 7 days 10–5
Winemaker John Loxton **Est.** 1969 **Cases** 10 000 **Vyds** 65 ha
For over 35 years this family-owned vineyard and relatively low-profile winery has produced
some outstanding wood-matured whites and pleasant, soft reds selling at attractive prices.
Shiraz takes the lion's share of the plantings, then cabernet sauvignon, sauvignon blanc,
chardonnay, riesling and semillon. It will be apparent from this that the essential part of the
grape production is sold. Exports to the UK, the US and China.

ŸŸŸŸŸ   The Viaduct Viognier Roussanne 2009 A wine with exceptional impact given
❂   its moderate alcohol, quince reflected in both its flavour and texture, with touches of
spice and a long, firm finish. Screwcap. 12.5% alc. Rating 92 To 2011 $17

ŸŸŸŸ   Water Ribbon Gewurztraminer 2009 Rating 88 To 2012 $17
Sedgeland Gris Blanc 2009 Rating 87 To 2010 $17
The Viaduct Viognier Roussanne 2008 Rating 87 To 2010 $17

Cuttaway Hill   ★★★★

PO Box 630, Mittagong, NSW 2575 **Region** Southern Highlands
T (02) 4871 1004 **F** (02) 4871 1005 **www**.cuttawayhillwines.com.au **Open** By appt
Winemaker Monarch Winemaking Services **Est.** 1998 **Cases** 15 000 **Vyds** 23.5 ha
Owned by the O'Neil family, Cuttaway Hill is one of the largest vineyard properties in
the Southern Highlands, with three vineyard sites. The original Cuttaway Hill vineyard at
Mittagong has chardonnay, merlot, cabernet sauvignon and shiraz. The Allambie vineyard, on

the light sandy loam soils of Ninety Acre Hill, is planted to sauvignon blanc, pinot gris and pinot noir. The third and newest vineyard, at Maytree, west of Moss Vale, in a relatively drier and warmer meso-climate, has cabernet sauvignon, merlot and pinot noir (and a small amount of chardonnay). The standard of both viticulture (headed by Mark Bourne) and contract winemaking is evident in the quality of the wines, not to mention the growth in production and sales. Exports to the UK, the US, Canada, Sweden and China.

ᵀᵀᵀᵀᵀ **Southern Highlands Chardonnay 2008** Bright colour; the bouquet is
✪   starting to build some bottle-developed complexity, the palate bringing grapefruit
        and white peach flavours to the fore, oak merely a whisper. Screwcap. 13% alc.
        Rating 93 **To** 2015 $20
✪   **Southern Highlands Sauvignon Blanc 2009** A zesty, lively wine on bouquet
        and palate alike, the flavours ranging through herb, citrus and gooseberry, the finish
        bright and crisp. Screwcap. 12% alc. **Rating** 92 **To** 2011 $20
        Southern Highlands Pinot Gris 2009 Spice, pear and fig aromas; genuine
        gris style, rich and mouthfilling, Alsace-like. Screwcap. 14.5% alc. **Rating** 91
        To 2012 $25

ᵀᵀᵀᵀ **Southern Highlands Pinot Noir 2008** **Rating** 88 **To** 2013 $25

d'Arenberg   ★★★★★
Osborn Road, McLaren Vale, SA 5171 **Region** McLaren Vale
T (08) 8329 4888 **F** (08) 8323 8423 **www.**darenberg.com.au **Open** 7 days 10–5
Winemaker Chester Osborn, Jack Walton **Est.** 1912 **Cases** 260 000 **Vyds** 197.2 ha
Nothing, they say, succeeds like success. Few operations in Australia fit this dictum better than d'Arenberg, which has kept its almost 100-year-old heritage while moving into the 21st century with flair and elan. As at last count the d'Arenberg vineyards, at various locations, have 24 varieties planted, as well as 120 growers in McLaren Vale. There is no question that its past, present and future revolve around its considerable portfolio of richly robed red wines: Shiraz, Cabernet Sauvignon and Grenache being the cornerstones, but with over 20 varietal and/or blend labels spanning the gulf between Roussanne and Mourvedre. The quality of the wines is unimpeachable, the prices logical and fair. It has a profile in both the UK and the US that far larger companies would love to have, underlined by *Wine & Spirits Magazine* (US) accolade of Winery of the Year in '09. Exports to all major markets.

ᵀᵀᵀᵀᵀ **The Feral Fox Adelaide Hills Pinot Noir 2008** Good hue, albeit light; follows
        in the footsteps of previous Feral Foxes, with impressive varietal character on both
        bouquet and palate, the savoury characters in balance with the plum fruit; has a
        long finish. Screwcap. 14.5% alc. **Rating** 94 **To** 2013 $30
        The Dead Arm Shiraz 2007 Deep, dark red-purple; a very powerful wine
        proclaiming its regional origin with a strong overlay of dark chocolate, licorice
        and earth to the underlying blackberry fruit; stringent selection of grapes/wine has
        paid dividends. Screwcap. 14.5% alc. **Rating** 94 **To** 2022 $65
        The Laughing Magpie Shiraz Viognier 2008 Good colour; highly perfumed
        bouquet, with an abundance of black fruits, savoury charcuterie, and a suggestion
        of violets; the palate is seamless and beautifully poised, with the acidity providing
        contrast to the lavish levels of fruit; a well-constructed example of the style.
        Screwcap. 14.5% alc. **Rating** 94 **To** 2016 $30 BE
✪   **The Cadenzia Grenache Shiraz Mourvedre 2008** Strong crimson-purple;
        as ever, the weight and fruit depth of McLaren Vale grenache comes to the
        fore; given the challenge of the vintage, this is a truly delicious wine. Screwcap.
        14.5% alc. **Rating** 94 **To** 2023 $25

ᵀᵀᵀᵀᵀ **The Wild Pixie McLaren Vale Shiraz Roussanne 2008** **Rating** 93
        To 2020 $30
✪   **The High Trellis McLaren Vale Cabernet Sauvignon 2008** Good colour;
        over the years, has often outperformed both its region and price point, and this
        is no exception; cassis and blackcurrant fruit drives through the medium-bodied
        palate to a long finish. Screwcap. 14.5% alc. **Rating** 93 **To** 2018 $19.95

✪ **The Last Ditch Adelaide Hills McLaren Vale Viognier 2008** An impressive example, and very well priced; it has varietal flavour, but also the freshness and zip that is so often lacking. Screwcap. 13.5% alc. **Rating** 92 **To** 2012 $19

✪ **d'Arry's Original McLaren Vale Shiraz Grenache 2007** A classic blend, showing the roots of its consistency, even in a challenging vintage; the bouquet straddles the line of fresh red fruits and savoury Provençal herbs beautifully; the palate is generous and soft, with an underlying structure providing freshness and contrast to the sweet fruit. Screwcap. 14.5% alc. **Rating** 92 **To** 2015 $19.95 BE
The Coppermine Road Cabernet Sauvignon 2007 **Rating** 92 **To** 2016 $65 BE

✪ **The Noble Wrinkled McLaren Vale Riesling 2008** Arguably the best of a fascinating trio, each in a different ratio of alcohol to sweetness; lacks riesling varietal character, but there is good acidity. Screwcap. 11.5% alc. **Rating** 92 **To** 2012 $19.95

✪ **The Noble Mud Pie Adelaide Viognier Pinot Gris Marsanne 2008** Deep gold; some very sophisticated winemaking lies behind this wine, with its lusciously sweet cinnamon, cumquat and apricot flavours; some Austrian trockenbeerenauslese characteristics. Screwcap. 8.5% alc. **Rating** 91 **To** 2010 $19.95
The Lucky Lizard Adelaide Hills Chardonnay 2008 **Rating** 90 **To** 2012 $25
The Love Grass McLaren Vale Shiraz 2008 **Rating** 90 **To** 2018 $25

✪ **The Footbolt McLaren Vale Shiraz 2008** Deep colour; licorice, bitter chocolate and a distinct aroma of candle wax combine on the bouquet; the palate is rich, warm and inviting, with lavish levels of sweet fruit the central theme of the wine. Screwcap. 14.5% alc. **Rating** 90 **To** 2015 $19.95 BE
The Derelict Vineyard McLaren Vale Grenache 2007 **Rating** 90 **To** 2015 $29
The Noble Prankster Adelaide Hills Chardonnay Semillon 2008 **Rating** 90 **To** 2010 $19.95

Dal Zotto Wines   ★★★★☆

Main Road, Whitfield, Vic 3733 **Region** King Valley
T (03) 5729 8321 **F** (03) 5729 8490 **www**.dalzotto.com.au **Open** 7 days 10–5
Winemaker Michael Dal Zotto **Est.** 1987 **Cases** 15 000 **Vyds** 48 ha
The Dal Zotto family is a King Valley institution; ex-tobacco growers, then contract grapegrowers, they are now primarily focused on their Dal Zotto range. Led by Otto and Elena, and with sons Michael and Christian handling winemaking and sales/marketing respectively, the family is producing increasing amounts of wine of exceptionally consistent quality from its substantial estate vineyard. The cellar door is in the centre of Whitfield, and is also home to their new Trattoria (open weekends). One of the first to produce Prosecco in Australia. Exports to the UK and China.

🍷🍷🍷🍷🍷 **King Valley Riesling 2009** Light straw-green; has excellent varietal expression
✪ on bouquet and palate alike, with ripe citrus flavours backed by good acidity. Screwcap. 12.5% alc. **Rating** 93 **To** 2018 $17.50
L'Immigrante Barbera 2006 Good colour; has developed slowly in bottle, the fruit still very fresh, sustained in part by distinctive acidity that also underpins the length of the finish. Screwcap. 13.5% alc. **Rating** 92 **To** 2016 $52.50

✪ **King Valley Chardonnay 2005** Glowing green-yellow; has developed exceptionally and unexpectedly well, nutty peach flavours coming together very nicely. Absolutely drink now. Screwcap. 13.5% alc. **Rating** 90 **To** 2012 $22
King Valley Arneis 2009 A less immediately expressive bouquet than the '08, but does have a vibrant palate that combines finesse with intensity and length; citrus and pear are the flavours. Screwcap. 12.5% alc. **Rating** 90 **To** 2013 $27

✪ **King Valley Rosato 2009** Pale salmon-pink; a clean but relatively inexpressive bouquet, the palate with red fruits and faintly citrussy acidity. Blue-gold Sydney International Wine Competition '10. Screwcap. 12.5% alc. **Rating** 90 **To** 2011 $17.50

✪   **Pucino King Valley Prosecco NV** Super-abundant mousse; one of the early
movers, if not the earliest, with Prosecco; the wine is fruity but dry, and ticks
all the boxes for the style: long, clean and crisp. Cork. 11.5% alc. **Rating** 90
To 2012 $18.50

Dalfarras   ★★★★

PO Box 123, Nagambie, Vic 3608 **Region** Nagambie Lakes
T (03) 5794 2637 **F** (03) 5794 2360 **Open** At Tahbilk
Winemaker Alister Purbrick, Alan George **Est.** 1991 **Cases** 9500 **Vyds** 20.97 ha
The personal project of Alister Purbrick and artist wife Rosa (née Dalfarra), whose paintings
adorn the labels of the wines. Alister, of course, is best known as winemaker at Tahbilk (see
separate entry), the family winery and home, but this range of wines is intended to (in Alister's
words) 'allow me to expand my winemaking horizons and mould wines in styles different
from Tahbilk'. Exports to Sweden.

🍷🍷🍷🍷🍷   **Cabernet Sangiovese 2008** Bright crimson-red; very attractive wine, with real
✪   synergy between the two varieties; a range of redcurrant, red cherry and sour cherry
flavours supported by fine tannins. Screwcap. 14% alc. **Rating** 92 **To** 2015 $14.95

🍷🍷🍷🍷   **Pinot Grigio Viognier 2008 Rating** 89 **To** 2012 $13.95

Dalrymple Estate   ★★★★

1337 Pipers Brook Road, Pipers Brook, Tas 7254 **Region** Northern Tasmania
T (03) 6382 7222 **F** (03) 6382 7222 **www**.dalrymplevineyards.com.au **Open** 7 days 10–5
Winemaker Natalie Fryar **Est.** 1987 **Cases** 4000 **Vyds** 15 ha
Dalrymple Estate was established many years ago by the Mitchell and Sundstrup families; the
vineyard and brand were acquired by Hill Smith Family Vineyards in late 2007. Plantings are
split between pinot noir and sauvignon blanc, and the wine is made at Jansz Tasmania.

🍷🍷🍷🍷🍷   **Estate Pinot Noir 2008** Bright, light colour; very similar to Barringwood
Park Forest Raven; supple, silky red fruits; clear, fresh finish. Vino-Lok. 13.5% alc.
Rating 90 **To** 2014 $44.95

Dalwhinnie   ★★★★★

448 Taltarni Road, Moonambel, Vic 3478 **Region** Pyrenees
T (03) 5467 2388 **F** (03) 5467 2237 **www**.dalwhinnie.com.au **Open** 7 days 10–5
Winemaker David Jones, Gary Baldwin (Consultant) **Est.** 1976 **Cases** 4500
David and Jenny Jones are making wines with tremendous depth of fruit flavour, reflecting
the relatively low-yielding but very well-maintained vineyards. It is hard to say whether the
Chardonnay, the Cabernet Sauvignon or the Shiraz is the more distinguished. A further 8 ha
of shiraz (with a little viognier) were planted in 1999 on a block acquired on Taltarni Road.
A 50-tonne contemporary high-tech winery now allows the wines to be made onsite, with
three single-vineyard Shirazs in the pipeline under the Eagles Series, South West Rocks and
Goddess labels. On the other side of the ledger, the Pinot Noir has been discontinued. Exports
to the UK and other major markets.

🍷🍷🍷🍷🍷   **Southwest Rocks Shiraz 2008** Piercing red fruits dominate the almost pinot-
like bouquet, with cinnamon, clove and a touch of orange rind adding complexity;
the striking palate is superfine, with wonderful silky tannins, and loaded with pure,
focused and poised red fruit, again showing elements more akin to pinot than
shiraz, something rarely seen outside of France; very long and racy on the finish.
Screwcap. 14% alc. **Rating** 96 **To** 2025 $75 BE
Moonambel Chardonnay 2007 Deep colour; a complex wine striving for
(and finding) the complete gamut of aromas and flavours the winemaker can get
out of the wine; sizzling bacon fat, grilled cashew, grapefruit and a little toasty oak
combine to great effect; the palate vibrates with flavour, and the line is precise,
long and wonderfully fresh and complex; challenging for some, but ideal for
others. Screwcap. 13% alc. **Rating** 95 **To** 2020 $38 BE

Moonambel Shiraz 2008 Attractive colour; the bouquet has a seductive offering of black fruits, dark spices and minerals; the palate is loaded with sweet fruits, with redcurrant providing light to the blackberry shade; the texture is engaging, with plentiful fine-grained tannins, and a lingering mineral complexity to the finish. Screwcap. 13.5% alc. **Rating** 95 **To** 2025 $60 BE

The Pinnacle Shiraz 2008 At the dark end of the shiraz spectrum, with fresh and confit blackberry and mulled spices on offer; the palate is unctuous and rich, with plenty of sweet dark fruit given lift by a subtle dollop of black pepper; soft and generous on the finish. Screwcap. 15% alc. **Rating** 94 **To** 2020 $75 BE

The Eagle Shiraz 2005 Still pristine and fresh, with more of everything providing plenty of stuffing; redcurrant, blackberry, sage and a touch of mint are all evident; the texture appears to be the key, with all of the elements working together harmoniously; still oaky, but with plenty of time ahead to enjoy witnessing its evolution. Cork. 14.5% alc. **Rating** 94 **To** 2025 $135 BE

ΥΥΥΥΥ **Moonambel Cabernet 2008** **Rating** 93 **To** 2020 $50 BE

Dandelion Vineyards   ★★★★★

PO Box 138, McLaren Vale, SA 5171 **Region** McLaren Vale/Barossa Valley
T (08) 8556 6099 **F** (08) 8556 6609 **www**.dandelionvineyards.com.au **Open** Not
Winemaker Elena Brooks **Est.** 2007 **Cases** 4000 **Vyds** 124.2 ha
This is a highly impressive partnership between Peggy and Carl Lindner (40%), Elena and Zar Brooks (40%), and Fiona and Brad Rey (20%). It brings together vineyards spread across the Adelaide Hills, Eden Valley, Langhorne Creek, McLaren Vale, Barossa Valley and Fleurieu Peninsula. Elena is not only the beautiful wife of industry dilettante Zar, but also an exceptionally gifted winemaker. It may be a dauntingly competitive marketplace, but there can be few more promising new ventures than this one.

ΥΥΥΥΥ **Wishing Clock of the Adelaide Hills Sauvignon Blanc 2009** Impressive
✪ wine; bell clear varietal expression on both bouquet and palate, and a gloriously supple mouthfeel seamlessly welding tropical and grassy/minerally flavours. Screwcap. 12.5% alc. **Rating** 96 **To** 2011 $26.95

✪ **Wonderland of the Eden Valley Riesling 2009** Brilliant light green – exceptional colour; a wine of great purity and finesse, with an interplay of lime, apple and mineral through to a perfectly balanced finish; 98-year-old vines, whole-bunch-pressed grapes, unfined/unfiltered; 233 cases made. Screwcap. 12% alc. **Rating** 95 **To** 2020 $26.95

✪ **Lionheart of the Barossa Shiraz 2008** Deep crimson colour; must surely have been picked before the heatwave, its medium-bodied frame charged with supple plum, blackberry and black cherry fruit; French oak handling exemplary, as are the tannins. Screwcap. 14% alc. **Rating** 95 **To** 2020 $25

✪ **Twilight of the Adelaide Hills Chardonnay 2008** Yet another very well made wine from Dandelion; fragrant white peach, nectarine and citrus fruit flavours have largely absorbed the generous use of quality French oak; good length and balance. Screwcap. 13% alc. **Rating** 94 **To** 2015 $25

ΥΥΥΥΥ **Pride of the Fleurieu Peninsula Cabernet Sauvignon 2007** **Rating** 92 **To** 2018 $25

ΥΥΥΥ **Lion's Tooth of McLaren Vale Shiraz Riesling 2007** **Rating** 89 **To** 2013 $25

Darling Park   ★★★★★

232 Red Hill Road, Red Hill, Vic 3937 **Region** Mornington Peninsula
T (03) 5989 2324 **F** (03) 9012 4348 **www**.darlingparkwinery.com **Open** 7 days11–5
Winemaker Judy Gifford **Est.** 1989 **Cases** 2000 **Vyds** 1.3 ha
Josh and Karen Liberman have energetically expanded the range of Darling Park's wines while maintaining a high-quality standard. The Art of Wine club offers back vintages, as well as previews of upcoming releases. Wine labels feature artworks from the owners' collections;

artists include Sidney Nolan, Arthur Boyd, John Perceval and Charles Blackman. The most important source of grapes for the venture come from Hugh Robinson, who produces some of the best grapes available for sale on the Mornington Peninsula. The arrangement with Darling Park is a permanent one, with purchase by area, rather than by tonnes of grapes produced.

ŸŸŸŸŸ **Reserve Chardonnay 2007** Similar brilliant colour to the varietal; a complex bouquet redolent of rich fruit, then a sumptuous palate with creamy/nutty nuances alongside the deep stone fruit flavours. Screwcap. 13.5% alc. **Rating** 95 To 2017 $35
Chardonnay 2007 Brilliant straw-green; an elegant, precisely balanced wine, white peach and oak playing tag with each other on the long palate; in radically different style to the Reserve. Screwcap. 13.5% alc. **Rating** 94 To 2016 $26

ŸŸŸŸŸ **Shiraz 2007 Rating** 92 To 2014 $32
Pinot Gris 2009 Rating 90 To 2011 $25

Darlington Vineyard   ★★★★☆

Holkam Court, Orford, Tas 7190 **Region** Southern Tasmania
T (03) 6257 1630 **F** (03) 6257 1630 **Open** Thurs–Mon 10–5
Winemaker Frogmore Creek **Est.** 1993 **Cases** 600
Peter and Margaret Hyland planted a little under 2 ha of vineyard in 1993, located on the Freycinet coast. The first wines were made from the 1999 vintage, forcing retired builder Peter to complete their home so that the small building in which they had been living could be converted into a cellar door. The vineyard looks out towards the settlement of Darlington on Maria Island, the site of Diego Bernacchi's attempt to establish a vineyard in the 1880s and lure investors by attaching artificial bunches of grapes to his vines.

ŸŸŸŸŸ **TGR Riesling 2008** Light green-straw; lovely lime juice aromas and flavours, intense yet fine; the barest hint of sugar is perfectly balanced by acidity. Has improved dramatically since January '09. Screwcap. 10.5% alc. **Rating** 94 To 2016 $19

ŸŸŸŸŸ **Sauvignon Blanc 2009 Rating** 90 To 2012 $22

David Franz   ★★★★★

PO Box 677, Tanunda, SA 5352 **Region** Barossa Valley
T (08) 8563 0705 **F** (08) 8563 0708 **www**.david-franz.com **Open** Not
Winemaker David Franz Lehmann **Est.** 1998 **Cases** 2700 **Vyds** 17.8 ha
How do you distil down 10 well-typed pages of background into a meagre few lines when it involves a cast of characters that are the very essence of all that is great about the Barossa Valley? It's about a guy who first tried his hand at graphic design at university, switching to an architecture interior design course for two years (equally unfulfilling), then working around Australia, before spending three successful years gaining a diploma in hospitality business management. Next he headed overseas with his new wife Nicki, working a traumatic vintage in South Africa, then escaping to England to work anywhere, as backpackers do, with side trips to Europe. Their third and final trip to France was cut short by the discovery that Nicki was pregnant, forcing a return to Australia. So who is David Franz? Well, he is one of Margaret and Peter Lehmann's sons, who has finally acknowledged that wine is in his blood. With help from his parents along the way, including some financial help, he established David Franz. And I personally know what it is like making wine with stainless-steel dairy mini-vats, plastic tubs, a hand-operated basket press and a one-inch mono pump. End of page one. Exports to the UK, the US, Canada, Singapore, Japan, Indonesia, Hong Kong and China.

ŸŸŸŸŸ
✪ **Eden Valley Riesling 2008** Bright straw-green; mineral, slate and apple aromas, then an intense and incisive palate, with a long, bracing finish. Great cellaring potential. Screwcap. 11.4% alc. **Rating** 95 To 2020 $27
✪ **Benjamin's Promise Shiraz 2004** Colour remarkably fresh and bright; the lively bouquet is fragrant, the palate with a display of delicious, juicy red fruits and fine tannins. Cork. 14.7% alc. **Rating** 94 To 2019 $34

Larrikin III Blend NV The colour reflects 73% younger components; the bouquet is fragrant, with spicy red fruits to the fore, the palate full of energy and drive to its flavours. An audacious assemblage that is surprisingly convincing. Grenache/Shiraz/Cabernet Sauvignon/Mataro, 40% '06/33% '07/ 27% '05–'03. Cork. 14.5% alc. **Rating** 94 **To** 2019 $42

Georgie's Walk Cabernet Sauvignon 2005 Good hue for age; the fragrant bouquet offers more varietal expression than many '05 Barossa cabernets, and the silky palate does not disappoint – indeed it is a handsome surprise. Cork. 13% alc. **Rating** 94 **To** 2015 $36

Alexander's Reward 2004 Good retention of colour; has very attractive, juicy red and black fruit aromas and flavours ranging from cherry to plum to blackberry; unmarked high-quality cork; ageing with considerable grace. Cabernet Sauvignon (55%)/Shiraz (45%). 14.6% alc. **Rating** 94 **To** 2016 $34

Museum Release AD 2000 Shiraz Cabernet VP 1979 A well-remembered port originally released under the Peter Lehmann label; has matured very well; chocolate, mocha and spice, with a marvellously dry finish. Cork. 17.4% alc. **Rating** 94 **To** 2015 $42

Old Redemption Tawny NV The golden tawny colour is an immediate indicator of age, as is the Christmas cake and toffee bouquet; the palate is very complex, with a strong brandy snap biscuit character. Diam. 20.1% alc. **Rating** 94 **To** 2011 $42

ϼϼϼϼϼ **Stonewell Hill Semillon 2008 Rating** 93 **To** 2018 $32
Brother's Ilk Adelaide Hills Chardonnay 2008 Rating 93 **To** 2018 $38
Benjamin's Promise Shiraz 2005 Rating 93 **To** 2020 $36
Alexander's Reward 2005 Rating 93 **To** 2020 $36
POP Wine Issue 3 Stockwell Road Cabernet 2006 Rating 93 **To** 2026 $46
Georgie's Walk Cabernet Sauvignon 2004 Rating 92 **To** 2018 $34
POP Wine Issue 1 CSG 2006 Rating 92 **To** 2016 $46

✪ **Red Rose 2008** Fresh and lively from start to finish, in spite of, or because of (I don't know which) the extraordinary varietal assemblage (six red, nine white) co-fermented in barrel and taken through mlf. Screwcap. 12% alc. **Rating** 91 **To** 2010 $19

Larrikin II Blend NV Rating 91 **To** 2014 $42
POP Wine Issue 2 Greenock Grenache 2007 Rating 90 **To** 2015 $46

ϼϼϼϼ **Sticky Late Harvest Riesling 2008 Rating** 88 **To** 2012 $18

David Hook Wines ★★★★★

Cnr Broke Road/Ekerts Road, Pokolbin, NSW 2320 **Region** Hunter Valley
T (02) 4998 7121 www.davidhookwines.com.au **Open** 7 days 10–5
Winemaker David Hook **Est.** 1984 **Cases** 10 000 **Vyds** 8 ha
David Hook has 25 years' experience as a winemaker for Tyrrell's and Lake's Folly, also doing the full Flying Winemaker bit with jobs in Bordeaux, the Rhône Valley, Spain, the US and Georgia. He and his family began establishing the vineyard in 1984. The estate-owned Pothana Vineyard has been in production for 25 years, and the wines made from it are given the 'Old Vines' banner. This vineyard is planted on the Belford Dome, an ancient geological formation that provides red clay soils over limestone on the slopes, and sandy loams along the creek flats; the former for red wines, the latter for white. Exports to the US and Japan.

ϼϼϼϼϼ ✪ **Orange Riesling 2009** A clean, fragrant bouquet leads into a joyous palate, with elfin dances of lime, acid and residual sugar constantly interweaving, none dominating. Perfect summer wine, beautifully made. Screwcap. 10.2% alc. **Rating** 95 **To** 2016 $25

✪ **Pothana Vineyard Old Vines Belford Semillon 2009** Bright light straw-green; a fragrant, flowery bouquet with blossom and fresh cut grass aromas, the palate very intense and very long. Will develop superbly for 20+ years. Screwcap. 11% alc. **Rating** 95 **To** 2029 $25

🍷🍷🍷🍷🍷 Pothana Vineyard Old Vines Belford Shiraz 2007 Rating 93 To 2022 $40
Pothana Vineyard Old Vines Belford Chardonnay 2009 Rating 91
To 2014 $30
Hunter Valley Viognier 2009 Rating 90 To 2012 $25
Hunter Valley Barbera 2008 Rating 90 To 2012 $25
Hunter Valley Barbera 2007 Rating 90 To 2013 $25

🍷🍷🍷🍷 Hunter Valley Mosto 2009 Rating 88 To 2011 $25
Hunter Valley + Shiraz Viognier 2008 Rating 87 To 2013 $18

De Beaurepaire Wines ★★★☆

182 Cudgegong Road, Rylstone, NSW 2849 **Region** Mudgee
T (02) 6379 1473 **F** (02) 6379 1474 **www**.debeaurepairewines.com
Open At Bridgeview Inn, Rylstone
Winemaker Michael Slater (Contract) **Est.** 1998 **Cases** 2000 **Vyds** 52.4 ha
This is the retirement business of former clinical psychologist Janet de Beaurepaire and
investment banker Richard de Beaurepaire. Beaurepaire Ridge Vineyard is situated on the
200-ha Woodlawn property, one of the oldest properties west of the Blue Mountains, at an
altitude of 570–600 m. While part of the Mudgee GI, the Rylstone climate is significantly
cooler than other parts of the region. The vineyard is planted to shiraz, merlot, cabernet
sauvignon, chardonnay, semillon, viognier, petit verdot, verdelho and pinot gris. The property
is bounded on two sides by the Cudgegong River, which provides irrigation. Exports to
Malaysia and Singapore.

🍷🍷🍷🍷🍷 Captain Starlight Series Semillon Sauvignon Blanc 2009 Citrussy, grassy
✪ semillon is both the foundation and the framework for a tightly structured wine of
considerable length, with the potential to grow over the next 2–3 years. Screwcap.
12% alc. **Rating** 91 To 2013 $19

🍷🍷🍷🍷 Captain Starlight Series Chardonnay 2009 Rating 88 To 2012 $19

De Bortoli ★★★★★

De Bortoli Road, Bilbul, NSW 2680 **Region** Riverina
T (02) 6966 0100 **F** (02) 6966 0199 **www**.debortoli.com.au **Open** Mon–Sat 9–5, Sun 9–4
Winemaker Darren De Bortoli, Julie Mortlock, John Coughlan **Est.** 1928 **Cases** 3 million
Vyds 300 ha
Famous among the cognoscenti for its superb Noble One, which in fact accounts for only a
minute part of its total production, this winery turns around low-priced varietal and generic
wines that are invariably competently made and equally invariably provide value for money.
These come in part from estate vineyards, but also from contract-grown grapes. The rating
is in part a reflection of the exceptional value for money offered across the range. Exports to
all major markets.

🍷🍷🍷🍷🍷 Noble One 2008 Bright yellow-gold; the vast experience of De Bortoli with
this style results in a wine with the rich, opulent and sweet fruit balanced by the
acidity missing from lesser wines; cumquat, mandarin, honey and vanilla are all part
of the package. 375 ml. Screwcap. 10% alc. **Rating** 95 To 2014 $32
Noble One 2007 Brilliant green-gold; has all the luscious intensity expected,
ranging through citrus, cumquat and vanilla bean, yet is not over the top. Its best
features are its balance, line and extreme length, similar to that of the '02. 375 ml.
Screwcap. 10% alc. **Rating** 95 To 2013 $33.90

🍷🍷🍷🍷🍷 Deen De Bortoli Vat 1 Durif 2008 Deep crimson-purple; this simply has to be
✪ one of the most durable and flexible red varieties in the world, it keeps its colour
and rich plummy fruit regardless of how and where it is grown, or how heavily it
is cropped. Screwcap. 14% alc. **Rating** 90 To 2013 $12.90

🍷🍷🍷🍷 Deen De Bortoli Vat 2 Sauvignon Blanc 2009 Well priced given its generous
✪ tropical/passionfruit aromas and flavours, then the crisp finish. Screwcap. 12% alc.
Rating 88 To 2010 $12.90

✪ **Montage Semillon Sauvignon Blanc 2009** De Bortoli seems best able to create surprises with wines under $10; the lemony/grassy semillon has considerable thrust and intensity, carrying the light tropical characters of the sauvignon blanc along in its wake. Screwcap. 12% alc. **Rating** 88 **To** 2011 $9.50

✪ **Deen De Bortoli Vat 7 Chardonnay 2008** Has that extra bit of elegance that lifts it out of the ruck, some oak maturation adding to the texture, not the flavour. Screwcap. 12.5% alc. **Rating** 88 **To** 2011 $12.90

✪ **Sacred Hill Cabernet Merlot 2008** Vibrant colour; juicy young fruited style; redcurrant and a touch of cedar; clean and vibrant on the finish. Has developed a few savoury characters, which add to the interest and length. Screwcap. 13.5% alc. **Rating** 88 **To** 2012 $7.50

✪ **Deen De Bortoli Vat 6 Verdelho 2008** Punches above its weight, with positive tropical fruit aromas and flavours on a generous palate. Screwcap. 13.5% alc. **Rating** 87 **To** 2011 $12.90

✪ **Montage Cabernet Merlot 2008** Fresh, clear red-purple; a light-bodied, well-balanced wine with good varietal expression of black fruits and plums; impossible to expect more at this price. Screwcap. 13.5% alc. **Rating** 87 **To** 2012 $9.50

✪ **Deen De Bortoli Vat 9 Cabernet Sauvignon 2008** Good colour; a very well made wine at this price point, with plenty of blackcurrant and plum fruit supported by soft, fine tannins. Screwcap. 14.5% alc. **Rating** 87 **To** 2013 $12.90

✪ **Emeri Chardonnay Pinot Noir NV** Best mousse; the best of the three Emeri sparklings, which should come as no surprise; good balance to the stone fruit and citrus flavours; clean, dry finish. Cork. 11.5% alc. **Rating** 87 **To** 2010 $13

De Bortoli (Hunter Valley) ★★★★☆

532 Wine Country Drive, Lovedale, NSW 2325 **Region** Hunter Valley
T (02) 4993 8800 **F** (02) 4993 8899 **www.**debortoli.com.au **Open** 7 days 10–5
Winemaker Steve Webber **Est.** 2002 **Cases** 10 000
De Bortoli extended its wine empire in 2002 with the purchase of the former Wilderness Estate, giving it an immediate and significant presence in the Hunter Valley courtesy of the 26 ha of established vineyards; this was expanded significantly by the subsequent purchase of an adjoining 40-ha property. Exports to all major markets.

♟♟♟♟♟ **Murphy's Vineyard Semillon 2005** Quite a restrained and delicate bouquet, with lemon curd and anise on show; the palate is fine, almost ethereal, with crisp acidity providing a clean and focused conclusion. Screwcap. 11.5% alc. **Rating** 95 **To** 2020 $35 BE

♟♟♟♟♟ **Will's Hill Vineyard Shiraz 2008 Rating** 90 **To** 2014 $40 BE

De Bortoli (Victoria) ★★★★★

Pinnacle Lane, Dixons Creek, Vic 3775 **Region** Yarra Valley
T (03) 5965 2271 **F** (03) 5965 2464 **www.**debortoli.com.au **Open** 7 days 10–5
Winemaker Steve Webber **Est.** 1987 **Cases** 350 000 **Vyds** 228.86 ha
The quality arm of the bustling De Bortoli group, run by Leanne De Bortoli and husband Steve Webber, ex-Lindemans winemaker. The top label (De Bortoli), the second (Gulf Station) and the third label (Windy Peak) offer wines of consistently good quality and excellent value – the complex Chardonnay and the Pinot Noirs are usually of outstanding quality. The volume of production, by many times the largest in the Yarra Valley, simply underlines the quality/value for money ratio of the wines. This arm of the business has vineyards in the Yarra Valley, and in the King Valley. Viticultural resources to one side, Steve was *Gourmet Traveller* Winemaker of the Year '07, recognition he thoroughly deserved. Exports to all major markets.

♟♟♟♟♟ **Estate Grown Yarra Valley Shiraz Viognier 2008** Bright, clear crimson; a fragrant bouquet of red and black fruits, then a captivating burst of energy and intensity to the beautifully weighted palate, the tannin texture exemplary. Screwcap. 13.5% alc. **Rating** 96 **To** 2020 $30

Melba Reserve 2007 Deep crimson; a cabernet blend from vineyards dating back to 1971, and has the silken polish that winemaker Steve Webber prizes so highly; no one flavour or aroma jumps out, and the line of the palate is superb. Screwcap. 13% alc. **Rating** 96 **To** 2023 $60

Reserve Release Yarra Valley Chardonnay 2007 A particularly distinguished interpretation of the Yarra Valley, oak providing no more than a fermentation medium, the grapes picked to precisely provide the stone fruit and fig flavours supported by natural acidity. Screwcap. 12% alc. **Rating** 95 **To** 2017 $45

✪ **Estate Grown Yarra Valley Pinot Noir 2008** Clear colour; a fragrant and pure bouquet has distinct Burgundian overtones, the palate showing all the precision that Steve Webber works so hard to achieve, and remarkable for its length. Screwcap. 13% alc. **Rating** 95 **To** 2015 $38

Reserve Release Yarra Valley Pinot Noir 2007 A very expressive bouquet, with elements of spice, cedar and smoke; the palate has great length and outstanding texture, line and length; very attractive red fruits at the core. Screwcap. 13% alc. **Rating** 95 **To** 2016 $50

✪ **Melba Lucia 2007** A fragrant bouquet of cassis and black fruits, then an elegantly poised, medium-bodied palate that has particularly good line and length; a winemaker in complete command. Cabernet Sauvignon/Merlot/Sangiovese/Petit Verdot. Screwcap. 13% alc. **Rating** 95 **To** 2027 $31

Reserve Release Yarra Valley Sauvignon 2008 A textured and (to use Steve Webber's description) detailed wine with strong French overtones; in a different universe to conventional sauvignon blanc; the late Didier Dageneau would approve. Screwcap. 13.5% alc. **Rating** 94 **To** 2013 $38

Estate Grown Yarra Valley Chardonnay 2008 Bright colour; has a very fragrant and fresh bouquet, doubtless thanks in part to its low alcohol; the resulting delicate fruit has been protected from new oak; has early picking has been taken a little too far? Screwcap. 12.5% alc. **Rating** 94 **To** 2015 $31

✪ **Gulf Station Yarra Valley Chardonnay 2008** The oak contribution has been deliberately suppressed in a subtle wine, with very harmonious fruit, oak and acidity; the flavours are ripe without threatening the elegance of the palate, nor obscuring its length. Screwcap. 13% alc. **Rating** 94 **To** 2016 $19

✪ **Gulf Station Yarra Valley Pinot Noir 2008** A serious pinot at this price, aromatic and spicy, with excellent texture and structure; the flavours halfway between plum and cherry, and a savoury finish; subtle oak. Screwcap. 13.5% alc. **Rating** 94 **To** 2015 $19

Estate Grown Yarra Valley Syrah 2008 Bright hue; a highly floral and fragrant bouquet with spicy dark berry aromas, then a long palate with strong spicy/savoury nuances from the inclusion of whole bunches in the ferment. Screwcap. 14% alc. **Rating** 94 **To** 2020 $30

Reserve Release Yarra Valley Syrah 2007 Light colour; a very expressive bouquet, almost perfumed; the palate also walks along a path of its choosing, intense yet with spicy/savoury components; has elements of the Northern Rhône Valley in its make-up. Screwcap. 13% alc. **Rating** 94 **To** 2019 $50

Melba Mimi Yarra Valley Cabernet Sauvignon Syrah Nebbiolo 2008 Hits all the right notes, with an understated elegance to the ensemble of black fruits, with bass notes of cedar, and fine tannins as the finale. Screwcap. 13.5% alc. **Rating** 94 **To** 2023 $31

♔♔♔♔♔ **Estate Grown Yarra Valley Sauvignon 2008 Rating** 93 **To** 2012 $25

✪ **Gulf Station Yarra Valley Shiraz Viognier 2008** Typically bright and lifted red cherry aromas and flavours; superfine tannins lengthen the finish, as does the French oak. Seductive style. Screwcap. 14.5% alc. **Rating** 93 **To** 2016 $19

✪ **Windy Peak Chardonnay 2008** Bright pale green; has vibrantly juicy grapefruit and stone fruit flavours, which have largely absorbed the barrel ferment inputs; very elegant wine. Screwcap. 12.5% alc. **Rating** 92 **To** 2014 $14.90

Estate Grown Yarra Valley Viognier 2008 Rating 92 **To** 2013 $24

Estate Grown Yarra Valley Shiraz Viognier 2007 Rating 90 **To** 2014 $35

Rococo Yarra Valley Blanc de Blancs NV Rating 90 **To** 2013 $22

♟♟♟♟ **Windy Peak Pinot Noir Chardonnay NV** Good mousse, and salmon-pink
❍   colour; obvious care in selection of base wine, most from the Yarra Valley; the
      strawberry fruit notes are, of course, pinot-derived, backed up by citrussy acidity.
      Cork. 11.5% alc. **Rating** 89 **To** 2010 $14.90
❍   **Windy Peak Sangiovese 2008** Bright hue for sangiovese; doubtless primarily
      from the King Valley; light-bodied, with cherry fruit neatly balanced by typical
      tannins. Screwcap. 13.5% alc. **Rating** 89 **To** 2012 $14

De Iuliis   ★★★★★
21 Broke Road, Pokolbin, NSW 2320 **Region** Hunter Valley
T (02) 4993 8000 **F** (02) 4998 7168 **www.**dewine.com.au **Open** 7 days 10–5
Winemaker Michael De Iuliis **Est.** 1990 **Cases** 10 000 **Vyds** 45 ha
Three generations of the De Iuliis family have been involved in the establishment of their
45-ha vineyard. The family acquired the property in 1986 and planted the first vines in 1990,
selling the grapes from the first few vintages to Tyrrell's but retaining increasing amounts for
release under the De Iuliis label. Winemaker Michael De Iuliis has completed postgraduate
studies in oenology at the Roseworthy campus of Adelaide University and was a Len Evans
Tutorial scholar. He has lifted the quality of the wines into the highest echelon.

♟♟♟♟♟ **Hunter Valley Semillon 2009** Light, bright straw-green; expressive bouquet
❍   with notes of citrus, grass and a touch of herb; beautifully balanced palate,
      with very good line and length to the fruit, which has echoes of lime in the
      background. Now or later. Screwcap. 10.5% alc. **Rating** 95 **To** 2017 $18
      Sunshine Vineyard Semillon 2009 Bright but pale straw-green; a finely
      tempered and tightly focused bouquet and palate; all the ingredients of grass, lime,
      lemon, mineral and acid; very fresh, it definitely needs time to open up and for
      the talc in the mouth to soften. It is on soil similar to the great Sunshine Vineyard
      once owned by Lindemans, but is a different property. Screwcap. 10.1% alc.
      Rating 95 **To** 2020 $25
❍   **Aged Release Hunter Valley Semillon 2004** Still pale, bright straw-green;
      the bouquet and palate are in perfect harmony, both displaying pure semillon fruit
      with a seamless chord of mineral, sweet lime/grapefruit fruit and acidity. Screwcap.
      11% alc. **Rating** 94 **To** 2020 $25
      Limited Release Hunter Valley Chardonnay 2009 Pale quartz-green; an
      ultra-elegant wine, hand-picked and sorted, whole-bunch-pressed and wild yeast,
      barrel fermented; flinty and citrussy, it could come from anywhere, Tasmania
      included. Needs time to fully display its wares. Screwcap. 12.5% alc. **Rating** 94
      To 2015 $25
      Limited Release Hunter Valley Shiraz 2007 Deeply coloured, with excellent
      hue; this is a thoroughly impressive, full-bodied wine, saturated with black fruits,
      and precise tannin and oak support. Given another five years in bottle, it will start
      the long path towards full maturity, when it will undoubtedly be a great wine.
      Screwcap. 14.3% alc. **Rating** 94 **To** 2034 $50

♟♟♟♟♟ **Show Reserve Hunter Valley Chardonnay 2009** Rating 92 **To** 2014 $20
      Shiraz 2008 Rating 90 **To** 2020 $30

Dead Horse Hill   ★★★★☆
Myola East Road, Toolleen, Vic 3551 **Region** Heathcote
T (03) 5433 6214 **F** (03) 5433 6164 **Open** By appt
Winemaker Jencie McRobert **Est.** 1994 **Cases** 500 **Vyds** 4 ha
Jencie McRobert (and husband Russell) 'did a deal with Dad' for approximately 65 ha of
her parents' large sheep and wheat farm at Toolleen, 20 km north of Heathcote. It took a
number of years for the dry-grown shiraz vines to achieve reasonable yields, but they are now
yielding between 3.7 and 5 tonnes per ha of high-quality fruit. Jencie's introduction to wine
came partly through the family dining table and partly from meeting Steve Webber, then
working for Lindemans at Karadoc, when she was working in soil conservation and salinity
management in the Mallee. She subsequently completed a course at CSU and makes the wine
at De Bortoli in the Yarra Valley, with the odd bit of assistance from Webber.

ŢŢŢŢŢ **Heathcote Shiraz 2008** Bright colour; lifted and fragrant, with black fruits the
driving aroma of the bouquet; lively and pure on the palate, with the bright acidity
picking up the red highlights and showing a touch of bay leaf, while the chewy
tannins provide the muscle. Screwcap. 14.5% alc. **Rating** 93 $26 BE

Deakin Estate ★★★★

Kulkyne Way, via Red Cliffs, Vic 3496 **Region** Murray Darling
T (03) 5018 5555 **F** (03) 5018 5565 www.deakinestate.com.au **Open** Not
Winemaker Dr Phil Spillman **Est.** 1980 **Cases** 400 000 **Vyds** 350 ha
Part of the Katnook Estate, Riddoch and Deakin Estate triumvirate, which constitutes the
Wingara Wine Group, now fully owned by Freixenet of Spain. Deakin Estate draws from its
own vineyards, making it largely self-sufficient, and produces wines of consistent quality and
impressive value, thanks in no small part to the skills and expertise of winemaker Phil Spillman.
Exports to all major markets.

ŢŢŢŢŢ **Rose 2009** Bright pale pink; made from Cabernet Sauvignon/Petit Verdot, it has
✪   a very fragrant bouquet of cool red fruits; finishes refreshingly dry, yet with good
fruit on the mid-palate. Screwcap. 12.5% alc. **Rating** 90 **To** 2011 $10

✪   **Moscato 2009** This is one of the very few super-low alcohol examples that has
intensity of flavour, and more importantly considerable length. Its high residual
sugar (100 grammes per litre) is largely masked by its low pH of 2.92 rather
than its middle of the road (6.5 grammes per litre) of acidity. Screwcap. 4.5% alc.
Rating 90 **To** 2011 $10

ŢŢŢŢ **Shiraz 2008** Clear red; the wine has a fragrant bouquet of black and red cherry,
✪   the light- to medium-bodied palate encapsulating those flavours in a fine web
of gently savoury tannins. Continues a tradition of excellent value for this label.
Screwcap. 13.5% alc. **Rating** 89 **To** 2013 $10

✪   **Sauvignon Blanc 2009** Amazingly, leads Deakin Estate's sales (of all varieties)
in NZ. It has a mix of grassy/herbal characters plus some tropical notes, and
has a commendably dry finish, which makes it food friendly. Screwcap. 11% alc.
Rating 88 **To** 2010 $10

✪   **Chardonnay 2008** Has developed unexpected well in bottle, growing in flavour,
without becoming broad, just ripe, gently mouthfilling stone fruit. Screwcap.
13.5% alc. **Rating** 88 **To** 2010 $10

✪   **Merlot 2007** Savoury smoky spicy aromas give way to a palate with surprising
varietal character in a savoury black olive mode, supported by well-judged tannins.
Over delivers. Screwcap. 13.5% alc. **Rating** 88 **To** 2011 $10

Chardonnay 2009 Rating 87 **To** 2010 $10
Brut NV Rating 87 **To** 2010 $10

Deep Woods Estate ★★★★☆

Commonage Road, Yallingup, WA 6282 **Region** Margaret River
T (08) 9756 6066 **F** (08) 9756 6366 www.deepwoods.com.au **Open** Tues–Sun 11–5,
7 days during hols
Winemaker Travis Clydesdale **Est.** 1987 **Cases** 20 000
The Gould family acquired Deep Woods Estate in 1992, when the first plantings were four
years old. In 2005 the business was purchased by Perth businessman Peter Fogarty and family,
who also own Lake's Folly in the Hunter Valley, and Millbrook in the Perth Hills. The 32-ha
property has 16-ha plantings of cabernet sauvignon, shiraz, merlot, cabernet franc, chardonnay,
sauvignon blanc, semillon and verdelho. Vineyard and cellar door upgrades are underway.
Exports to Switzerland, Belgium, Denmark and Ireland.

ŢŢŢŢŢ **Reserve Margaret River Cabernet Sauvignon 2008** Strong crimson-purple;
a classy, full-bodied cabernet, the bouquet with blackcurrant, cassis and cedary oak,
the medium- to full-bodied palate a replay, sustained by firm, but balanced, tannins.
Screwcap. 14% alc. **Rating** 94 **To** 2028 $40.50

ΨΨΨΨΨ   **Margaret River Sauvignon Blanc 2009** A wine designed from the ground up
✪   to maximise its early drinking appeal; passionfruit, citrus and snow pea flavours
       have been given texture by partial barrel fermentation. Screwcap. 12.5% alc.
       Rating 93 To 2012 $22
       Block 7 Margaret River Shiraz 2008 Rating 93 To 2023 $25

ΨΨΨΨ   **Harmony Margaret River Rose 2009** Rating 89 To 2011 $14.95
       Ivory Margaret River Semillon Sauvignon Blanc 2009 Rating 88
       To 2010 $14.95

Deetswood Wines   ★★★

Washpool Creek Road, Tenterfield, NSW 2372 **Region** New England
T (02) 6736 1322 **F** (02) 6736 1322 **www**.deetswoodwines.com.au
Open Fri–Mon 10–5, or by appt
Winemaker Contract **Est.** 1996 **Cases** 2000 **Vyds** 2.4 ha
Deanne Eaton and Tim Condrick established their micro-vineyard in 1996, planting semillon,
chardonnay, pinot noir, shiraz, merlot, viognier and cabernet sauvignon. At the end of the
19th century, German immigrant Joe Nicoll planted vines here and made wines for family
use, and there is still one vine surviving on the site today from those original plantings. The
wines are normally consistent both in quality and style, offering further proof that this is a
very interesting area.

Deisen   ★★★★★

PO Box 61, Tanunda, SA 5352 **Region** Barossa Valley
T (08) 8563 2298 **F** (08) 8563 2298 **www**.deisen.com.au **Open** Not
Winemaker Sabine Deisen **Est.** 2001 **Cases** 1000
Deisen (owned by Sabine Deisen and Les Fensom) once again proves the old adage true that
nothing succeeds like success. In the first year, 3.5 tonnes of grapes produced five barrels of
Shiraz and two of Grenache. Since that time, production has grown slowly but steadily with
bits and pieces of traditional winemaking equipment (small crushers, open tanks and hand-
plunging, now housed in a slightly larger tin shed). The number of wines made and the tiny
quantities of some (20 dozen is not uncommon) is staggering. The style of all the wines is
remarkably similar: sweet and luscious fruit; soft, ripe tannins; and a warmth from the alcohol
(toned down in recent releases). Exports to the US.

ΨΨΨΨΨ   **Sweetheart Barossa Shiraz 2006** Slightly more aromatic and spicy on the
       bouquet than Backblock, and with more thrust on the palate, yet still well and
       truly in the family style. Quality cork. 15% alc. Rating 95 To 2021 $40
       Backblock Barossa Shiraz 2006 In typical rich, dense Deisen style, with
       luscious black fruits, yet neither alcoholic nor in any way clumsy on the finish.
       High-quality cork, properly inserted. 15% alc. Rating 94 To 2018 $65
       Barossa Shiraz 2005 Strong colour; full of flavour, albeit without any confit or
       dead fruit components; dark chocolate and mocha surround the black fruit flesh
       of the mid-palate. Cork. 14.8% alc. Rating 94 To 2015 $56

ΨΨΨΨΨ   **Barossa GSM 2006** Rating 91 To 2016 $40
       Barossa Mataro 2006 Rating 90 To 2015 $37

Delamere Vineyard   ★★★★

Bridport Road, Pipers Brook, Tas 7254 **Region** Northern Tasmania
T (03) 6382 7190 **F** (03) 6382 7250 **www**.delamerevineyards.com.au **Open** 7 days 10–5
Winemaker Shane Holloway **Est.** 1983 **Cases** 2500 **Vyds** 6.9 ha
Delamere produces elegant, rather light-bodied wines that have a strong following. The
Chardonnay has been most successful; a textured, complex wine.

ΨΨΨΨΨ   **Chardonnay 2008** Light straw-green; very intense, pure and long; complex
       barrel ferment inputs to grapefruit and white peach flavours; a long finish with
       slightly high acidity. Screwcap. 12.5% alc. Rating 92 To 2014 $35

Delatite ★★★★★

26 High Street, Mansfield, Vic 3722 **Region** Upper Goulburn
T (03) 5775 2922 **F** (03) 5775 2911 **www**.delatitewinery.com.au **Open** 7 days 11–5
Winemaker Andy Browning **Est.** 1982 **Cases** 12 000 **Vyds** 18.5 ha
With its sweeping views across to the snow-clad Alps, this is uncompromising cool-climate viticulture, and the wines naturally reflect that. Increasing vine age (many of the plantings are well over 25 years old), the adoption of organic (and partial biodynamic) viticulture seems also to have played a role in providing the red wines with more depth and texture; the white wines as good as ever. Exports to Denmark, China, Japan and Malaysia.

ΨΨΨΨΨ **Riesling 2008** Lime and lemon blossom aromas lead into a brilliantly fresh palate,
✪   where green apple joins the lime of the bouquet; perfectly balanced acidity draws
      out the long finish. Screwcap. 13% alc. **Rating** 96 **To** 2020 $23

✪   **Late Harvest Riesling 2008** Glowing yellow-green; lime blossom aromas
      introduce an utterly, totally delicious lime juice palate, sweetness and acidity perfectly
      balanced on the lingering finish. Screwcap. 11% alc. **Rating** 96 **To** 2023 $23

      Pinot Noir 2008 Bright, clear crimson; plum, black cherry and spice aromas are
      repeated on the palate, which has excellent texture and structure, with savoury
      Burgundian tannins; 500 cases made. Screwcap. 14% alc. **Rating** 94 **To** 2015 $28

      Devils River 2006 Light, bright crimson; bubbling with a basket of fresh-picked
      berry fruits (cherry/raspberry/mulberry) backed by superfine tannins and good
      acidity. Lovely light-bodied red. Cabernet Sauvignon/Merlot/Malbec/Cabernet
      Franc. Screwcap. 14% alc. **Rating** 94 **To** 2014 $30

      Devils River 2008 Bright crimson hue; a time-honoured wine that has thrown
      off the strong minty characters it once had, now with attractive cassis fruit and
      fine-grained tannins on the long finish. Merlot/Cabernet Sauvignon. Screwcap.
      13.5% alc. **Rating** 94 **To** 2018 $30

      Late Harvest Riesling 2009 Pale bright quartz-green; the sure touch of Delatite
      is there from the word go, with a wonderfully pure and delicate wine; it cries out
      for several years in bottle and is guaranteed to repay those with faith and patience.
      Screwcap. 9% alc. **Rating** 94 **To** 2017 $23

ΨΨΨΨΨ **Rose 2009 Rating** 93 **To** 2011 $18
      Shiraz 2008 Rating 93 **To** 2016 $30
      RJ Limited Edition 2006 Rating 92 **To** 2016 $55
      Dungeon Gully 2008 Rating 90 **To** 2016 $25
      Donald Tempranillo 2008 Rating 90 **To** 2014 $30
      Demelza Sparkling Pinot Noir 2008 Rating 90 **To** 2013 $30

ΨΨΨΨ   **Dead Man's Hill Gewurztraminer 2009 Rating** 89 **To** 2014 $25
      Unwooded Chardonnay 2008 Rating 89 **To** 2011 $23

Delbard ★★★☆

'Spring Hill', 577 Springs Road, at the Crystal Brook, Caveat, Vic 3660
Region Strathbogie Ranges
T (03) 5790 4006 **Open** By appt
Winemaker Ross MacLean **Est.** NA **Cases** 500 **Vyds** 5 ha
Ross and Christine MacLean have established their vineyard, planted to 1 ha each of pinot noir, chardonnay, merlot, sauvignon blanc and shiraz, on a rolling granite plateau at an elevation of 600 m, complete with lichen-covered granite boulders and bubbling springs (drought permitting). The wine is made onsite in small, hand-plunged vats and basket-pressed. Exports the UK, The Netherlands and Singapore.

ΨΨΨΨΨ **Premium Reserve Strathbogie Ranges Shiraz 2007** Good hue; a well-
      balanced, medium-bodied shiraz with notes of spice and cedar; a wine with
      deceptive length that is easy to miss first up; the oak and tannins have been well
      handled. Diam. 14% alc. **Rating** 90 **To** 2017 $30

Derwent Estate ★★★★★
329 Lyell Highway, Granton, Tas 7070 **Region** Southern Tasmania
T (03) 6263 5802 **F** (03) 6263 5802 **www**.derwentestate.com.au
Open Mon–Fri 10–4 (Oct–Easter), Sun 10–4 (Dec–Jan)
Winemaker Winemaking Tasmania (Julian Alcorso) **Est.** 1992 **Cases** 2000 **Vyds** 10 ha
Three generations of the Hanigan family are involved in the management of their historic Mt Nassau property, owned by the family since 1913. Given that over the last 100 years or so the property has at various times been involved with sheep, cattle, vegetable production, seed crops, poppies, quarrying and the production of lime, the addition of viticulture in 1992 was not surprising. The vineyard has grown in stages, doubling to 10 ha in 2003, the grapes bound for Bay of Fires wines and Penfolds Yattarna. The grapes retained by Derwent Estate have produced consistently good wines.

ΨΨΨΨΨ **Chardonnay 2007** Bright, light straw-green; white peach and grapefruit; subtle oak; good length and balance; great finesse. Has blossomed over the past 15 months. Trophy Tas Wine Show '10. Screwcap. 12% alc. **Rating** 96 **To** 2015 $32
Chardonnay 2008 Bright straw-green; a fragrant and complex bouquet, fruit to the fore, oak in the background; the palate borders on the electric, so intense is it and its incumbent citrussy acidity; very long, lingering finish. Screwcap. 13% alc. **Rating** 94 **To** 2016 $32

ΨΨΨΨΨ **Riesling 2009 Rating** 93 **To** 2024 $25
Pinot Noir 2008 Rating 93 **To** 2018 $32

ΨΨΨΨ **Sauvignon Blanc 2009 Rating** 89 **To** 2011 $26

Deviation Road ★★★★★
214 Scott Creek Road, Longwood, SA 5153 **Region** Adelaide Hills
T (08) 8339 2633 **F** (08) 8331 1360 **www**.deviationroad.com **Open** W'ends & public hols, or by appt
Winemaker Kate and Hamish Laurie **Est.** 1999 **Cases** 5500 **Vyds** 11.05 ha
Deviation Road was created in 1998 by Hamish Laurie, great-great-grandson of Mary Laurie, SA's first female winemaker. He initially joined with father Dr Chris Laurie in 1992 to help build the Hillstowe Wines business; the brand was sold to Banksia Wines in 2001, but the Laurie family retained the vineyard, which now supplies Deviation Road with its grapes. Wife Kate joined the business in 2001, having studied winemaking and viticulture in Champagne, then spending four years at her family's Stone Bridge winery in Manjimup. All the wines come from the family vineyards, but only account for a small portion of the annual grape production of those vineyards. It also has 3 ha of pinot noir and shiraz at Longwood, where its new cellar door is situated. Exports to the UK, the US, Switzerland and Hong Kong.

ΨΨΨΨΨ **Adelaide Hills Sauvignon Blanc 2009** Interesting aromas, part tropical, part
✪ pear, even apricot, then a zesty palate with considerable thrust; bracing acidity adds to the length. Screwcap. 12% alc. **Rating** 94 **To** 2011 $18.95
Adelaide Hills Pinot Noir 2008 Strong colour; an aromatic spice, black cherry and plum bouquet leads into a full, soft and flavoursome palate, with just a touch of warmth on the finish not detracting from the overall appeal. Screwcap. 14.5% alc. **Rating** 94 **To** 2015 $32

ΨΨΨΨΨ **Adelaide Hills Pinot Gris 2009** What else but partial barrel fermentation? All
✪ the smartest winemakers are using this to add interest, although here early picking has invested the wine with a high-tensile, stainless-steel backbone of acidity. Screwcap. 13% alc. **Rating** 93 **To** 2012 $22.95
Adelaide Hills Methode Champenoise Brut 2008 Rating 92 **To** 2012 $28

Devil's Lair ★★★★★
Rocky Road, Forest Grove via Margaret River, WA 6285 **Region** Margaret River
T (08) 9757 7573 **F** (08) 9757 7533 **www**.devils-lair.com **Open** Not
Winemaker Oliver Crawford **Est.** 1981 **Cases** NFP **Vyds** 130 ha

Having rapidly carved out a high reputation for itself through a combination of clever packaging and impressive wine quality, Devil's Lair was acquired by Southcorp in 1996. The estate vineyards have been substantially increased since, now with sauvignon blanc, semillon, chardonnay, cabernet sauvignon, merlot, shiraz, cabernet franc and petit verdot, supplemented by grapes purchased from contract growers. An exceptionally successful business; production has increased from 40 000 cases to many times greater, in no small measure due to its second label, Fifth Leg. Exports to the UK, the US and other major markets.

ŸŸŸŸŸ **Margaret River Chardonnay 2008** A surprisingly elegant wine despite the generous use of fine French oak involved; pure grapefruit, seasoned delicately with cinnamon and clove from the oak, seamlessly entwined on the bouquet; while rich, the palate is light and fine on entry, and then the regional power of the variety shines through on a generous and complex conclusion. Screwcap. 13.5% alc. **Rating** 95 **To** 2018 $45 BE

✪ **Fifth Leg White 2009** Pungent and racy, with the sauvignon blanc and semillon components driving the flavours, chardonnay playing a minor role in filling out the mid-palate a little; crisp acid provides a clean, dry finish. Gold medal Sydney Wine Show '10. Screwcap. 12% alc. **Rating** 94 **To** 2012 $20

ŸŸŸŸ **Fifth Leg Chardonnay 2009** Tightly wound with nectarine and grapefruit
✪ coming to the fore; the acidity is very high and certainly at the crisp end, resulting in a finish that is distinctly lemony; super on a hot day. Screwcap. 11.5% alc. **Rating** 88 **To** 2012 $20 BE

Fifth Leg Red 2007 **Rating** 88 **To** 2012 $20

Dexter Wines   ★★★★☆

210 Foxeys Road, Merricks North, Vic 3926 (postal) **Region** Mornington Peninsula
T (03) 5989 7007 **F** (03) 5989 7009 **www**.dexterwines.com.au **Open** Not
Winemaker Tod Dexter **Est.** 2006 **Cases** 600 **Vyds** 7.1 ha
Tod Dexter was introduced to wine through a friendship between his parents and then leading Melbourne retailer Doug Crittenden. A skiing trip to the US indirectly led to Tod becoming an apprentice winemaker at Cakebread Cellars, a well-known Napa Valley winery, in 1979. After seven years he returned to Australia and the Mornington Peninsula, and began the establishment of the vineyard, planted to pinot noir (4 ha) and chardonnay (3.1 ha). To keep the wolves from the door he became winemaker at Stonier, and leased his vineyard to Stonier, the grapes always used in the Stonier Reserve range. Having left Stonier to become Yabby Lake winemaker, and spurred on by turning 50 in 2006 (and at the urging of friends), he and wife Debbie decided to establish the Dexter label. Exports to the UK.

ŸŸŸŸŸ **Mornington Peninsula Pinot Noir 2008** Bright and clear colour; a fragrant red fruit bouquet, then a fresh and lively light-bodied palate, the red fruits surging through to a lingering finish with fine tannins. A restrained winemaking hand at work. Screwcap. 13% alc. **Rating** 94 **To** 2015 $49

ŸŸŸŸŸ **Mornington Peninsula Chardonnay 2008** **Rating** 93 **To** 2015 $38

Di Fabio Estate   ★★★★

5 Valleyview Drive, McLaren Vale, SA 5171 (postal) **Region** McLaren Vale
T (08) 8383 0188 **F** (08) 8383 0168 **www**.difabioestatewines.com.au **Open** Not
Winemaker Goe Di Fabio **Est.** 1994 **Cases** 6000 **Vyds** 38.91 ha
Di Fabio Estate is the venture of brothers Goe and Tony Di Fabio. Their parents Giovanni and Maria Di Fabio purchased their first vineyard in McLaren Vale in 1966 (with a tradition stretching back further to Italy) and became long-term contract grapegrowers for other winemakers. The business carried on by their sons has a 56-ha property at McLaren Vale, and 8.5 ha at Waikerie. The plantings are dominated by 12.5 ha of grenache, 10.5 ha of shiraz, and 3.6 ha of mourvedre. Petit verdot, merlot, chardonnay, cabernet franc, sauvignon blanc and semillon are also grown. Exports to Macau, Singapore and China.

🍷🍷🍷🍷🍷 The Old House McLaren Vale Merlot 2004 Exceptional colour for a five-year-old merlot from anywhere, let alone McLaren Vale; the palate, too, is fresh and vibrant, the varietal expression right on the money; has eaten 31 months in new oak. A major surprise packet. Diam. 14% alc. **Rating** 94 To 2019 $30

🍷🍷🍷🍷 The Old House McLaren Vale Cabernet Franc 2004 **Rating** 88 To 2014 $30

di Lusso Estate ★★★★★

Eurunderee Lane, Mudgee, NSW 2850 **Region** Mudgee
T (02) 6373 3125 **F** (02) 6373 3128 **www**.dilusso.com.au **Open** Wed–Mon 10–5
Winemaker Julia Conchie, Robert Paul (Consultant) **Est.** 1998 **Cases** 4000 **Vyds** 6.5 ha
Rob Fairall and partner Luanne Hill have brought to fruition their vision to establish an Italian 'enoteca' operation, offering Italian varietal wines and foods. When they began to plant their vineyard in 1998, the Italian varietal craze was yet to gain serious traction. They now have a thoroughly impressive range of barbera, sangiovese, vermentino, aleatico, lagrein, greco di tufo, picolit and nebbiolo. The estate also produces olives for olive oil and table olives, and the range of both wine and food will increase over the years. The decision to focus on Italian varieties has been a major success, the quality of the wines, however, rather than passing popularity, the key to that success.

🍷🍷🍷🍷🍷 Pinot Grigio 2009 Pale blush pink; strong spiced pear aromas and even a hint of strawberry; the palate has both character and length. Practice makes perfect. Screwcap. 12.7% alc. **Rating** 94 To 2012 $26

✪ Passito 2006 Grapes rack-dried for two months, then barrel aged for three years; intensely sweet and very complex; spicy brandy snap overtones. One of a handful made in Australia. Screwcap. 9.5% alc. **Rating** 94 To 2011 $55

🍷🍷🍷🍷🍷 Vermentino 2009 A highly aromatic bouquet of citrus, pear, apple and spice
✪ leads into an intensely tangy palate, with noticeable acidity. Screwcap. 10.7% alc. **Rating** 92 To 2012 $21

✪ Vino Rosato 2009 Bright, light crimson; a fragrant bouquet of ripe cherry and spices, then a firm, brisk and long palate, tailor-made for food. Lagrein. Screwcap. 12.9% alc. **Rating** 91 To 2011 $19
Mudgee Picolit 2007 **Rating** 91 To 2013 $23
Mudgee Nebbiolo 2008 **Rating** 90 To 2014 $26

🍷🍷🍷🍷 Moscato 2009 **Rating** 88 To 2010 $18

Diamond Creek Estate ★★★

Diamond Fields Road, Mittagong, NSW 2575 **Region** Southern Highlands
T (02) 4872 3311 **F** (02) 4872 3311 **www**.diamondcreekestate.com.au **Open** By appt
Winemaker Eddy Rossi, Nick Spence **Est.** 1997 **Cases** 2400 **Vyds** 6 ha
Helen Hale purchased Diamond Creek Estate in late 2002, by which time the chardonnay, sauvignon blanc, riesling, pinot noir and cabernet sauvignon planted in 1997 by the prior owner had come into bearing. The vineyard is established at 680 m on rich basalt soil, the north-facing slope being relatively frost-free. Since Helen acquired the property, some of the grapes have been sold to Southern Highlands Winery, but most have been retained for release under the Diamond Creek Estate label: these include Riesling, Sauvignon Blanc, Pinot Noir, Cabernet Sauvignon and a highly successful Noble Diamond Botrytis Chardonnay.

🍷🍷🍷🍷 Pinot Noir 2007 Light colour, similar to rose; while far from rich, shows once
✪ again not to judge a pinot by its colour, for there are neatly expressed spicy savoury varietal flavours running through a long palate. Screwcap. 13% alc. **Rating** 89 To 2012 $20

Sauvignon Blanc 2008 Has developed a glowing green hue; a crisp, lively grassy lemony palate follows the similar bouquet; good length, but drink asap. Screwcap. 12% alc. **Rating** 88 To 2010 $16

Chardonnay 2008 Good greenish colour; a light-bodied citrussy chardonnay that has been matured in American oak, presumably in an effort to add softer, sweeter notes. I think the cure is worse than the illness. Screwcap. 12.5% alc. **Rating** 87 **To** 2013 $22

Diamond Island Wines

PO Box 56, Bicheno, Tas 7215 **Region** East Coast Tasmania
T 0409 003 988 **Open** Not
Winemaker Winemaking Tasmania (Julian Alcorso) **Est.** 2002 **Cases** 500 **Vyds** 2 ha
Owner Derek Freeman has planted pinot noir, and is the personal full-time viticulturist, helped out during peak periods by a part-time employee. It may not seem much, but successfully growing pinot noir (or any other variety, for that matter) in Tasmania requires an enormous degree of attention to debudding, leaf plucking, wire raising and (in the winter months) pruning. Not surprisingly, Freeman says he has no plans to extend the vineyard at the moment.

ŸŸŸŸŸ **Bicheno Pinot Noir 2008** Colour bright and light; lively, medium- to full-bodied with good intensity to red cherry/berry fruits; very good fine tannins. Screwcap. 13.3% alc. **Rating** 92 **To** 2014 $22

Diggers Bluff ★★★☆

PO Box 34, Tanunda, SA 5352 **Region** Barossa Valley
T 0417 087 566 **F** (08) 8563 1613 **www**.diggersbluff.com **Open** By appt
Winemaker Timothy O'Callaghan **Est.** 1998 **Cases** 1000 **Vyds** 1.9 ha
Timothy O'Callaghan explains that his family crest is an Irish hound standing under an oak tree; the Diggers Bluff label features his faithful hound Digger, under a Mallee tree. He is a third-generation O'Callaghan winemaker, and – reading his newsletter – it's not too hard to guess who the second generation is represented by. Diggers Bluff has cabernet sauvignon, shiraz, grenache, alicante and mataro, all old vines. Exports to the UK, Canada, Singapore and Hong Kong.

DiGiorgio Family Wines ★★★★☆

Riddoch Highway, Coonawarra, SA 5263 **Region** Coonawarra
T (08) 8736 3222 **F** (08) 8736 3233 **www**.digiorgio.com.au **Open** 7 days 10–5
Winemaker Peter Douglas, Vanessa Marsden **Est.** 1998 **Cases** 25 000 **Vyds** 278 ha
Stefano DiGiorgio emigrated from Abruzzi, Italy, in 1952. Over the years, he and his family gradually expanded their holdings at Lucindale. In 1989 he began planting cabernet sauvignon (100 ha), chardonnay (10 ha), merlot (9 ha), shiraz (6 ha) and pinot noir (2 ha). In 2002 the family purchased the historic Rouge Homme winery, capable of crushing 10 000 tonnes of grapes, and its surrounding 13.5 ha of vines, from Southcorp. Since that time the Coonawarra plantings have been increased to 126 ha, the lion's share cabernet sauvignon. The enterprise is offering full winemaking services to vignerons in the Limestone Coast Zone. The ownership of the properties has now passed to former lawyer Frank DiGiorgio, who gave up his law practice when he and his family moved to Coonawarra full-time. Exports to the UK and other major markets.

ŸŸŸŸŸ **Coonawarra Shiraz 2006** Deep colour; bright blackberry fruit bouquet, with
✪ a fairly healthy dose of high-quality oak; the palate is generous and shows fine-grained tannins and fruit in abundance; surprisingly fresh and unevolved, there is plenty of life ahead. ProCork. 14% alc. **Rating** 92 **To** 2020 $23 BE

✪ **Coonawarra Cabernet Sauvignon 2006** Rich and essency bouquet of cassis and mint; pushing the envelope of ripeness with a slight confiture aspect to the fruit; the tannin/acid balance pulls the fruit somewhat back into line, to leave a long and savoury finish. ProCork. 14.5% alc. **Rating** 92 **To** 2018 $23 BE

Francesco Reserve Cabernet Sauvignon 2002 Restrained bouquet of cedar, olive, redcurrant and spice from oak usage; complex and layered, with an appropriate level of development for its age; long, fine and savoury to conclude. Cork. 13.7% alc. **Rating** 92 **To** 2018 $50 BE

❂ **Lucindale Merlot 2006** Retains good hue; spice, earth and olive notes on the bouquet set the scene for a medium-bodied wine with good varietal character, cassis and spice running through the long palate. Screwcap. 14% alc. **Rating** 90 **To** 2016 $20

Emporio Coonawarra Merlot Cabernet Sauvignon Cabernet Franc 2006 Spicy cassis with a touch of earthy complexity; the palate is quite deep and compelling, with the components working together to deliver a well-balanced array of dark fruits and savoury complexity; long, chewy and a little toasty to finish. ProCork. 14.5% alc. **Rating** 90 **To** 2016 $23 BE

Coonawarra Fortified Shiraz 2006 Fresh mulberry, blackberry, cinnamon and sandalwood; the palate is lively and there is a good balance between ripe shiraz fruit, clean spirit and structure; well made. ProCork. 19% alc. **Rating** 90 **To** 2025 $33 BE

♈♈♈♈ **Sauvignon Blanc 2009** Rating 88 **To** 2012 $18 BE
Lucindale Chardonnay 2009 Rating 88 **To** 2012 $18
Traditional Method Coonawarra Sparkling Pinot Noir 2008 Rating 88 **To** 2012 $26

Dinny Goonan

880 Winchelsea-Deans Marsh Road, Bambra, Vic 3241 **Region** Geelong
T 0438 408 420 **F** (03) 5288 7100 **www.**dinnygoonan.com.au **Open** 7 days Jan, w'ends & public hols Nov–Jun, or by appt
Winemaker Dinny and Angus Goonan **Est.** 1990 **Cases** 1000 **Vyds** 5.5 ha
The establishment of Dinny Goonan dates back to 1988 when Dinny Goonan bought a 20-ha property near Bambra, in the hinterland of the Otway Coast. Dinny had recently completed a viticulture diploma at CSU, and initially a wide range of varieties was planted in what is now known as the Nursery block to establish those best suited to the area. As these came into production Dinny headed back to CSU, where he completed a wine science degree. Ultimately, it was decided to focus production on shiraz and riesling, with more extensive planting of these varieties. In '07 a 'sticky' block was added.

♈♈♈♈♈ **Riesling 2009** Pale straw-green; a very tight and precise wine folded in on itself with lemon and apple flavours enhanced by minerally acidity. Demands time. Screwcap. 12.5% alc. **Rating** 91 **To** 2024 $22

Early Harvest Riesling 2009 Water white; a bold experiment in super-early picking, barely off-dry and with delicate lime flavours. Has to be drunk as an aperitif, although will fill out with a few years in bottle. Screwcap. 9.5% alc. **Rating** 90 **To** 2019 $27

♈♈♈♈ **Blanc de Bambra 2009** Rating 88 **To** 2012 $25
Shiraz 2008 Rating 87 **To** 2014 $23

Dionysus Winery ★★★★

1 Patemans Lane, Murrumbateman, NSW 2582 **Region** Canberra District
T (02) 6227 0208 **F** (02) 6227 0209 **www.**dionysus-winery.com.au **Open** W'ends & public hols 10–5, or by appt
Winemaker Michael O'Dea **Est.** 1998 **Cases** 1000 **Vyds** 4 ha
Michael and Wendy O'Dea are both public servants in Canberra, seeking weekend and holiday relief from their everyday life at work. They purchased their property at Murrumbateman in 1996, and planted chardonnay, sauvignon blanc, riesling, viognier, merlot, pinot noir, cabernet sauvignon and shiraz between 1998 and 2001. Michael has completed an associate degree in winemaking at CSU, and is responsible for viticulture and winemaking; Wendy has completed

various courses at the Canberra TAFE and is responsible for wine marketing and (in their words) 'nagging Michael and being a general slushie'.

ΨΨΨΨΨ **Canberra District Shiraz 2008** Good colour; a complex bouquet with dark
✪ berry, spice, licorice and game aromas, the savoury palate following suit, and
finishing well. Screwcap. 14.5% alc. **Rating** 91 **To** 2017 $22
Canberra District Cabernet Sauvignon 2008 Bright colour and attractive
blackcurrant fruit aromas are a good start, and introduce medium-bodied palate
flavours tracking the bouquet; all is well until the finish and aftertaste, which
warms up because of its alcohol. Screwcap. 15% alc. **Rating** 90 **To** 2018 $22

ΨΨΨΨ **Canberra District Sauvignon Blanc 2009 Rating** 89 **To** 2010 $19
Canberra District Riesling 2009 Rating 88 **To** 2013 $19
Canberra District Merlot 2008 Rating 88 **To** 2013 $22

Disaster Bay Wines ★★★★

133 Oaklands Road, Pambula, NSW 2549 **Region** South Coast Zone
T (02) 6495 6869 **www**.disasterbaywines.com **Open** Not
Winemaker Dean O'Reilly, Capital Wines (Andrew McEwen) **Est.** 2000 **Cases** 450
Vyds 1.2 ha
Dean O'Reilly has a 10-year background in the distribution of fine table wines, culminating
in employment by Möet Hennessy Australia. He has accumulated the UK-based WSET
Intermediate and Advanced Certificates, completed various other programs and competitions,
and has been associate judge and judge at various Canberra district events. He has also
travelled through the wine regions of NZ, Champagne, Bordeaux, Chablis, Piedmont and
Tuscany. In 2009 he was one of 12 wine professionals selected to participate in the week-
long Len Evans Tutorial. The wines are made at Kyeema, with Andrew McEwen overseeing
Dean's apprenticeship; the grapes come from the block owned by Dean adjacent to the
Pambula River.

ΨΨΨΨΨ **Barrel Matured Sauvignon Blanc Semillon 2008** Oak is the dominant
character, but it has been handled well; guava, peach and touch of straw all
combine with a pleasant cinnamon seasoning added from the oak; the palate is
fresh and clean, with added texture and weight provided by the winemaking; a
good effort. Screwcap. 13% alc. **Rating** 92 **To** 2013 $30 BE

djinta djinta Estate ★★★

10 Stevens Road, Kardella South, Vic 3951 **Region** Gippsland
T (03) 5658 1163 **F** (03) 5658 1928 **www**.djintadjinta.com.au **Open** W'ends 12–5, or by appt
Winemaker Marcus Satchell, Mal Stewart **Est.** 1991 **Cases** 600 **Vyds** 5 ha
djinta djinta had several changes of ownership before being acquired by Alex and Eleonor Biro
in late 2004. The vineyard is planted to sauvignon blanc, semillon, marsanne, roussanne, viognier,
cabernet sauvignon and cabernet franc. Nestled among the Strezlecki Ranges, the property
takes its name from the indigenous Willy Wagtails that populate the surrounding country.

ΨΨΨΨ **South Gippsland Chardonnay 2007** Still pale green-straw; a well-made wine
benefiting from its low alcohol; fresh and crisp citrussy fruit, with a subtle twist of
oak. Screwcap. 12.5% alc. **Rating** 89 **To** 2013 $22
South Gippsland Rose 2009 Salmon-pink; an easy-access style, made with
merlot from Phillip Island Vineyard; a fragrant bouquet and soft palate. Screwcap.
13% alc. **Rating** 89 **To** 2011 $18

🍇 Dog Trap Vineyard ★★★★

262 Dog Trap Road, Yass, NSW 2582 **Region** Canberra District
T (02) 6226 5898 **www**.dogtrapvineyard.com.au **Open** By appt
Winemaker Dr Dennis Hart, Dr Roger Harris, Brian Sinclair **Est.** 1996 **Cases** 650
Vyds 6.35 ha

The somewhat ghoulish name and label illustration is a reminder of bygone days when wild dogs were caught in traps in much the same way as rabbits. It certainly means the name of the venture will be remembered. Planting of the vineyard began in 1996, with a smaller addition in '98. The property was purchased by Dr Dennis Hart and Ms Julian White in December 2003, and until '06 the grapes were sold to Constellation's Kamberra winery. In '07 the crop was completely destroyed by a violent but localised hailstorm, so the first wines were not made until '08. Shiraz and cabernet sauvignon were the initial plantings, and more recently, riesling and pinot gris were added.

♀♀♀♀♀ **Lyn Canberra District Shiraz 2008** An opulent full-bodied shiraz, with blackberry, licorice, vanilla and mocha aromas and flavours, ripe tannins and American oak to the fore; carries its alcohol burden slightly better than Tony. Screwcap. 15.5% alc. **Rating** 91 **To** 2020 $27
Tony Canberra District Shiraz 2008 Deeper purple than Lyn; an extremely powerful, very ripe wine, the flavour and mouthfeel seemingly amplified by the French oak, the alcohol slightly stripping the back-palate. Screwcap. 15.5% alc. **Rating** 90 **To** 2020 $27
Canberra District Cabernet Sauvignon 2008 Very good colour; a luscious and ripe cabernet that shows its alcohol, yet largely gets away with it; blackcurrant and Ribena flavours along with a touch of cedary French oak work well. Diam. 15% alc. **Rating** 90 **To** 2015 $21

♀♀♀♀ **Canberra District Shiraz 2008 Rating** 89 **To** 2017 $18

DogRidge Wine Company   ★★★★★
RSD 195 Bagshaws Road, McLaren Flat, SA 5171 **Region** McLaren Vale
T (08) 8383 0140 **F** (08) 8383 0430 **www**.dogridge.com.au **Open** 7 days 11–5
Winemaker Fred Howard, Nick Bourke (Consultant) **Est.** 1991 **Cases** 10 000 **Vyds** 45 ha
Dave and Jen Wright had a combined background of dentistry, art and a CSU viticultural degree when they moved from Adelaide to McLaren Flat to become vignerons. They inherited vines planted in the early 1940s as a source for Chateau Reynella fortified wines, and their viticultural empire now ranges from 2001 plantings to some of the oldest vines remaining in the immediate region today. At the McLaren Flat vineyards, DogRidge has 60+-year-old shiraz, as well as 60-year-old grenache. Part of the grape production is retained, but most is sold to other leading wineries. Exports to the UK, the US and other major markets.

♀♀♀♀♀ **Most Valuable Player McLaren Vale Shiraz 2005** Retains good colour hue and depth; a powerful testament to the region, redolent of dark chocolate and black fruits; the palate has excellent texture, structure and length, fruit characters winning the day on the finish and aftertaste. Screwcap. 14.5% alc. **Rating** 96 **To** 2030 $65
Most Valuable Player McLaren Vale Shiraz 2007 Good hue and depth for age; a world apart from Shirtfront, with all the attributes the '07 Shirtfront was short on, most notably rich blackberry fruit, supple, ripe tannins and a dash of dark chocolate. Screwcap. 14.5% alc. **Rating** 94 **To** 2027 $65
✪ **Shirtfront McLaren Vale Shiraz 2006** Good colour; the great '06 vintage to the fore; excellent regional typicity, with blackberry fruit, dark chocolate, spice and oak seamlessly welded on the long, medium- to full-bodied palate. Screwcap. 14% alc. **Rating** 94 **To** 2026 $25

♀♀♀♀♀ **Square Cut McLaren Vale Cabernet 2006 Rating** 93 **To** 2021 $25
Square Cut McLaren Vale Cabernet 2007 Rating 92 **To** 2017 $25
Cadenzia McLaren Vale Grenache 2006 Rating 90 **To** 2014 $25

♀♀♀♀ **Shirtfront McLaren Vale Shiraz 2007 Rating** 89 **To** 2015 $25
The Pup Cabernet Merlot 2008 Rating 89 **To** 2015 $18
The Pup Cabernet Merlot 2007 Rating 89 **To** 2014 $18
The Pup Sauvignon Blanc 2009 Rating 88 **To** 2010 $18
Digs Vineyard McLaren Vale Viognier 2009 Rating 88 **To** 2011 $20

The Pup Shiraz 2007 Rating 88 To 2014 $18
The Pup Shiraz 2008 Rating 87 To 2014 $18

DogRock Winery ★★★★☆

114 De Graves Road, Crowlands, Vic 3377 **Region** Pyrenees
T (03) 5354 9201 **www**.dogrock.com.au **Open** W'ends 11–5
Winemaker Allen Hart **Est.** 1999 **Cases** 500 **Vyds** 6.2 ha
This is the micro-venture (but with inbuilt future growth to something slightly larger) of Allen (now full-time winemaker) and Andrea (viticulturist) Hart. Having purchased the property in 1998, planting shiraz, riesling, tempranillo, grenache, chardonnay and marsanne began in 2000. Given Allen's former post as research scientist/winemaker with Foster's, the attitude taken to winemaking is unexpected. The estate-grown wines are made in a low-tech fashion, without gas cover or filtration. The one concession to technology, say the Harts, is that 'all wine will be sealed with a screwcap and no DogRock wine will ever be released under natural cork bark'.

ŸŸŸŸŸ Degraves Road 2008 Excellent crimson-purple; the blend of Grenache/Shiraz/
        Tempranillo is one of those that doesn't always work – this wine does so in spades,
        the fragrant bouquet good, the medium-bodied palate brilliantly counterpoising
        the red and black fruit flavours in a fine web of tannins, the finish and aftertaste
        terrific. Screwcap. 14% alc. Rating 96 To 2030 $68

ŸŸŸŸŸ Pyrenees Chardonnay 2008 Rating 91 To 2013 $25
        Pyrenees Tempranillo 2007 Rating 90 To 2014 $25

ŸŸŸŸ Pyrenees Riesling 2009 Rating 89 To 2018 $20
        Pedro's Pyrenees Sparkling Red 2008 Rating 88 To 2014 $32

🍇 Doherty Wines ★★★★☆

Box 6101, Cromer, Vic 3193 **Region** Various
T (03) 9585 7828 **F** (03) 9585 0887 **www**.dohertywines.com **Open** Not
Winemaker Kilikanoon (Kevin Mitchell), Carlei (Sergio Carlei), Stella Bella (Janice McDonald), Gibson (Rob Gibson) **Est.** 2006 **Cases** 5000
This is a virtual winery with a twist. Bede Doherty has a background in chemistry, strategic marketing, viticulture and oenology, and has pulled these threads together as a negociant. He has secured the services of highly regarded winemakers from the Barossa Valley, Clare Valley, Yarra Valley, Central Victoria and Margaret River to make wines for his brand, The Doherty Signature Collection. He says the Collection features the winemakers, signatures both on the label and in the bottle, a neat summary. A common price point of $25 for five of the six wines ($30 for the Janice McDonald Cabernet Merlot) has the virtue of simplicity. Exports to China.

ŸŸŸŸŸ The Doherty Signature Collection Cabernet Merlot 2008 Excellent
        crimson-purple; a rich, complex bouquet and medium- to full-bodied palate
        showing all that Margaret River so easily achieves with this blend; sumptuous
        blackcurrant, plum and cassis fruit, with excellent tannin structure and length.
        Janice McDonald. Cork. 14.3% alc. Rating 95 To 2023 $32

ŸŸŸŸŸ The Doherty Signature Collection Pinot Noir 2008 Rating 90 To 2014 $25
        The Doherty Signature Collection Shiraz Cabernet 2008 Rating 90
        To 2016 $25
        The Doherty Signature Collection Cabernet Sauvignon 2006 Rating 90
        To 2016 $25

ŸŸŸŸ The Doherty Signature Collection Shiraz 2006 Rating 87 To 2014 $25

Domain Barossa ★★★★

25 Murray Street, Tanunda, SA 5352 **Region** Barossa Valley
T (08) 8563 2170 **F** (08) 8563 2164 **www**.domainbarossa.com **Open** W'ends 11–5.30
Winemaker Todd Riethmuller **Est.** 2002 **Cases** 3000

Todd Riethmuller and family are long-term residents of the Barossa Valley and have the inside running, as it were, when it comes to buying grapes from local growers. Thus they have been able to dispense with the expensive and often frustrating business of having their own winery, yet can make wines of exceptional quality.

ŸŸŸŸ♀ **Black Tongue Shiraz 2008** Good hue; a complex Barossa Valley shiraz that
✪ seems to have had a brief liaison with McLaren Vale and come home with a distinct touch of chocolate to add to its black fruits, fine-grained tannins and plentiful oak. Screwcap. 14.5% alc. **Rating** 90 **To** 2016 $19
Sticky Cane Dried Semillon 2009 Bright yellow-gold; extremely rich and luscious cane-cut and dried style; honey, marmalade and cumquat flavours are balanced by good acidity. Screwcap. 11% alc. **Rating** 90 **To** 2012 $15

ŸŸŸŸ **Toddler GSM 2009 Rating** 89 **To** 2013 $21
Ruth Miller Eden Valley Riesling 2009 Rating 88 **To** 2017 $17
Merlot 2008 Rating 88 **To** 2014 $21

Domain Day ★★★★☆

24 Queen Street, Williamstown, SA 5351 **Region** Barossa Valley
T (08) 8524 6224 **F** (08) 8524 6229 **www.**domainday.com.au **Open** W'ends & public hols 10–5
Winemaker Robin Day **Est.** 2000 **Cases** 8000 **Vyds** 15.1 ha
This is a classic case of an old dog learning new tricks, and doing so with panache. Robin Day had a long and distinguished career as winemaker, chief winemaker, then technical director of Orlando; he participated in the management buy-out, and profited substantially from the on-sale to Pernod Ricard. He hastened slowly with the establishment of Domain Day, but there is nothing conservative about his approach in his vineyard at Mt Crawford, high in the hills (at 450 m) of the southeastern extremity of the Barossa Valley, two sides of the vineyard bordering the Eden Valley, and moving to positive biological controls. While the mainstream varieties are merlot, pinot noir and riesling, he has trawled Italy, France and Georgia for the other varieties: viognier, nebbiolo, sangiovese, saperavi, lagrein, garganega, sagrantino and nebbiolo. Robin Day says, 'Years of writing descriptions for back labels have left me convinced that this energy is more gainfully employed in growing grapes and making wine.' Robin provides tutored tastings in the vineyard, showcasing alternative varieties (by appointment). Exports to the UK and Canada.

ŸŸŸŸ♀ **One Serious Mt Crawford Riesling 2008** Offers a fragrant, flowery apple
blossom bouquet, then a firm, fresh palate; good length and balance. Screwcap. 12% alc. **Rating** 92 **To** 2016 $20

Domaine A ★★★★★

Tea Tree Road, Campania, Tas 7026 **Region** Southern Tasmania
T (03) 6260 4174 **F** (03) 6260 4390 **www.**domaine-a.com.au **Open** Mon–Fri 9–4, w'ends by appt
Winemaker Peter Althaus **Est.** 1973 **Cases** 5000 **Vyds** 10.7 ha
The striking black label of the premium Domaine A wine, dominated by the single, multi-coloured 'A', signified the change of ownership from George Park to Swiss businessman Peter Althaus many years ago. The wines are made without compromise, and reflect the low yields from the immaculately tended vineyards. They represent aspects of both Old World and New World philosophies, techniques and styles. Exports to the UK, Denmark, Switzerland, Germany, France, Belgium, Canada, NZ, China, Japan and Singapore.

ŸŸŸŸŸ **Cabernet Sauvignon 2004** Every bit as youthful as the '05; a very fragrant
bouquet with hallmark blackcurrant fruit and a finely framed palate; these cabernets are by far the best in Tasmania, but are not for lovers of Barossa cabernets. Cork. 13% alc. **Rating** 95 **To** 2019 $70

Pinot Noir 2006 Exceptionally deep purple-red; as heroically concentrated as the bouquet suggests, and still needing years for its black fruits to open up, its tannins to soften. In the unique Domain A style. High-quality, perfectly inserted cork should do the job. 14.3% alc. Rating 94 To 2018 $70

ￜￜￜￜￜ Stoney Vineyard Sauvignon Blanc 2009 Rating 93 To 2014 $35
Cabernet Sauvignon 2005 Rating 93 To 2017 $70
Stoney Vineyard Pinot Noir 2008 Rating 92 To 2015 $35

Domaine Asmara   ★★★★★

Gibb Road, Toolleen, Vic 3551 **Region** Heathcote
T 0432 501 135 **www**.domaineasmara.com **Open** 7 days 9–6.30
Winemaker Sanguine Estate, Dominique Portet **Est.** 2008 **Cases** 3000 **Vyds** 12 ha
Chemical engineer Andreas Greiving had a lifelong dream to own and operate a vineyard, and the opportunity came along with the global financial crisis. He was able to purchase a 12-ha vineyard planted to shiraz, cabernet sauvignon, cabernet franc, durif and viognier, and have the wines contract-made. The venture is co-managed by dentist wife Hennijati Greiving.

ￜￜￜￜￜ Infinity Heathcote Shiraz 2008 Dense, impenetrable purple; both the bouquet and full-bodied palate are all about power and concentration, yet the wine is not unduly extractive, and there is no doubt about its long fermentation; luscious black fruits are tempered by ripe tannins and oak, the finish long and satisfying. Screwcap. 14.8% alc. Rating 95 To 2023 $75
Private Collection Heathcote Shiraz 2008 Similar colour to the Reserve; a complex bouquet of blackberry, plum, licorice, warm spice and oak leads into a medium-bodied palate with plentiful, maybe too plentiful, oak and a spicy, savoury finish punctuated by tannins. Screwcap. 14.5% alc. Rating 94 To 2018 $40
Reserve Heathcote Shiraz 2008 Crimson-purple; all three shiraz back labels say, 'This shiraz is rich and complex and will repay cellaring'; a potent bouquet of black fruits, spice and licorice is followed by a full-bodied palate loaded with dark fruits, the oak – while obvious – is balanced by the fruit and tannins. Screwcap. 14.8% alc. Rating 94 To 2023 $45

ￜￜￜￜￜ Private Collection Heathcote Cabernet Sauvignon 2008 Rating 90 To 2015 $35

Domaine Chandon   ★★★★★

Green Point, Maroondah Highway, Coldstream, Vic 3770 **Region** Yarra Valley
T (03) 9738 9200 **F** (03) 9738 9201 **www**.chandon.com.au **Open** 7 days 10.30–4.30
Winemaker Matt Steel, Glenn Thompson, Andrew Santarossa, Adam Keath **Est.** 1986
Cases 120 000 **Vyds** 78 ha
Established by Möet & Chandon, this is one of the two most important wine facilities in the Yarra Valley; the tasting room has a national and international reputation, having won a number of major tourism awards in recent years. The sparkling wine product range has evolved, and there has been increasing emphasis placed on the table wines, now released under the Domaine Chandon label. An energetic young winemaking team has maintained the high-quality standards set by ex-CEO and mentor Dr Tony Jordan, who continues to consult to the winery. Exports to all major markets.

ￜￜￜￜￜ Barrel Selection Yarra Valley Chardonnay 2008 A truly classy chardonnay, taking the move to brighter fruit, lower alcohol and less oak started some years ago to another level; the finesse of the wine, with its delicate white peach and citrus flavours, is exceptional. Screwcap. 13% alc. Rating 96 To 2015 $49.95

✿ Heathcote Shiraz 2007 Full crimson-purple; a wine that brings out all the best features of Heathcote, the fragrant aromas of cherry and spice leading into a beautifully balanced, elegant, medium-bodied palate that flows across the tongue, finishing with succulent tannins. Screwcap. 14% alc. Rating 96 To 2022 $32

Prestige Cuvee 2002 Pale, bright green-straw; a reflection of the coolest ever vintage, spending seven years on lees prior to disgorgement; wonderfully fine and balanced, the mouthfeel only coming with such a long time on lees. Available only from cellar door. Diam. 12.5% alc. **Rating** 96 **To** 2013 $65

○ **Yarra Valley Chardonnay 2008** A very modern style of chardonnay, the low alcohol resulting in a fragrant bouquet and an elegant but intense palate, driven by white peach and a hint of citrus, oak evident but only in the background. Screwcap. 13% alc. **Rating** 95 **To** 2014 $28

Tasmanian Cuvee 2006 Bright straw-green, good mousse; from the Coal River region, with 30 months on lees prior to disgorgement; has an incisive zest unique to this wine, coupled with a minerality all of its own. Diam. 12.5% alc. **Rating** 95 **To** 2013 $39.95

Z*D Blanc de Blancs 2006 Glowing green-yellow; a remarkable combination of elegance and complexity, with fine citrussy components alongside white and yellow peach notes; the absence of dosage is simply not obvious. Crown seal. 12.5% alc. **Rating** 94 **To** 2013 $39.95

○ **Brut Rose Non Vintage NV** Pale salmon-pink; it is a delicious rose constructed from pinot noir and chardonnay, with a small amount of pinot noir red wine adding a distinct strawberry influence; the length, balance and finish are particularly good. A sparkler to be drunk with gusto. Cork. 12.5% alc. **Rating** 94 **To** 2010 $29

○ **Sparkling Pinot Shiraz NV** The move from McLaren Vale to cool-grown Vic shiraz (and Yarra Valley pinot) has resulted in a much finer and better balanced sparkling wine – indeed, the finest on the market, and excellent value. Diam. 14% alc. **Rating** 94 **To** 2014 $29

🍷🍷🍷🍷🍷 **Brut NV Rating** 93 **To** 2013 $29
Cuvee Riche NV Rating 93 **To** 2013 $39.95
Pinot Gris 2009 Rating 91 **To** 2011 $27.95

🍷🍷🍷🍷 **Sauvignon Blanc 2009 Rating** 89 **To** 2011 $24.95

🍇 Domaines & Vineyards ★★★★

PO Box 803, West Perth, WA 6872 **Region** Pemberton & Margaret River
T 0400 880 935 **F** (08) 9324 2155 **www.dandv.com.au Open** Not
Winemaker Rob Bowen **Est.** 2009 **Cases** 4500
One of the best known winemakers in WA is Rob Bowen, with over 35 years' experience with several of WA's leading wineries, most recently Houghton. In 2009 he joined forces with a team of viticulturists led by David Rado and other agricultural experts, who collectively furnish the project with an extensive range of knowledge and expertise. The theme is to produce premium wines with a strong sense of place through a virtual winery exercise, all grapes to be handpicked from the best available vineyards in the Margaret River and Pemberton regions of southern WA. A second range under the Robert N Bowen label will follow the same strategy, except for pricing, which will be at 'an affordable level'. So long as the grape surplus continues, it is highly likely all of the wines will provide excellent value for money. At the present time sauvignon blanc, chardonnay and pinot noir are sourced from Pemberton, sauvignon blanc, semillon, cabernet sauvignon and merlot from Margaret River. Exports to the UK, the US and Hong Kong.

🍷🍷🍷🍷🍷 **Pemberley Pemberton Sauvignon Blanc 2009** A precise and linear sauvignon blanc, the aromas and flavours basically in a tropical spectrum, but tied together on the finish by a bow of citrussy acidity. Screwcap. 13.2% alc. **Rating** 92 **To** 2011 $24.95

Pemberley Mt Barker Shiraz 2004 Developed colour; spicy black fruits are swathed in French oak on both the bouquet and palate, the latter with fine, savoury tannins adding texture. Cork. 13.5% alc. **Rating** 90 **To** 2014 $30.60

Dominique Portet ★★★★★

870-872 Maroondah Highway, Coldstream, Vic 3770 **Region** Yarra Valley
T (03) 5962 5760 **F** (03) 5962 4938 **www**.dominiqueportet.com **Open** 7 days 10–5
Winemaker Ben Portet **Est.** 2000 **Cases** 6000 **Vyds** 4.3 ha

Dominique Portet was bred in the purple. He spent his early years at Chateau Lafite (where his father was regisseur) and was one of the very first Flying Winemakers, commuting to Clos du Val in the Napa Valley, where his brother was winemaker. He then spent over 20 years as managing director of Taltarni and the Clover Hill vineyard in Tasmania. After retiring from Taltarni, he moved to the Yarra Valley, a region he had been closely observing since the mid-1980s. In 2001 he found the site he had long looked for and in the twinkling of an eye built his winery and cellar door, planting a quixotic mix of viognier, sauvignon blanc and merlot next to the winery. Son Ben is now executive winemaker, leaving Dominique with a roving role as de facto consultant and brand marketer. Ben (28) has a winemaking CV of awesome scope, covering all parts of France, South Africa, California and four vintages at Petaluma. I have made allowances for all Yarra Valley wineries in the wake of the catastrophic '09 vintage. Exports to Canada, The Netherlands, Denmark, Dubai, Hong Kong, Singapore, Malaysia, China and NZ.

ŸŸŸŸŸ **Heathcote Shiraz 2008** Strong crimson; a very appealing bouquet of dark berry and plum fruit and some oak; the medium- to full-bodied palate has black fruits, a dash of dark chocolate, persistent but ripe tannins and quality oak. Diam. 14.5% alc. **Rating** 95 **To** 2020 $50

ŸŸŸŸŸ **Gippsland Pinot Noir 2009 Rating** 93 **To** 2016 $35
✪ **Fontaine Yarra Valley Pyrenees Rose 2009** Salmon-pink; has more structure and texture than most, with a sprinkle of dusty tannins to add interest. Cabernet/Merlot/Shiraz. Screwcap. 14% alc. **Rating** 92 **To** 2011 $20
Yarra Valley Sauvignon Blanc 2009 Rating 91 **To** 2012 $28
Yarra Valley Cabernet Sauvignon Merlot 2008 Rating 90 **To** 2020 $45
Yarra Valley Brut Rose LD NV Rating 90 **To** 2012 $28

Donny Goodmac ★★★★☆

PO Box 467, Healesville, Vic 3777 **Region** Yarra Valley
T (03) 5962 3779 **F** (03) 5962 3779 **www**.donnygoodmac.com.au **Open** Not
Winemaker Kate Goodman **Est.** 2002 **Cases** 500

The improbable name is a typically whimsical invention of the three proprietors: Donny is contributed by Stuart Gregor, whose marketing and PR prowess has hitherto prevented an entry for the venture in the *Wine Companion*. Kate Goodman is the (genuinely) good part of the team, while Cameron MacKenzie is the 'mac'. Goodman and MacKenzie both work full-time at Punt Road, where Kate is chief winemaker. What started as a little bit of fun in 2002 (less than 50 cases made) has grown to the dizzy heights of 600 cases, utilising old vine shiraz from the Pyrenees, and chardonnay and cabernet sauvignon from a couple of old vineyards in the Coldstream area of the Yarra Valley.

ŸŸŸŸŸ **Yarra Valley Chardonnay 2008** A distinctly complex bouquet courtesy of wild fermentation and moderately low alcohol, with some French oak adding substantially; the Coldstream-region grapes were picked at precisely the right moment; 250 dozen made. Screwcap. 13% alc. **Rating** 94 **To** 2013 $28

ŸŸŸŸŸ **Pyrenees Shiraz 2007 Rating** 93 **To** 2017 $36.50
Yarra Valley Shiraz Viognier 2008 Rating 92 **To** 2018 $33
Yarra Valley Cabernet Sauvignon 2007 Rating 92 **To** 2017 $33

Doonkuna Estate ★★★☆

3182 Barton Highway, Murrumbateman, NSW 2582 **Region** Canberra District
T (02) 6227 5811 **F** (02) 6227 5085 **www**.doonkuna.com.au **Open** 7 days 10–4
Winemaker Bruce March **Est.** 1971 **Cases** 4000 **Vyds** 19.2 ha

Following the acquisition of Doonkuna by Barry and Maureen Moran in late 1996, the plantings were increased to almost 20 ha, and include shiraz, chardonnay, cabernet sauvignon, sauvignon blanc, zinfandel, sangiovese, riesling, merlot and pinot noir. A wide range of vintages of many of the wines is available at cellar door at modest prices.

ΥΥΥΥΥ **Sauvignon Blanc 2009** A restrained bouquet is followed by a palate with unexpected thrust and drive to its mix of tropical and citrus fruit, the finish clean and uncluttered. Screwcap. 11.8% alc. **Rating** 90 **To** 2011 $18

ΥΥΥΥ **Shiraz 2008 Rating** 89 **To** 2015 $25

Dorrien Estate ★★★★★
Cnr Barossa Valley Way/Siegersdorf Road, Tanunda, SA 5352 **Region** Barossa Valley
T (08) 8561 2200 **F** (08) 8561 2262 **www**.cellarmasters.com.au **Open** Not
Winemaker Mark Robertson (Chief), Julie Montgomery, Neil Doddridge **Est.** 1982
Cases 750 000
Dorrien Estate is the physical base of the vast Cellarmasters network that, wearing its retailer's hat, is by far the largest direct-sale outlet in Australia. It also makes wine for many producers across Australia at its modern winery, which has a capacity of 14.5 million litres of wine in tank and barrel; however, a typical make of each wine will be little more than 1000 cases. Most of the wines made for others are exclusively distributed by Cellarmasters. (Chateau Dorrien is an entirely unrelated business.) Purchased by private equity firm Archer Capital in 2007. Exports to the UK and NZ.

ΥΥΥΥΥ **Dorrien Estate Bin 1A Chardonnay 2007** Pale, bright straw-green; like the '08, a blend of Mount Benson/Coal River, the percentages not specified; a vibrantly fresh bouquet and equally fresh palate of white peach, nectarine and grapefruit, oak present but little more. Screwcap. 13.5% alc. **Rating** 95 **To** 2016 $36
Black Wattle Black Label Shiraz 2006 Healthy colour; a fragrant bouquet of spice, black fruits and oak, then a seductively juicy and long palate adding some plummy notes, the tannins silky. Screwcap. 15% alc. **Rating** 95 **To** 2021 $54
Dorrien Estate Bin 1A Chardonnay 2008 A blend of Mount Benson (70%)/ Coal River, Tasmania (30%) produces a fruit-driven yet complex wine, with citrus and nectarine fruit interwoven with quality barrel ferment oak; good length. Screwcap. 13.5% alc. **Rating** 94 **To** 2015 $36
Dorrien Estate Bin 1 Barossa Valley Shiraz 2007 Deep purple; the wine makes its quality stand around its admirable texture; here all the strands of plum, blackberry, vanillan oak and expertly handled tannins come together. Screwcap. 14.5% alc. **Rating** 94 **To** 2022 $42
Black Wattle Icon Mt Benson Cabernet Sauvignon 2007 Has a strongly spicy, cedary bouquet; the full-bodied palate is another thing again, intense, tightly focused and long, with blackcurrant and cigar box flavours. Screwcap. 14% alc. **Rating** 94 **To** 2027 $54
Black Wattle Mt Benson Cabernet Sauvignon 2007 While a junior brother to the Icon, is no shrinking violet; has excellent varietal characters and even better balance and mouthfeel, thanks to supple tannins. Screwcap. 14% alc. **Rating** 94 **To** 2020 $41

ΥΥΥΥΥ **Krondorf Symmetry Eden Valley Chardonnay 2008 Rating** 93 **To** 2012 $49
Krondorf Symmetry Eden Valley Chardonnay 2006 Rating 93 **To** 2015 $49
Black Wattle Mount Benson Chardonnay 2008 Rating 92 **To** 2014 $28
Avon Brae New Eden Vineyards Shiraz 2007 Rating 92 **To** 2017 $33.65
Dorrien Estate The Growers Barossa Valley Cabernet Sauvignon 2007 Rating 91 **To** 2017 $26
Dorrien Estate The Growers Barossa Valley Shiraz 2007 Rating 90 **To** 2017 $26
Krondorf Symmetry Barossa Valley Shiraz 2007 Rating 90 **To** 2020 $49

○   **Krondorf Barossa Valley Merlot 2009** Bright crimson-purple; very respectable varietal expression on both bouquet and palate, the ripe redcurrant and plum fruit easy on the gums (using the immortal words of Sir James Hardy). Screwcap. 14.5% alc. **Rating** 90 **To** 2012 $20

♀♀♀♀   **Krondorf Growers Heidenreich & Rohrlach Barossa Valley Chardonnay 2008 Rating** 89 **To** 2011 $26
       Dorrien Estate The Valleys Shiraz 2008 Rating 87 **To** 2011 $20

Dos Rios   ★★★☆

PO Box 343, Nyah, Vic 3594 **Region** Swan Hill
T (03) 5030 3005 **F** (03) 5030 3006 **www**.dosrios.com.au **Open** Fri–Mon 9–9
Winemaker Cobaw Ridge (Alan Cooper), Kilchurn Wines (David Cowburn) **Est.** 2003
Cases 1200 **Vyds** 1.05 ha
Bruce Hall entered the wine business as a small contract grower for McGuigan Simeon Wines. From this point on, the story goes in reverse: instead of McGuigan Simeon saying it no longer required the grapes, it purchased the vineyard in 2003. In the meantime, Hall had hand-picked the grapes left at the end of the rows after the mechanical harvester had passed through, and had the wines made by Alan Cooper of Cobaw Ridge. In 2004 he purchased a small property northwest of Swan Hill with plantings of 20-year-old shiraz, which has been extended by small areas of viognier, tempranillo, verdelho and moscato giallo. Exports to Japan.

♀♀♀♀♀ **Reserve Swan Hill Shiraz Viognier 2006** Excellent crimson colour and the
○   lifted aromas from the co-fermentation of shiraz and viognier; remarkably, 30 months in used barriques has not diminished the fresh fruit. Screwcap. 13.5% alc. **Rating** 90 **To** 2014 $20

♀♀♀♀   **Swan Hill Lagrein 2007 Rating** 88 **To** 2015 $20
       Swan Hill Viognier 2007 Rating 87 **To** 2009 $15
       Swan Hill Shiraz 2006 Rating 87 **To** 2014 $20

Dowie Doole   ★★★★☆

Cnr McMurtrie Road/Main Road, McLaren Vale, SA 5171 **Region** McLaren Vale
T (08) 8323 7428 **F** (08) 8323 8895 **www**.dowiedoole.com **Open** 7 days 10–5
Winemaker Brian Light (Contract) **Est.** 1996 **Cases** 20 000 **Vyds** 44.35 ha
Dowie Doole was born of the frustration following the 1995 vintage, which led friends and grapegrowers Norm Doole and Drew Dowie to form a partnership to take control over the destiny of their grapes. In '98, Leigh Gilligan, a McLaren Vale veteran, was appointed to take overall control of the business, and joined the partnership. Right from the outset the wines have been made by Brian Light at Boar's Rock, while Norm oversees the Norjan Vineyard in McLaren Vale, and Drew's wife, Lulu Lunn, is in charge of viticultural operations at Tintookie Vineyard at Blewitt Springs. Dowie Doole has direct or indirect interest in five vineyards, all of which are managed using sustainable viticultural practices. Exports to the UK, the US and other major markets.

♀♀♀♀♀ **Reserve McLaren Vale Shiraz 2008** Deep purple-crimson; the bouquet speaks equally strongly about the variety and the region, black fruits wrapped in a light coat of dark chocolate; the palate has more finesse, structure and length than California Road. Diam. 14.5% alc. **Rating** 95 **To** 2020 $50

♀♀♀♀♀ **Second Nature Adelaide Hills Sauvignon Blanc 2009** A very fragrant
○   bouquet, with passionfruit and gooseberry playing tag, then a fine and elegant palate, with similar fruit plus lemony acidity. Screwcap. 13% alc. **Rating** 93 **To** 2011 $19
       California Road McLaren Vale Shiraz 2008 Rating 93 **To** 2020 $35
       McLaren Vale Shiraz 2008 Rating 91 **To** 2020 $25
       McLaren Vale Cabernet Sauvignon 2007 Rating 91 **To** 2016 $25

ŸŸŸŸ McLaren Vale Chenin Blanc 2009 Rating 89 To 2012 $17
G&T McLaren Vale Garnacha & Tempranillo 2009 Rating 89 To 2012 $25

Downing Estate Vineyard ★★★★☆
19 Drummonds Lane, Heathcote, Vic 3523 **Region** Heathcote
T (03) 5433 3387 **F** (03) 5433 3389 **www**.downingestate.com.au **Open** Long w'ends &
public hols 11.30–4.30, or by appt
Winemaker Don Lewis **Est.** 1994 **Cases** 1000 **Vyds** 10 ha
Bob and Joy Downing purchased 24 ha of undulating land in 1994, and have since established
a dry-grown vineyard planted to shiraz (6.5 ha), cabernet sauvignon (2.5 ha) and merlot
(0.5 ha). At any one time, a number of vintages of each wine is available for sale. Exports to
Canada, Singapore and China.

ŸŸŸŸŸ Heathcote Cabernet Sauvignon 2006 Impressive crimson-purple; rich
blackcurrant and cassis aromas, then a classically proportioned and structured
palate, the flavours correct. Screwcap. 15% alc. **Rating** 94 To 2021 $39

ŸŸŸŸŸ Heathcote Shiraz 2006 Rating 91 To 2016 $39

Drayton's Family Wines ★★★★★
55 Oakey Creek Road, Cessnock, NSW 2321 **Region** Hunter Valley
T (02) 4998 7513 **F** (02) 4998 7743 **www**.draytonswines.com.au **Open** Mon–Fri 8–5,
w'ends & public hols 10–5
Winemaker Max Drayton, John Drayton, William Rikard-Bell **Est.** 1853 **Cases** 75 000
Vyds 72 ha
This long-established, substantial, but low-profile Hunter Valley producer gained national
headlines on 17 Jan 2007 for all the wrong reasons when winemaker Trevor Drayton was
killed in an explosion at the winery, believed to be caused by sparks from welding being
carried out, igniting ethanol in an adjoining room. It was a horrific example of third-time
unlucky, following the 1979 death of Barry Drayton, overcome by chlorine in a tank he was
cleaning, and that of Reg and Pam Drayton in the 1994 Seaview air disaster on the way to
Lord Howe Island. Happily, the family, its winery and winemaker William (Will) Rikard-Bell
(badly injured in the explosion) are in fine fettle, Will responsible for the trophy-winning '09
Chardonnay. Exports to Ireland, Vietnam, Singapore, Taiwan and China.

ŸŸŸŸŸ Susanne Semillon 2006 Produced from 100-year-old semillon planted by
William Drayton; intense, fine and delicate, it has great length and balance; very
hard to guess how long the wine will live for, so slow is its development to this
point, but it will be a long way off. Screwcap. 11% alc. **Rating** 95 To 2013 $35
Vineyard Reserve Pokolbin Semillon 2006 Bright, light straw-green;
interesting wine; has more citrus fruit on both bouquet and palate than Susanne,
and will reach its peak earlier; the track record with semillon and cork strongly
suggests you should make hay while the sun shines. 11% alc. **Rating** 95
To 2015 $30
Vineyard Reserve Pokolbin Chardonnay 2009 Bright straw-green; a lively
and fresh wine, with nectarine and white peach fruit having largely absorbed six
months in new oak. Gold medal Sydney Wine Show '10, trophy Hunter Valley
Wine Show '09 (Current Vintage Chardonnay). Screwcap. 12.5% alc. **Rating** 94
To 2014 $30
❂ Hunter Valley Chardonnay 2006 Bright green-yellow; has developed
considerable richness despite its modest alcohol; white peach, rock melon and a
caress of oak, before a bright finish. Screwcap. 12.5% alc. **Rating** 94 To 2014 $20

ŸŸŸŸŸ Hunter Valley Semillon 2008 Bright straw-green; already shows the first signs
❂ of toast and honey that will emerge with age; for now, lemon and grass flavours
dominate the long palate. Screwcap. 11% alc. **Rating** 93 To 2020 $20

○ **Hunter Valley Cabernet Merlot 2007** Good purple-red; pokes a stick in the eye of those (myself included) who decry this blend in the Hunter Valley; the '07 vintage was good to be sure, but the blackcurrant fruit and energy, texture and structure of this wine can't be denied. Screwcap. 13.5% alc. **Rating** 92 **To** 2020 $20

♈♈♈♈ **Bin 5555 Hunter Valley Shiraz 2007** Rating 89 To 2015 $20
Hunter Valley Cabernet Sauvignon 2007 Rating 89 To 2015 $20
Vineyard Reserve Pokolbin Verdelho 2009 Rating 88 To 2012 $30
Hunter Valley Semillon Sauvignon Blanc 2009 Rating 87 To 2012 $20
Hunter Valley Verdelho 2008 Rating 87 To 2011 $20
Vineyard Reserve Pokolbin Shiraz 2007 Rating 87 To 2015 $26

Dromana Estate   ★★★★☆

555 Old Moorooduc Road, Tuerong, Vic 3933 **Region** Mornington Peninsula
T (03) 5974 4400 **F** (03) 5974 1155 **www**.dromanaestate.com.au **Open** Wed–Sun 11–5
Winemaker Duncan Buchanan **Est.** 1982 **Cases** 30 000 **Vyds** 53.9 ha
Since it was established by Garry Crittenden (who exited some years ago), Dromana Estate has always been near or at the cutting edge, both in marketing terms and in terms of development of new varietals, most obviously the Italian range under the 'i' label. Dromana Estate is owned by the investors of a publicly listed company and operates under the name of Mornington Winery Group Limited. It includes the Dromana Estate, Mornington Estate and David Traeger (see separate entry) labels. Expanded production has seen export markets increase. Exports to the UK, Canada and China.

♈♈♈♈♈ **Mornington Peninsula Chardonnay 2008** A crisp and lively wine in the new style, early picking resulting in white peach and nectarine fruit supported by subtle oak; shortens fractionally on the finish. Early picking is a double-edged sword. Screwcap. 12.7% alc. **Rating** 93 **To** 2014 $29.95

○ **Mornington Estate Pinot Noir 2007** Light bright red; has an intriguing aromatic bouquet of red fruits, and a quite piercing and tangy palate. You get plenty of pinot bang for your buck. Screwcap. 13% alc. **Rating** 93 **To** 2014 $19.95

○ **Mornington Estate Chardonnay 2008** A classy wine at the price, with ripe stone fruit and melon, well-integrated French oak, and good acidity running through a notably long palate. Screwcap. 13% alc. **Rating** 92 **To** 2014 $19.95

i Mornington Peninsula Pinot Grigio 2009 Light quartz; has more juiciness to the fruit than many of its competitors; sourced from vineyards across Vic, some warm, some cool; an early mover with the variety, and it shows. Screwcap. 13.1% alc. **Rating** 90 **To** 2011 $15.95

Mornington Estate Pinot Gris 2009 Presents a true gris face, with part barrel fermented to produce a more textured character to cool-grown fruit; well made. Screwcap. 13.5% alc. **Rating** 90 **To** 2011 $19.95

Mornington Peninsula Pinot Noir 2008 Good hue, although light; has zest and life, the red cherry with a savoury/stemmy twist that works well; good balance and length. Screwcap. 13% alc. **Rating** 90 **To** 2014 $29.95

Mornington Estate Shiraz Viognier 2008 Typical vivid crimson colour; while only light-bodied, has drive and thrust to its display of red cherry, plum and spice fruit; co-fermentation has worked its magic well. Screwcap. 13.6% alc. **Rating** 90 **To** 2015 $19.95

♈♈♈♈ **Mornington Estate Pinot Noir 2006** Rating 88 To 2011 $19.95
Mornington Estate Shiraz Viognier 2006 Rating 88 To 2014 $19.95
i Heathcote Sangiovese 2008 Rating 88 To 2012 $15.95

Drummonds Corrina Vineyard   ★★★★☆

85 Wintles Road, Leongatha South, Vic 3953 **Region** Gippsland
T (03) 5664 3317 **Open** W'ends 12.30–4.30
Winemaker Bass Phillip **Est.** 1983 **Cases** NA **Vyds** 3 ha

The Drummond family organically grow 1 ha each of pinot noir and sauvignon blanc, and 0.5 ha each of cabernet sauvignon and merlot, all established slowly without the aid of irrigation. The viticultural methods are those practised by Phillip Jones, who makes the wines for Drummonds: north–south row orientation, leaf plucking on the east side of the rows, low yields, and all fruit picked by hand. Similarly restrained winemaking methods (no pumping, no filters and low SO_2) follow in the winery.

🍷🍷🍷🍷🍷 **South Gippsland Pinot Noir 2006** Faintly hazy colour (no filtration used); exemplary pinot flavours in a deliciously juicy and rich cherry and satsuma plum spectrum; flows effortlessly across the mouth into a long finish; a touch of mint is the only downside. Diam. 12.5% alc. **Rating** 94 **To** 2015 $39

Dryridge Estate   ★★★
The Six Foot Track, Megalong Valley, NSW 2785 **Region** Central Ranges Zone
T (02) 4787 5625 **F** (02) 4787 5626 **www**.dryridge.com.au **Open** Sun from 11 am, or by appt
Winemaker Madrez Wine Services (Chris Derrez, Lucy Maddox) **Est.** 1999 **Cases** 675 **Vyds** 4.7 ha
Bob and Barbara Tyrrell (no relation to Tyrrell's of the Hunter Valley) have pioneered commercial viticulture in the Megalong Valley, adjacent to the Blue Mountains National Park. They have 1.8 ha of riesling, 1.1 ha of shiraz and 0.9 ha of cabernet sauvignon, and a further 0.9 ha to be planted (possibly fiano) in due course. The vines are set on typically east-facing rolling hillsides, with granitic-derived light, sandy clay loam soils of moderately low fertility. The first of two lodges on the vineyard has been opened, providing 4.5-star accommodation.

🍷🍷🍷🍷 **Blue Mountains Riesling 2009** Attractive perfume of ripe lime with a touch of slate; generous mouthfeel, with a soft yet assertive finish. Screwcap. 12% alc. **Rating** 88 $22 BE

Ducketts Mill   ★★★★☆
1678, Scotsdale Road, Denmark, WA 6333 **Region** Denmark
T (08) 9840 9844 **F** (08) 9840 9668 **www**.duckettsmillwines.com.au **Open** 7 days 10–5
Winemaker Harewood Estate (James Kellie) **Est.** 1997 **Cases** 1500 **Vyds** 8 ha
Ducketts Mill is a twin operation with Denmark Farmhouse Cheese, both owned and operated by Ross and Dallas Lewis. They have the only cheese factory in the Great Southern region, and rely on James Kellie to make the wines from the extensive estate plantings (riesling, chardonnay, semillon, sauvignon blanc, merlot, cabernet franc, ruby cabernet and cabernet sauvignon). Some of the grapes are sold, some made into Riesling, Late Harvest Riesling, Merlot and Three Cabernets. The handmade cheeses make an even wider choice.

🍷🍷🍷🍷🍷 **Denmark Riesling 2009** Green-straw; a highly floral passionfruit blossom
✪ bouquet leads into a palate of quite spectacular intensity and energy, the pure lime juice flavours drawing saliva from the mouth; tremendous length and style. Bargain of the century. Screwcap. 12% alc. **Rating** 96 **To** 2020 $16

🍷🍷🍷🍷🍷 **Denmark Shiraz 2008** Bright purple-crimson hue; the fragrant bouquet
✪ exudes spice, pepper and licorice aromas combined with French oak; the light- to medium-bodied palate has an open-weave texture, allowing the range of flavours free play; good tannin and oak management. Screwcap. 14.5% alc. **Rating** 92 **To** 2018 $18

✪ **Denmark Three Cabernets 2008** Good crimson colour; a blend of Cabernet Sauvignon/Cabernet Franc/Ruby Cabernet, the presence of ruby cabernet (cross bred in California, once popular in Australia for low-priced reds) a pity. That said, it's true the other components provide a convincingly ripe and well-structured cabernet palate. Screwcap. 14% alc. **Rating** 90 **To** 2015 $16

🍷🍷🍷🍷 **Reserve Denmark Cabernets 2007 Rating** 88 **To** 2017 $21

Dudley Wines

★★★★☆

Cnr North Terrace/Thomas Willson Street, Penneshaw, Kangaroo Island 5222
Region Kangaroo Island
T (08) 8553 1333 **F** (08) 8553 1567 **www**.dudleywines.com.au **Open** 7 days 10–5
Winemaker Jeff and Brodie Howard **Est.** 1994 **Cases** 3500 **Vyds** 12 ha
Jeff Howard, Alan Willson and Paul Mansfield have formed a partnership to bring together three vineyards on Kangaroo Island's Dudley Peninsula: the Porky Flat Vineyard, Hog Bay River and Sawyers. It is the quirky vineyard names that give the wines their distinctive identities. The partners not only look after viticulture, but also join in the winemaking process. Most of the wines are sold through licensed outlets on Kangaroo Island.

ΨΨΨΨΨ **Porky Flat Kangaroo Island Shiraz 2007** Retains strong crimson colour; the complex bouquet has spiced black fruits that provide the key flavours of the medium-bodied palate, but it is the silky mouthfeel and delicious cedary tannins that really cause this wine to sing. Screwcap. 14.5% alc. **Rating** 94 **To** 2017 $22

ΨΨΨΨΩ **MacDonnell Kangaroo Island Merlot 2008** This is an above-average merlot from start to finish, with nuances of spice to its raspberry and plum fruit, the medium-bodied palate supple and smooth, the finish long and with just a touch of varietal savoury characters. Screwcap. 14.5% alc. **Rating** 92 **To** 2015 $18

Island Chardonnay 2009 The slightly funky bouquet attests to the use of some oak, but the palate is energetically driven by its grapefruit and white peach; very good length. Screwcap. 13.5% alc. **Rating** 91 **To** 2012 $18

Hog Bay River Kangaroo Island Cabernet Sauvignon 2007 **Rating** 90 **To** 2017 $22

ΨΨΨΨ **Grassy Flat Kangaroo Island Sauvignon Blanc 2009** **Rating** 89 **To** 2011 $18
Shearing Shed Red Kangaroo Island Cabernet Shiraz Merlot 2006 **Rating** 89 **To** 2014 $18
Pink Bay Kangaroo Island Rose 2009 **Rating** 88 **To** 2010 $18

Duke's Vineyard

★★★★★

Porongurup Road, Porongurup, WA 6324 **Region** Porongurup
T (08) 9853 1107 **F** (08) 9853 1107 **www**.dukesvineyard.com **Open** 7 days 10–4.30
Winemaker The Vintage Wineworx **Est.** 1998 **Cases** 3000 **Vyds** 10 ha
When Hilde and Ian (Duke) Ranson sold their clothing manufacturing business in 1998, they were able to fulfil a long-held dream of establishing a vineyard in the Porongurup subregion of Great Southern with the acquisition of a 65-ha farm at the foot of the Porongurup Range. They planted shiraz and cabernet sauvignon (3 ha each) and riesling (4 ha). Hilde, a successful artist, designed the beautiful, scalloped, glass-walled cellar door sales area, with its mountain blue cladding. In the lead-up to the 2007 vintage the biggest bushfire ever seen in the Porongurup Range led to the loss of the entire vintage due to smoke taint. The closure of the National Park to tourists through to November 2007 meant almost no cellar door trade right through to Jan '08. Exports to the UK.

ΨΨΨΨΨ **Magpie Hill Reserve Riesling 2009** Pale quartz; still an infant, but you can easily see its breeding and length; superfine lime/citrus fruit and a touch of apple drive the long palate and lingering finish. Great future. Screwcap. 10.5% alc. **Rating** 95 **To** 2024 $26.70

Great Southern Shiraz 2008 Deep colour; it seems that once you have terroir such as that of Duke's Vineyard, the role of the winemaker becomes quality control at best; fragrant black fruits and spices stream effortlessly through the bouquet and palate alike, the finish long and sustaining. Screwcap. 13.9% alc. **Rating** 95 **To** 2020 $21.70

Great Southern Riesling 2009 Pale straw-green; floral aromas lead into a palate with exemplary poise, tension and precision; here lime and lemon flavours seamlessly meld with minerally acidity on the cleansing finish. Screwcap. 11.2% alc. **Rating** 94 **To** 2020 $20

Magpie Hill Reserve Shiraz 2007 Very good crimson-purple colour; the spicy bouquet and palate both show significant new French oak impact, but there are plenty of black fruits to absorb that oak as the wine matures, and ripe tannins to support the ageing process. Screwcap. 14.2% alc. **Rating** 94 **To** 2027 $35

✪ **Great Southern Cabernet Sauvignon 2008** Bright crimson-purple; a deliciously fragrant blackcurrant and cassis bouquet is precisely replayed on the juicy, medium-bodied palate; the oak is subtle, although present, the tannins perfect, balance likewise. Screwcap. 13% alc. **Rating** 94 **To** 2020 $20

Magpie Hill Reserve Cabernet Sauvignon 2007 Some colour development, but still deep; a classic medium-bodied cabernet, with black fruits, cigar box and fine but persistent tannins on the long palate; good balance. Screwcap. 13.2% alc. **Rating** 94 **To** 2022 $35

♟♟♟♟♟ **Sparkling Shiraz 2006 Rating** 92 **To** 2015 $35
✪ **Great Southern Rose 2009** Pale pink; a light, fresh-scented bouquet, then a cool, zesty, bone-dry palate with plenty of drive and energy. Cabernet Sauvignon/Shiraz. Screwcap. 12.2% alc. **Rating** 90 **To** 2011 $16.70

♟♟♟♟ **Great Southern Autumn Riesling 2009 Rating** 89 **To** 2015 $18.30

Dumaresq Valley Vineyard ★★★☆

Bruxner Highway, Tenterfield, NSW 2372 **Region** New England
T (02) 6737 5281 **F** (02) 6737 5293 www.dumaresqvalleyvineyard.com.au **Open** 7 days 9–5
Winemaker Peter Zappa, Contract **Est.** 1997 **Cases** 2500 **Vyds** 20 ha
Three generations of the Zappa family have been involved in the establishment of what is now a very large mixed farming property on 1600 ha, all beginning when the first generation arrived from Italy in the late 1940s to work as cane-cutters in Qld. Today, Martin and Amelia, with three of their sons and their wives, have a property sustaining 120 cattle, 5000 superfine wool Merino sheep, 140 ha of fresh produce, 250 ha of cereal crops and a 20-ha vineyard. The vineyard was progressively established between 1997 and 2000, with plantings of chardonnay, semillon, sauvignon blanc, shiraz, merlot, cabernet sauvignon, barbera and tempranillo. Exports to Japan.

♟♟♟♟♟ **Reserve Release Barbera 2008** Trademark dense colour; while full-bodied, is the least extractive of the '08 Dumaresq reds, with solid black cherry, plum and dark chocolate fruit, finishing with spicy tannins. Screwcap. 14% alc. **Rating** 90 **To** 2016 $22

Dunn's Creek Estate ★★★

137 McIlroys Road, Red Hill, Vic 3937 **Region** Mornington Peninsula
T 0413 020 467 **F** (03) 5989 2011 www.dunnscreek.com.au **Open** By appt
Winemaker Sandro Mosele (Contract) **Est.** 2001 **Cases** 500 **Vyds** 3.34 ha
This is the retirement venture of Roger and Hannah Stuart-Andrews, a former professional couple whose love of Italian and Spanish wines led them to their eclectic choice of varieties. Thus they have planted barbera, arneis, savagnin and pinot gris.

♟♟♟♟ **Mornington Peninsula Arneis 2009** Very pale straw-green; interesting wine that mimics the texture and structure of barrel fermentation in old French oak; has a distinctive crushed leaf and lemon flavour. Screwcap. 14% alc. **Rating** 88 **To** 2011 $18

Dutschke Wines ★★★★★

PO Box 107 Lyndoch, SA 5351 **Region** Barossa Valley
T (08) 8524 5485 **F** (08) 8524 5489 www.dutschkewines.com **Open** Not
Winemaker Wayne Dutschke **Est.** 1998 **Cases** 6000 **Vyds** 17.5 ha
Wayne Dutschke spent over 20 years working in Australia and overseas for companies large and small before joining his uncle (and grapegrower) Ken Semmler to form Dutschke Wines. In addition to outstanding table wines, he has a yearly release of fortified wines (doubtless

drawing on his time at Baileys of Glenrowan); these sell out overnight, and have received the usual stratospheric points from Robert Parker Jr. The quality of the wines is in fact exemplary. Exports to the UK, the US and other major markets.

ΨΨΨΨΨ GHR Neighbours Barossa Valley Shiraz 2008 Excellent crimson-purple; an opulent bouquet is matched by an equally opulent palate, with blackberry, prune, dark chocolate and licorice flavours, the tannins in balance. Screwcap. 14.7% alc. **Rating** 94 **To** 2018 $28

St Jakobi Single Vineyard Barossa Valley Shiraz 2008 Takes the aromas and flavours of GHR to another level, although one wonders whether the alcohol was dialled by the heatwave rather than viticulturist Ken Semmler or winemaker Wayne Dutschke. That said, the full-bodied wine has sufficient intrinsic power to largely carry the alcohol. Screwcap. 15.5% alc. **Rating** 94 **To** 2028 $40

The Tawny NV This is true tawny, 22 years old (some more than 30 years old), amber in colour, with a spice bouquet, fruitcake and butterscotch flavours and a clean, dry finish. No stale characters whatsoever. Screwcap. 20% alc. **Rating** 94 **To** 2011 $35

ΨΨΨΨΨ Sun-Dried Shiraz NV Rating 91 **To** 2011 $35
The Tokay NV Rating 90 **To** 2011 $25
The Muscat NV Rating 90 **To** 2011 $25

ΨΨΨΨ Willow Bend Barossa Valley Shiraz Merlot Cabernet Sauvignon 2008 Rating 89 **To** 2017 $22
Old Codger Fine Old Tawny NV Rating 87 **To** 2011 $18

Eagle Vale Estate   ★★★★☆

7087 Caves Road, Margaret River, WA 6285 **Region** Margaret River
T (08) 9757 6477 **F** (08) 9757 6199 **www**.eaglevalewine.com **Open** Mon–Fri 10–4.30, w'ends by appt
Winemaker Guy Gallienne **Est.** 1997 **Cases** 13 500 **Vyds** 11.5 ha
Eagle Vale is the venture of Colorado businessman Steve Jacobs, and the operator/winemaking team of Chantal and Guy Gallienne. The Galliennes come from the Loire Valley, although Guy secured his winemaking degree at Roseworthy College/Adelaide University. The vineyard is managed on a low-impact basis, without pesticides (guinea fowls do the work) and with minimal irrigation. All the wines are made from estate-grown grapes. Exports to the UK, the US, Seychelles, China and Hong Kong.

ΨΨΨΨΨ ⚪ **Margaret River Semillon Sauvignon Blanc 2009** Light straw-green; has a fragrant bouquet with grass and nettle plus a hint of gooseberry; the palate progressively gains intensity and velocity through to its vibrant, part juicy, part minerally, finish. No need of oak. Screwcap. 13% alc. **Rating** 94 **To** 2013 $18

ΨΨΨΨΨ Margaret River Cabernet Merlot 2007 Rating 90 **To** 2016 $20 BE
Whispering Lake Single Vineyard Margaret River Cabernet Sauvignon 2004 Rating 90 **To** 2014 $36 BE

ΨΨΨΨ Margaret River Shiraz 2008 Rating 88 **To** 2015 $20 BE

🍂 Earthworks Wines   ★★★☆

PO Box 551, Tanunda, SA 5352 **Region** Barossa Valley
T (08) 8561 3200 **F** (08) 8561 3465 **www**.earthworkswines.com **Open** Not
Winemaker Tyson Bitter, Andrew La Nauze **Est.** 2003 **Cases** 10 000 **Vyds** 15 ha
Earthworks was founded by the Lindner and Bitter families in 2003. Both have been centrally involved in the Barossa wine industry for many years, and were able to persuade the marketing arm of the Hill Smith Family/Yalumba, Negociants Australia, to handle the domestic distribution of the wine. When the arrangement extended internationally via Negociants International, part of the business was purchased by the Hill Smith Family, reinforcing their sales, winemaking and marketing efforts with an equity position in Earthworks.

ＹＹＹＹＹ **Barossa Valley Shiraz 2008** Bright colour; a particularly elegant wine, barely
○ medium–bodied, but with a clear varietal fruit profile in a plum and blackberry
spectrum, the finish fresh. Screwcap. 14% alc. **Rating** 91 **To** 2015 $15

Eastwell Estate ★★★★

129 Whitworth Road, Forest Hill, WA 6324 **Region** Great Southern
T 0410 161 221 www.eastwell.com.au **Open** By appt
Winemaker John Wade (Contract) **Est.** 2008 **Cases** 600 **Vyds** 6 ha
This is the venture of the Eastwell family; son Matt graduated from the viticulture and oenology
course at the Curtin Margaret River Campus in 2006. The following year he and his parents,
Adrian and Margaret, purchased the 40-ha property intending to focus on the viticulture side,
and initially sell the grapes to local wineries as the previous owner had done. The vineyard
had been planted in 1998 to sauvignon blanc, semillon, merlot, cabernet sauvignon and shiraz.
As so often happens, they are now producing wine under the Eastwell Estate label. The wines,
selling at mouth-watering prices, are made by industry stalwart John Wade.

ＹＹＹＹＹ **Great Southern Shiraz 2008** Good depth and hue; attractive plum, cherry,
○ spice and pepper aromas are an accurate portent of the medium- to full-bodied
palate; the flavours persist, and are supported by very good tannins and some
French oak. Screwcap. 13% alc. **Rating** 93 **To** 2020 $18
○ **Great Southern Merlot 2008** Strong red, very good for merlot, even if
fractionally advanced; the expressive bouquet has an unexpected element of
chocolate alongside the (expected) plum; the palate is medium- to full-bodied,
with impressive texture and structure. Screwcap. 13% alc. **Rating** 92 **To** 2018 $20
Great Southern Sauvignon Blanc 2009 What is the world coming to? A
sauvignon blanc priced higher than a seriously good shiraz? This wine certainly
has good structure, flavour (a mix of herbaceous and tropical fruit) and length, but
that's it. Screwcap. 12.5% alc. **Rating** 90 **To** 2012 $24

ＹＹＹＹ **Great Southern Semillon Sauvignon Blanc 2009** Rating 89 To 2012 $18

Echo Ridge Wines ★★★★☆

Lot 1 Oakey Creek Road, Pokolbin, NSW 2320 **Region** Hunter Valley
T (02) 4998 6714 **F** (02) 9986 3360 www.echoridgewines.com.au **Open** W'ends &
public hols 11–4
Winemaker Mark Woods **Est.** 2005 **Cases** 5000 **Vyds** 10.7 ha
When Greg and Anthony Ward purchased the 40-ha property now known as Echo Ridge, it
already had well-established vines, together with a 3000-tree olive plantation. They secured
Mark Woods (of Briar Ridge) as their contract winemaker, but have deliberately sold part of
the grape production, limiting the amount of each wine released to a maximum of 5000 cases.
They have also built and opened a sophisticated cellar door, which came on-stream in 2009.
The vineyard is planted to semillon, shiraz, verdelho, chardonnay and petit verdot.

ＹＹＹＹＹ **Hunter Valley Semillon 2007** Pale straw-green; a more traditional semillon
than the '09, with crisp lemon/lemongrass aromas and flavours built on a platform
of lingering acidity; bone-dry finish. Gold medal Hunter Valley Wine Show '08.
Screwcap. 11.5% alc. **Rating** 94 **To** 2022 $28

ＹＹＹＹＹ **Top Block Hunter Valley Chardonnay 2009** Rating 93 To 2019 $25
Hunter Valley Semillon 2009 Rating 91 To 2019 $28

ＹＹＹＹ **Hunter Valley Shiraz 2006** Rating 88 To 2016 $25

Eclectic Wines ★★★☆

687 Hermitage Road, Pokolbin, NSW 2320 (postal) **Region** Hunter Valley
T (02) 6574 7201 www.eclecticwines.com.au **Open** At Hunter Valley Winegrowers
Centre, Thurs–Mon 10–5
Winemaker Contract **Est.** 2001 **Cases** 1500 **Vyds** 16 ha

This is the venture of Paul and Kate Stuart, nominally based in the Hunter Valley, where they live and have a vineyard planted to shiraz and mourvedre; 'nominally', because Paul's 30 years in the wine industry have given him the marketing knowledge to sustain the purchase of grapes from various regions, including the Hunter Valley, Canberra and interstate. He balances the production and sale of his own wines under the Eclectic label while also acting as an independent marketing and sales consultant to other producers, avoiding a conflict of interest by selling his clients' wine in different markets from those in which he sells his own. Many of the wines under the Eclectic umbrella go to the Netherlands, for distribution throughout central Europe.

ŶŶŶŶŶ **Hunter Valley Verdelho 2008** A neat mix of tropical fruit offset by citrus/ grapefruit acidity produces a lively wine, with above average focus and length. Screwcap. 13% alc. **Rating** 90 **To** 2011 $28

ŶŶŶŶ **Canberra Shiraz Viognier 2006** Rating 87 To 2010 $28

Eddington Rise   ★★★☆

PO Box 190, Maryborough, Vic 3465 **Region** Central Victoria Zone
T 0408 578 141 **F** (03) 5461 4599 **Open** Not
Winemaker Welshmans Reef Vineyard (Ron Snep) **Est.** 1999 **Cases** 300 **Vyds** 1.21 ha
The Forbes family has been involved in cattle farming for over 120 years, and in partnership with Maryborough lawyer Kelvin Noonan, has established a small vineyard equally divided between shiraz and semillon. The block in question had been of no use for grazing, and with the assistance of many friends, the area was deep-ripped, large rocks removed, posts embedded, trellis completed and drip irrigation from dams on the property installed. The partners say they have 'a predisposition to wine tasting', so one wonders just how much of the wine will remain available for sale.

ŶŶŶŶŶ **Shiraz 2008** Red-purple; a full-bodied shiraz, reflecting its terroir and varietal character in equal proportions; blackberry, licorice and dark chocolate are all to be found on the generous palate; the tannins are ripe and balanced. Screwcap. 14.5% alc. **Rating** 91 **To** 2023 $16.65

ŶŶŶŶ **Botrytis Semillon 2006** Rating 87 To 2012 $25

Eden Hall   ★★★★★

36a Murray Street, Angaston, SA 5353 **Region** Eden Valley
T (08) 8562 4590 **F** (08) 8342 3950 **www.**edenhall.com.au **Open** 7 days 11–5
Winemaker Kym Teusner, Christa Deans (Contract) **Est.** 2002 **Cases** 2500 **Vyds** 32.3 ha
David and Mardi Hall purchased the historic Avon Brae property in 1996. The 120-ha property has been planted to cabernet sauvignon (the lion's share with 13 ha), riesling (9.24 ha), shiraz (5.75 ha) and smaller plantings of merlot and cabernet franc. The majority of the production is contracted to Yalumba, St Hallett and McGuigan Simeon, with 10% of the best grapes held back for the Eden Hall label. The Riesling, Shiraz Viognier and Cabernet Sauvignon are all excellent, the red wines outstanding. Exports to the US, Malaysia and Japan.

ŶŶŶŶŶ **Riesling 2009** Already bright green-yellow; a tight, complex and powerful
✪ riesling bursting with lime and mineral fruit that surges through the palate to the long finish. Screwcap. 11.5% alc. **Rating** 95 **To** 2019 $20
Shiraz 2006 Strong crimson-red; intense black fruits, licorice, spice and bitter chocolate drive bouquet and palate alike; the tannins are generous but fully ripe and balanced, as is the oak. Screwcap. 14.5% alc. **Rating** 95 **To** 2026 $44
Cabernet Sauvignon 2006 Very correct blackcurrant and cassis fruit allied with cedary oak on both bouquet and palate, and supported by ripe tannins; there are also some savoury/olivaceous notes. Screwcap. 14.5% alc. **Rating** 94 **To** 2026 $38

ŶŶŶŶŶ **CSV Cabernet Shiraz Viognier 2006** Rating 93 To 2021 $23

Eden Road Wines ★★★★★

Cnr Northbourne Ave/Flemington Road, North Lyneham, ACT 2602
Region Canberra District
T (02) 6220 8500 **F** (02) 6241 1166 **www**.edenroadwines.com.au **Open** Fri–Sun 10–6
Winemaker Nick Spencer, Hamish Young **Est.** 2006 **Cases** 5000
The name of this business, now entirely based in the Canberra District, reflects an earlier
stage of its development when it also had a property in the Eden Valley. That has now been
separated, and Eden Road's operations since 2008 centre on Hilltops, Canberra District and
Tumbarumba. The business utilises the Kamberra Winery built by Hardys to the highest
standards. At the Royal Melbourne Wine Show '09 Eden Road's The Long Road Hilltops
Shiraz '08 was awarded the Jimmy Watson Memorial Trophy; if it needed a higher profile, it
now has one.

ŶŶŶŶŶ **The Long Road Hilltops Shiraz 2008** Included as a reference point: the wine
won the Jimmy Watson Trophy '09, its price $18 and has long since sold out,
needless to say. Purple-crimson, its black fruits have the great poise and length
of good, cool-grown shiraz. A worthy winner of the trophy. Screwcap. 14.5% alc.
Rating 95 **To** 2020
Reserve Tumbarumba Chardonnay 2008 Brilliant pale green; a super-elegant
and fine chardonnay, with hallmark grapefruit and white peach to the fore, some
barrel ferment and lees notes adding to the impact of a wine with extreme length.
Screwcap. 12.8% alc. **Rating** 94 **To** 2015 $50

ŶŶŶŶŶ **Eden Valley Shiraz 2008 Rating** 93 **To** 2018 $35
✪ **The Long Road Barossa Shiraz 2008** Bright hue; attractive plum and red
cherry fruit courses through the bouquet and light- to medium-bodied palate
alike; 18 months in French oak has left the barest of imprints on this seriously
good wine. Screwcap. 14% alc. **Rating** 93 **To** 2016 $18
The Long Road Canberra Riesling 2009 Rating 91 **To** 2017 $18
✪ **The Long Road Hilltops Barbera & Nebbiolo 2008** The blend works better
than one might expect, the synergy obvious; floral aromas lead into a savoury/
spicy/tarry palate that accelerates through to the dark cherry fruits of the finish.
Screwcap. 13.5% alc. **Rating** 90 **To** 2015 $18

ŶŶŶŶ **The Long Road Canberra Sauvignon Blanc 2009 Rating** 89 **To** 2011 $18
The Long Road Tumbarumba Chardonnay 2008 Rating 89 **To** 2012 $18
The Long Road Hilltops Cabernet Sauvignon 2008 Rating 89 **To** 2015 $18

Eden Springs ★★★★★

Boehm Springs Road, Springton, SA 5235 **Region** Eden Valley
T (08) 8564 1166 **F** (08) 8564 1265 **www**.edensprings.com.au **Open** At Taste Eden Valley
Winemaker Jo Irvine, David Norman (Contract) **Est.** 1972 **Cases** 2000 **Vyds** 51.87 ha
When you read the hyperbole that sometimes accompanies the acquisition of an existing wine
business, about transforming it into a world-class operation, it is easy to sigh and move on.
When self-confessed wine lover Ray Gatt acquired Eden Springs, he proceeded to translate
words into deeds. As well as the 19.82-ha Eden Springs Vineyard, he also acquired the historic
Siegersdorf Vineyard (19.43 ha) on the Barossa floor, and the neighbouring Graue Vineyard
(11.4 ha). He then put contract winemakers Joanne Irvine and David Norman in charge,
tapping into their long-established credentials. It was hardly surprising that a string of wine
show medals should be bestowed on the wines, my personal appreciation of the wines also no
surprise. Perhaps the most obvious feature is the exceptional value for money they represent.
Exports to Hong Kong and other major markets.

ŶŶŶŶŶ **Barossa Shiraz 2007** Very good colour for vintage; a wine crammed full of
✪ supple blackberry, plum and black cherry fruit, mocha/vanillan oak and ripe
tannins on the long finish; exemplary alcohol; 260 dozen made. Screwcap. 14% alc.
Rating 94 **To** 2022 $24.90

High Eden Shiraz 2007 Slightly diffuse colour; a wine that creeps up on you, for a lot of the action occurs on the finish and aftertaste, which is slippery rather than tough (the latter an '07 character); the aromas and flavours are in a red and black fruit spectrum, the tannins fine. Screwcap. 14% alc. **Rating** 94 **To** 2022 $24.90

High Eden Cabernet Sauvignon 2007 Good colour; right in the mainstream of Eden Valley cabernet character, with gently savoury tannins woven through rippling blackcurrant and cassis fruit; a medium- to full-bodied wine with exemplary balance. Screwcap. 13.5% alc. **Rating** 94 **To** 2022 $24.90

ŶŶŶŶŶ
✪
High Eden Riesling 2009 Light straw-green; a highly perfumed, floral bouquet of crushed lime leaves, then a high-flavoured lime and lemon juice palate, an echo of the bouquet coming through as a hint of herb; very long finish. Screwcap. 11.5% alc. **Rating** 93 **To** 2019 $19.90

Edwards Wines   ★★★★★

687 Ellensbrook Road, Cowaramup, WA 6284 **Region** Margaret River
T (08) 9755 5999 **F** (08) 9755 5988 **www.**edwardswines.com.au **Open** 7 days 10.30–5
Winemaker Michael Edwards **Est.** 1993 **Cases** 11 500 **Vyds** 28.01 ha
Edwards Wines is a family-owned and operated winery, brothers Michael (formerly a wine-maker at Voyager Estate) and Christo are the winemaker and viticulturist, respectively. The vineyard includes cabernet sauvignon (13.15 ha), shiraz (5.95 ha), chardonnay (3.12 ha), semillon (2.5 ha), sauvignon blanc (2.29 ha) and merlot (1 ha). The consistency in the quality of the wines is admirable. Exports to all major markets.

ŶŶŶŶŶ
Margaret River Chardonnay 2008 The eastern states are not alone in reducing the alcohol of their chardonnays. Here the grapefruit and melon flavours are bright and crisp, the finish fine, the oak restrained. Just makes it over the line. Screwcap. 13% alc. **Rating** 94 **To** 2015 $32

Margaret River Shiraz 2008 Dense crimson-purple; a rich, full-bodied shiraz with layers of blackberry, blackcurrant and black cherry, with soft tannins running through the length of the palate; still to develop shape, but will do so. Screwcap. 14.5% alc. **Rating** 94 **To** 2023 $30

BCE Reserve Cabernet Sauvignon 2007 The hue is slightly better than the varietal, although not entirely convincing; curious that a lower alcohol wine can deliver more cassis and blackcurrant fruit, particularly on the fragrant bouquet; the palate is cedary but more elegant, the tannins finer. Screwcap. 14% alc. **Rating** 94 **To** 2022 $60

ŶŶŶŶŶ
✪
Tiger's Tale Margaret River Cabernet Sauvignon Merlot 2008 Crimson-red; a good example of Margaret River style, so suited to this blend; blackcurrant, cassis and fine, sweet tannins are supported by a touch of French oak. Screwcap. 14% alc. **Rating** 93 **To** 2015 $18

✪
Margaret River Semillon Sauvignon Blanc 2009 A tangy, citrus-predominant bouquet is reflected in the palate, which is fresh and breezy, introducing an extra touch of herb and tropical fruit; clean, well balanced, finish. Screwcap. 13% alc. **Rating** 92 **To** 2011 $23

Margaret River Cabernet Sauvignon 2008 Rating 92 **To** 2018 $35

✪
Tiger's Tale Margaret River Semillon Sauvignon Blanc 2009 While not particularly complex, has surprising intensity to its citrus and lemongrass palate, the finish zesty and long. Screwcap. 13% alc. **Rating** 90 **To** 2011 $18

Elan Vineyard   ★★★★

17 Turners Road, Bittern, Vic 3918 **Region** Mornington Peninsula
T (03) 5989 7209 **F** (03) 5989 7042 **www.**elanvineyard.com.au **Open** 1st w'end of month, public hols 11–5, or by appt
Winemaker Selma Lowther **Est.** 1980 **Cases** 500 **Vyds** 2.5 ha

Selma Lowther, then fresh from CSU (as a mature-age student) made an impressive debut with her spicy, fresh, crisp Chardonnay, and has continued to make tiny quantities of appealing and sensibly priced wines. Most of the grapes from the estate vineyards are sold; production remains minuscule. There is a rotunda and children's playground overlooking the vineyard.

ΨΨΨΨΨ   **Mornington Peninsula Shiraz 2008** Crimson-purple; has a fragrant bouquet
✪   with spicy cherry and satsuma plum, then an energetic and vibrant palate reflecting its modest alcohol and cool region. Diam. 12.5% alc. **Rating** 92 **To** 2019 $20
Cabernet Merlot 2008 A generous wine, with lots of ripe and luscious blackcurrant fruit; controlled tannins and oak. Diam. 12.5% alc. **Rating** 90 **To** 2018 $20

Elderton   ★★★★★

3-5 Tanunda Road, Nuriootpa, SA 5355 **Region** Barossa Valley
T (08) 8568 7878 **F** (08) 8568 7879 **www.**eldertonwines.com.au
Open Mon–Fri 8.30–5, w'ends & hols 11–4
Winemaker Richard Langford **Est.** 1982 **Cases** 32 000 **Vyds** 46 ha
The founding Ashmead family, with mother Lorraine supported by sons Allister and Cameron, continues to impress with its wines. The original source was 30 ha of fully mature shiraz, cabernet sauvignon and merlot on the Barossa floor; subsequently 16 ha of Eden Valley vineyards (shiraz, cabernet sauvignon, chardonnay, zinfandel, merlot and roussanne) were incorporated into the business. The Command Shiraz is justifiably regarded as its icon wine; energetic promotion and marketing both in Australia and overseas is paying dividends. Elderton has followed in the footsteps of Cullen by becoming carbon neutral. Exports to all major markets.

ΨΨΨΨΨ   **Command Single Vineyard Barossa Shiraz 2007** The bouquet delivers a
complex array of red and black fruit, with smoky tar and licorice on display; the palate is an experience in two parts; on entry vibrant perfume, and to conclude there is a lingering sense of black fruit, fresh leather and smoky tar all working seamlessly together. Screwcap. 14.5% alc. **Rating** 95 **To** 2025 $95 BE
Ode to Lorraine Barossa Cabernet Sauvignon Shiraz Merlot 2008 All components of this wine are in plain view; the spicy warm shiraz first; the slightly savoury merlot second and the structured and almost strict cabernet third; in time these components will amalgamate to form an impressive blend, supported by rich, toasty oak. Screwcap. 14.5% alc. **Rating** 95 **To** 2025 $50 BE
✪   **Eden Valley Cabernet Sauvignon 2009** Perfume is the pivotal element of this wine; redcurrant and a vein of quartz-like minerality run throughout the core of fleshy red fruits; really generous on the palate, and very serious in intent, this is extremely good value cabernet. Screwcap. 14% alc. **Rating** 94 **To** 2016 $19 BE
Ashmead Single Vineyard Barossa Cabernet Sauvignon 2008 A highly polished example of Barossa cabernet, dominated by red fruit on the bouquet, and a healthy dose of new oak; the essence of the wine lies in the tightness of the palate; the ample fine-grained tannins and tangy acid pull the fruit to a long, fine and even conclusion. Screwcap. 14.5% alc. **Rating** 94 **To** 2020 $90 BE

ΨΨΨΨΨ   **Eden Valley Riesling 2009** Quite a perfumed bouquet of bath talc and lemons,
✪   with a distinct mineral edge; generous on entry, with fleshy citrus fruit, the palate tightening on the finish, with pure citrus lingering for some time. Screwcap. 11.5% alc. **Rating** 92 **To** 2018 $19 BE
✪   **Eden Valley Shiraz 2009** Bright garnet; a highly perfumed floral bouquet with an attractive element of blueberry and just a pinch of spice; medium-bodied and full of fruit, the tannins are soft, plush and giving for such a young wine, and will be best enjoyed young. Screwcap. 14% alc. **Rating** 92 **To** 2014 $19 BE
Barossa Shiraz 2007 Rating 92 **To** 2016 $27 BE
✪   **Adelaide Hills Sauvignon Blanc 2009** The bouquet is clean and distinctly fragrant in the pea pod and grass end of the spectrum, the palate adding just a touch of citrussy minerality. Screwcap. 12.5% alc. **Rating** 91 **To** 2011 $19

ΨΨΨΨ   Eden Valley Chardonnay 2009 Rating 89 To 2013 $19
Friends Vineyard Series Shiraz 2008 Rating 89 To 2014 $19
Barossa Merlot 2008 Rating 89 To 2014 $27 BE
Friends Vineyard Series Cabernet Sauvignon 2008 Rating 89 To 2014 $19

Eldridge Estate of Red Hill ★★★★★

120 Arthurs Seat Road, Red Hill, Vic 3937 **Region** Mornington Peninsula
T (03) 5989 2644 www.eldridge-estate.com.au **Open** Mon–Fri 12–4, w'ends & hols 11–5
Winemaker David Lloyd **Est.** 1985 **Cases** 1000 **Vyds** 3 ha
The Eldridge Estate vineyard was purchased by Wendy and David Lloyd in 1995. Major
retrellising work has been undertaken, changing to Scott Henry, and all the wines are estate-
grown and made. David has also planted several Dijon-selected pinot noir clones (114, 115
and 777), which have been contributing since 2004, likewise the Dijon chardonnay clone 96.
An interesting move has been the development of the Euroa Creeks range (Early Harvest
Shiraz, Shiraz and Reserve Shiraz), made from contract-grown grapes (a long-term contract)
at the northern end of Heathcote. An interesting grafting of the skills of a cool-climate pinot
noir grower and maker onto the far bigger wine base of Heathcote shiraz.

ΨΨΨΨΨ   Single Clone 96 Chardonnay 2008 Brilliant green-gold; a more complex and
racy bouquet than the Estate, the palate likewise with more texture and bite, a
touch of grapefruit added to the mix. Screwcap. 14% alc. **Rating** 94 To 2018 $45
✪   North Patch Chardonnay 2008 Glowing green-yellow; an exercise in restraint
and balance from start to finish, the melon, fig and stone fruit interwoven with
nutty French oak; ready now. Screwcap. 14% alc. **Rating** 94 To 2013 $30
Gamay 2008 Bright crimson-purple; very well made, and shows clear-cut
varietal character from start to finish; bright cherry/strawberry fruit and perfectly
structured; closes with good acidity. Screwcap. 13.1% alc. **Rating** 94 To 2012 $35
Clonal Blend Pinot Noir 2008 Bright, light crimson; by far the most powerful
and savoury of the three '08 Pinot releases, introducing both plum and a strongly
textured palate, thanks to spicy/savoury tannins. Screwcap. 13.7% alc. **Rating** 94
To 2014 $75

ΨΨΨΨΨ   Chardonnay 2008 Rating 93 To 2016 $40
Pinot Noir 2008 Rating 93 To 2013 $50
Single Clone Pinot Noir 2008 Rating 93 To 2013 $45

Eleven Paddocks ★★★★

PO Box 829, Macleod, Vic 3084 **Region** Pyrenees
T (03) 9458 4997 **F** (03) 9458 5075 www.elevenpaddocks.com.au **Open** Not
Winemaker Gabriel Horvat, Gary Mills **Est.** 2003 **Cases** 1500 **Vyds** 8.1 ha
Eleven partners, under the direction of managing partner Danny Gravell, purchased a small
vineyard in 2002 in the foothills of the Pyrenees Ranges near Landsborough. The quality
of the first vintage was sufficient to encourage the partners to increase planting to 4 ha of
shiraz, 2 ha each of chardonnay and cabernet sauvignon and a dash of petit verdot. Exports
to Singapore and China.

ΨΨΨΨΨ   The McKinlay Shiraz 2008 Crimson-purple; a well-made wine from quality
grapes; the bouquet promises much, the medium-bodied palate delivering black
cherry and plum fruit in abundance; needed a touch more structure on the finish
for top points. Screwcap. 14.2% alc. **Rating** 93 To 2018 $28

ΨΨΨΨ   Yarra Valley Chardonnay 2009 Rating 89 To 2013 $20

Elgee Park ★★★★☆

Merricks Wine General Store, 3460 Frankston-Flinders Road, Merricks, Vic 3916
Region Mornington Peninsula
T (03) 5989 8088 **F** (03) 5989 7199 www.elgeeparkwines.com.au **Open** 7 days 9–5
Winemaker Geraldine McFaul, Kathleen Quealy (Contract) **Est.** 1972 **Cases** 1600
Vyds 4.5 ha

The pioneer of the Mornington Peninsula in its 20th-century rebirth, owned by Baillieu Myer and family. The vineyards are planted to riesling, chardonnay, viognier (some of the oldest vines in Australia), pinot gris, pinot noir, shiraz, merlot and cabernet sauvignon. The wines are made by Geraldine McFaul (Willow Creek), with the exception of Viognier and Pinot Gris, which are made by Kathleen Quealy (Balnarring Estate). Exports to China.

ɯɯɯɯɯ Family Reserve Mornington Peninsula Chardonnay 2008 Delicious wine; the aromas of white flowers and stone fruits of the bouquet flow into the elegant palate of white peach and nectarine, oak evident but not obtrusive; no problem with the alcohol. Screwcap. 14.5% alc. **Rating** 94 **To** 2015 $35

ɯɯɯɯɯ Family Reserve Mornington Peninsula Pinot Noir 2008 Rating 91 **To** 2015 $43
Family Reserve Cabernet Merlot 2007 Rating 91 **To** 2014 $30
○ **Family Reserve Mornington Peninsula Riesling 2009** Intense green-straw; an unusual and highly floral bouquet with some rose petal notes leads into a well-flavoured palate that reflects the maritime climate of the Peninsula. Screwcap. 13% alc. **Rating** 90 **To** 2014 $18
Mornington Peninsula Cuvee Brut 2006 Rating 90 **To** 2014 $45

Elgo Estate ★★★☆

2020 Upton Road, Upton Hill, via Longwood, Vic 3664 **Region** Strathbogie Ranges
T (03) 9328 3766 **F** (03) 9326 3358 **www**.elgoestate.com.au **Open** By appt
Winemaker Dennis Clarke, Craig Lewis **Est.** 1999 **Cases** 13 000 **Vyds** 54.6 ha
Elgo was purchased by the Taresch family in 1997, who immediately embarked upon an extensive program to improve the property. Part of its rejuvenation included the development of land for the planting of a vineyard on the slopes of Upton Hill at the top of Elgo Estate. This development commenced in 2000, with the winery commissioned in time for the '04 Vintage. Originating from Germany, Gunter and Hermine Taresch migrated to Australia in 1962 and have since raised a family. In addition they created a very successful graphic design business in Melbourne. The younger of two sons, Grant, now directs and manages the vineyard and winery at Elgo Estate.

ɯɯɯɯɯ Strathbogie Ranges Chardonnay 2006 Bright green-yellow; a firm, tangy chardonnay, fruit and barrel ferment inputs now welded together; has good length and a bright finish. Screwcap. 13% alc. **Rating** 91 **To** 2012 $22

ɯɯɯɯ Strathbogie Ranges Riesling 2006 Rating 89 **To** 2014 $22
○ **Allira Strathbogie Ranges Chardonnay 2008** Fresh straw-green; has good energy and drive to its white peach fruit framed by a touch of oak; positive finish. Screwcap. 13.5% alc. **Rating** 89 **To** 2013 $13

Ellender Estate ★★★☆

Leura Glen, 260 Green Gully Road, Glenlyon, Vic 3461 **Region** Macedon Ranges
T (03) 5348 7785 **F** (03) 5348 7784 **www**.ellenderwines.com.au **Open** W'ends & public hols 11–5, or by appt
Winemaker Graham Ellender **Est.** 1996 **Cases** 1000 **Vyds** 4.1 ha
Graham and Jenny Ellender have established pinot noir (2.7 ha), chardonnay (1 ha), sauvignon blanc (0.2 ha) and pinot gris (0.1 ha). Wine style is now restricted to those varieties true to the ultra-cool climate of the Macedon Ranges: Pinot Noir, Pinot Rose, Chardonnay and sparkling. Exports to the United Arab Emirates.

ɯɯɯɯɯ Macedon Ranges Chardonnay 2008 Bright green-yellow; a single-vineyard wine with a core of grapefruit/citrus giving the palate good length and grip, French oak well in the background. Screwcap. 13.3% alc. **Rating** 90 **To** 2013 $25

ɯɯɯɯ Rosetta Macedon Ranges Pinot Rose 2009 Rating 89 **To** 2011 $24
Macedon Ranges Pinot Noir 2008 Rating 89 **To** 2015 $35

Elmswood Estate   ★★★★

75 Monbulk-Seville Road, Wandin East, Vic 3139 **Region** Yarra Valley
T (03) 5964 3015 **F** (03) 5964 3405 **www.**elmswoodestate.com.au **Open** 7 days 10–5
Winemaker Paul Evans, Mal Stewart **Est.** 1981 **Cases** 3000 **Vyds** 8.5 ha
Elmswood Estate has planted cabernet sauvignon, chardonnay, merlot, sauvignon blanc, pinot
noir, shiraz and riesling on the red volcanic soils of the far-southern side of the Yarra Valley.
The cellar door operates from 'The Pavilion', a fully enclosed glass room, situated on a ridge
above the vineyard, with 180° views of the Upper Yarra Valley. It seats up to 110 guests, and is
a popular wedding venue. Music events are held on the third Sunday of each month. Exports
to China.

ŶŶŶŶŶ **Sauvignon Blanc 2009** Pale straw-green; an impressive wine, with a fragrant
✪   bouquet and lively palate, more or less equally poised between citrus/grassy and
           tropical flavours; also has good length. Screwcap. 13% alc. **Rating** 93 **To** 2012 $23
           Pinot Noir 2008 Light, bright crimson; some spicy savoury notes accompany the
           red cherry and raspberry fruit; has a long finish, the fruit unfurling through to the
           aftertaste. Screwcap. 13.5% alc. **Rating** 92 **To** 2014 $28

ŶŶŶŶ   **Riesling 2009 Rating** 89 **To** 2015 $20

🌿 Eloquesta   ★★★★

11 Stroud Avenue, Dubbo, NSW 2830 (postal) **Region** Mudgee
T 0458 525 899 **www.**eloquesta.com.au **Open** Not
Winemaker Stuart Olsen **Est.** 2008 **Cases** 600 **Vyds** 6 ha
The full name of the business is Eloquesta by Stuart Olsen, Stuart being the sole owner and
winemaker. He is a trained scientist and teacher, gaining winemaking experience since 2000,
variously working at Cirillo Estate, Lowe Family Wines and Torbreck, as well as a German
winery in the Rheinhessen. His aim in Mudgee is to make the two varieties that he believes
grow consistently well year after year in the cooler foothills of Mudgee and Rylestone: Shiraz
and Petit Verdot, with an occasional bucket of Viognier. He aims to make fragrant, well-
balanced and medium weight wines, and has succeeded in his aim.

ŶŶŶŶŶ **Mudgee Shiraz Petit Verdot 2008** Medium red-purple; a very complex
           and intense wine, with four batches of 0.5 tonnes each separately fermented,
           two batches with 2–3% viognier; shiraz is by a small margin the major variety,
           petit verdot just behind, but it is petit verdot that is the dominant player in a
           fragrant, black-fruited wine with persistent but ripe tannins. Highly individualistic.
           Screwcap. 14.5% alc. **Rating** 91 **To** 2018 $22

Emma's Cottage Vineyard   ★★★

Wilderness Road, Lovedale, NSW, 2320 **Region** Hunter Valley
T (02) 4998 7734 **F** (02) 4998 7209 **www.**emmascottage.com.au **Open** Fri–Mon,
public & school hols 10–5, or by appt
Winemaker David Hook (Contract) **Est.** 1987 **Cases** 1000 **Vyds** 3 ha
Rob and Toni Powys run a combined boutique winery and accommodation business on their
12-ha property at Lovedale; 3 ha of semillon, chardonnay, verdelho, merlot, pinot noir and
shiraz have been planted, and a range of varietals and vintages are on offer.

ŶŶŶŶ   **Hunter Valley Shiraz 2007** Good purple-red; a distinctly regional wine, with
           earthy/leathery overtones to the strong black fruits of the medium- to full-
           bodied palate. Should mature nicely over the next 5+ years. Screwcap. 13.5% alc.
           Rating 89 **To** 2016 $35
           Avalon 2009 A pleasant blend of Semillon/Chardonnay that reflects the good
           vintage, chardonnay given an armchair ride by the semillon. Screwcap. 11.8% alc.
           Rating 87 **To** 2015 $22

Hunter Valley Merlot 2007 Slightly dull/diffuse colour; a light- to medium-bodied merlot that has enough varietal expression to get it across the line, albeit in an uncompromisingly savoury mode. Screwcap. 12.5% alc. **Rating** 87 **To** 2013 $25
Perfect Dessert Wine 2009 Exceedingly sweet and simple ice wine style; needs more acidity; will charge out of the cellar door. Screwcap. 10% alc. **Rating** 87 **To** 2012 $25

 # Enigma Variations   ★★★★☆

Glenelg Highway, Dunkeld, Vic 3294 **Region** Grampians
T (03) 5332 2987 **Open** By appt
Winemaker Tamara Irish **Est.** 2008 **Cases** 250 **Vyds** 1 ha
This is the new venture of former Tarrington winemaker Tamara Irish, who had joined forces with NZ-born Julia Hailes (a Francophile, violinist and psychodramatist) to buy a small property near Dunkeld at the base of the Grampians mountain range. Tamara and Julia are fiercely committed to biodynamic grapegrowing, and are moving towards the establishment of a little over 1 ha of densely planted, low-yielding and multi-clonal shiraz, and a small winery, hopefully, to process shiraz to be purchased from the same source as that used for the former Artemesia label of Tarrington vineyards. The last of the Tarrington wines made by Tamara are being marketed under the Enigma Variations brand (the site and source acknowledged on the labels) and are being sold through Enigma, including 2006 and '07 Pinot Noir, and '07 Shiraz.

🍷🍷🍷🍷🍷 **Syrah 2007** Strong purple-crimson; vibrant and fresh cool-grown aromas and flavours with a fruit lift similar to that given by viognier (there is none so far as I know); the palate is juicy and long, tannins and oak in a dual support role. Stained cork a worry. 13.7% alc. **Rating** 94 **To** 2017 $49

🍷🍷🍷🍷🍷 **Pinot Noir 2007 Rating** 92 **To** 2014 $45

Eperosa   ★★★★☆

24 Maria Street, Tanunda, SA 5352 **Region** Barossa Valley
T 0428 111 121 **F** (08) 8563 1576 **www**.eperosa.com.au **Open** By appt
Winemaker Brett Grocke **Est.** 2005 **Cases** 650
Eperosa owner Brett Grocke qualified as a viticulturist in 2001, and, through Grocke Viticulture, consults and provides technical services to over 200 ha of vineyards spread across the Barossa Valley, Eden Valley, Adelaide Hills, Riverland, Langhorne Creek and Hindmarsh Valley. He is ideally placed to secure small parcels of grapes of the highest quality, and treats these with traditional, no-frills winemaking methods: de-stemmed, macerated prior to fermentation, open fermented, hand plunging, basket-pressed, then 18 months in used French oak barrels. The wines are of impeccable quality.

🍷🍷🍷🍷🍷 **Elevation 2007** Dense purple-red; an exceptionally rich and generous shiraz for '07, with layers of black fruits of all kinds; the tannin structure is exemplary, oak handling likewise. The name comes from the vineyard situated 300 m above sea level. High-quality cork. 14.5% alc. **Rating** 94 **To** 2022 $38

🍷🍷🍷🍷🍷 **Totality 2007 Rating** 90 **To** 2017 $35

Epsilon   ★★★★★

Moppa Springs Road, Greenock, SA 5360 **Region** Barossa Valley
T 0417 871 951 **F** (08) 8562 8597 **www**.epsilonwines.com.au **Open** Not
Winemaker Aaron Southern, Jaysen Collins **Est.** 2004 **Cases** 3000 **Vyds** 22 ha
Epsilon (the fifth-brightest star in a constellation) takes its name from the five generations of the Kalleske family's involvement in Barossa Valley grapegrowing; Julie Southern is née Kalleske. She and husband Aaron bought back this part of the family farm in 1994, initially selling the grapes, but in 2003 joined forces with close friends Dan Standish and Jaysen Collins to produce the Epsilon wines. Exports to the UK, the US, Canada and Southeast Asia.

ŸŸŸŸŸ **Barossa Valley Shiraz 2008** Strong crimson red; a complex bouquet of
✪   blackberry mixed with touches of licorice, bitter chocolate and oak, precisely
           replayed on the medium-bodied palate, the finish long and textured. Screwcap.
           14.5% alc. **Rating** 94 **To** 2023 $19.95

✪   **Barossa Valley Tempranillo Graciano 2008** The blend is synergistic,
           producing a totally delicious wine with black and red cherry fruits, spices and a
           savoury twist on the finish; quality tannins underline the texture and structure.
           Screwcap. 14% alc. **Rating** 94 **To** 2018 $25

ŸŸŸŸ **Barossa Valley Grenache Tempranillo Rose 2009 Rating** 89 **To** 2010 $17

`ese Vineyards   ★★★★★
1013/1015 Tea Tree Road, Tea Tree, Tas 7017 **Region** Southern Tasmania
T 0417 319 875 **Open** By appt
Winemaker Winemaking Tasmania (Julian Alcorso) **Est.** 1994 **Cases** 3500 **Vyds** 4.1 ha
`ese Vineyards was established by Elvio and Natalie Brianese in the Coal River Valley, 13 km
from the historic town of Richmond. The 6.5-ha property is planted to just over 4 ha of
closely planted vines in the traditional Italian manner, the Brianese family with centuries-old
viticultural roots in the Veneto region of northern Italy. The Pinot Noirs have been consistent
gold medal winners over the years. Exports to Italy and China.

ŸŸŸŸŸ **Pinot Noir 2008** Excellent colour; very fragrant red and black fruits on the
           bouquet and palate; juicy, fine, and a long, lingering finish. Gold medal Tas Wine
           Show '10. Screwcap. 13.4% alc. **Rating** 95 **To** 2015 $35

Evans & Tate   ★★★★★
Cnr Metricup Road/Caves Road, Wilyabrup, WA 6280 **Region** Margaret River
T (08) 9755 6244 **F** (08) 9755 6346 **www.**mcwilliamswinesgroup.com **Open** 7 days 10.30–5
Winemaker Matthew Byrne **Est.** 1970 **Cases** 450 000
The 40-year history of Evans & Tate has been one of constant change and, for decades,
expansion, moving to acquire large wineries in SA and NSW. For a series of reasons, nothing
to do with the excellent quality of its Margaret River wines, the empire fell apart in 2005;
however, it took an interminable time before McWilliam's (together with a syndicate of
local growers) finalised its acquisition of the Evans & Tate brand (although not the winery or
vineyards) in December '07. Remarkably, wine quality was maintained through the turmoil,
and shows no sign whatsoever of faltering. Exports to all major markets.

ŸŸŸŸŸ **Margaret River Chardonnay 2008** Vivid hue, star bright; quite a restrained
✪   bouquet, showing fine aromas of grapefruit, nectarine and just the merest hint
           of spice from well-handled oak; the palate is dominated by fresh citrus fruit,
           with the acidity driving the wine for a considerable time; a suggestion of oak
           follows through on the very long, and evenly balanced finish. Screwcap. 14% alc.
           Rating 95 **To** 2020 $23 BE
           Redbrook Cabernet Sauvignon 2007 Bright purple-crimson; here is
           the intensity and drive missing from the standard cabernet, with a chorus of
           blackcurrant, cassis, cedar and a touch of varietal astringency on the long finish.
           Screwcap. 14.2% alc. **Rating** 95 **To** 2022 $38

✪   **Margaret River Sauvignon Blanc 2009** Finer, more focused and more intense
           than the Gnangara, the flavours ranging through grapefruit, passionfruit and
           even stone fruit, pulled back into line by the streak of mineral running through
           the palate. Gold medal Sydney Wine Show '10. Screwcap. 12.5% alc. **Rating** 94
           To 2012 $23

✪   **Margaret River Semillon Sauvignon Blanc 2009** Here semillon demarcates
           the boundaries of the bouquet and palate, herb, grass and mineral dominant,
           although there are some tropical notes in the centre, and the certainty of
           development. Gold medal Sydney Wine Show '10. Screwcap. 12.5% alc. **Rating** 94
           To 2013 $23

Redbrook Chardonnay 2008 Seductive nectarine, white peach and hints of toast, fig and grilled nuts, all of which glide across the tongue in an unbroken stream; flavour and finesse. Screwcap. 14% alc. **Rating** 94 **To** 2015 $29.95

The Reserve Margaret River Chardonnay 2006 In the restrained and sophisticated style for which Evans & Tate is well known, achieved at higher than currently fashionable alcohol levels, proving that numbers tell only part of the story; this is all about citrus and mineral seamlessly married with French oak on the long palate. Screwcap. 14% alc. **Rating** 94 **To** 2014 $29.95

Wildberry Springs Estate Margaret River Chardonnay 2005 A restrained and elegant bouquet of grapefruit and spice, despite the lavish level of new oak; the fruit handles the wood with aplomb, and delivers a long and seamless finish of textbook chardonnay, admittedly at the larger end of the spectrum. Screwcap. 14.5% alc. **Rating** 94 **To** 2016 $45 BE

Redbrook Shiraz 2007 Crimson-purple; delicious plum, black cherry and blackberry fruit on the bouquet sweeps imperiously across the medium- to full-bodied palate; very good length and balance, oak used to advantage. Screwcap. 14.6% alc. **Rating** 94 **To** 2022 $38

✪ Margaret River Cabernet Merlot 2008 Crimson-purple; the aromatic bouquet has an abundance of blackcurrant, plum and cassis fruit, oak not threatening; the medium-bodied palate is long and distinguished, the fruit flavours perfectly ripened, oak and tannins very well handled. Screwcap. 14% alc. **Rating** 94 **To** 2020 $23

♈♈♈♈♈ Gnangara Cabernet Merlot 2008 Textbook WA cabernet blend, exhibiting
✪ ripe red fruits, hints of olives and a distinct note of dry leaf; the palate is surprisingly firm and full, and the serious intent of this wine is belied by the lowly price tag. Screwcap. 14.5% alc. **Rating** 93 **To** 2016 $14 BE

✪ Gnangara Sauvignon Blanc 2009 Offers abundant varietal flavour, and surprising life at its price point; tropical fruit is lengthened by citrussy acidity, the finish fresh. Screwcap. 13% alc. **Rating** 90 **To** 2011 $14

Stellar Ridge Vineyard Margaret River Chardonnay 2006 **Rating** 90 **To** 2014 $45 BE

Margaret River Shiraz 2007 **Rating** 90 **To** 2015 $23

Margaret River Cabernet Sauvignon 2008 **Rating** 90 **To** 2018 $23

Classic Margaret River Red 2008 **Rating** 90 **To** 2016 $20

Even Keel/Polperro ★★★★

76 Arthurs Seat Road, Red Hill, Vic 3937 **Region** Mornington Peninsula
T 0405 155 882 **www**.evenkeelwines.com **Open** Not
Winemaker Samuel Coverdale **Est.** 2006 **Cases** 1500
Sam Coverdale lives and works on the Mornington Peninsula, with a new brand called Polperro utilising two single vineyards at Shoreham and Red Hill, with 200 cases of Chardonnay and Pinot Noir to be released in 2011. He also has 4 ha on the Peninsula under a management contract. The rest of the Even Keel wines came from various parts of South Eastern Australia.

♈♈♈♈♈ Even Keel Tumbarumba Chardonnay 2008 Glowing yellow-green; fashioned from biodynamically grown grapes and wild yeast-fermented; a powerful and intense wine is the outcome, with a lifted finish. Screwcap. 13% alc. **Rating** 93 **To** 2012 $30

Even Keel Mornington Peninsula Pinot Noir 2008 Light red-purple; fragrant flowery/spicy red fruit aromas, then a light-bodied palate that scores more for length than depth; has a degree of savoury elegance. Screwcap. 13.5% alc. **Rating** 90 **To** 2013 $32

♈♈♈♈ Even Keel Canberra District Shiraz Viognier 2008 **Rating** 89 **To** 2013 $30

Evoi Wines ★★★★★

92 Dunsborough Lakes Drive, Dunsborough, WA 6281 (postal) **Region** Margaret River
T 0407 131 080 **F** (08) 9755 3742 **www**.evoiwines.com **Open** Not
Winemaker Nigel Ludlow **Est.** 2006 **Cases** 175

NZ-born, Flying Winemaker Nigel Ludlow has roosted in the Margaret River for the past eight years, and has no intention of leaving, the beaches, scenery, lifestyle and wine quality all reasons to stay. Evoi is in fact a busman's holiday from his other winemaking responsibilities in the region. Exports to Hong Kong.

� Reserve Margaret River Chardonnay 2009 Hand-picked, basket-pressed, partial wild yeast-fermented and mlf in new and one-year-old French barriques, and lees stirred. It retains elegance, precision and length, the white peach and grapefruit flavours complexed by nutty/creamy notes ex barrel fermentation; has great length. Screwcap. 13.5% alc. **Rating** 96 **To** 2018 $42

Eyre Creek ★★★★

Main North Road, Auburn, SA 5451 **Region** Clare Valley
T 0418 818 400 **F** (08) 8849 2555 **www**.eyrecreekwines.com.au **Open** W'ends & public hols 10–5, Mon–Fri as per sign
Winemaker Stephen John, O'Leary Walker Wines **Est.** 1998 **Cases** 2500 **Vyds** 2.9 ha

John and Glenise Osborne, well-known Auburn hoteliers, established Eyre Creek in 1998. In 2008 they opened their cellar door, a renovated 100-year-old dairy, just north of Auburn. They grow dryland shiraz and grenache; the production is sold at the cellar door, mail order and at selected bottle shops and restaurants in Adelaide and Sydney.

77777 **Clare Valley Grenache Rose 2009** Bright magenta; fragrant spice and Turkish
✪ delight aromas, then a crisp and long palate; attractive dry and long finish. Top food style. Screwcap. 12% alc. **Rating** 93 **To** 2011 $20
✪ **Semillon Sauvignon Blanc 2009** It is uncommon for a 100% Clare blend of these two varieties to work so well; early picking is part of the answer, for this is a very lively and fresh wine, the grassy/lemony contribution of semillon the key. Screwcap. 11% alc. **Rating** 91 **To** 2013 $20
✪ **Explorers Clare Valley Grenache 2008** While the flavours of spicy red fruits and vanilla are expected, this medium-bodied wine has more structure than most Clare Valley grenaches display. Screwcap. 15% alc. **Rating** 90 **To** 2014 $20

7777 **Clare Valley Riesling 2009** Rating 89 **To** 2019 $20
The Brookvale Clare Valley Shiraz 2008 Rating 89 **To** 2018 $30

Faber Vineyard ★★★★★

233 Haddrill Road, Baskerville, WA 6056 (postal) **Region** Swan Valley
T (08) 9296 0619 **F** (08) 9296 0681 **www**.fabervineyard.com.au **Open** Sun 10–4
Winemaker John Griffiths **Est.** 1997 **Cases** 2000 **Vyds** 4.5 ha

Former Houghton winemaker, now university lecturer and consultant, John Griffiths teamed with wife, Jane Micallef, to found Faber Vineyard. They have established shiraz, verdelho (1.5 ha each), brown muscat, chardonnay and petit verdot (0.5 ha each). Says John, 'It may be somewhat quixotic, but I'm a great fan of traditional warm-area Australian wine styles – those found in areas such as Rutherglen and the Barossa, wines made in a relatively simple manner that reflect the concentrated ripe flavours one expects in these regions. And when one searches, some of these gems can be found from the Swan Valley.' Possessed of an excellent palate, and with an impeccable winemaking background, the quality of John's wines is guaranteed, although the rating is also quixotic. A new cellar door, billed as a 'cellar door with a difference', opened in 2008.

77777 Reserve Swan Valley Shiraz 2007 Deep purple; a voluminous bouquet with black fruits and licorice in abundance, all of which cascade on the warm-hearted, rich and soft palate; 100% estate-grown; a style that John Griffiths lives for. Stained cork a worry. 14.5% alc. **Rating** 94 **To** 2017 $70

ΨΨΨΨΨ   Dwellingup Chardonnay 2009 Rating 92 To 2015 $32
Dwellingup Shiraz 2008 Rating 92 To 2018 $32
Dwellingup Malbec 2008 Rating 90 To 2015 $32

ΨΨΨΨ   Swan Valley Verdelho 2009 Produced from one of the Swan Valley's oldest
✪   vineyards; has focus and intensity, with length and texture more important than the
gentle fruit salad flavours; has time in front of it. Screwcap. 13.5% alc. Rating 89
To 2013 $17.50

Fabric Wines   ★★★★
1 Main North Road, Penwortham, SA 5453 Region Clare Valley Zone
T 0433 989 600 F (08) 8736 3090 www.fabricwines.com Open Wed–Sun 10–5
Winemaker Alana Langworthy Est. 2007 Cases 1000 Vyds 4 ha
Fabric Wines is the brainchild of Adelaide-born owner/winemaker Alana Langworthy. The
inspiration for the brand came from a London wine bar and the theme of interwoven wines
from Limestone Coast regions. A vineyard has been purchased in the Clare Valley, and came
into production in 2010. In late 2008 she left the security of employment with Coonawarra
Developments to work full-time on Fabric Wines. A cellar door is scheduled to open in
August 2010.

ΨΨΨΨΨ   Mt Gambier Sauvignon Blanc 2008 Bright green tinges; has a clean bouquet,
✪   then the palate progressively builds flavour and intensity as it moves through to the
clean, crisp finish. Screwcap. 12% alc. Rating 90 To 2011 $17
Mt Gambier Pinot Noir 2008 The clear varietal expression is yet more proof of
the potential of Mount Gambier for pinot noir; plum fruit is complexed by notes
of spice, stem and forest. Screwcap. 13% alc. Rating 90 To 2014 $23

ΨΨΨΨ   Wrattonbully Chardonnay 2008 Rating 89 To 2014 $18
Coonawarra Cabernet Shiraz 2006 Rating 88 To 2014 $25

Falls Wines   ★★★★
Belubula Way, Canowindra, NSW 2804 Region Cowra
T (02) 6344 1293 F (02) 6344 1290 www.fallswines.com Open 7 days 10–4
Winemaker Madrez Wine Services (Chris Derrez) Est. 1997 Cases 1500 Vyds 94 ha
Peter and Zoe Kennedy have established Falls Vineyard & Retreat (to give it its full name) on
the outskirts of Canowindra. They have planted shiraz, chardonnay, merlot, cabernet sauvignon
and semillon, with luxury B&B accommodation offering large spa baths, exercise facilities,
fishing and a tennis court.

ΨΨΨΨΨ   Squatter's Ghost Shiraz 2002 Has retained very good colour, especially with
a modest-quality cork; even more remarkable is the medium- to full-bodied
palate, with a multiple array of red and black fruits, tannins and oak all in balance.
14.5% alc. Rating 91 To 2017 $19.80

Farmer's Daughter Wines   ★★★
791 Ulan Road, Mudgee, NSW 2850 Region Mudgee
T (02) 6373 3177 F (02) 6373 3759 www.farmersdaughterwines.com.au
Open Mon–Fri 9–5, Sat 10–5, Sun 10–4
Winemaker Greg Silkman Est. 1995 Cases 12 000 Vyds 20 ha
The intriguingly named Farmer's Daughter Wines is a family-owned vineyard, run by the
daughters of a feed-lot farmer. Part of the production from the vineyard, planted to shiraz
(9.6 ha), cabernet sauvignon, merlot (3.2 ha each), chardonnay (2.5 ha), and semillon (1.5 ha),
is sold to other makers, the majority is made for the Farmer's Daughter label. Exports to the
US, Canada and Vietnam.

ΨΨΨΨ   Mudgee Chardonnay 2009 An attractive marriage of nectarine, melon and
citrus fruit aromas and flavours, with a subliminal touch of sweetness on the finish
for market appeal; little or no oak. Screwcap. 12.9% alc. Rating 89 To 2011 $18

Mudgee Rose 2009 Pale pink; fresh strawberry, cherry and raspberry drive a light but nicely proportioned palate. Screwcap. 12.5% alc. **Rating** 88 **To** 2010 $18
Mudgee Semillon Sauvignon Blanc 2009 A pleasant, well-made wine, largely driven by the crisp, grassy semillon, but with some tropical nuances from the sauvignon blanc. Screwcap. 12% alc. **Rating** 87 **To** 2010 $25

Farmer's Leap Wines ★★★

PMB 99, Naracoorte, SA 5271 (postal) **Region** Padthaway
T (08) 8765 6007 **F** (08) 8765 6020 **www.**farmersleap.com **Open** Not
Winemaker Contract **Est.** 2004 **Cases** 2500 **Vyds** 250 ha
Scott Longbottom and Cheryl Merrett are third generation farmers in the Padthaway region. They commenced planting the vineyard in 1995 on the family property, and there are now 120 ha shiraz (a further 12 ha being planted), 69 ha cabernet sauvignon, 49 ha chardonnay and 12 ha merlot. The majority of the grapes are sold, part going to make the Farmer's Leap wines using contract winemakers. Exports to China (Hong Kong and Shanghai).

Padthaway Shiraz 2004 Strong colour for age; does reflect its alcohol, but there is an abundance of ripe black fruits, plum and mocha; one of the least readable labels of all time, black on dark blackish-blue, breaking all the rules of label design. Screwcap. 15% alc. **Rating** 87 **To** 2014 $18

Farr Rising/by Farr ★★★★★

27 Maddens Road, Bannockburn, Vic 3331 **Region** Geelong
T (03) 5281 1733 **F** (03) 5281 1433 **www.**byfarr.com.au **Open** By appt
Winemaker Gary and Nick Farr **Est.** 1999 **Cases** 5000 **Vyds** 10 ha
Father Gary and son Nick Farr have merged their businesses, although the two labels (by Farr and Farr Rising) will continue. The estate plantings of pinot noir, chardonnay, shiraz and viognier cover the varieties made under the labels; whether Nick will continue to source grapes from the Mornington Peninsula remains to be seen. The combined production represents an even split for each of the two brands. The Farrs make exceptionally complex Pinot Noir and Chardonnay, the Shiraz/Syrah/Viognier equally meritorious. Exports to the Hong Kong, Singapore, Taiwan and Maldives.

by Farr Geelong Chardonnay 2008 Gold-green; a particularly rich and complex example of a chardonnay that is always built in layers, as deep as it is long; fully flavour ripe at 13%, it has seamlessly absorbed the oak inputs (and, so far, cork). Cork. 13% alc. **Rating** 96 **To** 2016 $62.90
by Farr Sangreal 2008 Takes Farrside up another notch in terms of intensity and length, although the bouquet and palate flavours are in the same spectrum except for a delicious twist of red cherry on the finish. Pinot Noir. Cork. 13% alc. **Rating** 96 **To** 2018 $66.90
by Farr Tout Pres Pinot Noir 2008 'Grown on a "very close" planted anatomically distinguished vineyard' is the verbose explanation on the back label, the other by Farr back labels contenting themselves with meeting boring legal requirements. Close planting doesn't always come off, but it certainly did in '08, producing an exceptionally long and intense wine. Cork. 13.5% alc. **Rating** 96 **To** 2020 $97.50
by Farr Geelong Shiraz 2008 Usual good colour; a shiraz made by a pinot noir maker, and harking to the affinity between the Northern Rhône and Burgundy. Perfumed and silky, it is no more than medium-bodied; is supple and long, fruits washing between red and black. Cork. 13.5% alc. **Rating** 96 **To** 2020 $62.90
Farr Rising Geelong Chardonnay 2008 Like the by Farr, has great colour; curiously, although this wine has higher alcohol, it is more elegant, grapefruit and nectarine running through to a fine, tangy finish. Chablis rather Puligny Montrachet. Cork. 13.5% alc. **Rating** 94 **To** 2015 $35

✪ **Farr Rising Geelong Saignee 2009** Bright pink, tinged with magenta; this isn't a rose so much as a high-quality, light-bodied pinot noir table wine, complexed by barrel fermentation; immaculate length and balance. It's a knockout bargain. Diam. 13.5% alc. **Rating** 94 **To** 2013 $21

by Farr Farrside Pinot Noir 2008 Another altogether different register to the Farr Rising wines, strong spicy/stemmy aromas, then a particularly intense palate, with tangy, spicy fruit flavours driving through to the long finish. Cork. 13.5% alc. **Rating** 94 **To** 2016 $64.50

Farr Rising Geelong Pinot Noir 2008 Good colour, although less bright than Mornington; a radically different wine both in terms of flavour (darker berries and plum) and texture (savoury tannins); it's simply a question of style preference, not quality. Cork. 14% alc. **Rating** 94 **To** 2016 $39

Farr Rising Mornington Pinot Noir 2008 Excellent purple hue typical of Mornington; a fragrant, almost flowery, bouquet of red cherry and wild strawberry; the palate is long and silky, carrying its delicious fruit flavours through to the finish and aftertaste. Cork. 13.5% alc. **Rating** 94 **To** 2017 $39

🍷🍷🍷🍷 **by Farr Geelong Viognier 2008** **Rating** 92 **To** 2014 $56.90

Farrawell Wines ★★★★

60 Whalans Track, Lancefield, Vic 3435 **Region** Macedon Ranges
T (03) 5429 2020 **www**.farrawellwines.com.au **Open** 4th Sat of each month 1–5, or by appt
Winemaker Trefor Morgan, David Cowburn (Contract) **Est.** 2000 **Cases** 300 **Vyds** 2 ha

Farrawell had a dream start to its commercial life when its 2001 Chardonnay was awarded the trophy for Best Chardonnay at the Macedon Ranges Wine Exhibition '03. Given that 1 ha each of chardonnay and pinot noir are the sole source of wines, production will always be limited. Trefor Morgan is the owner/winemaker of Mount Charlie Winery, but was perhaps better known as a Professor of Physiology at Melbourne University.

🍷🍷🍷🍷 ✪ **Macedon Ranges Chardonnay 2008** Interest provided by savoury complexity, foremost grilled almonds, lemon butter and a touch of clove; the palate revolves around linear acidity, with the toasty fruit and nutty character extending on the finish. Screwcap. 12.5% alc. **Rating** 91 **To** 2015 $22 BE

Feehans Road Vineyard ★★★★☆

50 Feehans Road, Mount Duneed, Vic 3216 **Region** Geelong
T (03) 5264 1706 **F** (03) 5264 1307 **www**.feehansroad.com.au **Open** W'ends 10–5
Winemaker Lethbridge Wines (Ray Nadeson, Maree Collis) **Est.** 2000 **Cases** 200 **Vyds** 1.2 ha

Peter Logan's interest in viticulture dates back to a 10-week course run by Denise Miller (at Dixons Creek in the Yarra Valley) in the early 1990s. This led to further formal studies, and the planting of a 'classroom' vineyard of 500 chardonnay and shiraz vines. A move from Melbourne suburbia to the slopes of Mt Duneed led to the planting of a vineyard, and to the appointment of Lethbridge Wines as winemaker.

🍷🍷🍷🍷🍷 **Geelong Shiraz 2008** Very good crimson-purple; delicious spice, anise and even a hint of dark chocolate on the bouquet, the generous medium- to full-bodied palate with supple, round black fruits and a twist of spice on the finish. Richly deserved gold medal Geelong Wine Show '09. Screwcap. 13.5% alc. **Rating** 95 **To** 2023 $32

Feet First Wines ★★★★☆

32 Parkinson Lane, Kardinya, WA 6163 (postal) **Region** Western Australia
T (08) 9314 7133 **F** (08) 9314 7134 **www**.feetfirstwines.com.au **Open** Not
Winemaker Contract **Est.** 2004 **Cases** 8000

This is the business of Ross and Ronnie (Veronica) Lawrence, who have been fine wine wholesalers in Perth since 1987, handling top-shelf Australian and imported wines. It is a virtual winery, with both grapegrowing and winemaking provided by contract, the aim being to produce easy-drinking, good-value wines under $20; the deliberately limited portfolio includes Semillon Sauvignon Blanc, Chardonnay and Cabernet Merlot.

ΨΨΨΨΨ **Shiraz 2008** Excellent crimson-purple; typical cool-grown medium-bodied shiraz of very good quality; spice, plum, blackberry and a touch of licorice, with ultrafine tannins. Frankland River. Gold medal Mt Barker Wine Awards '09. Screwcap. 14% alc. **Rating** 94 **To** 2016 $29.80

ΨΨΨΨΨ **Grenache Barbera 2008 Rating** 93 **To** 2015 $29.80

✪ **Semillon Sauvignon Blanc 2009** An unoaked 71/29 blend that has more texture to the mid-palate than many, the flavours tracking the bouquet as best they can, for there is a constantly shifting display of herb, ripe citrus and tropical fruits; very satisfying finish. Screwcap. 12.1% alc. **Rating** 92 **To** 2013 $17.75

✪ **Chenin Blanc 2009** A blend of Swan Valley (86%)/Geographe grapes provides a luscious fruit basket of flavours; striking wine, but needed a touch more acidity for top points. Screwcap. 12.5% alc. **Rating** 90 **To** 2012 $17.75

✪ **Cabernet Merlot 2009** Strong red-purple; a 75/25 blend, the bouquet and medium- to full-bodied palate offering a range of blackcurrant and plum fruits supported by cedary oak and substantial, although ripe, tannins. Screwcap. 14.1% alc. **Rating** 90 **To** 2017 $17.75

Fergusson ★★★★☆

Wills Road, Yarra Glen, Vic 3775 **Region** Yarra Valley
T (03) 5965 2237 **F** (03) 5965 2405 **www**.fergussonwinery.com.au **Open** 7 days 11–5
Winemaker Robert Paul (Consultant) **Est.** 1968 **Cases** 2000 **Vyds** 6 ha
One of the very first Yarra wineries to announce the rebirth of the Valley, now best known as a favoured destination for tourist coaches, offering hearty fare in comfortable surroundings and wines of both Yarra and non-Yarra Valley origin. For this reason the limited quantities of its estate wines are often ignored, but they should not be. Exports to the UK.

ΨΨΨΨΨ **Jeremy Yarra Valley Shiraz 2006** Retains good hue; succeeds where the Louis
✪ Pinot fails; spice, pepper and licorice nuances frame the black cherry and plum fruit, the tannins firm but fine, the length good. Screwcap. 14.5% alc. **Rating** 94 **To** 2021 $25

Fermoy Estate ★★★★★

838 Metricup Road, Wilyabrup, WA 6280 **Region** Margaret River
T (08) 9755 6285 **F** (08) 9755 6251 **www**.fermoy.com.au **Open** 7 days 11–4.30
Winemaker Liz Dawson **Est.** 1985 **Cases** 30 000 **Vyds** 17 ha
A long-established estate-based winery with 14 ha of semillon, sauvignon blanc, chardonnay, cabernet sauvignon and merlot. Notwithstanding its significant production, it is happy to keep a relatively low profile, however difficult that may be given the quality of the wines Liz Dawson is making. Exports to Europe and Asia.

ΨΨΨΨΨ **Margaret River Shiraz 2008** Bright crimson-purple; a fragrant bouquet of
✪ red and black cherry and plum aromas leads into a vibrant, incisive palate with background spice and pepper underlining the freshness of the wine. Impressive length. Screwcap. 14% alc. **Rating** 94 **To** 2023 $22

Margaret River Merlot 2008 Bright, clear crimson-purple; the bouquet is at once fragrant and complex, cassis and plum fruit with spicy/savoury notes; the medium-bodied palate has the supple red berry and plum fruit of the variety, tannins and oak in discreet support. Diam. 14% alc. **Rating** 94 **To** 2020 $30

Margaret River Cabernet Sauvignon 2008 Good hue; in the mainstream of the elegant Fermoy style, 25-year-old estate vines producing perfectly ripened cabernet, with blackcurrant, cedar and cigar box all intermingling, supported by exemplary tannins and French oak. Screwcap. 14% alc. **Rating** 94 **To** 2023 $30

ΨΨΨΨΨ **Reserve Margaret River Semillon 2008 Rating** 93 **To** 2016 $37

❂   **Margaret River Sauvignon Blanc 2009** Pale quartz; a very pure and restrained
rendition of sauvignon blanc, the aromas and flavours pitched halfway between
herbal and tropical; the palate is very long and finely balanced. Screwcap. 14% alc.
Rating 93 To 2012 $22
Yallingup Vineyards Margaret River Semillon Sauvignon Blanc 2009
Rating 93 To 2012 $20
Yallingup Vineyards Margaret River Cabernet Sauvignon Merlot 2008
Rating 91 To 2017 $20

Fernfield Wines   ★★★★☆

Rushlea Road, Eden Valley, SA 5235 **Region** Eden Valley
T (08) 8564 1041 **F** (08) 8564 1041 **www.**fernfieldwines.com.au **Open** 7 days 10–5
Winemaker Bronwyn Lillecrapp, Shannon Plummer **Est.** 2002 **Cases** 2000 **Vyds** 27.8 ha
The establishment date of 2002 might, with a little poetic licence, be shown as 1864. Bryce
Lillecrapp is the fifth generation of the Lillecrapp family, his great-great-great-grandfather
bought land in the Eden Valley in 1864, subdividing it in 1866, establishing the township of
Eden Valley and building the first house, Rushlea Homestead. Bryce restored this building and
opened it in 1998 as a bicentennial project, now serving as Fernfield Wines' cellar door. He
heads up Fernfield as grapegrower, with his wife Bronwyn chief winemaker, son Shannon
cellar hand and assistant winemaker, and daughter Rebecca the wine marketer. While all
members of the family have married grapegrowing and winemaking with other vocations,
they have moved inexorably back to Fernfield, where they have vines dating back three
generations of the family (riesling, pinot noir, shiraz, merlot, cabernet sauvignon, traminer and
cabernet franc). In 2002 they built a winery, and keep part of the crop for the Fernfield label.
Exports to Singapore.

♀♀♀♀♀   **Eden Valley Riesling 2009** A floral bouquet of lime blossom and crushed leaf
❂   intensifies on the classy palate, with lime juice and a touch of passionfruit; finishes
with crisp acidity. Screwcap. 11.5% alc. Rating 94 To 2019 $20

♀♀♀♀♀   **Pridmore Eden Valley Shiraz 2007** The colour is still dense and deep; a full-
❂   bodied shiraz with dense black fruits, dark chocolate and a splash of licorice;
the alcohol is part of the full-bodied make-up of the wine. Screwcap. 15.1% alc.
Rating 93 To 2022 $20

❂   **Triple C Eden Valley Cabernet Sauvignon 2007** Good colour for age and
vintage; there is a swirl of activity under the blackcurrant of the bouquet, spice and
licorice the most obvious; the palate has excellent mouthfeel and balance to the
multiple flavours of sweetly ripened cabernet fruit. Screwcap. 14.4% alc. Rating 93
To 2020 $15

Ferngrove   ★★★★★

276 Ferngrove Road, Frankland River, WA 6396 **Region** Frankland River
T (08) 9855 2378 **F** (08) 9855 2368 **www.**ferngrove.com.au **Open** 7 days 10–4
Winemaker Kim Horton **Est.** 1997 **Cases** 50 000 **Vyds** 225 ha
After 90 years of family beef and dairy farming heritage, Murray Burton ventured into
premium grapegrowing and winemaking in 1977. Today the venture he founded has two
large vineyards in Frankland River planted to the leading varieties, the lion's share to shiraz,
cabernet sauvignon, chardonnay, sauvignon blanc, merlot and semillon, with a small but
important planting of malbec. The operation centres around the Ferngrove Vineyard, where
a large rammed-earth winery and tourist complex was built in 2000. Part of the vineyard
production is sold as grapes, part as juice or must, part as finished wine, and the pick of the
crop is made for the Ferngrove label. The consistency of its wines across a wide range of price
points is wholly admirable. Acquired Killerby (Margaret River) in 2008. Exports to the UK,
the US and other major markets.

♀♀♀♀♀   **Cossack Frankland River Riesling 2009** Excellent example of a tried and
❂   true top performer in the Frankland River; apple and lime blossom aromas are
followed by a crisp, immaculately weighted palate, and a long finish. But why the
crass new label? Screwcap. 12.5% alc. Rating 95 To 2021 $23

The Stirlings Shiraz Cabernet Sauvignon 2007 Strong crimson-purple; a distinguished, full-bodied wine, cabernet firmly in control of proceedings; blackcurrant and blackberry fruits combine synergistically against a backdrop of ripe tannins that will underpin the wine as it ages. Screwcap. 14.5% alc. **Rating** 95 To 2027 $60

ΨΨΨΨΨ **Symbols Frankland River Cabernet Merlot 2008** Vivid purple-crimson;
✪ stacked full of exuberant blackcurrant, redcurrant and plum fruit, the tannins soft and ripe; I suppose oak is there, but it's subtle. Great bargain. Screwcap. 14% alc. **Rating** 92 To 2018 $16
Diamond Frankland River Chardonnay 2008 Rating 90 To 2013 $25

ΨΨΨΨ **Frankland River Sauvignon Blanc 2009** Rating 89 To 2010 $20
Symbols Frankland River Sauvignon Blanc Semillon 2009 Rating 88 To 2011 $16

🌿 5th Chapter Estate ★★★☆

217 Walkers Lane, Avoca, NSW 2577 **Region** Southern Highlands
T 0418 483 923 **F** (02) 4887 7041 **www.fifthchapter.com.au Open** By appt
Winemaker Cindy Manassen **Est.** 1999 **Cases** 600 **Vyds** 3.5 ha
Cindy and Roy Manassen have lost no time in establishing a Garden of Eden on their Southern Highlands property (which has the misleading name of Avoca, something outside their control, of course). It is a home away from their Mosman residence, and the extravagantly beautiful Japanese garden, French garden, silver birch grove and ornamental pond (tended by resident horticulturist Peter Hastings) are wholly remarkable. You might think this is just a plaything for a well-to-do Sydney family, but in fact Cindy completed her wine science degree from CSU in 2004, and both during her studies and since, has worked several vintages in Gevrey Chambertin in France. Pinot noir (1.5 ha) is the most important variety, supported by 1 ha each of shiraz and sauvignon blanc. The vineyard was planted in 1999, and subsequently pruned from 6.5 to 3.5 ha, to make it more manageable. The onsite winery was completed in March 2008, prior to which time Cindy made the wines at a local winery.

ΨΨΨΨΨ **Orange Southern Highlands Sauvignon Blanc 2008** A very well put together regional blend, the Orange component (70%) providing the tropical fruit base, Southern Highlands a streak of lemon mineral; good length and balance. Screwcap. 12% alc. **Rating** 90 To 2012 $18.50

ΨΨΨΨ **Southern Highlands Shiraz 2006** Rating 88 To 2013 $22

Fighting Gully Road ★★★★

319 Whorouly South Road, Whorouly South, Vic 3735 **Region** Beechworth
T (03) 5727 1434 **F** (03) 5727 1434 **Open** By appt
Winemaker Mark Walpole, Joel Pizzini **Est.** 1997 **Cases** 500 **Vyds** 8.3 ha
Mark Walpole (chief viticulturist for Brown Brothers) and partner Carolyn De Poi began the development of their Aquila Audax Vineyard in 1997, planting the first vines. It is situated between 530 and 580 m above sea level: the upper-eastern slopes are planted to pinot noir and the warmer western slopes to cabernet sauvignon; there are also small quantities of shiraz, tempranillo, sangiovese and merlot.

ΨΨΨΨΨ **Beechworth Pinot Noir 2008** Bright red-crimson; an attractive multi-clone pinot that has a fragrant and spicy bouquet; the palate has very good length and mouthfeel with a range of red fruits on display. Screwcap. 13% alc. **Rating** 92 To 2013 $27.50
Aquila 2008 A blend of Chardonnay/Viognier/Petit Manseng unique to Fighting Gully Road, fermented in used French barriques with a mix of indigenous and cultured yeasts; there are no dominant varietal characters other (perhaps) than chardonnay; the texture and weight define a well balanced, mouthfilling, dry white wine. Screwcap. 12.5% alc. **Rating** 90 To 2014 $27.50

Three Mile Tempranillo Cabernet Sauvignon 2008 Light but bright purple-crimson; an intense and tightly structured blend, the tannins firm and savoury, but not so much as to unbalance the dark fruits of the blend. Screwcap. 14% alc. **Rating** 90 **To** 2018 $45

Fire Gully   ★★★★★

Metricup Road, Wilyabrup, WA 6280 **Region** Margaret River
T (08) 9755 6220 **F** (08) 9755 6308 **Open** By appt
Winemaker Dr Michael Peterkin **Est.** 1988 **Cases** 5000 **Vyds** 13.3 ha
The Fire Gully vineyard has been established on what was first a dairy and then a beef farm. A 6-ha lake created in a gully ravaged by bushfires gave the property its name. In 1998 Mike Peterkin of Pierro purchased the property and manages the vineyard in conjunction with former owners Ellis and Margaret Butcher. He regards the Fire Gully wines as entirely separate from those of Pierro, being estate-grown: the vineyards are planted to cabernet sauvignon, merlot, shiraz, semillon, sauvignon blanc, chardonnay, viognier and chenin blanc, and have been increased by over 4 ha in recent years. Exports to all major markets.

♀♀♀♀♀ **Reserve Margaret River Cabernet Sauvignon 2007** Crimson-purple; blackcurrant, cedar and spice aromas slide effortlessly into the medium-bodied palate; here fine-grained tannins provide great texture and structure. Screwcap. 14.5% alc. **Rating** 96 **To** 2020 $45
Margaret River Sauvignon Blanc Semillon 2009 A wonderfully fragrant bouquet, with passionfruit and citrus aromas that in turn provide the no less delicious flavours of the light- to medium-bodied palate. Screwcap. 12.7% alc. **Rating** 94 **To** 2012 $27

♀♀♀♀♀ **Margaret River Chardonnay 2008** The fragrant bouquet and bright fruit of
❂ the palate reflect the major portion of the wine fermented in stainless steel, the touch of complexity from the smaller barrel ferment portion; the varietal fruit expression is pure Margaret River. Screwcap. 14.5% alc. **Rating** 93 **To** 2014 $29
❂ **Margaret River Shiraz 2007** Crimson-purple; an elegant medium-bodied wine typical of Margaret River; bright cherry and plum fruit is seasoned by a generous sprinkle of spice, the tannins long and refined. Screwcap. 14.5% alc. **Rating** 93 **To** 2020 $26

Fireblock   ★★★

St Vincent Street, Watervale, SA 5452 **Region** Clare Valley
T 0414 441 925 **F** (02) 9144 1925 **Open** Not
Winemaker O'Leary Walker **Est.** 1926 **Cases** 3000 **Vyds** 6 ha
Fireblock (formerly Old Station Vineyard) is owned by Alastair Gillespie and Bill and Noel Ireland, who purchased the 70-year-old vineyard in 1995. Watervale Riesling, Old Vine Shiraz and Old Vine Grenache are skilfully contract-made, winning trophies and gold medals at capital city wine shows. Exports to the US, Sweden and Malaysia.

♀♀♀♀ **Old Vine Clare Valley Shiraz 2007** A strange wine that should be much better than it is; vanillan oak is dominant, followed by spicy/savoury notes, shiraz fruit in third place. Screwcap. 15.5% alc. **Rating** 87 **To** 2014 $20

First Creek Wines   ★★★★★

Cnr McDonalds Road/Gillards Road, Pokolbin, NSW 2320 **Region** Hunter Valley
T (02) 4998 7293 **F** (02) 4998 7294 **www.**firstcreekwines.com.au **Open** 7 days 10–4
Winemaker Greg Silkman, Liz Jackson, Ryan McCann, Damien Stevens **Est.** 1984
Cases 35 000
First Creek is the shop front of Monarch Winemaking Services, which has acquired the former Allanmere wine business and offers a complex range of wines under both the First Creek and the Allanmere labels. Meticulous winemaking results in quality wines both for the contract clients and for the own-business labels. First Creek may have lost the services of Jim

Chatto (to Peppertree), but has secured an outstanding winemaker to take his place – Liz Jackson. Exports to the UK, the US and Canada.

ŸŸŸŸŸ **Winemaker's Reserve Hunter Valley Chardonnay 2009** Pale straw-green; a rare dry vintage and highly skilled winemaking have produced a truly fine chardonnay, with the white peach fruit more commonly associated with cool climates caressed by quality French oak. Screwcap. 12.5% alc. **Rating** 95 To 2020 $45

Winemaker's Reserve Canberra Shiraz 2008 A move to Canberra for shiraz in '08 was as much a matter of necessity as choice (rain-sodden Hunter vintage) but a very fine and elegant shiraz was the outcome, with totally beguiling red and black cherry fruit aromas and flavours on the long, light- to medium-bodied palate; a wine of great line and finesse. Screwcap. 13.5% alc. **Rating** 95 To 2020 $45

Winemaker's Reserve Hunter Valley Semillon 2009 Pale straw; an elegant, fine version of '09 semillon, marrying the vintage citrus and lemon tart flavours with more traditional grassy acidity on the finish. Will mature superbly. Screwcap. 11% alc. **Rating** 94 To 2025 $45

Orange Cabernet Sauvignon 2008 Bright crimson; has the fragrance and bright fruit flavours, cassis to the fore; a delicious palate, free from the sometimes forbidding tannins, but with a long finish. Screwcap. 13.5% alc. **Rating** 94 To 2020 $25

ŸŸŸŸ♀ **Canberra District Sauvignon Blanc 2009 Rating** 91 To 2012 $25
Winemaker's Reserve Tasmania Pinot Noir 2008 Rating 91 To 2015 $45

ŸŸŸŸ **Pinot Noir 2008 Rating** 88 To 2013 $25

First Drop Wines   ★★★★☆

PO Box 64, Williamstown, SA 5351 **Region** Barossa Valley
T 0420 971 209 **F** (08) 8389 7952 **www**.firstdropwines.com **Open** Not
Winemaker Matt Gant **Est.** 2005 **Cases** 3500
This is a virtual winery, with no vineyards and no winery of its own. What it does have are two owners with immaculate credentials to produce a diverse range of wines of significantly higher quality than those of many more conventional operations. Matt Gant was in his final year of a geography degree at the University of London in 1995 when lecturer Tim Unwin (a noted wine writer) contrived a course that involved tastings and ultimately a field trip of Burgundy and Champagne. Geography went out the window, and Matt did vintages in NZ, Spain, Italy, Portugal, the US and finally Australia. Working at St Hallett he won the Wine Society's Young Winemaker of the Year Award '04, and the Young Gun Wine Award for First Drop in '07. John Retsas has an equally impressive CV, working at St Hallett and Chain of Ponds, and is now general manager of Schild Estate. First Drop's portfolio includes Arneis, Nebbiolo, Barbera and Montepulciano (all from the Adelaide Hills), Barossa Savagnin and Trincadeira Rose, and a string of Barossa Shirazs ranging from $24 to $80 a bottle. Exports to the UK, the US, Canada, Denmark, Germany and NZ.

ŸŸŸŸŸ **Two Percent Barossa Shiraz 2007** Solid, bright colour; this is declassified The Cream and Fat of the Land that were not made in '07, and shows real integrity – and some very good black fruits and ripe tannins on the long, balanced palate. The label design and blurb is directed to the US market, and unlikely to win friends in Australia. Screwcap. 14.5% alc. **Rating** 94 To 2020 $36

ŸŸŸŸ♀ **Pintor Barossa Tempranillo 2008 Rating** 91 To 2020 $30
Minchia Adelaide Hills Montepulciano 2007 Rating 91 To 2022 $36
Mother's Milk Barossa Shiraz 2008 Rating 90 To 2016 $25
The Big Blind Adelaide Hills Nebbiolo Barbera 2008 Rating 90 To 2014 $30

ŸŸŸŸ **Bella Coppia Adelaide Hills Arneis 2009 Rating** 89 To 2012 $25
Lush Trincadeira Barossa Rose 2009 Rating 89 To 2011 $18
Home of the Brave Adelaide Hills Arneis 2008 Rating 88 To 2011 $30

5 Blind Mice ★★★☆

PO Box 243, Basket Range, SA 5138 **Region** Adelaide Hills
T (08) 8390 0206 **F** (08) 8390 3693 **www**.5blindmice.com.au **Open** Not
Winemaker Jodie and Hugh Armstrong **Est.** 2004 **Cases** 200
Owners Jodie and Hugh Armstrong say, 'What started out as an idea between friends and family to make something for themselves to drink at home during the week has blossomed into a quest for something to stand proudly on its own.' They purchase pinot noir from three sites in the Adelaide Hills, the vines over 15 years old. The wine is made in the boutique contract winery Red Heads Studio in McLaren Vale, with Jodie and Hugh making the wine under the eyes of Justin Lane and Adam Hooper, the winemakers at Red Heads.

ȲȲȲȲȲ **La Petite Souris Adelaide Hills Pinot Noir 2008** Clear, deep red; strong spiced plum aromas and flavour; there is substantial tannin structure, but in balance with the fruit; definitely needs 2–3 years minimum before consumption. Screwcap. **Rating** 92 **To** 2014 $25

ȲȲȲȲ **Adelaide Hills Pinot Noir 2007 Rating** 89 **To** 2014 $39

Five Geese ★★★★☆

RSD 587 Chapel Hill Road, Blewitt Springs, SA 5171 (postal) **Region** McLaren Vale
T (08) 8383 0576 **F** (08) 8383 0629 **www**.fivegeese.com.au **Open** Not
Winemaker Boar's Rock (Mike Farmilo) **Est.** 1999 **Cases** 1500 **Vyds** 24.84 ha
Sue Trott is passionate about her Five Geese wine, which is produced by Hillgrove Wines. The wines come from vines planted in 1927 and '65. The grapes were sold for many years, but in 1999 Sue decided to create her own label and make a strictly limited amount of wine from the pick of the vineyards. Exports to the UK, the US, Canada, Hong Kong and Singapore.

ȲȲȲȲȲ **McLaren Vale Shiraz 2007** Good hue, although not particularly deep; the
✪ bouquet immediately proclaims its regional birthplace, chocolate, plum and vanilla all on display, and rolling through the generous palate. Screwcap. 14.5% alc. **Rating** 92 **To** 2015 $20

5 Maddens Lane ★★★

PO Box 7001, McMahons Point, NSW 2060 **Region** Yarra Valley
T 0401 145 964 **F** (02) 9460 4194 **www**.5maddenslane.com.au **Open** Not
Winemaker Mac Forbes (Contract) **Est.** 2005 **Cases** 1000 **Vyds** 6 ha
5 Maddens Lane has been developed over a number of years. Four ha of cabernet sauvignon were planted between 1988 and '97, and the 2 ha of sauvignon blanc were planted in '87. Owner Marc de Cure lives in Sydney, and has secured the services of up-and-coming winemaker Mac Forbes as contract maker, and John Evans of Yering Station as vineyard manager. However, de Cure has his own qualifications, with a Master of Wine Quality (with distinction) from the University of Western Sydney.

ȲȲȲȲ **Mt Juliet Yarra Valley Sauvignon 2008** I'm not convinced the fruit was sufficiently intense to justify 10 months in (presumably old) French oak; half that time might have produced a top wine. As it is, good mid-ripe flavours are evident, even if shaded by the oak. Screwcap. 13% alc. **Rating** 89 **To** 2011 $30
Yarra Ranges Cabernet Sauvignon 2007 Light colour, although the hue is good; fresh, light-bodied, early-picked style, with blackcurrant and raspberry fruit, the raspberry presumably ex the 5% merlot. Screwcap. **Rating** 87 **To** 2013 $18

Five Sons Estate ★★★☆

85 Harrisons Road, Dromana, Vic 3936 **Region** Mornington Peninsula
T (03) 5987 3137 **F** (03) 5981 0572 **www**.fivesonsestate.com.au **Open** W'ends & public hols 11–5, 7 days in Jan
Winemaker Contract **Est.** 1998 **Cases** 2500 **Vyds** 18.82 ha

Bob and Sue Peime purchased the most historically significant viticultural holding on the Mornington Peninsula in 1998. Development of the 68-ha property began in the early 1930s, and was sold to a member of the Seppelt family, who planted riesling in '48. Two years later the property was sold to the Broadhurst family, close relatives of Doug Seabrook, who persisted with growing and making riesling until a 1967 bushfire destroyed the vines. Since 1998 (in descending order) pinot noir, chardonnay, shiraz, pinot gris and cabernet sauvignon have been planted.

🍷🍷🍷🍷🍷 **Mornington Peninsula Pinot Noir 2005** Very good hue for age; an aromatic and complex bouquet and palate, ranging from stewed, spiced plums to forest floor nuances; good balance and length. Screwcap. 13.5% alc. **Rating** 92 **To** 2013 $26

🍷🍷🍷🍷 **The Boyz Mornington Peninsula Pinot Noir 2005 Rating** 89 **To** 2011 $18

Flametree   ★★★★★

Cnr Caves Road/Chain Avenue, Dunsborough, WA 6281 **Region** Margaret River
T (08) 9756 8577 **F** (08) 9756 8572 www.flametreewines.com **Open** 7 days 10–5
Winemaker Cliff Royle **Est.** 2007 **Cases** 8000
Flametree, now owned solely by the Towner family (John, Liz, Jeremy and Rob), has had extraordinary success since its first vintage in 2007. The usual practice of planting a vineyard and then finding someone to make the wine was turned on its head: a state-of-the-art winery was built, and grape purchase agreements entered into with various growers in the region. Gold medal after gold medal, and trophy after trophy followed, topped by the winning of the Jimmy Watson Trophy with its first red wine, the 2007 Cabernet Merlot. If all this were not enough, Flametree has secured the services of former long-serving winemaker at Voyager Estate, Cliff Royle. Exports to the UK, Fiji and Singapore.

🍷🍷🍷🍷🍷 **Frankland River Shiraz 2008** Bright crimson; has a strong spicy component to
✪   the plummy bouquet, the medium-bodied palate adding licorice and dark cherry before fine, persistent tannins add a third dimension with their savoury character; oak present but not distracting. Screwcap. 14.5% alc. **Rating** 95 **To** 2020 $25

✪   **Margaret River Cabernet Merlot 2008** A pure lifted black fruit bouquet, showing touches of violet, cedar and regional leafiness; the palate has lovely texture and depth, showing generosity on the one hand and firmness of structure on the other; long and luscious, but restrained and poised; a beautifully crafted successor to the Jimmy Watson–winning '07. Screwcap. 14.5% alc. **Rating** 95 **To** 2020 $25 BE

✪   **Margaret River Sauvignon Blanc Semillon 2009** Plays the full scale of passionfruit, kiwi fruit, herb, apple and grass aromas and flavours, all encapsulated in an elegant but intense palate. Screwcap. 13% alc. **Rating** 94 **To** 2011 $19

🍷🍷🍷🍷🍷 **Margaret River Chardonnay 2008 Rating** 92 **To** 2015 $25

🍷🍷🍷🍷 **Embers Red 2008 Rating** 89 **To** 2012 $15

Flaxman Wines   ★★★★★

Lot 535 Flaxmans Valley Road, Angaston, SA 5353 **Region** Eden Valley
T 0411 668 949 **F** (08) 8565 3299 www.flaxmanwines.com.au **Open** By appt
Winemaker Colin Sheppard **Est.** 2005 **Cases** 500 **Vyds** 2 ha
After visiting the Barossa Valley for over a decade, and working during vintage with Andrew Seppelt at Murray Street Vineyards, Melbourne residents Colin and Fiona Sheppard decided on a seachange and found a small, old vineyard overlooking Flaxmans Valley. It consists of 1 ha of 40+-year-old riesling, 1 ha of 50+-year-old shiraz and a small planting of 40+-year-old semillon. The vines are dry-grown, hand-pruned and hand-picked, and treated – say the Sheppards – as their garden. Yields are restricted to under 4 tonnes per ha, and small amounts of locally grown grapes are also purchased.

🍷🍷🍷🍷🍷 **The Stranger Barossa Shiraz Cabernet 2008** Vivid crimson-purple; an unashamedly full-bodied wine, black fruits woven through a framework of tannins that are firm but balanced; comes together very well; 140 dozen made. Screwcap. 14% alc. **Rating** 96 **To** 2034 $35

Eden Valley Shiraz 2007 Winemaking in Lilliput, as only 70 dozen were made; has the hallmark Eden Valley elegance, the spicy red and black cherry fruit having a silky texture and mouthfeel, and a long, balanced finish. Screwcap. 14.5% alc. Rating 94 To 2017 $45

ŦŦŦŦŦ Eden Valley Riesling 2009 Rating 93 To 2019 $25
❂ Eden Valley Dessert Semillon 2009 Cordon-cut semillon that has a zesty twist often lost in the sweetness; good acidity also helps; 60 dozen half bottles made. Screwcap. 11% alc. Rating 91 To 2012 $20
❂ Barossa Shiraz VP 2008 Bright crimson; plum and blackberry fruit; clean spirit; still in its infancy but has balance and length; 60 dozen made. Deserves five years. Screwcap. 17.5% alc. Rating 90 To 2015 $20

ŦŦŦŦ Barossa Sparkling Shiraz NV Rating 89 To 2013 $35

Flinders Bay   ★★★★
Bussell Highway, Metricup, WA 6280 Region Margaret River
T (08) 9757 6281 F (08) 9757 6353 Open 7 days 10–4
Winemaker O'Leary Walker, Flying Fish Cove Est. 1995 Cases 10 000 Vyds 50 ha
A joint venture between Alastair Gillespie and Bill and Noel Ireland, Alastair a grapegrower and viticultural contractor in Margaret River for over 25 years, Bill and Noel Sydney wine retailers for an even longer period. The wines are made from grapes grown on the Karridale Vineyard (planted between 1995 and '98), with the exception of a Verdelho, which is purchased from northern Margaret River. Part of the grape production is sold, and part made under the Flinders Bay and Dunsborough Hills brands. Exports to the US, Sweden, Malaysia and China.

ŦŦŦŦŦ Margaret River Cabernet Sauvignon 2008 Bright crimson hue, although not
❂ deep; cassis and blackcurrant fruit on the bouquet and medium- to full-bodied palate is supported by serious tannins; coveted gold medal WA Wine Show '09. Good future. Screwcap. 14.6% alc. Rating 93 To 2023 $18
❂ Dunsborough Hills Margaret River Sauvignon Blanc Semillon 2009 Pale quartz; a spotlessly clean bouquet leads into a fresh, crisp and lively palate with light citrus and grass flavours; how this wine was top gold in Class 1 at the Perth Wine Show '09 is beyond my comprehension. Screwcap. 12.5% alc. Rating 90 To 2012 $15

ŦŦŦŦ Dunsborough Hills Margaret River Chardonnay 2009 I'm not convinced
❂ about the necessity for the touch of oak in the wine; it is only a touch, but there are sufficient grapefruit and stone fruit flavours to carry an unoaked wine. Carping criticism, for it's great value. Screwcap. 13% alc. Rating 89 To 2013 $15
❂ Dunsborough Hills Margaret River Shiraz 2008 Relatively light red-purple; predominant red berry fruits have spicy undertones, the finish savoury but fresh; a stylish wine at the price, ready to go now. Screwcap. 14.5% alc. Rating 89 To 2013 $15
Dunsborough Hills Margaret River Merlot Cabernet Sauvignon 2008 Rating 89 To 2014 $17
Dunsborough Hills Margaret River Cabernet Sauvignon 2008 Rating 89 To 2014 $17
Dunsborough Hills Geographe Margaret River Verdelho 2009 Rating 88 To 2013 $15
Margaret River Shiraz 2007 Rating 88 To 2014 $18

Flint's of Coonawarra   ★★★★
PO Box 8, Coonawarra, SA 5263 Region Coonawarra
T (08) 8736 5046 F (08) 8736 5146 www.flintsofcoonawarra.com.au Open Not
Winemaker Contract Est. 2000 Cases 2600 Vyds 84 ha

Six generations of the Flint family have lived and worked in Coonawarra since 1840. Damian Flint and his family began the development of 84 ha of cabernet sauvignon, shiraz and merlot in 1989 (65 ha leased for 20 years), but it was not until 2000 that they decided to have a small portion of cabernet sauvignon made at Majella, owned by their lifelong friends the Lynn brothers. The wine had immediate show success; another 10 tonnes were diverted from the 2001 vintage, and the first wines were released in '03. Exports to the UK and Hong Kong.

ΨΨΨΨΨ **Gammon's Crossing Cabernet Sauvignon 2007** A full-bodied cabernet that instantly makes its presence felt through its forceful but balanced mix of ripe blackcurrant fruit, oak, persistent tannins and alcohol; built for the long haul. Gold medal Sydney Wine Show '10. Screwcap. 15% alc. **Rating** 94 **To** 2015 $20

ΨΨΨΨ **Rostrevor Shiraz 2007 Rating** 89 **To** 2016 $18

Fluted Cape Vineyard ★★★★
128 Groombridge Road, Kettering, Tas 7155 **Region** Southern Tasmania
T (03) 6267 4262 **Open** 7 days 10–5
Winemaker Hood Wines **Est.** 1993 **Cases** 150
For many years Val Dell was the senior wildlife ranger on the central plateau of Tasmania, his wife Jan running the information centre at Liawenee. I met them there on trout fishing expeditions, staying in one of the park huts. They have now retired to the Huon Valley region, having established 0.25 ha each of pinot noir and chardonnay overlooking Kettering and Bruny Island, said to be a spectacularly beautiful site. The wines are made for them by Andrew Hood and are sold through the cellar door and Hartzview Cellars in Gardners Bay.

ΨΨΨΨΨ **Pinot Noir 2007** Has continued to evolve; bronze medal Tas Wine Show '08, silver medal '09; here the forest floor characters are less overt, a touch of mint making its presence felt; good mouthfeel and length. Screwcap. 13.8% alc. **Rating** 91 **To** 2014

ΨΨΨΨ **Pinot Noir 2008 Rating** 89 **To** 2015

🍇 Flyfaire ★★☆
1190 Tunnel Road, Woomargama, NSW 2644 (postal) **Region** Murray Darling
T 0407 908 499 **Open** Not
Winemaker Les Hanel **Est.** 1994 **Cases** 350 **Vyds** 5 ha
Les Hanel decided to diversify the production of what was a fine wool and beef cattle farm in 1993. Instead of simply jumping in at the deep end, as so many have done, he first enrolled at CSU to study viticulture and winemaking as a mature-age student. He began the plantings the following year on a southeast-facing hill slope at an altitude above 600 m. The degraded granite over red clay soil was acidic, and was deep-ripped to allow penetration of lime. Over the ensuing years riesling, chardonnay and merlot have been established at a deliberately slow pace; in September 2009 Les explained, 'Our cellar door is a work-in-progress and we should have the cladding on soon!'

Flying Fish Cove ★★★★☆
Caves Road, Wilyabrup, WA 6284 **Region** Margaret River
T (08) 9755 6600 **F** (08) 9755 6788 **www**.flyingfishcove.com **Open** 7 days 11–5
Winemaker Damon Eastaugh, Simon Ding, Ryan Aggiss **Est.** 2000 **Cases** 17 000
Vyds 25 ha
A group of 20 shareholders acquired the 130-ha property on which the Flying Fish Cove winery was subsequently built. It has two strings to its bow: contract winemaking for others, and the development of three product ranges (Upstream, Prize Catch and Margaret River varietals), partly based on 25 ha of estate plantings, with another 10 ha planned. Exports to the US, Singapore and Japan.

ⵢⵢⵢⵢⵢ Wildberry Estate Margaret River Chardonnay 2008 A very elegant
expression of Margaret River chardonnay; despite barrel fermentation in new
French oak, that oak does not obscure the fine, delicate nectarine and white peach
fruit; finishes with citrussy acidity. Screwcap. 13% alc. Rating 93 To 2015 $29

✪ Margaret River Chardonnay 2008 A crisp and incisive wine, with grapefruit
and white peach to the fore on bouquet and palate; lees contact has been
substituted for oak maturation, and works well. Screwcap. 13% alc. Rating 90
To 2014 $19.50

ⵢⵢⵢⵢ Margaret River Cabernet Sauvignon Merlot 2008 Rating 89 To 2016 $19.50
The Italian Job 2009 Rating 89 To 2014 $22

✪ Cuttlefish Margaret River Classic White 2008 In fact a blend of Semillon/
Sauvignon Blanc/Chardonnay, the chardonnay adding a touch of stone fruit to a
pleasant, if distinctly light-bodied wine, ever so easy to drink. Screwcap. 13% alc.
Rating 88 To 2010 $14

✪ Cuttlefish Classic Red Shiraz Cabernet 2007 Bright crimson-purple; this
is pretty remarkable value from Margaret River (and a touch of French oak),
although it is clearly engineered as a drink-today proposition with its lively red
fruit flavours and absence of tannins. Screwcap. 14.5% alc. Rating 88 To 2012 $14

Flynns Wines   ★★★★☆

Lot 5 Lewis Road, Heathcote, Vic 3523 **Region** Heathcote
T (03) 5433 6297 **F** (03) 5433 6297 **www.**flynnswines.com **Open** W'ends 11.30–5
Winemaker Greg and Natala Flynn **Est.** 1999 **Cases** 2000 **Vyds** 4.04 ha
The Flynn name has a long association with Heathcote. In the 1970s John Flynn and Laurie
Williams established a 2-ha vineyard next door to Mount Ida Vineyard, on the rich, red
Cambrian soil. It produced some spectacular wines before being sold in 1983. Greg and
Natala Flynn (no relation to John Flynn) spent 18 months searching for their property, 13 km
north of Heathcote on the same red Cambrian soil. They have established shiraz, sangiovese,
verdelho, cabernet sauvignon and merlot. Greg is a Roseworthy marketing graduate, and has
had 22 years working on the coalface of retail and wholesale businesses, interweaving eight
years of vineyard and winemaking experience, supplemented by the two-year Bendigo TAFE
winemaking course. Just for good measure, wife Natala joined Greg for the last eight years of
vineyard and winemaking, and likewise completed the TAFE course.

ⵢⵢⵢⵢⵢ MC Heathcote Shiraz 2008 Bright hue of moderate depth; a fragrant bouquet
of red and black fruits, then a delicious, silky palate with lively fruit flavours and
well integrated and balanced (40% new) oak. MC stands for multi clone, not
maceration carbonique. Screwcap. 14.3% alc. Rating 95 To 2023 $35

ⵢⵢⵢⵢⵢ Heathcote Sangiovese 2007 Rating 92 To 2012 $33

Fonty's Pool Vineyards   ★★★★★

Seven Day Road, Manjimup, WA 6258 **Region** Pemberton
T (08) 9777 0777 **F** (08) 9777 0788 **www.**fontyspoolwines.com.au **Open** 7 days 12–4
Winemaker Melanie Bowater, Bernie Stanlake **Est.** 1989 **Cases** 20 000 **Vyds** 69.42 ha
The Fonty's Pool vineyards are part of the original farm owned by pioneer settler Archie
Fontanini, who was granted land by the government in 1907. In the early 1920s a large dam
was created to provide water for the intensive vegetable gardens that were part of the farming
activities. The dam became known as Fonty's Pool, and to this day remains a famous local
landmark and recreational facility. The first grapes were planted in 1989, and the vineyard
is one of the region's largest, supplying grapes to a number of leading WA wineries. An
increasing amount of the production is used for Fonty's Pool. Exports to all major markets.

ⵢⵢⵢⵢⵢ Single Vineyard Pemberton Chardonnay 2008 Bright straw-green; a
✪ chardonnay with the precision of a Swiss watch, a highly fragrant bouquet
ranging through citrus and white flesh stone fruit, the palate picking up those
flavours, then adding a fine veneer of oak and a mineral backbone to the package.
Screwcap. 13% alc. Rating 96 To 2017 $22

✪ **Lucia Limited Release Pemberton Sauvignon Blanc Semillon 2008** Bright quartz-green, a 50/50 blend with some oak infusion; a totally brilliant winemaking exercise, the wine building lemony flavour progressively through the length of the palate and aftertaste in the manner of a great Burgundy. Screwcap. 12% alc. **Rating** 95 **To** 2012 $22

Single Vineyard Pemberton Chardonnay 2007 Classic cool-grown chardonnay with a racy mix of grapefruit, mineral and stone fruit, oak somewhere in the mix, although never obvious. Screwcap. 13.5% alc. **Rating** 94 **To** 2017 $22

✪ **Single Vineyard Pemberton Pinot Noir 2009** Light crimson; fragrant red cherry and spice aromas, then a relatively light-bodied savoury/spicy/cherry palate that has excellent texture, structure and, above all, length. Screwcap. 13% alc. **Rating** 94 **To** 2015 $19.80

🍷🍷🍷🍷 **Single Vineyard Pemberton Merlot 2008 Rating** 92 **To** 2014 $22

✪ **Single Vineyard Pemberton Cabernet Merlot 2008** This is a convincing cool-region blend, with attractive cassis/blackcurrant flavours offset by fine, savoury tannins. A case of less is more. Screwcap. 13.5% alc. **Rating** 91 **To** 2016 $17

Single Vineyard Pemberton Sauvignon Blanc Semillon 2009 Rating 90 **To** 2012 $19.80

🍷🍷🍷🍷 **Puddle Jumper Pemberton Sauvignon Blanc Semillon 2009 Rating** 89 **To** 2012 $15

Puddle Jumper Pemberton Merlot Shiraz Malbec 2008 Rating 88 **To** 2013 $15

Lucia Pemberton Sparkling Brut Chardonnay 2008 Rating 87 **To** 2012 $26

Forest Hill Vineyard ★★★★★

Cnr South Coast Highway/Myers Road, Denmark, WA 6333 **Region** Great Southern
T (08) 9848 2199 **F** (08) 9848 0095 **www**.foresthillwines.com.au **Open** 7 days 10–5
Winemaker Clemence Haselgrove **Est.** 1965 **Cases** 35 000 **Vyds** 77 ha

This family-owned business is one of the oldest 'new' winemaking operations in WA, and was the site for the first grape plantings in Great Southern in 1965. The Forest Hill brand became well known, aided by the fact that a 1975 Riesling made by Sandalford from Forest Hill grapes won nine trophies. The quality of the wines made from the oldest vines on the property is awesome (released under the numbered vineyard block labels). Exports to the UK, Taiwan, Hong Kong and China.

🍷🍷🍷🍷🍷 **Block 1 Mount Barker Riesling 2009** Complex aromas reflecting wild fermentation of separate parcels from the oldest vines, dry-grown and hand-picked; an intense, long and powerful display of lime, apple, spice and mineral underwritten by natural acidity into future decades. Screwcap. 12.5% alc. **Rating** 96 **To** 2030 $35

Block 9 Mount Barker Shiraz 2007 Good hue; made from the oldest shiraz vines on the vineyard; a wonderfully perfumed bouquet, with spice, anise and a bed of black fruits, the medium-bodied palate positively silky and very long, the tannins superfine. Screwcap. 15% alc. **Rating** 96 **To** 2030 $50

✪ **Estate Chardonnay 2008** Bright green-gold; the expressive bouquet is an immediate alert to a very impressive chardonnay to come on the intense, long and harmonious palate; the wine is built around white peach, nectarine and grapefruit, the acidity perfect, quality French oak in support. Screwcap. 14% alc. **Rating** 95 **To** 2016 $26

Block 8 Mount Barker Chardonnay 2008 Pale green-gold; a complex bouquet and palate, each delivering a similar message: very fine white peach, apple and grapefruit flavours in a thin veil of oak; most surprising is the finesse achieved at this alcohol level. Screwcap. 14% alc. **Rating** 95 **To** 2018 $38

✪ **Great Southern Riesling 2009** More accessible than Block 1, especially on the back-palate and finish, where lime juice and lime blossom notes break free; a very pure and intense riesling, also born to stay, thanks to its great acidity. Screwcap. 12% alc. **Rating** 94 **To** 2025 $22

ŶŶŶŶŶ **Block 5 Mount Barker Cabernet Sauvignon 2007** Rating 93 To 2032 $55
✪   **Boobook Great Southern Sauvignon Blanc Semillon 2009** A bright and
fragrant bouquet with floral aromas ranging from herb to citrus sustained on the
long palate by minerally acidity and a twitch of lemon zest. Screwcap. 13.5% alc.
Rating 91 To 2011 $19
Great Southern Noble Riesling 2008 Rating 91 To 2013 $24
Boobook Great Southern Shiraz 2008 Rating 90 To 2017 $19
Boobook Great Southern Cabernet Merlot 2008 Rating 90 To 2014 $19

Forester Estate   ★★★★★

1064 Wildwood Road, Yallingup, WA 6282 **Region** Margaret River
T (08) 9755 2788 **F** (08) 9755 2766 **www.**foresterestate.com.au **Open** By appt
Winemaker Kevin McKay, Michael Langridge **Est.** 2001 **Cases** 25 000 **Vyds** 33.5 ha
The Forester Estate business partners are Kevin McKay and Redmond Sweeny. Winemaker
Michael Langridge has a Bachelor of Arts (Hons) in Psychology and a Bachelor of Applied
Science (wine science, CSU). As Kevin says, 'He is the most over-qualified forklift driver
in Australia'. They have built and designed a 500-tonne winery, half devoted to contract
winemaking, the other half for the Forester label. The estate vineyards are planted to sauvignon
blanc, semillon, chardonnay, cabernet sauvignon, shiraz, merlot, petit verdot, malbec and
alicante bouschet. Exports to Singapore, China and Japan.

ŶŶŶŶŶ **Yelverton Reserve Margaret River Cabernet 2007** Pristine bouquet of
cedar, cassis, sandalwood and a touch of redcurrant; the palate is poised and precise,
with a multi-dimensional personality of savoury characters coming to the fore,
especially black olive; the acidity is bright and the tannins super fine; long and bell-
like clarity to conclude. Screwcap. 14% alc. Rating 96 To 2025 $55 BE
Margaret River Chardonnay 2008 A complex chardonnay offering grapefruit,
nectarine and plenty of toasty oak on the bouquet; the palate is rich and deep,
with the grapefruit acidity providing freshness and line. Gold medal Sydney Wine
Show '10. Screwcap. 13% alc. Rating 94 To 2016 $28

ŶŶŶŶŶ **Margaret River Semillon Sauvignon Blanc 2009** A bright, fragrant and
✪   flowery mix of citrus and grass on the one hand, and more tropical on the other,
runs through the bouquet; the palate is punchy, crisp and dry, with good length.
Screwcap. 13% alc. Rating 93 To 2012 $20
✪   **Margaret River Cabernet Merlot 2008** Bright and focused redcurrant and
cassis notes run through the bouquet; young, fresh and a little raw with the oak
prominent, the quality of the fruit, firmness of the tannins and the length of the
palate put forward a convincing case for such an inexpensive wine. Screwcap.
13.5% alc. Rating 93 To 2018 $20 BE
Yelverton Reserve Margaret River Cabernet 2005 Rating 92 To 2015
$55 BE
Yelverton Reserve Margaret River Cabernet 2004 Rating 91 To 2015 $47
✪   **Margaret River Sauvignon Blanc 2009** On the herbal/grassy/mineral end
of the spectrum, but in a precise framework. Seafood style. Screwcap. 13.5% alc.
Rating 90 To 2010 $23
Home Block Margaret River Shiraz 2008 Rating 90 To 2016 $33 BE

ŶŶŶŶ **Margaret River Shiraz 2007** Rating 89 To 2014 $20 BE

Foster e Rocco   ★★★★☆

139 Williams Road, Myers Flat, Vic 3556 (postal) **Region** Heathcote
T 0434 365 504 **Open** Not
Winemaker Adam Foster, Lincoln Riley **Est.** 2008 **Cases** 750
Long-term sommeliers and friends, Adam Foster and Lincoln Riley have established a business
that has a very clear vision: food-friendly wine based on the versatility of sangiovese. They
make their wines at Syrahmi, building it from the ground up, with fermentation in both
stainless steel and a mixture of older French oak barrels.

ŦŦŦŦŦ Heathcote Sangiovese 2008 There is no question whatsoever, this has varietal character in spades, with flavour from ripe to sour cherries, and plentiful tannins which actually need to soften a little. Screwcap. 13.2% alc. **Rating** 94 **To** 2015 $29

ŦŦŦŦⵢ Heathcote Rose 2009 Rating 90 **To** 2011

Four Winds Vineyard ★★★☆

392 Murrumbateman Road, Murrumbateman, NSW 2582 **Region** Canberra District
T (02) 6226 8182 **www**.fourwindsvineyard.com.au **Open** Not
Winemaker Graeme and Jaime Lunney **Est.** 1998 **Cases** 1300 **Vyds** 14.1 ha
Graeme and Suzanne Lunney conceived the idea for Four Winds in 1997, planting the first vines in '98, moving to the property full-time in '99, and making the first vintage in 2000. Son Tom manages the day-to-day operations of the vineyard; daughter Sarah looks after events and promotions; and youngest daughter Jaime, complete with a degree in Forensic Biology, has joined Graeme in the winery. Graeme makes the wine, and Suzanne tends the gardens and the 100 rose bushes at the end of the vine rows.

ŦŦŦŦⵢ Alinga Canberra District Cabernet Merlot 2008 Deeper colour than the Merlot, accurately suggesting greater depth and more structure; blackcurrant and plum fruit are supported by persistent savoury tannins; again seems to have higher alcohol, but it barely matters. Screwcap. 13.5% alc. **Rating** 90 **To** 2016 $16

ŦŦŦŦ Alinga Canberra District Riesling 2009 Rating 89 **To** 2013 $16

Fox Creek Wines ★★★★☆

Malpas Road, McLaren Vale, SA 5171 **Region** McLaren Vale
T (08) 8556 2403 **F** (08) 8556 2104 **www**.foxcreekwines.com **Open** 7 days 10–5
Winemaker Scott Zrna **Est.** 1995 **Cases** 40 000 **Vyds** 21 ha
Fox Creek has made a major impact since coming on-stream late in 1995. It is the venture of the Watts family: Jim (a retired surgeon), wife Helen and son Paul (a viticulturist); and the Roberts family: John (a retired anaesthetist) and wife Lyn. Kristin McLarty (née Watts) is marketing manager and Paul Rogers (married to Georgy, née Watts) is general manager. Moves are afoot to introduce organic practices in the vineyards, with trials of an organically registered herbicide derived from pine oil for weed control. The wines have enjoyed considerable show success. Exports to all major markets.

ŦŦŦŦⵢ Reserve McLaren Vale Shiraz 2007 Strong dark red colour; an elegant, medium-bodied wine that has good texture, flavour and structural balance; blackberry, dark chocolate, vanilla and spice flow into each other. Good outcome for the vintage. Screwcap. 14.5% alc. **Rating** 93 **To** 2020 $70
Reserve McLaren Vale Cabernet Sauvignon 2008 Strong crimson-purple; made in the full-bodied fashion of all in the Fox Creek Reserve wines, oozing blackcurrant fruit, cedary oak, dark chocolate and substantial tannins. Will not reach its peak in less than 10 years. Screwcap. 14.5% alc. **Rating** 93 **To** 2023 $40.50
Reserve McLaren Vale Merlot 2008 McLaren Vale merlots are a breed unto themselves, the chocolate undertone of the region one marker, and a rugged density the other; these are merlots for died-in-the-wool cabernet drinkers; this, then, is typical of its region. Screwcap. 14.5% alc. **Rating** 92 **To** 2020 $40.50
✪ **Duet McLaren Vale Cabernet Merlot 2008** The impact of fruit selection and winery techniques are vividly demonstrated by this medium-bodied wine, which has classic varietal blackcurrant from the cabernet, and cassis and plum from the merlot, oak and tannins barely relevant. Screwcap. 14.5% alc. **Rating** 91 **To** 2015 $19
✪ **McLaren Vale Chardonnay 2008** Very much in the new lower alcohol style; from a single-estate vineyard, it has elegant nectarine and white peach fruit; barrel fermentation has added to the texture more than the flavour. Screwcap. 12% alc. **Rating** 90 **To** 2013 $17

✪ **Shadow's Run Shiraz Cabernet Sauvignon 2008** Good crimson hue; wow; this is a flavour bomb for the price, full of plush yet bright red and black fruits, the tannins soft, the balance good. Screwcap. 13.5% alc. **Rating** 90 **To** 2016 $12
Circle Barrel Selection McLaren Vale Grenache Mourvedre 2008 Oak is evident on the bouquet, but that is partly a function of an inherently light-bodied wine, with red fruits and a touch of varietal confection akin to that of Barossa grenache. Bottle 422 of 1250. Screwcap. 14.5% alc. **Rating** 90 **To** 2016 $25
Circle Puncheon 5302 pm McLaren Vale Grenache Mourvedre 2008 This is a drilling down to the far extreme, only leaving individual bottle selection; there does seem to be a little more substance to the fruit, even a hint of darker berry flavours. Very intimidating wines to point. Bottle 615 of 750. Screwcap. 14.5% alc. **Rating** 90 **To** 2017 $25

♟♟♟♟ **Shadow's Run Sauvignon Blanc 2009** A remarkable achievement for the hot
✪ '09 vintage, for the wine has freshness and zest in a grassy/lemony spectrum, and a clean, crisp finish. Screwcap. 13% alc. **Rating** 89 **To** 2011 $12
McLaren Vale Shiraz Grenache Mourvedre 2008 Rating 89 **To** 2014 $17.50
Vixen NV Rating 89 **To** 2012 $22.50
McLaren Vale Late Harvest Semillon 2008 Rating 89 **To** 2012 $20

Fox Gordon   ★★★★★

102 Main Street, Hahndorf, SA 5245 **Region** Barossa Valley/Adelaide Hills
T (08) 8388 7155 **F** (08) 8388 7522 **www.**foxgordon.com.au **Open** Not
Winemaker Natasha Mooney **Est.** 2000 **Cases** 12 000
This is the venture of three very well known figures in the wine industry: Jane Gordon, Rachel Atkins (née Fox) and Natasha Mooney. Natasha (Tash) has had first-class experience in the Barossa Valley, particularly during her time as chief winemaker at Barossa Valley Estate. The partners wanted to produce high-quality wine, but only small quantities, which would allow them time to look after their children; the venture was planned in the shade of the wisteria tree in Tash's back garden. The grapes come from dry-grown vineyards farmed under biodiversity principles, which, says Tash, makes the winemaker's job easy. Classy packaging adds the final touch. Exports to the UK, the US, Canada, Germany, India, Singapore and Hong Kong.

♟♟♟♟♟ **Sassy Adelaide Hills Sauvignon Blanc 2009** Offers the full spectrum of sauvignon blanc aromas and flavours – passionfruit, lychee, citrus and grass – running through an intense bouquet and equally intense palate; a black eye for Marlborough. Screwcap. 12.9% alc. **Rating** 94 **To** 2011 $15.95
✪ **Abby Adelaide Hills Viognier 2009** Fox Gordon has got the best out of this difficult variety, with fresh ginger among the mix of pear, apricot and orange zest; flavour is achieved without phenolic toughness, the acidity providing a pathway to food matching. Screwcap. 13.5% alc. **Rating** 94 **To** 2010 $19.95

♟♟♟♟ **Princess Adelaide Hills Fiano 2009** An incredibly fragrant and flowery
✪ bouquet, with some muscat-like notes alongside frangipani; the palate is a major disconnect, the grapefruit zest flavours bordering on sourness. Screwcap. 13.5% alc. **Rating** 89 **To** 2011 $19.95
✪ **Eight Uncles Barossa Valley Shiraz 2007** First signs of colour development; the gulf between the character of the opulent '08s and the leaner, more savoury '07s becomes more evident every day; here there is an element of spice under the red and black cherry fruit of the medium-bodied palate that will approach maturity over the next year or so. Screwcap. 13.5% alc. **Rating** 89 **To** 2015 $19.95

Foxeys Hangout   ★★★★☆

795 White Hill Road, Red Hill, Vic 3937 **Region** Mornington Peninsula
T (03) 5989 2022 **F** (03) 5989 2822 **www.**foxeys-hangout.com.au **Open** W'ends & public hols 11–5
Winemaker Tony Lee, Michael Lee **Est.** 1998 **Cases** 3000 **Vyds** 4.3 ha

This is the venture of Tony Lee and journalist wife Cathy Gowdie. Cathy explains where it all began in 1998. 'We were not obvious candidates for a seachange. When we talked of moving to the country, friends pointed out that Tony and I were hardly back-to-nature types. "Do you own a single pair of shoes without heels?" asked a friend. But at the end of a bleak winter, we bought an old farmhouse on 10 daffodil-dotted acres at Red Hill and planted a vineyard.' They planted pinot noir, chardonnay, pinot gris and shiraz on the north-facing slopes of the old farm. The name (and the catchy label) stems from the tale of two fox-hunters who began a competition with each other in 1936, hanging their kills on the branches of an ancient eucalypt tree to keep count. The corpses have gone, but not the nickname for the area.

ȚȚȚȚȚ **Mornington Peninsula Shiraz 2008** Bright colour; highly spicy with black
✪   pepper framing red fruits and a hint of violets; medium-bodied, with plenty of energy and a dark mineral core providing complexity pure and persistent on the savoury finish. Screwcap. 14.5% alc. **Rating** 93 **To** 2016 $25 BE
Mornington Peninsula Chardonnay 2008 A soft style, with melon, Meyer lemon and a little spice; crunchy acid provides light, with a distinct nutty character shining through on the finish. Screwcap. 13.5% alc. **Rating** 90 **To** 2014 $25 BE
Mornington Peninsula Pinot Noir 2008 Light colour; the bouquet exhibits cherry and cinnamon spice on the bouquet; acidity drives the palate, with tightly wound red fruits unravelling slowly; structured and firm on the finish. Screwcap. 13.5% alc. **Rating** 90 **To** 2014 $30 BE

Frankland Estate   ★★★★★

Frankland Road, Frankland, WA 6396 **Region** Frankland River
T (08) 9855 1544 **F** (08) 9855 1549 **www**.franklandestate.com.au **Open** Mon–Fri 10–4, public hols & w'ends by appt
Winemaker Elizabeth Smith, Hunter Smith **Est.** 1988 **Cases** 15 000 **Vyds** 34.5 ha
A significant Frankland River operation, situated on a large sheep property owned by Barrie Smith and Judi Cullam. The vineyard has been established progressively since 1988; the recent introduction of an array of single-vineyard Rieslings has been a highlight. The venture into the single-vineyard wines is driven by Judi's conviction that terroir is of utmost importance, and the soils are indeed different. The climate is not, and the difference between the wines is not as clear-cut as theory might suggest. The Isolation Ridge Vineyard is now organically grown. Frankland Estate has held several important International Riesling tastings and seminars over recent years. Exports to all major markets.

ȚȚȚȚȚ **Isolation Ridge Riesling 2009** A classic riesling with every detail perfectly proportioned and balanced; a mix of apple and citrus that glides across the tongue in a continuous line. Organically grown from old vines. Screwcap. 12% alc. **Rating** 95 **To** 2020 $30
Cooladerra Vineyard Riesling 2009 Lemon and apple blossom bouquet, with a distinctly regional mineral complexity to the fruit; the palate is disarmingly generous, showing plenty of flesh and cleansing acidity; there is a savoury edge to the finish that leaves the palate fresh, linear and long to conclude. Screwcap. 12.5% alc. **Rating** 95 **To** 2020 $27 BE
✪   **Isolation Ridge Vineyard Cabernet Sauvignon 2008** Lovely colour, very bright; essency cassis aromas come to the fore on the bouquet, but are underpinned beautifully by savoury ironstone minerality; the palate shows dark fruit in abundance, again underscored by savoury complexity and structure that can only be described as serious; certainly assured of a long and very bright future, this wine is a bargain for price. Screwcap. 14% alc. **Rating** 95 **To** 2020 $24 BE
Olmo's Reward 2008 Deep in colour, and serious in intent, the bouquet of this wine is all dark fruits, savoury complexity and some seriously good oak; the texture of the wine is remarkable, showing less of the overt minerality of the other wines, and more silk; fine-grained tannins are the key, ensuring the wine is long-lived and long on the palate; built for those who enjoy structure with their fruit. Screwcap. 14.5% alc. **Rating** 95 **To** 2025 $40 BE

○ **Isolation Ridge Vineyard Chardonnay 2008** Quite a tight and lemony bouquet, with a strong mineral underpinning providing contrast and complexity; the palate is zesty and full of life, with a quartz-like quality to the structure; extremely long, fresh and enticing. Screwcap. 13.5% alc. **Rating** 94 **To** 2016 $24 BE

Smith Cullam Shiraz Cabernet 2008 Vibrant colour; pristine fruit aromas of blackberry, blackcurrant, ironstone and a suggestion of oak; the complexity continues to unroll on the palate, with bitter chocolate offsetting the generous fruit; as expected the structure is firm, but the generosity shines through on the very long and even finish. Screwcap. 14.5% alc. **Rating** 94 **To** 2018 $55 BE

Olmo's Reward 2007 Very good colour; the bouquet offers cassis, spice and cedar, characters reappearing on the medium-bodied palate, which is notable for its texture and structure, fine-grained tannins lengthening and strengthening the finish. Merlot/Cabernet Franc/Malbec. Screwcap. 14% alc. **Rating** 94 **To** 2027 $40

♟♟♟♟♙ **Poison Hill Riesling 2009 Rating** 92 **To** 2015 $27
Isolation Ridge Vineyard Shiraz 2008 Rating 91 **To** 2018 $27 BE

♟♟♟♟ **Rocky Gully Sauvignon Blanc 2009 Rating** 88 **To** 2012 $18 BE
Rocky Gully Cabernet Franc Merlot Cabernet Sauvignon 2007 Rating 88 **To** 2015 $17

Frankland Grange Wines ★★★★☆

Lot 71 Frankland/Kojonup Road, Frankland, WA 6396 **Region** Frankland River
T (08) 9388 1288 **F** (08) 9388 1020 www.franklandgrange.com **Open** By appt
Winemaker Alkoomi (Michael Staniford) **Est.** 1995 **Cases** 1000 **Vyds** 4 ha
Frank Keet used cuttings from Alkoomi when he planted 2.5 ha of shiraz in 1995, followed by 1.5 ha of chardonnay (also locally sourced) in '98. Given the quality of fruit coming from the Frankland River subregion, it seems highly likely that the number of wine producers will steadily increase in the years ahead.

♟♟♟♟♟ **Shiraz 2008** Bright crimson-purple; a fragrant and spicy red cherry bouquet, the
○ vibrant and perfectly balanced medium-bodied palate full of very well ripened shiraz fruit. Screwcap. 13.9% alc. **Rating** 94 **To** 2023 $25

♟♟♟♟♙ **Shiraz 2007 Rating** 92 **To** 2020 $25
○ **Unwooded Chardonnay 2008** Bright green-straw; nectarine and grapefruit aromas and flavours run through a fresh, light-bodied palate. Good unwooded chardonnay. Screwcap. 13% alc. **Rating** 90 **To** 2012 $16

♟♟♟♟ **Shiraz 2006 Rating** 89 **To** 2014 $26

Fraser Gallop Estate ★★★★★

547 Metricup Road, Wilyabrup, WA 6280 **Region** Margaret River
T (08) 9755 7553 **F** (08) 9755 7443 www.frasergallopestate.com.au **Open** By appt
Winemaker Clive Otto, Kate Morgan **Est.** 1999 **Cases** 8000 **Vyds** 18.55 ha
Nigel Gallop began the development of the vineyard in 1999, planting cabernet sauvignon, semillon, petit verdot, cabernet franc, malbec, merlot and multi-clone chardonnay. The vines are dry-grown with modest yields, followed by kid-glove treatment in the winery. The first vintage was 2002, the wine being contract-made offsite, but with Clive Otto (formerly of Vasse Felix) on board, a 300-tonne winery was built onsite for the '08 vintage. As well as wines under the Fraser Gallop Estate label, limited amounts of contract wine are made for others. Exports to the UK, Canada and Hong Kong.

♟♟♟♟♟ **Margaret River Chardonnay 2009** A very fine and delicate chardonnay at the dawn of its life; white peach fruit is in a gentle gauze of French oak and the mouthfeel is exceptionally good, likewise the balance; will flower with time in bottle. Screwcap. 13.5% alc. **Rating** 94 **To** 2017 $30

⊗   **Margaret River Cabernet Merlot 2008** Excellent hue; an altogether superior wine, displaying both varietal and regional typicity; blackcurrant, cassis, black olive, quality oak and balanced savoury tannins all play their part. Screwcap. 13.5% alc. **Rating** 94 **To** 2018 $20

Margaret River Cabernet Sauvignon 2008 Bright crimson-purple; has a totally seductive bouquet filled with red and black small berry aromas; the palate quickly changes pace, with persistent but high-quality tannins and oak. Has a great future, for there is no doubt the bouquet and palate will come together. Screwcap. 14.5% alc. **Rating** 94 **To** 2028 $34

ᵀᵀᵀᵀᵀ **Margaret River Semillon Sauvignon Blanc 2009** Two-thirds semillon and
⊗   partial barrel ferment takes the focus away from sauvignon blanc into an altogether more complex and mouthfilling mode, the balance is good, the style likewise. Screwcap. 12.9% alc. **Rating** 92 **To** 2014 $20

🍇 Fratelli   ★★★☆

12 Melbourne Road, Yea, Vic 3717 (postal) **Region** Victoria
T 0419 117 858 **F** (03) 5797 2932 **www**.fratelliwines.com.au **Open** Not
Winemaker Andrew Santarossa **Est.** 2007 **Cases** 600
This is the virtual winery operation of three brothers of Italian heritage with a love of wine: Andrew, Michael and Anthony Santarossa. Andrew, the eldest, is a winemaker with 10 years' experience making wines in Oregon, the Margaret River and the Yarra Valley. The handsomely packaged wines are sourced from various regions across Victoria; it's a small business as yet, but has the capacity to grow.

ᵀᵀᵀᵀᵀ **Yarra Valley Sauvignon Blanc 2009** A crisp, clean and correct bouquet leads
⊗   into a commendably intense palate with a mix of citrus and tropical fruit, and a lingering lemony finish. Screwcap. 13% alc. **Rating** 91 **To** 2011 $20

ᵀᵀᵀᵀ   **Heathcote Primitivo 2008 Rating** 89 **To** 2013 $30

Freshy Bay Wines   ★★★☆

PO Box 4170, Mosman Park, WA 6012 **Region** South West Australia Zone
T (08) 9384 9916 **F** (08) 9284 5964 **www**.freshybay.com **Open** Not
Winemaker Simon Ding, Nigel Ludlow **Est.** 2000 **Cases** 1400
Freshy Bay Wines is owned by Colin and Judy Evans, its establishment part of a winding-down process from their prior professional careers. In 2000 they planted 2 ha of shiraz and produced five vintages from '03 to '07 inclusive, which enjoyed show success and critical acclaim. Finding the responsibility of caring for the vineyard too onerous, it was sold, and the business now operates as a virtual winery, chardonnay being purchased from growers in the Margaret River region.

ᵀᵀᵀᵀᵀ **Margaret River Chardonnay 2008** Pale straw-green; a light- to medium-
⊗   bodied fresh and clean chardonnay, with gentle white flesh stone fruit and the barest hint of oak; good balance and length, and ready to go right now. Screwcap. 13% alc. **Rating** 90 **To** 2012 $16

Freycinet   ★★★★★

15919 Tasman Highway via Bicheno, Tas 7215 **Region** East Coast Tasmania
T (03) 6257 8574 **F** (03) 6257 8454 **www**.freycinetvineyard.com.au **Open** 7 days 9.30–4.30
Winemaker Claudio Radenti, Lindy Bull **Est.** 1980 **Cases** 5000 **Vyds** 9.08 ha
The Freycinet vineyards are beautifully situated on the sloping hillsides of a small valley. The soils are brown dermosol on top of Jurassic dolerite, and the combination of aspect, slope, soil and heat summation produces red grapes with unusual depth of colour and ripe flavours. One of Australia's foremost producers of pinot noir, with a wholly enviable track record of consistency – rare in such a temperamental variety. The Radenti (sparkling), Riesling and Chardonnay are also wines of the highest quality. Exports to the UK and Sweden.

♀♀♀♀♀ **Pinot Noir 2007** Even deeper purple-crimson than Louis; the pure fruit of the bouquet is but foreplay for the palate, charged with luscious plum and black cherry, then reined in and given great texture and structure by a whisk of fine tannins on the finish. Gold medal Tas Wine Show '10. Screwcap. 14% alc. **Rating** 96 **To** 2017 $70

Riesling 2008 Has a very fragrant, flowery and complex bouquet; the palate opens with lime and tropical fruit, then an almost savoury minerally acidity takes over the back-palate and draws out the palate to an extremely long finish and aftertaste. Screwcap. 13% alc. **Rating** 95 **To** 2020 $27

✪ **Louis Pinot Noir 2007** Typical strong Tasmanian colour, headed well into purple; the bouquet is redolent of satsuma plum, the palate silky, round and very long; great line and balance. Trophy Tas Wine Show '10. Screwcap. 14.5% alc. **Rating** 95 **To** 2017 $35

Riesling 2009 A spice and lime zest bouquet leads into a richly fruited palate where Tasmanian acidity is enveloped by ripe, varietal citrus flavours before a touch of mineral brings the wine to its conclusion. Screwcap. 13% alc. **Rating** 94 **To** 2021 $27

Chardonnay 2008 High-quality chardonnay that achieves vibrancy and finesse without the loss of varietal fruit characters; while peach and melon are in the front seat, oak is in the back seat. A harmonious and balanced wine. Screwcap. 13.5% alc. **Rating** 94 **To** 2018 $38

✪ **Radenti Chardonnay Pinot Noir 2000** Very complex wine; toasty dried fruits, figs, brioche; long finish. Cork. 12.5% alc. **Rating** 94 **To** 2015 $50

♀♀♀♀♀ **Louis Chardonnay 2008 Rating** 92 **To** 2014 $24
Cabernet Sauvignon Merlot 2006 Rating 90 **To** 2020 $38

Frog Rock Wines   ★★★☆

Edgell Lane, Mudgee, NSW 2850 **Region** Mudgee
T (02) 6372 2408 **F** (02) 6372 6924 **www**.frogrockwines.com **Open** 7 days 10–5
Winemaker David Lowe, Jane Wilson, Simon Gilbert (Contract) **Est.** 1973 **Cases** 7000
Vyds 40 ha
The Frog Rock label was launched in 1997 by the Turner family, named after local frog-shaped granite boulders on land granted to famous explorer and grazier William Lawson in 1823. The vineyard, on deep alluvial clay soils, employs minimal irrigation and sprays; plantings include cabernet sauvignon (13 ha), shiraz (12 ha) and chardonnay (4.5 ha), with lesser amounts of merlot, semillon, petit verdot and chambourcin. Exports to Hong Kong.

♀♀♀♀♀ **Sticky Frog 2009** Bright green-gold; has plenty of flavour, sweetness and acidity and is well balanced; some botrytis; matured in French oak, and has overall elegance. Semillon. Screwcap. 10.6% alc. **Rating** 90 **To** 2013 $20

♀♀♀♀ **Sauvignon Blanc 2009** Intelligent winemaking and the '09 vintage combine
✪ to produce a sauvignon blanc with clear varietal character, not common with this variety in Mudgee; a strong line of citrus and lemon runs through the palate and brisk finish. Screwcap. 11.5% alc. **Rating** 89 **To** 2011 $18

Mudgee Pinot Gris 2009 Rating 89 **To** 2011 $18
Rick's Mudgee Merlot 2006 Rating 89 **To** 2014 $20

Frogmore Creek   ★★★★★

20 Denholms Road, Cambridge, Tas 7170 **Region** Southern Tasmania
T (03) 6248 5844 **F** (03) 6248 5855 **www**.frogmorecreek.com.au
Open W'ends 10–5 Aug–Apr, w'ends 11–4 May–Jul
Winemaker Alain Rousseau, Nick Glaetzer, Andrew Hood (Consultant) **Est.** 1997
Cases 18 000 **Vyds** 28.6 ha
Frogmore Creek is a Pacific Rim joint venture, the owners being Tony Scherer of Tasmania and Jack Kidwiler of California. The partners have developed an organically grown vineyard, and have acquired the Hood/Wellington wine business previously owned by Andrew Hood,

who continues his involvement as a consultant. Winemaking has been consolidated at Cambridge, where the Frogmore Creek and 42° South brands are made, as well as a thriving contract winemaking business. Exports to the US, Japan, Indonesia and South Korea.

ΨΨΨΨΨ **42°S Unwooded Chardonnay 2008** Light green–straw; lively, fresh, crisp
✪ grapefruit and some white peach; has length and personality; excellent example of unwooded chardonnay. Gold medal Tas Wine Show '10. Screwcap. 12.7% alc. Rating 94 To 2013 $21.50
Chardonnay 2008 Bright green-gold; has a complex bouquet without any single factor dominating; intense flavours, with seamless grapefruit and white peach woven through subtle oak. Gold medal Tas Wine Show '10. Screwcap. 13.7% alc. Rating 94 To 2016 $30
✪ **Iced Riesling 2008** Andrew Hood pioneered tank-frozen Iced Rieslings in Tasmania and passed his knowledge on to the Frogmore Creek wine crew. This has classic lime juice, on a potent and long palate, with very good balancing acidity. Screwcap. 8% alc. Rating 94 To 2016 $26

ΨΨΨΨΨ **Riesling 2008** Rating 93 To 2019 $24
✪ **FGR Riesling 2009** Strong lime and orange blossom aromas; the wine that set the path for this Mosel style, with its complex sweetness balanced by Tasmanian acidity; very rich and satisfying. FGR means 40 grammes per litre of residual sugar. Screwcap. 9.5% alc. Rating 93 To 2020 $24
Riesling 2009 Rating 90 To 2016 $24
42°S Pinot Grigio 2009 Rating 90 To 2012 $24 BE
Pinot Noir 2008 Rating 90 To 2014 $36

ΨΨΨΨ **Reserve Pinot Noir 2008** Rating 89 To 2015 $60
42° S Sauvignon Blanc 2009 Rating 87 To 2011 $24

Gabriel Horvat Wines   ★★★

No 9, 37-39 East Street, Daylesford, Vic 3460 **Region** Macedon Ranges
T 0429 585 129 **www**.wineisa4letterword.com **Open** Mon–Tues 11–5, Fri–Sat 11–late, Sun 12–4
Winemaker Gabriel Horvat **Est.** 2005 **Cases** 1000
Gabriel Horvat grew up in the Pyrenees town of Landsborough, and after finishing school, worked for several years in local vineyards before beginning a winemaking degree in 2000 at CSU. He subsequently decided to discontinue studying for that degree, instead gaining practical and philosophical education in traditional methods in his father's winery (Horvat). He began developing his own labels, and eventually moved to set up his own small winery in Daylesford. Situated in the middle of town, his venture extends to a boutique wine store focusing on the wines of western Vic, wine bar and music venue. The premises are named 'W.I.N.E is a 4 letter word', his operating company called Liberated Winemakers.

ΨΨΨΨ **Pyrenees Shiraz 2007** More successful than the Grampians Shiraz; aromas of black fruits and licorice, then a light- to medium-bodied palate with savoury notes developing. Screwcap. 14.3% alc. Rating 89 To 2015 $35

Gaelic Cemetery Wines   ★★★★★

PO Box 54, Sevenhill, SA 5453 **Region** Clare Valley
T (08) 8843 4370 **F** (08) 8843 4353 **www**.gaelic-cemetery-wines.com **Open** Not
Winemaker Neil Pike, John Trotter **Est.** 2005 **Cases** 500 **Vyds** 6.5 ha
This is a joint venture between winemaker Neil Pike, viticulturist Andrew Pike and Adelaide retailers Mario and Ben Barletta. It hinges on a single vineyard owned by Grant Arnold, planted in 1996, adjacent to the historic cemetery of the region's Scottish pioneers. Situated in a secluded valley of the Clare hills, the low-cropping vineyard, say the partners, 'is always one of the earliest ripening shiraz vineyards in the region and mystifyingly produces fruit with both natural pH and acid analyses that can only be described as beautiful numbers'. The result is hands-off winemaking and maturation for 24 months in new and used Burgundian barriques. Exports to the UK, the US, Singapore and NZ.

🍷🍷🍷🍷🍷 **Clare Valley Shiraz 2007** Deep purple-crimson; a very concentrated and powerful full-bodied shiraz with blackberry, dark chocolate, licorice and mocha flavours, the tannins ripe; carries its alcohol; 280 cases made. High-quality cork. 15% alc. **Rating** 94 **To** 2022 $120

Galafrey ★★★★
Quangellup Road, Mount Barker, WA 6324 **Region** Mount Barker
T (08) 9851 2022 **F** (08) 9851 2324 **www.**galafreywines.com.au **Open** 7 days 10–5
Winemaker Paul Nelson **Est.** 1977 **Cases** 5000 **Vyds** 12.82 ha
Relocated to a purpose-built but utilitarian winery after previously inhabiting the exotic surrounds of the old Albany wool store, Galafrey makes wines with plenty of robust, if not rustic, character, drawing grapes in the main from estate plantings. Following the death of husband/father/founder Ian Tyrer, Kim and Linda Tyrer have taken up the reins, announcing, 'There is girl power happening at Galafrey Wines!' There is a cornucopia of back vintages available, some superb and underpriced, at the cellar door. The arrival of Paul Nelson as winemaker bodes well for the future. Exports to China and Japan.

🍷🍷🍷🍷🍷 ✪ **Semillon Sauvignon Blanc 2009** Pale straw-green; a fragrant and aromatic bouquet with gooseberry, guava and citrus sets the scene for a palate with good drive and length to its positive fruit flavours. Screwcap. 13.5% alc. **Rating** 93 **To** 2012 $18
Dry Land Reserve Mount Barker Riesling 2009 Some spicy notes on the bouquet, then moves decisively to mouthfilling, lime-accented flavours, surprisingly full given the modest alcohol. Screwcap. 11.5% alc. **Rating** 91 **To** 2016 $20
Reserve Dry Grown Mount Barker Shiraz 2006 Good colour; a fragrant bouquet with a mix of red and black fruits, spice and a hint of pepper; the light-to medium-bodied palate has good length and balance. Screwcap. 12.5% alc. **Rating** 91 **To** 2016 $35
Mount Barker Unoaked Chardonnay 2009 Offers more than the majority in this style, with tangy grapefruit and stone fruit flavours running through the generous palate. Screwcap. 13% alc. **Rating** 90 **To** 2012 $18

🍷🍷🍷🍷 **Reserve Semillon 2009 Rating** 89 **To** 2014 $22
Sauvy Mount Barker Sauvignon Blanc 2009 Rating 89 **To** 2011 $18

Gallagher Wines ★★★☆
2770 Dog Trap Road, Murrumbateman, NSW 2582 **Region** Canberra District
T (02) 6227 0555 **F** (02) 6227 0666 **www.**gallagherwines.com.au **Open** W'ends & public hols 10–5
Winemaker Greg Gallagher **Est.** 1995 **Cases** 2750 **Vyds** 2 ha
Greg Gallagher was senior winemaker at Taltarni for 20 years, working with Dominique Portet. He began planning a change at much the same time as did Portet, and started establishing a small vineyard at Murrumbateman in 1995, now planted to 1 ha each of chardonnay and shiraz.

🍷🍷🍷🍷🍷 ✪ **Canberra District Sauvignon Blanc 2009** A generous helping of ripe, tropical fruits on bouquet and palate alike, ranging from passionfruit to pineapple; avoids phenolic heaviness on the finish. Screwcap. 12.3% alc. **Rating** 90 **To** 2012 $17.95
Canberra District Sparkling Duet 2008 Identical techniques to those of the Brut Rose; here Pinot Noir (55%)/Chardonnay (45%); a slightly funky bouquet, then a brisk citrussy palate with good drive and length. Zork SPK an interesting closure, especially its reseal capacity. 12.7% alc. **Rating** 90 **To** 2012 $25

🍷🍷🍷🍷 **Canberra District Riesling 2009 Rating** 89 **To** 2014 $17.95
Canberra District Shiraz 2008 Rating 89 **To** 2015 $21.95
Canberra District Sparkling 2008 Rating 89 **To** 2012 $25
Canberra District Merlot 2008 Rating 88 **To** 2013 $21.95
Canberra District Brut Rose 2008 Rating 87 **To** 2012 $24.95

Galli Estate ★★★★★

1507 Melton Highway, Rockbank, Vic 3335 **Region** Sunbury
T (03) 9747 1444 **F** (03) 9747 1481 **www**.galliestate.com.au **Open** 7 days 11–5
Winemaker Ben Ranken **Est.** 1997 **Cases** 8000 **Vyds** 149 ha
Galli Estate, founded in 1997 by (the late) Lorenzo and Pam Galli, is located at Rockbank in Sunbury, with 40 ha of vines (chardonnay, shiraz, pinot grigio, cabernet sauvignon and merlot) planted on rich red volcanic soil. The second Camelback Vineyard at Heathcote has 109 ha planted to a mix of mainstream and Mediterranean varieties (shiraz, cabernet sauvignon, chardonnay, sangiovese, viognier, tempranillo, nebbiolo, merlot, grenache and petit verdot). All wines are estate-grown. Following the death of Lorenzo a decision has been taken to substantially downsize the operation by reducing the make, and selling more of the grapes. Exports to the UK, the US, Canada, Denmark, Japan, Singapore, China, Taiwan and Hong Kong.

ҰҰҰҰҰ **Artigiano Sunbury Chardonnay 2009** Pale, bright colour, takes all the elements of the La Famiglia, but hones and fines them on its very long and perfectly balanced palate, grapefruit and white flesh stone fruit in a near-invisible web of oak. Screwcap. 12.5% alc. **Rating** 94 **To** 2017 $30

✪ **Artigiano Heathcote Viognier 2009** Straw-green; while the bouquet is restrained, the palate is not, with unusual thrust to its peach, apricot and citrus flavours, yet devoid of unwanted phenolics. Screwcap. 13.5% alc. **Rating** 94 **To** 2013 $26

✪ **Heathcote Sangiovese Shiraz 2008** The blend works very well indeed, plum, red cherry and sour cherry coming together on a lively and fresh palate, the tannins savoury yet fine. Screwcap. 13.8% alc. **Rating** 94 **To** 2017 $20

ҰҰҰҰҰ **Artigiano Sunbury Shiraz 2008 Rating** 93 **To** 2017 $26
Artigiano Block Two Heathcote Shiraz 2007 Rating 93 **To** 2020 $30

✪ **La Famiglia Sunbury Chardonnay 2009** Light straw-green; a crisp and lively wine showcasing chardonnay varietal fruit flavours ripened in a cool climate, its grapefruit and nectarine fruit making such oak as there is irrelevant. Screwcap. 13% alc. **Rating** 92 **To** 2015 $18

✪ **Heathcote Shiraz Viognier 2008** Light but bright crimson; only light- to medium-bodied, but is in very good balance, and the flavours are delicious; spiced cherry and plum, with fine tannins. Screwcap. 14.9% alc. **Rating** 92 **To** 2015 $18
Artigiano Heathcote Sangiovese 2008 Rating 92 **To** 2013 $30

✪ **Sunbury Sauvignon Blanc 2009** An easy access style, with a gentle mix of tropical and more herbal/grassy components; good balance and length. Screwcap. 12% alc. **Rating** 90 **To** 2011 $18
Sunbury Pinot Grigio 2009 Rating 90 **To** 2011 $20

✪ **La Famiglia Sunbury Cabernet Sauvignon 2008** Bright hue; an aromatic bouquet of blackcurrant and red berries is followed by a more savoury palate with ingrained tannins running through to the finish. Screwcap. 13.5% alc. **Rating** 90 **To** 2023 $18

ҰҰҰҰ **Heathcote Tempranillo Grenache Mourvedre 2008 Rating** 89 **To** 2015 $20
Artigiano Heathcote Nebbiolo 2008 Rating 89 **To** 2020 $30
Artigiano Block Two Heathcote Shiraz 2008 Rating 87 **To** 2015 $30

🍇 Gallows Wine Co ★★★☆

Lennox Road, Carbunup River, WA 6280 **Region** Margaret River
T (08) 9755 1060 **F** (08) 9755 1060 **www**.gallows.com.au **Open** 7 days 10–5
Winemaker Charlie Maiolo **Est.** 2008 **Cases** 10 000 **Vyds** 27 ha
This is the venture of the Maiolo family, headed by winemaker Charlie, the macabre name that of one of the most famous surf breaks on the Margaret River coast. The vineyard is planted to semillon, sauvignon blanc, chardonnay, pinot noir, shiraz, merlot and cabernet sauvignon. The site-climate is strongly influenced by Geographe Bay, 5 km to the north, and facilitates the production of wines with a large spectrum of differing flavours and characteristics.

ŶŶŶŶ♀ **Car Park Margaret River Sauvignon Blanc Semillon 2009** Bright pale
❍   straw; a very fragrant bouquet sets the scene for a lively palate, with distinctive zesty
       lemony fruit and considerable length. Screwcap. 12.5% alc. **Rating** 92 **To** 2011 $20

ŶŶŶŶ **Margaret River Semillon Sauvignon Blanc 2009 Rating** 89 **To** 2012 $24

Garbin Estate   ★★★☆

209 Toodyay Road, Middle Swan, WA 6056 **Region** Swan Valley
T (08) 9274 1747 **F** (08) 9274 1747 **www**.garbinestatewines.com.au
Open 7 days 10.30–5.30
Winemaker Peter Garbin **Est.** 1956 **Cases** 3500 **Vyds** 7 ha
Duje Garbin, winemaker and fisherman from a small island near the Dalmatian coast in the
Adriatic Sea, migrated to WA in 1937; in '56 he purchased the Middle Swan property on
which Garbin Estate stands. When he retired in the early 1990s, son Peter took over what was
a thoroughly traditional and small business, and embarked on a massive transition: a new cellar
door and processing area, upgraded major plant and equipment, and the establishment of a
vineyard in Gingin. A former design draughtsman, Peter is now full-time winemaker, backed
up by wife Katrina, assistant winemaker, and sons Joel and Adam. Exports to China.

ŶŶŶŶ♀ **Reserve Basket Pressed Shiraz 2009** Good red–purple; a medium- to full-
       bodied shiraz with abundant blackberry and plum fruit, the texture and structure
       from good tannins and oak extraction. Screwcap. 14% alc. **Rating** 92 **To** 2017 $25

ŶŶŶŶ **Reserve Chardonnay 2009 Rating** 87 **To** 2012 $17

Gardners Ground   ★★★

444 Rivers Road, Canowindra, NSW 2804 **Region** Cowra
T (02) 6344 3135 **F** (02) 6344 3175 **www**.gardnersground.com.au **Open** Not
Winemaker Graeme Kerr, Chris Derrez (Contract) **Est.** 2001 **Cases** 2000 **Vyds** 14 ha
Jenny and Herb Gardner chose their property, situated on the southern bank of the Belubula
River, back in 1996. It was the culmination of an extensive search over southeastern Australia,
meeting the requirements of appropriate soil structure as well as natural beauty. It was always
their intention that the vineyard (7.5 ha of shiraz, 6.5 ha of chardonnay) would be run
organically, and the use of chemicals ceased in 1996 before planting began. Chardonnay and
Shiraz are made by contract winemakers Graeme Kerr (at Canowindra) and Chris Derrez (at
Orange). Most of the wine, labelled under the Hawkewind brand, is exported to Japan.

ŶŶŶŶ **Canowindra Shiraz 2008** Blackberry, cherry and plum fruit has distinct
       earth and spice nuances, the light- to medium-bodied palate with good balance.
       Organic. Screwcap. 14.6% alc. **Rating** 88 **To** 2013 $19.95

Garners   ★★★

54 Longwood/Mansfield Road, Longwood East, Vic 3666 **Region** Strathbogie Ranges
T (03) 5798 5513 **F** (03) 5798 5514 **www**.garnerswine.com.au **Open** W'ends 10–4, or
by appt 0410 649 030
Winemaker Plunkett Fowles (Lindsay Brown) **Est.** 2005 **Cases** 450 **Vyds** 1.8 ha
Former Professor of Optometry Leon Garner, and artist wife Rosie, returned to Australia
in 2005 after living in NZ since 1979. They intended to settle in Qld, but by pure chance
while driving along the Longwood/Mansfield Road, they noticed a 'for sale' sign. The granite
house was called Roseleigh (an eerie coincidence) and – when the surrounding scenery was
considered – it was too hard to resist. Having purchased the house, they quickly formed a close
friendship with Jenny Houghton of neighbouring Maygars Hill Winery, and she provided
them with sufficient cuttings to plant 1.8 ha of shiraz. Their first vintage followed in 2008.

ŶŶŶŶ **Strathbogie Ranges Shiraz 2008** Some colour development; savoury/spicy
       aromas, likewise flavours, on the light- to medium-bodied palate. Screwcap.
       14.1% alc. **Rating** 88 **To** 2014 $18

Gartelmann Hunter Estate ★★★★☆

701 Lovedale Road, Lovedale, NSW 2321 **Region** Hunter Valley
T (02) 4930 7113 **F** (02) 4930 7114 **www**.gartelmann.com.au **Open** 7 days 10–5
Winemaker Jorg Gartelmann, Liz Jackson **Est.** 1970 **Cases** 5000
In 1996 Jan and Jorg Gartelmann purchased what was previously the George Hunter Estate –
16 ha of mature vineyards, most established by Sydney restaurateur Oliver Shaul in '70. A
major change in the business model resulted in the sale of the vineyards after the 2006 vintage,
and the grapes are now sourced from other Hunter Valley vineyards, giving the business
maximum flexibility. Is now owned by Swish Wine (see separate entry), but retains its identity
(and cellar door). Exports to Germany.

ɀɀɀɀɀ **Reserve Semillon 2003** Brilliant green-straw; the grassy bouquet and palate
show why this semillon was held for six years before release; still pungently fresh
and lively, lemongrass coming through on the palate, it has years still left. Screwcap.
10.5% alc. **Rating** 94 **To** 2018 $30

ɀɀɀɀɀ **Wilhelm Shiraz 2007 Rating** 93 **To** 2017 $25
Classic Chardonnay 2009 Rating 90 **To** 2013 $30
Classic Cabernet Merlot 2008 Rating 90 **To** 2015 $25

ɀɀɀɀ **Benjamin Semillon 2009 Rating** 89 **To** 2013 $25

Geddes Wines ★★★★

PO Box 227, McLaren Vale, SA 5171 **Region** McLaren Vale
T (08) 8323 8814 **F** (08) 8323 8814 **www**.geddeswines.com **Open** Not
Winemaker Tim Geddes **Est.** 2004 **Cases** 1800
Owner/winemaker Tim Geddes and wife Amanda, a chef, bring considerable experience to
the venture. Tim's started in Hawke's Bay, NZ, with three vintages as a cellar hand, which led
to a move to Australia to complete the oenology degree at Adelaide University. Dual vintages
in the Barossa and Hunter valleys were woven in between settling down in McLaren Vale,
where he has been a contract winemaker for a number of clients since 2002. Tim's 2007 lease
of a 500-tonne winery means even greater contract work, while he slowly builds the Seldom
Inn range (made every vintage) and the Geddes label, which is only made in the best years.
The long-term aim is to make 3000 cases, relying on small parcels of fruit from a number of
selected McLaren Vale subregions. Exports to Canada.

ɀɀɀɀɀ **Seldom Inn McLaren Vale Shiraz 2008** Dense, impenetrable colour;
✪ interesting wine; has been able to absorb 40% new French and American oak,
and is not tannic or extractive. I suppose you can drink it now (as the back
label suggests) but I would would prefer to give it time to learn how to speak.
Screwcap. 14.5% alc. **Rating** 92 **To** 2020 $22
Wild Ferment Viognier 2009 A very powerful and very complex viognier, with
considerable texture to the stone fruit and nutty characters; slightly phenolic, but
not oily. Screwcap. 14% alc. **Rating** 91 **To** 2013 $30
✪ **Seldom Inn McLaren Vale Cabernet Sauvignon 2008** Strong red-purple;
rich, dense and opulent, flooded with blackcurrant fruit; more depth than length,
but has allure. Screwcap. 14.5% alc. **Rating** 91 **To** 2018 $22

ɀɀɀɀ **Seldom Inn McLaren Vale Viognier 2009 Rating** 89 **To** 2012 $20
Seldom Inn McLaren Vale Grenache Shiraz Mataro 2008 Rating 89
To 2015 $22
Seldom Inn McLaren Vale Petit Verdot 2008 Rating 89 **To** 2014 $22

Gelland Estate ★★★☆

PO Box 1148, Mudgee, NSW 2850 **Region** Mudgee
T (02) 6373 5411 **www**.gellandestate.com.au **Open** Not
Winemaker Rhys Eather (Contract) **Est.** 1999 **Cases** 500 **Vyds** 6 ha

Warren and Stephanie Gelland moved from Sydney to Mudgee in 1998 'to start a family with room to move'. They had no background in viticulture, but friends who had previously made the same move and established a vineyard suggested that the Gellands follow suit, which they duly did by planting 4 ha of cabernet sauvignon and 2 ha of chardonnay. More recently they have purchased small parcels of shiraz and viognier from Mudgee vineyards to add a Cabernet Shiraz, Viognier Chardonnay and Cabernet Rose to the portfolio.

ΨΨΨΨΨ **Mudgee Rose 2009** Deep pink; attractive cabernet rose; red berry/cassis, then a
✪   long, dry and crisp finish. Screwcap. 11.5% alc. **Rating** 90 **To** 2011 $18

Gembrook Hill ★★★★★

Launching Place Road, Gembrook, Vic 3783 **Region** Yarra Valley
T (03) 5968 1622 **F** (03) 5968 1699 **www**.gembrookhill.com.au **Open** By appt
Winemaker Timo Mayer, Andrew Marks **Est.** 1983 **Cases** 2500 **Vyds** 6 ha
Ian and June Marks established Gembrook Hill, one of the oldest vineyards in the coolest part of the upper Yarra Valley, usually harvested some four weeks later than the lower parts of the region. Son Andrew assists Timo Mayer on the winemaking front, each also having their own respective labels (see separate entries for The Wanderer and Mayer). The northeast-facing vineyard is in a natural amphitheatre and most vines are over 20 years old; the low-yielding vines are not irrigated, are hand-pruned and harvested (plantings consist of sauvignon blanc, chardonnay and pinot noir). The minimal approach to winemaking produces wines of a consistent style with finesse and elegance. Exports to the UK, Denmark, Japan and Malaysia.

ΨΨΨΨΨ **Yarra Valley Sauvignon Blanc 2008** Has a very complex bouquet, with exotic
        tropical fruit aromas of passionfruit, guava and gooseberry, custard apple joining
        the band on the expressive palate. Screwcap. 13% alc. **Rating** 94 **To** 2011 $35
        Yarra Valley Chardonnay 2006 Bright straw-green; right in the mainstream of
        modern Yarra Valley style, with modest alcohol and oak contributions to a notably
        long citrus and stone fruit palate. Diam. 13% alc. **Rating** 94 **To** 2014 $38
✪   **Mayer Vineyard Yarra Valley Pinot Noir 2008** Bright, light crimson; the
        bouquet is complex and exotic, with plum and spice aromas, the palate following
        closely behind; long and intense, it has a mix of red fruits and a strong, foresty
        background. Screwcap. 13.5% alc. **Rating** 94 **To** 2013 $28

ΨΨΨΨΨ **Yarra Valley Pinot Noir 2008 Rating** 90 **To** 2013 $50

ΨΨΨΨ **Blanc de Blancs 2005 Rating** 89 **To** 2013 $55

Gemtree Vineyards ★★★★★

PO Box 164, McLaren Vale, SA 5171 **Region** McLaren Vale
T (08) 8323 8199 **F** (08) 8323 7889 **www**.gemtreevineyards.com.au **Open** 7 days 10–5
at Salopian Inn
Winemaker Mike Brown **Est.** 1998 **Cases** 30 000 **Vyds** 133.16 ha
The Buttery family, headed by Paul and Jill, and with the active involvement of Melissa as viticulturist, have been grapegrowers in McLaren Vale since 1980, when they purchased their first vineyard. Today the family owns a little over 130 ha of vines. The oldest block, of 25 ha on Tatachilla Road at McLaren Vale, was planted in 1970. The wine portfolio is of high quality, and also full of interest. Exports to the the UK, the US and other major markets.

ΨΨΨΨΨ **Uncut McLaren Vale Shiraz 2008** Deep, dense colour; regional licorice and
✪   dark chocolate overtones to the blackberry fruit of the bouquet leap from the
        glass, the medium- to full-bodied palate providing more of the same, with 16
        months in French oak doing little more than rounding off the tannins. Screwcap.
        14.5% alc. **Rating** 95 **To** 2028 $22
✪   **Moonstone 2009** A fruit blossom bouquet is followed by an intense and zesty
        palate, with a range of citrus and green apple flavours that have tremendous thrust
        and vitality; very interesting wine. Savagnin. Screwcap. 12.5% alc. **Rating** 94
        To 2014 $25

White Lees McLaren Vale Shiraz 2007 Strong colour; the fragrant bouquet of spicy plum and black fruits leads into an intense, finely textured and very long palate; the wine spent 28 months in oak on chardonnay lees, with continuous battonage (lees stirring). Screwcap. 14.5% alc. **Rating** 94 **To** 2023 $45

The Phantom McLaren Vale Petit Verdot 2008 Typical dense colour; scented black fruit aromas lead into a full-bodied palate (what else?) with layers of fruit and ripe tannins, the latter a by-product of 12 weeks' maceration and 14 months in French oak. Screwcap. 14.5% alc. **Rating** 94 **To** 2023 $30

ŢŢŢŢŢ **Bloodstone McLaren Vale Shiraz 2008** Deep colour; a potent bouquet, with ✪ black fruits, licorice and dark chocolate all evident, foretells the medium- to full-bodied palate, where the fruit flavours are supple and welcoming. Attractive wine with plenty of attitude. Screwcap. 14.5% alc. **Rating** 92 **To** 2018 $16.50

Cadenzia McLaren Vale Grenache Tempranillo Shiraz 2008 Rating 92 **To** 2014 $25

✪ **Citrine McLaren Vale Chardonnay 2009** Light straw-green; very well made, part stainless-steel fermented and matured, part barrel-fermented and matured; this, coupled with moderately low alcohol, gives a bright and fresh flavour profile, the oak a definite contributor but in a restrained fashion. Screwcap. 13% alc. **Rating** 91 **To** 2014 $16

Tatty Road Cabernet Sauvignon Merlot Petit Verdot Cabernet Franc 2008 Rating 90 **To** 2015 $21

Geoff Merrill Wines   ★★★★

291 Pimpala Road, Woodcroft, SA 5162 **Region** McLaren Vale
T (08) 8381 6877 **F** (08) 8322 2244 **www**.geoffmerrillwines.com **Open** Mon–Fri 10–5, w'ends 12–5
Winemaker Geoff Merrill, Scott Heidrich **Est.** 1980 **Cases** 80 000 **Vyds** 132 ha
If Geoff Merrill ever loses his impish sense of humour or his zest for life, high and not-so-high, we shall all be the poorer. The product range consists of three tiers: premium (varietal); Reserve, being the older (and best) wines, reflecting the desire for elegance and subtlety of this otherwise exuberant winemaker; and, at the top, Henley Shiraz. Mount Hurtle wines are sold exclusively through Vintage Cellars/Liquorland. I am at a loss to explain why only the cheaper wines were submitted this year, however good their value. Exports to all major markets.

ŢŢŢŢŢ **McLaren Vale Shiraz Grenache Mourvedre 2006** Light colour; in the ✪ manner of Southern Rhône wines, the colour is no necessary guide, the warm, spicy red fruit flavours insidiously imposing themselves on an unexpectedly long finish. Screwcap. 14.5% alc. **Rating** 91 **To** 2014 $20

ŢŢŢŢ **Wickham Park Foothills Sauvignon Blanc 2009** Unusual wine; the texture ✪ suggests some barrel fermentation or maturation, but there is none, just gentle tropical fruits with some grassy edges. Screwcap. 12.5% alc. **Rating** 89 **To** 2011 $20

✪ **Bush Vine McLaren Vale Grenache Rose 2009** Vivid fuchsia; very well made given the vintage conditions; crisp and clean, but not much depth. Screwcap. 14% alc. **Rating** 89 **To** 2010 $20

Geoff Weaver   ★★★★★

2 Gilpin Lane, Mitcham, SA 5062 (postal) **Region** Adelaide Hills
T (08) 8272 2105 **F** (08) 8271 0177 **www**.geoffweaver.com.au **Open** Not
Winemaker Geoff Weaver **Est.** 1982 **Cases** 3500 **Vyds** 12.3 ha
This is the full-time business of former Hardys chief winemaker Geoff Weaver. He draws upon a little over 12 ha of vineyard established between 1982 and '88, and invariably produces immaculate Riesling and Sauvignon Blanc, and one of the longest-lived Chardonnays to be found in Australia, with intense grapefruit and melon flavour. The beauty of the labels ranks supreme with Pipers Brook. Exports to Germany and Singapore.

🍷🍷🍷🍷🍷 **Lenswood Sauvignon Blanc 2009** Fastidious winemaking puts this wine on
✪ another plane; the gooseberry and kiwi fruit flavours are intense and penetrating, the palate very long and the dry, almost savoury, aftertaste lingers long. Screwcap. 13.5% alc. **Rating** 96 **To** 2014 $24
Lenswood Chardonnay 2008 Has all the elegance and finesse that is the hallmark of the Weaver style; white peach, creamy/nutty nuances and balanced acidity give the wine harmony and length. Screwcap. 13.5% alc. **Rating** 94 **To** 2015 $38

🍷🍷🍷🍷🍷 **Lenswood Pinot Noir 2008 Rating** 90 **To** 2015 $38

Ghost Rock Vineyard ★★★☆

1055 Port Sorrell Road, Northdown, Tas 7307 **Region** Northern Tasmania
T (03) 6428 4005 **F** (03) 6428 4330 **www**.ghostrock.com.au **Open** Wed–Sun & public hols 11–5 (7 days Jan–Feb)
Winemaker Tom Ravech (Contract) **Est.** 2001 **Cases** 1500 **Vyds** 7 ha
Cate and Colin Arnold purchased the former Patrick Creek Vineyard (planted in 1989) in 2001. They run a printing and design business in Devonport and were looking for a suitable site to establish a vineyard. The vineyard (pinot gris, pinot noir, sauvignon blanc, chardonnay and riesling) is planted on a northeasterly aspect on a sheltered slope. The increase in plantings (and consequent production) has allowed the Arnolds to supply markets throughout the mainland.

🍷🍷🍷🍷🍷 **Ol' Man's Ghost Pinot Gris 2009** Highly perfumed, with musk and citrus in abundance; the palate is quite zesty, with the acidity giving way to a gentle boxwood honey finish. Screwcap. 13.5% alc. **Rating** 90 **To** 2012 $26 BE

🍷🍷🍷🍷 **Clairdown Estate Pinot Noir 2008 Rating** 88 **To** 2015 $29 BE

Giaconda ★★★★★

30 McClay Road, Beechworth, Vic 3747 **Region** Beechworth
T (03) 5727 0246 **F** (03) 5727 0246 **www**.giaconda.com.au **Open** By appt
Winemaker Rick Kinzbrunner **Est.** 1985 **Cases** NA
These wines have a super-cult status and, given the tiny production, are extremely difficult to find; they are sold chiefly through restaurants and by mail order. All have a cosmopolitan edge befitting Rick Kinzbrunner's international winemaking experience. The Chardonnay and Pinot Noir are made in contrasting styles: the Chardonnay tight and reserved, the Pinot Noir more variable, but usually opulent and ripe. Exports to the UK and the US.

🍷🍷🍷🍷🍷 **Chardonnay 2008** Bright straw-green; has all the textural complexity for which Giaconda is rightly revered, creamy/nutty characters held by perfectly balanced acidity, the mid-palate with pristine nectarine and melon fruit, oak at once omnipresent yet subtle. Screwcap. 13.5% alc. **Rating** 96 **To** 2020 $127

Giant Steps/Innocent Bystander ★★★★★

336 Maroondah Highway, Healesville, Vic 3777 **Region** Yarra Valley
T (03) 5962 6111 **F** (03) 5962 6199 **www**.giant-steps.com.au **Open** Mon–Fri 10–10, w'ends 8–10
Winemaker Phil Sexton, Steve Flamsteed, Dave Mackintosh **Est.** 1997 **Cases** 60 000
Vyds 35.3 ha
Phil Sexton made his first fortune as a pioneer micro-brewer, and invested part of that fortune in establishing Devil's Lair. Late in 1996 he sold Devil's Lair to Southcorp, which had purchased Coldstream Hills earlier that year. Two years later he purchased a hillside property less than 1 km from Coldstream Hills, and sharing the same geological structure and aspect. The name Giant Steps comes in part from his love of jazz and John Coltrane's album of that name, and in part from the rise and fall of the property across a series of ridges ranging from 120 m to 360 m. The vineyard is predominantly planted to pinot noir and chardonnay, but

with significant quantities of cabernet sauvignon and merlot, plus small plantings of cabernet franc and petit verdot. It also leases Tarraford Vineyard, with 8.5 ha of vines up to 20 years old. Innocent Bystander contributes 40 000 cases to the overall production of the venture. Exports to the UK, the US and other major markets.

ΨΨΨΨΨ **Giant Steps Tarraford Vineyard Yarra Valley Chardonnay 2008** Bright green-gold; a complex, multifaceted bouquet with fused French oak and fruit leads into an intense and very long palate, nectarine and grapefruit the drivers, perfect acidity on the finish. A long life ahead. Trophy Best Single Vineyard Wine Melbourne Wine Show '09, gold medal Sydney Wine Show '10. Screwcap. 13.5% alc. **Rating** 96 **To** 2016 $39.95

Giant Steps Tarraford Vineyard Yarra Valley Pinot Noir 2008 Light and clear colour; fragrant aromatics range from red fruits to forest; a correspondingly fine and delicate palate, perfectly balanced and with immaculate length; overall light-bodied but none the worse for that. Screwcap. 13% alc. **Rating** 94 **To** 2015 $44.95

Sexton Harry's Monster 2008 Crimson-red; a very harmonious bouquet leads into a strongly structured palate with the black fruits duelling with the tannins in an evenly matched contest over the next decade. Cabernet Sauvignon/Merlot/Petit Verdot/Cabernet Franc. Screwcap. 14.5% alc. **Rating** 94 **To** 2023 $44.95

ΨΨΨΨΨ **Giant Steps Sexton Vineyard Yarra Valley Pinot Noir 2008** **Rating** 93 **To** 2015 $39.95

Giant Steps Sexton Vineyard Yarra Valley Chardonnay 2008 **Rating** 92 **To** 2014 $34.95

Giant Steps Sexton Vineyard Yarra Valley Merlot 2008 **Rating** 91 **To** 2018 $34.95

✪ **Innocent Bystander Yarra Valley Chardonnay 2009** From contract-grown Yarra Valley grapes; aromatic grapefruit, white flesh stone fruit and crisp acidity. A good example of what unwooded chardonnay should look like. Screwcap. 13% alc. **Rating** 90 **To** 2012 $19.95

ΨΨΨΨ **Innocent Bystander Pinot Gris 2009** **Rating** 89 **To** 2011 $19.95

✪ **Innocent Bystander Shiraz 2008** Strong red-purple; from seven cool-climate Victorian vineyards 'owned by our grower partners'. A supremely honest medium-to full-bodied shiraz with abundant blackberry and plum fruit to sustain it for years to come. Screwcap. 13.9% alc. **Rating** 89 **To** 2020 $19.95

✪ **Innocent Bystander Sangiovese 2008** Quite strong purple hue; the Bystander strolled to McLaren Vale to find the grapes for this wine, with its persuasive mix of black cherry and sour (red) cherry. Screwcap. 13.7% alc. **Rating** 89 **To** 2014 $19.95

✪ **Innocent Bystander Moscato 2009** Vivid colour; has abundant vibrant red fruit flavours mixed with a dash of lemon juice; more attitude than most others. Crown seal. 5.5% alc. **Rating** 89 **To** 2011 $12.50

Innocent Bystander Pinot Noir 2009 **Rating** 88 **To** 2012 $19.95

Gibson Barossavale/Loose End   ★★★★★

Willows Road, Light Pass, SA 5355 **Region** Barossa Valley
T (08) 8562 3193 **F** (08) 8562 4490 **www.**gibsonwines.com.au **Open** 7 days 11–5
Winemaker Rob Gibson **Est.** 1996 **Cases** 15 000 **Vyds** 10 ha
Rob Gibson spent much of his working life as a senior viticulturist for Penfolds. While at Penfolds he was involved in research tracing the characters that particular parcels of grapes give to a wine, which left him with a passion for identifying and protecting what is left of the original vineyard plantings in wine regions around Australia. He has two vineyards in the Barossa Valley at Stockwell (shiraz, mataro and grenache) and Light Pass (merlot), and one in the Eden Valley (shiraz and riesling), and also purchases grapes from McLaren Vale and the Adelaide Hills. Loose End is an important 7000-case brand launched in 2007, offering wines at lower price points. Exports to the US, Japan, China and Singapore.

ŸŸŸŸŸ   **Gibson Reserve Shiraz 2006** Good colour; a fragrant and pure bouquet
✪   leads into an utterly delicious palate, with a fresh, lively and juicy display of
predominantly black fruits, the long finish marked by excellent acidity. Old vine
elegance. Screwcap. 14.9% alc. **Rating** 96 **To** 2031 $40
Gibson Reserve Merlot 2006 One of those tricky blends, Barossa Merlot
(75%)/Adelaide Hills Merlot (11%)/Barossa Cabernet Sauvignon (14%) could be
labelled Barossa Merlot; red berry, olive and a touch of mint on the bouquet, then
a vibrantly juicy palate, initially sweet, but concluding with a dry, slightly savoury,
finish. Screwcap. 14.6% alc. **Rating** 94 **To** 2020 $40

ŸŸŸŸŸ   **The Dirtman Shiraz 2006 Rating** 90 **To** 2015 $25 BE

ŸŸŸŸ   **Loose End Riesling 2009 Rating** 88 **To** 2016 $18 BE

Gibson Estate   ★★★☆
57 Tubbarubba Road, Merricks North, Vic 3926 **Region** Mornington Peninsula
T (03) 5989 7501 **www**.gibsonestate.com.au **Open** By appt
Winemaker Phil Kerney **Est.** 2001 **Cases** 400
Kate and Stuart Gibson say they spent 15 years searching for the perfect site to grow classic
pinot noir. They ultimately settled on a north-facing slope of the Red Hill area of the
Mornington Peninsula. It is 110 m above sea level, and is on a moderate (15°) incline, picking
up maximum sun interception, which allows them to pick a little earlier than vineyards further
up the Red Hill hillsides. The 2.5 ha of pinot noir is planted in three equal blocks of MV6,
114 and 115 clones, two-thirds planted on vigour-reducing rootstocks, thus limiting the yield
to 2 tonnes to the acre.

ŸŸŸŸŸ   **Reserve Pinot Noir 2005** Two years in French oak has largely smothered the
fruit; there are many things going on here: powerful, savoury dark fruits; the '04
varietal shows the wine can evolve well over a number of years. Diam. 14.5% alc.
Rating 90 **To** 2014 $60

Gilberts   ★★★★★
RMB 438 Albany Highway, Kendenup via Mount Barker, WA 6323 **Region** Mount Barker
T (08) 9851 4028 **F** (08) 9851 4021 **www**.gilbertwines.com.au **Open** Wed–Mon 10–5
Winemaker Plantagenet **Est.** 1980 **Cases** 4000 **Vyds** 14.5 ha
Once a part-time occupation for sheep and beef farmers Jim and Beverly Gilbert, but now
a full-time and very successful one. The mature vineyard (shiraz, chardonnay, riesling and
cabernet sauvignon), coupled with contract winemaking at Plantagenet, has long produced
very high-class Riesling, and now also makes excellent Shiraz. In 2000 a new red wine was
introduced into the range, named the Three Devils Shiraz in honour of their then nine- to
14-year-old sons. Exports to Hong Kong and Switzerland.

ŸŸŸŸŸ   **Mount Barker Riesling 2009** Similar colour to Alira; a flowery, aromatic bouquet
✪   of lime and crushed lime leaves; bright, fine and intense, with minerally acidity lifting
and lengthening the finish. Screwcap. 12.5% alc. **Rating** 94 **To** 2019 $19
Reserve Mount Barker Shiraz 2007 Vivid crimson-purple; a powerful, full-
bodied shiraz that has an abundance of black fruits, spice and licorice, French
oak evident but well integrated; carries its alcohol with ridiculous ease. Screwcap.
15% alc. **Rating** 94 **To** 2020 $30

ŸŸŸŸŸ   **Alira 2009** Bright straw-green; a succulent wine, citrus fruits with a tropical edge
✪   enhanced by some residual sweetness. No need for patience, although will cellar
well. Riesling. Screwcap. 12.5% alc. **Rating** 90 **To** 2013 $17
✪   **Three Devils Mount Barker Rose 2009** Pale fuchsia; a 'dash of riesling' added
to the cabernet base is detectable, adding to raciness of the flavour and mouthfeel;
a bold throw that comes off. Screwcap. 13% alc. **Rating** 90 **To** 2010 $18

ŸŸŸŸ   **Mount Barker Chardonnay 2009 Rating** 89 **To** 2014 $23

Gilligan ★★★☆

PO Box 235, Willunga, SA 5172 **Region** McLaren Vale
T (08) 8323 8379 **F** (08) 8323 8379 **www**.gilligan.com.au **Open** Not
Winemaker Mark Day, Leigh Gilligan **Est.** 2001 **Cases** 1000 **Vyds** 5.74 ha
Leigh Gilligan is a 20-year marketing veteran, mostly with McLaren Vale wineries (including
Wirra Wirra). The Gilligan family has just over 4 ha of shiraz and 0.4 ha each of grenache,
mourvedre, marsanne and roussanne, selling part of the production. In 2001 they persuaded
next-door neighbour Drew Noon to make a barrel of Shiraz, which they drank and gave
away. Realising they needed more than one barrel, they moved to Maxwell Wines, with help
from Maxwell winemaker Mark Day, and have now migrated to Mark's new Koltz Winery at
Blewitt Springs. Exports to the UK, the US, Canada, Germany, Denmark and Thailand.

ΨΨΨΨΨ **McLaren Vale Shiraz 2008** Dense, dark crimson; as the colour suggests, a
full-bodied shiraz with strong regional expression courtesy of a bitter chocolate
coating around blackberry and black cherry fruit; carries its alcohol bravely.
Screwcap. 15% alc. **Rating** 91 **To** 2023 $25

ΨΨΨΨ **McLaren Vale Marsanne Roussanne 2009** Rating 89 To 2013 $25

Gioiello Estate ★★★☆

PO Box 250, Tullamarine, Vic 3043 **Region** Upper Goulburn
T 0437 240 502 **www**.gioiello.com.au **Open** Not
Winemaker Steve Flamsteed, Scott McCarthy (Contract) **Est.** 1987 **Cases** 5000
Vyds 9.09 ha
The Gioiello Estate vineyard was established by a Japanese company and originally known as
Diawa Nar Darak. Planted between 1987 and '96, it accounts for fractionally more than 9 ha
on a 400-ha property of rolling hills, pastures, bushland, river flats, natural water springs and
billabongs. The wines produced were sold only in Japan, but the quality was demonstrated
by the 1994 Daiwa Nar Darak Chardonnay, which won the George Mackey Award for Best
Wine Exported from Australia in '95. It is now owned by the Schiavello family, which is
contemplating increasing the plantings with Italian varieties such as nebbiolo and arneis. The
gold medal won by the 2007 Reserve Chardonnay at the 18th Annual Concours des Vins du
Victoria in November '08 proves the Mackey Award was no fluke.

ΨΨΨΨΨ **Reserve Upper Goulburn Chardonnay 2008** Here the components come
together far more convincingly than they do with the red wines; attractive
nectarine and grapefruit has been embellished by barrel fermentation and
12 months' maturation in French oak; opens delicately, but gains power through to
the finish. Screwcap. 13% alc. **Rating** 90 **To** 2013 $40

GISA ★★★☆

3 Hawke Street, Linden Park, SA 5065 **Region** South Australia
T (08) 8338 2123 **F** (08) 8338 2123 **www**.gisa.com.au **Open** Not
Winemaker Mat Henbest **Est.** 2006 **Cases** 3000
Mat and Lisa Henbest have chosen a clever name for their virtual winery – GISA standing
for Geographic Indication South Australia – neatly covering the fact that their grapes come
variously from the Adelaide Hills (Sauvignon Blanc), McLaren Vale (Shiraz Viognier) and
Barossa Valley (Reserve Shiraz). It in turn reflects Mat's long apprenticeship in the wine
industry, as a child living on his parents' vineyard, then working in retail trade while he
pursued tertiary qualifications, and thereafter wholesaling wine to the retail and restaurant
trade. He then moved to Haselgrove, where he spent five years working closely with the small
winemaking team, refining his concept of style, and gaining experience on the other side of
the fence of the marketing equation.

ΨΨΨΨΨ **Round Adelaide Hills Sauvignon Blanc 2009** Has herb, asparagus and citrus
aromas and flavours; the palate has very good line and flow, finishing with citrussy
acidity and some mineral notes. Screwcap. 12.5% alc. **Rating** 92 **To** 2010 $18

Gisborne Peak   ★★★★

69 Short Road, Gisborne South, Vic 3437 **Region** Macedon Ranges
T (03) 5428 2228 **F** (03) 5428 4816 **www**.gisbornepeakwines.com.au **Open** 7 days 11–5
Winemaker John Ellis **Est.** 1978 **Cases** 1800 **Vyds** 4.55 ha
Bob Nixon began the development of Gisborne Peak way back in 1978, planting his dream
vineyard row-by-row. (Bob is married to Barbara Nixon, founder of Victoria Winery Tours.)
The tasting room has wide shaded verandahs, plenty of windows and sweeping views. The
vineyard is planted to chardonnay, pinot noir, semillon, riesling and lagrein.

ȲȲȲȲȲ **Mawarra Vineyard Macedon Ranges Unwooded Chardonnay 2009**
✪   Light straw-green; the bouquet is on the quiet side, but the palate has plenty to
            say with its nectarine, fig and citrus flavours; good example of the genre. Screwcap.
            13.3% alc. **Rating** 90 **To** 2013 $21.15
            Mawarra Vineyard Reserve Pinot Noir 2008 While clearly a sister of Two
            Blocks, this has more fruit weight, both cherry and plum coming into play, the
            mouthfeel a little more supple, but still having savoury/spicy notes to provide
            texture. Screwcap. 13.1% alc. **Rating** 90 **To** 2013 $29.70

ȲȲȲȲ **Mawarra Vineyard Duet Macedon Ranges Unwooded Chardonnay**
✪   **Semillon 2008** Bright, clear colour; the wine isn't green or even grassy, just clean
            and fresh, with white fruits and a touch of citrus; clean, balanced finish. Screwcap.
            13.3% alc. **Rating** 89 **To** 2012 $18
            Mawarra Vineyard Macedon Ranges Pinot Rose 2008 Rating 89
            To 2011 $21.60
            Mawarra Vineyard Two Blocks Blend Macedon Ranges Pinot Noir 2008
            Rating 89 **To** 2012 $25.20
            Mawarra Vineyard Allegro Semi-Sweet Semillon 2008 Rating 89
            To 2012 $19.80
            Mawarra Vineyard Macedon Ranges Sparkling Pinot Noir 2008
            Rating 87 **To** 2010 $26.55

Glaetzer Wines   ★★★★★

Lot 5 Gomersal Road, Tanunda, SA 5352 (postal) **Region** Barossa Valley
T (08) 8563 0947 **F** (08) 8563 3781 **www**.glaetzer.com **Open** Not
Winemaker Ben Glaetzer **Est.** 1996 **Cases** 15 000
Colin Glaetzer and son Ben are almost as well known in SA wine circles as Wolf Blass
winemaker John Glaetzer, Colin's twin brother. Glaetzer Wines purchases all its grapes from
the Ebenezer subregion of the Barossa Valley, principally from fifth-generation growers. Its
four wines (Amon-Ra Shiraz, Anaperenna Shiraz Cabernet Sauvignon, Bishop Shiraz and
Wallace Shiraz Grenache) are all made under contract at Barossa Vintners in what might be
termed a somewhat incestuous relationship because of the common links in ownership of the
very successful Barossa Vintners business. Exports to all major markets.

ȲȲȲȲȲ **Amon-Ra Unfiltered Barossa Valley Shiraz 2008** Dense purple-crimson; the
            bouquet is redolent of black fruits and licorice, the full-bodied palate a masterpiece
            of winemaking, rich and thickly textured on the mid-palate, then slimming
            down on the finish, with savoury notes inviting the next glass. Cork. 14.5% alc.
            Rating 96 **To** 2030 $90
✪   **Bishop Barossa Valley Shiraz 2008** Deep, dense purple; a more immediately
            complex bouquet has elements of spice and herb that come through on the lively
            medium- to full-bodied palate; there is a myriad of flavours to be found, yet
            they present a coherent whole through to the long finish. Screwcap. 14.5% alc.
            Rating 96 **To** 2023 $33
✪   **Wallace Barossa Valley Shiraz Grenache 2008** Strong crimson-purple; only
            Glaetzer would find Barossa Valley grenache of this quality and style, and blend it
            so synergistically with shiraz; the wine is ready to drink now, but will easily see out
            a decade or more. Screwcap. 14.5% alc. **Rating** 94 **To** 2020 $23

🍇 Glaetzer-Dixon Family Winemakers   ★★★★

197 Goulburn Street, West Hobart, Tas 7000 (postal) **Region** Southern Tasmania
T (03) 6248 5844 **F** (03) 6248 5855 **www**.gdfwinemakers.com **Open** Not
Winemaker Nick Glaetzer **Est.** 2008 **Cases** 900

History does not relate what Nick Glaetzer's high-profile Barossa Valley winemaker relatives thought of his decision to move to Tasmania in 2005, commencing a search for cool-grown, super-premium vineyards to make cutting-edge cool-climate styles. Obviously wife Sally approves, and Nick has a full-time job as one of the winemakers at Frogmore Creek. While his winemaking career began in the Barossa Valley, he then reached into scattered parts of the New World and Old World alike, working successively in Languedoc, the Pfaltz, Margaret River, Riverland, Sunraysia, Hunter Valley and Burgundy. It is a virtual winery operation, an eminently sensible first step. Exports to Hong Kong.

🍷🍷🍷🍷🍷 **Uberblanc Riesling 2009** Floral spice and talc aromas; the palate is full of energy, with lime, lemon and green apple; typically potent Tasmanian acidity, but not to the detriment of the wine; low alcohol adds drive. Screwcap. 11.9% alc. **Rating** 90 **To** 2017 $24
Reveur Pinot Noir 2008 Purple hue, although not intense; the structure of the wine is foremost, fine savoury tannins evident from start to finish, and carrying the black cherry and dark plum fruit. Screwcap. 13.5% alc. **Rating** 90 **To** 2013 $48

🍷🍷🍷🍷 **Avance Pinot Noir 2009 Rating** 88 **To** 2012 $28
Mon Pere Shiraz 2008 Rating 87 **To** 2012 $42

Glaymond/Tscharke Wines   ★★★★★

Seppeltsfield Road, Marananga, SA 5360 **Region** Barossa Valley
T 0438 628 178 **F** (08) 8562 4920 **www**.tscharke.com.au **Open** By appt
Winemaker Damien Tscharke **Est.** 2001 **Cases** 4000 **Vyds** 23.1 ha

Damien Tscharke grew up in the Barossa Valley among the vineyards at Seppeltsfield and Marananga. In 2001 he began the production of Glaymond, four estate-grown wines based on what he calls the classic varieties (following the trend of having catchy, snappy names), followed by wines under the Tscharke brand using the alternative varieties of tempranillo, graciano, zinfandel, montepulciano and savagnin. Like the Glaymond wines, these are estate-grown, albeit in very limited quantities. Exports to the US and other major markets.

🍷🍷🍷🍷🍷 **Glaymond Fortune Marananga Shiraz 2005** Deep colour; concentrated aromas of licorice, dark chocolate, red and black fruits and a generous dollop of toasty oak; the palate reveals the quality of the winemaking and the fruit, with a lovely expression of blackberry and lively acidity providing complexity, line and length; a show stopper, but not overdone. Cork. 15% alc. **Rating** 95 **To** 2025 $100 BE
Glaymond Distinction Barossa Valley Shiraz 2005 Licorice, polished leather and black fruit aromas lead into a profound, velvety palate with a near-identical array of flavours; supple finish. Cork. 15% alc. **Rating** 94 **To** 2018 $90

🍷🍷🍷🍷🍷 **Tscharke The Curse Barossa Valley Zinfandel 2008 Rating** 93 **To** 2015 $34 BE
Tscharke Lumberjack Vintage Fortified 2004 Rating 93 **To** 2014 $30
Glaymond The Distance Barossa Valley Shiraz 2007 Rating 92 **To** 2020 $30 BE
The Master Barossa Valley Montepulciano 2008 Rating 90 **To** 2018 $34
✪ **Eva Barossa Valley Savagnin 2009** The back label comes with what appears to be a marriage proposal by Damien to Eva. This apart, I prefer the acidity in this semi-sweet version to that of the dry. Screwcap. 8% alc. **Rating** 90 **To** 2014 $15

🍷🍷🍷🍷 **Tscharke Girl Talk 2009 Rating** 89 **To** 2011 $21
Tscharke The Potter Barossa Valley Garnacha 2008 Rating 89 **To** 2013 $25
Glaymond Asif Barossa Valley Cabernet Sauvignon 2007 Rating 88 **To** 2014 $30 BE

Glen Eldon Wines ★★★★☆

Lot 100 Hamiltons Road, Springton, SA 5235 **Region** Barossa Valley
T (08) 8568 2644 **F** (08) 8568 2144 **www**.gleneldonwines.com.au **Open** By appt
Winemaker Richard Sheedy **Est.** 1997 **Cases** 6000 **Vyds** 50 ha
Owners Richard and Mary Sheedy (and their four children) have established the Glen Eldon
property in the Eden Valley. The shiraz and cabernet sauvignon come from their vineyards in
the Barossa Valley; riesling, viognier and merlot from contract-grown fruit; the riesling from
the Eden Valley. Exports to the UK, the US, Canada, Switzerland and China.

ΨΨΨΨΨ **Dry Bore Barossa Shiraz 2006** Deep, dark colour; has a deep well of
✪ blackberry, plum and dark chocolate on both the bouquet and medium- to full-
bodied palate; the tannins and overall extract have been well controlled. Screwcap.
14.5% alc. **Rating** 94 **To** 2021 $25

ΨΨΨΨΨ **Barossa Cabernet Sauvignon 2006 Rating** 93 **To** 2021 $25

ΨΨΨΨ **Eden Valley Riesling 2008 Rating** 87 **To** 2014 $16 BE
Sparkling Cinnabar 2004 Rating 87 **To** 2012 $28

Glen Holme Vineyards ★★★★

White Park Road, Bangor via Wirrabara, SA 5481 **Region** Southern Flinders Ranges
T (08) 8666 5222 **F** (08) 8666 5222 **Open** Fri–Mon 10–5
Winemaker Stephen John Wines (red), University of Adelaide (white) **Est.** 1998 **Cases**
560 **Vyds** 11.73 ha
David and Margaret Blesing have slightly more than 11.5 ha of vineyards, with shiraz (8.35
ha) and cabernet sauvignon (2.35 ha) dominant. The remainder is planted to merlot, nebbiolo,
riesling, semillon and chardonnay. All but 5 tonnes of the shiraz is sold to Peter Lehmann
Wines, its quality attracting a substantial bonus payment on top of the base contract price. A
cellar door opened in 2008, adding to the range of cellar doors now available to visitors to
the beautiful Southern Flinders Ranges.

ΨΨΨΨΨ **Blesing's Garden Southern Flinders Ranges Shiraz 2008** Dense purple; the
bouquet is stacked with black fruits, as is the full-bodied palate, adding licorice and
dark chocolate to the blackberry and prune fruit; picked a little too late, but an
impressive barbecue style. Screwcap. 15% alc. **Rating** 90 **To** 2023
✪ **Blesing's Garden Southern Flinders Ranges Cabernet Sauvignon 2008**
Strong red-purple; an unequivocally full-bodied cabernet, with abundant black
fruits that have stood up well to the substantial oak; a little old-fashioned, but a big
bang of flavour for the buck. Screwcap. 14.5% alc. **Rating** 90 **To** 2018 $20

ΨΨΨΨ **Blesing's Garden Southern Flinders Ranges Riesling 2009 Rating** 87
To 2014 $18
Blesing's Garden Southern Flinders Ranges Chardonnay 2009 Rating 87
To 2013 $18
Blesing's Garden Southern Flinders Ranges Nebbiolo 2008 Rating 87
To 2014 $20

GlenAyr ★★★☆

Back Tea Tree Road, Richmond, Tas 7025 **Region** Southern Tasmania
T (03) 6260 2388 **F** (03) 6260 2691 **www**.glenayrwines.com.au **Open** Mon–Fri 8–5
Winemaker Contract **Est.** 1975 **Cases** 500
The now fully mature Tolpuddle Vineyard, managed by Warren Schasser, who is completing
a Bachelor of Applied Science (viticulture) at CSU, provides the grapes that go to make the
GlenAyr wines. The major part of the grape production continues to be sold to Domaine
Chandon and Hardys, with most going to make premium table wine, and a lesser amount to
premium sparkling.

ΨΨΨΨ̰ **Tolpuddle Vineyards Chardonnay 2008** Light straw-green; light, fine and
elegant; very good fruit, oak, acid, balance and length; citrussy; Chablis style.
Screwcap. 13% alc. **Rating** 90 **To** 2015 $23

ΨΨΨΨ **Tolpuddle Vintage Cuvee 2007 Rating** 89 **To** 2013 $29
Cabernet Sauvignon 2008 Rating 87 **To** 2015

Glendonbrook   ★★★☆

Lot 2 Park Street, East Gresford, NSW 2311 **Region** Upper Hunter Valley
T (02) 4938 9666 **F** (02) 4938 9766 **www**.glendonbrook.com **Open** W'ends &
public hols 10.30–4.30
Winemaker Geoff Broadfield **Est.** 2000 **Cases** 25 000 **Vyds** 12.5 ha
Sydney businessman Tom Smith and wife Terese purchased the Bingleburra homestead at East
Gresford in the mid-1990s. The 600-ha property raises beef cattle, but in 1997 vines were
planted (8.3 ha shiraz, 4.2 ha verdelho). This in turn led to the construction (in 2001) of a
$2 million, 300-tonne capacity winery. The estate production is supplemented by contract-
grown grapes, and the winery offers contract winemaking facilities for others. It marks a major
return to the Gresford area, where Dr Henry Lindeman established his Cawarra vineyards in
the mid-1800s.

ΨΨΨΨ̰ **Semillon 2008** Bright straw-green; a particularly intense palate, with grass, citrus
✪   and mineral characters carried along with a wave of brisk acidity; needs time to
settle down, but will do so. Screwcap. 12% alc. **Rating** 91 **To** 2023 $15

ΨΨΨΨ **Verdelho 2008** Has all the typical fruit salad and a drizzle of citrus characters
✪   that lead the appeal of the variety – modest appeal in my book, it must be said.
Screwcap. 13% alc. **Rating** 88 **To** 2012 $15

✪   **Cabernet Merlot 2006** Solid colour; a pleasant surprise, red and blackcurrant
fruits easily able to carry the regional nuances of leather and earth; some
development potential. Screwcap. 14% alc. **Rating** 88 **To** 2014 $15

✪   **Chardonnay 2007** Bright yellow-green; a generously flavoured palate riding
on peach and melon fruit, with just a touch of French oak. Screwcap. 13% alc.
Rating 87 **To** 2012 $15

Glenguin Estate   ★★★★★

Milbrodale Road, Broke, NSW 2330 **Region** Hunter Valley
T (02) 6579 1009 **F** (02) 6579 1009 **www**.glenguinestate.com.au **Open** 7 days 10–5
Winemaker Robin Tedder MW, Rhys Eather **Est.** 1993 **Cases** 3000 **Vyds** 10.3 ha
Glenguin Estate was established by the Tedder family, headed by Robin Tedder MW, close
to Broke and adjacent to Wollombi Brook. Here the backbone of the production comes
from 20-year-old plantings of semillon and shiraz. Small plantings of tannat, viognier and
chardonnay have since been added. Vineyard manager, Andrew Tedder, who has considerable
experience with organics and biodynamics, is overseeing the ongoing development of
Glenguin's organic program. Exports to the UK, Hong Kong, Singapore and NZ.

ΨΨΨΨΨ **Aristea Hunter Valley Shiraz 2007** Excellent crimson hue; an evocative
bouquet ranging through dominant black fruits and subtle regional earth and
leather notes, oak in the background, the medium- to full-bodied palate bringing
some licorice into play, tannins in great balance; 240 dozen made. Screwcap.
14% alc. **Rating** 96 **To** 2047 $54

School House Shiraz 2007 The twist of co-fermented viognier has taken
the colour to purple and lifted the fragrance of the bouquet; the medium-
bodied palate, too, has energy and drive, with spicy characters emerging with the
blackberry and plum fruit. A subtle nod to the Rhône Valley with the Burgundy-
shaped bottle. Screwcap. 14% alc. **Rating** 95 **To** 2027 $31.50

ΨΨΨΨ♀   **Stonybroke Shiraz 2007** Crimson-purple; this is the most powerful and
✪   concentrated of the '07 Glenguin Shirazs, albeit lacking the finesse and balance
of the Aristea or the fruit of School House. What it does have is layered black
fruits and no less layered tannins. Demands time. Screwcap. 14% alc. **Rating** 93
To 2032 $20.70
Protos Chardonnay 2009 Rating 92 To 2017 $27

ΨΨΨΨ   **Old Broke Block Semillon 2009 Rating** 89 To 2015 $18
Ironbark Tannat 2007 Rating 88 To 2027 $31.50

Glenwillow Vineyard   ★★★★☆

40 McIntyre Street, White Hills, Vic 3550 (postal) **Region** Bendigo
T 0428 461 076 **F** (03) 5434 1340 **www**.glenwillow.com.au **Open** Not
Winemaker Matt Hunter (Contract) **Est.** 1999 **Cases** 450 **Vyds** 2.8 ha
Peter and Cherryl Fyffe began their vineyard at Yandoit Creek, 10 km south of Newstead,
in 1999, planting 1.8 ha of shiraz and 0.3 ha of cabernet sauvignon, and branching out with
0.6 ha of nebbiolo and 0.1 ha of barbera. The choice of Cyclone Gully for the basic wines (the
Reserve wines are not made every year) might be considered a little ghoulish. In Jan 1978 a
cyclone moved up Sandon-Yandoit Creek Road, causing much property damage, and killing
two elderly travellers pulled from their car by the cyclone.

ΨΨΨΨΨ   **Bendigo Shiraz 2008** Good hue and depth; a very attractive wine, offering
✪   all the richness of Bendigo shiraz, yet with great elegance; the medium-bodied
palate has lifted fruit and excellent texture, plus admirable line, length and balance.
Screwcap. 14.5% alc. **Rating** 95 To 2020 $24

ΨΨΨΨ♀   **Reserve Bendigo Shiraz 2007 Rating** 90 To 2020 $30

Goaty Hill Wines   ★★★★☆

Auburn Road, Kayena, Tas 7270 **Region** Northern Tasmania
T 1300 819 997 **F** 1300 819 907 **www**.goatyhill.com **Open** 7 days 10–5 (Aug to May)
or by appt
Winemaker Fran Austin (Contract) **Est.** 1998 **Cases** 3000 **Vyds** 19.5 ha
The partners in Goaty Hill are six friends from two families who moved from Victoria to
Tasmania and, they say, 'were determined to build something for the future while having fun'.
The partners in question are Markus Maislinger, Natasha and Tony Nieuwhof, Kristine Grant,
and Margaret and Bruce Grant, and in 1998 they began the planting of pinot noir, riesling,
chardonnay and sauvignon blanc. Part of the grape production is sold to Bay of Fires and, in
return, the highly talented Bay of Fires winemaker, Fran Austin, makes the Goaty Hill wines
from that part of the annual crop retained by the partners. Goaty Hill's first wine show entries
yielded a string of medals.

ΨΨΨΨ♀   **Pinot Noir 2009** Good hue and depth; spiced plum aromas are replayed on the
palate; perfectly pitched tannins provide texture and length; in its infancy, but will
develop very well. Screwcap. 14% alc. **Rating** 93 To 2016 $31.95
Riesling 2009 Light green-straw; quite intense and focused; has an elegant
and pure stream of lime flavours; handles a touch of sweetness well. Screwcap.
11.9% alc. **Rating** 90 To 2017 $23.95
Sauvignon Blanc 2009 Well made; good fruit/acid balance; light touches of
gooseberry/tropical fruit aromas and flavours. Well above Tasmanian average.
Screwcap. 11.9% alc. **Rating** 90 To 2012 $25.95

God's Hill Wines   ★★★★

Lot 211 Gods Hill Road, Lyndoch, SA 5351 **Region** Barossa Valley
T 0412 836 004 **F** (08) 8331 9895 **www**.godshillwines.com **Open** By appt
Winemaker Charlie Scalzi **Est.** 1998 **Cases** 1400 **Vyds** 12 ha

Carmine (Charlie) Scalzi arrived in Australia with his parents in 1960, the family settling in Adelaide. His final education was mechanical engineering, and at the age of 24 he established Monza Motors, specialising in Italian cars such as Ferrari and Alfa Romeo. In 1998, having followed in the footsteps of grandfather and father with home winemaking, he purchased a 40-ha property near Lyndoch, planting 4.5 ha each of shiraz and cabernet sauvignon, 2 ha of merlot and 1 ha of chardonnay. Most of the grapes are taken by Dorrien Estate, with a small amount retained for the God's Hill label.

ÏÏÏÏÏ **Menzel Barossa Valley Shiraz 2006** Good hue and depth; a potent wine, with layers of black fruits, licorice, prune and dark chocolate; against all the odds, is not extractive, and doesn't seem alcoholic. Silver medal Great Australian Wine Challenge '09. Cork. 16% alc. **Rating** 92 **To** 2016 $39.50

Amo Rosso 2006 Bright crimson, preserved by the screwcap; a more convincing wine than Menzel, bordering on elegance, but not sacrificing length or intensity to its complex array of predominantly black fruits. Cabernet Sauvignon/Shiraz/Merlot. 14% alc. **Rating** 92 **To** 2021 $38

Black Olive Barossa Valley Merlot 2006 The '06 vintage has worked its magic here, with its mix of ripe plum, blackcurrant, spice and earth components; the texture is good, as is the balance, less clear is the varietal character. Screwcap. 15.1% alc. **Rating** 90 **To** 2015 $38

ÏÏÏÏ **Permanent Arm Barossa Valley Cabernet Sauvignon 2006** Rating 88 **To** 2014 $39.50

III Rows Barossa Valley Unwooded Chardonnay 2009 Rating 87 **To** 2011 $22

Golden Grove Estate ★★★★☆

Sundown Road, Ballandean, Qld 4382 **Region** Granite Belt
T (07) 4684 1291 **F** (07) 4684 1247 **www**.goldengroveestate.com.au **Open** 7 days 9–4
Winemaker Raymond Costanzo **Est.** 1993 **Cases** 3000 **Vyds** 12.4 ha
Golden Grove Estate was established by Mario and Sebastiana Costanzo in 1946, producing stone fruits and table grapes for the fresh fruit market. The first wine grapes (shiraz) were planted in 1972, but it was not until '85, when ownership passed to son Sam and his wife Grace, that the use of the property began to change. In 1993 chardonnay and merlot joined the shiraz, followed by cabernet sauvignon, sauvignon blanc and semillon. The baton has been passed down another generation to Ray Costanzo, who has lifted the quality of the wines remarkably, and has also planted tempranillo, durif, barbera, malbec, mourvedre, vermentino and nero d'Avola. Its trophies and gold medals from the Australian Small Winemakers Show '08 are to be taken seriously: this is a well-judged show with entries from all over Australia, and has been running for over 30 years.

ÏÏÏÏÏ **Nero d'Avola 2009** Bright youthful crimson; a strong bouquet with ultra-juicy plum and black cherry fruit flavours, then good tannins to close. Full of promise. Screwcap. 13.1% alc. **Rating** 94 **To** 2019 $40

ÏÏÏÏÏ **Granite Belt Tempranillo 2008** Bright crimson hue; a fragrant bouquet of red
✪ and black cherries is followed by a supple and juicy palate, the cherry fruit joined by restrained French oak. Screwcap. 14% alc. **Rating** 92 **To** 2015 $22

✪ **Accommodation Creek Mediterranean Red 2009** Bright purple-crimson; the blend of Tempranillo/Durif/Barbera comes together very well, the flavours bright and long, with an appealing crisp edge. Silver medal alternative Wines Show '09 well deserved. Screwcap. 14% alc. **Rating** 91 **To** 2016 $18

✪ **Granite Belt Barbera 2008** Bright crimson; has the juicy raspberry/red cherry fruit of barbera, and also good texture and structure to lift it out of the normal style. Screwcap. 14.5% alc. **Rating** 91 **To** 2016 $20

Granite Belt Durif 2008 Rating 91 **To** 2017 $28

Granite Belt Malbec 2008 Rating 90 **To** 2016 $28

♥♥♥♥ Granite Belt Sauvignon Blanc 2009 Rating 89 To 2011 $22
Accommodation Creek Granite Belt Semillon Sauvignon Blanc 2009
Rating 89 To 2011 $18
Granite Belt Shiraz 2008 Rating 89 To 2018 $20
Castalina 2009 Rating 88 To 2011 $18

Golders Vineyard ★★★★☆

Bridport Road, Pipers Brook, Tas 7254 **Region** Northern Tasmania
T (03) 6395 4142 **F** (03) 6395 4142 **Open** By appt
Winemaker Richard Crabtree **Est.** 1991 **Cases** 600
Richard Crabtree continues to make the Golders Vineyard wines at the Delamere winery as
he has in the past. The 2.5-ha vineyard established by Crabtree has in fact been sold, and since
2006 grapes have been purchased from the Pipers River region.

♥♥♥♥♀ Pinot Noir 2007 Bright crimson-purple; fragrant red berry fruits run through a
pure, lively and fresh palate; there are some slightly green nuances that I am happy
to ignore. Rating 92 To 2014

♥♥♥♥ Pinot Noir 2008 Rating 88 To 2017 $25

Golding Wines ★★★

Western Branch Road, Lobethal, SA 5241 **Region** Adelaide Hills
T (08) 8389 5120 **F** (08) 8389 5290 www.goldingwines.com.au **Open** 7 days 11–4
Winemaker Michael Sykes, Darren Golding **Est.** 2002 **Cases** 1500 **Vyds** 18.53 ha
The Golding family has lived in the Lobethal area of the Adelaide Hills for several generations,
and has trimmed its once larger viticultural holdings to concentrate on their Western Branch
Road vineyard, planted to sauvignon blanc, savagnin, chardonnay, pinot gris and pinot noir.
The Golding Wines brand was created in 2002, the owners being Darren and Lucy Golding.
In 2006 Darren secured some Marlborough sauvignon blanc through his brother-in-law,
who happens to be managing director of NZ's largest independent contract winemaking
company. This has resulted in three wines: The Local (100% estate-grown); The Tourist (100%
Marlborough); and The Leap (51% estate-grown/49% Marlborough). Exports to Hong Kong,
Philippines and China.

♥♥♥♥ La Francesca Adelaide Hills Savagnin 2009 Gleaming green-quartz; is
intense, almost to the point of aggression, with potent lemon zest flavours and
brisk acidity. Just where the vines/grapes will head when mature is anyone's guess.
Screwcap. 14% alc. Rating 89 To 2013 $25

Good Catholic Girl Wines ★★★★☆

Box 526, Clare, SA 5453 **Region** Clare Valley
T 0419 822 909 www.goodcatholicgirl.com.au **Open** Not
Winemaker Julie Ann Barry **Est.** 2005 **Cases** 460 **Vyds** 1 ha
Good Catholic Girl is the venture of Julie Ann Barry, one of the many children of the late
Jim Barry. She says, 'Having been born into a Catholic wine family, in vintage, my fate was
sealed. My Limerick Vineyard was planted in the Armagh area of the Clare Valley in 1997,
cuttings taken from my father's famed Armagh shiraz vines planted across the paddock.' The
Shiraz is named The James Brazill, Jim Barry's Christian names. She takes up the story thus:
'In 2008 I made my first Clare Valley Riesling "Teresa" named after my mother, who is the
true GCG (good catholic girl), and loves Clare Riesling, and who may in time consume my
entire production of 108 dozen!' Exports to the US.

♥♥♥♥♥ The James Brazill Clare Valley Shiraz 2007 Gains additional divine approval
✪ having been picked on St Patrick's Day (Mar 17), every bit as propitious as the
biodynamicacists' fruit day, for this is a most attractive medium-bodied wine;
very supple (not normally a Clare Valley feature) and has good length. Screwcap.
15% alc. Rating 94 To 2022 $30

♔♔♔♔♕ **Teresa Clare Valley Riesling 2009** Light straw-green; a clean but as yet reticent
✪ bouquet, the apple nuances gaining traction on the energetic palate where lime/
citrus joins the dalliance and provides a juicy finish. Could develop very well
indeed. Screwcap. 11.8% alc. **Rating** 92 **To** 2019 $25

Goombargona Park ★★★

Near Nug Nug, Vic 3737 (postal) **Region** Alpine Valleys
T (03) 5754 2224 www.goombargonapark.com.au **Open** Not
Winemaker Ian Black **Est.** 1996 **Cases** 300 **Vyds** 2 ha
What a tale to tell. Ian Black (with wife Clare Leeuwin-Clark) has myriad connections with
wine growers (and consumers), including a long-ago family relationship with Francois de
Castella, one of the heroes in the development of the Yarra Valley in the 19th century. Since
then, the contacts have become rather more direct, firstly through his two sons completing
oenology degrees at CSU, and – prior to that time – an on-again, off-again career as an
occasional weekend grapegrower. Goombargona Park (with its wonderful address, no fax, no
email and only a postcode to direct the delivery of mail) is his third and most serious wine
venture. The fortified wines are made by Ian, not purchased from others.

♔♔♔♔ **Pinot Noir 2008** Colour shows first signs of development; a quite fragrant and
spicy bouquet hinting at the tangy, slightly minty, palate that follows. Screwcap.
13% alc. **Rating** 88 **To** 2013 $30

Goona Warra Vineyard ★★★★☆

790 Sunbury Road, Sunbury, Vic 3429 **Region** Sunbury
T (03) 9740 7766 **F** (03) 9744 7648 www.goonawarra.com.au **Open** 7 days 10–5
Winemaker John Barnier, Adrian Sautolin **Est.** 1863 **Cases** 3000 **Vyds** 6.92 ha
A historic stone winery, originally established under this name by a 19th-century Victorian
premier. A brief interlude as part of The Wine Investment Fund in 2001 is over, the Barniers
having bought back the farm. Excellent tasting facilities, an outstanding venue for weddings
and receptions, and lunch on Sunday. Exports to Canada, China, Taiwan and Korea.

♔♔♔♔♔ **Sunbury Shiraz 2008** A beautifully balanced cool-climate shiraz that wraps its
power in a velvet glove. There are typical cool-climate pepper and spice notes to
both the bouquet and palate that is sustained by fine, lingering tannins. Trophy
Winewise '09. Screwcap. 13.5% alc. **Rating** 96 **To** 2023 $32

Gotham ★★★★☆

PO Box 343, Mona Vale, NSW 1660 **Region** South Australia
T 0412 124 811 **F** (02) 9973 3586 **Open** Not
Winemaker Bruce Clugston **Est.** 2004 **Cases** 45 000
Bruce Clugston, with a long involvement in the wine industry, purchases grapes from various
vineyards in Langhorne Creek, McLaren Vale, Barossa Valley and Clare Valley. It is one of the
larger virtual wineries in SA, and its production underlines its commercial success. The 2005
Shiraz was made from 5 tonnes of premium shiraz from Jon Pfeiffer's outstanding vineyard at
Marananga in the Barossa Valley. Exports to the US, Canada, Germany and Denmark.

♔♔♔♔♔ **Reserve Old Vine Barossa Shiraz 2007** From three vineyards, respectively
planted in the 1880s (Nuriootpa), 1926 (Greenock) and '29 (Eden Valley), the
wine spending 28 months in new French oak; it is plush and full-bodied, the
oak as obvious as expected, but curiously seems to tone down the impact of
the alcohol, the lingering tannins on the finish likewise. Screwcap. 15.7% alc.
Rating 94 **To** 2032 $25

♔♔♔♔♕ **Clare Valley Riesling 2009** Light straw-green; a fragrant lime-infused bouquet
✪ is reflected in the delicate, fresh palate; hasn't been sweetened for impact. Screwcap.
12% alc. **Rating** 91 **To** 2014 $14

✪ **Mastermind The Queen Tumbarumba Chardonnay 2008** Has all the characteristics of Tumbarumba chardonnay, ranging fluidly through white peach, melon and grapefruit; you don't notice the oak, which is all but irrelevant. Screwcap. 14% alc. **Rating** 91 To 2014 $12

✪ **McLaren Vale Shiraz 2008** Good hue and depth; again, a lot of oak (100% new American) but also an abundance of very ripe blackberry, prune and plum fruit; picked just in time. Screwcap. 14.9% alc. **Rating** 91 To 2018 $14
Stalking Horse Adelaide Hills Shiraz 2008 Rating 90 To 2018 $20

🍷🍷🍷🍷 **Adelaide Hills McLaren Vale Sauvignon Blanc Semillon 2008** Bright
✪ yellow-green; a 52/48 blend, the lifted fruits of the sauvignon blanc now in retreat, leaving the play to the semillon. Screwcap. 13% alc. **Rating** 89 To 2010 $14

✪ **Langhorne Creek Shiraz 2008** Medium red-purple; a shiraz with more or less equal proportions of fruit, dark chocolate and vanillan/mocha oak, the oak infusion through barrel fermentation and 10 months' maturation. Screwcap. 15.5% alc. **Rating** 89 To 2015 $14
Reserve Old Vine Barossa Valley Mataro 2007 Rating 89 To 2016 $25
Mastermind The Rook McLaren Vale Shiraz 2008 Rating 88 To 2018 $16
Reserve Old Vine Barossa Valley Grenache 2007 Rating 88 To 2012 $25
McLaren Vale Chardonnay 2008 Rating 87 To 2012 $14

Goulburn Terrace ★★★

340 High Street, Nagambie, Vic 3608 **Region** Nagambie Lakes
T (03) 5794 2828 **F** (03) 5794 1854 **www**.goulburnterrace.com.au **Open** By appt
Winemaker Dr Mike Boudry, Greta Moon **Est.** 1993 **Cases** 1000 **Vyds** 6.8 ha
Dr Mike Boudry and Greta Moon have established their vineyard on the west bank of the Goulburn River, 8 km south of Lake Nagambie. Planting began in 1993: 2.2 ha of chardonnay on the alluvial soils (10 000 years old, adjacent to the river), and 2.3 ha of cabernet sauvignon on a gravelly rise based on 400-million-year-old Devonian rocks; 1.2 ha of shiraz and 1.1 ha of marsanne followed later. The wines are made in small volumes, with open fermentation and hand-plunging of the reds; all are basket-pressed. Exports to Canada and Japan.

🍷🍷🍷🍷 **Nagambie Chardonnay 2008** Made from biodynamically grown grapes; a soft wine, with peachy fruit and obvious oak; earlier picking may have been a rewarding option. Cork. 14% alc. **Rating** 87 To 2011 $28

Goundrey ★★★★☆

Location 10460, Vasse Highway, Nannup, WA 6275 **Region** Western Australia Zone
T 1800 088 711 **F** (08) 8392 2202 **www**.goundreywines.com.au **Open** Not
Winemaker Garth Cliff **Est.** 1976 **Cases** NFP
Goundrey is part of the Constellation Wines Australia (CWA) empire. In 2008 it was put on the market by CWA, together with its 237 ha of estate vineyards. In 2009 it was purchased by comparative minnow West Cape Howe. The Goundrey brand name has been retained by CWA, and significant quantities of wine will continue to be made from its WA base, with 100% of the Goundrey-grown grapes sold back to CWA pursuant to an ongoing contract with West Cape Howe. Exports to all major markets.

🍷🍷🍷🍷🍷 **G Pemberton Sauvignon Blanc Semillon 2009** Vivid hue; citrus, tropical
✪ and pungent cut grass bouquet; plenty of depth on the palate, with the acidity providing freshness to finish. Gold medal Sydney Wine Show '10. Screwcap. 13% alc. **Rating** 94 To 2012 $21.50 BE

🍷🍷🍷🍷 **Homestead Sauvignon Blanc 2009** Rating 88 To 2010 $17.50
Homestead Cabernet Merlot 2008 Rating 87 To 2015 $17.50 BE

Gracebrook Vineyards ★★★★☆

4446 Wangaratta–Whitfield Road, King Valley, Vic 3678 **Region** King Valley
T (03) 5729 3562 **F** (03) 5729 3684 www.gracebrook.com.au **Open** 7 days 10–5
Winemaker David Maples, King Valley Wines (Gary Wall) **Est.** 1989 **Cases** 10 000
Vyds 35.75 ha
David and Rhonda Maples' vineyard is planted to merlot, shiraz, riesling, cabernet sauvignon, sangiovese, chardonnay, dolcetto, sagrantino and savagnin, plus trial rows of moscato giallo, muscadelle, muscat blanc, cabernet franc and muscat rouge. Their cellar door, housed in stables built in the 1880s, has panoramic views of the King Valley and can cater for functions/weddings for up to 100 people. Exports to Malaysia, Singapore, Hong Kong, China and NZ.

♀♀♀♀♀ **King Valley Savagnin 2009** A flowery and perfumed bouquet, with a line of
✪   chalk coming through on the palate providing contrast before a twist of lemon/citrus on the finish. Screwcap. 11.5% alc. **Rating** 90 $18

♀♀♀♀ **King Valley Rosato 2009 Rating** 89 To 2010 $18
King Valley Sagrantino 2008 Rating 89 To 2013 $18
Sunshine King Valley Sparkling White NV Rating 89 To 2010 $18
King Valley Dolcetto 2009 Rating 88 To 2012 $18

Grampians Estate ★★★★★

1477 Western Highway, Great Western, Vic 3377 **Region** Grampians
T (03) 5354 6245 **F** (03) 5354 6257 www.grampiansestate.com.au **Open** 7 days 12–5
Winemaker Hamish Seabrook, Don Rowe, Tom Guthrie **Est.** 1989 **Cases** 1200 **Vyds** 8.6 ha
Graziers Sarah and Tom Guthrie began their diversification into wine in 1989, but their core business continues to be fat lamb and wool production. Both activities were ravaged by the 2006 bushfires, but each has recovered, that of their grapegrowing and winemaking rising like a phoenix from the ashes. They have acquired the Garden Gully winery at Great Western, giving them a cellar door presence and a vineyard of 2.4 ha of 60-year-old shiraz, and 3 ha of 45-year-old riesling vines. A feature of the cellar door is wine tutorials that can be booked at any time; the cellar door offers the full range of Grampians Estate wines and specially chosen wines from smaller local boutique wineries.

♀♀♀♀♀ **Black Sunday Friends Sparkling Shiraz 2006** An echo of the great Seppelt sparkling shirazs of the '40s and '50s; this wine has absolutely wonderful sweet shiraz fruit – not sugar sweetness – on the finish, and will develop for up to 20 years if well cellared. Crown seal. 14.6% alc. **Rating** 94 To 2026 $35
Rutherford Sparkling Shiraz 2006 Presumably bottle-fermented, but no mention of this; is well balanced, neither oak nor sweetness obvious, just gently spicy shiraz, perhaps with a touch of licorice; good length and balance. Crown seal. 14% alc. **Rating** 94 To 2015 $35

♀♀♀♀ **Kelly's Welcome Pinot Chardonnay 2008 Rating** 87 To 2013 $35

Granite Hills ★★★★★

1481 Burke and Wills Track, Baynton, Vic 3444 **Region** Macedon Ranges
T (03) 5423 7273 **F** (03) 5423 7288 www.granitehills.com.au **Open** 7 days 11–6
Winemaker Llew Knight, Ian Gunter **Est.** 1970 **Cases** 6000 **Vyds** 10.8 ha
Granite Hills is one of the enduring classics, pioneering the successful growing of riesling and shiraz in an uncompromisingly cool climate. It is based on riesling, chardonnay, shiraz, cabernet sauvignon, cabernet franc, merlot and pinot noir (the last also used in its sparkling wine). After a quiet period in the 1990s, it has been reinvigorated, with its original two icons once again to the fore. The Rieslings age superbly, and the Shiraz is at the forefront of the cool-climate school in Australia. Exports to Canada, Germany, Mauritius, Hong Kong, Singapore and China.

ŶŶŶŶŶ **Knight Macedon Ranges Riesling 2008** Light bright green-yellow; flowery
✪   apple and citrus aromas lead into a light but gloriously juicy palate, the finish long
       and cleansing. Screwcap. 12% alc. **Rating** 95 **To** 2023 $20

✪   **Knight Macedon Ranges Shiraz 2004** Has the hallmark spicy/peppery
       nuances of Granite Hills, but is otherwise unusual, reaching 15% alcohol and
       spending three years in oak – neither of which are the least obvious. Screwcap.
       Rating 95 **To** 2019 $32

       Knight Macedon Ranges Vintage 2001 Persistent mousse; complex wine, lots
       of biscuit and brioche; good length, dried fruits, dry finish, very fine. Crown seal.
       12.5% alc. **Rating** 95 **To** 2013 $40

✪   **Knight Macedon Ranges Riesling 2009** Light green-straw; the power of
       40-year-old vines, and the cold and windswept site, invest the wine with intensity
       and purity, although often needing some years in bottle to express its quality; the
       palate has a rare depth and richness of flavour, and its natural acidity will sustain it
       for a decade or more. Screwcap. 12.5% alc. **Rating** 94 **To** 2020 $22

ŶŶŶŶŶ **Nardoo Pinot Noir 2008** Developed, light colour; the gently aromatic bouquet
✪   does not foretell the thrust and energy of the red berry and spice fruits of the
       palate. The classy label design is in another galaxy compared to prior Granite Hill
       labels; Nardoo is an aquatic fern that grows after seasonal rain. Screwcap. 14% alc.
       Rating 91 **To** 2014 $22

✪   **Knight Macedon Ranges Pinot Noir 2006** Well made; good colour, texture
       and structure; black cherry spice and bramble nuances to both bouquet and palate;
       shrugs off its alcohol. Screwcap. 15% alc. **Rating** 91 **To** 2013 $24

       Knight Heathcote Shiraz 2001 Rating 91 **To** 2016 $30

✪   **Nardoo Semillon Sauvignon Blanc 2008** A lively, crisp and punchy wine,
       both components from the Macedon Ranges; herb, mineral and lemon characters
       give no sign of development, the finish quite juicy. Screwcap. 13% alc. **Rating** 90
       To 2012 $20

✪   **Nardoo Chardonnay 2007** Bright straw-green; a very refined chardonnay, with
       mineral and citrus nuances along with stone fruit; oak is very subtle, if it's there at
       all; good length. Screwcap. 13.5% alc. **Rating** 90 **To** 2013 $20

ŶŶŶŶ   **Nardoo Semillon Sauvignon Blanc 2009 Rating** 89 **To** 2014 $18
       Knight Macedon Ranges Chardonnay 2008 Rating 89 **To** 2012 $22 BE
       Nardoo Shiraz 2004 Rating 89 **To** 2012 $26
       Nardoo Premium Cuvee Brut NV Rating 89 **To** 2013 $25

Granite Ridge Wines   ★★★

Sundown Road, Ballandean, Qld 4382 **Region** Granite Belt
T (07) 4684 1263 **F** (07) 4684 1250 **www**.graniteridgewines.com.au **Open** 7 days 9–5
Winemaker Dennis and Juliane Ferguson **Est.** 1995 **Cases** 2000 **Vyds** 5 ha
Formerly known as Denlana Ferguson Estate Wines, Granite Ridge had considerable success
in the mid-1990s. Its Goldies Unwooded Chardonnay was the first Qld wine to be chosen as
the official Parliamentary wine of the Qld Government. Most of the production comes from
its estate vineyard, which is planted to pinot gris, chardonnay, verdelho, merlot, shiraz, petit
verdot, tempranillo and cabernet sauvignon. Exports to Singapore.

ŶŶŶŶ   **Granite Rock Shiraz 2006** Light red-purple; a light-bodied, savoury/spicy wine
       with good length and balance, and a certain degree of elegance. Screwcap. 13% alc.
       Rating 89 **To** 2015 $21

       Top Block Cabernet Sauvignon 2006 Strong red-purple; a medium-bodied
       wine with a mix of ripe blackcurrant, cassis and mint fruit offset by powerful,
       dryish tannins; is developing slowly and will continue to do so. Screwcap. 14% alc.
       Rating 89 **To** 2016 $35

Grant Burge ★★★★★

Jacobs Creek, Barossa Valley, SA 5352 **Region** Barossa Valley
T (08) 8563 3700 **F** (08) 8563 2807 **www**.grantburgewines.com.au **Open** 7 days 10–5
Winemaker Grant Burge, Craig Stansborough **Est.** 1988 **Cases** 400 000 **Vyds** 440 ha
As one might expect, this very experienced industry veteran makes consistently good, full-flavoured and smooth wines based on the pick of the crop of his extensive vineyard holdings; the immaculately restored/rebuilt stone cellar door sales buildings are another attraction. The provocatively named The Holy Trinity joins Shadrach and Meshach at the top of the range. In 1999 Grant Burge repurchased the farm from Mildara Blass by acquiring the Krondorf winery in Tanunda (not the brand), in which he made his first fortune. He renamed it Barossa Vines and opened a cellar door offering casual food. A third cellar door (Illaparra) is open on Murray Street, Tanunda. Exports to all major markets.

🍷🍷🍷🍷🍷 **Meshach 2005** Deep crimson-purple; at this stage the wine is full-bodied, compact and thickly textured, the flavours deep and layered in a black fruit spectrum; the abundant tannins and oak are in perfect balance with the fruit, and a recent vertical tasting put beyond doubt the great future this wine has. Once past its tenth birthday (cork permitting) it will reach its plateau of supple perfection that will last at least another decade. Shiraz. 14.5% alc. **Rating** 96 **To** 2025 $129.95
Filsell Old Vine Barossa Valley Shiraz 2007 Strong crimson-red; aromas of blackberry and plum come through strongly on the medium- to full-bodied palate, fine but savoury tannins and oak on the finish tying the fruit up nicely. Cork. 14.5% alc. **Rating** 94 **To** 2020 $39

🍷🍷🍷🍷🍷 **East Argyle Pinot Gris 2009 Rating** 93 **To** 2012 $21
Miamba Barossa Shiraz 2007 Rating 91 **To** 2022 $24.95
○ **Thorn Eden Valley Riesling 2009** An aromatic bouquet with elements of chalk and spice, then a full-flavoured robust palate, with ripe citrus fruit flavours. Screwcap. 12.5% alc. **Rating** 90 **To** 2016 $21
○ **Daly Road Barossa Shiraz Mourvedre 2007** Another Grant Burge wine to defy the '07 odds, with a bright array of red fruits in a fluid, medium-bodied framework; appealing juicy finish. Screwcap. 14.5% alc. **Rating** 90 **To** 2015 $21.95

🍷🍷🍷🍷 **Moscato 2009 Rating** 89 **To** 2010 $18
Hillcot Barossa Merlot 2008 Rating 89 **To** 2016 $21.95
Cameron Vale Barossa Cabernet Sauvignon 2007 Rating 89 **To** 2015 $24.95
Barossa Vines Shiraz 2007 Rating 88 **To** 2015 $17
Lily Farm Barossa Frontignan 2009 Rating 88 **To** 2011 $15.95

Grassy Point Wines ★★★★

Coatsworth Farm, 145 Coatsworth Road, Portarlington, Vic 3223 **Region** Geelong
T 0409 429 608 **F** (03) 5251 3969 **www**.grassypointwines.com.au **Open** By appt
Winemaker Provenance (Scott Ireland) **Est.** 1997 **Cases** 600 **Vyds** 6.3 ha
Partners Dr David Smith, Robert Bennett and Kerry Jones purchased this 32-ha undeveloped grazing property in 1997. Coatsworth Farm includes a vineyard (pinot noir, chardonnay, sauvignon blanc, shiraz, cabernet franc, merlot and malbec), South Devon beef cattle and Perendale/White Suffolk-cross lambs.

🍷🍷🍷🍷🍷 **Bellarine Peninsula Pinot Noir 2008** Crimson-red; pure pinot from start to finish, bringing together plum and black cherry on a supple and smooth palate; has all the requisites to build complexity over the next few years and become a very good wine. Screwcap. 13.2% alc. **Rating** 93 **To** 2015
Bellarine Peninsula Shiraz 2008 Light purple-crimson; a fragrant, spicy bouquet leads into a light- to medium-bodied palate, with bright and juicy red fruit flavours and a tangy, although not green, finish. Very good early drinking style. Screwcap. 13.2% alc. **Rating** 90 **To** 2013

🍷🍷🍷🍷 **Bellarine Peninsula Chardonnay 2008 Rating** 89 **To** 2014
Bellarine Peninsula Sauvignon Blanc 2009 Rating 88 **To** 2011 $16

Greenstone Vineyard   ★★★★★

319 Whorouly South Road, Whorouly South, Vic 3735 (postal) **Region** Heathcote
T (03) 5727 1434 **F** (03) 5727 1434 **www**.greenstoneofheathcote.com **Open** Not
Winemaker Sandro Mosele (Contract), Alberto Antonini **Est.** 2002 **Cases** 3000 **Vyds** 20 ha
This is one of the most interesting ventures to emerge over the past few years, bringing
together David Gleave MW, born and educated in Canada, now a long-term UK resident,
who manages an imported wine business and writes widely about the wines of Italy; Alberto
Antonini, a graduate of the University of Florence, with postgraduate degrees from Bordeaux
and University of California (Davis), and Italian Flying Winemaker; and Mark Walpole, a
20-year veteran with Brown Brothers and now manager of their 700 ha of vineyards. The
partners have chosen what they consider an outstanding vineyard on the red soil of the
Heathcote region, planted to 17 ha of shiraz, 2 ha of sangiovese and 1 ha of monastrell
(mourvedre). Exports to the UK, the US and other major markets.

ΨΨΨΨΨ **Heathcote Sangiovese 2007** Bright clear red colour, very good for sangiovese;
has a particularly fragrant savoury cherry bouquet, then a lively palate with pure
varietal fruit expression coupled with wonderfully fine tannins; there is enough
sour cherry cut to add a stamp of authority. Screwcap. 13.5% alc. **Rating** 96
To 2014 $65

✪ **Heathcote Shiraz 2007** Bright colour; spicy notes to the black cherry fruit of
the bouquet accurately foretell the elegant, medium-bodied palate that follows,
the fruit expressing itself with great clarity thanks to the relatively low alcohol and
lively acidity. Screwcap. 13.5% alc. **Rating** 95 To 2020 $33

ΨΨΨΨΩ **Heathcote Monastrell 2007 Rating** 91 To 2017 $33
Heathcote Rose 2009 Rating 90 To 2011 $24

Greg Cooley Wines   ★★★★★

Lot 4 Seipelt Lane, Penwortham, SA 5453 (postal) **Region** Clare Valley
T (08) 8843 4284 **F** (08) 8843 4284 **www**.gregcooleywines.com.au **Open** Not
Winemaker Greg Cooley **Est.** 2002 **Cases** 2500
Greg Cooley says, 'I followed the traditional path to winemaking via accountancy, fraud
squad, corporate investigations, running a Wendy's Supa Sundaes franchise and then selling
residential property. I left the property market in Brisbane just as the boom started in 2001 and
moved to the beautiful Clare just about when the wine glut started. Things didn't look overly
promising when my first wine entered into the Clare Show in 2003. The Riesling came 97th
of a total of 97, a platform on which I have since built, having sought loads of advice from
local winemakers and subsequently winning a medal the following year.' He explains, 'All my
wines are named after people who have been of influence to me in my 45 years and their
influence is as varied as the wine styles – from pizza shop owners, to my greyhound's vet and
South Australian author Monica McInerney.' I have to confess that I am taken by Greg's path
to glory because my move through law to wine was punctuated by the part-ownership of two
greyhounds that always wanted to run in the opposite direction to the rest of the field.

ΨΨΨΨΨ **Valerie Beh Clare Valley Riesling 2009** Has a very complex bouquet with
✪ notes of toast lurking in the background, then a superbly focused and balanced
palate offering a basket of citrus and tropical fruits running through to a long,
lingering finish. Screwcap. 11.8% alc. **Rating** 94 To 2020 $18

Rehbein and Ryan Reserve Clare Valley Cabernet 2007 Deep purple-red;
95% Cabernet from a single vineyard, the remaining 5% a cocktail of Malbec/
Cabernet Franc/Merlot, all spending 20 months in French oak. It is in full-bodied
Clare Valley mode, but the components are in balance, and the wine has a long
future; 166 cases made. Screwcap. 15% alc. **Rating** 94 To 2027 $30

ΨΨΨΨΩ **Bennett and Byrne Reserve Clare Valley Shiraz 2007 Rating** 91
To 2022 $30

○   **Kelli Maree Clare Valley Classic Dry White 2009** A neat and lively blend of an odd couple (Semillon/Viognier), with an ode to another union on the back label; the blend works well, particularly the balance between full flavour and freshness. Screwcap. 12.1% alc. **Rating** 90 **To** 2012 $18

○   **Five Year Olds and Dogs Clare Valley Rose 2009** Vivid fuchsia-pink; a cleverly made rose with a great interplay between acidity and controlled sweetness drawing out the length and finish. Back label alone worth the price. Screwcap. 12.5% alc. **Rating** 90 **To** 2011 $18

♥♥♥♥   **Monica, Macca and Moo Clare Valley Shiraz 2007 Rating** 89 **To** 2017 $22
Terry and Suzi Clare Valley Cabernet Shiraz 2007 Rating 88 **To** 2015 $22

Grey Sands   ★★★★☆

Cnr Kerrisons Road/Frankford Highway, Glengarry, Tas 7275 **Region** Northern Tasmania
T (03) 6396 1167 **F** (03) 6396 1167 **www**.greysands.com.au **Open** By appt
(open 2nd w'end Nov 10–6)
Winemaker Fran Austin, Bob Richter **Est.** 1989 **Cases** 1000 **Vyds** 3.5 ha
Bob and Rita Richter began the establishment of Grey Sands in 1989, slowly increasing the plantings to the present total. The ultra-high density of 8900 vines per ha reflects the experience gained by the Richters during a three-year stay in England, when they visited many vineyards across Europe, as well as Bob's graduate diploma from Roseworthy College. Plantings include pinot noir, merlot, pinot gris and malbec. Exports to Canada.

♥♥♥♥♥   **Merlot 2006** Good hue; the bouquet is very fragrant, and the palate has clear varietal fruit in a cool-grown mode, with strong olive and herb notes encircling the red fruits; by any measure, Tasmania's best varietal merlot. Not for lovers of McLaren Vale nebbiolo. Diam. 13.7% alc. **Rating** 94 **To** 2014 $35

♥♥♥♥♀   **Pinot Noir 2008 Rating** 92 **To** 2014 $40

♥♥♥♥   **Pinot Gris 2008 Rating** 89 **To** 2012 $35
Chardonnay Viognier 2008 Rating 87 **To** 2012 $35

Griffin Wines   ★★★★☆

Tynan Road, Kuitpo, SA 5172 **Region** Adelaide Hills
T (08) 8239 2545 **F** (08) 8388 3557 **www**.griffinwines.com **Open** Not
Winemaker Phil Christiansen, Shaw & Smith **Est.** 1997 **Cases** 2400 **Vyds** 26.16 ha
The Griffins (Trevor, Tim, Mark and Val) planted pinot noir, merlot, chardonnay, sauvignon blanc and shiraz in 1997, having owned the property for over 30 years. Situated 3 km from Kuitpo Hall, its 350 m elevation gives sweeping views over the valley below.

♥♥♥♥♀   **No. 2 Adelaide Hills Sauvignon Blanc 2009** Light colour; an elegant, juicy
○   sauvignon blanc with passionfruit and gooseberry aromas and flavours to the fore; good length and balance. Screwcap. 13% alc. **Rating** 92 **To** 2011 $19.50
No. 3 Adelaide Hills Pinot Noir 2008 Strong colour, deep and clear; an aromatic bouquet of dark plum and black cherry, then a powerful and ripe palate of lush dark fruits; has balance and will repay short-term cellaring. Screwcap. 13.9% alc. **Rating** 91 **To** 2015 $26
No. 3 Adelaide Hills Pinot Noir 2007 Developed colour; the fruit aromas and flavours have moved into a spicy herbal range, but by no means decayed; the palate is long, the aftertaste good. Screwcap. 14.3% alc. **Rating** 90 **To** 2013 $28
No. 1 Adelaide Hills Shiraz 2007 Retains purple-crimson hue; a vibrant and spicy shiraz, predominantly driven by spicy red fruits and a dash of licorice, the tannins fine but savoury. Screwcap. 14% alc. **Rating** 90 **To** 2017 $23

♥♥♥♥   **No. 4 Adelaide Hills Merlot 2007 Rating** 88 **To** 2012 $20

Groom ★★★★☆

28 Langmeil Road, Tanunda, SA 5352 (postal) **Region** Barossa Valley
T (08) 8563 1101 **F** (08) 8563 1102 **www**.groomwines.com **Open** Not
Winemaker Daryl Groom **Est.** 1997 **Cases** 5350 **Vyds** 29.6 ha

The full name of the business is Marschall Groom Cellars, a venture owned by David and Jeanette Marschall and their six children, and Daryl and Lisa Groom and their four children. Daryl was a highly regarded winemaker at Penfolds before he moved to Geyser Peak in California. Years of discussion between the families came to a head with the purchase of a 35-ha block of bare land adjacent to Penfolds' 130-year-old Kalimna Vineyard. Shiraz was planted in 1997, giving its first vintage in '99, the wine blended with the output from two vineyards, one 100 years old, the other 50 years old. The next acquisition was an 8-ha vineyard at Lenswood in the Adelaide Hills, planted to sauvignon blanc. In 2000, 3.2 ha of zinfandel was planted on the Kalimna Bush Block, with the first vintage in '03. Not surprisingly, a substantial part of the production is exported to the US (and also to Hong Kong and Taiwan).

🍷🍷🍷🍷🍷 **Adelaide Hills Sauvignon Blanc 2009** Classic Adelaide Hills style, with herb, gooseberry and grass characters on both bouquet and palate; has good balance and length, and has no casual flourishes. Screwcap. 12.8% alc. **Rating** 93 **To** 2011 **$24**

Barossa Valley Shiraz 2008 Deep garnet, purple hue; a fresh bouquet of confit blackberry, and a touch of bitter chocolate; the palate is quite fleshy, with plenty of fresh fruit on offer; quite weighty on the finish, with some noticeable warmth from the alcohol, there is plenty of stuffing in this wine to enjoy. Cork. 14.9% alc. **Rating** 93 **To** 2015 **$48** BE

Bush Block Barossa Valley Zinfandel 2008 Has the typical lifted red berry fruit aromas of zinfandel, which have some similarity to pinot noir; however, the lush, sweet raspberry fruit of the palate ends that discussion; soft, mouthfilling and agreeable. Cork. 14.7% alc. **Rating** 91 **To** 2014 **$30**

Grosset ★★★★★

King Street, Auburn, SA 5451 **Region** Clare Valley
T (08) 8849 2175 **F** (08) 8849 2292 **www**.grosset.com.au **Open** Wed–Sun 10–5 from Sept for approx 6 weeks
Winemaker Jeffrey Grosset, Brent Treloar **Est.** 1981 **Cases** 95 000 **Vyds** 22 ha

Jeffrey Grosset has assumed the unchallenged mantle of Australia's foremost riesling maker in the wake of John Vickery stepping back to a consultancy role for Richmond Grove. Grosset's pre-eminence in riesling making is recognised both domestically and internationally; however, he merits equal recognition for the other wines in his portfolio: Semillon Sauvignon Blanc from Clare Valley/Adelaide Hills, Chardonnay and Pinot Noir from the Adelaide Hills; and Gaia, a Bordeaux blend from the Clare Valley. These are all benchmarks. His quietly spoken manner conceals a steely will, exemplified by his long and ultimately successful battle to prevent the use of 'riesling' on flagons and bottles as a generic description, rather than varietal, and his subsequent success in having the Clare Valley riesling makers migrate en masse to screwcaps, unleashing a torrent of change across Australia. Trial plantings (2 ha) of fiano aglianico, nero d'Avola and petit verdot suggest some new wines maybe gestating. Exports to all major markets.

🍷🍷🍷🍷🍷 **Springvale Watervale Riesling 2009** Fragrant lime, herb and spice aromas lead into an incisive and tightly focused palate, with delicious lime and green apple fruit coursing through to the finish. Screwcap. 12.5% alc. **Rating** 96 **To** 2020 $36

Piccadilly Adelaide Hills Chardonnay 2008 Pale yellow-green; the fragrant bouquet of white peach, citrus and subtle oak tells you what is to come on the long, elegant palate with its fusion of white peach, grapefruit and fine oak. Screwcap. 13.5% alc. **Rating** 96 **To** 2015 $53

Clare Valley Adelaide Hills Semillon Sauvignon Blanc 2009 A typically rich and complex wine, with a panoply of aromas and flavours running through from start to finish, but it is the lively farewell of ripe, citrus-flavoured acidity that is special. Screwcap. 12.5% alc. **Rating** 95 **To** 2013 $32

Adelaide Hills Pinot Noir 2008 Bright, clear colour; a pinot with very good tension and complexity to its mix of black cherry, spice and more foresty nuances; unusually good tannin structure. Screwcap. 14% alc. **Rating** 95 **To** 2016 $66
Gaia 2007 Retains good hue; an intense and complex blend (Cabernet Sauvignon/Cabernet Franc/Merlot), the bouquet with ripe blackcurrant fruit, the medium- to full-bodied palate with great structure for the display of black and red fruits running through to the long finish. Screwcap. 14% alc. **Rating** 95 **To** 2027 $60
Polish Hill Riesling 2009 Opens quietly on the bouquet and fore-palate before dramatically picking up the pace on the back-palate and finish, with spice, lime and some mineral. Screwcap. 13% alc. **Rating** 94 **To** 2017 $45

Grove Estate Wines   ★★★★★

Murringo Road, Young, NSW 2594 **Region** Hilltops
T (02) 6382 6999 **F** (02) 6382 4527 **www**.groveestate.com.au **Open** W'ends 10–5, or by appt
Winemaker Long Rail Gully Wines (Richard Parker) **Est.** 1989 **Cases** 5000 **Vyds** 55 ha
The Grove Estate partners of Brian Mullany, John Kirkwood and Mark Flanders purchased the then unplanted property situated on volcanic red soils at an elevation of 530 m with the intention of producing premium cool-climate wine grapes for sale to other winemakers. Over the ensuing years plantings included cabernet sauvignon, shiraz, merlot, zinfandel, barbera, sangiovese, petit verdot, chardonnay, semillon and nebbiolo. In 1997 a decision was taken to retain a small amount of cabernet sauvignon and have it vinified under the Grove Estate label, and the winemaking gathered pace thereafter.

♟♟♟♟♟ **The Cellar Block Hilltops Shiraz Viognier 2009** Highly aromatic and very attractive spiced blue and black fruit bouquet, accentuated by an elegant viognier lift; the palate is silky, medium-bodied and loaded with clearly defined fruit and powdery fine tannins; long, ample and quite succulent to conclude. Screwcap. 14.5% alc. **Rating** 95 **To** 2016 $38 BE
Sommita Hilltops Nebbiolo 2008 Bright colour for nebbiolo; the fragrant complexities of the bouquet do not prepare you for the sheer intensity of the palate and its array of warm spices, savoury berry fruits and perfect tannins. Small wonder the wine has had such acclaim. Screwcap. 15.5% alc. **Rating** 95 **To** 2016 $35
✪ **Sommita Hilltops Nebbiolo 2007** Remarkably tamed nebbiolo that retains clear varietal character yet is food (and taster) friendly. It has seductive berry and spice aromas and flavours, but it is the fine, soft tannins that make this something special. Trophy NSW Wine Awards '09, Blue-Gold Sydney International Wine Show '09, gold medal Sydney Wine Show '10. Screwcap. 14.5% alc. **Rating** 94 **To** 2017 $45
✪ **Reserve Hilltops Nebbiolo 2006** Has retained remarkable red hue; was a delicious (and superior) wine when first tasted in March '07, and has lost nothing in the intervening years, its fruit with more red notes than the '08, but the same structure. Screwcap. 15% alc. **Rating** 94 **To** 2014 $35

♟♟♟♟♟ **Tumbarumba Delicate White 2008** Light straw-green; what a bargain; flooded
✪ with nectarine and white peach fruit, with a drizzle of citrus, this predominantly chardonnay doesn't have the slightest need of oak to show its wares, nor time in bottle – although it will age well. Screwcap. 12.5% alc. **Rating** 93 **To** 2012 $15
Hilltops Cabernet Sauvignon 2008 Rating 91 **To** 2018 $25
The Italian Hilltops Sangiovese Barbera 2008 Rating 90 **To** 2014 $20

Growlers Gully   ★★★☆

354 Shaws Road, Merton, Vic 3715 **Region** Upper Goulburn
T (03) 5778 9615 **F** (03) 5778 9615 **www**.growlersgully.com.au **Open** W'ends & public hols 11–5, or by appt
Winemaker Les Oates **Est.** 1997 **Cases** NA **Vyds** 2.4 ha
Les and Wendy Oates have established the Growlers Gully vineyard (shiraz, cabernet sauvignon, viognier and sauvignon blanc) at an elevation of 375 m on fertile brown clay loam soil.

A rammed-earth cellar door sales outlet offers light meals and barbecue facilities. No harvest in 2007 due to smoke taint.

ΨΨΨΨ͠   **Upper Goulburn Shiraz 2008** Relatively light but bright hue; a light- to medium-bodied palate with a juicy display of spice, plum and blackberry fruit, the tannins fine and ripe, the finish supple. Screwcap. 14.4% alc. **Rating** 90 **To** 2018 $25

ΨΨΨΨ   **Upper Goulburn Pinot Noir 2008 Rating** 87 **To** 2013 $25

Guichen Bay Vineyards   ★★★★☆

PO Box 582, Newport, NSW 2106 **Region** Mount Benson
T (02) 9997 6677 **F** (02) 9997 6177 **www.**guichenbayvineyards.com.au **Open** At Mount Benson Tourist & Wine Information Centre
Winemaker Simon Greenleaf (White), Mark Day (Red) **Est.** 2003 **Cases** 1000 **Vyds** 120 ha
Guichen Bay Vineyards is one of three adjacent vineyards known collectively as the Mount Benson Community Vineyards. Chardonnay, sauvignon blanc, shiraz, merlot and cabernet sauvignon were planted between 1997 and 2001. While the major part of the production is sold, the owners have obtained a producer's licence, and a small quantity of grapes is held back and made by local winemakers under the Guichen Bay Vineyards label.

ΨΨΨΨΨ   **Reserve Mount Benson Shiraz 2007** Strong crimson; a fusion of plum,
✪   spice, licorice and cedar on the bouquet is precisely replayed on the medium-bodied palate, tannins in regimented support. Screwcap. 14.7% alc. **Rating** 94 **To** 2017 $27

ΨΨΨΨ͠   **Mount Benson Shiraz 2007 Rating** 93 **To** 2018 $27

ΨΨΨΨ   **Mount Benson Cabernet Sauvignon 2007 Rating** 89 **To** 2017 $20
Mount Benson Sauvignon Blanc 2009 Rating 87 **To** 2010 $16.50
Mount Benson Unwooded Chardonnay 2009 Rating 87 **To** 2011 $16.50

🍂 Guildford Vineyard   ★★★★

6720 Midland Highway, Guildford, Vic 3451 **Region** Macedon Ranges
T (03) 5476 4457 **F** (03) 5476 4421 **www.**guildfordvineyard.com.au **Open** W'ends & public hols 11.30–5
Winemaker Ron Snepp, Brian Jean **Est.** 2003 **Cases** 500 **Vyds** 4 ha
Brian and Mary Jean decided to establish a vineyard (and winery) in a region with similar growing conditions to the Rhône Valley, with 2.5 ha of shiraz and 0.5 ha each of viognier, chardonnay and cabernet sauvignon. While they are technically in the Macedon Ranges region, the style of the wines is more typical of the cool end of Bendigo. The winery is cut into the side of a stony ridge, covered by an insulated curved steel roof spanning over 16 m. Their property is roughly halfway between Castlemaine and Daylesford, with Malmsbury and Kyneton to the east. The website gives full details of the numerous attractions of this very pretty area.

ΨΨΨΨ͠   **Reserve Shiraz 2008** Significantly deeper and brighter colour than the varietal;
✪   riper fruit, more weight and more tannins merit more than a $2 difference in price; savoury, spicy dark berry aromas and flavours have good intensity and length. Screwcap. 14.5% alc. **Rating** 90 **To** 2016 $20
✪   **Shiraz 2007** Slightly hazy colour; attractive wine; spicy red and black berries on the bouquet and medium-bodied palate; fine, ripe tannins on the finish, along with integrated oak. Screwcap. 14.2% alc. **Rating** 90 **To** 2016 $20

ΨΨΨΨ   **Shiraz 2008 Rating** 87 **To** 2013 $18

🍂 Gumpara Wines   ★★★★

PO Box 3 Stockwell Road, Light Pass, SA 5355 **Region** Barossa Valley
T 0419 624 559 **F** (08) 8562 4557 **www.**gumpara.blogspot.com/ **Open** By appt
Winemaker Mark Mader, Alex Peel, Beville Falkenberg **Est.** 1999 **Cases** 650 **Vyds** 22 ha

In 1856 the Mader family, driven by religious persecution, left their homeland of Germany to settle in South Australia, acquiring a 25-ha property at Light Pass. Over the generations, farming and fruit growing gave way to 100% grape growing; six generations later, Mark Mader produced the first wine under the Gumpara label in 2000. After success with shiraz, Mark branched out into semillon made from a small parcel of almost 90-year-old estate semillon. It was judged the top '08 Semillon in the Barossa Wine Show of that year. The portfolio may be small, but it's certainly diverse, with a Vermentino made in '09 and a range of fortified wines, Tawny Grenache, Liqueur Semillon and Liqueur Frontignac made by Mark personally.

ŸŸŸŸŸ **Old Vine Barossa Valley Semillon 2008** Attractive semillon undefiled by oak;
✪ fresh lemon and apple fruit is supported by lively, zesty acidity; very much in the new style of Barossa Valley semillon, giving full opportunity for the near-90-year-old vines to express themselves. Screwcap. 12.5% alc. **Rating** 93 **To** 2020 $20
Liqueur Barossa Valley Frontignac NV Slightly deeper brown-gold than the Liqueur Semillon; sweeter and more complex towards Amontillado in weight and sweetness; similar clean, dry finish. Cork. 18% alc. **Rating** 91 **To** 2011 $32.50
✪ **Barossa Valley Vermentino 2009** Light straw-green; a fragrant bouquet with a whiff of tangerine, then a palate with considerable life and thrust. The first vermentino to be planted on the Barossa Valley floor. Screwcap. 11% alc. **Rating** 90 **To** 2013 $20
Barossa Valley Liqueur Semillon NV Very interesting wine; golden brown, and with some mouthfeel of a dryish Madeira; clean finish to the gentle toffee flavours. Cork. 18% alc. **Rating** 90 **To** 2011 $32.50

ŸŸŸŸ **Barossa Valley Tawny Grenache NV Rating** 89 **To** 2011 $32.50
Reserve Barossa Valley Shiraz 2006 Rating 88 **To** 2016 $32.50
Victor's Old Vine Barossa Valley Shiraz 2007 Rating 87 **To** 2014 $25

🍇 Gundog Estate ★★★★

PO Box 8729, Gundaroo, NSW 2620 **Region** Canberra District
T 0412 371 666 **www**.gundogestate.com.au **Open** Not
Winemaker Wandin Valley Estate (Matthew Burton) **Est.** 1996 **Cases** 1000 **Vyds** 5 ha
Owners Sharon Bell and Geoff Burton have had a long association with academia, filmmaking and the arts, their involvement with wine triggered by elder son Matthew Burton. With a winemaking degree from CSU and vintages in Alsace, Oregon and the Yarra Valley, he is now chief winemaker and general manager of Wandin Valley Estate, where the Gundog Estate wines are made. The grapes are grown on the family property at Gundaroo, with chardonnay and cabernet sauvignon; shiraz is purchased from a local grower. The label features the family cocker spaniel named Karl Marx, pheasant in his mouth a fiction given that he flees in the opposite direction at the sound of a gunshot.

ŸŸŸŸŸ **Gundaroo Shiraz 2008** Vivid crimson hue, although not especially deep; particularly fresh and lively, with a silky texture to its spicy red and black fruit flavours; tannin and oak management on the money. Screwcap. 13.5% alc. **Rating** 92 **To** 2020 $25
Canberra District Rose 2009 Clear pink; made from 100% estate-grown cabernet sauvignon; attractive dry style matching a wide array of foods; well made. Screwcap. 13% alc. **Rating** 90 **To** 2011 $20

Haan Wines ★★★★★

Siegersdorf Road, Tanunda, SA 5352 **Region** Barossa Valley
T (08) 8562 4590 **F** (08) 8562 4590 **www**.haanwines.com.au **Open** Not
Winemaker Mark Jamieson (Contract) **Est.** 1993 **Cases** 4500 **Vyds** 16.3 ha
Hans and Fransien Haan established their business in 1993 when they acquired a vineyard near Tanunda. The plantings are shiraz (5.3 ha), merlot (3.4 ha), cabernet sauvignon (3 ha), viognier (2.4 ha), cabernet franc (1 ha) and malbec, petit verdot and semillon (0.4 ha each).

Oak undoubtedly plays a role in the shaping of the style of the Haan wines, but it is perfectly integrated, and the wines have the fruit weight to carry the oak. Exports to the UK and other major markets.

Barossa Valley Shiraz Prestige 2006 In the heart of the Haan style, intense fruit lifted by co-fermented viognier on both bouquet and medium-bodied palate; delicious blackberry and plum fruit with soft but persistent tannins and French oak; shows the great '06 vintage to advantage. Cork. 14.5% alc. **Rating** 96 **To** 2020 $47.50

Barossa Valley Merlot Cabernet Franc 2008 The use of only French oak pays dividends with this elegant and seductive light- to medium-bodied wine; red fruits glide along the mouth, the tannins superfine – perhaps a little too much so. Screwcap. 14.5% alc. **Rating** 93 **To** 2018 $19.95
Barossa Valley Semillon Sauvignon Blanc 2009 Rating 90 **To** 2011 $19.95

Barossa Valley Shiraz Cabernet Sauvignon 2008 Rating 89 **To** 2016 $19.95

Hahndorf Hill Winery   ★★★★★
Lot 10 Pains Road, Hahndorf, SA 5245 **Region** Adelaide Hills
T (08) 8388 7512 **F** (08) 8388 7618 **www.**hahndorfhillwinery.com.au **Open** 7 days 10–5
Winemaker Geoff Weaver (Consultant) **Est.** 2002 **Cases** 4500 **Vyds** 6.5 ha
Larry Jacobs and Marc Dobson, both originally from South Africa, purchased Hahndorf Hill Winery in 2002. Larry gave up a career in intensive-care medicine in 1988 when he purchased an abandoned property in Stellenbosch, and established the near-iconic Mulderbosch Wines. When Mulderbosch was purchased at the end of 1996, the pair migrated to Australia and eventually found their way to Hahndorf Hill. In 2006, their investment in the winery and cellar door was rewarded by induction into the South Australian Great Tourism Hall of Fame, having won the award for Best Tourism Winery for three consecutive years. In 2007 they began the process of converting the vineyard to biodynamic status, and they were one of the first movers in implementing a carbon offset program. They have successfully imported three clones of gruner veltliner from Austria, and their first vintage was made in 2010; however, they were been beaten to the punch by Lark Hill. Exports to the UK, Singapore and China.

Adelaide Hills Sauvignon Blanc 2009 A delicious bouquet with citrus, passionfruit and gooseberry sets the scene for the long, lively and flavoursome palate, ending with a crisp finish. Screwcap. 12.5% alc. **Rating** 94 **To** 2011 $22
Adelaide Hills Shiraz 2007 Good depth and hue; typical cool-grown Adelaide Hills characters, with red and black berries, spice and licorice coming together seamlessly on both bouquet and palate before a final savoury twist on the finish provides emphasis. Screwcap. 14.5% alc. **Rating** 94 **To** 2020 $30

Adelaide Hills Blaufrankisch 2008 Rating 90 **To** 2014 $35

Adelaide Hills Chardonnay 2008 Rating 89 **To** 2014 $28
Adelaide Hills Pinot Grigio 2009 Rating 89 **To** 2011 $26
Adelaide Hills Rose 2009 Rating 89 **To** 2011 $20

Hamelin Bay   ★★★★★
McDonald Road, Karridale, WA 6288 **Region** Margaret River
T (08) 9758 6779 **F** (08) 9758 6779 **www.**hbwines.com.au **Open** 7 days 10–5
Winemaker Julian Scott **Est.** 1992 **Cases** 12 000 **Vyds** 24 ha
The Hamelin Bay vineyard was established by the Drake-Brockman family, pioneers of the region. Richard Drake-Brockman's great grandmother, Grace Bussell, is famous for her courage when, in 1876 aged 16, she rescued the survivors of a shipwreck not far from the mouth of the Margaret River. The initial releases were contract made, but a winery with cellar door sales facility was opened in 2000, which has enabled an increase in production. Exports to the UK, Canada, Malaysia and Singapore.

🍷🍷🍷🍷🍷 **Margaret River Semillon Sauvignon Blanc 2009** Pale straw; a restrained
✪ but intense and tight blend, lemony semillon leading the way on both bouquet
and palate, with a tropical twist on the very long finish. Trophies for Best White
Blend at both WA and Adelaide Wine Shows '09. Screwcap. 12.5% alc. **Rating** 95
To 2013 $22

✪ **Margaret River Sauvignon Blanc 2009** A slightly controversial wine that
won the trophy for Best Sauvignon Blanc at the Adelaide Wine Show '09
notwithstanding its faintly sweaty bouquet; it came romping home thanks to
its intense and very long palate, the finish clean and crisp. Screwcap. 13% alc.
Rating 94 To 2011 $22
Margaret River Chardonnay 2008 An understated but stylish wine, fruit and
oak impeccably balanced and integrated; grapefruit and nectarine are set against
nutty/creamy characters on the light- to medium-bodied palate. Gold medal
Hobart Wine Show '09. Screwcap. 13% alc. **Rating** 94 To 2015 $28
Margaret River Shiraz 2007 The slightly lower alcohol is reflected in the
purple-crimson hue; the fragrant bouquet and lively palate offer more at this stage
than Five Ashes, with juicy, spicy red and black cherry fruit supported by fine
tannins. Screwcap. 14.5% alc. **Rating** 94 To 2017 $31

🍷🍷🍷🍷🍷 **Five Ashes Reserve Margaret River Shiraz 2007** Rating 93 To 2022 $45
Margaret River Cabernet Sauvignon 2007 Rating 91 To 2016 $31

🍷🍷🍷🍷 **Five Ashes Reserve Margaret River Cabernet Sauvignon 2007** Rating 89
To 2017 $45

Hamiltons Bluff   ★★★☆

Longs Corner Road, Canowindra, NSW 2804 **Region** Cowra
T (02) 6344 2079 **F** (02) 6344 2165 www.hamiltonsbluff.com.au **Open** W'ends 10–4
Winemaker Chris Derrez (Contract) **Est.** 1995 **Cases** 500 **Vyds** 46.4 ha
Hamiltons Bluff is owned and operated by the Andrews family, which established 44 ha
of vines at their Canowindra vineyard, the largest planting that of chardonnay, but with
significant quantities of shiraz and cabernet sauvignon, followed by sangiovese and semillon.
More recently they embarked on a 2.4-ha vineyard at Orange, with 0.4 ha each of chardonnay,
riesling, viognier, shiraz, cabernet sauvignon and merlot.

🍷🍷🍷🍷🍷 **Sangiovese 2007** Slightly better hue than the '08; this is for lovers of Italian
✪ (home-grown) wines, winning a gold medal the Australian Alternative Varieties
Wine Show '08; its cherry fruit is more than matched by its tannins, and demands
food. Screwcap. 15.4% alc. **Rating** 90 To 2013 $25

🍷🍷🍷🍷 **Sangiovese 2002** Rating 89 To 2012 $25

🍇 Hamlet Vineyard   NR

55 Greatorex Road, Denmark, WA 6333 **Region** Denmark
T (08) 9840 8356 www.hamletvineyard.com.au **Open** By appt
Winemaker Harewood Estate (James Kellie) **Est.** 1998 **Cases** 3000 **Vyds** 8 ha
Andrew and Yvonne Bruce began the planting of their riesling, sauvignon blanc, shiraz,
merlot, cabernet franc and cabernet sauvignon in 1998. Andrew is a barrister, and Yvonne a
former operating theatre nurse, and say, 'We went into the enterprise as a retirement project
and with complete ignorance, something that is a requirement in this industry, because if you
know anything about it you won't even think of it.' That is somewhat disingenuous, because
they are determined to grow high-quality grapes to turn into high-quality wine. Moreover,
Yvonne's role as managing partner stems from her early life on her parents' farm in the
Murray Mallee, and the discipline subsequently learnt in hospital theatres.

Hanging Rock Winery

88 Jim Road, Newham, Vic 3442 **Region** Macedon Ranges
T (03) 5427 0542 **F** (03) 5427 0310 **www.**hangingrock.com.au **Open** 7 days 10–5
Winemaker John Ellis **Est.** 1982 **Cases** 40 000 **Vyds** 14.5 ha
The Macedon area has proved very marginal in spots, and the Hanging Rock vineyards, with their lovely vista towards the Rock, are no exception. John Ellis has thus elected to source additional grapes from various parts of Victoria to produce an interesting and diverse range of varietals at different price points. Exports to the UK, the US and other major markets.

🍷🍷🍷🍷🍷 **Heathcote Shiraz 2006** Dense, inky colour; a profound wine with intense blackberry fruit framed by vanillan oak, and complexed further by touches of licorice and spice; most remarkable is the softness of the tannins. Screwcap. 14.5% alc. **Rating** 95 **To** 2026 $70

🍷🍷🍷🍷 **Odd One Out Pinot Gris 2009 Rating** 87 **To** 2010 $19.95
Odd One Out Viognier 2008 Rating 87 **To** 2010 $19.95

Hanson-Tarrahill Vineyard ★★★

49 Cleveland Avenue, Lower Plenty, Vic 3093 (postal) **Region** Yarra Valley
T (03) 9439 7425 **F** (03) 9439 4217 **Open** Not
Winemaker Dr Ian Hanson **Est.** 1983 **Cases** 1000 **Vyds** 9.4 ha
Dental surgeon Ian Hanson planted his first vines in the late 1960s, close to the junction of the Yarra and Plenty rivers; in '83 those plantings were extended (by 3000 vines), and in '88 the Tarrahill property at Yarra Glen was established with a further 4 ha. The varieties planted are (in descending order) pinot noir, cabernet sauvignon, shiraz, cabernet franc, chardonnay and viognier. Exports to the UK.

🍷🍷🍷🍷 **Cabernet Franc 2008** There is no question about the varietal character, with its perfumed bouquet at odds with its dusty/savoury palate; you can see why it is usually blended with cabernet, merlot, etc. Diam. 14% alc. **Rating** 87 **To** 2013 $20

Happs

575 Commonage Road, Dunsborough, WA 6281 **Region** Margaret River
T (08) 9755 3300 **F** (08) 9755 3846 **www.**happs.com.au **Open** 7 days 10–5
Winemaker Erl Happ, Mark Warren **Est.** 1978 **Cases** 20 000 **Vyds** 37 ha
One-time schoolteacher, potter and winemaker Erl Happ is now the patriarch of a three-generation family. More than anything, Erl has been a creator and experimenter, building the self-designed winery from mudbrick, concrete form and timber, and designing and making the first crusher. In 1994 he began an entirely new vineyard at Karridale, planted to no less than 28 different varieties, including some of the earliest plantings in Australia of tempranillo. The Three Hills label is made from varieties grown at the 30-ha Karridale vineyard. Erl passed on to son Myles a love of pottery, and Happs Pottery now has four potters, including Myles. Exports to Denmark, Netherlands, Malaysia, Hong Kong, China and Japan.

🍷🍷🍷🍷🍷 **Three Hills Chardonnay 2008** Bright straw-green; a complex bouquet with a touch of smoky oak, the palate tighter and more focused than the standard wine, with grapefruit and nectarine flavours; good length and balance. Screwcap. 13.2% alc. **Rating** 94 **To** 2015 $27
Three Hills Nebbiolo 2008 Again, exceptional colour for nebbiolo, even if the wine is young; the palate builds on the expectation generated by the colour, with a Patrician presence typical of Barolo, the black cherry fruit easily carrying the tannins. Cork. 14.4% alc. **Rating** 94 **To** 2020 $40
Three Hills Malbec 2008 Vivid crimson-purple; arguably the best of the Three Hills wines simply because it brings out the best features of malbec: glossy red and black cherry and raspberry fruit (usual) and perfect texture and structure (very unusual). Cork. 13.4% alc. **Rating** 94 **To** 2016 $36

✪   **Fortis 2008** Intense, deep purple; it's been too long since I last tasted one of Happs Vintage Port style wines; this is brilliant, almost dry, yet intense and very well balanced. 500 ml. Cork. 18.5% alc. **Rating** 94 **To** 2020 $25

🍷🍷🍷🍷🍸 **Three Hills Petit Verdot 2008 Rating** 92 **To** 2018 $36
    Three Hills Eva Marie 2008 Rating 91 **To** 2012 $27

✪   **Margaret River Chardonnay 2008** Bright straw-green; has considerable depth of flavour to its nectarine and peach fruit, yet retains elegance courtesy of a line of acidity. Screwcap. 13% alc. **Rating** 91 **To** 2014 $20
    Three Hills Sangiovese 2008 Rating 91 **To** 2018 $36

✪   **Margaret River Semillon Sauvignon Blanc 2009** Attractive wine with gooseberry, citrus and grass components seamlessly welded, the juicy mouthfeel giving good length and balance. Screwcap. 13.5% alc. **Rating** 90 **To** 2011 $16

🍷🍷🍷🍷 **Muscat a Pink 2009 Rating** 89 **To** 2010 $22
    Three Hills Cabernet Franc 2008 Rating 88 **To** 2016 $36

Harbord Wines ★★★☆

PO Box 41, Stockwell, SA 5355 **Region** Barossa Valley
T (08) 8562 2598 **F** (08) 8562 2598 **www.**harbordwines.com.au **Open** Not
Winemaker Roger Harbord **Est.** 2003 **Cases** 2000
Roger Harbord is a well-known and respected Barossa winemaker, with over 20 years' experience, the last 10 as chief winemaker for Cellarmasters Wines, Normans and Ewinexchange. He has set up his own virtual winery as a complementary activity; the grapes are contract-grown, and he leases winery space and equipment to make and mature the wines. Exports to the US, France, Singapore and Hong Kong.

🍷🍷🍷🍷🍸 **The Tendril Barossa Shiraz 2008** Good colour and depth; well-constructed
✪   and full of flavour; has blackberry, plum and dark chocolate aromas and flavours supported by ripe tannins. Screwcap. 14% alc. **Rating** 90 **To** 2016 $18

🍷🍷🍷🍷 **Clare Valley Riesling 2009** Light straw-green; an attractive, lime-accented
✪   bouquet with a hint of toast on the bouquet; then a pleasant, gently fruited, palate. Screwcap. 12% alc. **Rating** 88 **To** 2014 $14

Harcourt Valley Vineyards ★★★★★

3339 Calder Highway, Harcourt, Vic 3453 **Region** Bendigo
T (03) 5474 2223 **www.**harcourtvalley.com.au **Open** 7 days 11–5
(11–6 during daylight savings)
Winemaker Kye and Quinn Livingstone **Est.** 1976 **Cases** 1500 **Vyds** 4 ha
Established by Ray and Barbara Broughton, the vineyard was handed over to John and Barbara Livingstone in 1988. Barbara's Shiraz was created by Barbara Broughton, but with the arrival of the 'new' Barbara it lives on as the flagship of the vineyard. The Livingstones planted a further 2 ha of shiraz on north-facing slopes with the aid of two sons, who, says Barbara, then 'bolted, vowing never to have anything to do with vineyards, but having developed fine palates'. John died in mid-2004, but Barbara continues her role of viticulturist; winemaking is now in the hands of sons Kye and Quinn (who have returned to the fold).

🍷🍷🍷🍷🍷 **Barbara's Reserve Bendigo Shiraz 2007** Near identical colour to the standard, and there is no question about it, this is another big step above the varietal, the flavours more intense, the profile and texture more precise and long. Screwcap. 13.5% alc. **Rating** 95 **To** 2027 $35
    Reserve Cabernet Sauvignon 2007 High-quality, medium-bodied cabernet; has clear varietal expression with particularly good length; not tricked up. Gold medal Winewise '09. Screwcap. 13.5% alc. **Rating** 94 **To** 2017 $35

🍷🍷🍷🍷🍸 **Barbara's Bendigo Shiraz 2007 Rating** 93 **To** 2020 $25
    Bendigo Cabernet Sauvignon 2007 Rating 92 **To** 2020 $25

⊘   **Sightings Cabernet Sauvignon 2008** Reddish purple; ripe black and red berry fruit on the bouquet flows through to the well-balanced, medium- to full-bodied palate; fine tannins support the finish. Screwcap. 14% alc. **Rating** 90 **To** 2017 $20

♥♥♥♥   **Sightings Shiraz 2008 Rating** 89 **To** 2017 $20
Limited Release Bendigo Malbec 2008 Rating 89 **To** 2013 $20

Hardys   ★★★★★

202 Main Road, McLaren Vale, SA 5171 **Region** McLaren Vale
T (08) 8329 4124 **F** (08) 8329 4155 **www.**hardys.com.au **Open** Mon–Fri 10–4.30,
Sat 10–4, Sun 11–4, closed public hols
Winemaker Paul Lapsley (Chief) **Est.** 1853 **Cases** NFP
The 1992 merger of Thomas Hardy and the Berri Renmano group may well have had some elements of a forced marriage when it took place, but the merged group prospered mightily over the next 10 years. So successful was it that a further marriage followed in early 2003, with Constellation Wines of the US the groom, and BRL Hardy the bride, creating the largest wine group in the world (the Australian arm of the business is known as Constellation Wines Australia, or CWA). The Hardys wine brands are headed by Eileen Hardy Chardonnay and Shiraz and Thomas Hardy Cabernet Sauvignon; then the Sir James range of sparkling wines; next the newly introduced HRB Riesling, Chardonnay, Shiraz and Cabernet; then the expanded Oomoo range; and at the bottom of the price pyramid, the Chronicles wines. Exports to all major markets.

♥♥♥♥♥   **Eileen Hardy Chardonnay 2008** Can fairly be said to represent the state of the art of chardonnay in Australia today, without in any way diminishing the stature of single-vineyard wines such as Leeuwin Estate and Giaconda; has exceptional focus and intensity without sacrificing elegance; fruit, oak and acidity are seamless, the palate of extreme length. Three trophies Sydney Wine Show '10. Screwcap. 13.1% alc. **Rating** 97 **To** 2018 $74
Eileen Hardy Chardonnay 2007 While there is a healthy dose of toasty oak, the hedonistic levels of grapefruit, grilled cashew, sizzling bacon fat and quartz-like minerals punch through with ease; the amount of flavour is staggering given the 12.1% alcohol and the rapier-like acidity provides marvellous intensity and drive from start to the almost elegant conclusion. Gold medal Sydney Wine Show '10. Screwcap. **Rating** 97 **To** 2025 $74 BE
Thomas Hardy Cabernet Sauvignon 2004 A rarely encountered fusion of finesse, length and intensity, and remarkable for its varietal purity and presence. Beautiful cassis and blackcurrant varietal fruit expression runs through the palate to its vibrant, surging finish. From Margaret River, not Coonawarra. Trophy Sydney Wine Show '10. Cork. 13.5% alc. **Rating** 97 **To** 2024 $107
Eileen Hardy Shiraz 2005 Deep, dense, purple-crimson, exceptional for a five-year-old wine; has everything expected of a great Australian red destined for a long life – other than a screwcap – with an opulent array of black fruits, ripe tannins and quality oak. Stains on the sides of the cork are unsettling, but ignored. Gold medal Sydney Wine Show '10. 14% alc. **Rating** 96 **To** 2030 $107
Thomas Hardy Cabernet Sauvignon 2006 Constellation's insistence on using cork for the top Hardys reds must drive the winemakers to the brink of suicide; this is a fascinating wine, the first icon in recent years to have an alcohol lower than 13%; the result is a very elegant wine with immaculate balance. 12.9% alc. **Rating** 95 **To** 2021 $107
HRB Chardonnay 2008 Still very pale colour; a complete and perfectly balanced chardonnay; fresh white stone fruit, grapefruit and rock melon flavours are couched in a fine web of high-quality French oak; the palate is long, the finish fresh. Screwcap. 13.2% alc. **Rating** 94 **To** 2015 $33

⊘   **Chronicle No. 1 Twice Lost Shiraz Cabernet Rose 2009** Vivid light crimson; the wine has a delicious burst of red cherry and raspberry on the very well-balanced palate, which has real length. High-quality rose. Screwcap. 12.5% alc. **Rating** 94 **To** 2010 $17

HRB Shiraz 2007 Bright purple-crimson; a very fine and elegant shiraz, its texture and structure guaranteeing a long life if you can keep your hands off it; supple black fruits have a dash of spice to add interest, oak balanced and integrated. Gold medal Sydney Wine Show '10. Screwcap. 13.9% alc. **Rating** 94 **To** 2030 $39

ŸŸŸŸŸ   **HRB Cabernet Shiraz 2007 Rating** 93 **To** 2027 $39

✪   **Sir James Brut de Brut NV** Fine mousse; very attractive stone fruit and citrus flavours have been given complexity by 23 months on yeast lees; the finish is long and quite soft (but not flabby). A lot of wine for the dollar. Cork. 12% alc. **Rating** 91 **To** 2012 $17

ŸŸŸŸ   **Nottage Hill Riesling 2008** Skilfully made, presenting an abundance of ripe
✪   citrus/tropical fruits enriched with a light touch of residual sugar. Ready right now. Screwcap. 12.5% alc. **Rating** 89 **To** 2010 $11

✪   **Nottage Hill Riesling 2009** Bright colour; vibrant bouquet of lime and bath talc; the palate is vibrant, zesty and as clean as a whistle; well constructed and very good value. Screwcap. 12.5% alc. **Rating** 88 **To** 2016 $10.50 BE

Harewood Estate   ★★★★★

Scotsdale Road, Denmark, WA 6333 **Region** Denmark
T (08) 9840 9078 **F** (08) 9840 9053 **www.**harewoodestate.com.au **Open** 7 days 10–4
Winemaker James Kellie, Luke Hipper **Est.** 1988 **Cases** 10 000 **Vyds** 10 ha
In 2003 James Kellie, for many years a winemaker with Howard Park, and responsible for the contract making of Harewood's wines since 1998, purchased the estate with his father and sister as partners. Events moved quickly thereafter: a 300-tonne winery was constructed, offering both contract winemaking services for the Great Southern region and the ability to expand the Harewood range to include subregional wines that demonstrate the differences in style across the region. Exports to the UK, Denmark, Hong Kong, China and Japan.

ŸŸŸŸŸ   **Great Southern Riesling 2009** Ripe pristine citrus aromas combine with a
✪   touch of green apple and slatey minerality; the palate is generous, almost juicy on entry, with the acidity and slate tightening up the finish and providing a fresh, focused and surprisingly long conclusion. Screwcap. 12.5% alc. **Rating** 95 **To** 2018 $19.95 BE

Great Southern Chardonnay 2008 Bright, light straw-green; elegant, but very intense; grapefruit and white peach caressed by barrel ferment French oak; the finish is long, as is the aftertaste. Screwcap. 13.5% alc. **Rating** 95 **To** 2018 $24.95

Reserve Great Southern Semillon Sauvignon Blanc 2009 Straw, lemon and gun flint are evident on the bouquet; the palate is deep and luscious on entry, moving through to fresh lemon to conclude; generous, poised and precise. Screwcap. 13% alc. **Rating** 94 **To** 2013 $25 BE

Great Southern Shiraz 2007 Has won top awards (in several lesser wine shows) and it's not hard to see why; crimson-purple, it weaves red and black fruits, French oak and silky tannins into a picture-perfect tapestry. Screwcap. 15% alc. **Rating** 94 **To** 2022 $34.95

ŸŸŸŸŸ   **Great Southern Shiraz Cabernet 2008** Elements of leafy cabernet and spicy
✪   shiraz combine with great effect; juicy red fruits on entry, with slightly stricter dark fruits coming through on the finish; lots of energy and life in this wine. Screwcap. 14.5% alc. **Rating** 92 **To** 2017 $19.95 BE

Great Southern Cabernet Sauvignon 2007 Rating 91 **To** 2018 $29.50 BE
Great Southern Shiraz 2008 Rating 90 **To** 2018 $29.50 BE

ŸŸŸŸ   **Great Southern Pinot Noir 2009** Deep colour and deeply fruited; savoury
✪   smoky bacon and black plum aromas are framed by a gentle lick of cinnamon; the palate is generous, varietal and quite soft to conclude. Screwcap. 14% alc. **Rating** 89 **To** 2013 $19.95 BE

Harmans Ridge Estate

Cnr Bussell Highway/Harmans Mill Road, Wilyabrup, WA 6284 **Region** Margaret River
T (08) 9755 7409 **F** (08) 9755 7400 www.harmansridge.com.au **Open** 7 days 10.30–5
Winemaker Paul Green, Dave Longden **Est.** 1999 **Cases** 25 000
Harmans Ridge Estate, with a crush capacity of 1600 tonnes, is primarily a contract maker for
larger producers in the Margaret River region who do not have their own winery/winemaker.
It does, however, make wines on its own account under three labels: Harmans Ridge Estate,
Howling Wolves and Mootown Range, albeit with no obvious price pattern across the three
ranges. Exports to the US, India, Hong Kong, China, Vietnam, Malaysia and Singapore.

ꝐꝐꝐꝐꝒ **Howling Wolves Small Batch Chardonnay 2008** Glowing yellow-green; a
classic example of chardonnay made to be enjoyed two or three years after vintage;
generous nectarine and peach flavours are framed by good acidity and a touch of
oak, all in balance. Screwcap. 13.5% alc. **Rating** 92 **To** 2012 $25

✪ **Howling Wolves Semillon Sauvignon Blanc 2009** Light-bodied, but has
plenty of focus to its flavours of lime, passionfruit and grass, the palate long and
fresh. Screwcap. 12.5% alc. **Rating** 90 **To** 2010 $14

ꝐꝐꝐꝐ **Howling Wolves Shiraz 2008** Good hue, although not very deep; spicy red and
✪ black berry aromas and flavours are augmented on the medium-bodied palate by
savoury/spicy tannins. Screwcap. 14% alc. **Rating** 89 **To** 2013 $14
Margaret River Shiraz Grenache Mourvedre 2007 **Rating** 88 **To** 2014 $20
✪ **Howling Wolves Cabernet Sauvignon 2008** Despite its moderately light
colour and body, the flavour of this wine surprises with its cassis and blackcurrant
fruit and its restrained tannins. Screwcap. 14% alc. **Rating** 88 **To** 2013 $14

Harris River Estate

Lot 1293 Harris River Road, Collie, WA 6225 **Region** Geographe
T (08) 9734 1555 **F** (08) 9734 1555 www.harrisriverestate.com.au **Open** Wed–Sun 11–4
Winemaker Jane Gilham **Est.** 2000 **Cases** 2000 **Vyds** 24 ha
Under the direction of principal owners Karl and Julie Hillier, Harris River Estate has rapidly
increased in size since its establishment in 2000. The estate vineyards are planted to verdelho,
viognier, chardonnay, merlot, shiraz and cabernet sauvignon, and all of the wines are estate-
grown and made – and offer excellent value. Exports to Singapore.

ꝐꝐꝐꝐꝒ **Verdelho 2009** Has the zesty intensity that marks Harris River Estate's white
✪ wines; fruit salad and pink grapefruit flavours drive the fresh palate. Screwcap.
14.3% alc. **Rating** 90 **To** 2013 $18

✪ **Viognier 2009** Radically different mouthfeel, as it should be, to the Verdelho;
ripe fruit with touches of fig, ginger and apricot, then a generous finish. Screwcap.
15% alc. **Rating** 90 **To** 2012 $18

ꝐꝐꝐꝐ **Classic White 2008** Whatever the varieties may be, they collectively provide
✪ more fruit weight and richness than most classic whites; ready to drink right
now before its succulent flavours blow out. Screwcap. 13.7% alc. **Rating** 89
To 2012 $16
Chardonnay 2009 **Rating** 87 **To** 2011 $18
Shiraz 2007 **Rating** 87 **To** 2013 $18
Classic Red 2007 **Rating** 87 **To** 2012 $16

Hartz Barn Wines

1 Truro Road, Moculta, SA 5353 **Region** Eden Valley
T 0408 857 347 **F** (08) 8563 9002 www.hartzbarnwines.com.au **Open** By appt
Winemaker David Barnett **Est.** 1997 **Cases** 1400
Hartz Barn Wines was formed in 1997 by Penny Hart (operations director), David Barnett
(winemaker/director), Katrina Barnett (marketing director) and Matthew Barnett (viticulture/
cellar director), which may suggest that the operation is rather larger than it in fact is. The
business name and label have an unexpectedly complex background, too, involving elements

from all the partners. The grapes come from the 11.5-ha Dennistone Vineyard, which is planted to merlot, shiraz, riesling, cabernet sauvignon, chardonnay and lagrein. Exports to Canada, Japan and NZ.

ΨΨΨΨ   **General Store Eden Valley Riesling 2009** Bright straw-green; a floral bouquet leads into a fresh, delicate palate with touches of lime and green apple along with good acidity. Screwcap. 11.5% alc. **Rating** 89 **To** 2017 $25

Hastwell & Lightfoot   ★★★

Foggos Road, McLaren Vale, SA 5171 **Region** McLaren Vale
T (08) 8323 8692 **F** (08) 8323 8098 www.hastwellandlightfoot.com.au **Open** By appt
Winemaker James Hastwell, Goe DiFabio (Contract) **Est.** 1990 **Cases** 5000 **Vyds** 16 ha
Established in 1988 by Mark and Wendy Hastwell and Jill Lightfoot with a focus on growing quality grapes for McLaren Vale wineries, it has now grown to 16 ha of vines and olive trees. Over the last 12 years they have moved to putting significant commitment being the Hastwell & Lightfoot brand producing wines from estate-grown varieties (Cabernet Sauvignon, Shiraz, Cabernet Franc, Tempranillo, Chardonnay and Viognier). They say that if the kangaroos stop eating the young vines they plan to add barbera to that list. Exports to the UK, Canada, Norway, Malaysia and Singapore.

ΨΨΨΨ   **McLaren Vale Viognier 2009** A respectable rendition of a recalcitrant variety, with a honeysuckle bouquet, then a nicely chalky (not oily) palate with nuances of pear and apricot, the finish crisp and dry. Screwcap. 13.5% alc. **Rating** 87 **To** 2011 $19
McLaren Vale Shiraz 2007 Retains red-purple hue; an unequivocally full-bodied wine, with blackberry and dark chocolate aromas that extend into the palate before pervasive tannins take their grip on proceedings; needed less extraction or more fining. Screwcap. 14.5% alc. **Rating** 87 **To** 2015 $22

Hat Rock Vineyard   ★★★☆

2330 Portarlington Road, Bellarine, Vic 3221 (postal) **Region** Geelong
T (03) 5259 1386 www.hatrockvineyard.com.au **Open** By appt
Winemaker Contract **Est.** 2000 **Cases** 300 **Vyds** 2 ha
Steven and Vici Funnell began the development of Hat Rock in 2000, planting pinot noir. The vineyard derives its name from a hat-shaped rocky outcrop on the Corio Bay shore, not far from the vineyard, a landmark named by Matthew Flinders when he mapped the southern part of Australia. The wines are available through the website.

ΨΨΨΨΨ   **Bellarine Peninsula Pinot Noir 2008** Slightly diffuse, slightly dull, purple; a very powerful pinot, presumably neither fined nor filtered; dark berry fruit is swathed in earthy/savoury characters. Needs time. Screwcap. 13.2% alc. **Rating** 90 **To** 2016 $30

Hatherleigh Vineyard   ★★★☆

35 Redground Heights Road, Laggan, NSW 2583 **Region** Southern New South Wales Zone
T (02) 6288 3505 www.nickbulleid.com/hatherleigh **Open** Not
Winemaker PJ Charteris, Nick Bulleid **Est.** 1996 **Cases** 250 **Vyds** 1 ha
This is the venture of long-term Brokenwood partner and peripatetic wine consultant Nick Bulleid. It has been a slowly, slowly venture, with all sorts of obstacles along the way, with 1 ha of pinot noir planted between 1996 and '99, but part thereafter grafted to a better clone, resulting in a clonal mix of MV6 (predominant) with two rows of clone 777 and a few vines of clone 115. The wines are made at Brokenwood under the joint direction of PJ Charteris and Nick, and are available though the website.

ΨΨΨΨΨ   **Pinot Noir 2006** Clear red; red berry fruit aromas have a touch of forest that becomes more evident on the light-bodied, complex, savoury palate. The cellaring has been done for you, ready now. Screwcap. 14% alc. **Rating** 90 **To** 2012 $39.90

Hay Shed Hill Wines   ★★★★★

511 Harmans Mill Road, Wilyabrup, WA 6280 **Region** Margaret River
T (08) 9755 6046 **F** (08) 9755 6083 **www**.hayshedhill.com.au **Open** 7 days 9–5
Winemaker Michael Kerrigan **Est.** 1987 **Cases** 20 000 **Vyds** 17.4 ha
The changes continue at Hay Shed Hill. Highly regarded former winemaker at Howard Park,
Mike Kerrigan acquired the business in late 2006 (with co-ownership by the West Cape
Howe syndicate) and is now the full-time winemaker. He had every confidence he could
dramatically lift the quality of the wines, which is precisely what he has done. Exports to the
US, Singapore, China and Hong Kong.

Block 6 Margaret River Chardonnay 2008 Bright straw-green; a complete
chardonnay in a style unique to Margaret River, although the low alcohol adds
another dimension; the fruit has a wonderful clarity undimmed by barrel ferment.
Screwcap. 12.2% alc. **Rating** 96 **To** 2016 $35

Block 2 Margaret River Cabernet Sauvignon 2007 Deep colour; a rich, full-
bodied wine bursting with blackcurrant fruit, the ripe tannins fitting like a glove,
the oak likewise. A 20-year minimum future. Screwcap. 14.6% alc. **Rating** 96
To 2027 $50

Block 6 Margaret River Chardonnay 2009 Vibrant hue; a highly perfumed
bouquet of nectarine and grapefruit, with a sprinkle of vanilla from the fine
French oak; the palate is incredibly fresh, and the acidity quite racy and fine, with
a long, fine and even finish to the wine; beautiful purity at just 12% alcohol.
Screwcap. **Rating** 95 **To** 2018 $35 BE

Block 2 Margaret River Cabernet Sauvignon 2008 The stellar 2008
Margaret River vintage is on full display in this wine; pure blackcurrant, olive
and tobacco leaf give over to a fleshy, full-bodied and generous mouthful of
pure cabernet fruit; couple this to a thrilling backbone of acidity, silky fine-
grained tannins and you have a wine that will excite at any stage of development.
Screwcap. 14% alc. **Rating** 95 **To** 2025 $50 BE

Block 1 Margaret River Semillon Sauvignon Blanc 2009 Offers a totally
seamless fusion of citrus, guava and lemongrass with subtle barrel ferment French
oak inputs, underwritten by mineral and lemon acidity; excellent length. Screwcap.
11.5% alc. **Rating** 94 **To** 2012 $28

Margaret River Chardonnay 2009 Rating 93 **To** 2015 $25 BE
Margaret River Shiraz Tempranillo 2008 Fragrant and perfumed, with a spicy
edge to the bouquet; medium-bodied with a fleshy mid-palate and abundant red
fruits marrying seamlessly with a touch of a roasted meat savoury character; fine
and fresh on the finish. Screwcap. 14% alc. **Rating** 92 **To** 2014 $20 BE

Margaret River Cabernet Merlot 2008 A highly polished bouquet of
redcurrant, blackcurrant and a touch of cedar; medium-bodied with plenty of
flesh, fine-grained tannins and satisfyingly persistent flavour. Screwcap. 14% alc.
Rating 92 **To** 2017 $20 BE

Margaret River Sauvignon Blanc Semillon 2009 Quite a pristine bouquet,
blending a touch of the tropical, nettle and a little citrus; the palate is fresh and
focused, with plenty of flavour and good line to conclude. Screwcap. 12.5% alc.
Rating 91 **To** 2012 $20 BE

Margaret River Cabernet Sauvignon 2008 Rating 91 **To** 2016 $25

Hazyblur Wines   ★★★★☆

Lot 5, Angle Vale Road, Virginia, SA 5120 **Region** Adelaide Plains
T (08) 8380 9307 **F** (08) 8380 8743 **www**.hazyblur.com **Open** By appt
Winemaker Ross Trimboli **Est.** 1998 **Cases** 4000 **Vyds** 5 ha
Robyne and Ross Trimboli hit the jackpot with their 2000 vintage red wines, sourced from
various regions in SA, including one described by Robert Parker Jr as 'Barotta, the most
northerly region in SA' (it is in fact Baroota, and is not the most northerly), with Parker
points ranging between 91 and 95. One of the wines was a Late Harvest Shiraz, tipping the

scales at 17% alcohol, and contract-grown at Kangaroo Island. It is here that the Trimbolis have established their own vineyard, planted to cabernet sauvignon, shiraz, pinot noir and pinot gris. Exports to the UK, the US, Canada, Denmark, Taiwan, Malaysia, Singapore, Hong Kong and Japan.

♥♥♥♥♥ **Barossa Valley Shiraz 2007** Has the best colour of the four Hazyblur Shirazs, but there's not much in it; a powerful medium- to full-bodied wine with considerable drive and focus to its blackberry fruit; well-balanced tannin and oak inputs. Will likely outlive the cork. 14.5% alc. **Rating** 94 **To** 2022 $45

♥♥♥♥♀ **McLaren Vale Shiraz 2007 Rating** 92 **To** 2020 $26
The Baroota Shiraz 2007 Rating 92 **To** 2022 $26
Kangaroo Island Shiraz 2007 Rating 90 **To** 2017 $24

Head Wines   ★★★★★

Lot 1, Stonewell Road, Stonewell, SA 5352 **Region** Barossa Valley
T 0413 114 233 **F** (02) 9211 2382 **www.**headwines.com.au **Open** By appt
Winemaker Alex Head **Est.** 2006 **Cases** 900
Head Wines is the intriguing, but highly focused, venture of Alex Head, who came into the wine industry in 1997 with a degree in biochemistry from Sydney University. Experience in fine wine retail stores, wholesale importers and an auction house was followed by vintage work at wineries he particularly admired: Tyrrell's, Torbreck, Laughing Jack and Cirillo Estate. The labelling and naming of the wines reflects his fascination with the Northern Rhône Valley, and, in particular, Côte-Rôtie. The two facing slopes in Côte-Rôtie are known as Côte Blonde and Côte Brune, sometimes combining grapes from the two slopes as Côte Brune et Blonde. Head's Blonde comes from an east-facing slope in the Stonewell subregion of the Barossa Valley, while The Brunette comes from a very low-yielding vineyard in the Moppa subregion. In each case, open fermentation (with whole bunches included) and basket pressing precedes 15 months in seasoned French hogsheads.

♥♥♥♥♥ **The Brunette Single Vineyard Syrah 2008** Vivid crimson sets the scene for similarly vivid aromas and flavours of cherry, raspberry and plum, the medium-bodied palate with superfine tannins, the oak balanced and integrated; 132 cases. Screwcap. 13.5% alc. **Rating** 96 **To** 2023 $35

✪ **The Blonde Barossa Valley Shiraz Viognier 2008** Dense purple-crimson; has a voluminous bouquet and very luscious palate of dark berry fruits shot through with wafts of spice and pepper; tannins and oak are in appropriate balance, indeed balance is the heart of the wine. Screwcap. 14.8% alc. **Rating** 96 **To** 2021 $30

✪ **Head Red Barossa Valley Shiraz Viognier 2008** Deep crimson-purple; it is hard to imagine how this can be declassified barrels of Head's single-vineyard wines; it has plush plum and black cherry fruits, the glossy mouthfeel due in part to the viognier. Ludicrously good value. Screwcap. 14% alc. **Rating** 95 **To** 2020 $20

✪ **Barossa Valley Rose 2009** Light, vivid puce; very pure, fresh and bright strawberry and raspberry fruits, with just a dusting of spice and perfect acidity. Screwcap. 13.5% alc. **Rating** 94 **To** 2010 $20

Heafod Glen Winery   ★★★★☆

8691 West Swan Road, Henley Brook, WA 6055 **Region** Swan Valley
T (08) 9296 3444 **F** (08) 9296 3555 **www.**heafodglenwine.com.au **Open** Wed–Sun 10–5
Winemaker Liam Clarke **Est.** 1999 **Cases** 2400 **Vyds** 3 ha
A combined vineyard and restaurant business, each set on outdoing the other, each with major accolades. Founder Neil Head taught himself winemaking, but in 2007 employed Liam Clarke (with a degree in viticulture and oenology) that has led to a string of significant show successes for Verdelho, Viognier and Reserve Chardonnay. The restaurant, originally set up by Paul Smith, was awarded Best Tourism Restaurant in '08 and Best Restaurant at a Winery – Perth and Surrounds '09, sous chef James Ward having taken over before those awards were gained. Exports to Japan.

ŢŢŢŢŢ Family Reserve Perth Hills Chardonnay 2008 Pale bright green; an elegant and particularly well-made chardonnay, both picking and winemaking decisions exactly right; part of the wine was barrel fermented and taken through mlf, the remainder in tank with lees contact. Gold medal Small Winemakers Show '09. Screwcap. 12.5% alc. **Rating** 94 **To** 2015 $50

ŢŢŢŢŢ Family Reserve Methode Champenoise Pinot Noir 2008 **Rating** 90 **To** 2012 $40

ŢŢŢŢ Swan Valley Viognier 2009 **Rating** 87 **To** 2011 $35

Heartland Wines ★★★★

Winehouse, Wellington Road, Langhorne Creek, SA 5255 **Region** Langhorne Creek
T (08) 8363 4456 **F** (08) 8363 4458 **www**.heartlandwines.com.au **Open** 7 days 10–5
Winemaker Ben Glaetzer **Est.** 2001 **Cases** 80 000
This is a joint venture of five industry veterans: winemakers Ben Glaetzer and Scott Collett, viticulturist Geoff Hardy, marketer Vicki Arnold and wine industry management specialist Grant Tilbrook. It uses grapes grown in the Limestone Coast and Langhorne Creek, predominantly from vineyards owned by the partners. It currently exports 70% of its make to 38 international markets, and 30% domestic. The wines are principally contract-made at Barossa Vintners and represent excellent value for money.

ŢŢŢŢŢ Director's Cut Shiraz 2007 No-holds-barred full-bodied wine, magnifying the flavours and (especially) tannins of the varietal version; why use a cork in this potentially long-lived wine (not even a Diam) beggars belief. Reverse the cork/screwcap closures with the Langhorne Creek Limestone Coast Shiraz. 15% alc. **Rating** 93 **To** 2017 $30

✪ Langhorne Creek Limestone Coast Shiraz 2007 Good retention of crimson-purple; exemplary winemaking brings together plum, spice, chocolate and blackberry fruit with ripe, soft tannins and a veneer of French oak, all in a medium-bodied palate. Screwcap. 14.5% alc. **Rating** 91 **To** 2015 $16

✪ Langhorne Creek Limestone Coast Cabernet Sauvignon 2008 Deep purple-crimson; has an expressive bouquet of cassis and blackcurrant, the medium-bodied palate with good texture, structure and length, tannins and oak cleverly manipulated. Screwcap. 14.5% alc. **Rating** 91 **To** 2018 $17

✪ Langhorne Creek Limestone Coast Shiraz 2008 Deep crimson-purple; the full range of plum, dark chocolate, spice and licorice run through bouquet and palate alike; mix-master tannins and oak have been blended in on the palate. Screwcap. 14.5% alc. **Rating** 90 **To** 2018 $17

ŢŢŢŢ Stickleback Red 2008 Strong colour; delivers a massive bang for its buck, with
✪ an array of red and black fruits on bouquet and palate alike; if looking to criticise, a little short on structure. Screwcap. 14.5% alc. **Rating** 89 **To** 2015 $12

Langhorne Creek Limestone Coast Pinot Grigio 2009 **Rating** 88 **To** 2012 $17

✪ Stickleback White 2009 A decidedly useful quaffer of Verdelho/Viognier/Semillon at the right price for any informal setting. Screwcap. 12% alc. **Rating** 87 **To** 2011 $12

Heaslip Wines ★★★★

PO Box 878, Clare, SA 5453 **Region** Clare Valley
T (08) 8842 3242 **F** (08) 8842 3233 **www**.heaslipwines.com.au **Open** Not
Winemaker Paulett Wines (Neil Paulett), Cardinham Estate (Scott Smith) **Est.** 2005
Cases 700 **Vyds** 4 ha
The Heaslip family, headed by Marie Heaslip, son Anthony and wife Philippa Stansell, pooled their resources to buy the vineyard (planted to cabernet sauvignon, shiraz and riesling) in 2004, after it had been on the market for some time. It is dry-grown, fertilised with organic fertilisers, all fungicides are organic, and no insecticides are used. The tough '07 vintage produced no grapes, but the organic approach, coupled with minimal use of tractors in the

vineyard, is paying dividends. Anthony and Philippa live and work in the Northern Territory for most of the year, leaving management of the property to Marie. The wines are contract-made, up to '08 by Paulett Wines, and from '09 by Cardinham Estate. Exports to the US, Europe and NZ.

ＹＹＹＹＹ Philly's Block Dry Grown Hand Picked Clare Valley Cabernet Sauvignon
✪ **2006** Retains excellent hue; has particularly good varietal expression through a combination of blackcurrant, cassis and a counterweight of fine, savoury/earthy tannins. Screwcap. 14% alc. **Rating** 92 **To** 2016 $10

✪ Dry Grown Hand Picked Clare Valley Shiraz Cabernet 2006 Deep colour; the cabernet component, while less than the shiraz, makes a major impact, adding zesty blackcurrant to the flavour range; good length and great value. Screwcap. 13.5% alc. **Rating** 90 **To** 2016 $10

ＹＹＹＹ Dayspring Dry Grown Hand Picked Clare Valley Shiraz 2006 You really
✪ have to wonder why a dry-grown, hand-picked shiraz from the Armagh district of the Clare Valley needs to be sold at this price; the vines are young, and the wine is no more than light- to medium-bodied, but the blackberry and blueberry fruit flavours are spot on. Screwcap. 13.5% alc. **Rating** 89 **To** 2015 $10

Heathcote Estate   ★★★★★

Level 1, 500 Chapel Street, South Yarra, Vic 3141 (postal) **Region** Heathcote
T (03) 9667 6541 **F** (03) 9827 3970 **www**.yabbylake.com **Open** Not
Winemaker Tom Carson, Chris Forge **Est.** 1988 **Cases** 6000 **Vyds** 34 ha
Heathcote Estate is a thoroughly professional venture, a partnership between Louis Bialkower, founder of Yarra Ridge, and Robert G. Kirby, owner of Yabby Lake Vineyards, Director of Escarpment Vineyards (NZ) and Chairman of Village Roadshow Ltd. They purchased a prime piece of Heathcote red Cambrian soil in 1999, planting shiraz (30 ha) and grenache (4 ha), the latter an interesting variant on viognier. The wines are matured exclusively in French oak (50% new). The arrival of the hugely talented Tom Carson as Group Winemaker can only add lustre to the winery and its wines. The rating is solely for the shiraz. Exports to the US, the UK, Canada, Sweden, Singapore, Hong Kong and China.

ＹＹＹＹＹ Shiraz 2007 Dense purple; blackberry, plum, cedar and dark chocolate aromas are
✪ repeated on the medium-bodied palate; immaculate handling of oak and tannins completes a high-quality package. Screwcap. 14.5% alc. **Rating** 96 **To** 2027 $40

Heathcote II   ★★★★☆

290 Cornella-Toolleen Road, Toolleen, Vic 3551 **Region** Heathcote
T (03) 5433 6292 **F** (03) 5433 6293 **www**.heathcote2.com **Open** W'ends 10–5
Winemaker Peder Rosdal **Est.** 1995 **Cases** 600 **Vyds** 6 ha
This is the venture of Danish-born, French-trained, Flying Winemaker (California, Spain and Chablis) Peder Rosdal and viticulturist Lionel Flutto. The establishment of the vineyard dates back to 1995, with new plantings in 2004 and '08 of shiraz (with the lion's share of 2.7 ha), cabernet sauvignon, cabernet franc, merlot and tempranillo. The vines are dry-grown on the famed red Cambrian soil, and the wines are made onsite using hand-plunging, basket press and (since 2004) French oak maturation. Exports to the US, Switzerland, Denmark, Germany, Japan and Singapore.

ＹＹＹＹＹ Myola 2007 Strong crimson-purple; has a very complex bouquet with a range of fruit aromas and a touch of coffee, as does Chateau Haut Brion; the medium- to full-bodied palate does finish with persistent tannins, but the fruit is there to balance them as the wine ages. Merlot/Cabernet Franc/Cabernet Sauvignon/Shiraz. Cork. 15% alc. **Rating** 94 **To** 2024 $65

ＹＹＹＹＹ HD Shiraz 2007 **Rating** 90 **To** 2015 $89

Heathcote Winery   ★★★★☆

183-185 High Street, Heathcote, Vic 3523 **Region** Heathcote
T (03) 5433 2595 **F** (03) 5433 3081 **www.**heathcotewinery.com.au **Open** 7 days 10–5
Winemaker Rachel Brooker **Est.** 1978 **Cases** 10 000 **Vyds** 15.25 ha
The Heathcote Winery was one of the first to be established in the region. The wines are produced predominantly from the estate vineyard (shiraz, viognier, chardonnay and marsanne), and some from local and other growers under long-term contracts; the tasting room facilities have been restored and upgraded. Exports to Poland and Hong Kong.

▼▼▼▼▼ **Curagee Shiraz 2008** Crimson-purple, slightly better hue than Mail Coach; the fragrant multi-berry bouquet leads into a very lively and attractive medium-bodied palate, with splashes of flavour popping up along its length. Screwcap. 14.5% alc. **Rating** 95 **To** 2023 $55

▼▼▼▼▽ **Slaughter House Paddock Shiraz 2008 Rating** 93 **To** 2023 $44
✪   **Mail Coach Shiraz 2008** Good hue; a brightly flavoured regional shiraz that has blackberry and black cherry fruit supported by fine tannins on a palate with considerable freshness achieved in the face of drought. Screwcap. 14.5% alc. **Rating** 93 **To** 2018 $27.50

▼▼▼▼ **Cravens Place MCV White 2008 Rating** 88 **To** 2011 $16.50 BE

Heathvale   ★★★★☆

Saw Pit Gully Road, via Keyneton, SA 5353 **Region** Eden Valley
T (08) 8564 8248 **F** (08) 8564 8248 **www.**heathvale.com
Open At Taste Eden Valley, Angaston
Winemaker Trevor March **Est.** 1987 **Cases** 1500 **Vyds** 10 ha
The origins of Heathvale go back to 1865 when William Heath purchased the property, building the home and establishing the vineyard. The wine was initially made in the cellar of the house, which still stands on the property (now occupied by owners Trevor and Faye March). The vineyards were re-established in 1987, and consist of shiraz (3 ha), cabernet sauvignon, chardonnay, riesling (2 ha each) and sagrantino (1 ha). A winery was completed in 2008. Exports to the US and China.

▼▼▼▼▼ **William Heath Eden Valley Shiraz 2008** Crimson-purple; a rich, powerful and concentrated full-bodied wine with lush black fruits, licorice and a dash of bitter chocolate; a long future ahead. Screwcap. 14% alc. **Rating** 94 **To** 2030 $50

▼▼▼▼▽ **Eden Valley Cabernet Sauvignon 2008** Slightly diffuse colour, although the
✪   hue is bright; has clear-cut varietal character, with a mix of blackcurrant, cassis and blackberry; the tannin balance is good, the oak likewise. Screwcap. 14% alc. **Rating** 93 **To** 2020 $25
✪   **Eden Valley Riesling 2009** Light straw-green; a clean but relatively subdued bouquet gives little clue to the intensely focused and long palate to come, with citrus, apple and mineral all thrusting through to the finish. Screwcap. 12% alc. **Rating** 92 **To** 2019 $20

▼▼▼▼ **The Angry Rabbit 2008 Rating** 88 **To** 2013 $20

Hedberg Hill   ★★★

701 The Escort Way, Orange, NSW 2800 **Region** Orange
T (02) 6365 3428 **F** (02) 6365 3428 **www.**hedberghill.com.au **Open** W'ends 11–5
Winemaker Simon Gilbert **Est.** 1998 **Cases** 500 **Vyds** 5.6 ha
Peter and Lee Hedberg have established their hilltop vineyard 4 km west of Orange, with 0.8 ha each of cabernet sauvignon, merlot, tempranillo, chardonnay, viognier, sauvignon blanc and riesling. The new cellar door opened in March 2010 and has great views of Mt Canobolas and the surrounding valleys.

♥♥♥♥ Lara's Orange Chardonnay 2008 Bright straw-green; the wine has potent grapefruit/citrus flavours that have an almost peppery finish, like Austrian gruner veltliner; it has eaten up 9 months' French oak maturation. Screwcap. 13.5% alc. **Rating** 89 **To** 2013 $17

Claudia's Orange Viognier 2008 A viognier that has intrinsic merit; the flavours span peach, citrus and a faint touch of ginger; the finish is positive, but not phenolic. Screwcap. 13.5% alc. **Rating** 89 **To** 2012 $17

Oscar's Orange Cabernet Sauvignon 2007 Blackcurrant and plum fruit is encircled by earthy/savoury characters on both the bouquet and light- to medium-bodied palate, then finishes with a subliminal touch of mint. Screwcap. 13.5% alc. **Rating** 89 **To** 2014 $17

Lee's Orange Tempranillo 2008 Medium purple-red; the cool climate gives the medium-bodied palate a savoury, spicy bite to the core of red and black cherry fruit and the twist of lemon on the finish; the texture is quite complex. Screwcap. 13.5% alc. **Rating** 89 **To** 2014 $17

Orange Sauvignon Blanc 2009 A highly aromatic bouquet that also has a trace of reduction, the palate crisp, with a mix of herb and citrus. Screwcap. 12.5% alc. **Rating** 88 **To** 2011 $17

🍇 Heemskerk ★★★★☆

131 Cascade Road, South Hobart, Tas 7004 (postal) **Region** Southern Tasmania
T 1300 651 650 **www**.heemskerk.com.au **Open** Not
Winemaker Anna Pooley **Est.** 1974 **Cases** NFP **Vyds** 5.2 ha
The Heemskerk brand established by Graham Wiltshire when he planted the first vines in 1965 (in the Pipers River region) is a very different business these days. It is part of the Foster's Wine Group, and sources its grapes from three vineyards: the Riversdale Vineyard in the Coal River Valley for riesling; the Lowestoft Vineyard in the Derwent Valley for pinot noir; and the Tolpuddle Vineyard in the Coal River Valley for chardonnay. Here there is a link with the past, for winemaker Anna Pooley was born in the Coal River region, where her parents have their own vineyard and winery, Pooley Wines, with brother Matt in charge of winemaking.

♥♥♥♥♥ Coal River Valley Chardonnay 2008 Pale straw-green; a superfine, tightly sculpted wine framed by the urgency of Tasmanian acidity and its citrus zest influences. In the modern style, just avoiding the crossover into sauvignon blanc territory. Gold medal Sydney Wine Show '10. Screwcap. 13% alc. **Rating** 94 **To** 2015 $50

♥♥♥♥♀ Derwent Valley Pinot Noir 2008 Rating 92 **To** 2015 $60
Tamar Valley Pinot Noir 2008 Rating 91 **To** 2017 $60

Heggies Vineyard ★★★★★

Heggies Range Road, Eden Valley, SA 5235 **Region** Eden Valley
T (08) 8565 3203 **F** (08) 8565 3380 **www**.heggiesvineyard.com **Open** At Yalumba
Winemaker Peter Gambetta **Est.** 1971 **Cases** 13 000 **Vyds** 62 ha
Heggies was the second of the high-altitude (570 m) vineyards established by the Hill Smith family. Plantings on the 120-ha former grazing property began in 1973; the principal varieties are riesling, chardonnay, viognier and merlot. There are then two special plantings: a 1.1-ha reserve chardonnay block, and 27 ha of various clonal trials. Exports to all major markets.

♥♥♥♥♥ Reserve 242 Botrytis Riesling 2007 Major botrytis infection, golden tinged with green; level of sweetness never previously achieved; incredibly rich, luscious and sweet, but has great acidity; 242 grammes per litre of residual sugar. Screwcap. 8.1% alc. **Rating** 96 **To** 2014 $34.95

✪ Eden Valley Riesling 2009 An expressive bouquet with ripe blossom aromas leads into a palate that gathers pace as it streams to a vital and intense conclusion, lime/citrus flavours sustained by excellent acidity. Screwcap. 12% alc. **Rating** 95 **To** 2019 $19.95

Reserve Eden Valley Chardonnay 2007 Gleaming green-yellow; an extra year in bottle, slightly riper and better quality fruit than the '08 varietal, gives this wine the edge, but there is a similarity about the message: controlled complexity, a meeting of New and Old World philosophies, with a multiplicity of flavours yet a pure finish. Screwcap. 13% alc. **Rating** 95 **To** 2014 $39.95

ㅜㅜㅜㅜㅜ **Eden Valley Chardonnay 2008 Rating** 93 **To** 2015 $26.95

Heidenreich Estate ★★★☆

PO Box 99, Tanunda, SA 5352 **Region** Barossa Valley
T (08) 8563 2644 **F** (08) 8563 1554 **www**.heidenreichvineyards.com.au **Open** Not
Winemaker Noel Heidenreich **Est.** 1998 **Cases** 2000 **Vyds** 45 ha
The Heidenreich family arrived in the Barossa in 1857, with successive generations growing grapes ever since. It is now owned and run by Noel and Cheryl Heidenreich who, having changed the vineyard plantings and done much work on the soil, were content to sell the grapes from their 45 ha (at three different sites) of shiraz, cabernet sauvignon, cabernet franc, viognier and chardonnay until 1998, when they and friends crushed a tonne in total of shiraz, cabernet sauvignon and cabernet franc. Since that time, production has increased to around 2000 cases, most exported to San Diego in the US, and a little sold locally.

ㅜㅜㅜㅜㅜ **The Old School Graduates Barossa Valley Cabernet Sauvignon 2006**
Deeply coloured; a full-bodied powerful cabernet that largely throws off the shackles of its alcohol, with a proud display of black fruits, a touch of dark chocolate and firm, but balanced, tannins. Screwcap. 15% alc. **Rating** 91 **To** 2021 $30

ㅜㅜㅜㅜ **The Old School Principals Barossa Valley Shiraz 2006 Rating** 88
To 2015 $30
The Old School Blackboard Blend Barossa Valley Semillon Sauvignon Blanc 2009 Rating 87 **To** 2010 $20

Helen's Hill Estate ★★★★★

16 Ingram Road, Lilydale, Vic 3140 **Region** Yarra Valley
T (03) 9739 1573 **F** (03) 9739 0350 **www**.helenshill.com.au **Open** 7 days 10–5
Winemaker Scott McCarthy **Est.** 1984 **Cases** 10 000 **Vyds** 53 ha
Helen's Hill Estate is named after the previous owner of the property, Helen Fraser. Venture partners, Andrew and Robyn McIntosh and Lewis, Roma and Allan Nalder, combined childhood farming experience with more recent careers in medicine and finance to establish and manage the day-to-day operations of the estate. The estate produces two labels: Helen's Hill Estate and Ingram Rd, both labels made onsite by Scott McCarthy. Scott started his career early by working vintages during school holidays before gaining diverse and extensive experience working in the Barossa and Yarra valleys, Napa Valley, Languedoc, Loire Valley and Marlborough. Commanding some of the best views in the valley, an elegant 140-seat restaurant was opened in 2005; a new winery and cellar door complex was opened in '06. Exports to Hong Kong.

ㅜㅜㅜㅜㅜ **Evolution Yarra Valley Sauvignon Blanc 2007** The Full winemaking Monty, wholly wild yeast barrel-fermented in seasoned French oak barriques followed by 18 months' maturation on lees. It has worked a treat, the tropical fruit still there to be seen and still fresh, but given texture by the oak handling. Screwcap. 13.4% alc. **Rating** 94 **To** 2012 $30
Single Vineyard Yarra Valley Chardonnay 2008 Bright straw-green; a fine and delicate wine that delivers the length and flavour typical of the Yarra Valley at its best, with persistent citrus and white peach flavours, good acidity and subtle oak. Smart new label design. Screwcap. 12.4% alc. **Rating** 94 **To** 2016 $30

✪ **Ingram Rd Yarra Valley Pinot Noir 2008** Bright, clear colour; fragrant aromas of cherry, plum and a touch of forest spice lead into a long palate that has very good thrust and drive, and a savoury twist on the finish and aftertaste. Sophisticated new labels. Screwcap. 13.7% alc. **Rating** 94 **To** 2015 $18

ŦŦŦŦ͡Q Ingram Rd Yarra Valley Sauvignon Blanc 2009 Pale green-straw; a very
✪ attractive wine at the price, with abundant tropical/passionfruit flavours balanced
by lemony acidity on the finish, restrained alcohol a further plus. Screwcap.
12.4% alc. **Rating** 92 **To** 2010 $15
Ingram Rd Shiraz Cabernet 2006 Rating 90 To 2016 $18

ŦŦŦŦ Ingram Rd Yarra Valley Pinot Grigio 2009 Rating 89 To 2010 $18

Helm ★★★★☆

19 Butt's Road, Murrumbateman, NSW 2582 **Region** Canberra District
T (02) 6227 5953 **F** (02) 6227 0207 **www**.helmwines.com.au **Open** Thurs–Mon 10–5
Winemaker Ken and Stephanie Helm **Est.** 1973 **Cases** 4000 **Vyds** 15.5 ha
Ken Helm, well known as one of the more stormy petrels of the wine industry, is an
energetic promoter of his wines and of the Canberra District generally. His wines have been
workmanlike at the least, but recent vintages have lifted the quality bar substantially, receiving
conspicuous show success and critical acclaim for the Rieslings. Plantings have steadily
increased, with riesling, traminer, chardonnay, pinot noir, cabernet sauvignon, merlot, shiraz
and cabernet franc. Exports to Singapore, Macau and Hong Kong.

ŦŦŦŦŦ Classic Dry Riesling 2009 A clean and expressive bouquet leads into a palate
✪ with considerable depth and intensity given its moderately low alcohol, with apple,
lime and lemon flavours; a long and penetrating finish. Gold medal Sydney Wine
Show '10. Screwcap. 11.7% alc. **Rating** 94 **To** 2019 $28

ŦŦŦŦ͡Q Canberra District Cabernet Sauvignon 2007 Rating 91 To 2017 $32

Henley Hill Wines ★★★

1 Mount Morton Road, Belgrave South, Vic 3160 (postal) **Region** Yarra Valley
T 0414 563 439 **F** (03) 9764 3675 **www**.henleyhillwines.com.au **Open** Not
Winemaker Travis Bush (Contract) **Est.** 2003 **Cases** 7000 **Vyds** 12 ha
The history of Henley Hill dates back to 1849 when Rowland Hill began growing crops in
the Yarra Valley; the home was built in the 1860s by David Mitchell, Dame Nellie Melba's
father. The property adjoined Gulf Station, but when that property was sold in the 1930s the
home was moved to Henley and re-erected by Clive and Hilda Hill. Clive then purchased an
80-ha property adjoining Gulf Station, completing a full circle for the origins of the Henley
name. In 2003 Debbie Hill (Clive's granddaughter), Errol Campbell (Debbie's father-in-law)
and Nick and Andrew Peters planted chardonnay, sauvignon blanc, pinot gris and shiraz.
Errol, Nick and Andrew are long-time partners in various business ventures in the hospitality
industry and property development. Exports to India and China.

ŦŦŦŦ Yarra Valley Chardonnay 2008 Stone fruit, citrus and mineral components in
a light-bodied frame; the finish is fractionally bitter. Screwcap. 13% alc. **Rating** 88
To 2013 $17.50
Yarra Valley Shiraz 2008 Crimson-red; clear-cut cool-grown shiraz aromas and
flavours that go a little too far down that track; despite the alcohol, there are fleeting
touches of green leaf/herb. Screwcap. 13.8% alc. **Rating** 88 **To** 2016 $22.50
Yarra Valley Cabernet Sauvignon 2008 Strong crimson; a solid, slightly four
square cabernet; does have varietal blackcurrant fruit and a touch of black olive,
but less finesse. Screwcap. 14.3% alc. **Rating** 88 **To** 2014 $22.50

Henry Holmes Wines ★★★★

Gomersal Road, Tanunda, SA 5352 **Region** Barossa Valley
T (08) 8563 2059 **F** (08) 8563 2581 **www**.woodbridgefarm.com **Open** By appt
Winemaker Robin Day **Est.** 1998 **Cases** 1500 **Vyds** 34 ha
The Holmes family's background runs from Samuel Henry Holmes (whose parents William
Henry and Penelope Jane Holmes are co-owners of the property) to Samuel Henry's great-
great-grandparents, whose son (and his great-grandfather) Henry Holmes was born en route

to Australia from England. A further distinction is that the property owned by the Holmes family today was first planted by the Henschke family in the 1860s. The label denotes the division of opinion between Bill and Penny (as they are known) on the merits of viticulture on the one hand and White Suffolk sheep on the other; shiraz, cabernet sauvignon, grenache, riesling and tempranillo are on one side of the property, sheep on the other (held at bay by a fence). Exports to the US.

ΨΨΨΨΨ **Shack 68 Barossa Valley Grenache Rose 2009** Bright fuchsia; has an
✪ exceptionally fruity palate with raspberries to the fore, but in no way relies on
sweetness. Very impressive. Screwcap. 13% alc. **Rating** 92 **To** 2011 $15

✪ **Blue House Barossa Riesling 2009** Straw-green; elegant and fresh, with lime
zest characters on the bouquet and long palate; good acidity underpins the wine, and
will sustain it as it develops in bottle. Screwcap. 12% alc. **Rating** 90 **To** 2019 $15

ΨΨΨΨ **Barossa Valley Shiraz 2007 Rating** 89 **To** 2013 $22

Henry's Drive Vignerons ★★★★

Hodgsons Road, Padthaway, SA 5271 **Region** Padthaway
T (08) 8765 5251 **F** (08) 8765 5180 **www**.henrysdrive.com **Open** 7 days 10–4
Winemaker Kim Jackson, Chris Ringland (Consultant). **Est.** 1998 **Cases** 170 000
Named after the proprietor of the 19th-century mail coach service that once ran through their property, Henry's Drive Vignerons is the wine operation established by Kim Longbottom and her late husband Mark. Kim is continuing to build the family tradition of winemaking with brands such as Henry's Drive, Parson's Flat, The Trial of John Montford, Dead Letter Office, Pillar Box, Morse Code and The Postmistress. Exports to the UK, the US and other major markets.

ΨΨΨΨΨ **Pillar Box Reserve 2007** Good colour; rich blackberry, prune and dark
✪ chocolate aromas are repeated on the palate; shiraz is Padthaway's trump card.
Doesn't show dead fruit. Screwcap. 15% alc. **Rating** 91 **To** 2017 $18

✪ **Morse Code Padthaway Shiraz 2008** Luscious blackberry, prune and licorice
fruit on the bouquet, then a medium- to full-bodied palate with sufficient tannins
to provide some discipline, although not ultimate length. Exceptional bargain.
Screwcap. 14.7% alc. **Rating** 90 **To** 2014 $10

ΨΨΨΨ **Pillar Box Reserve 2008 Rating** 89 **To** 2023 $18
Dead Letter Office Shiraz 2007 Rating 89 **To** 2015 $23
✪ **Morse Code Padthaway Chardonnay 2009** Light-bodied, fresh and crisp,
with some regional grapefruit nuances; no oak, of course, and enough length to
carry it over the line. Screwcap. 12.5% alc. **Rating** 88 **To** 2011 $10
Padthaway Shiraz 2007 Rating 88 **To** 2015 $32
✪ **Pillar Box Red 2007** Dense colour; licorice, prune and dark confit fruit aromas
and flavours; a huge amount of flavour for $14; less (i.e. earlier picking) might have
been better. Shiraz/Cabernet Sauvignon/Merlot. Screwcap. 15% alc. **Rating** 88
To 2013 $14
Parson's Flat Padthaway Shiraz Cabernet 2007 Rating 88 **To** 2014 $35
Pillar Box White 2009 Rating 87 **To** 2010 $14
Pillar Box White 2008 Rating 87 **To** 2010 $14
Pillar Box Red 2008 Rating 87 **To** 2012 $14
The Trial of John Montford Cabernet Sauvignon 2007 Rating 87
To 2011 $30

Henschke ★★★★★

Henschke Road, Keyneton, SA 5353 **Region** Eden Valley
T (08) 8564 8223 **F** (08) 8564 8294 **www**.henschke.com.au **Open** Mon–Fri 9–4.30,
Sat 9–12, public hols 10–3
Winemaker Stephen Henschke **Est.** 1868 **Cases** 30 000 **Vyds** 121.72 ha
Regarded as the best medium-sized red wine producer in Australia, Henschke has gone from strength to strength over the past three decades under the guidance of winemaker Stephen

and viticulturist Prue Henschke. The red wines fully capitalise on the very old, low-yielding, high-quality vines and are superbly made with sensitive but positive use of new small oak: Hill of Grace is second only to Penfolds Grange as Australia's red wine icon (since 2005 sold with a screwcap). Exports to all major markets.

ΨΨΨΨΨ **Hill of Grace 2006** Bright red-purple; highly fragrant spice, cedar, red and black berry aromas, oak evident but not excessive; it has a silky, velvety texture and mouthfeel to a beautifully balanced medium-bodied palate brimming with black fruits; wonderful length and finish. Surely one of the best Hill of Graces. Shiraz. Screwcap. 14.5% alc. **Rating** 97 **To** 2026 $600

✪ **Julius Eden Valley Riesling 2009** A flowery bouquet with hints of herb and spice, then a tight but very long palate with impressive finesse to the lime-accented palate, leaving the mouth fresh. Screwcap. 12.5% alc. **Rating** 96 **To** 2020 $28

Mount Edelstone 2007 Vivid colour; it has a rich and deep bouquet with licorice, spice, tar and black fruit aromas; the palate extremely rich and complex, layered fruit with plush tannins, yet is supple; very long finish to an outstanding '07 wine. Shiraz. Screwcap. 14% alc. **Rating** 95 **To** 2022 $105

Coralinga Adelaide Hills Sauvignon Blanc 2009 A finely crafted and delineated wine, with an appealing touch of tropical fruit behind both bouquet and palate; has excellent length, and a very classy, lingering finish. Screwcap. 13% alc. **Rating** 94 **To** 2011 $26

✪ **Eleanor's Cottage Eden Valley Adelaide Hills Sauvignon Blanc Semillon 2009** Has a notably fragrant bouquet, with tropical passionfruit aromas contributed by the sauvignon blanc, then a well-structured palate provided by the semillon; a very synergistic blend. Screwcap. 12% alc. **Rating** 94 **To** 2012 $22

Croft Lenswood Chardonnay 2008 Whole bunch pressed, wild yeast fermented and no mlf; fine, intense grapefruit and stone fruit; has a strong minerally streak, oak a minor player in a very pure wine. Screwcap. 13.5% alc. **Rating** 94 **To** 2015 $42

Giles Lenswood Pinot Noir 2008 Whole berry, whole bunch, wild yeast fermented; multiple clone base; relatively light-bodied but very well balanced and structured, with red cherry and strawberry fruit given complexity by a light touch of spice; a silky, long, finish. Screwcap. 14.5% alc. **Rating** 94 **To** 2015 $46

Henry's Seven 2008 Typical bright hue; a delicious medium-bodied wine, with its bright red fruits lifted by viognier; has length built partially around ripe but fine tannins. Shiraz/Grenache/Viognier. Screwcap. 14.5% alc. **Rating** 94 **To** 2020 $33

Lenswood Abbott's Prayer 2007 Relatively light but bright hue; a multi-red fruit array on bouquet and palate, the fruit gliding across the mouth; a tribute to Adelaide Hills' ability to ride the punches of hot years. Screwcap. 14.5% alc. **Rating** 94 **To** 2017 $77

Cyril Henschke 2007 The colour is more advanced than Mount Edelstone; olive, cedar, sage, herb and black fruits on the bouquet and palate; the tangy savoury finish is drawn out and lengthened by the fine tannins. Cabernet Sauvignon/Merlot/Cabernet Franc. Screwcap. 14% alc. **Rating** 94 **To** 2022 $130

ΨΨΨΨΩ **Green's Hill Lenswood Riesling 2009** Apple blossom aromas lead into a
✪ perfectly balanced palate, citrus to the fore, apple in the rear; good length and balance. Screwcap. 13% alc. **Rating** 93 **To** 2019 $22

Louis Eden Valley Semillon 2008 Rating 93 **To** 2016 $28

Kyneton Euphonium 2007 Rating 93 **To** 2020 $48

Hill of Roses 2007 Rating 92 **To** 2022 $210

Henry's Seven 2007 Rating 92 **To** 2015 $33

Peggy's Hill Eden Valley Riesling 2009 Rating 91 **To** 2018 $19.30

Joseph Hill Eden Valley Gewurztraminer 2009 Rating 90 **To** 2013 $33

✪ **Tilly's Vineyard 2008** A time-honoured blend (Semillon/Sauvignon Blanc/ Chardonnay/Pinot Gris) freed from unnecessary oak and benefiting from its three main components; juicy fruit flavours persist through the length of the palate. Screwcap. 13% alc. **Rating** 90 **To** 2012 $18

Johann's Garden 2008 Rating 90 **To** 2018 $41

Hentley Farm Wines   ★★★★★

Cnr Jenke Road/Gerald Roberts Road, Seppeltsfield, SA 5355 **Region** Barossa Valley
T (08) 8562 8427 **F** (08) 8562 8037 **www.**hentleyfarm.com.au **Open** 7 days 10–5
Winemaker Andrew Quin **Est.** 1999 **Cases** 10 000 **Vyds** 38.21 ha
Keith and Alison Hentschke purchased the Hentley Farm in 1997, then an old vineyard
and mixed farming property. Keith has thoroughly impressive credentials, having studied
agricultural science at Roseworthy, and then wine marketing, obtaining an MBA. During
the 1990s he had a senior production role with Orlando, before moving on to manage one
of Australia's largest vineyard management companies, and from 2002 to '06 he worked with
Nepenthe. Shiraz (26.83 ha), grenache (6.46 h), cabernet sauvignon (4 ha), zinfandel (0.78 ha)
and viognier (0.14 ha) are now in production. The vineyard, situated among rolling hills on
the banks of Greenock Creek, has red clay loam soils overlaying shattered limestone, lightly
rocked slopes and little top soil. Exports to the US and other major markets.

ⵦⵦⵦⵦⵦ The Beast Barossa Valley Shiraz 2008 Deep colour with as much purple as
crimson; whereas Clos Otto is basically wrapped up in itself, this wine has more
light and shade both in terms of aroma/flavour and texture/structure, unfolding
superbly on its spicy, slightly savoury, finish; full-bodied, to be sure, but with
elegance. Cork. 15% alc. **Rating** 96 To 2033 $75
Clos Otto Barossa Valley Shiraz 2008 Dense, deep purple-crimson; a
voluptuous, full-bodied wine that has achieved so much flavour without any
sign of dead fruit or over-extraction; layers of blackberry, plum, prune and dark
chocolate envelope the tannins and oak components that will appear with
time. The choice of cork is a tragedy for a wine built to last 40 years. 15% alc.
Rating 95 To 2048 $150
The Beauty Barossa Valley Shiraz 2008 Impenetrable colour; a hedonistic
array of dark fruits, fruitcake spice, licorice and mocha; the palate is thickly
textured, with staggering levels of dark fruit, cleaned up by a little savoury edge of
fresh bitumen and turned earth; massively proportioned for those in search of a big
style. Cork. 15% alc. **Rating** 94 To 2020 $60 BE
The Stray Mongrel 2009 A blend of estate-grown Grenache/Shiraz/Zinfandel,
each variety separately fermented and barrel matured prior to blending; the colour
is very bright crimson, the wine with a delicious array of red fruits, tannins and
oak fulfilling a pepper and salt role for the dish. A surprise packet, for these oddball
blends seldom excite. Screwcap. 15% alc. **Rating** 94 To 2014 $35

ⵦⵦⵦⵦⵦ Fools Bay Dirty Bliss Barossa Valley Grenache Shiraz 2009 Hentley
✪   Farm must have an exceptional vineyard, because few Barossa Valley grenache
blends share the bright colour and fresh fruit flavours of this wine; nor is it just an
upjumped rose, for its has subtle but positive tannin structure. Screwcap. 15% alc.
Rating 93 To 2014 $20
Barossa Valley Zinfandel 2008 **Rating** 92 To 2015 $34
Fools Bay Dusty's Desire Barossa Valley Shiraz 2008 **Rating** 91 To 2018 $34
Barossa Valley Shiraz 2008 **Rating** 91 To 2018 $32 BE
Barossa Valley Viognier 2009 **Rating** 90 To 2012 $41.50 BE
✪   Caretaker Shiraz 2009 Strong purple; a very dense wine from start to finish;
there must be some very powerful and rich shirazs to follow in due course; needs,
and will repay, some years in bottle. Screwcap. 15% alc. **Rating** 90 To 2020 $20

ⵦⵦⵦⵦ   Fools Bay Dirty Bliss Barossa Valley Grenache Shiraz 2008 **Rating** 89
To 2015 $20
Barossa Valley Zinfandel 2009 **Rating** 89 To 2014 $35
The Exception Eden Valley Riesling 2009 **Rating** 87 To 2015 $23 BE

Henty Estate   ★★★★☆

657 Hensley Park Road, Hamilton, Vic 3300 (postal) **Region** Henty
T (03) 5572 4446 **F** (03) 5572 4446 **www.**henty-estate.com.au **Open** Not
Winemaker Peter Dixon **Est.** 1991 **Cases** 1400 **Vyds** 7 ha

Peter and Glenys Dixon have hastened slowly with Henty Estate. In 1991 they began the planting of 4.5 ha of shiraz, 1 ha each of cabernet sauvignon and chardonnay, and 0.5 ha of riesling. In their words, 'we avoided the temptation to make wine until the vineyard was mature', establishing the winery in 2003. Encouraged by neighbour John Thomson, they have limited the yield to 3–4 tonnes per ha on the VSP-trained, dry-grown vineyard.

ŶŶŶŶŶ **Chardonnay 2008** Light straw-green; has a particularly expressive bouquet of
❂ grapefruit and white peach, replayed in turn on the palate; barrel ferment inputs are discernible, but no more, the finish crisp and minerally. Screwcap. 13.5% alc. Rating 94 To 2015 $20

ŶŶŶŶŶ **Riesling 2009** Rating 91 To 2018 $20

Herbert Vineyard ★★★★

Bishop Road, Mount Gambier, SA 5290 **Region** Mount Gambier
T 0408 849 080 **F** (08) 8724 9512 www.herbertvineyard.com.au **Open** By appt
Winemaker David Herbert **Est.** 1996 **Cases** 450 **Vyds** 2.4 ha
David and Trudy Herbert have planted 1.9 ha of pinot noir, and a total of 0.5 ha of cabernet sauvignon, merlot and pinot gris. The majority of the pinot noir is sold to Foster's for sparkling wine, and the Herberts have built a two-level (mini) winery overlooking a 1600-sq metre maze planted in 2000, which is reflected in the label logo.

ŶŶŶŶŶ **Mount Gambier Rose 2009** Bright fuchsia; a complex bouquet of sweet red
❂ berry fruit, then a full-flavoured, although not heavy, palate. Cabernet Sauvignon/ Merlot. Screwcap. 12.9% alc. Rating 90 To 2011 $16
Barrel Number 1 Mount Gambier Pinot Noir 2008 Slightly deeper colour than the standard wine, but substantially greater flavour structure, with plum joining the suite of flavours. Will develop. Screwcap. 13.5% alc. Rating 90 To 2015 $27

ŶŶŶŶ **Kangaroo Hill Shiraz Cabernet 2008** Rating 89 To 2013 $18
Mount Gambier Pinot Noir 2008 Rating 88 To 2013 $23
Mount Gambier Cabernet Plus 2008 Rating 88 To 2014 $18

Heritage Estate ★★★★

Granite Belt Drive, Cottonvale, Qld 4375 **Region** Granite Belt
T (07) 4685 2197 **F** (07) 4685 2112 www.heritagewines.com.au **Open** 7 days 9–5
Winemaker John Handy **Est.** 1992 **Cases** 5000 **Vyds** 8.75 ha
Bryce and Paddy Kassulke operate a very successful winery, showcasing their wines through a cellar door at Mt Tamborine in a converted old church, which has views over the Gold Coast hinterland, and includes a restaurant, barbecue area and art gallery. Estate plantings have been steadily expanded, now comprising chardonnay, shiraz, merlot, verdelho, cabernet sauvignon, durif and savagnin, with additional varieties purchased from local growers. Heritage Estate has been a prolific award winner in various Qld wine shows.

ŶŶŶŶŶ **Semillon 2009** Light straw-green; stood up to the heat, but the sauvignon blanc
❂ didn't (until '09 the two were blended), henceforth there will be 100 cases a year of semillon, a thoroughly justified decision, for this is a thoroughly good semillon, bursting with juicy citrus flavours, and a long, clean finish. Diam. 11.8% alc. Rating 90 To 2016 $16.50
Reserve Blend Granite Belt Verdelho 2009 A good vintage and astute winemaking (part barrel, part stainless-steel fermentation) have produced a verdelho that deserves the Reserve tag; it has excellent citrussy acidity and plenty of mid-palate flavour. Diam. 13.5% alc. Rating 90 To 2013 $25

ŶŶŶŶ **Patricia Granite Belt Shiraz 2008** Rating 89 To 2018 $22.50
Rabbit Fence Red Granite Belt Cabernet Shiraz 2009 Rating 88 To 2011 $16.50
Verdelho 2009 Rating 87 To 2011 $20
Fortified Shiraz 2008 Rating 87 To 2013 $18

Heritage Wines   ★★★★★

106a Seppeltsfield Road, Marananga, SA 5355 **Region** Barossa Valley
T (08) 8562 2880 **F** (08) 8562 2692 **www**.heritagewinery.com.au **Open** Mon–Fri 10–5,
w'ends & public hols 11–5
Winemaker Stephen Hoff **Est.** 1984 **Cases** 5500 **Vyds** 8.3 ha
A little-known winery that deserves a far wider audience, for veteran owner/winemaker
Stephen Hoff is apt to produce some startlingly good wines. At various times the Riesling
(from old Clare Valley vines), Cabernet Sauvignon and Shiraz (now the flag-bearer) have all
excelled. The vineyard is planted to cabernet sauvignon (5.5 ha), shiraz (2.5 ha) and malbec
(0.3 ha). No relevant tasting notes for the 2011 *Wine Companion*. Exports to the UK, the US,
Thailand, Hong Kong, Malaysia and Singapore.

Herons Rise Vineyard   ★★★☆

Saddle Road, Kettering, Tas 7155 **Region** Southern Tasmania
T (03) 6267 4339 **F** (03) 6267 4245 **www**.heronsrise.com.au **Open** By appt
Winemaker Contract **Est.** 1984 **Cases** 250
Sue and Gerry White run a small stone country guest house in the D'Entrecasteaux Channel
area and basically sell the wines produced from the surrounding hectare of vineyard to those
staying at the two self-contained cottages.

♟♟♟♟♟ **Pinot Noir 2007** Strong crimson-purple, bright and clear; rich plum fruit and
spice to a soft and generous wine; the trajectory does slow a little on the finish.
Screwcap. 14% alc. **Rating** 91 **To** 2014 $20

Hesketh Wine Company   ★★★★★

6 Blairgowrie Road, St Georges, SA 5064 **Region** Various
T 0419 003 144 **F** (08) 8344 9429 **www**.heskethwinecompany.com.au **Open** Not
Winemaker Various **Est.** 2006 **Cases** 4000
The Hesketh Wine Company is a New World version of the French Negociant Eleveur,
commonly known in Australia as a virtual winery, and owned by Jonathon Hesketh, wife
Trish and children. Jonathon spent seven years as the Global Sales & Marketing Manager
of Wirra Wirra, two and a half years as General Manager of Distinguished Vineyards in NZ
working with the Möet Hennessy wine and champagne portfolio, plus the Petaluma group,
and also had significant global responsibility for Mars Corporation over a four-year period. He
also happens to be the son of Robert Hesketh, one of the key players in the development of
many facets of the SA wine industry. The model for Hesketh Wine Company is to find wines
that best express the regions they come from and closely monitor their production, but own
neither vineyards nor a winery.

♟♟♟♟♟ **Perfect Stranger Krems Gruner Veltliner 2008** Lively and persuasive gruner
✪ at the alcohol level that I think best suits the style; made by Bert Salomon at the
Salomon winery in Austria. Screwcap. 12.5% alc. **Rating** 94 **To** 2018 $24.95
✪ **The Protagonist Barossa Valley Shiraz 2006** Has retained excellent hue;
another reminder of just how good the '06 vintage was, here effortlessly providing
shiraz flooded with opulent black fruits, ripe tannins and oak all in perfect balance,
an unexpected twist of spice on the aftertaste a bonus. Screwcap. 14.5% alc.
Rating 94 **To** 2020 $24.95

♟♟♟♟ **Hidden Garden Marlborough Sauvignon Blanc 2009** **Rating** 89
To 2011 $19.95
Usual Suspects McLaren Vale Shiraz 2008 **Rating** 89 **To** 2018 $19.95
Thirsty Dog Coonawarra Cabernet Sauvignon 2008 **Rating** 89
To 2016 $19.95

Hewitson ★★★★★

1 Seppeltsfield Road, Dorrien, SA 5355 **Region** Adelaide Zone
T (08) 8443 6466 **F** (08) 8443 6866 **www**.hewitson.com.au **Open** By appt
Winemaker Dean Hewitson **Est.** 1996 **Cases** 25 000 **Vyds** 4.5 ha
Dean Hewitson was a winemaker at Petaluma for 10 years, during which time he managed
to do three vintages in France and one in Oregon as well as undertaking his Masters at the
University of California (Davis). It is hardly surprising that the wines are immaculately made
from a technical viewpoint. Dean has managed to source 30-year-old riesling from the Eden
Valley and 70-year-old shiraz from McLaren Vale; he also makes a Barossa Valley Mourvedre
from vines planted in 1853 at Rowland Flat and a Barossa Valley Shiraz and Grenache from
60-year-old vines at Tanunda. Between 2008 and '10 Dean Hewitson progressively established
his own winery at Dorrien, completing it in time to process the '10 vintage. Exports to the
UK, the US and other major markets.

ᵀᵀᵀᵀᵀ **Private Cellar Barossa Valley Shiraz Mourvedre 2007** Good hue;
blackberry, blackcurrant, earth and dark chocolate all coalesce on the medium- to
full-bodied palate, which has outstanding texture and structure, oak and tannins
precisely controlled; 20 years cellaring suggestion on front label seems remarkably
modest. Magnum. Screwcap. 14% alc. **Rating** 96 **To** 2037 $150

✪ **LuLu Adelaide Hills Sauvignon Blanc 2009** Offers predominant citrus and
grass aromas on the bouquet, but there is also a touch of tropical fruit; all these
characters come through on the palate, which has thrust and drive to the cleansing
finish. Screwcap. 12.5% alc. **Rating** 94 **To** 2011 $22

Ned & Henry's Barossa Valley Shiraz 2008 Strong, dark crimson; attractive
medium-bodied wine, presumably picked before the heat; blackberry and plum
are the main drivers, with lesser licorice and dark chocolate nuances; good balance,
line and length. Screwcap. 14% alc. **Rating** 94 **To** 2023 $25

The Mad Hatter McLaren Vale Shiraz 2007 Still holding youthful colour; red
and black fruits, spice, a wisp of dark chocolate and mocha oak on the bouquet
lead into a vibrant palate that has just enough fruit to carry 20 months in 100%
new French oak. A modern interpretation of the Blewitt Springs subregion of
McLaren Vale. Screwcap. 14.5% alc. **Rating** 94 **To** 2027 $70

ᵀᵀᵀᵀᵀ **Miss Harry Dry Grown & Ancient 2008** Bright, light colour; a lusciously
✪ juicy wine, with cherry and raspberry flavours tempered by a slightly savoury
finish; good length and balance. Grenache/Shiraz/Mourvedre/Cinsaut. Screwcap.
14% alc. **Rating** 92 **To** 2015 $22

Baby Bush Barossa Valley Mourvedre 2008 Rating 91 **To** 2016 $28

ᵀᵀᵀᵀ **Gun Metal Eden Valley Riesling 2009 Rating** 88 **To** 2014 $22

🍇 Heydon Estate ★★★★☆

325 Harmans South Road, Wilyabrup, WA 6280 **Region** Margaret River
T (08) 9755 6995 **F** (08) 9755 6996 **www**.heydonestate.com.au **Open** Fri–Sun 10–5
Winemaker Mark Messenger, John Durham **Est.** 1988 **Cases** 1200 **Vyds** 10 ha
Margaret River dentist George Heydon (and wife Mary) have been involved in the region's
wine industry since 1995. They became 50% partners in Arlewood, and when that partnership
was dissolved in '04 the Heydons relinquished their interest in the Arlewood brand but
retained the property and the precious 2 ha of cabernet sauvignon and 2.5 ha of Gin Gin
clone chardonnay planted in '88. Additional plantings in '95 include Dijon chardonnay clones,
sauvignon blanc, semillon, shiraz and petit verdot. The first cabernet made under the Heydon
ownership, the '04 WG Grace Cabernet Sauvignon, won the trophy for Best Cabernet
Sauvignon at the Margaret River Wine Show '06 and the '05 The Willow Chardonnay
received a gold medal at the Perth Royal Wine Show '08. The estate is now biodynamic,
near-neighbour Vanya Cullen having no doubt inspired the decision. And if it wasn't already
very obvious, George is a cricket tragic. Exports to the UK.

ŶŶŶŶŶ **W.G. Grace Single Vineyard Margaret River Cabernet Sauvignon 2004**
Good hue, although not deep; an elegant medium-bodied wine with every
component precisely where it should be; blackcurrant, cassis, plum, cedar and
tannins on the long palate. Screwcap. 13.8% alc. **Rating** 94 **To** 2019 $45

ŶŶŶŶŶ **The Willow Single Vineyard Margaret River Chardonnay 2005** Rating 93
To 2015 $35
The Urn Single Vineyard Margaret River Botrytis Semillon 2006
Rating 91 **To** 2015 $25

Hidden Creek   ★★★☆
Eukey Road, Ballandean, Qld 4382 **Region** Granite Belt
T (07) 4684 1383 **F** (07) 4684 1355 **www**.hiddencreek.com.au **Open** Mon & Fri 11–3,
w'ends 10–4
Winemaker Jim Barnes **Est.** 1997 **Cases** 1000 **Vyds** 2 ha
A beautifully located vineyard and winery at 1000 m on a ridge overlooking the Ballandean
township and the Severn River Valley. The granite boulder–strewn hills mean that the 70-ha
property only provides 2 ha of vineyard, in turn divided into six different blocks planted to
shiraz and merlot. The business is owned by a group of Brisbane wine enthusiasts and Jim
Barnes, who also runs a contract winemaking business as well as making the Hidden Creek
wines. There are three labels: Hidden Creek, Red Bird and Rooklyn. Rooklyn is made from
Granite Belt grapes, which are either of outstanding quality, unusual styles, or are emerging
varieties, and have had overwhelming success in wine shows.

ŶŶŶŶŶ **Granite Belt Shiraz 2008** Deep red-purple; blackberry and plum fruit drives
the bouquet and the medium-bodied palate; has good texture and structure, fruit
lingering on the finish. Screwcap. 14% alc. **Rating** 90 **To** 2018 $28

ŶŶŶŶ **Girraween Granite Belt Cabernet Merlot Petit Verdot 2008** Rating 89
To 2016 $28
Granite Belt Petit Verdot 2008 Rating 89 **To** 2016 $25
Premium Granite Belt Verdelho 2009 Rating 88 **To** 2012 $22
Granite Belt Marsanne Viognier 2008 Rating 87 **To** 2012 $22

Higher Plane   ★★★★☆
165 Warner Glen Road, Forest Grove, WA 6286 **Region** Margaret River
T (08) 9258 9437 **F** (08) 9755 9100 **www**.higherplanewines.com.au **Open** Not
Winemaker Mark Messenger, Kym Eyres **Est.** 1996 **Cases** 2000 **Vyds** 19.68 ha
In late 2006 Higher Plane was purchased by Roger Hill and family (of Juniper Estate), but
kept as a stand-alone brand, with different distributors, etc. The Higher Plane vineyards are
planted to all of the key varieties, sauvignon blanc foremost, then chardonnay, semillon and
cabernet sauvignon (shiraz, merlot, cabernet franc, malbec, petit verdot and viognier make up
the rest of the plantings). Exports to Canada and Denmark.

ŶŶŶŶŶ **Margaret River Cabernet Sauvignon 2007** Strong crimson-purple; there is
no question about the integrity of the varietal character of this full-bodied wine,
with intense blackcurrant fruit and even more intense savoury tannins that need to
soften before the fruit does. Screwcap. 14% alc. **Rating** 92 **To** 2032 $35
Margaret River Chardonnay 2008 A super-elegant wine, perhaps just a touch
too elegant, for there is not a hair out of place; white peach and citrus fruit, a
gossamer benison of oak, and crisp acidity make up a light-bodied, fresh wine with
undoubted cellaring capacity. Screwcap. 14% alc. **Rating** 91 **To** 2016 $35
✪ **South by Southwest Margaret River Cabernet Merlot 2008** What you
see is what you get: a medium-bodied display of blackcurrant, redcurrant and
plum fruit, a substrate of tannins and a modicum of oak – pure Margaret River.
Screwcap. 14% alc. **Rating** 91 **To** 2018 $21

○　　South by Southwest Margaret River Shiraz 2007 Clear crimson-purple;
a small percentage of co-fermented viognier has made a major impact on the
bouquet and light- to medium-bodied palate, also highlighting the oak. Screwcap.
14% alc. **Rating** 90 **To** 2015 $21

ΨΨΨΨ　South by Southwest Margaret River Sauvignon Blanc Semillon 2009
Rating 89 **To** 2011 $21
South by Southwest Margaret River Chardonnay 2006 Rating 89
To 2013 $22

Hillbillé ★★★★

Blackwood Valley Estate, Balingup Road, Nannup, WA 6275 **Region** Blackwood Valley
T (08) 9481 0888 **F** (08) 9486 1899 **www**.hillbille.com **Open** By appt
Winemaker Woodlands Wines (Stuart Watson) **Est.** 1998 **Cases** 3000 **Vyds** 18 ha
Gary Bettridge has planted chardonnay shiraz, cabernet sauvignon, merlot, semillon, sauvignon
blanc and viognier on his 75-ha family property. The vineyard is situated in the Blackwood
Valley between Balingup and Nannup, which the RAC describes as 'the most scenic drive
in the southwest of WA'. A significant part of the grape production is sold to other makers,
but since 2003 part has been vinified for the Hillbillé label. Exports to Japan, Singapore and
Hong Kong.

ΨΨΨΨΨ　Estate Sauvignon Blanc Semillon 2009 A fragrant and lively bouquet with a
○　　range of aromas well beyond the usual square, bringing in both pear and apple to
join the citrus; the crisp, clean and well-balanced palate does not deviate from the
path laid down by the bouquet. Screwcap. 13.2% alc. **Rating** 91 **To** 2012 $18

Hillbrook Wines ★★★★

Cnr Hillbrook Road/Wheatley Coast Road, Quinninup, WA 6258 **Region** Pemberton
T (08) 9776 7202 **F** (08) 9776 6473 **www**.hillbrookwines.com.au **Open** By appt
Winemaker Castle Rock Estate **Est.** 1996 **Cases** 500 **Vyds** 7.1 ha
When Brian Eade and partner Anne Walsh left Alice Springs in 1996 to move to Pemberton,
they made (in their words) the ultimate tree change. As well as establishing sauvignon
blanc (3 ha), semillon (2 ha), merlot (17 ha) and a smattering of chardonnay, they have 600
olive trees.

ΨΨΨΨΨ　Pemberton Sauvignon Blanc 2009 Very pale straw-green; the bouquet is
○　　spotlessly clean and fresh, but doesn't prepare you for the intensity of the palate,
the flavours perfectly positioned between the herbaceous and tropical ends of
the spectrum. Trophy Cowra Wine Show '09. Screwcap. 12.5% alc. **Rating** 95
To 2012 $18

ΨΨΨΨ　Pemberton Merlot 2007 **Rating** 89 **To** 2014 $18

Hillcrest Vineyard ★★★★★

31 Phillip Road, Woori Yallock, Vic 3139 **Region** Yarra Valley
T (03) 5964 6689 **F** (03) 5961 5547 **www**.hillcrestvineyard.com.au **Open** By appt
Winemaker David and Tanya Bryant **Est.** 1970 **Cases** 800 **Vyds** 16.2 ha
The small, effectively dry-grown vineyard was established by Graeme and Joy Sweet, who
ultimately sold it to David and Tanya Bryant. The pinot noir, chardonnay, merlot and cabernet
sauvignon grown on the property have always been of the highest quality and, when
Coldstream Hills was in its infancy, were particularly important resources for it. Plantings
in 2000 have substantially increased the area under vine, and the wine available for sale will
steadily, although not dramatically, increase.

ΨΨΨΨΨ　Premium Yarra Valley Pinot Noir 2008 Bright and clear, despite no fining or
filtration; an extremely pure and fine wine, the bouquet adding a touch of plum
that comes through on the precise and very long palate. Three fascinating pinots.
Cork. 13% alc. **Rating** 96 **To** 2015 $55

Premium Yarra Valley Cabernet Sauvignon 2008 Dense purple-crimson; a full-bodied wine, with tremendous depth to the blackcurrant fruit and exceptional savoury yet fine and ripe tannins; oak also plays a role of some importance. Stained cork. 13.9% alc. **Rating** 96 **To** 2023 $55

Estate Yarra Valley Chardonnay 2008 Bright green-straw; a delicious, albeit understated, chardonnay, French oak gently woven through the white peach and melon fruit of the bouquet and palate, and supported by perfect acidity. Cork. 13% alc. **Rating** 94 **To** 2013 $37

Premium Yarra Valley Chardonnay 2008 Developed green-gold; a touch of grilled nuts ex barrel fermentation on the bouquet, the palate still tight, fresh and long; white peach and a little grapefruit; long finish. Quality cork, slightly distorted. 13% alc. **Rating** 94 **To** 2013 $55

Estate Yarra Valley Pinot Noir 2008 Bright, clear red; the bouquet is complex, with a core of black cherry fruit, the palate fine and long, fruit and forest equally balanced. Cork. 13% alc. **Rating** 94 **To** 2015 $37

ǄǄǄǄ **Reserve Merlot 2008 Rating** 93 **To** 2018 $100
Village Yarra Valley Pinot Noir 2008 Rating 90 **To** 2013 $20

Hillwood Vineyard ★★★

55 Innocent Street, Kings Meadows, Tas 7249 (postal) **Region** Northern Tasmania
T 0418 500 672 **Open** Not
Winemaker Geoff Carr **Est.** NA **Cases** NA
Geoff Carr, owner, viticulturist and winemaker, has established his vineyard on the east bank of the Tamar River, looking out over the river. He supplements his estate-grown grapes by purchasing some chardonnay and pinot gris from local growers.

ǄǄǄǄ **Sauvignon Blanc 2009** Clean and fresh nuances of passionfruit; finishes with crisp acidity. **Rating** 87 **To** 2011

Hirsch Hill Estate ★★★

2088 Melba Highway, Dixons Creek, Vic 3775 **Region** Yarra Valley
T 1300 877 781 **F** (03) 9640 0370 **www**.hirschhill.com **Open** Not
Winemaker Yering Farm (Alan Johns) **Est.** 1998 **Cases** 3500 **Vyds** 12 ha
The Hirsch family has planted a vineyard to pinot noir (predominantly), cabernet sauvignon, chardonnay, merlot and cabernet franc. (New plantings of 2.5 ha of sauvignon blanc, shiraz and viognier were lost in the Black Saturday bushfires.) The vineyard is part of a larger racehorse stud, situated in a mini-valley at the northern end of the Yarra Valley.

ǄǄǄǄ **Yarra Valley Cabernet Sauvignon 2008** Some colour development; has a quite fragrant bouquet and juicy blackcurrant flavours on the medium-bodied palate; good early drinking style. Screwcap. 13.5% alc. **Rating** 89 **To** 2014 $20

Hobbs of Barossa Ranges ★★★★☆

Cnr Flaxman's Valley Road/Randalls Road, Angaston, SA 5353 **Region** Barossa Valley
T 0427 177 740 **F** (08) 8565 3268 **www**.hobbsvintners.com.au **Open** By appt
Winemaker Pete Schell, Chris Ringland (Consultant) **Est.** 1998 **Cases** 1100 **Vyds** 6.22 ha
Hobbs of Barossa Ranges is a high-profile, if somewhat challenging, venture of Greg and Allison Hobbs. The estate vineyards revolve around 1 ha of shiraz planted in 1908, another ha planted in '88, a further ha planted in '97, and 1.82 ha planted in 2004. In 2009 0.4 ha of old white frontignac was removed, giving space for another small planting of shiraz. The viticultural portfolio is completed with 0.6 ha of semillon planted in the 1960s, and an inspired 0.6 ha of viognier ('88). All of the wines made by Peter Schell (at Spinifex) push the envelope. The only conventionally made wine is the Shiraz Viognier, with a production of 130 cases. Gregor, an Amarone-style Shiraz in full-blooded table wine mode, and a quartet of dessert wines are produced by cane cutting followed by further desiccation on racks. The Grenache comes from a Barossa floor vineyard, the Semillon, Viognier and White Frontignac from estate-grown grapes.

ŸŸŸŸŸ Viognier 2007 Full golden colour; more luscious and rich than the Semillon, and retains the apricot/stone fruit flavours it started with; sensual texture and lifted by lesser alcohol. Screwcap. 8.1% alc. **Rating** 94 To 2011 $39

ŸŸŸŸŸ Semillon 2007 **Rating** 93 To 2012 $39
Shiraz 2006 **Rating** 92 To 2016 $130
Gregor Shiraz 2007 **Rating** 90 To 2017 $130
Shiraz Viognier 2007 **Rating** 90 To 2014 $110

Hoddles Creek Estate ★★★★★

505 Gembrook Road, Hoddles Creek, Vic 3139 **Region** Yarra Valley
T (03) 5967 4692 **F** (03) 5967 4692 **www.**hoddlescreekestate.com.au **Open** By appt
Winemaker Franco D'Anna, Lucas Hoorn **Est.** 1997 **Cases** 15 000 **Vyds** 28.6 ha
In 1997, the D'Anna family decided to establish a vineyard on the property that had been in the family since 1960. The vineyards (chardonnay, pinot noir, sauvignon blanc, cabernet sauvignon, pinot gris, merlot and pinot blanc) are hand-pruned and hand-harvested. A 300-tonne, split-level winery was completed in 2003. Son Franco is the viticulturist and winemaker; he started to work in the family liquor store at 13, graduating to chief wine buyer by the time he was 21, then completed a Bachelor of Commerce degree at Melbourne University before studying viticulture at CSU. A vintage at Coldstream Hills, then consulting help from Peter Dredge of Red Edge and Mario Marson (ex Mount Mary), has put an old head on young shoulders. Exports to South Africa and Singapore.

ŸŸŸŸŸ Yarra Valley Chardonnay 2008 A delicious chardonnay, exemplifying the
✪ Yarra Valley style with its length and finesse; white peach and nectarine fruit flow smoothly across the palate, oak and acidity in perfectly balanced support. Screwcap. 13.5% alc. **Rating** 95 To 2014 $19
1er Yarra Valley Chardonnay 2008 Complex chardonnay, with a lot of winemaker influences lurking like unseen ghosts; nectarine, melon, fig and cashew characters are balanced by fresh acidity, oak the now discarded womb. Very harmonious. Screwcap. 13.2% alc. **Rating** 95 To 2016 $35

ŸŸŸŸŸ Wickhams Road Yarra Valley Chardonnay 2009 More complex than the
✪ Gippsland wine; here white and yellow flesh stone fruit comes to the fore, lemony acidity rounding up the lingering finish. Different style, same value for money. Screwcap. 13.5% alc. **Rating** 92 To 2014 $15
1er Yarra Valley Pinot Noir 2008 **Rating** 92 To 2015 $35
✪ Wickhams Road Gippsland Chardonnay 2009 Very different from the more opulent and oaky '08; tangy grapefruit and melon fruit aromas and flavours are the drivers of a delightfully crisp wine. Screwcap. 13% alc. **Rating** 91 To 2014 $15
✪ Yarra Valley Pinot Noir 2008 Relatively light colour; both the bouquet and palate have red fruits encased in a swathe of forest, herb and spice characters; has above-average length. Screwcap. 13.2% alc. **Rating** 91 To 2013 $19

ŸŸŸŸ Wickhams Road Yarra Valley Cabernet Merlot 2008 Bright colour; fresh,
✪ aromatic and lively, with abundant juicy red and black berry fruits and a clear, zesty finish. Screwcap. 14% alc. **Rating** 89 To 2013 $15

Hoeyfield ★★★★

17 Jetty Road, Birchs Bay, Tas 7162 **Region** Southern Tasmania
T (03) 6267 4149 **F** (03) 6267 4249 **Open** By appt
Winemaker Contract **Est.** 1995 **Cases** 110 **Vyds** 0.5 ha
Richard and Jill Pringle-Jones run a postage stamp–sized vineyard of 0.25 ha each of pinot noir and chardonnay, planted on a vine-by-vine basis. When they purchased Hoeyfield in 2004, plantings of chardonnay and pinot noir had spread over '98, '00, and '02; Richard and Jill added more pinot noir (the new Dijon clone 777) in '04 and '05. It is very much a weekend and holiday occupation, Richard's real job being with ABN AMRO Morgans Limited.

🍷🍷🍷🍷🍷 D'Entrecasteaux Channel Pinot Noir 2005 Light but bright hue; still has lovely red fruits and a silky, spicy palate, though won't go on forever. Screwcap. 13.5% alc. **Rating** 95 **To** 2013 $40

🍷🍷🍷🍷 D'Entrecasteaux Channel Chardonnay 2009 **Rating** 89 **To** 2013 $20

Hoffmann's ★★★

Ingoldby Road, McLaren Flat, SA 5171 **Region** McLaren Vale
T (08) 8383 0232 **F** (08) 8383 0232 www.hoffmannswine.com.au **Open** Thurs–Tues 11–5
Winemaker Hamish McGuire (Consultant) **Est.** 1996 **Cases** 2500 **Vyds** 4 ha
Peter and Anthea Hoffmann began the rehabilitation of their vineyard, replanting poor varieties with premium grapes (cabernet sauvignon and shiraz) at their property in 1978, and Peter has worked at various wineries in McLaren Vale since '79. Both he and Anthea have undertaken courses at the Regency TAFE Institute in Adelaide, and (in Peter's words), 'in 1996 we decided that we knew a little about winemaking and opened a small cellar door'. Prior to that time the grapes from the rejuvenated vineyard had been sold to other winemakers. Exports to the UK, the US and Germany.

🍷🍷🍷🍷 McLaren Vale Shiraz Cabernet 2008 A savoury bouquet, with fresh herbs and black fruits in evidence; fresh acidity drives the palate, with fine tannins providing structure and backbone. Screwcap. 14.5% alc. **Rating** 88 **To** 2014 $24 BE

Hollick ★★★★☆

Riddoch Highway, Coonawarra, SA 5263 **Region** Coonawarra
T (08) 8737 2318 **F** (08) 8737 2952 www.hollick.com **Open** 7 days 9–5
Winemaker Ian Hollick, Matthew Caldersmith **Est.** 1983 **Cases** 40 000 **Vyds** 80 ha
A family business owned by Ian and Wendy Hollick, and winner of many trophies (including the most famous of all, the Jimmy Watson), its wines are well crafted and competitively priced. The lavish cellar door and restaurant complex is one of the focal points for tourism in Coonawarra. The Hollicks have progressively expanded their vineyard holdings: the first is the Neilson's Block, one of the original John Riddoch selections, but used as a dairy farm from 1910 to '75, when the Hollicks planted cabernet sauvignon and merlot. The second is the Wilgha Vineyard, purchased in '87 with established dry-grown cabernet sauvignon and shiraz. The last is the Red Ridge Vineyard in Wrattonbully, which includes trial plantings of tempranillo and sangiovese. Exports to most major markets.

🍷🍷🍷🍷🍷 Coonawarra Cabernet Sauvignon 2008 Red-purple; a classic, elegant Coonawarra cabernet, the blackcurrant fruit of the bouquet and palate with an underlay of clean dark earth that will become more evident as the wine ages; balance and length are very good. Screwcap. 14% alc. **Rating** 94 **To** 2023 $28

🍷🍷🍷🍷☼ Wrattonbully Tempranillo 2008 Good colour introduces a tempranillo with
✪   attitude and conviction; black cherry and dark berry fruits on the palate have a typical flavour twist on the finish, a ghost of citrus/citrus peel; the tannin structure is exemplary. Screwcap. 13.5% alc. **Rating** 92 **To** 2018 $21
✪   Coonawarra Sauvignon Blanc Semillon 2009 Although this is a 90/10 blend, the bouquet and palate seem to have more in common with the semillon component than the sauvignon blanc; fresh and lively, with grassy/herbaceous flavours dominant, but there is a touch of tropical fruit on the finish. Screwcap. 12.5% alc. **Rating** 90 **To** 2012 $21
     Wrattonbully Shiraz 2008 **Rating** 90 **To** 2018 $24
✪   Stock Route Coonawarra Wrattonbully Shiraz Cabernet Sauvignon 2008 Red-purple hue; a well-balanced, medium-bodied wine with a touch of spice from the shiraz, and black fruits from the cabernet sauvignon; the tannins are very good, running the length of the palate. Screwcap. 14.5% alc. **Rating** 90 **To** 2017 $21

○   **Hollaia Wrattonbully Sangiovese Cabernet Sauvignon 2008** Good
crimson hue; sangiovese now accounts for 70% (previously 50%) of the blend;
savoury black fruits and sour cherry have the expected structure, especially the
extended tannins of the sangiovese. Screwcap. 14% alc. **Rating** 90 **To** 2015 $21

ŸŸŸŸ   **Coonawarra Savagnin 2009 Rating** 89 **To** 2011 $21
Tannery Block Coonawarra Cabernet Sauvignon Merlot 2008
Rating 89 $24

Holm Oak   ★★★★

11 West Bay Road, Rowella, Tas 7270 **Region** Northern Tasmania
T (03) 6394 7577 **F** (03) 6394 7350 **www**.holmoakvineyards.com.au
Open 7 days 11–5 Sept–June, Wed–Sun 11–4 Jun–Aug
Winemaker Rebecca Wilson **Est.** 1983 **Cases** 3500 **Vyds** 10.4 ha
Holm Oak takes its name from its grove of oak trees, planted around the beginning of the 20th
century, and originally intended for the making of tennis racquets. In 2004 Ian and Robyn
Wilson purchased the property. The vineyard is planted (in descending order) to pinot noir,
cabernet sauvignon, riesling, chardonnay, sauvignon blanc, pinot gris and cabernet sauvignon,
with small amounts of cabernet franc, merlot and arneis. In 2006 the Wilson's daughter
Rebecca (with extensive winemaking experience both in Australia and California) became
winemaker, and partner Tim Duffy (a viticultural agronomist) has taken over management of
the vineyard. A winery was completed just in time for the 2007 vintage.

ŸŸŸŸŸ   **Riesling 2008** Bright, light straw-green; citrus and apple blossom aromas;
lively juicy flavours; long and well-balanced. Screwcap. 12.3% alc. **Rating** 93
To 2016 $25

ŸŸŸŸ   **Sauvignon Blanc 2009 Rating** 89 **To** 2011 $28.95

Home Hill   ★★★★☆

38 Nairn Street, Ranelagh, Tas 7109 **Region** Southern Tasmania
T (03) 6264 1200 **F** (03) 6264 1069 **www**.homehillwines.com.au **Open** 7 days 10–5
Winemaker Peter Dunbavan **Est.** 1994 **Cases** 2000 **Vyds** 6 ha
Terry and Rosemary Bennett planted their first 0.5 ha of vines in 1994 on gentle slopes in
the beautiful Huon Valley. Between 1994 and '99 the plantings were increased to 3 ha of
pinot noir, 1.5 ha chardonnay and 0.5 ha sylvaner. Home Hill has had great success with its
exemplary Pinot Noir, a consistent wine show major award winner.

ŸŸŸŸŸ   **Pinot Noir 2008** Incredibly deep colour; the bouquet is a concentrated and
essency amalgam of black cherries, clove and cinnamon; the palate follows with
abundant rich dark fruit and quite plush tannins; a big, rich and juicy style set to
take on Central Otago at its own game. Gold medal Tas Wine Show '10. Screwcap.
13.8% alc. **Rating** 95 $35 BE

ŸŸŸŸŸ   **Kelly's Reserve Chardonnay 2008 Rating** 93 **To** 2015 $28
Kelly's Reserve Late Harvest Sticky 2009 Rating 90 $20 BE

Honey Moon Vineyard   ★★★★☆

PO Box 544, Echunga SA 5153 **Region** Adelaide Hills
T 0419 862 103 **F** (08) 8388 8384 **www**.honeymoonvineyard.com.au **Open** Not
Winemaker Jane Bromley, Hylton McLean **Est.** 2005 **Cases** 500 **Vyds** 0.8 ha
Jane Bromley and Hylton McLean planted 0.4 ha each of pinot noir (clones 777, 114 and 115)
and shiraz (selected from two old vineyards known for their spicy fruit flavours) in 2003. The
moon is a striking feature in the landscape, particularly at harvest time when, as a full moon, it
appears as a dollop of rich honey in the sky – hence the name. The first vintage was 2005, but
Jane has been making wine since '01, with a particular interest in Champagne, while Hylton
is a winemaker, wine science researcher and wine educator with over 20 years' experience.

ᵀᵀᵀᵀᵀ **Adelaide Hills Pinot Noir 2008** Bright red hue; the bouquet is packed with predominantly red berry fruit, the palate opening with more of the same before the second stanza brings savoury tannins into play. All the bells and whistles of Dijon clones 777, 115 and 114, hand-plunged open fermenters, some wild ferments, some whole bunches, then 17 months in old and new French barriques. Screwcap. 14.5% alc. **Rating** 94 **To** 2016 $42

ᵀᵀᵀᵀᵀ **Adelaide Hills Shiraz 2008 Rating** 92 **To** 2018 $42

ᵀᵀᵀᵀ **Early Bottled Vintage Shiraz 2009 Rating** 87 **To** 2015 $37

Honeytree Estate ★★★★

16 Gillards Road, Pokolbin, NSW 2321 **Region** Hunter Valley
T (02) 4998 7693 **F** (02) 4998 7693 **www**.honeytreewines.com
Open Wed–Fri 11–4, w'ends 10–5
Winemaker Monarch Winemaking Services **Est.** 1970 **Cases** 1200 **Vyds** 9.8 ha
The Honeytree Estate vineyard was first planted in 1970 and for a period of time wines were produced. It then disappeared, but the vineyard has since been revived by Dutch-born Henk Strengers and family. The vineyard includes semillon, cabernet sauvignon, shiraz and a little clairette. Jancis Robinson comments that the wine 'tends to be very high in alcohol, a little low in acid and to oxidise dangerously fast', but in a sign of the times, the first Honeytree Clairette sold out so quickly (in four weeks) that 2.3 ha of vineyard has been grafted over to clairette. Exports to The Netherlands.

ᵀᵀᵀᵀᵀ **Paul Alexander Old Vines Hunter Valley Shiraz 2007** Bright colour; a concentrated black fruit bouquet with oak and a touch of mineral; the palate shows firm tannins, with the fruit balancing the savoury finish with ease. Released July 2010. Screwcap. 13.2% alc. **Rating** 93 **To** 2015 $25 BE

ᵀᵀᵀᵀ **Veronica Hunter Valley Semillon 2009 Rating** 89 **To** 2013 $18
Hunter Valley Clairette 2009 Rating 89 **To** 2015 $20

Horvat Estate ★★★☆

2444 Ararat-St Arnaud Rd, Landsborough, Vic 3384 **Region** Pyrenees
T (03) 5356 9208 **F** (03) 5356 9208 **Open** 7 days 10–5
Winemaker Andrew and Gabriel Horvat **Est.** 1995 **Cases** 4000 **Vyds** 4.7 ha
The Horvat family (Janet, Andrew and Gabriel) began developing their shiraz vineyard in 1995, supplementing production with contract-grown grapes. The wines are made using traditional methods and ideas, deriving in part from the family's Croatian background. Exports to China.

ᵀᵀᵀᵀᵀ **Premium Family Reserve Pyrenees Shiraz 2009** Red-purple, slightly advanced; attractive medium-bodied shiraz, with fine, soft tannins providing good texture to the blackberry and plum fruit. Screwcap. 14% alc. **Rating** 90 **To** 2016 $35

Houghton ★★★★★

Dale Road, Middle Swan, WA 6065 **Region** Swan Valley
T (08) 9274 9540 **F** (08) 9274 5172 **www**.houghton-wines.com.au **Open** 7 days 10–5
Winemaker Ross Pamment **Est.** 1836 **Cases** NFP
Houghton's reputation was once largely dependent on its (then) White Burgundy, equally good when young or 10 years old. In the last 20 years its portfolio has changed out of all recognition, with a kaleidoscopic range of high-quality wines from the Margaret River, Frankland River, Great Southern and Pemberton regions to the fore. The Jack Mann and Gladstones red wines stand at the forefront, the Wisdom range covering all varietal bases in great style. Nor should the value-for-money brands (Stripe, The Bandit and others) be ignored. To borrow a saying of the late Jack Mann, 'There are no bad wines here.' Exports to all major markets.

🍷🍷🍷🍷🍷 Wisdom Margaret River Cabernet Sauvignon 2008 Lavish levels of high-quality oak have been used to frame superbly ripe and focused cabernet fruit; the palate has serious intent written all over it, with great depth, layers of texture and fruit, toasty oak, and a long succulent finish with attractive tannins drawing out to conclude. Screwcap. 14% alc. **Rating** 96 **To** 2025 $32 BE

✪ Wisdom Margaret River Cabernet Sauvignon 2007 Strong crimson-red; a gloriously balanced and silky wine in the mouth; has as much blackcurrant and cassis as you could ever wish for. Enough to seduce a pinot lover. Diam. 14% alc. **Rating** 96 **To** 2027 $32

Gladstones Margaret River Cabernet Sauvignon 2004 Colour still dense; a veritable powerhouse, as the wine usually is. This is deadly serious cabernet sauvignon, like a knight in full-body armour. Inside there is a wealth of blackcurrant/blackberry fruit, and tannins as a second line of defence. When and how to attack is the question. Gold medal Sydney Wine Show '10. Cork. 15% alc. **Rating** 96 **To** 2030 $60

Jack Mann 2004 Deep purple; a beautiful wine in every respect; purity of classic varietal fruit; texture, structure and length all perfect; fine tannins and integrated oak. Cabernet Malbec. Cork. 14.4% alc. **Rating** 96 **To** 2024 $110

Wisdom Great Southern Riesling 2009 Restrained bouquet, barely offering the full gamut of its personality, with slatey minerality and lemons lurking; the palate reveals the complex nature of the wine, with texture the central theme; lemon and mineral palate, fine and focused with a dry, chalky finish to conclude. Screwcap. 12.5% alc. **Rating** 94 **To** 2020 $28.50 BE

CW Ferguson Great Southern Cabernet Malbec 2007 Excellent crimson-purple colour; the malbec contribution is very obvious, adding plum/plum jam to the black fruits of the cabernet. Will be long lived. Mt Barker (Cabernet)/ Frankland River (Malbec). Screwcap. 14% alc. **Rating** 94 **To** 2032 $55

Wisdom Pemberton Chardonnay Pinot Noir 2006 The mousse is still fine and persistent; extended lees age has imparted a strong brioche/yeast overlay to the very fine fruit – indeed almost too fine, but that is a quibble. Cork. 12.5% alc. **Rating** 94 **To** 2015 $32

🍷🍷🍷🍷🍷 Wisdom Frankland River Shiraz 2008 **Rating** 93 **To** 2025 $32 BE

✪ Margaret River Cabernet Sauvignon 2008 Ripe cassis, olive, cedar and violet bouquet, with a truly complex array of aromas; the palate is generous on entry, providing fleshy black and red fruits, following with savoury leafy notes and focused tannins to conclude; once again excellent value. Screwcap. 13.5% alc. **Rating** 93 **To** 2020 $20 BE

✪ Margaret River Chardonnay 2009 Bright and vivid hue; the bouquet is full of grapefruit and spiced nectarine, with a delicate seasoning of high-quality French oak; this is followed by a lively acid-driven palate, revealing a trace of mineral and toasty oak on the finish. Screwcap. 13% alc. **Rating** 91 **To** 2016 $20 BE

✪ The Bandit Shiraz Tempranillo 2008 The left of centre blend works well, with lush blackberry and dark cherry fruit further enriched by oak and supple tannins. Should develop well. Screwcap. 14% alc. **Rating** 91 **To** 2018 $19

✪ Stripe Cabernet Sauvignon 2008 Varietal cassis, redcurrant and dried leaf bouquet; fleshy, precise and focused, this wine delivers a knockout punch of flavour for this price. Screwcap. 13.5% alc. **Rating** 91 **To** 2015 $14 BE

✪ Stripe White Classic 2009 Brisk and lively, the varietal mix a long way away from that of 40 years ago; clearly sauvignon blanc has invaded the once semi-secret recipe, increasing its drinkability now, but not in the future. Screwcap. 13% alc. **Rating** 90 **To** 2012 $14

🍷🍷🍷🍷 Margaret River Sauvignon Blanc 2009 **Rating** 89 **To** 2011 $20

✪ Sauvignon Blanc Semillon 2009 Has every bit as much to offer as the Sauvignon Blanc, with a delicately fragrant, gently tropical bouquet, then picking up pace on the palate, with gooseberry and citrus fruit to the fore. Screwcap. 12.5% alc. **Rating** 89 **To** 2012 $14

Museum Release White Classic 2002 **Rating** 89 **To** 2014 $32 BE
The Bandit Sauvignon Blanc Pinot Gris 2009 **Rating** 88 **To** 2012
$19.95 BE

Howard Park/MadFish   ★★★★★

Miamup Road, Cowaramup, WA 6284 **Region** Margaret River/Denmark
T (08) 9756 5200 **F** (08) 9756 5222 **www.**howardparkwines.com.au **Open** 7 days 10–5
Winemaker Tony Davis, Genevieve Stols (Margaret River), Andrew Milbourne
(Denmark) **Est.** 1986 **Cases** NFP **Vyds** 137 ha
In the wake of its acquisition by the Burch family and the construction of a large state-of-
the-art winery at Denmark, a capacious cellar door (incorporating Feng Shui principles) has
opened in the Margaret River, where there are also significant estate plantings. The Margaret
River flagships are the Leston Shiraz and Leston Cabernet Sauvignon, but the Margaret River
vineyards routinely contribute to all the wines in the range, from multi-region MadFish at
the bottom, to the iconic Cabernet Sauvignon Merlot at the top. MadFish is a second label,
itself with three price tiers: MadFish Gold Turtle, Sideways and (the original) MadFish. There
are also three vineyards: Leston and Block B in the Margaret River, and Mt Barrow in Mount
Barker. Howard Park also operates a cellar door at Scotsdale Road, Denmark (7 days 10–4).
Exports to all major markets.

♥♥♥♥♥ **Howard Park Great Southern Riesling 2009** Exceedingly pale colour; citrus
✪   blossom aromas announce an initially mouth-puckering (in the best possible way)
          palate, opening quickly to reveal a zesty lime and mineral range of flavours; the
          acid profile promises a very long life. Screwcap. 12.5% alc. **Rating** 96 **To** 2029 $25
          Howard Park Abercrombie Cabernet Sauvignon 2008 Beautifully poised
          bouquet, with unmistakable varietal leafiness and bucketloads of enticing cassis
          fruit; the bouquet moves into florals, with oak playing a minor role to the pristine
          and ample fruit; the palate displays an impeccable balance of fruit, acid and
          silky fine-grained tannins, revealing a long complex and wonderfully satisfying
          experience; while it will age gracefully, many simply won't wait, and they will not
          be disappointed. Screwcap. 14% alc. **Rating** 96 **To** 2025 $85 BE
          Howard Park Abercrombie Cabernet Sauvignon 2007 Excellent crimson;
          features a blend of 'old vine' cabernet from Great Southern (93%)/Margaret River
          (7%); a distinguished wine with very clearly articulated varietal fruit at the 'sweet
          spot' of maturity. Will age superbly. Screwcap. 14% alc. **Rating** 96 **To** 2027 $85
          Howard Park Scotsdale Great Southern Shiraz 2008 Deep crimson-purple;
          while not sacrificing elegance, has the greatest volume of fruit of the three Shirazs,
          with blackberry, licorice and plum, that has swallowed the oak; a complete wine in
          every respect. Screwcap. 14% alc. **Rating** 95 **To** 2023 $40
          Howard Park Sauvignon Blanc 2009 Pale straw-green; an intriguing wine
          from start to finish, with delicate fruit ranging from citrus to tropical, and a
          feathery touch of barrel ferment that might so easily have obscured, rather than
          enhanced, the fruit. Screwcap. 13% alc. **Rating** 94 **To** 2011 $25
          Howard Park Leston Margaret River Cabernet Sauvignon 2008 Bright
          colour; an elegant blend of red fruits and cassis, with alluring tones of cedar and
          a touch of violets; the perfume follows on the palate, delivering an understated
          mixture of structure, finesse and power, as the palate really builds to an harmonious
          crescendo; looks to have a healthy future ahead. Screwcap. 13.5% alc. **Rating** 94
          To 2020 $40 BE

♥♥♥♥♡ **Howard Park Leston Margaret River Shiraz 2008 Rating** 93 **To** 2018 $40
✪   **MadFish Sideways Cabernet Sauvignon Merlot 2008** Good colour; classic
          Margaret River style, tightly structured and focused, with hints of gravel among
          the blackcurrant and cassis fruit flavours; the tannins are well integrated, the oak
          likewise. Screwcap. 14.5% alc. **Rating** 93 **To** 2018 $20
✪   **MadFish Sideways Shiraz 2008** Bright crimson-red; a succulent medium-
          bodied shiraz from Margaret River, even though the front label does not disclose
          this; there is a cascade of red cherry, plum and spicy fruit, the tannins and oak
          playing a support role. Screwcap. 14.5% alc. **Rating** 92 **To** 2017 $20

○   **MadFish Premium Red 2008** Bright colour; skilfully constructed with all aspects working harmoniously; red and blackcurrant, cedar and a touch of leaf; super juicy and vibrant, with an underlying seriousness to the structure; a very good wine for the price. Cabernet Sauvignon/Merlot. Screwcap. 14.5% alc. **Rating** 92 **To** 2017 $17 BE
Howard Park Scotsdale Great Southern Cabernet Sauvignon 2008 Rating 92 **To** 2020 $40 BE
MadFish Gold Turtle Margaret River Cabernet Sauvignon 2007 Rating 92 **To** 2015 $28
MadFish Gold Turtle Pinot Noir 2009 Rating 91 **To** 2014 $30
MadFish Gold Turtle Tempranillo 2008 Rating 90 **To** 2015 $30

Howard Vineyard   ★★★★★

Lot 1, Bald Hills Road, Nairne, SA 5252 **Region** Adelaide Hills
T (08) 8188 0203 **F** (08) 8388 0623 **www**.howardvineyard.com **Open** Mon–Fri 12–4, w'ends 11.30–4.30
Winemaker Ian Northcott, Mark Swann, Michael Sykes **Est.** 2005 **Cases** 5000 **Vyds** 60 ha
This venture began in the late 1990s with the establishment of two vineyards at different locations in the Adelaide Hills. The Schoenthal Vineyard near Lobethal, at an elevation of 440–500 m, is planted primarily to sauvignon blanc and chardonnay, with smaller amounts of pinot noir and pinot gris. The Howard Vineyard is at a lower elevation, and the slightly warmer site has been planted (in descending order) to sauvignon blanc, chardonnay, semillon, cabernet sauvignon, shiraz, viognier and cabernet franc. The substantial quantities of grapes not required for the Howard Vineyard label are sold to other winemakers.

ΨΨΨΨΨ   **Adelaide Hills Chardonnay 2009** A deliciously crisp and lively chardonnay, with white peach and grapefruit dominant on both bouquet and palate, partial barrel ferment oak inputs in the background; excellent length and a zesty, clean finish. Screwcap. 14% alc. **Rating** 94 **To** 2015 $22
Amos Adelaide Hills Cabernet Sauvignon 2007 Good hue and depth; perfectly ripened cabernet sauvignon for a full-bodied style ex a cool climate; ripe blackcurrant aromas and flavours mix with savoury tannins and cedar/mocha oak. Screwcap. 15% alc. **Rating** 94 **To** 2025 $55

ΨΨΨΨΨ   **Frolic Adelaide Hills Semillon Sauvignon Blanc 2009 Rating** 90 **To** 2012 $22
Adelaide Hills Shiraz 2007 Rating 90 **To** 2015 $24

ΨΨΨΨ   **Adelaide Hills Sauvignon Blanc 2009 Rating** 89 **To** 2011 $22
Adelaide Hills Cabernet Franc Rose 2009 Rating 89 **To** 2010 $22
Adelaide Hills Cabernets 2006 Rating 89 **To** 2015 $25
Amos Adelaide Hills Cabernet Franc 2007 Rating 89 **To** 2016 $55

Hugh Hamilton Wines   ★★★★☆

McMurtrie Road, McLaren Vale, SA 5171 **Region** McLaren Vale
T (08) 8323 8689 **F** (08) 8323 9488 **www**.hughhamiltonwines.com.au **Open** 7 days 11–5
Winemaker Peter Leske **Est.** 1991 **Cases** 30 000 **Vyds** 31.05 ha
Hugh Hamilton is the fifth generation of the famous Hamilton family, who first planted vineyards at Glenelg in 1837. A self-confessed black sheep of the family, Hugh embraces non-mainstream varieties such as sangiovese, tempranillo, petit verdot and viognier, and is one of only a few growing saperavi. Production comes from estate plantings, which includes the original Church Block, home to McLaren Vale's oldest chardonnay vines, and a vineyard in Blewitt Springs of 85-year-old shiraz and 65-year-old cabernet sauvignon. The irreverent black sheep packaging was the inspiration of daughter Mary (CEO). The cellar door is lined with the original jarrah from Vat 15 from the historic Hamilton's Ewell winery, the largest wooden vat ever built in the southern hemisphere. Exports to the UK, the US, Canada, Korea, Japan and China.

ŸŸŸŸŸ **Jekyll & Hyde McLaren Vale Shiraz Viognier 2008** Good colour as expected from a co-fermented blend including 8% viognier; this is an extremely complex and intense wine even if correctly described as bipolar on the back label, with McLaren Vale black fruits and dark chocolate pulled in another direction by the bright viognier. Whatever, it certainly deserves better than its scrappy, stained cork. 14% alc. **Rating** 93 **To** 2020 $45

The Rascal McLaren Vale Shiraz 2007 Quintessential McLaren Vale with a coat of dark chocolate around black fruit flavours leavened by fine, spicy tannins and quality French oak. Screwcap. 15.5% alc. **Rating** 92 **To** 2017 $24.50

The Ratbag McLaren Vale Merlot 2008 Bright colour; McLaren Vale has always produced bouncy, juicy merlot, and this is no exception; the flavour is given complexity by a distinctly savoury, black olive, finish. Screwcap. 15% alc. **Rating** 91 **To** 2016 $24.50

✪ **The Loose Cannon McLaren Vale Viognier 2009** Partial barrel ferment and lees contact has been used to good effect; the peach, apricot and ginger character of viognier have been preserved, and the finish is not phenolic. Screwcap. 13.5% alc. **Rating** 90 **To** 2013 $22.50

✪ **The Floozie McLaren Vale Tempranillo Rose 2009** Bright, light fuchsia; an aromatic bouquet, then an interesting palate, with distinct red fruit sweetness (not sugar) ranging through strawberry, cherry and Turkish delight. Screwcap. 12.5% alc. **Rating** 90 **To** 2011 $22.50

The Villain McLaren Vale Cabernet Sauvignon 2007 Light colour, but good hue; a savoury, spicy manifestation of cabernet with some minty notes and a French oak push; scores for overall liveliness. Screwcap. 14.5% alc. **Rating** 90 **To** 2015 $24.50

ŸŸŸŸ **The Odd Ball McLaren Vale Saperavi 2007 Rating** 89 **To** 2014 $45
The Madam NV Rating 88 **To** 2013 $22.50

Hugo ★★★★

Elliott Road, McLaren Flat, SA 5171 **Region** McLaren Vale
T (08) 8383 0098 **F** (08) 8383 0446 **www**.hugowines.com.au **Open** Mon–Fri 9.30–5, Sat 12–5, Sun 10.30–5
Winemaker John Hugo **Est.** 1982 **Cases** 10 000 **Vyds** 25.2 ha
A winery that came from relative obscurity to prominence in the late 1980s with some lovely ripe, sweet reds, which, while strongly American oak-influenced, were quite outstanding. Has picked up the pace again after a dull period in the mid-1990s. There are over 25 ha of estate plantings (shiraz, cabernet sauvignon, chardonnay, grenache and sauvignon blanc), with part of the grape production sold to others. Exports to the UK, the US and Canada.

ŸŸŸŸŸ **McLaren Vale Chardonnay 2008** Has joined the mass migration of chardonnay to a brighter, lighter, fresher style expressed by the lower alcohol and crisp, citrus flavours; barrel ferment in French oak evident but not oppressive. Screwcap. 13% alc. **Rating** 90 **To** 2014 $19

McLaren Vale Shiraz 2008 Bright red-purple; a medium-bodied wine with black fruits, chocolate and vanillan oak driving both bouquet and palate; does have some light and shade. Screwcap. 14.5% alc. **Rating** 90 **To** 2017 $23

Humbug Reach Vineyard ★★★★

72 Nobelius Drive, Legana, Tas 7277 **Region** Northern Tasmania
T (03) 6330 2875 **F** (03) 6330 2739 **www**.humbugreach.com.au **Open** Not
Winemaker Paul McShane, Bass Fine Wines (Guy Wagner) **Est.** 1988 **Cases** 350 **Vyds** 1 ha
The Humbug Reach Vineyard was established in the late 1980s on the banks of the Tamar River with plantings of pinot noir; riesling and chardonnay followed. Since 1999 it has been owned by Paul and Sally McShane, who proudly tend the 6000 vines on the property. After frost decimated the 2007 vintage, Sally and Paul, wanting to become involved in winemaking, brought the process closer to home, with Guy Wagner making the Riesling and Chardonnay,

Paul making the Pinot Noir (commuting from the Sustainability Institute at Monash University in Melbourne to do so).

🍷🍷🍷🍷🍷 **Riesling 2009** A cleverly made wine with ripe, juicy lime flavours balanced by quite firm acidity that lengthens the finish and aftertaste. Screwcap. 11.7% alc. **Rating** 90 **To** 2016 $23
Pinot Noir 2008 Bright red–purple; a full-bodied and intense pinot with dark cherry and plum fruit on the mid-palate; has good structure and likewise future. Screwcap. 13.5% alc. **Rating** 90 **To** 2015 $35

🍂 Hundred of Comaum   ★★★★

48 Church Street, Penola, SA 5277 **Region** Coonawarra
T 0438 005 051 **F** (08) 8125 6766 **www**.hundredofcomaum.com.au **Open** 7 days 10–6
Winemaker Keith Wilkens **Est.** 1999 **Cases** 4000 **Vyds** 9.6 ha
Stephen Moignard sits defiantly on an ancient backhoe with the registration plate DAVNET, even though the backhoe is not registered, and the plate came from a Ferrari he once owned. He was briefly CEO of the publicly-listed DAVNET, rising from 4c a share in 1999 to $5 just before the tech wreck of 2002 took it back to 10c. He made the BRW Rich List for one year, which excited the interest of various regulators. He says, 'You would be right to ask whether eight years of fighting de factos, ASIC and the ATO has sent [me] around the twist. Who cares? I'll die here, and I can even dig the hole.' These days he has cabernet sauvignon, shiraz and riesling planted on Lot 1, Comaum School Road, Coonawarra, hence the brand name Hundred of Comaum. The Penola address is that of the Terra Rossa Wine Club Restaurant, which Stephen runs with business partner Tim Kidman of Woodblock Wines, and where Spanish-style tapas are available throughout the day, with Steve as chef. Exports to China.

🍷🍷🍷🍷🍷 **Reserve Coonawarra Shiraz 2006** A bright and intense shiraz with considerable length to its tangy fruit flavours, sweetened by a touch of oak; sets the world record for the smallest, completely indecipherable text of four of the five panels of the back label. ProCork. 14% alc. **Rating** 90 **To** 2016 $39
Reserve Coonawarra Cabernet Sauvignon 2006 Deep colour; has the blackcurrant and redcurrant fruit missing from the '07, ripe tannins and oak also adding to the overall appeal. ProCork. 13.5% alc. **Rating** 90 **To** 2020 $39

🍷🍷🍷🍷 **Coonawarra Shiraz 2008** **Rating** 88 **To** 2014 $27
Coonawarra Cabernet Sauvignon 2007 **Rating** 87 **To** 2014 $27

Hungerford Hill   ★★★★★

1 Broke Road, Pokolbin, NSW 2320 **Region** Hunter Valley
T (02) 4998 7666 **F** (02) 4998 7375 **www**.hungerfordhill.com.au
Open Sun–Thurs 10–5, Fri–Sat 10–6
Winemaker Michael Hatcher **Est.** 1967 **Cases** 50 000 **Vyds** 5 ha
Hungerford Hill, sold by Southcorp to the Kirby family in 2002, has emerged with its home base at the impressive winery previously known as One Broke Road. The development of the One Broke Road complex proved wildly uneconomic, and the rationalisation process has resulted in Hungerford Hill becoming the sole owner. The quality of the wines has seen production soar from 20 000 cases to 50 000 cases, reversing the pattern under prior Southcorp ownership. As the notes indicate, Hungerford Hill now focuses its attention on Tumbarumba and the Hunter Valley, with some wines coming from the Hilltops region. Exports to all major markets.

🍷🍷🍷🍷🍷 **Hunter Valley Semillon 2007** Glowing yellow-green, almost iridescent; has emerged from its promising start at the NSW Wine Awards '09 (where it won the trophy for Best Young Semillon) with all flags flying, lemon and mineral notes soaring across the palate. Screwcap. 11.5% alc. **Rating** 95 **To** 2017 $50
✪ **Hunter Valley Semillon 2009** Pale straw; a very fragrant bouquet right in the mainstream of the great '09 vintage, the palate adding some grass and herb to the citrus/lemon notes that mark the vintage. Screwcap. 10.5% alc. **Rating** 94 **To** 2020 $25

Higher Octave Tumbarumba Chardonnay 2008 Gleaming, bright straw-green; has that typical finesse and intensity of Tumbarumba chardonnay, grapefruit, white peach and nectarine; the oak handling is sure, and a ritzy label design completes the package. Screwcap. 13% alc. **Rating** 94 To 2015 $35

♀♀♀♀♀
✪
FishCage Southern NSW Shiraz 2009 Crimson-purple; highly aromatic spicy red and black fruits on the bouquet, then a palate with exceptional drive and intensity to its juicy, spicy flavours. The Southern NSW Zone takes in Canberra, Gundagai, Hilltops and Tumbarumba. Screwcap. 14.5% alc. **Rating** 93 To 2016 $18
Hunter Valley Shiraz 2009 Rating 93 To 2020 $30
Tumbarumba Sauvignon Blanc 2009 Rating 92 To 2011 $25
Tumbarumba Pinot Noir 2008 Rating 92 To 2014 $35
Tumbarumba Shiraz 2008 Rating 91 To 2020 $35

♀♀♀♀
FishCage Semillon Sauvignon Blanc 2009 Rating 89 To 2012 $18
Tumbarumba Pinot Noir 2009 Rating 88 To 2014 $30

Huntington Estate ★★★★☆

Cassilis Road, Mudgee, NSW 2850 **Region** Mudgee
T 1800 995 931 **F** (02) 6373 3730 **www**.huntingtonestate.com.au **Open** Mon–Sat 10–5, Sun & public hols 10–4
Winemaker Tim Stevens **Est.** 1969 **Cases** 20 000 **Vyds** 43.77 ha
Bob and Wendy Roberts invested a lifetime in Huntington Estate, joined in more recent years by daughter Susie as winemaker. When the time came to sell, it was to next-door neighbours Tim and Nicky Stevens of Abercorn. Stevens has deliberately remained faithful to the slightly rustic, traditional ageing style of Huntington, picking up from the '06 vintage. Another element of continuity is the music festival held at the winery each November. Transition issues have been overcome, and Huntington Estate is now headed back towards its pre-eminent position in Mudgee.

♀♀♀♀♀
Signature Cabernet Sauvignon 2006 Brighter hue than the standard, with more expressive blackcurrant fruit that has a distinct juicy touch on the well-balanced palate; has finesse and length, and the tannins to guarantee a long life. Screwcap. 13.2% alc. **Rating** 95 To 2026 $32.50

♀♀♀♀♀
✪
Shiraz 2006 Relatively light but bright colour; a very well balanced, medium-bodied palate that has clear-cut regional character to its supple red and black fruits, tannins and oak in secondary support roles. Screwcap. 13.2% alc. **Rating** 93 To 2016 $21
Special Reserve Shiraz 2006 Rating 92 To 2026 $31
Special Reserve Mudgee Cabernet Sauvignon 2006 Rating 92 To 2021 $32.50

♀♀♀♀
Signature Shiraz Cabernet Merlot 2005 Rating 89 To 2014 $39
Cabernet Sauvignon 2006 Rating 89 To 2016 $21

Hurley Vineyard ★★★★★

101 Balnarring Road, Balnarring, Vic 3926 **Region** Mornington Peninsula
T (03) 5931 3000 **F** (03) 5931 3200 **www**.hurleyvineyard.com.au **Open** By appt
Winemaker Kevin Bell **Est.** 1998 **Cases** 600
It's never as easy as it seems. Although Kevin Bell is now a Victorian Supreme Court judge, and his wife Tricia Byrnes has a busy legal life as a family law specialist in a small Melbourne law firm, they have done most of the hard work in establishing Hurley Vineyard themselves, with family and friends. Most conspicuously, Kevin has completed the Applied Science (Wine Science) degree at CSU, drawing on Nat White for consultancy advice, and occasionally from Phillip Jones of Bass Phillip and Domaine Fourrier in Gevrey Chambertin.

ΨΨΨΨΨ **Hommage Mornington Peninsula Pinot Noir 2008** Highly scented red fruit bouquet, with attractive spice notes of cinnamon and clove; the palate is fine and immediately generous, with a serious spine of structure lurking beneath the ample fruit; the tannins are superfine and the texture quite silky. Diam. 13.2% alc. **Rating** 94 **To** 2015 $55 BE
Garamond Mornington Peninsula Pinot Noir 2008 Attractive hue; deeply scented with plum and black cherry fruit; there is a savoury component reminiscent of fresh turned earth and ironstone; the palate is firm at first, then revealing an almost luscious core of dark fruit; long, complex and eventually quite silky to conclude. Diam. 13.8% alc. **Rating** 94 **To** 2016 $60 BE

ΨΨΨΨΨ **Lodestone Mornington Peninsula Pinot Noir 2008 Rating** 90 **To** 2015 $50 BE

Hutton Vale Vineyard   ★★★★☆

Stone Jar Road, Angaston, SA 5353 **Region** Eden Valley
T (08) 8564 8270 **F** (08) 8564 8385 **www**.huttonvale.com **Open** By appt
Winemaker Torbreck Vintners, Rockford **Est.** 1960 **Cases** 700 **Vyds** 26 ha
John Howard Angas (who arrived in SA in 1843, aged 19, charged with the responsibility of looking after the affairs of his father, George Fife Angas) named part of the family estate Hutton Vale. It is here that John Angas, John's great-great-grandson, and wife Jan tend a little over 26 ha of vines. Almost all the grapes are sold, but a tiny quantity has been made by the who's who of the Barossa Valley, notably David Powell of Torbreck and Chris Ringland of Rockford. Exports to Singapore and NZ.

ΨΨΨΨΨ **Eden Valley Shiraz 2004** Dark, deep purple-red; the bouquet is crammed with spice, licorice and black fruits, the palate simply providing a three-dimensional view of those aromas, but a great view; the capsule has been dipped in wax, giving an imprint of '04 on top. Screwcap. 14% alc. **Rating** 95 **To** 2024 $59

ΨΨΨΨΨ **Eden Valley Cabernet Sauvignon 2006 Rating** 93 **To** 2016 $29
Eden Valley Grenache Mataro 2006 Rating 90 **To** 2015 $29

ΨΨΨΨ **Eden Valley Riesling 2008 Rating** 88 **To** 2014 $19

Hutton Wines   ★★★★★

PO Box 1214, Dunsborough, WA 6281 **Region** Margaret River
T 0417 923 126 **F** (08) 9759 1246 **www**.huttonwines.com **Open** Not
Winemaker Dr Bradley Hutton **Est.** 2006 **Cases** 375
This is another venture of the Hutton family of Gralyn fame, with brothers (and sons) Bradley and Michael doing their own thing. Bradley became winemaker at Gralyn in 2001 following the completion of postgraduate studies in oenology at the University of Adelaide, so this is a busman's holiday. Cabernet sauvignon and chardonnay are made from grapes purchased from the family vineyard and other growers in the surrounding area.

ΨΨΨΨΨ **Triptych Margaret River Chardonnay 2008** Light straw-green; a fragrant and tangy bouquet accurately foretells the palate; here white peach, grapefruit and classy French oak come together harmoniously. Very good winemaking at work. Screwcap. 13.8% alc. **Rating** 94 **To** 2014 $40
Triptych Margaret River Cabernet Sauvignon 2007 Good crimson; a deliciously juicy, cassis-accented cabernet is ripe, but not the least overripe, its flavours perfectly supported by fine tannins and quality oak. Drink any time over the next 20 years. Screwcap. 13.9% alc. **Rating** 94 **To** 2027 $50

Idavue Estate   ★★★☆

470 Northern Highway, Heathcote, Vic 3523 **Region** Heathcote
T (03) 5433 3464 **F** (03) 5433 3049 **www**.idavueestate.com **Open** W'ends & public hols 10.30–5
Winemaker Andrew and Sandra Whytcross **Est.** 2000 **Cases** 600 **Vyds** 5.7 ha

Owners and winemakers Andrew and Sandra Whytcross both undertook a two-year wine-making course through the Bendigo TAFE; with assistance from son Marty, they also look after the vineyard, which is planted to shiraz (3 ha), cabernet sauvignon (1.9 ha), and semillon and chardonnay (0.4 ha each). The red wines are made in typical small-batch fashion with hand-picked fruit, hand-plunged fermenters and a basket press.

ŸŸŸŸŸ **Blue Note Heathcote Shiraz 2008** Although having the same alcohol as the varietal, is slightly deeper in colour, and has more black fruit flavours to the similarly savoury/earthy palate; an austere style, perhaps partly shaped by drought; a vinous replay of American blues indeed. Diam. 14.2% alc. **Rating** 90 **To** 2019 $32

ŸŸŸŸ **Heathcote Shiraz 2008** Rating 89 To 2016 $25
Heathcote Shiraz Cabernet 2008 Rating 88 To 2015 $25
Heathcote Semillon Chardonnay 2009 Rating 87 To 2014 $20

Indigo Ridge ★★★★☆
719 Icely Road, Orange, NSW 2800 **Region** Orange
T (02) 6362 1851 **F** (02) 6362 1851 **www**.indigowines.com.au **Open** W'ends & public hols 12–5
Winemaker Contract **Est.** 1994 **Cases** 2000 **Vyds** 6 ha
Paul Bridge and Trish McPherson describe themselves as the owners, labourers and viti-culturists at Indigo Ridge; they planted and tend every vine on the vineyard. The plantings are sauvignon blanc, cabernet sauvignon, shiraz and merlot. As at early 2010 was for sale. Exports to Malaysia and Singapore.

ŸŸŸŸŸ **Orange Shiraz 2008** Strong red-purple; has far greater depth and weight of plum and blackberry fruit than most Orange shirazs, however good they may be. This depth is doubtless reflected in the indecipherable number of trophies on the label; has remarkably pure fruit (not alcohol or sugar) sweetness; 150 cases made. Screwcap. 14.5% alc. **Rating** 94 **To** 2023 $40

ŸŸŸŸŸ **Orange Sauvignon Blanc 2009** Rating 91 To 2012 $25

Indigo Wine Company ★★★☆
1221 Beechworth-Wangaratta Road, Everton Upper, Vic 3678 **Region** Beechworth
T (03) 5727 0233 **F** (03) 5727 0580 **www**.indigovineyard.com.au **Open** Wed–Sun 11–4
Winemaker Brokenwood (PJ Charteris, Sarah Crowe) **Est.** 1999 **Cases** 1900 **Vyds** 46.15 ha
Indigo Wine Company has a little over 46 ha of vineyards planted to 11 varieties, including the top French and Italian grapes. The business was and is primarily directed to growing grapes for sale to Brokenwood, but since 2004 small parcels of grapes have been vinified for the Indigo label. The somewhat incestuous nature of the whole business sees the Indigo wines being made at Brokenwood.

ŸŸŸŸŸ **Beechworth Shiraz 2008** Relatively light colour; a complex, spicy wine, presently doing battle with the powdery tannins that run through the length of its medium-bodied palate, oak also playing a role; in some ways in a wine that pushes the envelope. Screwcap. 14% alc. **Rating** 91 **To** 2016 $27

ŸŸŸŸ **Beechworth Cabernet Sauvignon Sangiovese 2008** Rating 88 To 2014 $27
Beechworth Nebbiolo 2008 Rating 88 To 2014 $27

Inghams Skilly Ridge Wines ★★★★☆
Gillentown Road, Sevenhill via Clare, SA 5453 **Region** Clare Valley
T 0418 423 998 **F** (08) 8843 4330 **Open** W'ends 10–5, or by appt
Winemaker Clark Ingham, O'Leary Walker **Est.** 1994 **Cases** 3000 **Vyds** 25 ha
Clark Ingham has established shiraz, cabernet sauvignon, merlot, chardonnay, riesling, tempranillo and primitivo. Part of the production is made by contract winemaker David O'Leary (with input from Clark), the remaining grape production is sold. Exports to the UK, Germany and China.

🍷🍷🍷🍷🍷 **Reserve Clare Valley Shiraz 2005** Excellent colour for age; has plum, blackberry and vanilla aromas that feed through into the medium-bodied but quite intense palate, delicious flavour-sweet (not sugar-sweet) fruit coming through strongly on the finish, American oak in support. Screwcap. 14% alc. **Rating** 94 $48

🍷🍷🍷🍷 **Clare Valley Riesling 2009** **Rating** 92 **To** 2019 $22
Clare Valley Shiraz 2007 **Rating** 90 **To** 2020 $22

Ingoldby ★★★★☆

GPO Box 753, Melbourne, Vic 3001 **Region** McLaren Vale
T 1300 651 650 **F** (08) 8383 0790 **www**.ingoldby.com.au **Open** Not
Winemaker Kelly Healy **Est.** 1983 **Cases** NFP

Part of the Foster's group, with the wines now having a sole McLaren Vale source. Over the years, Ingoldby has produced some excellent wines, which can provide great value for money.

🍷🍷🍷🍷🍷 **McLaren Vale Shiraz 2008** Deep and rich, almost essency redcurrant and blackberry bouquet; the palate is warm, unctuous, inviting and surprisingly fresh and focused; long on chocolate and fruitcake spice to conclude. Screwcap. 14% alc. **Rating** 94 **To** 2018 $20 BE

🍷🍷🍷🍷 **McLaren Vale Cabernet Sauvignon 2008** **Rating** 91 **To** 2016 $20

Inkwell ★★★★

PO Box 404, McLaren Vale, SA 5171 **Region** McLaren Vale
T 0430 050 115 **www**.inkwellwines.com **Open** By appt
Winemaker Dudley Brown **Est.** 2003 **Cases** 800 **Vyds** 12 ha

Inkwell was born in 2003 when Dudley Brown and wife Karen Wotherspoon returned to Australia from California and bought a somewhat rundown vineyard on the serendipitously named California Road. They inherited 5 ha of neglected shiraz, and planted an additional 7 ha to viognier (2.5 ha), zinfandel (2.5 ha) and heritage shiraz clones (2 ha). The five-year restoration of the old vines and establishment of the new reads like the ultimate handbook for aspiring vignerons, particularly those who are prepared to work non-stop. The reward has been rich – almost all the grapes are sold, and the grapes go from a mid-range commercial rating to near the top of the tree. The first toe in the water of winemaking came in 2006 with 140 cases produced, rising to 400 cases in '08. Dudley is adamant the production will be capped at 2000 cases. Exports to the US and Canada.

🍷🍷🍷🍷 **McLaren Vale Shiraz 2007** Obviously made for the US market. Traditional McLaren Vale style, with lush black fruits tempered by a touch of chocolate; good mouthfeel and carries its alcohol. True to its heritage: 240 dozen made, hand bottled. Screwcap. 14.9% alc. **Rating** 92 **To** 2017 $25

Iron Pot Bay Wines ★★★★

766 Deviot Road, Deviot, Tas 7275 **Region** Northern Tasmania
T (03) 6394 7320 **F** (03) 6394 7346 **www**.ironpotbay.com.au **Open** By appt
Winemaker Dr Andrew Pirie **Est.** 1988 **Cases** 2400 **Vyds** 5 ha

Iron Pot Bay was established by the Cuthbert family and continues in family ownership. The vineyard takes its name from a bay on the Tamar River (now called West Bay) and is strongly maritime-influenced, producing delicate but intensely flavoured unwooded white wines. Over half of the vineyard is planted to chardonnay, the remainder semillon, sauvignon blanc, pinot gris, gewurztraminer and riesling.

🍷🍷🍷🍷🍷 **Unwooded Chardonnay 2008** Very pale and bright; juicy and vibrant; here is a very nice example of the unwooded style; grapefruit and white peach. Gold medal Tas Wine Show '10. Crown seal. 12.7% alc. **Rating** 94 **To** 2013 $22

🍷🍷🍷🍷 **Dessert Riesling 2008** **Rating** 89 **To** 2013 $16

Ironbark Hill Vineyard ★★★

694 Hermitage Road, Pokolbin, NSW 2321 **Region** Hunter Valley
T (02) 6574 7085 **F** (02) 6574 7089 **www.**ironbarkhill.com.au **Open** 7 days 10–5
Winemaker Will Rickard-Bell **Est.** 1990 **Cases** 7000 **Vyds** 12.5 ha
Ironbark Hill Estate is owned by Peter and Leesa Drayton and Michael and Julie Dillon.
Peter's father, Max Drayton, and brothers John and Greg, run Drayton's Family Wines. The
estate plantings include shiraz, chardonnay, semillon, cabernet sauvignon, tempranillo, merlot,
verdelho and tyrian. Peter is a commercial/industrial builder, so constructing the cellar door
was a busman's holiday. The hope is that the striking building and landscape surrounds will
bring more wine tourists to the Hermitage Road end of Pokolbin. Exports to China and
Hong Kong.

♈♈♈♈
✪   **Semillon 2009** A lively, crisp wine with plenty of energy; grass and mineral
      aromas and flavours are clear-cut, but there is little of the extra dimension of citrus
      of the '09 vintage. Screwcap. 11% alc. **Rating** 89 **To** 2014 $16
✪   **Chardonnay 2008** A lively and juicy wine, with zesty stone fruit, citrus and
      melon fruit and integrated French oak; has good length and persistence. Screwcap.
      13% alc. **Rating** 89 **To** 2012 $16
      Alfresco Unwooded Chardonnay 2009 An attractive unwooded chardonnay
      that is indeed in alfresco style, with juicy fruit flavours akin to a 50/50 blend of
      chardonnay/sauvignon blanc. Screwcap. 11% alc. **Rating** 87 **To** 2011 $18
      Merlot Rose 2009 Bright colour; some cherry cola/sarsaparilla flavours, but not
      overtly sweet, citrussy acidity providing freshness. Screwcap. 14% alc. **Rating** 87
      To 2011 $18
      Liqueur Shiraz 2007 Is not over-sweet, nor is the spirit fiery; should develop
      nicely in bottle – it is a vintage port style – but is accessible now. Screwcap.
      18% alc. **Rating** 87 **To** 2014 $17.50

Ironwood Estate ★★★★

2191 Porongurup Road, Porongurup, WA 6234 **Region** Porongurup
T (08) 9853 1126 **F** (08) 9853 1172 **Open** Wed–Mon 11–5
Winemaker Wignalls Wines (Mick Perkins) **Est.** 1996 **Cases** 2500 **Vyds** 5 ha
Ironwood Estate was established in 1996 under the ownership of Mary and Eugene (Gene)
Harma. An estate vineyard planted to riesling, sauvignon blanc, chardonnay, shiraz, merlot and
cabernet sauvignon (in more or less equal amounts) has been established on a northern slope
of the Porongurup Range. Exports to Japan and Singapore.

♈♈♈♈♉
✪   **Porongurup Shiraz 2008** Crimson-purple; vibrant red fruits, spice and pepper
      aromas leap from the glass, the medium-bodied palate adding a touch of licorice
      to the cherry fruit; fine tannins. Screwcap. 14.5% alc. **Rating** 93 **To** 2016 $20
✪   **Porongurup Merlot 2008** Fresh colour; a plum and spice bouquet, then a light-
      to medium-bodied palate with red fruits to the fore, some black olive nuances
      extending the finish; overall elegance. Screwcap. 13.8% alc. **Rating** 91 **To** 2015 $20

♈♈♈♈   **Reserve Porongurup Chardonnay 2009** **Rating** 88 **To** 2014 $20

Irvine

PO Box 308, Angaston, SA 5353 **Region** Eden Valley
T (08) 8564 1046 **F** (08) 8564 1314 **www.**irvinewines.com.au **Open** At Eden Valley Hotel
Winemaker James and Joanne Irvine **Est.** 1980 **Cases** 8000 **Vyds** 9.5 ha
Industry veteran Jim Irvine, who has successfully guided the destiny of so many SA wineries,
quietly introduced his own label in 1991. The vineyard from which the wines are sourced was
planted in 1983 to an eclectic mix of merlot (4.2 ha), chardonnay (3.1 ha), pinot gris (1 ha),
petit meslier, zinfandel (0.5 ha each) and tannat (0.2 ha). The flagship is the rich Grand Merlot.
Exports to the UK, Germany, Taiwan, Malaysia, Singapore, Hong Kong and China.

♟♟♟♟♟ **The Baroness 2008** Excellent crimson colour; a fragrant, indeed perfumed, bouquet with red fruits and violets leads into a lively, juicy palate awash with cassis and red fruits which carry through to the finish and aftertaste. Merlot/Cabernet Franc/Cabernet Sauvignon. Screwcap. 14.5% alc. **Rating** 95 **To** 2023 $48

James Irvine Eden Valley Grand Merlot 2006 If you must use a cork, it should be as long as, and as well inserted as the cork in this bottle; 23 months in (French) Allier oak, strong varietal fruit and bottle age all combine to make this an impressive wine with layers of plum and spice running through to the long finish. 14.5% alc. **Rating** 94 **To** 2016 $130

♟♟♟♟♡ **Savagnin 2009** Very different from the '09 Chapel Hill Savagnin, less flowery,
✪ but with more structure and flavour complexity on the palate, with potent ginger and citrus zest. Both wines show this is a variety with real potential. Screwcap. 12.5% alc. **Rating** 92 **To** 2015 $24

Estate Barossa Merlot 2007 **Rating** 90 **To** 2014 $25
Barossa Merlot Cabernet Franc 2006 **Rating** 90 **To** 2014 $25

♟♟♟♟ **Reserve Barossa Zinfandel 2006** **Rating** 89 **To** 2014 $35

J&J Wines
★★★☆

Lot 115 Rivers Lane, McLaren Vale, SA 5172 **Region** McLaren Vale
T (08) 8323 9888 **F** (08) 8323 9309 **www.**jjwines.com.au **Open** By appt
Winemaker Charles Whish **Est.** 1998 **Cases** 5000 **Vyds** 5.5 ha
This single-vineyard business began as a grapegrower in 1995, with 5.5 ha of shiraz. When part of the production was not purchased in 2004, owner Jeff Mason had wine made for private use. Since then volume has grown to the point where it is most definitely a commercial venture.

♟♟♟♟♡ **McLaren Vale Shiraz 2008** Good colour; the elegant medium-bodied palate
✪ shows the wine was picked before the heatwave, displaying both regional dark chocolate and varietal black fruits, a twist of spice on the finish. Screwcap. 13.9% alc. **Rating** 90 **To** 2018 $20

Jacob's Creek
★★★★★

Barossa Valley Way, Rowland Flat, SA 5352 **Region** Barossa Valley
T (08) 8521 3000 **F** (08) 8521 3003 **www.**jacobscreek.com **Open** 7 days 10–5
Winemaker Bernard Hickin **Est.** 1973 **Cases** NFP
Jacob's Creek is one of the largest selling brands in the world, and the global success of the basic Jacob's Creek range has had the perverse effect of prejudicing many critics and wine writers who fail (so it seems) to objectively look behind the label and taste what is in fact in the glass. Jacob's Creek has four ranges, and all the wines have a connection, direct or indirect, with Johann Gramp, who built his tiny stone winery on the banks of the creek in 1847. The four-tier range consists of Icon (Johann Shiraz Cabernet); then Heritage (Steingarten Riesling, Reeves Point Chardonnay, Centenary Hill Barossa Shiraz and St Hugo Coonawarra Cabernet); then Reserve (all of the major varietals); and finally Traditional (ditto). Exports to the UK, the US and other major markets.

♟♟♟♟♟ **Steingarten Barossa Riesling 2007** Named in honour of the 1962 planting orchestrated by Colin Gramp, this is a totally seductive wine, with lime and tropical fruit woven through background acidity from the tip of the tongue through to the finish; exceptional line and length, still very fresh. Gold medal Sydney Wine Show '10. Screwcap. 12.5% alc. **Rating** 96 **To** 2016 $32
✪ **Three Vines Shiraz Grenache Sangiovese 2009** Pale magenta; fragrant red fruit aromas, then an almost slippery palate; while dry, red fruits rise on the back-palate and finish. A complete rose with character and attitude. Gold medal Sydney Wine Show '10. Screwcap. 12.5% alc. **Rating** 94 **To** 2011 $15

ŶŶŶŶŶ **Reserve Riesling 2009** 'Made from selected parcels of grapes from SA's
♻   finest regions' says the front label. As ever, no thought of regionality here,
        notwithstanding its lovely juicy citrus flavours running through the length of the
        palate. Screwcap. 12% alc. **Rating** 91 **To** 2020 $18.50
♻   **Reserve Shiraz 2007** Bright, clear purple-red; a very well crafted, elegant red;
        I only wish it could be presented every time UK wine scribes start putting the
        dagger into Australian wines made by the big companies; this is not alcoholic, not
        oaky and not sweet. Screwcap. 14% alc. **Rating** 91 **To** 2014 $18.50
♻   **Reserve Chardonnay 2008** Like the Reserve Riesling, from SA's finest
        (unspecified) regions; the barrel ferment inputs are obvious in a stone fruit–
        dominated palate, with some grapefruit pointing at a Padthaway origin; buy it on
        special discount. Screwcap. 13.5% alc. **Rating** 90 **To** 2013 $18.50
        St Hugo Coonawarra Cabernet Sauvignon 2006 Rating 90 **To** 2016 $47

ŶŶŶŶ **Shiraz Rose 2009** Pale pink; a very lively and vibrant rose, the flavours coursing
♻   through the length of the dry palate; clean finish. Screwcap. 12.5% alc. **Rating** 89
        To 2011 $11.50
♻   **Semillon Sauvignon Blanc 2009** Particularly well made, giving a vibrant
        overtone to the bouquet and palate; juicy lemon and grass notes run through a well-
        balanced and quite long palate. Screwcap. 11.5% alc. **Rating** 88 **To** 2012 $11.50
♻   **Tempranillo 2008** Very hard to resist or criticise at the price; supple, gently sweet
        red berry fruits with just a hint of citrus in the mix, oak and tannins irrelevant.
        Screwcap. 13.5% alc. **Rating** 88 **To** 2012 $11.40
♻   **Pinot Grigio 2008** This has to be one of the best value pinot grigios on the
        market at this price; tangy and fresh, it has length, and is not sweet. Screwcap.
        12.5% alc. **Rating** 87 **To** 2010 $11.40
♻   **Grenache Shiraz 2009** Bright, clear colour; the bouquet is quite fragrant,
        the palate with fresh red fruits. Excellent value. Screwcap. 14% alc. **Rating** 87
        To 2012 $11.50
♻   **Cabernet Merlot 2007** Good colour; a light- to medium-bodied blend,
        the flavours varietally correct, as is the savoury twist on the finish; no heat, no
        sweetness. Screwcap. 13.5% alc. **Rating** 87 **To** 2012 $11.50

JAG Wines   ★★★

72 William Street, Norwood, SA 5067 (postal) **Region** Various
T (08) 8364 4497 **F** (08) 8364 4497 **www.**jagwines.com **Open** By appt
Winemaker Grant Anthony White **Est.** 2001 **Cases** 700
The name is doubtless derived from that of owners Julie and Grant White, but might cause
raised eyebrows in clothing circles. The project developed from their lifelong love of wine; it
started with a hobby vineyard (along with friends) in the Adelaide Hills, then more formal
wine studies, then highly successful amateur winemaking. The Whites purchase grapes from
major SA regions, bringing them to their suburban house to be fermented and pressed, and
then storing the wine offsite in French and American oak until ready for bottling and sale.

ŶŶŶŶ **Reuben Cabernet Sauvignon 2007** Some development in colour no surprise;
        a virtual winery operation, here using grapes from Langhorne Creek. Fruit,
        oak and tannins are all present in ample amounts, less finesse – but it's honest.
        Screwcap. 14% alc. **Rating** 87 **To** 2014 $35

🍇 JaJa   ★★★★☆

PO Box 3015, Strathmore, Vic 3041 **Region** Barossa Valley
T 0411 106 652 **www.**jaja.com.au **Open** Not
Winemaker Troy Kalleske (Contract) **Est.** 2003 **Cases** 1000
Brothers Bert and Pierre Werden are the faces behind www.winestar.com.au, which they
describe as Australia's leading online fine wine retailer. While it seemed a natural progression
for them to develop a family label, they say, 'Being in retail was a huge advantage in learning

what not to do'. On the positive side was the decision to concentrate on Barossa shiraz, the Stonewell subdistrict, 50-year-old vines, and the services of Troy Kalleske as winemaker.

ŸŸŸŸŸ Barossa Shiraz 2004 Deeper colour than the '05; darker fruit and more savoury tones on both bouquet and palate, but the texture and mouthfeel are similar; excellent balance and length. Screwcap. 14.5% alc. **Rating** 94 **To** 2024 $30

ŸŸŸŸŸ Barossa Shiraz 2005 Rating 93 **To** 2021 $30

Jamabro Wines   ★★★☆

PO Box 434, Tanunda, SA 5352 **Region** Barossa Valley
T 0437 633 575 **F** (08) 8563 3837 **www**.jamabro.com.au **Open** By appt
Winemaker David Heinze **Est.** 2003 **Cases** 300 **Vyds** 20.7 ha
Sixth-generation grapegrower David Heinze and wife Juli moved into winemaking in 2003, just as many of the major companies reduced their intake of Barossa grapes. With a little over 20 ha of vines planted to eight varieties, they started with a full suite of wines, using estate-grown grapes and carrying out all the winemaking (other than bottling) onsite. Real marketing skill is involved with the labelling (Jamabro is taken from a combination of family names), but it is the back labels that catch the eye. The Semillon takes the name of daughter Madison who, having just had her hair straightened for a school photograph, was doused in semillon when a bung came out unexpectedly, causing lengthy and messy re-straightening (and an aversion to the winery); and Mum's Spade Shiraz celebrates the spade given to David's mum when she turned 21. 'Wherever Mum went, so did her spade…When there was something to dig, out of the car boot came the spade. We lost Mum in 2006. Mum's Spade Shiraz is our tribute to Mum and all the other great Australian farming women, often the quiet achievers.'

ŸŸŸŸŸ Rough Cut Diamond Barossa Valley Viognier Moscato 2009 The rough cut diamond is Jamabro owner David Heinze; a thoroughly unusual wine that has won silver medals at the Barossa Valley Wine Show and the Japan Challenge in '09, heaven knows in what classes. The flavours are good, the wine is balanced, and the amount of gas is negligible, almost entirely in solution. Screwcap. 8.5% alc. **Rating** 90 **To** 2012 $20

ŸŸŸŸ
✪ Acappella Single Vineyard Barossa Valley Riesling 2009 Pale green-straw; a fresh, light-bodied riesling reflecting its early picking, with delicate lime fruit flavours and a well-balanced finish with some minerality. Screwcap. 11% alc. **Rating** 89 **To** 2013 $15

James Estate   ★★★☆

951 Bylong Valley Way, Baerami via Denman, NSW 2333 **Region** Upper Hunter Valley
T (02) 6547 5168 **F** (02) 6547 5164 **www**.jamesestatewines.com.au **Open** 7 days 10–4.30
Winemaker Graeme Scott, Daniela Neumann **Est.** 1997 **Cases** 25 000 **Vyds** 86 ha
James Estate has had an unsettled corporate existence at various times since 1997, but should enter distinctly calmer waters in the years ahead. Graeme Scott has been installed as senior winemaker, having previously worked with Jim Chatto and Ross Pearson at First Creek, and The Rothbury Estate before that. The newly appointed winemaking team has appreciably lifted the quality of the wines, with (I guess) more to come. Exports to China.

ŸŸŸŸŸ Reserve Hunter Valley Semillon 2009 Bright straw-green; the clean bouquet is grassy (traditional) rather than the citrussy notes of most '09 semillons; the long palate opens the door to some citrus; the wine will develop with grace. Screwcap. 11% alc. **Rating** 92 **To** 2020 $21

ŸŸŸŸ Reserve Hunter Valley Chardonnay 2008 Rating 89 **To** 2014 $21
Verdelho 2009 Rating 88 **To** 2012 $15
✪ Chardonnay 2008 Bright quartz-green; partial barrel fermentation has worked well with the fresh, light-bodied melon and stone fruit flavours; good overall balance. Screwcap. 12.5% alc. **Rating** 87 **To** 2012 $15

James Haselgrove Wines   ★★★☆

PO Box 271, McLaren Vale, SA 5171 **Region** McLaren Vale
T (08) 8383 0886 **F** (08) 8383 0887 www.haselgrovevignerons.com **Open** Not
Winemaker James Haselgrove **Est.** 1981 **Cases** 500
While in one sense this is now a virtual winery, Nick Haselgrove is quick to point out that
it has access to substantial vineyards and winemaking resources. He and James Haselgrove
(who founded this winery) are reluctant to see the business disappear, and intend to continue
making and releasing wines under the James Haselgrove label. In terms of both price and style
they differ from Blackbilly (see separate entry). Exports to the US, Canada and China.

YYYYY **Futures McLaren Vale Shiraz 2008** Impenetrable colour; lashings of oak
dominate the bouquet, with super ripe black fruit lurking beneath; the palate
is dense and chewy, and quite traditional in style; very warm and quite oaky to
conclude, this is for those who enjoy more of everything. Screwcap. 15% alc.
Rating 91 **To** 2020 $55

Jamieson Estate   ★★★★

PO Box 6598, Silverwater, NSW 2128 **Region** Mudgee
T (02) 9737 8377 **F** (02) 9737 9274 www.jamiesonestate.com.au **Open** Not
Winemaker Robert Paul **Est.** 1998 **Cases** 6000 **Vyds** 89.2 ha
Generations of the Jamieson family have been graziers in the region for 150 years, and were
able to select 100 ha of the most suitable soil from their property on which to establish their
vineyard. Beginning in 1998, they have planted over 32 ha of shiraz, almost 24 ha of cabernet
sauvignon and 12 ha of chardonnay, with smaller amounts of semillon, petit verdot, sauvignon
blanc, merlot and barbera. Until 2005 all of the grapes were sold to leading wineries in the
region, but beginning in '06 small amounts of chardonnay, sauvignon blanc, semillon, shiraz
and petit verdot were held back for the Jamieson Estate label.

YYYYY **Guntawang Shiraz 2009** Bright red-purple; while very young, the varietal
expression is bright and correct, black cherry, plum and spice enhanced by
good tannin structure; every reason to suppose the wine will develop very well,
reflecting a top Mudgee vintage. Screwcap. 13.6% alc. **Rating** 91 **To** 2017 $20
Springfield Lane Petit Verdot 2009 Deep purple-red, the signpost of the
variety; the full-bodied palate does not disappoint, with black berry fruits, prune
and confit plum; is not tannic or over-extracted; paradoxically, best when young,
but with a spit-roast ox. Screwcap. 14.8% alc. **Rating** 90 **To** 2014 $20

YYYY **Magpie Lane Cabernet Sauvignon 2009 Rating** 89 **To** 2015 $20
Galambine Chardonnay 2009 Rating 88 **To** 2012 $15

Jamiesons Run   ★★★★★

Coonawarra Wine Gallery, Riddoch Highway, Penola, SA 5277 **Region** Coonawarra
T (08) 8737 3250 **F** (08) 8737 3231 www.jamiesonsrun.com.au **Open** 7 days 10–5
Winemaker Andrew Hales **Est.** 1987 **Cases** NFP
The wheel has turned a full circle for Jamiesons Run. It started out as a single-label, mid-
market, high-volume brand developed by Ray King during his time as CEO of Mildara. It
grew and grew until Mildara, having many years since been merged with Wolf Blass, decided
to rename the Mildara Coonawarra winery as Jamiesons Run, with the Mildara label just
one of a number falling under the Jamiesons Run umbrella. Now the Jamiesons Run winery
is no more – Foster's has sold it, but retained the brand; the cellar door moved to shared
accommodation at the Coonawarra Wine Gallery. Exports to the UK.

YYYYY **Mildara Coonawarra Cabernet Shiraz 2006** Excellent colour for age; the
label lives on; if only I could have the '64 Cabernet Shiraz at four years of age ex a
time machine to put alongside this wine – I fancy the current-day version would
come out on top; black fruits, cedar, earth, tar and spice all come together on
the medium- to full-bodied and very long palate. Screwcap. 14% alc. **Rating** 95
To 2021 $30

Mildara Coonawarra Cabernet Sauvignon 2007 Dressed in the label made famous by the '63 Mildara Coonawarra Cabernet Sauvignon and nicknamed Peppermint Pattie; this is said to be an attempt to capture the distinctive characters of the '63; dodging the complex questions that aim creates, this is a high-quality Coonawarra cabernet, with blackcurrant, earth, dark chocolate, mint and cedar on the medium-bodied, long palate, tannins and French oak both positive. Screwcap. 14.5% alc. **Rating** 94 **To** 2022 $30

Jamsheed ★★★★★

157 Faraday Street, Carlton, Vic 3053 (postal) **Region** Yarra Valley
T 0409 540 414 **F** (03) 5967 3581 **www**.jamsheed.com.au **Open** Not
Winemaker Gary Mills **Est.** 2003 **Cases** 1000
Jamsheed is the venture of Gary Mills, proprietor of Simpatico Wine Services, a boutique contract winemaking company established at the Hill Paddock Winery in Healesville. The wines are sourced from a 30-year-old, low-yielding vineyard, and are made using indigenous/wild yeasts and minimal handling techniques. For the short-term future the business will focus on old vine sites in the Yarra Valley, but will also include a Grampians and Heathcote Shiraz. The name, incidentally, is that of a Persian king recorded in the Annals of Gilgamesh.

♟♟♟♟♟ **Westgate Great Western Riesling 2009** Bright quartz-green; here pushing the envelope has succeeded brilliantly; hand-picked, whole-bunch-pressed riesling was run straight to 800-litre old French oak barrels for fermentation and kept on lees for 8 months, bottled without any acidification. Has purity and intensity, with a great texture to its fresh lime fruit flavours. Screwcap. 12% alc. **Rating** 95 **To** 2024 $26.50
Garden Gully Great Western Syrah 2008 The single-vineyard/region Syrahs are made in the same way except for one thing: this wine is only 50% whole bunch (the others are 100%); wild yeast, 40 days' maceration, 20% new French oak, 10 months' lees contact, bottled without fining or filtration. This wine has the brightest hue, and a fragrant array of black and red fruits; the palate is deceptively light on entry to the mouth, positive tannins appearing on the back-palate and finish; 180 dozen made, 60-year-old vines. Diam. 13.5% alc. **Rating** 94 **To** 2023 $39

♟♟♟♟♟ **Gruyere Yarra Valley Syrah 2008 Rating** 93 **To** 2020 $39
La Syrah 2009 Rating 90 **To** 2013 $20
Silvan Yarra Valley Syrah 2008 Rating 90 **To** 2016 $39

Jane Brook Estate Wines ★★★★☆

229 Toodyay Road, Middle Swan, WA 6056 **Region** Swan Valley
T (08) 9274 1432 **F** (08) 9274 1211 **www**.janebrook.com.au **Open** 7 days 10–5
Winemaker Mark Baird **Est.** 1972 **Cases** 20 000 **Vyds** 18.2 ha
Beverley and David Atkinson have worked tirelessly to build up the Jane Brook Estate wine business over the past 40 years. The most important changes during that time have been the establishment of a Margaret River vineyard (11.7 ha), and sourcing grapes from other southern wine regions in WA. Exports to Hong Kong and Singapore.

♟♟♟♟♟ **David Atkinson Series Liqueur Verdelho NV** Extremely rich and viscous, its age obvious; successive cuvees have won gold medals at the Sheraton WA Wine Awards (only one gold is awarded) in '01, '04 and '09. Burnt toffee, Christmas cake and barley sugar flavours; the spirit is very powerful. Diam. 18.7% alc. **Rating** 94 **To** 2011 $120

♟♟♟♟♟ **Back Block Shiraz 2008 Rating** 93 **To** 2020 $25
Shovelgate Vineyard Margaret River Chardonnay 2009 Rating 92 **To** 2015 $35
✪ **Margaret River Sauvignon Blanc Semillon 2009** A very different wine (although similar label) to the Sauvignon Blanc; here very early picking has led to an intense lemon juice palate, acidity a given. Slightly left field, but tailor made for seafood. Screwcap. 11.2% alc. **Rating** 90 **To** 2012 $21

ΥΥΥΥ   Shovelgate Vineyard Margaret River Cabernet Sauvignon 2008
Rating 89 To 2014 $35

Jansz Tasmania ★★★★★

1216b Pipers Brook Road, Pipers Brook, Tas 7254 **Region** Northern Tasmania
T (03) 6382 7066 **F** (03) 6382 7088 **www.**jansztas.com **Open** 7 days 10–5
Winemaker Natalie Fryar **Est.** 1985 **Cases** 35 000 **Vyds** 30 ha
Jansz is part of Hill Smith Family Vineyards, and was one of the early sparkling wine labels in
Tasmania, stemming from a short-lived relationship between Heemskerk and Louis Roederer.
Its 15 ha of chardonnay, 12 ha of pinot noir and 3 ha of pinot meunier correspond almost
exactly to the blend composition of the Jansz wines. It is the only Tasmanian winery entirely
devoted to the production of sparkling wine under the Jansz Tasmania brand (although the
small amount of Dalrymple Estate wines are also made here), and is of high quality. Exports
to all major markets.

ΥΥΥΥΥ   **Premium Non Vintage Cuvee NV** Full yellow-gold, with some cashew aromas,
✪   followed by an intense mix of stone fruit, citrus and strawberries set in a creamy
mid-palate, the citrus-toned finish clean and fresh. Cork. 12.5% alc. **Rating** 94
To 2010 $24.95
Premium Vintage Rose 2006 Pale salmon-pink; a 100% pinot with three
years on yeast lees marries flavour with finesse, strawberry pinot with spices
and some brioche/cracked yeast; long, fresh finish. Cork. 11.5% alc. **Rating** 94
To 2013 $39.95

ΥΥΥΥႷ   **Premium Non Vintage Rose NV Rating** 93 To 2013 $24.95
Premium Vintage Late Disgorged 2002 Rating 90 To 2011 $49.95

Jarrah Ridge Winery ★★★

651 Great Northern Highway, Herne Hill, WA 6056 **Region** Perth Hills
T (08) 9296 6337 **F** (08) 9403 0800 **www.**jarrahridge.com.au **Open** 7 days 10–5
Winemaker Rob Marshall, John Griffiths (Contract) **Est.** 1998 **Cases** 10 000 **Vyds** 20.5 ha
Syd and Julie Pond have established their vineyard with shiraz the most important variety, the
remainder planted to chenin blanc, chardonnay, cabernet sauvignon, verdelho, viognier and
merlot. Children Michael and Lisa are also involved in the business. Most of the wines have
a degree of sweetness, which will doubtless appeal to cellar door and restaurant customers.
Exports to Canada and Hong Kong.

ΥΥΥΥ   **Marginata Perth Hills Rose 2009** Pale magenta; a fragrant bouquet with a hint
✪   of spice, the palate with cherry and strawberry fruit and a soft finish, with a faint
echo of sweetness. Screwcap. 13.4% alc. **Rating** 87 To 2010 $13

Jasper Hill ★★★★★

Drummonds Lane, Heathcote, Vic 3523 **Region** Heathcote
T (03) 5433 2528 **F** (03) 5433 3143 **www.**jasperhill.com **Open** By appt
Winemaker Ron and Emily Laughton **Est.** 1975 **Cases** 2500 **Vyds** 26.5 ha
The red wines of Jasper Hill are highly regarded and much sought after, invariably selling
out at the cellar door and through the mailing list within a short time of release. These are
wonderful wines in admittedly Leviathan mould, reflecting the very low yields and the care
and attention given to them. The oak is not overdone, and the fruit flavours show Heathcote
at its best. Exports to the UK, the US and other major markets.

ΥΥΥΥΥ   **Emily's Paddock Shiraz Cabernet Franc 2008** Lighter in colour than
Georgia's, which sets the tone for a thoroughly attractive wine, with savoury/
spicy nuances to both bouquet and the graceful, medium-bodied palate; fine, ripe
tannins add to the texture and structure. The spectre of a stained cork is a real
worry for the best Emily's Paddock yet. 14% alc. **Rating** 96 To 2028 $96

Georgia's Paddock Heathcote Shiraz 2008 Good crimson hue; given the protracted drought, this is a great outcome, plum, licorice and blackberry in a swirl of savoury/spicy tannins and oak; has length and authority. Impeccable cork. 15% alc. **Rating** 95 **To** 2020 $73

???? **Georgia's Paddock Heathcote Riesling 2009 Rating** 92 **To** 2014 $35
Cornella Vineyard Heathcote Grenache 2008 Rating 91 **To** 2016 $45

jb Wines ★★★
PO Box 530, Tanunda, SA 5352 **Region** Barossa Valley
T (08) 8563 0291 **F** (08) 8379 4359 **www**.jbwines.com **Open** By appt
Winemaker Joe Barritt, Tim Geddes **Est.** 2005 **Cases** 900 **Vyds** 18 ha
The Barritt family has been growing grapes in the Barossa since the 1850s, but this particular venture was established in 2005 by Lenore, Joe and Greg Barritt. It is based on shiraz, cabernet sauvignon and chardonnay (with tiny amounts of zinfandel, pinot blanc and clairette) planted between 1972 and 2003. Greg runs the vineyard operations; Joe, with a Bachelor of Agricultural Science degree from Adelaide University, followed by 10 years of winemaking in Australia, France and the US, is now the winemaker together with Tim Geddes at McLaren Vale, where the wines are made. Exports to Hong Kong.

???? **Joseph's Barossa Valley Clairette 2009** Pale colour; lemon and straw bouquet, with just a touch of mineral; fresh and lively and distinctly savoury, finishing with an attractive nutty edge to the fruit. Screwcap. 13% alc. **Rating** 89 **To** 2013 $25 BE

Jeanneret Wines ★★★★☆
Jeanneret Road, Sevenhill, SA 5453 **Region** Clare Valley
T (08) 8843 4308 **F** (08) 8843 4251 **www**.jeanneretwines.com **Open** Mon–Fri 9–5, w'ends & public hols 10–5
Winemaker Ben Jeanneret, Harry Dickinson **Est.** 1992 **Cases** 12 000 **Vyds** 6 ha
Ben Jeanneret has progressively built the range and quantity of wines made by him at the onsite winery. In addition to the vineyards, Jeanneret has contracts with owners of an additional 20 ha spread throughout the Clare Valley. All these vines are hand-pruned, hand-picked and dry-grown. Exports to the US, Canada and Japan.

????? **Doozie 2009** Textbook bath talc and fresh lime bouquet; the palate offers piercing acidity and great poise; tightly wound, fresh and focused on the extremely long finish. Riesling. Screwcap. 12.9% alc. **Rating** 94 **To** 2020 $40 BE

Jeir Creek ★★★★
122 Bluebell Lane, Murrumbateman, NSW 2582 **Region** Canberra District
T (02) 6227 5999 **F** (02) 6227 5900 **www**.jeircreekwines.com.au **Open** Thurs–Mon & hols 10–5 (w'ends only during Aug)
Winemaker Rob Howell **Est.** 1984 **Cases** 3000 **Vyds** 8 ha
Rob and Kay Howell, owner-founders of Jeir Creek, celebrated 25 years of involvement in 2009. Rob runs the technically advanced winery, while Kay looks after the cellar door. Predominantly an estate-based business, the plantings comprise chardonnay, cabernet sauvignon (2 ha each), riesling, sauvignon blanc, shiraz (1 ha each) and smaller plantings of pinot noir, viognier and muscat. Exports to Singapore and China.

????? ✪ **Canberra District Riesling 2009** Light straw-green; a riesling with plenty of structure and minerally grip to the lime and grapefruit flavours. Will undoubtedly cellar well. Screwcap. 11.5% alc. **Rating** 92 **To** 2020 $20

✪ **Canberra District Shiraz Viognier 2008** Good colour; a surprisingly robust wine given co-fermentation of what has to be at least 5% viognier (if less, cannot be shown on the front label) with black fruits, licorice and spice all present on the medium- to full-bodied palate. Screwcap. 14.5% alc. **Rating** 91 **To** 2023 $25

Canberra District Botrytis Semillon Sauvignon Blanc 2008 This classic Sauternes blend is rare in Australia, because sauvignon blanc doesn't seem to want to join the botrytis party; it is moderately sweet, with a nutty complexity and good length. Worth trying. Screwcap. 11% alc. **Rating** 90 **To** 2014 $25

🍷🍷🍷🍷 Canberra District Pinot Noir 2009 **Rating** 89 **To** 2014 $25
Canberra District Sparkling Shiraz Viognier 2006 **Rating** 89 **To** 2014 $30

Jester Hill Wines ★★★★

292 Mount Stirling Road, Glen Aplin, Qld 4381 **Region** Granite Belt
T (07) 4683 4380 **F** (07) 4683 4396 **www**.jesterhillwines.com.au **Open** 7 days 9–5
Winemaker James Janda **Est.** 1993 **Cases** 1300 **Vyds** 5.5 ha
A family-run vineyard situated in the pretty valley of Glen Aplin in the Granite Belt. The owners, John and Genevieve Ashwell, aim to concentrate on small quantities of premium-quality wines reflecting the full-bodied style of the region. Believing that good wine is made in the vineyard, John and Genevieve spent the first seven years establishing healthy, strong vines on well-drained soil.

🍷🍷🍷🍷🍷 Touchstone Granite Belt Cabernet Sauvignon 2008 Strong purple-crimson;
✪ a well-made wine, the medium-bodied palate with very good varietal fruit expression courtesy of blackcurrant and redcurrant flavours that are focused and persistent. Screwcap. 14.1% alc. **Rating** 91 **To** 2018 $25
✪ Touchstone Granite Belt Shiraz 2008 Strong crimson-purple; a quite vibrant and juicy shiraz, with blackberry, plum and spice on a well-balanced, medium-bodied palate; has good length. Screwcap. 14.6% alc. **Rating** 90 **To** 2018 $22

🍷🍷🍷🍷 Touchstone Vintner's Reserve Granite Belt Shiraz 2008 **Rating** 89 **To** 2016 $32
Touchstone Granite Belt Cabernet Sauvignon 2007 **Rating** 89 **To** 2020 $25
Touchstone Granite Belt Petit Verdot 2008 **Rating** 87 **To** 2015 $22

Jim Barry Wines ★★★★★

Craig's Hill Road, Clare, SA 5453 **Region** Clare Valley
T (08) 8842 2261 **F** (08) 8842 3752 **www**.jimbarry.com **Open** Mon–Fri 9–5, w'ends & hols 9–4
Winemaker Peter Barry (leads a team of five) **Est.** 1959 **Cases** 80 000 **Vyds** 250 ha
The patriarch of this highly successful wine business, Jim Barry, died in 2004, but the business continues under the active management of several of his many children. There is a full range of wine styles across most varietals, but with special emphasis on Riesling, Shiraz and Cabernet Sauvignon. The ultra-premium release is The Armagh Shiraz, with the McCrae Wood red wines not far behind. Jim Barry Wines is able to draw upon mature Clare Valley vineyards, plus a small holding in Coonawarra. Exports to all major markets.

🍷🍷🍷🍷🍷 The Florita Clare Valley Riesling 2008 Bright pale green; complex and fragrant herb and lime blossom aromas, then a complete change of pace with delicacy and purity taking over, some apple joining the citrus; precisely balanced acidity takes over on the finish. Screwcap. 11.5% alc. **Rating** 95 **To** 2023 $45
The Florita Clare Valley Riesling 2009 The purchase of the famed Leo Buring Florita Vineyard was a masterstroke; this, hand-picked from particular rows, is reticent on its bouquet, but the palate leaves no doubt about its sheer class and long future, with lime, apple and mineral in perfect harmony. The points are for today, not the future when they will be more. Screwcap. 12.1% alc. **Rating** 94 **To** 2030 $49.95
First Eleven Coonawarra Cabernet Sauvignon 2007 I know I keep banging on about it but my mind boggles at the sight of a second-rate cork in a wine of this price; it's not good enough to blame the export markets that demand this closure. This elegant and fragrant wine has utterly delicious cassis and blackcurrant fruit, and a silky palate, making it all the more susceptible to cork issues. 13.4% alc. **Rating** 94 **To** 2017 $60

ŦŦŦŦŦ   **The Lodge Hill Riesling 2009** From the high-elevation Lodge Hill Vineyard;
✪   some citrus blossom aromas, but the action really starts with the long palate and
    its rippling flavours of lime (predominantly) and apple. Screwcap. 12.2% alc.
    Rating 93 To 2023 $19.95
    The Armagh Shiraz 2007 Rating 93 To 2027 $230
    The PB Reserve Shiraz Cabernet Sauvignon 2005 Rating 93 To 2020 $100
✪   **The Lodge Hill Shiraz 2007** A rich and multi-layered full-bodied shiraz, with
    an array of black fruits, licorice and dark chocolate; fine but persistent tannins to
    finish. Striped screwcap a design feature that works well. 14.5% alc. Rating 92
    To 2020 $19.50
✪   **Riesling Project – Tank 8 Sweet Riesling 2009** Available at cellar door only;
    picked at 8.5° baume; the low pH and high acidity largely masks the residual
    sugar; Rheingau or dry Mosel, not the normal Kabinett style in Australia. Very
    interesting. Screwcap. 8% alc. Rating 92 To 2020 $19.95
✪   **The Lodge Hill Shiraz 2008** Good, deep colour; at 480 m, the Lodge Hill
    Vineyard is one of the highest in the Clare Valley, and the wine has more spicy/
    savoury characters than usual in the region; the medium- to full-bodied palate
    has good texture and structure to its black fruit flavours. Screwcap. 14.5% alc.
    Rating 91 To 2028 $19.95
✪   **The Cover Drive Coonawarra Cabernet Sauvignon 2007** An appealing
    cabernet that has run rings around the vintage, cassis and blackcurrant fruit set in a
    lively background; gently spicy oak notes bring the innings to a close. Coonawarra
    the twelfth man? Screwcap. 14% alc. Rating 91 To 2017 $19.50
✪   **Watervale Riesling 2009** Pale and bright straw-green; the delicate, fresh
    bouquet has lime and lemon characters that are precisely repeated on the palate;
    delicious now, but give it a few years to grow. Screwcap. 12% alc. Rating 90
    To 2015 $14.95

ŦŦŦŦ   **Silly Mid On Sauvignon Blanc Semillon 2009** Rating 89 To 2012 $19.95
    The Cover Drive Coonawarra Cabernet Sauvignon 2008 Rating 89
    To 2018 $19.95
    Three Little Pigs 2005 Rating 88 To 2014 $19.95

Jimbour Wines   ★★★

86 Jimbour Station Road, Jimbour, Qld 4406 **Region** Queensland Zone
T (07) 3236 2100 **F** (07) 3236 0110 **www**.jimbour.com **Open** Wed–Sun 10–4.30
Winemaker Peter Scudamore-Smith MW (Consultant) **Est.** 2000 **Cases** 4000 **Vyds** 19.3 ha
Jimbour Station was one of the first properties opened in the Darling Downs and the
heritage-listed homestead was built in 1876. The property, owned by the Russell family
since 1923, has diversified by establishing a vineyard (shiraz, chardonnay, verdelho, cabernet
sauvignon, viognier and merlot) and opening a cellar door on the property in a renovated
water tower built in 1870. In 2010 the family decided to suspend winemaking and mothball
the vineyard; the situation will be reviewed when (and if) market conditions improve. Exports
to Japan, Taiwan, Hong Kong, Korea and China.

ŦŦŦŦ   **Ludwig Leichhardt Summer Pruned Reserve Shiraz 2008** Deep colour; a
    rich bouquet of braised beef and confit blackberry; the palate is quite unctuous
    and fleshy, with a lively lick of acidity to finish. Screwcap. 16.5% alc. Rating 89
    To 2016 $29 BE
    Jimbour Station Shiraz 2008 A quite lifted bouquet; dried black fruits, with a
    distinct pastille edge; quite fleshy on entry, with the acidity showing prominently.
    Screwcap. 15% alc. Rating 87 To 2013 $16 BE

Jinks Creek Winery ★★★★

Tonimbuk Road, Tonimbuk, Vic 3815 **Region** Gippsland
T (03) 5629 8502 **F** (03) 5629 8551 **www**.jinkscreekwinery.com.au **Open** Sun 12–5
or by appt
Winemaker Andrew Clarke **Est.** 1981 **Cases** 2000 **Vyds** 3.52 ha
Planting of the Jinks Creek vineyard antedated the building of the winery by 11 years, but
all of the wines are made from estate-grown grapes. Perched above the vineyard with an
uninterrupted view of the Bunyip State Forest and Black Snake Ranges, a refurbished 100-
year-old wool shed has been renovated to house a restaurant, art gallery and cellar door. This
venue is constructed entirely from recycled materials sourced from Gippsland, including
old lining boards, a kauri pine dance floor and a perfectly preserved pressed-tin ceiling.
Huge industrial steel windows open onto an outer deck, next to the sculpture garden and
contemporary artworks by well-known Australian artists including Esther Erlich, Christopher
Lees, Willy Sheather and Mark Knight. Open on Sundays for wood-fired pizza and wine
tasting, the venue is available for private functions by arrangement, and a nearby Victorian
weatherboard cottage provides secluded accommodation above the vineyard. Exports to
the US.

ŶŶŶŶŶ **Longford Shiraz 2008** Good colour; spicy nuances on the bouquet attest to a
cool site, as does the drive of the medium-bodied palate, black cherry fruit with a
zesty finish. Diam. 13.5% alc. **Rating** 91 **To** 2020 $30

ŶŶŶŶ **Pinot Gris 2009 Rating** 89 **To** 2011 $26
Rose 2009 Rating 89 **To** 2015 $25

John Duval Wines ★★★★★

PO Box 622, Tanunda, SA 5352 **Region** Barossa Valley
T (08) 8562 2266 **F** (08) 8562 3034 **www**.johnduvalwines.com **Open** Not
Winemaker John Duval **Est.** 2003 **Cases** 6900
John Duval is an internationally recognised winemaker, having been the custodian of Penfolds
Grange for almost 30 years as part of his role as chief red winemaker at Penfolds. He remains
involved with Penfolds as a consultant, but these days is concentrating on establishing his own
brand, and providing consultancy services to other clients in various parts of the world. On
the principle 'if not broken, don't fix', he is basing his business on shiraz and shiraz blends
from old-vine vineyards in the Barossa Valley. The brand name Plexus denotes combining the
different elements of shiraz/grenache/mourvedre into a coherent structure. Exports to the
UK, the US and other major markets.

ŶŶŶŶŶ **Entity Barossa Valley Shiraz 2008** Intense, dark purple-crimson; a highly
✪ expressive and complex bouquet of black fruits, licorice and oak is followed by
a full-bodied palate that is savoury rather than jammy, notes of dark chocolate
joining the black fruits. A 30-year future is conservative. Screwcap. 14.5% alc.
Rating 96 **To** 2038 $47
Plexus Barossa Valley Shiraz Grenache Mourvedre 2008 Purple-red;
Barossa Valley blends of shiraz/grenache/mourvedre seldom have the poise,
conviction or richness of this wine; the flavours are multi-layered yet not the least
jammy, the tannins particularly good, the length all one can ask for. Screwcap.
14.5% alc. **Rating** 95 **To** 2028 $38

John Gehrig Wines ★★★☆

Oxley-Milawa Road, Oxley, Vic 3678 **Region** King Valley
T (03) 5727 3395 **F** (03) 5727 3699 **www**.johngehrigwines.com.au **Open** 7 days 9–5
Winemaker Ross Gehrig **Est.** 1976 **Cases** 5600 **Vyds** 6 ha
Parents John and Elizabeth Gehrig have effectively passed on the management (and the
winemaking) to son Ross, and now look after cellar door and marauding ducks and geese.
The estate vineyard is a patchwork quilt of riesling, chenin blanc, chardonnay, pinot meu-
nier, pinot noir, cabernet sauvignon, merlot, malbec, cabernet franc, ruby cabernet, petit

verdot, tempranillo, muscat, durif and gamay, allowing – indeed demanding – Ross to make wines in a wide variety of styles, continuing to enjoy particular success with Riesling and Chenin Blanc.

♥♥♥♥♀ **King Valley Cabernet Merlot 2006** A savoury style with fresh leather, cassis and a touch of olive on the bouquet; soft and fleshy, red fruits and ironstone come through on the finish. Screwcap. 14.3% alc. **Rating** 90 **To** 2014 $25 BE

John Kosovich Wines   ★★★★★
Cnr Memorial Avenue/Great Northern Highway, Baskerville, WA 6056 **Region** Swan Valley
T (08) 9296 4356 **F** (08) 9296 4356 **www**.johnkosovichwines.com.au **Open** 7 days 10–5.30
Winemaker Anthony Kosovich **Est.** 1922 **Cases** 3500 **Vyds** 12.5 ha
John Kosovich Wines operated as Westfield Wines until 2003, when it changed its name to honour John's 50th vintage. The name change did not signify any change in either philosophy or direction for this much-admired producer of a surprisingly elegant and complex Chardonnay. The other wines are more variable, but from time to time there have been attractive Verdelho and excellent Cabernet Sauvignon. Since 1998, wines partly or wholly from the family's planting at Pemberton have been made, the Swan Valley/Pemberton blends released under the Bronze Wing label. No relevant tasting notes for the 2011 *Wine Companion*.

John Siding Vintners   ★★★★
Barker Road, Mount Barker, SA 6324 **Region** Adelaide Hills
T 0418 713 947 **F** (08) 8398 2927 **Open** By appt
Winemaker John Gilbert **Est.** 1996 **Cases** 12 000
John Gilbert has a number of brands, led by Gilberts Siding with a flagship Erebus Shiraz and Earhart Cabernet from McLaren Vale, supported by Sangiovese Shiraz and a Grenache Shiraz. His Jardim do Bomfim wines come from the Thunderbird Vineyard at Middleton (Fleurieu Peninsula), Ironstone Ridge Vineyard in the Adelaide Hills (planted to Italian varieties, including a direct importation of a Sicilian white grillo brought in after the 2001 vintage), and the dry-grown XR-65 Vineyard at Langhorne Creek.

♥♥♥♥♀ **Jardim do Bomfim Barossa Valley Shiraz 2006** Very good purple-crimson; has a fragrant bouquet of plum, blackberry and well-balanced oak; the palate has a spicy zesty character that shows no sign whatsoever of dead fruit or alcohol; rather, there is a bright display of cherry and blackberry fruit and good oak ex 24 months' maturation. Screwcap. 14.8% alc. **Rating** 92 **To** 2016
Jardim do Bomfim Dry Grown Old Vine Langhorne Creek Shiraz 2004 Slightly brighter colour than Thunderbird, with more purple; has good intensity, focus and length, with plum, dark chocolate and spice flavours in a fine web of savoury tannins; good oak and tannin management; from 50-year-old vines. Screwcap. 14.5% alc. **Rating** 92 **To** 2017
Jardim do Bomfim Thunderbird Vineyard Shiraz 2005 Some colour development consistent with the vintage; ripe berry aromas and flavours, the long, medium-bodied palate with plum and spicy/savoury notes. Curious labelling, the front showing Thunderbird alone, the back label showing Thunderbird, Southern Fleurieu (60%)/Langhorne Creek vineyard (40%). Screwcap. 14.8% alc. **Rating** 91 **To** 2015
Gilberts Siding McLaren Vale Sangiovese Shiraz 2001 Despite the very large red typeface of the shiraz, the much smaller black script for sangiovese, this is a 50/50 blend; the sangiovese has imparted the savoury tannins of the variety, but there is just enough shiraz to provide balance, and there is abundant length. Cork. 14.5% alc. **Rating** 90 **To** 2015

♥♥♥♥ **Gilberts Siding Erebus McLaren Vale Shiraz 2002** Rating 88 To 2012
Jardim do Bomfim Zinfandel 2004 Rating 88 To 2012
Gilberts Siding McLaren Vale Shiraz Grenache 2002 Rating 87 To 2011

John's Blend ★★★★★

18 Neil Avenue, Nuriootpa, SA 5355 (postal) **Region** Langhorne Creek
T (08) 8562 1820 **F** (08) 8562 4050 **www**.johnsblend.com.au **Open** At The Winehouse,
Langhorne Creek
Winemaker John Glaetzer **Est.** 1974 **Cases** 2500 **Vyds** 23 ha
John Glaetzer was Wolf Blass' right-hand man almost from the word go, the power behind
the throne of the three Jimmy Watson trophies awarded to Wolf Blass Wines in 1974, '75 and
'76, and a small matter of 11 Montgomery trophies for the Best Red Wine at the Adelaide
Wine Show. This has always been a personal venture on the side, as it were, by John and wife
Margarete, officially sanctioned of course, but really needing little marketing effort. Exports to
the UK, Canada, Switzerland, Indonesia, Singapore and Hong Kong.

ΨΨΨΨΨ Individual Selection Langhorne Creek Cabernet Sauvignon 2006 No. 33.
Deep crimson-purple; the wine spent over three years in new oak, half French,
half Californian; the astonishing thing is the way the bounteous blackcurrant
fruit has managed to deal with that oak and not lose its identity. Cork. 14.5% alc.
Rating 95 **To** 2026 $35
Margarete's Shiraz 2007 No. 13. Deeply coloured; winemaking techniques and
philosophy fills in the gaps often evident with '07 reds; rich, luscious and supple
black fruits are seamlessly woven with oak and gently ripe tannins. A classic of its
genre. Cork. 14.5% alc. **Rating** 94 **To** 2017 $35

Johnston Oakbank ★★★☆

18 Oakwood Road, Oakbank, SA 5243 **Region** Adelaide Hills
T (08) 8388 4263 **F** (08) 8388 4278 **www**.johnston-oakbank.com.au **Open** Mon–Fri 8–5
Winemaker David O'Leary (Contract), Geoff Johnston **Est.** 1843 **Cases** 8000 **Vyds** 49 ha
The origins of this business, owned by the Johnston Group, date back to 1839, making it the
oldest family-owned business in SA. The vineyard at Oakbank is substantial, with plantings of
chardonnay, pinot noir, sauvignon blanc, shiraz, merlot and cabernet sauvignon.

ΨΨΨΨ Adelaide Hills Sauvignon Blanc 2009 Well made and balanced, but curiously
lacking flavour intensity given the age of the vines; there are notes of gooseberry,
and the minerally finish is long. Screwcap. 11.5% alc. **Rating** 89 **To** 2011 $17.95

Jones Road ★★★☆

2 Godings Road, Moorooduc, Vic 3933 **Region** Mornington Peninsula
T (03) 5978 8080 **F** (03) 5978 8081 **www**.jonesroad.com.au **Open** W'ends 11–5
Winemaker Sticks (Travis Bush) **Est.** 1998 **Cases** 8000 **Vyds** 26.5 ha
It's a long story, but after establishing a very large and very successful herb-producing business
in the UK, Rob Frewer and family migrated to Australia in 1997. By a circuitous route
they ended up with a property on the Mornington Peninsula, promptly planting pinot
noir and chardonnay, then pinot gris, sauvignon blanc and merlot, and have since leased
another vineyard at Mt Eliza, and purchased Ermes Estate in 2007. Production has increased
significantly in the wake of these purchases. Exports to the UK, Canada, Norway, Sweden,
Singapore and Japan.

ΨΨΨΨΨ Jr Jones Mornington Peninsula Pinot Grigio 2009 Thoroughly interesting,
✪ for this wine really does have the faintly grainy/gritty texture of grigio, standing
out in a sea of often bland gris. Screwcap. 13% alc. **Rating** 90 **To** 2011 $19

ΨΨΨΨ Mornington Peninsula Pinot Noir 2008 **Rating** 89 **To** 2015 $27

Josef Chromy Wines ★★★★☆

370 Relbia Road, Relbia, Tas 7258 **Region** Northern Tasmania
T (03) 6335 8700 **F** (03) 6335 8777 **www**.josefchromy.com.au **Open** 7 days 10–5
Winemaker Jeremy Dineen **Est.** 2004 **Cases** 18 000 **Vyds** 60 ha

Joe Chromy just refuses to lie down and admit the wine industry in Tasmania is akin to a financial black hole. After escaping from Czechoslovakia in 1950, establishing Blue Ribbon Meats, using the proceeds of sale to buy Rochecombe and Heemskerk Vineyards, then selling those and establishing Tamar Ridge before it, too, was sold, Joe is at it again; this time he's invested $40 million in a wine-based but multifaceted business, including a major building development in Launceston. If this were not remarkable enough, Joe has turned 80, and has recovered from a major stroke. Foundation of the new wine business was the purchase of the large Old Stornoway Vineyard at a receivership sale in 2003; in all, there are 60 ha of 10-year-old vines, the lion's share to pinot noir and chardonnay. He retained Jeremy Dineen (for many years winemaker at Hood/Wellington) as winemaker, the winery completed prior to the '07 vintage. Chromy's grandson Dean Cocker is guiding the development of a restaurant, function and equestrian centre, the latter on a scale sufficient to accommodate the Magic Millions yearling sales. Exports to Canada, Sweden, Singapore and Japan.

�♀♀♀ **ZDAR Riesling 2005** A well-rounded bouquet of ripe lemons, lime, candied orange and a touch of spice; the palate shows vitality and nerve, with green apple acidity, talc and slate all combining seamlessly on the savoury, complex and thoroughly satisfying finish. Screwcap. 12.5% alc. **Rating** 94 **To** 2016 $48 BE

♀♀♀♀♀ **DELIKAT SGR Riesling 2008** Pale hue; green apples are the central theme
✪ of the bouquet and the fruit purity is outstanding; the lime-sweetness is counterbalanced by piercing acidity, and the finish clean and almost chalky dry. Screwcap. 8.5% alc. **Rating** 93 **To** 2017 $25 BE
ZDAR Pinot Noir 2005 Rating 93 $48 BE
Pinot Noir Chardonnay 2005 Rating 92 **To** 2013 $45
Botrytis Riesling 2008 Rating 92 **To** 2015 $24
✪ **Riesling 2009** The bouquet is driven by savoury notes of slate and flint, making way for Meyer lemon rind; there is a strong bath talc element to the palate, with texture playing a key role and providing a distinct almond character to the finish; an unashamedly European style. Screwcap. 12.5% alc. **Rating** 91 **To** 2016 $25 BE
✪ **Pinot Noir 2008** A fragrant bouquet with red fruits and some stemmy characters; sweet red berry flavours are rounded off with touches of spice and stem on the finish. Screwcap. 14% alc. **Rating** 91 **To** 2015 $28
Sauvignon Blanc 2009 Rating 90 $25 BE
Pinot Gris 2009 Rating 90 $25 BE

♀♀♀♀ **PEPIK Chardonnay 2009 Rating** 89 **To** 2013 $19
Chardonnay 2008 Rating 89 $30 BE
PEPIK Pinot Noir 2008 Rating 89 **To** 2012 $19

Juniper Estate   ★★★★★

Harmans Road South, Cowaramup, WA 6284 **Region** Margaret River
T (08) 9755 9000 **F** (08) 9755 9100 **www**.juniperestate.com.au **Open** 7 days 10–5
Winemaker Mark Messenger, Kym Eyres **Est.** 1973 **Cases** 14 000 **Vyds** 19.52 ha
When Roger Hill and Gillian Anderson purchased the Wrights vineyard in 1998, the 10-ha vineyard was already 25 years old, but in need of retrellising and a certain amount of nursing to bring it back to health. All of that has happened, along with the planting of additional shiraz and cabernet sauvignon. The Juniper Crossing wines use a mix of estate-grown and purchased grapes from other Margaret River vineyards. The Juniper Estate releases are made only from the estate plantings. Exports to the UK, Ireland, Canada, Denmark, Hong Kong, Philippines and Singapore.

♀♀♀♀♀ **Margaret River Semillon 2008** Light straw-green; while barrel-fermented and
✪ matured, it is the varietal fruit that rules the roost, not oak, with classic grassy/lemony flavours, crisp acidity and a long finish. Screwcap. 13% alc. **Rating** 94 **To** 2020 $26

Margaret River Chardonnay 2008 Pale straw-green; a super-elegant and fragrant bouquet is reflected by the palate, with immaculate nectarine and white peach fruit, all in a subtle mode. Will develop a little more punch as it ages. Screwcap. 14% alc. **Rating** 94 **To** 2017 $35

Margaret River Cabernet Sauvignon 2007 Purple-crimson; typical of the somewhat severe but clear-cut expression of cabernet in Margaret River this vintage, with pure blackcurrant, earth and cassis fruit; here the tannins are evident but are ripe and in balance. Screwcap. 14% alc. **Rating** 94 **To** 2027 $45

♟♟♟♟♀ **Juniper Crossing Margaret River Semillon Sauvignon Blanc 2009** Rating 90 To 2010 $21

Juniper Crossing Margaret River Shiraz 2007 Rating 90 To 2014 $21

✪ **Juniper Crossing Margaret River Cabernet Sauvignon Merlot 2007** Retains crimson-purple hue; fragrant red fruit/cassis/plum aromas roll into the palate, here joined by some barrel ferment oak inputs lending a savoury touch and texture. Screwcap. 14% alc. **Rating** 90 **To** 2017 $21

Juul Wines   ★★★★

930 Merriwa Road, Denman, NSW 2328 **Region** Upper Hunter Valley
T (02) 6547 1243 **F** (02) 6547 1298 **www.**juulwines.com **Open** By appt
Winemaker Inwine (Barry Koorij) **Est.** NFP **Cases** 2000
Juul Wines has undergone signficant changes since its establishment, with divestment of the 40-ha vineyard, and a significant reduction in the production, contract made by Barry Koorij, taking it into the realm of a virtual winery. Exports to China and – wait for it – Lord Howe Island.

♟♟♟♟♟ **Hollydene Estate Semillon 2007** Pale straw-green; vibrantly fresh and juicy,
✪ with citrus and grass in more or less equal proportions, this wine is as lovely now as it will be in 10 or 20 years' time; the name Hollydene is a blast from the Hunter past. Screwcap. 11% alc. **Rating** 94 **To** 2022 $14

♟♟♟♟ **Giants Leap Sauvignon Blanc 2008** Tangy citrussy aromas and flavours,
✪ particularly on the back-palate and finish are a surprise packet from the Upper Hunter. Screwcap. 12% alc. **Rating** 88 **To** 2011 $14

Loaded Fox Rose 2007 Rating 88 To 2010 $15

Kabminye Wines   ★★★★☆

Krondorf Road, Tanunda, SA 5352 **Region** Barossa Valley
T (08) 8563 0889 **F** (08) 8563 3828 **www.**kabminye.com **Open** 7 days 11–5
Winemaker Rick Glastonbury **Est.** 2001 **Cases** 3500 **Vyds** 1.5 ha
Richard and Ingrid Glastonbury's cellar door is on land settled in the 1880s by Ingrid's ancestor Johann Christian Henschke. Kabminye is an Aboriginal word meaning 'morning star', and was given to the hamlet of Krondorf as a result of the anti-German sentiment during the Second World War (since changed back to the original Krondorf). The cellar door and café opened in 2003; SA Tourism has since used the building as a sustainable tourism case study. The vineyard is planted to durif, shiraz, mourvedre, carignan, cinsaut, princess black muscat and black frontignac. Exports to the UK, Malaysia, Hong Kong and China.

♟♟♟♟♟ **Hubert Barossa Valley Shiraz 2008** Strong, deep crimson; shares the same savoury elegance as the standard wine, dark fruits with touches of spice and dark chocolate, the tannins and oak on the medium-bodied palate well-balanced and integrated; 200 cases made. Screwcap. 14.5% alc. **Rating** 94 **To** 2023 $45

♟♟♟♟♀ **Barossa Valley Shiraz 2008** Rating 93 To 2020 $28
Durif Carignan Shiraz 2007 Rating 93 To 2027 $45
Ken & Neville 2008 Rating 92 To 2018 $23.50
Barossa Eden Valley Kerner 2009 Rating 90 To 2013 $22

Kaesler Wines

★★★★★

Barossa Valley Way, Nuriootpa, SA 5355 **Region** Barossa Valley
T (08) 8562 4488 **F** (08) 8562 4499 **www**.kaesler.com.au **Open** Mon–Sat 10–5,
Sun & public hols 11.30–4
Winemaker Reid Bosward, Stephen Dew **Est.** 1990 **Cases** 25 000 **Vyds** 50 ha

The Kaesler name originated in 1845, when the first members of the family settled in the Barossa Valley. The vineyards date back to 1893, but the Kaesler ownership ended in 1968. After several changes, the present (much-expanded) Kaesler Wines was acquired by a small group of investment bankers headed by Swiss-born, Singapore-resident, quietly spoken Ed Peter (who has since acquired Yarra Yering) in conjunction with former Flying Winemaker Reid Bosward and wife Bindy. Bosward's experience shows through in the wines, which now come from estate vineyards, 40 ha adjacent to the winery, and 10 ha in the Marananga area. The latter includes shiraz planted in 1899, with both blocks seeing plantings in the 1930s, '60s, then each decade through to the present. Exports to all major markets.

ㅜㅜㅜㅜㅜ **Alte Reben Barossa Valley Shiraz 2008** While Kaesler regards vines over 40 years as old, this wine comes from an estate vineyard at Marananga planted in 1899; striking crimson-purple colour, and has gorgeously pure blackberry and plum fruit, oak (French) and tannins perfectly balanced. Not fined or filtered. The one drawback is the choice of cork for a wine that would live for 50 years under screwcap. 14% alc. **Rating** 97 **To** 2038 $120
Reid's Rasp Semillon 2004 Brightly coloured, it has an uncommon degree of complexity, akin to white Bordeaux. Most compelling is its thrust and drive, no doubt assisted by the very low alcohol (by the standards of the Barossa Valley). Screwcap. 11% alc. **Rating** 95 **To** 2014 $35
Old Bastard Shiraz 2007 Deep colour; a hilarious new label depicting said old bastard does not herald any change in the style of this wine, made from a small estate block planted in 1893. Rich, supple and velvety, it is able to carry its alcohol; it is chock-full of dark berry flavours. Cork. 15.5% alc. **Rating** 95 **To** 2027 $160
Patel Barossa Valley Shiraz 2008 Derives its name from the ship that brought the first members of the Kaesler family to Australia in 1845; vines planted in 1961. Deep crimson-purple, it is an exuberantly full-bodied and luscious wine in radically different style to Alte Reben; well executed for those who gravitate to this end of the spectrum. Cork. 16% alc. **Rating** 94 **To** 2030 $120
The Bogan 2007 The equally deep colour has a better hue than Old Bastard; produced from estate vineyards planted in 1899 and 1965; aromas of licorice, boot polish and black fruits are followed by a distinctly savoury, spicy palate, oak and tannins playing a support role. Shiraz. Cork. 15.5% alc. **Rating** 94 **To** 2022 $50
Patel Barossa Valley Cabernet Sauvignon 2008 Good purple-red; made from 40-year-old estate plantings and matured in French oak for 18 months; there is no question the wine has clear varietal character and surprising finesse on the back-palate, which lengthens the finish, but I wish the wine was 14% alcohol, not 15%. Cork. **Rating** 94 **To** 2023 $120

ㅜㅜㅜㅜㅜ **Reid's Rasp Barossa Valley Shiraz 2009 Rating** 93 **To** 2019 $35
Old Vine Barossa Valley Shiraz 2007 Rating 93 **To** 2022 $70
Alte Reben Barossa Valley Mataro 2008 Rating 93 **To** 2020 $80
Barossa Valley Viognier 2008 Rating 90 **To** 2013 $25
Avignon 2007 Rating 90 **To** 2017 $30

ㅜㅜㅜㅜ **Stonehorse Barossa Valley Shiraz 2008 Rating** 89 **To** 2018 $22
Barossa Valley Cabernet Sauvignon 2007 Rating 89 **To** 2017 $25
Stonehorse Barossa Valley Grenache Shiraz Mourvedre 2007 Rating 87 **To** 2014 $18

Kahlon Estate Wines   ★★★

Lot 4 Airport Road, Renmark, SA 5341 **Region** Riverland
T (08) 8586 5744 **F** (08) 8586 5799 **www.**kahlonestatewine.com.au
Open Mon–Fri 8–5, w'ends 9–4
Winemaker Ashu Ashutosh **Est.** 2004 **Cases** 10 000 **Vyds** 158 ha
The roots of Kahlon Estate go back to 1990, when founder/owner Mohinder Kahlon
began the development of what ultimately became a substantial vineyard. Initially simply
a grapegrower, the business first diversified into volume wines sold in bulk, and ultimately
(in 2004) to cleanskin bottled wines selling for $33 per 12-bottle case, and varietal wines
under the Long Tail brand (Chardonnay, Sauvignon Blanc, Shiraz, Petit Verdot and Cabernet
Sauvignon) at $50 per case. Exports to the UK, Canada, Italy, Czech Republic, India, Malaysia,
Vietnam, China and NZ.

ŶŶŶŶ **Longtail Petit Verdot 2007** Petit verdot proves its resilience once again,
✪   retaining good colour and offering black fruits supported by firm, but balanced,
       tannins. Cork. 13.6% alc. **Rating** 87 **To** 2012 $7

Kalgan River Wines   ★★★★★

PO Box 5559, Albany, WA 6332 **Region** Albany
T (08) 9841 4413 **F** (08) 9841 6471 **www.**kalganriverwines.com.au **Open** Not
Winemaker Mike Garland **Est.** 2000 **Cases** 2000 **Vyds** 21 ha
John and Dianne Ciprian have brought different backgrounds to their Kalgan River property. John has grapegrowing in two generations of ancestral blood in his veins. However, it
was his success as a jeweller that provided the wherewithal for Kalgan River; Dianne started
as a mathematics teacher, and then became a jewellery valuer, both occupations requiring
intellectual rigour. Thanks to what they describe as 'hard yakka', they have established shiraz,
cabernet sauvignon (7 ha each), chardonnay, riesling (3 ha each) and viognier (1 ha). Exports
to the UK.

ŶŶŶŶŶ **Great Southern Shiraz Viognier 2008** A fragrant bouquet derives its perfume
       from the co-fermented viognier, while the palate reflects the cool climate without
       sacrificing generosity and complexity; spice, pepper, satsuma plum and blackberry;
       fine tannins. Screwcap. 14.5% alc. **Rating** 95 **To** 2023 $34.95
       Great Southern Cabernet Sauvignon 2008 Albany produced excellent
       cabernet sauvignons in '08, and this is a very good example. Brightly coloured, it
       has a supple parade of blackcurrant, cedar and a wisp of olive; the tannins and oak
       are perfectly pitched. Screwcap. 13.8% alc. **Rating** 95 **To** 2023 $24.95

ŶŶŶŶŶ **Ciprian Great Southern Shiraz 2008 Rating** 92 **To** 2017 $44.95
       Great Southern Rose 2009 Rating 90 **To** 2011 $22.95

Kalleske   ★★★★★

6 Murray Street, Greenock, SA 5360 **Region** Barossa Valley
T (08) 8563 4000 **F** (08) 8563 4001 **www.**kalleske.com **Open** By appt
Winemaker Troy Kalleske **Est.** 1999 **Cases** 10 000 **Vyds** 42 ha
The Kalleske family has been growing and selling grapes on a mixed farming property at
Greenock for over 100 years. Sixth-generation Troy Kalleske with brother Tony established
the winery and created the Kalleske label in 1999. The vineyard is planted to shiraz (27 ha),
grenache (6 ha), mataro (2 ha), chenin blanc, durif, viognier, zinfandel, petit verdot, semillon
and tempranillo (1 ha each). The vines vary in age with the oldest dating back to 1875, and an
overall average age of about 50 years, all grown organically. Exports to all major markets.

ŶŶŶŶŶ **Barossa Valley Rosina 2009** Largely made from 70-year-old estate grenache,
✪   early-picked and wild yeast–fermented, partly in old barriques; the wine justifies all
       the costly inputs, with vibrant cherry and Turkish delight flavours on a long finish.
       Screwcap. 12.5% alc. **Rating** 94 **To** 2012 $18

✪   **Pirathon by Kalleske Barossa Valley Shiraz 2008** Very interesting wine, seemingly sourced from top-quality subdistricts in the northwest corner of the Barossa, and which carries its alcohol well, the red and black fruits of the finish persistent and quite elegant. Screwcap. 15% alc. **Rating** 94 **To** 2018 $23

✪   **Moppa Barossa Valley Shiraz 2008** Dark dense purple; a rich, lifted and complex bouquet is followed by a full-bodied and no less complex palate, seemingly riper than the alcohol suggests. There is a lift to the flavour, but whether or not this is due to the trace of viognier and petit verdot is hard to say. Screwcap. 14.5% alc. **Rating** 94 **To** 2025 $28

�♔   **Old Vine Barossa Valley Grenache 2007 Rating** 92 **To** 2017 $45
Johann Georg Old Vine Barossa Valley Shiraz 2007 Rating 90
To 2016 $100

✪   **Clarry's Grenache Shiraz Mourvedre 2008** Would seem to have been picked before the March heatwave, for the fruit flavours are juicy, expressive and fresh on the mid-palate, followed by a more savoury finish. Screwcap. 14.5% alc. **Rating** 90 **To** 2014 $18

♔♔♔♔   **Florentine Barossa Valley Chenin Blanc 2009 Rating** 89 **To** 2014 $18

Kangarilla Road Vineyard   ★★★★★
Kangarilla Road, McLaren Vale, SA 5171 **Region** McLaren Vale
T (08) 8383 0533 **F** (08) 8383 0044 **www**.kangarillaroad.com.au **Open** Mon–Fri 9–5,
w'ends 11–5
Winemaker Kevin O'Brien **Est.** 1997 **Cases** 40 000 **Vyds** 14 ha
Kangarilla Road is owned and operated by long-time industry identity Kevin O'Brien and wife Helen. The estate plantings include shiraz, zinfandel, viognier, chardonnay and savagnin, intake supplemented by purchases from other vineyards in the region. Zinfandel is the winery speciality, other alternative varieties including Sangiovese, sold either under that name or as Primitivo. Exports to the UK, the US and other major markets.

♔♔♔♔♔   **Q McLaren Vale Shiraz 2007** Excellent colour, half suggesting the inclusion of viognier; prolonged oak ageing has not imposed itself on the wine, which is very intense, the quality particularly good for '07; lots of dark chocolate and fluffy tannins. Biodynamic. Screwcap. 15% alc. **Rating** 94 **To** 2022 $70
The Devil's Whiskers McLaren Vale Shiraz 2007 The elevated purple-crimson colour points to the 4% viognier inclusion, as does the aromatic bouquet; the palate has the dark chocolate and earth of the region, but there is a definite tweak from the viognier. Screwcap. 14% alc. **Rating** 94 **To** 2017 $30

♔♔♔♔♔   **McLaren Vale Sangiovese 2008 Rating** 90 **To** 2015 $24
Black St Peters McLaren Vale Zinfandel 2007 Rating 90 **To** 2017 $30

♔♔♔♔   **Good Intentions 2009 Rating** 89 **To** 2012 $24
McLaren Vale Chardonnay 2009 Rating 88 **To** 2012 $16
Fleurieu Primitivo 2007 Rating 88 **To** 2015 $21

Kara Kara Vineyard   ★★★☆
99 Edelsten Road, St Arnaud, Vic 3478 **Region** Pyrenees
T (03) 5496 3294 **F** (03) 5496 3294 **www**.karakarawines.com.au **Open** 7 days 10–6
Winemaker Steven Zsigmond Jr, Steve Zsigmond, Hanging Rock Winery **Est.** 1977
Cases 1200 **Vyds** 8 ha
Hungarian-born Steve Zsigmond comes from a long line of vignerons and sees Kara Kara as the eventual retirement occupation for himself and wife Marlene. He is a graduate of the Adelaide University (Roseworthy) wine marketing course, and worked for Yalumba and Negociants as a sales manager in Adelaide and Perth. He looks after sales and marketing from the Melbourne premises of Kara Kara, and the wine is made at Hanging Rock by Steve Zsigmond Jr, his father in semi-retirement, with consistent results.

ŶŶŶŶ♀ **Limited Release Black Label Pyrenees Shiraz 2005** Excellent hue, still with purple remaining; a luscious and rich wine, the density and depth of the black fruits coupled with licorice; there is a slight suggestion of volatility. Screwcap. 14.9% alc. **Rating** 90 **To** 2020 $33

Karanto Vineyards   ★★★

Box 12, Langhorne Creek, SA 5255 **Region** Langhorne Creek
T (08) 8537 3106 **F** (08) 8537 3106 **www**.karanto.com.au **Open** Not
Winemaker Briony Hoare **Est.** 2002 **Cases** 1500 **Vyds** 43.5 ha
The Karanto property was purchased in 1910 by PR Dodd, who established a mixed horticultural venture. In 1979 it came into the ownership of Dodd's granddaughter Zonda and husband Dennis Elliott, who progressively changed the 44-ha property into a single-purpose viticultural enterprise. Until 2002 all the grapes were sold to major wine companies, but in that year the Elliotts made their first Shiraz; both it and the '03 won significant accolades. The Shiraz continues, and the Elliotts have since established 0.5 ha each of aglianico, greco di tufo, primitivo, fiano and 2.5 ha of pinot grigio, the first vines made over the 2007 to '09 vintages. The wines are made by former Australian Young Winemaker of the Year, Briony Hoare.

ŶŶŶŶ **Langhorne Creek Pinot Grigio 2009** Pale straw; a crisp, clean and clear line of pear, apple and a smidgin of citrus; summer pleasure. Screwcap. 12% alc. **Rating** 89 **To** 2010 $17
Langhorne Creek Shiraz 2006 Strong crimson-purple; a curate's egg: it is not until you reach the back-palate that the dead fruit characters (and concomitant alcohol) become obvious; there is much to enjoy before this point. Diam. 15.5% alc. **Rating** 89 **To** 2015 $25

Karatta Wine Company   ★★★★

Lot 202 Robe-Penola Road, Bray, SA 5276 **Region** Robe
T (08) 8735 7255 **F** (08) 8215 0450 **www**.karattawines.com.au **Open** W'ends &
hols 11–4, or by appt
Winemaker Duane Coates **Est.** 1994 **Cases** NFP **Vyds** 39.6 ha
Owned by David and Peg Woods, Karatta Wine Company is named after Karatta House, one of Robe's well-known heritage-listed icons on the shores of Lake Butler. Built in 1858, Karatta House was occupied by the SA Governor Sir James Fergusson during the summers of 1868 to '71. Vineyards include 12 Mile Vineyard and Tenison Vineyard, both located in Robe.

ŶŶŶŶ♀ **12 Mile Vineyard Robe Shiraz Cabernet Sauvignon 2007** Bright red-
✪ purple; a fragrant, aromatic bouquet of zesty red and black fruits with multiple spices, the palate continuing the theme without a blink of the eye, but adding enough tannins to give texture and structure. Screwcap. 13.8% alc. **Rating** 92 **To** 2022 $22
12 Mile Vineyard Robe Shiraz 2007 Red-magenta hue just starting to fade; an attractive, medium-bodied shiraz with red cherry juicy fruit set within a finely wrought frame of spicy, savoury tannins; has good length and balance. Screwcap. 14.3% alc. **Rating** 90 **To** 2014 $22
12 Mile Vineyard Robe Cabernet Sauvignon 2007 Excellent purple-crimson; a harmonious bouquet, the dark fruits and oak in seamless union; the palate has marked drive and thrust, accenting the savoury olive notes and fine tannins. Screwcap. 13.4% alc. **Rating** 90 **To** 2020 $22

ŶŶŶŶ **Frog Island Selection Robe Rose 2009** Bright, light pink; the palate has more
✪ life than many, the cherry and strawberry fruit pronounced, the touch of sweetness balanced by crisp acidity. Screwcap. 13.6% alc. **Rating** 89 **To** 2010 $16

Karina Vineyard

35 Harrisons Road, Dromana, Vic 3936 **Region** Mornington Peninsula
T (03) 5981 0137 **F** (03) 5981 0137 www.karinavineyard.com.au **Open** W'ends 11–5,
7 days Jan
Winemaker Gerard Terpstra **Est.** 1984 **Cases** 2000 **Vyds** 3.1 ha
A typical family-owned (by Gerard and Joy Terpstra) Mornington Peninsula vineyard, situated
in the Dromana/Red Hill area on rising, north-facing slopes, just 3 km from the shores of Port
Phillip Bay, immaculately tended and with picturesque garden surrounds. Fragrant Riesling
and cashew-accented Chardonnay are usually its best wines from the organically certified
vineyard. Exports to Canada and Japan.

ŶŶŶŶŶ **Mornington Peninsula Pinot Noir 2008** Good depth and hue; an aromatic
bouquet of gently spicy red berry and plum leads into a long and expressive
palate with strong spicy/savoury/oaky overtones. Screwcap. 14% alc. **Rating** 91
To 2014 $25

ŶŶŶŶ **Terroir Mornington Peninsula Cabernet Merlot 2008** Rating 89
To 2018 $22.35
Creme de la Creme Mornington Peninsula Chardonnay 2009 Rating 88
To 2014 $22.35

Karra Yerta Wines ★★★★

Lot 534 Flaxman's Valley Road, Wilton, SA 5353 **Region** Eden Valley
T 0438 870 178 www.karrayertawines.com.au **Open** By appt
Winemaker James Linke, Peter Gajewski **Est.** 2006 **Cases** 350 **Vyds** 1.92 ha
The name Karra Yerta is derived from the local Aboriginal language, 'karra' the name for the
majestic red gum trees, and 'yerta' meaning country or ground. The landscape has changed
little (other than the patches of vineyard) since the ancestors of James and Marie Linke arrived
(separately) in SA in 1847. Both James and Marie were born in Angaston, but moved to the
Flaxmans Valley in 1985, and in '87 purchased one of the old stone cottages in the region.
Much time has been spent in reviving the largely abandoned vineyard, which provides most of
their grapes; plantings now include semillon, riesling, shiraz and frontignac. While most of the
grapes were sold, they indulged in home winemaking for many years, but have now moved
into commercial winemaking on a micro scale.

ŶŶŶŶŶ **Barossa Ranges Shiraz Cabernet 2007** Barossa Ranges is used for this varietal
and regional blend from the Eden and Barossa valleys, even though the word
'Ranges' is superfluous; the wine has an extremely attractive mix of blackberry,
blackcurrant and dark chocolate fruit, with more life and length than many '07s.
Screwcap. 14.5% alc. **Rating** 92 To 2017 $25
Eden Valley Riesling 2009 Pale straw-green; a very crisp, fresh and lively
riesling, with lime, lemon and apple on bouquet and palate alike; good length
sustained by fine acidity; 130 cases made from dry-grown estate vines. Screwcap.
13% alc. **Rating** 91 To 2017 $25
Barossa Ranges Shiraz Cabernet 2006 Like the '07, has very good colour;
this wine is more tangy and lively, but doesn't have the same degree of richness
and depth, a difference of style as much as quality; 170 dozen of each wine
produced. Screwcap. 14.5% alc. **Rating** 91 To 2016 $25

ŶŶŶŶ **Barossa Ranges Sparkling Shiraz NV** Rating 89 To 2015 $35

KarriBindi

RMB 111, Scott Road, Karridale, WA 6288 (postal) **Region** Margaret River
T (08) 9758 5570 **F** (08) 9758 5570 www.karribindi.com.au **Open** Not
Winemaker Naturaliste Vintners (Bruce Dukes) **Est.** 1997 **Cases** 1200 **Vyds** 32.25 ha
KarriBindi has been established by Kevin, Yvonne and Kris Wealand. The name is partly
derived from Karridale and the surrounding Karri forests, and from Bindi, the home town of

one of the members of the Wealand family. In Nyoongar, 'karri' means strong, special, spiritual, tall tree and 'bindi' means butterfly, hence the label's picture of a butterfly soaring through Karri trees. The Wealands have established sauvignon blanc (15 ha), chardonnay (6.25 ha), cabernet sauvignon (4 ha), semillon (3 ha), and shiraz and merlot (2 ha each). The major part of the grape production is sold under contract to Vasse Felix and Leeuwin Estate, with limited amounts released under the KarriBindi label. The core range includes Sauvignon Blanc, Semillon Sauvignon Blanc, Shiraz and Chardonnay Pinot.

ΨΨΨΨΨ **Margaret River Semillon Sauvignon Blanc 2009** A fragrant herbaceous bouquet proclaims the semillon component and leads the palate, joined there by kiwi fruit and a hint of passionfruit. Attractive wine. Screwcap. 12.5% alc. **Rating** 92 **To** 2011 $20

✪ **Margaret River Shiraz 2007** Light but bright colour; a fragrant, spicy bouquet, the fresh light- to medium-bodied palate with lively red fruits and spice. Delicious drink-now style. Screwcap. 13.7% alc. **Rating** 91 **To** 2014 $20

✪ **Margaret River Sauvignon Blanc 2009** A wine that creeps up on you, for it is not until the finish and aftertaste that the intensity of the citrus and grass flavours make their presence felt. Screwcap. 13% alc. **Rating** 90 **To** 2010 $20

ΨΨΨΨ **Margaret River Chardonnay Pinot Noir 2007** **Rating** 88 **To** 2011 $25

Kate Hill Wines   ★★★★★

PO Box 3052, West Hobart, Tas 7005 **Region** Southern Tasmania
T (03) 6223 5641 **F** (03) 9598 2226 **www**.katehillwines.com.au **Open** Not
Winemaker Kate Hill **Est.** 2008 **Cases** 1000
When Kate Hill (and husband Charles) came to Tasmania, Kate had worked as a winemaker in Australia and overseas for 10 years. They arrived in 2006, Kate to grow her winemaking consultancy business and to gradually establish her own label. In 2008 she made Riesling and Pinot Noir; the wines are made from a number of vineyards across southern Tasmania, the aim being to produce approachable, delicate wines. She achieved precisely that with the gold-medal-winning '08 Riesling entered in the Tasmanian Wines Show '09.

ΨΨΨΨΨ **Pinot Noir 2008** Outstanding colour; a full-bodied pinot, full of generous black fruits, reminiscent of some top-end Central Otago wines; will be very long-lived. Two trophies Tas Wine Show '10. Screwcap. 13.5% alc. **Rating** 95 **To** 2020 $32

ΨΨΨΨ **Riesling 2009** **Rating** 88 **To** 2015 $24

Katnook Estate   ★★★★☆

Riddoch Highway, Coonawarra, SA 5263 **Region** Coonawarra
T (08) 8737 0300 **F** (08) 8737 0330 **www**.katnookestate.com.au **Open** Mon–Sat 10–5, Sun 11–4
Winemaker Wayne Stehbens **Est.** 1979 **Cases** 90 000 **Vyds** 198 ha
One of the largest contract grapegrowers and suppliers in Coonawarra, selling more than half its grape production to others. The historic stone wool shed in which the second vintage in Coonawarra (1896) was made, and which has served Katnook since 1980, has been restored. Well over half the total estate plantings are cabernet sauvignon and shiraz, other varieties of importance being chardonnay, merlot, sauvignon blanc and pinot noir. The Odyssey Cabernet Sauvignon and Prodigy Shiraz are the icon duo at the top of a multi-tiered production. Freixenet, the Spanish Cava producer, now owns 100% of the business. Exports to all major markets.

ΨΨΨΨΨ **Coonawarra Shiraz 2007** The impact of 22 months in 20% new French and 80% second-use American oak barrels is immediately obvious, although there is a substantial well of plum and blackberry fruit to provide a balanced counter to that oak; the tannins are fine and ripe, and the wine has a long finish. Screwcap. 13.5% alc. **Rating** 94 **To** 2022 $40

ΨΨΨΨ♀ **Coonawarra Riesling 2009** Light straw-green; not surprisingly, has the floral
○   aromas and flavours that are particular to Coonawarra, a mix of green apple and
        citrus with a boney streak of mineral providing structure, and the certainty of a
        long life ahead. Screwcap. 12% alc. **Rating** 93 **To** 2020 $20
        Coonawarra Cabernet Sauvignon 2006 Rating 93 **To** 2020 $40
        Founder's Block Chardonnay Pinot Noir NV Rating 93 **To** 2012 $23
○   **Founder's Block Coonawarra Shiraz 2007** A much shorter time in oak has
        left this shiraz with a slightly better hue; a much more direct wine, the medium-
        bodied palate with fresh red and black fruit, good tannin structure and subtle oak.
        Screwcap. 13.5% alc. **Rating** 90 **To** 2017 $20
○   **Founder's Block Coonawarra Cabernet Sauvignon 2008** Good colour;
        yet another Coonawarra cabernet to underline the quality of the vintage, the heat
        having passed before the cabernet was ripe; has delicious red and blackcurrant
        fruit, supple tannins and subtle oak. Screwcap. 13.5% alc. **Rating** 90 **To** 2018 $20

ΨΨΨΨ   **Founder's Block Coonawarra Sauvignon Blanc 2009 Rating** 89
        To 2012 $18 BE
        Coonawarra Chardonnay 2006 Rating 89 **To** 2013 $28
        Coonawarra Sauvignon Blanc 2009 Rating 87 **To** 2012 $23

Kay Brothers Amery Vineyards   ★★★★★

Kay Road, McLaren Vale, SA 5171 **Region** McLaren Vale
T (08) 8323 8211 **F** (08) 8323 9199 **www**.kaybrothersamerywines.com
Open Mon–Fri 9–5, w'ends & public hols 12–5
Winemaker Colin Kay, Andy Coppard **Est.** 1890 **Cases** 14 000 **Vyds** 19.6 ha
A traditional winery with a rich history and just under 20 ha of priceless old vines; while
the white wines have been variable, the red wines and fortified wines can be very good. Of
particular interest is Block 6 Shiraz, made from 100-year-old vines; both vines and wines are
going from strength to strength. Exports to the UK, the US, Canada, Switzerland, France,
Hong Kong, Singapore, Japan and NZ.

ΨΨΨΨΨ **Block 6 Shiraz 2007** A particularly expressive bouquet of spiced plum and
        blackberry fruit, then an elegant savoury/spicy palate of considerable length; hand-
        picked, from 115-year-old vines. Screwcap. 13.5% alc. **Rating** 94 **To** 2022 $60
        Rare McLaren Vale Muscat NV Tawny hue, with no red hints remaining; is
        clearly very old, with a viscous texture and an array of Christmas cake, toffee,
        caramelised sugar and spice aromas and flavours; not the least stale, but you wonder
        whether a little more young material might lift it even further. Cork. 19.5% alc.
        Rating 94 **To** 2011 $60

ΨΨΨΨ♀ **Basket Pressed McLaren Vale Cabernet Merlot 2007 Rating** 90
        To 2017 $25

ΨΨΨΨ   **Basket Pressed McLaren Vale Mataro 2008 Rating** 88 **To** 2014 $25

Keith Tulloch Wine   ★★★★★

Hunter Ridge Winery, Hermitage Road, Pokolbin, NSW 2320 **Region** Hunter Valley
T (02) 4998 7500 **F** (02) 4998 7211 **www**.keithtullochwine.com.au
Open Wed–Sun 10–5, or by appt
Winemaker Keith Tulloch **Est.** 1997 **Cases** 13 500 **Vyds** 7.4 ha
Keith Tulloch is, of course, a member of the Tulloch family, which has played such a lead
role in the Hunter Valley for over a century. Formerly a winemaker at Lindemans and then
Rothbury Estate, he has developed his own label since 1997. There is the same almost
obsessive attention to detail, the same almost ascetic intellectual approach, the same refusal to
accept anything but the best as that of Jeffrey Grosset. Exports to the UK, the US, Canada,
Sweden, Hong Kong and Singapore.

ᵀᵀᵀᵀᵀ Field of Mars Hunter Valley Semillon 2009 Only 50 dozen bottles made
from 50-year-old dry-grown estate Field of Mars vineyard; the floral bouquet has
hints of talc and bath powder, the intense and very long palate with great semillon
flavours of citrus and herb; surely there should have been a greater price difference
from the standard wine. Screwcap. 11% alc. **Rating** 95 **To** 2024 $30
Museum Release Hunter Valley Semillon 2004 Brilliant green-straw; a dual
trophy winner at the Hunter Valley Wine Show '04, which amply demonstrates
great young semillon becomes great mature semillon, still vibrantly alive and fresh,
the long palate with perfect balance. Screwcap. 11% alc. **Rating** 95 **To** 2017 $42
Hunter Valley Semillon 2009 Bright, light straw-green; the bouquet is slightly
less floral and more citrussy/grassy than Field of Mars; it has very good focus and
length, with more mouthfeel than most, reflecting its marginally higher alcohol.
Screwcap. 11% alc. **Rating** 94 **To** 2024 $26
Field of Mars Hunter Valley Chardonnay 2009 Light straw-green; has
obvious barrel ferment inputs on the bouquet, possibly because both of the barrels
were new; there is an abundance of ripe fruit to sustain that oak; very good length
and intensity. Screwcap. 14% alc. **Rating** 94 **To** 2015 $40

ᵀᵀᵀᵀᵀ Field of Mars Hunter Valley Shiraz 2006 **Rating** 93 **To** 2021 $70

ᵀᵀᵀᵀ Hunter Valley Chardonnay 2009 **Rating** 89 **To** 2013 $28

Kellybrook ★★★★

Fulford Road, Wonga Park, Vic 3115 **Region** Yarra Valley
T (03) 9722 1304 **F** (03) 9722 2092 **www**.kellybrookwinery.com.au
Open Mon 11–5, Tues–Sat 10–5, Sun 11–5
Winemaker Philip and Darren Kelly **Est.** 1960 **Cases** 2800 **Vyds** 8.5 ha
The vineyard is at Wonga Park, one of the gateways to the Yarra Valley, and has a picnic area
and a full-scale restaurant. A very competent producer of both cider and apple brandy (in
Calvados style) as well as table wine. When it received its winery licence in 1960, it became
the first winery in the Yarra Valley to open its doors in the 20th century, a distinction often
ignored or forgotten (by this author as well as others). Exports to the UK and Denmark.

ᵀᵀᵀᵀᵀ Yarra Valley Sauvignon Blanc 2009 A well-made sauvignon blanc, the
tropical passionfruit lead balanced by grapefruit/citrus notes; the flavours expand
impressively on the finish. Screwcap. 12.5% alc. **Rating** 91 **To** 2010 $22
Yarra Valley Shiraz 2007 Retains good hue; has considerable depth to its spicy
blackberry and plum fruit; smoke taint has affected many '07 Yarra Valley reds, but
it's not evident here. Screwcap. 14.5% alc. **Rating** 90 **To** 2014 $27

ᵀᵀᵀᵀ Yarra Valley Pinot Noir 2007 **Rating** 89 **To** 2012 $27

Kelman Vineyard ★★★☆

2 Oakey Creek Road, Pokolbin, NSW 2320 **Region** Hunter Valley
T (02) 4991 5456 **F** (02) 4991 7555 **www**.kelmanvineyard.com.au **Open** 7 days 9–5
Winemaker Tower Estate **Est.** 1999 **Cases** 2000 **Vyds** 9 ha
Kelman Vineyard is a California-type development on the outskirts of Cessnock. A 40-ha
property has been subdivided into 80 residential development lots, with vines wending
between the lots, which are under common ownership. Part of the chardonnay has already
been grafted across to shiraz before coming into full production, and the vineyard has the
potential to produce 8000 cases of wine per year. In the meantime, each owner receives
12 cases a year.

ᵀᵀᵀᵀᵀ Hunter Valley Semillon 2009 Nice semillon, with some citrus notes
accompanying the herb, grass and mineral background expected of the variety;
plenty yet to come. Screwcap. 11.5% alc. **Rating** 90 **To** 2020 $22

ᵀᵀᵀᵀ Cate 2009 **Rating** 88 **To** 2016 $22

Kelvedon ★★★★☆

PO Box 126, Swansea, Tas 7190 **Region** East Coast Tasmania
T (03) 6257 8283 **F** (03) 6257 8179 **Open** Not
Winemaker Winemaking Tasmania (Julian Alcorso) **Est.** 1998 **Cases** 1200 **Vyds** 9 ha
Jack and Gill Cotton began the development of Kelvedon by planting 1 ha of pinot noir in
1998. The plantings were extended in 2000–01 by an additional 5 ha, half to pinot noir and
half to chardonnay, followed by a further 2 ha of chardonnay in '10. The '01 and '10 plantings
are under contract to CWA. One ha of sauvignon blanc has also been established to provide a
second wine under the Kelvedon label; the Pinot Noir can be of excellent quality.

🍷🍷🍷🍷🍷 **Pinot Noir 2008** Deep colour; a potent, powerful wine following the gold-
medal-winning '07, but with a bigger frame; black cherry and plum fruit is held
within a fine web of tannins, new oak also on display. A vin de garde still crying
out for time. Screwcap. 13.5% alc. **Rating** 94 **To** 2018 $28

🍷🍷🍷🍷 **Sauvignon Blanc 2009 Rating** 87 **To** 2011 $22

Kennedy ★★★☆

Maple Park, 224 Wallenjoe Road, Corop, Vic 3559 (postal) **Region** Heathcote
T (03) 5484 8293 **F** (03) 5484 8148 **www.**kennedyvintners.com.au **Open** Not
Winemaker Sandro Mosele (Contract) **Est.** 2002 **Cases** 1000 **Vyds** 29.2 ha
Having been farmers in the Colbinabbin area of Heathcote for 27 years, John and Patricia
Kennedy were on the spot when a prime piece of red Cambrian soil on the east-facing slope
of Mt Camel Range became available for purchase. They planted 20 ha of shiraz in 2002. As
they gained knowledge of the intricate differences within the site, and worked with contract
winemaker Sandro Mosele, further plantings of shiraz, tempranillo and mourvedre followed in
'07. The Shiraz is made in small open fermenters, using indigenous yeasts and gentle pigeage
before being taken to French oak (20% new) for 12 months' maturation prior to bottling.

🍷🍷🍷🍷 **Heathcote Shiraz 2007** Has some early-picked notes (notwithstanding the
alcohol) reflected in the spicy bouquet and lively, juicy red fruits of the palate.
Diam. 14% alc. **Rating** 89 **To** 2017 $25

Kennedy & Wilson ★★★★☆

15/4 North Gateway, Coldstream, Vic 3770 (postal) **Region** Port Phillip Zone
T (03) 9017 4746 **www.**kennedyandwilson.com.au **Open** Not
Winemaker Peter and James Wilson **Est.** 2005 **Cases** 1000
Kennedy & Wilson is a partnership between brothers James and Peter Wilson, and Juliana
Kennedy. James, previously a chemical engineer, completed his Master of Oenology degree at
Adelaide University in 2006, and is currently completing a PhD. Peter worked under Bailey
Carrodus at Yarra Yering from 1986–96, and established Kennedy & Wilson chocolates in '96
before joining Stuart Wines as chief winemaker in 2003. Juliana, ex-CEO of a smartcard/ sim
card company and the business mind behind the chocolate venture, now describes herself as
'manager of the worldwide Kennedy & Wilson conglomerate'. A sense of humour in this
business is an essential ingredient. The grapes come from the Quarry Ridge Vineyard in
Kilmore at an elevation of 400 m on the southern side of the Great Dividing Range. The
chardonnay and one of the pinot noir blocks are 20 years old; the balance of the vineyard
was planted in 1998. The climate is very cool indeed, the hand-picked fruit ripening between
April and May.

🍷🍷🍷🍷🍷 **Quarry Ridge Vineyard Semillon 2008** Genuinely cool climate semillons are
✪ few and far between, but this shows how rewarding they can be; delicate citrus
flavours are complexed by a hint of tropical fruit; the palate has drive and length.
Screwcap. 11.5% alc. **Rating** 94 **To** 2018 $20

🍷🍷🍷🍷🍷 **Quarry Ridge Vineyard Pinot Noir 2008** Bright, clear red; a fragrant and pure
✪ red fruit bouquet leads into a lively, fresh and supple palate, finishing with tangy
zest. Screwcap. 14% alc. **Rating** 93 **To** 2014 $20

🍷🍷🍷🍷 **Quarry Ridge Vineyard Shiraz 2007 Rating** 88 **To** 2014 $20

Kersbrook Hill ★★★★

Lot 102 Bagshaw Road, Kersbrook, SA 5231 **Region** Adelaide Hills
T 0419 570 005 **www**.kersbrookhill.com.au **Open** Tues–Sun 10–5.30
Winemaker Ben Jeanneret, Harry Dickenson **Est.** 1998 **Cases** 3000 **Vyds** 11 ha
Paul Clark purchased what is now the Kersbrook Hill property, then grazing land, in 1997, planting 0.4 ha of shiraz on a reality-check basis. Encouraged by the results, he increased the plantings to 3 ha of shiraz and 1 ha of riesling two years later. Yet further expansion of the vineyards sees the area under vine increased to 11 ha, cabernet sauvignon (with 6 ha) the somewhat unusual frontrunner. Mark Whisson is consultant viticulturist (Mark has been growing grapes in the Adelaide Hills for 20 years) and Ben Jeanneret was chosen as winemaker because of his experience with riesling. Exports to the US, China and Singapore.

ŸŸŸŸŸ **Adelaide Hills Riesling 2008** Light straw-green; right in the mainstream of modern riesling style, with both texture and structure to the lime, apple and mineral fruit, the finish displaying well-balanced acidity. Screwcap. 12% alc. **Rating** 93 **To** 2018 $29
Adelaide Hills Riesling 2009 Pale, vibrant green hue; ripe lime and a touch of fruit salad tropical notes; minerally palate, with citrus and pine needles lingering on the finish. Screwcap. 12% alc. **Rating** 90 **To** 2016 $25

Kidman Wines ★★★☆

Riddoch Highway, Coonawarra, SA 5263 **Region** Coonawarra
T (08) 8736 5071 **F** (08) 8736 5070 **www**.kidmanwines.com.au **Open** 7 days 10–5
Winemaker Sid Kidman **Est.** 1984 **Cases** 6000 **Vyds** 17 ha
One of the district pioneers, with a fully mature estate vineyard planted to cabernet sauvignon (6 ha), shiraz (5 ha), riesling (4 ha) and sauvignon blanc (2 ha). Limited retail distribution in Melbourne and Adelaide; exports through Australian Prestige Wines.

ŸŸŸŸŸ **The Ridge Coonawarra Shiraz 2008** Good crimson-red; the bouquet has
✿   attractive aromatic blackberry and plum fruit that continues through the lively, quite juicy, medium-bodied palate; tannins fine, oak subtle. Screwcap. 14.5% alc. **Rating** 91 **To** 2016 $23

ŸŸŸŸ **Coonawarra Shiraz 2006 Rating** 89 **To** 2014 $18
Coonawarra Cabernet Sauvignon 2006 Rating 89 **To** 2016 $20

Kies Family Wines ★★★★

Barossa Valley Way, Lyndoch, SA 5381 **Region** Barossa Valley
T (08) 8524 4110 **F** (08) 8524 4544 **www**.kieswines.com.au **Open** 7 days 9.30–4
Winemaker Wine Wise Consultancy **Est.** 1969 **Cases** 4000 **Vyds** 26.3 ha
The Kies family has been resident in the Barossa Valley since 1857; the present generation of winemakers is the fifth, their children the sixth. Until 1969 the family sold almost all their grapes, but in that year they launched their own brand, Karrawirra. The coexistence of Killawarra forced a name change in 1983 to Redgum Vineyard; this business was subsequently sold. Later still, Kies Family Wines opened for business, drawing upon vineyards (up to 100 years old) that had remained in the family throughout the changes, offering a wide range of wines through the 1880 cellar door. Exports to the UK, Singapore, Hong Kong, China and Japan.

ŸŸŸŸŸ **Barossa Valley Bastardo NV** Relatively youthful ruby-style port, full of interest
✿   with its fragrant spicy fruits and very long palate; especially pleasing is its relatively dry finish. A great bargain. Cork. 18.5% alc. **Rating** 93 **To** 2011 $20
Klauber Block Barossa Valley Shiraz 2005 Earth, spice, blackberry, dark chocolate and vanilla all coalesce on the bouquet, tannins joining in on the palate. High-quality cork does not appear to have spent much time in the bottle. 14.5% alc. **Rating** 91 **To** 2015 $25

ᵀᵀᵀᵀ   Monkey Nut Tree Barossa Valley Merlot 2007 Rating 89 To 2015 $25
        Chaff Mill Barossa Valley Cabernet Sauvignon 2007 Rating 89 To 2015 $25

Kilikanoon   ★★★★★

Penna Lane, Penworthan, SA 5453 **Region** Clare Valley
T (08) 8843 4206 **F** (08) 8843 4246 **www**.kilikanoon.com.au **Open** Thurs–Mon 11–5
Winemaker Kevin Mitchell **Est.** 1997 **Cases** 40 000 **Vyds** 330 ha
Kilikanoon has over 300 ha of vineyards, predominantly in the Clare Valley but spreading to
all regions around Adelaide and the Barossa Valley. It had the once-in-a-lifetime experience of
winning five of the six trophies awarded at the Clare Valley Wine Show '02, spanning Riesling,
Shiraz and Cabernet, and including Best Wine of Show. In August 2007 it purchased the
iconic Seppeltsfield in the Barossa Valley (see separate entry). It also has wines from the Loire
and Rhône Valleys specifically made for it, the labels reflecting its ownership of the wines.
Exports to all major markets.

ᵀᵀᵀᵀᵀ   Alliance Hermitage 2007 A touch of purple is added to the crimson; from
        the 'Grand Cru' (if there were one in the Rhône Valley) of Hermitage; the shiraz
        flavours are a little brighter, the palate a little longer and finer than the Crozes
        Hermitage. It's a better wine, but 300%? Cork. 13.5% alc. Rating 96 To 2022 $120
        Alliance Crozes-Hermitage 2007 Bright crimson; very interesting wine; the
        red cherry and plum fruit flavours are fresh and very expressive, superfine tannins
        extending the length of the medium-bodied, well balanced and constructed palate.
        Cork. 13.5% alc. Rating 95 To 2020 $44
        M McLaren Vale Shiraz 2006 Deep colour; a wine that mixes power with
        finesse on the bouquet and palate alike; regional bitter chocolate is present, but
        it is the blackberry and licorice fruit that lies at the heart of this full-bodied
        wine. Pity about the cork for such a potentially long life. 15% alc. Rating 95
        To 2023 $80
✪   Mort's Block Watervale Riesling 2009 A flowery bouquet leads into an
        elegant and fine palate, with flavours of lime, lemon and green apple neatly tied
        together with crisp acidity. Screwcap. 12.5% alc. Rating 94 To 2019 $22
        Mort's Reserve Watervale Riesling 2009 Follows the path of Mort's Block,
        simply adding extra depth and power; at the moment, less lively and expressive,
        although will flourish with time. Screwcap. 12.5% alc. Rating 94 To 2020 $35

ᵀᵀᵀᵀᵀ   Mort's Cut Watervale Riesling 2009 Rating 93 To 2014 $30
✪   Barrel Fermented Clare Valley Semillon 2009 Straw, pea pod and a hint
        of tropical fruit all work seamlessly with the oak element of the wine; the palate
        is lively and fine, with a slight charry edge to the finish. Screwcap. 12.5% alc.
        Rating 91 To 2015 $20 BE
        Alliance Hermitage Blanc 2007 Rating 90 To 2012 $80
        Covenant Clare Valley Shiraz 2007 Rating 90 To 2016 $44 BE
        Testament Barossa Valley Shiraz 2007 Rating 90 To 2016 $44 BE
        Prodigal Clare Valley Grenache 2007 Rating 90 To 2015 $30 BE

Killara Estate   ★★★★

773 Warburton Highway, Seville East, Vic 3139 **Region** Yarra Valley
T (03) 5961 5877 **F** (03) 5961 5629 **www**.killaraestate.com.au **Open** Tues–Sun 11–5
Winemaker David Bicknell **Est.** 1997 **Cases** 7000 **Vyds** 91.13 ha
The Palazzo family, one of the largest vineyard holders in the Yarra Valley, have two
distinct vineyards at different locations: Killara and Sunnyside. The varieties overlap with
two exceptions: 1.19 ha sangiovese on Sunnyside, and 1.11 ha viognier on Killara. The
shared varieties are cabernet sauvignon, chardonnay, merlot, pinot gris, shiraz, pinot noir
and sauvignon blanc; pinot noir (almost 33 ha) and chardonnay (over 19 ha) are the most
substantial. The largest part of production is sold to producers both within and without the
Yarra Valley, but Killara Estate retains sufficient to produce the Killara Estate and Racers &
Rascals ranges. Exports to the UK.

ΨΨΨΨ **Yarra Valley Pinot Noir 2008** Clear purple-crimson; an expressive bouquet of black cherry, plum and a hint of spice leads into a powerful palate with a strong foresty overlay to the fruit; a little disjointed, and needing a year or two. Screwcap. 13.5% alc. **Rating** 91 **To** 2015 $25
Yarra Valley Cabernet Merlot 2008 Crimson-purple; the bouquet is fragrant, with spicy elements to the blackcurrant and plum aromas; the medium-bodied palate has firm mouthfeel, the effect enhanced by roasted pepper on both bouquet and palate, in turn offset by red fruit flavours. Screwcap. 13.5% alc. **Rating** 91 **To** 2020 $25

ΨΨΨΨ **Yarra Valley Chardonnay 2008 Rating** 89 **To** 2014 $25
Yarra Valley Shiraz 2008 Rating 89 **To** 2014 $25
Yarra Valley Sparkling Shiraz 2007 Rating 89 **To** 2017 $30

Killerby   ★★★★

Caves Road, Wilyabrup, WA 6280 **Region** Margaret River
T 1800 655 722 **F** 1800 679 578 **www**.killerby.com.au **Open** Not
Winemaker Kim Horton **Est.** 1973 **Cases** 10 000 **Vyds** 13 ha
In June 2008, the winery established by the late Dr Barry Killerby 35 years ago was purchased by the Ferngrove wine group. Wines made from the estate plantings (shiraz, chardonnay, sauvignon blanc, semillon and cabernet sauvignon) will be made at Ferngrove, but sold through a new cellar door expected to be completed in 2010.

ΨΨΨΨ **Semillon 2009** Vibrant and fresh citrus and straw bouquet; the palate shows a touch of nettle adding complexity, and the texture is generous while remaining light and fresh. Screwcap. 13% alc. **Rating** 93 $20 BE
Margaret River Cabernet Sauvignon 2008 Deep colour; prominent dusty tones on the bouquet with almost essency cassis beneath; the palate is loaded with sweet fruit, and the tannins are assertive and acidity fresh; dark on the finish, with a black olive presence. Screwcap. 14% alc. **Rating** 90 $25 BE

ΨΨΨΨ **Chardonnay 2007 Rating** 89 $30 BE
Shiraz 2007 Rating 89 $25 BE

Killiecrankie Wines   ★★★★★

PO Box 6125, Lansell Plaza, Vic 3555 **Region** Bendigo
T (03) 5435 3155 **Open** Not
Winemaker Tony Winspear, John Monteath **Est.** 2000 **Cases** 100 **Vyds** 1 ha
This is the venture of John and Claire Monteath; John moved to the Bendigo region in 1999 to pursue his interest in viticulture and winemaking, and while helping to establish the vineyard from which the grapes are sourced, gained experience at Water Wheel, Heathcote Estate and Balgownie Estate wineries. The non-irrigated vineyard was planted in 2000 to four shiraz clones. The tiny crop is hand-picked, and the wine is made in true garagiste style by local winemaker Tony Winspear, with John his assistant. Further plantings within the Bendigo region, and parcels of premium fruit sourced from other meticulously tended vineyards, will be added to create a range of individual vineyard wines.

ΨΨΨΨ **Shiraz 2008** Deep purple-crimson; rich black fruits, licorice and spice fill the bouquet; the medium- to full-bodied palate displays similar flavours, the texture and structure wholly admirable. Diam. 14.5% alc. **Rating** 94 **To** 2023 $39

Kimbarra Wines   ★★★★★

422 Barkly Street, Ararat, Vic 3377 **Region** Grampians
T (03) 5352 2238 **F** (03) 5342 1950 **www**.kimbarrawines.com.au
Open Mon–Fri 9–4.30, or by appt
Winemaker Peter Leeke, Ian MacKenzie **Est.** 1990 **Cases** 900 **Vyds** 12 ha

Jim, Peter and David Leeke have established riesling, shiraz and cabernet sauvignon, varieties that have proved best suited to the Grampians region. The particularly well-made, estate-grown wines deserve a wider audience.

ŸŸŸŸŸ **Great Western Riesling 2009** An intriguing bouquet, with pine needle and wild herb nuances that disappear on the delicious lime juice palate with a lingering, pure finish. Screwcap. 12% alc. **Rating** 94 **To** 2019 $27
Great Western Shiraz 2008 Strong crimson-red; has an abundance of lively black and red berry fruit on the bouquet and palate; the finish is full of energy and drive, the tannins silky but active. Screwcap. 13.5% alc. **Rating** 94 **To** 2020 $33

ŸŸŸŸ **Great Western Riesling 2004 Rating** 89 **To** 2012 $25
Great Western Cabernet Sauvignon 2008 Rating 89 **To** 2017 $29

🍇 Kimbolton Wines ★★★★

The Winehouse Cellar Door, Lot 93 Wellington Road, Langhorne Creek, SA 5255
Region Langhorne Creek
T (08) 8537 3359 **F** (08) 8537 3349 **Open** 7 days 10–5
Winemaker Greg Follett, Simon Greenleaf (Contract) **Est.** 1998 **Cases** 500 **Vyds** 49.3 ha
The Kimbolton property originally formed part of the Potts Bleasdale estate; in 1946 it was acquired by Henry and Thelma Case (parents of the current owners, Len and wife Judy Case). Since that time the grapes from vineyard plantings of cabernet sauvignon, shiraz, chardonnay and sauvignon blanc have been sold to leading wineries. However, in '98 the decision was taken to retain a small amount of cabernet sauvignon and shiraz to supply the Kimbolton Wines label established in that year (the name comes from a medieval town in Bedfordshire, UK, from which some of Judy's ancestors emigrated). No more than 500 cases are contract-made, with input from Bradley Case; in '06 the total was 334 cases.

ŸŸŸŸŸ **The Rifleman Langhorne Creek Shiraz 2007** Good hue for age; a substantial wine with one foot in Langhorne Creek, the other in McLaren Vale (the dark chocolate component, together with the soft and generous fruit); good tannins for the long haul. Screwcap. 14.3% alc. **Rating** 92 **To** 2027 $42

✪ **Block 18 Langhorne Creek Sauvignon Blanc 2009** Pale straw-green; an impressively intense sauvignon blanc with vineyard and winery inputs of equal merit; gooseberry, snow pea and fresh tropical notes are all part of a persuasive wine with very good length. Screwcap. 12.5% alc. **Rating** 91 **To** 2012 $16

ŸŸŸŸ **Langhorne Creek Cabernet Sauvignon 2006 Rating** 89 **To** 2016 $20

King River Estate ★★★★

3556 Wangaratta-Whitfield Road, Wangaratta, Vic 3678 **Region** King Valley
T (03) 5729 3689 **F** (03) 5729 3688 **www.**kingriverestate.com.au **Open** 7 days 11–5
Winemaker Trevor Knaggs **Est.** 1996 **Cases** 3000 **Vyds** 16 ha
Trevor Knaggs, with the assistance of his father Collin, began the establishment of King River Estate in 1990, making the first wines in '96. The initial plantings were 3.3 ha each of chardonnay and cabernet sauvignon, followed by 8 ha of merlot and 3 ha of shiraz. More recent plantings have extended the varietal range to include verdelho, viognier, barbera and sangiovese. Biodynamic practices have been used in the vineyard since 2008. Exports to China and Singapore.

ŸŸŸŸŸ **Cuvee Sauvage King Valley Chardonnay 2009** No, this is not a sparkling wine, but one made using wild yeast and minimal winemaker intervention, other than barrel fermentation in French oak; a generously endowed chardonnay with ripe stone fruit and melon aromas and flavours caressed by oak. Screwcap. 14.2% alc. **Rating** 90 **To** 2013 $35
King Valley Shiraz 2008 Some colour development, partly high pH-driven; an opulent wine with vanilla, dark chocolate and black fruits coalescing; the alcohol doesn't heat the palate, but does sweeten the flavours, offset by fine tannins. Screwcap. 15.8% alc. **Rating** 90 **To** 2016 $28

✪   King Valley Merlot 2008 Strong colour; a generous medium-bodied wine, flush
with plum and blackcurrant fruit and good structure; should be longer lived than
the '05. Screwcap. 14.3% alc. Rating 90 To 2014 $20

♀♀♀♀   King Valley Vermentino 2009 Rating 88 To 2012 $25
King Valley Sangiovese 2008 Rating 88 To 2013 $30
King Valley Sauvignon Blanc 2009 Rating 87 To 2010 $20
King Valley Merlot 2005 Rating 87 To 2012 $20
King Valley Lagrein 2008 Rating 87 To 2013 $60

Kingsdale Wines   ★★★☆

745 Crookwell Road, Goulburn, NSW 2580 Region Southern New South Wales Zone
T (02) 4822 4880 F (02) 4822 4881 www.kingsdale.com.au Open W'ends &
public hols 10–5
Winemaker Howard Spark Est. 2001 Cases 1000 Vyds 2.5 ha
Howard and Elly Spark established their vineyard (shiraz, sauvignon blanc, chardonnay, merlot
and semillon) south of the burgeoning Southern Highlands region, falling in the Southern
NSW Zone. It sits 700 m above sea level on deep red soils with iron-rich sediments (doubtless
causing the colour) and limestone. The limestone-clad cellar door overlooks Lake Sooley,
7 mins drive from Goulburn.

♀♀♀♀♀   Goulburn Semillon Sauvignon Blanc 2009 Full, bright straw-green; a wine
✪   of considerable presence, offering a mix of tropical fruits supported by lively
lime/citrus on both bouquet and palate alike. Ready now. Screwcap. 12.5% alc.
Rating 90 To 2010 $20

♀♀♀♀   Goulburn Merlot Malbec 2006 Rating 88 To 2014 $20

Kingston Estate Wines   ★★★☆

Sturt Highway, Kingston-on-Murray, SA 5331 Region South Australia
T (08) 8243 3700 F (08) 8243 3777 www.kingstonestatewines.com Open By appt
Winemaker Bill Moularadellis, Brett Duffin, Helen Foggo, Donna Hartwig Est. 1979
Cases 300 000 Vyds 200 ha
Kingston Estate, under the direction of Bill Moularadellis, has its production roots in the
Riverland region, but has long-term purchase contracts with growers in the Clare Valley,
Adelaide Hills, Coonawarra, Langhorne Creek and Mount Benson. It has also spread its net
to take in a wide range of varietals, mainstream and exotic, under a number of different brands
at various price points. Exports the UK, the US and other major markets.

♀♀♀♀♀   Sarantos Soft Press Pinot Gris 2009 Pale pink; has a very good aromatic
✪   bouquet, with spice, pear and blossom to the fore; the palate is crisp, quite long,
and pleasingly dry. Well above average. Screwcap. 13% alc. Rating 90 To 2011 $15

♀♀♀♀   Adelaide Hills Mt Benson Sauvignon Blanc 2009 A remarkable price
✪   given its birth places; clean, well made, with a subliminal touch of residual sugar
to underpin the gentle tropical fruit flavours, and a twist of lemon. Screwcap.
13.5% alc. Rating 89 To 2010 $13
✪   Shiraz 2008 Dense crimson-purple; a full-flavoured shiraz from the Mount Lofty
Ranges/Limestone Coast; medium- to full-bodied with blackberry and licorice
the flavour drivers; does fall away a touch on the finish, but very good value.
Screwcap. 14.5% alc. Rating 89 To 2012 $13

Kinloch Wines   ★★★★

'Kainui', 221 Wairere Road, Booroolite, Vic 3723 Region Upper Goulburn
T (03) 5777 3447 F (03) 5777 3449 www.kinlochwines.com.au Open 7 days 10–4
Winemaker Al Fencaros (Contract) Est. 1996 Cases 2000 Vyds 4.42 ha
In 1996 Susan and Malcolm Kinloch began the development of their vineyard, at an altitude
of 400 m on the northern slopes of the Great Dividing Range, 15 mins from Mansfield. The

vineyard is planted to chardonnay, pinot noir, pinot meunier (primarily used for sparkling wines), sauvignon blanc, riesling and tempranillo, supplemented by purchases of other varieties from local growers. The grapes are hand-picked and contract-made in the Yarra Valley.

🍷🍷🍷🍷⚲ **Mansfield Chardonnay 2008** A well-made chardonnay, with white peach,
✪   nectarine and melon fruit enhanced by gentle oak nuances; good overall balance
     and length. Screwcap. 13.5% alc. **Rating** 91 **To** 2015 $22
     Mary Friend 2006 A distinctly savoury complexity runs through the wine,
     impacting on the array of red and black berry fruits of both bouquet and palate,
     the latter supported by fine tannins. Cabernet Sauvignon/Merlot/Cabernet Franc.
     Diam. 13.5% alc. **Rating** 91 **To** 2018 $50

🍷🍷🍷🍷 **Mansfield Merlot 2008 Rating** 89 **To** 2016 $26
     Don Kinloch Chardonnay Pinot Noir Pinot Meunier 2008 Rating 89
     To 2013 $32
     Mansfield Pinot Meunier 2008 Rating 88 **To** 2013 $23

Kirrihill Wines   ★★★★★
Wendouree Road, Clare, SA 5453 **Region** Clare Valley
T (08) 8842 4087 **F** (08) 8842 4089 **www.**kirrihillwines.com.au **Open** 7 days 10–4
Winemaker Donna Stephens, Marnie Roberts **Est.** 1998 **Cases** 30 000
A large development, with an 8000-tonne, $12 million winery making and marketing its own range of wines, also acting as a contract maker for several producers. Focused on the Clare Valley and Adelaide Hills, grapes are sourced from specially selected parcels of Kirribilly's 1300 ha of managed vineyards, as well as the Edwards and Stanway families' properties in these regions. The quality of the wines is thus no surprise. The Companions range comprises blends of both regions, while the Single Vineyard Series aims to elicit a sense of place from the chosen vineyards. Exports to all major markets.

🍷🍷🍷🍷🍷 **Clare Valley Shiraz 2008** Very good colour; opens with rich dark fruit aromas,
✪   then abundant plum and blackberry fruit on the medium- to full-bodied palate
     supported by ripe tannins and a modicum of French oak. Screwcap. 15% alc.
     Rating 94 **To** 2023 $15
✪   **Single Vineyard Tullymore Vineyard Clare Valley Shiraz 2008** Outstanding
     deep purple-crimson; the rich and complex dark berry fruits of the bouquet holds
     out the promise of a quality palate and the wine does not disappoint; layers of
     flavour in a spicy black berry fruit range, good tannins and oak completing the
     picture. Screwcap. 14.5% alc. **Rating** 94 **To** 2028 $19.95

🍷🍷🍷🍷⚲ **Clare Valley Cabernet Sauvignon 2008** Strong colour; a medium- to full-
✪   bodied cabernet, with layers of blackcurrant fruit interwoven with firm, ripe
     tannins and subtle oak; good balance and length. Screwcap. 14.5% alc. **Rating** 91
     To 2016 $15
     Single Vineyard Slate Creek Vineyard Clare Valley Riesling 2009
     Rating 90 **To** 2016 $19

🍷🍷🍷🍷 **Single Vineyard Tullymore Vineyard Clare Valley Cabernet Sauvignon**
     2008 Rating 88 **To** 2023 $19.95
     Celestial Clare Valley Riesling 2009 Rating 88 **To** 2014 $18

Knappstein   ★★★★★
2 Pioneer Avenue, Clare, SA 5453 **Region** Clare Valley
T (08) 8841 2100 **F** (08) 8841 2101 **www.**knappstein.com.au **Open** Mon–Fri 9–5,
Sat 11–5, Sun & public hols 11–4
Winemaker Julian Langworthy **Est.** 1969 **Cases** 35 000 **Vyds** 114 ha
Knappstein's full name is Knappstein Enterprise Winery & Brewery, reflecting its history before being acquired by Petaluma, and since then part of Lion Nathan's stable. The substantial mature estate vineyards in prime locations supply grapes both for the Knappstein brand and

for wider Petaluma use. Despite making seriously good wines, Knappstein can't seem to regularly get across the line to greatness. Exports to all major markets.

ŶŶŶŶŶ 8:8:18 Clare Valley Riesling 2009 Early picking has presented a wine with
✪   8% alcohol, 8 grammes per litre of acidity and 18 grammes per litre of residual
           sugar, which works very well indeed, the secret lying as much with the acidity as
           anything else. It is brilliantly pure and fine, with expressive lime juice and mineral
           flavours. Screwcap. **Rating** 96 **To** 2017 $22.95
           Ackland Vineyard Watervale Riesling 2009 Distinct flowery citrus blossom
           aromas; the palate has great thrust and urgency, lime and lemon intertwined with
           minerally acidity; retains finesse and delicacy in the midst of this power. Screwcap.
           12% alc. **Rating** 96 **To** 2029 $33

ŶŶŶŶŶ **Hand Picked Clare Valley Riesling 2009** The bouquet is as yet restrained,
✪   but the very lively, juicy, lime-accented palate promises much for the future; great
           finish and aftertaste. Screwcap. 12% alc. **Rating** 93 **To** 2020 $19.95
           Three Clare Valley Gewurztraminer Riesling Pinot Gris 2009 Rating 92
           To 2011 $22.95
           Clare Valley Cabernet Merlot 2007 Rating 92 **To** 2020 $22.95
           Clare Valley Shiraz 2007 Rating 90 **To** 2015 $22.95

ŶŶŶŶ   **Clare Valley Sauvignon Blanc Semillon 2009** Rating 88 **To** 2011 $19.95

Knee Deep Wines   ★★★★☆

Lot 61 Johnson Road, Wilyabrup, WA 6280 **Region** Margaret River
T (08) 9755 6776 **F** (08) 9755 6779 **www.**kneedeepwines.com.au **Open** 7 days 10–5
Winemaker Bruce Dukes, Bob Cartwright (Consultant) **Est.** 2000 **Cases** 8800
Perth surgeon and veteran yachtsman Phil Childs has found time to acquire a 34-ha farming property in Wilyabrup, and plant a little over 20 ha of chardonnay (3.16 ha), sauvignon blanc (4.1 ha), semillon (1.48 ha), chenin blanc (4.15 ha), cabernet sauvignon (6.34 ha) and shiraz (1.23 ha). The name, Knee Deep Wines, was inspired by absolute commitment to making premium wine (and its concomitant cost) and by a tongue-in-cheek acknowledgement of the grape glut building more or less in tune with the venture. It is as well that Childs has consultant winemaker Bob Cartwright (28 vintages as winemaker at Leeuwin Estate) and consultant viticulturist Greg Nikulinsky (seven years at Ferngrove) to oversee the vineyard management.

ŶŶŶŶŶ **Margaret River Shiraz 2008** Strong purple-crimson; black cherry, polished
✪   leather, spice and licorice all leap from the glass on the bouquet, and the palate
           delivers precisely what the bouquet suggests, plus fine but firm tannins. Screwcap.
           14.1% alc. **Rating** 94 **To** 2023 $26

ŶŶŶŶ⚲ **Margaret River Sauvignon Blanc 2009** Deliciously fresh and vibrant
✪   passionfruit and lychee aromas and flavours; is delicate, the type of wine that
           encourages you to drink, rather than sip. Screwcap. 12.8% alc. **Rating** 91
           To 2010 $22
           Margaret River Sauvignon Blanc Semillon 2009 Rating 90 **To** 2012 $22

Knots Wines   ★★★★

A8 Shurans Lane, Heathcote, Vic 3552 **Region** Heathcote
T (03) 5441 5429 **F** (03) 5441 5429 **www.**thebridgevineyard.com.au
Open Select w'ends, or by appt
Winemaker Lindsay Ross **Est.** 1997 **Cases** 1000 **Vyds** 4.75 ha
This venture of former Balgownie winemaker Lindsay Ross and wife Noeline is part of a broader business known as Winedrops, which acts as a wine production and distribution network for the Bendigo wine industry. The Knots wines are sourced from long-established vineyards, providing shiraz (4 ha), malbec (0.5 ha) and viognier (0.25 ha). The viticultural accent is on low-cropping, with concentrated flavours, the winemaking emphasis on flavour, finesse and varietal expression.

ŸŸŸŸŸ   **Starboard Liqueur Shiraz 2008** Deep, dark crimson-purple; a very intense savoury spicy wine, made in a refreshingly dry style, the sweetness only just apparent. Could age very well indeed. Diam. 18.5% alc. **Rating** 92 **To** 2023 $40
Sheepshank Bendigo Shiraz 2006 Good colour; the alcohol contributes to the sweetness of the black fruits on the palate, but doesn't heat the finish; soft tannins and controlled oak are also in balance. Diam. 15% alc. **Rating** 90 **To** 2020 $29
The Bridge Heathcote Shiraz 2006 Strong, clear crimson hue; a no-holds-barred full-bodied style; despite the intensity of the fruit and the presence of substantial tannins, alcohol does strike a light on the finish. Will greatly appeal to those who like heroic wines. Diam. 16% alc. **Rating** 90 **To** 2026 $50

ŸŸŸŸ   **The Bridge Heathcote Shiraz Malbec 2006** **Rating** 89 **To** 2021 $50
Rose Lashing Rose 2009 **Rating** 88 **To** 2011 $20

Kominos Wines   ★★★★
27145 New England Highway, Severnlea, Qld 4352 **Region** Granite Belt
T (07) 4683 4311 **F** (07) 4683 4291 **www.**kominoswines.com **Open** 7 days 9–5
Winemaker Tony Comino **Est.** 1976 **Cases** NFP **Vyds** 12 ha
Tony Comino, a dedicated viticulturist and winemaker, and wife Mary, took over ownership of the winery from his parents on its 21st vintage. Tony is proud of the estate-grown, -made and -bottled heritage of the winery and content to keep a relatively low profile, although the proud show record of the wines might suggest otherwise. In addition to the estate plantings, he manages an additional 7 ha. The varieties planted are sauvignon blanc, chenin blanc, semillon, chardonnay, shiraz, merlot, cabernet franc and cabernet sauvignon. Another Qld producer to make good wines, capable of holding their own against all-comers from the south (as Queenslanders refer to anyone not born in the state). Fifty per cent of production is exported to the US, Taiwan, Korea, China and Singapore.

ŸŸŸŸŸ   **Reserve Merlot 2008** While still full-bodied, this wine has better varietal expression, balance and mouthfeel to its mix of plum, blackcurrant and olive fruit than the Estate; silver medal NZ International Wine Show '09. Diam. 15% alc. **Rating** 91 **To** 2018 $24

ŸŸŸŸ   **Estate Merlot 2008** **Rating** 88 **To** 2017 $19

K1 by Geoff Hardy   ★★★★★
Tynan Road, Kuitpo, SA 5172 **Region** Adelaide Hills
T (08) 8388 3700 **F** (08) 8388 3564 **www.**k1.com.au **Open** W'ends & public hols 11–5
Winemaker Geoff Hardy, Shane Harris **Est.** 1980 **Cases** 8000 **Vyds** 36.5 ha
The ultra-cool Kuitpo vineyard in the Adelaide Hills was planted by Geoff Hardy in 1987 after searching the hills for an ideal location for premium wine production. As this was the first significant vineyard planted in the region it became known as the K1 vineyard. All fruit for Geoff Hardy's K1 brand is sourced from this vineyard, perched on the south-western ridge of the Adelaide Hills above McLaren Vale. Exports to the US, Canada, The Netherlands, Switzerland, Malaysia, Hong Kong and Singapore.

ŸŸŸŸŸ   **Gold Label Adelaide Hills Chardonnay 2008** Bright youthful colour; an impressive chardonnay that seamlessly brings together nectarine, white peach fruit and barrel ferment oak inputs, the mouthfeel supple and giving. Screwcap. 13.5% alc. **Rating** 94 **To** 2015 $35
Gold Label Adelaide Hills Shiraz 2008 Crimson-red; yet further evidence of the Adelaide Hills' ability to withstand hot vintages; here red and black cherry accompany plum on the medium-bodied palate, with just a tweak of spicy savoury notes on the finish. Screwcap. 14.5% alc. **Rating** 94 **To** 2020 $35

ŸŸŸŸ   **Adelaide Hills Merlot 2007** **Rating** 91 **To** 2017 $35
✪   **Silver Label Shiraz 2007** Good hue; a powerful, medium- to full-bodied shiraz with a fragrant bouquet lifted by a touch of viognier, the sturdy palate moving away on a path of its own, disavowing the viognier. Screwcap. 14.5% alc. **Rating** 90 **To** 2020 $18

ΥΥΥΥ   **Adelaide Hills Sauvignon Blanc 2009** Rating 89 To 2010 $20
✪   **Gold Label Adelaide Hills Arneis 2009** Has some herb and wild flower
aromas, then a positive herb and citrus palate, with good drive and length. Worth a
second (or third) look. Screwcap. 12.5% alc. Rating 89 To 2012 $20
✪   **Silver Label Cabernet Tempranillo 2007** Has retained very good purple
colour; the bouquet is attractive, with black fruits doing the talking, but not
preparing you for the Italianate tannins on the back-palate; can only be appreciated
with red meat dishes. Screwcap. 14.5% alc. Rating 89 To 2017 $18

Koonaburra Vineyard   ★★★

44 Summerhill Road, Bywong, NSW 2621 **Region** Canberra District
T (02) 6236 9019 **F** (02) 6236 9029 **www**.koonaburra.com.au **Open** Thurs–Mon 10–5
Winemaker Canberra Winemakers **Est.** 1998 **Cases** 230 **Vyds** 3.2 ha
Nicolaas (Nico) and wife Shawn Duynhoven left Sydney and purchased their block of land
'because we wanted to grow something'. Nico built the house and cellar door/café, and they
initially planted 280 hazelnut trees, followed by a little merlot and (progressively) 1 ha each
of riesling, sauvignon blanc and pinot noir. They achieved all this while holding down full-
time jobs, Nico in home building and Shawn in nursing. By producing a Sauvignon Blanc, a
Wooded Sauvignon Blanc, Riesling, Pinot Noir, Merlot, Sparkling Merlot and Riesling Ice
Wine, they have managed to expand the range of their wine portfolio notwithstanding its
small estate-grown basis.

ΥΥΥΥ   **Lightly Wooded Sauvignon Blanc 2009** A full-flavoured, full-bodied
sauvignon blanc with tropical fruits and nutty oak competing for attention; is there
a hint of residual sugar? Screwcap. 12.9% alc. Rating 89 To 2011 $28
Merlot 2005 Now largely developed, but has moved through to this point
without any problems; the hue is still good, and the savoury/olive notes
contrasting with the red and plum fruit are in balance. Screwcap. 14.2% alc.
Rating 88 To 2012 $20
Riesling Ice Wine 2006 Developed gold; has the same off-dry flavours as the
'09, here complexed into more nutty characters by bottle age. Screwcap. 11.9% alc.
Rating 88 To 2010 $22
Pinot Noir 2007 Light colour with some development; spicy foresty characters
are woven through the red berry fruits from start to finish; definitely drink soon
before the forest engulfs the fruit. Screwcap. 13.2% alc. Rating 87 To 2011 $20
Riesling Ice Wine 2009 It is obvious the temperature of the juice was not
far below zero, or the process was cut short, for this is only marginally off-dry.
Screwcap. 12.1% alc. Rating 87 To 2013 $22

Koonara   ★★★★

44 Main Street, Penola, SA 5277 **Region** Coonawarra
T (08) 8737 3222 **F** (08) 8737 3220 **www**.koonara.com **Open** 7 days 10–6
Winemaker Peter Douglas, Dru Reschke **Est.** 1988 **Cases** 5000 **Vyds** 8 ha
Koonara is a sister, or, more appropriately, a brother company to Reschke Wines. The latter is
run by Burke Reschke, Koonara by his brother Dru. Both are sons of Trevor Reschke, who
planted the first vines on the Koonara property in 1988. The initial planting was of cabernet
sauvignon, followed by shiraz in 1993 and additional cabernet sauvignon in '98. Peter Douglas,
formerly Wynns' chief winemaker before moving overseas for some years, has returned to the
district and is consultant winemaker. The Bay of Apostles range was released in 2008, with
four of the five wines under the label sourced from Vic. A Bay of Apostles cellar door has
been opened in the main street of Apollo Bay on the Great Ocean Road. Exports to Malaysia,
Singapore and China.

ΥΥΥΥΥ   **Bay of Apostles Coonawarra Cabernet Sauvignon 2006** Very good purple-
✪   crimson; has another dimension of fruit flavour, with abundant blackcurrant fruit
and purposeful tannins in support. Screwcap. 13.5% alc. Rating 92 To 2021 $20

✪ **The Seductress Coonawarra Shiraz 2006** There is nothing remarkable about the colour or bouquet, but there is decided interest to the palate, which is finely structured and tempered, the interplay between 80% new oak and 20% American a backdrop to the bright fruit flavours and long finish. Screwcap. 13.9% alc. **Rating** 90 **To** 2016 $19.95

🍷🍷🍷🍷 **Angel's Peak Coonawarra Cabernet Sauvignon 2006** **Rating** 89 **To** 2014 $15.95

Koonowla Wines ★★★★

PO Box 45, Auburn, SA 5451 **Region** Clare Valley
T (08) 8849 2080 **F** (08) 8849 2293 **www**.koonowla.com **Open** Not
Winemaker O'Leary Walker Wines **Est.** 1997 **Cases** 50000 **Vyds** 100 ha

It's not often that a light as large as this can be hidden under a bushel. Koonowla is a historic Clare Valley property; situated just east of Auburn, it was first planted with vines in the 1890s, and by the early 1900s was producing 60 000 litres of wine annually. A disastrous fire in 1926 destroyed the winery and wine stocks, and the property was converted to grain and wool production. Replanting of vines began in 1985, and accelerated after Andrew and Booie Michael purchased the property in '91; there are now 40 ha of cabernet sauvignon, 36 ha riesling, 20 ha of shiraz, and 2 ha each of merlot and semillon. In an all too familiar story, the grapes were sold until falling prices forced a change in strategy; now a major part of the grapes are vinified by the infinitely experienced David O'Leary and Nick Walker, with the remainder sold. Most of the wines are exported to the UK, the US, Scandinavia, Malaysia and NZ.

🍷🍷🍷🍷½ **Clare Valley Riesling 2009** Light, bright straw-green; lime, spice and sundry citrus notes drive both bouquet and palate; plenty on offer now, but will benefit from further time in bottle. Screwcap. 12% alc. **Rating** 92 **To** 2019 $19

✪ **The Ringmaster Clare Valley Shiraz 2007** Strong purple-crimson; an attractive bouquet of plum, spice, blackberry and balanced oak, then a medium- to full-bodied palate full of dark berry fruit, finishing with fine tannins. Screwcap. 14.5% alc. **Rating** 91 **To** 2020 $15

🍷🍷🍷🍷 ✪ **The Ringmaster Clare Valley Cabernet Sauvignon 2007** Is developing nicely, with spicy French oak (despite none new, just two- and three-year-old) seamlessly marrying with cassis-accented fruit; the tannins are fine and soft, the balance good. Screwcap. 14.5% alc. **Rating** 89 **To** 2015 $15

Kooyong ★★★★★

PO Box 153, Red Hill South, Vic 3937 **Region** Mornington Peninsula
T (03) 5989 4444 **F** (03) 5989 7677 **www**.kooyong.com **Open** At Port Phillip Estate
Winemaker Sandro Mosele **Est.** 1996 **Cases** 5000 **Vyds** 47.7 ha

Kooyong, owned by Giorgio and Dianne Gjergja, released its first wines in 2001. The vineyard is planted to pinot noir, chardonnay and, more recently, pinot gris. Winemaker Sandro Mosele is a graduate of CSU, and has a deservedly high reputation. He also provides contract winemaking services for others. The Kooyong wines are made at the spectacular new winery of Port Phillip Estate, also owned by the Gjergias. Exports to the UK, the US, Canada, Sweden and Singapore.

🍷🍷🍷🍷🍷 **Single Vineyard Selection Faultline Chardonnay 2008** This wine, with the same alcohol as Estate, has a far more intense personality, the lemon and grapefruit aromas framed by the right amount of barrel ferment oak, the palate with piercing fruit rather than piercing acidity, the length prodigious. Screwcap. 12.5% alc. **Rating** 96 **To** 2018 $58

Single Vineyard Selection Ferrous Pinot Noir 2008 As with all the Kooyong Pinots, excellent colour and clarity; a resplendent bouquet of sultry, dark berry fruits and an imperious palate driving through to an emphatic finish. Diam. 13.5% alc. **Rating** 96 **To** 2018 $66

Single Vineyard Selection Farrago Chardonnay 2008 This is a long way from traditional Mornington Peninsula chardonnay style; notwithstanding the complexity and nutty characters from barrel fermentation and maturation, the wine has a piercing nectarine/white peach/citrus fruit line that drives through the palate, finish and aftertaste. Screwcap. 12.5% alc. **Rating** 95 **To** 2016 $58

Single Vineyard Selection Haven Pinot Noir 2008 Here the thrust and character of the wine is built more around red fruits, especially red cherry, the texture more slinky, yet in no way effete, the finish drawn out by some foresty notes providing contrast. Diam. 13% alc. **Rating** 95 **To** 2017 $66

Single Vineyard Selection Meres Pinot Noir 2008 Provides the greatest harmony and continuity of line of the Kooyong Pinots; a totally delicious fusion of predominantly red fruits cut by some savoury nuances on the pure-bred finish. Diam. 13% alc. **Rating** 95 **To** 2017 $66

Estate Mornington Peninsula Chardonnay 2008 An exercise in extreme restraint, the alcohol the lowest yet for this label, and the winery handling aimed at preserving the elegance and finesse of the fruit flavours, not embellishing them; there is supple nectarine fruit in abundance, the citrus-tinged acidity perfect. Screwcap. 12.5% alc. **Rating** 94 **To** 2015 $39

Beurrot Mornington Peninsula Pinot Gris 2008 A pinot gris that has been given the full treatment, so much so its varietal origin is all but lost, but very good texture compensates. Screwcap. 13.5% alc. **Rating** 94 **To** 2012 $30

ŶŶŶŶŶ **Beurrot Mornington Peninsula Pinot Gris 2009 Rating** 93 **To** 2012 $30
Estate Mornington Peninsula Pinot Noir 2008 Rating 93 **To** 2014 $46

ŶŶŶŶ **Massale Mornington Peninsula Pinot Noir 2008 Rating** 89 **To** 2015 $30

Kopparossa Wines ★★★★

PO Box 26, Coonawarra, SA 5263 **Region** Coonawarra
T (08) 8736 3268 **F** (08) 8736 3363 **Open** By appt
Winemaker Gavin Hogg, Mike Press **Est.** 1996 **Cases** 5000 **Vyds** 22 ha
Of the many complicated stories, this is one of the most complicated of all. Founded by Gavin Hogg and Mike Press in 1996 and based on an 80-ha vineyard in the Wrattonbully region, the Kopparossa label was born in 2000. The vineyard was sold in '02, and Mike retired to pursue separate interests in his Adelaide Hills family vineyard. Various wine releases and events occurred until 2005, when a joint venture between Stentiford Pty Ltd (Kopparossa's parent company) and Estate Licensing Pty Ltd (Olivia Newton John's wine-naming rights company) was entered into. Says Gavin's newsletter, 'Put simply, Stentiford produces and packages wine for the Olivia Label, which is then marketed and sold by Estate Licensing.' Another complication followed in 2009, when Gavin purchased a 24-ha vineyard on the Murray River at Yelta, adjacent to his parents' vineyard; most of the 15 ha of shiraz is sold to Constellation, but from 2011 part will be retained for the Hoggies Estate brand. Exports to the UK, the US, Canada and Hong Kong.

ŶŶŶŶŶ **Hoggies Estate Chardonnay 2006** To add total confusion (in the context of
✪ the red wines) this is indeed an estate-grown wine from the Hoggs' Coonawarra vineyard; tight, long and intense citrus and nectarine fruit do the talking; still very youthful. Screwcap. 13.5% alc. **Rating** 90 **To** 2014 $9.95

✪ **Hoggies Estate Cabernet Sauvignon 2009** From a vineyard near Yelta, the vines managed by Gavin Hogg, and made in Coonawarra. Its crimson colour leads into a medium-bodied palate with a cascade of blackcurrant fruit. Amazing value. Screwcap. 14% alc. **Rating** 90 **To** 2015 $9.95

ŶŶŶŶ **Hoggies Estate Shiraz 2008** Like the '09 Hoggies Estate Cabernet, from
✪ a Sunraysia vineyard managed by Gavin Hogg. Red-purple, moderate depth; a medium- to full-bodied shiraz, full of flavour from start to finish; plum, blackberry and black cherry fruit is supported by ripe, unapologetic tannins and a hint of vanilla. Screwcap. 14% alc. **Rating** 89 **To** 2014 $9.95

Olivia Coonawarra Cabernet Sauvignon 2006 Rating 88 **To** 2014 $14.95

Krinklewood Biodynamic Vineyard ★★★★

712 Wollombi Road, Broke, NSW 2330 **Region** Hunter Valley
T (02) 6579 1322 **F** (02) 9986 2154 **www**.krinklewood.com **Open** W'ends &
public hols 10–5
Winemaker Liz Jackson, Rod Windrim **Est.** 1981 **Cases** 6500 **Vyds** 19.9 ha
A boutique, family-owned biodynamic vineyard, Krinklewood produces 100% estate-grown
wines reflecting the terroir of the Broke–Fordwich area of the Hunter Valley. The cellar door
is set among Provençal-style gardens that overlook the vineyard, with the Wollombi Brook and
Brokenback range providing a spectacular backdrop. Exports to Canada, Denmark and Japan.

ŸŸŸŸŸ **Chardonnay 2008** In the modern style, early picking conserving natural acidity
and introducing citrussy components to a wine with minimal oak impact; nectarine
fruit is at the core of the wine. Screwcap. 12.7% alc. **Rating** 93 **To** 2015 $24

Semillon 2009 Pale straw; a spotlessly clean, but as yet somewhat closed, bouquet;
the wine springs into life on the palate, incisively fresh and crisp, the early picking
showing the other face of an undoubtedly excellent vintage. Could well surprise
given several years in bottle. Screwcap. 9.8% alc. **Rating** 92 **To** 2016 $22

Spider Run Red 2005 Relatively light colour; distinctly regional earthy/leathery
overtones to the red fruits of the bouquet, the light- to medium-bodied palate
in similar vein. Spider Run is an allusion to the biodynamic viticulture. Shiraz.
Screwcap. 13.5% alc. **Rating** 91 **To** 2015 $45

Spider Run White 2007 Hmmm. A blend of Semillon/Chardonnay/Verdelho
with some pleasant bottle-developed flavours and a clean finish. It will need hand-
selling, methinks. Screwcap. 12.5% alc. **Rating** 90 **To** 2014 $45

Francesca Rose 2009 Light magenta; a quiet bouquet but plenty of red fruits
on the palate, balanced by firm acidity on the finish. Co-fermented Mourvedre/
Tempranillo blended with Shiraz. Screwcap. 12.3% alc. **Rating** 90 **To** 2010 $22

The Gypsy Sparkling Shiraz 2004 Bottle-fermented, but no further details;
however, has built complexity, most likely on lees, but possibly also cork. Good
regional base introduces slightly spicy/savoury components, and the dosage is well
balanced. 13% alc. **Rating** 90 **To** 2013 $45

ŸŸŸŸ **Verdelho 2009** **Rating** 89 **To** 2014 $22

KT & The Falcon ★★★★★

Mintaro Road, Leasingham, SA 5452 5415 **Region** Clare Valley
T 0419 855 500 **F** (08) 8843 0040 **www**.ktandthefalcon.com.au **Open** By appt
Winemaker Kerri Thompson **Est.** 2006 **Cases** 700
KT is winemaker Kerri Thompson and the Falcon is viticulturist Stephen Farrugia. Kerri
graduated with a degree in oenology from Roseworthy Agricultural College in 1993, and
thereafter made wine in McLaren Vale, Tuscany, Beaujolais and the Clare Valley, becoming well
known as the Leasingham winemaker in the Clare. Steve managed vineyards in McLaren Vale
and the Clare Valley before establishing the estate vineyard. Despite Kerri's former role within
a very large winemaking organisation, the two have unhesitatingly moved into biodynamic
management of their own vineyard (planted chiefly to riesling, but with some shiraz) and
one of the vineyards they manage (moving to biodynamic farming in 2003). Kerri resigned
from Hardys/Leasingham in 2006 after seven years at the helm, and made the first official
KT & The Falcon wines the following year. She makes these wines at Crabtree, where she is
winemaker. Exports to the UK.

ŸŸŸŸŸ **Melva Watervale Riesling 2009** Has the purity of great riesling, effortlessly
filling the bouquet and palate with waves of aromas and flavours in a citrus and
apple spectrum; there is a haunting sweetness throughout on both the mid-palate
and finish without compromising the balance; 210 dozen made. Screwcap. 12% alc.
Rating 96 **To** 2024 $29

Peglidis Vineyard Watervale Riesling 2009 This is the most powerful, tightly
focused and intense of the three Rieslings, made in classic dry style; it has the
balance and acidity to guarantee a very long life, and deserves a few years in bottle
for the fruit to open further. Screwcap. 12% alc. **Rating** 96 **To** 2030 $33

⊗   **Churinga Vineyard Watervale Riesling 2009** Immaculate grapegrowing and winemaking pay big dividends with all the KT & The Falcon wines; lime and a touch of passionfruit provide a sweet fruit mid-palate before finishing dry and crisp. Vines planted in the Great Depression in 1930; 210 dozen made. Screwcap. 13% alc. **Rating** 94 **To** 2019 $29

Kurrajong Downs   ★★★

Casino Road, Tenterfield, NSW 2372 **Region** New England
T (02) 6736 4590 **F** (02) 6736 1983 **www**.kurrajongdownswines.com **Open** Thurs–Mon 9–4
Winemaker Ravens Croft Wines (Mark Ravenscroft), Symphony Hill (Mike Hayes)
Est. 2000 **Cases** 2000 **Vyds** 5 ha
Jonus Rhodes arrived at Tenterfield in 1858, lured by the gold he mined for the next 40 years, until his death in 1898. He was evidently successful, for the family now runs a 2800-ha cattle-grazing property on which Lynton and Sue Rhodes began the development of their vineyard at an altitude of 850 m in 1996. Plantings include shiraz, cabernet sauvignon, merlot, pinot noir, chardonnay and pinot noir.

♟♟♟♟   **Black Duck Tenterfield Shiraz 2008** Light red-purple; an elegant, light-bodied shiraz with bright red fruits and spice on both bouquet and palate, the tannins deftly handled. No need for prolonged cellaring. Screwcap. 13% alc. **Rating** 89 **To** 2012 $21
All Nations Tenterfield Pinot Noir 2008 Strong crimson; the spicy cherry bouquet and palate are impressive, as is the silky texture of the mouthfeel; the only downside is green, minty notes on the back-palate and finish. Screwcap. 13% alc. **Rating** 87 **To** 2013 $18

Kurtz Family Vineyards   ★★★★★

PO Box 460, Nuriootpa, SA 5355 **Region** Barossa Valley
T 0418 810 982 **F** (08) 8564 3217 **www**.kurtzfamilyvineyards.com.au **Open** By appt
Winemaker Steve Kurtz **Est.** 1996 **Cases** 4000 **Vyds** 15.04 ha
The Kurtz family has a little over 15 ha of vineyard at Light Pass, with 9 ha of shiraz, the remainder planted to chardonnay, cabernet sauvignon, semillon, sauvignon blanc, petit verdot, grenache, mataro and malbec. Steve Kurtz has followed in the footsteps of his great-grandfather Ben Kurtz, who first grew grapes at Light Pass in the 1930s. After a career working first at Saltram and then Foster's until 2006, Steve gained invaluable experience from Nigel Dolan, Caroline Dunn and John Glaetzer among others. Exports to the US, India, Macau, Hong Kong and China.

♟♟♟♟♟   **Lunar Block Individual Vineyard Barossa Valley Shiraz 2006** Good, deep colour; a rich wine reflecting the outstanding vintage; delicious blackberry and licorice fruit runs the length of the supple, medium- to full-bodied palate. The wine will outlive the cork. 14% alc. **Rating** 96 **To** 2031 $45

Kyneton Ridge Estate   ★★★

90 Blackhill School Road, Kyneton, Vic 3444 **Region** Macedon Ranges
T (03) 5422 7377 **F** (03) 5422 3747 **www**.kynetonridge.com.au **Open** W'ends & public hols 10–5, or by appt
Winemaker John and Luke Boucher **Est.** 1997 **Cases** 700 **Vyds** 4 ha
Kyneton Ridge Estate has been established by a family team of winemakers, with winemaking roots going back four generations in the case of John and Ann Boucher. Together with Pauline Russell they found what they believe is a perfect pinot noir site near Kyneton, and planted 2.5 ha of pinot noir in 1997; 1.5 ha of chardonnay was added in '02. The crush is supplemented by small parcels of shiraz and cabernet sauvignon from vineyards in the Macedon Ranges and Heathcote regions.

ŸŸŸŸ   **Premium Macedon Ranges Pinot Noir 2006** Good colour, expected development; a fragrant bouquet of spicy dark berry fruits flows through to the spicy, savoury palate, fruit still holding on, although not for much longer. Has merit. Screwcap. 13.5% alc. **Rating** 89 **To** 2012 $36

Macedon Ranges Shiraz 2007 The bouquet has intense spice, black pepper and licorice overtones shrieking cool climate; the palate follows suit, but introduces a touch of astringency on the finish that would have been better avoided. Screwcap. 13.5% alc. **Rating** 88 **To** 2017 $25

Fortunate Land Macedon Ranges Wooded Chardonnay 2008 Bright straw-green; a mix of grass, citrus, stone fruit and strong grainy/minerally acidity; a little confronting, but food would deal with that. Screwcap. 12.5% alc. **Rating** 87 **To** 2011 $18

La Colline Wines   ★★★

42 Lake Canobolas Road, Orange, NSW 2800 **Region** Orange
T (02) 6365 3289 **F** (02) 6365 3289 **Open** Wed–Sun 10–5
Winemaker Madrez Wine Services **Est.** 1999 **Cases** 1500 **Vyds** 14.5 ha
Aline and Philippe Prudhomme combine a vineyard (selling most of the grapes, but having some contract-made for La Colline) and a 70-seat licensed restaurant featuring the French provincial cuisine from the land of their birth. The cellar door and restaurant are 6 km from Orange, with views of the Towac Valley.

ŸŸŸŸ   **Sparkling of Orange NV** Pronounced mousse; lively, indeed vibrant, juicy citrus flavours; all about fruit, not complexity. Cork. 11.5% alc. **Rating** 87 **To** 2010 $19

La Curio   ★★★★☆

11 Sextant Avenue, Seaford, SA 5169 (postal) **Region** McLaren Vale
T (08) 8327 1442 **F** (08) 8327 1442 **www**.lacuriowines.com **Open** Not
Winemaker Adam Hooper **Est.** 2003 **Cases** 1400
La Curio has been established by Adam Hooper, who purchases small parcels of grapes from vineyards in McLaren Vale with an average age of 40 years, the oldest 80 years. The wines are made at Redheads Studio, a boutique winery in McLaren Vale that caters for a number of small producers. The manacles depicted on the striking label are those of Harry Houdini, and the brand proposition is very cleverly worked through. Winemaking techniques, too, are avant-garde, and highly successful. Exports to the UK, the US, Canada and Sweden.

ŸŸŸŸŸ   **Reserve Bush Vine McLaren Vale Grenache 2008** Typical light colour; grenache at its best, mocking the alcohol with its vibrant bouquet and lively palate; there is a cascade of red fruit flavours, and a fine, supple palate. Cork. 15% alc. **Rating** 94 **To** 2018 $27

ŸŸŸŸŸ   **Reserve McLaren Vale Shiraz 2008 Rating** 92 **To** 2028 $31

La Linea   ★★★★★

36 Shipsters Road, Kensington Park, SA 5068 (postal) **Region** Adelaide Hills
T (08) 8431 3556 **www**.lalinea.com.au **Open** Not
Winemaker Peter Leske **Est.** 2007 **Cases** 1000
Partners Peter Leske and Jason Quin bring vast experience to this venture. After a number of years with the Australian Wine Research Institute, interacting with many wine businesses, large and small, Peter became chief winemaker at Nepenthe for the better part of a decade. Jason Quin spent years at T'Gallant, one of the pioneers of pinot gris. Working exclusively with tempranillo to produce a serious Rose from a cooler part of the Adelaide Hills, and a dry red (tempranillo) from a separately owned vineyard in the warmer and drier northern end of the Hills, marks the start of the business. La Linea, Spanish for 'the line', reflects the partners' aim to hold the line in style and quality.

ŸŸŸŸŸ   Vertigo TRKN Adelaide Hills Riesling 2009 Very pale quartz; TRKN is morse
✪   code for trocken (German for dry) and that is precisely what this wine is, although
far from devoid of fruit, citrus, lime and apple are present as much on the finish as
the mid-palate. Screwcap. 12% alc. **Rating** 95 **To** 2015 $27

✪   Vertigo 25GR Adelaide Hills Riesling 2009 Similar label to TRKN; here
25GR means 25 grammes per litre of residual sugar, beautifully balanced by lime-
juicy acidity; another of the ever-growing band of Mosel rieslings, and a good
wine. Screwcap. 10.5% alc. **Rating** 94 **To** 2016 $23

ŸŸŸŸŸ   Adelaide Hills Tempranillo 2008 **Rating** 91 **To** 2018 $26

La Pleiade ★★★★★
c/- Jasper Hill, Drummonds Lane, Heathcote, Vic 3523 **Region** Heathcote
T (03) 5433 2528 **F** (03) 5433 3143 **Open** By appt
Winemaker Ron Laughton, Michel Chapoutier **Est.** 1998 **Cases** 600 **Vyds** 9 ha
This is the joint venture of Michel and Corinne Chapoutier and Ron and Elva Laughton. In
spring 1998 a vineyard using Australian and imported French shiraz clones was planted. The
vineyard is run biodynamically, and the winemaking is deliberately designed to place maximum
emphasis on the fruit quality. Exports to the UK, the US and other major markets.

ŸŸŸŸŸ   Heathcote Shiraz 2007 Excellent purple-crimson colour, deep but clear; an
unashamedly full-bodied wine, black fruits in a girdle of grippy tannins; long-term
cellaring should resolve those tannins, but the wine stains along two channels of
the cork cause concern. Pray. 15% alc. **Rating** 94 **To** 2027 $68

🍇 La Violetta Wines ★★★☆
PO Box 798, Denmark, WA 6333 **Region** Great Southern
T 0402 373 723 **F** (08) 9848 3842 **www**.lavioletta.com.au **Open** Not
Winemaker Andrew Hoadley **Est.** 2008 **Cases** 600
La Violetta is owned by husband and wife team Andrew Hoadley and Hanna Reichel, who
first met in Canberra and worked several vintages together at Constellation's Kamberra
Winery. Andrew had majored in history at the University of Queensland, and completed
a wine science degree from CSU in 2003. Rhineland-born Hanna Reichel has a PhD in
entomology, and completed three-quarters of the CSU wine science degree before children
intervened. Andrew's first wine experience was pruning for De Bortoli in the Yarra Valley
in 1997, before going on to work at Bay of Fires, Cumulus Wines, Dominion Wines and
Kamberra, also winemaking in Piedmont and Washington State. The couple has now settled
in Denmark, where Andrew is winemaker with Castelli Estate, and able to make the small
amounts of La Violetta wines at that winery. Exports to the UK.

ŸŸŸŸŸ   La Ciornia Shiraz 2008 Another La Violetta wine to walk on the wild side;
savoury tannins make an impact right from the outset, giving the wine some Old
World/Rhône nuances; the black fruits at its core will hold the wine for years.
Screwcap. 14% alc. **Rating** 91 **To** 2023 $46

ŸŸŸŸ   Das Sakrileg Riesling 2008 **Rating** 89 **To** 2014 $19

Laanecoorie ★★★★☆
4834 Bendigo/Maryborough Road, Betley, Vic 3472 **Region** Bendigo
T (03) 5468 7260 **F** (03) 5468 7388 **www**.laanecoorievineyard.com **Open** W'ends &
public hols 11–5, Mon–Fri by appt
Winemaker Graeme Jukes, John Ellis (Contract) **Est.** 1982 **Cases** 1000
John and Rosa McQuilten's vineyard (shiraz, cabernet franc, merlot and cabernet sauvignon)
produces grapes of high quality, and competent contract winemaking does the rest. The '08
Reserve was a great comeback after the '07 crop was destroyed.

ᵀᵀᵀᵀᵀ **McQuilten's Reserve Shiraz 2008** Deep colour; a complex and satisfying medium- to full-bodied shiraz, the aromas of black fruits, spice and licorice repeated on the well-balanced and long palate; long future ahead. Diam. 15% alc. **Rating** 94 **To** 2028 $39.50

Lake Barrington Vineyard   ★★★☆

1133-1136 West Kentish Road, West Kentish, Tas 7306 **Region** Northern Tasmania
T (03) 6491 1249 **F** (03) 9662 9553 www.lbv.com.au **Open** Wed–Sun 11–4 (Nov–Apr)
Winemaker Frogmore Creek, White Rock, Julian Alcorso **Est.** 1986 **Cases** 350 **Vyds** 1 ha
Charles and Jill Macek purchased the vineyard from founder Maree Tayler in 2005. Charles is a distinguished company director (Telstra, Wesfarmers). Lake Barrington's primary focus is on high-quality sparkling wine, which has won many trophies and gold medals over the years at the Tasmanian Wine Show, with lesser quantities of high-quality chardonnay and pinot noir. There are picnic facilities at the vineyard and, needless to say, the scenery is very beautiful.

ᵀᵀᵀᵀᵀ **Alexandra 2006** Pale straw-green; fresh and crisp, has length, acidity at upper end, but works. Three years on yeast lees prior to disgorgement. Diam. 12.5% alc. **Rating** 90 **To** 2014 $40

Lake Breeze Wines   ★★★★★

Step Road, Langhorne Creek, SA 5255 **Region** Langhorne Creek
T (08) 8537 3017 **F** (08) 8537 3267 www.lakebreeze.com.au **Open** 7 days 10–5
Winemaker Greg Follett **Est.** 1987 **Cases** 15 000 **Vyds** 90 ha
The Folletts have been farmers at Langhorne Creek since 1880, and grapegrowers since the 1930s. Most of the grape production is sold, but the quality of the Lake Breeze wines has been exemplary, with the red wines particularly appealing. Lake Breeze also owns and makes the False Cape wines from Kangaroo Island. Exports to the US and other major markets.

ᵀᵀᵀᵀᵀ **Arthur's Reserve Cabernet Sauvignon Petit Verdot Malbec 2006** Retains excellent crimson colour; this 82/9/9 blend spent 22 months in new French oak and absorbed it all; the flavours are those of a cool region, dark and savoury, but very long; 270 dozen made. Screwcap. 14.5% alc. **Rating** 95 **To** 2026 $35

✪ **Langhorne Creek Shiraz 2008** Crimson-purple; a medium-bodied and very stylish shiraz, with supple black fruits, oak and tannins in excellent balance; the clarity of line on the back-palate and finish is particularly good. Screwcap. 14.5% alc. **Rating** 94 **To** 2018 $21

ᵀᵀᵀᵀᵀ **False Cape Ship's Graveyard Shiraz 2007** Excellent purple hue; spicy red
✪ and black fruit aromas come through strongly on the medium-bodied palate, especially the spicy element; a wine with real personality. Screwcap. 14.5% alc. **Rating** 92 **To** 2015 $18

✪ **Bullant Langhorne Creek Cabernet Merlot 2008** Good colour; a medium-bodied wine that is all about blackcurrant and plum fruit supported by fine, gently savoury tannins. Screwcap. 14.2% alc. **Rating** 92 **To** 2016 $15

✪ **Bullant Langhorne Creek Shiraz 2008** Vivid, deep crimson-purple; a rich, medium- to full-bodied shiraz replete with black fruits and dark chocolate; a slight kick on the finish (alcohol?) is eminently forgivable at this price; worth cellaring. Screwcap. 14.5% alc. **Rating** 90 **To** 2018 $15

✪ **False Cape Unknown Sailor Cabernet Merlot 2007** Good colour; another appealing Kangaroo Island wine; somehow the terroir invests these wines with a bright, vinous heart to sustain the more spicy savoury components. Screwcap. 14% alc. **Rating** 90 **To** 2017 $18

ᵀᵀᵀᵀ **Langhorne Creek Chardonnay 2009** **Rating** 89 **To** 2015 $18
Bernoota Langhorne Creek Shiraz Cabernet 2007 **Rating** 89 **To** 2015 $21
Langhorne Creek Cabernet Sauvignon 2007 **Rating** 89 **To** 2015 $23
False Cape The Captain Cabernet Sauvignon 2006 **Rating** 88 **To** 2016 $28

Lake Cairn Curran Vineyard ★★★★

'Park Hill', Leathbridge Road, Welshman's Reef, Vic 3462 **Region** Bendigo
T (03) 5476 2523 **F** (03) 5476 2523 www.lakecairncurranvineyard.com.au **Open** By appt
Winemaker Sarah Ferguson, Moorooduc Estate (Richard McIntyre) **Est.** 1987
Cases 800 **Vyds** 5.4 ha
When Ross and Sarah Ferguson purchased what is now known as Lake Cairn Curran Vineyard in 1999, they acquired not only the vineyard (chardonnay, pinot noir and shiraz), but also a slice of history, evoked by the beautiful labels. The Park Hill homestead dates back to the establishment of the Tarrengower Run in the 1840s, and the mudbrick cellar door is located adjacent to the homestead, overlooking the Cairn Curran Reservoir and Loddon River Valley. Notwithstanding that, Sarah has a wine science (oenology) degree from CSU, and having worked several vintages at Moorooduc Estate, makes small batches of wine at the newly renovated onsite winery. However, Rick McIntyre will continue to make the major table wine releases, David Cowburn of Kilchurn the sparkling wines.

🍷🍷🍷🍷🍷 **Shiraz 2008** Strong purple-crimson; a complex medium-bodied wine bringing
✪   spice, pepper and licorice into a garden of vibrant and juicy black and red fruits; the savoury backdrop works well. Screwcap. 13.5% alc. **Rating** 91 **To** 2020 $20
✪   **Wild Yeast Chardonnay 2008** Glowing yellow-green; a complex wine, with (self-described) 'funky wild yeast characters' that come through strongly on the low-alcohol chardonnay foundation. Screwcap. 12.1% alc. **Rating** 90 **To** 2014 $20

🍷🍷🍷🍷 **Emma Sparkling 2008 Rating** 87 **To** 2012 $25

Lake George Winery ★★★★☆

Old Federal Highway, Lake George, NSW 2581 **Region** Canberra District
T (02) 9948 4676 **F** (02) 9949 2873 www.lakegeorgewinery.com.au **Open** 7 days 10–5
Winemaker Alex McKay, Nick O'Leary **Est.** 1971 **Cases** 4000 **Vyds** 20 ha
Lake George Winery was sold by founder Dr Edgar Riek some years ago. The plantings of 37-year-old chardonnay, pinot noir, cabernet sauvignon, semillon and merlot have been joined by shiraz and tempranillo, and yet more plantings of pinot gris, viognier, pinot noir and malbec. In March 2008 Lake George acquired the Madew vineyard, providing yet more grape resources. The winemaking techniques include basket pressing and small batch barrel maturation under the expert eyes of consultant winemakers Alex McKay and Nick O'Leary.

🍷🍷🍷🍷🍷 **Reserve Chardonnay 2008** A very elegant chardonnay in the modern style, with restrained alcohol and oak entirely appropriate for the delicate, although quite intense white peach, melon and citrus fruit, the oak influence as much subliminal as subtle. Screwcap. 13% alc. **Rating** 95 **To** 2016 $35

🍷🍷🍷🍷🍷 **Reserve Shiraz 2008 Rating** 93 **To** 2020 $49

🍷🍷🍷🍷 **Tempranillo 2008 Rating** 89 **To** 2014 $29

Lake Moodemere Vineyards ★★★☆

McDonalds Road, Rutherglen, Vic 3685 **Region** Rutherglen
T (02) 6032 9449 **F** (02) 6032 7002 www.moodemerewines.com.au **Open** Mon, Thurs, Fri, Sun 10–4, Sat & public hols 10–5
Winemaker Michael Chambers **Est.** 1995 **Cases** 2000 **Vyds** 20.74 ha
Michael, Belinda, Peter and Helen Chambers are members of the famous Chambers family of Rutherglen. The vineyards (tended by Peter), include the Italian grape variety biancone, a vineyard speciality made in a light-bodied late-harvest style. The cellar door sits high above Lake Moodemere, and gourmet hampers can be arranged with 24 hours' notice.

🍷🍷🍷🍷🍷 **Concord Rutherglen Shiraz & Cinsaut 2008** Made by Michael Chambers and youngest son Joel; the wine has bright red fruit aromas and flavours of cherry and strawberry, the tannin impact negligible, although it has a long finish; an elegant wine from Rutherglen. Screwcap. 14% alc. **Rating** 90 **To** 2015 $26

🍷🍷🍷🍷 **Rutherglen Chardonnay 2006 Rating** 88 **To** 2014 $18

Lake's Folly ★★★★★

2416 Broke Road, Pokolbin, NSW 2320 **Region** Hunter Valley
T (02) 4998 7507 **F** (02) 4998 7322 **www**.lakesfolly.com.au **Open** 7 days 10–4 while
wine available
Winemaker Rodney Kempe **Est.** 1963 **Cases** 5000 **Vyds** 12.2 ha
The first of the weekend wineries to produce wines for commercial sale, long revered for its
Cabernet Sauvignon and nowadays its Chardonnay. Very properly, terroir and climate produce
a distinct regional influence and thereby a distinctive wine style. The winery continues to
enjoy an incredibly loyal clientele, with much of each year's wine selling out quickly by mail
order. Lake's Folly no longer has any connection with the Lake family, having been acquired
some years ago by Perth businessman Peter Fogarty. Peter's family company previously
established the Millbrook Winery in the Perth Hills, so is no stranger to the joys and agonies
of running a small winery. Curiously, it is the Chardonnay that justifies the rating (and the
historic nature of the winery).

♀♀♀♀♀ Hunter Valley Chardonnay 2009 Bright green-straw; the sheer class of
this wine is immediately apparent when the bouquet is first encountered,
continuing in a seamless line through to the finish and aftertaste; it has many of
the characteristics of a cool-grown wine, notably its length. Screwcap. 14% alc.
Rating 96 To 2020 $60

Lambert Vineyards ★★★★

810 Norton Road, Wamboin, NSW 2620 **Region** Canberra District
T (02) 6238 3866 **F** (02) 6238 3855 **www**.lambertvineyards.com.au
Open Thurs–Sun 10–5, or by appt
Winemaker Steve and Ruth Lambert **Est.** 1998 **Cases** 4000 **Vyds** 10 ha
Ruth and Steve Lambert have established riesling (2.5 ha), pinot noir, pinot gris (2 ha each),
merlot (1.5 ha), chardonnay (1 ha), cabernet sauvignon and shiraz (0.5 ha each). Steve makes
the many wines onsite, and does so with skill and sensitivity. Definitely a winery to watch.

♀♀♀♀♀ Canberra District Pinot Gris 2008 Plenty of colour; slight candied fruit
bouquet, with ginger and orange on show; the palate shows some sweetness, and
the wine fits neatly into the 'gris/Alsace' mould. Screwcap. 14% alc. Rating 90
To 2013 $22 BE
Canberra District Shiraz 2008 Bright colour; concentrated aromas of
blueberry, tar and ironstone; medium- to full-bodied with real depth to the fruit;
vibrant, almost crisp acidity and supple, silky fine-grained tannins conclude with
true harmony. Screwcap. 14.4% alc. Rating 90 To 2016 $25 BE

♀♀♀♀ Canberra District Riesling 2009 Rating 88 To 2016 $22 BE
Canberra District Chardonnay 2007 Rating 88 To 2014 $25 BE
Canberra District Pinot Noir 2008 Rating 88 To 2013 $30 BE
Union 2008 Rating 88 To 2015 $25 BE

Landhaus Estate ★★★★★

PO Box 2135, Bethany SA 5352 **Region** Barossa Valley
T (08) 8353 8442 **F** (08) 8353 0542 **www**.landhauswines.com **Open** Not
Winemaker Kane Jaunutis **Est.** 2002 **Cases** 4200
The Jaunutis family (John, Barbara and son Kane) purchased Landhaus Estate in November
2002, and the following month bought 'The Landhaus' cottage and 1-ha vineyard at Bethany.
Bethany is the oldest German-established town in the Barossa (1842) and the cottage was
one of the first to be built. Kane has worked vintages for Mitolo and Trevor Jones, as well as
managing East End Cellars, one of Australia's leading fine wine retailers, while John brings
decades of owner/management experience and Barbara 20 years in sales and marketing.
Rehabilitation of the estate plantings and establishing a grower network has paid handsome
dividends. Exports to Singapore.

🍷🍷🍷🍷🍷 **Reserve Barossa Valley Shiraz 2008** Very good crimson-purple; a highly expressive wine, the bouquet offering black fruits, dark chocolate and licorice, the super-elegant and long palate following suit; the best five barrels from old vineyards in the Ebenezer/Bethany subregions. Screwcap. 14.2% alc. **Rating** 95 **To** 2028 $45

Barossa Valley Shiraz Mourvedre 2008 Bright hue; the percentage of mourvedre is not shown, but adds spicy/savoury characters to the wine, and also contributes to the texture of the medium-bodied palate; has a long, evenly balanced back-palate and finish. Screwcap. 14% alc. **Rating** 94 **To** 2023 $36

🍷🍷🍷🍷🍷 **The Siren Barossa Valley Rose 2009** **Rating** 92 **To** 2013 $22
The Saint 2008 **Rating** 92 **To** 2020 $22
Barossa Valley Grenache 2008 **Rating** 92 **To** 2018 $26
Barossa Valley Mourvedre Grenache Shiraz 2008 **Rating** 90 **To** 2013 $28

🍷🍷🍷🍷 **The Sinner 2008** **Rating** 89 **To** 2012 $22

Landscape Wines   ★★★★☆

383 Prossers Road, Richmond, Tas 7025 **Region** Southern Tasmania
T (03) 6260 4216 **F** (03) 6260 4016 **Open** By appt
Winemaker Contract **Est.** 1998 **Cases** 120
Knowles and Elizabeth Kerry run the Wondoomarook mixed farming and irrigation property in the heart of the Coal River Valley. In 1998–99 they decided to undertake a small scale diversification, planting 0.5 ha each of riesling and pinot noir. The labels, depicting Antarctic scenes by Jenni Mitchell, hark back to the Kerrys' original occupation in Antarctic scientific research. No new wines available in 2010 owing to one year of drought, and another of frost.

🍷🍷🍷🍷🍷 **Riesling 2007** Straw-green; lime/apple blossom aromas; the palate has very good line, length and balance. Has positively flowered over the past two years. Screwcap. 12.5% alc. **Rating** 94 **To** 2016 $28

Langmeil Winery   ★★★★★

Cnr Para Road/Langmeil Road, Tanunda, SA 5352 **Region** Barossa Valley
T (08) 8563 2595 **F** (08) 8563 3622 **www.**langmeilwinery.com.au **Open** 7 days 10.30–4.30
Winemaker Paul Lindner, Tyson Bitter **Est.** 1996 **Cases** 42 000 **Vyds** 25.3 ha
Vines were first planted at Langmeil (which possesses the oldest block in Australia) in the 1840s, and the first winery on the site, known as Paradale Wines, opened in 1932. In '96, cousins Carl and Richard Lindner with brother-in-law Chris Bitter formed a partnership to acquire and refurbish the winery and its 5-ha vineyard (planted to shiraz, and including 2 ha planted in 1843). Another vineyard was acquired in 1998, which included cabernet sauvignon and grenache. Exports to all major markets.

🍷🍷🍷🍷🍷 **Barossa Old Vine Company Shiraz 2006** Youthful hue; a wonderfully expressive wine showing true depth of Barossa character with red and black fruits entwined seamlessly, and complemented by an array of complex aromas of tar, chocolate and turned earth; the palate is dense and rich, but there is a lightness that belies the 15.5% alcohol; long, supple and seamless. Cork. **Rating** 95 **To** 2025 $100 BE

The 1843 Freedom Barossa Valley Shiraz 2007 Colour good, although not especially so; a very distinct change of pace from the '06, the palate only medium-bodied, and in harmony with the red and black fruits of the bouquet, the two-thirds new French oak also stamping its mark. As usual, an echo of sweetness evident. Screwcap. 15% alc. **Rating** 94 **To** 2022 $100

Jackaman's Barossa Cabernet Sauvignon 2007 Deep crimson colour, excellent for the vintage; a well-made wine, with juicy blackcurrant fruit and no heat; the house style hint of sweetness works well here, leading to a rising cadence on the finish. Screwcap. 14% alc. **Rating** 94 **To** 2016 $50

ㅜㅜㅜㅜᲧ Dry Eden Valley Riesling 2009 Bright straw-green; attractive lime and a little
○   green apple aromas and flavours; the restrained alcohol gives the wine freshness
     and crisp acidity. Screwcap. 11.5% alc. **Rating** 93 **To** 2017 $19.50
○   **Bella Rouge 2009** Attractive wine; 24 hours skin contact with cabernet
     sauvignon has worked well, with bright flavours and a pleasing touch of tannin to
     strengthen the finish. Screwcap. 13% alc. **Rating** 93 **To** 2010 $20
     Valley Floor Barossa Shiraz 2008 Rating 93 **To** 2023 $28.50
     The Fifth Wave Barossa Grenache 2007 Rating 93 **To** 2017 $35
     Liqueur 20 Year Old Shiraz Tawny NV Rating 93 **To** 2011 $35
     Barossa Valley Sparkling Shiraz Cuvee NV Rating 92 **To** 2013 $35
     Orphan Bank Barossa Valley Shiraz 2007 Rating 91 **To** 2017 $50
     Barossa Valley Vintage Shiraz 2003 Rating 91 **To** 2023 $25

ㅜㅜㅜㅜ Live Wire Eden Valley Riesling 2009 **Rating** 89 **To** 2016 $20
     Blacksmith Barossa Cabernet Sauvignon 2007 Rating 89 **To** 2014
     $28.50 BE
     Ten Year Old Barossa Tawny NV Rating 89 **To** 2011 $18.50
     Hangin' Snakes Barossa Valley Shiraz Viognier 2008 Rating 88 **To** 2015 $20
     Barossa Late Harvest Riesling 2008 Rating 88 **To** 2013 $25
     Eden Valley Chardonnay 2009 Rating 87 **To** 2011 $15

Lark Hill   ★★★★★

521 Bungendore Road, Bungendore, NSW 2621 **Region** Canberra District
T (02) 6238 1393 **F** (02) 6238 1393 **www**.larkhillwine.com.au **Open** Wed–Mon 10–5
Winemaker Dr David, Sue and Chris Carpenter **Est.** 1978 **Cases** 3000 **Vyds** 6.5 ha
The Lark Hill vineyard is situated at an altitude of 860 m, level with the observation deck
on Black Mountain Tower, and offers splendid views of the Lake George escarpment. The
Carpenters have made wines of real quality, style and elegance from the start, but have defied
all the odds (and conventional thinking) with the quality of their Pinot Noirs in favourable
vintages. Significant changes have come in the wake of son Christopher gaining three degrees,
including a double in wine science and viticulture through CSU: the progression towards
biodynamic certification of the vineyard and the opening of a restaurant in 2007. They have
also planted 1 ha of gruner veltliner; it is hard to understand why there have been so few
plantings of this high-quality variety calling Austria its home. Exports to the UK.

ㅜㅜㅜㅜㅜ Canberra District Riesling 2009 A complex bouquet and palate, with notes of
     citrus rind, a hint of tropical fruit and a whisper of honeysuckle; fills the mouth
     with flavour. Screwcap. 12% alc. **Rating** 94 **To** 2017 $30
     Canberra District Gruner Veltliner 2009 At long last, a gruner veltliner to
     write about. In Austria it is planted in precisely the same regions as riesling, so it
     was doubly pleasing it should appear in the Canberra District. Is strongly varietal,
     with a waft of white pepper on the bouquet adding complexity to the fig and ripe
     pear fruit; best of all is the texture and mouthfeel. Screwcap. 12.5% alc. **Rating** 94
     To 2019 $45

Larry Cherubino Wines   ★★★★★

15 York Street, Subiaco, WA 6000 **Region** Western Australia
T (08) 9382 2379 **F** (08) 9382 2397 **www**.larrycherubino.com **Open** Not
Winemaker Larry Cherubino **Est.** 2005 **Cases** 6000 **Vyds** 20 ha
Larry Cherubino has had a particularly distinguished winemaking career, first at Hardys
Tintara, then Houghton, and thereafter as consultant/Flying Winemaker in Australia, NZ,
South Africa, the US and Italy. In 2005 he started Larry Cherubino Wines and has developed
three ranges: at the top is Cherubino (Riesling, Sauvignon Blanc, Shiraz and Cabernet
Sauvignon); next The Yard, five single-vineyard wines from WA; and at the bottom another
five wines under the Ad Hoc label, all single-region wines. The range and quality of his wines
is extraordinary, the prices irresistible. Exports to the UK, the US, Canada, The Netherlands
and Switzerland. Winery of the year 2011 *Wine Companion*.

ŶŶŶŶŶ **Cherubino Porongurup Riesling 2009** An exercise in restraint on the bouquet, which hides the quite remarkable intensity and drive of the palate, with lime and lemon juice on the mid-palate framed by lingering minerally acidity. Gold-plated 20-year development potential. Screwcap. 12.2% alc. **Rating** 97 **To** 2030 $35

✪ **The Yard Porongurup Riesling 2009** As with all the '09 Larry Cherubino Rieslings, virtually devoid of colour; the bouquet, however, is expressive, the palate beautifully defined and balanced, the aftertaste lingering. Five years will see it come into full flower. Screwcap. 12.3% alc. **Rating** 96 **To** 2027 $25

✪ **The Yard Kalgan River Riesling 2009** Hints of wild flowers, even sage, on the bouquet lead into a lip-smacking juicy palate with flavours from lemon to mandarin driving through to an emphatic finish. Screwcap. 12.8% alc. **Rating** 96 **To** 2024 $25

✪ **Cherubino Pemberton Sauvignon Blanc 2009** Pale green-straw; citrus and herb, rather than tropical, aromas precede a blaze of flavour on the highly charged, intense and long palate. The barrel fermentation is not the least obvious. Screwcap. 13% alc. **Rating** 96 **To** 2013 $35

Cherubino Frankland River Shiraz 2008 Smoky oak, violets, roasted meat, blackberry and Asian all-spice blend to form a beguiling bouquet; the palate is multi-layered and amazingly silky with black fruits swamping the considerable oak with ease; incredibly complex, lacy and engaging from start to finish. Cork. 14% alc. **Rating** 96 $65 BE

✪ **The Yard Mount Barker Riesling 2009** Evanescent blossom aromas from apple to lime foreshadow an elegant and precisely pitched palate, with citrus and green apple flavours running through to the crisp finish. From the Whispering Hill Vineyard. Screwcap. 12% alc. **Rating** 95 **To** 2024 $25

✪ **The Yard Pannoo Porongurup Riesling 2009** Has the intensity and acidity usually restricted to Tasmania, with almost searing green lime and apple fruit encased in a fine-spun web of acidity; dry finish. Screwcap. 12.3% alc. **Rating** 95 **To** 2020 $25

The Yard Pemberton Sauvignon Blanc 2009 Pale straw-green; while grassy/citrussy notes are dominant, there are whispers of tropical fruits; has excellent line, length and balance. Screwcap. 12.6% alc. **Rating** 94 **To** 2012 $25

Cherubino Margaret River Chardonnay 2009 A complex yet restrained bouquet of grilled cashews, grapefruit and toasty oak; the palate is quite tightly wound, showing white nectarine and grapefruit, combined with lively acidity and a touch of grip; unevolved, but with a bright future. Screwcap. 13.2% alc. **Rating** 94 $49 BE

The Yard 24 Road Vineyard Chardonnay 2009 Pale, bright straw-green; a wine made with great skill to reflect the more elegant side of Margaret River chardonnay, nectarine fruit in a silken web of quality oak, fruit always dominating the oak. Screwcap. 13% alc. **Rating** 94 **To** 2019 $30

Cherubino Margaret River Cabernet Sauvignon 2008 Bright colour; unevolved bouquet with layers of cigar box, rolled leaf, cassis and fine seasoning from new French oak; the palate is layered and almost silky in texture, with a sweet spot of dark fruit concluding with extremely fine-grained tannins; needs time, but should reward amply. Cork. 13.5% alc. **Rating** 94 $75 BE

ŶŶŶŶ⚲ **The Yard Pedestal Vineyard Margaret River Semillon Sauvignon Blanc 2009 Rating** 93 **To** 2015 $28 BE

✪ **Ad Hoc Tree Hugger Margaret River Chardonnay 2009** Pale straw, bright hue; lemon and grapefruit bouquet, showing a slight steely/flinty edge; incredibly fresh, zesty and focused, with a lingering lemon character; demanding of seafood to complement. Screwcap. 13% alc. **Rating** 92 **To** 2016 $20 BE

✪ **Ad Hoc Hen & Chicken Chardonnay 2008** Bright green-gold; a very elegant wine, with white peach and nectarine doing the talking aided by perfectly balanced acidity; if there is oak, it is not obvious. Screwcap. 13.5% alc. **Rating** 92 **To** 2014 $19.95

The Yard Acacia Vineyard Frankland River Shiraz 2008 Rating 92 $35

✪ Ad Hoc Wallflower Riesling 2009 Has a highly toned and expressive bouquet with perfumed white flower aromas, then a bright but quite tight palate with touches of apple and citrus. Screwcap. 12.3% alc. Rating 91 To 2017 $18 BE

✪ Ad Hoc Straw Man Sauvignon Blanc Semillon 2009 Attractive, easy-drinking style; gooseberry and citrus flavours dominate proceedings; has good balance and length. Screwcap. 13.5% alc. Rating 91 To 2012 $20

The Yard Orondo Vineyard Dwellingup Mourvedre Grenache Shiraz 2009 Rating 91 To 2016 $25 BE

✪ Ad Hoc Etcetera Cabernet Merlot 2008 'A blend of Cabernet, Merlot ... and the rest.' A full-bodied and rich array of black fruits complexed by notes of briar and spice, and supported by ripe tannins. Good cellaring potential. Screwcap. 14.2% alc. Rating 91 To 2020 $20

Ad Hoc Hen & Chicken Chardonnay 2009 Rating 90 To 2014 $20 BE

✪ Ad Hoc Red Wine 2008 Bright, clear colour; filled to the gills with plush red (dominant) and black fruits; oak and tannins largely irrelevant; shortens fractionally on the finish. Cherubino's summary: 'Mix Master. Well mixed red.' Screwcap. 14% alc. Rating 90 To 2015 $18

Ad Hoc Sparkling Chardonnay Pinot Noir NV Rating 90 To 2013 $20

🍷🍷🍷🍷 Ad Hoc Middle of Everywhere Shiraz 2008 Rating 89 To 2015 $20

🌿 Last Word Wines ★★★

12 Main North Road, Clare, SA 5453 **Region** Clare Valley
T 0458 434 000 **F** (08) 8842 2695 **www**.lastwordwines.com **Open** 7 days 9–8
Winemaker Donna Stephens (Contract) **Est.** 2009 **Cases** 7000 **Vyds** 110 ha
Founder and owner Con Lymberopoulos is a former PE teacher who built himself a house in the Clare Valley before deciding to plant 1 ha of vacant land next door to vines. Together with one of his closest friends, and a collection of other partners, he began buying land and vineyards in the Clare Valley, building the holdings to an impressive 20 ha at Watervale, and 90 ha at Quarry Road, Clare. The labels and wine styles are different to most, as is the Last Word Inn, a combined café, restaurant, take away and cellar door, open 7 days for prodigiously long hours, particularly on the weekend.

🍷🍷🍷🍷 Intellectual Riesling 2009 Pale straw-green; lime, lemon, apple and spice aromas, then a pleasant palate that does chop off somewhat on the finish. Screwcap. 12.9% alc. Rating 87 To 2015 $14

Laughing Jack ★★★★★

Cnr Parbs Road/Boundry Road, Greenock, SA 5360 **Region** Barossa Valley
T 0427 396 928 **F** (08) 8562 3878 **www**.laughingjackwines.com **Open** By appt
Winemaker Mick Schroeter, Shawn Kalleske **Est.** 1999 **Cases** 3000 **Vyds** 35 ha
The Kalleske family has many branches in the Barossa Valley. Laughing Jack is owned by Shawn, Nathan, Ian and Carol Kalleske, and Linda Schroeter. They have 35 ha of vines, the lion's share to shiraz (22 ha), with lesser amounts of semillon, chardonnay, riesling and grenache. Vine age varies considerably, with old dry-grown shiraz the jewel in the crown. A small part of the shiraz production is taken for the Laughing Jack Shiraz. As any Australian knows, the kookaburra is also called the laughing jackass, and there is a resident flock of kookaburras in the stands of blue and red gum eucalypts surrounding the vineyards. Exports to the UK, the US and Switzerland.

🍷🍷🍷🍷🍷 Greenock Barossa Valley Shiraz 2007 Deep crimson-purple; an unashamedly full-bodied wine, with black fruits (blackberry, plum, prune) surrounded by firm tannins and some savoury characters; needs considerable patience, but will repay it. Screwcap. 14.5% alc. Rating 94 To 2022 $38

ŶŶŶŶŶ **Jack's Barossa Valley Shiraz 2008** Deep crimson-purple; filled to the gills
✪   with a cascade of plum, prune and blackberry fruit, the mouthfeel supple and
       smooth. There is a hint of sweetness, but I'm not sure whether it's simply fruit
       or a touch of residual sugar; given the benefit of the doubt. Screwcap. 14.5% alc.
       Rating 93 To 2018 $20

✪   **Jack's Barossa Valley Shiraz 2007** Good colour; not typical of '07, with ripe,
       gently sweet black fruits to the fore, the tannins well balanced and integrated.
       Impressive wine at the price. Screwcap. 14.5% alc. **Rating** 92 To 2016 $20

Laurance of Margaret River   ★★★★☆

3518 Caves Road, Wilyabrup, WA 6280 **Region** Margaret River
T (08) 9755 5199 **F** (08) 9755 6188 **www**.laurancewines.com **Open** 7 days 10–5
Winemaker Naturaliste Vintners (Bruce Dukes) **Est.** 2001 **Cases** 5000 **Vyds** 21.83 ha
Founder and chairwoman Dianne Laurance is the driving force behind this family-owned
and run business, with sons Brendon (Executive Director) and Danny (Special Events
Manager) representing the next generation. The 100-ha property has just under 22 ha of vines
(planted in 1996 to three clones of chardonnay, sauvignon blanc, shiraz, cabernet sauvignon,
semillon and merlot), beautiful gardens, artwork and sculptures. The quality of the wines can
be lost behind the oddly shaped bottles reminiscent of Perrier-Jouet's Belle Epoque deluxe
Champagne. Exports to Singapore, Hong Kong, Malaysia, Thailand, China and Japan.

ŶŶŶŶŶ **Icon Cabernet Sauvignon 2007** Deep purple-red; an altogether serious
       cabernet, with intense blackcurrant fruit supported by fine tannins; quality cedary
       French oak. Screwcap. 13.5% alc. **Rating** 94 To 2027 $40

ŶŶŶŶŶ **Chardonnay 2008 Rating** 93 To 2020 $38
       White 2009 Rating 91 To 2012 $31

ŶŶŶŶ   **Semillon Sauvignon Blanc 2009 Rating** 88 To 2010 $26

Laurel Bank   ★★★★

130 Black Snake Lane, Granton, Tas 7030 **Region** Southern Tasmania
T (03) 6263 5977 **F** (03) 6263 3117 **www**.laurelbankwines.com.au **Open** By appt
Winemaker Winemaking Tasmania (Julian Alcorso) **Est.** 1987 **Cases** 900 **Vyds** 3.5 ha
Laurel (hence Laurel Bank) and Kerry Carland began planting their vineyard in 1986 to
sauvignon blanc, riesling, pinot noir, cabernet sauvignon and merlot. They delayed the first
release of their wines for some years and (by virtue of the number of entries they were able
to make) won the trophy for Most Successful Exhibitor at the Hobart Wine Show '95. Things
have settled down since; wine quality is very reliable.

ŶŶŶŶŶ **Pinot Noir 2008** Exceptional colour, deep and strong; another full-bodied pinot
       flooded with black fruits, but also some juicy, slippery notes. Silver medal Tas Wine
       Show '10. Screwcap. 13.6% alc. **Rating** 93 To 2014 $33

ŶŶŶŶ   **Sauvignon Blanc 2009 Rating** 87 To 2012 $22 BE

Lavina Wines   ★★★

263 Main Road, McLaren Vale, SA 5171 **Region** McLaren Vale
T (08) 8323 9646 **F** (08) 8323 8300 **www**.lavinawines.com.au **Open** Mon–Fri 10–5,
w'ends 11–5
Winemaker Matt Rechner, Mike Brown **Est.** 2004 **Cases** 55 000
Lavina Wines is owned by Sam and Victoria Daw, who continue to rapidly build and expand
the Lavina brand along with its sub-brands, private label and bulk wine divisions to both
domestic and overseas markets. Mike Brown and Matt Rechner are responsible for producing
the new Grand Royale and existing Select Series wines. To maintain 'elasticity and diversity',
associated export company Lavina World Wine Export handles the bulk division, which now
ships close to 1 million litres and 50 000 dozen bottles annually. Exports to Europe and Asia.

ρρρρ   **McLaren Vale Shiraz 2008** A big juicy ripe and ultimately friendly wine; fresh
✪   and confit blackberry bouquet with a little bitter chocolate to conclude; fleshy and
       forward. Cork. 14% alc. **Rating** 88 **To** 2014 $15 BE

Leabrook Estate   ★★★★★

Cnr Greenhill Road/Reserve Road, Balhannah, SA 5242 **Region** Adelaide Hills
T (08) 8398 0421 **F** (08) 8398 0421 **www**.leabrookestate.com **Open** W'ends &
public hols 11–5, or by appt
Winemaker Colin Best **Est.** 1998 **Cases** 4000 **Vyds** 2.75 ha
With a background as an engineer and having dabbled in home winemaking for 30 years,
Colin (and Chris) Best took the plunge and moved into commercial winemaking in 1998.
His wines are found in a who's who of restaurants, and in some of the best independent wine
retailers on the east coast. Best says, 'I consider that my success is primarily due to the quality
of my grapes (2.25 ha of pinot noir, 0.5 ha of chardonnay), since they have been planted
on a 1.2 m x 1.2 m spacing and very low yields.' The business has continued to grow, with
contract-grown grapes coming from here, there and everywhere. In 2008 the Bests took over
the former Spur Creek winery, with a consequent move of cellar door. Exports to the UK,
Ireland, Singapore and Hong Kong.

ρρρρρ **Reserve Adelaide Hills Chardonnay 2008** Considerable colour development,
       although is bright; a wine with a passing nod to Burgundy, for it is as much about
       texture and structure as varietal fruit flavour; stone fruit and toasty oak flavours are
       held together by good acidity on the long finish. Screwcap. 13% alc. **Rating** 94
       To 2014 $35
       Adelaide Hills Chardonnay 2007 Similar bright colour to the '08; has
       a complex, slightly funky (in the good sense) bouquet, then a palate with
       considerable intensity, drive and focus to its citrus and white flesh stone fruit;
       finishes fresh and crisp. Screwcap. 13% alc. **Rating** 94 **To** 2014 $30
       Adelaide Hills Pinot Gris 2009 Pale straw; has infinitely more intensity and
       varietal character than the majority of pinot gris, the palate mouthfilling yet
       fine, the flavours coursing through citrus, pear, apple and strawberry. Screwcap.
       12.9% alc. **Rating** 94 **To** 2012 $26

ρρρρρ **George 2008 Rating** 93 **To** 2018 $42
       Reserve Adelaide Hills Pinot Noir 2007 Rating 92 **To** 2014 $33
       Adelaide Hills Riesling 2008 Rating 90 **To** 2014 $22
       Adelaide Hills Semillon 2008 Rating 90 **To** 2015 $22
       Adelaide Hills Sauvignon Blanc 2009 Rating 90 **To** 2011 $22
       Adelaide Hills Cabernet Franc 2006 Rating 90 **To** 2016 $26

ρρρρ   **Adelaide Hills Cabernet Merlot 2003 Rating** 88 **To** 2012 $25

Leasingham   ★★★★★

PO Box 57, Clare, SA 5453 **Region** Clare Valley
T 1800 088 711 **F** (08) 8392 2202 **www**.leasingham-wines.com.au **Open** Not
Winemaker Paul Lapsley **Est.** 1893 **Cases** NFP
In 2009 CWA sold a large part of its Clare vineyard holdings to Tim Adams and, so far
unable to sell the Leasingham winery, has closed it. CWA still retains the Provis Vineyard as its
viticultural headquarters, and the Leasingham wines are made in the CWA group winery in
McLaren Vale. Exports to all major markets.

ρρρρρ **Individual Vineyard Watervale Riesling 2008** A toasty bouquet, with fresh
       lemon fruit and slatey minerality on show; the palate is fresh on entry, and builds
       to a powerful crescendo of fruit and almost chewy, chalky acidity to conclude;
       serious in intent and delivery. Screwcap. 12% alc. **Rating** 95 **To** 2020 $48 BE
       Classic Clare Riesling 2006 A toasted lemon curd bouquet with fresh lime
       playing a supporting role; quite a rich palate, steely and dry, with a long, toasty and
       complex finish to the fruit. Screwcap. 12.6% alc. **Rating** 95 **To** 2016 $39 BE

Classic Clare Cabernet 2005 Very powerful and full-bodied, with a long life ahead; the power comes from its great length, or is it the other way around? Either way, strong blackcurrant fruit has sidelights of spice, cedar and dark chocolate, the tannins lining up in regimental support. Cork. 13.5% alc. **Rating** 95 **To** 2025 $55

✪ **Bin 7 Clare Valley Riesling 2009** A racy bouquet of freshly squeezed limes and green apple; the palate is full of zesty fruit, and is drawn out to a long and even conclusion by fine rapier-like acidity. Screwcap. 12.5% alc. **Rating** 94 **To** 2025 $23 BE

Classic Clare Riesling 2008 A highly aromatic and intense bouquet, leads into a strong palate with spice and mineral notes; a very dry, almost savoury, finish, which lingers in the mouth. Gold medal National Wine Show '08. Screwcap. 10.9% alc. **Rating** 94 **To** 2018 $30

Classic Clare Shiraz 2007 Vibrant hue; quite prominent oak on the bouquet, with blackberry, licorice and a little mint in the background; the palate is fleshy and very firm, with the plentiful tannins showing roundness to them; long, supple and poised on the finish. Cork. 13.7% alc. **Rating** 94 **To** 2020 $57 BE

✪ **Bin 61 Clare Valley Shiraz 2007** Bright colour; the fragrant bouquet offers spice, dark chocolate and berry fruit; unexpectedly fresh and lively on the palate, with well-weighted tannins and oak. Screwcap. 13.5% alc. **Rating** 94 **To** 2020 $26

✪ **Bin 56 Clare Valley Cabernet Malbec 2008** A label with a rich history, the '71 was a beautiful wine drinking well into the '90s (cork permitting). Bright crimson-red, the black fruits of the cabernet fleshed out by the confit fruit of the malbec. A sentimental vote, perhaps, but worth it. Screwcap. 13.9% alc. **Rating** 94 **To** 2023 $26

Classic Clare Sparkling Shiraz 2004 Engaging red mousse, with deep purple beneath; a rich and savoury bouquet of fresh blackberry, mint and a touch of leathery complexity; mouth filling and savoury, with plenty of structure lurking beneath the ample fruit; dark, complex and a profound example of the style. Cork. 14% alc. **Rating** 94 **To** 2018 $55 BE

Leayton Estate
★★★☆

PO Box 325, Healesville, Vic 3777 **Region** Yarra Valley
T (03) 5962 3042 **F** (03) 5962 4674 **www.**leaytonestate.com.au **Open** Not
Winemaker Graham Stephens **Est.** 1997 **Cases** 280 **Vyds** 1.6 ha
Yet another partnership between medicine and winemaking: Dr Graham Stephens is a GP in Healesville, and together with wife Lynda, has established a vineyard (split evenly between chardonnay and pinot noir) and a supplementary olive plantation on a 12-ha property west of Healesville. Two-thirds of the grapes are sold to Sergio Carlei, and one-third retained for the Leayton Estate label. Graham is still working full-time as a doctor, but intends to gradually wind back his medical hours and spend more time in the vineyard and winemaking.

🍷🍷🍷🍷🍷 **Yarra Valley Chardonnay 2008** Light straw-green; hand-picked and basket-pressed, then nine months in French oak; light-bodied and minerally, the varietal fruit expression is neatly controlled given its Chablis style. ProCork. 12.9% alc. **Rating** 90 **To** 2012 $20

Leconfield
★★★★☆

Riddoch Highway, Coonawarra, SA 5263 **Region** Coonawarra
T (08) 8737 2326 **F** (08) 8737 2285 **www.**leconfieldwines.com **Open** Mon–Fri 9–4.30, w'ends & public hols 11–4.30
Winemaker Paul Gordon, Tim Bailey (Assistant) **Est.** 1974 **Cases** 20 000 **Vyds** 44.5 ha
Sydney Hamilton purchased the unplanted property that was to become Leconfield in 1974, having worked in the family wine business for over 30 years until his retirement in the mid-'50s. When he acquired the property and set about planting it, he was 76, and reluctantly bowed to family pressure to sell Leconfield to nephew Richard in '81. Richard progressively increased the vineyards to their present level, over 75% to cabernet sauvignon, for long the winery's speciality. Exports to the UK, Japan, Malaysia, Hong Kong, Singapore and NZ.

ŸŸŸŸŸ **Coonawarra Cabernet Sauvignon 2008** Dense purple-red; has similar power and intensity to other '08 Coonawarra cabernets, with a classy tension between rich black fruits and more savoury/earthy notes. Gold medal Sydney Wine Show '10. Screwcap. 14.5% alc. **Rating** 94 **To** 2023 $30.95

ŸŸŸŸŸ **Coonawarra Chardonnay 2008** **Rating** 93 **To** 2018 $24.95
McLaren Vale Shiraz 2008 **Rating** 93 **To** 2023 $24.95
Coonawarra Merlot 2008 **Rating** 92 **To** 2018 $24.95
Coonawarra Cabernet Sauvignon 2007 **Rating** 90 **To** 2017 $30.95

Leeuwin Estate ★★★★★

Stevens Road, Margaret River, WA 6285 **Region** Margaret River
T (08) 9759 0000 **F** (08) 9759 0001 **www**.leeuwinestate.com.au **Open** 7 days 10–5
Winemaker Paul Atwood **Est.** 1974 **Cases** 60 000 **Vyds** 121 ha
This outstanding winery and vineyard is owned by the Horgan family, with parents Denis and Tricia at the helm, son Justin as general manager. The Art Series Chardonnay is, in my opinion, Australia's finest example, based on the wines of the last 28 vintages. The decision to move to screwcap in 2004 brought a large smile to the faces of those who understand just how superbly the wine ages, unless sabotaged by sporadic oxidation (caused by cork). The large estate plantings, coupled with strategic purchases of grapes from other growers, provide the base for high-quality Art Series Cabernet Sauvignon and Shiraz; a hugely successful, quick-selling Art Series Riesling and Sauvignon Blanc; and lesser priced wines such as Prelude Chardonnay and Siblings Sauvignon Blanc Semillon. Exports to all major markets.

ŸŸŸŸŸ **Art Series Margaret River Sauvignon Blanc 2009** Pale straw-green; is an exceptionally fine and elegant rendition of sauvignon blanc, falling largely on the nettle, herb and snow pea side, but also capturing a delicate waft of passionfruit and stone fruit; perfectly balanced acidity. Screwcap. 12.5% alc. **Rating** 96 **To** 2012 $32

Art Series Margaret River Chardonnay 2007 Pale, bright straw-green; fragrant grapefruit, melon and white peach aromas, the oak subtle and integrated, are followed by an exceptionally intense and long palate, the alcohol lost in the sea of flavour. Screwcap. 14.5% alc. **Rating** 96 **To** 2022 $96

✪ **Siblings Margaret River Sauvignon Blanc Semillon 2009** A 62/38 blend, the varieties seamlessly joined in a never-ending circle of herb, grass, citrus and lemongrass, the finish alluringly fresh and crisp. Screwcap. 12.5% alc. **Rating** 94 **To** 2012 $24

Prelude Vineyards Margaret River Chardonnay 2008 A second label equal to most producers' best, although the price (inevitably) reflects the quality; fragrant white peach and grapefruit aromas and flavours drive the wine, having soaked up the barrel ferment oak in the process; long, complete and perfectly balanced. Screwcap. 14.5% alc. **Rating** 94 **To** 2018 $33

Art Series Margaret River Shiraz 2008 Light, bright crimson; the fragrant bouquet of spicy red fruits is closely tracked on the light- to medium-bodied palate that is all about finesse, line and length, the red cherry fruit with spicy nuances, the oak reserved. Screwcap. 13.5% alc. **Rating** 94 **To** 2016 $38

Art Series Margaret River Cabernet Sauvignon 2005 A super-elegant and refined wine, with few of the flourishes that many of its regional counterparts exhibit; the fragrant, dark fruits of the bouquet are precisely replayed on the palate with its sombre flavours and tannins. Screwcap. 13.5% alc. **Rating** 94 **To** 2030 $60

ŸŸŸŸŸ ✪ **Siblings Margaret River Shiraz 2008** A touch more purple in colour to the Art Series; interesting wine, with more black fruit characters and more depth, but not so much finesse perhaps; should develop well and is a bargain in the Leeuwin context. Screwcap. 13.5% alc. **Rating** 92 **To** 2018 $24

✪ **Siblings Margaret River Shiraz 2007** Bright crimson-purple; lively and zesty red fruits run through the bouquet and medium-bodied palate; attractive touches of spice add to the appeal and length of the palate. Screwcap. 13% alc. **Rating** 92 **To** 2017 $24

Prelude Vineyards Margaret River Cabernet Merlot 2005 **Rating** 92
To 2015 $30
Art Series Margaret River Riesling 2009 **Rating** 91 To 2020 $23

ΨΨΨΨ   Art Series Margaret River Riesling 2008 **Rating** 89 To 2012 $25

Lengs & Cooter ★★★★
24 Lindsay Terrace, Belair, SA 5042 **Region** Adelaide Zone
T (08) 8278 3998 **F** (08) 8278 3998 **www**.lengscooter.com.au **Open** Not
Winemaker Colin Cooter & Contract **Est.** 1993 **Cases** 3000
Karel Lengs and Colin Cooter began making wine as a hobby in the early 1980s. Each had (and has) a full-time occupation outside the wine industry, so it was all strictly for fun. One thing led to another, and although they still possess neither vineyards nor what might truly be described as a winery, the wines have graduated to big-boy status, winning gold medals at national wine shows and receiving critical acclaim from writers across Australia. The wines come from McLaren Vale and the Clare Valley. Exports to the UK, the US, Canada, Singapore, Malaysia and Japan.

ΨΨΨΨΨ   **Watervale Riesling 2009** Good colour; lime and bath talc bouquet; plenty of
✪   weight and richness, with drying acidity cleaning up the palate. Screwcap. 12% alc. **Rating** 90 To 2016 $18 BE
Old Vines Clare Valley Shiraz 2005 Bright colour; the evolution is evident, with turned earth, leather and warm blackberry fruit on offer; the palate is vibrant and savoury, with earthy notes to finish. Screwcap. 14.5% alc. **Rating** 90 To 2015 $26 BE
Swinton McLaren Vale Cabernet Sauvignon 2005 Oaky and completely unevolved, with cassis and toast the dominant factors; full-bodied and impressively structured, there is a healthy dose of fruit to go with the generous level of oak. Screwcap. 14.5% alc. **Rating** 90 To 2020 $24 BE

Lenton Brae Wines ★★★★★
Wilyabrup Valley, Margaret River, WA 6285 **Region** Margaret River
T (08) 9755 6255 **F** (08) 9755 6268 **www**.lentonbrae.com **Open** 7 days 10–6
Winemaker Edward Tomlinson **Est.** 1983 **Cases** NFP **Vyds** 9 ha
Former architect and town planner Bruce Tomlinson built a strikingly beautiful winery (now heritage listed by the Shire of Busselton), which is now in the hands of winemaker son Edward, who consistently makes elegant wines in classic Margaret River style. Exports to the UK, Canada, Singapore, Vietnam and Hong Kong.

ΨΨΨΨΨ   **Margaret River Semillon Sauvignon Blanc 2009** A particularly fragrant bouquet and elegant palate; in Lenton Brae style, the fruit components contributed by each variety flow seamlessly into each other, grass, citrus, gooseberry and passionfruit all quietly murmuring. A wine with cellaring potential. Screwcap. 12% alc. **Rating** 94 To 2013 $24
Wilyabrup Semillon Sauvignon Blanc 2009 Light straw-green; a 60/40 blend, barrel-fermentation and maturation (used for the first time) in new French oak has added to, not detracted from, a wine with a proud track record, citrus and mineral flavours still foremost on a long, crisp palate. Screwcap. 12.5% alc. **Rating** 94 To 2014 $45
✪   **Wilyabrup Semillon Sauvignon Blanc 2008** Somewhat richer and fuller-bodied than prior vintages, flavour achieved without reliance on alcohol; this is an unashamedly French oak barrel-fermented and matured style in classic White Bordeaux style. Screwcap. 12% alc. **Rating** 94 To 2013 $35
✪   **Margaret River Cabernet Merlot 2008** Crimson-purple; a pure and fragrant bouquet, then a vibrantly fresh palate, with redcurrant, blackcurrant, cherry and raspberry flavours, the finish lingering for a long time. Screwcap. 13.5% alc. **Rating** 94 To 2023 $24

ΨΨΨΨΨ   **Margaret River Shiraz 2008** **Rating** 93 To 2018 $40

Leo Buring   ★★★★★

Sturt Highway, Nuriootpa, Sa 5355 **Region** Eden Valley/Clare Valley
T 1300 651 650 **www**.leoburing.com.au **Open** Not
Winemaker Peter Munro **Est.** 1931 **Cases** NFP
Australia's foremost producer of rieslings over a 35-year period, with a rich legacy left by former winemaker John Vickery. After veering away from its core business with other varietal wines, it has now been refocused as a specialist riesling producer. The top of the range is the Leonay Eden Valley Riesling under a changing DW bin no. (DWL for 2008, DWM for '09 etc), supported by Clare Valley Riesling and Eden Valley Riesling at significantly lower prices, and expanding its wings to Tasmania and WA.

ΨΨΨΨΨ **Medium Sweet Eden Valley Riesling 2009** The wheel turns full circle with
✪   this wine, recalling the John Vickery spatlese rieslings of the early 1970s; no-holds-barred aromas and flavours of lime and green apple with excellent acidity. Screwcap. 10.5% alc. **Rating** 94 **To** 2019 $22
        Leonay Riesling 2008 DWL17 Green-quartz; has more on offer at this stage than '09 DWM18, doubtless in part due to the extra year in bottle, but also to the clear granny smith apple aromas and flavours, and lingering lime/citrus acidity on the long finish. High Eden. Screwcap. 11.5% alc. **Rating** 94 **To** 2018 $40

ΨΨΨΨΨ **Leonay Riesling 2009 Rating** 93 **To** 2020 $40

Lerida Estate   ★★★★★

The Vineyards, Old Federal Highway, Lake George, NSW 2581 **Region** Canberra District
T (02) 6295 6640 **F** (02) 6295 6676 **www**.leridaestate.com **Open** 7 days 10–5
Winemaker Malcolm Burdett **Est.** 1999 **Cases** 5000 **Vyds** 19.42 ha
Lerida Estate owes a great deal to the inspiration of Dr Edgar Riek, planted as it is immediately to the south of the Lake George vineyard. The initial plantings of 7.4 ha were dominated by pinot noir; here, too, Edgar Riek was the inspiration. The vineyard has now more than doubled, with 9.58 ha of pinot noir, and smaller quantities of pinot gris, chardonnay, shiraz, merlot, cabernet franc and viognier. The Glenn Murcutt–designed winery, barrel room, cellar door and café complex has spectacular views over Lake George. Lerida Estate won four trophies, and 56 gold, silver and bronze medals in the 2009 wine show season. Equally remarkable is the fact that every wine entered in wine shows in '09 won at least one medal.

ΨΨΨΨΨ **Canberra District Shiraz 2008** Crimson-purple; very good example of cool-
✪   grown shiraz, with a spice, cracked pepper and black cherry bouquet; the medium-bodied palate has immaculate length, texture, line and balance. Screwcap. 14% alc. **Rating** 95 **To** 2023 $28
        Josephine Lake George Pinot Noir 2008 Some first stage colour development; an aromatic and spicy bouquet, then a palate with excellent drive and length, offering spicy/savoury nuances woven through black cherry and plum fruit. Screwcap. 14.1% alc. **Rating** 94 **To** 2014 $59.50
        Lake George Shiraz Viognier 2008 Bright hue; the viognier component works its magic on the colour, bouquet and palate, lifting the aromas and investing the plum and black cherry fruit with a juicy character offset by superfine tannins. Screwcap. 13.9% alc. **Rating** 94 **To** 2020 $59.50

ΨΨΨΨΨ **Lake George Pinot Gris 2009 Rating** 93 **To** 2011 $28
✪   **Lake George Pinot Rose 2009** Very pale magenta; a fragrant strawberry bouquet, then a brightly flavoured palate with particularly good length and mouthfeel. Screwcap. 11.2% alc. **Rating** 93 **To** 2011 $18
        Lake George Chardonnay 2008 Rating 92 **To** 2015 $25
        Lake George Viognier 2009 Rating 91 **To** 2013 $28
        Cullerin Lake George Pinot Noir 2008 Rating 90 **To** 2014 $35 BE

ΨΨΨΨ **Lake George Unwooded Chardonnay 2009 Rating** 89 **To** 2013 $19
       Lake George Merlot Cabernet Franc 2008 Rating 89 **To** 2015 $35 BE

Lethbridge Wines   ★★★★★

74 Burrows Road, Lethbridge, Vic 3222 **Region** Geelong
T (03) 5281 7279 **F** (03) 5281 7221 **www.**lethbridgewines.com **Open** Thurs–Sun &
public hols10.30–5, or by appt
Winemaker Ray Nadeson, Maree Collis **Est.** 1996 **Cases** 2500
Lethbridge was founded by scientists Ray Nadeson, Maree Collis and Adrian Thomas. In
Ray's words, 'Our belief is that the best wines express the unique character of special places.'
As well as understanding the importance of terroir, the partners have built a unique straw-bale
winery, designed for its ability to recreate the controlled environment of cellars and caves in
Europe. Winemaking is no less ecological: hand-picking, indigenous yeast fermentations, small
open fermenters, pigeage (foot-stamping) and minimal handling of the wines throughout
the maturation process are all part and parcel of the highly successful Lethbridge approach.
Nadeson also has a special touch with chardonnay, and has a successful contract winemaking limb to the business.

ΨΨΨΨΨ **Dr Nadeson Portland Riesling 2009** From the Henty region, seldom
✪   mentioned in dispatches when riesling is discussed, despite Crawford River and
            Seppelt Drumborg being among Australia's best. This is made with a deliberate
            touch of sweetness in Mosel style, the sweetness balanced by awesome drive and
            acidity; 30 years won't seriously challenge it. Screwcap. 11.5% alc. **Rating** 97
            To 2039 $30
✪   **Geelong Shiraz 2008** Strong purple-crimson; the complex bouquet and palate
            march in unison with an array of spice, pepper and blackberry aromas and flavours;
            the texture of the palate is outstanding, giving the wine wonderful line and length.
            Screwcap. 14% alc. **Rating** 96 To 2023 $35
            Chardonnay 2008 Bright straw-green; the bouquet encompasses fruit, cashew
            and oak, but the real character of the wine only makes itself manifest on the
            mid-palate through to the vibrant citrussy finish; here fresh, crisp nectarine fruit
            establishes the platform for the wine. Screwcap. 13.5% alc. **Rating** 94 To 2016 $35
            Geelong Pinot Noir 2008 Light, slightly developed colour; spicy, savoury notes
            and sweet red fruit flavours are evenly balanced on both bouquet and palate, the
            finish long and clean. A wine of finesse, but don't wait too long. Screwcap. 14% alc.
            Rating 94 To 2013 $35

ΨΨΨΨΨ **Allegra Geelong Chardonnay 2007 Rating** 93 To 2015 $55
            Pinot Gris 2009 Rating 93 To 2013 $30
            C'est la Gris Pinot Gris 2009 Rating 91 To 2011 $25
            Que Syrah Syrah Geelong Shiraz 2008 Rating 91 To 2016 $25
            Geelong Shiraz 2007 Rating 91 To 2016 $35

Leura Park Estate   ★★★★★

1400 Portarlington Road, Curlewis, Vic 3222 **Region** Geelong
T (03) 5253 3180 **F** (03) 5248 3466 **www.**leuraparkestate.com.au **Open** W'ends &
public hols 10.30–5, 7 days Jan, or by appt
Winemaker Stephen Webber, Ray Nadeson **Est.** 1995 **Cases** 4000 **Vyds** 15.7 ha
Leura Park Estate's vineyard, planted to chardonnay, pinot noir, pinot gris, sauvignon blanc
and shiraz, was established in 1995. New owners David and Lyndsay Sharp are committed to
maintaining minimal interference in the vineyard, and have expanded the estate-grown wine
range (Sauvignon Blanc, Pinot Gris, Chardonnay, Pinot Noir and Shiraz) to include Vintage
Grand Cuvee (Pinot Noir Chardonnay). The next step was the erection of an onsite winery
prior to the 2010 vintage, leading to increased production.

ΨΨΨΨΨ **Limited Release Block 1 Reserve Chardonnay 2008** Brilliant colour, green-
            tinted; has zest and drive from the outset through to the finish; nectarine, white
            peach and grapefruit are the principal drivers, oak contributing more to texture
            than flavour. Screwcap. 13.5% alc. **Rating** 95 To 2018 $32

❂   Bellarine Peninsula Sauvignon Blanc 2009 Bright and light colour; a wine that bursts into song on its very intense and long palate, the fruit flavours exactly pitched at perfect ripeness, with citrus, passionfruit and herb running through to the lingering finish. Screwcap. 12% alc. **Rating** 94 **To** 2012 $19.50

♟♟♟♟♀   Bellarine Peninsula Chardonnay 2008 **Rating** 92 **To** 2015 $24.50
Bellarine Peninsula Pinot Noir 2008 **Rating** 92 **To** 2014 $28.95
Shiraz 2008 **Rating** 90 **To** 2017 $28.95
Limited Release Yublong Cabernet Sauvignon 2008 **Rating** 90
To 2016 $28.95

♟♟♟♟   Voix de la Terre Reserve Sauvignon Blanc 2008 **Rating** 89 **To** 2011 $21.50
Vintage Grande Cuvee Pinot Chardonnay 2008 **Rating** 89 **To** 2012 $24.95

Lewood Estate   ★★★

80 Shotton Road, Mt Eliza, Vic 3930 **Region** Mornington Peninsula
T (03) 5975 6912 **F** (03) 5975 6912 **Open** By appt
Winemaker Gavin Perry **Est.** 1996 **Cases** 300 **Vyds** 2 ha
Robert and Dale Lee were inspired to plant shiraz on their property after attending a wine dinner at which Port Phillip Estate Cabernet Sauvignon and Shiraz were served. To the Lees, the Shiraz stood out as quite special, and they were able to obtain 350 cuttings from Port Phillip Estate, which were planted in September 1996. Experimental Shirazs made from these vines in 1999 and 2000 both won medals in the amateur winemaking classes at the Victorian Wines Show, which encouraged the Lees to expand the vineyard by taking further cuttings from the Port Phillip–sourced shiraz. Well down the track, 25 of the original cuttings were found to be merlot, and, quite accidentally, the 1.5 ha of shiraz is accompanied by 0.5 ha of merlot. They thus have two varietal releases, and a Rose for good measure.

♟♟♟♟   Luella's Mornington Peninsula Classic White 2007 Crisp, fresh and moderately minerally, its citrus/lime characters from the riesling, the dominant partner in this three-varietal blend; had good length and thrust. Screwcap. 11.3% alc. **Rating** 88 **To** 2014 $15

🍇 Liffey Valley Vineyard   ★★★

191 Myrtle Creek Road, Liffey, Tas 7301 (postal) **Region** Northern Tasmania
T (03) 6397 3470 **Open** Not
Winemaker Bass Fine Wines (Guy Wagner) **Est.** 1999 **Cases** 350 **Vyds** 2 ha
Caryl and Ian Cairns own what may well be the greenest vineyard in the world – greenest in terms of the overall purity of the site. It is situated at an altitude of 300 m on the eastern foothills of Tasmania's Cluan Tier, surrounded by native forest and overlooking the beautiful Liffey Valley. Protected by mountains and escarpments to the south and west, and open to the north and east, it escapes most damaging winds and experiences few severe frosts. Warm summer days and cool nights see vintage in late April or early May. The property has been farmed using organic and biodynamic methods since 1991, and the soils have no chemical history. Cape Grim (measured as the world's purest air) is to windward, and the Cairns are the first users of gravity-fed water from a pristine mountain stream. The wines are made with the least amount of sulphur dioxide needed to avoid barrel spoilage.

♟♟♟♟   Bye's Pinot Noir 2008 Light, clear colour; a light-bodied pinot with savoury/foresty/spicy nuances on both bouquet and palate; while the wine is not powerful, it does have length. Organic. Screwcap. 13% alc. **Rating** 88 **To** 2013 $30

Light's View/Pure Vision Organic Wines ★★★★

PO Box 258, Virginia, SA 5120 **Region** Adelaide Plains
T 0412 800 875 **F** (08) 8380 9501 **www.lightsviewwines.com.au** **Open** Not
Winemaker David Norman, Jim Irvine, Ken Carypidis **Est.** 2001 **Cases** 12 000

The Carypidis family runs two brands: Pure Vision has 15 ha of certified organically grown grapes, and there's a much larger Light's View (www.lightsviewwines.com.au) planting of 54 ha of conventionally grown grapes. If you are to grow grapes under a certified organic regime, it makes the task much easier if the region is warm to hot and dry, conditions unsuitable for botrytis and downy mildew. You are still left with weed growth (no herbicides are allowed) and powdery mildew (sulphur sprays are permitted) but the overall task is a much easier one. The Adelaide Plains, where Pure Vision's vineyard is situated, is such a region, and owner Ken Carypidis has been clever enough to secure the services of Jim Irvine as co-winemaker. Exports to the US, Canada and China.

ΨΨΨΨΨ **Nature's Step Wild Ferment Chardonnay 2009** Fresh and aromatic, with nectarine and citrus providing tension to the bouquet and crisp palate; bright acidity to close; no sign of oak. Screwcap. 12.5% alc. **Rating** 91 **To** 2013 $10
Nature's Step Wild Ferment Rose 2009 Intriguingly, made from early-picked petit verdot, hardly the variety one would first think of, nor imagine giving attractive strawberry and raspberry fruit flavours on the long palate. Screwcap. 12.7% alc. **Rating** 91 **To** 2011 $10

Nature's Step Wild Ferment Sauvignon Blanc 2009 Unexpectedly vibrant and pungent given the vintage; has a zesty, almost crystalline palate, minerally acidity to the fore, touches of lemon and capsicum attesting to the variety. Screwcap. 11% alc. **Rating** 90 **To** 2011 $10

ΨΨΨΨ **Pure Vision Organic Shiraz 2007 Rating** 87 **To** 2013 $18

Lightfoot & Sons ★★★★☆

Myrtle Point Vineyard, 717 Calulu Road, Bairnsdale, Vic 3875 (postal) **Region** Gippsland **T** (03) 5156 9205 **www**.lightfootwines.com **Open** Not
Winemaker Alastair Butt, Tom Lightfoot **Est.** 1995 **Cases** 2000 **Vyds** 30 ha
Brian and Helen Lightfoot have established pinot noir, shiraz, chardonnay, cabernet sauvignon and merlot, the lion's share to pinot noir and shiraz. The soil bears a striking resemblance to that of Coonawarra, with terra rossa over limestone. The vines are irrigated courtesy of a licence allowing the Lightfoots to pump water from the Mitchell River, and most of the grapes are sold (as originally planned) to other Vic winemakers. With the arrival of Alastair Butt (formerly of Brokenwood and Seville Estate), supported by son Tom, production has increased, and may well rise further. Second son Rob has also come on board with 10 years' experience in sales and marketing.

ΨΨΨΨΨ **Myrtle Point Vineyard Chardonnay 2008** Bright green-straw; a particularly attractive wine, marrying nutty/cashew barrel ferment characters with elegant nectarine and white peach fruit, citrus-tinged acidity to close. Screwcap. 12.5% alc. Rating 94 To 2014 $19

ΨΨΨΨΨ **Myrtle Point Vineyard Cabernet Sauvignon 2006** Good colour; a wine with abundant personality in a cedary/savoury mode, texture and length of flavour its strong points; cassis and mint are the flavour drivers. Screwcap. 14.9% alc. Rating 90 To 2014 $19

ΨΨΨΨ **Myrtle Point Vineyard Shiraz 2006 Rating** 89 **To** 2015 $19
Myrtle Point Vineyard Pinot Noir 2009 Rating 88 **To** 2014 $24.90

Lillian ★★★★

Box 174, Pemberton, WA 6260 **Region** Pemberton
T (08) 9776 0193 **F** (08) 9776 0193 **Open** Not
Winemaker John Brocksopp **Est.** 1993 **Cases** 450 **Vyds** 3.2 ha
Long-serving (and continuing consultant) viticulturist to Leeuwin Estate, John Brocksopp established 2.8 ha of the Rhône trio of marsanne, roussanne and viognier, and 0.4 ha of shiraz. The varietal mix may seem à la mode, but it in fact comes from John's early experience working for Seppelt at Barooga in NSW, and his formative years in the Barossa Valley. Exports to the UK and Japan.

ŶŶŶŶŶ Pemberton Viognier 2008 A rich and hedonistic style, full of apricot flesh, candied pear and plenty of spice; thickly textured, with a touch of bitterness providing contrast; luscious, but best consumed early. Screwcap. 14% alc. **Rating** 90 **To** 2013 $26 BE

Pemberton Marsanne Roussanne 2008 Honeysuckle and white flower bouquet, with a savoury undercurrent; the palate is fleshy and generous, with layers of stone fruits and melon coming to the fore; clean and complex to conclude. Screwcap. 14.5% alc. **Rating** 90 **To** 2014 $19.20 BE

Lillydale Estate   ★★★★★

45 Davross Court, Seville, Vic 3139 **Region** Yarra Valley
T (02) 9722 1299 **F** (02) 9722 1260 **www**.mcwilliamswinesgroup.com **Open** Not
Winemaker Russell Cody **Est.** 1975 **Cases** NFP **Vyds** 13.4 ha
Lillydale Estate was acquired by McWilliam's in 1994. The major part of the production comes from the two estate vineyards, Morning Light and Sunnyside, planted in 1976. The names have been given by McWilliam's: the former is that of the ship that brought Samuel McWilliam from Ireland to Melbourne in 1857, and Sunnyside is the name of the first winery and vineyard he established at Corowa in NSW in 1877. The estate production is bolstered by contract-grown fruit from other growers in the Valley. Exports to Fiji and Singapore.

ŶŶŶŶŶ Yarra Valley Chardonnay 2008 Light straw-green; a deliciously understated style, the typical length of Yarra Valley chardonnay doing the talking; white peach and grapefruit to the fore, fine French oak in the background. Screwcap. 13% alc. **Rating** 94 **To** 2016 $27

Yarra Valley Pinot Noir 2008 Clear, vivid crimson hue; pure, light, bright red berry aromas, then a bright and clear palate, again with red cherry and strawberry fruit. Gold medal Sydney Wine Show '10. Screwcap. 13.5% alc. **Rating** 94 **To** 2015 $27

Lillypilly Estate   ★★★★☆

Lillypilly Road, Leeton, NSW 2705 **Region** Riverina
T (02) 6953 4069 **F** (02) 6953 4980 **www**.lillypilly.com **Open** Mon–Sat 10–5.30,
Sun by appt
Winemaker Robert Fiumara **Est.** 1982 **Cases** 15 000 **Vyds** 27.8 ha
Botrytised white wines are by far the best offering from Lillypilly, with the Noble Muscat of Alexandria unique to the winery; these wines have both style and intensity of flavour and can age well. However, table wine quality is always steady. Exports to the UK, the US, Canada, Korea and China.

ŶŶŶŶŶ Family Reserve Noble Blend 2002 Glowing gold; has matured with more grace than many in this category, winning double gold medals at the Sydney International Wine Competition '06; notes of cumquat and caramel are balanced by good acidity. Screwcap. 12.5% alc. **Rating** 94 **To** 2012 $38.50

ŶŶŶŶŶ Noble Harvest 2006 **Rating** 92 **To** 2012 $18.50

ŶŶŶŶ Shiraz 2007 **Rating** 87 **To** 2012 $16.50

Limbic   ★★★★☆

295 Morrison Road, Pakenham Upper, Vic 3810 **Region** Port Phillip Zone
T (03) 5942 7723 **F** (03) 5942 7723 **www**.limbicwines.com.au **Open** By appt
Winemaker Michael Pullar **Est.** 1997 **Cases** 600 **Vyds** 7 ha
Jennifer and Michael Pullar have established a vineyard on the hills between Yarra Valley and Gippsland, overlooking the Mornington Peninsula and Westernport Bay (thus entitled only to the Port Phillip Zone GI). They have planted pinot noir, chardonnay and sauvignon blanc, increasingly using organic and thereafter biodynamic practices. 'Limbic' is the word for a network of neural pathways in the brain that link smell, taste and emotion.

ŶŶŶŶŶ Sauvignon Blanc 2009 A fragrant bouquet of passionfruit and citrus, then a
✪   vibrant palate with citrus to the fore, the finish long and crisp; some very good
          white wines made despite the vintage. Screwcap. 13% alc. Rating 94 To 2011 $20

ŶŶŶŶŶ Chardonnay 2008 Rating 91 To 2014 $30

Lindemans (Coonawarra/Padthaway) ★★★★★

Coonawarra Wine Gallery, Riddoch Highway, Coonawarra, SA 5263 **Region** Coonawarra
T (08) 8737 3250 **F** (08) 8737 3231 www.lindemans.com **Open** 7 days 10–5
Winemaker Brett Sharpe **Est.** 1908 **Cases** NFP
Lindemans' Limestone Coast vineyards are of increasing significance because of the move
toward regional identity in the all-important export markets, which has led to the emergence
of a range of regional/varietal labels. After a quiet period, the wines are on the march again.
Exports to the UK, the US, Canada and NZ.

ŶŶŶŶŶ Limestone Ridge Vineyard Shiraz Cabernet 2008 Deep purple-crimson; a
          particularly luscious and rich Limestone Ridge, flush with blackcurrant, blackberry
          and licorice fruit, the full-bodied palate weaving positive oak and ripe tannins into
          its excellent texture. Screwcap. 14.5% alc. Rating 96 To 2030 $55
          St George Coonawarra Cabernet Sauvignon 2006 Very good depth to
          the colour; a died-in-the-wool classic Coonawarra cabernet, with both bouquet
          and palate exuding blackcurrant and blueberry fruit sustained and complexed by
          persistent but silky tannins and judicious use of French oak (70% new). Screwcap.
          14% alc. Rating 96 To 2031 $55
          Limestone Ridge Vineyard Shiraz Cabernet 2006 Holding hue well,
          still bright and clear crimson; unequivocally good wine, with blackberry and
          blackcurrant fruit interwoven with fine but persistent tannins and positive
          American oak. Gold medals at Adelaide Wine Show '08 and Queensland Wine
          Show. Screwcap. 14% alc. Rating 94 To 2021 $55
          Pyrus Cabernet Sauvignon Cabernet Franc Merlot 2006 Slightly lighter
          and more developed colour to a wine that is more savoury and lighter bodied than
          the St George; spicy red fruits are accompanied by a touch of Coonawarra earth;
          the line and length are good; 100% French oak (80% new). Screwcap. 14% alc.
          Rating 94 To 2021 $55

Lindemans (Karadoc) ★★★

Edey Road, Karadoc, Vic 3496 **Region** Murray Darling
T (03) 5051 3285 **F** (03) 5051 3390 www.lindemans.com **Open** 7 days 10–4.30
Winemaker Wayne Falkenberg, Hayden Donohue **Est.** 1974 **Cases** NFP
Now the production centre for all the Lindemans and Leo Buring wines, with the exception
of special lines made in Coonawarra. The very large winery allows all-important economies
of scale, and is the major processing centre for Foster's beverage wine sector (casks, flagons and
low-priced bottles). Exports to all major markets.

ŶŶŶŶ   Early Harvest Semillon Sauvignon Blanc 2009 The early picking has worked
✪   well; the suite of aromas and flavours are delicate, all varietal (grass, herb, citrus,
          tropical) and are sufficiently intense to hold interest in a food context. Screwcap.
          8.5% alc. Rating 89 To 2011 $14
✪   Bin 95 Sauvignon Blanc 2009 Fights the good fight against the lower priced
          sector of the Marlborough invasion, albeit in a low key minerally mode that won't
          frighten the horses; freshness is its main virtue. Screwcap. 12% alc. Rating 87
          To 2011 $10
✪   Bin 65 Chardonnay 2009 Yellow-green hues have already developed; a
          mainstream commercial chardonnay with ample stone fruit flavours that do not
          rely on sweetness nor oak; drink now. Screwcap. 13% alc. Rating 87 To 2011 $10
✪   Early Harvest Rose 2009 Light shocking pink; Lindemans was an early mover
          in the early harvest stakes; citrus raspberry flavours; close your eyes and you would
          think it was a tangy white wine. Screwcap. 8.5% alc. Rating 87 To 2011 $14

❂   **Bin 50 Shiraz 2009** Vibrant colour; juicy blueberry and spice bouquet; medium-bodied, spicy, fresh and focused, with the impression of sweet fruit to conclude. Screwcap. 13.5% alc. **Rating** 87 **To** 2013 $10 BE

Lindenderry at Red Hill ★★★★☆
142 Arthurs Seat Road, Red Hill, Vic 3937 **Region** Mornington Peninsula
T (03) 5989 2933 **F** (03) 5989 2936 **www.**lindenderry.com.au **Open** W'ends 11–5
Winemaker Paringa Estate **Est.** 1999 **Cases** 2000 **Vyds** 3.35 ha
Lindenderry at Red Hill is a sister operation to Lancemore Hill in the Macedon Ranges and Lindenwarrah at Milawa. It has a 5-star country house hotel, conference facilities, a function area, day spa and à la carte restaurant on 16 ha of park-like gardens, but also has a little over 3 ha of immaculately maintained vineyards, planted equally to pinot noir and chardonnay 15 years ago. The wines are made by the famed Lindsay McCall, using similar techniques to those he uses for his Paringa Estate wines.

♆♆♆♆♆ **Mornington Peninsula Pinot Noir 2008** Bright, light red-crimson; the fragrant bouquet ranges through red berry fruits and oak, the palate with beautiful mouthfeel, supple and silky, perfectly framing the lingering red fruit flavours. Screwcap. 13.9% alc. **Rating** 94 **To** 2013 $35

♆♆♆♆♀ **Chardonnay 2007 Rating** 93 **To** 2014 $28
Mornington Peninsula Pinot Noir 2007 Rating 93 **To** 2015 $40

♆♆♆♆ **Mornington Peninsula Pinot Rose 2009 Rating** 89 **To** 2012 $19

Lindenton Wines ★★★☆
102 High Street, Heathcote, Vic 3523 **Region** Heathcote
T (03) 5433 3246 **F** (03) 5433 3246 **Open** 7 days 10–4 by appt
Winemaker Adrian Munari, Greg Dedman (Contract) **Est.** 2003 **Cases** 1000 **Vyds** 4 ha
Jim Harrison's Lindenton Wines is a semi-retirement occupation. His business plan is based on the purchase of grapes from smaller growers in the region who do not have access to winemaking facilities or outlets for their fruit. From the word go there has been an extensive range of wines available, running through Verdelho, Chardonnay, Viognier, Marsanne, Merlot, Shiraz, Shiraz Viognier and top-of-the-tree Melange. Jim's longer range plan is to make the wines himself.

♆♆♆♆♀ **Limited Release Shiraz 2008** Strong red-purple; a powerful, full-bodied wine with a range of blackberry, licorice, spice and plum fruit on both bouquet and palate, and almost chocolatey tannins on the finish. A wine sure to develop well. Screwcap. 14.5% alc. **Rating** 91 **To** 2020 $30

♆♆♆♆ **Limited Release Shiraz Cabernet 2008 Rating** 89 **To** 2014 $25

Linfield Road Wines ★★★★
65 Victoria Terrace, Williamstown, SA 5351 **Region** Barossa Valley
T (08) 8524 7355 **F** (08) 8524 6132 **www.**linfieldroadwines.com **Open** 7 days 10–5
Winemaker David Norman **Est.** 2002 **Cases** 2000 **Vyds** 19 ha
The Wilson family has been growing grapes at their estate vineyard for over 100 years; Steve and Deb Wilson are fourth-generation vignerons. The vineyard is in one of the coolest parts of the Barossa Valley, in an elevated position near the Adelaide Hills boundary. The estate vineyard is planted to riesling (5.2 ha), cabernet sauvignon (3.1 ha), semillon, shiraz, merlot and grenache (2.4 ha each), and chardonnay (1.1 ha). In 2002 the Wilsons decided to vinify part of the production. Within 12 months of the first release, the wines had accumulated three trophies and five gold medals. A much anticipated ambition to open a cellar door finally came to pass in mid-2008. Exports to the US, Canada, Hong Kong, South Korea, Singapore, Japan and China.

♟♟♟♟♀ **Edmund Major Reserve 100 Year Old Vines Barossa Shiraz 2006**
Relatively light and slightly diffuse colour; a light- to medium-bodied wine, with
strongly savoury nuances that initially disappoint before the line and excellent
length of the palate becomes obvious, likewise the lingering aftertaste. Screwcap.
14.9% alc. **Rating** 93 **To** 2016 $65

The Stubborn Patriarch Shiraz 2005 Has the generous soft fruit markers of
the '05 vintage, with spicy plum/plum cake flavours, soft tannins and good overall
balance. Screwcap. 14.8% alc. **Rating** 91 **To** 2018 $25

✪   **The Black Hammer Cabernet Sauvignon 2005** Normally one would not
expect Barossa cabernet to get away with this level of alcohol, but this does
so, with a fresh array of red and black berry fruits and good balance. Screwcap.
14.8% alc. **Rating** 90 **To** 2015 $22

♟♟♟♟ **The Man About Town Harvest Aged White Tawny 2006 Rating** 89
To 2011 $15
Dear Nellie Single Vineyard Barossa Semillon 2009 Rating 88 **To** 2013 $15
The Stubborn Patriarch Shiraz 2008 Rating 88 **To** 2016 $25
Ratafia Riesling 2008 Rating 87 **To** 2011 $22

Lirralirra Estate   ★★★☆

15 Paynes Road, Chirnside Park, Vic 3116 **Region** Yarra Valley
T (03) 9735 0224 **F** (03) 9735 0224 www.lirralirraestate.com.au **Open** W'ends & hols 10–6
Winemaker Alan Smith **Est.** 1981 **Cases** 200 **Vyds** 2.5 ha
Alan and Jos Smith, stalwarts of the Yarra Valley for 30 years, have decided that the 2010
vintage would be their last. The decision came in the wake of '07 (frost, no vintage); '08
(drought and heat, only pinot noir made but sold in bulk); and '09 (drought, heat and smoke).
The cellar door will remain open for several years until the '10 wines and some prior stock is
sold. Thereafter it will be closed, but the Johns will continue to live on the property 'with or
without vines for as long as possible'.

♟♟♟♟♀ **Reserve Sauvignon Blanc 2009** Light straw-green; a substantial wine that
might be confused with semillon (or a blend); in a grassy/herbal (although not
unripe) mode; has good length and balance, and a clean finish. Screwcap. 13% alc.
Rating 90 **To** 2012 $22

♟♟♟♟ **Reserve Pinot Noir 2009 Rating** 87 **To** 2012 $30

Lister Wines   ★★★

c/- 15a Rodney Avenue, Tranmere, SA 5073 (postal) **Region** Adelaide Hills/Langhorne Creek
T 0401 524 539 **F** (08) 8361 2399 **Open** Not
Winemaker Cate Lister **Est.** 2001 **Cases** 200 **Vyds** 1 ha
This is a micro-operation run by Cate Lister, with estate plantings of chardonnay, roussanne,
viognier and marsanne, the grapes for Soliloquy continuing to be purchased 'until the perfect
spot is found'. The tiny production means the wines are mainly sold through word of mouth
and mail order, and small retail outlets in SA.

♟♟♟♟ **Soliloquy Adelaide Hills Merlot 2006** A complex, cedary/savoury bouquet;
the leaf, olive and savoury inflections on the finish are varietal, but a little too
much so for comfort. Screwcap. 13% alc. **Rating** 88 **To** 2013 $19.95

 ## Lithostylis   ★★★

17 Church Street, Leongatha, Vic 3953 (postal) **Region** Gippsland
T (03) 5662 2885 **F** (03) 5662 2128 www.lithostylis.com **Open** Not
Winemaker Dean Roberts **Est.** 2006 **Cases** 150 **Vyds** 2.25 ha
Dean and Dayna Roberts purchased a vineyard in 2006, which had been planted in 1997 on
a very close spacing of 1 m x 1 m. They say 'organic and biodynamic practices are preferred,
but not dogmatically pursued. Winemaking is limited to essential interventions.' Dean began

his career with a viticulture diploma from Swinburne University, Lilydale, in 2002, becoming vineyard manager for Diamond Valley Vineyards, simultaneously undertaking further wine-making studies. He then completed a vintage at Ponzi Wines in Oregon, and on returning to Australia had a short, but intense, period of employment with Bass Phillip. He now works as a vineyard management contractor, and on the winemaking front receives assistance from Dayna, who has a biomedical science degree from Monash University.

ΨΨΨΨ **Chardonnay 2007** Light, bright straw-green; crisp and tight, with strong lemon overtones to the underlying white fruits. Not complex, but has merit. Diam. 12% alc. **Rating** 89 **To** 2012 $28
Pinot Noir 2008 Good hue; early picking has delivered brightness, but also some green notes and edgy acidity; curate's egg. Diam. 12.5% alc. **Rating** 88 **To** 2013 $44

Little Bridge ★★★

106 Brooks Road, Bywong, NSW 2621 **Region** Canberra District
T (02) 6226 6620 **F** (02) 6226 6842 **www.**littlebridgewines.com.au **Open** By appt
Winemaker Canberra Winemakers, Mallaluka Winemakers **Est.** 1996 **Cases** 1000
Vyds 5.5 ha
Little Bridge is a partnership between long-term friends John Leyshon, Rowland Clark, John Jeffrey and Steve Dowton. There are 2 ha of chardonnay, pinot noir, riesling and merlot planted at Folly Run; 2 ha of shiraz, cabernet sauvignon, sangiovese, cabernet franc and malbec planted at Mallaluka; and 1.5 ha of riesling, chardonnay and mourvedre at Brooks Creek. Canberra Winemakers makes the white wines, and the reds are made at Mallaluka. Steve Dowton purchased Brooks Creek Vineyard in 2009 (largely derelict, and being rehabilitated), and it is here that the Little Bridge cellar door will be situated. Exports to Singapore.

ΨΨΨΨ **Canberra District Cabernet Sauvignon 2007** Strong purple hue; strong red fruit bouquet with a little touch of cinnamon spice; the palate is vibrant and juicy, medium-bodied and full of red fruits. Screwcap. 13.8% alc. **Rating** 88 **To** 2014 $20 BE
Canberra District Shiraz 2008 Bright colour; quite a spicy bouquet, with red fruits and a touch of orange rind; medium-bodied, with lively fruit to conclude. Screwcap. 13.9% alc. **Rating** 87 **To** 2014 $20 BE

Littles ★★★★

Cnr Palmers Lane/McDonalds Road, Pokolbin, NSW 2321 **Region** Hunter Valley
T (02) 4998 7626 **F** (02) 4998 7867 **www.**littleswinery.com.au **Open** Fri–Mon 10–4.30
Winemaker Peter Orr (Contract) **Est.** 1984 **Cases** 2000 **Vyds** 21.6 ha
Littles is managed by the Kindred family, the ownership involving a number of investors. The winery has mature vineyards planted to shiraz (7.3 ha), cabernet sauvignon (4.5 ha), semillon (4.3 ha), pinot noir (3.4 ha), chardonnay (1.3 ha) and marsanne (0.8 ha). Exports to Germany, Taiwan and Japan.

ΨΨΨΨΨ **Hunter Valley Semillon 2009** Light straw-green; has an almost blossom-scented
✪ bouquet, then the citrus overtones that '09 gave to most semillons of the vintage. Screwcap. 11% alc. **Rating** 91 **To** 2018 $17
✪ **Hunter Valley Chardonnay 2009** Very pale straw-green; follows the trend to early-picked chardonnay in the Hunter Valley, with strong citrus and white flesh stone fruit, and no obvious oak. Screwcap. 12% alc. **Rating** 90 **To** 2013 $22
Reserve Hunter Valley Cabernet Sauvignon 2007 Good red-purple; cabernet isn't an easy variety in the Hunter Valley, but red vintages such as '09 can give good results, as in this case; the medium-bodied palate has blackcurrant fruit, ripe tannins and touches of earth that are regional, but add complexity. Screwcap. 14% alc. **Rating** 90 **To** 2020 $24

ΨΨΨΨ **Hunter Valley Semillon Sauvignon Blanc 2009** **Rating** 88 **To** 2012 $17
Hunter Valley Marsanne 2009 **Rating** 88 **To** 2017 $17
Reserve Hunter Valley Shiraz 2007 **Rating** 87 **To** 2017 $24

Littore Family Wines ★★★

265 Ballan Road, Moorabool, Vic 3221 **Region** Geelong
T (03) 5228 4888 **F** (03) 5276 1537 **www.**littorewines.com.au **Open** 7 days 10–5
Winemaker David Thompson, Toby Wanklyn, Daniel Greene **Est.** 1997
Cases 1.5 million **Vyds** 1416 ha

Littore Family Wines was founded by Mario and Aurora Littore on the Murray River near Mildura, the first vineyard named Jindalee, meaning 'bare hill'. A decade later the winery capacity was increased from 3 million to 13 million litres (15 000 tonnes). Sons Vince and David had purchased the Idyll Vineyard (now Jindalee Estate) near Geelong, which is now the headquarters of the group, and oversaw the expansion in the Riverland (here the group owns 1400 ha planted to 23 varieties; the Geelong vineyards a paltry 16 ha). The wines now come under a number of labels for its domestic and numerous export markets. Exports to the UK, the US and other major markets.

ŸŸŸŸ   **Pinot Grigio 2008** A well-made and very cleverly packaged wine at such a
✪   low price – looks more like a $20 bottle; there is a sufficient level of varietal pear
       and apple aroma and fruit not to need the panacea of residual sugar. Screwcap.
       11.5% alc. **Rating** 88 **To** 2011 $9.95
✪   **Tempranillo 2008** The packaging, trendy variety and the wine in the glass all
       make fun of the price; juicy black cherry fruit and that twist of citrus point in the
       same direction; lack of structure only criticism. Screwcap. 13.5% alc. **Rating** 88
       To 2012 $9.95

Lloyd Brothers ★★★★

34 Warners Road, McLaren Vale, SA 5171 **Region** McLaren Vale
T (08) 8323 8792 **F** (08) 8323 8833 **www.**lloydbrothers.com.au **Open** 7 days 10–5
Winemaker Hugh Thomson **Est.** 2002 **Cases** 2500 **Vyds** 19 ha

The business is owned by David Lloyd (nephew of Mark Lloyd, and son of the late Guy Lloyd of Lloyd Aviation). It has 14 ha of shiraz, and shares a property with a planting of old olive trees, which produces high-quality table olives and extra-virgin olive oil sold through The Olive Grove at McLaren Vale. Lloyd Brothers sells a significant part of its grape production (inter alia to d'Arenberg) and sells the entire crop in years where the standard is not considered high enough to warrant an estate release. Brother Matthew also has an Adelaide Hills vineyard planted to 5 ha of chardonnay, verdelho and pinot noir; the Adelaide Hills cellar door is at 94 Main St, Hahndorf.

ŸŸŸŸŸ **Bonvale Adelaide Hills Chardonnay 2008** Gleaming green-gold; generous
✪   stone fruit flavours have a nice bite to the finish; wild yeast, barrel-fermented wine
       with only 230 dozen made. Screwcap. 13.5% alc. **Rating** 90 **To** 2013 $16
✪   **McLaren Vale Rose 2009** Bright, light magenta; a fragrant, spicy bouquet is
       followed by a red berry palate purely driven by its shiraz base, the grapes picked
       early specifically for this wine. Screwcap. 13% alc. **Rating** 90 **To** 2011 $16
       Single Vineyard McLaren Vale Fortified Shiraz 2008 Traditional Australian
       vintage port style (terminology no longer allowed by the EU), with spicy black
       fruits, dark chocolate and licorice, tradition coming in the degree of fruit sweetness
       left unfermented. Cork. 19.5% alc. **Rating** 90 **To** 2020 $25

ŸŸŸŸ   **McLaren Vale Shiraz 2007 Rating** 88 **To** 2016 $20

Lobethal Road Wines ★★★★☆

Lot 1, Lobethal Road, Mount Torrens, SA 5244 **Region** Adelaide Hills
T (08) 8389 4595 **F** (08) 8389 4596 **www.**lobethalroad.com **Open** Thurs–Sun &
public hols 11–5
Winemaker Michael Sykes (Contract) **Est.** 1998 **Cases** 1500 **Vyds** 5.1 ha

Dave Neyle and Inga Lidums bring diverse but very relevant experience to the Lobethal Road vineyard, which has shiraz (2.6 ha), chardonnay (1.5 ha), riesling (0.6 ha) and sauvignon blanc (0.4 ha). Dave has been in vineyard development and management in SA and Tasmania since

1990, and is currently managing 60 ha in the Adelaide Hills. Inga brings 25 years' experience in marketing and graphic design both in Australia and overseas, with a focus on the wine and food industries. The property is managed with minimal chemical input, and the use of solar power in the pursuit of an environmentally sustainable product and lifestyle.

ΨΨΨΨΨ **Bacchant Adelaide Hills Shiraz 2007** Excellent crimson-purple; so this is where the legacy of the '06 went, with its spicy, peppery black fruit bouquet, and medium-bodied but firm and long palate, the tannins and oak in support. Screwcap. 14.5% alc. **Rating** 95 **To** 2022 $42

ΨΨΨΨΨ **Adelaide Hills Sauvignon Blanc 2009** Bright straw-green; an aromatic
❂ bouquet with a mix of passionfruit and gooseberry aromas, the palate finer and more citrus-oriented; good line, length and balance. Screwcap. 12% alc. **Rating** 93 **To** 2011 $20

ΨΨΨΨ **Adelaide Hills Botrytis Riesling 2009** **Rating** 89 **To** 2012 $20
Adelaide Hills Pinot Gris 2009 **Rating** 88 **To** 2013 $20
Adelaide Hills Shiraz 2007 **Rating** 87 **To** 2014 $20

Lofty Valley Wines   ★★★★☆

PO Box 55, Summertown, SA 5141 **Region** Adelaide Hills
T (08) 8390 0053 **F** (08) 8239 2329 **www.loftyvalleywines.com.au Open** Not
Winemaker Sam Scott **Est.** 2004 **Cases** 400 **Vyds** 3 ha
Medical practitioner Brian Gilbert began collecting wine when he was 19, flirting with the idea of becoming a winemaker before being headed firmly in the direction of medicine by his parents. Thirty or so years later he purchased a blackberry- and gorse-infested 12-ha property in the Adelaide Hills, eventually obtaining permission to establish a vineyard. Chardonnay (2 ha) was planted in 2004, and 1 ha of pinot noir in '07, both on steep slopes. A single barrel of (over-oaked) Chardonnay was made in 2007 from the first crop of a little over one-third of a tonne, the '08 Chardonnay bypassing oak altogether.

ΨΨΨΨΨ **Adelaide Hills Shiraz 2008** Deep crimson-purple; the bouquet is rich and
❂ profound, and the palate lives up to is promise; black cherry, blackberry, licorice and cracked pepper flow seamlessly on the medium-bodied palate. Screwcap. 14% alc. **Rating** 94 **To** 2018 $19.95

ΨΨΨΨΨ **Adelaide Hills Unwooded Chardonnay 2009** If you are seeking to sell
❂ unwooded chardonnay, this is precisely the style you should aim for: bright and juicy, with grapefruit, nectarine and other citrus notes dancing along the palate and finish. Screwcap. 13.5% alc. **Rating** 90 **To** 2012 $14.95

Logan Wines   ★★★★

Castelreagh Highway, Apple Tree Flat, Mudgee, NSW 2850 **Region** Mudgee
T (02) 6373 1333 **F** (02) 6373 1390 **www.loganwines.com.au Open** 7 days 10–5
Winemaker Peter Logan, Andrew Ling **Est.** 1997 **Cases** 45 000
Logan is a family-owned and operated business with emphasis on cool-climate wines from Orange and Mudgee. The business is run by husband and wife team Peter (winemaker) and Hannah (sales and marketing). Wines are released from three ranges: Logan (from Orange), Weemala and Apple Tree Flat. Exports to the UK, the US, Japan and other major markets.

ΨΨΨΨΨ **Orange Chardonnay 2008** A very elegant chardonnay, with considerable
❂ brightness and purity to the varietal expression; distinctly light-bodied, and needs time, but will repay it. Screwcap. 14% alc. **Rating** 92 **To** 2017 $22
❂ **Orange Cabernet Merlot 2007** Bright crimson; a fresh and bright wine with a posy of red fruits on the bouquet and medium-bodied palate; superfine tannins are on the money. Screwcap. 14.5% alc. **Rating** 92 **To** 2015 $25
❂ **Weemala Orange Riesling 2009** Pale straw-green; lively citrus and apple blossom aromas are precisely reflected in the crisp, light and well-balanced palate. Screwcap. 12% alc. **Rating** 90 **To** 2016 $18

Orange Sauvignon Blanc 2009 Aromas of gooseberry, kiwi fruit and guava lead into a crisp, clean palate, the flavours waiting until the back-palate and long, dry finish to re-emerge. Screwcap. 13.5% alc. **Rating** 90 **To** 2010 $22

Hannah Orange Rose 2009 Light, clear colour; interesting flavours, quite tangy and spicy, albeit with a core of cherry fruit. Screwcap. 12.5% alc. **Rating** 90 **To** 2011 $22

Orange Shiraz 2007 Despite its high alcohol, has the lively, spicy fruit on the mid-palate for which Orange is becoming so well known. Nonetheless, might have been even better if picked earlier. Screwcap. 15% alc. **Rating** 90 **To** 2017 $25

ioioioio **Orange Pinot Noir 2008 Rating** 89 **To** 2014 $30
Weemala Orange Gewurztraminer 2009 Rating 88 **To** 2013 $18
Weemala Orange Pinot Gris 2009 Rating 88 **To** 2010 $18

✪ **Apple Tree Flat Shiraz 2008** A particularly impressive wine at this price, its origins unspecified, but its black fruit flavours and structure making discussion superfluous. Screwcap. 14.5% alc. **Rating** 88 **To** 2014 $11

✪ **Apple Tree Flat Merlot 2008** Exceptional purple-red; in a way, is too much of a good thing, for the depth and tannin extract require some patience, or a thick barbecued rump. Impressive value. Screwcap. 14.5% alc. **Rating** 87 **To** 2013 $11

Longleat Wines ★★★☆

105 Old Weir Road, Murchison, Vic 3610 **Region** Goulburn Valley
T (03) 5826 2294 **F** (03) 5826 2510 **www**.murchisonwines.com.au **Open** W'ends & most public hols 10–5, or by appt
Winemaker Guido Vazzoler **Est.** 1975 **Cases** 4000 **Vyds** 8.1 ha
Sandra (ex–kindergarten teacher turned cheesemaker) and Guido Vazzoler (ex–Brown Brothers) acquired the long-established Longleat Estate vineyard in 2003 (renaming it Murchison Wines), after living on the property (as tenants) for some years. The mature vineyard comprises 3.2 ha of shiraz, 2.3 ha of cabernet sauvignon, 0.8 ha each of semillon, sauvignon blanc and chardonnay, and 0.2 ha petit verdot. Exports to Hong Kong.

ioioioioio **Shiraz 2008** Developed red, with just a hint of purple remaining; a traditional, earthy/leathery/blackberry bouquet is repeated on the medium- to full-bodied palate; the tannins are ripe, the vanillan oak evident but not excessive. Screwcap. 14.6% alc. **Rating** 93 **To** 2023 $22

ioioioio
✪ **Semillon 2009** Bright and clear colour; lemony fruit runs through the bouquet and lively palate, which has an almost juicy texture; should develop well over the next few years. Screwcap. 11.5% alc. **Rating** 89 **To** 2016 $15
Cabernet Sauvignon 2008 Rating 87 **To** 2016 $22

Longview Creek Vineyard ★★★

150 Palmer Road, Sunbury, Vic 3429 **Region** Sunbury
T (03) 9740 2448 **F** (03) 9740 2495 **www**.longviewcreek.com.au **Open** W'ends 11–5, or by appt
Winemaker Bill Ashby **Est.** 1988 **Cases** 400 **Vyds** 2.2 ha
Bill and Karen Ashby purchased the Longview Creek Vineyard from founders Dr Ron and Joan Parker in 2003. It is situated on the brink of the spectacular Longview Gorge, the bulk of the plantings of chardonnay (0.8 ha), pinot noir (0.6 ha) and chenin blanc (0.4 ha) were made between 1988 and '90. Thereafter a little cabernet franc and riesling were planted.

ioioioio **Cabernet Franc 2006** Is in no way a generous wine, but does have some of the fragrance expected of cabernet franc, likewise some of the spicy red fruits. For lovers of St Emilion, Bordeaux. Screwcap. 13% alc. **Rating** 88 **To** 2013 $25

Longview Vineyard   ★★★★☆

Pound Road, Macclesfield, SA 5153 **Region** Adelaide Hills
T (08) 8388 9694 **F** (08) 8388 9693 **www.**longviewvineyard.com.au **Open** 7 days 11–5
Winemaker Ben Glaetzer (Contract) **Est.** 1995 **Cases** 17 000 **Vyds** 70 ha

Longview Vineyard came to be through the success of Two Dogs, the lemon-flavoured
alcoholic drink created by Duncan MacGillivray and sold in 1995 to the Pernod Ricard
Group (also the owners of Orlando). Shiraz and cabernet sauvignon have been planted
(accounting for a little over half the total), plus significant amounts of chardonnay and merlot,
and smaller plantings of viognier, semillon, riesling, sauvignon blanc, zinfandel, nebbiolo,
pinot gris and savagnin. A significant part of the production is sold, but $1.2 million has been
invested in a cellar door and function area, barrel rooms and an administration centre for
the group's activities. All the buildings have a spectacular view over the Coorong and Lake
Alexandrina. In 2008 the Saturno family of Adelaide, with brothers Peter and Mark leading
the way, acquired Longview. Exports to the UK, the US, Canada and Hong Kong.

♟♟♟♟♟ **Devils Elbow Adelaide Hills Cabernet Sauvignon 2007** A particularly
good cabernet, transcending the vintage and its alcohol, for it is a cedary, medium-
bodied wine with delicious blackcurrant fruit and persistent but superfine tannins.
Screwcap. 14.9% alc. **Rating** 94 **To** 2020 $30

♟♟♟♟♟ **Red Bucket Adelaide Hills Shiraz Cabernet 2008** Bright, deep crimson-
❂ purple; there is a lot of juicy wine for the price, with a cascade of vibrant black
fruits, spice and pepper, the tannins fine and well balanced. Screwcap. 14.5% alc.
Rating 91 **To** 2018 $16

Whippet Adelaide Hills Sauvignon Blanc 2009 Rating 90 **To** 2011 $19
❂ **Boat Shed Adelaide Hills Nebbiolo Rose 2009** Very pale pink, typical
of nebbiolo rose; while the bouquet doesn't give much away, the palate is
entertaining, with cherry, citrus and a subliminal touch of sweetness. Good food
rose. Screwcap. 13% alc. **Rating** 90 **To** 2011 $18

❂ **Red Bucket Adelaide Hills Shiraz Cabernet 2007** A fresh, lively and friendly
blend, with some spicy elements; gold medal Perth '08 and trophy at the Houston
International Wine Show '09 (for shiraz/cabernet blends) represent an odd
double; the wine is supple and has good length. Screwcap. 14.5% alc. **Rating** 90
To 2012 $15

♟♟♟♟ **Iron Knob Adelaide Hills Riesling 2009 Rating** 89 **To** 2015 $19
❂ **Red Bucket Adelaide Hills Semillon Sauvignon Blanc 2009**
Uncompromisingly intense, reflecting the low alcohol and underlining the green
lemon zest and mineral flavours. Would be very good with spicy Chinese/Asian
food. Screwcap. 11.5% alc. **Rating** 89 **To** 2011 $15
Riserva Nebbiolo 2006 Rating 89 **To** 2013 $75
Epitome Late Harvest Riesling 2008 Rating 88 **To** 2012 $19

Loom Wine.   ★★★★

90 Chalk Hill Road, McLaren Vale, SA 5171 **Region** McLaren Vale
T (08) 8323 8623 **F** (08) 8323 8694 **www.**loomwine.com **Open** By appt
Winemaker Steve Grimley, Adam Hooper **Est.** 2005 **Cases** 300 000

Steve Grimley runs a substantial offsite winemaking business, which includes the Loom Wine
and Willundry Road Shirazs, and contract winemaking services for others. All of the grapes
used are contract-grown. The large production reflects contract-made wines for various
private label customers. The wines made under the Loom banner are a tiny part, usually less
than 500 cases in each lot. Exports to the UK, the US and other major markets.

♟♟♟♟♟ **Ranger & Apprentice Clare Valley Riesling 2009** Bath talc, lime juice and
❂ a touch of musk are all evident on the bouquet; the palate is zesty and linear,
finishing with a dry and chalky conclusion. Screwcap. 13.5% alc. **Rating** 91
To 2015 $15 BE

○ **Long Yarn Clare Valley Riesling 2009** Vibrant hue; generous lemon bouquet with a touch of straw and chalk; the palate is juicy and generous on entry, tightening to a fine and quite linear finish. Screwcap. 12.5% alc. **Rating** 90 To 2014 $11 BE

♀♀♀♀ **Long Yarn McLaren Vale Shiraz 2009** Deep and vibrant colour; the bouquet
○ offers generous levels of sweet, dark blackberry fruit; bitter chocolate provides contrast on the fleshy, fruit-forward palate. Screwcap. 14% alc. **Rating** 89 To 2014 $11 BE

Lou Miranda Estate   ★★★★

Barossa Valley Way, Rowland Flat, SA 5352 **Region** Barossa Valley
T (08) 8524 4537 **F** (08) 8524 4066 **www**.loumirandaestate.com.au
Open Mon–Fri 10–4, w'ends 11–4
Winemaker Lou Miranda **Est.** 2005 **Cases** 15 000 **Vyds** 23.29 ha
Lou Miranda's daughters Lisa and Victoria are the driving force behind the estate, albeit with continuing hands-on involvement from Lou. The jewels in the crown of the estate plantings are 1 ha of shiraz and 0.5 ha of mourvedre planted in 1898, plus 1.5 ha of shiraz planted in 1907. The remaining vines have been planted gradually since '95, the varietal choice widened by cabernet sauvignon, merlot, chardonnay and pinot grigio. The cellar door works on the principle that there should be a wine for every conceivable taste. Exports to the UK and other major markets.

♀♀♀♀♀ **Individual Vineyard Old Vine Barossa Valley Shiraz 2008** Lighter colour than the Cordon Cut; an altogether different wine, of course, the spices more savoury, the palate medium-bodied and long; there is a faint touch of what appears to be sweetness on the finish; 100-year-old vines. Cork. 14.5% alc. **Rating** 93 To 2020 $34.95
Leone Riverina Botrytis Semillon 2008 Bright brassy-gold; a complex cumquat and crystallised peach bouquet, the palate luscious but, in relative terms, showing some restraint. Screwcap. 10% alc. **Rating** 93 To 2012 $16.95
Individual Vineyard Cordon Cut Barossa Valley Shiraz 2008 Strong purple-red; an unusually strong array of warm spices on the blood plum bouquet leads into a rich and well-textured full-bodied palate that carries its alcohol well; I don't know quite why it was decided to use the cordon cut method to partially desiccate the grapes. Cork. 15% alc. **Rating** 91 To 2023 $29.95
○ **Leone Adelaide Hills Sauvignon Blanc 2009** A clean and gently fragrant bouquet with a mix of tropical and grassy aromas, then a palate that opens quietly accelerates on the zesty, citrussy finish and aftertaste. Screwcap. 13% alc. **Rating** 90 To 2012 $16.95
○ **Individual Vineyard Aged Cobweb NV** Pretty useful tawny; has some rancio and nutty complexity, the aged component freshened with a small amount of young material. Screwcap. 17% alc. **Rating** 90 To 2011 $19.95

♀♀♀♀ **Leone Adelaide Hills Pinot Grigio 2009** Rating 89 To 2010 $16.95
Leone Barossa Valley Sparkling Shiraz 2007 Rating 87 To 2010 $21.95

Lowe Family Wines   ★★★★☆

Tinja Lane, Mudgee, NSW 2850 **Region** Mudgee
T (02) 6372 0800 **F** (02) 6372 0811 **www**.lowewine.com.au **Open** 7 days 10–5
Winemaker David Lowe, Jane Wilson **Est.** 1987 **Cases** 7000 **Vyds** 11 ha
Business partners David Lowe and Jane Wilson have consolidated their operations in Mudgee, moving back from the Hunter Valley. They have started a new business, Mudgee Growers, at the historic Fairview winery. The main business is here, and they have spread their wings, successfully introducing less well-known varieties, and looking to other regions more suited for both mainstream styles (e.g. Orange for pinot gris and sauvignon blanc) and alternative varieties (e.g. Orange roussanne). Since 2006, all wines have been classified as organic. Exports to the UK, Singapore and Japan.

🍷🍷🍷🍷🍷 **Tinja Mudgee Riesling 2009** Mudgee riesling has been a star performer in the last couple of years, this zesty, lime-juicy wine another example; has very good length and balance, kicking again on the finish, perhaps with subliminal sweetness. Top vintage, too. Screwcap. 12.2% alc. **Rating** 94 **To** 2020 $23

🍷🍷🍷🍷🍷 **Tinja Mudgee Botrytis Semillon 2008** Has already developed a golden hue;
✪   is very complex and rich, although not particularly sweet – no bad thing; the flavours are of cumquat and mandarin balanced by acidity. Screwcap. 12.2% alc. **Rating** 92 **To** 2011 $20

🍷🍷🍷🍷 **Preservative Free Mudgee Merlot 2009 Rating** 88 **To** 2010 $20

Lucas Estate   ★★★☆

329 Donges Road, Severnlea, Qld 4352 **Region** Granite Belt
T (07) 4683 6365 **F** (07) 4683 6356 **www**.lucasestate.com.au **Open** 7 days 10–5
Winemaker Louise Samuel **Est.** 1999 **Cases** 1500 **Vyds** 2.7 ha
Louise Samuel and her late husband Colin Sellers purchased Lucas Estate in 2003. The wines are made from the estate vineyard (at an altitude of 825 m), which is planted to chardonnay, cabernet sauvignon, muscat hamburg, merlot, verdelho and shiraz, and also from purchased grapes. A new winery was completed in time for the 2008 vintage, with a pneumatic press for the white wines, leaving the basket press for reds. Later that year Colin succumbed to cancer; after it had been diagnosed 18 months earlier, he and Louise agreed that Lucas Estate should continue, and that is what she is doing.

🍷🍷🍷🍷🍷 **The Gordon Estate Granite Belt Shiraz 2008** Good purple-red; a DIY and largely indecipherable lab label does bear a trophy symbol for Best Qld Shiraz at the Australian Small Winemakers Show, doubtless scoring for racy, savoury flavour and texture on its long, medium-bodied palate. Screwcap. 14% alc. **Rating** 92 **To** 2018 $40

🍷🍷🍷🍷 **Granite Belt Petit Verdot 2008 Rating** 89 **To** 2015 $32

🍇 Lucinda Estate Vineyard   ★★★★

108 Parr Street, Leongatha, Vic 3953 **Region** Gippsland
T 0417 337 270 **www**.lucindaestate.com.au **Open** Thurs–Mon 11–4
Winemaker Andrew Gromotka **Est.** 1990 **Cases** 700 **Vyds** 3.64 ha
Owners Lucinda and Andrew Gromotka planted their vineyard in 1990, the lion's share to pinot noir, with 0.4 ha each of shiraz and chardonnay. It is an east-facing block, the soil ancient volcanic deep red clay loam, with buckshot giving a high ironstone content. Andrew is both winemaker and viticulturist, describing himself as vigneron.

🍷🍷🍷🍷🍷 **The Natural South Gippsland Pinot Noir 2008** Similar colour to the standard wine despite lower alcohol; a purer and brighter wine, with attractive cherry and plum fruit aromas and flavours, the palate with good line and length. Screwcap. 13% alc. **Rating** 92 **To** 2014 $40
✪   **Reserve South Gippsland Chardonnay 2007** Retains bright green-yellow; has developed nicely, oak and fruit now welded together in a light- to medium-bodied frame, citrussy acidity extending the length. Screwcap. 13.5% alc. **Rating** 90 **To** 2013 $25

🍷🍷🍷🍷 **South Gippsland Syrah 2008 Rating** 89 **To** 2014 $25
Reserve South Gippsland Syrah 2007 Rating 89 **To** 2015 $35
South Gippsland Pinot Noir 2008 Rating 88 **To** 2013 $25

Lucy's Run   ★★★☆

1274 Wine Country Drive, Rothbury, NSW 2335 **Region** Hunter Valley
T (02) 4938 3594 **F** (02) 4938 3592 **www**.lucysrun.com **Open** 7 days 10–5
Winemaker David Hook (Contract) **Est.** 1998 **Cases** 800 **Vyds** 3.9 ha

The Lucy's Run business has a variety of offerings of wine, cold-pressed extra-virgin olive oil and self-catered farm accommodation. The wines are made from estate-grown shiraz (1.9 ha), verdelho and merlot (1 ha each). The feisty label design is the work of local artist Paula Rengger, who doubles up as the chef at the nearby Shakey Tables Restaurant, itself the deserving winner of numerous awards.

ŸŸŸŸŸ **Shiraz 2007** That ever-so-typical veneer of polished leather drives the bouquet, retreating into the background of the full-bodied palate with its display of black fruits and touches of earth. For the long haul. Screwcap. 13.5% alc. **Rating** 90 To 2022 $25

ŸŸŸŸ **Sweet Sophie's Dessert Verdelho 2008 Rating** 88 To 2012 $20
Verdelho 2009 Rating 87 To 2012 $18
Verdelho 2008 Rating 87 To 2011 $18

Luke Lambert Wines   ★★★★☆

PO Box 1297, Healesville, Vic 3777 **Region** Yarra Valley
T 0448 349 323 **F** (03) 5962 5337 **www**.lukelambertwines.com.au **Open** By appt
Winemaker Luke Lambert **Est.** 2003 **Cases** 800 **Vyds** 3 ha
Luke Lambert graduated from CSU's wine science course in 2002, aged 23, cramming in wine-making experience at Mount Pleasant, Coldstream Hills, Mount Prior, Poet's Corner, Palliser Estate in Martinborough, and Badia di Morrona in Chianti. With this background he has established a virtual winery, purchasing grapes from quality-conscious growers in the Yarra Valley and Heathcote. After several trial vintages, the first wines were released from the 2005 vintage. He has now settled in the Yarra Valley, leasing slightly less than 1 ha of Heathcote nebbiolo, and similar amounts of Yarra Valley shiraz and Yarra Valley nebbiolo (newly grafted). The wines are wild yeast-fermented and bottled without fining or filtration. Exports to the UK.

ŸŸŸŸŸ **Yarra Valley Syrah 2008** Like the Reserve, of single-vineyard origin, and bottled without fining or filtration; the hue is fractionally less vibrant, but the aroma and flavour are more expressive at this stage, with tangy, spicy notes to the dark fruits of the bouquet and palate. The Reserve will overtake it in the future, but right now this is the better wine. Diam. 13% alc. **Rating** 94 To 2018 $38

ŸŸŸŸŸ **Reserve Yarra Valley Syrah 2008 Rating** 92 To 2023 $65

M. Chapoutier Australia   ★★★★★

11 Nicholson Place, Melbourne, Vic 3000 (postal) **Region** Mount Benson
T (03) 5433 2411 **F** (03) 5433 2400 **www**.chapoutier.com **Open** Not
Winemaker Benjamin Darnault, Anthony Terlato **Est.** 1998 **Cases** 10 000
M. Chapoutier Australia is the offshoot of the famous Rhône Valley producer. It has established three vineyards in Australia: Domaine Tournon at Mount Benson (17 ha shiraz, 10 ha cabernet sauvignon, 4 ha marsanne, 3 ha viognier), Domaine Terlato Chapoutier in the Pyrenees (30 ha shiraz, 2 ha viognier) and a third at Heathcote (10 ha shiraz). It seems likely that increasing emphasis will be placed on the Victorian vineyards. The business has also established operations in Heathcote. The Domaine Terlato and Chapoutier wines are made by Anthony Terlato, a Napa Valley winemaker. Most recently, Chapoutier has purchased the 20-ha vineyard of Landsborough Valley Estate. Exports to all major markets.

ŸŸŸŸŸ **Domaine Terlato & Chapoutier lieu-dit Malakoff Pyrenees Shiraz 2008** Strong red-purple; proclaims its class from the very start; the bouquet is aromatic, and the black fruits of the full-bodied palate manage to combine power and elegance, no mean feat; oak and tannins have been judged to perfection. A rock-hard cork is a major concern for the long-term cellaring the wine deserves. 14% alc. **Rating** 96 To 2028 $35

❂ **Domaine Tournon Western Victoria Syrah 2008** Good depth of colour; an expertly made shiraz, the winemaker content to allow the fruit to fully express its quality and character; medium- to full-bodied, it has supple tannins, excellent balance and length. Cork. 14.5% alc. **Rating** 94 To 2020 $18

ᵼᵼᵼᵼ♀ Domaine Tournon Mount Benson Shiraz 2007 Rating 93 To 2020 $23
Domaine Terlato & Chapoutier lieu dit Malakoff Pyrenees Viognier
2009 Rating 91 To 2013 $32

ᵼᵼᵼᵼ Domaine Tournon Landsborough Valley Estate Chardonnay 2009
Rating 88 To 2012 $23

McAdams Lane   ★★★★

90 McAdams Lane, Bellarine, Vic 3223 (postal) **Region** Geelong
T 1300 651 485 **F** (03) 9602 3388 www.mcadamslane.com.au **Open** Not
Winemaker Anthony Brain **Est.** 2003 **Cases** 1000 **Vyds** 4.6 ha
Retired quantity surveyor Peter Slattery bought the 48-ha property in 2001, intending to
plant the vineyard, make wine and develop a restaurant. He has achieved all of this (with help
from others, of course), planting shiraz (0.5 ha), pinot noir (1.8 ha), pinot gris (1 ha), picolit
(0.6 ha), chardonnay (0.4 ha) and zinfandel (0.3 ha). Picolit is the most interesting, a highly
regarded grape in northern Italy where it makes small quantities of high-quality sweet wine.
It has proved to be very temperamental here, as in Italy, with very unreliable fruitset.

ᵼᵼᵼᵼ♀ Terindah Estate Bellarine Peninsula Pinot Noir 2008 Bright and clear
❂   colour; the expression of varietal character is razor sharp and clear through both
the bouquet and palate, turning primarily on red cherry/berry fruit flavours; good
length. Screwcap. 13.8% alc. **Rating** 92 To 2015 $20
❂   Terindah Estate Bellarine Peninsula Shiraz 2008 Bright crimson; attractive
cool-climate shiraz, the red cherry and plum fruit laced with spice and pepper, the
finish long and juicy. Screwcap. 14.4% alc. **Rating** 92 To 2016 $20
Terindah Estate Bellarine Peninsula Pinot Gris 2008 Almost water-white;
interesting wine, pure, linear and focused, with mineral and nashi pear flavours
just peeping through. Vinous minimalism. Screwcap. 13.2% alc. **Rating** 90
To 2010 $20

ᵼᵼᵼᵼ Bellarine Peninsula Pinot Noir 2008 Rating 89 To 2014 $20

Macaw Creek Wines   ★★★

Macaw Creek Road, Riverton, SA 5412 **Region** Mount Lofty Ranges Zone
T (08) 8847 2237 **F** (08) 8847 2237 www.macawcreekwines.com.au **Open** By appt
Winemaker Rodney Hooper **Est.** 1992 **Cases** 5000 **Vyds** 10 ha
The property on which Macaw Creek Wines is established has been owned by the Hooper
family since the 1850s, but development of the estate vineyards did not begin until 1995.
The Macaw Creek brand was established in 1992 with wines made from grapes from other
regions, including the Preservative-Free Yoolang Cabernet Shiraz. Rodney Hooper is a highly
qualified and skilled winemaker with experience in many parts of Australia and in Germany,
France and the US. Exports to the UK, the US, Canada and China.

macforbes   ★★★★☆

770 Healesville-Koo Wee Rup Road, Healesville. Vic 3777 **Region** Yarra Valley
T (03) 9818 8099 **F** (03) 9818 8299 www.macforbes.com **Open** By appt
Winemaker Mac Forbes, Tony Fikkers **Est.** 2004 **Cases** 2000
Mac Forbes cut his vinous teeth at Mount Mary, where he was winemaker for several years
before heading overseas in 2002. He spent two years in London working for Southcorp in
a marketing liaison role, then travelled to Portugal and Austria to gain further winemaking
experience. He returned to the Yarra Valley prior to the 2005 vintage, purchasing grapes
for the two-tier portfolio: first, the Victorian range (employing unusual varieties or unusual
winemaking techniques); and, second, the Yarra Valley range of multiple terroir-based offerings
of Chardonnay and Pinot Noir. The business has grown steadily, with Tony Fikkers joining the
winemaking team, and Dylan Grigg as viticulturist guiding the contract grapegrowers upon
whom macforbes relies. Exports to the UK, the US, Dubai and Japan.

ΨΨΨΨΨ **Yarra Valley Chardonnay 2008** Has slightly deeper colour, and a slightly softer profile than the Woori Yallock, suggesting some oak influence – slight; citrus and nectarine fruit softens the acidity and fills the profile. Screwcap. 12% alc. **Rating** 93 **To** 2015 $28

Coldstream Pinot Noir 2008 Light-coloured and light-bodied, it has ripe plum aromas, and a high-fidelity supple palate precisely tracking the bouquet; its length and balance are precisely calibrated; only 20% to 25% new oak was used, no acid additions were made, nor enzymes added. A west-facing vineyard with lean clay and gravel soils. Screwcap. 13% alc. **Rating** 93 **To** 2013 $44

Dixons Creek Pinot Noir 2008 Bright, clear red; a highly perfumed bouquet, with tangy/menthol overtones to the red fruits; the palate picks up the tangy notes of the bouquet; has thrust and intensity. Screwcap. 12.5% alc. **Rating** 93 **To** 2014 $34

Yarra Glen Pinot Noir 2008 Clear, bright, red-purple; it has a spicy, perfumed bouquet but the fruit profile is significantly diminished; instead, it has a finer, almost mineralic structure, with spice and briar to the fore. The minimalist approach in the winery (no cold soak, no whole bunches) inevitably means these wines are light-bodied, low alcohol amplifying the style. An east-facing, close-planted block with shallow clay/loam over a granitic base. Screwcap. 12% alc. **Rating** 92 **To** 2013 $40

Woori Yallock Pinot Noir 2008 Bright, clear but very light colour; attractive spicy strawberry and cherry fruits on a very pure but very light-bodied palate. Don't delay. South facing, healthy silty clay loam over clay. Screwcap. 13% alc. **Rating** 91 **To** 2013 $48

Tradition Riesling 2008 Deep straw-yellow colour; it is a red wine masquerading as a white wine except for its minerally acidity. It is bone-dry, and has tannins normally only found in reds; in some ways it has a Manzanilla-like quality. Definitely needs food. Screwcap. 12% alc. **Rating** 90 **To** 2012 $44

Woori Yallock Chardonnay 2008 A startlingly crisp and vibrant palate, with razor-sharp acidity cutting through its length from start to finish. Such oak as there may be is irrelevant to the main agenda of the wine. There can be too much of a good thing. Screwcap. 12.5% alc. **Rating** 90 **To** 2014 $38

Yarra Valley Pinot Noir 2008 A similarly light-bodied wine, the colour fractionally more advanced, the flavours a little more savoury, the palate a touch longer. Screwcap. 12.5% alc. **Rating** 90 **To** 2013 $28

Gruyere Pinot Noir 2008 Slight colour development; foresty/briary/spicy aromas, the palate with hints of mint and earth; the most severe of the '08 Pinots. Dry-grown on healthy clay loam and silt soil. Screwcap. 12.5% alc. **Rating** 90 **To** 2013 $44

ΨΨΨΨ **Hugh 2007** **Rating** 89 **To** 2014 $48

McGlashan's Wallington Estate ★★★★☆

225 Swan Bay Road, Wallington, Vic 3221 **Region** Geelong
T (03) 5250 5760 **F** (03) 5250 5760 **www**.mcglashans.com.au **Open** W'ends & public hols 11–5, 7 days in Jan
Winemaker Robin Brockett (Contract) **Est.** 1996 **Cases** 1500 **Vyds** 10 ha
Russell and Jan McGlashan began the establishment of their vineyard in 1996. Chardonnay and pinot noir (4 ha each) make up the bulk of the plantings, the remainder shiraz and pinot gris (1 ha each); the wines are made by Robin Brockett, with his usual skill and attention to detail. Local restaurants around Geelong and the Bellarine Peninsula take much of the wine, although a newly opened cellar door offering food and music will see an increase in direct sales.

ΨΨΨΨΨ **Bellarine Peninsula Shiraz 2008** Good purple hue; the bouquet and palate loudly proclaim its cool-grown origin, with fragrant spice, red and black fruits and nervosity (French for nervous energy); lovely palate, feel and length, oak judged to perfection. Screwcap. 14% alc. **Rating** 94 **To** 2020 $28

ŸŸŸŸꞍ Bellarine Peninsula Chardonnay 2008 Rating 90 To 2014 $24

ŸŸŸŸ Bellarine Peninsula Pinot Noir 2008 Rating 89 To 2014 $26

McGrath Wines ★★★★☆

101 Burkes Lane, Brewongle via Bathurst, NSW 3795 **Region** Central Ranges Zone
T (02) 6337 5501 www.mcgrathwines.com.au **Open** By appt
Winemaker Peter McGrath **Est.** 1999 **Cases** 1000 **Vyds** 3.5 ha
Peter McGrath has endured all the hard knocks of establishing an isolated vineyard (no near vigneron-neighbours to give friendly advice), coinciding with a drought and the failure of irrigation equipment to arrive when promised. This led to his enrolment in a viticulture course. His first attempt at winemaking produced what he describes as 'nondescript vinegar', which led to the decision to enrol in a winemaking course. All this transpired between 1999 and '03, and thereafter he achieved modest show success in cool-climate and small-maker wine shows. His estate-grown shiraz, cabernet and riesling is supplemented by chardonnay from a grower in the Bathurst region.

ŸŸŸŸŸ Shiraz 2007 Retaining very good hue; well made, the winemaker's fingerprints subtle, and enhancing the spicy black fruit flavours of the palate, rather than smothering them in oak or tannins. Trophy National Cool Climate Wine Show '09. Screwcap. 14% alc. Rating 94 To 2017 $25

ŸŸŸŸꞍ Riesling 2009 Brilliant green hue; well made, with clear-cut riesling varietal
✪   character framed by chalky/slatey/minerally acidity driving the long palate. Screwcap. 12.5% alc. Rating 90 To 2019 $15
✪   Chardonnay 2009 A light- to medium-bodied chardonnay grown at an elevation of 1000 m, and which, despite its delicacy, has been able to absorb six months in new French oak barriques. Screwcap. 13% alc. Rating 90 To 2012 $15

ŸŸŸŸ Cabernet Sauvignon 2008 Rating 89 To 2015 $20
      Shiraz 2006 Rating 87 To 2012 $15

McGuigan Wines ★★★★☆

Cnr Broke Road/McDonald Road, Pokolbin, NSW 2321 **Region** Hunter Valley
T (02) 4998 7400 **F** (02) 4998 7401 www.mcguiganwines.com.au **Open** 7 days 9.30–5
Winemaker Peter Hall **Est.** 1992 **Cases** 1.5 million
A publicly listed company – the ultimate logical expression of Brian McGuigan's marketing drive and vision, which is on a par with that of Wolf Blass in his heyday. The overall size of the company has been measurably increased by the acquisition of Simeon Wines; Yaldara and Miranda, now also part of the business, made wine industry headlines in 2006 when it terminated a large number of grape purchase contracts. In 2007 McGuigan Simeon acquired Nepenthe Vineyards, a move that surprised many. In 2008 the group was renamed Australian Vintage Limited, a slightly curious moniker. Under its more friendly name, it won four major trophies at the International Wine & Spirit Competition, London '09. Exports to all major markets.

ŸŸŸŸŸ The Shortlist Adelaide Hills Chardonnay 2009 Bright green-straw; wild
✪   yeast-fermented in new French hogsheads; lees stirred for eight months, yet it is the white peach and nectarine fruit that drives the long palate of a very impressive wine. Screwcap. 13% alc. Rating 94 To 2019 $26

ŸŸŸŸꞍ Bin 9000 Hunter Valley Semillon 2004 A mature bouquet, with straw and
✪   lemon the centrepiece; the palate is still fresh, but certainly at the peak of its powers; drink up and enjoy. Screwcap. 11% alc. Rating 90 To 2013 $20 BE
      The Shortlist Barossa Valley GSM 2008 Rating 90 To 2016 $25 BE

ŸŸŸŸ Handmade Langhorne Creek Shiraz 2008 Rating 89 To 2014 $45 BE
      The Shortlist Eden Valley Riesling 2009 Rating 88 To 2014 $25 BE
      The Shortlist Barossa Valley Shiraz 2008 Rating 88 To 2014 $25 BE

Vineyard Select Hunter Valley Shiraz 2007 Rating 88 To 2014 $20 BE
Personal Reserve Botrytis Semillon 2005 Rating 88 To 2012 $26 BE
Bin 7000 Hunter Valley Chardonnay 2008 Rating 87 To 2013 $13 BE

McGuigan Wines (Barossa Valley)   ★★★★☆
Chateau Yaldara, Hermann Thumm Drive, Lyndoch, SA 5351 **Region** Barossa Valley
T (08) 8524 0200 **F** (08) 8524 0240 **www**.mcguiganwines.com.au **Open** 7 days 9.30–5
Winemaker James Evers **Est.** 1947 **Cases** 5000
At the end of 1999, Yaldara became part of the publicly listed Simeon Wines, the intention
being that it (Yaldara) should become the quality flagship of the group. Despite much
expenditure and the short-lived stay of at least one well-known winemaker, the plan failed to
deliver the expected benefits. In 2002 McGuigan Wines made a reverse takeover for Simeon,
and the various McGuigan brands will (presumably) fill the role intended for Yaldara. Exports
to all major markets.

♀♀♀♀♀ **Farms Barossa Valley Shiraz 2008** Dark fruits, licorice, dark chocolate
and mulled spices co-exist on the bouquet; the palate is full and luscious, with
hedonistic levels of sweet fruit on display; chewy and impressively proportioned to
conclude. Cork. 14.5% alc. **Rating** 94 **To** 2018 $70 BE

McHenry Hohnen Vintners   ★★★★☆
McHenrys Farm Shop, 5962 Caves Road, Margaret River, WA 6285 **Region** Margaret River
T (08) 9757 9684 **F** (08) 9757 9176 **www**.mchv.com.au **Open** 7 days 10–5
Winemaker Freya Hohnen, Ryan Walsh **Est.** 2004 **Cases** 8000 **Vyds** 120 ha
McHenry Hohnen is owned by the McHenry and Hohnen families, sourcing grapes from
four vineyards owned by various members of the families. In all, 120 ha of vines have been
established on the McHenry, Calgardup Brook, Rocky Road and McLeod Creek properties.
A significant part of the grape production is sold to others (including Cape Mentelle), but
McHenry Hohnen have 18 varieties to choose from in fashioning their wines. The family
members with direct executive responsibilities are leading Perth retailer Murray McHenry,
Cape Mentelle founder and former long-term winemaker David Hohnen, and Freya Hohnen,
who shares the winemaking duties with partner Ryan Walsh. In 2007 David received the
inaugural Len Evans Award for Leadership. Not helped by lack of samples submitted for this
edition. Exports to the UK, Japan, Singapore, Hong Kong and NZ.

♀♀♀♀♀ **Rolling Stone 2007** Generously proportioned, with exuberant fruits matched
by calm tannins, oak an onlooker. Best leave the wine to sort itself out for a
minimum of five years before the long plateau of optimum drinkability arrives.
Malbec/Cabernet Sauvignon/Merlot/Petit Verdot. Screwcap. 14.5% alc. **Rating** 95
To 2032 $37

♀♀♀♀♀ **Tiger Country Margaret River Tempranillo Petit Verdot Cabernet
Sauvignon 2006** Rating 90 **To** 2015 $37

McIvor Estate   ★★★★☆
80 Tooborac-Baynton Road, Tooborac, Vic 3522 **Region** Heathcote
T (03) 5433 5266 **F** (03) 5433 5358 **www**.mcivorestate.com.au **Open** W'ends &
public hols 10–5, or by appt
Winemaker Various contract **Est.** 1997 **Cases** 2000
McIvor Estate is situated at the base of the Tooborac Hills, at the southern end of the
Heathcote wine region, 5 km southwest of Tooborac. Gary and Cynthia Harbor have planted
5.3 ha of marsanne, roussanne, shiraz, cabernet sauvignon, merlot, nebbiolo and sangiovese.

♀♀♀♀♀ **Nebbiolo 2008** Very good bright crimson; a major surprise, with delicious
✪   flowery, small berry fruit flavours and, best of all, fine-grained, balanced tannins.
Screwcap. 13% alc. **Rating** 94 **To** 2016 $25

ŸŸŸŸŸ Shiraz 2008 Rating 93 To 2023 $35
Heathcote Sangiovese 2007 Rating 91 To 2014 $25
Heathcote Marsanne Roussanne 2009 Rating 90 To 2013 $25
Heathcote Sangiovese 2008 Rating 90 To 2015 $25

McKellar Ridge Wines   ★★★★

Point of View Vineyard, 2 Euroka Avenue, Murrumbateman, NSW 2582
Region Canberra District **T** (02) 6258 1556 **F** (02) 6258 9770
www.mckellarridgewines.com.au **Open** Sun 12–5, or by appt Sept–Jun
Winemaker Dr Brian Johnston **Est.** 2000 **Cases** 600 **Vyds** 5.5 ha
Dr Brian Johnston and his wife Janet are the partners in McKellar Ridge Wines. Brian has
completed a postgraduate diploma in science at CSU, focusing on wine science and wine
production techniques. The wines come from low-yielding, mature vines and have had
significant show success (shiraz, cabernet sauvignon, chardonnay, merlot and viognier). They
are made using a combination of traditional and new winemaking techniques, the emphasis
being on fruit-driven styles.

ŸŸŸŸŸ Trio Canberra District Cabernet Sauvignon Cabernet Franc Merlot
2008 Brilliant crimson hue; a fragrant bouquet of redcurrant, red cherry and
blackcurrant, then an elegant medium-bodied palate, the flavours mainly in the
red spectrum and fully ripe, the fine tannins ditto. Screwcap. 14.5% alc. **Rating** 94
To 2017 $28

ŸŸŸŸ Basket Press Canberra District Shiraz Viognier 2008 Rating 88 To 2013 $28

McLaren Ridge Estate   ★★★

Whitings Road, McLaren Vale, SA 5171 **Region** McLaren Vale
T (08) 8383 0504 **F** (08) 8383 0504 www.mclarenridge.com **Open** 7 days 11–5
Winemaker Brian Light **Est.** 1997 **Cases** 5000 **Vyds** 6 ha
Peter and Heather Oliver have 4 ha of shiraz and 2 ha of grenache, planted over 50 years ago
on the ridge that now gives their estate its name. The cellar door opened in 2007, and luxury
vineyard accommodation is available. Exports to the UK and Canada.

ŸŸŸŸ GSM 2007 Quite lively, with some freshness and savoury spice provided by this
traditional Rhône blend; medium-bodied, with red fruits and a touch of Provincial
herbs. ProCork. 14% alc. **Rating** 87 To 2013 $20 BE

McLaren Vale III Associates   ★★★★★

130 Main Road, McLaren Vale, SA 5171 **Region** McLaren Vale
T 1800 501 513 **F** (08) 8323 7422 www.associates.com.au **Open** Mon–Fri 9–5,
tasting by appt
Winemaker Brian Light **Est.** 1999 **Cases** 14 000 **Vyds** 34 ha
The three associates in question all have a decade or more of wine industry experience;
Mary Greer is managing partner, Reginald Wymond chairing partner, and Christopher Fox
partner. The partnership has two vineyards, one owned by Mary and John Greer, the other
by Reg and Sue Wymond. An impressive portfolio of affordable quality wines has been the
outcome, precisely as the partners wished. Exports to the US, Canada, Germany, Hong Kong
and Singapore.

ŸŸŸŸŸ Descendant of Squid Ink Shiraz 2008 Strong crimson-purple; viewed
against the other Squid Ink wines (present and past vintages), this is a particularly
elegant and harmonious wine, the regional black fruits given free expression, oak
and tannins with a lesser role; trophy McLaren Vale Wine Show '09. Screwcap.
14.5% alc. **Rating** 94 To 2020 $35

Squid Ink Reserve Shiraz 2008 Slightly deeper colour than Descendant; an undoubtedly full-bodied wine, with a peacock's tail display of blackberry fruit, dark chocolate and vanillan oak, and with impeccable balance and line, the finish supple. Screwcap. 14.5% alc. **Rating** 94 **To** 2023 $50

ƟƟƟƟƟ Four Score Grenache 2008 **Rating** 92 **To** 2016 $30
Squid Ink Sparkling Shiraz NV **Rating** 90 **To** 2014 $50

ƟƟƟƟ Memento Cabernet Sauvignon 2008 **Rating** 89 **To** 2014 $30

McLean's Farm   ★★★★☆

barr-Eden Vineyard, Menglers Hill Road, Tanunda, SA 5352 **Region** Eden Valley
T (08) 8564 3340 **F** (08) 8564 3340 **www**.mcleansfarm.com **Open** W'ends 10–5, or by appt
Winemaker Bob McLean **Est.** 2001 **Cases** 6000
Bob McLean has gone perilously close to being a marketing legend in his own lifetime, moving from Orlando to Petaluma and then St Hallett. The farm shed on the home property produces 1000 cases of red wine; the remainder of the production is contract made by some very savvy winemakers. There are now three brands: barr-Eden from the estate vineyard and sold only ex cellar for private buyers and some trade; second, McLean's Farmgate is made in lots of 250–300 cases each when special parcels of grapes become available from 'a few old chums'; and, thirdly, McLean's Farm, 100% Barossa fruit and now made through the Dorrien Estate facility. These wines are sold through Cellarmasters, but with some restaurant listings. The barr-Eden Vineyard, with an altitude of around 500 m, is one of the highest in the Eden Valley. Exports to the UK.

ƟƟƟƟƟ barr-Eden Riesling 2009 The colour is bright, the bouquet good, but it is the tension and structure of the strongly minerally palate that gives this riesling its quality, and will underpin the growth in intensity of the lime fruit at its core. Screwcap. 12% alc. **Rating** 94 **To** 2020 $35

ƟƟƟƟƟ barr-Eden Mataro Shiraz Grenache 2007 **Rating** 93 **To** 2016 $35
Reserve Barossa Valley Grenache Shiraz Mataro 2007 **Rating** 93 **To** 2015 $32
Eden Valley Cabernet Sauvignon 2006 **Rating** 93 **To** 2020 $35

ƟƟƟƟ Barossa Chardonnay 2009 **Rating** 88 **To** 2012 $26
Barossa Valley Semillon 2008 **Rating** 87 **To** 2013 $23

McLeish Estate   ★★★★★

462 De Beyers Road, Pokolbin, NSW 2320 **Region** Hunter Valley
T (02) 4998 7754 **F** (02) 4998 7754 **www**.mcleishhunterwines.com.au
Open 7 days 10–5, or by appt
Winemaker Andrew Thomas (Contract) **Est.** 1985 **Cases** 8000 **Vyds** 14 ha
Bob and Maryanne McLeish began planting their vineyard in 1985, and now have semillon, chardonnay, verdelho, shiraz, merlot and cabernet sauvignon. They have also opened their cellar door, having accumulated a number of gold medals for their wines, thanks in no small measure to the winemaking skills of Andrew Thomas. Exports to the UK and the US.

ƟƟƟƟƟ Hunter Valley Semillon 2009 Pale straw-green; a very intense and expressive
✪   bouquet of citrus, lemon to the fore, then an equally intense and pervasive palate, with almost freakish intensity of citrus fruit; the finish lingers long. Screwcap. 11% alc. **Rating** 96 **To** 2020 $23
✪   Reserve Hunter Valley Chardonnay 2009 Light green-straw; a prime example of early picking that has not killed the varietal fruit; intense white peach and grapefruit flavours run through the long palate, oak at once present yet largely irrelevant. Screwcap. 12.8% alc. **Rating** 94 **To** 2015 $25
Reserve McLaren Vale Shiraz 2008 Strong crimson-red; has an exceptional array of black cherry, plum and black berry fruits allied with ripe tannins, a touch of dark chocolate and positive oak; a medium-bodied, mouthfilling wine. Screwcap. 15% alc. **Rating** 94 **To** 2023 $45

ΥΥΥΥ♀   **Hunter Valley Semillon Chardonnay 2009** A 50/50 blend which is a
❂   marriage of opportunity rather than convenience; citrus and white peach aromas
        and flavours dance around each other, the chardonnay most obvious on the back-
        palate and finish. Screwcap. 11.8% alc. **Rating** 92 **To** 2014 $18
❂   **Hunter Valley Orange Semillon Sauvignon Blanc 2009** Although the
        Orange sauvignon blanc component accounts for only 40% of the blend, its
        tropical fruit leads the mid-palate flavours, citrussy acidity on the finish from the
        semillon. Screwcap. 12% alc. **Rating** 90 **To** 2011 $18
        Jessica's Hunter Valley Botrytis Semillon 2009 Rating 90 To 2012 $25

ΥΥΥΥ   **Hunter Valley Verdelho 2009** Rating 88 To 2011 $16

McPherson Wines   ★★★★☆

PO Box 767, Hawthorn, Vic 3122 **Region** Nagambie Lakes
T (03) 9832 1700 **F** (03) 9832 1750 **www**.mcphersonwines.com **Open** Not
Winemaker Geoff Thompson, Joanne Nash **Est.** 1993 **Cases** 420 000 **Vyds** 262 ha
McPherson Wines is not well known in Australia but is, by any standards, a substantial business.
Its wines are largely produced for the export market, with some sales in Australia. Made at
various locations from the estate vineyards and supplemented with contract-grown grapes,
they represent very good value. For the record, McPherson Wines is a joint venture between
Andrew McPherson and Alister Purbrick (Tahbilk), both of whom have had a lifetime of
experience in the industry. Exports to all major markets.

ΥΥΥΥΥ   **Basilisk Shiraz Mourvedre 2008** Very well made, the spicy red and black
❂   cherry fruit of the shiraz working synergistically with the tannins of the
        mourvedre, which are fine rather than robust. All in all, a notably elegant wine.
        Gold medal Sydney Wine Show '10. Screwcap. 14.5% alc. **Rating** 94 **To** 2016 $18

ΥΥΥΥ♀   **Chapter Three Shiraz Viognier 2007** Rating 90 To 2014 $30
❂   **Cabernet Sauvignon 2009** Bright crimson-purple; a lively palate with
        extremely good varietal fruit flavours ranging from red and blackcurrant to plum;
        ridiculously good value. Cork. 14% alc. **Rating** 90 **To** 2014 $11

ΥΥΥΥ   **Basilisk Cabernet Merlot 2008** Rating 89 To 2016 $18
❂   **Sauvignon Blanc 2009** You can't expect any more from a sauvignon blanc at
        this price; while not intense, the aromas and flavours are authentic in a gentle
        tropical mode, the finish clean and well balanced. Screwcap. 12% alc. **Rating** 87
        To 2011 $11
❂   **Shiraz 2009** Bright colour; blue and blackberry fruit bouquet, with a slight briny
        edge; the palate is fleshy and forward, with a few rough edges; good concentration
        and flavour for the price. Screwcap. 14.5% alc. **Rating** 87 **To** 2014 $11 BE

McWilliam's   ★★★★★

Jack McWilliam Road, Hanwood, NSW 2680 **Region** Riverina
T (02) 6963 3400 **F** (02) 6963 3444 **www**.mcwilliamswinesgroup.com
Open Mon–Fri 10–4, Sat 10–5
Winemaker Jim Brayne, Corey Ryan **Est.** 1916 **Cases** NFP **Vyds** 445 ha
The best wines to emanate from the Hanwood winery are from other regions, notably the
Barwang Vineyard at Hilltops (see separate entry), Coonawarra (Brand's Laira), Yarra Valley,
Tumbarumba and Eden Valley. As McWilliam's viticultural resources have expanded, they have
been able to produce regional blends from across Australia of startlingly good value. The 2006
sale of McWilliam's Yenda winery to Casella has led to a major upgrade in both the size and
equipment at the Hanwood winery, now the nerve centre of the business. Exports to all major
markets via a major distribution joint venture with Gallo.

ΥΥΥΥΥ   **1877 Cabernet Sauvignon Shiraz 2004** Festooned with gold, top gold
        medals and a trophy, this multi-regional, two-varietal blend is as good an example
        of the quality of wines as you are ever likely to find. It is supremely elegant
        and beautifully balanced. Pity about the cork (for the US market, one assumes).
        14% alc. **Rating** 96 **To** 2014 $95

Morning Light Riverina Botrytis Semillon 2007 Glowing gold; the making of these wines has become steadily more sophisticated over time; French oak maturation, picking at less than maximum botrytis to provide a finer and more balanced wine has worked well, and all the honey and cumquat marmalade one expects is there. Screwcap. 12% alc. **Rating** 94 **To** 2013 $29.95

ΨΨΨΨΩ **Catching Thieves Margaret River Chardonnay 2008** Vivid green hue;
✪   quite a savoury bouquet, indicating interesting winemaking, employing solids for complexity; the palate shows a distinctly lemony personality, with a touch of honey to conclude; very good savoury drinking for the price. Screwcap. 13% alc. **Rating** 92 **To** 2014 $17 BE
Catching Thieves Margaret River Semillon Sauvignon Blanc 2009 **Rating** 91 **To** 2009 $17

✪   **Hanwood Estate Cabernet Sauvignon 2008** Cleverly made; there are substantial cool-climate contibutions in addition to the Riverina component; is a considerable WA component; has good savoury structure and texture under-pinning red and blackcurrant fruit. Screwcap. 13.5% alc. **Rating** 91 **To** 2014 $13

✪   **Hanwood Estate Sauvignon Blanc 2009** Doubtless draws on McWilliam's Australia-wide grape resources; has lively passionfruit and gooseberry flavours backed by crisp acidity that leaves the mouth clean and fresh. Screwcap. 12% alc. **Rating** 90 **To** 2010 $13

✪   **Hanwood Estate Cabernet Merlot 2008** Significantly over delivers, using grapes from the Limestone Coast/Yarra Valley/Hilltops/Riverina; blackcurrant fruit is counterbalanced by some savoury/olive notes ex the merlot; the texture and structure are both impressive. Screwcap. 13.5% alc. **Rating** 90 **To** 2013 $13

ΨΨΨΨ **Hanwood Estate Chardonnay 2008** Nectarine and spice bouquet, with a
✪   little citrus providing lift; juicy and fine, with persistent varietal character playing across the palate; excellent quality for the price. Screwcap. 13.5% alc. **Rating** 89 **To** 2014 $13 BE

✪   **Hanwood Estate Crisp Chardonnay 2009** Vibrant green hue; green pear and nectarine bouquet, striving for freshness; the palate is lively and shows nectarine and zesty acidity to finish. Screwcap. 13% alc. **Rating** 88 **To** 2013 $13 BE

✪   **Hanwood Estate Shiraz 2007** A well-crafted wine, with above-average structure and complexity for this price point in a black fruit spectrum; good balance. Screwcap. 13.5% alc. **Rating** 88 **To** 2013 $13

✪   **Inheritance Shiraz Cabernet 2009** Pure juicy red fruit bouquet and palate, with a little drying firmness provided by the cabernet; reasonably persistent on the finish. Screwcap. 13.5% alc. **Rating** 88 **To** 2013 $7.50 BE

✪   **Hanwood Estate Pinot Noir Chardonnay Brut NV** A far cry from the Brut of days gone by, reflecting McWilliam's far reach across Australia's warm and cool regions alike; good balance, line and length, the finish fine and dry. Cork. 11.5% alc. **Rating** 88 **To** 2012 $13

✪   **Inheritance Fruitwood Pink NV** Surprisingly like the back label claims: fruit salad in a glass; fresh, lively and sure to be popular with many. Screwcap. 8% alc. **Rating** 88 **To** 2012 $7.50 BE

✪   **Inheritance Fruitwood Red NV** Bright cherry fruit, delivered on a semisweet platform; quite refreshing when chilled properly. Screwcap. 9% alc. **Rating** 88 **To** 2012 $7.50 BE

✪   **Inheritance Riesling 2009** Clean and varietal, with lemon and grapefruit on the bouquet and palate; vibrant, juicy and generous; made for early consumption. Screwcap. 11.5% alc. **Rating** 87 **To** 2013 $7.50 BE

✪   **Hanwood Estate Chardonnay 2007** A supremely honest, full-flavoured, commercial chardonnay, with ripe peachy fruit to the fore, and no excessive sweetness. Screwcap. 13.5% alc. **Rating** 87 **To** 2010 $13

✪   **Inheritance Shiraz Merlot 2009** Bright and juicy, with spiced plum fruit; light, juicy palate, forward and quite fleshy; easy-drinking style. Screwcap. 13.5% alc. **Rating** 87 **To** 2012 $7.50 BE

McWilliam's Mount Pleasant ★★★★★

Marrowbone Road, Pokolbin, NSW 2320 **Region** Hunter Valley
T (02) 4998 7505 **F** (02) 4998 7761 **www**.mcwilliamswinegroup.com **Open** 7 days 10–5
Winemaker Phillip Ryan, Andrew Leembruggen **Est.** 1921 **Cases** NFP **Vyds** 119 ha
McWilliam's Elizabeth and the glorious Lovedale Semillon are generally commercially available with four to five years of bottle age; they are undervalued treasures with a consistently superb show record. The individual vineyard wines, together with the Maurice O'Shea memorial wines, add to the lustre of this proud name. Exports to many countries, the most important being the UK and Canada.

♟♟♟♟♟ **Maurice O'Shea Shiraz 2007** Youthful hue; an unevolved bouquet, redolent of fresh crushed blackberries, redcurrant and an ironstone minerality running through the core; there is plenty of very good oak evident marrying with the fruit with apparent ease; medium-bodied with superfine tannins and vibrant almost crunchy acidity; long and deserving of some time in the cellar to show full potential. Screwcap. 14.8% alc. **Rating** 96 **To** 2028 $65 BE
Lovedale Limited Release Hunter Valley Semillon 2005 Pale straw-green; still crawling on all fours, so youthful is it; long live the screwcap, although the price comes as a shock after decades of underpricing; lemon citrus and grass still do the talking, with no sign of honey, which will come with time. 11.5% alc. **Rating** 95 **To** 2030 $65
Elizabeth Semillon 2002 Museum. Bright, light green-gold; still has obvious CO_2 present, making it obvious this was always intended to be a late release, with a last hurrah for the cork; this bottle was absolutely delicious, with lemon and vanilla nuances, toast yet to appear. 10.5% alc. **Rating** 95 **To** 2014 $40
✪ **Elizabeth Semillon 2005** Classic lemon curd bouquet, with the merest hint of toast providing interest; zesty, lively and textbook Hunter semillon, thankfully under a screwcap; a healthy life ahead. 11.5% alc. **Rating** 94 **To** 2020 $22 BE
Original Vineyard Rosehill Hunter Valley Shiraz 2007 Quite a lifted almost floral bouquet, with black cherry and a gentle spice aspect to the fruit; warm, rich and generous palate, with fine tannins and an almost slippery quality to the fruit; seamless on the finish. Screwcap. 13.6% alc. **Rating** 94 **To** 2020 $34 BE

♟♟♟♟♟ **Original Vineyard OP&OH Hunter Valley Shiraz 2007** **Rating** 92 **To** 2020 $40 BE
✪ **Philip Hunter Valley Shiraz 2008** Vibrant and pure red fruit bouquet, with a thin veil of cinnamon and clove adding interest; the palate is medium-bodied, with a huge sweet spot on the mid-palate; quite silky and precise to conclude. Screwcap. 14% alc. **Rating** 91 **To** 2016 $18 BE
Philip Hunter Valley Shiraz 2007 **Rating** 90 **To** 2014 $18

Mad Dog Wines ★★★★☆

PO Box 166, Tanunda, SA 5352 **Region** Barossa Valley
T (08) 8563 2758 **F** (08) 8563 2027 **www**.maddogwines.com **Open** Not
Winemaker Jeremy Holmes, Matthew Munzberg **Est.** 1999 **Cases** 400 **Vyds** 35 ha
Geoff (aka Mad Dog) Munzberg, a third-generation grapegrower, has joined with Jeremy and Heidi Holmes, Aaron and Kirsty Brasher and son Matthew to create Mad Dog Wines. The principal wine, Shiraz, comes from vines with an average age of 35 years; most of the grapes are sold, with the best kept for the Mad Dog label. The purchase of a neighbouring vineyard in 2006 has led to the inclusion of some 100-year-old vine fruit, and the range has been extended with small amounts of Moscato and Sangiovese. Exports to the UK.

♟♟♟♟♟ **Barossa Valley Sangiovese 2008** Attractive cherry/sour cherry/spice aromas
✪ and flavours are classic varietal indicators; the tannins have been expertly handled, the oak (French) likewise. Screwcap. 14% alc. **Rating** 94 **To** 2015 $26

♟♟♟♟♟ **Barossa Valley Shiraz 2006** **Rating** 90 **To** 2014 $26

Maddens Rise ★★★☆

Cnr Maroondah Highway/Maddens Lane, Coldstream, Vic 3770 **Region** Yarra Valley
T (03) 8608 2560 **F** (03) 8608 1115 **www**.maddensrise.com **Open** Fri–Mon 11–5
Winemaker Luke Lambert **Est.** 1996 **Cases** 2500 **Vyds** 24 ha
Justin Fahey has established a vineyard planted to pinot noir, chardonnay, cabernet sauvignon, merlot, shiraz, viognier and nebbiolo. Planting began in 1996, although the first wines were not released until 2004. The vines are grown using organic/biological farming practices that focus on soil and vine health, low yields and hand picking to optimise the quality. Part of the grape production is sold to other Yarra Valley wineries.

♟♟♟♟   **Yarra Valley Chardonnay 2009** Light straw-green; surprisingly juicy, given its very low alcohol and its citrus-dominated aromas and flavours; wild-fermented, little oak evident; not fined or filtered. Screwcap. 11.2% alc. **Rating** 88 **To** 2012 $25

Madeleines Wines ★★★★★

PO Box 778, McLaren Vale, SA 5171 **Region** Southern Fleurieu
T 0447 009 795 **F** (08) 8370 5737 **www**.vincognita.com.au **Open** Not
Winemaker Peter Belej, Chris Dix **Est.** 1999 **Cases** 4000 **Vyds** 42.3 ha
This is the former Vincognita, jointly owned by Peter Belej and Chris Dix. The business was in fact founded by Chris, who had been winemaker with Lindemans for six years, and chief winemaker at Fox Creek Wines for five years. In 2002 Peter joined the business, with primary responsibility for the vineyards, but also with an executive winemaking role. The estate plantings are substantial, and the wines have accumulated an extraordinary number of gold medals and other awards since 2006. Exports to China.

♟♟♟♟♟   **Macclesfield Single Vineyard Musque Adelaide Hills Chardonnay 2009**
✪   A sophisticated wine with wild ferment of cloudy juice in aged French barriques of the so-called Musque (musk) chardonnay clone, often heard of in France, but not Australia. The result is a complex, powerful, tangy and convincing wine. Screwcap. 13% alc. **Rating** 94 **To** 2013 $24
✪   **Nangkita Single Vineyard Viognier 2008** Remarkably intense palate combining peach, stone fruit and grapefruit; very good balance and length. Gold medal Sydney Wine Show '09. Screwcap. 13% alc. **Rating** 94 **To** 2013 $19.50
✪   **Willunga Single Vineyard McLaren Vale Shiraz 2008** Deep colour, with a good hue; the full-bodied palate is powerful and dense, with blackberry, licorice, plum and dark chocolate flavours, the texture supple and smooth, and easily carrying its alcohol. Screwcap. 15% alc. **Rating** 94 **To** 2023 $24
         NSX Nangkita Shiraz 2007 Good hue, still with some crimson; has some flavour similarities to Madeleines, but much more dark berry flavour intensity and structure, the tannins equivalently more powerful; 110 dozen made. Screwcap. 15% alc. **Rating** 94 **To** 2022 $48

♟♟♟♟♀   **Nangkita Single Vineyard Shiraz 2008** Fair colour; a very complex and
✪   fragrant bouquet, and an intriguing palate, spicy, tangy and savoury flavours suggesting a wine with 13% alcohol, not 15%, its future uncertain. Screwcap. **Rating** 93 **To** 2023 $19.90
✪   **Nangkita Single Vineyard Gewurztraminer 2009** Bright and clear colour; faint touches of spice and rose petal establish the wine's varietal credentials, and it has considerable length, the flavours growing on retasting. Screwcap. 14% alc. **Rating** 92 **To** 2014 $15
✪   **Willunga Single Vineyard McLaren Vale Shiraz 2007** Dense crimson-purple; massively concentrated yet not over-extracted; multiple layers of blackberry and satsuma plum fruit; from the oldest vines in the Willunga district. Screwcap. 15% alc. **Rating** 92 **To** 2027 $19.90
✪   **Nangkita Single Vineyard Instinct Chardonnay 2009** Cool-grown and seemingly unoaked, with a bright mix of nectarine and grapefruit aromas and flavours; good mouthfeel and length. Screwcap. 13.5% alc. **Rating** 90 **To** 2012 $15
         Nangkita Single Vineyard Viognier 2009 Rating 90 **To** 2012 $19.50

🍷🍷🍷🍷 ✪ **Nangkita Single Vineyard Sauvignon Blanc 2009** An aromatic mix of tropical, grass and citrus notes lay the way for the palate, with its neat array of flavours and balanced finish. Screwcap. 12.5% alc. **Rating** 89 **To** 2010 $15
Nangkita Single Vineyard Shiraz 2007 **Rating** 89 **To** 2014 $19.50
Nangkita Single Vineyard Primitivo 2008 **Rating** 89 **To** 2018 $19.90
Shiraz 2007 **Rating** 88 **To** 2015 $19.50
Nangkita Single Vineyard Essencia Sweet Viognier 2009 **Rating** 88 **To** 2011 $15

Magpie Estate ★★★★★

PO Box 126, Tanunda, SA 5352 **Region** Barossa Valley
T (08) 8562 3300 **F** (08) 8562 1177 **Open** Not
Winemaker Rolf Binder, Noel Young **Est.** 1993 **Cases** 5000

This is a partnership between Rolf Binder and Cambridge (UK) wine merchant Noel Young. It came about in 1993 when there was limited demand for or understanding of Southern Rhône–style blends based on shiraz, grenache and mourvedre. Initially a small, export-only brand, the quality of the wines was such that it has grown over the years, although the intention is to limit production. The majority of the wines are reasonably priced, the super-premiums more expensive. Exports to the UK, the US, Canada, Austria, Finland, Belgium and the Bahamas.

🍷🍷🍷🍷🍷 **The Election Barossa Shiraz 2006** Good hue; a complex bouquet of black cherry, spice and oak; the medium-bodied palate has excellent line and length, plum and black cherry, spice and oak (ex 22 months' maturation). Cork. 14.5% alc. **Rating** 94 **To** 2020 $70

The Malcolm Barossa Valley Shiraz 2006 Deeper colour than The Election, with more purple; a deep, full-bodied wine, saturated with black fruits, licorice and a hint of dark chocolate, tannins and a surge of barrel ferment American oak; all these characters manage to largely carry the alcohol. Power is the key word here, with no pretence of elegance. High-quality cork. 15.5% alc. **Rating** 94 **To** 2026 $150

✪ **The Schnell Barossa Valley Shiraz Grenache 2007** Light, bright red; a fragrant and complex bouquet, with red fruits of quite different registers, one ex the shiraz, one ex the grenache; the medium-bodied palate does not disappoint, adding fine tannins to impressively extend the length. Screwcap. 14% alc. **Rating** 94 **To** 2015 $20

The Gomersal Barossa Grenache 2006 Deeper, more purple hue than The Fakir, despite an extra year in bottle; the excellent vintage, and the addition of a small amount of shiraz, has given the wine stature and texture akin to that of the best McLaren Vale grenache; delicious red and black fruits, spice and fine, persistent tannins are the mark of a very good grenache. Cork. 14% alc. **Rating** 94 **To** 2015 $50

🍷🍷🍷🍷½ **The Sack Barossa Valley Shiraz 2007** **Rating** 92 **To** 2015 $30

✪ **The Fakir Barossa Valley Grenache 2007** Bright, relatively light colour; a lively, fresh, red-fruited Barossa Valley grenache, with spices denoting the variety rather than confection/Turkish delight; I enjoy the restraint in flavour, achieved without sacrificing length. Screwcap. 14% alc. **Rating** 91 **To** 2017 $25

✪ **The Salvation Gewurztraminer 2009** Bright green-gold; interesting wine; abundant ripe fruit flavour without phenolics intruding; however, there are as many riesling flavours as gewurztraminer, albeit with some lychee on the finish. Screwcap. 13% alc. **Rating** 90 **To** 2014 $20

The Call Bag Mourvedre Grenache 2007 **Rating** 90 **To** 2015 $25

🍷🍷🍷🍷 **The Black Sock Barossa Valley Mourvedre 2007** **Rating** 89 **To** 2015 $30

Magpie Springs   ★★★☆

RSD 1790 Meadows Road, Hope Forest, SA 5172 **Region** Adelaide Hills
T (08) 8556 7351 **F** (08) 8556 7351 www.magpiesprings.com.au **Open** Fri–Sun &
public hols 11–5
Winemaker Adrian Kenny, Reg Wilkinson **Est.** 1991 **Cases** 1000 **Vyds** 15.3 ha
Stuart Brown and Rosemary (Roe) Gartelmann purchased the property on which Magpie
Springs is now established in 1983, for growing flowers commercially and grazing cattle.
Chardonnay was planted experimentally, and were among the earliest vines in the area. In
1991 the commencement of the vineyard proper led to the planting of a little over 15 ha of
semillon, chardonnay, sauvignon blanc, pinot noir, merlot, shiraz, riesling and gewurztraminer.
Roe paints professionally from the Magpie Springs studio, and many classes and workshops
have been held over the years; her studio can be visited during cellar door hours.

Adelaide Hills Shiraz 2007 Proclaims its cool-grown origin from the word go;
has vibrant black fruits, spice, licorice and pepper all making their presence felt on
the light- to medium-bodied, long palate; best while fresh and youthful. Screwcap.
14.5% alc. **Rating** 91 **To** 2014 $18

Main Ridge Estate   ★★★★★

80 William Road, Red Hill, Vic 3937 **Region** Mornington Peninsula
T (03) 5989 2686 **F** (03) 5931 0000 www.mre.com.au **Open** Mon–Fri 12–4, w'ends 12–5
Winemaker Nat White **Est.** 1975 **Cases** 1200 **Vyds** 2.8 ha
Quietly spoken and charming founder/owners Nat and Rosalie White preside over their
immaculately maintained vineyard, and equally meticulously run winery. Their site is a
particularly cool one, and if global warming proves to be a permanent part of the landscape,
they say they will not be complaining.

Half Acre Mornington Peninsula Pinot Noir 2007 Deeper colour than usual;
a totally delicious array of vibrant red fruits with fine-grained, spicy tannins adding
appropriate authority; great balance and length. Screwcap. 13.5% alc. **Rating** 96
To 2015 $65
Mornington Peninsula Chardonnay 2008 Bright straw-green; as usual, a very
complex and strongly textured chardonnay, reflecting 100% wild yeast, 100% barrel
fermentation, and 100% mlf, all adding up to rich, creamy, nutty characters joining
the nectarine and white peach fruit. Screwcap. 13.5% alc. **Rating** 95 **To** 2014 $52

Mainbreak Wines   ★★★★☆

199 McDonald Road, Karridale, WA 6288 (postal) **Region** Margaret River
T (08) 9758 6779 **F** (08) 9758 6779 www.mainbreak.net.au **Open** Not
Winemaker Contract **Est.** 2009 **Cases** 3000
This is a small side venture to Hamelin Bay, also owned by Mainbreak Wines proprietors
Richard and Roslyn Drake-Brockman. The grapes are sourced from the southern end of
the Margaret River and the business has grown under the direction of winemaker and keen
surfer Julian Scott. The label underlines the association between the region and its outstanding
surf beaches.

Margaret River Sauvignon Blanc Semillon 2009 Not in the least flamboyant,
and has an attractive precision to its bouquet and palate that earned it a gold medal
at the Qantas WA Wine Show '09; the citrus and grass flavours drive a long palate
and clean finish. Screwcap. 12.5% alc. **Rating** 94 **To** 2012 $18

Margaret River Cabernet Merlot 2008 Good colour; an effusive bouquet of
black fruits, spice and herbs leads into a palate full of thrust and vigour to its mix
of black and red fruits plus savoury nuances. Gold medal Hobart International
Wine Show '09. Screwcap. 14% alc. **Rating** 92 **To** 2023 $18

❦ Maipenrai Vineyard & Winery   ★★★★

1516 Sutton Road, Sutton, NSW 2620 (postal) **Region** Canberra District
T (02) 8588 1217 **F** (02) 8588 1217 **www.**maipenrai.com.au **Open** Not
Winemaker Brian Schmidt **Est.** 2000 **Cases** 250 **Vyds** 1.1 ha
What a story this is, far too rich for just a few lines. It begins at Harvard, in 1992–93, where American-born Brian Schmidt and (now) wife (Australian) Jennifer Gordon were both working on their PhDs. Brian is presently a Laureate Fellow at the Australian National University's Mount Stromlo Observatory. Prior to emigrating to Canberra in '95, he had formed a research team of 20 astronomers on five continents who used distant exploding stars to trace the expansion of the universe back in time; between then and now he has been awarded a constellation of awards and fellowships, undeterred by the tragic destruction of Mount Stromlo in the Canberra bushfires in '03. In 1999 he and Jennifer purchased a property with a beautiful sloped hillside, and planted six clones of pinot noir; he was 33 at the time, and figured that by the time he was ready to retire, the vineyard would be well and truly into the prime of its life. An astronomer's view indeed. In 2004 the first barrel of wine was made, followed by three barrels in '05 and two barrels in '06; in '07 all the wine was declassified into the Amungula Creek label, also used for wine made from small amounts of pinot grapes purchased from time to time from local growers.

♟♟♟♟♟ **Canberra District Pinot Noir 2005** More youthful colour than the '06; there is also substantially more fruit, in a spiced plum spectrum; good mouthfeel and balance. One of the first wines in Australia to adopt the Vino-Lok. 13% alc. **Rating** 90 **To** 2013 $28

Majella   ★★★★★

Lynn Road, Coonawarra, SA 5263 **Region** Coonawarra
T (08) 8736 3055 **F** (08) 8736 3057 **www.**majellawines.com.au **Open** 7 days 10–4.30
Winemaker Bruce Gregory **Est.** 1969 **Cases** 15 000 **Vyds** 60 ha
Majella is one of the foremost grapegrowers in Coonawarra, with important vineyards, principally shiraz and cabernet sauvignon, and with a little riesling and merlot. The Malleea is one of Coonawarra's greatest wines, The Musician one of Australia's most outstanding red wines selling for less than $20. Exports to the UK, the US and other major markets.

♟♟♟♟♟ **Coonawarra Cabernet Sauvignon 2007** Purple-red; a fragrant mix of
✪   cedar, cassis and earth on the bouquet is replayed on the long, medium- to full-bodied palate, which is pure Coonawarra in every respect; fine tannins, long and harmonious. Screwcap. 14.5% alc. **Rating** 96 **To** 2022 $33

✪   **The Musician Coonawarra Cabernet Shiraz 2008** Good hue; delivers as much as ever, with an abundance of blackcurrant and blackberry fruit supported by ripe tannins that give excellent balance. Screwcap. 14.5% alc. **Rating** 94 **To** 2015 $17

♟♟♟♟♟ **Coonawarra Merlot 2008 Rating** 93 **To** 2018 $28
Coonawarra Sparkling Shiraz 2005 Rating 93 **To** 2014 $28
Coonawarra Riesling 2009 Rating 90 **To** 2018 $16
Coonawarra Sparkling Shiraz 2006 Rating 90 **To** 2013 $28

Malcolm Creek Vineyard   ★★★★

Bonython Road, Kersbrook, SA 5231 **Region** Adelaide Hills
T (08) 8389 3619 **F** (08) 8389 3542 **www.**malcolmcreekwines.com.au **Open** W'ends & public hols 11–5, or by appt
Winemaker Peter Leske **Est.** 1982 **Cases** 700 **Vyds** 2 ha
Malcolm Creek was set up as the retirement venture of Reg Tolley, who decided to upgrade his retirement by selling the venture to Bitten and Karsten Pedersen in 2007. They intend to continue making the wines in the same age-worthy style. The wines are invariably well made

and develop gracefully; they are worth seeking out, and are usually available with some extra bottle age at a very modest price. Exports to the UK, the US and Denmark.

ŸŸŸŸ♀ **Ashwood Estate Adelaide Hills Chardonnay 2008** Light straw-green; a
✪ distinctly restrained and elegant style, with a backbone of minerality providing its structure, 10 months in oak providing the texture. Screwcap. 14% alc. **Rating** 90 To 2014 $18

Malone Wines   ★★★★

PMB 47, Naracoorte, SA 5271 **Region** Wrattonbully
T (08) 8764 6075 **F** (08) 8764 6060 **www**.malonewines.com.au **Open** Not
Winemaker Paulett Wines **Est.** 2005 **Cases** 500 **Vyds** 23 ha
The third and fourth generations of the Malone family continue to farm the Talinga property, owned by the family since 1930. The planting of vines in '98 was a minor diversification from the core businesses of producing prime lamb, hay and pasture seed. The decision was taken to focus on shiraz and cabernet sauvignon, with most of the grapes being sold, and limited amounts made under the Malone label. The results have been impressive, to say the least.

ŸŸŸŸ♀ **Wrattonbully Shiraz 2007** Deep, dark red; while (only) medium-bodied, is packed with plum, blackberry and black cherry fruit, complexed by a touch of spice; the palate is long and well balanced, the vanillan oak appropriate for the fruit flavours. Screwcap. 14.5% alc. **Rating** 93 To 2020 $25
Wrattonbully Cabernet Sauvignon 2007 Malone obviously has a good vineyard site; medium-bodied, the wine has clear varietal expression and compelling elegance and length, the fruit and tannins are well balanced. Screwcap. 13.5% alc. **Rating** 91 To 2017 $25

Mandala   ★★★★★

1568 Melba Highway, Dixons Creek, Vic 3775 **Region** Yarra Valley
T (03) 5965 2016 **F** (03) 5965 2147 **www**.mandalawines.com.au **Open** 7 days 10–5
Winemaker Scott McCarthy (Contract) **Est.** 2007 **Cases** 7000 **Vyds** 27.4 ha
Mandala was officially opened in July 2008 by owner Charles Smedley. The estate vineyard has vines up to 20 years old, but the spectacular restaurant and cellar door complex is entirely new. The vineyards are primarily at the home base, Dixons Creek, with chardonnay (8.7 ha), sauvignon blanc, cabernet sauvignon and pinot noir (a little over 4 ha each), shiraz (1.7 ha) and merlot (0.4 ha), and a separate 4-ha vineyard of pinot noir at Yarra Junction with an impressive clonal mix. The restaurant has deservedly achieved considerable praise.

ŸŸŸŸŸ **Prophet Yarra Valley Pinot Noir 2008** Strong, clear colour; has a fragrant bouquet centred on cherry, plum and raspberry aromas; the palate is silky and juicy, with very good mouthfeel and length. Screwcap. 14% alc. **Rating** 95 To 2015 $50
Yarra Valley Chardonnay 2008 Bright green-straw; very much in the modern idiom, early picked and subtle French oak; flavours of nectarine, white peach and grapefruit drive the palate through to its long conclusion. Screwcap. 12.3% alc. **Rating** 94 To 2016 $25
Yarra Valley Cabernet Sauvignon 2008 An elegant wine, with cedar and spice nuances rippling through the base of blackcurrant and cassis, the texture very fine, tannins and oak simply providing background. Screwcap. 13.7% alc. **Rating** 94 To 2016 $25

ŸŸŸŸ♀ **Margaret River Sauvignon Blanc Semillon 2009 Rating** 92 To 2011 $20
Yarra Valley Shiraz 2008 Rating 92 To 2016 $25
Yarra Valley Cabernet Sauvignon 2007 Rating 92 To 2020 $25
Yarra Valley Pinot Noir 2008 Rating 90 To 2014 $25

Mandalay Estate

Mandalay Road, Glen Mervyn via Donnybrook, WA 6239 **Region** Geographe
T (08) 9732 2006 **F** (08) 9732 2006 **www**.mandalayroad.com.au **Open** 7 days 11–5
Winemaker Fermoy Estate (Liz Dawson) **Est.** 1997 **Cases** 1000 **Vyds** 4.2 ha
Tony and Bernice O'Connell left careers in science and education to establish plantings of
shiraz, chardonnay, zinfandel and cabernet sauvignon on their property in 1997. What started
off as a fun venture has quickly turned into serious grapegrowing and winemaking. A hands-
on approach with low yields has brought out the best characteristics of the grape varieties and
the region. Exports to the US.

Mandalay Road Geographe Shiraz 2007 Good red–purple hue; a fragrant
spicy bouquet, then an elegant, medium-bodied palate, red berry fruits supported
by fine tannins. Trophy Geographe Wine Show '09. Screwcap. 14.5% alc.
Rating 91 **To** 2017 $20

Mandalay Road Geographe Chardonnay 2009 Bright, pale straw–green; an
elegant wine, partial barrel ferment adding more to texture than flavour, the latter
with a mix of citrus and white peach fruit; just a little light on, perhaps. Screwcap.
13.9% alc. **Rating** 89 **To** 2012 $16

Mandalay Road Geographe Shiraz 2008 Light, but bright colour; a spicy red
and black fruit bouquet leads into a light- to medium-bodied palate, with juicy
fruit flavours and fine tannins; early-drinking style. Screwcap. 14.1% alc. **Rating** 89
To 2013 $15

Mandalay Road Cabernet Sauvignon 2007 Rating 87 **To** 2013 $16

Mansfield Wines ★★★

201 Eurunderee Lane, Mudgee, NSW 2850 **Region** Mudgee
T (02) 6373 3871 **F** (02) 6373 3708 **www**.mansfieldwines.com.au **Open** Thurs–Tues &
public hols 10–5, or by appt
Winemaker Bob Heslop **Est.** 1975 **Cases** 2000 **Vyds** 10 ha
Family-owned Mansfield Wines has moved with the times, taking the emphasis from fortified
wines to table wines (though still offering some fortifieds) and expanding the product range
to take in new-generation varieties such as savagnin, vermentino, petit manseng, parellada,
tempranillo, touriga, zinfandel and tinta cao, supported by grenache, mourvedre and pedro
ximinez.

Touriga Nacional 2008 Bright purple-red; has good mouthfeel and balance to
the black fruits and a hint of tobacco somewhere in the background; fine, ripe
tannins. Interesting varietal play. Diam. 13% alc. **Rating** 89 **To** 2016 $18

Vermentino 2009 Pale straw–green; ultra-early picking has resulted in a very
fresh wine, citrus notes to the fore, but would you guess the variety if served blind?
I couldn't. Screwcap. 10.5% alc. **Rating** 87 **To** 2011 $17

Marchand & Burch ★★★★★

PO Box 180, North Fremantle, WA 6159 **Region** Great Southern
T (08) 9336 9600 **F** (08) 9336 9622 **www**.marchandburchwines.com.au
Open At Howard Park
Winemaker Pascal Marchand, Jeff Burch **Est.** 2006 **Cases** 1100
This is the first stage of a joint venture between Canadian-born and Burgundian-trained
Pascal Marchand and the Burch family, which owns Howard Park. The first releases are of
Chardonnay and Pinot Noir sourced from the Porongurup and Mount Barker subregions
of the Great Southern and Shiraz from Frankland River/Margaret River. The Chardonnay,
in particular, is outstanding. In late 2009, two Burgundies from '07 were released: Gevrey
Chambertin ($99) and Chambertin Clos de Beze ($475), both under screwcap. Exports to the
UK, the US and Canada.

7777 **Chambertin Clos de Beze Pinot Noir 2007** Clear crimson-purple; stands apart from the best Australian pinots with its extra dimension of ripe tannins, and the way the flavours swell on the finish and aftertaste. Screwcap. 13% alc. **Rating** 96 **To** 2020 $475

Margaret River Shiraz 2008 From a single site at Wilyabrup, this is a distinguished wine, its texture and structure superb; the flavours are in a dark plum and black cherry spectrum, lifting and lilting on the finish and aftertaste, oak and tannins in perfect unison. Screwcap. 14.5% alc. **Rating** 96 **To** 2028 $65

Meursault 2007 Quite fascinating how the screwcap has kept the wine so vibrantly fresh – and (perhaps) Pascal Marchand's experience in Australia has ever-so-slightly fined the more normal exuberance of Meursault. Chardonnay. 13% alc. **Rating** 95 **To** 2020 $88

Gibraltar Rock Porongurup Pinot Noir 2009 Full red-purple, bright and clear; a powerful pinot with undeniable black plum varietal character and unusually complex structure on the long finish; in a perfect world, would have been aged for two years prior to release. Screwcap. 14% alc. **Rating** 94 **To** 2020 $70

Mount Barrow Mount Barker Pinot Noir 2009 Good hue, although lighter in depth than Gibraltar Rock; the aromatic red cherry bouquet sets the scene for a radically different wine, although no less varietal; red fruits and spices carry the long, fine palate; perfectly judged extract. Screwcap. 14.5% alc. **Rating** 94 **To** 2016 $70

Gevrey Chambertin Pinot Noir 2007 Distinctly deeper colour than the Clos de Beze; rich and generous, awash with plum and black cherry fruit and may appeal to some more than the Clos de Beze, but it isn't in the same ultimate class – just very good. Screwcap. 13% alc. **Rating** 94 **To** 2017 $99

Marcus Hill Vineyard   ★★★

560 Banks Road, Marcus Hill, Vic 3222 (postal) **Region** Geelong
T (03) 5222 5764 **www**.marcushillvineyard.com.au **Open** Not
Winemaker Darren Burke (Contract), Richard Harrison **Est.** 2000 **Cases** 1000 **Vyds** 3 ha
In 2000, Richard and Margot Harrison, together with 'gang pressed friends', planted 2 ha of pinot noir overlooking Port Lonsdale, Queenscliffe and Ocean Grove, a few kilometres from Bass Strait and Port Phillip Bay. Since then chardonnay, shiraz and pinot noir have been added. The vineyard is run with minimal sprays, and the aim is to produce elegant wines that truly express the maritime site.

7777 **Bellarine Peninsula Chardonnay 2008** Light-bodied, very much in the citrus/grapefruit aroma and flavour range, and has been well made, the use of French oak restrained, and only partial mlf. Screwcap. 12.5% alc. **Rating** 89 **To** 2013 $25

Bellarine Peninsula Shiraz 2008 Very light but bright crimson; an early-picked shiraz full of spicy/peppery red fruits, and avoids green or minty flavours. Best enjoyed soon. Screwcap. 12.5% alc. **Rating** 88 **To** 2012 $20

Bellarine Peninsula Pinot Noir 2007 Normal colour development; very savoury wine, reflecting its early picking and has probably passed its best; length is its redeeming feature. Screwcap. 12.4% alc. **Rating** 87 **To** 2011 $25

Margan Family   ★★★★★

1238 Milbrodale Road, Broke, NSW 2330 **Region** Hunter Valley
T (02) 6579 1317 **F** (02) 6579 1267 **www**.margan.com.au **Open** 7 days 10–5
Winemaker Andrew Margan **Est.** 1997 **Cases** 30 000 **Vyds** 98 ha
Andrew Margan, following in his father's footsteps, entered the wine industry over 20 years ago, and has covered a great deal of territory since, working as a Flying Winemaker in Europe, then for Tyrrell's. Andrew and wife Lisa now have almost 100 ha of fully mature vines at their Ceres Hill property at Broke, and lease the nearby Vere Vineyard. Wine quality is consistently good. The rammed-earth cellar door and restaurant are highly recommended. Exports to the UK, the US and other major markets.

ŸŸŸŸŸ Hunter Valley Semillon 2009 A good example of a family of splendid semillons
✪ from the Hunter Valley in '09; tasting immediately after a run of rieslings (from cool regions) confirms the view these '09 semillons have exceptional flavour, with some similarities to riesling from the citris nuances in most. Screwcap. 12.5% alc. Rating 94 To 2024 $18

Aged Release Semillon 2003 Bright yellow-green; a great demonstration of the ability of semillon to mature with grace under screwcap; the lemongrass and mineral flavours are underpinned by perfect acidity, the wine still with years to go. 10.5% alc. Rating 94 To 2023 $35

ŸŸŸŸŸ Aged Release Shiraz 2003 Rating 92 To 2023 $65
✪ Hunter Valley Cabernet Sauvignon 2007 Speaks as much of the region as it does of the variety, with some nuances of earth and leather, but delicious silky texture to the medium-bodied palate and its slinky red fruit flavours. Jekyll & Hyde, but good. Screwcap. 13.5% alc. Rating 92 To 2017 $20

✪ Hunter Valley Merlot 2007 A medium- to full-bodied wine with as much varietal expression as is possible from the warm Hunter environment; the palate is long, and the strength of the wine emerges on the finish and aftertaste. Very well made. Screwcap. 13.5% alc. Rating 91 To 2017 $20

✪ Hunter Valley Chardonnay 2009 Traditional Hunter Valley style, with stone fruit and melon partially barrel fermented and matured in French oak; the oak is well integrated and balanced; finishes with good acidity; 40-year-old vines play their part. Screwcap. 13.5% alc. Rating 90 To 2016 $18

✪ Hunter Valley Shiraz 2007 The mix of earth and leather leaps out of the glass in a strident expression of variety and place, the palate continuing the theme. Definitely needs time to calm down, but will do so. Screwcap. 13.5% alc. Rating 90 To 2020 $20

ŸŸŸŸ Hunter Valley Verdelho 2009 Rating 88 To 2011 $18

Marienberg/Fern Hill Estate ★★★

2 Chalk Hill Road, McLaren Vale, SA 5171 **Region** McLaren Vale
T (08) 8323 9666 **F** (08) 8323 9600 **www**.marienberg.com.au **Open** 7 days 10–5
Winemaker Graeme Scott, Daniela Neumann **Est.** 1966 **Cases** 10 000
Marienberg (founded by Australia's first female owner/vigneron, Ursula Pridham), along with Fern Hill Estate and Basedow (see separate entry), became part of the James Estate empire in 2003. A revamping of the packaging and labelling, plus acquisition of grapes from the Adelaide Hills to supplement those from McLaren Vale, has been accompanied by a move away from retail to restaurant/on-premises sales. The Marienberg Centre includes a restored 1850s cottage that incorporates the cellar door, wine bar and Limeburner's Restaurant. Exports to Canada.

ŸŸŸŸ Marienberg Reserve Shiraz 2006 Good hue; in the mainstream of traditional McLaren Vale shiraz, with black fruits, dark chocolate and vanillan oak; flavoursome, but how much better would it have been with 1% less alcohol. Screwcap. 15.5% alc. Rating 87 To 2016 $22

Maritime Estate ★★★★☆

65 Tucks Road, Red Hill, Vic 3937 **Region** Mornington Peninsula
T 0432 931 890 **Open** Not
Winemaker Sandro Mosele **Est.** 1988 **Cases** 1000 **Vyds** 4.5 ha
John and Linda Ruljancich and Kevin Ruljancich have enjoyed great success since their first vintage in 1994, no doubt due in part to skilled winemaking but also to the situation of their vineyard, looking across the hills and valleys of the Red Hill subregion.

ŸŸŸŸŸ BJRS Mornington Peninsula Chardonnay 2006 Still brilliant green; a complex bouquet offers nectarine fruit and positive and balanced barrel ferment inputs; the palate is very lively and focused, with delicious nectarine and grapefruit flavours. Diam. 14% alc. Rating 95 To 2014 $32

ŸŸŸŸŸ DJS Mornington Peninsula Pinot Noir 2006 Rating 90 To 2013 $36

Marius Wines   ★★★★★

PO Box 545, Willunga, SA 5172 **Region** McLaren Vale
T 0402 344 340 **F** (08) 8121 7656 **www**.mariuswines.com.au **Open** By appt
Winemaker Roger Pike, James Hastwell **Est.** 1994 **Cases** 1000 **Vyds** 1.8 ha
Roger Pike says he has loved wine for over 30 years; that for 15 years he has had the desire to
add a little bit to the world of wine; and that over a decade ago he decided to do something
about it, ripping the front paddock and planting shiraz in 1994. He sold the grapes from
the 1997–99 vintages, but when the '98 vintage became a single-vineyard wine (made by
the purchaser of the grapes), selling in the US at $40, the temptation to make his own wine
became irresistible. Exports to the US and Denmark.

🍷🍷🍷🍷🍷 Symphony Single Vineyard McLaren Vale Shiraz 2008 Fruit selection (the
best rows of the home vineyard shared with Simpatico) and 100% French oak add
to both the texture and flavour of the wine, as well as giving it greater length on
the medium- to full-bodied palate. Screwcap. 14.5% alc. **Rating** 95 **To** 2023 $35
End Play 2008 Enigmatic labelling, but the wine shrieks McLaren Vale on both
bouquet and palate, delicious plum and blackberry fruit in a light embrace of
dark chocolate; the tannins are fine, the length and line good. Screwcap. 14% alc.
Rating 94 **To** 2018 $35

🍷🍷🍷🍷🍷 Simpatico Single Vineyard McLaren Vale Shiraz 2008 **Rating** 93
To 2020 $25

Markwood Estate   ★★★★

135 Morris Lane, Markwood, Vic 3678 **Region** King Valley
T (03) 5727 0361 **Open** 7 days 9–5
Winemaker Rick Morris **Est.** 1971 **Cases** 200 **Vyds** 3 ha
A member of the famous Morris family, Rick Morris shuns publicity and relies virtually
exclusively on cellar door sales for what is a small output. He may shun publicity, but does so
with grace, and his Old Tawny (he won't be able to used the adjunct Port for much longer)
is a very good wine.

🍷🍷🍷🍷🍷 Select Limited Edition 30 Year Blend Old Tawny Port NV Almost into
⊘   olive on the rim; this is very old material, almost viscous; it has penetrating aromas
and flavours that Michael Broadbent might (approvingly) describe as 'swingeing'.
Cork. 19% alc. **Rating** 93 **To** 2011 $40

Marri Wood Park   ★★★★

Caves Road, Yallingup, WA 6282 **Region** Margaret River
T 0438 525 580 **F** (08) 9755 2343 **www**.marriwoodpark.com.au **Open** 7 days 11–5
Winemaker Ian Bell, Bob Cartwright, Cliff Royle **Est.** 1993 **Cases** 1800 **Vyds** 6.5 ha
With plantings commencing in 1993, Marri Wood Park has 2 ha of chenin blanc, 1.5 ha
each of sauvignon blanc and cabernet sauvignon, with 1.5 ha of semillon, malbec and merlot
making up the total; part of the grape production is sold to other makers. The budget-priced
Guinea Run range takes its name from the guinea fowl, which are permanent vineyard
residents, busily eating the grasshoppers, weevils and bugs that cluster around the base of
the vines, thus reducing the need for pesticides. The vineyard is certified 'In Conversion
Biodynamic' and commencing with the 2009 vintage, the wines will be biodynamic. The
premium Marri Wood Park range takes its name from the giant Marri gum tree depicted on
the label. Exports to Japan.

🍷🍷🍷🍷🍷 Reserve Margaret River Cabernet Sauvignon 2007 Strong colour; has all
the concentration and power typical of good Margaret River cabernets from '07;
deep black fruits are matched by strong, although ripe, tannins to sustain it for the
long haul. Screwcap. 14.5% alc. **Rating** 93 **To** 2020 $32

Marsh Estate   ★★★★☆

Deasy's Road, Pokolbin, NSW 2321 **Region** Hunter Valley
T (02) 4998 7587 **F** (02) 4998 7884 **www**.marshestate.com.au **Open** Mon–Fri 10–4.30,
w'ends 10–5
Winemaker Andrew Marsh **Est.** 1971 **Cases** 6000 **Vyds** 32 ha
Through sheer consistency, value for money and unrelenting hard work, the Marsh family has
built up a sufficiently loyal cellar door and mailing list clientele to allow all the production
to be sold direct. Wine style is always straightforward, with oak playing a minimal role, and
prolonged cellaring paying handsome dividends.

🍷🍷🍷🍷🍷 Holly's Block Hunter Valley Semillon 2009 Vibrant green hue; attractive
bouquet of straw, lemon and lime; the palate is super fresh and focused, with lovely
energy and drive, but enough generosity to be enjoyed as a young wine; will age
gracefully for years to come. Screwcap. 11% alc. **Rating** 95 **To** 2025 $29.50 BE

🍷🍷🍷🍷🍷 Hunter Valley Semillon 2009 **Rating** 92 **To** 2018 $26.50 BE

Martins Hill Wines   ★★★

1179 Castlereagh Highway, Mudgee, NSW 2850 **Region** Mudgee
T (02) 6373 1248 **F** (02) 6373 1248 **www**.martinshillwines.com.au **Open** Not
Winemaker Pieter Van Gent (Contract) **Est.** 1985 **Cases** 800 **Vyds** 4 ha
Janette Kenworthy and Michael Sweeny are both committed organic grapegrowers and
are members of the Organic Vignerons Association. Their small operation is growing, with
shiraz (2 ha), sauvignon blanc (1.5 ha), cabernet sauvignon (1 ha) and pinot noir (0.5 ha) in
productions. The vineyard is carbon neutral, with solar electricity and plantings of native trees
and shrubs. Organic vineyard tours and talks can be arranged by appointment.

🍷🍷🍷🍷 Mudgee Shiraz 2007 Despite an extremely stained cork, the hue is still good,
and the wine still fresh, perhaps sustained in part by its substantial bank of tannins
and good acidity. 14% alc. **Rating** 88 **To** 2012 $19

Mason Wines   ★★★★

27850 New England Highway, Glen Aplin, Qld 4381 **Region** Granite Belt
T (07) 4684 1341 **www**.masonwines.com.au **Open** 7 days 11–4
Winemaker Jim Barnes **Est.** 1998 **Cases** 5000 **Vyds** 30.5 ha
Robert and Kim Mason set strict criteria when searching for land suited to viticulture: a long
history of commercial stone fruit production with well-drained, deep soil. The first property
was purchased in 1997, the vines planted thereafter. A second property was purchased in 2000,
and a cellar door was constructed. They have planted cabernet sauvignon, chardonnay, shiraz,
merlot, viognier, semillon, sauvignon blanc and petit verdot. Yet another Queenslander on the
ascent. Exports to Japan.

🍷🍷🍷🍷 Granite Belt Petit Verdot 2008 Typical dense colour; lush black fruit aromas
✪ announce a full-bodied palate with similar black fruits, and excellent tannin
structure – the latter as unexpected as it is pleasing. Screwcap. 15% alc. **Rating** 94
To 2023 $18

🍷🍷🍷🍷 Granite Belt Verdelho 2009 Light straw-green; the strong citrus element in
✪ both bouquet and palate brightens the fruit salad flavours and extends the length
of the wine. Screwcap. 13.7% alc. **Rating** 89 **To** 2012 $17
Granite Belt Viognier 2009 **Rating** 88 **To** 2012 $18

Massena Vineyards   ★★★★★

PO Box 54, Tanunda, SA 5352 **Region** Barossa Valley
T (08) 8564 3037 **F** (08) 8564 3038 **www**.massena.com.au **Open** By appt
Winemaker Dan Standish, Jaysen Collins **Est.** 2000 **Cases** 5000 **Vyds** 4 ha

Massena Vineyards draws upon 1 ha each of mataro (mourvedre), saperavi, primitivo (petite syrah) and tannat at Nuriootpa, also purchasing grapes from other growers. It is an export-oriented business, although the wines can be purchased by mail order, which, given both the quality and innovative nature of the wines, seems more than ordinarily worthwhile. Exports to the UK, the US and other major markets.

ŸŸŸŸŸ **The Eleventh Hour Barossa Valley Shiraz 2008** Impenetrable colour; an opulent array of essency black fruits, dark chocolate, mulled spices and mocha; the palate is unctuous, showing deep levels of concentrated sweet fruit, followed by chewy tannins to conclude; a rich wine, perfect for a cold night. Cork. 14.5% alc. Rating 94 To 2018 $35 BE

The Looting Duke Barossa Valley Shiraz 2007 More purple tinges to the colour than Eleventh Hour, and there is more structure; the mix of blackberry, plum and bitter chocolate is supported by fine, ripe tannins and balanced oak; the alcohol is less overt, too. Cork. 14.5% alc. Rating 94 To 2022 $60

✪ **The Moonlight Run 2008** Blackberry pastille bouquet, with licorice, spice and a touch of ginger; the palate is warm, unctuous and in complete balance with all its parts; a very attractive undercurrent of Provençal herbs comes through on the finish, providing savoury complexity. Grenache/Shiraz/Mataro/Cinsaut. Cork. 14.5% alc. Rating 94 To 2015 $25 BE

ŸŸŸŸŸ
✪ **The Surly Muse Barossa Valley Viognier 2009** A rich and hedonistic offering of apricot, peach and spice; thickly textured, but with grapefruit-like acidity, providing a fresh twist to the tail; best enjoyed in its youth. Screwcap. 13.5% alc. Rating 90 To 2011 $18 BE

ŸŸŸŸ **The Eleventh Hour Barossa Valley Shiraz 2007** Rating 89 To 2017 $35

Massoni

PO Box 11036, Frankston Central, Vic 3199 **Region** Pyrenees/Mornington Peninsula **T** 1300 131 175 **F** 1300 131 185 **www**.massoniwines.com **Open** Not
Winemaker Robert Paul (Consultant) **Est.** 1984 **Cases** NA
Massoni, under the joint ownership of the Pellegrino and Ursini families, has regained control of its destiny after a proposed public share issue was terminated. The main grape source for Massoni is the very large GlenKara vineyard in the Pyrenees, with a yield well in excess of 1000 tonnes. However, the Mornington Peninsula is where Massoni started, and where it gained its reputation.

ŸŸŸŸŸ
✪ **Mornington Peninsula Pinot Noir 2008** Bright and clear crimson hue; a fragrant bouquet of red cherry and wild strawberry leads into a totally seductive palate, with vivid red fruit flavours neatly harnessed by balanced acidity; excellent length. Outstanding value. Screwcap. 13.5% alc. Rating 96 To 2015 $25

Chardonnay 2008 Pale straw-green; an estate-grown, elegant wine with white peach fruit on an extremely long and fine palate, French oak held in restraint. Screwcap. 13.5% alc. Rating 95 To 2016 $25

ŸŸŸŸŸ
✪ **Sangiovese 2006** Light colour, although the hue is holding very well; a very attractive sangiovese, with fresh cherry fruit to the fore, silky tannins gliding over the palate. Major surprise. From GlenKara Estate in the Pyrenees. Screwcap. 13.6% alc. Rating 93 To 2014 $25

Mornington Peninsula Sauvignon Blanc 2009 Rating 92 To 2011 $25
Lectus Cuvee NV Rating 92 To 2013 $27
GlenKara Estate Pyrenees Shiraz 2006 Rating 91 To 2018 $25

ŸŸŸŸ **Barbera 2005** Rating 88 To 2013 $25

Maverick Wines ★★★★★

Lot 141 Light Pass Road, Vine Vale, Moorooroo, SA 5352 **Region** Barossa Valley
T (08) 8563 3551 **F** (08) 8563 3554 **www**.maverickwines.com.au **Open** By appt
Winemaker Ronald Brown **Est.** 2004 **Cases** 8000 **Vyds** 20.8 ha
This is the very successful venture of Ronald Brown, Jeremy Vogler and Adrian Bell. Taking advantage of excess grape production in Australia, the partners have acquired four vineyards in key areas of the Eden Valley and Barossa Valley. With vines ranging in age from 40 to over 100 years. The wines are made in small batches in tanks of half a tonne to 3-tonne capacity, and are then matured in French oak. Maverick has achieved listings in top restaurants and fine wine retailers in Australia, a dazzling array of hotels and restaurants in Tokyo, and the Hilton Hotel in Osaka. Exports to the UK, the US, Canada, Scandinavia, Thailand, Singapore, Hong Kong, Japan and China.

Trial Hill Eden Valley Riesling 2009 Light straw-green; a distinguished and particularly intense wine from a single, low-yielding vineyard; the citrus and apple flavours course through to a long, lingering finish. Screwcap. 13% alc. **Rating** 95 To 2022 $24

Twins Barossa Shiraz 2008 Deep crimson; ripe blackberry and plum fruit on the bouquet, the medium- to full-bodied palate showing very good restraint; the finish is full of character; likely picked before the heatwave. Screwcap. 14% alc. **Rating** 94 To 2023 $27

Twins Eden Valley Chardonnay 2008 Rating 90 To 2015 $27 BE

Paraview Barossa Valley Shiraz 2007 Rating 89 To 2016 $40 BE
Twins Barossa Grenache Shiraz Mourvedre 2008 Rating 88 To 2014 $27 BE
Breechens Blend Barossa Red 2008 Rating 88 To 2013 $18

Maximus Wines ★★★☆

Cnr Foggo Road/Penny's Road, McLaren Vale, SA 5171 **Region** McLaren Vale
T (08) 8323 8777 **F** (08) 8323 8977 **www**.maximuswinesaustralia.com.au
Open 1st w'end of month 11–4, or by appt
Winemaker Tim Geddes **Est.** 2007 **Cases** NA **Vyds** 1.82 ha
Successful sailing master Rowland Short, having run one of Australia's most successful sailing schools, decided (in his words) 'to brave the choppy waters of the Australian wine industry' by establishing Maximus Wines in partnership with wife Shelley. They purchased an already-planted shiraz vineyard, and built a cellar door using sandstone blocks, with western red cedar doors and windows. It is built into the side of a hill, and has a barrel store underneath for maturing cask and bottled wine. Grapes are purchased from other vineyards in McLaren Vale, and the wines are contract-made by well-known local winemaker, Tim Geddes.

Adelaide Hills Pinot Gris 2009 Pale straw; a quite intense bouquet of pear and citrus leads into an even more intense palate, which retains its grip through to the finish. Screwcap. 13.5% alc. **Rating** 91 To 2011 $25

McLaren Vale Grenache Tempranillo Rose 2009 Rating 89 To 2011 $20

Maxwell Wines ★★★★☆

Olivers Road, McLaren Vale, SA 5171 **Region** McLaren Vale
T (08) 8323 8200 **F** (08) 8323 8900 **www**.maxwellwines.com.au **Open** 7 days 10–5
Winemaker Alexia Roberts, Mark Maxwell **Est.** 1979 **Cases** 15 000 **Vyds** 19 ha
Over the past 30 years Maxwell Wines has carved out a reputation as a premium producer in McLaren Vale. The brand has produced some excellent red wines in recent years, making the most of the solid limestone hill in the Seaview area on which the winery and vineyards are situated. The majority of the vines on the estate were planted in 1972, and include 19 rows

of the highly regarded Reynella Selection cabernet sauvignon. The Ellen Street shiraz block in front of the winery was planted in 1953. During vintage, visitors to the elevated cellar door can watch the gravity-flow operations in the winery as the winemaking team plunge and pump-over the red ferments. Owned and operated by Mark Maxwell. Exports to all major markets.

ΨΨΨΨΨ **Ellen Street McLaren Vale Shiraz 2007** The fragrant and complex bouquet has black fruits, earth and spice, all of which appear on the generous palate, which has an intriguing twist on the finish. Screwcap. 14.5% alc. **Rating** 93 **To** 2020 $32

✪ **Silver Hammer McLaren Vale Shiraz 2008** Dense purple-red; the hallmark regional dark chocolate is present on both bouquet and palate, along with ripe blackberry fruit and mocha oak; the tannins are supple and prolong the finish; no issue at all with the alcohol. Screwcap. 14.9% alc. **Rating** 92 **To** 2023 $19.95

Lime Cave McLaren Vale Cabernet 2007 Slightly uncertain colour, then a basically savoury mix of black fruits, cedar, earth and some dark chocolate, all attesting to the vintage; pleasant tannins a partial redemption. Screwcap. 14% alc. **Rating** 90 **To** 2019 $32

ΨΨΨΨ **Silver Hammer McLaren Vale Shiraz 2007** Faintly hazy colour; has a complex
✪ array of aromas and flavours, with black fruits, spice, dark chocolate and mocha all present, but doesn't entirely escape the clutches of '07. Screwcap. 14.5% alc. **Rating** 89 **To** 2015 $19.95

✪ **Four Roads McLaren Vale Shiraz Grenache Viognier 2007** A perfumed bouquet leads into a light- to medium-bodied and quite fresh palate; the 5% viognier was co-fermented with the shiraz, the 10% grenache blended later. The blend is doubtless based on the Rhône parentage of the varieties, and works quite well. Screwcap. 14.5% alc. **Rating** 89 **To** 2016 $19.95

Little Demon McLaren Vale Cabernet Merlot 2008 Rating 88 **To** 2013 $16.95

Mayer ★★★★★

66 Miller Road, Healesville, Vic 3777 **Region** Yarra Valley
T (03) 5967 3779 **www.**timomayer.com.au **Open** By appt
Winemaker Timo Mayer **Est.** 1999 **Cases** 600
Timo Mayer, also winemaker at Gembrook Hill Vineyard, teamed with partner Rhonda Ferguson to establish Mayer Vineyard on the slopes of Mt Toolebewoong, 8 km south of Healesville. The steepness of those slopes is presumably 'celebrated' in the name given to the wines (Bloody Hill). There is just under 2.5 ha of vineyard, the lion's share to pinot noir, and smaller amounts of shiraz and chardonnay – all high-density plantings. Mayer's winemaking credo is minimal interference and handling, and no filtration.

ΨΨΨΨΨ **Bloody Hill Yarra Valley Chardonnay 2008** Light straw-green; a very complex chardonnay, putting ripe nectarine and white peach fruit against a background of slightly funky barrel ferment characters, then accelerating across the palate to an imperious finish. Diam. 13% alc. **Rating** 95 **To** 2016 $35

Close Planted Yarra Valley Pinot Noir 2008 Even better colour and shares many flavour and textural characters with Bloody Hill, but in a finer, more precisely calibrated, livery. Has great length, although whether this justifies the use of Rousseau's Chambertin label design is doubtful. Diam. 13.5% alc. **Rating** 94 **To** 2015 $50

Big Betty Yarra Valley Shiraz 2008 Bright crimson, clear rather than deep; a lively, aromatic bouquet and commensurately lively palate, with flavours running from black fruits to briar to stem, and – in particular – spice; a highly personalised example of cool-climate shiraz. Diam. 14% alc. **Rating** 94 **To** 2018 $35

ΨΨΨΨΨ **Bloody Hill Yarra Valley Pinot Noir 2008 Rating** 92 **To** 2014 $28

Mayfield Vineyard ★★★★☆

Icely Road, Orange, NSW 2800 **Region** Orange
T (02) 6365 9292 **F** (02) 6365 9281 **www.**mayfieldvineyard.com **Open** Wed–Sun 10–4
Winemaker Jon Reynolds, Richard Palmer, Phil Kearney, Usher Tinkler (Contract)
Est. 1998 **Cases** 7000 **Vyds** 40 ha

The property – including the house in which owners Richard and Kathy Thomas now live, and its surrounding arboretum – has a rich history as a leading Suffolk sheep stud, founded upon the vast fortune accumulated by the Crawford family via its biscuit business in the UK. The Thomases planted the vineyard in 1998, with merlot (12 ha) leading the way, followed (in descending order) by cabernet sauvignon, sauvignon blanc, chardonnay, pinot noir, riesling and sangiovese. The wines are marketed under the Mayfield Vineyard and Icely Road brands. Exports to the UK, Scandinavia and Asia.

Icely Rd Orange Chardonnay 2008 Bright, pale straw-green; an elegant chardonnay with melon, white peach and nectarine fruit, barrel ferment inputs exactly calibrated; has very good line and length. Screwcap. 14% alc. **Rating** 94 To 2015 $20

Single Vineyard Orange Chardonnay 2007 Rating 93 To 2014 $28
Single Vineyard Orange Riesling 2009 Rating 92 To 2019 $28
Icely Rd Orange Merlot 2008 Good colour; attractive plum, cherry and cassis aromas drive the well-balanced, medium-bodied palate, which also has good line and length. Screwcap. 14.5% alc. **Rating** 91 To 2016 $20

Icely Rd Sauvignon Blanc 2009 Rating 89 To 2011 $20
Private Reserve Orange Pinot Noir 2008 Rating 89 To 2013 $35
Icely Rd Orange Riesling 2009 Rating 87 To 2016 $20

Maygars Hill Winery ★★★★★

53 Longwood-Mansfield Road, Longwood, Vic 3665 **Region** Strathbogie Ranges
T 0402 136 448 **F** (03) 5798 5457 **www.**strathbogieboutiquewines.com **Open** By appt
Winemaker Plunkett Fowles **Est.** 1997 **Cases** 1100 **Vyds** 3.2 ha

Jenny Houghton purchased this 8-ha property in 1994, planting shiraz (1.9 ha) and cabernet sauvignon (1.3 ha), and establishing a stylish B&B cottage. The name comes from Lieutenant Colonel Maygar, who fought with outstanding bravery in the Boer War in South Africa in 1901, and was awarded the Victoria Cross. In World War I he rose to command the 8th Light Horse Regiment, winning yet further medals for bravery. He died on 1 November 1917. Exports to Fiji.

Reserve Shiraz 2009 Intense crimson-purple; luscious and rich, but not jammy, fruit is the foundation of a very good medium- to full-bodied wine with a great future. Exceptional for the vintage. Screwcap. 14.5% alc. **Rating** 95 To 2030 $34
Reserve Shiraz 2008 The hue is good, although not the spectacular depth of the '09 Reserve; here the wine relies on the complex interaction of savoury/spicy notes with red and black cherry fruit; has good length and balance. Screwcap. 14% alc. **Rating** 94 To 2018 $34

Reserve Cabernet Sauvignon 2008 Rating 90 To 2018 $34

Mayhem & Co ★★★★☆

Lot 2 Sydney Road, Nairne, SA 5252 **Region** Adelaide Hills
T (08) 8188 0011 **www.**mayhemandcowines.com.au **Open** Fri–Sun 11–5
Winemaker Brendon Keys **Est.** 2009 **Cases** 6200 **Vyds** 2.5 ha

This is the venture of farmer Andrew Taylor and Peter Michelmore, with significant involvement of winemaker Brendon Keys. They say, 'Why would you launch a new wine brand now? … It is nothing short of madness – sheer mayhem, in fact!' But Andrew had long harvested an ambition to build a winery in the Adelaide Hills, and Brendon, having worked vintages in NZ, Australia, the US and Argentina, was only too happy to join the venture. The estate vineyard is planted to sauvignon blanc; the remaining wines are made from grapes purchased from various local growers.

🍷🍷🍷🍷🍷 **Sauvignon Blanc 2009** From estate-grown fruit; 10% barrel fermented with lees
✪ stirring (battonage) for 4 months has worked to perfection, adding to the texture of the wine without diminishing its varietal expression in a crisp, herbal spectrum. Screwcap. 12.6% alc. **Rating** 94 **To** 2011 $19

🍷🍷🍷🍷 **Viognier 2009** Six months lees contact after fermentation has added weight to
✪ the mid-palate without hitting the finish with phenolics; apricot, spice and a touch of ginger are the flavour drivers. Screwcap. 14% alc. **Rating** 90 **To** 2013 $17
Pinot Noir 2009 Rating 90 **To** 2015 $24

🍷🍷🍷🍷 **Riesling 2009 Rating** 89 **To** 2015 $17
Chardonnay 2009 Rating 89 **To** 2013 $19

🌿 Meadow Croft Wines ★★★

221 Woodlands Road, Mittagong, NSW 2575 **Region** Southern Highlands
T (02) 4878 5344 **Open** By appt
Winemaker Jonathan Holgate **Est.** 1998 **Cases** NA **Vyds** 1.2 ha
Carl and Linda Bahls have 20 ha of prime grazing country, but decided on a minor diversification by planting 0.6 ha each of chardonnay and cabernet sauvignon. 'Whilst chardonnay was a natural choice of fruit for a cool climate, cabernet sauvignon was a gamble, albeit a calculated one.' The gamble was fully justified when the 2007 Cabernet Sauvignon was placed first at the Southern Highlands Wine Show, the result of meticulous work in the vineyard, and the winemaking team of Jonathan Holgate at High Range Vintners (overseen by Nick Bulleid MW).

🍷🍷🍷🍷 **Southern Highlands Chardonnay 2008** Has been well made within the limitations of the fruit, presumably ex young vines, and early picked; no attempt to overdo the flavours. Screwcap. 12% alc. **Rating** 87 **To** 2013 $15

Meadowbank Estate ★★★★★

699 Richmond Road, Cambridge, Tas 7170 **Region** Southern Tasmania
T (03) 6248 4484 **F** (03) 6248 4485 **www**.meadowbankwines.com.au **Open** 7 days 10–5
Winemaker Contract **Est.** 1974 **Cases** 6000
An important part of the Ellis family business on what was once a large grazing property on the banks of the Derwent. Increased plantings are under contract to Hardys, and a splendid winery has been built to handle the increased production. The winery complex has expansive entertainment and function facilities, plus a large restaurant, and presents an arts and music program. Exports to Germany, Sweden, the Netherlands and Hong Kong.

🍷🍷🍷🍷🍷 **FGR Riesling 2009** The bouquet offers a strong slatey personality, with a suggestion of lemon and green apple; the palate delivers a stunning blow of fresh cut green apple fruit, vibrant, almost crunchy, acidity, and the sweetness of the residual sugar disappears alongside rapier-like acidity; the impression on the finish is almost dry and chalky. Screwcap. 10.8% alc. **Rating** 95 **To** 2020 $31 BE
Henry James Pinot Noir 2008 Colour good; there is activity and complexity from the outset, great life and length to the black cherry, plum and spice flavours; oak is very much in evidence, but will integrate with time. Screwcap. 13.6% alc. **Rating** 94 **To** 2015 $49.50

🍷🍷🍷🍷 **Grace Elizabeth Chardonnay 2006 Rating** 92 **To** 2016 $36.50 BE

🍷🍷🍷🍷 **Riesling 2009 Rating** 89 **To** 2016 $29
Sauvignon Blanc 2009 Rating 89 **To** 2011 $31
Mardi 2006 Rating 88 **To** 2014 $45

Medhurst ★★★★

24–26 Medhurst Road, Gruyere, Vic 3770 **Region** Yarra Valley
T (03) 5964 9022 **F** (03) 5964 9033 **www**.medhurstwines.com.au
Open Fri–Sun & public hols 10–5
Winemaker Matt Steel **Est.** 2000 **Cases** 2500 **Vyds** 14 ha
The wheel has come full circle for Ross and Robyn Wilson. In the course of a very distinguished corporate career, Ross was CEO of Southcorp during the time it brought the Penfolds, Lindemans and Wynns businesses under the Southcorp banner. For her part, Robyn spent her childhood in the Yarra Valley, her parents living less than a kilometre away as the crow flies from Medhurst. Immaculately sited and tended vineyard blocks, most on steep, north-facing slopes, promise much for the future. The vineyard is planted to sauvignon blanc, chardonnay, pinot noir, cabernet sauvignon and shiraz, all running on a low-yield basis. Red Shed is the newly introduced second label, taking its name from the recently opened café.

ŶŶŶŶŶ **Red Shed Yarra Valley Cabernet Sauvignon 2007** Bright red-purple;
✪   fresh blackcurrant fruit on the bouquet and juicy palate is the primary driver
        of an attractive, light- to medium-bodied wine at a very good price. Screwcap.
        13.5% alc. **Rating** 92 **To** 2015 $17.50
        Yarra Valley Cabernet Sauvignon 2006 Good hue; a complex, yet elegant,
        wine with tightly focused red and black fruits, and fine, savoury tannins on a long
        finish. Cork. 14% alc. **Rating** 92 **To** 2018 $25
✪   **Red Shed Yarra Valley Shiraz 2007** Bright colour; tangy, fresh red and black
        cherry aromas are matched by the medium-bodied palate, which has good length
        and tannin support. Screwcap. 13.5% alc. **Rating** 90 **To** 2014 $17.50

ŶŶŶŶ   **Yarra Valley Chardonnay 2009 Rating** 89 **To** 2013 $22.50
        Yarra Valley Rose 2009 Rating 89 **To** 2011 $18.50

Meerea Park ★★★★★

188 Palmers Lane, Pokolbin, NSW 2320 **Region** Hunter Valley
T (02) 4998 7474 **F** (02) 4998 7974 **www**.meereapark.com.au **Open** At The Boutique
Wine Centre, Pokolbin
Winemaker Rhys Eather **Est.** 1991 **Cases** 10 000
All the wines are produced from grapes purchased from growers primarily in the Pokolbin area, but also from the Upper Hunter, and as far afield as Young. It is the brainchild of Rhys Eather, a great-grandson of Alexander Munro, a leading vigneron in the mid-19th century; he makes the wine at the former Little's Winery at Palmers Lane in Pokolbin, which was purchased in 2007 and is now named Meerea Park. Exports to the UK, the US and other major markets.

ŶŶŶŶŶ **Terracotta Semillon 2005** Glowing green-gold; richer and fuller than Alexander
✪   Munro, with generous lemon and lemon tart flavours braced by typical acidity; any
        time over the next five years. Screwcap. 11% alc. **Rating** 96 **To** 2015 $30
        Alexander Munro Individual Vineyard Hunter Valley Shiraz 2007
        Crimson-purple hue; a particularly distinguished single vineyard wine, featuring
        the Hunter Valley at its very best; dark plum, cherry and blackberry fruit is framed
        by supple tannins and perfectly balanced oak. Screwcap. 14% alc. **Rating** 96
        To 2027 $70
✪   **XYZ Canberra District Shiraz 2008** Dense purple-crimson; a fragrant and
        spicy bouquet leads into a supple palate reflecting whole bunch fermentation,
        although not the least stemmy; 250 cases made of a delicious wine. Screwcap.
        14.5% alc. **Rating** 95 **To** 2020 $22
✪   **Hell Hole Hunter Valley Semillon 2009** For once vintage rain did not force
        early picking, and the '09 semillons (this wine included) have an unusually intense
        citrus (lime and lemon) framework, which offers great drinking now without
        threatening a sure-fire, 10-year future, thanks to the acidity and the screwcap.
        10.5% alc. **Rating** 94 **To** 2020 $25

Alexander Munro Individual Vineyard Hunter Valley Semillon 2005
Bright pale straw-green; has developed slowly but surely, still youthful and built around lemony acidity; is still building flavour, with another 5+ years to go to get close to its peak. Screwcap. 11% alc. **Rating** 94 **To** 2020 $35

Hell Hole Hunter Valley Shiraz 2007 Good hue; the fruit aromas and flavours are led by blackberry, with plum and a touch of spice in support; the medium-bodied palate has impeccable balance, and all the wine needs is a few more years to soften and open up. Screwcap. 13.5% alc. **Rating** 94 **To** 2022 $55

Terracotta Hunter Valley Shiraz 2007 The vintage produced powerful red wines, and this is no shrinking violet. But the viognier (less than 5%) has added what I call 'light and shade' highlights in both the red-fruit-'tinged flavour, and a touch of finesse to the structure. Screwcap. 14% alc. **Rating** 94 **To** 2022 $50

Aged Release Alexander Munro Individual Vineyard Hunter Valley Shiraz 1999 A well-inserted, quality cork has done its job well, carrying the wine through to the start of its plateau of maturity, with earthy Hunter flavours running through the black fruits, the tannins present but fine; has a particularly long finish. 13.5% alc. **Rating** 94 **To** 2014 $100

ŸŸŸŸŸ Alexander Munro Individual Vineyard Hunter Valley Chardonnay 2009 **Rating** 93 **To** 2014 $35

✪ XYZ Hunter Valley Chardonnay 2009 Bright yellow-green; touches of smoky/funky characters (borrowed from Burgundy, perchance) lift the nectarine, fig and cashew characters of the palate; 250 cases made. Screwcap. 13.5% alc. **Rating** 93 **To** 2015 $22

✪ Shiraz 2008 A blend of Hunter Valley/Hilltops which comes together very well, the Hilltops cooler-grown fruit adding elegance to a light- to medium-bodied palate that has persistent black fruits, licorice and leather notes. Gold medal Winewise '09. Screwcap. 14% alc. **Rating** 93 **To** 2018 $15

The Aunts Shiraz 2007 **Rating** 93 **To** 2022 $26
XYZ Hunter Valley Semillon 2009 **Rating** 90 **To** 2018 $22

Melia Grove Vineyards **NR**
55 Gibbs Lane, Majorca, Vic 3953 **Region** Bendigo
T (03) 5367 8275 **Open** W'ends 10–5, or by appt
Winemaker Mount Beckworth (Paul Lesock) **Est.** 1990 **Cases** 135 **Vyds** 1.6 ha
This has been a slow-growing venture owned by Anne and David Ferguson based on vines planted between 1990 and '94. No fungicides or pesticides are used, and only minimal drip irrigation. The first significant grape production in 2003 was sold to Cleveland, and the first Melia Grove wine was made in '04.

Mermerus Vineyard ★★★☆
60 Soho Road, Drysdale, Vic 3222 **Region** Geelong
T (03) 5253 2718 **F** (03) 5251 1555 **www**.mermerus.com.au **Open** Sun 11–4
Winemaker Paul Champion **Est.** 2000 **Cases** 600 **Vyds** 2.5 ha
Paul Champion has established pinot noir, chardonnay and riesling at Mermerus since 1996. The wines are made from the small but very neat winery on the property, with small batch handling and wild yeast fermentation playing a major part in the winemaking, oak taking a back seat. Paul also acts as contract winemaker for small growers in the region.

ŸŸŸŸ ✪ Bellarine Peninsula Chardonnay 2008 Pale quartz-green; a vibrantly fresh wine with grapefruit and white peach fruit doing all the talking. Screwcap. 13.5% alc. **Rating** 90 **To** 2012 $20

ŸŸŸŸ Bellarine Peninsula Pinot Noir 2008 **Rating** 89 **To** 2013 $22
Bellarine Peninsula Riesling 2009 **Rating** 87 **To** 2014 $18

Merops Wines ★★★★★

5992 Caves Road, Margaret River, WA 6825 **Region** Margaret River
T (08) 9757 9195 **F** (08) 9757 3193 **www**.meropswines.com.au **Open** By appt
Winemaker Flying Fish Cove (Elizabeth Reed), Jurg Muggli **Est.** 2000 **Cases** 1000
Vyds 6.3 ha
Jim and Yvonne Ross have been involved in horticulture for over 25 years, in production, retail nurseries and viticulture. They established a nursery and irrigation business in the Margaret River township in 1985 before establishing a rootstock nursery. In 2000 they removed the nursery and planted cabernet sauvignon, cabernet franc, merlot and shiraz on the laterite gravel over clay soils. They use the practices developed by Professor William Albrecht in the US 50 years ago, providing mineral balance and thus eliminating the need for insecticides and toxic sprays. Organic pre-certification was completed in 2007, which resulted in the '08 vintage being certified organic. Over the years the wines have won numerous bronze medals at Australian wine shows, Ornatus having particular success at the International Wine & Spirit Competition (London), with Best in Class silver medals.

🍷🍷🍷🍷🍷 **Margaret River Shiraz 2008** Bright crimson; a fragrant bouquet with a mix of black and red fruits plus a sprinkle of spice leads into an elegant, medium-bodied palate with a similar array of flavours sustained by fine but firm tannins. Trophy Margaret River Wine Show '09. Screwcap. 14.5% alc. **Rating** 94 **To** 2018 $27.95
Ornatus 2008 Light, bright crimson-purple; an elegant, fragrant blend of Cabernet Sauvignon (60%)/Merlot (40%) with similarities to the structure of the '08 Shiraz, particularly its powdery, full tannins. Gold medal WA Wine Show '09. Screwcap. 14.5% alc. **Rating** 94 **To** 2020 $27.95

🍷🍷🍷🍷🍷 **Margaret River Cabernet Merlot 2008 Rating** 91 **To** 2018 $27.95

Merricks Creek Wines ★★★★★

44 Merricks Road, Merricks, Vic 3916 **Region** Mornington Peninsula
T (03) 5989 8868 **F** (03) 5989 9070 **www**.pinot.com.au **Open** Not
Winemaker Nick Farr **Est.** 1998 **Cases** 650 **Vyds** 2 ha
The pinot noir vineyard established by Peter and Georgina Parker has consistently produced grapes of exceptional quality. It is planted to a sophisticated collection of pinot noir clones, and includes a small planting at an ultra-high density of 500 mm spacing, which produces the Close Planted Pinot Noir. Gary Farr, the notable Geelong-based viticulturist and winemaker, was retained on a consultancy basis to advise on all aspects of the establishment and subsequent training of the vineyard. Son Nick Farr has been the winemaker, the third part of a notably successful operation. Exports to the UK.

🍷🍷🍷🍷🍷 **Close Planted Mornington Peninsula Pinot Noir 2007** Bright colour; highly fragrant; has a vibrant palate replete with red and black fruits, and a strikingly long finish; lovely pinot. Diam. 13.5% alc. **Rating** 96 **To** 2017 $57
Close Planted Mornington Peninsula Pinot Noir 2006 Light colour showing some development; the spicy/savoury fragrance flows through onto the palate, which is seriously long and very fine. Cork. 13.5% alc. **Rating** 95 **To** 2016 $57
Mornington Peninsula Pinot Noir 2007 Slightly deeper colour than Close Planted; an altogether bigger wine, with luscious plum and black cherry; good line and length. Diam. 13.5% alc. **Rating** 94 **To** 2016 $46

Merricks Estate ★★★★★

Thompsons Lane, Merricks, Vic 3916 **Region** Mornington Peninsula
T (03) 5989 8416 **www**.merricksestate.com.au **Open** 1st w'end of month, daily
26–31 Dec, every w'end in Jan & public hol w'ends 12–5
Winemaker Paul Evans **Est.** 1977 **Cases** 750 **Vyds** 4 ha
Melbourne solicitor George Kefford, with wife Jacky, runs Merricks Estate as a weekend and holiday enterprise. Right from the outset it has produced distinctive, spicy, cool-climate Shiraz, which has accumulated an impressive array of show trophies and gold medals.

ŸŸŸŸŸ **Thompson's Lane Chardonnay 2008** Classic Mornington Peninsula style, with
✪ white peach fruit to the fore on the bouquet and palate, barrel ferment oak in a
supporting role. Has impeccable balance and length. Screwcap. 14% alc. **Rating** 94
To 2015 $20
Thompson's Lane Shiraz 2007 Bright crimson; classic cool-grown style from
vines planted in 1978; Merricks was the pace setter for a decade; red and black
cherry fruit liberally sprinkled with spice and pepper, the texture and balance
good. Screwcap. 14% alc. **Rating** 94 **To** 2017 $20
✪ **Mornington Peninsula Shiraz 2005** The pungent spice and pepper of three
years ago (when first tasted) has receded somewhat, complex secondary characters
starting to emerge, the length and balance intact. Diam. 13.5% alc. **Rating** 94
To 2015 $25

ŸŸŸŸŸ **Mornington Peninsula Chardonnay 2007 Rating** 93 **To** 2017 $25
✪ **Thompson's Lane Pinot Noir 2008** Bright colour; fragrant red cherry and
spice aromas, then a long and well-balanced palate, with ample red fruits and
tannins to match. Screwcap. 13.5% alc. **Rating** 92 **To** 2014 $22

ŸŸŸŸ **Mornington Peninsula Pinot Noir 2006 Rating** 89 **To** 2013 $27

Metcalfe Valley   ★★★★☆
283 Metcalfe-Malmsbury Road, Metcalfe, Vic 3448 **Region** Macedon Ranges
T (03) 5423 2035 **F** (03) 5423 2035 **www**.metcalfevalleywines.com.au **Open** By appt
Winemaker Matt Pattison **Est.** 1994 **Cases** 900 **Vyds** 7.2 ha
Ian Pattison, who has a PhD in metallurgy and a diploma in horticultural science and
viticulture from Melbourne University/Dookie College, purchased Metcalfe Valley from the
Frederiksens in 2003. The vineyard is planted to shiraz (5.6 ha) and sauvignon blanc (1.6 ha).
He has been joined by son Matt, who has a BAgSci from the University of Melbourne, has
made wine at De Bortoli (Yarra Valley) and is currently a winemaker at Carlei Estate.

ŸŸŸŸŸ **Sauvignon 2008** Straw-green; an extremely successful and adventurous blend of
85% Macedon Ranges Sauvignon Blanc, plus 12% Semillon and 3% Chardonnay
from the Yarra Valley and Port Phillip Zone; citrus is the main player, with some
nutty notes (presumably oak is in play) and yet a vibrantly fresh and long finish.
Screwcap. 12.4% alc. **Rating** 94 **To** 2013 $19.50

ŸŸŸŸ **Shiraz 2006 Rating** 88 **To** 2014 $22

Miceli   ★★★★
60 Main Creek Road, Arthurs Seat, Vic 3936 **Region** Mornington Peninsula
T (03) 5989 2755 **F** (03) 5989 2755 **Open** 1st w'end of month 12–5, by appt public hols,
every w'end & in Jan
Winemaker Anthony Miceli **Est.** 1991 **Cases** 3000 **Vyds** 4 ha
This may be a part-time labour of love for general practitioner Dr Anthony Miceli, but that
hasn't prevented him taking the whole venture very seriously. He acquired the property in
1989 specifically to establish a vineyard, planting 1.8 ha in 1991, followed by a further ha of
pinot gris in '97. Between '91 and '97 Dr Miceli completed the wine science course at CSU
and now manages both vineyard and winery. One of the top producers of sparkling wine on
the Peninsula.

ŸŸŸŸŸ **Michael Mornington Peninsula Brut 2004** Still has a vibrant green colour;
over three years on yeast lees and further time on cork are barely apparent, partly
because of the low dosage, partly the low alcohol. Pinot Noir/Chardonnay/Pinot
Gris. Gold medal Melbourne Wine Show '08. 11% alc. **Rating** 93 **To** 2012 $32
Lucy's Choice Mornington Peninsula Pinot Noir 2006 Very good hue for
age, still bright red; an elegantly structured pinot, the black cherry fruit on the
bouquet and palate framed by spicy, foresty elements; good length. Screwcap.
14% alc. **Rating** 92 **To** 2015 $26

Iolanda Mornington Peninsula Pinot Grigio 2008 Has good intensity and depth to its display of pear, apple and lemony acidity; the line and length are good. Screwcap. 13.5% alc. **Rating** 90 **To** 2011 $23

♟♟♟♟ **Dry Pinot Noir Rose 2007 Rating** 89 **To** 2011 $20

Michael Hall Wines ★★★★★
10 George Street, Tanunda, SA 5352 (postal) **Region** Mount Lofty Ranges Zone
T 0419 126 290 **F** (08) 8563 0913 **www**.michaelhallwines.com **Open** Not
Winemaker Michael Hall **Est.** 2008 **Cases** 900
For reasons no longer relevant (however interesting) Michael Hall was once a jewellery valuer for Sotheby's in Switzerland. He came to Australia in 2001 to pursue winemaking, a lifelong interest, and undertook the wine science degree at CSU, graduating as dux in '05. His vintage work in Australia and France is a veritable who's who: in Australia with Cullen, Giaconda, Henschke, Shaw & Smith, Coldstream Hills and Veritas; in France with Domaine Leflaive, Meo-Camuzet, Vieux Telegraphe and Trevallon. He now works for Rocland Estate in Nuriootpa, but has the right to make his own wines in the Rocland winery, sourced from four small blocks. They are as impressive as his CV suggests they should be. Exports to the UK.

♟♟♟♟♟ **Piccadilly Valley Chardonnay 2008** Bright colour; a fragrant bouquet of nectarine and citrus leads into a vibrant and incisive palate with white peach and nectarine fruit, the oak subtle, the acidity natural; 250 cases made. Diam. 13.8% alc. **Rating** 96 **To** 2015 $45

✪ **Sang de Pigeon Barossa Shiraz Saignee 2009** Vivid light crimson-purple, astonishing given the winemaking techniques; the fragrant bouquet leads into a palate full of red fruits, with great texture and length to its vibrant red fruit flavours; 20 hours' skin contact, 16-day wild yeast fermentation, six months in seasoned French barriques, one month in tank; blended with 5% sauvignon blanc. Succeeds brilliantly. Screwcap. 13.5% alc. **Rating** 95 **To** 2012 $20

Michael Unwin Wines ★★★★
2 Racecourse Road, on the Western Highway, Beaufort, Vic 3373
Region Western Victoria Zone
T (03) 5349 2021 **F** (03) 5349 2032 **www**.michaelunwinwines.com.au
Open Mon–Fri 8.30–5, Sat 11–4.30, Sun 12–4.30
Winemaker Michael Unwin **Est.** 2000 **Cases** 2000 **Vyds** 8 ha
Michael Unwin, a veteran of 28 vintages, learned the art of winemaking around the world with some of the most influential and forward-thinking winemakers of our time. The winery location was chosen because it is the geographical centre of the best viticultural areas in Western Victoria. The grapes are grown in up to six mature vineyards, all with different site climates. In all, approximately 2 ha of shiraz and 1 ha each of cabernet sauvignon, sangiovese, barbera, durif, riesling and chardonnay are grown or contracted.

♟♟♟♟♀ **Acrobat Umbrella Man Sangiovese 2006** Good colour; fragrant black and red cherry aromas are replayed on the quite juicy palate, but drink asap. Zork. 13.5% alc. **Rating** 90 **To** 2012 $26
Acrobat Umbrella Man Barbera 2005 Amazing retention of purple hue; the spicy berry aromas of the bouquet are neatly contrasted by the supple mouthfeel of the palate; good length and balance. Screwcap. 14% alc. **Rating** 90 **To** 2015 $26

♟♟♟♟ **Tattooed Lady Shiraz 2004 Rating** 88 **To** 2014 $45

Michelini Wines ★★★★
Great Alpine Road, Myrtleford, Vic 3737 **Region** Alpine Valleys
T (03) 5751 1990 **F** (03) 5751 1410 **www**.micheliniwines.com.au **Open** 7 days 10–5
Winemaker Greg O'Keefe **Est.** 1982 **Cases** 10 000 **Vyds** 34.5 ha
The Michelinis are among the best known grapegrowers in the Buckland Valley of Northeast Victoria. Having migrated from Italy in 1949, they originally grew tobacco, diversifying into

vineyards in 1982. The vineyard, on terra rossa soil, is at an altitude of 300 m, mostly with frontage to the Buckland River. The winery can handle 1000 tonnes of fruit, which eliminates the problem of moving grapes out of a declared phylloxera area. Exports to China.

ΨΨΨΨΩ · ✪　**Alpine Valleys Sangiovese 2008** Attractive red, bright and clear hue; a very well made wine flooded with juicy sour cherry flavours and tangy acidity on the finish; absolutely classic varietal character from vines now having some age. Screwcap. 13.5% alc. **Rating** 93 **To** 2012 $18.50

✪　**Chardonnay Pinot Cuvee NV** Very pale colour; has been well made, and the quality of the base wine is reflected in the long palate, with a positive mix of stone fruit and cherry flavours. Cork. 12.5% alc. **Rating** 90 **To** 2012 $20

ΨΨΨΨ　**Alpine Valleys Sauvignon Blanc 2009** **Rating** 89 **To** 2010 $17.50
Alpine Valleys Barbera 2008 **Rating** 89 **To** 2012 $18.50
Alpine Valleys Marzemino 2008 **Rating** 88 **To** 2013 $18.50

Mihi Creek Vineyard ★★★☆

1292 Enmore Road, Mihi via Uralla, NSW 2358 (postal) **Region** New England
T (02) 6778 2166 **www**.home.bluepin.net.au/mihicreek **Open** Not
Winemaker Merilba Estate (Shaun Cassidy) **Est.** 2003 **Cases** NFP **Vyds** 1.8 ha
Andrew and Belle Close purchased 180 ha of what was part of the large Mihi Station sheep and cattle property in 2001. Situated at an elevation of 1000 m, the first plantings in 2003 (sauvignon blanc, viognier, pinot noir, cabernet sauvignon and merlot) performed well, with the first vintage in '06. Since then, there have been further plantings of sauvignon blanc, with removal of the cabernet sauvignon making way for further sauvignon blanc.

ΨΨΨΨΩ · ✪　**New England Merlot 2009** Deep purple-crimson; pushes the right buttons for merlot, with plum and cassis fruit supported by savoury/olive nuances; the oak is on the generous side. Screwcap. 12.8% alc. **Rating** 90 **To** 2015 $20

ΨΨΨΨ　**New England Sauvignon Blanc 2009** **Rating** 88 **To** 2011 $20
New England Merlot 2008 **Rating** 87 **To** 2012 $22

Mike Press Wines ★★★★★

PO Box 224, Lobethal, SA 5241 **Region** Adelaide Hills
T (08) 8389 5546 **F** (08) 8389 5548 **www**.mikepresswines.com.au **Open** Not
Winemaker Mike Press **Est.** 1998 **Cases** 10 000 **Vyds** 23.2 ha
Mike and Judy Press established their Kenton Valley Vineyards in 1998, when they purchased 34 ha of land in the Adelaide Hills at an elevation of 500 m. Over the next two years they planted mainstream, cool-climate varieties (merlot, shiraz, cabernet sauvignon, sauvignon blanc, chardonnay and pinot noir), intending to sell the grapes to other wine producers. Even an illustrious 42-year career in the wine industry did not prepare Mike for the downturn in grape prices that followed, and that led to the development of the Mike Press wine label. They produce Sauvignon Blanc, Chardonnay, Pinot Noir, Merlot, Shiraz, Cabernet Merlot and Cabernet Sauvignon, which, despite accumulating gold medals and trophies, are sold at low prices.

ΨΨΨΨΨ · ✪　**Adelaide Hills Chardonnay 2009** Elegant, vibrant and supremely fresh, it runs the gamut of grapefruit, green apple, white peach and nectarine flavours with perfectly judged acidity. No oak evident, and none needed. Screwcap. 12.5% alc. **Rating** 94 **To** 2013 $11

✪　**Adelaide Hills Shiraz 2008** Vivid crimson; the wine exudes black cherry, blackberry, licorice and spice through every pore; just enough tannins to underwrite development. Screwcap. 14.9% alc. **Rating** 94 **To** 2015 $14

Adelaide Hills Cabernet Sauvignon 2008 Deep crimson-red; a luscious cabernet crammed to the gills with roughly equal blackcurrant and cassis fruit; despite all this flavour, is not the least extractive, the tannins fine. Screwcap. 14.9% alc. **Rating** 94 **To** 2018 $14

Miles from Nowhere ★★★★

PO Box 197, Belmont, WA 6984 **Region** Margaret River
T (08) 9267 8555 **F** (08) 9267 8599 **www.**milesfromnowhere.com.au **Open** Not
Winemaker Jodie Opie **Est.** 2007 **Cases** 6000 **Vyds** 20 ha
Miles from Nowhere is the born-again business of Franklin (Frank) and Heather Tate;
Frank was CEO of Evans & Tate for many years. The demise of Evans & Tate has been well
chronicled, but has not prevented the Tates from doing what they know best. The plantings of
petit verdot, chardonnay, shiraz, sauvignon blanc, semillon, viognier, cabernet sauvignon and
merlot are scattered across the Margaret River region, miles from nowhere.

ŶŶŶŶŶ ✪ **Margaret River Cabernet Merlot 2008** Purple-crimson; a full-bodied blend
in traditional Margaret River style, the black and red fruits with a savoury/gravelly
backbone, tannins ripe and adding to the texture. Screwcap. 13.9% alc. **Rating** 91
To 2018 $18

✪ **Margaret River Sauvignon Blanc Semillon 2009** A potent bouquet, with
a strong waft of asparagus and ripe citrus fruit; the focused palate follows suit,
strengthened by acidity; can age for a year or two. Screwcap. 13% alc. **Rating** 90
To 2012 $18

Milhinch Wines ★★★★

PO Box 655, Greenock, SA 5360 **Region** Barossa Valley
T (08) 8563 4003 **F** (08) 8563 4003 **www.**seizetheday.net.au **Open** At Barossa Small
Winemakers, Chateau Tanunda
Winemaker Contract **Est.** 2003 **Cases** 1200 **Vyds** 4 ha
Peter Milhinch and Sharyn Rogers have established 2 ha each of shiraz and cabernet
sauvignon near the Greenock Creek, which (sometimes) flows through their Seppeltsfield
property. At the foot of their vineyard is Seppeltsfield Vineyard Cottage, a restored German
settler's cottage offering luxury accommodation for one couple. The Cottage has won three
successive SA Tourism Awards, two National Tourism Awards and was inducted into the SA
Tourism Hall of Fame in 2007. The Cottage project and Peter and Sharyn's wine production
began in 2003 when Peter was recovering from cancer. They gained inspiration and hope from
legendary American cyclist Lance Armstrong's own cancer journey, so much so that the Seize
the Day phrase on their wine labels has been borrowed from Lance's book, *It's Not About the
Bike*. Exports to Singapore.

ŶŶŶŶŶ **Seize the Day Single Vineyard Barossa Valley Shiraz 2007** Strong colour;
a full-bodied shiraz, with a wide range of black fruits, licorice, leather and oak
aromas and flavours giving the wine length. Screwcap. 14.9% alc. **Rating** 92
To 2020 $30

ŶŶŶŶ **Seize the Day Single Vineyard Barossa Valley Rose 2009 Rating** 88
To 2011 $20

Millamolong Estate ★★★★

Millamolong Road, Mandurama, NSW 2792 **Region** Orange
T 0429 635 191 **F** (02) 6367 4088 **www.**millamolong.com **Open** 7 days 9–4
Winemaker Madrez Wine Services **Est.** 2000 **Cases** NFP **Vyds** 24.05 ha
This is a book about wine, not polo, but it so happens that Millamolong Estate has been the
centrepiece of Australian polo for over 80 years. For an even longer period, generations of
James Ashton (differentiated by their middle name) have been at the forefront of a dynasty to
make *Rawhide* or *McLeod's Daughters* seem tame. In the context of this, 24 ha of chardonnay,
riesling, cabernet, shiraz and merlot may seem incidental, but it happens to add to the luxury
accommodation at the main homestead, which caters for up to 18 guests. Exports to the UK.

ŶŶŶŶŶ ✪ **56 Miles Orange Shiraz 2008** An elegant, medium-bodied wine with spicy/
pepper overtones to its predominantly red fruit flavours, the tannins fine, the oak
well integrated. Screwcap. 14.5% alc. **Rating** 90 **To** 2015 $20

Millbrook Winery

Old Chestnut Lane, Jarrahdale, WA 6124 **Region** Perth Hills
T (08) 9525 5796 **F** (08) 9525 5672 www.millbrookwinery.com.au **Open** 7 days 10–5
Winemaker Damian Hutton, Josh Uren **Est.** 1996 **Cases** 20 000 **Vyds** 7.8 ha
The strikingly situated Millbrook Winery is owned by highly successful Perth-based
entrepreneur Peter Fogarty and wife Lee. They also own Lake's Folly in the Hunter Valley and
Deep Woods Estate in Margaret River, and have made a major commitment to the quality
end of Australian wine. Millbrook draws on vineyards in the Perth Hills, planted to sauvignon
blanc, semillon, chardonnay, viognier, cabernet sauvignon, merlot, shiraz and petit verdot. The
wines (Millbrook and Barking Owl) are of consistently high quality. Exports to Belgium,
Germany, Denmark, Singapore, Malaysia, Hong Kong, China and Japan.

♆♆♆♆♆ **LR Chardonnay 2009** Attractive bouquet of grilled cashews, grapefruit and
nectarine; good intensity of fruit, with plenty of spice and char from the oak in
evidence; long and harmonious. Screwcap. 14% alc. **Rating** 94 **To** 2016 $45 BE

♆♆♆♆♀ **LR Chardonnay 2008 Rating** 92 **To** 2014 $42
LR Viognier 2009 Rating 92 **To** 2013 $45 BE
Estate Shiraz Viognier 2006 Rating 92 **To** 2014 $35
✪ **Barking Owl Shiraz Viognier 2008** The aromatic lift and edge of intensity
to the fruit on the palate is due to the viognier; the origins of the grapes not
disclosed, but the wine seems to have spicy cool-grown components, adding zest.
Screwcap. 14% alc. **Rating** 91 **To** 2015 $17.95
LR Shiraz Cabernet 2007 Rating 91 **To** 2016 $45 BE
Sauvignon Blanc 2009 Rating 90 **To** 2011 $22

♆♆♆♆ **Estate Shiraz Viognier 2007 Rating** 88 **To** 2015 $35 BE
Estate Viognier 2009 Rating 87 **To** 2012 $35 BE

Miller's Dixons Creek Estate   ★★★★

1620 Melba Highway, Dixons Creek, Vic 3775 **Region** Yarra Valley
T (03) 5965 2553 **F** (03) 5965 2320 www.graememillerwines.com.au **Open** 7 days 10–5
Winemaker Graeme Miller, Shaun Crinion **Est.** 2004 **Cases** 7000 **Vyds** 30.4 ha
Graeme Miller is a Yarra Valley legend in his own lifetime, having established Chateau Yarrinya
(now De Bortoli) in 1971, and as a virtual unknown winning the Jimmy Watson Trophy in '78
with the '77 Chateau Yarrinya Cabernet Sauvignon. He sold Chateau Yarrinya in 1986 and,
together with wife Bernadette, established a vineyard that has steadily grown to over 30 ha,
with chardonnay, pinot gris, cabernet sauvignon, cabernet franc, carmanere, shiraz, pinot noir,
sauvignon blanc, petit verdot and merlot. A significant part of the production is sold, but the
opening of the winery in 2004, and a cellar door thereafter, has seen production increase.

♆♆♆♆♀ **Yarra Valley Sauvignon Blanc 2009** The freakish '09 vintage had very good
✪ growing conditions either side of the 10 days' hellfire and brimstone at the start of
Feb, and some very good white wines were made, as smoke taint has no impact on
whites. Here an 8% barrel-fermented portion has added to the flavour and texture,
the flavour taking in grass, gooseberry and some tropical notes. Screwcap. 12% alc.
Rating 90 **To** 2012 $16
Yarra Valley Chardonnay 2009 Whole bunch pressed, barrel fermented in
new French (Nevers) oak, restrained lees stirring and 25% mlf; has considerable
intensity to its grapefruit and melon flavours, and a long palate; a faint question
about the quality of the oak. Screwcap. 13.4% alc. **Rating** 90 **To** 2015 $28
Yarra Valley Petit Verdot 2007 Good red-purple; a typically robust wine,
albeit with a touch of restraint; shoot and bunch thinning to very low crop levels
have resulted in ripe fruit flavours in the cool Yarra Valley climate, oak handling
appropriate. Perfect cork. 13.4% alc. **Rating** 90 **To** 2029 $25

Milton Vineyard   ★★★★

14635 Tasman Highway, Cranbrook, Tas 7190 **Region** East Coast Tasmania
T (03) 6257 8298 **F** (03) 6257 8297 **www.**miltonvineyard.com.au **Open** 7 days 10–5
Winemaker Winemaking Tasmania (Julian Alcorso) **Est.** 1992 **Cases** 2840 **Vyds** 6.3 ha
Michael and Kerry Dunbabin have one of the most historic properties in Tasmania, dating
back to 1826. The property is 1800 ha, meaning the vineyard (2.7 ha of pinot noir, 1.4 ha of
riesling, 1.2 ha of pinot gris and 1 ha of gewurztraminer) has plenty of room for expansion.
Michael says, 'I've planted some of the newer pinot clones in 2001, but have yet to plant what
I reckon will prove to be some of the best vineyard sites on the property.' Initially the grapes
were sold to Hardys, but since 2005 much of the production has been retained for the Milton
Vineyard label. Exports to Japan.

ŶŶŶŶŶ **Freycinet Coast Pinot Noir 2008** Bright colour; a fragrant red fruit bouquet;
very attractive and elegant palate, with juicy red berry fruits, almost angelica-like.
Screwcap. 13.4% alc. **Rating** 93 **To** 2014 $28
Iced Riesling 2008 Pale straw-green; very sweet and unctuous; layers of fruit still
bundled up, but will unwind with time. Screwcap. 9% alc. **Rating** 90 **To** 2014 $23

Milvine Estate Wines   ★★★☆

108 Warren Road, Heathcote, Vic 3523 **Region** Heathcote
T (03) 5433 2772 **F** (03) 5433 2769 **www.**milvineestatewines.com.au **Open** W'ends &
public hols 11–5
Winemaker Graeme Millard, Wes Vines **Est.** 2002 **Cases** 300 **Vyds** 2 ha
Jo and Graeme Millard planted clonally selected shiraz (90%) and cabernet sauvignon (10%)
in 1995, picking their first grapes in '98; in that and the ensuing four vintages the grapes were
sold to Heathcote Winery, but in 2003 part of the production was vinified by Heathcote
Winery for the Millards, and in '06 all production moved onsite to Milvine Estate. The
Millards support and use the principles of sustainable, minimal chemical intervention in
the vineyard and during wine production. The wines are handcrafted, the grapes receiving
minimal irrigation during the growing period (the main irrigation is at budburst, and again at
veraison), when the vines sometimes receive a small amount of seaweed-based fertiliser.

ŶŶŶŶŶ **Puddlers Gully Heathcote Shiraz 2008** Deep, dense purple-crimson; rich and
intense black fruits, licorice and pepper on the bouquet are replayed on the richly
fruited, medium- to full-bodied palate; good length and overall structure. Diam.
14.7% alc. **Rating** 93 **To** 2020 $38

ŶŶŶŶ **Heathcote Marsanne 2009 Rating** 87 **To** 2012 $25

Minko Wines   ★★★★☆

13 High Street, Willunga, SA 5172 **Region** Southern Fleurieu
T (08) 8556 4987 **F** (08) 8556 2688 **www.**minkowines.com **Open** Wed–Mon 11–5
Winemaker James Hastwell (red), Adrian Kenny (white) **Est.** 1997 **Cases** 1500 **Vyds** 11.2 ha
Mike Boerema (veterinarian) and Margo Kellet (ceramic artist) established the Minko vineyard
on their cattle property at Mt Compass. The vineyard is planted to pinot noir, merlot, cabernet
sauvignon, chardonnay and pinot gris, and managed using sustainable eco-agriculture; 60 ha
of the 160-ha property is heritage listed. Exports to the UK.

ŶŶŶŶŶ **Southern Fleurieu Pinot Noir 2008** Slightly diffuse colour; a fragrant bouquet
✪   and decisive palate, with a range of plum, cherry and delicate spice flavours;
excellent length to a wine of breed and class. Screwcap. 13% alc. **Rating** 95
To 2015 $25

ŶŶŶŶ **Merlot 2006** Impressive colour; reaching towards maturity, with texture, structure
✪   and weight all good, the varietal fruit is correct too; just falters at the finish line.
Screwcap. 13.8% alc. **Rating** 90 **To** 2013 $20

⚙ **Cabernet Sauvignon 2006** Good colour; a neatly put together medium-bodied cabernet, blackcurrant fruit supported by quite gentle tannins; good balance and length. Screwcap. 13.8% alc. **Rating** 90 **To** 2016 $20

♀♀♀♀ **Southern Fleurieu Pinot Grigio 2009** **Rating** 89 **To** 2010 $18

Minnow Creek   ★★★☆

5 Hillside Road, Blackwood, SA 5051 (postal) **Region** McLaren Vale
T 0404 288 108 **F** (08) 8278 8248 **www**.minnowcreekwines.com.au **Open** Not
Winemaker Tony Walker **Est.** 2005 **Cases** 1500
Former Fox Creek winemaker Tony Walker has set up Minnow Creek in partnership with William Neubauer, the grapes grown by Don Lopresti at vineyards just west of Willunga. The name of the venture reflects the intention of the partners to keep the business focused on quality rather than quantity, and to self-distribute much of the wine through the large number of highly regarded Adelaide restaurants. Exports to the US, Canada and Germany.

♀♀♀♀♀ **McLaren Vale Shiraz 2008** Good hue and depth; solid McLaren Vale shiraz, black fruits, licorice, dark chocolate and tannins interwoven; apparently picked before the heat struck, and has good length. Screwcap. 14.5% alc. **Rating** 90 **To** 2018 $27

♀♀♀♀ **McLaren Vale Shiraz 2007** **Rating** 89 **To** 2014 $26
The Silver Minnow Sauvignon Blanc Semillon 2009 **Rating** 88 **To** 2011 $19.50
McLaren Vale Rose 2009 **Rating** 88 **To** 2010 $17.50
The Black Minnow McLaren Vale Sangiovese Cabernet Sauvignon Malbec 2008 **Rating** 87 **To** 2011 $19.50

Minot Vineyard   ★★★★

Lot 4 Harrington Road, Margaret River, WA 6285 **Region** Margaret River
T (08) 9757 3579 **F** (08) 9757 2361 **www**.minotwines.com.au **Open** By appt 10–5
Winemaker Clive Otto **Est.** 1986 **Cases** 2500 **Vyds** 4.2 ha
Minot, which takes its name from a small chateau in the Loire Valley, is the husband and wife venture of the Miles family. It produces just two wines from the plantings of semillon, sauvignon blanc and cabernet sauvignon. Exports to the UK and Singapore.

♀♀♀♀♀
⚙ **Margaret River Sauvignon Blanc Semillon 2009** Pale straw-green; a fragrant, scented bouquet of citrus blossom and a more herbal underlay sets the scene for the long, quite intense palate, the flavours pure and persistent. Screwcap. 13.9% alc. **Rating** 91 **To** 2013 $15

⚙ **Margaret River Cabernet Sauvignon 2008** Bright crimson; an aromatic and lively wine, with cassis and blackcurrant fruit cradled in French oak (14 months), the palate given texture and length by fine, persistent tannins. Screwcap. 14.4% alc. **Rating** 91 **To** 2020 $25

Mintaro Wines   ★★★☆

Leasingham Road, Mintaro, SA 5415 **Region** Clare Valley
T (08) 8843 9150 **F** (08) 8843 9050 **www**.mintarowines.com.au **Open** Thurs–Mon 10–4.30
Winemaker Peter Houldsworth **Est.** 1984 **Cases** 4000 **Vyds** 10 ha
Has produced some very good Rieslings over the years, developing well in bottle. The red wines, too, have improved significantly. The labelling is nothing if not interesting, from the depiction of a fish drinking like a fish, not to mention the statuesque belles femmes. Exports to Singapore.

♀♀♀♀♀ **Leckie Window Clare Valley Cabernet Sauvignon 2006** Holding purple-red hue; powerful and intense black fruits on the bouquet translate into a strict palate, the blackcurrant fruit held in the grip of savoury tannins; has length, and should blossom with a thick steak. Screwcap. 14.5% alc. **Rating** 90 **To** 2021 $28

♟♟♟♟   Clare Valley Shiraz 2007 Rating 89 To 2013 $23
Clare Valley Cabernet Sauvignon 2006 Rating 89 To 2014 $23
Clare Valley Late Picked Riesling 2009 Rating 89 To 2013 $16
Clare Valley Riesling 2009 Rating 88 To 2016 $19.90

Mistletoe Wines   ★★★★★

771 Hermitage Road, Pokolbin, NSW 2320 **Region** Hunter Valley
T (02) 4998 7770 **F** (02) 4998 7792 **www.**mistletoewines.com **Open** 7 days 10–6
Winemaker Nick Paterson **Est.** 1989 **Cases** 7000 **Vyds** 5.5 ha
Mistletoe Wines, owned by Ken and Gwen Sloan, can trace its history back to 1909, when
a vineyard was planted on what was then called Mistletoe Farm. The Mistletoe Farm brand
made a brief appearance in the late 1970s. The wines are made onsite by Nick Paterson, who
has had significant experience in the Hunter Valley. The quality and consistency of these wines
is irreproachable, as is their price. Mistletoe has also been steadily building museum stock for
sale, with four years' bottle age.

♟♟♟♟♟   Grand Reserve Hunter Valley Shiraz 2007 Great colour, deep and intense
crimson-purple; an outstanding wine, combining richness with grace and elegance;
layers of plum and blackberry fruit, the tannins ripe and balanced, oak subtle. From
low-yielding, dry-grown 40-year-old vines. Will be a great Hunter shiraz in the
decades to come. Screwcap. 14% alc. **Rating** 97 To 2040 $40

✪   Home Vineyard Hunter Valley Semillon 2009 A delicious wine, showing
the best features of the striking '09 vintage, the fruit flavours crossing into riesling
territory, or even cool-climate chardonnay courtesy of lime and grapefruit nuances;
long, crisp finish. Screwcap. 10% alc. **Rating** 95 To 2020 $19

Reserve Hunter Valley Semillon 2009 Bright pale green-quartz; while the
bouquet is sulking, the palate has those supercharged citrus and mineral flavours
of the '09 vintage; from a single vineyard in the Belford area. Screwcap. 10.6% alc.
Rating 95 To 2025 $24

Reserve Hunter Valley Semillon 2008 Here, too, the bouquet is still
developing; the racy, intense palate has potent lemon and lime flavours; like the '09,
extended lees contact has given the wine extra power, although the technique is
not generally used with semillon. Screwcap. 10% alc. **Rating** 95 To 2025 $24

Reserve Hunter Valley Semillon 2004 Re-released Jul '10. Still vibrant
pale green-straw; is strolling leisurely towards maturity some way – a long way
perhaps – down the track. Given 93 points in Aug '05, and has always been a very
good wine. Screwcap. 10.5% alc. **Rating** 95 To 2020 $30

✪   Hilltops Shiraz Viognier 2008 Lively and juicy, the red fruit flavours almost
tingling, so fresh are they; the finish, too, leaves the mouth echoing the messages
of the bouquet and mid-palate. Top gold medal Winewise '09. Screwcap. 14% alc.
Rating 95 To 2014 $20

Reserve Hunter Valley Chardonnay 2009 Bright green-straw; whole bunch
pressing and fermentation in French puncheons takes the wine out of traditional
Hunter Valley style; intense grapefruit and white flesh stone fruit drive the wine's
long palate, not oak. Screwcap. 13.5% alc. **Rating** 94 To 2016 $35

Reserve Hunter Valley Shiraz 2005 Re-release July '10. Medium red-purple,
holding hue well for age; has now had time to fully reflect its regional character; a
medium-bodied wine with plum, blackberry, leather, spice and sweet earth notes
all intermingling. Screwcap. 13% alc. **Rating** 94 To 2020 $40

♟♟♟♟♡   Hunter Valley Chardonnay 2008 Light straw-green, still bright and pale;
✪   hand-picked, whole bunch pressed and fermented in French oak puncheons; still
very fresh and precise, with grapefruit and white peach fruit to the fore. Screwcap.
13.5% alc. **Rating** 93 To 2016 $20

Hunter Valley Shiraz 2007 Rating 91 To 2017 $25
Hunter Hilltops Shiraz Cabernet 2008 Rating 90 To 2014 $22

♟♟♟♟   Hunter Valley Mozcato 2009 Rating 87 To 2010 $22

Mitchell ★★★★★

Hughes Park Road, Sevenhill via Clare, SA 5453 **Region** Clare Valley
T (08) 8843 4258 **F** (08) 8843 4340 **www**.mitchellwines.com **Open** 7 days 10–4
Winemaker Andrew Mitchell **Est.** 1975 **Cases** 20 000 **Vyds** 69 ha
One of the stalwarts of the Clare Valley, producing long-lived Rieslings and Cabernet
Sauvignons in classic regional style. The range now includes very creditable Semillon,
Grenache and Shiraz. A lovely old stone apple shed provides the cellar door and upper section
of the compact winery. Exports to the UK, Canada, Singapore, Hong Kong and NZ.

ŸŸŸŸŸ **Watervale Riesling 2009** Classic freshly squeezed lime, bath talc and a touch
✪ of spring flowers on the bouquet; pristine, precise and showing great energy and
drive, with an ultimately fulfilling, fine and focused conclusion. Screwcap. 13% alc.
Rating 94 To 2020 $22 BE
McNicol Clare Valley Shiraz 2002 Vibrant colour; for an aged release it has a
fresh and unevolved bouquet, showing blackberry confiture, a touch of mint and
baked spices; the palate is fleshy and approachable, with an abundance of warm
dark fruit, plentiful fine-grained tannins and a long and savoury finish. Screwcap.
14.5% alc. Rating 94 To 2016 $40 BE

ŸŸŸŸŸ **Peppertree Vineyard Clare Valley Shiraz 2007** Rating 91 To 2016 $26 BE
GSM Clare Valley Grenache Sangiovese Mourvedre 2006 Rating 91
To 2016 $21 BE
Sevenhill Vineyard Clare Valley Cabernet Sauvignon 2006 Rating 90
To 2020 $26 BE

Mitchell Harris Wines ★★★★★

515 Havelock Street, Soldiers Hill, Vic 3350 (postal) **Region** Pyrenees
T 0438 301 471 **www**.mitchellharris.com.au **Open** Not
Winemaker John Harris **Est.** 2008 **Cases** 500
Mitchell Harris Wines is a partnership between Alicia and Craig Mitchell and Shannyn and
John Harris, the latter winemaker for this little producer and for the somewhat larger Mount
Avoca winery. John began his career at Mount Avoca, then spent eight years as winemaker
at Domaine Chandon in the Yarra Valley, cramming in northern hemisphere vintages in
California and Oregon. The Mitchells grew up in the Ballarat area, and have an affinity for
the Macedon and Pyrenees ranges districts. While the total make is not large, a lot of thought
has gone into the creation of each of the wines.

ŸŸŸŸŸ **Pyrenees Shiraz 2008** Purple-red; a perfumed bouquet attests to the presence
of some viognier, the silky/savoury/spicy palate with distinctive whole bunch
fermentation characters; very much à la mode. Screwcap. 13.5% alc. Rating 95
To 2020 $34.95
✪ **Pyrenees Cabernet Sauvignon 2007** Good colour, crimson-purple hue; given
the drought conditions, a remarkably pure varietal wine, with medium-bodied
but intense blackcurrant fruit and a fine veil of supporting tannins; picked at the
optimum moment. Screwcap. 13.5% alc. Rating 94 To 2022 $21.95

ŸŸŸŸŸ **Pyrenees Sauvignon Blanc Fume 2009** Rating 93 To 2012 $21.95

Mitchelton ★★★★☆

Mitchellstown via Nagambie, Vic 3608 **Region** Nagambie Lakes
T (03) 5736 2222 **F** (03) 5736 2266 **www**.mitchelton.com.au **Open** 7 days 10–5
Winemaker Ben Haines **Est.** 1969 **Cases** 220 000
Acquired by Petaluma in 1994 (both now part of Lion Nathan), having already put the runs
on the board in no uncertain fashion with gifted winemaker Don Lewis (who retired in '04).
His successor, Ben Haines, won the Wine Society Winemaker of the Year Award '08 (from a
pool of Australian and NZ winemaking talent). Mitchelton, which celebrated its 40th birthday
in 2009, boasts an array of wines across a broad spectrum of style and price, each carefully
aimed at a market niche. Exports to all major markets.

ΨΨΨΨΨ **Marsanne 2007** Bright yellow-green; the aromatic bouquet introduces peach
✪   and apricot to the play, the palate picking up some honeysuckle, and a very good
       citrussy tang to the finish. Screwcap. 14% alc. **Rating** 94 **To** 2015 $22

ΨΨΨΨΨ **Blackwood Park Riesling 2009** Firm, crisp, crunchy/minerally; doesn't have
✪   quite enough citrussy fruit to convince, but will develop well. Screwcap. 13% alc.
       Rating 93 **To** 2019 $18
       Crescent Mourvedre Shiraz Grenache 2006 Rating 92 **To** 2014 $28
✪   **Preece Merlot 2008** Bright crimson-red; has enough varietal character on
       bouquet and palate to satisfy, particularly given the fresh cassis flavours, enhanced by
       a crisp finish, the tannins ultrafine. Screwcap. 14.5% alc. **Rating** 90 **To** 2013 $16

ΨΨΨΨ   **Preece Chardonnay 2008 Rating** 89 **To** 2014 $16
       Preece Shiraz 2008 Rating 88 **To** 2014 $16

Mitolo Wines   ★★★★★
PO Box 520, Virginia, SA 5120 **Region** McLaren Vale
T (08) 8282 9012 **F** (08) 8282 9062 **www**.mitolowines.com.au **Open** Not
Winemaker Ben Glaetzer **Est.** 1999 **Cases** 20 000
Frank Mitolo began making wine in 1995 as a hobby, and soon progressed to undertaking
formal studies in winemaking. His interest grew year by year, and in 2000 he took the plunge
into the commercial end of the business, retaining Ben Glaetzer to make the wines. Since that
time, a remarkably good series of wines has been released. Imitation being the sincerest form
of flattery, part of the complicated story behind each label name is pure Torbreck, but Mitolo
then adds a Latin proverb or saying to the name. Exports to all major markets.

ΨΨΨΨΨ **Jester McLaren Vale Cabernet Sauvignon 2008** Black fruits, leather and
       dark chocolate aromas jump from the glass, and are the drivers on the palate, which
       is more elegant than prior Jesters. Screwcap. 14.5% alc. **Rating** 94 **To** 2018 $28

ΨΨΨΨΨ **Jester McLaren Vale Sangiovese Rose 2009 Rating** 92 **To** 2011 $24

Molly Morgan Vineyard   ★★★★
496 Talga Road, Rothbury, NSW 2320 **Region** Hunter Valley
T (02) 4930 7695 **F** (02) 4006 3004 **www**.mollymorgan.com
Open W'ends 10–5 (summer), w'ends 10–4.30 (winter), or by appt
Winemaker Simon Miles **Est.** 1963 **Cases** 600 **Vyds** 6.3 ha
Molly Morgan has been acquired by Andrew and Hady Simon, who established the
Camperdown Cellars Group in 1971, which became the largest retailer in Australia, before
moving on to other pursuits. They were joined by Grant Breen, their former general manager
at Camperdown Cellars. The property includes unirrigated semillon vines over 40 years old
(used for the Old Vines Semillon), 2 ha of chardonnay, 3.7 ha shiraz and a few riesling vines.

ΨΨΨΨΨ **Hunter Valley Semillon 2009** Bright pale straw; the bouquet is spotlessly clean,
✪   the palate tightly focused and long; attractive citrus flavours, then a bright and crisp
       finish. At the start of a long and prosperous journey. Screwcap. 11% alc. **Rating** 93
       To 2020 $20
✪   **Chardonnay 2009** The grapes were picked at precisely the right time, retaining
       freshness yet not compromising varietal expression; little or no evidence of oak
       is no hindrance to the nectarine and white peach flavours of the wine. Screwcap.
       13% alc. **Rating** 90 **To** 2014 $20
       Hunter Valley Rose 2009 Bright magenta; a fresh and lively burst of red fruits
       on bouquet and palate alike; good length and a crisp finish. Screwcap. 12% alc.
       Rating 90 **To** 2011 $20

Momentum Wines ★★★★

8 Canal Rocks Road, Yallingup, WA 6282 **Region** Margaret River
T (08) 9755 2028 **F** (08) 9755 2101 **www.**winemomentum.com **Open** W'ends & hols 10–5
Winemaker Egidijus Rusilas, Siobhan Lynch **Est.** 1978 **Cases** 2800 **Vyds** 4 ha
The vineyard, planted to semillon, cabernet sauvignon and sauvignon blanc, was established by
David Hunt in 1978. Originally called Sienna Estate, it has now passed into the ownership of
the Rusilas family, which has significantly enhanced its legacy. Exports to Lithuania.

♈♈♈♈♈ **Momentum of Passion Margaret River Semillon Sauvignon Blanc 2009**
A fresh-fruited and smoky bouquet; the palate has attractive texture with chalky
acidity. Screwcap. 13% alc. **Rating** 90 **To** 2012 $14.90 BE

Mongrel Creek Vineyard ★★★☆

109 Hayes Road, Yallingup Siding, WA 6281 **Region** Margaret River
T 0417 991 065 **F** (08) 9755 5708 **Open** W'ends & public hols 10–5
Winemaker Tony Davis, Genevieve Stols **Est.** 1996 **Cases** 1000 **Vyds** 2.8 ha
Larry and Shirley Schoppe both have other occupations, Larry as vineyard supervisor at
Howard Park's Leston Vineyard, Shirley as a full-time nurse. Thus the vineyard, planted to
shiraz, semillon and sauvignon blanc in 1996, is still a weekend and holiday business. Given the
viticultural and winemaking expertise of those involved, it is hardly surprising that the wines
have been consistent show medal winners.

♈♈♈♈♈ **Margaret River Merlot Cabernet Franc 2008** Good purple-crimson;
✪   attractive raspberry, black cherry and plum aromas and flavours; light- to medium-
bodied, but with very good texture courtesy of fine tannins. Screwcap. 14% alc.
Rating 93 **To** 2018 $19

♈♈♈♈ **Margaret River Shiraz 2007 Rating** 88 **To** 2015 $20

Montalto Vineyards ★★★★★

33 Shoreham Road, Red Hill South, Vic 3937 **Region** Mornington Peninsula
T (03) 5989 8412 **F** (03) 5989 8417 **www.**montalto.com.au **Open** 7 days 11–5
Winemaker Simon Black **Est.** 1998 **Cases** 6000 **Vyds** 11.1 ha
John Mitchell and family established Montalto Vineyards in 1998, but the core of the vineyard
goes back to '86. There are 5.6 ha of pinot noir, 3 ha of chardonnay, 1 ha of pinot gris, and
0.5 ha each of semillon, riesling and pinot meunier. Intensive vineyard work opens up the
canopy, with yields ranging between 1.5 and 2.5 tonnes per acre. Wines are released under
two labels, the flagship Montalto and Pennon, the latter a lower-priced, second label. In 2010
Montalto opened its own winery in a converted coolstore in Merricks North, ending a long
period of skilled contract winemaking by Robin Brockett of Scotchmans Hill.

♈♈♈♈♈ **Mornington Peninsula Pinot Noir 2008** An exceptional wine, combining
power with finesse; has great balance, line and length, its black cherry fruit making
the tannins and oak all but irrelevant now; their day to come when the burst of
primary fruit diminishes. Screwcap. 14% alc. **Rating** 96 **To** 2018 $45
Lake Block Pinot Noir 2008 Bright clear colour; the pure bouquet announces
a palate with effortless power and precise length to the mix of black cherry and
plum fruit that will evolve superbly over the next five years; 80 cases made from
the oldest block on the vineyard. Screwcap. 14% alc. **Rating** 96 **To** 2018 $65
The Eleven Chardonnay 2007 Green-gold; a selection within a selection: the
best four barriques from the total number produced from 11 rows of the oldest
chardonnay vines; has developed some extra depth from bottle age, but is still
youthful and immaculately balanced. Screwcap. 13.5% alc. **Rating** 95 **To** 2014 $55
Mornington Peninsula Chardonnay 2008 Elegant and impeccably balanced,
with nectarine fruit in a subtle oak framework; a touch of French funk adds
interest and complexity. Screwcap. 13.5% alc. **Rating** 94 **To** 2018 $36

✪   **Pennon Hill Mornington Peninsula Pinot Noir 2008** Good hue and
      limpidity; a very stylish wine with excellent line and length to the plum and
      cherry fruit; lovely mouthfeel, finish and aftertaste. Screwcap. 14% alc. **Rating** 94
      To 2015 $28

♟♟♟♟♟ **Pennon Hill Rose 2009** A highly fragrant blend of Pinot Noir/Pinot Meunier;
✪   strawberries leaping from the glass; the bone-dry and long palate adds a touch of
      red cherry to a very good rose. Screwcap. 13.5% alc. **Rating** 93 To 2011 $22
      Pennon Hill Mornington Peninsula Shiraz 2008 Rating 93 To 2023 $28
      Cuvee One 2006 Rating 93 To 2014 $35
      Mornington Peninsula Riesling 2008 Rating 92 To 2017 $23
      Pennon Hill Pinot Grigio 2009 Rating 92 To 2011 $24
✪   **Pennon Hill Chardonnay 2008** This provides maximum varietal impact per
      dollar, with generous stone fruit on the bouquet and palate alike, oak merely a
      vehicle for the white and yellow peach flavours. Screwcap. 13.5% alc. **Rating** 91
      To 2014 $21

Montgomery's Hill   ★★★★☆

South Coast Highway, Upper Kalgan, Albany, WA 6330 **Region** Albany
T (08) 9844 3715 **F** (08) 9844 3819 **www**.montgomeryshill.com.au **Open** 7 days 11–5
Winemaker The Vintage Wineworx, Bill Crappsley (Consultant) **Est.** 1996 **Cases** 6000
Montgomery's Hill is 16 km northeast of Albany on a north-facing slope on the banks of the
Kalgan River. Previously used as an apple orchard; it is a diversification for the third generation
of the Montgomery family. Chardonnay, cabernet sauvignon, cabernet franc, sauvignon blanc,
shiraz and merlot were planted in 1996–97. The wines are made with a gentle touch.

♟♟♟♟♟ **Albany Sauvignon Blanc 2009** Light straw-green; the flavours capture the best
✪   of both sauvignon worlds: grass and citrus on one hand, passionfruit and tropical
      on the other; remarkably, the flavours are seamless, the line unbroken. Gold medal
      WA Wine Show '09, silver medal Perth Wine Show '09. Screwcap. 13% alc.
      Rating 94 To 2011 $18

♟♟♟♟♟ **Albany Cabernet Sauvignon 2007** Deep red-purple; interesting wine;
✪   despite its modest alcohol, it is fully ripe and has a medium- to full-bodied palate,
      blackcurrant and cassis fruit supported by ripe tannins and subtle oak. Screwcap.
      13% alc. **Rating** 93 To 2022 $20
      Albany Chardonnay 2008 Rating 90 To 2016 $22

Moody's Wines   ★★★

'Fontenay', Stagecoach Road, Orange, NSW 2800 **Region** Orange
T (02) 6365 9117 **F** (02) 6391 3650 **www**.moodyswines.com **Open** W'ends 10–5, or by appt
Winemaker Madrez Wine Services (Chris Derrez) **Est.** 2000 **Cases** 150 **Vyds** 2 ha
Tony Moody's great-grandfather started a retail chain of shops in Merseyside, England, under
the banner Moody's Wines. The business was ultimately sold in 1965 to a brewery seeking to
minimise off-licence competition. Tony planted 1 ha of shiraz 'in a promising sheep paddock'
in 2000, and has subsequently added 1 ha of sauvignon blanc.

♟♟♟♟ **Orange Shiraz 2009** Light colour, good hue; a light-bodied shiraz that has good
      cool-grown characteristics, its fresh cherry fruit dusted with spice and pepper
      notes. Drink sooner than later. Screwcap. 13.5% alc. **Rating** 88 To 2012 $20
      Orange Shiraz 2008 Light but bright crimson; very fresh, with some mint
      and eucalypt characters throughout; a wine seemingly picked a little too early.
      Screwcap. 13% alc. **Rating** 87 To 2013 $20

Moombaki Wines   ★★★★★

341 Parker Road, Kentdale via Denmark, WA 6333 **Region** Denmark
T (08) 9840 8006 **F** (08) 9840 8006 **www**.moombaki.com **Open** 7 days 11–5
Winemaker Harewood Estate (James Kellie) **Est.** 1997 **Cases** 1200 **Vyds** 2.4 ha

David Britten and Melissa Boughey (with three young sons in tow) established vines on a north-facing gravel hillside, with picturesque Kent River frontage. Not content with establishing the vineyard (cabernet sauvignon, shiraz, cabernet franc and malbec), they put in significant mixed tree plantings to increase wildlife habitats. It is against this background that they chose Moombaki as their vineyard name: a local Aboriginal word meaning 'where the river meets the sky'. Exports to the UK, Switzerland, Malaysia and Singapore.

ΨΨΨΨΨ **Reserve 2007** Relatively light but good hue; a fragrant, complex bouquet is driven by the Bordeaux half of the blend of Shiraz/Cabernet Sauvignon/Cabernet Franc/Malbec, and the savoury flavours and tannins of the medium- to full-bodied palate do not shift the balance of power; cedary characters will emerge with time; 1050 bottles produced from the best barrels in the cellar. Screwcap. 14% alc. Rating 94 To 2027 $55
Cabernet Sauvignon Cabernet Franc Malbec 2004 Good colour, although not as bright as the '05; a very expressive bouquet of blackcurrant and some floral notes from the cabernet franc and malbec; very good fruit flavours with blackcurrant and cassis, the long palate sustained by fine, persistent tannins. Screwcap. 14% alc. Rating 94 To 2017 $45

ΨΨΨΨΨ **Chardonnay 2008** Rating 93 To 2015 $25
Shiraz 2007 Rating 92 To 2015 $29 BE
Cabernet Sauvignon Cabernet Franc Malbec 2005 Rating 92 To 2015 $40
Chardonnay 2007 Rating 90 To 2012 $28

Moonbark Estate Vineyard ★★★★
Lot 11, Moonambel-Natte Yallock Road, Moonambel, Vic 3478 (postal) **Region** Pyrenees
T 0439 952 263 **F** (03) 9873 7876 **www.**moonbark.com.au **Open** Not
Winemaker Contract **Est.** 1998 **Cases** 500 **Vyds** 1.75 ha
This small family-owned and operated vineyard is located on a 17.1-ha property in the Pyrenees region. Rod Chivers and his family have slowly established their vineyard with 1 ha of shiraz, 0.5 ha of merlot and 0.25 ha of cabernet sauvignon planted on the red clay soils intermingled with quartz typical of the region.

ΨΨΨΨΨ **Merlot 2008** Bright hue; merlot has lost its magic, but this is a very attractive
✪ and true-to-variety wine; medium-bodied, it has cassis and black olive flavours supported by fine, spicy tannins. Screwcap. 14% alc. Rating 94 To 2018 $18

ΨΨΨΨ **Shiraz 2008** Rating 89 To 2014 $20
Shiraz 2006 Rating 87 To 2015 $16

Moondah Brook ★★★★
Dale Road, Middle Swan, WA 6056 **Region** Swan Valley
T (08) 9274 9540 **F** (08) 9274 5172 **www.**moondahbrook.com.au **Open** Not
Winemaker Courtney Treacher **Est.** 1968 **Cases** NFP
Part of Constellation Wines Australia, Moondah Brook has its own special character, as it draws part of its fruit from the large Gingin vineyard, 70 km north of the Swan Valley, and part from the Margaret River and Great Southern. From time to time it has excelled even its own reputation for reliability with some quite lovely wines, in particular honeyed, aged Chenin Blanc, generous Shiraz and finely structured Cabernet Sauvignon. Exports to the UK and other major markets.

ΨΨΨΨΨ **Shiraz 2008** Strong crimson-red; black fruit aromas intermingle with oak on the
✪ bouquet, the palate following suit but with substantial tannins added to the mix. Will reward patience. Screwcap. 14% alc. Rating 91 To 2020 $18
Cabernet Rose 2009 Pale bright pink; a time-honoured style, clean, fresh and crisp, with redcurrant fruit, but needing a little more depth. Screwcap. 12.5% alc. Rating 90 To 2010 $18

○   **Cabernet Sauvignon 2008** A large-volume wine that reflects Constellation's
spread of cabernet resources across the southern part of the state; vibrant purple-
crimson, it has clear-cut varietal cabernet ripened to the precise point, and good
texture and structure. Screwcap. 14% alc. **Rating** 90 **To** 2018 $18

♉♉♉♉   **Verdelho 2009 Rating** 88 **To** 2013 $18 BE

Moondarra   ★★★

45 Grange Road, Sandringham, Vic 3191 (postal) **Region** Gippsland
T 0408 666 348 **F** (03) 9598 0677 **www**.moondara.com.au **Open** Not
Winemaker Neil Prentice **Est.** 1991 **Cases** 3200 **Vyds** 14 ha
In 1991 Neil Prentice and family established their Moondarra Vineyard in Gippsland,
eventually focusing on the 2 ha of low-yielding pinot noir. Subsequently, they began planting
their Holly's Garden vineyard at Whitlands in the King Valley, where they have 12 ha of pinot
gris and pinot noir. It is from this vineyard that all but 200 cases of their wines come, sold
under the Holly's Garden label. Exports to the US, Singapore, Hong Kong, Philippines, Korea
and Japan.

♉♉♉♉   **Holly's Garden Whitlands Pinot Noir 2008** Clear colour, fractionally
advanced; has a fragrant and scented bouquet (a hint of violet?), but the palate
moves decisively into a savoury/leafy spectrum with a slightly bitter finish.
Screwcap. 13.5% alc. **Rating** 89 **To** 2013 $25
Holly's Garden Pinot Gris 2009 More colour (greenish) than most young
pinot gris; brown pear, apple and spice aromas, then slightly phenolic palate with
ample flavour. Screwcap. 13.5% alc. **Rating** 88 **To** 2011 $29

Moorabool Ridge   ★★★★☆

23 Spiller Road, Lethbridge, Vic 3332 **Region** Geelong
T (03) 5281 9240 **F** (03) 5281 9240 **Open** W'ends & public hols 11–5
Winemaker Ray Nadeson **Est.** 1991 **Cases** 400 **Vyds** 2.25 ha
Tim Harrop and Katarina Romanov-Harrop planted their first vines in 1990, and the first
olive trees in 2001 (the latter now extended to 800 trees and a commercial olive oil and olive
business). Despite the name, the vines are planted on the floor of the Moorabool Valley on
the bank of Moorabool River; there are 2 ha of shiraz and 1 ha each of semillon, chardonnay,
cabernet sauvignon, cabernet franc and merlot. For the first 10 years the grapes were sold, but
thereafter part of the production was retained for the Moorabool Ridge label, sold through
the cellar door situated in the historic Sheppard's Hut dating from 1856.

♉♉♉♉♉   **Sofia Reserve Shiraz 2008** Strong crimson-purple; spiced red and black cherry
○   aromas lead into a medium-bodied palate with similar flavours, backed by fine but
warm and spicy tannins and oak inputs. Harmonious wine. Screwcap. 14% alc.
Rating 94 **To** 2016 $20

♉♉♉♉♉   **Cynthia Chardonnay 2008** Bright straw-green; a most attractive light- to
○   medium-bodied, fruit-driven style, flavours running from ripe peach to gentle
citrus/grassy notes; seemingly unoaked. Screwcap. 13% alc. **Rating** 91 **To** 2014 $18

Moorebank Vineyard   ★★★☆

150 Palmers Lane, Pokolbin, NSW 2320 **Region** Hunter Valley
T (02) 4998 7610 **F** (02) 4998 7367 **www**.moorebankvineyard.com.au **Open** 7 days 10–5
Winemaker Gary Reed **Est.** 1977 **Cases** 12 500 **Vyds** 6 ha
Ian Burgess and Debra Moore own a mature vineyard planted to chardonnay (3 ha),
semillon, gewurztraminer and merlot (1 ha each), with a small cellar door operation offering
immaculately packaged wines in avant-garde style. Exports to Singapore, China and Japan.

♉♉♉♉♉   **Private Vineyard Late Harvest Semillon 2007** Glowing yellow-green; the
Hunter Valley can do this style well when aided by vintage/late-vintage rain; a
mix of cumquat, honey and lemon zest acidity; good balance. Screwcap. 9.5% alc.
Rating 90 **To** 2012 $29.50

Moores Hill Estate ★★★★

3343 West Tamar Highway, Sidmouth, Tas 7270 **Region** Northern Tasmania
T (03) 6394 7649 **F** (03) 6394 7647 **www**.mooreshill.com.au **Open** 7 days 10–5
Winemaker Winemaking Tasmania (Julian Allpart) **Est.** 1997 **Cases** 2500 **Vyds** 4.5 ha
Rod and Karen Thorpe established Moores Hill Estate in 1997 on the gentle slopes of the
West Tamar Valley. It has riesling, chardonnay, pinot noir, merlot and cabernet sauvignon.
The vineyard represents a full circle for the Thorpes, who bought the farm 30 years ago and
ripped out a small vineyard. The Wine Centre (built in 2002 mainly from timber found on
the property) overlooks the vineyard.

🍷🍷🍷🍷🍷 **Riesling 2009** Light straw-green; an elegant, flowery bouquet; very attractive lime
and passionfruit flavours; good length and finish. Gold medal Tas Wine Show '10.
Screwcap. 12% alc. **Rating** 95 **To** 2019 $30

🍷🍷🍷🍷 **Premium Pinot Noir 2007 Rating** 87 **To** 2012 $27

Moorilla Estate ★★★★

655 Main Road, Berriedale, Tas 7011 **Region** Southern Tasmania
T (03) 6277 9900 **F** (03) 6249 4093 **www**.moorilla.com.au **Open** 7 days 10–5
Winemaker Conor van der Reest **Est.** 1958 **Cases** 8000 **Vyds** 21.9 ha
Moorilla Estate was the second winery to be established in Tasmania in the 20th century, Jean
Miguet's La Provence beating it to the punch by two years. However, through much of the
history of Moorilla Estate, it was the most important winery in the state, if not in size but as
the icon. Magnificently situated on a mini-isthmus reaching into the Derwent River, and a
20-min drive from the Hobart CBD, it has always been a must-visit for wine lovers and tourists.
A new winery, due for completion in October 2010, will see a decrease of 80% from peak
production to around 90 tonnes per year sourced entirely from the vineyards around Moorilla,
and its St Matthias Vineyard (Tamar Valley). It's almost incidental that the new winery is part
of an overall development said by observers (not Moorilla) to cost upwards of $100 million. It
will also house the boutique brewery Moo Brew, but its raison d'être is the establishment of an
art gallery that will have the highest accreditation of any gallery in the Southern Hemisphere,
housing both the extraordinary art collection owned by Moorilla, and visiting exhibitions from
major art museums around the world. I'm inclined to say the elaborative winemaking, with the
winemakers' fingerprints everywhere, is appropriate for the venue. Exports to the US.

🍷🍷🍷🍷🍷 **Praxis Chardonnay 2009** Amazingly, chardonnay varietal fruit comes through
on the long palate, with a mix of grapefruit and stone fruit flavours. Screwcap.
14% alc. **Rating** 93 **To** 2016 $28
Praxis Chardonnay 2008 Sourced from three blocks on the St Matthias
Vineyard (two removed since vintage due to eutypa infection). Hand picked,
crushed, some skin contact; 32 barrels of different sizes were each treated as a
separate ferment with different regimes, Muse and Fraxis ultimately selected
from these barrels. There is more fruit to be found here, and the lower alcohol is
quite evident with more citrus and mineral elements; extremely long finish and
aftertaste. Screwcap. 13.2% alc. **Rating** 92 **To** 2016 $28
Muse Pinot Noir 2008 Bright clear colour; fragrant red and black fruits; has
line and nervosity, with some stemmy notes adding complexity. Eleven separate
vineyard blocks were given a total of 42 different treatments; includes 4% shiraz.
Screwcap. 14.4% alc. **Rating** 92 **To** 2015 $45
Muse Sauvignon 2008 A blend of Sauvignon Blanc (93%)/Pinot Noir
(3%)/Viognier/Chardonnay (2% each) from two vineyards and a multitude of
fermentation techniques, including 15% solids fermentation in oak – the list
goes on. The result is downplayed fruit aromas and flavours, the focus on texture
and complexity. One man's meat; points for effort. Screwcap. 13% alc. **Rating** 90
To 2014 $29
Muse Chardonnay 2008 Obviously, an extremely complex wine, the emphasis
on texture and structure, not varietal fruit. Screwcap. 13.6% alc. **Rating** 90
To 2015 $45

Praxis Pinot Noir 2009 Brilliantly clear crimson; a pure expression of the variety, with bell-clear plummy fruit; good line and length. Screwcap. 14.7% alc. **Rating** 90 **To** 2016 $28

Muse Syrah 2008 Crimson-purple; shows why Tasmania in general is better off chasing syrah than cabernet; its generous alcohol is balanced by almost 7.5 grammes per litre of acidity, giving the wine a light touch; lots of spice and pepper to accompany the cherry fruit; 56 dozen made; 4% merlot. Screwcap. 15.1% alc. **Rating** 90 **To** 2018 $75

♟♟♟♟ **Muse Botrytis Riesling 2008 Rating** 89 **To** 2012 $40

Moorooduc Estate   ★★★★★
501 Derril Road, Moorooduc, Vic 3936 **Region** Mornington Peninsula
T (03) 5971 8506 **F** (03) 5971 8550 **www**.moorooducestate.com.au **Open** W'ends 11–5, Mon, Thurs–Fri 11–4
Winemaker Dr Richard McIntyre **Est.** 1983 **Cases** 5000 **Vyds** 6.5 ha
Richard McIntyre has taken Moorooduc Estate to new heights, having completely mastered the difficult art of gaining maximum results from wild yeast fermentations. While the Chardonnays remain the jewels in the crown, the Pinot Noirs are also very impressive. Viticulturist Hugh Robinson tends the vines with the same attention to detail he bestows on his own vineyard. Jill's Restaurant and accommodation has been closed, but food and coffee are available at the newly renovated and much-improved cellar door, including sour dough wood-fired pizza on weekends. Exports to Hong Kong and Singapore.

♟♟♟♟♟ **The Moorooduc Chardonnay 2008** Light straw-green; this wine brings together the best of the McIntyre and Robinson Vineyard wines: complexity, sheer intensity and an extremely long palate with great energy and drive. Close to perfection. Screwcap. 13.5% alc. **Rating** 97 **To** 2029 $55

McIntyre Vineyard Chardonnay 2008 Light straw; here great complexity has been achieved without loss of finesse; the nectarine, white peach and integrated barrel ferment oak of the bouquet lead into a palate with excellent texture and structure, grainy acidity running through the intense fruit flavours, oak just where it should be. Screwcap. 13.5% alc. **Rating** 96 **To** 2018 $35

The Moorooduc Pinot Noir 2008 As usual, the most powerful, complex and age-worthy pinot in the Moorooduc range, the bouquet with dark plum and briar aromas, the palate with tremendous drive, and an unexpected juicy red fruit burst on the finish and aftertaste. Screwcap. 14% alc. **Rating** 96 **To** 2019 $55

Robinson Vineyard Chardonnay 2008 Light straw-green; a wonderful display of single-vineyard contrasting terroir; here the palate is supple, smooth and introduces a touch of grapefruit to accompany the stone fruit components, oak relegated to the shadows. Screwcap. 13.5% alc. **Rating** 95 **To** 2018 $35

McIntyre Vineyard Pinot Noir 2008 Clear, strong colour; a fragrant bouquet with blood plum and cherry aromas, the palate with life and drive to its red fruits and silky, lingering tannins. Delicious now, but has years in front of it. Screwcap. 14% alc. **Rating** 95 **To** 2017 $35

Robinson Vineyard Pinot Noir 2008 The bouquet has spice, red cherry and mulled strawberry aromas, then a strongly spicy/savoury palate with considerable texture and complexity, the line and length very good. Screwcap. 14% alc. **Rating** 95 **To** 2018 $35

Garden Vineyard Pinot Gris 2008 Wild yeast, cloudy juice, barrel fermentation and estate-grown grapes all add up to a complex, textured pinot gris with a distinct savoury twist. More than a nod to Alsace. Screwcap. 13.8% alc. **Rating** 94 **To** 2012 $35

McIntyre Vineyard Shiraz 2007 Good colour; an appropriately elegant shiraz, no more than medium-bodied, but with fluid cherry fruits and fresh acidity; oak inputs nicely controlled, the length admirable. Screwcap. 14% alc. **Rating** 94 **To** 2020 $35

ɉɉɉɉɉ Devil Bend Creek Chardonnay 2008 Rating 93 To 2015 $25
Devil Bend Creek Pinot Noir 2008 Rating 93 To 2016 $25

ɉɉɉɉ Moorooduc Blanc 2008 Rating 88 To 2012 $16

Moppity Vineyards ★★★★☆

Moppity Road, Young, NSW 2594 (postal) **Region** Hilltops
T (02) 6382 6222 **F** (02) 6382 6222 **www.**moppity.com.au **Open** Not
Winemaker Nick Spencer; **Est.** 1973 **Cases** 30 000 **Vyds** 73 ha
Jason Brown (and wife Alecia), with backgrounds in fine wine retail and accounting, purchased Moppity Vineyards in 2004, then already 31 years old. Initially they were content to sell the grapes to other makers, but that changed with the release of the '06 Shiraz, which won top gold in its class at the London International Wine & Spirit Competition, thereafter adding another two gold medals. In Nov '09 the '08 Eden Road Long Road Hilltops Shiraz, made from Moppity Vineyards grapes, won the Jimmy Watson Trophy. Moppity Vineyards' own Reserve Shiraz from '08 won the trophy for Best Medium Bodied Dry Red at the Sydney International Winemakers Competition '10. These awards are among a cascade of golds for its Shirazs, Riesling, Tumbarumba Chardonnay and Cabernet Sauvignon. The consequence has been that production (and sales) have soared, and all of the grapes from the estate are now used for the Moppity Vineyards brand. Exports to the UK and China.

ɉɉɉɉɉ Reserve Hilltops Shiraz 2008 Bright crimson; a perfumed bouquet with spice and licorice alongside the dark berry fruits; excellent structure and texture to the medium-bodied palate, with very good cool-grown spice and licorice flavours; good length. Trophy Sydney International Wine Competition '10. Screwcap. 14.5% alc. Rating 94 To 2020 $50

ɉɉɉɉɉ Hilltops Riesling 2009 Light straw-green; an attractive bouquet with a range
✪ of citrus and tropical aromas, the hyper-intense palate driven by lemony acidity, needing to back off a little – which it will do over the next 5+ years. Screwcap. 12% alc. Rating 93 To 2024 $20

✪ Lock & Key Single Vineyard Hilltops Riesling 2009 This is in lock-step with its more expensive brother, and is the wine to drink now, while the latter begins to relax; it has the same crunchy, crisp lemony acidity. If 'commonly $9.99 on special' as claimed, a great buy. Screwcap. 12.5% alc. Rating 90 To 2019 $15
Hilltops Cabernet Sauvignon 2008 Rating 90 To 2018 $20
Reserve Hilltops Sparkling Shiraz NV Rating 90 To 2013 $50

ɉɉɉɉ Hilltops Shiraz 2008 Rating 89 To 2014 $20
✪ Lock & Key Single Vineyard Hilltops Shiraz 2008 Lighter coloured than Hilltops, also lighter-bodied, yet paradoxically has better structure and balance; if discounted to $9.99, exceptional drinking over the next two years. Screwcap. 14.5% alc. Rating 88 To 2011 $15

Morambro Creek Wines ★★★★☆

PMB 98, Naracoorte, SA 5271 (postal) **Region** Padthaway
T (08) 8765 6043 **F** (08) 8765 6011 **www.**morambrocreek.com.au **Open** Not
Winemaker Ben Riggs **Est.** 1994 **Cases** 30 000 **Vyds** 170.5 ha
The Bryson family has been involved in agriculture for more than a century, moving to Padthaway in 1955 as farmers and graziers. Since the 1990s, they have progressively established large plantings of shiraz (88.5 ha), cabernet sauvignon (47.5 ha) and chardonnay (34.5 ha), lifting production from 6000 cases and establishing export markets, including the UK and the US. The wines have been consistent winners of bronze and silver medals.

ɉɉɉɉɉ Padthaway Shiraz 2007 Has four gold medals awarded in Sydney, London, San
✪ Francisco and NZ, and indeed it is a flashy, show style, with masses of blackberry and plum fruit, lots of American oak and plenty of tannins. I'm not disposed to spoil the party. Screwcap. 14.5% alc. Rating 94 To 2022 $22

♀♀♀♀♀ Jip Jip Rocks Shiraz Cabernet 2008 A 55/45 blend, with good crimson
✪   colour, and attractive blackcurrant and dark cherry fruits, the tannins fine and
          persistent, driving the long finish. Screwcap. 14.5% alc. **Rating** 90 **To** 2016 $18

♀♀♀♀ Jip Jip Rocks Unoaked Chardonnay 2009 **Rating** 89 **To** 2011 $18
          Jip Jip Rocks Shiraz 2008 **Rating** 89 **To** 2014 $18
✪   Mt Monster Cabernet 2008 Mt Monster is a local outcrop of pink granite,
          at odds with the sandy limestone soil around it, but not monstrous in real time
          observation. Medium-bodied, with classic cassis and blackcurrant fruit, and fine,
          ripe tannins in support. Great value. Screwcap. 14.5% alc. **Rating** 89 **To** 2016 $14
          Jip Jip Rocks Sparkling Shiraz NV **Rating** 87 **To** 2012 $18

Morgan Simpson   ★★★★
PO Box 39, Kensington Park, SA 5068 **Region** McLaren Vale
T 0417 843 118 **F** (08) 8364 3645 **www**.morgansimpson.com.au **Open** Not
Winemaker Richard Simpson **Est.** 1998 **Cases** 1000 **Vyds** 30.2 ha
Morgan Simpson was founded by South Australian businessman George Morgan (since
retired) and winemaker Richard Simpson, who is a graduate of CSU. The grapes are sourced
from the Clos Robert Vineyard (where the wine is made) planted to shiraz (10.2 ha), cabernet
sauvignon (7.1 ha), chardonnay (3.5 ha), mourvedre (3.5 ha), sauvignon blanc (2.5 ha),
semillon (1.8 ha) and pinot noir (1.6 ha), established by Robert Allen Simpson in 1972. Most
of the grapes are sold, the remainder used to provide the reasonably priced, drinkable wines
for which Morgan Simpson has become well known.

♀♀♀♀♀ Basket Press McLaren Vale Shiraz 2008 Dark, dense colour; the regional
✪   imprint is evident from the first whiff, with dark chocolate wrapped around
          blackberry fruit; a luscious and succulent palate. Screwcap. 14.9% alc. **Rating** 93
          To 2018 $23
✪   Basket Press McLaren Vale Shiraz 2007 Good colour; absolutely classic
          regional expression, with its opening stanza of dark chocolate on the bouquet,
          then supple and juicy black fruits on the medium-bodied palate. Attractive wine.
          Screwcap. 13.5% alc. **Rating** 91 **To** 2017 $22

♀♀♀♀ New Territories McLaren Vale Shiraz 2006 **Rating** 88 **To** 2026 $15

MorganField   ★★★★
104 Ashworths Road, Lancefield, Vic 3435 **Region** Macedon Ranges
T (03) 5429 1157 **www**.morganfield.com.au **Open** W'ends & public hols 11–5, or by appt
Winemaker John Ellis (Contract) **Est.** 2003 **Cases** 2000 **Vyds** 4 ha
The vineyard (then known as Ashworths Hill) was first planted in 1980 to pinot noir,
shiraz, pinot meunier and cabernet sauvignon. When purchased by Mark and Gina Morgan,
additional plantings increased the area under vine to 4 ha (after removal of the shiraz and pinot
meunier), with equal amounts of cabernet sauvignon, pinot noir and chardonnay. The wines
are deliberately made in a light-bodied, easy-access fashion.

♀♀♀♀♀ Macedon Ranges Pinot Noir 2007 Excellent retention of purple-red hue;
          a powerful pinot, with dark plum and black cherry fruit building to a savoury
          finish; more depth than the alcohol would suggest. Screwcap. 12.5% alc. **Rating** 91
          To 2014 $25
✪   Macedon Ranges Unwooded Chardonnay 2008 Bright green-quartz;
          a highly fragrant bouquet with grapefruit, citrus zest and white peach; very
          good unoaked style thanks to its fresh acidity and flavours. Screwcap. 12.5% alc.
          Rating 90 **To** 2012 $18

Morning Sun Vineyard   ★★★
337 Main Creek Road, Main Ridge, Vic 3928 **Region** Mornington Peninsula
T (03) 5989 6571 **F** (03) 5989 6572 **www**.morningsunvineyard.com.au **Open** 7 days 10–5
Winemaker Michael Kyberd **Est.** 1995 **Cases** 1500 **Vyds** 5.96 ha

When Mario Toniolo retired, aged 70, and purchased a property on the hills of Main Ridge, he had ideas for a yabby farm and a few cattle on what was an abandoned apple orchard. His Italian blood got the better of him, and he now has 5 ha of pinot noir, pinot grigio and chardonnay, and a 1.8-ha olive grove. In late 2009 Michael Kyberd, after over a decade with Red Hill Estate, took over the reins as vineyard manager/winemaker.

ŢŢŢŢ   **Mornington Peninsula Chardonnay 2007** Some development to the green-yellow colour; gentle nectarine and melon fruit is joined with some barrel ferment oak; not overmuch intensity, but what is there is good. Screwcap. 13.6% alc. **Rating** 89 **To** 2013 $29

Morningside Vineyard   ★★★★★

711 Middle Tea Tree Road, Tea Tree, Tas 7017 **Region** Southern Tasmania
T (03) 6268 1748 **F** (03) 6268 1748 **www**.morningsidevineyard.com.au **Open** By appt
Winemaker Peter Bosworth **Est.** 1980 **Cases** 600 **Vyds** 3 ha
The name Morningside was given to the old property on which the vineyard stands because it gets the morning sun first; the property on the other side of the valley was known as Eveningside. Consistent with the observation of the early settlers, the Morningside grapes achieve full maturity with good colour and varietal flavour. Production will increase as the vineyard matures, and as recent additions of clonally selected pinot noir (including 8104, 115 and 777) come into bearing. The Bosworth family, headed by Peter and wife Brenda, do all the vineyard and winery work, with conspicuous attention to detail.

ŢŢŢŢŢ   **Riesling 2009** Pale, bright straw-green; as sometimes happens, the retention of some residual sugar seems to mute the bouquet, the wonderfully lime-juicy and lively palate a complete contrast. Great Mosel look-alike. Screwcap. 11% alc. **Rating** 94 **To** 2020 $22
Riesling 2008 Light straw-green; lime, apple and mineral notes are interwoven on bouquet and palate alike; long, balanced finish. Screwcap. 11.5% alc. **Rating** 94 **To** 2016 $22

ŢŢŢŢ   **Pinot Noir 2008 Rating** 89 **To** 2013 $34

Morris   ★★★★★

Mia Mia Road, Rutherglen, Vic 3685 **Region** Rutherglen
T (02) 6026 7303 **F** (02) 6026 7445 **www**.morriswines.com **Open** Mon–Sat 9–5, Sun 10–5
Winemaker David Morris **Est.** 1859 **Cases** 100 000 **Vyds** 96 ha
One of the greatest of the fortified winemakers, ranking with Chambers Rosewood. Morris has changed its labelling system for its sublime fortified wines, with a higher-than-average entry point with the Classic Liqueur Muscat and Topaque, and the ultra premium wines are being released under the Old Premium Rare Liqueur label. The oldest components of the Old Premium Rare are entered in a handful of shows, but the trophies and stratospheric gold medal points they receive are not claimed for the Old Premium Rare wines. The art of these wines lies in the blending of very old and much younger material. They have no equivalent in any other part of the world.

ŢŢŢŢŢ   **Old Premium Liqueur Muscat NV** Deep olive-brown, coating the sides of the glass briefly when it is swirled; needless to say, is exceptionally rich and luscious, but – even more – complex, with a dense array of oriental sweet spices, dried raisins, and (for me) childhood memories of mother's Christmas pudding laced with brandy. And, yes, this really does go with dark, bitter chocolate in any form. Screwcap. 17.5% alc. **Rating** 97 **To** 2011 $65

✪   **Old Premium Liqueur Tokay NV** Mahogany, with an olive rim; aromas of Christmas cake and tea; incredibly viscous and rich, with layer upon layer of flavours ranging through ginger snap, burnt butterscotch, and every imaginable spice, the length and depth of the palate is as extraordinary as is that of the aftertaste. Released in tiny quantities each year, which maintain the extreme average age of each release. Even more viscous than the Grand. Screwcap. 18% alc. **Rating** 96 **To** 2011 $72

✪   **Grand Cellar Reserve Rutherglen Tokay NV** So viscous, rich, concentrated and complex it is hard to imagine there is a level higher than the Grand, but the magnificent Old Premium (all but in name Rare) delivers it. Screwcap. 17% alc. Rating 95 To 2011 $35

✪   **Grand Rutherglen Muscat NV** Golden brown; all remnants of red long since gone; it is extraordinary how such power and complexity can be so perfectly balanced; as easy to gulp (sacrilege) as sip (correct). Screwcap. 17.5% alc. **Rating** 95 To 2011 $35

✪   **Rutherglen Durif 2007** Deep purple-red; a full-bodied wine, as befits the variety and old vines; has very good balance and structure, the black fruit and licorice flavours easily matching the tannins. Screwcap. 14.5% alc. **Rating** 94 To 2017 $25

♈♈♈♈♈   **Liqueur Tokay NV** Golden brown; highly perfumed classic aromas of cold tea,
✪   rose petals and Christmas cake; excellent spirit and balance. Screwcap. 17.5% alc. **Rating** 93 To 2011 $19.60

✪   **Liqueur Muscat NV** More touches of red-brown than the Liqueur Tokay, precisely as it should be; fragrant raisin varietal fruit luring you into the second glass; perfect balance. Screwcap. 17.5% alc. **Rating** 93 To 2011 $19.60

Mosquito Hill Wines   ★★★☆

18 Trinity Street, College Park, SA 5069 (postal) **Region** Southern Fleurieu
T 0448 802 950 **F** (08) 8632 3954 **www**.mosquitohillwines.com.au **Open** Not
Winemaker Glyn Jamieson, Peter Leske **Est.** 2004 **Cases** 1200 **Vyds** 4.2 ha
In 1994, Glyn and Elizabeth Jamieson bought their small property on Mosquito Hill Road at Mt Jagged on the Fleurieu Peninsula. Glyn is yet another of the innumerable tribe of doctors who combine two professions; he just happens to be the prestigious Dorothy Mortlock Professor and Chairman of the Department of Surgery of the University of Adelaide. He and wife Elizabeth's interest in wine goes back for decades, and in 1990 they lived in France for a year, where he received both vinous and medical recognition. In 1994 Glyn commenced the part-time (distance) degree at CSU and says that while he never failed an exam, it did take him 11 years to complete the course. His year in France directed him to Burgundy, rather than Bordeaux, hence the planting of chardonnay, pinot blanc and savagnin on the slopes of Mt Jagged on the Magpies Song Vineyard and pinot noir (clones 114 and MV6) on the Hawthorns Vineyard. Exports to the US, China and Hong Kong.

♈♈♈♈♈   **Southern Fleurieu Rose 2009** Bright pink; makes no bones about a fact others
✪   don't disclose (there is no obligation to do so): namely a blend of red and white wine, Pinot Noir/Chardonnay, a time-honoured sparkling wine base, and which works well here with spicy savoury flavours and a dry finish. Screwcap. 12% alc. **Rating** 90 To 2012 $18

♈♈♈♈   **Southern Fleurieu Chardonnay 2008** Rating 89 To 2013 $19
    Alexandrina Hills The Hawthorns Pinot Noir 2008 Rating 89 To 2014 $21

Moss Brothers   ★★★★☆

3857 Caves Road, Wilyabrup, WA 6280 **Region** Margaret River
T (08) 9755 6270 **F** (08) 9755 6298 **www**.mossbrothers.com.au **Open** 7 days 10–5
Winemaker Navneet Singh **Est.** 1984 **Cases** 12 000 **Vyds** 9.6 ha
Patriarch Jeff Moss began his wine career in 1947, first with Mildara, then the Victorian Government, while simultaneously developing a 20-ha vineyard, followed by a five-year stint with Seppelt. In 1978 he and his family moved to WA, where he became vineyard manager for Houghton, part of his job entailing the identification of worthwhile vineyards in the cooler south of the state. The family took its first step in 1984 when it purchased the Caves Road property, planting commencing the following year. With various children involved in differing roles over the years, Moss Brothers has grown, most significantly with the construction of a 400-tonne winery in 1992, which both processes estate-grown and purchased grapes for the Moss Brothers label, and provides contract winemaking services. Exports to Canada, Germany, Hong Kong, Singapore and China.

♈♈♈♈♈ Single Vineyard Margaret River Chardonnay 2008 Bright straw-green; attractive stone fruit and melon are complexed by some creamy/nutty characters ex barrel ferment; good length. Screwcap. 13.5% alc. **Rating** 93 **To** 2015 $35
Margaret River Cabernet Sauvignon 2008 Youthful hue; a young, reserved and backward bouquet, showing glimpses of its future; the palate reveals a full-bodied muscular wine, with ample levels of cassis, cedar and gravelly tannins; the finish is long, savoury and complex, but time is needed to see this wine achieve its zenith. Screwcap. 14% alc. **Rating** 93 **To** 2020 $25 BE
Margaret River Cabernet Sauvignon 2007 Bright colour; the bouquet shows attractive redcurrant and cedar aromas; medium-bodied with fleshy fruit on entry, the palate reveals pristine fruit and an elegant nature to the finish; fine and supple. Screwcap. 14% alc. **Rating** 92 **To** 2016 $24 BE
Margaret River Semillon 2009 Classic pea pod, nettle and tropical fruit bouquet; clean, fresh, vibrant and juicy, with chalky acidity providing texture and length. Screwcap. 13.5% alc. **Rating** 91 **To** 2012 $25 BE
Margaret River Sauvignon Blanc 2009 Ripe varietal bouquet, with tropical fruit the central theme, complemented by a suggestion of green nettle; the palate shows lemon, with focused yet gentle acidity providing freshness. Screwcap. 13% alc. **Rating** 90 **To** 2012 $25 BE

♈♈♈♈ **Margaret River Shiraz 2007 Rating** 89 **To** 2016 $35 BE

Moss Wood ★★★★★
Metricup Road, Wilyabrup, WA 6284 **Region** Margaret River
T (08) 9755 6266 **F** (08) 9755 6303 **www.**mosswood.com.au **Open** By appt
Winemaker Keith Mugford, Josh Bahen, Amanda Shepherdson **Est.** 1969 **Cases** 15 000
Widely regarded as one of the best wineries in the region, capable of producing glorious Semillon in both oaked and unoaked forms, unctuous Chardonnay and elegant, gently herbaceous, superfine Cabernet Sauvignon, which lives for many years. In 2000 Moss Wood acquired the Ribbon Vale Estate; the Ribbon Vale wines are now treated as vineyard-designated within the Moss Wood umbrella. Exports to all major markets.

♈♈♈♈♈ **Amy's 2008** As expected, deep colour; likewise the blend of Cabernet
✪ Sauvignon/Petit Verdot/Malbec/Merlot produces a complex but very well balanced array of black fruits, cedar and spice; immaculate texture and structure is outstanding. Screwcap. 14% alc. **Rating** 96 **To** 2023 $33
✪ **Ribbon Vale Vineyard Margaret River Semillon Sauvignon Blanc 2009** Bright green-straw; a fragrant lemon zest bouquet leads into a tightly focused, intense and long palate, with an extra degree of fruit integrity. Screwcap. 14% alc. **Rating** 95 **To** 2013 $26
Margaret River Chardonnay 2008 Brilliant green-straw; a tightly wound, highly focused chardonnay with the fruit depth that is the mark of Margaret River, and that has easily absorbed the oak. Will have a long life (for chardonnay). Screwcap. 14.5% alc. **Rating** 95 **To** 2018 $57
Margaret River Semillon 2009 Very tightly focused and structured, with herb, grass and mineral characters dominant on both bouquet and palate; long and lean, with years to go. Screwcap. 14% alc. **Rating** 94 **To** 2019 $35
Mornington Peninsula Pinot Noir 2008 A courageous but entirely laudable decision to look so far afield for its pinot noir, made at Dromana Estate under the direction of Keith and Clare Mugford. Has everything a young pinot should have: bright red fruits and a long, silky palate, finishing on a rising cadence. Screwcap. 13.5% alc. **Rating** 94 **To** 2013 $45

♈♈♈♈♈ **Margaret River Pinot Noir 2007 Rating** 90 **To** 2013 $53
Margaret River Cabernet Sauvignon 2006 Rating 90 **To** 2013 $112

Motton Terraces

119 Purtons Road, North Motton, Tas 7315 **Region** Northern Tasmania
T (03) 6425 2317 **www**.cradlecoastwines.info **Open** Tues–Sun 10–5
Winemaker Flemming Aaberg **Est.** 1990 **Cases** 140 **Vyds** 1.5 ha
Another of the micro-vineyards, which seem to be a Tasmanian speciality; Flemming and
Jenny Aaberg planted slightly less than 0.5 ha of chardonnay and riesling in 1990, and have
now increased that with more riesling and some tempranillo. The exercise in miniature is
emphasised by the permanent canopy netting to ward off possums and birds.

🍷🍷🍷🍷 **Riesling 2009** Pale quartz; very attractive modern Kabinett/Mosel style, with
✪ sweet lime juice and apple blossom balanced by crisp, lively acidity; long, lingering
finish. Diam. 9.9% alc. **Rating** 92 **To** 2016 $15

🍷🍷🍷🍷 **Riesling 2008 Rating** 89 **To** 2013 $15
Chardonnay 2009 Rating 89 **To** 2011 $15

Mount Alexander Winery ★★★★☆

410 Harcourt Road, Sutton Grange, Vic 3448 **Region** Bendigo
T (03) 5474 2567 **www**.mawine.com.au **Open** W'ends & public hols 11–5, or by appt
Winemaker Bill Blamires **Est.** 2001 **Cases** 1200 **Vyds** 7.4 ha
Bill and Sandra Blamires acquired their property after a two-year search of the southern
Bendigo area for what they considered to be an ideal location. They have firmly planted their
faith in shiraz (6 ha), with merlot, cabernet sauvignon, chardonnay and viognier contributing
another hectare. The winery was previously called Blamires Butterfly Crossing (because of the
butterfly population on Axe Creek, which runs through the property), but has been changed
due to confusion with Angove's Butterfly Ridge.

🍷🍷🍷🍷🍷 **Cabernet Shiraz 2008** Dense, inky purple-crimson; a 75/25 blend, with the
lush blackcurrant fruit of the cabernet utterly dominant; from left field, because,
although the colour suggests heavy extraction and alcohol the possibility of
heat, the wine is no more than medium- to full-bodied; should live for decades.
Screwcap. 14.9% alc. **Rating** 94 **To** 2040 $20

🍷🍷🍷🍷 **Shiraz 2008 Rating** 89 **To** 2028 $16.50

Mount Avoca

Moates Lane, Avoca, Vic 3467 **Region** Pyrenees
T (03) 5465 3282 **F** (03) 5465 3544 **www**.mountavoca.com **Open** 7 days 10–5
Winemaker John Harris, Cameron McPherson **Est.** 1970 **Cases** 12 000 **Vyds** 22.3 ha
A winery that has long been one of the stalwarts of the Pyrenees region, owned by Matthew
and Lisa Barry. The estate vineyards (shiraz, sauvignon blanc, cabernet sauvignon, chardonnay,
merlot, cabernet franc and semillon) are organically managed, and provide the total intake of
the winery. Exports to China.

🍷🍷🍷🍷🍷 **Pyrenees Shiraz 2007** An excellent expression of the Pyrenees terroir; has a mix
✪ of black fruits, licorice, dark chocolate and earth, good tannins seamlessly woven
throughout the full-bodied palate. Screwcap. 14.5% alc. **Rating** 93 **To** 2022 $20
✪ **Pyrenees Shiraz 2008** Vibrant hue; black and blue fruit, framed by orange rind,
sage and cinnamon; medium-bodied, with fine-grained tannins providing extension
to the bright fruits on offer; the delicate spicy character of the wine lingers
harmoniously on the finish. Screwcap. 13.5% alc. **Rating** 91 **To** 2015 $22.95 BE

🍷🍷🍷🍷 **Pyrenees Chardonnay 2008 Rating** 88 **To** 2014 $19.95 BE
Pyrenees Merlot 2008 Rating 88 **To** 2013 $22.95 BE
Pyrenees Cabernet Sauvignon 2008 Rating 88 **To** 2014 $22.95 BE

Mt Bera Vineyards ★★★

PO Box 372, Gumeracha, SA 5233 **Region** Adelaide Hills
T (08) 8389 2433 **F** (08) 8389 2418 **www**.mtberavineyards.com.au **Open** Not
Winemaker Jeanneret Wines **Est.** 1997 **Cases** 600 **Vyds** 12 ha
In 2008 Greg and Katrina Horner (plus four kids and a growing collection of animals) purchased Mt Bera from Louise Warner. Both Greg and Katrina grew up on farms, and the 75-ha property, with its homestead built in the 1880s, was irresistible. The property is located in a sanctuary overlooking the Torrens Valley, looking out to Adelaide, 45 mins drive away. For the time being, at least, most of the production is sold to Penfolds, but the intention is to increase the range and quantity of wines available. Exports to the UK.

♟♟♟♟ **3.13 Adelaide Hills Pinot Noir 2007** Very good colour; dark cherry/plum aromas lead into a very powerful palate, sweet notes in contrast to strong tannins; big wine. Screwcap. 13.5% alc. **Rating** 89 **To** 2014 $25

Mt Billy ★★★★★

18 Victoria Street, Victor Harbor, SA 5211 (postal) **Region** Southern Fleurieu
T 0416 227 100 **F** (08) 8552 8333 **www**.mtbillywines.com.au **Open** Not
Winemaker Dan Standish, Peter Schell **Est.** 2000 **Cases** 2000 **Vyds** 2.4 ha
Having been an avid wine collector and consumer since 1973, John Edwards (a dentist) and wife Pauline purchased a 3.75-ha property on the hills behind Victor Harbor, planting chardonnay and pinot meunier. There have been various viticultural peregrinations since that time, involving the progressive grafting of all of the original plantings so that the vineyard (named 'No Secrets') now comprises 0.7 ha each of shiraz and tempranillo, the balance to petite syrah, sangiovese and viognier from which both varietal and blended wines will be made. John intends to personally make these wines, as he has been involved in the making of Circe and Tempranillo for several vintages. Exports to the US, Canada, Japan and China.

♟♟♟♟♟ **Willie John Shiraz 2007** Bright crimson-purple; a very complex and stylish shiraz, its 100% new French oak woven through and around the quite spicy black fruits, fine tannins likewise seamlessly integrated. All in all, a singular achievement from the '07 vintage. Diam. 13.8% alc. **Rating** 96 **To** 2022 $95
Destiny Barossa Valley Shiraz 2006 Strong crimson-red; a potent and powerful shiraz, punching well above its price weight; plum, fruitcake, mocha aromas and flavours fill the glass, with a final dash of dark chocolate for good measure. Screwcap. 15% alc. **Rating** 94 **To** 2021 $28

♟♟♟♟♟ **Harmony Barossa Valley Shiraz Mataro Grenache 2007** **Rating** 92 **To** 2017 $28
Reserve Antiquity Barossa Valley Shiraz 2006 **Rating** 91 **To** 2016 $75
Barossa Valley Shiraz VP 2006 **Rating** 90 **To** 2015 $25

Mount Broke Wines ★★★★

130 Adams Peak Road, Broke, NSW 2330 **Region** Hunter Valley
T (02) 6579 1314 **F** (02) 6579 1314 **www**.mtbrokewines.com.au **Open** Fri–Sun 10–5
Winemaker Jim Chatto **Est.** 1997 **Cases** 1000 **Vyds** 8 ha
Phil McNamara began planting the vineyard to shiraz, barbera, chardonnay, tempranillo, semillon and verdelho in 1997 on the west side of Wollombi Brook. Over the years since coming into production, the wines have been prolific medal winners in regional and boutique wine shows. Most of the grapes are sold, with limited production under the Mount Broke label.

♟♟♟♟♟ ✪ **Quince Tree Paddock Hunter Valley Semillon 2009** Pale straw-green; has that juicy energy (the French say nervosity) that is the mark of '09 semillon from all parts of the Hunter Valley; the finish is long and satisfying. Screwcap. 11% alc. **Rating** 93 **To** 2020 $18

River Bank Shiraz 2007 Deep, dark purple-red; a powerful full-bodied Hunter shiraz that will be long lived; black fruits drive the bouquet and palate, with leathery/savoury nuances waiting to develop as the wine slowly matures. Screwcap. 14% alc. **Rating** 93 **To** 2030 $30

♟♟♟♟   **Quince Tree Paddock Barbera 2007 Rating** 89 **To** 2014 $20

Mount Camel Ridge Estate   ★★★★

473 Heathcote-Rochester Road, Heathcote, Vic 3523 **Region** Heathcote
T (03) 5433 2343 **www**.mountcamelridgeestate.com **Open** By appt
Winemaker Ian and Gwenda Langford **Est.** 1999 **Cases** 350 **Vyds** 17 ha
Ian and Gwenda Langford commenced planting their vineyard in 1999, the majority to shiraz (8.5 ha), cabernet sauvignon (3.4 ha) and merlot (3.4 ha), with a little over 0.5 ha each of petit verdot, viognier and mourvedre. The vineyard operates using sustainable principles: prunings are mulched and returned to the vineyard rows along with bunch stalks and pressings. The wines are made in open half-tonne vats, basket-pressed and matured in French oak. Natural (wild) yeast fermentation is employed to capture the uniqueness of the terroir. The wines appear on the wine lists of many prestigious Melbourne restaurants. Exports to the US.

♟♟♟♟♟   **Heathcote Shiraz 2008** The colour is good, although not as brilliant as the 5% viognier might suggest; the fragrant, spicy bouquet does show its viognier lift, as does the elegant, wild yeast–fermented, medium-bodied palate. Diam. 14% alc. **Rating** 92 **To** 2020 $45

Mount Cathedral Vineyards   ★★★☆

125 Knafl Road, Taggerty, Vic 3714 **Region** Upper Goulburn
T 0409 354 069 **F** (03) 9374 4286 **www**.mtcathedralvineyards.com **Open** By appt
Winemaker Oscar Rosa, Nick Arena **Est.** 1995 **Cases** 900 **Vyds** 5 ha
The Rosa and Arena families established Mount Cathedral Vineyards in 1995, at an elevation of 300 m on the north face of Mt Cathedral. The first plantings were of 1.2 ha of merlot and 0.8 ha of chardonnay, followed by 2.5 ha of cabernet sauvignon and 0.5 ha of cabernet franc in 1996. No pesticides or systemic chemicals are used in the vineyard. Oscar Rosa, chief winemaker, has completed two TAFE courses in viticulture and winemaking, and completed a Bachelor of Wine Science course at CSU in 2002, and gained practical experience working at Yering Station in the late '90s. The 2009 Victorian bushfires miraculously spared the vineyard, but smoke taint meant no wine was made.

♟♟♟♟♟   **Reserve Merlot 2005** Riper, richer and fuller than the varietal, but not necessarily better; more flavour but slightly less verve; for the longer haul, perhaps. Diam. 14.9% alc. **Rating** 90 **To** 2016 $35

♟♟♟♟   **Merlot 2005 Rating** 89 **To** 2014 $20
Upper Goulburn Cabernet Merlot 2005 Rating 89 **To** 2020 $22
Upper Goulburn Cabernet 2005 Rating 89 **To** 2020 $22
Chardonnay 2006 Rating 87 **To** 2015 $20

Mount Charlie Winery   ★★★☆

228 Mount Charlie Road, Riddells Creek, Vic 3431 **Region** Macedon Ranges
T (03) 5428 6946 **F** (03) 5428 6946 **www**.mountcharlie.com.au **Open** Most w'ends
11–3, or by appt
Winemaker Trefor Morgan **Est.** 1991 **Cases** 800 **Vyds** 3 ha
Mount Charlie's wines are sold principally by mail order and through selected restaurants. A futures program encourages mailing-list sales, with a substantial discount to the eventual release price. Owner/winemaker Trefor Morgan is perhaps better known as Professor of Physiology at Melbourne University. He also acts as a contract maker for others in the region.

♀♀♀♀♀ **Chardonnay 2008** Glowing green-yellow; has very good texture and mouthfeel
✪ to the white and yellow stone fruit flavours, oak well integrated; well above-
average character for the region. Screwcap. 13.9% alc. **Rating** 92 **To** 2014 $20

♀♀♀♀ **Tempranillo 2008 Rating** 88 **To** 2011 $22

Mount Coghill Vineyard ★★★

Cnr Pickfords Road/Coghills Creek Road, Coghills Creek, Vic 3364 **Region** Ballarat
T (03) 5343 4329 **F** (03) 5343 4329 **Open** W'ends 10–5
Winemaker Owen Latta **Est.** 1993 **Cases** 160 **Vyds** 0.7 ha
Ian and Margaret Pym began planting their tiny vineyard in 1995 with 1280 pinot noir
rootlings, adding 450 chardonnay rootlings the next year. Since 2001 the wine has been made
and released under the Mount Coghill Vineyard label. Ian is an award-winning photographer,
and his photographs are on display at the cellar door.

♀♀♀♀ **Ballarat Pinot Noir 2008** Strong red-purple; plum and dark berry aromas are
replayed on the quite generous palate; a warm summer welcome here. Screwcap.
13.5% alc. **Rating** 89 **To** 2013 $22

Mount Cole Wineworks ★★★★☆

6669 Western Highway, Buangur, Vic 3375 **Region** Grampians
T (03) 5352 2311 **F** (03) 5354 3279 **www.**mountcolewineworks.com.au **Open** 7 days 10–5
Winemaker Dr Graeme Bertuch **Est.** 1998 **Cases** 800 **Vyds** 8.5 ha
Dr Graeme Bertuch's involvement in grapegrowing and winemaking goes back far further
than the establishment of Mount Cole Wineworks. In 1977 he established Cathcart Ridge, but
found the time demands on a rural doctor-cum-vigneron were too much. He sold Cathcart
Ridge in '93, but did not sell the itch to grow grapes and make wine. He now has 3.5 ha
of shiraz and 1 ha of viognier planted since 1998, and in 2007 purchased the Mt Chalambar
Vineyard previously owned by Trevor Mast, with 2 ha each of riesling and chardonnay planted
in the 1980s.

♀♀♀♀♀ **Fenix Rising Shiraz Viognier 2008** Bright, light crimson; a fragrant bouquet
and a lively, lifted palate pay homage to the viognier influence; very attractive
juicy red fruit flavours run through the long palate. Screwcap. 13% alc. **Rating** 93
To 2018 $40

Mount Eyre Vineyards ★★★★☆

173 Gillards Road, Pokolbin, NSW 2321 **Region** Hunter Valley
T 0438 683 973 **F** (02) 6842 4513 **www.**mounteyre.com **Open** Tues–Sun 11–5
Winemaker Stephen Hagan, Aniello Iannuzzi, Rhys Eather **Est.** 1970 **Cases** 5000
Vyds 33 ha
This is the venture of two families whose involvement in wine extends in an unbroken line
back several centuries: the Tsironis family in the Peleponese, Greece, and the Iannuzzi family
in Vallo della Lucania, Italy. Their vineyards are at Broke (the largest) and a smaller vineyard
at Pokolbin. The three principal varieties planted are chardonnay, shiraz and semillon, with
small amounts of merlot, viognier and chambourcin. Exports to Mexico, Thailand, Maldives,
Malaysia, China and Hong Kong.

♀♀♀♀♀ **Warrumbungle Shiraz 2008** Bright crimson; an unexpectedly fragrant and
✪ spicy bouquet, the palate in similar mode, more suggestive of cool-grown fruit
than that of Coonabarabran, where the grapes were grown. Altogether fascinating,
and very well made. Screwcap. 13.5% alc. **Rating** 94 **To** 2018 $24.95

♀♀♀♀♀ **Three Ponds Hunter Valley Semillon 2009** A good wine that progressively
✪ builds flavour and texture as it moves through the palate to the finish and
aftertaste, but without the flamboyant citrus characters of many from this vintage.
Undoubted cellaring potential. Screwcap. 10.5% alc. **Rating** 90 **To** 2016 $20

Mt Franklin Estate   ★★★☆

2 Whybrow Street, Franklinford, Vic 3461 **Region** Macedon Ranges
T (03) 5476 4475 **www**.mtfranklinwines.com.au **Open** By appt
Winemaker Scott McGillivray, Colin Mitchell **Est.** 2000 **Cases** 700 **Vyds** 4.04 ha
Owner Lesley McGillivray was well ahead of her time when, in 1988, she planted two test
rows of Italian varieties on rich volcanic soil situated near the foothills of Mt Franklin. The
varieties to succeed best were dolcetto and pinot gris, and with family and friends they planted
the first third of their vineyard with dolcetto and pinot gris in 2000. Since then, the vineyard
has been completed with more dolcetto, pinot gris and a little nebbiolo.

ꚜꚜꚜꚜꚜ **Pinot Grigio 2008** An interesting bouquet, with a hint of ginger; pear comes
in on the palate, which is long and well balanced. Impressive cool-grown style.
Screwcap. 13% alc. **Rating** 90 **To** 2010 $20

ꚜꚜꚜꚜ **Dolcetto 2007 Rating** 89 **To** 2013 $20
Pinot Grigio 2009 Rating 87 **To** 2011 $20

Mount Horrocks   ★★★★★

The Old Railway Station, Curling Street, Auburn, SA 5451 **Region** Clare Valley
T (08) 8849 2243 **F** (08) 8849 2265 **www**.mounthorrocks.com **Open** W'ends & public
hols 10–5
Winemaker Stephanie Toole **Est.** 1982 **Cases** 4500 **Vyds** 9.4 ha
Mount Horrocks has well and truly established its own identity in recent years, aided by
positive marketing and, equally importantly, wine quality, which has resulted in both show
success and critical acclaim. Stephanie Toole has worked long and hard to achieve this, and
I strongly advise you (or anyone else) not to get in her way. Exports to the UK, the US and
other major markets.

ꚜꚜꚜꚜꚜ **Watervale Riesling 2009** A rock of ages among all the activity of off-dry
rieslings and single-vineyard releases from here, there and everywhere. Firm and
strongly structured, it has ripe apple and citrus flavours on a long, even palate.
Screwcap. 13% alc. **Rating** 94 **To** 2020 $29.95
Clare Valley Semillon 2009 Bright straw-green; a 100% barrel-fermented wine
that breaks all the rules: has more freshness than any other Clare Valley semillon,
and the impact of the barrel fermentation is secondary to the fruit expression; has
excellent length, too. Screwcap. 13.5% alc. **Rating** 94 **To** 2017 $27
Clare Valley Cabernet Sauvignon 2007 Good hue and clarity; as close to
classic (Bordeaux style of yesteryear) cabernet as you are likely to find in the Clare
Valley; the blackcurrant fruit has a fine savoury edge or, as the French would say,
nervosity. Screwcap. 14% alc. **Rating** 94 **To** 2022 $35
Cordon Cut 2009 An impossible-to-resist wine, the purity of riesling not
compromised by the cane cutting; however, the sweetness is potent, and the wine
needs food company or (heretically) a jab of soda water. Screwcap. 11.5% alc.
Rating 94 **To** 2012 $35

Mt Jagged Wines   ★★★★

Main Victor Harbor Road, Mt Jagged, SA 5211 **Region** Southern Fleurieu
T (08) 8554 9520 **F** (08) 8554 9520 **www**.mtjaggedwines.com.au **Open** 7 days 11–5
Winemaker Duane Coates **Est.** 1989 **Cases** 10 000 **Vyds** 27.5 ha
Mt Jagged's vineyard was established in 1989 by the White family, with close-planted semillon,
chardonnay, merlot, cabernet sauvignon and shiraz. The vineyard sits at 350 m above sea level
on a diversity of soils ranging from ironstone/clay for the red varieties to sandy loam/clay
for the whites. The cool-climate vineyard (altitude and proximity to the ocean) produces
fresh, crisp, zingy white wines and medium-bodied savoury reds of complexity and depth.
The vineyard has good rainfall and natural spring water in abundance, and is currently in the
process of conversion to organic/biodynamic viticulture principles. Exports to the UK, the
US, Canada and China.

♟♟♟♟♟ Single Vineyard Reserve Shiraz 2007 Bright colour; a savoury bouquet redolent of redcurrant, blackberry, minerals and spice; medium-bodied, with cinnamon and clove making their presence felt; slippery tannins and fine acidity clean up the finish harmoniously. Screwcap. 14% alc. **Rating** 92 **To** 2020 $36 BE

Mount Langi Ghiran Vineyards ★★★★★

Warrak Road, Buangor, Vic 3375 **Region** Grampians
T (03) 5354 3207 **F** (03) 5354 3277 www.langi.com.au **Open** Mon–Fri 9–5, w'ends 10–5
Winemaker Dan Buckle, Kate Petering **Est.** 1969 **Cases** 60 000
A maker of outstanding cool-climate peppery Shiraz, crammed with flavour and vinosity, and very good Cabernet Sauvignon. The Shiraz points the way for cool-climate examples of the variety. The business was acquired by the Rathbone family group in 2002, and hence the marketing has been integrated with the Yering Station, Parker Coonawarra and Xanadu Estate wines, a synergistic mix with no overlap. Exports to all major markets.

♟♟♟♟♟ Langi Shiraz 2007 Near-identical deep crimson colour to all six releases; has the multi-layered flavours promised by the bouquet, and more texture from the fine, ripe tannins that run through the medium- to full-bodied palate and lingering aftertaste. Screwcap. 14.5% alc. **Rating** 96 **To** 2022 $75
Riesling 2009 A wolf in sheep's clothing: the alcohol prepares you for a Mosel Kabinett style with significant fruit sweetness; in fact it is barely off-dry, driven by its crystalline acidity on a feather-light palate, lime making a curtain call at the end. Screwcap. 10% alc. **Rating** 95 **To** 2020 $35
Langi Cabernet Sauvignon 2005 Colour development attests to a wine starting to show its wares through a spicy, red-fruited bouquet then a silky palate that lifts on the finish and aftertaste; oak and tannins perfectly judged. Screwcap. 15% alc. **Rating** 95 **To** 2025 $50
Cliff Edge Riesling 2009 So beautifully balanced in its mouthfeel, it's easy to overlook the inherent complexity; apple, lime, pear and mineral all take turns to strut their stuff, the finish long and complete. Screwcap. 11.5% alc. **Rating** 94 **To** 2020 $25
Bradach Vineyard Pinot Noir 2008 From a small, single very cool vineyard in the Moyston area; a skilfully made wine with gently spicy red and black fruits on a supple palate; good line and length. Screwcap. 12% alc. **Rating** 94 **To** 2018 $40

♟♟♟♟♟ Bradach Vineyard Pinot Noir 2009 **Rating** 92 **To** 2016 $38
✪ Billi Billi Shiraz 2008 Highly perfumed red and blue fruit bouquet, with orange and cinnamon playing a pivotal role; the palate is fresh, lovely and lithe, with the spice coming to the fore on the medium-bodied finish. Screwcap. 14.5% alc. **Rating** 92 **To** 2020 $18 BE
Cliff Edge Pinot Gris 2009 **Rating** 90 **To** 2011 $25

Mt Lofty Ranges Vineyard ★★★☆

Harris Road, Lenswood, SA 5240 **Region** Adelaide Hills
T (08) 8389 8339 **F** (08) 8389 8349 www.mtloftyrangesvineyard.com.au
Open W'ends 11–5, or by appt Aug–May
Winemaker Adelaide Hills Fine Wine Centre, Simon Greenleaf, Peter Leske (Consultants) **Est.** 1992 **Cases** 1000 **Vyds** 4.6 ha
Film industry executive Sharon Pearson and partner Garry Sweeney, a wine industry veteran, searched for more than six years for their ideal vineyard. Finding their vinous El Dorado meant leaving Sydney's northern beaches, a v-change of some magnitude, but they did not hesitate in buying the property from founders Alan Herath and Jan Reed. The vineyard is planted to pinot noir, sauvignon blanc, chardonnay and riesling; skilled contract winemaking has brought rewards and recognition to the brand.

♟♟♟♟ Lenswood Chardonnay 2008 Nuances of apple and nutty characters running alongside grapefruit and melon can have a number of origins (including slight oxidation), but seem to be part of the Mt Lofty Ranges Vineyard chardonnay style. Screwcap. 14% alc. **Rating** 89 **To** 2012 $23

Old Pump Shed Lenswood Pinot Noir 2008 Dark purple-red; a powerful, rich and very ripe pinot, with strong dark plum fruit and savoury tannins, made from 12 clones of pinot; a heroic style not for the faint hearted. Screwcap. 14.5% alc. **Rating** 89 **To** 2013 $25

Mount Majura Vineyard ★★★★★

RMB 314 Majura Road, Majura, ACT 2609 (postal) **Region** Canberra District
T (02) 6262 3070 **F** (02) 6262 4288 **www**.mountmajura.com.au **Open** Thurs–Mon 10–5
Winemaker Dr Frank van de Loo **Est.** 1988 **Cases** 3000 **Vyds** 9.31 ha
The first vines were planted in 1988 by Dinny Killen on a site on her family property that had been especially recommended by Dr Edgar Riek; its attractions were red soil of volcanic origin over limestone, with reasonably steep east and northeast slopes providing an element of frost protection. The tiny vineyard established in '88 has been significantly expanded since it was purchased in '99. The pre-existing blocks of pinot noir, chardonnay and merlot have all been increased, and have been joined by pinot gris, shiraz, tempranillo, riesling, graciano, cabernet franc and touriga. In additional, there has been an active planting program for the pinot noir, introducing Dijon clones 114, 155 and 777.

Canberra District Riesling 2009 Bright, green-tinged colour; after a quiet bouquet, the palate takes off like an express train hurtling through to a long and lingering finish, lime, lemon and mineral providing the rails. Screwcap. 11.9% alc. Rating 94 To 2020 $21

Canberra District Chardonnay 2008 Bright green-yellow; high-quality wine, nectarine and white peach driving the initial impetus, grapefruit and acidity the finish; controlled barrel ferment oak the clincher. Gold medal Winewise '09. Screwcap. 13.2% alc. **Rating** 94 To 2014 $21

TSG Canberra District Tempranillo Shiraz Graciano 2008 Bright crimson; tempranillo is the major partner (56%) and shows its dominance on the fragrant cherry and plum bouquet and the tangy/spicy palate, its length bolstered by fine, savoury tannins. Gold medal Winewise '09. Screwcap. 14% alc. Rating 94 To 2016 $21

Canberra District Tempranillo 2008 A thoroughly impressive example of this variety, for it has the structure and texture so often missing; its flavour, too, is exemplary, with black cherry, a hint of licorice and a twist of citrus peel. Screwcap. 14% alc. Rating 94 To 2018 $35

Canberra District Pinot Noir 2008 Fashioned within a savoury, earthy, foresty spectrum, but there is just enough red fruit at the heart of the wine to fully convince. Impressive effort. Screwcap. 14% alc. Rating 92 To 2013 $21

Canberra District Pinot Gris 2009 Rating 89 To 2011 $21
Canberra District Rose 2009 Rating 89 To 2011 $19
Canberra District Shiraz 2008 Rating 89 To 2017 $26

Mount Mary ★★★★★

Coldstream West Road, Lilydale, Vic 3140 **Region** Yarra Valley
T (03) 9739 1761 **F** (03) 9739 0137 **www**.mountmary.com.au **Open** Not
Winemaker Rob Hall **Est.** 1971 **Cases** 3500 **Vyds** 9.6 ha
Superbly refined, elegant and intense Cabernets and usually outstanding and long-lived Pinot Noirs fully justify Mount Mary's exalted reputation. The Triolet blend is very good; more recent vintages of Chardonnay are even better. Founder and long-term winemaker, the late Dr John Middleton, was one of the great, and truly original, figures in the Australian wine industry. He liked nothing more than to tilt at windmills, and would do so with passion. His annual newsletter grew longer as each year passed, although the paper size did not. The only change necessary was a reduction in font size, and ultimately very strong light or a magnifying glass (or both) to fully appreciate the barbed wit and incisive mind of this great character. The determination of the family to continue the business is simply wonderful, even if the 2007 vintage was severely reduced by frost, and the wines will not be commercially released.

Limited quantities of the wines are sold through the wholesale/retail distribution system in Vic, NSW, Qld and SA. Exports to the UK, the US, Denmark, Hong Kong, Singapore, Korea and China.

ŶŶŶŶŶ **Yarra Valley Pinot Noir 2006** Clear colour, yet to lose primary hue; a beautifully constructed pinot, lithe and silky on the mid-palate, then stretching out on the long finish, the sweet red fruits of the mid-palate reappearing on the aftertaste. Diam. 13.3% alc. **Rating** 96 **To** 2016 $100
Yarra Valley Chardonnay 2008 Bright green-yellow; absolutely in the mainstream of Mount Mary style, the French oak seamlessly moulded with the melon and nectarine fruit that flows through to the finish and aftertaste. Diam. 13.6% alc. **Rating** 94 **To** 2016 $70
Triolet 2008 Immaculate balance to this blend of Sauvignon Blanc/Semillon/Muscadelle; extreme length and a gloriously fresh finish and aftertaste, the fruit and oak components seamless. Diam. 12.9% alc. **Rating** 94 **To** 2014 $70
Quintet 2006 All about subtlety and finesse; while medium-bodied, has deceptive intensity and length, the five varieties seamlessly moulded into a mix of black and red fruits, fine tannins and a gently savoury finish. Oak? Yes, it's there, but you don't notice it. Diam. 12.9% alc. **Rating** 94 **To** 2021 $100

Mount Monument Winery ★★★★☆

1399 Romsey Road, Romsey, Vic 3434 **Region** Macedon Ranges
T 0407 291 449 **F** (03) 9329 6879 **Open** By appt
Winemaker Keith Brien **Est.** 2008 **Cases** 1500 **Vyds** 3.7 ha
Prominent Melbourne architect Nonda Katsalidis and wife Jane acquired the pre-existing vineyard in 2008, and embarked on major trellis redesign for the existing chardonnay, pinot noir and riesling, while undertaking major terracing works on a new site on the north face of Mt Monument where 1 ha of nebbiolo (with three clones) will be planted. All of these changes, and the future winemaking, will be under the direction of Keith Brien.

ŶŶŶŶŶ **Riesling 2009** Pale quartz-green; a citrus blossom bouquet, then a fine and elegant, exceptionally youthful, palate; has the balance and length to develop over 20 years. Screwcap. 11% alc. **Rating** 93 **To** 2030 $25
Macedon Ranges Pinot Noir 2008 Bright and clear purple-red; a scented red fruit bouquet, followed by an elegant, lissom and long palate with black and red cherry flavours, and particularly fine tannins. Holds much promise. Diam. 13% alc. **Rating** 92 **To** 2014 $33
Macedon Ranges Chardonnay 2008 Bright green-gold; citrus aromas and flavours, ranging from lemon to grapefruit, drive the wine reflecting the high natural acidity; pure but severe, and needs time (two years or so) to begin to soften. Diam. 13.5% alc. **Rating** 91 **To** 2016 $28

Mt Moriac Estate/Waurn Ponds Estate ★★★★

580 Hendy Main Road, Mt Moriac, Vic 3240 **Region** Geelong
T (03) 5266 1116 **F** (03) 5266 1116 **www**.kurabana.com **Open** Not
Winemaker Lee Evans **Est.** 1987 **Cases** 7000 **Vyds** 35.3 ha
The development of the quite extensive Kurabana Vineyard, west of Geelong in the foothills of Mt Moriac, began in 1987. Pinot noir (7.8 ha) is the largest portion, followed by (in descending order) shiraz, chardonnay, sauvignon blanc, pinot gris and viognier. In 2009 there were a number of major changes: the name of the business was changed, and it purchased the Waurn Ponds Estate label and all current wine from Deakin University. It also leased the Waurn Ponds vineyard from Deakin, lifting the aggregate area to 35.3 ha. The two brands continue, but have a common headquarters and ownership.

ŶŶŶŶŶ **Mt Moriac Estate Shiraz 2008** Strong purple-crimson; a supple and juicy shiraz, with plum and black fruits neatly supported by fine tannins, oak well balanced and integrated. Screwcap. 13.5% alc. **Rating** 93 **To** 2020 $25.95

Mt Moriac Estate Chardonnay 2008 Has distinctly more precision, focus and drive than the Geelong chardonnay; the fine fruits run from grapefruit to nectarine and melon; any oak used is not obvious. Screwcap. 13% alc. **Rating** 92 **To** 2014 $25.95

☻ **Mt Moriac Shiraz 2007** Retains good hue; a generous wine full of cool-grown characters, spice, pepper and licorice to the fore, but backed by attractive plum and black cherry fruit. Screwcap. 13% alc. **Rating** 92 **To** 2017 $17.95

☻ **Waurn Ponds Estate Chardonnay 2008** Light straw-green; the bouquet is fragrant, the palate elegant; white peach, citrus and nectarine fruit have good length and balance; any oak used is incidental to the main game. Screwcap. 13.5% alc. **Rating** 90 **To** 2014 $18.95

Mt Moriac Pinot Noir 2008 Moderately deep purple-red; a fragrant red fruit bouquet, the palate with ripe cherry fruit flavours and a hint of spice; good length. Screwcap. 13.5% alc. **Rating** 90 **To** 2014 $17.95

♥♥♥♥ **Waurn Ponds Estate Sauvignon Blanc 2008** Pale quartz; herb and grass
☻ aromas lead into a light-bodied, crisp and crunchy palate adding a touch of citrus zest. Classy label design adds to the total package. Screwcap. 13.5% alc. **Rating** 88 **To** 2011 $13.95

Mt Moriac Geelong Chardonnay 2008 **Rating** 88 **To** 2012 $17.95

Mount Pierrepoint Estate ★★★★☆

271 Pierrepoint Road, Tarrington, Vic 3301 (postal) **Region** Henty
T (03) 5572 5553 **F** (03) 5572 5553 www.mountpierrepoint.com **Open** Not
Winemaker Scott Ireland (Contract) **Est.** 1997 **Cases** 300 **Vyds** 5 ha
Mount Pierrepoint Estate was established by Andrew and Jennifer Lacey on the foothills of Mt Pierrepoint between Hamilton and Tarrington. The vineyard is planted to pinot noir, pinot gris (2 ha each) and chardonnay (1 ha).

♥♥♥♥♀ **Alexandra Chardonnay 2008** Bright, pale green; this chardonnay has an
☻ intensity and power derived from yields of 1 tonne per acre, and the very cool climate; the power is almost forbidding, and the wine needs time to soften a little in bottle. Screwcap. 13.5% alc. **Rating** 93 **To** 2018 $25

Pinot Noir 2008 A little colour development, but good hue; a complex bouquet of dark plum and black cherry, sweet plum fruit flavours capturing the palate, with a few spicy, savoury notes on the long finish. Screwcap. 13.5% alc. **Rating** 93 **To** 2015 $30

Mt Samaria Vineyard ★★★

3231 Midland Highway, Lima South, Vic 3673 **Region** Upper Goulburn
T (03) 5768 2550 **F** (03) 5768 2637 www.mtsamaria.com.au **Open** By appt
Winemaker Roger Cowan, Ros Ritchie Wines, Auldstone Cellars **Est.** 1992 **Cases** 600 **Vyds** 2.8 ha
The Mt Samaria Vineyard, with shiraz (1.6 ha) and tempranillo (0.8 ha) having the lion's share, accompanied by a little cabernet and pinot gris, is owned and operated by Judy and Roger Cowan. Plantings took place over an eight-year period, and in the early days the grapes were sold to Delatite until the Cowans ventured into wine production in 1999. Striking labels are a distinct plus, although wombats are not normally welcome visitors in vineyards.

♥♥♥♥ **Shiraz Cabernet 2008** Bright hue; while little more than light-bodied, curiously has riper fruit flavours than the Shiraz (cabernet should be more difficult to ripen); also has more oak. Diam. 14.5% alc. **Rating** 87 **To** 2014 $20

Mount Stapylton Vineyard ★★★

14 Cleeve Court, Toorak, Vic 3142 (postal) **Region** Grampians
T (03) 9824 6680 www.mtsv.com.au **Open** Not
Winemaker Don McRae **Est.** 2002 **Cases** 80 **Vyds** 1 ha

Mount Stapylton Vineyard forms part of the historic Goonwinnow Homestead farming property at Laharum on the northwest side of the Grampians in front of Mt Stapylton. Owners Howard and Samantha Staehr began the development of the shiraz vineyard (two-thirds Great Western Old Block clone and one-third clone 1654) in 2002, after Howard completed a viticulture course. It's still an embryonic business, as the Staehrs live in Melbourne and commute to the homestead whenever they can.

ΨΨΨΨ **Sophia Grampians Shiraz 2008** Dense purple; a decidedly curious bouquet, with licorice, black fruits, but also a silage character; the palate is powerful, with obvious American oak and an echo of that hard-to-define aroma of the bouquet. Stained cork. 13.8% alc. **Rating** 88 **To** 2018 $40

Mount Tamborine Vineyards & Winery ★★★☆

128 Long Road, Eagle Heights, Qld, 4271 **Region** Granite Belt
T (07) 5545 3506 **F** (07) 5545 3068 **www**.mttamborinewinery.com **Open** 7 days 10–4
Winemaker Jim Barnes **Est.** 1990 **Cases** NA **Vyds** 17 ha
The Mount Tamborine name has caused no small degree of confusion over the years between several wineries in that region. This venture had its birthplace in the Tamborine region, but has now migrated to the Granite Belt, where its vineyard and winery are located. Here there is shiraz (7.6 ha), cabernet sauvignon (3.6 ha), chardonnay (3 ha) and merlot (2.8 ha).

ΨΨΨΨΨ **Granite Belt Shiraz Cabernet 2007** Good hue; an unusual wine with strong cinnamon, clove and spice on both bouquet and palate alike, although there are blackberry and black cherry fruit flavours coupled with fine tannins. A 60/40 blend that won gold medals in the Australian Small Winemakers Show '09. Badly stained twin top. 14% alc. **Rating** 90 **To** 2017 $45

ΨΨΨΨ **RJH Range Black Shiraz 2008 Rating** 88 To 2015 $35

Mount Torrens Vineyards ★★★★★

PO Box 1679, Mt Torrens, SA 5244 **Region** Adelaide Hills
T 0418 822 509 **www**.solstice.com.au **Open** Not
Winemaker Torbreck (David Powell) **Est.** 1996 **Cases** 1000
Mount Torrens Vineyards has 2.5 ha of shiraz and viognier, and the distinguished team of Mark Whisson as viticulturist and David Powell as contract winemaker. The excellent wines are available by mail order and selected retailers, but are chiefly exported to the UK, the US and other major markets. The marketing is handled by owner and founder, David Thompson.

ΨΨΨΨΨ **Solstice Adelaide Hills Shiraz Viognier 2007** Curiously, less vibrant colour than the shiraz; fermented on 10% viognier skins and aged for 20 months in French oak; the bouquet is certainly fragrant and the medium-bodied palate is juicy and supple, with spicy fruit and a long finish. Cork. 14.5% alc. **Rating** 95 To 2015 $38
Solstice Adelaide Hills Shiraz 2007 Deep colour; has spicy savoury/peppery black fruit aromas and flavours; the medium- to full-bodied palate has very good length, tannins and oak both adding to the overall package. Top-quality cork. 14.5% alc. **Rating** 94 To 2017 $38

Mount Towrong ★★★☆

10 Taylors Road, Mount Macedon, Vic 3441 (postal) **Region** Macedon Ranges
T (03) 5426 3050 **F** (03) 5426 3050 **www**.mounttowrong.com.au **Open** Not
Winemaker Kilchurn Wines **Est.** 1996 **Cases** 500 **Vyds** 2 ha
When George and Deirdre Cremasco commenced the establishment of their vineyard (chardonnay, nebbiolo and prosecco), they did so with the help of George's father and grandfather. Strongly influenced by their Italian heritage, the vineyard has been terraced, with Chardonnay the first wine in production, and some commendable Nebbiolo and Prosecco following in its footsteps.

ŶŶŶŶŶ   **Macedon Rosso 2008** Bright pale red-purple; plays direct tribute to the
✪   organoleptic links said to exist between (mature) nebbiolo and pinot noir, and this
        delicious, fragrant, light-bodied wine – little more than rose in weight – achieves
        just that. Screwcap. 12.5% alc. **Rating** 91 **To** 2014 $25

ŶŶŶŶ   **Macedon Ranges Chardonnay 2008 Rating** 89 **To** 2014 $20
        Macedon Ranges Nebbiolo 2007 Rating 88 **To** 2013 $25
        Macedon Ranges Prosecco 2008 Rating 88 **To** 2012 $30
        Macedon Ranges Chardonnay 2007 Rating 87 **To** 2012 $22
        Macedon Rosso 2007 Rating 87 **To** 2013 $22
        Macedon Ranges Nebbiolo 2008 Rating 87 **To** 2015 $25

Mount Trio Vineyard ★★★★

2534 Porongurup Road, Mount Barker WA 6324 **Region** Porongurup
T (08) 9853 1136 **F** (08) 9853 1120 **www**.mounttriowines.com.au **Open** By appt
Winemaker Gavin Berry **Est.** 1989 **Cases** 5000 **Vyds** 7.8 ha
Mount Trio was established by Gavin Berry and Gill Graham shortly after they moved to
the Mount Barker area in late 1988. They have slowly built up the business, increasing estate
plantings with shiraz (2.5 ha), riesling (2.1 ha), pinot noir (2 ha) and sauvignon blanc (1.4 ha).
Exports to the UK, Denmark, Japan and Singapore.

ŶŶŶŶŶ   **Gravel Pit Great Southern Riesling 2009** A classic example of Great
✪   Southern riesling, still in its swaddling clothes and yet to crawl, let alone walk.
        But give it five years and it will do all of that and more as flesh builds around its
        mineral frame. Screwcap. 12% alc. **Rating** 93 **To** 2024 $19.50
✪   **Gravel Pit Great Southern Shiraz 2008** Good colour; strongly, almost
        stridently, proclaims its cool-grown origins, with spice and pepper woven through
        its red and black cherry fruit. Given a year or two, will be a delicious wine.
        Screwcap. 14.5% alc. **Rating** 91 **To** 2018 $19.50

ŶŶŶŶ   **Great Southern Sauvignon Blanc 2009** Lemony herbaceous aromas and
✪   flavours, rather than tropical fruit, drive the wine, which is decidedly fresh.
        Screwcap. 12.5% alc. **Rating** 89 **To** 2011 $16
        Gravel Pit Great Southern Pinot Noir 2008 Rating 88 **To** 2014 $19.50

Mount View Estate ★★★★★

Mount View Road, Mount View, NSW 2325 **Region** Hunter Valley
T (02) 4990 3307 **F** (02) 4991 1289 **www**.mtviewestate.com.au **Open** Mon–Sat 10–5,
Sun 10–4
Winemaker Phillip Halverson **Est.** 1971 **Cases** 3000 **Vyds** 16 ha
John and Polly Burgess became the owners of Mount View Estate (8 ha) in 2000, and in '04
purchased the adjoining Limestone Creek Vineyard (8 ha); planted in 1982, it fits seamlessly
into the Mount View Estate production.

ŶŶŶŶŶ   **Reserve Hunter Valley Semillon 2009** A somewhat different register of
        aromas, this with apple blossom and bath powder, although the palate is more
        typical of this exceptional semillon vintage, with citrus flavours and a penetrating
        finish. Screwcap. 12% alc. **Rating** 95 **To** 2020 $24
        Reserve Hunter Valley Chardonnay 2008 Bright green-gold; unusually juicy
        and fine for the Hunter Valley, with some cool-climate characters to the white
        peach and nectarine palate; good acidity prolongs the palate and finish, oak merely
        a vehicle. Screwcap. 13% alc. **Rating** 94 **To** 2017 $25

ŶŶŶŶ   **Reserve Hunter Valley Chardonnay 2009 Rating** 89 **To** 2014 $25
        Reserve Hunter Valley Merlot 2008 Rating 89 **To** 2013 $24 BE
        Hunter Valley Verdelho 2009 Rating 88 **To** 2012 $19 BE
        Basalt Hill 2008 Rating 88 **To** 2013 $19 BE
        Limestone Creek Vineyard Hunter Valley Chardonnay 2009 Rating 87
        To 2012 $21 BE

Mount William Winery

Mount William Road, Tantaraboo, Vic 3764 **Region** Macedon Ranges
T (03) 5429 1595 **www**.mtwilliamwinery.com.au **Open** W'ends & public hols 11–5
Winemaker David Cowburn (Contract), Murray Cousins **Est.** 1987 **Cases** 2000 **Vyds** 7.5 ha
Adrienne and Murray Cousins purchased a 220-ha grazing property in 1985; the sheep and
Angus cattle remain the principal part of the general farming program, but between '87 and
'99 they established pinot noir, chardonnay, cabernet franc, semillon and merlot. The quality
of the wines has been consistently good, and are sold through a stone cellar door, as well as at
a number of fine wine retailers around Melbourne.

ᵀᵀᵀᵀᵀ Special Late Disgorged 10 Years on Lees Macedon Blanc de Blancs
1998 Disgorged August '08, and needed no dosage; quite remarkably fresh, fine
and elegant, the palate with great line and length; a special Australian sparkling.
Diam. 12% alc. **Rating** 97 **To** 2014 $70
Macedon 2003 Gleaming green-gold; persistent, fine mousse; a high-quality
blanc de blanc (chardonnay) with a lovely display of white peach and creamy
brioche notes from over five years on lees, and a long, citrussy finish. Cork.
12.5% alc. **Rating** 96 **To** 2012 $35
Jorja-Alexis Pinot Rose 2003 Salmon-pink; intense spicy red fruits gain velocity
on the long palate, travelling through to the finish and aftertaste; marked acidity
might trouble some tasters. Sparkling. Diam. 13% alc. **Rating** 94 **To** 2013 $35

ᵀᵀᵀᵀᵀ Louise Clare NV **Rating** 92 **To** 2013 $45

Mountadam   ★★★★★

High Eden Road, Eden Valley, SA 5235 **Region** Eden Valley
T (08) 8564 1900 **F** (08) 8564 1999 **www**.mountadam.com.au **Open** By appt
Winemaker Con Moshos **Est.** 1972 **Cases** 35 000 **Vyds** 80 ha
Founded by the late David Wynn for the benefit of winemaker-son Adam, Mountadam was
(somewhat surprisingly) purchased by Cape Mentelle (doubtless under the direction of Möet
Hennessy Wine Estates) in 2000. Rather less surprising has been its sale in '05 to Adelaide
businessman David Brown, who has extensive interests in the Padthaway region. The arrival
of Con Moshos (long-serving senior winemaker at Petaluma) has already made a significant
impact in lifting the quality of the wines. One should hope so, because Con eats (well,
almost), drinks and sleeps Mountadam. Exports to the UK, France, Switzerland, Poland and
Hong Kong.

ᵀᵀᵀᵀᵀ The Red 2007 Healthy colour leads into a very elegant and fine wine, with
✪ vibrant blackcurrant, cassis and cherry fruit running through the long finish; it is
amazing how easily the wine has absorbed two years in new French oak barriques,
and how polished the tannins are. Cabernet Sauvignon/Merlot/Cabernet Franc.
Cork. 13.5% alc. **Rating** 96 **To** 2030 $35
Eden Valley Riesling 2009 Pale green-straw; fragrant lime and green apple
aromas, then a long, finely structured palate with a core of minerally acidity and a
touch of talc. Screwcap. 13.5% alc. **Rating** 95 **To** 2020 $25
High Eden Marble Hill Chardonnay 2006 Pale, bright straw-green; a
marvellously tight, youthful and lively bouquet, and an elegant, mineral-based
palate, nectarine and citrus fruit accompanied by fine barrel ferment oak. Still a
baby, and one would never guess 100% mlf had been employed. Screwcap. 13.5%
alc. **Rating** 95 **To** 2016 $85
High Eden Estate Chardonnay 2008 A wine with as much focus on structure
as on fruit flavour; 60% barrel ferment and taken through mlf in new French
barriques; notable savoury minerality to the back-palate and finish; will develop
very well in bottle. Screwcap. 14% alc. **Rating** 94 **To** 2020 $35

ᵀᵀᵀᵀᵀ Patriarch High Eden Shiraz 2007 **Rating** 93 **To** 2017 $35
✪ Barossa Chardonnay 2009 A very fragrant and elegant unoaked chardonnay, the
flavours of white peach and citrus, the length and balance impeccable. Encompasses
both Barossa and Eden valleys. Screwcap. 14.5% alc. **Rating** 92 **To** 2014 $15

Eden Valley Pinot Gris 2009 Rating 90 To 2013 $25
Barossa Cabernet Merlot 2008 Good colour; an 80/20 blend that spent 14 months in French oak and carries its alcohol well; savoury blackcurrant and plum fruit flavours pay homage to both varieties; the length and balance of fruit, oak and tannins is good. Screwcap. 15% alc. Rating 90 To 2015 $18

Barossa Shiraz 2008 Rating 89 To 2015 $18
Eden Valley Shiraz Viognier 2008 Rating 88 To 2015 $25

Mountain X Wine Co ★★★★☆

6864 Great Alpine Road, Porepunkah, Vic 3740 (postal) **Region** Hunter Valley/Yarra Valley
T (02) 9492 4140 **F** (02) 9492 4199 **www**.mountainx.com.au **Open** Not
Winemaker Rhys Eather, Franco d'Anna (Contract) **Est.** 2006 **Cases** 150
Mountain X Wine Co is a modest and loose partnership between part-time wine writer Gary Walsh and friend and full-time wine writer Campbell Mattinson. It is more or less the direct outcome of Campbell's research for and writing of *The Wine Hunter*, the story of Maurice O'Shea of Mt Pleasant. Says Campbell, 'It's no secret that during the research and writing of the Maurice O'Shea story I came not only to love the man, the land he worked on and his wines, but Hunter Valley reds fullstop.' Discussions over appropriate glasses of wine with Gary made them wonder why shiraz/pinot blends were so rarely made, and the only rational conclusion was that they should have wines made for them to their own specifications: the best possible grapes, large format French puncheons (only 25% new) and a percentage of pinot, which could only be obtained outside the Hunter Valley. In a fine display of flexibility, Campbell has released a Hilltops blend of Shiraz/Cabernet Sauvignon.

Hunter Shiraz 2007 Crimson-red; very few Hunter shirazs missed the mark in '07, and this wine certainly didn't; the bouquet is perfectly pitched with its black berry fruits and a hint of the leather to come as it ages, the powerful palate with a fascinating tweak on the finish, explained (after I tasted the wine) by the addition of some pinot noir; 140 dozen made. Diam. 13.2% alc. Rating 93 To 2022 $29.95
Jack Mattinson's Deluxe Dry Red Hilltops Shiraz Cabernet 2009 Medium red-purple; a fragrant bouquet has a mix of blackberry, blackcurrant, plum and spice that comes through strongly on the medium-bodied palate; the tannins are particularly good, providing both texture and structure, French oak another string to the bow. The back label alone is worth $14.95. Screwcap. 14.5% alc. Rating 92 To 2020 $14.95

Mr Riggs Wine Company ★★★★★

Main Road, McLaren Vale, SA 5171 **Region** McLaren Vale
T (08) 8556 4460 **F** (08) 8556 4462 **www**.mrriggs.com.au **Open** At Penny's Hill
Winemaker Ben Riggs **Est.** 2001 **Cases** 20 000 **Vyds** 7.5 ha
After a quarter of a century of winemaking experience, Ben Riggs is well established under his own banner. Ben sources the best fruit from individual vineyards in McLaren Vale, Clare Valley, Adelaide Hills, Langhorne Creek, Coonawarra, and from his own Piebald Gully Vineyard (shiraz and viognier). Each wine is intended to express the essence of not only the vineyard, but also the region's terroir. The vision of the Mr Riggs brand is unpretentious and personal, 'to make the wines I love to drink'. Exports to the US, Canada, Denmark, Sweden, Germany, The Netherlands, China, Hong Kong, Singapore and NZ.

Adelaide Hills Riesling VOR-GS 2009 A very well balanced and structured wine with a restrained touch of residual sugar offset by quite firm acidity, the flavours a mix of ripe apple and citrus. Screwcap. 10.5% alc. Rating 94 To 2019 $22
McLaren Vale Shiraz 2008 Dense purple-red; a voluminous bouquet and full-bodied palate are stacked with regional black fruits, dark chocolate and quality oak; despite the power, has a lighter savoury twist to the finish, which adds to the appeal. Diam. 14.5% alc. Rating 94 To 2028 $50

Piebald Adelaide Shiraz Viognier 2008 As much red as crimson in colour; a very vibrant and lively wine, with much flavour activity in the bouquet and in the mouth, with high-toned spices, hints of earth and leather, and juicy black fruits. Screwcap. 14.5% alc. Rating 94 To 2018 $27

Yacca Paddock Adelaide Hills Tempranillo 2008 Brightly coloured; has impressive focus, length and intensity to its display of spicy black cherry fruit, and convincing tannins on the finish. Screwcap. 14.5% alc. Rating 94 To 2016 $25

Watervale Riesling 2009 Rating 91 To 2017 $22
Cold Chalk Adelaide Hills Chardonnay 2009 Rating 90 To 2014 $22
Adelaide Viognier 2009 Rating 90 To 2012 $25 BE
Outpost Coonawarra Cabernet 2008 Rating 90 To 2017 $25

The Gaffer McLaren Vale Shiraz 2008 Rating 89 To 2015 $22
Sticky End McLaren Vale Viognier 2009 Rating 89 To 2012 $22

Mulyan ★★★★

North Logan Road, Cowra, NSW 2794 **Region** Cowra
T (02) 6342 1336 **F** (02) 6341 1015 **www**.mulyanwines.com.au **Open** W'ends & public hols 10–5, or by appt
Winemaker Chris Derez (Contract) **Est.** 1994 **Cases** 2000 **Vyds** 51 ha
Mulyan is a 1350-ha grazing property purchased by the Fagan family in 1886 from Dr William Redfern, a leading 19th-century figure in Australian history. The current-generation owners, Peter and Jenni Fagan, began planting in 1994, and intend the vineyard area to be 100 ha in all. Presently there are 28.5 ha of shiraz, 14.5 ha of chardonnay, and 4 ha each of merlot and viognier. The label features a statue of the Roman god Mercury, which has stood in the homestead garden since being brought back from Italy in 1912 by Peter's grandmother. Exports to the UK and China.

Bush Rangers Bounty Cowra Chardonnay 2007 Excellent wine, particularly given its price; the portion that went through barrel fermentation has added authority to the palate, which has clear varietal fruit in a citrus and nectarine mould; good line and length. Screwcap. 13.1% alc. Rating 91 To 2013 $15
Block 9 Shiraz Viognier 2007 Excellent colour; slightly left of centre, with the viognier seemingly adding an edge to the texture and flavour of the wine, with black fruits at its core and charry oak on the finish. Screwcap. 14.2% alc. Rating 90 To 2015 $25

Munari Wines ★★★★☆

Ladys Creek Vienyard, 1129 Northern Highway, Heathcote, Vic 3523 **Region** Heathcote
T (03) 5433 3366 **F** (03) 5433 3905 **www**.munariwines.com **Open** Tues–Sun 11–5
Winemaker Adrian Munari **Est.** 1993 **Cases** 3000 **Vyds** 6.9 ha
Established on one of the original Heathcote farming properties, Ladys Creek Vineyard is situated on the narrow Cambrian strip 11 km north of the town. Adrian Munari has harnessed traditional winemaking practices with New World innovation to produce complex, fruit-driven wines that marry concentration and elegance. They are produced from estate plantings of shiraz, cabernet sauvignon, merlot, cabernet franc and malbec. Exports to France, Denmark, Taiwan and China.

Black Lady Shiraz 2006 Dense, inky colour; mouthfilling, luscious plum, black cherry and chocolate; harmonious and supple tannins; intense and long; not the least heavy; 50% made by Glen Eldon, 50% by Munari Wines, and sold by each. Barossa/Heathcote. Cork. 14.5% alc. Rating 95 To 2017 $110

Schoolhouse Red 2007 Rating 92 To 2020 $25
The Beauregard 2007 Rating 90 To 2017 $20

Murdoch Hill ★★★★★

Mappinga Road, Woodside, SA 5244 **Region** Adelaide Hills
T (08) 8389 7081 **F** (08) 8389 7991 **www**.murdochhill.com.au **Open** By appt
Winemaker Brian Light (Contract), Michael Downer **Est.** 1998 **Cases** 5100 **Vyds** 20.5 ha
A little over 20 ha of vines were established on the undulating, gum-studded countryside of Charlie and Julie Downer's 60-year-old Erinka property, 4 km east of Oakbank. In descending order of importance, the varieties planted are sauvignon blanc, shiraz, cabernet sauvignon and chardonnay. Son Michael, with a Bachelor of Oenology degree from Adelaide University, is assistant winemaker. Exports to the UK and Canada.

ΨΨΨΨΨ **Adelaide Hills Chardonnay 2009** The epitome of correctness: low-yielding estate vines, whole bunch pressed, wild yeast fermented and lees stirred. It has worked to provide a fine, elegant wine with a streak of minerality to keep the palate tight and focused. Screwcap. 13% alc. **Rating** 94 **To** 2016 $25

✪ **Adelaide Hills Cabernet Sauvignon 2008** Good red-crimson hue; it's an ill wind, they say; the very warm '08 vintage meant Adelaide Hills cabernet reached full ripeness, the luscious blackcurrant cassis fruit showing through in this wine. Screwcap. 14% alc. **Rating** 94 **To** 2018 $19

ΨΨΨΨΨ **The Cronberry Adelaide Hills Shiraz 2007** **Rating** 92 **To** 2017 $22

ΨΨΨΨ **Adelaide Hills Sauvignon Blanc 2009** **Rating** 89 **To** 2010 $19
The Cronberry Adelaide Hills Shiraz 2008 **Rating** 89 **To** 2015 $19

Murphy Wines ★★★★

PO Box 1418, Nagambie, Vic 3608 **Region** Strathbogie Ranges
T (03) 5792 2074 **F** (03) 5794 2165 **www**.murphywines.com **Open** Not
Winemaker Arran Murphy **Est.** 2004 **Cases** 200
The story of Arran Murphy has a fairytale ring to it. He began as an unqualified cellarhand at Tahbilk in 2000, and in '03 was offered the opportunity of a traineeship at Plunkett Wines. He began studying wine production, and in 2004 received a scholarship that enabled him to do a harvest in the Sonoma Valley. Since 2000 he had been making small batches of wine collecting grapes from the end of rows picked by mechanical harvesters, using chicken wire as a destemmer, and using a three-generation-old basket press. In 2004 he decided to purchase a few tonnes of grapes and make his first commercial wine. With next to no capital, he was unable to afford any new oak, so experimented with inner staves, chips and oak cubes. This resulted in three batches of wine in 2004, which he called Hazel Shiraz, honouring his late grandmother Hazel Murphy who had constantly encouraged him to strive to better himself and aim high. The '04 won a gold medal at the Strathbogie Ranges Wine Show '07, and the '05 is a worthy follow-on.

ΨΨΨΨΨ **Hazel Shiraz 2005** A very dodgy, stained cork isn't a great start, but the wine is full of ripe black fruits on the bouquet and palate; quality oak is a plus. 14.5% alc. **Rating** 91 **To** 2020 $50

Murray Street Vineyard ★★★★★

Murray Street, Greenock, SA 5360 **Region** Barossa Valley
T (08) 8562 8373 **F** (08) 8562 8414 **www**.murraystreet.com.au **Open** 7 days 10–4.30
Winemaker Andrew Seppelt **Est.** 2001 **Cases** 10 000 **Vyds** 46 ha
Andrew Seppelt has moved with a degree of caution in setting up Murray Street Vineyard, possibly because of inherited wisdom and the business acumen of partner Bill Jahnke, a successful investment banker with Wells Fargo. Andrew is a direct descendant of Benno and Sophia Seppelt, who built Seppeltsfield and set the family company bearing their name on its path to fame. The partnership has 46 ha of vineyards, one block at Gomersal, the other at Greenock, with the lion's share going to shiraz, followed by grenache, mourvedre, viognier, marsanne, semillon and zinfandel. Most of the grapes are sold, with an increasing amount retained for the Murray Street Vineyard brand. Unusually good point of sale/propaganda material. Exports to the UK, the US, Canada and Denmark.

ŸŸŸŸŸ **Benno 2006** Deep, dark colour; like the Rhône blend, it is a very impressive wine, with highly focused black fruits and excellent structure; will live for decades. Mataro/Shiraz. Screwcap. 15% alc. **Rating** 96 **To** 2026 $80

Gomersal 2008 Significantly deeper colour than the standard wine, with more purple, attesting to the lower pH; while full-bodied, has a juicy elegance and supple texture; long life ahead. Shiraz. Screwcap. 13.9% alc. **Rating** 95 **To** 2038 $55

Sophia 2007 Deep purple-red; the bouquet and full-bodied palate abound with luscious black fruits, a commodity not common in '07; the alcohol simply doesn't show, and the fruit has not been over-extracted; the oak, too, is in good balance. Shiraz. Screwcap. 15% alc. **Rating** 95 **To** 2038 $75

Shiraz Cabernet 2005 Holding its hue very well; this is a lusciously rich, soft but full-bodied wine; the two-thirds shiraz, one-third cabernet works to perfection and (if all corks are as good as the one in this bottle) has a great future. 15.1% alc. **Rating** 95 **To** 2020 $100

Cabernet Sauvignon 2008 Crimson-purple; stacked to the gills with luscious blackcurrant fruit supported by integrated tannins throughout, before fruit surges again on the finish; great length. Screwcap. 14.1% alc. **Rating** 95 **To** 2030 $35

Greenock 2008 Deep colour, slightly less vibrant than Gomersal; masses of black fruits, licorice and tar on the full-bodied palate that dodges both the tannin and alcohol bullets; will be very long lived. Shiraz. Screwcap. 14.6% alc. **Rating** 94 **To** 2033 $55

Red Label Shiraz 2008 Deep, bright colour; surprisingly neither the bouquet or palate show any adverse impact from the higher alcohol; blackberry, plum, prune, dark chocolate and licorice are intertwined with quality tannins; very good overall balance. Screwcap. 15% alc. **Rating** 94 **To** 2030 $35

Greenock 2007 Fractionally more developed colour than the Gomersal, and much more expressive, the alcohol better integrated into the quite lively palate, with supple black fruits and balanced tannins. Very good outcome for the vintage. Shiraz. Screwcap. 15% alc. **Rating** 94 **To** 2020 $60

Sophia 2006 Deep colour, good hue; a very powerful, yet controlled wine with none of the uncertainties of ASW; oceans of blackberry and licorice fruit, alcohol the only question as the tannins and oak are well balanced and integrated. Shiraz. Screwcap. 15% alc. **Rating** 94 **To** 2026 $80

The Barossa 2008 Light colour, good hue; the bouquet is full of plum warm spices, and the palate has drive and energy to its peacock's display of cherry/cherry jam/plum/Turkish delight. Shiraz/Mataro/Grenache. Screwcap. 14.5% alc. **Rating** 94 **To** 2016 $35

The Barossa 2007 A very attractive Rhône Valley blend, light- to medium-bodied and smooth, the varieties combining synergistically on the splashy red palette cleverly used by the winemaker. Shiraz/Grenache/Mataro/Cinsaut. Screwcap. 15% alc. **Rating** 94 **To** 2017 $40

ŸŸŸŸŸ
✪ **Barossa Valley Shiraz 2008** Dense, dark purple-red; blackberry, prune and licorice aromas drive the fragrant bouquet and medium- to full-bodied palate; the tannins and oak, while evident, are in balance. Screwcap. 14.7% alc. **Rating** 93 **To** 2023 $25

Benno 2007 Rating 93 **To** 2020 $75

ŸŸŸŸ **Gomersal 2007 Rating** 89 **To** 2015 $60

ASW Shiraz 2006 Rating 89 **To** 2026 $50

Murrindindi Vineyards ★★★★

30 Cummins Lane, Murrindindi, Vic 3717 **Region** Upper Goulburn
T (03) 5797 8217 **F** (03) 5797 8448 **www**.murrindindivineyards.com **Open** Not
Winemaker Hugh Cuthbertson **Est.** 1979 **Cases** 3000 **Vyds** 15 ha
This small winery is owned and run by the Cuthbertson family, established by Alan and Jan as a minor diversification from their cattle property. Plantings began in 1978, increasing in '82 and '95 to their present level. Son Hugh, himself with a long and high-profile wine career,

has overseen the marketing of the wines, including the Family Reserve and Don't Tell Dad brands. Exports to the UK, the US, Finland, Estonia and China.

🍷🍷🍷🍷♀ **Family Reserve Yea Valley Chardonnay 2008** A lively, crisp and vibrant wine, driven by nectarine and grapefruit aromas and flavours, oak precisely positioned. Will age gracefully. Screwcap. 13.5% alc. **Rating** 93 **To** 2016 $28

Family Reserve Yea Valley Cabernet Sauvignon 2006 Retains good hue; has distinctly savoury herbal overtones to the black fruit flavours, but these don't extend to the tannins, which are fine. Screwcap. 14% alc. **Rating** 91 **To** 2016 $27

Don't Tell Dad Yea Valley Riesling 2008 Has good overall intensity and varietal character; ripe citrus notes on the bouquet intensify on the well-balanced palate. Screwcap. 13% alc. **Rating** 90 **To** 2015 $18.80

Myrtaceae   ★★★☆

53 Main Creek Road, Main Ridge, Vic 3928 **Region** Mornington Peninsula
T (03) 5989 2045 **F** (03) 5989 2845 **www**.myrtaceae.com.au **Open** W'ends & public hols 12–5, 7 days 27 Dec to end Jan
Winemaker Julie Trueman **Est.** 1985 **Cases** 300 **Vyds** 1 ha
Owners John Trueman (viticulturist) and wife Julie (winemaker) began the planting of Myrtaceae in 1985, intending to make a Bordeaux-style red blend. It became evident that these late-ripening varieties were not well suited to the site, so the vineyard was converted to chardonnay (0.6 ha) and pinot noir (0.4 ha) in 1998. Part of the property is devoted to the Land for Wildlife Scheme; the integrated Australian garden is a particular feature.

🍷🍷🍷🍷♀ **Mornington Peninsula Pinot Noir 2007** Brilliantly clear crimson; a fragrant and expressive bouquet of small red fruits with a foresty underlay, characters faithfully reproduced on the still-fresh, light- to medium-bodied palate; all up elegance. Screwcap. 13.5% alc. **Rating** 90 **To** 2013 $30

🍷🍷🍷🍷 **Mornington Peninsula Chardonnay 2008 Rating** 88 **To** 2013 $30

Naked Run Wines   **NR**

36 Parawae Road, Salisbury Plain, SA 5109 (postal) **Region** Clare Valley/Barossa Valley
T 0408 807 655 **F** (08) 8347 3366 **www**.nakedrunwines.com.au **Open** Not
Winemaker Steven Baraglia **Est.** 2005 **Cases** 1000
Naked Run Wines is the virtual winery of university graduates Jayme Wood, Bradley Currie and Steven Baraglia, their skills ranging from viticulture through to production, and also all-important sales and marketing. The riesling is sourced from Clare Valley, grenache from the Williamstown area of the Barossa Valley, and shiraz from Greenock.

Narkoojee   ★★★★☆

170 Francis Road, Glengarry, Vic 3854 **Region** Gippsland
T (03) 5192 4257 **F** (03) 5192 4238 **www**.narkoojee.com **Open** 7 days 10.30–4.30
Winemaker Harry and Axel Friend **Est.** 1981 **Cases** 4000
Narkoojee Vineyard (originally a dairy farm owned by the Friend family) is within easy reach of the old gold-mining town of Walhalla and looks out over the Strzelecki Ranges. The wines are produced from a little over 10 ha of estate vineyards, with chardonnay accounting for half the total. Former lecturer in civil engineering and extremely successful amateur winemaker Harry Friend changed horses in 1994 to take joint control, with Axel Friend, of the family vineyard and winery, and hasn't missed a beat since; their skills show through with all the wines, none more so than the Chardonnay. Exports to Canada, Ireland, Maldives, Japan, Hong Kong and Singapore.

🍷🍷🍷🍷♀ **Reserve Gippsland Chardonnay 2008** Has a precocious display of nectarine, peach (white and yellow), grapefruit, cashew and oak, all adding up to a high-flavoured wine. Diam. 14% alc. **Rating** 93 **To** 2015 $32

✪ **Gippsland Pinot Noir 2008** Bright, clear red-purple; black cherry and plum aromas with a whiff of French oak lead into an energetic palate that surges on the finish and aftertaste, supported by fine, foresty tannins. Diam. 13.7% alc. **Rating** 92 **To** 2014 $25

✪ **Gippsland Sparkling Harriet Chardonnay 2008** Pale straw-green; bottle-fermented; a delicate and extremely well balanced wine that will only get better as it ages; this is the second disgorgement, with more to follow. Diam. 12% alc. **Rating** 91 **To** 2014 $25

♀♀♀♀ **Cuvee Robert Fordham Gippsland Sparkling Merlot 2006** Rating 89 **To** 2014 $30

Nashwauk   ★★★★

PO Box 852, Nuriootpa, SA 5355 **Region** McLaren Vale
T (08) 8562 4488 **F** (08) 8562 4499 **www**.nashwaukvineyards.com.au **Open** Not
Winemaker Reid Bosward, Stephen Dew **Est.** 2005 **Cases** 5000 **Vyds** 20 ha
This is an estate-based venture, with 18 ha of shiraz and 1 ha each of cabernet and tempranillo, all except the tempranillo between 13 and 40+ years old. It is a stand-alone business of the Kaesler family, and the first time it has extended beyond the Barossa Valley. The striking label comes from satellite photos of the vineyard, showing the contour planting; the name Nashwauk comes from Canada's Algonquin indigenous language meaning 'land between'. The property is situated in the (unofficial) Seaview subregion, with Kays, Chapel Hill and Coriole as its neighbours, which all benefit from sea breezes and cooler nights. Exports to the US, Singapore, Malaysia and China.

♀♀♀♀♀ **McLaren Vale Tempranillo 2008** In theory, tempranillo is best suited to cool climates as it is an early ripening variety, tannins an issue in warm climates. Here the wine has excellent texture and structure, with very appealing spice, cherry and plum fruits, the tannins fine and soft. Cork. 15.5% alc. Rating 94 To 2016 $25

♀♀♀♀ **McLaren Vale Shiraz 2007** Rating 88 **To** 2015 $25

Nazaaray   ★★★☆

266 Meakins Road, Flinders, Vic 3929 **Region** Mornington Peninsula
T (03) 5989 0126 **F** (03) 5989 0495 **www**.nazaaray.com.au **Open** 1st weekend of month, or by appt
Winemaker Paramdeep Ghumman **Est.** 1996 **Cases** 800 **Vyds** 2.28 ha
Paramdeep Ghumman is, as far as I am aware, the only Indian-born winery proprietor in Australia. He and his wife migrated from India over 20 years ago, and purchased the Nazaaray vineyard property in 1991. An initial trial planting of 400 vines in 1996 was gradually expanded to the present level of 1.6 ha of pinot noir, 0.44 ha of pinot gris and 0.12 ha each of sauvignon blanc and shiraz. Notwithstanding the micro size of the estate, all the wines are made and bottled onsite.

♀♀♀♀♀ **Reserve Mornington Peninsula Pinot Noir 2006** Bright clear crimson-red; still very youthful, seemingly less ripe than the alcohol would suggest; light- to medium-bodied, with fresh cherry and plum fruit, fine tannins and minimal oak influence. Screwcap. 13.7% alc. **Rating** 90 **To** 2014 $31.50

♀♀♀♀ **Mornington Peninsula Pinot Gris 2009** Rating 89 **To** 2010 $27
Reserve Mornington Peninsula Pinot Noir 2008 Rating 89 **To** 2013 $40
Mornington Peninsula Shiraz 2008 Rating 89 **To** 2016 $38.50

Neagles Rock Vineyards   ★★★★★

Lot 1 & 2 Main North Road, Clare, SA 5453 **Region** Clare Valley
T (08) 8843 4020 **F** (08) 8843 4021 **www**.neaglesrock.com **Open** Mon–Sat 10–5, Sun 11–4
Winemaker Ang Meaney **Est.** 1997 **Cases** 11 000 **Vyds** 16.1 ha

Founding partners Jane Willson and Steve Wiblin went their separate ways in 2009, with a new equity partner joining Jane as owner. This to one side, it is business as usual, both in the winery and restaurant-cum-cellar door. Exports to the UK, the US and other major markets.

ΨΨΨΨΨ **One Black Dog Reserve Clare Valley Cabernet Shiraz 2006** Excellent hue; high-quality parcels of the two varieties have been seamlessly joined to provide a fragrant bouquet and luscious black fruits on the palate; good oak and tannin management also impressive. ProCork. 14.5% alc. **Rating** 95 **To** 2026 $60
Clare Valley Shiraz 2008 Strong red-crimson; a wine stacked with an array of black fruits from blackberry to licorice and a sprinkling of spice and black pepper; the texture and structure promise a long life. Screwcap. 14.5% alc. **Rating** 94 **To** 2028 $25
Clare Valley Cabernet Sauvignon 2008 Strong red-purple; a well-crafted cabernet, with ripe (not jammy) blackcurrant, cassis and plum fruit, well-integrated oak (some new) and supple tannins. Screwcap. 14.5% alc. **Rating** 94 **To** 2023 $25

ΨΨΨΨ **Misery Clare Valley Grenache Shiraz 2008 Rating** 88 **To** 2012 $20

Neil Hahn Wines   ★★★

PO Box 64, Stockwell, SA 5355 **Region** Barossa Valley
T (08) 8562 3002 **F** (08) 8562 1111 **www**.hahnbarossa.com **Open** Not
Winemaker Mark Jamieson **Est.** 1885 **Cases** 3500 **Vyds** 45.68 ha
Neil Hahn Wines has a very long history. On 25 January 1839 Johann Christian Hahn and wife Maria Elizabeth left their home in Silesia to travel to SA on the sailing ship *Catharina*. They were among the earliest white settlers to arrive, and in 1846 Johann purchased 32 ha of land in the Barossa Valley. In 1885 son Johann Christian II bought land of his own, situated on Light Pass Road. Mixed farming and viticulture were common and now, after being in the Hahn family for five generations, the property is totally planted to vines under the care and ownership of Neil and Sandy Hahn. There are 19.6 ha at this vineyard, and a further 30 ha in the Ebenezer Vineyard. The wines, contract-made by Mark Jamieson, overflow with luscious red and black fruit flavours and copious amounts of American oak. Exports to Singapore, Hong Kong, China, Japan and South Korea.

ΨΨΨΨ **Yanyarrie Shiraz Cabernet 2007** The strong point of the wine is its texture and structure, and its melange of mocha, black cherry and spice works well. Screwcap. 14.1% alc. **Rating** 89 **To** 2015 $17.95
✪ **Madcap Cabernet Merlot 2008** Good colour; clear-cut savoury/foresty edges to the juicy blackcurrant fruit; a simple but lively varietal blend. Twin top. 14% alc. **Rating** 87 **To** 2011 $9.95

Neilson Estate Wines   ★★★

63 Logue Road, Millendon, WA 6056 **Region** Swan Valley
T (08) 9296 4849 **F** (08) 9296 4849 **www**.neilsonestate.com.au **Open** By appt
Winemaker John Griffiths, Jim Neilson **Est.** 1998 **Cases** 100 **Vyds** 2 ha
Jim and Jenny Neilson planted their vineyard of shiraz and merlot (1 ha each) in 1998. Jim has undertaken the viticulture and oenology degree course at Curtin University, but since 2006 has worked in conjunction with John Griffiths at Faber Wines to produce the wines. Jenny, daughter Sarah and son Ben are all involved in the business.

ΨΨΨΨ **Reserve Swan Valley Shiraz 2008** Light, clear red-purple; ripe plum fruit on the bouquet and light- to medium-bodied palate is supported by a dash of vanillan oak and soft tannins. No need to wait. Screwcap. 14% alc. **Rating** 88 **To** 2014 $29

Nelwood Wines   ★★★

PO Box 196, Paringa, SA 5340 **Region** Riverland
T (08) 8595 8042 **F** (08) 8595 8182 **www**.nelwood.com **Open** By appt
Winemaker Boar's Rock (Mike Farmilo) **Est.** 2002 **Cases** 5000

The wines (released under the Red Mud label) come from 45-ha plantings of shiraz, chardonnay, petit verdot and cabernet sauvignon near Nelwood, 32 km east of Renmark near the South Australian border. The grapegrowers who are shareholders in the company have been growing grapes for up to three generations in the Riverland. Exports to the US.

ȚȚȚȚ **Red Mud Signature Series Petit Verdot 2006** Typical Riverland petit verdot, which retains colour and flavour integrity regardless of the challenges; dark berry fruit is nicely balanced by ripe tannins. Diam. 14.5% alc. **Rating** 89 **To** 2014 $36

Nepenthe ★★★★★

Jones Road, Balhannah, SA 5242 **Region** Adelaide Hills
T (08) 8398 8888 **F** (08) 8388 1100 **www.**nepenthe.com.au **Open** 7 days 10–4
Winemaker Andre Bondar **Est.** 1994 **Cases** 70 000 **Vyds** 93.92 ha
Nepenthe has almost 100 ha of close-planted vineyards in the Adelaide Hills, with an exotic array of varieties. It quickly established its reputation as a producer of high-quality wines, but founder Ed Tweddell died unexpectedly in 2006. In March '07 son James announced that McGuigan Simeon had purchased the winery, causing many industry observers to scratch their heads. In '09 the Adelaide Hills winery was closed, and winemaking operations transferred to Australian Vintage (aka McGuigan Simeon's principal SA winery). The transfer hasn't impacted on wine quality; if anything, the reverse. Exports to the UK, the US and other major markets.

ȚȚȚȚȚ **Ithaca Adelaide Hills Chardonnay 2008** Bright straw-green; a complex, slightly funky bouquet gives way to a razor-sharp palate, the fruit flavours arresting and remarkably intense as they power through to the long finish. Screwcap. 13% alc. **Rating** 95 **To** 2016 $28.90
Ithaca Adelaide Hills Chardonnay 2007 Light straw-green; still bright and focused; nectarine and white peach fruit are encircled by vibrant citrus acidity; oak provides some nutty notes and lengthens the finish. Screwcap. 13.5% alc. **Rating** 94 **To** 2014 $28.90
Gate Block Adelaide Hills Shiraz 2008 Light, bright purple-crimson; the cool-climate impact on the wine is marked, with vibrant spicy overtones to the red fruit aromas and flavours mimicking the effect of viognier; a spicy/savoury and long finish. Screwcap. 14.5% alc. **Rating** 94 **To** 2023 $38.90
Gate Block Adelaide Hills Shiraz 2007 Strong colour; elegant, medium-bodied cool-grown wine with a fragrant bouquet and a supple, slinky palate offering plum, cherry, a sprinkle of spice and cedary oak. Screwcap. 14.5% alc. **Rating** 94 **To** 2020 $38.90

ȚȚȚȚȚ **Adelaide Hills Sauvignon Blanc 2009** Everything in its place, a gently tropical
✪   and citrus blend of aromas and flavours, the palate lengthened and cleansed by crisp acidity. Screwcap. 13.5% alc. **Rating** 92 **To** 2011 $19.90
Petraea Sauvignon Blanc 2009 Rating 92 **To** 2011 $28
The Good Doctor Adelaide Hills Pinot Noir 2008 Rating 92 **To** 2014 $38.90
✪   **Tryst Adelaide Hills Sauvignon Blanc Semillon 2009** A well-made 60/40 blend, with citrussy/lemony components to the fore, and just an echo of tropical fruit ex the sauvignon blanc. Screwcap. 12.5% alc. **Rating** 90 **To** 2012 $14.90

ȚȚȚȚ **Adelaide Hills Unoaked Chardonnay 2009 Rating** 89 **To** 2012 $18.90
Adelaide Hills Savagnin 2009 Rating 89 **To** 2012 $25.90
Charleston Adelaide Hills Pinot Noir 2008 Rating 89 **To** 2013 $22.90
Adelaide Hills Pinot Gris 2009 Rating 88 **To** 2011 $22.90
✪   **Tryst 2008** Bright purple-crimson; the wine is all about fresh red and black fruit flavours, and not concerned about structure. Cabernet Sauvignon (73%)/ Tempranillo (27%), also taking in fruit from Adelaide Hills/Limestone Coast/ Barossa Valley. Screwcap. 14% alc. **Rating** 88 **To** 2013 $14.90

New Era Vineyards ★★★★☆

PO Box 391, Woodside SA 5244 **Region** Adelaide Hills
T (08) 8389 7715 **F** (08) 8389 7715 **www**.neweravineyards.com.au **Open** Not
Winemaker Robert Baxter, Reg Wilkinson **Est.** 1988 **Cases** 600 **Vyds** 12.5 ha
The New Era vineyard is situated over a gold reef that was mined for 60 years until all recoverable gold had been extracted (mining ceased in 1940). The vineyard was originally planted to chardonnay, shiraz, cabernet sauvignon, merlot and sauvignon, mostly contracted to Foster's. Recently 2 ha of cabernet sauvignon and 1.1 ha of merlot have been grafted over to sauvignon blanc. The small amount of wines made has been the subject of favourable reviews, and it's not hard to see why.

ＹＹＹＹＹ **Basket Pressed Adelaide Hills Shiraz 2003** The colour is still remarkably deep; potent black fruits, licorice, spice and pepper are evident from the word go; a wine of great power and intensity and sold at a price bordering on silly. Cork. 13.5% alc. **Rating** 94 **To** 2023 $25

ＹＹＹＹＹ **Adelaide Hills Merlot 2003 Rating** 93 **To** 2013 $22

ＹＹＹＹ **Adelaide Hills Cabernet Sauvignon 2003 Rating** 89 **To** 2014 $22

Newbridge Wines ★★★★★

18 Chelsea Street, Brighton, Vic 3186 (postal) **Region** Bendigo
T (03) 9591 0330 **F** (03) 9591 0330 **www**.newbridgewines.com.au **Open** At Newbridge Hotel, Newbridge
Winemaker Greg Dedman, Mark Matthews, Andrew Simpson **Est.** 1996 **Cases** 250
Vyds 1 ha
The Newbridge property was purchased by Ian Simpson in 1979 partly for sentimental family history reasons, and partly because of the beauty of the property situated on the banks of the Loddon River. It was not until 1996 that he decided to plant shiraz, and up to and including the 2002 vintage the grapes were sold to several local wineries. He retained the grapes and made wine in 2003, and Ian lived to see that and the following two vintages take shape before his death. The property is now run by his son Andrew and wife Kayleen, the wines contract-made by Greg Dedman and Mark Matthews, with enthusiastic support from Andrew.

ＹＹＹＹＹ **Bendigo Shiraz 2008** Dense, inky purple-crimson; a complex bouquet of black fruits, licorice and just a hint of spice leads into a full-bodied palate that miraculously retains lovely juicy fruit at its heart; only 98 cases made due to continuing drought after frost destroyed the '07 crop, the Loddon River not coming to the rescue, thanks to a zero water allocation. Screwcap. 14.5% alc. **Rating** 94 **To** 2023 $27

Newtons Ridge ★★★★☆

1170 Cooriemungle Road, Timboon, Vic 3268 **Region** Geelong
T (03) 5598 7394 **F** (03) 5598 7396 **www**.newtonsridge.com.au **Open** 7 days 11–5 Nov–Apr, or by appt
Winemaker David Newton **Est.** 1998 **Cases** 1500 **Vyds** 4 ha
David and Dot Newton say that after milking cows for 18 years, they decided to investigate the possibility of planting a northeast-facing block of land that they also owned. Their self-diagnosed mid-life crisis also stemmed from a lifelong interest in wine. They planted 2 ha of chardonnay and pinot noir in 1998, and another 2 ha of pinot gris, pinot noir and sauvignon blanc the following year. Having done a short winemaking course at Melbourne University (Dookie Campus), the Newtons completed a small winery in 2003. Originally called Heytesbury Ridge, the winery had a speedy name change to Newtons Ridge after a large legal stick was waved in their direction.

ＹＹＹＹＹ **Lila's Chardonnay 2008** Light, bright straw-green; a chardonnay that combines complexity with delicacy, intensity with subtlety; stone fruit and citrus flavours are caressed by light French oak, the finish long and clear. Gold medal Vic Wines Show '09. Screwcap. 13.5% alc. **Rating** 94 **To** 2018 $28

ŸŸŸŸŸ Sauvignon Blanc 2009 Bright straw-green; a lively wine with very attractive
☼   juicy fruit in a tropical spectrum driving the long palate; good balance. Screwcap.
            13.3% alc. **Rating** 90 **To** 2011 $20
☼   Taisha's Sparkling Trio 2006 Salmon-pink; vibrant and fresh, with strawberry
            and spice joining citrus components. Chardonnay/Pinot Noir/Pinot Meunier.
            Diam. 13% alc. **Rating** 90 **To** 2012 $22

Ngeringa   ★★★★★

91 Williams Road, Mount Barker, SA 5251 **Region** Adelaide Hills
T (08) 8398 2867 **F** (08) 8398 2867 **www**.ngeringa.com **Open** By appt
Winemaker Erinn and Janet Klein **Est.** 2001 **Cases** 2000
Erinn and Janet Klein say, 'As fervent practitioners of biodynamic wine growing, we respect
biodynamics as a sensitivity to the rhythms of nature, the health of the soil and the connection
between plant, animal and cosmos. It is a pragmatic solution to farming without the use of
chemicals and a necessary acknowledgement that the farm unit is part of a great whole.' It is
not an easy solution, and the Kleins have increased the immensity of the challenge by using
ultra-close vine spacing of 1.5 m x 1 m, necessitating a large amount of hand training of the
vines plus a tiny crawler tractor. Lest it be thought they have stumbled onto biodynamic
growing without understanding wine science, they teamed up while studying at Adelaide
University in 2000 (Erinn – oenology, Janet – viticulture/wine marketing), and then spent
time looking at the great viticultural regions of the Old World, with a particular emphasis
on biodynamics. The thick straw-bale walls of the winery result in a constant temperature
throughout the year. The JE label is used for the basic wines, Ngeringa only for the very best.
Exports to the UK, Canada, Germany, China, Taiwan and NZ.

ŸŸŸŸŸ Adelaide Hills Chardonnay 2008 Good colour; a very complex bouquet,
            with barrel ferment and intense cool-grown fruit in a grapefruit and white peach
            spectrum; has great length and thrust. Screwcap. 13.5% alc. **Rating** 96 **To** 2015 $35
            JE Adelaide Hills Pinot Noir 2007 Light colour, but retains good hue; in
            mainstream Adelaide Hills style, with delicate red fruits supported (or challenged)
            by spicy, foresty tannins; has good length and aftertaste. Screwcap. 13.5% alc.
            Rating 94 **To** 2015 $35

ŸŸŸŸŸ Adelaide Hills Pinot Noir 2007 **Rating** 93 **To** 2014 $35
            Adelaide Hills Syrah 2007 **Rating** 93 **To** 2017 $50
            Adelaide Hills Pinot Noir 2008 **Rating** 91 **To** 2014 $35

ŸŸŸŸ Adelaide Hills Viognier 2008 **Rating** 89 **To** 2011 $40
            Adelaide Hills Rose 2009 **Rating** 89 **To** 2010 $28
            JE Assemblage Red 2007 **Rating** 89 **To** 2013 $25
            JE Adelaide Hills Assemblage White 2008 **Rating** 87 **To** 2011 $25

Nicholson River   ★★★★

57 Liddells Road, Nicholson, Vic 3882 **Region** Gippsland
T (03) 5156 8241 **F** (03) 5156 8433 **www**.nicholsonriverwinery.com.au **Open** 7 days
10–4 during hols, or by appt
Winemaker Ken Eckersley **Est.** 1978 **Cases** 2000 **Vyds** 8 ha
Nicholson River's fierce commitment to quality in the face of the temperamental Gippsland
climate and frustratingly small production has been handsomely repaid by some massive
Chardonnays and impressive red wines (from estate plantings). Ken Eckersley refers to
his Chardonnays not as white wines but as gold wines, and lists them accordingly in his
newsletter. Exports to the US.

ŸŸŸŸŸ Montview Chardonnay 2008 Bright straw-green; a complex nutty bouquet,
            then a finer palate with nectarine and melon fruit kept in line by citrussy acidity;
            old vines, but not old style. Screwcap. 13.5% alc. **Rating** 93 **To** 2016 $25

Montview Syrah 2007 Medium red-purple; a fragrant light- to medium-bodied, cool-grown shiraz, with lively red fruits, spice and licorice supported by superfine tannins and a touch of oak; good mouthfeel, line and length. Screwcap. 13.5% alc. Rating 91 To 2014 $25

♥♥♥♥ **Merlot 2006** Rating 89 To 2013 $22
Cabernet Merlot 2006 Rating 89 To 2018 $22
Semillon Sauvignon Blanc 2009 Rating 88 To 2012 $19
Unwooded Chardonnay 2009 Rating 88 To 2012 $22

Nick O'Leary Wines ★★★★☆

129 Donnelly Road, Bungendore, NSW 2621 **Region** Canberra District
T (02) 6161 8739 **F** (02) 6166 0572 **www**.nickolearywines.com.au **Open** By appt
Winemaker Nick O'Leary **Est.** 2007 **Cases** 1250 **Vyds** 0.5 ha
At the ripe old age of 28 years, Nick O'Leary had been involved in the wine industry for over a decade, working variously in retail, wholesale, viticulture and winemaking. Two years earlier he had laid the foundation for Nick O'Leary Wines, purchasing shiraz from local vignerons (commencing in 2006) and riesling following in '08. His wines have had extraordinarily consistent success in local wine shows and competitions since the first vintages.

♥♥♥♥♥ **Shiraz 2008** A gloriously fragrant, complex and stylish red, with luscious black cherry, plum and blackberry fruit; well-handled tannins and oak; manages to combine full flavour while retaining elegance. Screwcap. 13.5% alc. Rating 94 To 2020 $28

♥♥♥♥♡ **Riesling 2009** Rating 91 To 2017 $25

Nillumbik Estate ★★★☆

PO Box 24, Smiths Gully, Vic 3760 **Region** Yarra Valley
T (03) 9710 1773 **www**.nillumbikestate.com.au **Open** Not
Winemaker John Tregambe **Est.** 2001 **Cases** 500 **Vyds** 1.6 ha
In establishing Nillumbik Estate, John and Chanmali Tregambe drew on the multi-generational winemaking experience of John's parents, Italian immigrants who arrived in Australia in the 1950s. The estate plantings of pinot noir are supplemented by cabernet sauvignon, chardonnay, shiraz and nebbiolo variously purchased from Sunbury, Heathcote and the King Valley.

♥♥♥♥♡ **Domenico & Francesca Yarra Valley Rose 2009** Well made from estate-grown pinot; salmon-pink, it has spicy strawberry fruit on both bouquet and palate, giving good length; pleasingly dry finish. Screwcap. 13% alc. Rating 92 To 2011 $17

♥♥♥♥ **Shiraz 2008** Rating 89 To 2018 $24.50
Yarra Valley Pinot Noir 2005 Rating 88 To 2013 $24
Yarra Valley Pinot Noir 2006 Rating 87 To 2013 $24

Nine Fingers ★★★☆

PO Box 212, Lobethal, SA 5241 **Region** Adelaide Hills
T (08) 8389 6049 **Open** By appt
Winemaker Contract **Est.** 1999 **Cases** 200 **Vyds** 1 ha
Simon and Penny Cox established their sauvignon blanc vineyard after encouragement from local winemaker Robb Cootes of Leland Estate. The small vineyard has meant that they do all the viticultural work, and meticulously tend the vines. They obviously have a sense of humour, which may not be shared by their youngest daughter Olivia. In 2002 two-year-old Olivia's efforts to point out bunches that needed to be thinned resulted in Penny's secateurs cutting off the end of Olivia's finger. A race to hospital and successful microsurgery resulted in the full restoration of the finger; strangely, Olivia has shown little interest in viticulture ever since, but will be reminded of the incident by the name of the business and the design of the label.

🍷🍷🍷🍷 **Adelaide Hills Sauvignon Blanc 2009** Firmly anchored on the grassy side of the sauvignon blanc spectrum, although not the least green; light-bodied, but well balanced, with a crisp, clean finish. Screwcap. 13% alc. **Rating** 88 **To** 2011 $19

919 Wines

★★★★☆

Section 919, Hodges Road, Berri, SA 5343 **Region** Riverland
T (08) 8582 4436 **F** (08) 8582 4478 **www**.919wines.com.au **Open** Wed–Sun & public hols 10–5
Winemaker Eric and Jenny Semmler **Est.** 2002 **Cases** 5000 **Vyds** 2.8 ha

Eric and Jenny Semmler have been involved in the wine industry since 1986, and have a special interest in fortified wines. Eric previously made fortified wines for Hardys at Berri Estates, and worked at Brown Brothers. Jenny has worked for Strathbogie Vineyards, Pennyweight Wines, St Huberts and Constellation. They have planted micro-quantities of varieties specifically for fortified wines: palomino, durif, tempranillo, muscat a petits grains, tinta cao, shiraz, tokay and touriga nacional. Notwithstanding their Riverland GI, they use minimal water application and deliberately reduce the crop levels, practising organic and biodynamic techniques where possible. Grapes are purchased from other growers if the need arises; the grapes are hand-picked, fermented in open fermenters and basket-pressed before the juice is fortified.

🍷🍷🍷🍷🍷 **Vintage 2006** Still vibrantly coloured in crimson spectrum; a stylish wine deserving its trophy at Winewise '08 and gold medal at the Riverland Wine Show '08. Has good fragrance and overall elegance. Touriga/Tinta Roriz/Tinta Cao/Shiraz/Durif. Screwcap. 18% alc. **Rating** 94 **To** 2016 $35

🍷🍷🍷🍷🍷 (half) **Classic Muscat NV Rating** 93 **To** 2011 **$35**
Tempranillo 2007 Rating 92 **To** 2017 **$33**
Petit Manseng 2009 Rating 91 **To** 2013 **$33**
Classic Tawny NV Rating 91 **To** 2011 **$25**
Sangiovese 2008 Rating 90 **To** 2015 **$33**
Fino NV Rating 90 **To** 2011 **$25**

🍷🍷🍷🍷 **Shiraz 2008 Rating** 88 **To** 2013 **$33**
Durif 2005 Rating 88 **To** 2015 **$30**
Redemption Ruby NV Rating 88 **To** 2011 **$15**
Vermentino 2009 Rating 87 **To** 2011 **$33**

Nintingbool

★★★

56 Wongerer Lane, Smythes Creek, Vic 3351 (postal) **Region** Ballarat
T (03) 5342 4393 **F** (03) 5342 4393 **www**.nintingbool.com **Open** Not
Winemaker Peter Bothe **Est.** 1998 **Cases** 320 **Vyds** 2 ha

Peter and Jill Bothe purchased the Nintingbool property in 1982 and built the home in which they now live in '84, using old bluestone dating back to the goldrush period. They established an extensive Australian native garden and home orchard, but in 1998 diversified with the planting of pinot noir, a further planting the following year lifting the total to 2 ha; a small amount of the property remains to be planted with pinot gris. This is one of the coolest mainland regions, and demands absolute attention to detail (and a warm growing season) for success. In 2002 and '03 the grapes were sold to Ian Watson, the wine made and released under the Tomboy Hill label but with the Nintingbool Vineyard shown on the label (the '02 was quite a beautiful wine). In '04 they decided to make the wines themselves, the opening vintage producing a tiny 44 cases.

🍷🍷🍷🍷 **Ballarat Pinot Noir 2008** Shows its very cool grown origin; complex whole bunch and stem characters, but distinctly savoury/stemmy on the finish, and really needs a little more sweet fruit on the mid-palate. Screwcap. 13.9% alc. **Rating** 89 **To** 2013 $30

No Regrets Vineyard ★★★★☆

40 Dillons Hill Road, Glaziers Bay, Tas 7109 **Region** Southern Tasmania
T (03) 6295 1509 **F** (03) 6295 1509 **Open** By appt, also at Salamanca Market (Hobart) most Saturdays
Winemaker Contract **Est.** 2000 **Cases** 350 **Vyds** 1 ha
Having sold Elsewhere Vineyard, Eric and Jette Phillips have planted the former flower gardens around the old Elsewhere homestead, where they still live, exclusively to pinot noir, and renamed this 1-ha 'retirement' vineyard No Regrets. After a slow restart, their Pinots are now resembling those of Elsewhere.

♥♥♥♥♥   Pinot Noir 2007 Still strong purple; has the same concentration and structure as the '08, the fruit more plush (a low-yielding vintage), sweet spiced plum flavours in the ascendant. Screwcap. 13% alc. **Rating** 94 To 2015 $30

♥♥♥♥♀   Pinot Noir 2008 **Rating** 93 To 2016 $30

Nocton Park ★★★☆

373 Colebrook Road, Richmond, Tas 7025 **Region** Southern Tasmania
T (03) 6260 2088 **F** (03) 6260 2880 **www.**noctonpark.com.au **Open** By appt
Winemaker Winemaking Tasmania (Julian Alcorso) **Est.** 1998 **Cases** 7000 **Vyds** 31.6 ha
Prior to the 2010 vintage, Nocton Park emerged from two years' administration following the financial demise of its founders. Jerry Adler and viticulturist Richard Meyman now run the business, the 100-ha property planted to pinot noir, chardonnay, merlot and sauvignon blanc. The site was originally earmarked by Peter Althaus of Domaine A (see separate entry) who, back in 1995, described it as the best vineyard land in the Coal River Valley. Exports to China.

♥♥♥♥♀   Pinot Noir 2008 Vivid purple-crimson, the type of hue only Tasmania achieves; very bright and firm varietal fruit, dark cherry and plum carrying the line, tannins and oak welded to the fruit. Screwcap. 13.5% alc. **Rating** 92 To 2017 $25

♥♥♥♥   Sauvignon Blanc 2009 **Rating** 89 To 2011 $25
Merlot 2008 **Rating** 88 To 2014 $25

Nolan Vineyard ★★★

217 Badger Creek Road, Badger Creek, Vic 3777 **Region** Yarra Valley
T (03) 5962 3435 **www.**nolanvineyard.com.au **Open** Fri–Mon & public hols 11–5
Winemaker Paul Evans (Contract) **Est.** 2000 **Cases** 300 **Vyds** 1.8 ha
John and Myrtle Nolan have established low-yielding, non-irrigated pinot noir using clones 114, 115 and MV6. Myrtle had worked in Yarra Valley vineyards for 10 years across all sectors of the Valley, and (one assumes it is Myrtle who says), 'John is a faithful supporter of the vineyard endeavours and is highly valued at picking time because of his large and extended family.' The vineyard, incidentally, is very close to the Healesville Sanctuary. Smoke taint caused huge problems for Yarra Valley pinot in '09.

♥♥♥♥   Yarra Valley Pinot Rose 2009 Light pink; spicy cherry/strawberry aromas, then a savoury, fractionally bitter palate. Screwcap. 12.5% alc. **Rating** 87 To 2010 $18

Noonji Estate ★★★★★

386 Wilderness Road, Lovedale, NSW 2321 **Region** Hunter Valley
T 0413 996 624 **www.**noonji.com.au **Open** W'ends & public hols 10–4
Winemaker Chateau Pato (Nick Patterson) **Est.** 2004 **Cases** 500 **Vyds** 5.5 ha
Self-described wine tragics Peter and Barbara Jensen chose to leave Sydney to pursue their dream of owning a small vineyard in an idyllic setting in the Hunter Valley. In 2004 they found a block of 40-year-old vines and began the long task of completely rejuvenating the vineyard, securing the services of Nick Patterson as contract winemaker. The 2.5 ha of chardonnay included in the plantings are among the oldest in the Hunter Valley.

ＹＹＹＹＹ
✪
Old Vine Hunter Valley Semillon 2006 Pale, bright straw-green; deliciously intense semillon just starting to unfurl its wings, citrus, grass and herbs starting to show green shoots. Screwcap. 10.8% alc. **Rating** 94 **To** 2021 $15
Reserve Hunter Valley Shiraz 2007 Good colour; the bouquet is distinctly regional, with warm earth and leather overtones that have nothing to do with brett or sulphide issues; the medium-bodied palate is well balanced and structured, the dark fruits supported by fine tannins. Screwcap. 13.6% alc. **Rating** 94 **To** 2022 $25

ＹＹＹＹＹ
✪
Old Vine Hunter Valley Semillon 2008 Pale straw; classic tight minerally semillon, the acidity cleansing and, until the fruit starts to develop, dominant. There are no fears for the future of the wine, particularly having tasted the '06. Screwcap. 10% alc. **Rating** 93 **To** 2020 $15

✪
Isabella Botrytis Semillon 2006 Glowing green-gold, spectacular; of spatlese sweetness, and in a weird way, half reminiscent of an older Rheingau spatlese; has a firm, fresh finish. Screwcap. 11.4% alc. **Rating** 91 **To** 2013 $15

✪
Old Vine Hunter Valley Chardonnay 2007 In the Noonji chardonnay style, punching well above its 12.4% alcohol weight; white and yellow peach fruit offset by spritely acidity. Screwcap. 12.4% alc. **Rating** 90 **To** 2012 $18

ＹＹＹＹ
Old Vine Hunter Valley Chardonnay 2008 Rating 89 **To** 2012 $18

Norfolk Rise Vineyard ★★★

Limestone Coast Road, Mount Benson, SA 5265 **Region** Mount Benson
T (08) 8768 5080 **F** (08) 8768 5083 **www.**kreglingerwineestates.com **Open** Not
Winemaker Daniel Berrigan **Est.** 2000 **Cases** 85 000 **Vyds** 130.3 ha
This is by far the largest and most important development in the Mount Benson region. It is ultimately owned by a privately held Belgian company, G & C Kreglinger, established in 1797. In early 2002 Kreglinger acquired Pipers Brook Vineyard; it will maintain the separate brands of the two ventures. The Mount Benson development commenced in 2000, with a large vineyard and a 2000-tonne winery, primarily aimed at the export market. It has to be said that the large investment in the winery and vineyards has not been supported by the quality of the wines so far made. Exports to the UK, the US and other major markets.

ＹＹＹＹ
Dai Gum San Limestone Coast Shiraz 2006 Relatively light colour showing some development; a light- to medium-bodied palate, distinctly spicy/savoury, with fine tannins. Seems older than it is, but not on the downhill run. Screwcap. 14.5% alc. **Rating** 88 **To** 2014 $15

✪
Mount Benson Merlot 2007 Light colour; has clear varietal expression with cassis/red fruits offset by fresh acidity; good balance and length to a light-bodied wine. Screwcap. 14% alc. **Rating** 88 **To** 2012 $16

Norton Estate ★★★★

758 Plush Hannans Road, Lower Norton, Vic 3401 **Region** Western Victoria Zone
T (03) 5384 8235 **F** (03) 5384 8235 **www.**nortonestate.com.au **Open** Wed–Sun 10–5
Winemaker Best's Wines **Est.** 1997 **Cases** 1300 **Vyds** 4.32 ha
In 1996 the Spence family purchased a run-down farm at Lower Norton and, rather than farming the traditional wool, meat and wheat, trusted their instincts and planted vines on the elevated, frost-free, buckshot rises. The surprising vigour of the initial planting of shiraz prompted further plantings of shiraz, cabernet sauvignon and sauvignon blanc. The vineyard is halfway between the Grampians and Mt Arapiles, 6 km northwest of the Grampians GI and will have to be content with the Western Victoria Zone, but the wines show regional Grampians character and style. A traditional Wimmera ripple-iron barn has been converted into a cellar door.

ＹＹＹＹＹ
Shiraz 2006 Like the '07, has developed (as predicted) nicely in bottle over the past year; nicely balanced light- to medium-bodied shiraz, with very good colour and attractive spicy components. Screwcap. 14% alc. **Rating** 91 **To** 2016 $22

Arapiles Run Shiraz 2007 The tannins that need to soften have duly done so in the year that has passed since first tasted; now an elegant, well-balanced, medium-bodied shiraz. Screwcap. 13.5% alc. **Rating** 90 **To** 2017 $35

ꖎꖎꖎ Cabernet Sauvignon 2006 **Rating** 89 **To** 2013 $22

Norton Summit Vineyards   ★★★☆

59 Nicholls Road, Norton Summit, SA 5136 **Region** Adelaide Hills
T (08) 8390 1986 **F** (08) 8390 1986 www.nsv.net.au **Open** By appt
Winemaker Kenn Fisher **Est.** 1998 **Cases** 500 **Vyds** 1.5 ha
Dr Kenn Fisher and partner Meredyth Taylor planted pinot noir and chardonnay in 1998. The vineyard has five blocks, each with its own mesoclimate, orientation and soil type. To add further complexity, four clones have been utilised. With additional vine age, the use of new French oak has been increased to 30%. Kenn makes the wines using traditional Burgundian methods of open fermenters and a basket press.

ꖎꖎꖎꖎ Estate Adelaide Hills Pinot Noir 2007 Red-purple; a complex bouquet and palate have contrasting dark plum and savoury characters, the latter expressed on the long, lingering finish, with superfine tannins at work. Screwcap. 13.5% alc. **Rating** 92 **To** 2013 $30

ꖎꖎꖎ Adelaide Hills Chardonnay 2008 **Rating** 89 **To** 2014 $27.50

Nova Vita Wines   ★★★★★

GPO Box 1352, Adelaide, SA 5001 **Region** Adelaide Hills
T (08) 8356 0454 **F** (08) 8356 1472 www.novavitawines.com.au **Open** Not
Winemaker Peter Leske, Mark Kozned **Est.** 2005 **Cases** 14 500 **Vyds** 46 ha
Mark and Jo Kozned spent months of painstaking research before locating the property on which they have now established their vineyard. Situated 4 km outside of Gumeracha, it has gentle slopes, plenty of water and, importantly, moderately fertile soils. Here the 30-ha Woodlands Ridge Vineyard is planted (in descending order of size) to chardonnay, sauvignon blanc, pinot gris and shiraz. They have subsequently established the Tunnel Hill Vineyard near Forreston, with 16 ha planted to pinot noir, shiraz, cabernet sauvignon, sauvignon blanc, semillon, verdelho, merlot and sangiovese. The name Nova Vita reflects the beginning of the Kozneds' new life, the firebird on the label coming from their Russian ancestry. It is a Russian myth that only a happy or lucky person may see the bird or hear its song. The increased vineyard resources have led to the Mad Russian range, exclusive to Cellarmasters in Australia, but also exported. Exports to the US and Singapore.

ꖎꖎꖎꖎꖎ Firebird Adelaide Hills Chardonnay 2009 Has the complexity and structure
✪   the Mad Russian lacks; a mix of wild and inoculated ferments of batches of wine from different vineyards all add to the package; retains good balance. Screwcap. 13.5% alc. **Rating** 94 **To** 2015 $25
          Barrel Selection Chardonnay 2009 Light, bright green-straw; has an intense, perfectly poised palate with grapefruit and white peach the major contributors, French oak certainly there but in restraint. Screwcap. 13% alc. **Rating** 94 **To** 2015 $40
✪   Firebird Adelaide Hills Pinot Gris 2009 It's not often a pinot gris stops you in your tracks; this not only has plenty of varietal fruit, but has great texture from barrel fermentation and lees maturation in (old) oak; a brilliant piece of winemaking. Screwcap. 13.5% alc. **Rating** 94 **To** 2011 $25
✪   Mad Russian Adelaide Hills Shiraz 2009 Light, bright crimson; a fragrant and juicy wine, with a rainbow of red and black fruit aromas offset by spice, licorice and fine tannins on the medium-bodied palate. Best fresh. Screwcap. 14.5% alc. **Rating** 94 **To** 2015 $26
✪   Firebird Adelaide Hills Shiraz 2008 Bright red-purple; a fragrant red cherry, blackberry and spice bouquet, then a complex palate with strong berry fruit and spice flavours backed up by equally powerful tannins, French oak in the background. Screwcap. 14.5% alc. **Rating** 94 **To** 2020 $25

ŸŸŸŸŸ Mad Russian Adelaide Hills Chardonnay 2009 Rating 92 To 2013 $23
Firebird Adelaide Hills Pinot Noir 2008 Rating 92 To 2014 $25
Mad Russian Adelaide Hills Shiraz 2008 Rating 92 To 2020 $26
Mad Russian Adelaide Hills Sauvignon Blanc 2009 Rating 91 To 2011 $24
Mad Russian Adelaide Hills Cabernet Merlot 2009 Rating 90 To 2014 $26
Mad Russian Adelaide Hills Cabernet Merlot 2008 Rating 90 To 2013 $26

ŸŸŸŸ Firebird Adelaide Hills Sauvignon Blanc 2009 Rating 89 To 2011 $20
Mad Russian Adelaide Hills Pinot Noir 2009 Rating 89 To 2016 $26
Firebird Cuvee NV Rating 89 To 2013 $25
Mad Russian Adelaide Hills Pinot Grigio 2009 Rating 88 To 2011 $23
Firebird Adelaide Hills Rose 2009 Rating 88 To 2010 $20

Nugan Estate ★★★★★

60 Banna Avenue, Griffith, NSW 2680 **Region** Riverina
T (02) 6962 1822 **F** (02) 6962 6392 **www**.nuganestate.com.au **Open** Mon–Fri 9–5
Winemaker Darren Owers **Est.** 1999 **Cases** 400 000 **Vyds** 590 ha
Nugan Estate arrived on the scene like a whirlwind. It is an offshoot of the Nugan Group
headed by Michelle Nugan, inter alia the recipient of an Export Hero Award in 2000. In
the mid-1990s the company began developing vineyards, and is now a veritable giant, with
310 ha at Darlington Point, 52 ha at Hanwood and 120 ha at Hillston (all in NSW), 88 ha
in the King Valley and 11 ha in McLaren Vale. In addition, it has contracts in place to buy
1000 tonnes of grapes per year from Coonawarra. It sells part of the production as grapes,
part as bulk wine and part under the Cookoothama and Nugan Estate labels. Both brands are
having considerable success in wine shows, large and small. Today the wine business is in the
energetic hands of Matthew and Tiffany Nugan, Michelle's children. Exports to the UK, the
US and other major markets.

ŸŸŸŸŸ Alcira Vineyard Coonawarra Cabernet Sauvignon 2006 Bright colour;
✪ attractive cedar and spice in part derived from 30 months in new and second-use
French oak; there are very attractive cassis notes throughout; the palate has good
drive and a long finish; the tannins are very fine. Screwcap. 14% alc. Rating 94
To 2021 $22.95
Cookoothama Darlington Point Botrytis Semillon 2007 Full gold colour;
intensely rich and luscious, with peach, cumquat and vanilla flavours; has sufficient
acidity. Screwcap. 11.5% alc. Rating 94 To 2014 $21

ŸŸŸŸŸ Cookoothama King Valley Riesling 2009 Bright colour; the bouquet is clean
✪ but somewhat closed, the lively, gently lime-juicy palate on another planet; good
length and a crisp finish. Screwcap. 12.5% alc. Rating 90 To 2015 $15
McLaren Parish Vineyard McLaren Vale Shiraz 2007 Rating 90
To 2017 $22.95
Manuka Grove Vineyard Riverina Durif 2008 Rating 90 To 2014 $22.95

ŸŸŸŸ Frasca's Lane Vineyard King Valley Chardonnay 2008 Rating 89
To 2013 $19.95
Cookoothama Darlington Point Chardonnay 2008 Rating 89
To 2012 $14.95
Cookoothama King Valley Sauvignon Blanc Semillon 2009 Rating 88
To 2011 $14.95
Frasca's Lane King Valley Pinot Grigio 2009 Rating 88 To 2011 $20
Cookoothama Darlington Point Shiraz 2008 Rating 88 To 2013 $14.95
Frasca's Lane Vineyard King Valley Sauvignon Blanc 2009 Rating 87
To 2010 $20
Cookoothama King Valley Sauvignon Blanc Semillon 2009 Rating 87
To 2010 $14.95
Talinga Park Chardonnay 2009 Rating 87 To 2011 $10
Cookoothama Darlington Point Cabernet Merlot 2007 Rating 87
To 2013 $14.95

Nuggetty Vineyard   ★★★

280 Maldon-Shelbourne Road, Nuggetty, Vic 3463 **Region** Bendigo
T (03) 5475 1347 **F** (03) 5475 1647 **www.**nuggettyvineyard.com.au **Open** W'ends &
public hols (10–5 winter, 10–6 summer), or by appt
Winemaker Greg Dedman **Est.** 1993 **Cases** 2000 **Vyds** 6 ha
This family-owned business is managed by Greg Dedman and daughter Meisha; Greg has
a formidable array of degrees: biology, aquatic biology, CSU oenology, and finally business
administration from Deakin University. He has 25 vintages under his belt, spreading from
Jaboulet in the Rhône Valley to Seppelt Great Western, Lindemans Karadoc and Best's,
before joining Blue Pyrenees in 1997. Apart from Nuggetty Vineyard, his principal present
occupation is that of senior winemaker at Bendigo Institute of TAFE. Exports to the UK
and China.

ŸŸŸŸ   **Barrel Fermented Semillon 2009** Ripe lemon and toast bouquet; loose-knit
       texture, but has good overall flavour. Screwcap. 12.5% alc. **Rating** 87 **To** 2014
       $18 BE

O'Leary Walker Wines   ★★★★★

Main Road, Leasingham, SA 5452 (PO Box 49, Watervale, SA 5452) **Region** Clare Valley
T (08) 8843 0022 **F** (08) 8843 0156 **www.**olearywalkerwines.com **Open** Mon–Fri 10–7,
w'ends by appt
Winemaker David O'Leary, Nick Walker **Est.** 2001 **Cases** 18 000 **Vyds** 35 ha
David O'Leary and Nick Walker together had more than 30 years' experience as winemakers
working for some of the biggest Australian wine groups when they took the plunge in 2001
and backed themselves to establish their own winery and brand. Initially the principal focus
was on the Clare Valley, with 10 ha of riesling, shiraz, cabernet sauvignon and semillon the
main plantings; thereafter attention swung to the Adelaide Hills, where they now have 25 ha
of chardonnay, cabernet sauvignon, pinot noir, shiraz, sauvignon blanc and merlot. Exports to
the UK, Ireland and Singapore.

ŸŸŸŸŸ **Drs' Cut Polish Hill River Riesling 2008** Made from 35-year-old vines, and
       effortlessly establishes itself on the palate. It has an extra dimension of lime and
       spice flavour that persists through the finish and into the satisfyingly dry aftertaste.
       Screwcap. 12% alc. **Rating** 96 **To** 2023 $35
       Claire Reserve Shiraz 2006 Retains good hue, still holding red-purple;
       produced from low-yielding, dry-grown, 100-year-old vines, it combines the
       concentration of juicy black fruits with great balance, line and length, the tannins
       and oak immaculately balanced. Screwcap. 14.5% alc. **Rating** 96 **To** 2031 $90
   ✪   **Clare Valley McLaren Vale Shiraz 2008** Dark crimson-purple; the bouquet
       immediately signals the synergy of the blend, a message reinforced by the
       medium- to full-bodied palate; the black fruits and a touch of licorice inhabit
       the mid-palate, before a delicious juicy and spicy twist on the finish. Screwcap.
       14.5% alc. **Rating** 95 **To** 2023 $23
   ✪   **Polish Hill River Riesling 2009** Dyed in the wool Polish Hill River style, with
       slate and mineral nuances woven through the lime and apple blossom fruit, the
       finish authoritative and long. Screwcap. 12% alc. **Rating** 94 **To** 2017 $18.50
   ✪   **Adelaide Hills Chardonnay 2008** Bright green-yellow; the suave bouquet
       balances complexity and finesse, the palate likewise; the flavours are layered,
       stone fruit foremost, but with a background of barrel ferment oak, lees and mlf
       components. Screwcap. 13.5% alc. **Rating** 94 **To** 2015 $23
   ✪   **Clare Valley Cabernet Sauvignon 2008** Dense colour; plush dark berry fruits
       and a decent slash of dark chocolate borrowed from McLaren Vale fill the palate;
       the tannins are soft, adding to the drinkability and excellent balance of the wine.
       Gold medal Sydney Wine Show '10. Screwcap. 14.5% alc. **Rating** 94 **To** 2018 $24

ΨΨΨΨ♀ **Adelaide Hills Sauvignon Blanc 2009** The bouquet takes a second or two
✪   to start sending its message of citrus, apple and passionfruit, the crisp, lively
       and intense palate setting the saliva glands to work through to the long finish.
       Screwcap. 11.5% alc. **Rating** 93 **To** 2011 $18.50
       Watervale Riesling 2009 Rating 90 **To** 2016 $17.50

ΨΨΨΨ **Blue Cutting Road Clare Valley Adelaide Hills Semillon Sauvignon Blanc
       2009 Rating** 88 **To** 2012 $15

Oakdene Vineyards   ★★★★★
255 Grubb Road, Wallington, Vic 3221 **Region** Geelong
T (03) 5256 3886 **F** (03) 5256 3881 **www.**oakdene.com.au **Open** Sun–Tues 12–5,
Wed–Sat 12–late
Winemaker Ray Nadeson, Robin Brockett **Est.** 2001 **Cases** 1500 **Vyds** 10.4 ha
Bernard and Elizabeth Hooley purchased Oakdene in 2001. Bernard focused on planting the
vineyard (shiraz, pinot gris, sauvignon blanc, pinot noir, chardonnay, merlot, cabernet franc and
cabernet sauvignon), while Elizabeth worked to restore the 1920s homestead. Ray Nadeson
makes Chardonnay, Pinot Noir and Shiraz; Robin Brockett makes the Sauvignon Blanc.
Much of the wine is sold through the award-winning Oakdene Restaurant and cellar door.

ΨΨΨΨ **Shiraz 2008** Good crimson hue; bright, lively, spicy overtones to plum fruit; the
       medium-bodied palate has lovely supple texture, the tannins fine, the finish juicy.
       Screwcap. 13.5% alc. **Rating** 94 **To** 2020 $28
       Shiraz 2007 Good hue, although not deep; an elegant, light- to medium-bodied
       shiraz with clear, cool-grown spice and pepper lifting the savoury finish. Gold
       medals Victoria and Melbourne wine shows. Screwcap. 14.5% alc. **Rating** 94
       To 2016 $28

ΨΨΨΨ♀ **Yvette Pinot Noir Chardonnay Brut 2006 Rating** 91 **To** 2013 $35

ΨΨΨΨ **Jessica Single Vineyard Bellarine Peninsula Sauvignon 2009 Rating** 89
       To 2011 $28
       Pinot Noir 2008 Rating 89 **To** 2013 $32

Oakover Wines   ★★★
14 Yukich Close, Middle Swan, WA 6056 **Region** Swan Valley
T (08) 9374 8000 **F** (08) 9250 7544 **www.**oakoverwines.com.au **Open** 7 days 11–4
Winemaker Rob Marshall **Est.** 1990 **Cases** 50 000 **Vyds** 100 ha
Oakover Wines is a family-operated winery located in the Swan Valley. Formerly part of
Houghton, in 1990 it came under the Yukich family's control as Oakover Estate. Prominent
Perth funds manager Graeme Yukich and his family have been involved in the region since
Nicholas Yukich purchased his first block of land in 1929. In 2002 Oakover Estate became
Oakover Wines and Rob Marshall joined the team as chief winemaker and general manager,
overseeing the construction of a new winery and managing the extensive vineyard operations
on the property. Today, Oakover is the third-largest winery in the Swan Valley. Oakover's
White Label brand is currently sold in over 500 independent liquor outlets in WA and Vic,
with expansion into NSW and Qld planned. Exports to China, Indonesia, Malaysia and
Singapore.

ΨΨΨΨ **White Label Margaret River Cabernet Merlot 2008** A light-bodied,
✪   juicy red-fruited wine, well made and very well priced; does lack depth and
       concentration, hardly surprising given its price. Drink now. Screwcap. 13.2% alc.
       Rating 88 **To** 2012 $12
✪   **White Label Swan Valley Sauvignon Blanc Semillon 2009** A wine that
       shows both sides of early picking: fresh and crisp, but not overmuch varietal fruit.
       Screwcap. 10.8% alc. **Rating** 87 **To** 2010 $12

Oakridge   ★★★★★

864 Maroondah Highway, Coldstream, Vic 3770 **Region** Yarra Valley
T (03) 9738 9900 **F** (03) 9739 1923 **www.**oakridgewines.com.au **Open** 7 days 10–5
Winemaker David Bicknell **Est.** 1978 **Cases** 15 000 **Vyds** 8.9 ha
The long, dark shadow of Evans & Tate's ownership is now totally dispelled. Life is never easy,
but winemaker (and now CEO) David Bicknell has proved his worth time and again as an
extremely talented winemaker. At the top of the brand tier is 864, all Yarra Valley vineyard
selections, and only released in the best years (Chardonnay, Shiraz, Cabernet Sauvignon,
Riesling); next is the Oakridge core label (the Chardonnay, Pinot Noir and Sauvignon Blanc
come from the cooler Upper Yarra Valley; the Shiraz, Cabernet Sauvignon and Viognier from
the Lower Yarra); and the Over the Shoulder range, drawn from all of the sources available to
Oakridge (Sauvignon Blanc, Pinot Grigio, Pinot Noir, Shiraz Viognier, Cabernet Sauvignon).
Exports to the UK, Papua New Guinea, Indonesia, Singapore, Hong Kong and NZ.

🍷🍷🍷🍷🍷 **864 Van der Meulen Vineyard Chardonnay 2009** The Van der Meulen
Vineyard is near Seville on the red soil of the Upper Yarra, and is dry-grown,
cropping at 5 tonnes per ha; David Bicknell seeks to push the envelope to
extremes with 864, but the intensity of the fruit – particularly on the finish –
overrides the pushing; very likely, Bicknell is pleased with the outcome. Screwcap.
13% alc. **Rating** 96 **To** 2019 $60
864 Yarra Valley Syrah 2008 A typically elegant example of the 864 icon
series; healthy colour, a complex and spicy bouquet, then a medium-bodied palate
that has fine tannins throughout, giving good texture, the flavours of spiced plum
and blackberry with a juicy farewell on the finish. Screwcap. 14% alc. **Rating** 96
To 2020 $60
Limited Release Yarra Valley Fume 2009 A blend of Sauvignon Blanc
(80%)/Semillon (20%) whole bunch pressed, the juice taken directly to old oak
puncheons for fermentation; an alternative approach that succeeds brilliantly, the
tangy and fresh flavours running right through the very long palate. Will age well.
Screwcap. 11.5% alc. **Rating** 95 **To** 2016 $32
Lieu-dit The Other Vineyard Chardonnay 2009 Bright straw-green; the
bouquet is less obviously complex than the Mackay Vineyard, and the palate
initially seems smooth and rounded before it literally takes off on the long, super-
intense finish; oak plays a minimal role in the flavours of the wine. Screwcap.
12.5% alc. **Rating** 95 **To** 2017 $40
Yarra Valley Chardonnay 2009 A pure expression of Yarra Valley chardonnay,
whole bunch pressed and taken directly to puncheons for wild yeast fermentation;
white peach and grapefruit zest, together with a strong minerally streak, drive the
bouquet and palate alike. Screwcap. 13% alc. **Rating** 95 **To** 2018 $32
864 Yarra Valley Cabernet Sauvignon 2006 Good crimson hue; blackcurrant
and cedar aromas lead into a medium-bodied, long and refined palate, the flavours
subtle yet multidimensional, ranging through black fruits to earth and spices.
Screwcap. 13% alc. **Rating** 95 **To** 2021 $60
Lieu-dit Mackay Vineyard Chardonnay 2009 The vineyard is at Hesketh,
near Mt Macedon, cropping at 4 tonnes per ha; a fine, yet complex bouquet,
with some affinities with Burgundy, or perhaps Chablis; has great thrust and drive,
mineral and lemon pouring through on the finish. Screwcap. 13.5% alc. **Rating** 94
To 2017 $40
Yarra Valley Pinot Noir 2009 Good colour; a complex pinot, both in terms
of flavour and texture, the tannins of exemplary quality; dark berry fruits are
the drivers, coupled with touches of forest floor. Quo Vadis? Screwcap. 13% alc.
Rating 94 **To** 2016 $32
Yarra Valley Cabernet Sauvignon 2008 Crimson hue; a fragrant, perfumed
bouquet of red and blackcurrant fruit, spice and cedar leads into a finely tuned
and structured palate, the finish sustained by fine tannins and cedary oak. Screwcap.
13.5% alc. **Rating** 94 **To** 2015 $32

Limited Release Yarra Valley Viognier 2009 Whole bunches picked from two local vineyards were frozen to -10°C and pressed at that temperature; lovely peach and apricot flavours with excellent acidity. Screwcap. 11% alc. Rating 94 To 2013 $40

ΨΨΨΨΨ 864 Yarra Valley Pinot Noir 2008 Rating 93 To 2015 $60
Limited Release Yarra Valley Blanc de Blancs 2006 Rating 92 To 2012 $40
✪ Over the Shoulder Chardonnay 2009 Bright crystal green; strong citrussy elements reflect its early picking; the long and tangy palate is almost certainly unoaked; for sauvignon blanc lovers. Screwcap. 12.5% alc. Rating 90 To 2014 $20
✪ Over the Shoulder Pinot Grigio 2009 Spicy, crunchy, grainy acidity underlies the primary pear fruit flavours; the finish is long and crisp, the acidity cleansing, not scarifying. Screwcap. 12.5% alc. Rating 90 To 2011 $20

ΨΨΨΨ Over the Shoulder Pinot Noir 2009 Rating 89 To 2014 $20

Oakvale ★★★★★

1596 Broke Road, Pokolbin, NSW 2320 Region Hunter Valley
T (02) 4998 7088 F (02) 4998 7077 www.oakvalewines.com.au Open 7 days 10–5
Winemaker Steve Hagan Est. 1893 Cases 12 000 Vyds 13.9 ha
For three-quarters of a century Oakvale was in the ownership of the founding Elliot family, whose original slab hut homestead is now a museum. In 2010 it was purchased by the Becker family, experienced grapegrowers and owners of the famed Steven's Vineyard. One of the 'must see' destinations in the Hunter. Exports to the US, Mexico and Japan.

ΨΨΨΨΨ Limited Release Rack Dried Shiraz 2006 Heavily and unusually stained Diam rings a warning bell; to this point, however, the wine has not suffered, the medium-bodied palate with great length and texture, perfect tannins bolstering the finish. 14.5% alc. Rating 95 To 2021 $65
Reserve Block 37 Verdelho 2009 Bright, quite deep, green-yellow; has exceptional depth of flavour for this variety, without departing from its core varietal expression of tropical fruit salad; is not phenolic but has the weight of a mature chardonnay. Screwcap. 12.5% alc. Rating 94 To 2013 $22.50

ΨΨΨΨΨ Reserve Peach Tree Chardonnay 2009 Rating 91 To 2015 $27
ΨΨΨΨ Barrel Select Reserve Shiraz 2006 Rating 89 To 2015 $45

Oakway Estate ★★★☆

575 Farley Road, Donnybrook, WA 6239 Region Geographe
T (08) 9731 7141 F (08) 9731 7190 www.oakwayestate.com.au Open By appt
Winemaker Stuart Pierce Est. 1998 Cases 1500 Vyds 2 ha
Ria and Wayne Hammond run a vineyard, beef cattle and sustainable blue gum plantation in undulating country on the Capel River in the southwest of WA. The grapes are grown on light gravel and loam soils that provide good drainage, situated high above the river, giving even sun exposure to the fruit and minimising the effects of frost. Varieties include shiraz, merlot, cabernet sauvignon and chardonnay, and have won a number of medals at wine shows. A cellar door is planned for 2010.

ΨΨΨΨΨ Sauvignon Blanc Semillon 2009 Pale quartz; a gently floral-scented bouquet
✪ leads into a fresh, well-balanced palate with a mix of citrus and tropical fruits; on much surer ground with its white wines than its reds. Screwcap. 12.5% alc. Rating 90 To 2012 $16

ΨΨΨΨ Unwooded Chardonnay 2009 Rating 89 To 2012 $16

Observatory Hill Vineyard   ★★★★

107 Centauri Drive, Mt Rumney, Tas 7170 **Region** Southern Tasmania
T (03) 6248 5380 **Open** By appt
Winemaker Frogmore Creek **Est.** 1991 **Cases** 1000 **Vyds** 3.1 ha
Glenn and Chris Richardson's Observatory Hill Vineyard has been developing since 1991,
when Glenn and his late father-in-law Jim Ramsey planted the first of the 8500 vines that
now make up the estate. Together with the adjoining property owned by Chris' brother Wayne
and his wife Stephanie, the vineyard now covers just over 3 ha, new plantings having been
made each year. The name 'Observatory Hill' comes from the state's oldest observatory, which
is perched on the hill above the vineyard.

♀♀♀♀♀ **Pinot Noir 2008** Good colour; complex aromas and flavours; a medium-bodied
wine with clever use of oak; some forest floor notes add complexity; good
development potential. Silver medal Tas Wine Show '10. Screwcap. 13.8% alc.
Rating 91 **To** 2015 $29
Chardonnay 2008 Glowing green-gold; complex bouquet with some barrel
ferment inputs; firm and precise palate; good length but not so complex as the
bouquet. Screwcap. 13.7% alc. **Rating** 90 **To** 2013 $26

♀♀♀♀ **Cabernet Sauvignon Merlot 2008 Rating** 88 **To** 2016 $29

Occam's Razor   ★★★☆

c/- Jasper Hill, Drummonds Lane, Heathcote, Vic 3523 **Region** Heathcote
T (03) 5433 2528 **F** (03) 5433 3143 **Open** By appt
Winemaker Emily Laughton **Est.** 2001 **Cases** 300 **Vyds** 2.5 ha
Emily Laughton has decided to follow in her parents' footsteps after first seeing the world
and having a range of casual jobs. Having grown up at Jasper Hill, winemaking was far from
strange, but she decided to find her own way, buying the grapes from a small vineyard owned
by Jasper Hill employee Andrew Conforti and his wife Melissa. She then made the wine
'with guidance and inspiration from my father'. The name comes from William of Ockham
(1285–1349), also spelt Occam, a theologian and philosopher responsible for many sayings,
including that appearing on the back label of the wine: 'what can be done with fewer is done
in vain with more'. Exports to the UK, the US, Canada and NZ.

♀♀♀♀ **Heathcote Shiraz 2008** Good hue; a very powerful wine in every respect;
abundant black fruits and some alcohol impact, then strong, drying tannins;
hopefully, but not certainly, these will soften before the fruit fades. Cork. 15.5% alc.
Rating 89 **To** 2020 $42

Ocean Eight Vineyard & Winery   ★★★★★

271 Tucks Road, Shoreham, Vic 3916 **Region** Mornington Peninsula
T (03) 5989 6471 **F** (03) 5989 6630 **www**.oceaneight.com **Open** 1st w'end each month
Winemaker Michael Aylward **Est.** 2003 **Cases** 4000 **Vyds** 16 ha
Chris, Gail and Michael Aylward were involved in the establishment of Kooyong vineyard and
winery, and after selling Kooyong in 2003, retained their 6-ha pinot gris vineyard at Shoreham.
After careful investigation, they purchased another property, where they have now planted
7 ha of pinot noir and 3 ha of chardonnay. A small winery has been set up, and the focus will
always be on estate-grown grapes. Exports to Canada and Hong Kong.

♀♀♀♀♀ **Aylward Pinot Noir 2007** Excellent hue; crammed with ripe, spicy cherry fruit
on the bouquet and palate, with a neat counterplay of a touch of forest floor; the
length and balance are impeccable. Distinguished wine. Diam. 13% alc. **Rating** 96
To 2018 $73.50
Mornington Peninsula Pinot Noir 2008 Clear red-crimson; the bouquet is
fragrant and slightly spicy, the palate with a savoury/minerally/stemmy coat around
its core of plum and black cherry fruit; good drive and length. Diam. 13% alc.
Rating 94 **To** 2015 $40

ΨΨΨΨ⍨ Mornington Peninsula Pinot Gris 2008 Rating 92 To 2011 $28
Verve Mornington Peninsula Chardonnay 2008 Rating 91 To 2014 $35

Oceans Estate   ★★★★

Courtney Road, Karridale, WA 6288 (postal) **Region** Margaret River
T (08) 9758 2240 **F** (08) 9758 2240 **www**.oceansestate.com.au **Open** Not
Winemaker Frank Kittler **Est.** 1999 **Cases** 6000 **Vyds** 21 ha
Oceans Estate was purchased by the Tomasi family (headed by Frank and Attilia Tomasi) in
1995, and, between '99 and 2007, chardonnay, sauvignon blanc, semillon, pinot noir, merlot
and cabernet sauvignon were planted. Since 2006 the wines have been made at the onsite
winery, adequate to handle the 180 to 220 tonnes of grapes that will come once the vineyards
are in full bearing.

ΨΨΨΨ⍨ **Margaret River Sauvignon Blanc Semillon 2009** Curiously, more fragrant
than the Sauvignon Blanc, and likewise with flavours extending into the tropical
spectrum; slightly riper fruit has to be the answer, and most certainly worth the
extra dollar. Screwcap. 13% alc. **Rating** 90 **To** 2011 $15

Nouveau Margaret River Pinot Noir 2008 Bright pale colour; while light in
body, has more (true) varietal character than many other Margaret River pinots,
reflecting its extreme southern end of the region; has spicy red fruits and foresty
notes. Screwcap. 12.9% alc. **Rating** 90 **To** 2013 $15

ΨΨΨΨ **Margaret River Sauvignon Blanc 2009** Does not need any winemaker
embellishments to convey its pure citrus and gooseberry flavours that run
through the bouquet and long palate, the finish juicy but dry. Screwcap. 12.5% alc.
Rating 89 **To** 2011 $14
Pemberton Vineyard Chardonnay 2008 Rating 89 To 2012 $21
Tomasi Vineyard Margaret River Merlot 2007 Rating 88 To 2014 $30

Oddfellows Wines   ★★★★

PO Box 88, Langhorne Creek, SA 5255 **Region** Langhorne Creek
T (08) 8537 3326 **F** (08) 8537 3319 **www**.oddfellowswines.com.au **Open** Not
Winemaker David Knight **Est.** 1997 **Cases** 6000 **Vyds** 41.6 ha
Oddfellows is the name taken by a group of five individuals who decided to put their
expertise, energy and investments into making premium wine. Langhorne Creek vignerons
David and Cathy Knight were two of the original members, and in 2007 took over ownership
and running of the venture. David worked with Greg Follett from Lake Breeze to produce
the wines, gradually taking over more responsibility, and is now both winemaker and
viticulturist for the estate's vineyard. This vineyard also produces the Winners Tank label (in
conjunction with Reid Bosward of Kaesler Wines in the Barossa); the first two vintages were
made for export only (Canada), with limited domestic distribution of the '06 vintage. Since
then, production has trebled. Exports to the UK, Canada, Singapore, Indonesia, Hong Kong
and China.

ΨΨΨΨ⍨ **Langhorne Creek Shiraz 2007** Vibrant hue; blackberry coulis and fruitcake are
the prominent theme, with a dose of new oak; the palate is quite chewy and dense,
and delivers an abundance of ripe and fresh black fruits, oak taking the front seat
to conclude. Screwcap. 14.8% alc. **Rating** 93 **To** 2020 $25 BE

🍇 Oenotria Vintners   ★★★★☆

82 Ridge Street, Northgate, Qld 4013 (postal) **Region** Yarra Valley/McLaren Vale
T 0409 570 694 **F** (07) 3266 8552 **Open** Not
Winemaker Paul Evans, Redheads Studio, Kurt Brill **Est.** 2008 **Cases** 200
This is the venture of Kurt Brill, who began his involvement in the wine industry having just
turned 30 (in 2003), largely through the encouragement of his wife Gillian. He commenced
the wine marketing course at the University of Adelaide, but ultimately switched from that to
the winemaking degree at CSU. His main business is the distribution company Grace James
Fine Wines, but he also runs a virtual winery operation, purchasing Yarra Valley chardonnay

(made by contract winemaker Paul Evans) and cabernet sauvignon (made at Redheads Studio under the eyes of Adam Hooper and Peter Kennedy). Needless to say, he participates as far as possible in the winemaking process. The Oenotria Vintners name comes from a Dorian word meaning 'land of the trained vines'; the Dorians migrated from northern Greece to Taranto in southern Italy in the 11th century, and Kurt believes that many of the techniques used today in viticulture are derived from the practices of the Dorians.

♟♟♟♟♟ **Land of the Vines Yarra Valley Chardonnay 2008** Bright straw-green; a faint touch of Burgundian funk on the bouquet gives way to a nectarine and citrus palate that has great thrust and length. Impressive. Screwcap. 13.5% alc. **Rating** 94 To 2016 $21

♟♟♟♟ **Land of the Vines McLaren Vale Cabernet Sauvignon 2008** Rating 88 To 2012 $23

Old Kent River   ★★★★

1114 Turpin Road, Rocky Gully, WA 6397 **Region** Frankland River
T (08) 9855 1589 **F** (08) 9855 1660 **www**.oldkentriver.com.au
Open At Kent River, Denmark
Winemaker Alkoomi (Contract), Michael Staniford **Est.** 1985 **Cases** 3000 **Vyds** 17 ha
Mark and Debbie Noack have earned much respect from their neighbours and from the other producers to whom they sell more than half the production from the vineyard on their sheep property. The quality of their wines has gone from strength to strength, Mark having worked particularly hard with his Pinot Noir. The Noacks have added a 2-ha vineyard at Denmark to their much older 15-ha vineyard at Rocky Gully. Exports to the UK, the US, Hong Kong, Malaysia and Singapore.

♟♟♟♟♀ **Backtrack Frankland River Pinot Noir 2008** Quite developed colour, fractionally hazy; the wine has distinct foresty/savoury notes, but a core of red cherry and strawberry fruit gives balance. Overall, no question about its varietal typicity. Screwcap. 12% alc. **Rating** 90 To 2014 $17

Old Plains   ★★★★☆

6 Winser Avenue, Seaton, SA 5023 (postal) **Region** Adelaide Plains
T 0407 605 601 **F** (08) 8355 3603 **www**.oldplains.com **Open** Not
Winemaker Domenic Torzi, Tim Freeland **Est.** 2003 **Cases** 2500 **Vyds** 11 ha
Old Plains is a partnership between Tim Freeland and Domenic Torzi, who have located and acquired small parcels of old vine shiraz (8 ha), grenache (2 ha) and cabernet sauvignon (1 ha) in the Adelaide Plains region. A portion of the wines, sold under the Old Plains, Longhop and Raw Power labels, are exported to the US, Denmark, Hong Kong, Singapore and China.

♟♟♟♟♟ **Longhop Mount Lofty Ranges Shiraz 2008** The bouquet is bursting with
✪   spice, hay, licorice and dark chocolate over the core of black fruits, taking on a more savoury character on the palate, black fruits again to the fore. Exceptional value. Screwcap. 14.5% alc. **Rating** 94 To 2016 $15

Olivers Taranga Vineyards   ★★★★

Seaview Road, McLaren Vale, SA 5171 **Region** McLaren Vale
T (08) 8323 8498 **F** (08) 8323 7498 **www**.oliverstaranga.com **Open** 7 days 10–4
Winemaker Corrina Wright **Est.** 1841 **Cases** 6000 **Vyds** 85.42 ha
William and Elizabeth Oliver arrived from Scotland in 1839 to settle at McLaren Vale. Six generations later, members of the family are still living on the Whitehill and Taranga farms. The Taranga property has 15 grape varieties planted (the lion's share to shiraz and cabernet sauvignon, with lesser quantities of chardonnay, chenin blanc, durif, fiano, grenache, mataro, merlot, petit verdot, sagrantino, semillon, tempranillo, viognier and white frontignac); grapes from the property have been sold, but since 1994 a portion has been made under the Olivers Taranga label. Since 2000 the wine has been made by Corrina Wright (the Oliver family's

first winemaker and a sixth-generation family member). No red wines were submitted for this edition. Exports to the US, Canada, Belgium, Singapore and Thailand.

ŸŸŸŸŸ **Small Batch McLaren Vale Fiano 2009** Has less textural baggage than the Coriole, which makes it more fragrant and lighter on its feet even though it has a little more alcohol. Here some citrus pith/zest is a definite marker, although time will tell whether this is a lasting guide. Screwcap. 13% alc. **Rating** 90 **To** 2013 $24

Olsen ★★★★

RMB 252 Osmington Road, Osmington, WA 6285 **Region** Margaret River
T (08) 9757 4536 **F** (08) 9757 4114 **www**.olsen.com.au **Open** At Margaret River Regional Wine Centre
Winemaker Jarrad Olsen **Est.** 1986 **Cases** 4000 **Vyds** 13.5 ha
Steve and Ann Marie Olsen have planted cabernet sauvignon, sauvignon blanc, chardonnay, semillon, verdelho and merlot, which they tend with the help of their four children. It was the desire to raise their children in a healthy country environment that prompted the move to establish the vineyard, coupled with a long-standing dream to make their own wine. Not to be confused with Olsen Wines in Melbourne. Exports to Canada.

ŸŸŸŸŸ **Margaret River Semillon Sauvignon Blanc 2009** Light straw-green; a
✪ vibrantly fresh and high-flavoured mix of all the tropical fruits one can imagine, and Jarrad Olsen has wisely let these aromas and flavours do the talking. Wak screwcap. 12.4% alc. **Rating** 92 **To** 2011 $19.95
✪ **Tom's Margaret River Merlot 2007** Bright hue; attractive plum and redcurrant fruit on the bouquet and palate provide the structure for the wine, oak and tannins the framework; has good length and mouthfeel. Screwcap. 14% alc. **Rating** 91 **To** 2022 $19.95
✪ **Margaret River Cabernet Sauvignon 2007** Good retention of hue; a nicely weighted and structured cabernet, with black fruits supported by fine but persistent tannins and good oak. Screwcap. 13.8% alc. **Rating** 91 **To** 2015 $19.95
Margaret River Verdelho 2009 Light straw-green; while the bouquet is not particularly expressive, the palate has abundant fruit ranging from banana to citrus, stone fruit along the way. Will develop into a full-bodied dry white. Wak screwcap. 13.5% alc. **Rating** 90 **To** 2014 $19.95

Olsen Wines Victoria ★★★☆

131 Koornang Road, Carnegie, Vic 3163 **Region** Port Phillip Zone
T (03) 9569 2188 **F** (03) 9563 5038 **www**.vin888.com **Open** Mon–Thurs 10.30–8,
Fri–Sat 10.30–9
Winemaker Glenn Olsen **Est.** 1991 **Cases** 55 000
Glenn Olsen, a science and engineering graduate of the University of Melbourne, has been involved in the wine industry since 1975, initially importing wines and spirits from Europe, then moving into retailing. In 1991, he and Angie Joso-Olsen started Olsen Wines, claiming to be Melbourne's first inner-suburban winery. Several others may dispute this claim, but that is perhaps neither here nor there. Most of the wines come either from grapes grown on the Murray River in Northeast Victoria for the full-bodied Big Fella range, or from the Yarra Valley. Exports to the US, Canada, Philippines, Korea, Singapore, Hong Kong and China.

ŸŸŸŸ **Big Fella Preservative Free Shiraz 2008** Full red-purple; a rich, full-bodied red that relies on its screwcap and abundant tannins to prevent oxidation; while robust, has good balance and sets the bar for sulphur-free red wines. 14.8% alc. **Rating** 89 **To** 2012 $24

Olssens of Watervale ★★★★☆

Sollys Hill Road, Watervale, SA 5452 **Region** Clare Valley
T (08) 8843 0065 **F** (08) 8843 0065 **Open** Thurs–Sun & public hols 11–5, or by appt
Winemaker Contract **Est.** 1994 **Cases** 3500 **Vyds** 31.6 ha

Kevin and Helen Olssen first visited the Clare Valley in 1986. Within two weeks they and their family decided to sell their Adelaide home and purchased a property in a small, isolated valley 3 km north of the township of Watervale. As a result of the acquisition of the Bass Hill Vineyard, estate plantings have risen to almost 32 ha, including unusual varieties such as carmenere and primitivo di Gioia. The Bass Hill project is a joint venture between parents Kevin and Helen and children David and Jane Olssen. Exports to the US, Sweden and Hong Kong.

ŸŸŸỴ̈ **Second Six 2007** A fragrant blend of red fruits and plenty of spice; the palate displays a sweet core of bright red fruits, with a soft and generous conclusion; a well-constructed blend. Merlot/Petit Verdot/Cabernet Sauvignon/Malbec/Carmenere/Cabernet Franc. Screwcap. 13.5% alc. **Rating** 92 $25 BE
Clare Valley Riesling 2009 Restrained bouquet of bath talc and lime; tight and linear palate with a little grip on the finish; good concentration and length. Screwcap. 12.5% alc. **Rating** 91 $20 BE

ŸŸŸŸ **Bass Hill Vineyard Shiraz 2006 Rating** 89 $30 BE

Onannon   ★★★★★
PO Box 190, Flinders, Vic 3929 **Region** Port Phillip Zone
T 0448 900 229 **Open** Not
Winemaker Sam Middleton, Kaspar Hermann, Will Byron **Est.** 2008 **Cases** 80
Onannon is the venture of Sam Middleton, Kaspar Hermann and Will Byron, who donated the last two or three letters of their surnames to come up with Onannon. They share many things in common, not the least working vintages at Coldstream Hills, Will for six years, Sam for two (before ultimately returning to the family's winery, Mount Mary) and Kaspar for one. Since then they have bounced between vintages in Burgundy and Australia, Will accumulating the most frequent flyer points. Strictly speaking, I should disqualify myself from making any comment about them or their wine, but you would have to go a long way to find three more open-hearted and utterly committed winemakers; the world is their oyster, their ambitions unlimited.

ŸŸŸŸŸ **Gippsland Pinot Noir 2009** Bright crimson-purple; a highly fragrant bouquet of red and black cherries, the palate a very pure expression of high-quality pinot noir; the whole purpose of the winemakers has been to allow the wine to express its variety and terroir. Diam. 12.5% alc. **Rating** 95 **To** 2016 $32
Mornington Pinot Noir 2009 More purple hints than Gippsland, slightly less bright; a more complex bouquet and palate, both in terms of texture/structure and flavours; savoury touches of forest and stem. Diam. 13% alc. **Rating** 94 **To** 2015 $40

145°02′23″E 37°11′16″S   ★★★★
27 Hilltop Road, Clareville, NSW 2107 (postal) **Region** Central Victoria Zone
T 0414 246 564 **Open** Not
Winemaker Steve Fitzmaurice **Est.** 2008 **Cases** 500 **Vyds** 2.02 ha
Steve Fitzmaurice was a professional yachtsman who, aged 40, had a 'typical mid-life crisis and uprooted the family from Sydney and headed to Wagga (CSU) to study oenology', an academic experience he didn't find altogether rewarding. A complicated turn of events led him to Adrian Munari's vineyard and winery in Heathcote, where he became involved in the making of the Sugarloaf Creek Shiraz from 2001, notwithstanding that Sugarloaf Creek is in fact in the Goulburn Valley, not Heathcote. He continued to learn pruning in the vineyard and winemaking in the winery, which led to his securing a three-year-plus-three-year option lease of Sugarloaf Creek, and making his 2008 Broadford Shiraz. The tasting note that follows was made before I read the life story and winemaking aims, and it would seem he has succeeded in making a wine precisely as he wished. That is a happy ending; however, one of these days he will get tired of restaurants and retailers throwing up their hands at the yachting-inspired name, which is the exact GPS position of the vineyard. No wine was made in 2009.

ΨΨΨΨΨ **Broadford Shiraz 2008** Strong colour; luscious, but not overripe or jammy, fruit in a blackberry and plum spectrum, with notes of pepper, spice and licorice; good oak integration. Still youthful and still good. Retasted '10. Screwcap. 14.5% alc. **Rating** 92 **To** 2018 $29

Optimiste   ★★★☆

PO Box 4214, Castlecrag, NSW 2068 **Region** Mudgee
T (02) 9967 3294 **F** (02) 9967 3295 **www**.optimiste.com.au **Open** Not
Winemaker Michael Slater, Barry Kooij **Est.** 1998 **Cases** 1500 **Vyds** 11 ha
Steven and Sharlene Dadd had been growing grapes for over a decade before realising a long-held dream to launch their own wines under the Optimiste label. The name is inspired by their son's struggle with deafness and a quote by Helen Keller: 'Optimism is the faith that leads to achievement. Nothing can be done without hope and confidence.' The first vines planted were cabernet sauvignon, petit verdot and merlot, with more recent plantings of viognier, semillon, tempranillo and pinot gris (chardonnay is purchased). A cellar door is planned to open in late 2010. Exports to Singapore.

ΨΨΨΨΨ **Limited Release Mudgee Semillon 2009** Light straw-green; has a very fragrant bouquet of grass, citrus and bath powder, the palate fixed around the grassy flavours; backs off a little on the finish. Screwcap. 11.3% alc. **Rating** 90 **To** 2017 $20

ΨΨΨΨ **Limited Release Mudgee Tempranillo 2009 Rating** 89 **To** 2012 $20
Mudgee Shiraz 2007 Rating 87 **To** 2014 $20

Orange Mountain Wines   ★★★★

Cnr Forbes Road/Radnedge Lane, Orange, NSW 2800 **Region** Orange
T (02) 6365 2626 **www**.orangemountain.com.au **Open** W'ends & public hols 9–5
Winemaker Terry Dolle **Est.** 1997 **Cases** 3000
Terry Dolle has a total of 5.5 ha of vineyards, part at Manildra (established 1997) and the remainder at Orange (in 2001). The Manildra climate is distinctly warmer than that of Orange, and the plantings reflect the climatic difference, with pinot noir and sauvignon blanc at Orange, shiraz, cabernet sauvignon, merlot and viognier at Manildra.

ΨΨΨΨΨ **Viognier 2009** While it has varietal character, it also has strong citrus components which lift the bouquet and palate and provide considerable length, acidity just within the bounds of comfort. Screwcap. 14% alc. **Rating** 90 **To** 2013 $22

✪ **Manildra Merlot 2006** Has retained good colour, and also clear varietal character at the savoury end of the spectrum, but with enough cassis to give overall balance. Screwcap. 14% alc. **Rating** 90 **To** 2014 $18

Mountain Ice 2009 Freeze concentration has done its work well; all the characters of Viognier/Chardonnay are intensified; sweetness and acidity well balanced. Screwcap. 11% alc. **Rating** 90 **To** 2012 $22

Mountain Ice 2008 Attractive citrussy acidity gives the wine added life and length, the sweet and luscious fruit neatly balanced. Viognier/Chardonnay. Screwcap. 10% alc. **Rating** 90 **To** 2011 $22

ΨΨΨΨ **CharVio 2008 Rating** 89 **To** 2012 $22
Pinot Noir 2006 Rating 88 **To** 2014 $25
Manildra Cabernet Sauvignon Merlot 2006 Rating 87 **To** 2015 $16

Oranje Tractor   ★★★★☆

198 Link Road, Albany, WA 6330 **Region** Albany
T (08) 9842 5175 **F** (08) 9842 5175 **www**.oranjetractor.com **Open** Fri–Sun & hols 11–5
Winemaker Rob Diletti, Mike Garland (Contract) **Est.** 1998 **Cases** 1000 **Vyds** 3 ha
The name celebrates the 1964 vintage, orange-coloured, Fiat tractor, acquired when Murray Gomm and Pamela Lincoln began the establishment of the vineyard. Murray was born next

door, but moved to Perth to work in physical education and health promotion. Here he met nutritionist Pamela, who completed the wine science degree at CSU in 2000, before being awarded a Churchill Fellowship to study organic grape and wine production in the US and Europe. When the partners established their vineyard, they went down the organic path.

ΨΨΨΨΨ Albany Riesling 2009 Bright, pale quartz-green; a wine with a proven track
✪   record of fragrant mineral, lime and passionfruit aromas and flavours; the past tells
      the future for this wine, developing wonderfully over five or more years. Screwcap.
      12% alc. Rating 94 To 2024 $19

ΨΨΨΨΨ Albany Sauvignon Blanc 2009 Rating 92 To 2011 $22.50

ΨΨΨΨ Albany Rose 2009 Rating 89 To 2011 $17.50
      Albany Merlot 2007 Rating 89 To 2014 $20.50

Orlando   ★★★★

Barossa Valley Way, Rowland Flat, SA 5352 **Region** Barossa Valley
T (08) 8521 3111 **F** (08) 8521 3100 **www**.orlandowines.com **Open** 7 days 10–5
Winemaker Bernard Hickin **Est.** 1847 **Cases** NFP **Vyds** 1600 ha
Orlando is the parent who has been divorced by its child, Jacob's Creek (see separate entry). While Orlando is 163 years old, Jacob's Creek is little more than 37 years. For what are doubtless sound marketing reasons, Orlando aided and abetted the divorce, but the average consumer is unlikely to understand the logic, and – if truth be known – care about it even less. The vineyard holding is for all brands (notably Jacob's Creek) and for all regions across SA, Vic and NSW; it will likely be less in coming years.

ΨΨΨΨΨ Gramp's Botrytis Semillon 2006 Gold-yellow; has considerable textural
✪   complexity, the honey and cumquat marmalade with an almost biscuity overlay
      coming from bottle development. Screwcap. 11.5% alc. Rating 93 To 2012 $20
✪   Trilogy Cuvee Brut NV Well put together bottle-fermented wine with a
      considerable pedigree; there are layers of flavour (including lees characters)
      achieved without coarseness; aperitif or with meal. Cork. 12.5% alc. Rating 90
      To 2010 $16.50

ΨΨΨΨ Trilogy Sparkling Rose NV Rating 89 To 2010 $16.50
      St Helga Eden Valley Riesling 2009 Rating 88 To 2015 $21
      Chardonnay Pinot Brut Cuvee NV Rating 87 To 2011 $14

Otway Estate   ★★★★

20 Hoveys Road, Barongarook, Vic 3249 **Region** Geelong
T (03) 5233 8400 **F** (03) 5233 8343 **www**.otwayestate.com.au **Open** Mon–Fri 11–4.30, w'ends 10–5
Winemaker Matthew di Sciascio **Est.** 1983 **Cases** 1800 **Vyds** 6.4 ha
The history of Otway Estate dates back to 1983 when the first vines were planted by Stuart and Eileen Walker. The current group of six family and friends have expanded the scope of the business: the vineyard is planted primarily to chardonnay (3 ha) and pinot noir (1 ha) with small patches of riesling, semillon, sauvignon blanc and gewurztraminer. Current winemaker Matthew di Sciascio (who also makes the Bellbrae/Longboard wines) believes the climate is much cooler than the norm for Geelong, closer to parts of Tasmania. Thus the future direction will focus on sparkling wines, Chardonnay, Pinot Noir and aromatic white wines.

ΨΨΨΨΨ Fortified Cabernet Sauvignon 2008 Strong colour; has attractive cabernet
✪   varietal fruit, and excellent balance, the finish elegant and dry; 375 ml. Screwcap.
      18% alc. Rating 93 To 2018 $20
      Pinot Noir 2008 Clear, bright colour; light-bodied, but has clarity of varietal
      expression in a red cherry and strawberry spectrum, the finish with good balance.
      Screwcap. 13% alc. Rating 90 To 2014 $29

ΨΨΨΨ Reserve Chardonnay 2008 Rating 88 To 2014 $32
      Chardonnay 2008 Rating 87 To 2012 $22

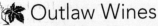 Outlaw Wines ★★★

1 Barossa Street, Nuriootpa, SA 5355 (postal) **Region** Barossa Valley
T 0407 471 772 **F** (08) 8564 2982 **www**.outlawwines.com.au **Open** Not
Winemaker Damon de Ruiter, Nigel Thiele **Est.** 2005 **Cases** 500 **Vyds** 3.2 ha
Damon de Ruiter and Nigel Thiele are winemakers at Barossa Vintners; together with their respective wives Patti and Ali, they have embarked on producing strictly limited quantities of shiraz from the Ebenezer and Lyndoch regions of the Barossa Valley. Somewhere along the way F.G.B. comes into the picture, and one does not need to be especially imaginative to guess what these letters might stand for. In 2009 the venture became rather more serious when the partners purchased 3.2 ha of a 110-year-old vineyard planted to shiraz and semillon; the grapes from this vineyard were incorporated in the 2010 vintage wines (semillon a new arrival).

🍷🍷🍷🍷 **Barossa Shiraz 2006** Designed to make an easy-drinking style, and succeeds; the only lack is length. Screwcap. 14.9% alc. **Rating** 88 **To** 2012 $20
Barossa Shiraz 2007 The label design and language is (presumably) aimed at the US market; honest, but unremarkable and short, shiraz produced by Good Booze Pty Ltd. Screwcap. 14.9% alc. **Rating** 87 **To** 2014 $20

Outlook Hill ★★★

97 School Lane, Tarrawarra, Vic 3777 **Region** Yarra Valley
T (03) 5962 2890 **F** (03) 5962 2890 **www**.outlookhill.com.au **Open** Fri–Sun 11–4.45
Winemaker Al Fencaros, Peter Snow **Est.** 2000 **Cases** 1600 **Vyds** 5.4 ha
After several years overseas, former Melbourne professionals Peter and Lydia Snow returned in 1997 planning to open a wine tourism business in the Hunter Valley. However, they had second thoughts, and in 2000 moved to the Yarra Valley, where they have now established three tourist B&B cottages, a vineyard, a terrace restaurant and adjacent cellar door outlet, backed by a constant temperature wine storage cool room. Exports to China and Japan.

Oxford Landing Estate ★★★

Pipeline Road, Nuriootpa, SA 5355 **Region** Riverland
T (08) 8561 3200 **F** (08) 8561 3393 **www**.oxfordlanding.com.au **Open** By appt
Winemaker Matthew Pick **Est.** 1958 **Cases** NA **Vyds** 250 ha
Oxford Landing Estate is, so the website tells us, 'A real place, a real vineyard. A place distinguished by clear blue skies, rich red soil and an abundance of golden sunshine.' In the 50+ years since the vineyard was planted, the brand has grown to reach all corners of the world. Success has been due to over-delivery against expectations at its price points, and has largely escaped the scorn of the UK wine press. In 2008 a five-year experiment began to determine whether a block of vines could survive and produce an annual crop with only 10% of the normal irrigation. This apart, there is now 1 ha of native vegetation for every ha of vineyard. I have no idea why so few Oxford Landing wines were submitted this year. Exports to the UK, the US and NZ.

🍷🍷🍷🍷 ✪ **Oxford Landing Merlot 2008** The hue is bright and clear, and the winemaking has not sought to extract what is not there, nor to cover up the light-bodied nature of the wine. All this means a bright and breezy wine without pretensions. Screwcap. 13.5% alc. **Rating** 87 **To** 2010 $8.95

Pages Creek ★★★★☆

624 Middle Teatree Road, Teatree, Tas 7017 **Region** Southern Tasmania
T (03) 6260 2311 **F** (03) 6331 9884 **www**.pagescreekwine.com.au **Open** By appt
Winemaker Winemaking Tasmania (Julian Alcorso) **Est.** 1999 **Cases** 150 **Vyds** 4 ha
In 1999 Peter and Sue Lowrie planted a vineyard on their 20-ha Pages Creek property, named after the creek that runs through it. They have 1.6 ha of cabernet sauvignon, 1 ha each of pinot noir and chardonnay and 0.4 ha of merlot. The tiny first vintage (2002) was consumed at their wedding; the first full vintage was '03, and the Pages Creek label was launched in '04. Exports to the US.

🍷🍷🍷🍷🍷 Pinot Noir 2006 Good colour retention; a complex spicy, savoury bouquet, then a very long and intense palate with lovely fruit/spice/forest balance. Trophy Tas Wine Show '10. Diam. 12.7% alc. **Rating** 95 **To** 2014 $30

Palmara ★★★☆

1314 Richmond Road, Richmond, Tas 7025 **Region** Southern Tasmania
T (03) 6260 2462 **F** (03) 6260 2943 **www**.palmara.com.au **Open** Sept–May 7 days 12–6
Winemaker Allan Bird **Est.** 1985 **Cases** 250 **Vyds** 0.9 ha
Allan Bird makes the Palmara wines in tiny quantities (the vineyard is slightly less than 1 ha, planted to pinot noir, chardonnay, cabernet sauvignon, ehrenfelser and siegerrebe). The Pinot Noir has performed consistently well since 1990. The Exotica Siegerrebe blend is unchallenged as Australia's most exotic and unusual wine, with pungent jujube/lanolin aromas and flavours.

🍷🍷🍷🍷🍷 Coal River Valley Chardonnay 2008 Bright straw-green; stone fruit and grapefruit aromas are mirrored on the palate, which has a richness belied by the low alcohol. Unoaked style works. Zork. 12.5% alc. **Rating** 90 **To** 2012 $22.50

🍷🍷🍷🍷 Coal River Valley Pinot Noir 2005 **Rating** 89 **To** 2010 $24.50
Coal River Valley Cabernet Sauvignon 2005 **Rating** 87 **To** 2012 $32.50

Palmer Wines ★★★★☆

1271 Caves Road, Dunsborough, WA 6281 **Region** Margaret River
T (08) 9756 7034 **F** (08) 9756 7399 **www**.palmerwines.net.au **Open** 7 days 10–5
Winemaker Mark Warren **Est.** 1977 **Cases** 6000 **Vyds** 45.2 ha
Stephen and Helen Palmer began the planting of their vineyard in 1977; with encouragement and direction from Dr Michael Peterkin of Pierro, the plantings have been increased over the years, and are now headed by cabernet sauvignon, sauvignon blanc, shiraz, merlot, chardonnay and semillon, with smaller amounts of malbec and cabernet franc. Exports to Indonesia (Bali).

🍷🍷🍷🍷🍷 Reserve Margaret River Shiraz 2008 Highly perfumed bouquet redolent of redcurrant, blackberry and framed by clove; the palate shows off the ample fruit in the best light, with fine-grained tannins drawing out the finish and providing a long, almost chewy finish. Screwcap. 14.9% alc. **Rating** 94 **To** 2025 $48 BE

🍷🍷🍷🍷🍷 Margaret River Chardonnay 2008 **Rating** 92 **To** 2016 $27.50 BE
Margaret River Shiraz 2008 **Rating** 90 **To** 2020 $24.50 BE
Margaret River Merlot 2008 **Rating** 90 **To** 2015 $24.50 BE

🍷🍷🍷🍷 Margaret River Semillon Sauvignon Blanc 2009 **Rating** 89 **To** 2013 $24.50 BE
Crackerjack 2008 **Rating** 89 **To** 2016 $19.50 BE
Crackerjack 2007 **Rating** 88 **To** 2014 $18.50

Pankhurst ★★★

'Old Woodgrove', Woodgrove Road, Hall, NSW 2618 **Region** Canberra District
T (02) 6230 2592 **F** (02) 6230 2592 **www**.pankhurstwines.com.au **Open** W'ends, public hols, or by appt
Winemaker Lark Hill, Brindabella Hills **Est.** 1986 **Cases** 2000 **Vyds** 5 ha
Agricultural scientist and consultant Allan Pankhurst and wife Christine (with a degree in pharmaceutical science) have established a split-canopy vineyard (pinot noir, chardonnay, cabernet sauvignon, merlot, sangiovese, tempranillo, semillon and sauvignon blanc). The first wines produced showed considerable promise. Pankhurst has had success with Pinot Noir and Chardonnay. Exports to China.

🍷🍷🍷🍷 Canberra District Unwooded Chardonnay 2008 The bouquet shows citrus, anise and a touch of earth; the prominent acidity drives the palate, ending up with a slightly nutty, oxidative finish. Screwcap. 13% alc. **Rating** 88 **To** 2012 $28 BE

Paracombe Wines ★★★★★

Main Road, Paracombe, SA 5132 **Region** Adelaide Hills
T (08) 8380 5058 **F** (08) 8380 5488 **www**.paracombewines.com **Open** By appt
Winemaker Paul Drogemuller **Est.** 1983 **Cases** 10 000 **Vyds** 17.7 ha
Paul and Kathy Drogemuller established Paracombe following the devastating Ash Wednesday bushfires in 1983. It has become a successful business, producing a range of wines that are never less than good, often very good. The wines are made onsite in the 250-tonne winery, with every part of the production process through to distribution handled from the winery. Exports to Canada, Sweden, Switzerland, Singapore, Taiwan, Hong Kong, Malaysia and India.

 careful ♀♀♀♀♀
✪ **Adelaide Hills Pinot Gris 2009** Distinct pink blush; highly fragrant and effusive blossom aromas of musk, pear, spice and apple are followed by a more sedate and controlled palate, albeit with echoes of the bouquet. Very example of pinot gris. Screwcap. 13% alc. **Rating** 95 **To** 2011 $19

✪ **Holland Creek Adelaide Hills Riesling 2009** A floral, flowery bouquet leads into a sleek and supple palate with beguiling lime and passionfruit flavours running through to the long finish; gets better each time retasted. Screwcap. 12% alc. **Rating** 94 **To** 2019 $21

♀♀♀♀♀
✪ **Adelaide Hills Sauvignon Blanc 2009** Scented gooseberry and lychee aromas flow into a palate that provides a good framework courtesy of minerally acidity; the contrast works well. Screwcap. 13% alc. **Rating** 93 **To** 2010 $21

✪ **Adelaide Hills Shiraz 2006** Very good retention of red–purple hue; reflects the excellent vintage with its array of black cherry, plum and blackberry, a hint of dark chocolate accompanying the French oak (20 months). Screwcap. 14.5% alc. **Rating** 93 **To** 2016 $21

✪ **The Reuben 2006** The eclectic blend of Cabernet Sauvignon/Merlot/Cabernet Franc/Malbec/Shiraz works well in this vintage, with a smooth and supple array of red and black fruits, a touch of chocolate and ripe, although gentle, tannins. Ready now, but will hold. Screwcap. 14.5% alc. **Rating** 91 **To** 2016 $21

✪ **Adelaide Hills Chardonnay 2007** Bright straw–green; has unusually sweet white peach/nectarine flavours that are attractive and not obscured by the French oak in which it was fermented. Screwcap. 13% alc. **Rating** 90 **To** 2013 $21
Adelaide Hills Cabernet Franc 2007 Rating 90 **To** 2015 $27

♀♀♀♀ **Adelaide Hills Pinot Noir 2008 Rating** 89 **To** 2015 $21

Paradigm Hill ★★★★★

26 Merricks Road, Merricks, Vic 3916 **Region** Mornington Peninsula
T (03) 5989 9000 **F** (03) 5989 8555 **www**.paradigmhill.com.au **Open** 1st w'end of month, public hols, or by appt
Winemaker Dr George Mihaly **Est.** 1999 **Cases** 1300 **Vyds** 4.2 ha
Dr George Mihaly (with a background in medical research, biotech and pharmaceutical industries) and wife Ruth (a former chef and caterer) have realised a 30-year dream of establishing their own vineyard and winery, abandoning their previous careers to do so. George had all the necessary scientific qualifications, and built on those by making the 2001 Merricks Creek wines, moving to home base at Paradigm Hill in '02, all along receiving guidance and advice from Nat White of Main Ridge Estate. The vineyard, under Ruth's control with advice from Shane Strange, is planted to 2.1 ha of pinot noir, 0.9 ha of shiraz, 0.8 ha of riesling and 0.4 ha of pinot gris. Exports to Singapore, Indonesia, Malaysia and China.

♀♀♀♀♀ **Les Cinq Mornington Peninsula Pinot Noir 2008** Similar colour and intensity to L'Ami Sage; less obvious spice and slightly rounder fruit flavours introducing black cherry and a touch of plum alongside the red cherry; single Dijon clone 115; only 600 bottles made. Screwcap. 13.5% alc. **Rating** 95 **To** 2018 $61
Mornington Peninsula Pinot Gris 2009 The audacity to barrel ferment pinot gris in 50% new/50% seasoned French oak and five months' maturation has paid off in prior vintages, and does so here. This is a real pea and thimble trick, elevating pinot gris to the level of real wine. Screwcap. 13.6% alc. **Rating** 94 **To** 2012 $43

ᵭᵭᵭᵭᵭ L'Ami Sage Mornington Peninsula Pinot Noir 2008 Rating 93 To 2015 $53
Col's Block Mornington Peninsula Shiraz 2008 Rating 92 To 2014 $40

Paradise IV   ★★★★★
45 Dog Rocks Road, Batesford, Vic 3221 (postal) **Region** Geelong
T (03) 5276 1536 **F** (03) 5276 1665 **Open** By appt
Winemaker Douglas Neal **Est.** 1988 **Cases** 600 **Vyds** 3.1 ha
The former Moorabool Estate has been renamed Paradise IV for the very good reason that it is the site of the original Paradise IV Vineyard planted in 1848 by Swiss vigneron Jean-Henri Dardel. It is owned by Ruth and Graham Bonney in partnership with former school teacher and wine lover Douglas Neal, who has the agency for various French barrel makers in Australia and South Africa. Neal is also a self-trained winemaker, and his role in the partnership is to make and sell the wines, with Graham and Ruth responsible for the vineyard. In practice, the functions overlap to a degree, as one would expect with a relatively small business. The winery has an underground barrel room, and the winemaking turns around wild yeast fermentation, natural mlf, gravity movement of the wine and so forth.

ᵭᵭᵭᵭᵭ Dardel Shiraz 2008 Slightly deeper colour, although similar to Bates' Ford; once again, a highly lifted and fragrant bouquet, the palate with lovely mouthfeel and a long, fluid drive complexed by touches of spice and pepper. Diam. 13.5% alc. Rating 96 To 2025 $45
Moorabool Estate Geelong Chardonnay 2008 Bright straw-green; a smoky, complex bouquet leads into a beautifully modulated palate, with grapefruit, white peach fruit and creamy/nutty nuances ex oak. Screwcap. 13% alc. Rating 95 To 2020 $43
The Bates' Ford Geelong Shiraz 2008 Strong crimson-purple; a fragrant and deliciously spicy bouquet leads into a svelte palate, red berry fruit supported by superfine tannins and quality French oak; 10% cabernet sauvignon. Diam. 13.5% alc. Rating 94 To 2020 $30
The Bates' Ford Geelong Shiraz 2007 Bright crimson-purple; an elegant, light- to medium-bodied wine with lively and fresh red berry, cherry and spice fruit, oak and tannins backstage. Drink whenever you wish. Diam. 13.5% alc. Rating 94 To 2015 $29.95

ᵭᵭᵭᵭᵭ Chaumont 2008 Rating 92 To 2014 $45

Paramoor Wines   ★★★★☆
439 Three Chain Road, Carlsruhe via Woodend, Vic 3442 **Region** Macedon Ranges
T (03) 5427 1057 **F** (03) 5427 3927 **www**.paramoor.com.au **Open** 7 days 10–5
Winemaker William Fraser **Est.** 2003 **Cases** 1200 **Vyds** 1.6 ha
Paramoor Wines is the retirement venture of Will Fraser, formerly Managing Director of Kodak Australasia. To be strictly correct, he is Dr Will Fraser, armed with a PhD in chemistry from Adelaide University. Much later he added a diploma of wine technology from the University of Melbourne (Dookie Campus) to his qualifications. Paramoor's winery is set on 17 ha of beautiful country not far from Hanging Rock, originally a working Clydesdale horse farm, with a magnificent heritage-style barn now used for cellar door sales and functions. Will has planted 0.8 ha each of pinot noir and pinot gris, and leases 2.6 ha of vines in the lower Goulburn Valley (1.3 ha shiraz, 0.9 ha cabernet sauvignon, 0.4 ha merlot). He also receives regular supplies of pinot noir and chardonnay grapes from another Macedon Ranges vineyard owned by friends.

ᵭᵭᵭᵭᵭ The Fraser Shiraz Cabernet Sauvignon 2007 Mislabelled, because the cabernet is 59% of the blend; the bouquet is fragrant and complex, with scented black fruits and some spicy notes; the palate is vibrant and long, reflecting the advantages of the modest alcohol. Diam. 13.8% alc. Rating 94 To 2017 $30

ᵭᵭᵭᵭᵭ Joan Picton Pinot Noir 2007 Rating 93 To 2014 $38
Mister Jack Pinot Noir 2007 Rating 90 To 2014 $30

Paringa Estate ★★★★★

44 Paringa Road, Red Hill South, Vic 3937 **Region** Mornington Peninsula
T (03) 5989 2669 **F** (03) 5931 0135 **www**.paringaestate.com.au **Open** 7 days 11–5
Winemaker Lindsay McCall **Est.** 1985 **Cases** 16 000 **Vyds** 24 ha
Schoolteacher-turned-winemaker Lindsay McCall has shown an absolutely exceptional gift for winemaking across a range of styles, but with immensely complex Pinot Noir and Shiraz leading the way. The wines have an unmatched level of success in the wine shows and competitions Paringa Estate is able to enter, the limitation being the relatively small production of the top wines in the portfolio. His skills are no less evident in contract winemaking for others. Winery of the Year 2007 Wine Companion. Exports to the UK, Denmark, South Korea, Singapore, Taiwan, Hong Kong and China.

ρρρρρ **The Paringa Single Vineyard Pinot Noir 2008** Deep, dark and almost mysterious, the concentration of black fruits is staggering; few pinots could chase such ripeness and maintain varietal integrity, yet this does; there is plenty of oak with mocha spice evident, but the palate actually provides a soft and fruitful journey from beginning to end; the tannins are plush and velvet-like to conclude. Formerly labelled Reserve. Screwcap. 14% alc. **Rating** 96 **To** 2020 $90 BE
Reserve Special Barrel Selection Mornington Peninsula Shiraz 2007 Strong crimson-purple; an elegant yet intense spray of spices, pepper, plum and red cherry fruit on the bouquet and fore-palate, then fine-grained savoury tannins on the finish; oak balanced and integrated. Screwcap. 14.5% alc. **Rating** 96 **To** 2020 $80
Estate Pinot Noir 2008 As ever, undeniable concentration, with red and black fruit framed amply by lavish levels of toasty oak; the fruit handles it with aplomb, as the palate is lively, fresh and ample; charry oak, layers of fruit and spice, and firm structure are the essence of this Mornington stalwart. Screwcap. 14% alc. **Rating** 95 **To** 2017 $60 BE
Peninsula Pinot Noir 2009 Bright, clear crimson-purple; Lindsay McCall does it again, the wine is fresh, rich plum and cherry fruit offset by foresty, but balanced, tannins and oak. Screwcap. 13.5% alc. **Rating** 94 **To** 2015 $28
Estate Shiraz 2008 The highly perfumed bouquet of blackberry, clove and smoked meat is framed by the generous level of high-quality toasty oak; the palate is loaded with dark fruits and moving towards full-bodied, but holds back with vibrancy and spice to conclude. Screwcap. 14.5% alc. **Rating** 94 **To** 2020 $50 BE

ρρρρϙ **The Paringa Single Vineyard Chardonnay 2008 Rating** 91 **To** 2016 $50 BE

ρρρρ **Peninsula Shiraz 2007 Rating** 89 **To** 2016 $25 BE
Estate Riesling 2009 Rating 88 **To** 2015 $15 BE
Peninsula Chardonnay 2008 Rating 88 **To** 2014 $22 BE

Parker Coonawarra Estate ★★★★★

Riddoch Highway, Coonawarra, SA 5263 **Region** Coonawarra
T (08) 8737 3525 **F** (08) 8737 3527 **www**.parkercoonawarraestate.com.au **Open** 7 days 10–4
Winemaker Peter Bissell (Contract) **Est.** 1985 **Cases** 7000
Parker Coonawarra Estate is at the southern end of Coonawarra, on rich terra rossa soil over limestone. Cabernet sauvignon is the predominant variety (17.45 ha), with minor plantings of merlot and petit verdot. Acquired by the Rathbone family in 2004. For current release red wine tasting notes see www.winecompanion.com.au. Exports to all major markets.

ρρρρρ **Favourite Son Chardonnay 2008** Pale colour, vibrant hue; restrained blanched almond and lemon bouquet, with a touch of nectarine; fresh, vibrant, focused and distinctly mineral in character, the finish is toasty and harmonious. Screwcap. 13% alc. **Rating** 94 **To** 2015 $23 BE

Parri Estate ★★★

Sneyd Road, Mount Compass, SA 5210 **Region** Southern Fleurieu/McLaren Vale
T (08) 8554 9660 **F** (08) 8554 9694 **www**.parriestate.com.au **Open** W'ends & public
hols, or by appt
Winemaker Linda Domas **Est.** 1998 **Cases** 15 000 **Vyds** 32 ha
Alice, Peter and John Phillips have established a business with a clear marketing plan and an
obvious commitment to quality. The vineyard is planted to chardonnay, viognier, sauvignon
blanc, semillon, pinot noir, cabernet sauvignon and shiraz, using modern trellis and irrigation
systems. In 2004 a second property on Ingoldby Road, McLaren Vale was acquired, with a
second cellar door, and shiraz, grenache and cabernet sauvignon plantings up to 60 years old.
Exports to the UK, the US, Canada, Mexico, Hong Kong, Singapore and China.

ŸŸŸŸ   **Southcote Southern Fleurieu Cabernet Shiraz 2006** Fractionally diffuse
✪   colour; struggled for ripeness, but against the odds, largely achieved it; while there's
          not much structure, the fruit flavours are not overtly green, just spicy and fresh.
          Will live. Cork. 12.5% alc. **Rating** 89 **To** 2015 $14
          Pangkarra McLaren Vale Shiraz 2006 Slightly hazy colour, although the
          hue is good; has strong regional typicity, with dark berry fruits and chocolate, but
          doesn't fulfil the expectations of the vintage; half-suspicion of random oxidation ex
          the cork. 14% alc. **Rating** 88 **To** 2013 $24

Passing Clouds ★★★★

Daylesford-Trentham Road, Musk, Vic 3461 **Region** Macedon Ranges
T 0408 120 376 **www**.passingclouds.com.au **Open** By appt
Winemaker Graeme and Cameron Leith **Est.** 1974 **Cases** 3000 **Vyds** 12 ha
In 1974, Graeme Leith and Sue Mackinnon planted the first vines at Passing Clouds, 60 km
northwest of Bendigo. Graeme is one of the great personalities of the wine industry, with
a superb sense of humour, and he makes lovely regional reds with cassis, berry and mint
fruit. With the passing of years (and clouds), Graeme is gradually handing over winemaking
responsibilities to son Cameron. Just as the *Wine Companion* was going to press we received
this newsletter from Graeme and Cameron: 'We're moving to Daylesford (Musk), but it's not
really a case of all good things coming to an end, it's more a case of everything changes –
nothing is forever. We'll be making wine at Daylesford and not at Kingower. Sue has passed
away and many of the Kingower vines also, so we move on, taking our pots and pans, our
crusher and press and our winemaking skills with us.'

ŸŸŸŸŸ **Two Mates Shiraz 2005** Showing a little development and a lot of
          concentration; deep and dark fruited, with elements of bay and thyme on the
          bouquet; delving into the full-bodied and full-blooded spectrum, the benefit of
          age has seen a little silk evolve to complement the sheer power of fruit. Diam.
          15.5% alc. **Rating** 93 **To** 2020 $40 BE

ŸŸŸŸ   **Pinot Noir 2008 Rating** 89 **To** 2014 $24 BE
          Graeme's Blend Shiraz Cabernet 2006 Rating 88 **To** 2015 $25 BE

Patina

109 Summerhill Lane, Orange, NSW 2800 **Region** Orange
T (02) 6362 8336 **F** (02) 6361 2949 **www**.patinawines.com.au **Open** W'ends 11–5, or by appt
Winemaker Gerald Naef **Est.** 1999 **Cases** 2500 **Vyds** 3 ha
Gerald Naef's home in Woodbridge in the Central Valley of California was surrounded by
the vast vineyard and winery operations of Gallo and Robert Mondavi. It would be hard to
imagine a more different environment than that provided by Orange. Gerald and wife Angie
left California in 1981, initially establishing an irrigation farm in the northwest of NSW; 20
years later they moved to Orange, and by 2006 Gerald was a final-year student of wine science
at CSU. He set up a micro-winery at the Orange Cool Stores, and his first wine was a 2003
Chardonnay, made from vines he planted in '99. At its first show entry it won the trophy for

Best White Wine of Show at the Orange Wine Show '06, of which I was Chairman. Dream starts seldom come better than this.

Orange Sauvignon Blanc 2008 The fragrant bouquet foretells the vibrant and lively palate, with its delicious mix of passionfruit and citrus; excellent line and length. Screwcap. 12.2% alc. Rating 94 To 2011 $19

Orange Pinot Gris 2008 Rating 90 To 2012 $22
Sticky Tea Orange Riesling 2009 Rating 90 To 2011 $22

Patrick T Wines ★★★★☆

Cnr Ravenswood Lane/Riddoch Highway, Coonawarra, SA 5263 **Region** Coonawarra
T (08) 8737 3687 **F** (08) 8737 3689 www.patricktwines.com **Open** 7 days 10–5
Winemaker Pat and Luke Toccaciu **Est.** 1996 **Cases** 5000 **Vyds** 50.5 ha
Patrick Tocaciu is a district veteran, setting up Patrick T Winemaking Services after prior careers at Heathfield Ridge Winery and Hollick Wines. He and his partners have over 40 ha of vines at Wrattonbully, and another 8 ha of cabernet sauvignon in Coonawarra. The Wrattonbully plantings cover all the major varieties, while the Coonawarra plantings give rise to the Home Block Cabernet Sauvignon. Also carries out contract winemaking for others. Pat has been joined by son Luke in the winery. Exports to Chile, Korea and NZ.

Limited Release Coonawarra Cabernet Sauvignon 2004 Holding its colour well; this is a particularly elegant wine that spent no less than four years in new French oak; over time, the oak and the fundamentally juicy fruit flavours dissolved into each other, the tannins contributed by both fruit and oak. Only 200 dozen made from old vines grapes. Badly stained ProCork is alarming. 14% alc. Rating 95 To 2024 $80

Estate Grown Mount Gambier Pinot Noir 2008 Rating 92 To 2014 $27
Estate Grown Wrattonbully Riesling 2009 Rating 90 To 2019 $20
Mother of Pearl Sauvignon Blanc 2009 Pale straw-green; the bouquet is rich with tropical fruits that come through strongly on the palate; good length and density. Coonawarra. Screwcap. 11.5% alc. Rating 90 To 2011 $16
Home Block Coonawarra Cabernet Sauvignon 2006 Rating 90 To 2018 $35
Reserve Estate Grown Coonawarra Cabernet Sauvignon 2005 Rating 90 To 2015 $29

Paul Bettio Wines ★★★

145 Upper King River Road, Cheshunt, Vic 3678 **Region** King Valley
T (03) 5729 8101 **F** (03) 5729 8405 www.paulbettiowines.com.au **Open** Mon–Fri 10–4, w'ends 10–5
Winemaker Damien Star **Est.** 1995 **Cases** 12 000 **Vyds** 27.2 ha
Paul and Helen Bettio have been growing grapes in the King Valley since 1988. The plantings include cabernet sauvignon, merlot, sauvignon blanc, pinot noir, pinot grigio, barbera and chardonnay (the latter three grown by Paul's father Joe).

King Valley Pinot Grigio 2009 Savoury lemon bouquet, with a touch of slatey minerality; the palate shows some oxidative complexity, but maintains freshness and energy; drink young and fresh. Screwcap. 12% alc. Rating 88 To 2012 $18 BE
King Valley Barbera 2008 Bright blue fruit bouquet, clean and fresh, with a soft core of fruit; fleshy and forward, best for early consumption. Screwcap. 12.8% alc. Rating 88 To 2012 $18 BE

Paul Conti Wines ★★★★☆

529 Wanneroo Road, Woodvale, WA 6026 **Region** Greater Perth Zone
T (08) 9409 9160 **F** (08) 9309 1634 www.paulcontiwines.com.au **Open** Mon–Sat 10–5, Sun by appt
Winemaker Paul and Jason Conti **Est.** 1948 **Cases** 6000 **Vyds** 15.5 ha

Third-generation winemaker Jason Conti has assumed control of winemaking, although father Paul (who succeeded his father in 1968) remains involved in the business. Over the years Paul challenged and redefined industry perceptions and standards; the challenge for Jason is to achieve the same degree of success in a relentlessly and increasingly competitive market environment, and he is doing just that. Plantings at the Carabooda Vineyard have been expanded with tempranillo, petit verdot and viognier, and pinot noir is purchased from Manjimup. In a further extension, a property has been acquired at Cowaramup in Margaret River, with sauvignon blanc, shiraz, cabernet sauvignon and semillon; muscat and malbec yet to come into full production. The original 2 ha vineyard (shiraz) of the Marginiup Vineyard remains the cornerstone. Exports to the UK, Malaysia and Japan.

ŸŸŸŸŸ **Medici Ridge Pinot Noir 2009** Bright crimson; the bouquet is complex, with Asian spices sprinkled through red and black cherry fruit; the palate has thrust and drive to the long finish. Thoroughly impressive. Screwcap. 14% alc. **Rating** 93 To 2015 $30

✪ **Medici Ridge Chardonnay 2009** Part barrel-fermented and matured, and from the South West Australia Zone, this is a very well made chardonnay, the fruit and oak balance judged to perfection, the varietal flavours of melon and white flesh stone fruit, the palate long. Screwcap. 13.5% alc. **Rating** 92 To 2015 $20

Mariginiup Shiraz 2008 For several decades before shiraz assumed cult status, was the flagship wine of Paul Conti; has very good colour and excellent balance; the black fruits of the medium-bodied palate are supple and fine, tannins in perfectly judged support. Screwcap. 14.5% alc. **Rating** 92 To 2018 $28

✪ **Tuart Vineyards Chenin Blanc 2009** A high-toned, floral, honeysuckle bouquet and a fresh, flavoursome palate; has more intensity and character than the vast majority. Screwcap. 13.5% alc. **Rating** 90 To 2014 $16

✪ **Roccella Grenache Shiraz 2009** Bright colour; the sweet red fruit flavours of the grenache are the dominant part of the wine, other than the structure that is supplied by the shiraz; a synergistic blend, all from WA. Screwcap. 14.5% alc. **Rating** 90 To 2015 $16

✪ **Tuart Vineyards Cabernet Sauvignon 2008** Bright red-purple; a relatively warm-grown cabernet with a relatively cool-grown personality; the medium-bodied palate has cassis and plum fruit, good tannins and a subtle intrusion of French oak from eight months in barrel. Screwcap. 14% alc. **Rating** 90 To 2015 $18

🍃 Paul Nelson Wines   ★★★★★

11 Kemsley Place, Denmark, WA 6333 (postal) **Region** Mount Barker
T 0406 495 066 **Open** Not
Winemaker Paul Nelson **Est.** 2009 **Cases** 290
Paul Nelson has a remarkably youthful face for someone who started making wine with one foot in the Swan Valley, the other in the Great Southern region of Denmark, while completing a bachelor's degree in viticulture and oenology at Curtin University. He then worked successively at Houghton in the Swan Valley, Goundrey in Mount Barker, Santa Ynez in California, South Africa (for four vintages), hemisphere hopping to the Rheinhessen, three vintages in Cyprus, then moving to a large Indian winemaker in Mumbai before returning to work for Houghton at Nannup. Thereafter he was approached by Galafrey to become chief winemaker, where he is now, but able to make (in partnership with wife Bianca Swart) 290 cases of fume blanc, a Provençal-style rose following in 2010.

ŸŸŸŸŸ **Mount Barker Fume Blanc 2009** A classy wine made with skill and a clear plan for its construction; intense citrus and lychee flavours run through the long palate, French oak adding to the integrity of the structure, but leaving the fruit to fully express itself. Screwcap. 13% alc. **Rating** 95 To 2012 $30

Paul Osicka   ★★★★☆

Majors Creek Vineyard at Graytown, Vic 3608 **Region** Heathcote
T (03) 5794 9235 **F** (03) 5794 9288 **Open** By appt
Winemaker Paul Osicka **Est.** 1955 **Cases** NFP **Vyds** 14 ha

The Osicka family arrived in Australia from Czechoslovakia in the early 1950s. Vignerons in their own country, they settled at Graytown and commenced planting vines in 1955. Their vineyard was the first new venture in Central and Southern Victoria for over half a century. It keeps a low profile, but produces consistently good shiraz from the 11 ha of estate plantings (the remainder cabernet sauvignon, merlot, riesling and roussanne). Exports to Canada, Ireland and Hong Kong.

ŸŸŸŸŸ **Majors Creek Vineyard Heathcote Shiraz 2008** Ripe blueberry, mint, sage and black fruits are on display, surrounded by a forest of new wood; full-bodied and luscious, with tar, mint, bay and a healthy dose of toasty oak; needs time, but the style is true to the house. Diam. 15% alc. **Rating** 93 **To** 2020 $35 BE
Shiraz Roussanne 2008 Fragrant blue fruit, spice and dried herb bouquet; medium-bodied, fleshy and attractive, with zesty acidity providing life and nerve to the ample fruit. Diam. 14.7% alc. **Rating** 92 **To** 2018 $45 BE

Paulett ★★★★★
Polish Hill Road, Polish Hill River, SA 5453 **Region** Clare Valley
T (08) 8843 4328 **F** (08) 8843 4202 **www.**paulettwines.com.au **Open** 7 days 10–5
Winemaker Neil Paulett **Est.** 1983 **Cases** 14 000 **Vyds** 26 ha
The Paulett story is a saga of Australian perseverance, commencing with the 1982 purchase of a property with 1 ha of vines and a house, promptly destroyed by the terrible Ash Wednesday bushfires of the following year. Son Matthew has joined Neil and Alison Paulett as a partner in the business, responsible for viticulture on a much-expanded property holding of 147 ha. The winery and cellar door have wonderful views over the Polish Hill River region, the memories of the bushfires long gone. Exports to the UK, the US, Denmark, China and NZ.

ŸŸŸŸŸ **Antonina Polish Hill River Riesling 2009** Whereas the standard of '09 riesling is all about immediate enjoyment and generosity, this is all about finesse, intensity and extreme length. A great riesling that cries out for time in bottle. Screwcap. 12.5% alc. **Rating** 96 **To** 2029 $44
Polish Hill River Aged Release Riesling 2005 Bright green–gold; perfect lime, toast and spice aromas do not show a scintilla of kerosene, the palate with the same pure equanimity, perfectly balanced as it enters a decade of perfection. Screwcap. 13% alc. **Rating** 96 **To** 2025 $30
Andreas 2006 Excellent hue; an altogether more subtle wine than the standard shiraz; here blackberry, dark plum and just a whisper of licorice are wrapped in a fine gauze of tannins; has particularly good length. Shiraz. Screwcap. 14.5% alc. **Rating** 95 **To** 2026 $48
Polish Hill River Riesling 2009 A delicious riesling, with an aromatic citrus bouquet, then a juicy palate, where lime takes centre stage. Good now, but will cellar well. Screwcap. 12.5% alc. **Rating** 94 **To** 2019 $22
Polish Hill River Shiraz 2006 Has a fragrant, multifaceted bouquet of spiced plum, polished leather and licorice, the medium-bodied palate precisely following suit, tannins and oak in support roles; carries its alcohol without complaint. Screwcap. 15% alc. **Rating** 94 **To** 2021 $22

ŸŸŸŸ **Polish Hill River Cabernet Merlot 2006 Rating** 89 **To** 2015 $22
Stone Cutting Clare Valley No Oak Chardonnay 2008 Rating 87 **To** 2011 $16

Paxton ★★★★★
Wheaton Road, McLaren Vale, SA 5171 **Region** McLaren Vale
T (08) 8323 9131 **F** (08) 8323 8903 **www.**paxtonvineyards.com **Open** 7 days 10–5
Winemaker Michael Paxton **Est.** 1979 **Cases** 15 000 **Vyds** 74.5 ha
David Paxton is one of Australia's best known viticulturists and consultants. He founded Paxton Vineyards in McLaren Vale with his family in 1979, and has since been involved in various capacities in the establishment and management of vineyards in several leading regions

across the country. Former Flying Winemaker, son Michael (with 14 years' experience in Spain, South America, France and Australia), is responsible for making the wines. There are five vineyards in the family holdings: the Thomas Block (28 ha), the Jones Block (22 ha), Quandong Farm (19 ha), Landcross Farm (2 ha) and Maslin Vineyard (3.5 ha). By 2006 all of the five vineyards were managed using full biodynamic principles. Paxton has become the first member of 1% For the Planet (www.onepercentfortheplanet.org). An underground barrel store has been completed and a cellar door opened in the original shearing shed. Exports to the UK, the US, Canada, Denmark, Sweden, Germany and Taiwan.

ppppp **Quandong Farm McLaren Vale Shiraz 2008** Very rich, intense black fruits and dark chocolate on the bouquet lead into a finely tempered medium-bodied palate with a delicious array of fruit, spice and gently savoury notes; excellent line and length; neither fined nor filtered. Screwcap. 14% alc. **Rating** 96 To 2023 $30

✪ **AAA McLaren Vale Shiraz Grenache 2008** Bright, light clear red-purple; a beautifully modulated and balanced wine with delicious red fruits to the fore, free of any confection characters whatsoever; the structure is outstanding, built on the foundations of silky tannins. Screwcap. 14.5% alc. **Rating** 94 To 2020 $23

ppppp **Thomas Block McLaren Vale Chardonnay 2008 Rating** 93 To 2015 $29
Jones Block McLaren Vale Shiraz 2006 Rating 93 To 2020 $39
The Vale McLaren Vale Cabernet Sauvignon 2008 Rating 92 To 2018 $30
McLaren Vale Pinot Gris 2009 Rating 90 To 2012 $23 BE
MV McLaren Vale Shiraz 2008 Rating 90 To 2018 $23
McLaren Vale Tempranillo 2008 Rating 90 To 2014 $23 BE

pppp **McLaren Vale Shiraz Rose 2009 Rating** 89 To 2010 $20

Payne's Rise ★★★★

10 Paynes Road, Seville, Vic 3139 **Region** Yarra Valley
T 0408 618 346 **F** (03) 5961 9383 **www**.paynesrise.com.au **Open** By appt
Winemaker Franco D'Anna (Contract) **Est.** 1998 **Cases** 700 **Vyds** 4 ha
Tim and Narelle Cullen have progressively established 1 ha each of cabernet sauvignon, shiraz, chardonnay and sauvignon blanc since 1998, supplemented by grapes purchased from local growers. They carry out all the vineyard work; Tim is also a viticulturist for a local agribusiness, and Narelle is responsible for sales and marketing. The contract-made wines have won several awards at the Victorian Wines Show.

ppppp **Yarra Valley Sauvignon Blanc 2009** Bright colour; has an equally balanced array of grassy/citrus and gooseberry/tropical fruit characters complexed by barrel fermentation in used oak; good acidity cleans up the finish. Screwcap. 13% alc. **Rating** 90 To 2011 $18

Peccavi Wines ★★★★★

1121 Wildwood Road, Yallingup Siding, WA 6282 (postal) **Region** Margaret River
T 0404 873 093 **F** (08) 6311 7435 **www**.peccavi-wines.com **Open** Not
Winemaker Various contract **Est.** 2006 **Cases** 4000 **Vyds** 16 ha
Owner Jeremy Muller was introduced to the great wines of the world by his father when he was young, and says he spent many years searching New and Old World wine regions (even looking at the sites of ancient Roman vineyards in England) and did not find what he was looking for until one holiday in Margaret River. There he found a vineyard in Yallingup that was available for sale, and he did not hesitate. He quickly put together a very impressive contract-winemaking team, and appointed Colin Bell as chief viticulturist. The wines are released under two labels: Peccavi, for 100% estate-grown fruit (all hand-picked) and No Regrets, for wines produced including contract-grown grapes blended with estate material. The quality of the wines is very good, reflecting the skills and experience of Brian Fletcher, Amanda Kraemer and Bruce Dukes as contract/consultant winemakers. Exports to the UK, Germany, Malaysia, Singapore and Dubai.

♟♟♟♟♟ **Margaret River Chardonnay 2007** The brilliant colour sets the antennae waving, and doesn't deceive; a beautifully crafted chardonnay with flawless balance between perfectly ripened fruit, barrel fermentation and maturation inputs. No need to describe every flavour nuance – it's got it all. Screwcap. 14.3% alc. **Rating** 96 **To** 2020 $45
No Regrets Margaret River Cabernet Merlot 2007 Crimson-purple; has the intensity and focus expected from Margaret River in a vintage such as this; black fruits have a spicy/savoury twist that gives emphasis to the finish, lengthening the palate; firm tannins are in balance. Screwcap. 14.5% alc. **Rating** 94 **To** 2020 $28

♟♟♟♟♟ **Margaret River Shiraz 2007 Rating** 92 **To** 2017 $40
Margaret River Cabernet Sauvignon 2007 Rating 92 **To** 2022 $45
No Regrets Margaret River Sauvignon Blanc Semillon 2008 Rating 91 **To** 2013 $24

🍇 Pedestal Vineyard Wines ★★★★★

PO Box 871, Canning Bridge, WA 6153 **Region** Margaret River
T 0405 232 890 **www.**pedestalwines.com.au **Open** Not
Winemaker Larry Cherubino **Est.** 2008 **Cases** 1000 **Vyds** 14 ha
This is a joint venture between land (and vineyard) owners Greg and Kerilee Brindle, and winemaker Larry Cherubino and wife Edwina. The vineyard (cabernet sauvignon, merlot, sauvignon blanc and semillon) was planted in 1998, the grapes being sold over the ensuing years to other winemakers in the region. In 2008 a small quantity of semillon and sauvignon blanc was retained for the Pedestal label, vinified along with an '08 Cabernet Merlot; '09 saw a second Semillon Sauvignon Blanc vintage, and future growth will depend on market demand. Distribution by Bibendum on the eastern seaboard is testimony to the skills of Larry Cherubino, and this is a venture worth watching.

♟♟♟♟♟ **Margaret River Sauvignon Blanc Semillon 2009** A 55/45 blend, partially
✪   barrel-fermented, that underscores what a great vintage this was for white wines, and especially this blend; its drive and intensity is outstanding, fruit dominant, the oak adding texture and structure, also contributing to the length. Screwcap. 13% alc. **Rating** 95 **To** 2014 $25
Reserve Margaret River Cabernet 2008 Strong red-purple; very much in the mould of the Cabernet Merlot, except that all the components are that little bit more intense and pronounced; blackcurrant fruit, a touch of tar, bold but ripe tannins, and French oak all contribute in a logical pattern. Screwcap. **Rating** 94 **To** 2033 $55

♟♟♟♟♟ **Margaret River Cabernet Merlot 2008 Rating** 93 **To** 2030 $25

Peel Estate ★★★★

290 Fletcher Road, Karnup, WA 6171 **Region** Peel
T (08) 9524 1221 **F** (08) 9524 1625 **www.**peelwine.com.au **Open** 7 days 10–5
Winemaker Will Nairn, Mark Morton **Est.** 1974 **Cases** 4500 **Vyds** 16 ha
The icon wine is the Shiraz, a wine of considerable finesse and with a remarkably consistent track record. Every year Will Nairn holds a Great Shiraz Tasting for 6-year-old Australian shirazs, and pits Peel Estate (in a blind tasting attended by 100 or so people) against Australia's best. It is never disgraced. The wood-matured Chenin Blanc is another winery speciality, although not achieving the excellence of the Shiraz. Exports to the UK, Ireland, China and Japan.

♟♟♟♟♟ **Shiraz 2003** Good colour retention despite heavily stained cork; has abundant flavour, with blackberry and plum fruit set in a warm savoury/vanilla cocoon, the tannins soft and ripe. 14.5% alc. **Rating** 92 **To** 2018 $33

Chardonnay 2007 Light straw-green; partial barrel fermentation was the correct response to the sotto voce fruit aroma and flavour; the result is a well-balanced wine that carries its alcohol well. Screwcap. 14.5% alc. **Rating** 90 **To** 2014 $22

ŸŸŸŸ   **Verdelho 2009 Rating** 89 **To** 2013 $17
Shiraz Cabernet NV Rating 88 **To** 2015 $20
Vintage Quattro 2005 Rating 87 **To** 2015 $21

Penfolds   ★★★★★

Tanunda Road, Nuriootpa, SA 5355 **Region** Barossa Valley
T (08) 8568 9408 **F** (08) 8568 9217 **www.**penfolds.com **Open** 7 days 10–5
Winemaker Peter Gago **Est.** 1844 **Cases** NFP
Senior among the numerous wine companies or stand-alone brands of Foster's, and undoubtedly one of the top wine companies in the world in terms of quality, product range and exports. The consistency of the quality of the red wines and their value for money has long been recognised worldwide; the white wines, headed by the ultra-premium Yattarna Chardonnay, are now on a par with the red wines. Exports to all major markets.

ŸŸŸŸŸ   **Yattarna Chardonnay 2007** Brilliant green-quartz; the bouquet instantaneously proclaims its intensity with the first whiff, and the palate repeats the performance; this has some of the hallmarks of Grand Cru Chablis from a good vintage; small wonder it has had such outstanding show success. Screwcap. 13% alc. **Rating** 97 **To** 2020 $130
Bin 51 Eden Valley Riesling 2009 Has a gently floral bouquet, then a fine and elegant palate ranging through lime, apple and pear, with perfectly balanced acidity providing length and a gloriously fresh aftertaste. Screwcap. 12.5% alc. **Rating** 96 **To** 2020 $32
Bin 311 Tumbarumba Chardonnay 2009 Light straw-green; a wine with exceptional drive and intensity spontaneously drawing saliva from the mouth in the aftertaste; white peach, nectarine and grapefruit contest each other for primacy, but the outcome is a draw; oh, and there is oak, but you barely notice it. Gold medal Sydney Wine Show '10. Screwcap. 13% alc. **Rating** 96 **To** 2015 $40
St Henri 2006 Strong purple-crimson; has the focus, intensity and class expected of the '06 vintage; blackberry, blackcurrant and savoury spices are supported and complexed by firm, ripe tannins on the medium- to full-bodied, long palate. Shiraz. Screwcap. 14.5% alc. **Rating** 96 **To** 2031 $90
Grange 2005 Protocol prevented me retasting this wine prior to its release date of 1 May '10, notwithstanding that no one will have read these words prior to the release of this book in late July '10. So this is my tasting note from the Rewards of Patience tasting held in Sept '07. Colour little different to the '04; tighter, more compact than the '04, yet the fruit line is glossy and smooth, the tannins (and acidity) acting as the brake and giving tightness. These are a different pair, and it will be fascinating to watch their development. Cork. 14.5% alc. **Rating** 96 **To** 2045 $650
Cellar Reserve Barossa Valley Cabernet Sauvignon 2008 The Cellar Reserve wines (sold only through cellar door and the Magill Restaurant) are of genuinely high quality and made in limited quantities, the latter being the reason why an '08 cabernet could be made from Barossa fruit; this has a tremendous volume of blackcurrant fruit, but is fresh, not dead, and has excellent structure. Screwcap. 15% alc. **Rating** 96 **To** 2038 $200
Great Grandfather Rare Old Liqueur Tawny NV Rich, but by no means heavy; great balance of rancio and fruit; long and very fine. Cork. 19.5% alc. **Rating** 96 **To** 2011 $350

✪   **Reserve Bin Aged Release Eden Valley Riesling 2005** Light green-straw; still incredibly fresh and tight; has fine apple and lime flavours with minerally acidity much in play on the long palate. Dual trophy winner Qld Wine Show '09. Screwcap. 11.5% alc. **Rating** 95 **To** 2020 $40

RWT Barossa Valley Shiraz 2007 Excellent crimson-purple; an unapologetic full-bodied shiraz, with waves of blackberry, plum and licorice; tannins and oak, too, are in abundance. Extremely rigourous selection has paid big dividends. Screwcap. 14.5% alc. **Rating** 95 **To** 2027 $175

✪ **Thomas Hyland Adelaide Chardonnay 2008** An altogether stylish wine with cool-grown grapefruit and white peach aromas and flavours; subtle French oak adds to the texture and mouthfeel; long, harmonious finish. Prolific gold medal winner; trophy Sydney Wine Show '10. Screwcap. 13% alc. **Rating** 94 **To** 2015 $20

Cellar Reserve Adelaide Chardonnay 2007 From the high-altitude Piccadilly vineyard; a supple palate with fruit flavours that seem fully ripe in a nectarine/white peach spectrum. Has evened out the bumps in the road. Screwcap. 12% alc. **Rating** 94 **To** 2015 $34

Koonunga Hill Seventy Six Shiraz Cabernet 2008 The special, on-premise version of Koonunga Hill with its original label; has good crimson-purple colour and abundant blackberry, plum and fruitcake flavours on the full-bodied palate; well-balanced, with typical Penfolds tannins to conclude. Gold medal Sydney Wine Show '10. Screwcap. 14.5% alc. **Rating** 94 **To** 2023 $35

Bin 138 Barossa Valley Shiraz Mourvedre Grenache 2008 Good colour for the blend; leather, spice, licorice and chocolate are all present, along with fruit on the bouquet; the palate has more luscious fruit in a darker register than usual, an unqualified success. Screwcap. 14.5% alc. **Rating** 94 **To** 2018 $30

Bin 707 Cabernet Sauvignon 2007 Deep purple-crimson; a brooding, powerful wine, black fruits, tannins, tar and earth dominant, the normally sweetening impact of the American oak to no avail. I'm not practising as I preach in giving the wine 94 points for tomorrow not today. Screwcap. 14.4% alc. **Rating** 94 **To** 2022 $190

Bin 389 Cabernet Shiraz 2007 Strong colour; has the strength of all the '07 Penfolds' reds, with an array of black fruits, dark chocolate and vanilla/mocha; the tannin structure is particularly good for the vintage. Screwcap. 14.5% alc. **Rating** 94 **To** 2022 $65

Cellar Reserve Barossa Valley Sangiovese 2008 Bright, deep hue; has an abundance of ripe, red and black cherry fruit that carries the tannins and oak with ease; the texture is exemplary, as is the length. Cork. 15% alc. **Rating** 94 **To** 2021 $50

Grandfather Fine Old Liqueur Tawny NV The colour almost indistinguishable from Great Grandfather, but on the one hand has more power, yet on the other, less of the silky smoothness of the older wine. Cork. 20.5% alc. **Rating** 94 **To** 2011 $100

♟♟♟♟♟ **Thomas Hyland Adelaide Chardonnay 2009 Rating** 93 **To** 2014 $22
Bin 128 Coonawarra Shiraz 2008 Rating 93 **To** 2023 $34
Kalimna Bin 28 Shiraz 2007 Rating 93 **To** 2022 $34
Bin 2 Shiraz Mourvedre 2008 Rating 93 **To** 2014
Bin 407 Cabernet Sauvignon 2007 Rating 92 **To** 2020 $55
Cellar Reserve McLaren Vale Tempranillo 2008 Rating 92 **To** 2023 $50
Cellar Reserve McLaren Vale Tempranillo 2007 Rating 91 **To** 2013 $50
Thomas Hyland Adelaide Sauvignon Blanc 2009 Rating 90 **To** 2012 $22
Thomas Hyland Cabernet Sauvignon 2008 Rating 90 **To** 2018 $22
Bluestone Grand Tawny NV Rating 90 **To** 2011 $25

Penfolds Magill Estate   ★★★★★

78 Penfold Road, Magill, SA 5072 **Region** Adelaide Zone
T (08) 8301 5569 **F** (08) 8301 5588 **www.**penfolds.com **Open** 7 days 10.30–5
Winemaker Peter Gago **Est.** 1844 **Cases** NFP **Vyds** 5.2 ha
This is the birthplace of Penfolds, established by Dr Christopher Rawson Penfold in 1844, his house still part of the immaculately maintained property. It includes 5.2 ha of precious shiraz used to make Magill Estate; the original and subsequent winery buildings, most still

in operation or in museum condition; and the much-acclaimed Magill Restaurant, with panoramic views of the city, a great wine list and fine dining. All this is a 20-min drive from Adelaide's CBD. Exports to the UK, the US and other major markets.

♟♟♟♟♟ **Shiraz 2007** Dense purple-red; has, as usual, a very different register, with life and movement to the spice and berry fruit aromas and flavours; the tannins are finer, the oak likewise. Screwcap. 14.5% alc. **Rating** 94 **To** 2020 $115

Penley Estate   ★★★☆
McLeans Road, Coonawarra, SA 5263 **Region** Coonawarra
T (08) 8736 3211 **F** (08) 8736 3124 **www**.penley.com.au **Open** 7 days 10–4
Winemaker Kym Tolley, Greg Foster **Est.** 1988 **Cases** 40 000 **Vyds** 111 ha
Owner winemaker Kym Tolley describes himself as a fifth-generation winemaker, the family tree involving both the Penfolds and the Tolleys. He worked 17 years in the industry before establishing Penley Estate and has made every post a winner since, producing a succession of rich, complex, full-bodied red wines and stylish Chardonnays. These are made from precious estate plantings. Exports to all major markets.

♟♟♟♟ **Aradia Coonawarra Chardonnay 2008** A fragrant and altogether pretty wine, with nectarine, white peach and grapefruit aromas and flavours, then a crisp finish; subtle oak, drink while young. Screwcap. 14.5% alc. **Rating** 89 **To** 2011 $20

Penmara   ★★★★☆
Suite 42, 5-13 Larkin Street, Camperdown, NSW 2050 (postal) **Region** Hunter Valley/Orange
T (02) 9517 4429 **F** (02) 9517 4439 **www**.penmarawines.com.au **Open** Not
Winemaker Hunter Wine Services (John Horden) **Est.** 2000 **Cases** 28 000 **Vyds** 120 ha
Penmara was formed with the banner 'Five Families: One Vision', pooling most of their grapes, with a central processing facility, and marketing focused exclusively on exports. The six sites are Lilyvale Vineyards in New England; Tangaratta Vineyards at Tamworth; Birnam Wood, Rothbury Ridge and Martindale Vineyards in the Hunter Valley; and Highland Heritage at Orange. In all, these vineyards give Penmara access to 120 ha of shiraz, chardonnay, cabernet sauvignon, semillon, verdelho and merlot, mainly from the Hunter Valley and Orange. Exports to the US and other major markets.

♟♟♟♟♟ **Reserve Orange Shiraz 2007** Bright crimson; the cool climate is reflected
✪   in the fragrant bouquet, the spicy/peppery notes to the black fruits and the fine tannins that give texture to the well-balanced, medium-bodied palate. Has a strong market in Ontario, Canada. Screwcap. 14% alc. **Rating** 94 **To** 2020 $20

♟♟♟♟♟ **Reserve Orange Sauvignon Blanc 2009** Rating 90 **To** 2011 $20

♟♟♟♟ **Five Families Riesling 2009** Rating 88 **To** 2013 $15

Penna Lane Wines   ★★★★☆
Lot 51, Penna Lane, Penwortham via Clare, SA 5453 **Region** Clare Valley
T (08) 8843 4364 **F** (08) 8843 4349 **www**.pennalanewines.com.au **Open** Thurs–Sun &
public hols 11–5, or by appt
Winemaker Ray Klavins, Paulett Wines **Est.** 1998 **Cases** 3000 **Vyds** 4.5 ha
A seachange brought Ray Klavins and Stephen Stafford-Brookes together. Ray ran a land-scaping business in Adelaide and Stephen was a sales rep in the UK. Both decided to get into wine production and, with enormous support from their wives, began studying oenology and viticulture at Roseworthy College in 1991. Ray and wife Lynette purchased their 14-ha property in the Skilly Hills in '93; it was covered with rubbish, Salvation Jane, a derelict dairy and tumbledown piggery. They spent all their spare time clearing up the property, living in a tent and the old shearing shed, and planted the first vines in '94. In '98 the Klavins and Stafford-Brookes families formed a partnership to produce and sell wine under the Penna Lane label. Exports to Hong Kong and Korea.

🍷🍷🍷🍷🍷 **Clare Valley Riesling 2009** Fresh citrus blossom aromas lead into a bright and
✪ lively palate, with intense but fine citrus and apple flavours; delicious finish to an
elegant wine. Screwcap. 12.5% alc. **Rating** 94 **To** 2019 $21

Penny's Hill ★★★★★

Main Road, McLaren Vale, SA 5171 **Region** McLaren Vale
T (08) 8556 4460 **F** (08) 8556 4462 **www.**pennyshill.com.au **Open** 7 days 10–5
Winemaker Ben Riggs **Est.** 1988 **Cases** 15 000 **Vyds** 44 ha
Penny's Hill is owned by Adelaide advertising agency businessman Tony Parkinson and Ben
Riggs. The 18.4-ha Penny's Hill vineyard, unusually for McLaren Vale, is close-planted with
a thin vertical trellis/thin vertical canopy, the work of consultant viticulturist David Paxton.
A group of small-volume, high-quality shirazs headed by The Holotype, The Footprint, The
Skeleton Key lead the way for the main shiraz, Cracking Black. The Malpas Road Vineyard
(15 ha) is planted to shiraz, cabernet sauvignon and merlot; and Goss Corner (10.6 ha) has
viognier, shiraz and merlot. Through a complicated ownership structure, the large-volume
Woop Woop and Black Chook wines are also in the camp. The innovative red dot packaging
was the inspiration of Tony Parkinson, recalling the red dot 'sold' sign on pictures and giving
rise to the Red Dot Art Gallery at Penny's Hill. The restaurant was named as Australia's Best
Restaurant in a Winery for 2007/08. Exports to the UK, the US, Canada, Sweden, Denmark,
Germany, Switzerland, Singapore and NZ.

🍷🍷🍷🍷🍷 **The Skeleton Key McLaren Vale Shiraz 2008** By a considerable margin, the
most profound of the Penny's Hill Shirazs, built on a precise 92 weeks in barrel
and 37 weeks in bottle prior to release; the aromas and flavours are all in a black
fruit range, with strong licorice and dark chocolate notes adding complexity to the
structure of the full-bodied palate. Screwcap. 14.5% alc. **Rating** 95 **To** 2028 $30
Veteran Very Old Fortified NV The brown colour attests to the average age of
over 20 years; the biscuity rancio is also very strong, the palate long and spicy, the
finish virtually dry. Screwcap. 18.5% alc. **Rating** 94 **To** 2011 $27

🍷🍷🍷🍷🍷 **Cracking Black McLaren Vale Shiraz 2008** The expressive bouquet has the
✪ full array of regional shiraz characters, the juicy and long medium-bodied palate
giving these characters dimension; plum and black cherry fruit with notes of spice
and dark chocolate run through a fluid finish. Screwcap. 14.5% alc. **Rating** 93
To 2018 $22

✪ **The Agreement Adelaide Hills Sauvignon Blanc 2009** Attractive wine,
with a positive array of tropical fruit aromas that gain intensity on the palate
without compromising balance, the twist of lemon on the finish a plus. Screwcap.
12.5% alc. **Rating** 91 **To** 2010 $18
The Specialized McLaren Vale Shiraz Cabernet Merlot 2008 **Rating** 91
To 2018 $22

✪ **The Black Chook Free Range Grenache Shiraz Viognier 2008** A 50/45/5
blend that works surprisingly well, providing a cascade of red and black fruit
flavours in a supple medium-bodied palate, ready to drink right now. Screwcap.
15% alc. **Rating** 91 **To** 2013 $17

✪ **The Black Chook Shiraz Viognier 2008** The substantial (6%) viognier
component is obvious on the bouquet, but slides back into the wine on its plush
palate, with plum and black cherry fruit, the tannins soft, the oak subtle. Screwcap.
14.5% alc. **Rating** 90 **To** 2014 $17
The Experiment McLaren Vale Grenache 2008 **Rating** 90 **To** 2014 $22

🍷🍷🍷🍷 **Red Dot McLaren Vale Shiraz 2008** Curiously, slightly more purple in its
✪ colour than Crackling Black; the light- to medium-bodied palate with good
mouthfeel thanks to the skein of fine tannins that support the black cherry fruit.
The price is a sign of the times. Screwcap. 14.5% alc. **Rating** 89 **To** 2014 $12

✿ Penrice Estate Wines ★★★★

93 Penrice Road, Angaston, SA 5353 (postal) **Region** Eden Valley
T (08) 8564 2935 **F** (08) 8564 2935 **www**.penriceestatewines.com.au **Open** Not
Winemaker Russell Johnson **Est.** 2005 **Cases** 1000 **Vyds** 4 ha
This is a partnership between Russell and Diane Johnson, and Jon and Sally Dean. It started life
as an export-only brand, selling wines direct to restaurants, boutique retailers and distributors
in the UK. The business focuses on single-vineyard wines, starting with the Dusty Dog Eden
Valley Riesling from the small O'Brien family vineyard in that region. With the range now
including a Cabernet Sauvignon and Chardonnay, with a single-vineyard Barossa Valley Shiraz,
the time arrived for the wines to be distributed within Australia. It is sold via the web.

♀♀♀♀♀ **Dusty Dog Reserve Eden Valley Riesling 2009** Excellent hue, bright and
green-tinged; has all the expected indicia of Eden Valley riesling, with fine lime, apple
and mineral notes on the long palate. Screwcap. 12% alc. **Rating** 92 **To** 2019 $21

Pepper Tree Wines ★★★★★

Halls Road, Pokolbin, NSW 2321 **Region** Hunter Valley
T (02) 4998 7539 **F** (02) 4998 7746 **www**.peppertreewines.com.au **Open** Mon–Fri 9–5,
w'ends 9.30–5
Winemaker Jim Chatto **Est.** 1991 **Cases** 50 000 **Vyds** 172.1 ha
The Pepper Tree winery is part of a complex that also contains The Convent guest house
and Roberts Restaurant. In 2002 it was acquired by a company controlled by Dr John Davis,
who owns 50% of Briar Ridge. The appointment of Jim Chatto as chief winemaker in 2007
brought the expertise of the best young wine judge on the Australian wine show circuit, with
winemaking talents to match, and should bring further improvement (vintage conditions
accepted). It sources the majority of its Hunter Valley fruit from its Tallavera Grove vineyard
at Mt View, but also has premium vineyards at Orange, Coonawarra and Wrattonbully, which
provide its Grand Reserve and Reserve (single-region) wines. Self-evidently, the wines are of
exceptional value for money. Exports to the US, Canada, Singapore, China and NZ.

♀♀♀♀♀
✪ **Alluvius Semillon 2009** Bright straw-green, it has a classic bouquet in the
main stream of high-quality, young semillon. The palate has tremendous thrust,
drive and exceptional length, minerally acidity running alongside mouth-tingling,
lemony fruit. Gold medal Sydney Wine Show '10. Screwcap. 10.5% alc. **Rating** 96
To 2020 $30

✪ **Limited Release Hunter Valley Semillon 2009** Light but vivid green-straw; a
wonderfully fragrant bouquet, at once precocious yet very fine; the palate delivers
on the promise of the bouquet, with intense highly focused flavour in a grass/
lemon/citrus spectrum. A great clean and refreshing finish and aftertaste. Screwcap.
11.2% alc. **Rating** 96 **To** 2022 $22

✪ **The Gravels Single Vineyard Reserve Wrattonbully Shiraz Viognier 2008**
Vivid crimson-purple ex co-fermented viognier (5%); a beautifully made, elegant
medium-bodied wine that is all about perfume and fruit finesse; has effortless
length and a superb aftertaste. Screwcap. 14.5% alc. **Rating** 96 **To** 2023 $35

✪ **Elderslee Road Single Vineyard Reserve Wrattonbully Cabernet
Sauvignon 2008** Improbably, the colour is even better than that of the regional
blend, deeper and more vibrant; this sets the scene for a more opulent, richly
textured wine with waves of sumptuous blackcurrant fruit, ripe tannins and oak; a
wine for your grandchildren. Screwcap. 14.5% alc. **Rating** 96 **To** 2040 $35

✪ **Calcare Single Vineyard Reserve Coonawarra Cabernet Sauvignon
2008** Strong colour; a distinguished cabernet by any standards, the bouquet with
high-toned cassis and blackcurrant aromas, the medium- to full-bodied palate with
similar fruit characters framed by exemplary tannins and high-quality French oak.
Gold medal Sydney Wine Show '10. Screwcap. 14.8% alc. **Rating** 96 **To** 2028 $35

✪ **Venus Block Single Vineyard Reserve Orange Chardonnay 2009** Light green-straw; the far greater intensity, structure, texture and power of this wine sets it apart; stone fruit, melon and integrated oak are present from the bouquet to the finish, none dominant; gives a nod in the direction of Burgundy. Screwcap. 13.5% alc. **Rating** 95 **To** 2017 $30

✪ **The Pebbles Limited Release Single Vineyard Wrattonbully Shiraz Viognier 2008** Vibrant crimson; a highly aromatic bouquet of spicy black fruits, the medium-bodied palate building with licorice, pepper and spice as ornaments to the platform of opulent fruit and fine, persistent tannins. Screwcap. 14.5% alc. **Rating** 95 **To** 2023 $25

✪ **Wrattonbully Shiraz 2008** Bright purple-crimson; a fragrant bouquet of red cherry, plum and spice leads fluidly into a vibrant medium-bodied palate, fine tannins and spicy notes supporting the fruit. Screwcap. 14.5% alc. **Rating** 94 **To** 2020 $18

✪ **Wrattonbully Coonawarra Cabernet Sauvignon 2008** Bright crimson-purple; a fragrant and pure bouquet and palate offer beautifully balanced blackcurrant and cassis fruit, oak and tannins on the medium-bodied palate; a long, refined finish. Screwcap. 14.5% alc. **Rating** 94 **To** 2020 $18

Strandlines Single Vineyard Grand Reserve Wrattonbully Cabernet Shiraz 2008 Good depth to the colour; a more robust, full-bodied style than Jim Chatto normally makes, but it comes together in the end, as the depth of the blackcurrant and blackberry fruits does carry the challenge of the tannins. Patience will be rewarded. Screwcap. 14.5% alc. **Rating** 94 **To** 2028 $65

♟♟♟♟♗ **Hunter Valley Marlborough Semillon Sauvignon Blanc 2009** Bright
✪ colour; you know the semillon contributes at least half of the blend, but it's so seamless and balanced you don't know how much; the citrus flavours of the semillon are tweaked (but no more) by the tropical notes of the sauvignon blanc. Screwcap. 11.5% alc. **Rating** 93 **To** 2012 $18

✪ **Limited Release Single Vineyard Hunter Valley Chardonnay 2009** The aromas and flavours are fresh and lively, although less exotic than the regional blend; balance is the key to a wine that has a splash of oak in the background, the melon and white flesh stone fruit with the ability to age. Screwcap. 13% alc. **Rating** 93 **To** 2015 $22

14 Shores Single Vineyard Reserve Wrattonbully Merlot 2008 **Rating** 93 **To** 2015 $35

Elderslee Road Single Vineyard Reserve Wrattonbully Cabernet Sauvignon 2006 **Rating** 93 **To** 2026 $35

✪ **Hunter Wrattonbully Orange Chardonnay 2009** Quartz-green; an extremely zesty and vibrant fruit-driven wine, albeit with subliminal barrel ferment characters; white peach and nectarine, even a hint of green pineapple, rocket through the bouquet and palate. Screwcap. 13% alc. **Rating** 92 **To** 2014 $18

♟♟♟♟ **Wrattonbully Merlot 2008** **Rating** 89 **To** 2012 $18
Wrattonbully Pinot Gris 2009 **Rating** 88 **To** 2011 $18

Pepperilly Estate Wines   ★★★★☆

18 Langham Street, Nedlands, WA 6009 (postal) **Region** Geographe
T 0401 860 891 **F** (08) 9389 6444 **www**.pepperilly.com **Open** Not
Winemaker The Vintage Wineworx **Est.** 1999 **Cases** 2500 **Vyds** 11 ha
Partners Geoff and Karyn Cross, and Warwick Lavis, planted their vineyard in 1991 with 2 ha each of cabernet sauvignon and shiraz, and 1 ha each of semillon, sauvignon blanc, chardonnay, viognier, merlot, mourvedre and grenache. The vineyard has views across the Ferguson Valley to the ocean, with sea breezes providing good ventilation.

♟♟♟♟♟ **Sauvignon Blanc Semillon 2009** A complex and contrasting bouquet of herbal
✪ and tropical components leads into a lushly yet tight flavoured palate, the flavours crossing a full band of tropical notes from pineapple to guava and passionfruit. Screwcap. 12.5% alc. **Rating** 94 **To** 2011 $17

ŸŸŸŸŲ   Ferguson Valley Shiraz 2007 Rating 90 To 2017 $25
          Ferguson Valley Grenache 2007 Rating 90 To 2014 $25
✪   Purple Patch 2007 A very interesting wine, this blend of Grenache (80%)/
          Mourvedre (15%)/Shiraz (5%) coming from a cooler climate than the regions in
          the eastern states that provide it; the gentle confection character of the grenache is
          freshened by good acidity and fine tannins. Well worth a look. Screwcap. 14% alc.
          Rating 90 To 2015 $25

ŸŸŸŸ   Cabernet Merlot 2007 Rating 89 To 2017 $17

Peregrine Ridge   ★★★★☆

19 Carlyle Street, Moonee Ponds, Vic 3039 (postal) **Region** Heathcote
T 0411 741 772 **F** (03) 9326 2885 **www**.peregrineridge.com.au **Open** Not
Winemaker Graeme Quigley, Sue Kerrison **Est.** 2001 **Cases** 900 **Vyds** 5.5 ha
Graeme Quigley and Sue Kerrison were wine lovers and consumers before they came to
growing and making their own wine. Having purchased a property high on the Mt Camel
Range (the name comes from the peregrine falcons that co-habit the vineyard and the
ridgeline that forms the western boundary of the property), they progressively planted their
vineyard solely to shiraz. Irrigation is used sparingly, with the yields restricted to 2.5 to
3.5 tonnes per ha; the grapes are hand-picked into small baskets, transported direct to small
open fermenters and made in small batches.

ŸŸŸŸŸ   Winemaker's Reserve Heathcote Shiraz 2006 Bright colour; quite dark and
          savoury aromas with leather, spice and chocolate framing red and blue fruit; the
          palate is very fresh, and belies the slightly forward nature of the bouquet; bright
          acid, and fine, almost slippery, tannins on the finish. Cork. 15.2% alc. **Rating** 94
          To 2016 $60 BE

ŸŸŸŸŲ   American Oak II Heathcote Shiraz 2007 Rating 90 To 2017 $40
          Limited Release Heathcote Shiraz 2006 Rating 90 To 2020 $35

ŸŸŸŸ   Winemaker's Reserve Heathcote Sparkling Shiraz 2005 Rating 88
          To 2014 $55 BE

Perri's Winery   **NR**

495 River Road, Kialla, Vic 3631 **Region** Goulburn Valley
T (03) 5827 1292 **Open** W'ends 10–5, or by appt
Winemaker Dom Perri **Est.** 1999 **Cases** 60 **Vyds** 2 ha
Dom and Dianne Perri purchased their 4-ha property (with secure water rights) in 1978,
intending to grow grapes. Raising three daughters caused the grape project to be delayed,
and it was not until 1997 that they established their vineyard of cabernet sauvignon, shiraz,
cabernet franc and frontignac. The direct inspiration was Dom's father, Antonio, who made
wine for consumption by the family. Dom produced his first wine in 2000, and in '04 was the
most successful exhibitor (and trophy winner) at the Victorian Wines Show's amateur classes
(for a cabernet sauvignon), two years later winning the award for Best White Wine in the
amateur section of the show, doing even better at the Dookie Wine Show, winning the trophy
for Best White Wine in Show. His skill as a winemaker was a result of completing a four-year
diploma of wine technology course at the Dookie Campus of Melbourne University, wife
Dianne also completing a post-fermentation short course at Dookie.

Pertaringa   ★★★★☆

Cnr Hunt Road/Rifle Range Road, McLaren Vale, SA 5171 **Region** McLaren Vale
T (08) 8323 8125 **F** (08) 8323 7766 **www**.pertaringa.com.au **Open** Mon–Fri 10–5,
w'ends & public hols 11–5
Winemaker Shane Harris, Ben Riggs **Est.** 1980 **Cases** 23 000 **Vyds** 25.2 ha
Pertaringa has been owned and operated for three decades by viticulturists Geoff Hardy
and Ian Leask, with Ben Riggs complementing the creative team as consultant winemaker.

The vineyard in the foothills of McLaren Vale was first established in 1969. In 2006, Ian's son Richard Leask took over the day-to-day management of the vineyard and since then there has been a 'back to the future' approach, with the introduction of biodynamics and biological farming techniques, as well as 15 ha of shiraz being carefully regenerated to its original early '70s shape. Although not always grammatically correct, the Two Gentlemen farmers will continue to pour their experience into Pertaringa. Exports to the UK, the US and other major markets.

ΥΥΥΥΥ **Undercover McLaren Vale Shiraz 2008** Medium- to full-bodied, the bouquet
❂ is brimming with mocha, licorice and black fruits; the palate is full of fleshy fruits, with the chewy tannins bringing up the rear; regional and well balanced. Screwcap. 15% alc. **Rating** 92 **To** 2020 $22 BE

❂ **Scarecrow Adelaide Sauvignon Blanc 2009** Fresh and crisp, citrus, tropical and mineral bouquet; the palate is clearly defined, with crunchy acid and vibrant fruit to conclude. Screwcap. 12% alc. **Rating** 90 **To** 2012 $18 BE

ΥΥΥΥ **Bonfire Block Adelaide Semillon 2009 Rating** 89 **To** 2014 $18
Over The Top McLaren Vale Shiraz 2008 Rating 89 **To** 2020 $39 BE

Petaluma ★★★★★

Spring Gully Road, Piccadilly, SA 5151 **Region** Adelaide Hills
T (08) 8339 9300 **F** (08) 8339 9301 **www**.petaluma.com.au **Open** At Bridgewater Mill, Bridgewater
Winemaker Andrew Hardy, Mike Mudge, Penny Jones **Est.** 1976 **Cases** 60 000 **Vyds** 240 ha
The Lion Nathan group (owned by Kirin of Japan) comprises Petaluma, Knappstein, Mitchelton, Stonier and Smithbrook. The Petaluma range has been expanded beyond the core group of Croser Sparkling, Clare Valley Riesling, Piccadilly Chardonnay and Coonawarra (Cabernet Sauvignon/Merlot). Newer arrivals of note include Adelaide Hills Viognier and Adelaide Hills Shiraz. Bridgewater Mill is the second label, which consistently provides wines most makers would love to have as their top label. The South Australian plantings in the Clare Valley, Coonawarra and Adelaide Hills provides a more than sufficient source of estate-grown grapes and wines. Exports to all major markets.

ΥΥΥΥΥ **Hanlin Hill Clare Valley Riesling 2009** The mature vineyard is the key to the consistency of this wine. The palate has considerable depth and intensity to its array of ripe citrus fruit flavours, the finish well balanced. Screwcap. 12.5% alc. **Rating** 94 **To** 2019 $30
Coonawarra 2007 Pure cassis bouquet, highlighted by cigar box and a suggestion of florals; elegantly structured, with ample levels of sweet red fruit and quite slippery tannins to conclude; certainly a sleeper and a very good example from the vintage. Cabernet Sauvignon/Merlot/Shiraz/Petit Verdot. Screwcap. 14.5% alc. **Rating** 94 **To** 2020 $55 BE
Croser Piccadilly Valley Pinot Noir Chardonnay 2006 Delicious flavour and balance marks one of the best vintages of this wine for some years; let's hope they keep some back for later disgorgement; citrus-tinged fruit and a fine touch of brioche are the keys. Cork. 13% alc. **Rating** 94 **To** 2013 $35
Croser Late Disgorged Piccadilly Valley Pinot Noir Chardonnay 1999 Glowing gold; has achieved all the complexity expected from 10 years on lees, with nutty/brioche notes, but the overarching characters come from the lemony citrussy finish and aftertaste. Cork. 13% alc. **Rating** 94 **To** 2012 $50
Bridgewater Mill Adelaide Hills Pinot Noir Chardonnay NV Salmon-pink; the pinot noir influence shows throughout, with red fruits and spicy notes; the wine has very good mouthfeel and balance, the long finish with perfectly calibrated dosage, one second sweet, the next dry. Cork. 13% alc. **Rating** 94 **To** 2012 $24
Croser Non Vintage Pinot Noir Chardonnay NV Has more exuberant fruit than the traditional Croser style; stone fruit, citrus and a hint of strawberry are held in a basket of brioche, dosage spot on, the length impressive. Cork. 13.5% alc. **Rating** 94 **To** 2014 $29

ΨΨΨΨ˅ Adelaide Hills Viognier 2009 Rating 93 To 2013 $40
Coonawarra 2003 Rating 93 To 2016 $60 BE
Bridgewater Mill Adelaide Hills Sauvignon Blanc 2009 Rating 92
To 2011 $22
Piccadilly Valley Chardonnay 2008 Rating 90 To 2014 $40 BE
Bridgewater Mill Adelaide Hills Pinot Grigio 2009 Rating 90 To 2011 $22
Croser Piccadilly Valley Pinot Noir Chardonnay 2007 Rating 90
To 2014 $40

ΨΨΨΨ Bridgewater Mill Adelaide Hills Chardonnay 2008 Rating 89 To 2013 $20
Bridgewater Mill Adelaide Hills Shiraz 2007 Rating 87 To 2013 $24

Peter Lehmann   ★★★★★

Para Road, Tanunda, SA 5352 **Region** Barossa Valley
T (08) 8563 2100 **F** (08) 8563 3402 **www**.peterlehmannwines.com **Open** Mon–Fri 9.30–5,
w'ends & public hols 10.30–4.30
Winemaker Andrew Wigan, Ian Hongell, Kerry Morrison, Phil Lehmann **Est.** 1979
Cases 750 000
Under the benevolent ownership of the Swiss/Californian Hess Group, Peter Lehmann has
continued to flourish, making wines from all the major varieties at multiple price points, the
common link being over-delivery against expectations. Its record with its Reserve Eden Valley
Riesling (usually released when five years old) is second to none, and it has refined its semillons
to the point where it can take on the Hunter Valley at its own game with five-year-old releases,
exemplified by the recent Reserve releases. At the base level, the Semillon is the largest seller
in that category in the country. Yet it is as a red winemaker that Peter Lehmann is best known
in both domestic and export markets, with some outstanding wines leading the charge. Grapes
are purchased from 150 growers in the Barossa and Eden Valleys, and the quality of the wines
has seen production soar. Exports to all major markets.

ΨΨΨΨΨ Wigan Eden Valley Riesling 2005 Glowing yellow-green; a very complex
❂   bouquet with ripe lemon blossom and a touch of kerosene; the palate is much
         tighter but no less intense, still to fully unfurl its wings. Screwcap. 11.5% alc.
         Rating 94 To 2015 $40
❂   Margaret Barossa Semillon 2005 A complex wine; when compared to Hunter
         semillons it has a different DNA code; tasted separately, it seems as much Hunter as
         Barossa; manages to combine ripe citrus flavour with delicacy; long, satisfying finish.
         Screwcap. 11.5% alc. Rating 94 To 2020 $30
         Stonewell Shiraz 2005 The bouquet offers dark, dense, mocha fruit with a
         notable fruitcake spice presence; the palate is full and rich, almost brutish at first,
         but the fruit comes to the fore late in the piece while the charry oak also provides
         lift; has a harmonious finish. Screwcap. 14.5% alc. Rating 94 To 2024 $90 BE
❂   Black Queen Sparkling Shiraz 2005 From small Barossa Valley vineyards
         including one owned by Peter and Margaret Lehmann; 1 year in barrel before
         being tiraged and bottled, then 2 years (minimum) on lees. Elegant and very well
         balanced wine. Cork. 14% alc. Rating 94 To 2020 $40

ΨΨΨΨ˅ Eden Valley Shiraz 2007 Rating 93 To 2022 $30
         The King Vintage Port 1998 Rating 93 To 2028 $25
❂   Barossa Shiraz 2008 Highly polished red and black fruit bouquet, with a
         touch of licorice for interest; the palate is quite fleshy, with the tannins asserting
         themselves on the finish; warm and rich to conclude. Screwcap. 14.5% alc.
         Rating 91 To 2018 $18 BE
❂   Cabernet Merlot 2006 An elegant light- to medium-bodied wine that reflects
         the great vintage and (apparently) a significant Eden Valley contribution to the
         fresh cassis and blackcurrant fruits; the structure is particularly fine. Screwcap.
         14% alc. Rating 91 To 2014 $18
         Chardonnay Pinot Noir 2006 Rating 91 To 2012 $25
         Light Pass Shiraz 2007 Rating 90 To 2015 $30

ΨΨΨΨ Clancy's Shiraz Cabernet Sauvignon Merlot 2005 While light, the hue is
⊗   still good; a light-bodied wine that is fully mature, juicy fruit to the fore, tannins
and oak irrelevant. Screwcap. 14% alc. **Rating** 88 **To** 2012 $13

Pettavel   ★★★★

65 Pettavel Road, Waurn Ponds, Vic 3216 **Region** Geelong
T (03) 5266 1120 **F** (03) 5266 1140 **www**.pettavel.com **Open** 7 days 10–5.30
Winemaker Peter Flewellyn **Est.** 2000 **Cases** 15 000 **Vyds** 66.2 ha
Pettavel is a major landmark in the Geelong region. Mike and wife Sandi Fitzpatrick sold
their large Murray Darling winery and vineyards and moved to Geelong, and in 1990 began
developing vineyards at Sutherlands Creek. They have been joined by daughter Robyn (who
manages the overseas business) and son Reece (who co-ordinates the viticultural resources). A
striking winery/restaurant complex was opened in 2002. In February '10 negotiations for the
sale of the business were underway. Exports to the UK, the US and other major markets.

ΨΨΨΨΨ Evening Star Geelong Shiraz 2008 Bright clear crimson; a lively, cool-grown
shiraz, the fragrant bouquet in a spicy red berry spectrum, the medium-bodied
palate providing more of the same, a savoury finish adding further interest. Picked
at precisely the right time. Screwcap. 13.5% alc. **Rating** 93 **To** 2020 $20
Evening Star Geelong Late Harvest Riesling 2009 Already gleaning gold-
green; lusciously rich and sweet, but not particularly complex; fermented in four-
year-old French oak; no obvious oak influence. Screwcap. 11.5% alc. **Rating** 90
To 2012 $20

ΨΨΨΨ Evening Star Geelong Chardonnay 2008 **Rating** 89 **To** 2013 $20

Pewsey Vale   ★★★★★

Browns Road, Eden Valley, SA 5353 (postal) **Region** Eden Valley
T (08) 8561 3200 **F** (08) 8561 3393 **www**.pewseyvale.com **Open** At Yalumba
Winemaker Louisa Rose **Est.** 1847 **Cases** 20 000 **Vyds** 48 ha
Pewsey Vale was a famous vineyard established in 1847 by Joseph Gilbert, and it was
appropriate that when the Hill Smith family began the renaissance of the Adelaide Hills
plantings in 1961, it should do so by purchasing Pewsey Vale and establishing 40 ha of riesling
and 4 ha each of gewurztraminer and pinot gris. The Riesling has also finally benefited from
being the first wine to be bottled with a Stelvin screwcap in 1977. While public reaction
forced the abandonment of the initiative for almost 20 years, Pewsey Vale never lost faith in
the technical advantages of the closure. A quick taste (or better, a share of a bottle) of five- to
seven-year-old Contours Riesling will tell you why. Exports to all major markets.

ΨΨΨΨΨ The Contours Museum Reserve Eden Valley Riesling 2004 Intense lime
and apple aromas show the first signs of developing some toasty notes, the palate
brilliantly fresh, with a hint of CO_2; citrus, spice and minerally acidity run through
the lingering finish. Screwcap. 12.5% alc. **Rating** 96 **To** 2019 $27.95
⊗   Prima Eden Valley Riesling 2009 The glass closure is striking, but the contents
even more so; made in a distinctly Germanic style, picked young to enhance
natural acidity, and with residual sugar left to balance the wine's assertive acidity;
green apple fruit with a lemony edge is refreshing, long, even and absolutely
poised, exhibiting the winemaker's rare talent for this variety. Vino-Lok. 9.5% alc.
Rating 95 **To** 2025 $24.95 BE
⊗   Eden Valley Riesling 2009 The bouquet has a very aromatic display of citrus
blossom, the palate with delicious lime juice flavours backed by fine acidity; has
considerable length. Screwcap. 12.5% alc. **Rating** 94 **To** 2020 $22.95

ΨΨΨΨΨ Individual Vineyard Selection Eden Valley Pinot Gris 2009 **Rating** 92
To 2013 $24.95 BE
Individual Vineyard Selection Eden Valley Gewurztraminer 2009
Rating 90 **To** 2013 $24.95 BE

Pfeiffer Wines   ★★★★★

167 Distillery Road, Wahgunyah, Vic 3687 **Region** Rutherglen
T (02) 6033 2805 **F** (02) 6033 3158 **www.**pfeifferwines.com.au **Open** Mon–Sat 9–5,
Sun 10–5
Winemaker Chris and Jen Pfeiffer **Est.** 1984 **Cases** 20 000 **Vyds** 32 ha
Family-owned and run, Pfeiffer Wines occupies one of the historic wineries (built in 1880)
that abound in Northeast Victoria, and which is worth a visit on this score alone. The fortified
wines are good, and the table wines have improved considerably over recent vintages, drawing
upon estate plantings. In 2009 Pfeiffer celebrated its 25th vintage in fine style. Exports to the
UK, the US and other major markets.

🍷🍷🍷🍷🍷 **Rare Rutherglen Muscat NV** Not the most concentrated example, but
beautifully balanced and poised; the old material is held in check by winemaking
that maintains precision, and it is not until you taste the wine that its full force is
revealed; wonderfully long and complex, this once again shows why these wines
are national treasures. Screwcap. 17.5% alc. **Rating** 96 **To** 2011 $123 BE
Grand Rutherglen Muscat NV Deep colour, with toffee, raisins, grilled nuts
and lip smacking floral fruit; the palate is rich yet lithe, also focused with a seamless
and effortless grace; there is great freshness to the beautiful old material held
within. Screwcap. 17.5% alc. **Rating** 95 **To** 2011 $83.50 BE
Gamay 2009 Light crimson-purple; an inviting cherry bouquet, then a long
palate that is dry, but has deep red berry fruit and a spider web of tannins that
provide texture and structure. Screwcap. 12% alc. **Rating** 94 **To** 2015 $17

🍷🍷🍷🍷🍷 **Cabernet Sauvignon 2008** Good depth to colour; has good texture from
✪ built-in, gently savoury tannins, which add a pleasing touch of austerity to the
blackcurrant fruit and toasty oak. Screwcap. 14.5% alc. **Rating** 93 **To** 2020 $21
Christopher's VP 2006 Rating 93 **To** 2026 $24.50
Carlyle Shiraz 2008 Rating 92 **To** 2023 $18.50
Classic Rutherglen Muscat NV Rating 92 **To** 2011 $29 BE
Rutherglen Topaque NV Rating 91 **To** 2011 $19.90
Shiraz 2008 Rating 90 **To** 2017 $21

Pfitzner   ★★★★

PO Box 1098, North Adelaide, SA 5006 **Region** Adelaide Hills
T (08) 8332 4194 **Open** Not
Winemaker Petaluma **Est.** 1996 **Cases** 750 **Vyds** 5.55 ha
The subtitle to the Pfitzner name is Eric's Vineyard. The late Eric Pfitzner purchased and
aggregated a number of small, subdivided farmlets to protect the beauty of the Piccadilly Valley
from ugly rural development. His three sons inherited the vision, with the vineyard planted
principally to chardonnay and pinot noir, plus small amounts of sauvignon blanc and merlot.
Half the total property has been planted, the remainder preserving the natural eucalypt forest.
Roughly half the production is sold in the UK, no surprise given the bargain-basement prices
asked for these lovely wines.

🍷🍷🍷🍷🍷 **Eric's Vineyard Piccadilly Valley Chardonnay 2006** Grapefruit aromas and a
little struck match complexity add to the interest; fresh and vibrant on the palate,
with plenty of grapefruit and grilled nuts to conclude; quite soft on the finish.
Screwcap. 14% alc. **Rating** 90 **To** 2014 $28 BE

Phaedrus Estate   ★★★★

220 Mornington-Tyabb Road, Moorooduc, Vic 3933 **Region** Mornington Peninsula
T (03) 5978 8134 **F** (03) 5978 8134 **www.**phaedrus.com.au **Open** W'ends &
public hols 11–5
Winemaker Ewan Campbell, Maitena Zantvoort **Est.** 1997 **Cases** 2500 **Vyds** 2.5 ha
Since Maitena Zantvoort and Ewan Campbell established Phaedrus Estate, they have gained a
reputation for producing premium cool-climate wines. Their winemaking philosophy brings

art and science together to produce wines showing regional and varietal character with minimal winemaking interference. Exports to Hong Kong.

ŸŸŸŸŸ **Mornington Peninsula Pinot Noir 2009** Bright garnet; young and fresh bouquet, showing a prominent lick of new charry oak; dark fruits and attractive spice follow through on the quite fleshy and generous palate; while oaky early, the quality of the fruit promises to fulfil an interesting future. Screwcap. 13.4% alc. Rating 90 To 2014 $25 BE

ŸŸŸŸ **Reserve Mornington Peninsula Pinot Noir 2007** Rating 89 To 2013 $45

PHI   ★★★★★

Lusatia Park Vineyard, Owens Road, Woori Yallock, Vic 3139 **Region** Yarra Valley
T (03) 5964 6070 **www.phiwines.com Open** By appt
Winemaker Steve Webber **Est.** 2005 **Cases** 1300 **Vyds** 18 ha
This is a joint venture between two very influential wine families: De Bortoli and Shelmerdine. The key executives are Stephen Shelmerdine and Steve Webber (and their respective wives). It has a sole viticultural base: the Lusatia Park vineyard of the Shelmerdine family. Unusually, however, it is of specific rows of vines, not even blocks, although the rows are continuous. They are pruned and managed quite differently from the rest of the block, with the deliberate aim of strictly controlled yields. While the partnership was entered into in 2005, De Bortoli has been buying grapes from the vineyard since '02, and has had the opportunity to test the limits of the grapes. The outcome has been wines of the highest quality, and a joint venture that will last for many years. The name, incidentally, is derived from the 21st letter of the ancient Greek alphabet, symbolising perfect balance and harmony. It's courageous pricing for a new kid on the block, but reflects the confidence the families have in the wines. Exports to the UK.

ŸŸŸŸŸ **Lusatia Park Vineyard Yarra Valley Chardonnay 2008** Pale straw-green; an exercise in restraint from start to finish; gentle stone fruit and rock melon flavours are given texture (but minimal flavour) from barrel ferment and maturation. Needs a few years to open up more. Screwcap. 13% alc. Rating 94 To 2016 $50
Lusatia Park Vineyard Yarra Valley Pinot Noir 2008 Clear reddish-purple; a fragrant bouquet leads into a strongly textured palate, with spicy tannins woven through the black cherry and plum fruit; fine finish. Screwcap. 13% alc. Rating 94 To 2017 $60

Philip Lobley Wines   ★★★★☆

1084 Eucalyptus Road, Glenburn, Vic 3717 (postal) **Region** Upper Goulburn
T (03) 5797 8433 **F** (03) 5797 8433 **Open** Not
Winemaker Philip Lobley **Est.** 2008 **Cases** 400 **Vyds** 3.4 ha
The micro, patchwork quilt vineyard was first planted by Philip Lobley in 1995 with pinot noir, merlot and cabernet sauvignon. In 2008 nebbiolo, semillon, sauvignon blanc and moscato giallo (or gold muskateller, thought to be a version of muscat a petits grains) were added. These are high-density plantings and, with shoot and crop thinning, yield is kept to 600–800 grammes per vine. The red wines are wild yeast-fermented and neither filtered nor fined; the Yarra Valley Sauvignon Blanc (purchased) is whole bunch pressed and wild yeast fermented. The 2008 plantings were destroyed by the Black Saturday bushfires, and nebbiolo and moscato giallo have been replanted; 80% of the older wines recovered thanks to the good spring/ summer rainfall of '10.

ŸŸŸŸŸ **Reserve Sauvignon Blanc 2008** An austere style, albeit with no shortage of focused and concentrated flavours in a mineral and citrus pith spectrum; has exceptional length, and should open up very well in a couple of years. Screwcap. 12.5% alc. Rating 91 To 2013 $32

🌼 Philip Murphy Estate   ★★★★☆

484 Purves Road, Main Ridge, Vic 3928 (postal) **Region** Mornington Peninsula
T (03) 5989 6609 **F** (03) 5989 6615 **www**.philipmurphyestate.com.au **Open** Not
Winemaker Philip Murphy **Est.** 2004 **Cases** 200 **Vyds** 1 ha

Few would know the challenges facing small, start-up wineries better than Philip Murphy.
After the sale of his very substantial retail wine business to Coles, he and wife Jennifer decided
to have a seachange and move down to the Mornington Peninsula. He then happened to meet
Supreme Court Justice Kevin Bell of Hurley Vineyard, who gave him the confidence to enrol
in wine science at CSU in 2003. The Murphys built a new house, incorporating a winery
and cellar door underneath. They planted chardonnay and pinot noir (the latter French clones
and MV6), and the first experimental vintage followed in '07, the '08 'a big step forward' says
Philip, and he's not wrong. And, of course, he has completely circumvented the sale challenges
with the tiny make (although it may be expanded) by selling most of the wine through the
mailing list and small amounts through the Pinot Shop in Launceston, the Prince Wine Store
and Como Wines & Spirits in Melbourne.

🍷🍷🍷🍷🍷 Mornington Peninsula Pinot Noir 2008 Clear, bright red-purple; a fine but
complex bouquet, the palate headed in the same direction; perfectly ripened pinot
flavours of red and black cherry are supported by superfine tannins; very good line,
length and mouthfeel unfurling. Cork. 13.5% alc. **Rating** 94 **To** 2014 $43

Philip Shaw Wines   ★★★★★

Koomooloo Vineyard, Caldwell Lane, Orange, NSW 2800 **Region** Orange
T (02) 6365 2334 **F** (02) 6365 2449 **www**.philipshaw.com.au **Open** W'ends 12–5, or by appt
Winemaker Philip Shaw **Est.** 1989 **Cases** 15 000 **Vyds** 456.2 ha

Philip Shaw, former chief winemaker of Rosemount Estate and then Southcorp, first became
interested in the Orange region in 1985. In 1988 he purchased the Koomooloo Vineyard and
began extensive plantings, the varieties including shiraz, merlot, pinot noir, sauvignon blanc,
cabernet franc, cabernet sauvignon and viognier. Exports to the UK, the US, Sweden, Korea
and Indonesia.

🍷🍷🍷🍷🍷 No. 11 Orange Chardonnay 2008 The decades of experience Philip Shaw has
in making chardonnay making comes to the fore in this effortless wine, beautiful
flavours of white peach and nectarine married with subtle French oak; immaculate
line, length and balance. Screwcap. 12.5% alc. **Rating** 95 **To** 2016 $30
No. 11 Orange Chardonnay 2007 Bright straw-green; an elegant, intense wine
with great focus and precision; white peach and some citrus flavours drive the long
palate, oak in the background. Screwcap. 13% alc. **Rating** 95 **To** 2020 $30
No. 89 Orange Shiraz 2008 Much deeper crimson than The Idiot, the
colour and intensity of the bouquet and palate in part explained by the viognier
mentioned on the back label; has great structure and texture to the dark fruits of
the long, full-bodied palate. Seriously good wine. Screwcap. 13.7% alc. **Rating** 95
To 2028 $44

🍷🍷🍷🍷🍷 No. 19 Orange Sauvignon Blanc 2009 An interesting and complex sauvignon
✪ blanc with the suggestion of some barrel fermentation inputs; its flavours are
full and intense, but largely in a grassy/herbal/asparagus spectrum. Refreshingly
different. Screwcap. 13% alc. **Rating** 93 **To** 2012 $23

🍷🍷🍷🍷 The Idiot Orange Shiraz 2008 **Rating** 89 **To** 2014 $20
No. 8 Orange Pinot Noir 2007 **Rating** 88 **To** 2011 $49

Phillips Brook Estate   ★★★★☆

118 Redmond-Hay River Road, Redmond, WA 6332 **Region** Albany
T (08) 9845 3124 **www**.phillipsbrook.com.au **Open** Wed–Sun 11–4
Winemaker Harewood Estate (James Kellie) **Est.** 1975 **Cases** 1200 **Vyds** 12 ha

Bronwen and David Newbury first became viticulturists near the thoroughly unlikely town of Bourke in western NSW, but in 2001 they moved back to the Great Southern region. The name comes from the adjoining Phillips Brook Nature Reserve and the permanent creek on their property. Riesling and cabernet sauvignon (2 ha each) had been planted in 1975, but thoroughly neglected. The Newburys have rehabilitated the old plantings, and have added chardonnay (5 ha), merlot, cabernet franc and sauvignon blanc (1 ha each).

ŸŸŸŸŸ **Albany Riesling 2009** Light straw-green; a fragrant lime and passionfruit
✪ blossom bouquet, then a perfectly balanced and textured palate, citrus/lime interwoven with mineral notes. Screwcap. 12% alc. **Rating** 94 **To** 2019 $20

ŸŸŸŸŸ **Albany Sauvignon Blanc 2009** A fragrant bouquet of citrus and passionfruit,
✪ the finely balanced and crafted palate providing more of the same, the finish bright and fresh. Screwcap. 12.5% alc. **Rating** 93 **To** 2011 $18

✪ **Albany Chardonnay 2008** Green-straw; sensitive winemaking has allowed the white peach and citrus fruit free rein, yet added a touch of barrel ferment complexity; the palate is long, the finish clean. Screwcap. 13% alc. **Rating** 93 **To** 2014 $20

ŸŸŸŸ **Albany Cabernet Sauvignon 2007** **Rating** 89 **To** 2015 $20

Piano Gully ★★★☆

Piano Gully Road, Manjimup, WA 6258 **Region** Pemberton
T (08) 9316 0336 **F** (08) 9316 0336 **www.**pianogully.com.au **Open** By appt
Winemaker Naturaliste Vintners **Est.** 1987 **Cases** 3500 **Vyds** 6 ha
The Piano Gully vineyard, established in 1987 on rich Karri loam, 10 km south of Manjimup (but in the Pemberton region), includes chardonnay, sauvignon blanc, cabernet sauvignon, viognier, shiraz and merlot. The name of the road (and the winery) commemorates the shipping of a piano from England by one of the first settlers in the region. The horse and cart carrying the piano on the last leg of the long journey were within sight of their destination when the piano fell from the cart and was destroyed.

ŸŸŸŸŸ **Sauvignon Blanc 2009** Exceedingly pale colour; crisp, clean and fresh, with
✪ predominant herb, grass and citrus notes accompanied by subtle tropical fruits. Screwcap. 13% alc. **Rating** 90 **To** 2011 $18

ŸŸŸŸ **Sauvignon Blanc Semillon 2009** Exceedingly pale colour; a delicate but
✪ flavoursome blend, with passionfruit woven through grass and citrus components; good length and balance. Screwcap. 13% alc. **Rating** 89 **To** 2011 $18

Picardy ★★★★☆

Cnr Vasse Highway/Eastbrook Road, Pemberton, WA 6260 **Region** Pemberton
T (08) 9776 0036 **F** (08) 9776 0245 **www.**picardy.com.au **Open** By appt
Winemaker Bill and Dan Pannell **Est.** 1993 **Cases** 6000 **Vyds** 10 ha
Picardy is owned by Dr Bill Pannell, wife Sandra, son Daniel and daughter Jodie; Bill and Sandra founded Moss Wood winery in Margaret River in 1969. Picardy initially reflected Bill's view that the Pemberton area was one of the best regions in Australia for pinot noir and chardonnay, but it is now clear Pemberton has as much Rhône and Bordeaux as Burgundy in its veins. The Pannell Family wines are a separate venture to Picardy. Exports to the UK, the US and other major markets.

ŸŸŸŸŸ **Pannell Family Pemberton Merlot Cabernet Sauvignon Cabernet Franc**
✪ **2007** Bright colour; a most attractive and fragrant wine, with fresh cassis notes giving a juicy cast to the palate, supported by fine tannins and quality French oak. Cork. 14% alc. **Rating** 94 **To** 2015 $25

ŸŸŸŸŸ **Pannell Family Pemberton Shiraz 2007** **Rating** 90 **To** 2015 $25

ŸŸŸŸ **Pannell Family Pemberton Pinot Noir 2007** **Rating** 88 **To** 2012 $35

Pierro   ★★★★★

Caves Road, Wilyabrup via Cowaramup, WA 6284 **Region** Margaret River
T (08) 9755 6220 **F** (08) 9755 6308 **www**.pierro.com.au **Open** 7 days 10–5
Winemaker Dr Michael Peterkin **Est.** 1979 **Cases** 10 000 **Vyds** 8.65 ha
Dr Michael Peterkin is another of the legion of Margaret River medical practitioners; for
good measure, he married into the Cullen family. Pierro is renowned for its stylish white
wines, which often exhibit tremendous complexity; the Chardonnay can be monumental in
its weight and texture. That said, its red wines from good vintages can be every bit as good.
Exports to the UK, the US, Japan and Indonesia.

♀♀♀♀♀ Margaret River Chardonnay 2008 A first-class example of Margaret River
          chardonnay, offering finesse, depth and complexity of flavours that expand on
          the back-palate and finish in the manner of great pinot noir. Screwcap. 14% alc.
          Rating 96 To 2015 $76
          Margaret River LTC 2009 The semillon and sauvignon blanc (the major
          components) have disappeared from the front label, leaving the 'little touch
          of chardonnay' initials. What has not changed is the subtle fusion of the three
          varieties, the palate length and the crisp, lively finish. Screwcap. 13.5% alc.
          Rating 94 To 2013 $31
          Margaret River Cabernet Sauvignon Merlot LTCf 2007 Light but bright
          hue; a stylish, medium-bodied wine that establishes a tension between its bright
          fruits and fine, savoury/spicy tannins, the long palate well balanced and complete.
          Screwcap. 14.5% alc. Rating 94 To 2019 $37

Pike & Joyce   ★★★★★

PO Box 54, Sevenhill, SA 5453 **Region** Adelaide Hills
T (08) 8843 4370 **F** (08) 8843 4353 **www**.pikeandjoyce.com.au **Open** Not
Winemaker Neil Pike, John Trotter, Steve Baraglia **Est.** 1998 **Cases** 5000 **Vyds** 18.5 ha
This is a partnership between the Pike family (of Clare Valley fame) and the Joyce family,
related to Andrew Pike's wife, Cathy. The Joyce family have been orchardists at Lenswood for
over 100 years, but also have extensive operations in the Riverland. Together with Andrew
they have established a vineyard planted to sauvignon blanc (5.9 ha), pinot noir (5.73 ha), pinot
gris (3.22 ha), chardonnay (3.18 ha) and semillon (0.47 ha). The wines are made at Pikes Clare
Valley winery. Exports to the UK, Canada, The Netherlands, Taiwan, Singapore and Japan.

♀♀♀♀♀ Adelaide Hills Chardonnay 2008 Light straw-green; an impressively
          fragrant bouquet with white peach and grapefruit leads into a palate with very
          good mouthfeel to the fruit and French oak. Screwcap. 13.5% alc. Rating 95
          To 2018 $35
✪   Adelaide Hills Pinot Gris 2009 This is a pinot gris with real attitude, the
          flavours positive rather than apologetic, ranging from the expected pear to
          the unexpected stone fruit and a drizzle of lemon juice. Screwcap. 13.5% alc.
          Rating 94 To 2011 $20

♀♀♀♀♀ Adelaide Hills Sauvignon Blanc 2009 Rating 93 To 2011 $20
          Adelaide Hills Pinot Noir 2008 Rating 93 To 2016 $35
          W.J.J. Reserve Adelaide Hills Pinot Noir 2007 Rating 93 To 2014 $65
          The Bleedings Adelaide Hills Pinot Noir Rose 2009 Rating 90 To 2011 $20

Pikes   ★★★★★

Polish Hill River Road, Sevenhill, SA 5453 **Region** Clare Valley
T (08) 8843 4370 **F** (08) 8843 4353 **www**.pikeswines.com.au **Open** 7 days 10–4
Winemaker Neil Pike, John Trotter, Steve Baraglia **Est.** 1984 **Cases** 35 000 **Vyds** 69.41 ha
Owned by the Pike brothers: Andrew was for many years the senior viticulturist with
Southcorp, Neil was a winemaker at Mitchell. Pikes now has its own winery, with Neil
presiding. In most vintages its white wines, led by Riesling, are the most impressive. Planting
of the vineyards has been an ongoing affair, with a panoply of varietals, new and traditional,

reflected in the 2007 plantings of an additional 4.3 ha of riesling (26 ha in total), 3.5 ha of shiraz and a first-up planting of 1.24 ha of savagnin. The Merle is Pikes' limited production, flagship Riesling. A recent mini-vertical tasting shows just how good the wine is. Exports to Canada, The Netherlands, Switzerland, Cyprus, Singapore, Malaysia, Hong Kong, Taiwan, South Korea, Japan and China.

ΨΨΨΨΨ **The Merle Reserve Clare Valley Riesling 2009** Pale straw-green; a more expressive bouquet than Traditionale, the palate with beautifully modulated, but very intense, juicy lime flavours and exceptional thrust to the long finish thanks to perfect acidity; every component in balance. Screwcap. 12.5% alc. **Rating** 96 To 2025 $38

✪ **Traditionale Clare Valley Riesling 2009** Pale straw-green; a gently flowery bouquet then a very precise, pure and penetrating palate, lime, lemon and slatey mineral notes driving through to the finish. Screwcap. 12% alc. **Rating** 94 To 2022 $23

✪ **Valley's End Clare Valley Sauvignon Blanc Semillon 2009** Bright colour; a powerful and focused blend, with great energy and concentration to the long palate with its seamless mix of herb, citrus and passionfruit; good style, with time in front of it. Screwcap. 12% alc. **Rating** 94 To 2012 $18

ΨΨΨΨΩ **The Dogwalk Clare Valley Cabernet Merlot 2007** A well-made wine, with
✪ good balance and structure; black fruits with hints of leather, earth and olive run through the long medium- to full-bodied palate. Screwcap. 14% alc. **Rating** 91 To 2015 $19
The Hill Block Clare Valley Cabernet 2007 Rating 91 To 2015 $28
Luccio Clare Valley Pinot Grigio 2009 Rating 90 To 2011 $17

ΨΨΨΨ **The Assemblage Clare Valley Shiraz Mourvedre Grenache 2007**
Rating 89 To 2014 $20
✪ **Luccio Clare Valley Sangiovese Merlot Cabernet Sauvignon 2007** Has the light colour expected of sangiovese, but the hue is still red; the light-bodied wine has distinct sour cherry aromas that are reflected on the light palate, the other two varieties making no impact. Screwcap. 13.5% alc. **Rating** 89 To 2012 $17
✪ **The Red Mullet Clare Valley Shiraz Grenache Mourvedre Tempranillo 2007** Holding colour; a wine almost entirely driven by fruit rather than tannins or oak; has pleasing red and black fruits, and a soft finish. Screwcap. 14.5% alc. **Rating** 88 To 2011 $15
The White Mullet Clare Valley Riesling Viognier Chenin Blanc Sauvignon Blanc 2009 Rating 87 To 2012 $15
Eastside Clare Valley Shiraz 2007 Rating 87 To 2014 $25

🍂 Pimpernel Vineyards ★★★★☆

6 Hill Road, Coldstream, Vic 3770 **Region** Yarra Valley
T 0457 326 436 **F** (03) 9817 3787 **www.**pimpernelvineyards.com.au **Open** By appt
Winemaker Mark Horrigan, Damien Archibald **Est.** 2001 **Cases** 1000 **Vyds** 6 ha
Lilydale-based cardiologist Mark Horrigan's love affair with wine started long before he had heard about either the Yarra Valley or his family's links centuries ago in Condrieu, France. He is a direct descendant of the Chapuis family, his ultimate ancestors first buried in the Church of St Etienne in 1377. In a cosmopolitan twist, his father came from a Welsh mining village, but made his way to university and found many things to enjoy, not the least wine. When the family moved to Australia in 1959, wine remained part of everyday life and, as Mark grew up in the 1970s, the obsession passed from father to son. In 1997, while working at Prince Alfred Hospital (Sydney), Mark was offered a job in Melbourne and within weeks of arriving had started looking for a likely spot in the Yarra Valley. In 2001 he and wife Fiona purchased the property on which they have built a (second) house, planted a vineyard, and erected a capacious winery designed by WA architect Peter Moran. In the course of doing so they became good friends of near-neighbour, the late Bailey Carrodus. A cellar door is planned for mid-2010.

ΨΨΨΨΨ Chardonnay 2008 Extremely good glowing green; a chardonnay bursting with flavour and character, more aligned to Margaret River than traditional Yarra Valley, yet all the power comes from the concentrated nectarine and peach fruit, not barrel ferment French oak, although it is there. Great first up wine. Diam. 13.5% alc. Rating 94 To 2014 $36

ΨΨΨΨΨ Pinot Noir 2008 Rating 92 To 2013 $36
Barrel Selection Pinot Noir 2008 Rating 91 To 2014 $42

ΨΨΨΨ Shiraz 2008 Rating 89 To 2016 $35

Pinelli Wines ★★★★

30 Bennett Street, Caversham, WA 6055 **Region** Swan District
T (08) 9279 6818 **F** (08) 9377 4259 **www.**pinelliwines.com.au **Open** Mon–Sat 9–5,
Sun & public hols 10–5
Winemaker Robert and Daniel Pinelli **Est.** 1980 **Cases** 20 000 **Vyds** 9.78 ha
Domenic and Iolanda Pinelli emigrated from Italy in the mid-1950s, and it was not long before Domenic became employed by Waldeck Wines, then one of the Swan Valley's more important wineries. With the benefit of 20 years' experience gained with Waldeck, in 1980 he purchased a 2.8-ha vineyard that had been established many years previously. It became the site of the Pinelli family winery, cellar door and home vineyard, subsequently significantly expanded to its present level, with cabernet sauvignon, colombard, merlot and shiraz. Son Robert graduated with a degree in oenology from Roseworthy in 1987, and has been the winemaker at Pinelli for over 20 years. His brother Daniel obtained a degree in civil engineering from the University of Western Australia in '94, but eventually the lure of the family winery became too strong, so he joined his brother in '02, and (using the distance education program) obtained his oenology degree from CSU in '07. He graduated with distinction, and was awarded the Domaine Chandon Sparkling Wine Award for best sparkling wine production student.

ΨΨΨΨΨ Family Reserve Swan Valley Semillon Sauvignon Blanc 2009 Unstated
✪ percentages of Swan Valley Semillon/Margaret River Sauvignon Blanc work well together to provide plenty of depth of ripe flavours notwithstanding moderate alcohol, which in turn gives acidity to the finish. Gold medal Swan Valley Wine Show '09. Screwcap. 12.5% alc. Rating 90 To 2011 $16

✪ Family Reserve Swan Valley Verdelho 2009 A very well made wine, with clean fruit salad and citrus aromas and flavours, finishing dry and fresh. Trophy Swan Valley Wine Show '09. Screwcap. 12.6% alc. Rating 90 To 2011 $14

ΨΨΨΨ Family Reserve Swan Valley Chenin Blanc 2009 Pale straw-green; mainline
✪ Swan Valley chenin blanc style, with abundant, ripe, tropical fruit flavours, and clever winemaking to keep the alcohol at a low level. Screwcap. 11.7% alc. Rating 88 To 2011 $14
Family Reserve Swan Valley Shiraz 2007 Rating 88 To 2013 $21
Swan Valley Late Harvest 2009 Rating 87 To 2010 $14

Pipers Brook Vineyard ★★★★★

1216 Pipers Brook Road, Pipers Brook, Tas 7254 **Region** Northern Tasmania
T (03) 6382 7527 **F** (03) 6382 7226 **www.**kreglingerwineestates.com **Open** 7 days 10–5
Winemaker René Bezemer **Est.** 1974 **Cases** 100 000 **Vyds** 185 ha
The Pipers Brook Tasmanian empire has 185 ha of vineyard supporting the Pipers Brook and Ninth Island labels, with the major focus, of course, being on Pipers Brook. Fastidious viticulture and winemaking, immaculate packaging and enterprising marketing create a potent and effective blend. Pipers Brook operates two cellar door outlets, one at headquarters, the other at Strathlyn. In 2001 it was acquired by Belgian-owned sheepskin business Kreglinger, which has also established a large winery and vineyard (Norfolk Rise) at Mount Benson in SA. Exports to the UK, the US and other major markets.

ΨΨΨΨΨ Estate Riesling 2009 A floral bouquet with some blossom aromas leads into a palate with intense, layered fruit flavours running from citrus to full-on tropical, offset against equally intense natural acidity. Striking wine. Screwcap. 13% alc. Rating 95 To 2020 $27.50

Reserve Pinot Noir 2005 Particularly good hue for its age; a wine with considerable power and intensity, especially for Pipers Brook; has vibrant red fruits on the mid-palate, then a very long, tangy, savoury finish. Classic style. Cork. 13.5% alc. Rating 95 To 2014 $75

Estate Pinot Noir 2008 The bright red fruits of this wine are dominated by lavish oak-handling, assuredly of the highest quality; however, the palate tells the true story, with liqueur cherry, clove and a perceptible ironstone character; treads the line between sweet fruit and savoury complexity with aplomb, and will deliver real pleasure when the oak further integrates with the fruit. Screwcap. 13.5% alc. Rating 94 To 2016 $41.50 BE

The Lyre Pinot Noir 2005 Showing some maturity, with secondary gamey notes giving way to plum and spiced mulberry fruit; there is strong oak on entry, but the fleshy fruit, and gamey nuances emerge triumphant in the end; firm and chewy tannins remain in abundance on the finish; the price may be a sticking point, but there is plenty of wine here. Cork. 13.5% alc. Rating 94 To 2014 $125 BE

Kreglinger Vintage Brut 2003 Five or so years on lees is what most Tasmanian sparkling wines need to fully show their wings; this wine has perfectly counterbalanced freshness and complexity, and (of course) great length. Cork. 12.5% alc. Rating 94 To 2014 $50

ΨΨΨΨΨ Estate Gewurztraminer 2009 Rating 93 To 2014 $27.50 BE
Estate Chardonnay 2008 Rating 93 To 2018 $34 BE
Kreglinger Blanc de Blancs 2003 Rating 93 To 2016 $65 BE
Reserve Chardonnay 2005 Rating 92 To 2020 $45
Kreglinger Vintage Brut 2004 Rating 92 To 2015 $50 BE
Ninth Island Pinot Grigio 2009 Rating 90 To 2011 $21.50
Ninth Island Chardonnay Pinot Noir Pinot Meunier NV Rating 90 To 2014 $27 BE

Pirie Tasmania ★★★★★

1a Waldhorn Drive, Rosevears, Tas 7277 **Region** Northern Tasmania
T (03) 6335 5480 **F** (03) 6335 5490 **www.**pirietasmania.com.au **Open** 7 days 10–5
Winemaker Andrew Pirie **Est.** 2004 **Cases** 12 000 **Vyds** 82.9 ha
Andrew Pirie has had a lifetime of experience growing grapes and making wine in northern Tasmania. He established Pipers Brook Vineyard in 1974, and was responsible for making it the best-known Tasmanian winery in the 1980s and much of the '90s, before he relinquished what was then part-ownership. He has since become increasingly involved with Tamar Ridge Estates (owned by Gunns Limited, the controversial Tasmanian timber company), of which he is CEO, and which owns Pirie Tasmania in conjunction with Andrew Pirie. The cellar door is now located at the spectacularly situated Rosevears Vineyard, which is also home to Estelle Restaurant, with its panoramic views over the Tamar River. Some will no doubt find it ironic that one of Rosevears' attractions is said to be eco-retreats. This is peripheral to the quality of the wines, which has always been very good. Exports to the UK, the US and other major markets.

ΨΨΨΨΨ Chardonnay 2007 A very good example of perfume and power, with pure
✪ citrus, almonds and hazelnuts on display; the palate takes it up a notch by providing layers of flavour, vibrant acidity and loads of complex grilled nut character that persists for an age; this should age gracefully, but is super in its youth. Screwcap. 13.5% alc. Rating 95 To 2016 $39 BE

Pinot Noir 2008 Decidedly reserved bouquet, with a strong savoury aspect reminiscent of graphite and showing hints of dark cherries; the fruit makes an appearance on the palate, but the mineral edge remains, and there is a firmness of tannin that is ultimately very satisfying, drawing the palate out to a long and even conclusion. Screwcap. 14% alc. **Rating** 94 **To** 2015 $39 BE

ΥΥΥΥΥ South Chardonnay 2008 **Rating** 92 **To** 2015 $22 BE
Non Vintage NV **Rating** 92 **To** 2013 $32 BE

ΥΥΥΥ South Estelle 2007 **Rating** 89 **To** 2012 $19 BE
South Riesling 2008 **Rating** 88 **To** 2014 $20 BE

Pirramimma   ★★★★★

Johnston Road, McLaren Vale, SA 5171 **Region** McLaren Vale
T (08) 8323 8205 **F** (08) 8323 9224 **www**.pirramimma.com.au **Open** Mon–Fri 10–5,
w'ends & public hols 10.30–5
Winemaker Geoff Johnston **Est.** 1892 **Cases** 50 000 **Vyds** 192 ha
A long-established, family-owned company with outstanding vineyard resources. It is using those resources to full effect, with a series of intense old-vine varietals including Semillon, Sauvignon Blanc, Chardonnay, Shiraz, Grenache, Cabernet Sauvignon and Petit Verdot, all fashioned without over-embellishment. There are two quality tiers, both offering excellent value, the packaging significantly upgraded recently. Exports to the US and other major markets.

ΥΥΥΥΥ McLaren Vale Petit Verdot 2006 One of the first producers of quality petit
✪   verdot in Australia; this is an aristocratic wine, with lovely cedary overtones to
         its blackcurrant fruits, the tannins perfectly balanced. Cork. 14.5% alc. **Rating** 95
         To 2021 $25
✪   McLaren Vale Shiraz 2006 Colour showing the first phase of development, but
         good; a complex yet harmonious and supple shiraz, with a cascade of dark berry,
         spice, vanilla and a whisk of dark chocolate, the tannins fine. Pity this had the cork
         rather than Stock's Hill. 14.5% alc. **Rating** 94 **To** 2020 $25

ΥΥΥΥ Katunga Shiraz 2008 **Rating** 90 **To** 2014 $19.95

ΥΥΥΥ 12 Year Old McLaren Vale Liqueur Tawny NV Red-brown; Christmas cake,
✪   toffee, raisin and dark chocolate flavours are finished with drying toasty/biscuity
         characters. Cork. 18.5% alc. **Rating** 89 **To** 2011 $15
✪   Stock's Hill McLaren Vale Shiraz 2006 Similar colour to the standard; a mix
         of savoury, earthy, chocolatey aromas and flavours to a light- to medium-bodied
         wine. For all occasions. Screwcap. 14% alc. **Rating** 88 **To** 2013 $16
         Katunga GTS 2006 **Rating** 88 **To** 2016 $19.95
         Scarlet Sparkling NV **Rating** 88 **To** 2012 $18
✪   Greg Nomad McLaren Vale Sparkling Shiraz 2008 Deep colour; despite the
         extreme youth of the base material, has avoided excessive sweetness and has length.
         Cork. 13% alc. **Rating** 87 **To** 2011 $15

Pizzini   ★★★★☆

175 King Valley Road, Whitfield, Vic 3768 **Region** King Valley
T (03) 5729 8278 **F** (03) 5729 8495 **www**.pizzini.com.au **Open** 7 days 10–5
Winemaker Joel and Alfred Pizzini **Est.** 1980 **Cases** 21 000 **Vyds** 38 ha
Fred and Katrina Pizzini have been grapegrowers in the King Valley for over 25 years, with a substantial vineyard. Originally much of the grape production was sold, but today 80% is retained for the Pizzini brand, and the focus is on winemaking, which has been particularly successful. Their wines rank high among the many King Valley producers. It is not surprising that their wines should span both Italian and traditional varieties, and I can personally vouch for their Italian cooking skills. The Vino e Vita cooking school is due to open in 2010, the date yet to be fixed at the time of going to press. Exports to Japan.

ŢŢŢŢŢ Whitefields King Valley Pinot Grigio 2009 Pale straw, vibrant green hue; savoury anise and pear bouquet, supported by a delicate underpinning of lemon; the palate is zesty and quite savoury, with depth of flavour and plenty of personality. Screwcap. 13.4% alc. **Rating** 92 **To** 2013 $25 BE

✪ King Valley Arneis 2009 Fresh pear and straw fairly leap out of the glass, with an attractive edge of nectarine; the palate shows plenty of weight, yet maintains freshness through lively acidity and a touch of grip to conclude; a good example of the variety and style. Screwcap. 13.5% alc. **Rating** 92 **To** 2012 $20 BE

ŢŢŢŢ King Valley Shiraz 2008 **Rating** 89 **To** 2014 $20 BE

✪ King Valley Sauvignon Blanc 2009 Interesting grapefruit and pear bouquet; the citrus element drives through on the palate, sitting comfortably alongside a savoury/mineral quality; light, fresh, crisp and dry. Screwcap. 11.2% alc. **Rating** 88 **To** 2012 $16 BE

Rosetta 2008 **Rating** 88 **To** 2010 $16.50

King Valley Nebbiolo 2005 **Rating** 88 **To** 2014 $45 BE

Plan B ★★★★

679 Calgardup Road, Forest Grove, WA 6286 **Region** Margaret River
T 0413 759 030 **F** (08) 9755 6267 **www**.planbwines.com **Open** At Arlewood Estate
Winemaker Bill Crappsley **Est.** 2005 **Cases** 6000 **Vyds** 8 ha
This is a joint venture between Bill Crappsley, a 43-year veteran winemaker/consultant; Martin Miles, who has a wine distribution business in the southwestern part of the state; Gary Gosatti, of Arlewood Estate; and Terry Chellappah, wine consultant and now also in partnership with Gary. The shiraz is sourced from Bill's Calgardup Vineyard, the remaining wines from Arlewood, and all are single-vineyard releases. Releases of Chardonnay, Shiraz and a white blend, Mental Blanc, were not bottled in time for this edition, but will be released at the end of 2010. Exports to the UK, Canada, Sweden, Norway, Singapore, Hong Kong and China.

ŢŢŢŢŢ Frankland River Shiraz 2007 Strong crimson-purple; a dense and powerful
✪ wine, with strong licorice and spicy black fruits, finishing with ripe tannins and oak. Will live for decades. Screwcap. 15% alc. **Rating** 93 **To** 2027 $19

✪ Frankland River Chardonnay 2007 Charged with masses of nectarine, melon and grapefruit on the medium-bodied palate, oak irrelevant (if, indeed, present). Screwcap. 14.5% alc. **Rating** 90 **To** 2013 $19

Plantagenet ★★★★★

Albany Highway, Mount Barker, WA 6324 **Region** Mount Barker
T (08) 9851 3131 **F** (08) 9851 1839 **www**.plantagenetwines.com **Open** 7 days 9–5
Winemaker John Durham, Andries Mostert **Est.** 1974 **Cases** 90 000 **Vyds** 130 ha
Plantagenet was established by Tony Smith, who continues to be involved in its management 35 years later, and notwithstanding that it has been owned by Lionel Samson & Son for many years. During his long stewardship, he established five vineyards: Bouverie in 1968, Wyjup in '71, Rocky Horror I in '88, Rocky Horror 2 in '99 and Rosetta in 2001. These vineyards are the cornerstone of the substantial production of the consistently high quality wines that have always been the mark of Plantagenet: highly aromatic Riesling, tangy citrus-tinged Chardonnay, glorious Rhône-style Shiraz and ultra-stylish Cabernet Sauvignon. Exports to all major markets.

ŢŢŢŢŢ Great Southern Riesling 2009 A flowery, almost spicy, bouquet, then a finely
✪ chiselled and precise palate, lime and mineral flavours intertwined; long-term future assured. Screwcap. 11.5% alc. **Rating** 94 **To** 2024 $22

Mount Barker Cabernet Sauvignon 2008 Bright and clear red-purple; a perfectly weighted wine with classic cool-grown varietal character; blackcurrant and nuances of olive, briar and earth; the finish is long and firm, as befits the variety. Screwcap. 14% alc. **Rating** 94 **To** 2020 $37

ŢŢŢŢŢ   Great Southern Brut 2006 Rating 92 To 2013 $27
         Great Southern Chardonnay 2008 Rating 91 To 2012 $28
✪   Omrah Shiraz 2007 Bright crimson; a fragrant black fruit and spice bouquet,
         then a lively medium-bodied palate tracking the bouquet, adding fine tannins on
         the finish. Screwcap. 14.5% alc. Rating 91 To 2015 $18
✪   Omrah Sauvignon Blanc 2009 Light straw-green; a pungent bouquet of
         herb, asparagus and grass predictably leads into a zesty palate, with lemon/lime
         characters taking the driver's seat. Screwcap. 13% alc. Rating 90 To 2011 $18
✪   Hazard Hill Semillon Sauvignon Blanc 2009 A bright and fragrant bouquet
         is a promising start, and the citrus and tropical palate does not disappoint; finishes
         with refreshing lemony acidity. Screwcap. 12.5% alc. Rating 90 To 2011 $13
✪   Omrah Cabernet Merlot 2007 Good crimson; a thoroughly enjoyable upper-
         level commercial wine, with a juicy display of black and redcurrant fruits, supple
         tannins and good balance. Screwcap. 14.5% alc. Rating 90 To 2015 $18
         Ringbark Riesling 2009 Rating 90 To 2014 $25

ŢŢŢŢ   Omrah Sangiovese 2008 Good colour; a sangiovese that pulls no punches,
✪   the black cherry/sour cherry/red cherry fruit corralled by unrelenting tannins;
         food and time may reveal a very interesting wine. Screwcap. 14% alc. Rating 89
         To 2015 $18
         Omrah Unoaked Chardonnay 2009 Rating 87 To 2011 $19

Plunkett Fowles   ★★★★★

Cnr Hume Freeway/Lambing Gully Road, Avenel, Vic 3664 **Region** Strathbogie Ranges
T (03) 5796 2150 **F** (03) 5796 2147 **www.plunkettfowles.com.au Open** 7 days 9–5
Winemaker Sam Plunkett, Victor Nash, Lindsay Brown, Michael Clayden **Est.** 1968
Cases 30 000 **Vyds** 193.64 ha
Plunkett Fowles is the new face for two families committed to building a prominent international wine business. The co-managers, Sam Plunkett and Matt Fowles, are in their late
30s and late 20s, with both winemaking and business skills. The two families have had a long
association with this dry, cool, granitic region, which has given them a deep understanding
of their extensive vineyards (chardonnay, shiraz, cabernet sauvignon, sauvignon blanc, pinot
noir, merlot, riesling, semillon, viognier, gewurztraminer, verdelho, savagnin, tempranillo and
lagrein). They are committed to a strategy of selling wine that exceeds the expectations for
any given price point. Exports to the UK, the US and other major markets.

ŢŢŢŢŢ   Stone Dwellers Strathbogie Ranges Chardonnay 2008 Still very light
✪   colour; an elegant wine, with a lingering, drawn-out finish emphasising the length
         of the palate; citrussy acidity also comes to the party, the oak very well integrated
         and balanced. Screwcap. 13.5% alc. Rating 94 To 2016 $24.95
         Ladies Who Shoot Their Lunch Strathbogie Ranges Shiraz 2007 Strong
         crimson-purple; an attractive bouquet of black fruits, the medium-bodied, supple
         palate providing more of the same, with a light spicy/savoury twist on the finish;
         carries its alcohol well. Screwcap. 15% alc. Rating 94 To 2017 $34.95
         Exception Stone Dwellers Strathbogie Ranges Shiraz 2004 Amazingly
         deep colour, still with a crimson-purple rim; the complex foresty black fruits of
         the bouquet lead into a massively concentrated full-bodied palate, fruit, tannins
         and oak all striving for supremacy. A wine that will outlive the cork. 14.5% alc.
         Rating 94 To 2030 $125
✪   Stone Dwellers Strathbogie Ranges Cabernet Sauvignon 2008 Deep
         colour; a powerful, medium- to full-bodied wine, ample black fruits and firm
         tannins marching arm in arm down the long palate and into the aftertaste; balance
         is the key. Screwcap. 15% alc. Rating 94 To 2020 $24.95

ŢŢŢŢŢ   Ladies Who Shoot Their Lunch Strathbogie Ranges Chardonnay 2008
         Rating 92 To 2014 $34.95
         Stone Dwellers Strathbogie Ranges Shiraz 2007 Rating 92 To 2015 $24.95
         Stone Dwellers Strathbogie Ranges Merlot 2008 Rating 92 To 2016 $24.95

Ladies Who Shoot Their Lunch Riesling 2008 Rating 91 To 2016 $34.95
Ladies Who Shoot Their Lunch Strathbogie Ranges Shiraz 2006
Rating 91 To 2015 $34.95
Stone Dwellers Museum Release Strathbogie Ranges Riesling 2004
Rating 90 To 2013 $29.95

Poacher's Ridge Vineyard ★★★★★

1630 Spencer Road, Narrikup, WA 6326 **Region** Mount Barker
T (08) 9857 6066 **F** (08) 9857 6077 **www**.prv.com.au **Open** Fri–Sun 10–4, or by appt
Winemaker Robert Diletti (Contract) **Est.** 2000 **Cases** 2200 **Vyds** 6.7 ha
Alex and Janet Taylor purchased the Poacher's Ridge property in 1999; before then it had
been used for cattle grazing. The vineyard includes shiraz, cabernet sauvignon, merlot, riesling,
marsanne and viognier. The first small crop came in 2003, a larger one in '04, together making
an auspicious debut. However, winning the Tri Nations merlot class against the might of
Australia, NZ and South Africa in 2007 with its '05 Louis' Block Great Southern Merlot was
a dream come true.

Louis' Block Great Southern Riesling 2009 Pure citrus bouquet of ripe
lemon, underpinned by mineral complexity; the palate is very fine and the acidity
linear, finishing with clean, vibrant and generous fruit. Screwcap. 11.6% alc.
Rating 94 $19 BE

Sophie's Yard Great Southern Shiraz Viognier 2008 Aromatic blue fruit
profile, layered with spice; attractive and full of ripe juicy fruit; bright acid is
prominent on the finish, drawing the light- to medium-bodied palate out to an
even and harmonious conclusion. Screwcap. 13.1% alc. Rating 94 $26 BE

Louis' Block Great Southern Cabernet Sauvignon 2008 Strong crimson-
purple; has an aromatic bouquet, with cassis and a touch of French oak; the
medium-bodied palate is intense and long, with a replay of the cassis and
blackcurrant of the bouquet, the finish with fine tannins and cedary French oak.
Screwcap. 13.5% alc. Rating 94 To 2020 $20

Sophie's Yard Great Southern Shiraz 2008 Rating 90 To 2016 $24

Point Leo Road Vineyard ★★★★

214 Point Leo Road, Red Hill South, Vic 3937 **Region** Mornington Peninsula
T 0406 610 815 **F** (03) 5989 2935 **www**.pointleoroad.com.au **Open** By appt
Winemaker Phillip Kittle, Andrew Thomson, David Cowburn **Est.** 1996 **Cases** 1000
Vyds 5.7 ha
John Law and family planted 1.9 ha of pinot noir and 1.5 ha of chardonnay in 1996 as contract
growers for several leading Mornington Peninsula wineries. Plantings have been progressively
expanded with small amounts of pinot gris, lagrein, sauvignon blanc and gewurztraminer.
Some of the grapes are now contract-made, and they have two labels: Point Leo Road for
premium wines, and Point Break the second label.

Mornington Peninsula Pinot Noir 2007 Shows the first stage of colour
development; a complex bouquet and palate with an anchor of ripe, dark fruits
allowing a textural interplay between the fruit, tannins and oak. Long-lived style.
Screwcap. 13.5% alc. Rating 93 To 2016 $30

Point Break Mornington Peninsula Pinot Noir 2007 Paradoxically, brighter
hue than its big brother; the aromas and flavours are more linear and precise,
although less complex; an attractive wine to drink while the main pinot matures.
Screwcap. 13.5% alc. Rating 91 To 2013 $22

Mornington Peninsula Lagrein 2007 Fresh and lively, with a juicy array of
cherry, plum and blackberry fruits on the light- to medium-bodied palate; fresh
acidity also helps. Estate grown. Screwcap. 13.5% alc. Rating 90 To 2013 $30

Pokolbin Estate ★★★★★

McDonalds Road, Pokolbin, NSW 2321 **Region** Hunter Valley
T (02) 4998 7524 **F** (02) 4998 7765 **www**.pokolbinestate.com.au **Open** 7 days 9–5
Winemaker Andrew Thomas (Contract) **Est.** 1980 **Cases** 4000 **Vyds** 17 ha

If you go to the lengths that Pokolbin Estate has done to hide its light under a bushel, you end up with something like seven vintages of Semillon, six of Riesling, eight of Shiraz, three of Tempranillo, three each of Nebbiolo and Sangiovese and sundry other wines adding up to more than 40 in total. Between 1998 and 2000 Neil McGuigan and Gary Reid shared the winemaking tasks; since '01 Andrew Thomas has skilfully made the wines from vineyards planted between 1960 and the early '70s.

🍷🍷🍷🍷🍷 **Reserve Hunter Valley Shiraz 2007** Deep colour; a seriously good Hunter shiraz that is absolutely certain to age wonderfully well for 40 years or more; it has a deep well of varietal fruit, great texture and structure, and even better line and length. Screwcap. 14.4% alc. **Rating** 97 **To** 2047 $50

✪ **Ken Bray Hunter Valley Semillon 2009** Yet another semillon to underline what a great vintage it was for the Hunter, a riesling cross-dresser with its delicious citrus flavour and long finish. Now or in 15 years. Screwcap. 11% alc. **Rating** 96 **To** 2024 $25

✪ **Phil Swannell Hunter Valley Semillon 2009** A delicious semillon, lighter and crisper than the Ken Bray, albeit with less fruit intensity; grass and mineral notes accompany some citrus. Definitely a wine for the cellar. Screwcap. 11% alc. **Rating** 95 **To** 2024 $25

✪ **Ken Bray Hunter Valley Semillon 2008** Immediately shows the extra dimension of flavour from the Ken Bray Vineyard; luscious citrus flavours will slowly pick up toast and honey over the next 10 years if you can keep your hands off it. Screwcap. 9.9% alc. **Rating** 95 **To** 2023 $25

✪ **Phil Swannell Hunter Valley Semillon 2006** As bright and as fresh as a daisy, still showing primary fruit and its single vineyard origin; grass, mineral and herb, finished with citrussy acidity. Screwcap. 10.7% alc. **Rating** 94 **To** 2021 $25

🍷🍷🍷🍷½ ✪ **Belebula Hunter Valley Sangiovese 2007** Excellent colour; no-holds-barred sour cherry varietal character on both the bouquet and remarkably intense and long palate. Great Italian food red. Screwcap. 13.9% alc. **Rating** 93 **To** 2015 $22
Hunter Valley Riesling 2008 **Rating** 90 **To** 2016 $25

🍷🍷🍷🍷 **Hunter Valley Riesling 2009** **Rating** 89 **To** 2016 $25
Hunter Valley Shiraz Viognier 2007 **Rating** 89 **To** 2015 $24
Hunter Valley Riesling Solera NV **Rating** 89 **To** 2011 $35
Belebula Hunter Valley Tempranillo 2007 **Rating** 87 **To** 2013 $28

Polin & Polin Wines ★★★☆

Mistletoe Lane, Pokolbin, NSW 2230 **Region** Hunter Valley
T 0422 511 348 **F** (02) 9969 9665 **www**.polinwines.com.au **Open** Not
Winemaker Peter Orr, Patrick Auld **Est.** 1997 **Cases** 2000 **Vyds** 10 ha

The first of the two vineyards of the business was established by Lexie and Michael Polin (and family) in 1997 near Denman, in the Upper Hunter. An additional 4 ha was acquired in Pokolbin in 2003, and all of the wines have been produced from single-vineyard sites. The name was chosen to honour forebears Peter and Thomas Polin, who migrated from Ireland in 1860, operating a general store in Coonamble. Limb of Addy has a distinctly Irish twist to it, but is in fact a hill immediately to the east of the vineyard. Subsequent wine names directly or indirectly reflect movement to Australia by 19th-century migrants.

🍷🍷🍷🍷½ **Limb of Addy Hunter Valley Shiraz 2006** Good colour; a very generous and supple wine, the medium- to full-bodied palate with flavours that might easily be taken for cool climate, with fresh spice and licorice over blackberry fruit; very good texture. Twin top. 13.5% alc. **Rating** 93 **To** 2016 $32

🍷🍷🍷🍷 **John Rook's Limited Release Hunter Valley Rose 2009** **Rating** 87 **To** 2011 $18

Pondalowie Vineyards ★★★★★

21 Wellsford Drive, Bendigo East, Vic 3550 **Region** Bendigo
T (03) 5437 3332 **F** (03) 5437 3332 **www**.pondalowie.com.au **Open** By appt
Winemaker Dominic Morris, Krystina Morris **Est.** 1997 **Cases** 2500 **Vyds** 10 ha
Dominic and Krystina Morris both have strong winemaking backgrounds gained from working in Australia, Portugal and France. Dominic has worked alternate vintages in Australia and Portugal since 1995, and Krystina has also worked at St Hallett and at Boar's Rock. They have established 5.5 ha of shiraz, 2 ha each of tempranillo and cabernet sauvignon, and a little viognier and malbec. Incidentally, the illustration on the Pondalowie label is not a piece of barbed wire, but a very abstract representation of the winery kelpie dog. Exports to the UK, Singapore, Macau, Hong Kong and Japan.

🍷🍷🍷🍷🍷 **Special Release Malbec 2006** An alluring concoction of freshly crushed blackberries and violets, supplemented with a little spice; completely fresh and unevolved, the life and energy in this wine is thoroughly engaging; medium-bodied, long and luscious. Screwcap. 14% alc. **Rating** 95 **To** 2016 $40 BE

🍷🍷🍷🍷🍷 **MT Tempranillo 2008** Good colour; has considerable flavour and structure,
✪   at odds with the wine never seeing oak; black cherry and touches of licorice and spice supported by grape-derived tannins. Screwcap. 13.5% alc. **Rating** 93 **To** 2016 $26

✪   **Pinga Tempranillo et al 2008** Vibrant colour; highly aromatic, with smoked meats, red fruits and a delicate seasoning of spice; medium-bodied, fleshy and fun, the packaging reflects the message of the wine; to be enjoyed in abundance, without too much concern. Tempranillo/Cabernet Sauvignon/Petit Syrah/Shiraz. Screwcap. 14% alc. **Rating** 92 **To** 2014 $25 BE
        Shiraz 2007 Rating 91 **To** 2016 $25 BE
        Cabernet Sauvignon 2007 Rating 90 **To** 2015 $25 BE

Poole's Rock/Cockfighter's Ghost ★★★★★

DeBeyers Road, Pokolbin, NSW 2321 **Region** Hunter Valley
T (02) 4993 3633 **F** (02) 4998 6866 **www**.poolesrock.com.au **Open** 7 days 10–5
Winemaker Usher Tinkler **Est.** 1988 **Cases** NFP **Vyds** 33 ha
Sydney merchant banker David Clarke has had a long involvement with the wine industry. The Poole's Rock vineyard, planted purely to chardonnay, is his personal venture; it was initially bolstered by the acquisition of the larger, adjoining Simon Whitlam Vineyard. However, the purchase of the Glen Elgin Estate, upon which the 2500-tonne former Tulloch winery is situated, takes Poole's Rock (and its associated brands, Cockfighter's Ghost and Firestick) into another dimension. Exports to the UK, the US and other major markets.

🍷🍷🍷🍷🍷 **Poole's Rock Hunter Valley Semillon 2009** A pure-bred semillon with tremendous thrust and drive through the long palate and lingering aftertaste; the focus is enhanced by the touch of minerality that accompanies the lemon citrus fruit. Screwcap. 10.9% alc. **Rating** 96 **To** 2030 $41.95
        Poole's Rock Hunter Valley Shiraz 2007 Excellent crimson-purple hue; typical of the excellent '07 red wine vintage in the Hunter Valley; there is abundant savoury leathery regional character underpinning the long palate of tangy black fruits. Screwcap. 13.6% alc. **Rating** 94 **To** 2027 $41.95

🍷🍷🍷🍷🍷 **Poole's Rock Hunter Valley Semillon 2007 Rating** 93 **To** 2027 $41.95
        Cockfighter's Ghost Adelaide Hills Sauvignon Blanc 2009 Rating 93 **To** 2011 $24.95
        Cockfighter's Ghost Premium Reserve Adelaide Hills Chardonnay 2008 Rating 93 **To** 2018 $40
        Cockfighter's Ghost Clare Valley Riesling 2008 Rating 92 **To** 2020 $24.95
✪   **Cockfighter's Ghost Hunter Valley Semillon 2009** Bright straw-green; a precocious young semillon already flaunting its wares, and will provide enjoyment now or at any time over the next decade thanks to its citrussy boost. Screwcap. 11% alc. **Rating** 92 **To** 2020 $18.95

Poole's Rock Hunter Valley Chardonnay 2007 Rating 91 To 2013 $41.95
Cockfighter's Ghost Tasmania Pinot Noir 2008 Rating 90 To 2016 $40

♈♈♈♈
✪ Firestick Chardonnay 2007 A Hunter Valley chardonnay made with
considerable skill; the fruit flavours are delicate but varietal, and the touch of oak
is perfectly balanced. Good now or over the next two years. Screwcap. 12.9% alc.
Rating 89 To 2012 $12.95
Cockfighter's Ghost Premium Reserve Coonawarra Cabernet
Sauvignon 2006 Rating 89 To 2021 $40
✪ Firestick Cabernet Merlot 2008 The cool climate of Orange is immediately
obvious in the mix of cassis, leaf and black olive that drives the bouquet and palate,
with a twist of mint on the finish. Screwcap. 14.5% alc. Rating 88 To 2010 $12.95

Pooley Wines   ★★★★★
Cooinda Vale Vineyard, Barton Vale Road, Campania, Tas 7026 **Region** Southern Tasmania
T (03) 6260 2895 **F** (03) 6260 2895 **www.pooleywines.com.au** **Open** 7 days 10–5
Winemaker Matt Pooley **Est.** 1985 **Cases** 2600 **Vyds** 10.2 ha
Three generations of the Pooley family have been involved in the development of Pooley
Wines, although the winery was previously known as Cooinda Vale. Plantings have now
reached over 10 ha in a region that is warmer and drier than most people realise. In 2003
the family planted 1.2 ha of pinot noir and 1.3 ha of pinot grigio at Belmont Vineyard,
1431 Richmond Road, Richmond, a heritage property with an 1830s Georgian home and a
second cellar door in the old sandstone barn and stables.

♈♈♈♈♈ Family Reserve Pinot Noir 2008 Colour good; very lively red and black
cherry fruit aromas; supple, silky, long lingering flavours, with an extra dimension
of sweet cherry fruit. Gold medal Tas Wine Show '10. Screwcap. **Rating** 95
To 2015 $60
Coal River Late Harvest Riesling 2008 Glowing yellow-green; strong botrytis
orange peel complexity fills the very sweet palate, which needs a luscious dessert
to pull back that richness (if you are Socrates dissatisfied). Gold medal Tas Wine
Show '10. Screwcap. 10.7% alc. **Rating** 94 To 2015 $28

♈♈♈♈♉ Butchers Hill Pinot Noir 2008 Rating 90 To 2014 $32

♈♈♈♈ Coal River Late Harvest Riesling 2009 Rating 89 To 2012 $28
Margaret Pooley Tribute Riesling 2008 Rating 87 To 2014
Coal River Valley Pinot Noir 2008 Rating 87 To 2013 $28

Poonawatta Estate   ★★★★★
PO Box 340, Angaston, SA 5353 **Region** Eden Valley
T (08) 8565 3248 **F** (08) 8565 3248 **www.poonawatta.com** **Open** Not
Winemaker Reid Bosward, Jo Irvine, Andrew Holt **Est.** 1880 **Cases** 1000 **Vyds** 3.6 ha
The Poonawatta Estate story is complex, stemming from 1.8 ha of shiraz planted in 1880. When
Andrew Holt's parents purchased the Poonawatta property, the vineyard had suffered decades
of neglect, and a slow process of restoration began. While that was underway, the strongest
canes available from the winter pruning of the 1880s block were slowly and progressively dug
into the stony soil of the site. It took seven years to establish the matching 1.8 ha, and the yield
is even lower than that of the 1880s block. In 2004 Andrew and wife Michelle were greeted
with the same high yields that were obtained right across South Eastern Australia, and this
led to declassification of part of the production, giving rise to a second label, Monties Block,
which sits underneath The Cuttings (from the 'new' vines) and, at the top, The 1880. In 2005
a Riesling was introduced, produced from a single vineyard of 2 ha hand-planted by the Holt
family in the 1970s. Exports to the US, France, Denmark, Hong Kong and China.

♈♈♈♈♈ The 1880 Eden Valley Shiraz 2008 A complex, warm and inviting bouquet
of black fruits, florals, roasted meat and iron minerality; full-bodied, deep and
compelling, the lavish levels of fruit are only trumped by the complexity on offer;
chewy, savoury and incredibly long to conclude, a question must be asked of the
closure. Cork. 15% alc. **Rating** 95 To 2030 $90 BE

The Eden Riesling 2009 Ripe Meyer lemon and mineral bouquet, with ginger and candle wax on show; the palate is generous and quite deep on entry, cleaning up on the finish with lively lemon curd acidity. Screwcap. 11.5% alc. **Rating** 94 To 2016 $25 BE

ΨΨΨΨϘ **The Cuttings Eden Valley Shiraz 2008 Rating** 90 To 2018 $49 BE

ΨΨΨΨ **The Four Corners of Eden Valley Shiraz 2008 Rating** 89 To 2016 $29 BE

Port Phillip Estate ★★★★★

263 Red Hill Road, Red Hill, Vic 3937 **Region** Mornington Peninsula
T (03) 5989 4444 **F** (03) 5989 3017 **www.**portphillipestate.com.au **Open** 7 days 11–5
Winemaker Sandro Mosele **Est.** 1987 **Cases** 4000 **Vyds** 9.37 ha
Port Phillip Estate has been owned by Giorgio and Dianne Gjergja since 2000. The ability of the site (enhanced, it is true, by the skills of Sandro Mosele) to produce outstanding Syrah, Pinot Noir, Chardonnay, and very good Sauvignon Blanc, is something special. Whence climate change? Quite possibly the estate may have answers for decades to come. A futuristic, multimillion-dollar restaurant, cellar door and winery complex was opened prior to the 2010 vintage. Exports to the UK, Canada and Singapore.

ΨΨΨΨΨ **Mornington Peninsula Pinot Noir 2008** Rich plum and cherry fruit on the bouquet appears first on the palate, soon followed by spicy, savoury tannins that give length and authority. Diam. 14% alc. **Rating** 96 To 2019 $37
Single Vineyard Selection Morillon Pinot Noir 2008 Great colour and clarity; while the spicy, dark-fruited bouquet is complex (and fragrant), this pinot is all about the texture imparted by superfine but obvious tannins that run through the length of the palate, guaranteeing a long life. Diam. 13.5% alc. **Rating** 95 To 2018 $46

✪ **Mornington Peninsula Sauvignon Blanc 2009** Follows in the footsteps of prior releases, with complex aromas and texture added by partial barrel fermentation; the palate swells on retasting, reaching towards White Bordeaux in character. Screwcap. 13.5% alc. **Rating** 94 To 2013 $25
Mornington Peninsula Chardonnay 2008 One of those wines that hangs together with disarming simplicity and harmony; nectarine, fig, cashew and French oak all coalesce on the seamless palate. Screwcap. 13.5% alc. **Rating** 94 To 2016 $30

✪ **Salasso 2009** Pale salmon-pink; a spicy red fruit bouquet, then a fresh strawberry-infused palate that has excellent drive and length; from 14-year-old vines, whole bunch-pressed with minimal skin contact, then barrel-fermented in older oak barrels to dryness using native yeast, and bottled early to preserve freshness. Screwcap. 13.5% alc. **Rating** 94 To 2011 $22

ΨΨΨΨϘ **Mornington Peninsula Shiraz 2007 Rating** 93 To 2020 $30
✪ **Quartier Mornington Peninsula Barbera 2008** Purple-crimson; in some ways a quixotic choice but the cool climate does energise the variety, with a bright and crisp berry finish. Screwcap. 14.5% alc. **Rating** 90 To 2014 $26
Quartier Mornington Peninsula Barbera 2007 Rating 90 To 2015 $25

ΨΨΨΨ **Quartier Mornington Peninsula Arneis 2008 Rating** 89 To 2012 $25
Quartier Mornington Peninsula Shiraz 2008 Rating 89 To 2012 $18

Portsea Estate ★★★★

PO Box 3148, Bellevue Hill, NSW 2023 **Region** Mornington Peninsula
T (02) 9328 6359 **F** (02) 9326 1984 **www.**portseaestate.com **Open** Not
Winemaker Paringa Estate (Lindsay McCall) **Est.** 2000 **Cases** 700
Warwick Ross and sister (and silent partner) Caron Wilson-Hawley may be relative newcomers to the Mornington Peninsula (the first vintage was 2004), but they have had exceptional success with their Pinot Noir, the '05 winning top gold medal at the Ballarat Wine Show '07,

and the '06 taking Champion Wine of the Show of the National Cool Climate Wine Show '07 (against all varietal comers). The vines are planted on calcareous sand and limestone (the chardonnay is in fact on the site of a 19th-century limestone quarry) only 700 m from the ocean. Warwick has been a very successful film producer and says, 'I'm not sure if that makes me a filmmaker with a passion for wine, or a vigneron with a passion for film. Either way, I'm very happy with the collision of the two.'

ΨΨΨΨ **Mornington Peninsula Pinot Noir 2008** Slightly opaque colour; a massively powerful bouquet and palate, with the opulent, sweet fruit that seems to be the style of this vineyard (and, perhaps, the winemaker). A love it or leave it wine, the points a compromise. Screwcap. 14% alc. **Rating** 90 **To** 2015 $32

Possums Vineyard ★★★★

Adams Road, Blewitt Springs, SA 5171 **Region** McLaren Vale
T (08) 8272 3406 **F** (08) 8272 3406 **www**.possumswines.com.au **Open** By appt
Winemaker Pieter Breugem **Est.** 2000 **Cases** 10 000 **Vyds** 60 ha
Possums Vineyard is owned by Dr John Possingham and Carol Summers. They have two vineyards in McLaren Vale – one at Blewitt Springs, the other at Willunga – covering shiraz (23.5 ha), cabernet sauvignon (17 ha), chardonnay (9 ha), viognier (2 ha), pinot gris (1.2 h), sauvignon blanc (1 ha) and malbec (0.7 ha). In 2007 they completed construction of a 500-tonne winery at Blewitt Springs and sell both bottled and bulk wine. Pieter Breugem, the winemaker, has come from South Africa via the US and Constellation Wines. Exports to the UK, Denmark, Germany and Hong Kong.

ΨΨΨΨ **McLaren Vale Cabernet Sauvignon 2005** Has retained good hue; it's hard
❂   to imagine a McLaren Valley cabernet with more chocolate on the bouquet and palate, yet it doesn't become a caricature thanks to its great balance and texture; really delicious, ready now. Screwcap. 14% alc. **Rating** 91 **To** 2013 $20
❂   **Willunga Shiraz 2008** Has abundant plum, blackberry and dark chocolate aromas and flavours; the medium-bodied palate is relatively soft. Drink sooner than later. Screwcap. 14.5% alc. **Rating** 90 **To** 2015 $15

ΨΨΨ **The Pink Possum McLaren Vale Rose 2009** **Rating** 89 **To** 2011 $15

Postcode Wines ★★★★★

PO Box 769, Cessnock, NSW 2325 **Region** Various
T (02) 4998 7474 **F** (02) 4998 7974 **www**.postcodewines.com.au **Open** At The Boutique Wine Centre, Pokolbin
Winemaker Rhys Eather **Est.** 2004 **Cases** 2000
This is a new and separate venture for Rhys and Garth Eather (of Meerea Park), taking as its raison d'être wines that clearly show their postcode by exhibiting true regional character. The initial releases were two Shirazs from the Hunter Valley (2320) with a Cabernet Sauvignon from Hilltops (2587), and with several white wines in the future mix. After a slow and opaque state, there is now clarity to the focus.

ΨΨΨΨ **2320 Reserve Shiraz 2007** Fractionally brighter colour than the varietal; a
❂   much more complex bouquet introducing some leather, spice and more overt oak; the palate has more spice, and first-class texture and structure. Screwcap. 14% alc. **Rating** 95 **To** 2032 $25
❂   **2582 Canberra Shiraz 2008** Crimson-purple; has a dusting of spice and pepper on the plum and blackberry fruit of the bouquet; the palate has very good texture and length, the fruit flavours enhanced by spot-on picking. Screwcap. 14% alc. **Rating** 94 **To** 2020 $20
❂   **2320 Hunter Shiraz 2007** Vivid crimson-purple; the aromas of blackberry and quality oak are followed by a long palate adding some fresh red cherry nuances and finishes with fine tannins. Screwcap. 13.5% alc. **Rating** 94 **To** 2027 $20

Poverty Hill Wines ★★★★☆

PO Box 76, Springton, SA 5235 **Region** Eden Valley
T (08) 8568 2220 **F** (08) 8568 2220 **www.**povertyhillwines.com.au **Open** Fri–Mon 10–5
Winemaker John Eckert **Est.** 2002 **Cases** 5000 **Vyds** 29 ha
I'm not sure whether there is a slight note of irony in the name, but Poverty Hill Wines brings together men who have had a long connection with the Eden Valley. Robert Buck owns a small vineyard on the ancient volcanic soils east of Springton, producing both Shiraz and Cabernet Sauvignon. Next is Stuart Woodman, who owns the vineyard with the riesling that produced glorious wines in the early 1990s, and also has high-quality, mature-vine cabernet sauvignon. Finally, there is John Eckert, who once worked at Saltram. He not only works as winemaker at Poverty Hill, but manages Rob Buck's vineyard and his own small block of young riesling in the highlands of Springton. Exports to the US, Hong Kong and NZ.

♟♟♟♟♟ **Eden Valley Riesling 2008** Bright straw-green; a fleeting touch of kerosene
✪ on the bouquet disappears on the lively crisp palate, with lime, toast and mineral combining in a coherent whole; very good finish. Screwcap. 12.5% alc. **Rating** 94 To 2016 $18

♟♟♟♟♀ **Eden Valley Riesling 2009** Light straw-green; has an aromatic bouquet of lime
✪ blossom and unexpected honeysuckle, then a crisp and tight palate with a strong backbone of minerally acidity. All in front of it. Screwcap. 12.5% alc. **Rating** 91 To 2020 $20

✪ **Eden Valley Cabernet Sauvignon 2007** Bright crimson-red; a powerful and intense wine with potent blackcurrant and redcurrant fruit, oak no more than a vehicle; considerable length. Screwcap. 15% alc. **Rating** 91 To 2020 $24

♟♟♟♟ **Eden Valley Merlot 2007 Rating** 89 To 2014 $24

Prancing Horse Estate ★★★★★

39 Paringa Road, Red Hill South, Vic 3937 **Region** Mornington Peninsula
T (03) 5989 2602 **F** (03) 9827 1231 **www.**prancinghorseestate.com **Open** 1st w'end of month, or by appt
Winemaker Sergio Carlei, Pascal Marchand, Patrick Piuze **Est.** 1990 **Cases** 1000 **Vyds** 6 ha
Anthony and Catherine Hancy acquired the Lavender Bay Vineyard in early 2002, renaming it the Prancing Horse Estate and embarking on increasing the estate vineyards, with 2 ha each of chardonnay and pinot noir, and 0.5 ha of pinot gris. The vineyard moved to organic farming in '03, progressing to biodynamic in '07. They appointed Sergio Carlei as winemaker, and the following year became joint owners with Sergio in Carlei Wines. An additional property 150 m west of the existing vineyard has been purchased, and 2 ha of vines will be planted in the spring of '10. Prancing Horse has become one of a number of a strange group including Foster's, Howard Park, and now Prancing Horse, having wines specifically made for them in Burgundy. Winemaker Pascal Marchand is involved with Howard Park and Prancing Horse, making the '06 Morey-St-Denis Clos des Ormes Premier Cru; two '08 Grand Cru Chablis and a vineyard-specific '08 Chablis are made for Prancing Horse by Patrick Piuze. In all, 400 dozen bottles come from Burgundy. Exports to the UK, the US, France and Sweden.

♟♟♟♟♟ **Mornington Peninsula Chardonnay 2008** Bright quartz-green; the bouquet is aromatic, but the magic of the wine comes from its super-intense palate, with waves of white peach and grapefruit that have swallowed the barrel ferment French oak contributions. Screwcap. 13.5% alc. **Rating** 96 To 2017 $55
Les Clos Chablis Grand Cru 2008 Pale gold, with glints of green; here is that effortless intensity and purity of top-class Chablis, fruit aromatics subordinate to its minerally expression of place; has great length and style. Cork is the sword of Damocles once past 2012, even though the wine should flourish much longer. 12.5% alc. **Rating** 95 To 2012 $160

Bougros Chablis Grand Cru 2008 It is oxymoronic to point out the gulf between the two Grand Crus and the Les Rosiers; this wine has great strength and also focus, line and extreme length, the finish with mineral and citrus acidity that lingers long. Cork. 13% alc. **Rating** 94 **To** 2012 $125

Mornington Peninsula Pinot Noir 2008 Bright crimson, some purple; a fragrant bouquet of red cherry and plum, the palate fine and supple with a long, lingering finish. Screwcap. 12.5% alc. **Rating** 94 **To** 2015 $65

ΨΨΨΨΩ **Clos des Ormes Morey-Saint-Denis 1er Cru 2006** **Rating** 93 **To** 2014 $125
Les Rosiers Chablis 2008 **Rating** 91 **To** 2012 $48

Pressing Matters   ★★★★★

PO Box 2119, Lower Sandy Bay Road, Tas 7005 **Region** Southern Tasmania
T 0439 022 988 **F** (03) 6227 8803 **Open** Not
Winemaker Winemaking Tasmania (Julian Alcorso), Paul Smart **Est.** 2002 **Cases** 1000
Vyds 6.9 ha
Greg Melick simultaneously wears more hats than most people manage in a lifetime. He is a top-level barrister (Senior Counsel), a Major General (thus the highest ranking officer in the Australian Army Reserve) and has presided over a number of headline special commissions and enquiries into subjects as diverse as cricket match fixing allegations against Mark Waugh and others, to the Beaconsfield mine collapse. Yet, if asked, he would probably nominate wine as his major focus in life. Having built up an exceptional cellar of the great wines of Europe, he has turned his attention to grapegrowing and winemaking, planting riesling (2.9 ha) at his vineyard on Middle Tea Tree Road in the Coal River Valley. It is a perfect north-facing slope, the Mosel-style Rieslings sweeping all before them. It is moderately certain Greg is waiting impatiently for his multi-clone pinot noir block to perform in a similar manner.

ΨΨΨΨΨ **R69 Riesling 2008** Bright green-straw; a vibrant, intense and luscious wine, the substantial residual sugar (69 grammes per litre) balanced by perfectly judged acidity. Trophy Tas Wine Show '09. Screwcap. 9.1% alc. **Rating** 95 **To** 2014 $29
R69 Riesling 2009 Bright straw-green; excellent balance; very pure and intense sweet lime juice; lingering acidity provides a clean finish. Gold medal Tas Wine Show '10. Screwcap. 10.5% alc. **Rating** 94 **To** 2016 $29

ΨΨΨΨΩ **R9 Riesling 2008** **Rating** 92 **To** 2018 $29
R139 Riesling 2009 **Rating** 92 **To** 2015 $26
R9 Riesling 2009 **Rating** 90 **To** 2018 $29

ΨΨΨΨ **Pinot Noir 2008** **Rating** 88 **To** 2013 $39

Preston Peak   ★★★☆

31 Preston Peak Lane, Toowoomba, Qld 4352 **Region** Darling Downs
T (07) 4630 9499 **F** (07) 4630 9499 **www.**prestonpeak.com **Open** Wed–Sun 10–5
Winemaker Various contract **Est.** 1994 **Cases** 5000 **Vyds** 9.25 ha
Dentist owners Ashley Smith and Kym Thumpkin have a substantial wine and tourism business. The large, modern cellar door accommodates functions of up to 150 people, and is used for weddings and other events. It is situated less than 10 mins drive from the Toowoomba city centre, with views of Table Top Mountain, the Lockyer Valley and the Darling Downs. The main estate vineyard is in the Granite Belt.

ΨΨΨΨΩ **Single Vineyard Reserve Shiraz 2008** Strong purple; a very powerful and complex syrah, with an array of black fruits, licorice and plum; good length and intensity. Screwcap. 15% alc. **Rating** 93 **To** 2018 $38

ΨΨΨΨ **Reserve Chardonnay 2008** **Rating** 89 **To** 2014 $32
Single Vineyard Syrah Viognier Mourvedre 2008 **Rating** 89 **To** 2016 $38
Leaf Series Merlot 2008 **Rating** 88 **To** 2014 $24

Preveli Wines ★★★★☆

Bessell Road, Rosa Brook, Margaret River, WA 6285 **Region** Margaret River
T (08) 9757 2374 **F** (08) 9757 2790 **www.**preveliwines.com.au **Open** At Prevelly
General Store, 7 days 10–8
Winemaker Vasse River Wines (David Johnson, Sharna Kowakzak) **Est.** 1998
Cases 5000 **Vyds** 7.5 ha
The Home family, led by Greg, have turned a small business into a larger one, with a vineyard
at Rosabrook (supplemented by contracts with local growers). The wines are of consistently
impressive quality. The Prevelly General Store (owned by the Homes) is the main local outlet.

♀♀♀♀♀ **Margaret River Chardonnay 2008** A very harmonious and balanced
✪   chardonnay, covering all the bases; a whiff of oak on the bouquet is the main
       indicator of 11 months in French barrels, for the white flesh stone fruit and
       grapefruit of the palate are the dominant drivers of the wine. A worthy successor
       to the '09. Screwcap. 13.5% alc. **Rating** 94 **To** 2014 $23.95

♀♀♀♀♀ **Margaret River Cabernet Merlot 2007** **Rating** 93 **To** 2017 $25.95

♀♀♀♀ **Margaret River Semillon Sauvignon Blanc 2009** **Rating** 89 **To** 2012 $18.95

Prime Premium Wines ★★★

Lot 2, Rivers Lane, McLaren Vale, SA 5171 **Region** McLaren Vale
T (08) 8323 8297 **www.**primepremiumwine.com.au **Open** By appt
Winemaker Longwood Wines (Phil Christiansen) **Est.** 2002 **Cases** 200 **Vyds** 4.1 ha
This is the business of Warwick, Jenny and Robert Prime, who acquired a block on the
fringe of McLaren Vale township first farmed by the Aldersey family in the mid-19th century.
The philosophy in choosing the block worked on the principle that the early settlers had
first choice of the best land. The Prime family believes they made the right decision, the
production from the 3.4 ha of cabernet sauvignon, 0.5 ha of shiraz and 0.2 ha of grenache is
contracted to Mollydooker Wines and finding its way to an enthusiastic market in the US. A
very small amount of grapes is held back for the Prime Premium Wines label, and the quantity
made will not exceed 300 to 400 cases per year.

♀♀♀♀ **Rivers Lane McLaren Vale Shiraz 2007** Abounds with savoury, earthy,
       chocolatey mocha characters expressive of the region and, of course, the variety;
       if there is a fault, it's the amount of mocha/vanillan oak, but at the price, that's a
       quibble. Screwcap. 15% alc. **Rating** 88 **To** 2015 $16.50

Primo Estate ★★★★★

McMurtie Road, McLaren Vale, SA 5171 **Region** McLaren Vale
T (08) 8323 6800 **F** (08) 8323 6888 **www.**primoestate.com.au **Open** 7 days 11–4
Winemaker Joseph Grilli, Daniel Zuzdo **Est.** 1979 **Cases** 30 000 **Vyds** 34 ha
One time Roseworthy dux Joe Grilli has always produced innovative and excellent wines.
The biennial release of the Joseph Sparkling Red (in its tall Italian glass bottle) is eagerly
awaited, the wine immediately selling out. Also unusual and highly regarded are the vintage-
dated extra-virgin olive oils. However, the core lies with the La Biondina, the Il Briccone
Shiraz Sangiovese and the Joseph Cabernet Merlot. The business has expanded to take in
both McLaren Vale and Clarendon, with plantings of colombard, shiraz, cabernet sauvignon,
riesling, merlot, sauvignon blanc, chardonnay, pinot gris, sangiovese, nebbiolo and merlot.
Exports to all major markets.

♀♀♀♀♀ **Joseph Sparkling Red NV** As ever, very complex; as ever, very well-balanced
       and long, with cedar, spice and the different flavour from the cabernet merlot
       barrel added each year. Disgorged June '09. Cork. 13.5% alc. **Rating** 95
       To 2015 $70
       Joseph Angel Gully Clarendon Shiraz 2007 Deep, dark colour; has layer
       upon layer upon layer of black fruit flavours on the full-bodied, but velvety palate,
       with gently ripe tannins in support. Wine penetration around the corner of cork.
       ProCork. 14.5% alc. **Rating** 94 **To** 2022 $65

✪   **Il Briccone McLaren Vale Shiraz Sangiovese 2008** Bright red-purple; both the bouquet and medium-bodied palate bring a mix of juicy fruits and spicy/savoury characters, the former from shiraz, the latter from sangiovese. Very attractive wine, all the components, including tannins, in balance, the finish fresh. Screwcap. 14.5% alc. **Rating** 94 **To** 2016 $22

Joseph Moda McLaren Vale Cabernet Sauvignon Merlot 2007 Initially seemed tough, but an extra year has transformed it; a rich ripe bouquet with black fruits and dark chocolate to the fore; the palate is also luscious, soaring above the limitations of the vintage; ripe tannins and quality oak complete the picture. ProCork. 14.5% alc. **Rating** 94 **To** 2022 $65

🍷🍷🍷🍷🍷 **Joseph Pinot Grigio d'Elena 2009 Rating** 93 **To** 2012 $25
Zamberlan McLaren Vale Cabernet Sauvignon Sangiovese 2007 **Rating** 93 **To** 2020 $28

✪   **Primo & Co The Tuscan Shiraz Sangiovese 2007** Bright light crimson; the spicy, earthy aromas are magnified on the medium-bodied palate, with black cherry and plum in the centre surrounded by spicy characters and savoury tannins. True food style. ProCork. 14% alc. **Rating** 92 **To** 2015 $25

Joseph McLaren Vale Nebbiolo 2007 Rating 91 **To** 2017 $75

✪   **La Biondina Colombard 2009** Seems in archetypal Biondina style: ie with a touch of sauvignon blanc, which isn't there; early picking plays a role, leaving the wine with zesty, cleansing acidity on the long finish. Screwcap. 12.5% alc. **Rating** 90 **To** 2011 $15

Primo & Co The Venetian Garganega Bianco 2008 Rating 90 **To** 2011 $25

🍷🍷🍷🍷
✪   **Merlesco McLaren Vale Merlot 2009** Colour little more than rose depth, but very bright; the flavour profile and structure likewise akin to rose, but provides extra. Drink now, slightly chilled in summer. Screwcap. 12.5% alc. **Rating** 89 **To** 2011 $15

Prince Albert   ★★★★

100 Lemins Road, Waurn Ponds, Vic 3216 **Region** Geelong
T (03) 5241 8091 **F** (03) 5241 8091 **Open** By appt
Winemaker Bruce Hyett, Fiona Purnell **Est.** 1975 **Cases** 250 **Vyds** 2 ha
In 2007 Dr David Yates, with a background based on a degree in chemistry, purchased the pinot noir–only Prince Albert vineyard from founder Bruce Hyett. David's plans are to spend 6–12 months running the vineyard and winery exactly as it has been, with advice from Bruce on winemaking and Steve Jones in the vineyard. So far as the latter is concerned, Yates is firmly committed to retaining the certified organic status for Prince Albert, and at this juncture sees no reason to change the style of the wine, which he has always loved. Exports to the UK.

🍷🍷🍷🍷🍷 **Geelong Pinot Noir 2008** Has the usual Prince Albert light, clear purple-red colour; the tangy/foresty/savoury palate utterly belies the alcohol; firm, fresh flavours of dark cherry and some stalk run through to the finish. Screwcap. 14.2% alc. **Rating** 90 **To** 2014 $30

Prince Hill Wines   ★★★☆

1220 Sydney Road, Mudgee, NSW 2850 **Region** Mudgee
T (02) 6373 1245 **F** (02) 6373 1350 **www.**princehillwines.com **Open** Mon–Sat 9–5, Sun 10–4
Winemaker Michelle Heagney **Est.** 1993 **Cases** 20 000 **Vyds** 25.5 ha
Prince Hill Wines has become the new name and identity for Simon Gilbert Wines. It is now associated with the Watson Wine Group, which has the difficult task of returning the business to profit. One might have thought the large, well-designed winery was well placed to take grapes from the various regions along the western side of the Great Dividing Range of NSW, but observers have questioned whether this can become a reality. In the meantime, the estate plantings of shiraz, merlot, petit verdot, cabernet sauvignon, zinfandel and sangiovese, all in reasonably significant amounts, provide the estate-grown wines. A proposal for the sale of

Prince Hill Wines by its owner, the Coonawarra Australia Property Trust, collapsed in March 2010. The failure of the sale to proceed leaves Prince Hill with an uncertain future. Exports to the UK, the US, Canada, Sweden, Dubai, China and NZ.

ᵠᵠᵠᵠᵠ **Card Collection Cabernet Sauvignon 2009** Good hue; made from estate-grown cabernet, and over-delivers for the region; the medium-palate has very good blackcurrant fruit, the mouthfeel supple, the tannins and oak in muted support. Screwcap. 14% alc. **Rating** 91 **To** 2018 $15

ᵠᵠᵠᵠ **Clare Valley Riesling 2009 Rating** 89 **To** 2015 $19
Mudgee Barbera 2009 Rating 89 **To** 2013 $19
Mudgee Botrytis Sauvignon Blanc 2009 Rating 89 **To** 2012 $19
Card Collection Merlot Sangiovese 2009 Rating 88 **To** 2013 $15
Eighty Links Reserve Mudgee Chardonnay 2009 Rating 87 **To** 2013 $27

Principia ★★★★

139 Main Creek Road, Red Hill, Vic 3937 (postal) **Region** Mornington Peninsula
T (03) 5931 0010 www.principiawines.com.au **Open** By appt
Winemaker Darrin Gaffy **Est.** 1995 **Cases** 450 **Vyds** 3.5 ha
Darrin and Rebecca Gaffy spent their honeymoon in SA, and awakened their love of wine. In due course they gravitated to Burgundy and began the search in Australia for a suitable cool-climate site to grow pinot noir and chardonnay. In 1995 they began to develop their vineyard, planting pinot noir and chardonnay. Darrin continues to work full-time as a toolmaker (and in the vineyard on weekends and holidays); Rebecca's career as a nurse took second place to the Bachelor of Applied Science (Wine Science) course at CSU, and she graduated in 2002. Along the way she worked at Red Hill Estate, Bass Phillip, Virgin Hills and Tuck's Ridge, and as winemaker at Massoni Homes.

ᵠᵠᵠᵠᵠ **Mornington Peninsula Pinot Noir 2008** Light red; a light-bodied pinot, with red cherry fruit on both bouquet and palate; not easy to understand 21 months in oak, although it is true the fruit is fresh, the finish long. Diam. 14.2% alc. **Rating** 92 **To** 2014 $36
Reserve Mornington Peninsula Pinot Noir 2008 Light red; a fresh red berry bouquet, then a light-bodied palate where more savoury characters take charge; has good length, but is a cerebral pinot. Diam. 14.2% alc. **Rating** 90 **To** 2014 $49

Printhie Wines ★★★★★

489 Yuranigh Road, Molong, NSW 2866 **Region** Orange
T (02) 6366 8422 **F** (02) 6366 9328 www.printhiewines.com.au **Open** Mon–Sat 10–4, or by appt
Winemaker Drew Tuckwell **Est.** 1996 **Cases** 20 000 **Vyds** 33 ha
Owned by the Swift family, Printhie has established itself at the forefront of quality viticulture and winemaking in Orange. The estate vineyards have matured and fruit intake is supplemented by contract growers, avoiding the fruit salad vineyard approach by sourcing fruit from the best growers in the best sites with the best varietal match. The new generation at Printhie continues to make its mark, with Ed Swift serving as President of the Orange Region Vignerons Association and as a participant of the Future Leaders Program. Winemaker Drew Tuckwell is a Len Evans Tutorial scholar and participant in the Wine Communicators of Australia Young Guns and Gurus program (as a young gun). The wine portfolio has been consolidated: the entry level Mountain Range now comprises just six wines (three white, three red), the Mount Canobolas Collection range is a quasi-reserve range, and the Swift Family Heritage flagship range has been trimmed to just one red wine (a Cabernet Sauvignon/Shiraz blend). Exports to the US, Denmark, Ivory Coast and China.

ᵠᵠᵠᵠᵠ **Mount Canobolas Collection Orange Riesling 2009** A delicious wine, with
✪ a floral bouquet, then a remarkably intense palate that somehow retains delicacy, its lime juice fruit set within a filigree of acidity, the finish fresh and vibrant. Screwcap. 11.5% alc. **Rating** 94 **To** 2019 $23

✪   **Orange Sauvignon Blanc 2009** This is another example of the synergy between Orange and sauvignon blanc; while there are abundant passionfruit, lychee and tropical aromas and flavours, the acidity is fresh and cleansing, giving both drive and balance. Screwcap. 12.5% alc. **Rating** 94 **To** 2011 $17

Swift Family Heritage 2008 Good crimson; a blend of Cabernet Sauvignon/ Shiraz, with spicy black and red fruit aromas, the flavours with more cool-climate cherry and cassis; has good purity, line and length. Screwcap. 14% alc. **Rating** 94 To 2020 $50

♟♟♟♟♟   **Orange Chardonnay 2009** Light straw-green; a crisp, fruit-driven bouquet and
✪   palate, with tangy grapefruit nuances to the white flesh stone fruit flavours; good line and length. Screwcap. 13% alc. **Rating** 93 **To** 2017 $17

Orange Pinot Gris 2009 Rating 90 **To** 2012 $17

✪   **Mountain Range Orange Cabernet Sauvignon 2009** Vibrant colour; red fruits dominate the bouquet, with a generous dollop of toasty oak; medium-bodied with fresh, juicy and vibrant red fruits. Screwcap. 12.5% alc. **Rating** 90 To 2014 $18 BE

♟♟♟♟   **Mountain Range Orange Shiraz 2009 Rating** 89 **To** 2013 $18 BE
Mountain Range Orange Shiraz 2008 Rating 89 **To** 2015 $17
Orange Merlot 2009 Rating 87 **To** 2012 $17

Provenance Wines   ★★★★★

870 Steiglitz Road, Sutherlands Creek, Vic 3331 **Region** Geelong
T (03) 5281 2230 **F** (03) 5281 2205 **www**.provenancewines.com.au **Open** By appt
Winemaker Scott Ireland, Kirilly Gordon, Sam Vogel **Est.** 1995 **Cases** 1500
Scott Ireland and partner Jen Lilburn established Provenance Wines in 1997 as a natural extension of Scott's years of winemaking experience, both here and abroad. Located in the Moorabool Valley, the winery team of Scott, Kirilly Gordon and Sam Vogel focuses on the classics in a cool-climate sense – Pinot Gris, Chardonnay, Pinot Noir in particular, as well as Shiraz. Fruit is sourced both locally within the Geelong region and further afield (when the fruit warrants selection). They are also major players in contract making for the Geelong region.

♟♟♟♟♟   **Geelong Pinot Noir 2008** A fragrant bouquet leads into a palate of quite beautiful line and length, with cherry and just a hint of forest; elegance personified. Screwcap. 13.5% alc. **Rating** 96 **To** 2015 $29

Turas Pinot Noir 2007 Holding bright crimson hue; the red fruit bouquet has a dusting of spice, the palate with juicy red fruits and a whisper of mint; this delicious wine's silky, supple texture and excellent length are its strongest points. A 50/50 blend of Geelong/Ballarat grapes with 25% whole bunches. Screwcap. 13.5% alc. **Rating** 95 **To** 2014 $45

✪   **Geelong Chardonnay 2008** Bright green-gold; the complexity and mouthfeel of the wine show just what can be achieved with alcohol under 13%; the flavours are ripe, with nectarine, melon and white peach, the barrel ferment oak carried by the fruit. Screwcap. 12.8% alc. **Rating** 94 **To** 2015 $28

✪   **Geelong Shiraz 2007** Crimson-purple; the spicy bouquet comes through on the palate, but the main theme is the juicy sweet red fruits (fruit-sweet, not sugar-sweet) and fresh acidity that make this wine so easy to enjoy. Screwcap. 13.5% alc. **Rating** 94 **To** 2017 $30

Providence Vineyards

236 Lalla Road, Lalla, Tas 7267 **Region** Northern Tasmania
T (03) 6395 1290 **F** (03) 6395 2088 **www**.providence.com.au **Open** 7 days 10–5
Winemaker Frogmore Creek, Bass Fine Wines **Est.** 1956 **Cases** 750 **Vyds** 2.6 ha
Providence incorporates the pioneer vineyard of Frenchman Jean Miguet, now owned by the Bryce family, who purchased it in 1980. The original 1.3-ha vineyard has been doubled, and unsuitable grenache and cabernet (from the original plantings) have been grafted over to chardonnay, pinot noir and riesling. Miguet called the vineyard 'La Provence', reminding him

of the part of France he came from, but after 40 years the French authorities forced a name change. The cellar door offers 70 different Tasmanian wines.

ŸŸŸŸŸ Monet Riesling 2009 Ripe, full-flavoured; a rich and generous wine that improves dramatically on re-tasting; has excellent balance and length. Screwcap. 11.4% alc. **Rating** 94 **To** 2017 $21

Puddleduck Vineyard ★★★★☆
992 Richmond Road, Richmond, Tas 7025 **Region** Southern Tasmania
T (03) 6260 2301 **F** (03) 6260 2301 **www**.puddleduckvineyard.com.au **Open** 7 days 10–5
Winemaker Frogmore Creek **Est.** 1997 **Cases** 1500 **Vyds** 3.5 ha
After working the majority of their adult lives at vineyards in southern Tasmania, Darren and Jackie Brown bought land in 1996 with the dream of one day having their own label and cellar door. The dream is now reality, with the vineyard planted to pinot noir, riesling, chardonnay and sauvignon blanc, and the next step is a small cheesery making cheese from their small goat herd to complement the wines, which are sold exclusively through the cellar door.

ŸŸŸŸŸ Chardonnay 2008 Very good green tints to colour; a decidedly complex bouquet, then a highly focused palate; grapefruit and white peach; subtle oak. Gold medal Tas Wine Show '10. Screwcap. 14% alc. **Rating** 94 **To** 2014 $30

ŸŸŸŸŸ Pinot Noir 2008 **Rating** 93 **To** 2015 $42
Bazil's Sweet Riesling 2009 **Rating** 91 **To** 2020 $26
Riesling 2009 **Rating** 90 **To** 2019 $28
Rose 2009 **Rating** 90 **To** 2010 $28
Bubbleduck 2007 **Rating** 90 **To** 2012 $47

ŸŸŸŸ Cabernet Sauvignon 2008 **Rating** 89 **To** 2015 $38
Sauvignon Blanc 2009 **Rating** 88 **To** 2011 $28
Muddleduck 2008 **Rating** 87 **To** 2011 $42

Pulpit Rock ★★★★★
2877 Wombeyan Caves Road, Bullio, NSW 2575 (postal) **Region** Southern Highlands
T 0418 242 045 **F** (02) 4872 2165 **www**.pulpitrockestate.com.au **Open** Not
Winemaker Rhys Eather (Contract) **Est.** 1998 **Cases** 600 **Vyds** 4 ha
Pulpit Rock brings together a team of professionals covering the field from grape to glass. Dr Richard Smart was the consultant viticulturist to give the venture his blessing; the wine is made by well-known Hunter Valley winemaker Rhys Eather; it is distributed by co-owner Carol-Ann Martin, with more than 20 years' experience as owner of a fine wine distribution business; and the wine is consumed wherever possible by her architect husband Philip Martin. The 2 ha each of chardonnay and pinot noir are managed on a minimal intervention basis, never easy in the Southern Highlands climate, but with obvious success.

ŸŸŸŸŸ Southern Highlands Chardonnay 2008 Bright hue; sophisticated winemaking
✪ is very evident in this polished wine, nectarine and citrus fruit enhanced rather than obscured by barrel ferment; good balance and length. Screwcap. 13.5% alc. **Rating** 94 **To** 2014 $28
✪ Southern Highlands Chardonnay 2007 Developed yellow-gold; an elegant, harmonious wine with the same bloodline as the '08; has considerable length to its citrus and nectarine fruit, oak merely a whisper in the background. Screwcap. 13% alc. **Rating** 94 **To** 2013 $28
✪ Southern Highlands Chardonnay 2006 Glowing yellow-green; still very fresh, showing no signs whatsoever of breaking down; has slightly more stone fruit in its make-up than the '07, but this is no criticism. Screwcap. 13% alc. **Rating** 94 **To** 2012 $28

ŸŸŸŸŸ Southern Highlands Pinot Noir 2007 **Rating** 90 **To** 2014 $49
Southern Highlands Pinot Noir 2006 **Rating** 90 **To** 2013 $49

ŸŸŸŸ Southern Highlands Pinot Noir 2005 **Rating** 88 **To** 2012 $49

Punch ★★★★★

2130 Kinglake Road, St Andrews, Vic 3761 (postal) **Region** Yarra Valley
T (03) 9710 1155 **F** (03) 9710 1369 **www.**punched.com.au **Open** Not
Winemaker James Lance **Est.** 2004 **Cases** 600 **Vyds** 3.45 ha
In the wake of Graeme Rathbone taking over the brand (but not the real estate) of Diamond Valley, the Lances' son James and his wife Claire leased the vineyard and winery from David and Catherine Lance, including the 0.25-ha block of close-planted pinot noir. In all, Punch has 2.25 ha of pinot noir (including the close-planted), 0.8 ha of chardonnay and 0.4 ha of cabernet sauvignon.

♟♟♟♟♟ **Lance's Vineyard Close Planted Yarra Valley Pinot Noir 2008** Bright, light crimson-purple, admirable given that the wine was neither fined nor filtered; the ultra-close planting (1.2 m x 1 m) has worked wonders with this vintage, the very intense, yet fine, dark berry flavours driving through the long palate and lingering finish; 80 dozen made. Screwcap. 13.5% alc. **Rating** 96 **To** 2018 $80
Lance's Vineyard Yarra Valley Pinot Noir 2008 Similar colour and clarity to Close Planted; an elegant and highly fragrant bouquet, then a delicious stream of red and black cherry fruit running seamlessly along the palate; superb line and length; 210 dozen made. Screwcap. 13.5% alc. **Rating** 96 **To** 2016 $50
Lance's Vineyard Yarra Valley Chardonnay 2008 Bright green-quartz, almost glowing; the bouquet is very fragrant and pure, the palate at once concentrated yet elegant; white peach, nectarine and melon are all to be found, oak in its place; 180 dozen made. Screwcap. 14% alc. **Rating** 95 **To** 2015 $40
Easdown Vineyard Kinglake Pinot Noir Chardonnay 2001 Fascinating wine; zero dosage was precisely the right way to go, for the wine has great balance to its nutty brioche characters from seven years on lees. Crown seal. 13% alc. **Rating** 94 **To** 2011 $40

♟♟♟♟♟ **Berrys Creek Vineyard Gippsland Noble Riesling 2008** Rating 92
To 2015 $25

Punt Road ★★★★☆

10 St Huberts Road, Coldstream, Vic 3770 **Region** Yarra Valley
T (03) 9739 0666 **F** (03) 9739 0633 **www.**puntroadwines.com.au **Open** 7 days 10–5
Winemaker Kate Goodman **Est.** 2000 **Cases** 20 000 **Vyds** 75 ha
Commencing in 2007, Punt Road began to change the focus of its business, a move triggered by the Napoleone family acquiring full ownership of the winery. The annual crush has decreased by two-thirds to 1200 tonnes, and the amount of contract winemaking significantly curtailed. The emphasis is now on wines produced from vines owned by the Napoleone family; this has resulted in the introduction of the Airlie Bank range, a sub-$20 Yarra Valley range made in a fruit-driven, lightly oaked style. While these plans will stay in place for the foreseeable future, the '07 vintage was frost-ravaged, and '09 significantly affected by smoke taint. Exports to the UK, the US and other major markets.

♟♟♟♟♟ **Napoleone Vineyards Yarra Valley Cabernet Sauvignon 2008** Bright
✪   purple; a fragrant, flowery bouquet of red and black berry fruits leads into an elegant, medium-bodied palate with crystal clear varietal fruit definition. Screwcap. 13% alc. **Rating** 94 **To** 2020 $28

♟♟♟♟♟ **Botrytis Semillon 2008** Rating 93 To 2014 $32
Napoleone Vineyards Yarra Valley Chardonnay 2008 Rating 92
To 2015 $25
Napoleone Vineyards Yarra Valley Pinot Noir 2008 Rating 92 To 2015 $30
Napoleone Vineyards Yarra Valley Shiraz 2008 Rating 92 To 2020 $28
Napoleone Vineyards Yarra Valley Viognier 2009 Rating 91 To 2013 $25

♟♟♟♟ **Airlie Bank Yarra Valley Sauvignon Blanc 2009** Rating 89 To 2010 $19
Yarra Valley Viognier 2009 Rating 89 To 2013 $24
Airlie Bank Yarra Valley Shiraz Viognier 2008 Rating 89 To 2012 $19

Airlie Bank Yarra Valley Chardonnay 2008 Rating 88 To 2011 $19
Napoleone Vineyards Yarra Valley Merlot 2008 Rating 88 To 2013 $28

Punters Corner ★★★★★

Cnr Riddoch Highway/Racecourse Road, Coonawarra, SA 5263 **Region** Coonawarra
T (08) 8737 2007 **F** (08) 8737 3138 **www.**punterscorner.com.au **Open** 7 days 10–5
Winemaker Balnaves (Peter Bissell) **Est.** 1988 **Cases** 8000
Punters Corner started its life in 1975 as James Haselgrove, but in '92 was acquired by a group of investors who evidently had few delusions about the uncertainties of viticulture and winemaking, even in a district as distinguished as Coonawarra. The arrival of Peter Bissell as winemaker at Balnaves paid immediate (and continuing) dividends. Sophisticated packaging and label design add to the appeal of the wines. Exports to Canada, The Netherlands, Malaysia, Singapore, Japan and China.

♟♟♟♟♟ **Coonawarra Cabernet Sauvignon 2006** Bright colour; a classic, slightly
✪ earthy, slightly austere, but oh-so-correct Coonawarra cabernet; medium-bodied, with blackcurrant fruit, cedary oak and fine but firm tannins. This is a past-the-post winner. Screwcap. 15% alc. **Rating** 95 **To** 2021 $30
Single Vineyard Coonawarra Chardonnay 2008 Picked before the March heatwave; an elegant and fresh wine with nectarine, grapefruit and white peach fruit, the French oak playing second fiddle; immaculate balance and length. Screwcap. 13% alc. **Rating** 94 **To** 2016 $26
✪ **Single Vineyard Coonawarra Chardonnay 2007** Light straw-green; skilled winemaking very obvious; while the wine has an abundant array of stone fruit flavours, it also has finesse and extreme length. Screwcap. 13% alc. **Rating** 94 **To** 2017 $26
Sovereign Reserve Cabernet Sauvignon 2006 Excellent colour; full-bodied, rich and complete, with multi-layers of black fruits, French oak and tannins all interwoven; needs much patience. ProCork. 15% alc. **Rating** 94 **To** 2026 $59.50

♟♟♟♟♟ **Coonawarra Shiraz 2006** Good crimson hue still apparent; a medium-
✪ bodied wine with a bright array of blackberry, spice and licorice fruit offset by mocha/vanillan oak nuances; finely textured tannins a feature. Screwcap. 15% alc. **Rating** 92 **To** 2016 $20

♟♟♟♟ **Triple Crown 2006** Bright crimson; a fragrant bouquet of red and black fruits
✪ and a touch of spice leads into a medium-bodied palate with savoury tannins that are just a little dry. Cabernet Sauvignon/Shiraz/Merlot. Screwcap. 14.5% alc. **Rating** 89 **To** 2015 $17

Pyren Vineyard ★★★☆

22 Errard Street North, Ballarat, Vic 3350 (postal) **Region** Pyrenees
T (03) 5467 2352 **F** (03) 5021 0804 **www.**pyrenvineyard.com **Open** By appt
Winemaker Andrew Davey **Est.** 1999 **Cases** 4500 **Vyds** 34 ha
Brian and Kevyn Joy have planted 23 ha of shiraz, 5 ha of cabernet sauvignon, 3 ha of viognier, 1 ha of durif and 2 ha comprising cabernet franc, malbec and petit verdot on the slopes of the Warrenmang Valley near Moonambel. Yield is restricted to between 1.5 and 2.5 tonnes per acre.

♟♟♟♟♟ **Block E Pyrenees Shiraz 2007** Medium- to full-bodied, with blackberry, plum
and spice on the lively, almost juicy, mid-palate, before the tannins on the finish introduce a more savoury note. Screwcap. 14.2% alc. **Rating** 91 **To** 2017 $28

♟♟♟♟ **Broken Quartz Pyrenees Shiraz 2007** Rating 89 To 2017 $18
Broken Quartz Pyrenees Cabernet Sauvignon 2007 Rating 89 To 2014 $18

Pyrenees Ridge Winery ★★★★☆

532 Caralulup Road, Lamplough via Avoca, Vic 3467 **Region** Pyrenees
T (03) 5465 3320 **F** (03) 5465 3710 **www**.pyreneesridge.com.au **Open** Thurs–Mon &
public hols 10–5
Winemaker Graeme Jukes **Est.** 1998 **Cases** 4000 **Vyds** 15.3 ha

Notwithstanding the quite extensive winemaking experience (and formal training) of Graeme
Jukes, this started life as small-scale winemaking in the raw version of the French garagiste
approach. Graeme and his wife Sally-Ann now have 10 ha of shiraz, 3 ha cabernet sauvignon,
with lesser amounts of chardonnay, merlot and a hatful of viognier. There are plans to plant a
further 3–4 ha of shiraz. After a fire in 2007 destroyed the winery and cellar door, the facility
has been rebuilt, bigger and better than before. Exports to Germany, Denmark, Singapore,
Hong Kong, China and Japan.

ΨΨΨΨΨ **Reserve Shiraz 2008** Deep and bright colour; a rich, voluptuous wine with
an array of aromas and flavours ranging from ripe black fruits through to more
savoury spicy notes; the tannins are ripe and balanced. Diam. 15% alc. **Rating** 94
To 2023 $50

ΨΨΨΨΨ **Shiraz 2008 Rating** 93 To 2023 $27

ΨΨΨΨ **Ridge Red 2008 Rating** 89 To 2015 $16
Cabernet Merlot 2008 Rating 89 To 2017 $26
Chardonnay 2008 Rating 88 To 2012 $19
Cabernet Sauvignon 2008 Rating 88 To 2016 $26

Quarisa Wines ★★★★

743 Slopes Road, Tharbogang, NSW 2680 (postal) **Region** South Eastern Australia
T (02) 6963 6222 **F** (02) 6963 6473 **www**.quarisa.com.au **Open** Not
Winemaker John Quarisa **Est.** 2005 **Cases** 20 000

Quarisa Wines was established by John and Josephine Quarisa (plus their three young
children). John has had a distinguished career as a winemaker spanning 22 years, working
for some of Australia's largest wineries including McWilliam's, Casella and Nugan Estate. He
was also chiefly responsible for winning the Jimmy Watson Trophy in 2004 (Melbourne) and
the Stodart Trophy (Adelaide). In a busman's holiday venture, they have set up a small family
business using grapes from various parts of NSW and SA, made in leased space. After a slightly
uncertain start, the current releases offer exemplary value for money, and it is no surprise that
leading national distributor Domaine Wine Shippers has taken on the brand. Exports to the
UK, Canada, Sweden, Indonesia, Israel, China, Hong Kong and NZ.

ΨΨΨΨΨ **Treasures Coonawarra Cabernet Merlot 2006** Distinctly Coonawarra, with
✪   abundant red and black fruits, framed by a mere suggestion of eucalypt; medium-
bodied and quite fleshy, the finish is harmonious and warm. Screwcap. 14.5% alc.
Rating 90 To 2016 $15 BE

✪   **Treasures Coonawarra Cabernet Sauvignon 2006** Redcurrant, tobacco,
mint and a touch of cassis feature; full-bodied fresh and lively, with plenty of
time ahead; the finish has fine-grained tannins in abundance. Screwcap. 14.5% alc.
Rating 90 To 2016 $15 BE

ΨΨΨΨ **30 Mile Shiraz 2008** Clean, fresh, vibrant and juicy red fruit bouquet; quite
✪   succulent palate with good acidity providing line; excellent quality for the price,
and best enjoyed in the full flush of youth. Screwcap. 14.5% alc. **Rating** 89
To 2014 $9 BE

✪   **30 Mile Chardonnay 2008** Struck match sulphide, melon fruit and a fleshy
palate provide interesting drinking at this price; plenty of flavour. Screwcap.
13.5% alc. **Rating** 88 To 2012 $9 BE

Quarry Hill Wines   ★★★☆

8 Maxwell Street, Yarralumla, ACT 2600 (postal) **Region** Canberra District
T 0414 574 460 **F** (02) 6100 6174 **www**.quarryhill.com.au **Open** Not
Winemaker Collector Wines (Alex McKay) **Est.** 1999 **Cases** 500 **Vyds** 5 ha
Owner Dean Terrell is the ex-Vice Chancellor of the Australian National University and a
Professor of Economics. The acquisition of the property, originally used as a quarry for the
construction of the Barton Highway and thereafter as a grazing property, was the brainchild
of his family, who wanted to keep him active in retirement from full-time academic and
administrative life. The vineyard was established in 1999, with further plantings in '01 and '06;
there are 2 ha of shiraz, 1 ha each of sauvignon blanc and pinot noir, and 1 ha split between
savagnin and tempranillo. The first commercial vintage followed in '06 after two trial vintages;
small plantings of other alternative varieties have followed. Since '08 Alex McKay of Collector
Wines has become winemaker, which bodes well for the future. Only part of the production
is released under the Quarry Hill label, as grapes are sold to wineries including Clonakilla
and Collector Wines.

♛♛♛♛♛ **Pinot Noir 2006** Holding hue particularly well; the spicy bouquet has begun to
show some bottle-developed complexity; the palate has notes of plum of morello/
glace cherry, again with some development. Drink sooner rather than later.
Screwcap. 13.8% alc. **Rating** 90 **To** 2013 $18

Quattro Mano   ★★★★☆

PO Box 189, Hahndorf, SA 5245 **Region** Barossa Valley
T 0430 647 470 **F** (08) 8388 1736 **www**.quattromano.com.au **Open** Not
Winemaker Anthony Carapetis, Christopher Taylor, Philippe Morin **Est.** 2006
Cases 1400 **Vyds** 1 ha
Anthony Carapetis, Philippe Morin and Chris Taylor have a collective experience of over
50 years working in various facets of the wine industry, Morin as a leading sommelier for
25 years, and presently as Director of French Oak Cooperage, Carapetis and Taylor as long-
serving winemakers. The dream of Quattro Mano began in the mid-1990s, but only became
a reality in '06. They now have an eclectic range of wines, tempranillo the cornerstone,
extending at one extreme to the multi-Iberian Peninsula Duende, to La Defi Pinot Noir
and La Hada Barossa Valley Mourvedre at the other. It's an impressive, albeit small, business.
Exports to Japan.

♛♛♛♛♛ **Le Defi Adelaide Hills Pinot Noir 2008** Very good clarity of colour; a
✪ fragrant bouquet and decisive palate, with a range of plum, cherry and delicate
spice flavours; excellent length to a wine of breed and class. Screwcap. 13% alc.
Rating 95 **To** 2015 $20

♛♛♛♛♛ **Duende 2009** Bright crimson hue; a singularly interesting wine, exhibiting a
✪ tapestry of bright red fruit flavours and little or no oak influence. Touriga/Tinta
Amarela/Tinta Cao/Cinsaut. Screwcap. 13% alc. **Rating** 91 **To** 2014 $20
La Reto Barossa Valley Tempranillo 2008 **Rating** 91 **To** 2017 $26
La Reto Barossa Valley Tempranillo 2007 **Rating** 90 **To** 2016 $26

Quealy   ★★★★★

Merricks Wine General Store, 3460 Frankston-Flinders Road, Merricks, Vic 3916
Region Mornington Peninsula
T (03) 5989 8088 **www**.quealy.com.au **Open** 7 days 9–5
Winemaker Kathleen Quealy **Est.** 1982 **Cases** 5000 **Vyds** 8 ha
Kathleen Quealy and husband Kevin McCarthy lost no time after their ties with T'Gallant
(purchased from them by Foster's in 2003) were finally severed. As they were fully entitled to
do, they already had their ducks set up in a row, and in short order acquired Balnarring Estate
winery (being significantly upgraded) and leased Earl's Ridge Vineyard near Flinders. In a
move reminiscent of Janice McDonald at Stella Bella/Suckfizzle in the Margaret River, they

launched their business with Pobblebonk (a white blend) and Rageous (a red blend), plus a Pinot Noir and a Pinot Gris with a passing nod to convention. The estate plantings are 2 ha each of pinot noir, tocai friulano and pinot gris, and 1 ha each of chardonnay and muscat giallo. Kathleen (with five children) is a human dynamo; this is a business sure to succeed. Balnarring Vineyard is Kathleen's second label, available exclusively at Balnarring Vineyard, 62 Bittern-Dromana Road, Balnarring, tel (03) 5983 2483. Exports to the UK.

ΥΥΥΥΥ **Seventeen Rows Pinot Noir 2008** Good clear crimson-purple; by a considerable distance, the best balanced wine of the Quealy pinots, with a strong and supple palate of plum, black cherry fruit framed by gently savoury nuances; very good finish. Screwcap. 14% alc. **Rating** 96 **To** 2018 $50

✪ **Balnarring Vineyard Chardonnay 2008** Bright straw-green; an intense fruit-driven wine, nectarine and grapefruit flavours with considerable textural complexity despite the absence of oak, and drive through the long finish. Unoaked chardonnay doesn't come better than this. Screwcap. 13.5% alc. **Rating** 94 **To** 2014 $18

ΥΥΥΥΥ **Musk Creek Pinot Noir 2008 Rating** 93 **To** 2015 $35
Pinot Grigio 2009 Rating 91 **To** 2011 $25
Senza Nome 2009 Rating 90 **To** 2010 $20

✪ **Balnarring Vineyard Pinot Noir 2008** Bright purple-crimson; a very fragrant bouquet leads into a fresh, zesty palate, all pointing to its modest alcohol. Great summer pinot. Screwcap. 12.9% alc. **Rating** 90 **To** 2014 $18

ΥΥΥΥ **Musk Creek Pinot Gris 2008 Rating** 89 **To** 2012 $30
Balnarring Vineyard Late Harvest Muscat a Petits Grains Blanc 2009 Rating 88 **To** 2010 $18

Racecourse Lane Wines   ★★★☆

28 Racecourse Lane, Pokolbin, NSW 2320 **Region** Hunter Valley
T 0408 242 490 **F** (02) 9949 7185 **www**.racecourselane.com.au **Open** By appt
Winemaker David Fatches (Contract) **Est.** 1998 **Cases** 1000 **Vyds** 5.3 ha
Mike and Helen McGorman purchased their 15-ha property in 1998. They have established shiraz, sangiovese, semillon, verdelho and viognier. Consultancy viticultural advice from Brian Hubbard, and winemaking by David Fatches (a long-term Hunter Valley winemaker, who also makes wine in France each year), has paid dividends. Exports to the UK.

ΥΥΥΥΥ **Hunter Valley Semillon 2003** Glowing green-yellow; in the context of semillon, a generous full-bodied style that has coasted through the seven years since it was made; bottle development will also mean bottle variation (due to the cork), so good luck. 12% alc. **Rating** 90 **To** 2013 $19

ΥΥΥΥ **Hunter Valley Verdelho 2009 Rating** 87 **To** 2012 $19

Radford Wines   ★★★★★

RSD 355, Eden Valley, SA 5235 (postal) **Region** Eden Valley
T (08) 8565 3256 **F** (08) 8565 3244 **www**.radfordwines.com **Open** Not
Winemaker Gill and Ben Radford **Est.** 2003 **Cases** 1100 **Vyds** 4 ha
I first met Ben Radford when he was working as a head winemaker at the Longridge/ Winecorp group in Stellenbosch, South Africa. A bevy of international journalists grilled Ben, a French winemaker and a South African about the wines they were producing for the group. The others refused to admit there were any shortcomings in the wines they had made (there were), while Ben took the opposite tack, criticising his own wines even though they were clearly the best. He and wife Gill are now the proud owners of a vineyard in the Eden Valley, with 1.2 ha of riesling planted in 1930, another 1.1 ha planted in '70, and 1.7 ha of shiraz planted in 2000. Following Ben's appointment as winemaker at Rockford in '07, executive winemaking responsibilities are now Gill's. Exports to the UK, the US, Denmark and South Africa.

♀♀♀♀♀ Bio-Dynamically Grown Eden Valley Riesling 2009 Vivid green-yellow; from
an 80-year-old estate block, the wine is deceptively powerful, only revealing itself
as it slowly uncoils on the back-palate and finish. Vino-Lok. 12% alc. **Rating** 94
To 2029 $39

❍   Eden Valley Riesling 2009 Seemingly also estate-grown old vines are the
source, although not biodynamic; either way, the wine is more immediately
expressive, with lime juice notes on the bouquet and palate. Screwcap. 12% alc.
Rating 94 To 2023 $23
Eden Valley Shiraz 2007 Strong purple-red; spicy peppery aromas to the
bouquet are reflected in the lively medium-bodied palate, helping lift the finish,
and showing none of the toughness of many '07s; excellent line and length.
Screwcap. 14% alc. **Rating** 94 To 2022 $36

♀♀♀♀♀ Eden Valley Botrytis Riesling 2006 **Rating** 93 To 2014 $31
Eden Valley Fortified Riesling NV **Rating** 90 To 2011 $29

Rahona Valley Vineyard   ★★★
6 Ocean View Avenue, Red Hill South, Vic 3937 **Region** Mornington Peninsula
T (03) 5989 2924 **F** (03) 5989 2924 **www**.rahonavalley.com.au **Open** By appt
Winemaker John Salmons **Est.** 1991 **Cases** 300 **Vyds** 1.6 ha
John and Leonie Salmons have one of the older and more interesting small vineyards on the
Mornington Peninsula, on a steep north-facing slope of a small valley in the Red Hill area.
The area takes its name from the ancient red basalt soils. Five clones of pinot noir are planted
(MV6, D5V12, G5V15, 115 and D2V5) totalling 1.2 ha, and a few hundred vines each of
pinot meunier and pinot gris.

♀♀♀♀ Reserve Red Hill Pinot Noir 2008 Light but slightly better hue than the
standard wine; while has many of the savoury characters of the standard pinot,
there is more fruit evident. Screwcap. **Rating** 88 To 2014 $35
Red Hill Pinot Noir 2008 Light and somewhat developed colour; a spicy, meaty
bouquet leads into a very savoury/briary palate that does have some length, albeit
a trifle bitter. Screwcap. **Rating** 87 To 2012 $26

 # Raidis Estate   ★★★★
147 Church Street, Penola, SA 5277 **Region** Coonawarra
T (08) 8737 2966 **F** (08) 8737 2443 **www**.raidis.com.au **Open** Thurs–Sun 12–6, or by appt
Winemaker Amelia Anderson **Est.** 2006 **Cases** 2000 **Vyds** 23 ha
The Raidis family has lived and worked in Coonawarra for over 40 years. Chris Raidis was
only three years old when he arrived in Australia with his parents, who were market gardeners
in Greece before coming here. In 1994 he planted just under 5 ha of cabernet sauvignon,
while son Steven significantly expanded the vineyard in 2003 with sauvignon blanc, riesling,
pinot gris, merlot and shiraz. A cellar door was opened by Deputy Prime Minister Julia Gillard
in Nov '09, an impressive example of pulling power.

♀♀♀♀♀ The Kid Riesling 2008 Bright straw-green; very pure and tightly focused, with
❍   that trademark green apple of Coonawarra riesling, the finish long and penetrating.
Screwcap. 12.7% alc. **Rating** 91 To 2016 $14
❍   Billy Cabernet Sauvignon 2006 Attractive regional cabernet, with sweet cassis
and mulberry fruit doing the talking on a medium-bodied palate, which has good
length and balance, the tannins fine and supple. Screwcap. 14.9% alc. **Rating** 91
To 2016 $21

♀♀♀♀ The Pup Sauvignon Blanc 2009 **Rating** 87 To 2010 $15

Ramsay's Vin Rose   ★★★★
30 St Helier Road, The Gurdies, Vic 3984 **Region** Gippsland
T (03) 5997 6531 **F** (03) 5997 6158 **www**.vinrosewinery.com **Open** 7 days 11–5
Winemaker Dianne Ramsay **Est.** 1995 **Cases** 500 **Vyds** 1.65 ha

The slightly curious name (which looks decidedly strange in conjunction with Riesling and Cabernet Sauvignon) stems from the original intention of Alan and Dianne Ramsay to grow roses on a commercial scale on their property. Frank Cutler, at Western Port Winery, persuaded them to plant wine grapes instead; the plantings comprise pinot noir, chardonnay, cabernet sauvignon, merlot and riesling. They opened their micro-winery in 1999, and have four self-contained units set around their 800-bush rose garden.

ŸŸŸŸŸ **Cabernet Sauvignon 2005** Has retained excellent hue (despite indifferent cork); 4+ years on, the tannins are still to fully soften, but the judges at the Gippsland Wine Show '08 awarded it a gold medal, and the benefit of doubt. Pray the cork will hold. 13.5% alc. **Rating** 91 **To** 2015 $20

Ravens Croft Wines ★★★★

274 Spring Creek Road, Stanthorpe, Qld 4380 **Region** Granite Belt
T (07) 4683 3252 **www**.ravenscroftwines.com.au **Open** Thurs–Mon 10.30–4.30
Winemaker Mark Ravenscroft **Est.** 2002 **Cases** 1000 **Vyds** 1.21 ha
Mark Ravenscroft was born in South Africa, and studied oenology there. He moved to Australia in the early 1990s, and in '94 became an Australian citizen. His wines come from estate plantings of verdelho and pinotage, supplemented by contract-grown grapes from other vineyards in the region. A new winery has recently been completed. Exports to Japan.

ŸŸŸŸŸ **Petit Verdot 2008** Clear red-purple; black fruits and cedar aromas lead into a fresh, well-balanced medium-bodied palate with blackberry and cherry fruit, the tannins benign rather than aggressive. Screwcap. 14% alc. **Rating** 91 **To** 2018 $35
Verdelho 2009 A deliberately pure and unadorned rendition of verdelho, tropical fruit salad given freshness by a twist of lemon juice; good balance and development potential. Screwcap. 13% alc. **Rating** 90 **To** 2013 $22

ŸŸŸŸ **Chardonnay 2009 Rating** 88 **To** 2014 $25
Cabernet Sauvignon 2008 Rating 88 **To** 2016 $28
Gewurztraminer 2009 Rating 87 **To** 2012 $25

Ravensworth ★★★★★

312 Patemans Lane, Murrumbateman, ACT 2582 **Region** Canberra District
T (02) 6226 8368 **F** (02) 6226 8378 **www**.ravensworthwines.com.au **Open** Not
Winemaker Bryan Martin **Est.** 2000 **Cases** 2000
Winemaker, vineyard manager and partner Bryan Martin (with dual wine science and wine growing degrees from CSU) has a background of wine retail, food and beverage in the hospitality industry, and teaches part-time in that field. He is also assistant winemaker to Tim Kirk at Clonakilla, after seven years at Jeir Creek. Judging at wine shows is another string to his bow. Ravensworth has two vineyards: Rosehill planted in 1998 to cabernet sauvignon, merlot and sauvignon blanc; and Martin Block planted in 2000–01 to shiraz, viognier, marsanne and sangiovese.

ŸŸŸŸŸ **Murrumbateman Shiraz Viognier 2009** A little reduction on opening, but beneath lie layers of dark fruit, spice and attractive floral nuances; the palate is fresh and lively, with acid driving the core and black and red fruits, with a strong, roasted meat character, accentuating the savoury finish; a generous, yet medium-bodied style. Screwcap. 14.5% alc. **Rating** 94 **To** 2018 $27 BE
Murrumbateman Shiraz Viognier 2007 A most attractive wine, with lifted red fruit contribution from the viognier component; the tannins (briefly an issue) are fine, and the oak perfectly balanced and integrated. All in all elegance. Retasted at Winewise '09 (from whence this note originates), top gold medal in its class. Screwcap. 14% alc. **Rating** 94 **To** 2017 $40

ŸŸŸŸŸ **Murrumbateman Shiraz Viognier 2008 Rating** 91 **To** 2014 $27

ŸŸŸŸ **Murrumbateman Marsanne 2009 Rating** 88 **To** 2015 $21 BE
Murrumbateman Sangiovese 2009 Rating 88 **To** 2013 $21 BE

Red Earth Estate ★★★

18L Camp Road, Dubbo, NSW 2830 **Region** Western Plains Zone
T (02) 6885 6676 **F** (02) 6882 8297 **www**.redearthestate.com.au **Open** Thurs–Tues 10–5
Winemaker Ken Borchardt **Est.** 2000 **Cases** 2500 **Vyds** 6.2 ha
Red Earth Estate, owned by Ken and Christine Borchardt, is the focal point of grapegrowing
and winemaking in the Western Plains Zone. They have planted riesling, verdelho, frontignac,
grenache, shiraz, cabernet sauvignon and a small amount of torrentes. The winery has a
capacity of 14 000 cases, and the Borchardts also offer contract winemaking facilities for
others in the region.

🍷🍷🍷🍷🍷 **Borchardt Bordeaux Blend Cabernet Sauvignon Petit Verdot Merlot
2008** Clear purple-red; a well-made, light- to medium-bodied blend of Cabernet
Sauvignon/Petit Verdot/Merlot; in particular, has not been over-extracted or over-
oaked; to be released in October '10, the 10th anniversary of the winery, and a
worthy testament. Screwcap. 13% alc. **Rating** 90 **To** 2018 $28

Red Edge ★★★★☆

Golden Gully Road, Heathcote, Vic 3523 **Region** Heathcote
T 0407 422 067 **F** (03) 9337 7550 **Open** By appt
Winemaker Peter Dredge **Est.** 1971 **Cases** 1500 **Vyds** 15 ha
Red Edge is a relatively new name on the scene, but the vineyard dates back to 1971, and the
renaissance of the Victorian wine industry. In the early 1980s it produced the wonderful wines
of Flynn & Williams and has now been rehabilitated by Peter and Judy Dredge, producing two
quite lovely wines in their inaugural vintage and continuing that form in succeeding vintages.
Exports to the US, Canada and China.

🍷🍷🍷🍷🍷 **Heathcote Shiraz 2007** Impressively deep crimson-purple colour; in the
full-bodied style of Red Edge, and a very good one. Layers of lush blackberry
fruit and licorice are supported by ripe tannins and balanced oak. One-quarter
whole bunch foot-stamped; neither fined nor filtered. Deserves at least a decade.
Screwcap. 15% alc. **Rating** 96 **To** 2035 $45

🍷🍷🍷🍷☆ **Degree Heathcote Shiraz 2007 Rating** 92 **To** 2020 $25
Heathcote Cabernet Sauvignon 2006 Rating 90 **To** 2016 $42

Red Hill Estate ★★★★★

53 Shoreham Road, Red Hill South, Vic 3937 **Region** Mornington Peninsula
T (03) 5989 2838 **F** (03) 5931 0143 **www**.redhillestate.com.au **Open** 7 days 11–5
Winemaker Michael Kyberd, Luke Curry **Est.** 1989 **Cases** 40 000 **Vyds** 84 ha
Red Hill Estate was established by Sir Peter Derham and family, and has three vineyard
sites: Range Road, Red Hill Estate (the home vineyard), and The Briars. Taken together, the
three vineyards make Red Hill Estate one of the larger producers of Mornington Peninsula
wines. The tasting room and ever-busy restaurant have a superb view across the vineyard to
Westernport Bay and Phillip Island. In 2007 it (surprisingly) merged with Arrowfield Estate
in the Hunter Valley; one can only assume marketing synergies are expected to drive the new
InWine Group Australia. Exports to the US, Canada, Ireland, Poland, Sweden, Singapore, Japan
and Hong Kong.

🍷🍷🍷🍷🍷 **Mornington Peninsula Shiraz 2008** Bright crimson; the enticing bouquet
✪ does not disappoint on the palate; a lovely example of medium-bodied cool-
grown shiraz with a panoply of red and black cherry fruit, spice and silky tannins.
Screwcap. 13.7% alc. **Rating** 96 **To** 2023 $30
Reserve Mornington Peninsula Chardonnay 2007 Bright straw; still very
tightly focused and youthful, the intensity and purity of the fruit excellent,
doubtless partly reflecting the alcohol; grapefruit, melon and nectarine to the fore.
Screwcap. 12.8% alc. **Rating** 95 **To** 2016 $35

❂   **Mornington Peninsula Chardonnay 2008** Light straw-green; archetypal Red Hill style, fine, highly focused and pure fruits ranging from nectarine to grapefruit, and every point in between; controlled oak adds a minor dimension. Screwcap. 13.6% alc. **Rating** 94 **To** 2015 $22
Reserve Mornington Peninsula Pinot Noir 2007 Retains good hue and brightness; fragrant cherry and plum on the bouquet, the palate with considerable drive and energy, bringing some spicy savoury notes into play; good length and finish. Screwcap. 13.3% alc. **Rating** 94 **To** 2015 $35

🍷🍷🍷🍷♀   **Cellar Door Release Mornington Peninsula Sauvignon Blanc 2009** **Rating** 90 **To** 2011 $22
Cellar Door Release Mornington Peninsula Rose 2009 Rating 90 **To** 2011 $22

🍷🍷🍷🍷   **Mornington Peninsula Pinot Grigio 2009** Rating 89 **To** 2011 $22
Mornington Peninsula Pinot Noir 2008 Rating 89 **To** 2012 $22

Redden Bridge Wines   ★★★

PO Box 1223, Naracoorte, SA 5271 **Region** Wrattonbully
T (08) 8762 1588 **F** (08) 8762 1688 **www**.reddenbridge.com **Open** Not
Winemaker Robin Moody (Contract) **Est.** 2002 **Cases** 1900 **Vyds** 28 ha
This is the venture of Greg and Emma Koch, Greg with a quarter-century of viticultural experience, first in Coonawarra (17 years) and thereafter turning his attention to Wrattonbully, buying land there in 1995 and setting up Terra Rossa Viticultural Management to assist growers across the Limestone Coast. Greg and Emma now have 23 ha of cabernet sauvignon and 5 ha of pinot gris, and retain the services of the immensely experienced Robin Moody to oversee the making of the Redden Bridge wines at Cape Jaffa Estate.

🍷🍷🍷🍷   **Gully Wrattonbully Shiraz 2006** Plum black cherry, spice and vanilla are at the core of a savoury, almost briary, palate; a little lean on the finish. Screwcap. 14.4% alc. **Rating** 89 **To** 2015 $22

Redesdale Estate Wines   ★★★★☆

Redesdale Hotel, 2640 Kyneton-Heathcote Road, Redesdale, Vic 3444 **Region** Heathcote
T (03) 5425 3236 **F** (03) 5425 3122 **www**.redesdale.com **Open** Tues–Wed 2–8, Thurs–Sun 11–late
Winemaker Tobias Ansted (Contract) **Est.** 1982 **Cases** 800 **Vyds** 4 ha
Planting of the Redesdale Estate vines began in 1982 on the northeast slopes of a 25-ha grazing property, fronting the Campaspe River on one side. The rocky quartz and granite soil meant the vines had to struggle, and when Peter Williams and wife Suzanne Arnall-Williams purchased the property in 1988 the vineyard was in a state of disrepair. They have rejuvenated the vineyard, planted an olive grove, and, more recently, erected a two-storey house surrounded by a garden, which is part of the Victorian Open Garden Scheme (and cross-linked to a villa in Tuscany).

🍷🍷🍷🍷♀   **Heathcote Cabernet Sauvignon Cabernet Franc 2006** Good hue; a severe cabernet, the fruit and tannins joining together to cause a mouth-puckering reaction; after the initial jolt, the pure varietal expression of the two cabernets is obvious; one assumes that time will soften the impact without diminishing the fruit. Screwcap. 14.1% alc. **Rating** 92 **To** 2016 $40

Redgate   ★★★★☆

659 Boodjidup Road, Margaret River, WA 6285 **Region** Margaret River
T (08) 9757 6488 **F** (08) 9757 6308 **www**.redgatewines.com.au **Open** 7 days 10–5
Winemaker Simon Keall **Est.** 1977 **Cases** 7500 **Vyds** 20.28 ha
Founder and owner of Redgate, Bill Ullinger, chose the name not simply because of the nearby eponymous beach, but also because – so it is said – a local farmer (with a prominent

red gate at his property) had run an illegal spirit-still 100 or so years ago, and its patrons would come to the property and ask whether there was any 'red gate' available. True or not, Ullinger, one of the early movers in the Margaret River, now has over 20 ha of mature estate plantings (the majority to sauvignon blanc, semillon, cabernet sauvignon, cabernet franc, shiraz and chardonnay, with smaller plantings of chenin blanc and merlot). Exports to the US, Switzerland, Denmark, Japan and Singapore.

ΨΨΨΨΨ **Margaret River Cabernet Sauvignon 2008** The bouquet exhibits essency red and blackcurrant fruit, with a delicate seasoning of cigar box and black olive; the palate is full of sweet fruit, but is quite serious in its intent, with a long, firm and well-balanced finish to conclude. Screwcap. 13.5% alc. **Rating** 94 **To** 2020 $35 BE

ΨΨΨΨΨ **Reserve Oak Matured Margaret River Sauvignon Blanc 2008** Rating 92 To 2014 $29 BE
Margaret River Chardonnay 2008 Rating 91 To 2015 $35 BE

❂ **Bin 588 2008** Bright colour; the bouquet exhibits cassis and olive with a touch of toasty oak on display; the palate is medium-bodied, with good flavour and plenty of oak in evidence, certainly harmonious with the fruit. Cabernet Sauvignon/Merlot. Screwcap. 13.5% alc. **Rating** 90 **To** 2014 $22.50 BE

ΨΨΨΨ **Margaret River Sauvignon Blanc Semillon 2009** Rating 87 To 2012 $21 BE

Redman ★★★☆

Main Road, Coonawarra, SA 5263 **Region** Coonawarra
T (08) 8736 3331 **F** (08) 8736 3013 **www**.redman.com.au **Open** Mon–Fri 9–5, w'ends 10–4
Winemaker Bruce, Malcolm and Daniel Redman **Est.** 1966 **Cases** 18 000 **Vyds** 32 ha
In March 2008 the Redman family celebrated 100 years of winemaking in Coonawarra. The 2008 vintage also marked the arrival of Daniel as the fourth-generation Redman winemaker. Daniel gained winemaking experience in Central Victoria, the Barossa Valley and the US before taking up his new position. It was felicitous timing, for the 2004 Cabernet Sauvignon and '04 Cabernet Merlot were each awarded a gold medal from the national wine show circuit in '07, the first such accolades for a considerable time. However, there hasn't been a lot of follow-up.

ΨΨΨΨΨ **Coonawarra Cabernet Sauvignon 2007** Good crimson-purple; an aromatic bouquet, then a medium-bodied palate with strongly varietal blackcurrant and cassis fruit; ripe tannins provide the framework. Cork. 14% alc. **Rating** 92 To 2023 $34

ΨΨΨΨ **Coonawarra Shiraz 2007** Rating 88 To 2014 $23.50

Reilly's Wines ★★★★

Cnr Hill Street/Burra Street, Mintaro, SA 5415 **Region** Clare Valley
T (08) 8843 9013 **F** (08) 8843 9275 **www**.reillyswines.com.au **Open** 7 days 10–4
Winemaker Justin Ardill **Est.** 1994 **Cases** 25 000 **Vyds** 125 ha
What began as a hobby for cardiologist Justin Ardill and wife Julie in 1993 has grown rapidly. The plantings are spread over five vineyards in Watervale, Leasingham and Mintaro. The oldest vineyard (1919 Block in Leasingham) is planted to bush vine grenache, the work of a returned serviceman from the First World War. The other vineyards have vines ranging between 10 and 90 years, including 43-year-old cabernet sauvignon and 40-year-old riesling. The cellar door and restaurant have an even longer history, built between 1856 and 1866 by Irish immigrant Hugh Reilly, 140 years later restored by the Ardills, distant relatives of Hugh Reilly. Exports to the US, Canada, Ireland, Malaysia, China and Singapore.

ΨΨΨΨΨ **RCV Clare Valley Shiraz 2006** Dark colour with some development, coffee, dark chocolate and prune all inhabit this unusual wine, which spent 27 months in French oak; the alcohol doesn't burn. Screwcap. 15.8% alc. **Rating** 91 To 2020 $45

✪   **Clare Valley Shiraz 2008** Dark red; an unashamedly full-bodied shiraz, with masses of black fruits, some tar, firm but ripe tannins and vanillan oak. Deserves a chance to soften and open up. Screwcap. 15% alc. **Rating** 90 **To** 2020 $18
Dry Land Old Bush Vine Clare Valley Grenache 2007 Despite coming from a 1919 block of bush-pruned vines, hand-picked and open-fermented, the colour remains stubbornly light, although the hue is good; the palate is a similar conundrum, full of flavour, yet distinctly hot on the finish; it has to be respected, even if not loved. Screwcap. 15.5% alc. **Rating** 90 **To** 2015 $22

♟♟♟♟   **Watervale Riesling 2009 Rating** 89 **To** 2016 $19
Dry Land Clare Valley Shiraz 2006 Rating 89 **To** 2020 $27
✪   **Clare Valley Cabernet Sauvignon 2008** There is an exceptional consistency to all the Reilly's red wines; a robust, full-bodied style that is all about maximum flavour extraction; here there is a suber-abundance of ripe black fruits and ripe tannins alike. Screwcap. 15% alc. **Rating** 88 **To** 2019 $18
Dry Land Clare Valley Cabernet Sauvignon 2005 Rating 88 **To** 2017 $27

Remarkable View Wines   ★★★★☆

Main North Road, Murray Town, SA 5481 **Region** Southern Flinders Ranges
T (08) 8667 2223 **F** (08) 8667 2165 **www.**remarkableview.com.au **Open** W'ends &
public hols 11–4.30, or by appt (closed Jan)
Winemaker Contract **Est.** 1997 **Cases** 100 **Vyds** 18 ha
Karen and the late Malcolm Orrock (and their family) began the establishment of the vineyard in 1997, and have progressively established shiraz, sangiovese, cabernet sauvignon, grenache, tempranillo and petit verdot. The bulk of the production is sold to Peter Lehmann Wines, with limited amounts made for sale under the Remarkable View brand, the interesting label of which is a grape vine leaf with the image of a Clydesdale horse's head within the veins of the leaf.

♟♟♟♟♟   **Southern Flinders Ranges Shiraz 2005** Holding crimson-purple hue
✪   remarkably well; a more powerful and rich wine than the '06 (unusual), with a similar mix of spice, licorice and black fruits that are given a savoury twist on the long finish. Screwcap. 14% alc. **Rating** 94 **To** 2020 $20

♟♟♟♟♟   **Southern Flinders Ranges Shiraz 2006** Good hue; a scented bouquet of
✪   gently spicy red fruits leads into a lively, spicy, medium-bodied palate that has an attractively savoury edge, taking the wine more to black fruits; good length and balance. Striking gold-embossed abstract leaf on the label. Screwcap. 14% alc.
Rating 93 **To** 2020 $20

Renards Folly   ★★★☆

PO Box 499, McLaren Vale, SA 5171 **Region** McLaren Vale
T (08) 8556 2404 **F** (08) 8556 2404 **Open** Not
Winemaker Tony Walker **Est.** 2005 **Cases** 1500
The dancing foxes on the label, one with a red tail, give a subliminal hint that this is a virtual winery, owned by Linda Kemp (who looks after the marketing and sales) and Mark Dimberline, who has spent 16 years in the wine industry. Aided by friend and winemaker Tony Walker, they source grapes from McLaren Vale, and allow the Vale to express itself without too much elaboration, the alcohol nicely controlled. Exports to the US, Canada, Germany and Singapore.

♟♟♟♟♟   **McLaren Vale Sauvignon Blanc Semillon 2009** Unexpectedly fresh, juicy and
✪   flavoursome, the tropical fruits of the sauvignon blanc playing the soprano role, the citrus of the semillon the tenor. Screwcap. 13% alc. **Rating** 90 **To** 2011 $16.95

♟♟♟♟   **McLaren Vale Shiraz 2008 Rating** 89 **To** 2018 $19.95
McLaren Vale Sangiovese Cabernet 2008 Rating 89 **To** 2012 $16.95

 Repertoire ★★★★

PO Box 293, Cowaramup, WA 6284 **Region** Margaret River
T 0404 987 417 **www**.repertoirewines.com.au **Open** Not
Winemaker Richard Tattam, Mark Warren **Est.** 2008 **Cases** 800
Repertoire is the virtual winery venture of Richard Tattam, who has turned his attention from sculpting bronze artworks to winemaking. He learnt to craft wines by working three vintages at Cullen Wines, two at Happs Three Hills winery, and two in France. The influence of Vanya Cullen has no doubt played a role in the decision of the business to be carbon neutral, while Tattam's artistic credentials comes through in the highly unusual labels and background stories of each of the wines to be found on the website. It is, indeed, the website that constitutes the retail sales outlet, apart from the numerous Margaret River restaurants and wine shops that list or stock the wines.

🍷🍷🍷🍷🍷 **Margaret River Sauvignon Blanc Semillon 2009** Light straw; grass, herb and asparagus aromas lead into a powerful, punchy and long palate. Screwcap. 13.5% alc. **Rating** 90 **To** 2012 $20
Skimpy But Buxom Margaret River Sauvignon Blanc Semillon 2007 Bright straw-green; has now developed to the point where waiting longer is not likely to be profitable; that said, has built on the flavours of the '09 varietal with greater citrussy fruit. Screwcap. 13.6% alc. **Rating** 90 **To** 2010 $25

🍷🍷🍷🍷 **Shim Margaret River Chardonnay 2007 Rating** 89 **To** 2014 $25
Strongman Margaret River Shiraz 2006 Rating 88 **To** 2013 $25
Venturous Margaret River Grenache 2006 Rating 87 **To** 2013 $25
Tall & Short Margaret River Cabernet Merlot 2006 Rating 87 **To** 2012 $25

Reschke Wines ★★★★☆

Level 1, 183 Melbourne Street, North Adelaide, SA 5006 (postal) **Region** Coonawarra
T (08) 8239 0500 **F** (08) 8239 0522 **www**.reschke.com.au **Open** Not
Winemaker Peter Douglas (Contract) **Est.** 1998 **Cases** 10 000 **Vyds** 143.86 ha
It's not often that the first release from a new winery is priced at $100 per bottle, but that was precisely what Reschke Wines achieved with its 1998 Cabernet Sauvignon. The family has been a landholder in Coonawarra for 100 years, with a large holding that is partly terra rossa, part woodland. Cabernet sauvignon (with 108 ha) takes the lion's share of the plantings, with merlot, shiraz and petit verdot making up the balance. Exports to the UK, the US and other major markets.

🍷🍷🍷🍷🍷 **Bos Coonawarra Cabernet Sauvignon 2005** High-quality Coonawarra cabernet, redolent of blackcurrant, mulberry and fresh earth; the texture, structure and oak handling are likewise admirable. Cork. 14% alc. **Rating** 94 **To** 2020 $40

🍷🍷🍷🍷🍷
✪ **Bull Trader Coonawarra Cabernet Merlot 2006** An unequivocally good example of the blend, with an almost chocolatey richness folded within the blackcurrant and cassis fruit; ripe, fine tannins and balanced oak. Screwcap. 14% alc. **Rating** 91 **To** 2016 $19

🍷🍷🍷🍷
✪ **Bull Trader Coonawarra Shiraz 2006** A light- to medium-bodied wine with spicy aromas and a fresh, tangy palate with a mix of black fruits and spice. Stylish packaging. Screwcap. 14% alc. **Rating** 89 **To** 2015 $19
Coonawarra Sauvignon Blanc 2009 Rating 88 **To** 2011 $19

Resolution Vineyard ★★★☆

4 Glen Street, South Hobart, Tas 7004 (postal) **Region** Southern Tasmania
T (03) 6224 9497 **www**.theresolutionvineyard.com **Open** Not
Winemaker Frogmore Creek **Est.** 2003 **Cases** 150 **Vyds** 0.8 ha
Owners Charles and Alison Hewitt live in England and entrust the care of the property and vineyard to Alison's father Peter Brown, with support from former Parks & Wildlife ranger Val Dell, who also has a small vineyard. A love of red burgundy and fishing was sufficient

for Charles to establish the vineyard planted to three clones of pinot noir in Tasmania, where Alison had spent most of her formative years. The vineyard is on a north-facing slope overlooking the D'Entrecasteaux Channel. Exports to the UK.

🍷🍷🍷🍷♀ **Pinot Noir 2007** Slightly lighter than the '08, but holding hue well; a finer wine,
○ with red fruits on the aromatic bouquet flowing through to the silky/slippery palate, the finish punctuated by fine tannins. Screwcap. 13.8% alc. **Rating** 92 **To** 2014 $25

🍷🍷🍷🍷 **Pinot Noir 2008 Rating** 89 **To** 2015 $20

Reynella ★★★★★

Reynell Road, Reynella, SA 5161 **Region** McLaren Vale/Fleurieu Peninsula
T (08) 8392 2300 **F** (08) 8392 2202 **Open** Mon–Sat 10–4
Winemaker Paul Lapsley **Est.** 1838 **Cases** NFP
John Reynell laid the foundations for Chateau Reynella in 1838; over the next 100 years the stone buildings and cellars, with patches of lawn and leafy gardens were constructed. Thomas Hardy's first job in SA was with Reynella, noting in his diary that he would be able to better himself soon. He did just that, becoming by far the largest producer in SA by the end of the 19th century; 150 or so years after Chateau Reynella's foundation CWA completed the circle by acquiring it and making it corporate headquarters, while preserving the integrity of the Reynell brand in no uncertain fashion. In a sign of the times, 'Chateau' has been dropped from its name.

🍷🍷🍷🍷🍷 **Basket Pressed McLaren Vale Shiraz 2007** Deep colour; heavily toasted oak comes to the fore, supported by generous levels of deep black fruit and dark chocolate; full-bodied, full-blooded and full of chewy tannins and dark fruit; completely unevolved, time is needed for all parts to come together. Cork. 14% alc. **Rating** 94 **To** 2025 $54 BE
Basket Pressed McLaren Vale Cabernet Sauvignon 2007 A powerful expression of cabernet, with essency cassis fruit and toasty oak in abundance; the palate delivers a full-bodied and powerful mouthful of flavour, with dark chocolate and black olives on the long and expressive finish. Cork. 13.6% alc. **Rating** 94 **To** 2025 $54 BE

🍷🍷🍷🍷 **McLaren Vale Grenache 2007 Rating** 89 **To** 2014 $37 BE

Richard Hamilton ★★★★★

Cnr Main Road/Johnston Road, McLaren Vale, SA 5171 **Region** McLaren Vale
T (08) 8323 8830 **F** (08) 8323 8881 **www**.leconfieldwines.com **Open** Mon–Fri 10–5, w'ends & public hols 11–5
Winemaker Paul Gordon, Tim Bailey **Est.** 1972 **Cases** 25 000 **Vyds** 73.09 ha
Richard Hamilton has outstanding estate vineyards, some of great age, all fully mature. The arrival of former Rouge Homme winemaker Paul Gordon has allowed the full potential of those vineyards to be realised. The quality, the style and the consistency of both red and white wines has reached a new level; being able to keep only the best parcels for the Richard Hamilton is an enormous advantage. Exports to the UK, the US, Canada, Malaysia, Hong Kong, Singapore, Japan and NZ.

🍷🍷🍷🍷🍷 **Gumprs' McLaren Vale Shiraz 2008** Good colour and bouquet, but it is the
○ palate that shows why this wine won trophies at the Adelaide (Best Shiraz) and McLaren Vale Wine Shows; it is bursting with spicy black fruits, but best of all is its outstanding drive and length. Screwcap. 14.5% alc. **Rating** 96 **To** 2023 $17.95
Hamilton Centurion Old Vine McLaren Vale Shiraz 2008 Deep purple-crimson; a deep, profound bouquet lazily unwinds itself into a long palate with ripe plum and spice fruit, no more than medium-bodied, the tannins marvellously soft; there is no hint of overripe fruit, and the wine will live forever, so perfect is its balance. From vines 116 years old. Screwcap. 14.5% alc. **Rating** 96 **To** 2050 $59.95

⊘ **Hamilton McLaren Vale Shiraz 2008** Bright purple-crimson; the junior brother of the Centurion, but with much going for it; a pristine bouquet then a lively, perfectly balanced, medium-bodied palate with plum, spice, raspberry and a hint of chocolate running through to a tangy finish. Successive trophies at McLaren Vale and Adelaide Wine Shows '09. Great bargain. Screwcap. 14.5% alc. **Rating** 94 **To** 2023 $17.95

Burton's Vineyard Old Bush Vine McLaren Vale Grenache Shiraz 2006 Produced from 62-year-old bush-trained interplanted vines on a single-vineyard block; it has retained excellent hue, and the palate is correspondingly fresh and lively, with cherry and raspberry fruit, rather than cosmetic/Turkish delight; the spicy components run right through to the finish. This is sheer enjoyment. Screwcap. 14.% alc. **Rating** 94 **To** 2020 $39.95

⊘ **Hut Block McLaren Vale Cabernet Sauvignon 2008** Good hue; has the same drive and flourish to the blackcurrant and cassis palate as the Shiraz, bringing it two trophies at the McLaren Vale Wine Show '09. Screwcap. 14% alc. **Rating** 94 **To** 2018 $17.95

🍷🍷🍷🍷 **Slate Quarry McLaren Vale Riesling 2009 Rating** 89 **To** 2014 $14.95
Almond Grove McLaren Vale Chardonnay 2009 Rating 89 **To** 2011 $14.95
⊘ **Lot 148 McLaren Vale Merlot 2008** Good red-purple; plum, cherry and raspberry fruits drive the bouquet and palate alive on a relatively full-bodied palate for merlot; honest flavour. Screwcap. 14% alc. **Rating** 89 **To** 2014 $17.95
Jette's McLaren Vale Viognier 2009 Rating 87 **To** 2011 $17.95

Richfield Estate ★★★★★

Bonshaw Road, Tenterfield, NSW 2372 **Region** New England
T (02) 6737 5488 **F** (02) 6737 5598 **www.**richfieldvineyard.com.au **Open** By appt 10–4
Winemaker John Cassegrain **Est.** 1997 **Cases** 4500 **Vyds** 30 ha
Singapore resident Bernard Forey is the chairman and majority shareholder of Richfield Estate. The 500-ha property, at an altitude of 720 m, was selected after an intensive survey by soil specialists. Shiraz, cabernet sauvignon, verdelho, merlot, semillon and chardonnay are planted. Winemaker John Cassegrain is a shareholder in the venture, and much of the wine is exported to Canada and Malaysia.

🍷🍷🍷🍷 **Richfields Semillon Sauvignon Blanc 2009** A blend of Lower Hunter
⊘ Valley/Hastings River/Mudgee that works very well, the grassy/herbal notes of the semillon augmented by ripe citrus nuances. Screwcap. 11.5% alc. **Rating** 89 **To** 2012 $11.65
⊘ **Richfields Sangiovese Shiraz 2008** Light, bright colour; has attractive light red cherry fruits with distinct spice and briar nuances; the tannins are no issue. Mudgee/New England. Screwcap. 14% alc. **Rating** 88 **To** 2012 $11.65
⊘ **Richfields Chardonnay 2008** A Tumbarumba/Gundagai/New England blend that is fresh and quite juicy; the absence of oak is no loss, for the wine has good length. Screwcap. 13.5% alc. **Rating** 87 **To** 2012 $11.65

Richmond Grove ★★★★

Para Road, Tanunda, SA 5352 **Region** Barossa Valley
T (08) 8563 7303 **www.**richmondgrovewines.com **Open** 7 days 10.30–4.30
Winemaker Steve Clarkson **Est.** 1983 **Cases** 100 000
Owned by Orlando Wyndham, Richmond Grove draws its grapes from diverse sources. The Richmond Grove Barossa Valley and Watervale Rieslings, a legacy of master winemaker John Vickery, represent excellent value for money year in, year out. Exports to the UK and Sweden.

🍷🍷🍷🍷🍷 **Limited Release Barossa Vineyards Shiraz 2007** Bright red-purple, particularly good for its age and the vintage; there is plenty going on in the mouth, with blackberry and plum fruit supported by fine tannins and a controlled touch of oak. Screwcap. 14.5% alc. **Rating** 90 **To** 2020 $22

Limited Release Coonawarra Vineyards Cabernet Sauvignon 2007 An elegant, medium-bodied cabernet with gentle blackcurrant, cedar and mocha notes supported by fine, ripe tannins. Screwcap. 14.5% alc. **Rating** 90 **To** 2017 $22

Rickety Gate   ★★★★☆

1949 Scotsdale Road, Denmark, WA 6333 **Region** Great Southern
T (08) 9840 9503 **F** (08) 9840 9502 **www**.ricketygate.com.au **Open** Fri–Mon 11–4
Winemaker John Wade **Est.** 2000 **Cases** 2500 **Vyds** 3.3 ha
The Rickety Gate vineyard is situated on north-facing slopes of the Bennet Ranges, in an area specifically identified by Dr John Gladstones as highly suited to cool-climate viticulture. The property was purchased by Russell and Linda Hubbard at the end of 1999, and 2 ha of merlot, 1 ha of riesling, 0.3 ha of pinot noir and 0.1 ha of chardonnay have been planted. John Wade contract-makes the wines at the small onsite winery.

♟♟♟♟♟ **Denmark Riesling 2003** Glowing green-straw; a beautifully pure and intense
✪   lime and passionfruit-accented riesling that has developed with extreme grace, and
            has a decade or more in front of it, although it's hard to think of a reason why it
            shouldn't be drunk now. Screwcap. 11% alc. **Rating** 96 **To** 2020 $30

♟♟♟♟♟ **Denmark Shiraz 2006 Rating** 91 **To** 2016 $24
            Denmark Merlot Cabernet Sauvignon 2003 Rating 91 **To** 2015 $30

Ridgemill Estate   ★★★☆

218 Donges Road, Severnlea, Qld 4352 **Region** Granite Belt
T (07) 4683 5211 **F** (07) 4683 5211 **www**.ridgemillestate.com **Open** Thurs–Mon 10–5
Winemaker Martin Cooper, Peter McGlashan **Est.** 1998 **Cases** 1000 **Vyds** 2.1 ha
Martin Cooper and Dianne Maddison acquired what was then known as Emerald Hill Winery in 2004. In '05 they reshaped the vineyards, which now have plantings of chardonnay, tempranillo, shiraz, merlot and cabernet sauvignon, saperavi, shiraz, verdelho and viognier, setting a course down the alternative variety road. The 2005 Chardonnay was the first Qld wine to win an international gold medal (at the International Chardonnay Challenge '05 in Gisborne, NZ). Its best wines are part of the Qld charge to recognition against all-comers.

♟♟♟♟♟ **Pedigree Granite Belt Shiraz Mourvedre Grenache 2008** Good purple-
            crimson hue; a pleasing bouquet of red and black fruits points to the 60/30/10
            blend; dark plum and red berry flavours mingle on the palate before some tannins
            on the finish; 168 cases made. Screwcap. 14% alc. **Rating** 90 **To** 2016 $25

♟♟♟♟ **Ella Granite Belt Verdelho 2009** A mix of freshness and layered fruit flavours
✪   helps build both mouthfeel and flavour; success in local wine shows no surprise.
            Screwcap. 13.5% alc. **Rating** 89 **To** 2012 $18
            Pedigree Granite Belt Shiraz 2008 Rating 87 **To** 2014 $25

RidgeView Wines   ★★★★☆

273 Sweetwater Road, Rothbury, NSW 2335 **Region** Hunter Valley
T 0419 475 221 **F** (02) 9534 5468 **www**.ridgeview.com.au **Open** Wed–Sun 10–5
Winemaker Cameron Webster, Darren Scott, Gary MacLean **Est.** 2000 **Cases** 2500
Vyds 9 ha
Darren and Tracey Scott (plus their four children and extended family) have transformed a 40-ha timbered farm into a vineyard, together with self-contained accommodation and cellar door. The lion's share of the plantings are 4.5 ha of shiraz, with cabernet sauvignon, chambourcin, merlot, pinot gris, viognier and traminer making up a somewhat eclectic selection of varieties. In 2010 the family celebrated ten years in business by opening a cellar door and restaurant. Exports to Japan.

ŸŸŸŸŸ **Generations Reserve Hunter Valley Shiraz 2006** Good varietal and regional expression; a mix of plum, blackberry, spice and earth, the tannins ripe and giving both texture and structure. Has developed well over the past 20 months. Trophy NSW Wine Awards '09, gold medal Sydney Wine Show '10. Screwcap. 15% alc. Rating 94 To 2021 $40

ŸŸŸŸŸ **Generations Reserve Hunter Valley Semillon 2009** Rating 93 To 2020 $25 BE

ŸŸŸŸ **Hunter Valley Verdelho 2009** Rating 87 To 2012 $20 BE
Generations Reserve Hunter Valley Shiraz 2007 Rating 87 To 2020 $40

Rileys of Eden Valley ★★★☆

PO Box 71, Eden Valley, SA 5235 **Region** Eden Valley
T (08) 8564 1029 **F** (08) 8564 1029 **www**.rileysofedenvalley.com.au **Open** Not
Winemaker Jo Irvine (Contract) **Est.** 2006 **Cases** 350 **Vyds** 7.7 ha
Rileys of Eden Valley is owned by father Terry, mother Jan and son Peter Riley, who way back in 1982 purchased 32 ha of a grazing property that they believed had potential for quality grape production. The first vines were planted in that year and over the next 16 years plantings extended to 7.2 ha. Minimal planting has occurred since, but in '08 0.8 ha of merlot were grafted to savagnin (in the belief that it was albarino). In '98 Terry retired from his position of Professor of Mechanical Engineering at the University of South Australia, allowing him to concentrate on the vineyard, and, more recently, winemaking activities, but the whole family (including granddaughter Maddy) have been involved in the development of the property. It had always been intended that the grapes would be sold, but when not all the grapes were contracted in '06, the Rileys decided to produce some wine (even though they ended up with buyers for all of the production that year).

ŸŸŸŸŸ ✪ **The Family Riesling 2009** Light green-straw; attractive regional lime and lemon blossom aromas, the palate building on those with lime juice to the fore; possibly a subliminal touch of sweetness. Screwcap. 12.5% alc. Rating 92 To 2019 $19

ŸŸŸŸ **Peter's Chardonnay 2009** Rating 88 To 2014 $19
Jump Ship Shiraz 2008 Rating 87 To 2014 $25.50
The Engineer Merlot 2008 Rating 87 To 2013 $24.75

Riposte ★★★★☆

PO Box 256, Lobethal, SA 5241 **Region** Adelaide Hills
T (08) 8389 8149 **F** (08) 8389 8178 **www**.timknappstein.com.au **Open** Not
Winemaker Tim Knappstein **Est.** 2006 **Cases** 8000
It's never too late to teach an old dog new tricks when the old dog in question is Tim Knappstein. With 40 years of winemaking and more than 500 wine show awards under his belt, Tim has started yet another new wine life with Riposte, a subtle response to the various vicissitudes he has suffered in recent years. While having no continuing financial interest in Lenswood Vineyards, established many years ago, Tim is able to source grapes from this vineyard, and also makes selections from other prime sites in surrounding areas. Exports to the UK and other major markets.

ŸŸŸŸŸ **The Sabre Adelaide Hills Pinot Noir 2008** Bright, clear red; a fragrant bouquet of red berry and spice leads into a very well proportioned and structured palate, black cherry also joining the party, as does a subtle carpet of French oak; very well made. Screwcap. 14% alc. Rating 94 To 2015 $29

ŸŸŸŸŸ **The Foil Adelaide Hills Sauvignon Blanc 2009** Rating 93 To 2011 $19.90

River Park   ★★★

River Park Road, Cowra, NSW 2794 **Region** Cowra
T (02) 6342 3596 **F** (02) 6341 3711 **www**.riverparkwines.com.au **Open** Mon–Fri 9–5,
w'ends 10–5
Winemaker Hunter Wine Services, Thistle Hill **Est.** 1994 **Cases** 2000 **Vyds** 20 ha
Bill and Chris Murphy established River Park with 13 ha of chardonnay and cabernet
sauvignon on the banks of the Lachlan River, on the outskirts of Cowra, in 1994. The
vineyard has since been expanded, and includes cabernet sauvignon (10 ha), chardonnay (5 ha)
and a recent planting of pinot gris (5 ha). Part of the wine made from the estate plantings is
sold (in bulk) to major wine companies, but an increasing amount is being reserved for the
River Park label.

⟡⟡⟡⟡ **Cowra Rose 2009** Bright magenta; very fresh, strawberry/raspberry fruit flavours
✪   with exemplary acidity to finish. Screwcap. 13.5% alc. **Rating** 89 **To** 2010 $17
        Cowra Cabernet Sauvignon 2007 Some colour development, although not
        excessive; continues the improvement in Cowra's red wines, with light but focused
        black and redcurrant fruit; the only thing lacking is structure. Screwcap. 13.5% alc.
        Rating 87 **To** 2012 $18

Riversands Vineyards   ★★★

Whytes Road, St George, Qld 4487 **Region** Queensland Zone
T (07) 4625 3643 **F** (07) 4625 5043 **www**.riversandswines.com **Open** Mon–Sat 8–5.30,
Sunday 9–4
Winemaker Ballandean Estate **Est.** 1990 **Cases** 4000 **Vyds** 20 ha
Riversands is on the banks of the Balonne River in the southwest corner of Qld. It is a mixed
wine grape and table grape business, acquired by present owners Alison and David Blacket
in 1996. Its extensive vineyards are planted to sauvignon blanc, semillon, chardonnay, white
muscat, black muscat, shiraz, cabernet sauvignon and merlot.

⟡⟡⟡⟡ **Golden Liqueur Muscat NV** Clean fortifying spirit no doubt earned the wine
        its trophy; the spirit cuts across the otherwise cloying finish; no obvious signs of
        age, solera must be young. Screwcap. 18% alc. **Rating** 88 **To** 2013 $24

 # Riversdale Estate   ★★★★

222 Denholms Road, Cambridge, Tas 7170 **Region** Southern Tasmania
T (03) 6248 5666 **F** (03) 6248 5492 **www**.riversdaleestate.com.au **Open** By appt
Winemaker Nick Badrice **Est.** 1991 **Cases** 10 000 **Vyds** 23 ha
Ian Roberts purchased the Riversdale property in 1980 while a university student, and says
he paid a record price for the district. The unique feature of the property is its front edge
to the Pittwater waterfront that acts as a buffer against frost, and also moderates the climate
during the ripening phase. The vines are planted on a gentle, easterly facing slope. It is a very
large property, with 23 ha of vines (not all in production) and one of the largest olive groves
in Tasmania, producing 50 olive-based products. Five families live permanently on the estate,
providing all the labour for the various operations, which also include four 5-star French
Provincial cottages overlooking the vines. Wine quality is consistently good.

⟡⟡⟡⟡⟡ **Centaurus Coal River Valley Pinot Noir 2008** Bright crimson-purple;
        decidedly more fragrant than the varietal, the palate with red and black fruits;
        the tannins have some of the savoury characters of that wine. Screwcap. 14% alc.
        Rating 93 **To** 2016 $29.65
        Coal River Valley Riesling 2009 Bright pale green; a very fragrant bouquet,
        lime, apple and pear followed by a palate driven by Tasmanian acidity that has
        a particular focus; needs several years to begin to open up. Screwcap. 12.5% alc.
        Rating 91 **To** 2019 $22

Crater Coal River Valley Chardonnay 2008 Pale, bright straw-green; an elegant, if slightly understated, wine with white peach and grapefruit flavours gently harnessed in French oak; crisp acidity helps drive the long finish; will age well. Screwcap. 13.5% alc. **Rating** 90 **To** 2015 $30

Coal River Valley Pinot Noir 2008 Good red-purple; warm spice and plum aromas lead into a powerful palate, the dark plum fruit woven with ripe tannins; overall quite savoury. Screwcap. 13.5% alc. **Rating** 90 **To** 2015 $24.85

ΨΨΨΨ **Coal River Valley Sauvignon Blanc 2009 Rating** 87 **To** 2011 $23
Crux Sparkling NV Rating 87 **To** 2012 $44

Robert Channon Wines ★★★☆

32 Bradley Lane, Stanthorpe, Qld 4380 **Region** Granite Belt
T (07) 4683 3260 **F** (07) 4683 3109 **www.**robertchannonwines.com **Open** Mon–Fri 11–4, w'ends & public hols 10–5
Winemaker Mark Ravenscroft **Est.** 1998 **Cases** 3000 **Vyds** 8 ha
Peggy and Robert Channon have established verdelho, chardonnay, pinot gris, shiraz, cabernet sauvignon and pinot noir under permanent bird protection netting. The initial cost of installing permanent netting is high, but in the long term it is well worth it: it excludes birds and protects the grapes against hail damage. Also, there is no pressure to pick the grapes before they are fully ripe. The winery has established a particular reputation for its Verdelho.

ΨΨΨΨΨ **Verdelho 2009** Nectarine and lime bouquet and palate; quite fresh and zesty on entry; a distinct mineral character lengthens the palate and finish. Screwcap. 13.5% alc. **Rating** 90 $24.50 BE

Robert Oatley Vineyards ★★★★★

Craigmoor Road, Mudgee, NSW 2850 **Region** Mudgee
T (02) 6372 2208 **F** (02) 9433 0456 **www.**robertoatley.com.au **Open** 7 days 10–4
Winemaker James Manners, Chris Hancock, Larry Cherubino, Trent Nankivell
Est. 2006 **Cases** NFP **Vyds** 461.83 ha
Robert Oatley Vineyards is the venture of the Oatley family, previously best known as the owners of Rosemount Estate until it was sold to Southcorp. The chairman is Bob Oatley; the new venture is run by son Sandy, with considerable hitting power added by deputy executive chairman Chris Hancock. Wild Oats, as anyone with the remotest interest in yachting and the Sydney–Hobart Yacht Race will know, has been the name of Bob Oatley's racing yachts. The family has long owned vineyards in Mudgee, but the new business has been rapidly expanded by the acquisition of the Montrose winery, the Craigmoor cellar door and restaurant, and vineyards spread across Mudgee. The family has completed a $10 million upgrade of the Montrose winery. The recruitment of Larry Cherubino as a consultant has given the business a major foothold in the southern regions of WA, resulting in east-meets-west regional blends, and also single-region wines. While there is a plethora of wines, stripped to its essentials, the portfolio is easy to understand: at the bottom, James Oatley Tic Tok ($18); next Wild Oats ($18); then Robert Oatley ($26–28); and at the top, Robert Oatley Family, with three prices: $32, $38 and $45. Exports to the US.

ΨΨΨΨΨ **Robert Oatley Family Margaret River Chardonnay 2009** Pale, bright green-quartz; very much in the modern style, early picked to maximise freshness and zest; grapefruit and white peach aromas and flavours are dominant, oak contributing as much to the texture as the flavour; will grow with bottle age. Screwcap. 12.5% alc. **Rating** 94 **To** 2017 $38

Robert Oatley Family Margaret River Cabernet Sauvignon 2009 Crimson-red; a very elegant medium-bodied cabernet that fully reflects one face of Margaret River with this variety; the black fruit flavours are long and fine, the tannins fine and silky, the oak evident but restrained. Screwcap. 13.8% alc. **Rating** 94 **To** 2020 $45

ҮҮҮҮҮ **Robert Oatley Family Margaret River Sauvignon Blanc Semillon 2009**
Rating 93 To 2014 $32
Robert Oatley Family Mudgee Chardonnay 2009 Rating 93 To 2016 $38
Robert Oatley Family Ovens Valley Shiraz 2009 Rating 92 To 2019 $45
Robert Oatley Margaret River & Mudgee Cabernet Merlot 2008
Rating 91 To 2016 $26
❂ **James Oatley Tic Tok Chardonnay 2008** Light straw-green; unexpectedly,
there is considerable synergy between the Mudgee and Pemberton components,
perhaps due to riper Mudgee stone fruit and a citrussy shaft from Pemberton.
Whatever, works well. Screwcap. 12.8% alc. Rating 90 To 2012 $18
Robert Oatley Frankland River & Mudgee Shiraz 2008 Rating 90
To 2018 $26

ҮҮҮҮ **James Oatley Tic Tok Shiraz 2008** Good colour; a rich and ripe shiraz, with a
❂ display of plum, black cherry, blackberry and dark chocolate reflecting its regional
components. Well made. Frankland River/Mudgee/McLaren Vale. Screwcap.
14% alc. Rating 89 To 2017 $18

Robert Stein Vineyard ★★★★★

Pipeclay Lane, Mudgee, NSW 2850 **Region** Mudgee
T (02) 6373 3991 **F** (02) 6373 3709 **www**.robertstein.com.au **Open** 7 days 10–4.30
Winemaker Andrew and Jacob Stein **Est.** 1976 **Cases** 10 000 **Vyds** 17.15 ha
While three generations of the family have been involved since Robert (Bob) Stein began
the establishment of the vineyard, the chain stretches even further back, going to Bob's great-
great-grandfather, Johann Stein, who was brought to Australia by the Macarthur family to
supervise the planting of the Camden Park vineyard. Robert's son Drew and grandson Jacob
have now taken over winemaking responsibilities. Jacob worked vintages in Italy, Canada,
Margaret River and Avoca, but more particularly, in the Rheingau and Rheinhessen regions of
Germany. It is no doubt the experience he gained there that led to the 2008 Riesling winning
three trophies at the Mudgee Wine Show '09, and the 2009 winning the Riesling Trophy at
the Winewise Small Winemakers Competition '09, and Best Riesling Trophy at the Cowra
Wine Show '09. Exports to Germany, Hong Kong, Singapore and China.

ҮҮҮҮҮ **Mudgee Riesling 2009** A beautifully aromatic wine, with citrus blossom aromas
❂ and delicate yet intense lime fruit flavours, the balance between fruit, a touch
of residual sugar and acidity perfect. Yet another wine reminiscent of German
Kabinett rieslings. Screwcap. 11% alc. Rating 95 To 2019 $25
Reserve Mudgee Shiraz 2007 A very well made wine, the texture and
structure particularly impressive thanks to the balance and integration of tannins
and oak into the blackberry and plum fruit. Made by Drew Stein prior to the
return of his son Jacob. Screwcap. 13.5% alc. Rating 94 To 2020 $35
Harvest Gold 2009 Glowing gold; intense mandarin and cumquat aromas
are replayed on the lusciously sweet palate, there balanced by acidity; a botrytis
semillon briefly exposed to French oak, it has great length and intensity. Screwcap.
8.5% alc. Rating 94 To 2014 $25

ҮҮҮҮҮ **Reserve Mudgee Cabernet Sauvignon 2008** Rating 91 To 2018 $30
❂ **Mudgee Cabernet Rose 2009** Pale, light magenta; small red berry fruit aromas,
then a red fruit palate with a touch of sweetness on the finish smuggled in; well
made. Screwcap. 12% alc. Rating 90 To 2010 $15

ҮҮҮҮ **Mudgee Cabernet Sauvignon 2007** Rating 89 To 2015 $20

Robertson of Clare ★★★★☆

PO Box 149, Killara, NSW 2071 **Region** Clare Valley
T (02) 9499 6002 **www**.rocwines.com.au **Open** Not
Winemaker Simon Gilbert, Leigh Eldredge **Est.** 2004 **Cases** NFP

This is a venture of Simon Gilbert, established after he ceased to have an executive position with Simon Gilbert Wines in Mudgee. He has joined with Clare Valley vigneron Leigh Eldredge to produce limited quantities of Clare Valley wines. The first release, MAX V, was sourced from three growers in the Clare Valley, utilising the five grapes of Bordeaux: cabernet sauvignon, cabernet franc, merlot, malbec and petit verdot. Lavish oak is the hallmark of this most unusual wine. Exports to the UK, the US, Denmark, The Maldives and Singapore.

🍷🍷🍷🍷🍷 MAX V 2007 Medium red-purple; a five-variety Bordeaux blend, one-third of which was fermented in new French 400-litre 'vinification integrale' barrels; the other two-thirds in Mintaro slate open fermenters; the wine then spent 30 months in 19 variations of new French barriques from five forests. And guess what? It smells and tastes very oaky; the points are for effort. Cork. 14.5% alc. **Rating** 94 To 2037 $75

Robyn Drayton Wines ★★★★

Cnr McDonalds Road/Pokolbin Mountain Road, Pokolbin, NSW 2321
Region Hunter Valley
T (02) 4998 7523 **F** (02) 4998 7523 **www**.robyndraytonwines.com.au **Open** 7 days 10–5
Winemaker Robyn Drayton, Andrew Spanazi **Est.** 1989 **Cases** 5000 **Vyds** 14 ha
In 1994 Robyn Drayton inherited the business started by her parents following their death in a plane crash. Together with her sons, Justin, Liam and Taylor, she has grown the business exponentially. The cellar door has been expanded twice, a new café and function centre opened, and an additional 6 ha of vines planted. Robyn is a fifth-generation Drayton, and continues the proud tradition of over 150 years of Drayton winemaking in the Hunter Valley.

🍷🍷🍷🍷🍷 Reginald Reserve Hunter Valley Semillon 2008 Super fresh and focused bouquet of lemon sherbert and a suggestion of straw; the palate is zesty as a young wine, but has a fine sweet spot of fruit on the mid-palate, providing an even and seamless conclusion. Screwcap. 10.2% alc. **Rating** 94 $30 BE

🍷🍷🍷🍷 Liam Reserve Hunter Valley Verdelho 2008 **Rating** 88 $25 BE

Rochford Wines ★★★★☆

Cnr Maroondah Highway/Hill Road, Coldstream, Vic 3770 **Region** Yarra Valley
T (03) 5962 2119 **F** (03) 5962 5319 **www**.rochfordwines.com **Open** 7 days 10–5
Winemaker Andrew Leitch **Est.** 1988 **Cases** 20 000 **Vyds** 45.26 ha
Following the acquisition of the former Eyton-on-Yarra by Helmut Konecsny, major changes occurred. Most obvious is the renaming of the winery and brand, slightly less so the move of the winemaking operations of Rochford from the Macedon Ranges to the Yarra Valley. Rochford has 30.55 ha of vineyards in the Macedon Ranges, and just under 15 ha in the Yarra Valley, with a heavy focus on chardonnay and pinot noir. The large restaurant is open 7 days for lunch and Rochford is well-known for the numerous concerts it stages in its lakeside amphitheatre. Exports to the UK, the US, Canada, Sweden, Philippines, Singapore, Hong Kong and China.

🍷🍷🍷🍷🍷 Macedon Ranges Chardonnay 2007 Bright green-straw; very much in the modern style, relying on the intensity and length of its citrussy cool-grown fruit more than artefact, although French oak has, of course, added to the structure of the wine. Screwcap. 13.5% alc. **Rating** 94 To 2014 $30

🍷🍷🍷🍷🍷 Macedon Ranges Pinot Noir 2007 **Rating** 93 To 2014 $40
Macedon Ranges Pinot Gris 2009 **Rating** 91 To 2010 $28

🍷🍷🍷🍷 Macedon Ranges Blanc de Noirs NV **Rating** 88 To 2012 $40

RockBare ★★★★

102–104 Main St, Hahndorf, Sa 5245 **Region** McLaren Vale
T (08) 8388 7155 **F** (08) 8388 7522 **www**.rockbare.com.au **Open** Not
Winemaker Marty O'Flaherty **Est.** 2000 **Cases** 50 000 **Vyds** 47 ha

A native of WA, Tim Burvill moved to SA in 1993 to do the winemaking course at the Adelaide University Roseworthy campus. Having completed an honours degree in oenology, he was recruited by Southcorp and quickly found himself in a senior winemaking position responsible for super-premium whites including Penfolds Yattarna. He oversees the team that makes the RockBare wines under lend-lease arrangements with other wineries. Has moved to a new cellar door in the centre of Hahndorf. Exports to all major markets.

ŶŶŶŶŶ **McLaren Vale Shiraz 2008** Prominent oak dominates the bouquet, giving the ample dark fruits a distinct cola edge; the palate too is quite charry, but there is plenty of fruit to push through with a little more time. Screwcap. 14.5% alc. **Rating** 90 **To** 2014 $21.95 BE

ŶŶŶŶ **Mojo Shiraz 2008 Rating** 89 **To** 2013 $17 BE
Mojo Sauvignon Blanc 2009 Rating 88 **To** 2012 $17 BE

Rockfield Estate ★★★★★
Rosa Glen Road, Margaret River, WA 6285 **Region** Margaret River
T (08) 9757 5006 **F** (08) 9757 5006 **www**.rockfield.com.au **Open** 7 days 11–5, or by appt
Winemaker Cliff Royle (Consultant), James Kalleske **Est.** 1997 **Cases** 6000 **Vyds** 11 ha
Rockfield Estate Vineyard is very much a family affair. Dr Andrew Gaman wears the hats of chief executive officer and co-marketing manager, wife Anne is a director, son Alex is the viticulturist, and Anna Walter (née Gaman) helps with the marketing. Chapman Brook meanders through the property, the vines running from its banks up to the wooded slopes above the valley floor. Exports to the UK and China.

ŶŶŶŶŶ ✪ **Margaret River Semillon Sauvignon Blanc 2009** Light straw-green; has an abundance of citrus, gooseberry and lychee aromas and flavours, partial barrel ferment adding to texture more than flavour; has great richness and persistence. Screwcap. 12.5% alc. **Rating** 94 **To** 2013 $19
Margaret River Cabernet Sauvignon 2007 Good red-purple; a medium-bodied but stylish, intense and long cabernet that reflects the good '07 vintage; blackcurrant fruit is the core of the wine, with cedar, spice and earth spun around that core, coupled with positive, ripe tannins. Screwcap. 14% alc. **Rating** 94 **To** 2022 $48

ŶŶŶŶŶ **Margaret River Merlot 2008 Rating** 93 **To** 2023 $39

Rockford ★★★★★
Krondorf Road, Tanunda, SA 5352 **Region** Barossa Valley
T (08) 8563 2720 **F** (08) 8563 3787 **www**.rockfordwines.com.au **Open** 7 days 11–5
Winemaker Robert O'Callaghan, Ben Radford **Est.** 1984 **Cases** NFP
Rockford can only be described as an icon, no matter how overused that word may be. It has a devoted band of customers who buy most of the wine through the cellar door or mail order (Rocky O'Callaghan's entrancing annual newsletter is like no other). Some wine is sold through restaurants, and there are two retailers in Sydney, and one each in Melbourne, Brisbane and Perth. Whether they will have the Basket Press Shiraz available is another matter; it is as scarce as Henschke Hill of Grace (and less expensive). Exports to the UK, Canada, Switzerland, Korea, Singapore, Japan, Hong Kong, China and NZ.

ŶŶŶŶŶ **Black Shiraz NV** One of the best sparkling shirazs available today, and always on strict allocation. This bottle was disgorged in Sept '09, and has immaculate balance in a light- to medium-bodied mode, the spicy black fruits needing minimal dosage. Cork. 13.5% alc. **Rating** 95 **To** 2015 $56
Rifle Range Barossa Valley Cabernet Sauvignon 2007 The brown, high-waisted, branded bottle is pure Rockford; the restrained use of oak and gentle extraction pays big dividends for this cabernet, its blackcurrant fruits beautifully offset, indeed enhanced, by ripe but fine tannins. Cork. 14.5% alc. **Rating** 94 **To** 2022 $35

Rod & Spur Barossa Valley Cabernet Shiraz 2006 Very good colour, typical of '06; the two varieties join synergistically, the shiraz providing blackberry and plum for the mid-palate, the cabernet the fresh blackcurrant fruit and tannins of the finish. Cork. 14.5% alc. **Rating** 94 **To** 2021 $29.50

ŶŶŶŶŶ Moppa Springs Barossa Valley Grenache Mataro Shiraz 2005 **Rating** 93 **To** 2020 $23.50
Basket Press Barossa Valley Shiraz 2007 **Rating** 92 **To** 2022 $51

✪ Frugal Farmer 2008 An entirely new take, with early picked grenache/ mourvedre crushed onto the pressed, but not fermented, skins of Alicante Bouchet; a bridge between rose and light dry red, distinctly spicy and crisp, and works very well. Screwcap. 12.5% alc. **Rating** 90 **To** 2011 $19.50

ŶŶŶŶ Handpicked Eden Valley Riesling 2007 **Rating** 89 **To** 2011 $19
Barossa Valley Alicante Bouchet 2009 **Rating** 89 **To** 2011 $17
Barossa Valley White Frontignac 2009 **Rating** 87 **To** 2010 $15.50

Rocky Passes Estate ★★★☆

1590 Highlands Road, Whiteheads Creek, Vic 3660 **Region** Upper Goulburn
T (03) 5796 9366 **F** (03) 5796 9366 **www**.rockypasses.com.au **Open** Sun by appt
Winemaker Vitto Oles **Est.** 2000 **Cases** 500 **Vyds** 2 ha
Vitto Oles and Candi Westney run this tiny, cool-climate vineyard situated at the southern end of the Strathbogie Ranges, which in fact falls in the Upper Goulburn region. They have planted 1.6 ha of shiraz and 0.4 ha of viognier, growing the vines with minimal irrigation and preferring organic and biodynamic soil treatments. Vitto is also a fine furniture designer and maker, with a studio at Rocky Passes.

ŶŶŶŶ Syrah Cabernet 2008 Tangy, spicy, minty characters run through the bouquet and palate, attesting to the cool climate; savoury, herbal tannins on the finish accentuate the impact. Diam. 15% alc. **Rating** 89 **To** 2018 $25

Rocland Estate ★★★☆

PO Box 679, Nuriootpa, SA 5355 **Region** Barossa Valley
T (08) 8562 2142 **F** (08) 8562 2182 **www**.roclandestate.com **Open** By appt
Winemaker Peter Gajewski, Michael Hall **Est.** 2000 **Cases** 10 000 **Vyds** 6 ha
Rocland Estate is primarily a bulk winemaking facility for contract work, but Frank Rocca does have 6 ha of shiraz to make the Rocland wines, largely destined for export markets, but with retail distribution in Adelaide. Rocland releases wines under the Lot 147, Kilroy Was Here, Duck Duck Goose, Chocolate Box, and the charmingly named Ass Kisser labels. Exports to the US, Singapore, China and NZ.

ŶŶŶŶŶ McLaren Vale Marsanne Viognier Roussanne 2009 Bright colour; a very
✪ creditable blend of these northern Rhône varieties, each playing off the other and leaving a juicy freshness on the aftertaste. Screwcap. 13.5% alc. **Rating** 90 **To** 2013 $22

ŶŶŶŶ Barossa Valley Grenache 2008 **Rating** 89 **To** 2013 $22
Chocolate Box Cherry Chocolate GSM 2007 **Rating** 88 **To** 2011 $20

Roennfeldt Wines ★★★

13 Augusta Street, Maylands, SA 5069 (postal) **Region** Barossa Valley
T 0411 180 960 **F** (08) 8363 9431 **Open** Not
Winemaker David Heinze **Est.** 2005 **Cases** 600 **Vyds** 18.2 ha
The Roennfeldt family emigrated from Germany in 1849 and has been growing grapes in the Barossa Valley for five generations. The vineyards, currently owned by Brett and Ruth Roennfeldt, are mainly 12–20 years old, with small sections of 50-year-old shiraz, mourvedre and grenache; 60% of the plantings are shiraz. The vineyard produces around 120 tonnes of grapes a year, almost all of which are sold to leading Barossa wineries. In 2005 5 tonnes

of seven- and 12-year-old shiraz were vinified to make the first release under the Roennfeldt label, marketed as 2005 Genesis Barossa Shiraz. No wine was made in the excellent 2006 vintage because the Roennfeldts were waiting to see how the '05 would be received. When it was placed sixth out of the 416 entries in the Visy Great Australian Shiraz Challenge '07 they had their answer, and production promptly resumed. The wine will always be a single-vineyard, estate-grown shiraz.

ΨΨΨΨ **Genesis Barossa Shiraz 2008** Deep, dark crimson-purple; powerful black fruit aromas follow through to the palate, the alcohol not hot, simply shortening the finish; I'm not sure where this will head. Screwcap. 15.5% alc. **Rating** 89 **To** 2016 $37

🍇 Rogers & Rufus ★★★

c/- Samuel Smith & Son, 6–8 Crewe Place, Rosebery, NSW 2018 **Region** Barossa Valley
T (02) 8344 8244 **F** (02) 8344 8246 **www.**samsmith.com.au **Open** Not
Winemaker Robert Hill Smith **Est.** 2009 **Cases** NFP
This is a decidedly under the bedcover partnership between Robert Hill Smith and his immediate family, and Rupert and Jo Clevely, Rupert the former Veuve Clicquot director in Australia, but now running gastro pub group Geronimo Inns in London. Late in 2008 the Hill Smiths and Clevelys decided (in their words) 'to do something fun together with a serious dip at Euro styled dry and savoury delicate rose using three site specific, old, low-yielding, dry-grown grenache sites from the Barossa floor'. Most of the production is sold in the US, with a small allocation marketed in Australia by Samuel Smith & Son.

ΨΨΨΨ **Barossa Grenache Rose 2009** Very pale colour; crisp, clean and bright, with some red fruit and Turkish delight flavours; modest, but does the job. Screwcap. 12% alc. **Rating** 87 **To** 2010 $17

Rohrlach Family Wines ★★★★★

PO Box 864, Nuriootpa, SA 5355 **Region** Barossa Valley
T (08) 8562 4121 **F** (08) 8562 4202 **www.**rohrlachfamilywines.com.au **Open** Not
Winemaker Peter Schell (Contract) **Est.** 2000 **Cases** 1000 **Vyds** 160.6 ha
Brothers Kevin, Graham and Wayne Rohrlach, with wives Lyn, Lynette and Kaylene, are third-generation owners of prime vineyard land, the first plantings made back in 1930 by their paternal grandfather. Until 2000 the grapes were sold to two leading Barossa wineries, but (in a common story) in that year some of the grapes were retained to make the first vintage of what became Rohrlach Family Wines. In '03 the family received the ultimate local accolade when the Barons of the Barossa gave them the title of 'Vignerons of the Year'.

ΨΨΨΨΨ **Mum's Block Barossa Valley Shiraz 2006** Good hue, although not entirely clear; a fragrant and elegant shiraz, the blackberry and cherry fruit effortlessly running through the long palate and finish. Screwcap. 14% alc. **Rating** 95 **To** 2031 $43
Mum's Block Barossa Valley Shiraz 2007 Impressive red-crimson; a deeply flavoured shiraz that steps around the usual toughness of '07, the 100-year-old vines providing a wine full of supple black fruits, the palate long and balanced. Screwcap. 14% alc. **Rating** 94 **To** 2027 $43

ΨΨΨΨ
❂ **Barossa Shiraz 2006** Rich, ripe and luscious full-bodied wine with a big fruitcake finish; all this achieved without high alcohol. Screwcap. 14.5% alc. **Rating** 89 **To** 2016 $20
Barossa Cabernet Merlot 2006 **Rating** 89 **To** 2014 $20

Rolf Binder Veritas Winery ★★★★☆

Cnr Seppeltsfield Road/Stelzer Road, Tanunda, SA 5352 **Region** Barossa Valley
T (08) 8562 3300 **F** (08) 8562 1177 **www.**rolfbinder.com **Open** Mon–Sat 10–4.30
Winemaker Rolf Binder, Christa Deans **Est.** 1955 **Cases** 30 000 **Vyds** 36 ha

The change of accent from Veritas to Rolf Binder came with the 50th anniversary of the winery, established by the parents of Rolf and sister Christa Deans. The growth in production and sales is due to the quality of the wines rather than the (hitherto) rather laid-back approach to marketing. The winery produces a full range of all the main white and red wines sourced from the Barossa and Eden valleys. It has had conspicuous success with semillon at the Barossa Valley Wine Show, but the red wines are equally commendable. Exports to the UK, the US and other major markets.

ΨΨΨΨΨ **Eden Valley Riesling 2009** Light straw-green; an intense and rich expression
✪ of Eden Valley riesling; floods the mouth with lime flavours; good length and persistence. Screwcap. 12.5% alc. **Rating** 93 **To** 2017 $17

Heysen Barossa Valley Shiraz 2007 Clear, bright red-purple; the plum and blackberry bouquet leads into a medium- to full-bodied palate that has good structure, texture and length, with an interplay between black fruits, licorice and ripe tannins. Cork. 14.5% alc. **Rating** 92 **To** 2015 $70

Rolf Binder's Bull's Blood Shiraz Mataro Pressings 2007 A marvellous retro label, even if Bull's Blood is in lighter typeface; the wine is very intense, very savoury and very individualistic – and also very enjoyable. Cork. 14.5% alc. **Rating** 91 **To** 2015 $45

✪ **Barossa Valley Cabernet Sauvignon Merlot 2008** Light, bright red-purple; surely picked before the heat on the basis of its colour and flavour; regardless, this is an elegant wine with blackcurrant, plum and spice flavours running through a finely pitched, medium-bodied palate. Screwcap. 14% alc. **Rating** 91 **To** 2016 $20

✪ **Barossa Valley Shiraz 2008** Medium red-purple; some smoky bacon notes on the bouquet (ex oak?) are followed by a medium-bodied palate, with spicy/savoury flavours running alongside the black fruits; has deceptive length. Screwcap. 14% alc. **Rating** 90 **To** 2017 $20

Heinrich Barossa Valley Shiraz Mataro Grenache 2007 Light colour; a light- to medium-bodied blend that is particularly successful in marrying the three components, spicy red fruits with balanced tannins and a touch of warm oak. Screwcap. 14% alc. **Rating** 90 **To** 2016 $35

ΨΨΨΨ **Barossa Valley Viognier 2008 Rating** 89 **To** 2012 $20

Romney Park Wines ★★★★★

Lot 100, Johnson Road, Balhannah, SA 5242 **Region** Adelaide Hills
T (08) 8398 0698 **F** (08) 8398 0698 **www.**romneyparkwines.com.au **Open** By appt
Winemaker Rod and Rachel Short **Est.** 1997 **Cases** 500 **Vyds** 3 ha
Rod and Rachel Short began the planting of chardonnay, shiraz and pinot noir in 1997. The first vintage was in 2002, made from 100% estate-grown grapes. Yields are limited to 3.7–5 tonnes per hectare for the red wines, and 2–3 tonnes for the chardonnay. The vineyard is managed organically, with guinea fowl cleaning up the insects, all vines hand-picked and hand-pruned. In every way (including the wines) has the beauty of a hand-painted miniature.

ΨΨΨΨΨ **Adelaide Hills Pinot Noir 2008** Very good hue; a delicious wine that has more
✪ purity of pinot expression than the majority of Adelaide Hills pinots, with sweet red cherry fruit and enough tannins to ensure authority. Diam. 14% alc. **Rating** 96 **To** 2015 $39

Adelaide Hills Shiraz 2008 Vivid crimson-purple; a highly attractive fragrant bouquet of spiced black fruits leads into a vibrantly textured palate, with spice, blackberry, plum, French oak and glorious tannins. Diam. 14.5% alc. **Rating** 96 **To** 2028 $36

Reserve Adelaide Hills Merlot 2007 Clear crimson-red; exemplary merlot varietal character throughout the bouquet and palate; plum and a touch of black olive are supported by fine, lingering tannins on the medium-bodied palate, the finish long and balanced. Diam. 13.7% alc. **Rating** 94 **To** 2017 $38

Adelaide Hills Blanc de Blancs 2004 Bright green-gold; an exceptionally fine
and fresh wine, even with five years on lees prior to disgorgement in July '09; the
balance is good, the dosage minimal. Will not suffer from further time in bottle.
Crown seal. 12.5% alc. **Rating** 94 **To** 2013 $65

Rookery Wines ★★★★

PO Box 132, Kingscote, Kangaroo Island, SA 5223 **Region** Kangaroo Island
T (08) 8553 9099 **F** (08) 8553 9201 www.rookerywines.com.au **Open** By appt
Winemaker Garry Lovering **Est.** 1999 **Cases** 800 **Vyds** 8 ha
Garry and Gael Lovering have established 3.2 ha of cabernet sauvignon and 1.6 ha of shiraz,
with smaller plantings of sauvignon blanc, tempranillo, saperavi, sangiovese, chardonnay,
merlot, petit verdot, riesling and zinfandel. Kangaroo Island is one of SA's best-kept secrets,
a place of genuine magic with its aquatic life, amazing coastline sculpture, wild flowers and
prolific native fauna.

ΨΨΨΨΨ Kangaroo Island Sauvignon Blanc 2009 Full of tropical passionfruit varietal
✪ expression on both bouquet and palate; has achieved this without moving into
a flabby, overripe mode; drink soon, however. Screwcap. 13% alc. **Rating** 91
To 2011 $18
Kangaroo Island Zinfandel 2008 Strong purple-red; aged in 100% new
American oak, but I'm not persuaded that was the right course; there is some
pretty useful fruit here, presently entombed in that oak – I hope it escapes, because
there's lot of potential here. Screwcap. 13% alc. **Rating** 90 **To** 2018 $18

ΨΨΨΨ Kangaroo Island Riesling 2009 **Rating** 88 **To** 2015 $18

Rosabrook Margaret River Wine ★★★★☆

Yungarra Estate, Lot 68 Yungarra Drive, Quedjinup, WA 6281 **Region** Margaret River
T (08) 9368 4553 **F** (08) 9368 4566 www.rosabrook.com.au **Open** 7 days 10–4
Winemaker Brian Fletcher **Est.** 1980 **Cases** 8000 **Vyds** 8 ha
Mike and Sally Calneggia have been at the forefront of vineyard development in the Margaret
River over the past decade, but also have various winemaking interests. The Rosabrook Estate
vineyards were established progressively between 1984 and '96, with semillon, chardonnay,
shiraz, merlot and cabernet sauvignon. The cellar door is housed in what was Margaret River's
first commercial abattoir, built in the early 1930s, hence the icon red is named Slaughterhouse
Block. Exports to Dubai, Hong Kong and Japan.

ΨΨΨΨΨ Cabernet Sauvignon 2007 Crimson-purple; a fragrant bouquet with perfectly
✪ ripened cabernet fruit on the cusp of cassis and blackcurrant tells you precisely
what to expect on the medium-bodied palate; the tannin texture and structure is a
bonus. Screwcap. 14.5% alc. **Rating** 94 **To** 2020 $24

ΨΨΨΨΨ Chardonnay 2009 An elegant, medium-bodied chardonnay with nectarine,
✪ white peach and citrus fruit couched in a fine web of French oak, and just a touch
of creamy/nutty character. Screwcap. 13.5% alc. **Rating** 92 **To** 2014 $22
Sauvignon Blanc Semillon 2009 **Rating** 90 **To** 2012 $20

Rose Hill Estate Wines ★★★

1400 Oxley Flats Road, Milawa, Vic 3678 **Region** King Valley
T (03) 5727 3930 **F** (03) 5727 3930 www.rosehillstatewines.com.au **Open** Fri–Mon 10–5
Winemaker Jo Hale **Est.** 1996 **Cases** 250 **Vyds** 2 ha
The Rose Hill vineyard, winery and house are all the work of Milawa cabinetmaker Stan
Stafford (and friends). The house, using 150-year-old bricks from a former chapel at Everton,
came first, almost 30 years ago. Then came the vineyard, with merlot planted in 1987, and
durif planted in 2002 to fill in the gaps where the merlot had died. It's a strange mix of
bedfellows, but it's easy to tell which is which. In '04, after many sleepless nights weighing up
the pros and cons, Jo Hale and Kevin de Henin purchased the estate from Stan. They knew

what they were doing: Jo had helped Stan in both vineyard and winery in the last few years while studying wine science at CSU, and working for Brown Brothers, Gapsted Wines and Sam Miranda; Kevin had also worked at many regional vineyards and wineries.

♀♀♀♀ King Valley Merlot 2008 Good depth of colour for the variety; the varietal expression on the bouquet is good, but the alcohol tends to take hold on the palate; for hearty stews on a cold winter's night. Screwcap. 15% alc. **Rating** 88 To 2014 $18

Durif 2008 The lighter than normal colour is at odds with the stated alcohol, as is the palate (which is a good thing); savoury, multi-spice flavours drive the palate and there is no undue heat. Screwcap. 16% alc. **Rating** 88 To 2017 $29

Rosedale Wines   ★★★☆

PO Box 308, Greenock, SA 5360 **Region** Barossa Valley
T (08) 8562 8562 **F** (08) 8562 8229 www.rosedalewines.com.au **Open** Not
Winemaker Matt Reynolds **Est.** 2006 **Cases** 40 000 **Vyds** 800 ha
This is the venture of Luciano (Luc) Signore, whose family wine roots are in the Campania region of Italy, but who has had over two decades of financial and company management consultancy work in Australia. Rosedale Wines is, he says 'strategically aligned' with Barossa Vines Ltd, which has 800 ha of vines situated west of Lyndoch and Greenock planted in 1998. The wines are made under the direction of the experienced Matt Reynolds at the Dorrien Estate and Barossa Valley Estate wineries. The focus for the modestly priced and stylishly packaged wines is exports to the US, Canada, Denmark, Germany, Hong Kong and Indonesia.

♀♀♀♀♀ Cat Amongst The Pigeons Nine Lives Shiraz 2007 A striking wine right
✪   from the first whiff, with spice, licorice, blackberry, dark chocolate and leather all clamouring for attention; happily, the wine is more relaxed on the back-palate and finish. Screwcap. 15% alc. **Rating** 91 To 2017 $17

♀♀♀♀ Cat Amongst The Pigeons Fat Cat Shiraz Cabernet 2007 Rating 87
To 2014 $17

Rosemount Estate   ★★★★☆

Chaffeys Road, McLaren Vale, SA 5171 **Region** McLaren Vale
T (08) 8323 8250 **F** (08) 8323 9308 www.rosemountestate.com.au **Open** Mon–Sat
10–5, Sun & public hols 11–4
Winemaker Matthew Koch **Est.** 1888 **Cases** 3 million **Vyds** 325 ha
Rosemount Estate has vineyards in the Upper Hunter Valley, Coonawarra and McLaren Vale that are the anchor for its top-of-the-range wines. It also has access to other Foster's estate-grown grapes, but the major part of its intake for the Diamond Label wines is supplied by contract growers across NSW, Vic and WA. Rosemount's Hunter Valley cellar door (open 7 days 10-5) is located at McDonalds Road, Pokolbin. Exports to all major markets.

♀♀♀♀♀ Show Reserve Coonawarra Cabernet Sauvignon 2008 Impressive colour
✪   and an essay of Coonawarra cabernet; essency cassis is framed by clearly defined mint and cedar; the palate is rich and chock full of black fruits, delivering a long finish full of black olive complexity; chewy, dark and tannic to conclude. Gold medal Sydney Wine Show '10. Screwcap. 14.5% alc. **Rating** 94 To 2020 $20 BE

♀♀♀♀♀ Show Reserve Cool Climate Release Robe Chardonnay 2009 Robe
✪   can produce chardonnay with classic cool-climate characters, undisturbed by heat spikes. This has flowery aromas and delicate but satisfying grapefruit, apple and white peach flavours; no obvious oak. Screwcap. 13.5% alc. **Rating** 92
To 2012 $20

Roxburgh Chardonnay 2007 Rating 90 To 2012 $42
✪   **Diamond Label Merlot 2008** Good colour, clear and bright; the aroma, flavour, texture and structure are all as they should be, with plum and blackcurrant doing the talking. Screwcap. 13.5% alc. **Rating** 90 To 2013 $16

○   **Show Reserve Traditional 2007** Highly polished bouquet of plush fruit and toasty oak; international in appeal, the underlying complexity of the fruit is somewhat shaded by the oak; fleshy, long and quite chewy to conclude. Cabernet Sauvignon/Merlot/Petit Verdot. Screwcap. 14.5% alc. **Rating** 90 **To** 2016 $20

♟♟♟♟   **Diamond Label Shiraz 2008 Rating** 89 **To** 2014 $16
Diamond Label Unoaked Chardonnay 2009 Rating 87 **To** 2010 $20 BE
Diamond Label Chardonnay 2008 Rating 87 **To** 2011 $16

Rosenthal Wines ★★★★

PO Box 1458, South Perth, WA 6951 **Region** Blackwood Valley
T 0407 773 966 **F** (08) 9368 6445 **www**.rosenthalwines.com.au **Open** Not
Winemaker Matilda's Estate (Toby Ladwig) **Est.** 2001 **Cases** 1000 **Vyds** 4 ha
Perth medical specialist Dr John Rosenthal heads Rosenthal Wines, which is a small part of the much larger 180-ha Springfield Park cattle stud situated between Bridgetown and Manjimup. He acquired the property from Gerald and Marjorie Richings, who in 1997 had planted a small vineyard as a minor diversification. The Rosenthals extended the vineyard, which is equally divided between shiraz and cabernet sauvignon. All of the wines have had significant show success, chiefly in WA-based shows.

♟♟♟♟♟   **The Naomi Shiraz Cabernet 2008** Good colour; a 70/30 blend of estate-grown fruit; the bouquet has aromatic berry fruits that expand their range on the palate from red cherry through to blackberry, oak inputs very evident. Screwcap. 14% alc. **Rating** 91 **To** 2018 $27.50

Rosenvale Wines ★★★★

Lot 385 Railway Terrace, Nuriootpa, SA 5355 **Region** Barossa Valley
T 0407 390 788 **F** (08) 8565 7206 **www**.rosenvale.com.au **Open** By appt
Winemaker James Rosenzweig, Mark Jamieson, Chris Taylor **Est.** 1999 **Cases** 4000
Vyds 105 ha
The Rosenzweig family vineyards, some old and some new, are planted to riesling, semillon, chardonnay, grenache, shiraz, merlot and cabernet sauvignon. Most of the grapes are sold to other producers, but since 2000 select parcels have been retained and vinified for release under the Rosenvale label. Exports to the UK and other major markets.

♟♟♟♟♟   **Old Vines Reserve Barossa Valley Cabernet Sauvignon 2006** Dense, dark colour; as the colour suggests, a seriously full-bodied wine, with an armada of black fruits, licorice and ripe tannins; at the outer end of ripeness and extraction, perhaps, but gets away with it. Diam. 14.5% alc. **Rating** 91 **To** 2030 $40
Estate Barossa Valley Shiraz 2008 Rich fruitcake and spice bouquet, followed by a generous and warm mouthful of blackberry fruit; a well-balanced example. Diam. 14.5% alc. **Rating** 90 **To** 2016 $24 BE

Rosily Vineyard ★★★★★

Yelveton Road, Wilyabrup, WA 6284 **Region** Margaret River
T (08) 9755 6336 **F** (08) 9221 3309 **www**.rosily.com.au **Open** W'ends 10–5 during hols
Winemaker Mike Lemmes **Est.** 1994 **Cases** 6500 **Vyds** 12.28 ha
The partnership of Mike and Barb Scott and Ken and Dot Allan acquired the Rosily Vineyard site in 1994, and the vineyard was planted over the next three years to sauvignon blanc, semillon, chardonnay, cabernet sauvignon, merlot, shiraz, grenache and cabernet franc. The first crops were sold to other makers in the region, but in 1999 Rosily built a winery with 120-tonne capacity, and it now handles the estate-grown fruit. Exports to the UK, Hong Kong and Singapore.

♟♟♟♟♟   **Margaret River Chardonnay 2008** A great example of the complexity
○   Margaret River can achieve with overtones of (good) Burgundy; the intense yet fine array of fruit aromas and flavours are the cornerstone, oak merely a vehicle. Will develop very well. Screwcap. 13.5% alc. **Rating** 95 **To** 2014 $23

❂ **Margaret River Semillon Sauvignon Blanc 2009** Takes the approach of the
sauvignon blanc one step further, due in part to the 65% semillon component, and
also maturation in oak. Has good length, structure and persistence of flavour in a
white Bordeaux style. Screwcap. 13.5% alc. **Rating** 94 **To** 2013 $21

♟♟♟♟♟ **Margaret River Sauvignon Blanc 2009** Part of a move away from anything
❂ remotely resembling Marlborough sauvignon blanc; partial barrel ferment supports
an intense bouquet and palate, with gooseberry and herb notes to the fore, grass
and citrus in the background. Gold medals Margaret River Wine Show and
Adelaide Wine Show '09. Screwcap. 13% alc. **Rating** 93 **To** 2011 $20
Margaret River Cabernet Sauvignon 2007 Rating 90 **To** 2015 $23

♟♟♟♟ **Margaret River Merlot 2007 Rating** 89 **To** 2014 $20

Rosnay Organic Wines   ★★★
Rivers Road, Canowindra, NSW 2804 **Region** Cowra
T (02) 6344 3215 **F** (02) 6344 3229 **www**.organicfarms.com.au **Open** By appt
Winemaker Various contract **Est.** 2002 **Cases** 3000
Rosnay Organic Wines is an interesting business venture of the Statham family, which
moved onto the property in 1995. There are 30 ha of vineyard on the 140-ha property, part
of which has been divided into 12 blocks along with 10 housing blocks, each of 5000 m².
The viticulture is organic, and the management company provides active growers or absentee
investors with a range of specialist organic farming machinery and contract management.
Winemaking is split between John Cassegrain of Cassegrain Wines, Kevin Karstrom of
Botobolar and Rodney Hooper, each one of whom has expertise in organic grapegrowing
and organic winemaking.

♟♟♟♟ **Cowra Triple Blend 2006** Light colour, but has retained good hue; a very
pleasant light- to medium-bodied wine, with cassis, plum and red and black cherry
fruit flavours, tannins out of the frame. Drink asap. Shiraz/Cabernet Sauvignon/
Merlot. Cork. 14% alc. **Rating** 88 **To** 2013 $18
Central Ranges Semillon Sauvignon Blanc 2009 A blend of estate-grown
Semillon (70%)/Orange Sauvignon Blanc (30%), all the fruit certified organic
and biodynamic; has a mix of broad flavours ex the semillon, given a tangy lift by
the sauvignon blanc, but the semillon comes again on the slightly tough finish.
Screwcap. 13.5% alc. **Rating** 87 **To** 2011 $18

Ross Estate Wines   ★★★★☆
Barossa Valley Way, Lyndoch, SA 5351 **Region** Barossa Valley
T (08) 8524 4033 **F** (08) 8524 4533 **www**.rossestate.com.au **Open** 7 days 10–4
Winemaker Alex Peel **Est.** 1999 **Cases** 15 000 **Vyds** 43 ha
Darius and Pauline Ross laid the foundation for Ross Estate Wines when they purchased
a vineyard that included two blocks of 75- and 90-year-old grenache. Also included were
blocks of 30-year-old riesling and semillon, and 13-year-old merlot; plantings of chardonnay,
sauvignon blanc, cabernet sauvignon, cabernet franc, shiraz and tempranillo have followed.
Exports to the UK, the US and other major markets.

♟♟♟♟♟ **Reserve Barossa Valley Shiraz 2006** If you must put a cork in a bottle, it
should be as good as the one in this bottle, a purple disc on the bottom, no wine
stains along the sides, and with no pock marks. Perfectly ripened fruit from the
best parcels of estate grapes grown in the ideal '06 vintage, the ensuing wine
aged in American oak gives a classic Barossa Valley shiraz. 14.5% alc. **Rating** 94
To 2021 $45

♟♟♟♟♟ **Single Vineyard Barossa Valley Cabernets Merlot 2006** Very good colour;
❂ the magic of the '06 vintage is immediately obvious, the red and black berry
fruits with freshness and precision, and perfectly balanced spicy/savoury tannins in
support, the oak also well handled. Screwcap. 14.5% alc. **Rating** 93 **To** 2021 $25

⚫ **ROSS Barossa Tempranillo 2008** Bright hue; while only light- to medium-bodied, has good structure to the red berry and mulberry fruit flavours, the tannins fine and well balanced. Gold medal Cowra, silver medal Rutherglen '09. Screwcap. 13% alc. **Rating** 90 **To** 2012 $18

♟♟♟♟ **ROSS Barossa Shiraz 2007 Rating** 88 **To** 2017 $18
ROSS Cabernet Merlot 2008 Rating 88 **To** 2016 $18
Single Vineyard Barossa Valley Cabernet Sauvignon 2008 Rating 88 **To** 2016 $25

Ross Hill Wines   ★★★★☆

134 Wallace Lane, Orange, NSW 2800 **Region** Orange
T (02) 6353 3223 **F** (02) 6363 1674 **www**.rosshillwines.com.au **Open** W'ends & public hols 10–4, or by appt
Winemaker Phil Kerney **Est.** 1994 **Cases** 8000 **Vyds** 17 ha
Owned by the Robson and James families. Chardonnay, merlot, sauvignon blanc, cabernet franc, shiraz and pinot noir have been established on north-facing, gentle slopes at an elevation of 800 m. No insecticides are used in the vineyard, the grapes are hand-picked and the vines are hand-pruned. The arrival of Phil Kerney from the Mornington Peninsula is significant, as is the increase from 12 ha to 17 ha of estate vineyards, production increasing from 300 cases to its present level. Ross Hill also has an olive grove with Italian and Spanish varieties. Exports to the UK, Hong Kong and China.

♟♟♟♟♟ **Orange Sauvignon Blanc 2009** Similar colour to Lily; earlier picking has diminished the fruit salad characters, but given the wine more focus, length and precision to a mix of citrus, gooseberry and mineral; wild yeast fermentation also used. Screwcap. 12.7% alc. **Rating** 94 **To** 2011 $30

♟♟♟♟♟ **Orange Chardonnay 2009 Rating** 93 **To** 2014 $30
Orange Pinot Noir 2009 Rating 93 **To** 2016 $35
Orange Shiraz 2008 Rating 92 **To** 2020 $35

♟♟♟♟ **Lily Orange Sauvignon Blanc 2009 Rating** 89 **To** 2010 $20
Maya Orange Chardonnay 2009 Rating 89 **To** 2013 $20
Orange Pinot Gris 2009 Rating 89 **To** 2011 $30
Thomas Orange Cabernet Sauvignon 2008 Rating 89 **To** 2016 $20
Isabelle Cabernet Franc Merlot 2008 Rating 89 **To** 2015 $20
Orange Cabernet Franc 2008 Rating 89 **To** 2016 $35
Shed No 8 Orange Sauvignon Blanc 2009 Rating 88 **To** 2010 $12
Orange Cabernet Sauvignon 2008 Rating 88 **To** 2014 $35

Rowanston on the Track   ★★★★

2710 Burke & Wills Track, Glenhope, Vic 3444 **Region** Macedon Ranges
T (03) 5425 5492 **F** (03) 5425 5493 **www**.rowanston.com **Open** Thurs–Sun 9–5, or by appt
Winemaker John Frederiksen **Est.** 2003 **Cases** 2500 **Vyds** 9.3 ha
John (a social worker) and Marilyn (a former teacher turned viticulturist) Frederiksen are no strangers to grapegrowing and winemaking in the Macedon Ranges. They founded Metcalfe Valley Vineyard in 1995, planting 5.6 ha of shiraz, going on to win gold medals at local wine shows. They sold the vineyard in early 2003 and moved to their new property, which now has over 9 ha of vines (shiraz, merlot, riesling, and sauvignon blanc) in the same year. The heavy red soils and basalt ridges hold moisture, which allows watering requirements to be kept to a minimum. Exports to the US.

♟♟♟♟♟ **Shiraz 2006** Retains hue, but slightly diffuse; a spicy bouquet is a promising start;
⚫ the palate has the same spicy nuances, adding black cherry and licorice flavours; good length. Screwcap. 13% alc. **Rating** 93 **To** 2016 $20
⚫ **Riesling 2009** Light straw-green; an attractive floral bouquet of lime blossom leads into a fresh, open palate with gentle lime flavours; well balanced, but not as intense as the very best. Screwcap. 12.5% alc. **Rating** 92 **To** 2017 $20

Ruane Winery   **NR**

110 Finn's Road, Menangle, NSW 2568 **Region** Sydney Basin
T (02) 4636 6249 **F** (02) 9896 1171 **Open** 3rd Sun each month
Winemaker Vicarys **Est.** 2000 **Cases** 400 **Vyds** 1.62 ha

Marilyn and John Baxter purchased their 32-ha property 30 years ago, when it was a bare block. The primary purpose was the establishment of a thoroughbred racehorse stud, and it has enjoyed outstanding success, with yearlings sold to the US, South Africa, NZ and the UK (as well as Australia). In 2000 they decided to plant a vineyard on a spare paddock, building on their pre-existing love of wine. They sourced sangiovese, pinot gris and chardonnay from Yalumba, and successfully established the vineyard with appropriate consultancy advice. Extensive rose gardens add to the beauty of the block, named in honour of John's mother (or, to be precise, her maiden name) who at the age of 93 still welcomes visitors on the third Sunday of each month.

Russell Wines   ★★★★☆

45 Murray Street, Angaston, SA 5353 **Region** Barossa Valley
T (08) 8564 2511 **F** (08) 8564 2533 **www.**russellwines.com.au **Open** By appt
Winemaker Shawn Kalleske **Est.** 2001 **Cases** 3500 **Vyds** 32.47 ha

John Russell (and wife Rosalind) came to the Barossa in 1990 to create the Barossa Music Festival. The winemaking bug soon bit, and in '94 they planted vines at Krondorf (expanded over the years) and on three vineyards at St Vincent, Augusta and Greenock Farm, which in turn give rise to the three labels. The cellar door is situated in the old Angaston Court House, where wine, food, music and art exhibitions are all on offer. Shawn Kalleske not only makes the wine, but oversees both his and Russell Wines' vineyards; part of the grape production from the latter is sold to other Barossa wineries. Exports to Switzerland.

♥♥♥♥♥ **Museum Release Augusta Old Vine Barossa Valley Grenache 2002** In
the Barossa Valley, grenache seldom acquires the degree of authority this wine has
in abundance; the very cool vintage, a perfect cork and eight years to (partially)
tame the alcohol all operate synergistically. 16.8% alc. **Rating** 94 **To** 2015 $80

♥♥♥♥ **Augusta Barossa Valley Shiraz 2007 Rating** 89 **To** 2015 $25

Rusticana   ★★★★

Lake Plains Road, Langhorne Creek, SA 5255 **Region** Langhorne Creek
T (08) 8537 3086 **F** (08) 8537 3220 **www.**rusticanawines.com.au **Open** 7 days 10–5
Winemaker John Glaetzer (Consultant) **Est.** 1998 **Cases** 1200 **Vyds** 10 ha

Brian and Anne Meakins are also owners of Newman's Horseradish, which has been on the SA market for over 80 years. Increasing demand for the horseradish forced a move from Tea Tree Gully to Langhorne Creek in 1985. It wasn't until 1997 that they succumbed to the urging of neighbours and planted 4.5 ha each of shiraz and cabernet sauvignon, adding 0.5 ha each of durif and zinfandel several years later.

♥♥♥♥♀ **Langhorne Creek Durif 2008** Dense, impenetrable purple; saturated with
blackberry and licorice and prune fruit; while not extractive, needs more light and
shade for top points. Screwcap. 14.9% alc. **Rating** 91 **To** 2016 $30

Hidden Gem 2007 Remarkably dense purple colour for an '07; there is a wealth
of black fruits, licorice and sweet leather on the bouquet and full-bodied palate;
the tannins are not tough, the oak balanced. Shiraz/Cabernet Sauvignon/Durif.
Screwcap. 15% alc. **Rating** 90 **To** 2030 $28

✪ **Langhorne Creek Cabernet Sauvignon 2007** Good purple hue; an aromatic
cassis-accented bouquet, then a quite complex palate both in terms of flavour and
texture, and escapes the alcohol trap. Screwcap. 15% alc. **Rating** 90 **To** 2017 $20

Rutherglen Estates   ★★★☆

Cnr Great Northern Road/Murray Valley Highway, Rutherglen, Vic 3685 **Region** Rutherglen
T (02) 6032 7999 **F** (02) 6032 7998 **www**.rutherglenestates.com.au **Open** At Tuileries
Building, Rutherglen 7 days 10–6
Winemaker Marc Scalzo **Est.** 2000 **Cases** 30 000 **Vyds** 30 ha
Rutherglen Estates was established in 1977 and remains one of the larger growers in the
region. The focus of the business has changed in recent times by slightly reducing its own fruit
intake while maintaining its contract processing. Production has turned to table wine made
from selected parcels of fruit hand-selected from the five Rutherglen vineyard sites. Rhône
and Mediterranean varieties such as durif, viognier, shiraz and sangiovese are a move away
from traditional varieties, as are alternative varieties including zinfandel, fiano and savagnin.
Exports to the UK, the US and other major markets.

ŶŶŶŶŶ **Sangiovese 2007** Typical light and slightly hazy colour; a very savoury rendition
✪   of sangiovese that won a gold medal at the Alternative Varieties Show '09; sorely
           needs food. Screwcap. 13.5% alc. **Rating** 90 **To** 2013 $19.95

ŶŶŶŶ **Fiano 2009 Rating** 89 **To** 2011 $21.95
✪   **Red 2008** Good crimson-purple; this 85/15 blend of Shiraz/Durif has attractive
       red and black fruit flavours, quite possibly unoaked, but offering a lot of wine for
       the price. Screwcap. 14.5% alc. **Rating** 88 **To** 2015 $12.95
       Renaissance Petit Sirah 2006 Rating 88 **To** 2020 $39.95
✪   **Savagnin 2009** Fresh and crisp, with delicate citrus and apple blossom aromas
       and flavours, then faintly chalky acidity on the finish. Screwcap. 12.5% alc.
       Rating 87 **To** 2010 $16.95
✪   **Red 2007** Bright clear colour; despite the Shiraz/Durif blend, is a light-
       bodied wine, with fresh fruit the driver; three silver medals. Screwcap. 14.5% alc.
       Rating 87 **To** 2011 $13.95

Rymill Coonawarra   ★★★★

Riddoch Highway, Coonawarra, SA 5263 **Region** Coonawarra
T (08) 8736 5001 **F** (08) 8736 5040 **www**.rymill.com.au **Open** 7 days 10–5
Winemaker Sandrine Gimon **Est.** 1974 **Cases** 35 000 **Vyds** 144 ha
The Rymills are descendants of John Riddoch and have long owned some of the finest
Coonawarra soil, upon which they have grown grapes since 1970. The promotion of
Champagne-trained Sandrine Gimon to chief winemaker (after three years as winemaker at
Rymill) is interesting. Sandrine is a European version of a Flying Winemaker, having managed
a winery in Bordeaux, and made wine in Champagne, Languedoc, Romania and WA. Given
the size of the vineyards, and the onsite winery, Rymill has never quite lived up to the high
expectations it engenders. Exports to all major markets.

ŶŶŶŶŶ **The Yearling Sauvignon Blanc 2009** A notably fragrant and flowery bouquet
✪   foreshadows a crisp, lively and expressive palate with a juicy mix of citrus and
           passionfruit flavours. Screwcap. 12% alc. **Rating** 92 **To** 2011 $15
✪   **The Yearling Shiraz 2008** Strong crimson; more depth and weight than many
       Rymill wines of previous vintages, entirely driven by luscious plum and blackberry
       fruit. Outstanding value. Screwcap. 13.5% alc. **Rating** 91 **To** 2013 $15
✪   **SBS Sauvignon Blanc Semillon 2009** Highly aromatic, with a flowery citrus-
       accented bouquet, then a more grassy palate, partial barrel ferment impacting on
       both flavour and texture. Screwcap. 12% alc. **Rating** 90 **To** 2011 $17.50
       Shiraz 2005 Very good crimson-red hue; dark berry and licorice fruit is
       supported by a touch of mocha oak on the supple medium-bodied palate; good
       balance and length. Diam. 14% alc. **Rating** 90 **To** 2015 $24.95
       Chardonnay Pinot Noir Pinot Meunier 2006 Made using the full Methode
       Champenoise technique including 25 months on yeast lees. Intriguing low-alcohol
       style that enhances the freshness, although not the complexity. Diam. 11.5% alc.
       Rating 90 **To** 2012 $24

ŶŶŶŶ **Cabernet Sauvignon 2006 Rating** 88 **To** 2014 $29.95

Saddlers Creek ★★★★★
Marrowbone Road, Pokolbin, NSW 2320 **Region** Hunter Valley
T (02) 4991 1770 **F** (02) 4991 2482 **www**.saddlerscreek.com **Open** 7 days 10–5
Winemaker Nick Flanagan, David Flett **Est.** 1989 **Cases** 6000 **Vyds** 10 ha
Made an impressive entrance to the district with full-flavoured and rich wines, and has continued on in much the same vein, with good wines across the spectrum. Estate plantings include shiraz (5 ha), cabernet sauvignon (3 ha) and merlot (2 ha). Exports to Sweden and the Pacific region.

TTTTT **Classic Hunter Semillon 2005** Bright straw-green; on the long march towards total maturity, marrying freshness with complexity; five years (and the '05 vintage in particular) sees a distinct stage in the development of semillon, and there is a strong argument for enjoying the wine now, notwithstanding yet further complexity lies further down the track. Screwcap. 11% alc. **Rating** 95 **To** 2015 $34
Reserve Chardonnay 2009 Light straw-green; a wine that really comes into its own on its lively, zesty palate; here white flesh stone fruit and citrus are the drivers, French oak a minor road sign; finishes crisp and clean. Screwcap. 13% alc. **Rating** 94 **To** 2015 $34
Reserve Shiraz 2005 Good hue, although light; neither the colour nor the bouquet give any clue about the power and length of the palate, where plum and blackberry fruit is swathed in vanillan oak (24 months in American barriques). Langhorne Creek. Screwcap. 15% alc. **Rating** 94 **To** 2020 $42

TTTTY **Classic Hunter Semillon 2009 Rating** 93 **To** 2019 $23
Reserve Semillon 2003 Rating 92 **To** 2013 $36

TTTT **Reserve Merlot 2007 Rating** 89 **To** 2015 $42

St Aidan ★★★☆
754 Ferguson Road, Dardanup, WA 6236 **Region** Geographe
T (08) 9728 3007 **F** (08) 9728 3006 **www**.saintaidan.com **Open** Mon–Tues, Thurs–Fri 11–4, w'ends & public hols 11–5
Winemaker Mark Messenger (Contract) **Est.** 1996 **Cases** 1200 **Vyds** 2.6 ha
Phil and Mary Smith purchased their property at Dardanup in 1991, a 20-min drive from the Bunbury hospitals where Phil works. They first ventured into Red Globe table grapes, planting 1 ha in 1994–2005, followed by 1 ha of mandarins and oranges. With this experience, and with Mary completing a TAFE viticulture course, they extended their horizons by planting 1 ha each of cabernet sauvignon and chardonnay in 1997, half a hectare of muscat in 2001, and semillon and sauvignon blanc thereafter.

TTTTY **Geographe Chardonnay 2008** Straw-green; despite its alcohol, has a strong citrus streak that runs through the long palate and finish. Trophy for Best Chardonnay Geographe Wine Show '09. Screwcap. 14% alc. **Rating** 90 **To** 2015 $20

TTTT **Geographe Sauvignon Blanc Semillon 2009 Rating** 87 **To** 2010 $14
Geographe Sparkling Chardonnay 2008 Rating 87 **To** 2012 $25
Cassie Geographe Moscato NV Rating 87 **To** 2010 $14

St Hallett ★★★★★
St Hallett Road, Tanunda, SA 5352 **Region** Barossa Valley
T (08) 8563 7000 **F** (08) 8563 7001 **www**.sthallett.com.au **Open** 7 days 10–5
Winemaker Stuart Blackwell, Toby Barlow **Est.** 1944 **Cases** 100 000
Nothing succeeds like success. St Hallett merged with Tatachilla to form Banksia Wines, which was then acquired by NZ's thirsty Lion Nathan. St Hallett understandably continues to ride the shiraz fashion wave, with Old Block the ultra-premium leader of the band (using grapes from Lyndoch and the Eden Valley) supported by Blackwell (taking its grapes from Greenock, Ebenezer and Seppeltsfield). It has also had conspicuous success with its Eden Valley Rieslings, and its big-volume Poacher's range. Exports to all major markets.

ŸŸŸŸŸ **Eden Valley Riesling 2009** A spotlessly clean floral bouquet leads into a dancing, light on its feet, palate, the low alcohol liberating what is a delicate but dry style; a classic now or much later drinking span. Screwcap. 11% alc. **Rating** 95 To 2019 $25

Old Block Barossa Shiraz 2007 Good hue; an extremely complex bouquet with black fruits, spice and licorice not common in the Barossa Valley (or previous vintages of Old Block) on both bouquet and the long, well-balanced palate. Screwcap. 14.5% alc. **Rating** 95 To 2027 $80

Blackwell Barossa Shiraz 2008 Strong crimson-purple; a very rich, traditional full-bodied Barossa Valley shiraz, with luscious black fruits on the bouquet, augmented there as well as on the palate by 20 months in American oak; the texture is velvety, the tannins ripe. A new type of screwcap with a silicone interior. Wak screwcap. 14.5% alc. **Rating** 94 To 2030 $35

ŸŸŸŸŸ ✪ **Gamekeeper's Reserve Barossa Shiraz Grenache 2008** A very good example of the blend, with juicy cherry and raspberry fruit flavours undiminished by tannins or oak. No need to wait for this. Gold medal Sydney Wine Show '10. Screwcap. 13.5% alc. **Rating** 93 To 2013 $16

Barossa GST Grenache Shiraz Touriga 2008 Rating 92 To 2020 $30

✪ **Faith Barossa Shiraz 2008** Good colour; although in radically different style to Blackwell, with attractive spice, chocolate and mocha components to its cherry and blackberry fruits; ever so slightly sweet. Screwcap. 14.5% alc. **Rating** 90 To 2018 $19

✪ **Gamekeeper's Reserve Barossa Shiraz Cabernet 2008** An extremely dense and powerful wine, with some rustic edges to its rich black fruits, which will settle down with a few more years in the bottle. A dark horse for the cellar. Screwcap. 14% alc. **Rating** 90 To 2018 $16

ŸŸŸŸ **Gamekeeper's Barossa Shiraz 2008 Rating** 88 To 2013 $16

St Huberts ★★★★★

Cnr Maroondah Highway/St Huberts Road, Coldstream, Vic 3770 **Region** Yarra Valley
T (03) 9739 1118 **F** (03) 9739 1096 **www.**sthuberts.com.au **Open** Mon–Fri 9.30–5, w'ends 10.30–5.30
Winemaker Greg Jarratt **Est.** 1966 **Cases** NFP
A once famous winery (in the context of the Yarra Valley) that is now part of Foster's. The wines are now made at Coldstream Hills, and on an upwards trajectory. (I have no part in their making.)

ŸŸŸŸŸ **Yarra Valley Cabernet Sauvignon 2008** Classic Yarra Valley cabernet from a warm vintage; highly aromatic, and almost succulent in the mouth, flavours seemingly achieved effortlessly; very fine tannins and French oak round off an impressive wine. Screwcap. 14.5% alc. **Rating** 95 To 2028 $33

Yarra Valley Chardonnay 2008 A complex bouquet has a hint of Burgundian funk, and the palate has multiple layers of complexity; slightly unusual for the Yarra Valley, depth is as important as length. Screwcap. 13.5% alc. **Rating** 94 To 2016 $27

Yarra Valley Pinot Noir 2008 Good hue and depth; has the aroma, structure, texture and length of quality pinot noir; dark plum fruits on the mid-palate flow through to a gently savoury and long finish sustained by fine tannins. Screwcap. 14% alc. **Rating** 94 To 2015 $34

ŸŸŸŸŸ ✪ **Hubert the Stag Yarra Valley Pinot Noir 2009** Good colour depth, purple hue; a fragrant bouquet with dark plum aromas; the palate is complex with sous bois/foresty notes; excellent length; no sign of smoke taint. Screwcap. 12.5% alc. **Rating** 93 To 2014 $24

Yarra Valley Cabernet Merlot 2008 Rating 93 To 2020 $27

St Imre Vineyard ★★★

6902 Huon Highway, Dover, Tas 7117 **Region** Southern Tasmania
T (03) 6298 1781 **www**.stimrevineyard.blogspot.com **Open** Wed–Sun 10–5
Winemaker Paul Molnar **Est.** 1999 **Cases** 450 **Vyds** 2 ha

Paul and Kat Molnar arrived in Australia in 1988, 10 years after they were married in their native Hungary. For the next 10 years they lived and worked in Pemberton, Paul as a fine woodcraft and furniture maker, Kat working in local vineyards. In 1998 they moved once again, this time to a tiny property in the Huon Valley where they planted predominantly pinot noir, some chardonnay and a thoroughly esoteric mix of baco noir, gamay, pinot gris, gewurztraminer and siegerrebe. Pinot and chardonnay are their main production; the other varieties have been blended into a red wine called Tiger Blood, and a white with the dubious name of Possum Piss.

ŸŸŸŸ   **Pinot Noir 2007** Some colour development, but bright and clear; has good
texture and structure thanks to balanced tannins; slight citrus/green notes don't
destroy the wine. Zork. 13.6% alc. **Rating** 89 **To** 2013 $22
Pinot Noir 2008 Good colour and clarity; offers a mix of plum and more
savoury/spicy notes on a light- to medium-bodied palate; needs more thrust. Zork.
13% alc. **Rating** 88 **To** 2014 $22

St Isidore ★★★★☆

1 Adelaide Lobethal Road, Lobethal, SA 5241 **Region** Adelaide Hills
T 0431 245 668 **www**.stisidoreadelaidehills.com **Open** Fri–Sun 11–4
Winemaker Simon Greenleaf **Est.** 2007 **Cases** 1000

After 15 years winemaking in Australia (Petaluma, Tatachilla and Red Hill Estate), France (Domaine Lafage), Chile (Santa Rita) and Spain (Bodegas Borsao), Simon Greenleaf established a small winery in the old Onkaparinga Woollen Mills building in the Adelaide Hills. St Isidore (the Catholic patron saint of farmers) makes single-vineyard wines from sites in the Adelaide Hills that produce high-quality fruit of distinct character.

ŸŸŸŸŸ   **Adelaide Hills Riesling 2009** Bright quartz-green; a fragrant and expressively
floral bouquet of lime and apple blossom, then a crisp, clean and energetic palate.
Screwcap. 12% alc. **Rating** 91 **To** 2016 $22

ŸŸŸŸ   **Adelaide Hills Gewurztraminer 2009** Rating 88 **To** 2013 $22
Adelaide Hills Late Harvest Pinot Gris Gewurztraminer 2008 Rating 88
To 2014 $25

St John's Road ★★★★☆

PO Box 311, Greenock, SA 5360 **Region** Barossa Valley
T (08) 8423 0272 **F** (08) 8423 0272 **www**.stjohnsroad.com **Open** Not
Winemaker Peter Schell, Kim Jackson (Contract) **Est.** 2002 **Cases** 5000

Following the tragic death of founder Martin Rawlinson from motor neurone disease, there was a period of inactivity before Adelaide wine identity, Alister Mibus, and two partners, purchased the St John's Road label. Winemaking remains with Peter Schell of Spinifex, with assistance from Kim Jackson (of Henry's Drive and Shirvington). The policy of selecting the best possible parcels of fruit from the Barossa and Eden valleys continues. Exports to Canada.

ŸŸŸŸŸ   **Peace of Eden Riesling 2009** Glowing green-yellow; has the abundance of
❸   ripe lime juice, bordering on tropical, promised by the colour, but falters slightly
on the finish. Screwcap. 12.5% alc. **Rating** 91 **To** 2017 $18

ŸŸŸŸ   **Blood & Courage Barossa Valley Shiraz 2008** Rating 89 **To** 2017 $22
Motley Bunch GSM 2008 Rating 87 **To** 2013 $22

St Leonards Vineyard ★★★★

St Leonards Road, Wahgunyah, Vic 3687 **Region** Rutherglen
T 1800 021 621 **F** (02) 6035 2200 **www**.stleonardswine.com.au **Open** W'ends 11–4
Winemaker Dan Crane **Est.** 1860 **Cases** 4000 **Vyds** 17.6 ha

An old favourite, relaunched in late 1997 with a range of premium wines cleverly marketed through a singularly attractive cellar door and bistro at the historic winery on the banks of the Murray. It is essentially a satellite operation of All Saints, and is under the same family ownership and management.

ᵀᵀᵀᵀᵀ **Wahgunyah Shiraz 2008** Purple-red; the striking bouquet makes sense once you find the Italian Ripasso technique has been used, with the '08 shiraz pumped into a tank containing the just-pressed and very ripe '09 shiraz skins and then re-fermented. It has worked well to deliver a genuinely different and generous wine. Screwcap. 15% alc. **Rating** 94 **To** 2018 $50

ᵀᵀᵀᵀ **Semillon Sauvignon Blanc 2009 Rating** 87 **To** 2010 $19

St Regis ★★★☆

35 Princes Highway, Waurn Ponds, Vic 3216 **Region** Geelong
T (03) 5241 8406 **F** (03) 5241 8946 **www**.stregis.com.au **Open** 7 days 11–5
Winemaker Peter Nicol **Est.** 1997 **Cases** 300 **Vyds** 5 ha

St Regis is a family-run boutique winery focusing on estate-grown shiraz, chardonnay and pinot noir. Each year the harvest is hand-picked by members of the family and friends, with Peter Nicol (assisted by wife Viv) the executive, onsite winemaker. While Peter has a technical background in horticulture, he is a self-taught winemaker, and has taught himself well, also making wines for others.

ᵀᵀᵀᵀᵀ **The Reg Geelong Shiraz 2008** Good hue; like the Pinot Noir, had eight weeks' maceration on skins that works better on shiraz; having spent the time (and assumed the risk) there is no point in aggressively fining the wine, and in truth there is little need when a few years in bottle will bring balance. Screwcap. 14.8% alc. **Rating** 90 **To** 2020 $25

ᵀᵀᵀᵀ **Geelong Chardonnay 2008 Rating** 89 **To** 2014 $20
Wild Reserve Geelong Pinot Noir 2008 Rating 89 **To** 2016 $25

Salitage ★★★★☆

Vasse Highway, Pemberton, WA 6260 **Region** Pemberton
T (08) 9776 1771 **F** (08) 9776 1772 **www**.salitage.com.au **Open** 7 days 10–4
Winemaker Patrick Coutts **Est.** 1989 **Cases** 15 000 **Vyds** 21.4 ha

Owned and operated by John and Jenny Horgan, Salitage is a showpiece of Pemberton. John had worked and studied under the guidance of Robert Mondavi in California, and also acquired a share in the famous Burgundy winery, La Pousse D'or (with other Aussie investors, all of whom have since sold out). Together with Bill and Sandra Pannell's Picardy, it is a bellwether for the reputation of the region. Exports to the UK and other major markets.

ᵀᵀᵀᵀᵀ **Pemberton Pinot Noir 2008** Clear purple; a complex bouquet with nuances of spice and herb along with the dark cherry and berry fruits that drive the palate; a touch of foresty tannin helps build the finish. Screwcap. 13.5% alc. **Rating** 94 **To** 2015 $40

ᵀᵀᵀᵀᵀ **Treehouse Pemberton Sauvignon Blanc 2009** An interesting decision
✪ to see the higher alcohol and bigger-flavoured wine under this label, although the minimal difference in price puts a different light on the choice; this wine does have the length missing in the top wine. Screwcap. 13.5% alc. **Rating** 90 **To** 2011 $20
Pemberton 2007 Rating 90 **To** 2017 $33

🍷🍷🍷🍷 **Pemberton Sauvignon Blanc 2009 Rating** 89 **To** 2010 $22
Pemberton Chardonnay 2008 Rating 89 **To** 2013 $35
Treehouse Pemberton Shiraz 2007 Rating 89 **To** 2014 $20
Treehouse Pemberton Chardonnay 2009 Rating 88 **To** 2011 $17
Treehouse Pemberton Pinot Noir 2008 Rating 88 **To** 2011 $20
Treehouse Pemberton Merlot Cabernet Sauvignon Cabernet Franc 2007 Rating 88 **To** 2012 $20

Sally's Paddock ★★★★☆

Redbank Winery, 1 Sally's Lane, Redbank, Vic 3478 **Region** Pyrenees
T (03) 5467 7255 **F** (03) 5467 3478 **www**.sallyspaddock.com.au **Open** Mon–Sat 9–5, Sun 10–5
Winemaker Neill Robb **Est.** 1973 **Cases** 2500 **Vyds** 18.5 ha

The Redbank brand and stocks (Long Paddock, etc) were acquired by the Hill Smith Family Vineyards (aka Yalumba) several years ago. The winery and surrounding vineyard that produces Sally's Paddock were retained by Neill and Sally Robb, and continue to produce (and sell) this single-vineyard, multi-varietal red wine and the Sally's Hill range. Exports to the US, Germany, Czech Republic, Thailand, Hong Kong, Singapore, Japan and China.

🍷🍷🍷🍷🍷 **2008 Sally's Paddock** Good colour; a luscious array of gently spicy black fruits and licorice on the bouquet and palate; has the tannin structure to underpin a decade-plus in bottle. Diam. 14.8% alc. **Rating** 94 **To** 2020 $59.20

🍷🍷🍷🍷🍷 **2007 Sally's Paddock Rating** 90 **To** 2014 $59.20

🍷🍷🍷🍷 **Sally's Hill Cabernet Franc 2008 Rating** 89 **To** 2016 $21.90

Salomon Estate ★★★★☆

PO Box 829, McLaren Vale, SA 5171 **Region** Southern Fleurieu
T 0417 470 590 **F** (08) 8323 8668 **www**.salomonwines.com **Open** Not
Winemaker Bert Salomon, Mike Farmilo **Est.** 1997 **Cases** 8000 **Vyds** 12.1 ha

Bert Salomon is an Austrian winemaker with a long-established family winery in the Kremstal region, not far from Vienna. He became acquainted with Australia during his time with import company Schlumberger in Vienna; he was the first to import Australian wines (Penfolds) into Austria in the mid-1980s, and later became head of the Austrian Wine Bureau. He was so taken by Adelaide that he moved his family there for the first few months each year, sending his young children to school and setting in place an Australian red winemaking venture. He retired from the Bureau and is a full-time travelling winemaker, running the family winery in the northern hemisphere vintage, and overseeing the making of the Salomon Estate wines at Boar's Rock in the first half of the year. The circle closes as Mike Farmilo, former Penfolds chief red winemaker, now makes Salomon Estate wines at Boar's Rock. Exports to the UK, the US and other major markets.

🍷🍷🍷🍷🍷 **Norwood Shiraz Cabernet 2008** Deep colour; seems to have dodged the bullet of the '08 heatwave, although it has a stack of black fruits, a splash of dark chocolate and handsome tannins. Cork used for export market, one assumes. 14.5% alc. **Rating** 94 **To** 2018 $18

🍷🍷🍷🍷🍷 **Finniss River Shiraz 2007 Rating** 93 **To** 2022 $30
Fleurieu Peninsula Syrah Viognier 2007 Rating 92 **To** 2017 $23
Altus Red 2003 Rating 91 **To** 2015 $95

✪ **Bin 4 Baan Shiraz & Company 2008** The '& Company' seems to be merlot; very good purple-crimson; a rich, but not the least jammy wine, with blackberry and plum fruit and soft, ripe tannins. Twin top. 14.5% alc. **Rating** 90 **To** 2015 $16

Saltram ★★★★★

Nuriootpa Road, Angaston, SA 5353 **Region** Barossa Valley
T (08) 8561 0200 **F** (08) 8561 0232 www.saltramwines.com.au **Open** 7 days 10–5
Winemaker Shavaugn Wells, Richard Mattner **Est.** 1859 **Cases** 150 000
There is no doubt that Saltram has taken giant strides towards regaining the reputation it held 30 or so years ago. Under Nigel Dolan's stewardship, grape sourcing came back to the Barossa Valley for the flagship wines, a fact of which he was rightly proud. The red wines, in particular, have enjoyed great show success over the past few years, with No. 1 Shiraz, Mamre Brook and Metala leading the charge. Nigel left Foster's in late 2007, and is now chief winemaker for Wyndham Estate. Exports to the UK, the US and other major markets.

ΨΨΨΨΨ **Vintage Rare Tawny 1959** A warm glow of tawny-orange grading almost to olive on the rim; sets the antennae waving: this is a remarkable tawny, with sweet Christmas cake and orange cake flavours, the spirit wonderfully smooth and integrated. 500 ml. Cork. 20% alc. **Rating** 98 **To** 2011 $200
The Journal Shiraz 2005 Deep purple-red hue; has great equilibrium and harmony, partly reflecting its blend of Barossa/Eden Valley grapes and its 20 months in French oak, partly due to moderate alcohol, and a clear decision in the winery not to over-elaborate a wine of considerable beauty; 50 years under screwcap, half that under cork. Cork. 14.5% alc. **Rating** 96 **To** 2030 $125

ΨΨΨΨΩ **Mamre Brook Eden Valley Riesling 2009** Rating 93 To 2019 $23
Metala Langhorne Creek Shiraz Cabernet 2008 Rating 92 To 2020 $22
Pepperjack Barossa Grenache Rose 2008 Rating 90 To 2010 $25
Pepperjack Barossa Cabernet Sauvignon 2008 Rating 90 To 2017 $25

ΨΨΨΨ **Pepperjack Barossa Shiraz 2008** Rating 89 To 2016 $25

Sam Miranda of King Valley ★★★★

1019 Snow Road, Oxley, Vic 3678 **Region** King Valley
T (03) 5727 3888 **F** (03) 5727 3853 www.sammiranda.com.au **Open** 7 days 10–5
Winemaker Sam Miranda **Est.** 2004 **Cases** 15 000 **Vyds** 15 ha
Sam Miranda, grandson of Francesco Miranda, joined the family business in 1991, striking out on his own in '04 after Miranda Wines was purchased by McGuigan Simeon. The High Plains Vineyard is in the Upper King Valley at an altitude of 450 m; estate plantings are supplemented by some purchased grapes. In 2005 Sam purchased the Symphonia Wines business, and intends to keep its identity intact and separate from the Sam Miranda brand. Exports to China.

ΨΨΨΨΩ **Riesling 2006** Mid-gold, green hue; showing plenty of toasty development, a
✿ bright core of lemon and a touch of spice unravel on the palate; still lively and with plenty of life to come. Screwcap. 12.5% alc. **Rating** 90 **To** 2016 $20 BE
Barbera Shiraz 2008 Lifted purple fruit bouquet, with a little spice for harmony; medium-bodied with prominent acidity, the drive from the Barbera really shines through in the blend; well constructed. Screwcap. 14.5% alc. **Rating** 90 **To** 2013 $30 BE

ΨΨΨΨ **Girls Block Cabernet Sauvignon Petit Verdot 2008** Rating 89 To 2015 $34 BE
Super King No. 1 Sangiovese Cabernet 2008 Rating 89 To 2014 $30 BE
Chardonnay 2008 Rating 88 To 2014 $28 BE
Semillon 2009 Rating 87 To 2016 $20 BE
Limited Release Trial 3 Botrytis Riesling 2009 Rating 87 To 2013 $25 BE

Samuel's Gorge ★★★★☆

Lot 10 Chaffeys Road, McLaren, SA 5171 **Region** McLaren Vale
T (08) 8323 8651 **F** (08) 8323 8673 www.gorge.com.au **Open** 1st w'end of spring until sold out, or by appt
Winemaker Justin McNamee **Est.** 2003 **Cases** 1250 **Vyds** 10 ha

After a wandering winemaking career in various parts of the world, Justin McNamee became a winemaker at Tatachilla in 1996, where he remained until 2003, leaving to found Samuel's Gorge. He has established his winery in a barn built in 1853, part of a historic property known as the old Seaview Homestead. The property was owned by Sir Samuel Way, variously Chief Justice of the South Australian Supreme Court and Lieutenant Governor of the state. The grapes come from small contract growers spread across the ever-changing (unofficial) subregions of McLaren Vale, and are basket-pressed and fermented in old open slate fermenters lined with beeswax – with impressive results. Exports to the UK, the US and Canada.

🍷🍷🍷🍷🍷 **McLaren Vale Shiraz 2007** Dense, inky purple-crimson; utterly consistent regional expression through both bouquet and palate; black fruits, dark chocolate and coffee/mocha. The palate is supple and the outcome excellent given the vintage. Pity about the cork. 14.5% alc. **Rating** 94 **To** 2020 $45

🍷🍷🍷🍷♀ **McLaren Vale Tempranillo 2008 Rating** 93 **To** 2015 $45

Sandalford   ★★★★★

3210 West Swan Road, Caversham, WA 6055 **Region** Margaret River
T (08) 9374 9374 **F** (08) 9274 2154 **www.**sandalford.com **Open** 7 days 10–5
Winemaker Paul Boulden, Hope Metcalf **Est.** 1840 **Cases** 100 000 **Vyds** 105 ha
Sandalford is one of Australia's oldest and largest privately owned wineries. In 1970 it moved beyond its original Swan Valley base, purchasing a substantial property in Margaret River that is now the main source of its premium grapes. With most of the vines now 40 years old, and with the highly experienced and former Flying Winemaker Paul Boulden in charge, it is no surprise that the quality of the wines is consistently excellent. Exports to all major markets.

🍷🍷🍷🍷🍷 **Prendiville Reserve Margaret River Shiraz 2008** Crimson-purple; sourced from the oldest (1970), dry-grown Margaret River shiraz; reflects the benefits of finishing the primary fermentation in new French oak (100%), with consequent integration of the oak and the tannin texture of the wine; the palate is long and fine, with all the spicy black fruits necessary for a long life. Outstanding wine; 300 dozen made. Screwcap. 14% alc. **Rating** 96 **To** 2025 $90

✪ **Estate Reserve Margaret River Cabernet Sauvignon 2008** Good colour; a classic cabernet in every sense of the term, all about texture, structure and length, rather than opulence, weight and extract/oak; the flavours are at the optimum point of ripeness, the tannins likewise. Screwcap. 14.5% alc. **Rating** 96 **To** 2030 $39.95

Estate Reserve Margaret River Chardonnay 2008 Bright green-gold; nectarine and white peach waft from the bouquet, but don't prepare you for the drive and energy of the palate; grapefruit acidity accelerates through the finish and on to the lingering aftertaste. Screwcap. 13.5% alc. **Rating** 95 **To** 2018 $35

✪ **Estate Reserve Margaret River Chardonnay 2009** Shows that elegance and fruit freshness can be achieved with ripe grapes and 10 months in oak following barrel fermentation; white peach and nectarine flavours course through the long palate and bright finish. Screwcap. 14% alc. **Rating** 94 **To** 2015 $29.95

✪ **Estate Reserve Margaret River Verdelho 2009** A clean and fresh bouquet of tropical fruit leads into the fore-palate, then citrussy acidity takes over, driving the wine through to a very long and intense finish. Screwcap. 13.5% alc. **Rating** 94 **To** 2019 $25

Estate Reserve Margaret River Shiraz 2007 Good depth of colour; a very complex wine that finished its primary fermentation in a mix of French and American oak of various ages; an array of warm spices, cedar and vanilla all add interest to a medium-bodied wine with good balance. Screwcap. 14% alc. **Rating** 94 **To** 2022 $33.95

Estate Reserve Margaret River Cabernet Sauvignon 2007 Attractive wine, although it makes no concessions to the autocratic nature of good Margaret River cabernet; the bouquet is pure blackcurrant fruit and cedary oak, the powerful black fruits on the palate with a flying wedge of tannins to knock the weak of spirit onto their knees. Screwcap. 14% alc. **Rating** 94 **To** 2030 $45

ŢŢŢŢŢ **Estate Reserve Margaret River Sauvignon Blanc Semillon 2009**
Rating 93 To 2011 $25

✪ **Classic Dry White Margaret River Semillon Sauvignon Blanc 2009**
A fragrant bouquet with intense herb, grass and passionfruit aromas precisely
foreshadows the palate, which has good length. Screwcap. 12.5% alc. **Rating** 90
To 2011 $18.95
Margaret River Rose 2009 Rating 90 To 2010 $18.95

✪ **Element Shiraz Cabernet 2008** Deep crimson-purple; has an extra touch of
class/style unexpected at this price point; red and black fruits, spice, black pepper
and a hint of oak all coalesce on the palate. Screwcap. 14.5% alc. **Rating** 90
To 2015 $13.95

ŢŢŢŢ **Element Classic White 2009** A zesty, clean and fresh mix of citrussy/grassy/
✪ herbal aromas and flavours provides an all-purpose, drink-now style. Screwcap.
12.5% alc. **Rating** 89 To 2011 $13.95

✪ **Margaret River Shiraz 2009** Bright, although light, crimson-purple hue; a
fragrant, gently spiced, bouquet leads into an elegant medium-bodied palate that
doesn't show its heat until the aftertaste, and then only slightly. Screwcap. 15% alc.
Rating 89 To 2017 $19

Sandhurst Ridge   ★★★★

156 Forest Drive, Marong, Vic 3515 **Region** Bendigo
T (03) 5435 2534 **F** (03) 5435 2548 **www.**sandhurstridge.com.au **Open** 7 days 11–5
Winemaker Paul and George Greblo **Est.** 1990 **Cases** 3000 **Vyds** 7.1 ha
The Greblo brothers (Paul and George), with combined experience in business, agriculture,
science and construction and development, began the establishment of Sandhurst Ridge in
1990, planting the first 2 ha of shiraz and cabernet sauvignon. Plantings have increased to over
7 ha, principally cabernet and shiraz, but also a little merlot and nebbiolo. As the business has
grown, the Greblos have supplemented their crush with grapes grown in the region. Exports
to Canada, Norway, Taiwan, Hong Kong, Japan and China.

ŢŢŢŢŢ **Bendigo Cabernet Sauvignon 2008** As with all the Sandhurst Ridge red
wines, open-fermented and basket-pressed; here estate-grown cabernet has been
picked at exactly the right time, the bouquet distinctly fragrant, the medium-bodied
palate well balanced; cassis-accented fruit does much of the talking; French oak and
tannins are in the second row. Screwcap. 14.7% alc. **Rating** 93 To 2018 $28
Bendigo Merlot 2008 Vivid crimson-purple, unusual for merlot; intriguing
wine, finishing fermentation in French oak followed by 20 months' maturation; has
bright red fruit flavours balanced by black olive tones on the finish; good overall
length and balance. Screwcap. 13.5% alc. **Rating** 92 To 2018 $28

✪ **Bendigo Sauvignon Blanc 2009** A no-frills, crisp and correct wine in a
strongly grassy mode, finishing with minerally acidity; has deceptive length, subtle
French barrel ferment characters, and is a far cry from the Sandhurst Ridge white
wines of years gone by. Screwcap. 13.6% alc. **Rating** 90 To 2012 $20

✪ **Bendigo Rose 2009** Pale pink-salmon; firm, precise, dry and long, reflecting
its Nebbiolo/Cabernet Sauvignon base; good food style. Screwcap. 13.3% alc.
Rating 90 To 2011 $20
Bendigo Shiraz 2008 Deep purple-red; a powerful, full-bodied regional shiraz
with brooding black fruit aromas and flavours augmented by licorice and a touch
of bitter chocolate; 18 months in French and American oak. Screwcap. 14.5% alc.
Rating 90 To 2023 $28
Bendigo Nebbiolo 2008 As long as you think pinot when looking at the
colour (pale) and palate (light cherry) the wine works well, with clear-cut varietal
characters and no excessive tannins. Screwcap. 13.8% alc. **Rating** 90 To 2014 $28

ŢŢŢŢ **Fringe Bendigo Shiraz Cabernet 2008 Rating** 88 To 2018 $22

Sanguine Estate ★★★★☆

77 Shurans Lane, Heathcote, Vic 3523 **Region** Heathcote
T (03) 9646 6661 **F** (03) 9646 1746 **www**.sanguinewines.com.au **Open** By appt
Winemaker Mark Hunter **Est.** 1997 **Cases** 3500 **Vyds** 21.57 ha

The Hunter family – parents Linda and Tony at the head, their children Mark and Jodi, with their respective partners Melissa and Brett – began establishing the vineyard in 1997. It has grown to 20.16 ha of shiraz, with smaller plantings of chardonnay, viognier, merlot, tempranillo, petit verdot, cabernet sauvignon and cabernet franc. Low-yielding vines and the magic of the Heathcote region have produced Shiraz of exceptional intensity, which has received rave reviews in the US, and led to the 'sold out' sign being posted almost immediately upon release. With the ever-expanding vineyard, Mark has become full-time vigneron, and Jodi Marsh part-time marketer and business developer. Exports to the UK, Denmark, Singapore and Hong Kong.

♟♟♟♟♟ **Heathcote Cabernet Sauvignon Cabernet Franc Petit Verdot 2007**
✪ Good colour; perfectly ripened and balanced fruit, coupled with sympathetic oak, results in a harmonious and supple wine. Like all Sanguine Estate wines, wild yeast-fermented and moved by gravity, not pumped. Diam. 13.5% alc. **Rating** 94 To 2022 $25

♟♟♟♟♀ **Progeny Heathcote Shiraz 2008** Healthy, full colour; a full-flavoured and rich
✪ wine with an array of dark plum, black cherry and blackberry aromas and flavours; the medium- to full-bodied palate has ripe, soft tannins that cosset the juicy fruit on the finish. Great value. Screwcap. 14.8% alc. **Rating** 93 To 2020 $20
✪ **Heathcote Chardonnay 2008** Deep green-gold; a complex full-bodied chardonnay with considerable texture and structure; some Burgundy connotations into the bargain. Screwcap. 13.8% alc. **Rating** 92 To 2013 $20
D'Orsa Heathcote Shiraz 2007 Rating 92 To 2040 $60
Heathcote Shiraz 2007 Rating 92 To 2027 $40
Heathcote Tempranillo 2007 Rating 91 To 2017 $30

Saracen Estates ★★★★☆

3517 Caves Road, Wilyabrup, WA 6280 **Region** Margaret River
T (08) 9755 6000 **F** (08) 9755 6011 **www**.saracenestates.com.au **Open** 7 days 11–5
Winemaker Bob Cartwright (Consultant) **Est.** 1998 **Cases** 7000 **Vyds** 16.96 ha

Luke and Maree Saraceni's first foray into the wine industry came via a small import business. The next step was the establishment of Saracen Estates; today they have almost 17 ha of vines on their 80-ha property, with a striking restaurant and cellar door (opened in 2007). This was followed by a visitor facility in 2008, incorporating a wine education centre, craft brewery, a beer garden and restaurant.

♟♟♟♟♟ **Margaret River Sauvignon Blanc 2009** Pale green-straw; a complex fruit
✪ bouquet of green pea, passionfruit and a touch of spice; the palate is fine and crisp, in a lemon, herb and apple spectrum; surges on the finish and aftertaste. Screwcap. 13% alc. **Rating** 94 To 2012 $24

♟♟♟♟♀ **Margaret River Sauvignon Blanc Semillon 2009** Pale green-quartz; a tightly
✪ structured and focused blend, with some of the green pea of the sauvignon blanc, lemon citrus added by the semillon; has good drive and length. Screwcap. 12.5% alc. **Rating** 93 To 2013 $22
Margaret River Chardonnay 2007 Rating 93 To 2015 $35
Margaret River Cabernet Sauvignon 2008 Rating 93 To 2028 $40
Margaret River Cabernet Sauvignon 2007 Rating 92 To 2020 $40 BE
✪ **Margaret River Cabernet Merlot 2007** Bright hue; a medium-bodied blend, with good aromatics to its blackcurrant, cassis and spice fruit that also underpin the juicy palate. Screwcap. 13.5% alc. **Rating** 91 To 2015 $22

♟♟♟♟ **Reserve Margaret River Shiraz 2008 Rating** 89 To 2016 $55 BE
Margaret River Shiraz 2007 Rating 89 To 2017 $35

Sarsfield Estate   ★★★☆

345 Duncan Road, Sarsfield, Vic 3875 **Region** Gippsland
T (03) 5156 8962 **F** (03) 5156 8970 **www**.sarsfieldestate.com.au **Open** By appt
Winemaker Dr Suzanne Rutschmann **Est.** 1995 **Cases** 1200 **Vyds** 2 ha
Owned by Suzanne Rutschmann, who has a PhD in Chemistry, a Diploma in Horticulture
and a BSc (Wine Science) from CSU, and Swiss-born Peter Albrecht, a civil and structural
engineer who has also undertaken various courses in agriculture and viticulture. For a part-
time occupation, these are exceptionally impressive credentials. Their vineyard (pinot noir,
cabernet, shiraz, cabernet franc and merlot) was planted between 1991 and '98. Sarsfield Pinot
Noir has enjoyed conspicuous success in both domestic and international wine shows over the
past few years. No insecticides are used in the vineyard, the winery runs on solar and wind
energy and relies entirely on rain water. No Pinot Noir was made in 2007 owing to smoke
taint. The previously released 2006 Pinot Noir won a gold medal at the Mondial du Pinot
Noir competition, held in Switzerland and attracting 1100 wines from 19 countries, judged
by 53 international wine judges, who thus had 40 wines for each panel to taste. Exports
to Ireland.

ㅜㅜㅜㅜ   **Pinot Noir 2008** Good colour and fragrance; a firm and precise wine, red fruits
mixed with savoury/briary elements, the latter controlling the finish; why play
Russian roulette with a modest-quality, one-piece cork? 14.1% alc. **Rating** 89
To 2012 $25

Sautjan Vineyards   ★★★★

PO Box 1317, Kyneton, Vic 3444 **Region** Macedon Ranges
T 0400 582 747 **F** (03) 5024 7401 **www**.s17.com.au **Open** Not
Winemaker John Ellis (Contract), Damien Pitt **Est.** 2006 **Cases** 500 **Vyds** 3.2 ha
Owner and founder Damien Pitt was looking for a cool-climate site, and he certainly found
one. The vineyard, situated on a north-facing slope of Mt Jim Jim at an elevation of 650 m,
has close-planted chardonnay, viognier and pinot gris. Until they come into bearing, grapes
are being purchased from various Victorian cool-climate vineyards.

ㅜㅜㅜㅜ°   **Three Chain Road Shiraz 2008** Deep, clear crimson-purple; blackberry,
plum, licorice and spice all appear on the medium-bodied palate; firm tannins
on the finish need to soften; Kilmore Ranges (70%)/Heathcote (30%). Screwcap.
13.8% alc. **Rating** 91 To 2020 $22.50
Three Chain Road Chardonnay 2008 Bright straw-green; has an abundance
of melon and white peach fruit, oak evident; 100% Macedon fruit is a surprise.
Screwcap. 12.5% alc. **Rating** 90 To 2015 $22.50

ㅜㅜㅜㅜ   **Three Chain Road Sauvignon Blanc 2008** A modest but well-balanced
✪   and structured sauvignon blanc from the Strathbogie Ranges, herbal fruit and
some minerally acidity making it food friendly. Screwcap. 12.5% alc. **Rating** 88
To 2010 $12
Three Chain Road Pinot Gris 2009 Rating 88 To 2010 $15

SC Pannell   ★★★★★

Box 1159, Unley BC, SA 5061 **Region** McLaren Vale
T (08) 8271 7118 **F** (08) 8271 7113 **www**.scpannell.com.au **Open** Not
Winemaker Stephen Pannell **Est.** 2004 **Cases** 3000
The only surprising piece of background is that it took (an admittedly still reasonably
youthful) Stephen Pannell (and wife Fiona) so long to cut the painter from Constellation/
Hardys and establish their own winemaking and consulting business. Steve radiates intensity,
and extended experience backed by equally long experimentation and thought has resulted
in wines of the highest quality right from the first vintage. At present the focus of their virtual
winery (they own neither vineyards nor winery) is grenache and shiraz grown in McLaren
Vale. This is a label well on its way to icon status. Exports to the UK, the US and Singapore.

ŦŦŦŦŦ McLaren Vale Arido Rose 2009 Vivid light crimson-purple; a highly fragrant bouquet of small red berry fruits, then a long, elegantly focused palate, with varietal Turkish delight nuances offset by excellent acidity. Screwcap. 13% alc. Rating 95 To 2010 $27
McLaren Vale Shiraz Grenache 2007 Bright crimson; an exercise in restrained elegance, with spicy/savoury elements to the fore, and a long, perfectly balanced palate, co-fermentation and French oak wrapping up the parcel to perfection. Screwcap. 14% alc. Rating 94 To 2020 $55

ŦŦŦŦŦ Adelaide Hills Sauvignon Blanc 2009 Rating 93 To 2011 $26
Pronto Tinto 2008 Rating 93 To 2014 $27
Adelaide Hills Pronto Bianco 2009 Rating 90 To 2012 $27

Scaffidi Wines ★★★

Talunga Cellars, Adelaide-Mannum Road, Gumeracha, SA 5233 **Region** Adelaide Zone
T (08) 8389 1222 **F** (08) 8389 1233 **www**.talunga.com.au **Open** Wed–Sun & public hols 10.30–5
Winemaker Vince Scaffidi **Est.** 1994 **Cases** 3000 **Vyds** 236 ha
Owners Vince and Tina Scaffidi have sold their interest in the 80-ha Gumeracha Vineyards, but have retained 2.8 ha of sauvignon blanc and chardonnay at their Gumeracha house property. They also have a little over 93 ha on their One Tree Hill Vineyard, planted to shiraz, cabernet sauvignon, merlot, sangiovese, nebbiolo, petit verdot, tempranillo and chardonnay, the majority of the grape production being sold. The cellar door and restaurant is named Talunga Cellars. The wines are exceptionally well priced.

ŦŦŦŦ Adelaide Hills Unwooded Chardonnay 2009 Pale straw-green; light, fresh
✪   and zesty, with white flesh stone fruits and potent citrussy acidity; good length; why drink Marlborough sauvignon blanc when you can have this for the same price? Screwcap. 13.5% alc. Rating 89 To 2012 $15
✪   Blushing Bride Adelaide Hills Rose 2009 Unusually (for the Adelaide Hills) made from grenache; a fragrant bouquet of cherries and small red berries is followed by a long, dry palate; a touch of alcohol warmth is the only issue. Screwcap. 14% alc. Rating 88 To 2011 $12
One Tree Hill That's Amore Sangiovese 2009 Light colour, but the hue is good; bright red and sour cherry fruit with spicy tannins in support; for short-term cellaring. Screwcap. 14.5% alc. Rating 88 To 2013 $15
One Tree Hill St Vincent Gulf Breeze Shiraz 2008 Deep crimson-purple; a substantial full-bodied shiraz, a little rustic, perhaps, but crammed full of ripe black fruits and licorice, with chewy but ripe tannins; finishes a little short. Screwcap. 15% alc. Rating 87 To 2018 $15.50

Scarborough Wine Co ★★★★★

179 Gillards Road, Pokolbin, NSW 2320 **Region** Hunter Valley
T (02) 4998 7563 **F** (02) 4998 7786 **www**.scarboroughwine.com.au **Open** 7 days 9–5
Winemaker Ian and Jerome Scarborough **Est.** 1985 **Cases** 20 000 **Vyds** 14 ha
Ian Scarborough honed his white winemaking skills during his years as a consultant, and has brought all those skills to his own label. He makes three different styles of Chardonnay: the Blue Label is a light, elegant, Chablis style for the export market; a richer barrel-fermented wine (Yellow Label) is primarily directed to the Australian market; the third is the White Label, a cellar door–only wine made in the best vintages. However, the real excitement for the future lies with the portion of the old Lindemans Sunshine Vineyard, which he purchased (after it lay fallow for 30 years) and planted with semillon and (quixotically) pinot noir. The first vintage from the legendary Sunshine Vineyard was made in 2004. Exports to the UK and the US.

ŦŦŦŦŦ White Label Hunter Valley Semillon 2009 Gloriously effusive and intense aromas into a lime, lemon spectrum; the palate is more discreet, indeed bordering on delicate, but with a framework of mineral/talc acidity. Screwcap. 10.5% alc. Rating 94 To 2014 $25

Yellow Label Chardonnay 2007 Bright green-gold; elegant wine with clear varietal character, yet in a pleasingly restrained persona; nectarine and fig fruit and good acidity illuminate a very good wine. Available only from cellar door. Screwcap. 13% alc. Rating 94 To 2014 $30

✪ Late Harvest Semillon 2009 An interesting contrast with the Mount Horrocks Cane Cut (riesling), for it is no less sweet, but seems to have more acidity. Classy wine. Screwcap. 12% alc. Rating 94 To 2013 $20

♟♟♟♟♟ Green Label Semillon 2009 The promise of the floral, aromatic bouquet is
✪ fulfilled by the palate, with its juicy mix of lemon juice, herb and mineral flavours. Has impeccable length and balance. Screwcap. 11% alc. Rating 93 To 2019 $18
White Label Hunter Valley Chardonnay 2008 Rating 93 To 2018 $30
Yellow Label Chardonnay 2006 Rating 93 To 2012 $24

♟♟♟♟ Blue Label Chardonnay 2008 Rating 88 To 2013 $19

Scarpantoni Estate ★★★★★
Scarpantoni Drive, McLaren Flat, SA 5171 Region McLaren Vale
T (08) 8383 0186 F (08) 8383 0490 www.scarpantoniwines.com Open Mon–Fri 9–5, w'ends & public hols 11–5
Winemaker Michael and Filippo Scarpantoni Est. 1979 Cases 30 000 Vyds 40 ha
With 20 ha of shiraz, 11 ha of cabernet sauvignon, 3 ha each of chardonnay and sauvignon blanc, 1 ha each of merlot and gamay, and 0.5 ha of petit verdot, Scarpantoni has come a long way since Domenico Scarpantoni purchased his first property in 1958. He was working for Thomas Hardy at its Tintara winery and subsequently became vineyard manager for Seaview Wines. In 1979 his sons Michael and Filippo built the winery, which has now been extended to enable all the grapes from the estate plantings to be used to make wine under the Scarpantoni label. Exports to the UK and other major markets.

♟♟♟♟♟ Block 3 McLaren Vale Shiraz 2008 Textbook expression of the region with dark chocolate, fruitcake spice and generous levels of black fruit and oak on display; the palate is rich and thickly textured, but displays life and energy with an attractive licorice note to conclude on the warm finish. Screwcap. 15% alc. Rating 94 To 2022 $30 BE
Brothers' Block McLaren Vale Cabernet Sauvignon 2008 Mocha notes derived from oak work with the blackcurrant fruit; the palate shows plenty of toast, with the tannins providing a very dry and chewy finish; big-boned and impressive. Screwcap. 15% alc. Rating 94 To 2020 $30 BE

♟♟♟♟♟ Sauvignon Blanc 2009 Fresh pea pod bouquet, with a suggestion of tropical
✪ fruit in the background; the palate is fleshy and forward, with fine acid cut providing persistence on the finish. Screwcap. 11.5% alc. Rating 90 To 2012 $18 BE
Reserve Cabernet Shiraz 2008 Rating 90 To 2016 $36 BE

♟♟♟♟ Pedler Creek Sauvignon Blanc 2009 Rating 88 To 2012 $14
Oxenberry Jack of all Trades 2009 Rating 88 To 2012 $22
Oxenberry The Right Nut 20 Year Old Liqueur Muscat NV Rating 88 To 2011 $30

Schild Estate Wines ★★★★
Cnr Barossa Valley Way/Lyndoch Valley Road, Lyndoch, SA 5351 Region Barossa Valley
T (08) 8524 5560 F (08) 8524 4333 www.schildestate.com.au Open 7 days 10–5
Winemaker Scott Hazeldine Est. 1998 Cases 30 000 Vyds 159.5 ha
Ed Schild is a Barossa Valley grapegrower who first planted a small vineyard at Rowland Flat in 1952, steadily increasing his vineyard holdings over the next 50 years to their present level. Currently 12% of the production from these vineyards (now managed by son Michael Schild) is used to produce Schild Estate wines, and the plan is to increase this percentage. The flagship wine is made from 150-year-old shiraz vines on the Moorooroo Block. The cellar door is in

the old ANZ Bank at Lyndoch, and provides the sort of ambience that can only be found in the Barossa Valley. A \$4 million winery was constructed and opened in time for the 2010 vintage; it is situated among the vines, and close to the existing cellar door. Exports to the UK, the US and other major markets.

Moorooroo Limited Release Barossa Valley Shiraz 2006 Some colour development; the aromas are of black fruits, plum, chocolate and vanilla, the medium-bodied palate providing a replay with the addition of creamy mocha notes; the cork is of high quality and has been perfectly inserted. 14.5% alc. Rating 93 To 2026 \$85

Barossa Adelaide Hills Semillon Sauvignon Blanc 2009 Intelligently made wine; it is surprising more Barossans haven't followed down this track; grassy/lemony aromas are amplified to the right degree on the long palate with its gentle tropical notes. Screwcap. 13% alc. Rating 91 To 2012 \$15

Old Bush Vine GMS Barossa Grenache Mourvedre Shiraz 2009 A 55/25/20 blend from vines with an average age of 70 years – how can such a wine be sold for \$16? It's made without the use of oak, a ploy that enhances the vibrancy of the red cherry, plum and spice flavours; best of all, its alcohol is moderate. A splendid bargain for immediate enjoyment. Screwcap. 14.5% alc. Rating 91 To 2013 \$16

Alma Schild Reserve Barossa Chardonnay 2009 Rating 88 To 2011 \$20
Barossa Shiraz 2007 Rating 88 To 2013 \$20
Barossa Chardonnay 2009 Rating 87 To 2010 \$15
Alma Schild Reserve Barossa Chardonnay 2008 Rating 87 To 2012 \$20
Barossa Cabernet Sauvignon 2008 Rating 87 To 2012 \$20
Three Springs 2009 Rating 87 To 2010 \$16

Schiller Vineyards ★★★

Light Pass Road, Light Pass, SA 5355 **Region** Barossa Valley
T (08) 8562 1258 **F** (08) 8562 2560 **www**.schillervineyards.com.au **Open** By appt
Winemaker Neville Falkenberg (Contract) **Est.** 1864 **Cases** 500 **Vyds** 72.55 ha
How can it be that a business established in 1864 was a new entry in the *2009 Wine Companion*? The answer is simple: Carl Freidrich Schiller arrived in SA in 1855, purchasing his first property in 1864 at Light Pass and soon thereafter establishing the first vines for the Schiller family. For six generations the Schiller family has been producing premium grapes for the best wineries of the Barossa; very few wineries in Bordeaux, Burgundy or California can claim to have had six generations of continuous viticulture under the same family name (a point often missed by distinguished wine writers from other parts of the world). To ram the point home, the underground cellar for the Schiller wines is situated below the original 1860 Schiller homestead (built on leased land in 1855). Only a tiny quantity of the estate vineyards (shiraz, mataro, grenache, semillon, chardonnay, savagnin, riesling, merlot and cabernet sauvignon) is vinified under the Schiller Vineyards label.

Barossa Shiraz 2006 Light colour, good hue; has bright fruit and good length, although there is a suggestion of lift; only 150 cases made. Screwcap. 14.5% alc. Rating 88 To 2015 \$20

Schindler Northway Downs ★★★

437 Stumpy Gully Road, Balnarring, Vic 3926 **Region** Mornington Peninsula
T (03) 5983 1945 **F** (03) 5983 1987 **www**.northwaydowns.com.au **Open** 1st w'end of month
Winemaker Sandro Mosele, Phillip Kittle (Contract) **Est.** 1996 **Cases** 250 **Vyds** 6 ha
The Schindler family planted the first 2 ha of pinot noir and chardonnay in 1996. A further 4 ha of pinot noir was planted on an ideal north-facing slope in 1999, and the first vintage followed in 2000. The cellar door offers Austrian food and live Austrian music on Sundays.

ŸŸŸŸ   **Mornington Peninsula Chardonnay 2008** Bright, light straw-green; a tightly bound wine, with a slightly sharp citrus edge needing to soften a little. Diam. 13.1% alc. **Rating** 89 **To** 2014 **$20**

Schubert Estate   ★★★★☆
Roennfeldt Road, Marananga, SA 5355 **Region** Barossa Valley
T (08) 8562 3375 **F** (08) 8562 4338 **www**.schubertestate.com.au **Open** Not
Winemaker Steve Schubert **Est.** 2000 **Cases** 600 **Vyds** 14 ha
Steve and Cecilia Schubert are primarily grapegrowers, with 13 ha of shiraz and 1 ha of viognier. They purchased the 25-ha property in 1986, when it was in such a derelict state that there was no point trying to save the old vines. Both were working in other areas, so it was some years before they began replanting, at a little under 2 ha per year. Almost all the production is sold to Torbreck. In 2000 they decided to keep enough grapes to make a barrique of wine for their own (and friends') consumption. They were sufficiently encouraged by the outcome to venture into the dizzy heights of two hogsheads a year (since increased to four or so). The wine is made with wild yeast, open fermentation, basket pressing and bottling without filtration. Found the 2007 vintage difficult – as did most. Exports to the UK, the US, Canada, Germany and Holland.

ŸŸŸŸŸ   **Goose-yard Block Barossa Valley Shiraz 2007** Deep and bright colour; a classy medium-bodied shiraz, with a seductive array of blackberry and plum fruit supported by fine, ripe tannins and well integrated; very high-quality cork, perfectly inserted. 14.5% alc. **Rating** 94 **To** 2020 **$65**

ŸŸŸŸŸ   **The Gosling Barossa Valley Shiraz 2007 Rating** 91 **To** 2015 **$24.50**

Schulz Vignerons   ★★★★☆
PO Box 121, Nuriootpa, SA 5355 **Region** Barossa Valley
T (08) 8565 6257 **F** (08) 8565 6257 **Open** By appt
Winemaker David Powell (Contract) **Est.** 2003 **Cases** 500 **Vyds** 58.5 ha
Marcus and Roslyn Schulz are the fifth generation of one of the best known wine families (or, rather, extended families) in the Barossa Valley. Four generations of grapegrowing and winemaking precede them, but they went down a new path by initiating biological farming in 2002. They have moved from irrigation and extensive spraying to the situation where the vines are now virtually dry-grown, producing generous yields of high-quality grapes, using natural nitrogen created by the active soil biology, and minimal chemical input. The vineyard is planted to 12 varieties, shiraz, mourvedre, grenache and cabernet sauvignon leading the band. They are also actively involved in a local co-operative campaign to protect blocks of native vegetation to encourage biodiversity. As might be imagined, the lion's share of the grapes are sold to other producers (some finding its way to Torbreck).

ŸŸŸŸŸ   **Marcus Barossa Valley Old Shiraz 2005** Has a strikingly complex bouquet of black fruits, prune, licorice and oak, the full-bodied palate taking those characters into another dimension. It's all too much for me, but will surely knock the socks off American critics; 60-year-old vines. Screwcap. 15.5% alc. **Rating** 94 **To** 2025 **$70**

ŸŸŸŸŸ   **Benjamin Barossa Valley Shiraz 2006 Rating** 90 **To** 2021 **$25**
✪   **Julius Barossa Valley Merlot 2006** Whether the Barossa Valley is the right place to grow merlot is a matter for debate, but the combination of a great vintage and the winemaking skills of David Powell have produced a luscious and well-balanced wine. Screwcap. 14.2% alc. **Rating** 90 **To** 2016 **$20**

ŸŸŸŸ   **Anthony Barossa Valley Cabernet Sauvignon 2006** A vintage that smiled
✪   on cabernet in the Barossa Valley, and there is no lack of generosity; however, a little less oak and slightly more focus on the fruit profile would have been better. Screwcap. 14% alc. **Rating** 89 **To** 2016 **$20**
✪   **Johann Barossa Valley Zinfandel 2006** Has the correct structure and red fruit profile of warmer climate zinfandel, with spiced, cooked red cherries and minimal tannins. Screwcap. 13% alc. **Rating** 89 **To** 2013 **$20**

Schutz Barossa ★★★

Stonewell Road, Marananga, SA 5355 **Region** Barossa Valley
T 0409 547 478 **F** (08) 8563 3472 **www.schutzbarossa.com Open** Not
Winemaker Troy Kalleske **Est.** 1997 **Cases** 1400 **Vyds** 9.5 ha
Tammy Schutz (nee Pfeiffer) may be a sixth-generation grapegrower, but she was only 19 when in 1997 she purchased the 27-ha property now known as Schutz Barossa. At that time there were 2.4 ha of shiraz plantings, the remainder was grazing land with a beautiful view towards the Seppeltsfield palm avenue. The existing shiraz had been sourced from 80-year-old vines grown in the Moppa district, and Tammy has since added more shiraz and 2 ha of cabernet sauvignon. She carries out much of the work on the vineyards herself, using sustainable vineyard practices wherever possible. The Stonewell area, in which the vineyard is situated, is well known for its high-quality shiraz fruit. The winemaking is done by her good friend and cousin Troy Kalleske. Exports to France, Denmark, The Netherlands, Ireland, Israel and Asia.

ΨΨΨΨ **Red Nectar Barossa Valley Shiraz 2007** A strongly built, full-bodied wine with blackberry, licorice and earth, plus plenty of oak; positive flavours, but less finesse. Screwcap. 15% alc. **Rating** 89 **To** 2015 $25
Red Nectar Barossa Valley Cabernet Sauvignon 2007 Good colour and hue; fully ripe cassis and blackcurrant fruit does the work, oak and tannins bystanders. Screwcap. 14% alc. **Rating** 88 **To** 2015 $25

Scion Vineyard & Winery ★★★☆

74 Slaughterhouse Road, Rutherglen, Vic 3685 **Region** Rutherglen
T (02) 6032 8844 **www.scionvineyard.com Open** W'ends & public hols 10–5, or by appt
Winemaker Jan and Rowland Milhinch **Est.** 2002 **Cases** 1000 **Vyds** 3.75 ha
Former audiologist Jan Milhinch is a great-great-granddaughter of GF Morris, founder of the most famous Rutherglen wine family. She was in her 50s and at the height of her professional career when she decided to take what she describes as a 'vine change', moving from Melbourne to establish a little over 3 ha of durif, orange muscat, brown muscat and viognier on a quartz-laden red clay slope, planted in 2002, but with a viticultural history stretching back to 1890. Son Rowland has joined the winemaking team.

ΨΨΨΨΨ **Rutherglen Durif 2008** Deep crimson-purple; as usual, flooded with black fruit flavours, but not so much as to obscure the good texture and structure of the palate, built around fine, persistent tannins. Screwcap. 13.9% alc. **Rating** 93 **To** 2018 $32

ΨΨΨΨ **Rutherglen Rose 2009 Rating** 89 **To** 2010 $19
Rutherglen Rose Muscat 2009 Rating 88 **To** 2011 $29

Scorpiiion ★★★★☆

32 Waverley Ridge Road, Crafers, SA 5152 (postal) **Region** Barossa
T 0409 551 110 **F** (08) 8353 1562 **www.scorpiiionwines.com.au Open** Not
Winemaker Pete Schell **Est.** 2002 **Cases** 800
Scorpiiion Wines was the concept of Mark Herbertt who decided to buy a small quantity of McLaren Vale and Barossa grapes in 2002 and have the wine made for himself, friends and family. In 2004 Paddy Phillips and Michael Szwarcbord – like Mark Herbertt, they share the Scorpio birth sign – joined the partnership. It is a virtual winery, with the grapes purchased, and the wines contract-made by the brilliant Peter Schell. They say, 'We share a number of likes and dislikes in relation to Australian red wines – apart from that, we don't really agree on anything … We aim for a fruit-driven style with elegant oak, rather than a big, oak-driven style.' Oh, and they are united in their insistence on using screwcaps rather than corks.

ΨΨΨΨΨ **Barossa Valley Shiraz 2008** Dense purple-crimson; a rich, opulent and complex ✪ shiraz with waves of black fruits and exemplary tannin management; fruit complexity from three subregions; given the benefit of a question of alcohol warmth that won't be noticed with food. Screwcap. 15% alc. **Rating** 94 **To** 2023 $24

ŢŢŢŢ♀ **Single Vineyard Barossa Valley Cabernet Sauvignon 2008** With no viable
✪   McLaren Vale fruit available, this became a single-vineyard wine (from Strait Gate)
     picked before the fruit was cooked; may be a little one-dimensional, but has really
     appealing flavours – and price. Screwcap. 14.5% alc. **Rating** 90 **To** 2015 $19
✪   **The Sting Barossa Valley Vintage Fortified Shiraz 2008** The combined
     effect of high baume fruit to start with, then the fortifying spirit, takes this into
     a serious echelon of alcohol, which may, however, sneak by unnoticed; there
     is a touch of elegance to the wine, and it is not overly sweet. I'm not sure the
     anti-alcohol lobby would approve of the come-hither price. Screwcap. 20% alc.
     Rating 90 **To** 2016 $12

Scorpo Wines   ★★★★★

23 Old Bittern-Dromana Road, Merricks North, Vic 3926 **Region** Mornington Peninsula
T (03) 5989 7697 **F** (03) 5989 7697 **www.**scorpowines.com.au **Open** By appt
Winemaker Paul Scorpo, Sandro Mosele (Contract) **Est.** 1997 **Cases** 3000 **Vyds** 9.64 ha
Paul Scorpo has a background as a horticulturist/landscape architect, working on major
projects ranging from private gardens to golf courses in Australia, Europe and Asia. His
family has a love of food, wine and gardens, all of which led to them buying a derelict apple
and cherry orchard on gentle rolling hills between Port Phillip and Westernport bays. Part
of a ridge system that climbs up to Red Hill, it offers north and northeast-facing slopes on
red-brown, clay loam soils. They have established pinot gris (4.84 ha), pinot noir (2.8 ha),
chardonnay (1 ha) and shiraz (1 ha). Exports to Singapore and Hong Kong.

ŢŢŢŢŢ **Mornington Peninsula Chardonnay 2008** Light, bright green; while the
     bouquet doesn't give too much away, the palate has a superb tactile quality that
     incites saliva to flow; the citrus component in the spectrum of stone fruit flavours
     lies at the heart of that tactile quality, for it is sweet, not sour. Diam. 13.5% alc.
     Rating 95 **To** 2015 $38
     Mornington Peninsula Pinot Noir 2008 Excellent colour and clarity; an
     exercise in the simultaneous delivery of purity and power, the red and black plum
     and cherry fruits integrated with fine, ripe tannins on the long and satisfying
     palate. Diam. 14% alc. **Rating** 95 **To** 2015 $43
     Noirien Mornington Peninsula Pinot Noir 2009 Bright crimson-purple;
     voluminous spiced cherry and blood plum on bouquet and palate alike; intended
     for early consumption, but has the structure and fruit to justify a drink some, keep
     some strategy. Diam. 13.5% alc. **Rating** 94 **To** 2015 $30

ŢŢŢŢ♀ **Mornington Peninsula Pinot Gris 2009** **Rating** 93 **To** 2012 $34
     Mornington Peninsula Rose 2009 **Rating** 91 **To** 2011 $30

Scotchmans Hill   ★★★★★

190 Scotchmans Road, Drysdale, Vic 3222 **Region** Geelong
T (03) 5251 3176 **F** (03) 5253 1743 **www.**scotchmanshill.com.au **Open** 7 days 10.30–5.30
Winemaker Robin Brockett, Marcus Holt **Est.** 1982 **Cases** 70 000
Situated on the Bellarine Peninsula, southeast of Geelong, with a well-equipped winery and
first-class vineyards. It is a consistent performer with its Pinot Noir and has a strong following
in Melbourne and Sydney for its astutely priced, competently made wines. The second
label, Swan Bay, has been joined at the other end of the spectrum with top-end individual
vineyard wines. The Ferryman brand was added in 2009, using contract-grown grapes from
the Mornington Peninsula. Exports to the UK and other major markets.

ŢŢŢŢŢ **Cornelius Bellarine Peninsula Chardonnay 2007** Glowing green-straw; has
     the Robin Brockett signature of elegant complexity; the bouquet has the first hints
     of secondary development, with gently nutty/toasty notes, but the long palate is
     bright, fresh and pure. Screwcap. 14% alc. **Rating** 95 **To** 2017 $50
     Bellarine Peninsula Shiraz 2007 Dense purple-crimson; a rich and dense full-
     bodied shiraz with blackberry, licorice and a touch of dark chocolate; has layers
     of flavour and good tannin structure, French oak controlled. An immensely long
     future. Screwcap. 14.5% alc. **Rating** 95 **To** 2030 $25

Cornelius Bellarine Peninsula Syrah 2007 Deep crimson-purple; a distinguished cool-climate shiraz, with fragrant spice, pepper and black fruit aromas, then a medium- to full-bodied palate with great drive and length, tannins and oak in unison with the fruit. Screwcap. 15% alc. **Rating** 95 **To** 2022 $50

Cornelius Bellarine Peninsula Sauvignon 2008 Bright green-straw; 100% barrel-fermented and lees stirred for six months before bottling; has retained vibrant fruit at the core of a complex and textured palate, the finish long and zesty. Screwcap. 14% alc. **Rating** 94 **To** 2011 $37

Bellarine Peninsula Chardonnay 2008 Very much in the usual tightly calibrated and focused style of Scotchmans Hill, barrel ferment oak and maturation largely absorbed by lively fruit (no mlf) in the white peach to citrus spectrum. Screwcap. 13.5% alc. **Rating** 94 **To** 2015 $25

Cornelius Bellarine Peninsula Pinot Gris 2008 Barrel-fermented and aged for six months in a range of new and used French oak barriques, doubtless part of the reason for the price; part, because this wine has managed to absorb that oak and retain fresh varietal fruit flavours and a clean, bright finish. Screwcap. 14% alc. **Rating** 94 **To** 2012 $37

Bellarine Peninsula Pinot Noir 2008 Strong clear colour; good expression of pinot varietal character from start to finish, with plum, spice and a touch of black cherry characters; very good mouthfeel and balance. Screwcap. 14% alc. **Rating** 94 **To** 2017 $32

Cornelius Bellarine Peninsula Pinot Noir 2007 Retains bright, clear hue; a spice and red berry fruit bouquet, then a finely structured, long and well-balanced palate with a particularly good finish and aftertaste. Screwcap. 14.5% alc. **Rating** 94 **To** 2015 $50

ŸŸŸŸŸ **Ferryman Mornington Peninsula Pinot Noir 2008 Rating** 92 **To** 2014 $24.50

Bellarine Peninsula Sauvignon Blanc 2009 Rating 90 **To** 2010 $22

✪ **Swan Bay Shiraz 2008** Bright colour; red and black fruit bouquet, with a touch of clove; the palate is laden with sweet fruit, is medium-bodied, fleshy, generous and quite engaging; very good quality for the price. Screwcap. 14.5% alc. **Rating** 90 $18

Seabrook Wines ★★★★★

Lot 350 Light Pass Road, Tanunda, SA 5352 **Region** Barossa Valley
T 0427 224 353 **F** (08) 8563 0349 **Open** By appt
Winemaker Hamish Seabrook **Est.** 2004 **Cases** 1000 **Vyds** 2 ha
Hamish Seabrook is the youngest generation of a proud Melbourne wine family once involved in wholesale and retail distribution, and as leading show judges of their respective generations. Hamish, too, is a wine show judge, but was the first to venture into winemaking, working with Best's and Brown Brothers in Vic before moving to SA with wife Joanne. Here they have a small planting of shiraz (recently joined by viognier) but also continue to source small amounts of shiraz from the Barossa and Pyrenees. In 2008 Hamish set up his own winery, located on the family property in Vine Vale, having previously made the wines at Dorrien Estate and elsewhere. Exports to the UK.

ŸŸŸŸŸ
✪ **The Merchant Barossa Valley Shiraz 2007** The colour is every bit as good as that of the Pyrenees; a lifted bouquet with black fruits, spice and oak nuances, the medium- to full-bodied palate built around fine, almost juicy, blackberry fruits, endowing it with elegance. Screwcap. 14% alc. **Rating** 95 **To** 2020 $35

✪ **The Judge Clare Valley Eden Valley Riesling 2009** Light straw-green; the bouquet is yet to fully flower, but the sheer intensity, power and length of the palate guarantees the medium- and long-term future of the wine; cleansing acidity on the finish is also part of a complex message. Screwcap. 12% alc. **Rating** 94 **To** 2024 $22

✪ **Pyrenees Shiraz 2007** Purple-crimson-red; a mix of spicy, savoury, earthy aromas underlie the black fruits of the bouquet; the palate adds licorice to the blackberry fruit, and not insubstantial tannins; overall, distinctly savoury. Screwcap. 14.5% alc. **Rating** 94 **To** 2017 $28

Seaforth Estate ★★★★☆

520 Arthurs Seat Road, Red Hill,Vic 3937 **Region** Mornington Peninsula
T (03) 5989 2362 **F** (03) 5989 2506 **www.**seaforthwines.com.au **Open** 1st w'end of month 11–5, or by appt
Winemaker Phillip Kittle (Contract) **Est.** 1994 **Cases** 2000 **Vyds** 4.1 ha
Seaforth Estate is a family-owned and operated business. Andrew and Venetia Adamson continue to undertake much of the management of their vineyard, which is planted on red volcanic soil at the top of Red Hill. At 300 m above sea level, Seaforth Estate is one of the highest vineyards on the Mornington Peninsula, sited on a north-facing slope overlooking Port Phillip Bay to the distant Melbourne skyline. Wines marketed under the Seaforth Estate label are 100% estate- grown and the Pinot Noir, Chardonnay and Pinot Gris have consistently performed well. In Oct '09 100 chardonnay vines (still leaving 2.4 ha) were removed and replaced with three clones of pinot noir, two new to Australia.

ŸŸŸŸŸ Mornington Peninsula Chardonnay 2008 Bright straw-green; a lively and
✪   intense chardonnay with classic white peach, nectarine and grapefruit aromas
         and flavours; the oak has been well handled, and the wine has length. Screwcap.
         13.2% alc. **Rating** 94 **To** 2015 $26

ŸŸŸŸ Mornington Peninsula Pinot Gris 2008 **Rating** 89 **To** 2011 $24
       Mornington Peninsula Wild Rose 2008 **Rating** 88 **To** 2011 $18
       Mornington Peninsula Pinot Noir 2008 **Rating** 87 **To** 2012 $28

Sedona Estate ★★★★☆

182 Shannons Road, Murrindindi,Vic 3717 **Region** Upper Goulburn
T (03) 9730 2883 **F** (03) 9730 2583 **www.**sedonaestate.com.au **Open** W'ends & public hols 11–5, or by appt
Winemaker Paul Evans **Est.** 1998 **Cases** 2000 **Vyds** 4 ha
The Sedona Estate vineyard was chosen by Paul and Sonja Evans after a long search for what they considered to be the perfect site. Situated on north-facing and gently undulating slopes, with gravelly black soils, it is planted (in descending order) to shiraz, cabernet sauvignon, merlot and sangiovese. Paul (former Oakridge winemaker) also contract-makes wines for a number of other small Yarra Valley producers.

ŸŸŸŸŸ Chardonnay 2009 Gleaming colour; a very elegant wine, with fine white peach
         and grapefruit flavours reflecting the whole bunch pressing, the barrel ferment
         inputs appropriately subtle; good balance and length. Screwcap. 13% alc. **Rating** 94
         To 2015 $18

ŸŸŸŸŸ Yea Valley Cabernet Merlot 2008 **Rating** 90 **To** 2017 $18

ŸŸŸŸ Yea Valley Shiraz 2008 **Rating** 89 **To** 2016 $20

See Saw ★★★★

PO Box 611, Manly, NSW 1655 **Region** Hunter Valley
T (02) 8966 9020 **F** (02) 8966 9021 **www.**seesawwine.com **Open** Not
Winemaker Hamish MacGowan, Andrew Margan **Est.** 2006 **Cases** 8000
This is another venture of Hamish MacGowan, the winemaker-cum-marketer who is responsible for Angus the Bull. While working in the Hunter Valley he met Andrew Margan and Sarah-Kate Dineen, then winemaker at Tempus Two. She has now returned to NZ (with winemaker husband Dan Dineen) to make sauvignon blanc, and Andrew remains in the Hunter with his own substantial winery and business. See Saw is a blend of 85% Hunter Valley Semillon and 15% Marlborough Sauvignon Blanc. Exports to the UK.

ŸŸŸŸŸ Hunter Valley Marlborough Semillon Sauvignon Blanc 2009 Bright
✪   straw-green; the Hunter Valley Semillon component provides the structure and
         length, the Marlborough Sauvignon Blanc fills the mid- and back-palate with
         appealing tropical fruits. A synergistic exercise. Screwcap. 12.5% alc. **Rating** 92
         To 2012 $18.95

Seppelt ★★★★★

Moyston Road, Great Western, Vic 3377 **Region** Grampians
T (03) 5361 2239 **F** (03) 5361 2328 **www.seppelt.com.au Open** 7 days 10–5
Winemaker Joanna Marsh, Emma Wood, Dougal Herd **Est.** 1865 **Cases** NFP
Australia's best known producer of sparkling wine, always immaculate in its given price range but also producing excellent Great Western–sourced table wines, especially long-lived Shiraz and Australia's best Sparkling Shirazs. The glitzy labels of the past have rightly been consigned to the rubbish bin, and the product range has been significantly rationalised and improved. Following the sale of Seppeltsfield to Kilikanoon, this is the sole operating arm of Seppelt under Foster's ownership. Exports to the UK, the US and other major markets.

🍷🍷🍷🍷🍷 **Drumborg Riesling 2009** The track record of this wine leaves no doubt it will
✪ develop slowly but superbly; it is perfectly balanced and has extreme length, with lime and apple flavours building to a crescendo on the finish. Screwcap. 12.5% alc.
Rating 96 **To** 2024 $32

✪ **Drumborg Vineyard Chardonnay 2008** Light straw-green; the extremely cool region is very obvious in this high-class wine, the flavours intense and pure, with citrus, apple and white peach caressed by oak but no more; has a very long palate and will develop superbly. Gold medal Sydney Wine Show '10. Screwcap. 13% alc.
Rating 96 **To** 2013 $45

Drumborg Vineyard Pinot Noir 2008 Good hue; the bouquet is delicately perfumed, the palate with elegance and finesse defining its style; it has a convincing mix of savoury and black cherry flavours. Screwcap. 13.5% alc. **Rating** 95
To 2015 $53

St Peters Grampians Shiraz 2008 Purple-crimson; a complex bouquet with fragrant blackberry, plum and licorice aromas and flavours; the medium-bodied palate has very good texture and structure. Screwcap. 14% alc. **Rating** 95
To 2028 $60

✪ **Chalambar Shiraz 2008** Deep crimson-purple; the expressive black fruits and spices of the bouquet are followed by a full-bodied palate, with fruit, oak and tannins all having their say, but none obscuring the others. Will coast through two decades at least. Grampians/Bendigo. Screwcap. 13.5% alc. **Rating** 95 **To** 2030 $27

🍷🍷🍷🍷🍷 **Salinger Pinot Noir Chardonnay 2006** Rating 92 To 2012 $35
Silverband Grampians Sparkling Shiraz NV Rating 91 To 2015 $35
Grampians Chardonnay 2008 Rating 90 To 2014 $18

🍷🍷🍷🍷 **Fleur de Lys Chardonnay Pinot NV NV** Rating 89 To 2012 $13

Seppeltsfield ★★★★★

1 Seppeltsfield Road, Seppeltsfield via Nuriootpa, SA 5355 **Region** Barossa Valley
T (08) 8568 6200 **F** (08) 8562 8333 **www.seppeltsfield.com.au Open** 7 days 10.30–5
Winemaker Fiona Donald **Est.** 1851 **Cases** 150 000
In August 2007 this historic property and its treasure trove of great fortified wines dating back to 1878 was purchased by the Kilikanoon group. A series of complicated lease-back arrangements and supply agreements were entered into between Kilikanoon and vendor Foster's, further complicated by Foster's keeping the Seppelt brand for table and sparkling wines (mostly produced at Great Western, Vic; see separate entry), but the Seppelt brand for fortified wines vesting in purchaser Kilikanoon. The winery has been recommissioned, including the gravity-flow system designed by Benno Seppelt in 1878.

🍷🍷🍷🍷🍷 **100 Year Old Para Liqueur 100 ml 1909** Almost into black, so dark is the
✪ burnt umber colour; paints the sides of the glass when swirled, the aromas of burnt toffee and raisin Christmas cake; anything more than a micro-sip is superfluous (although a number of micro-sips isn't); the sheer intensity of the impact of the wine in the mouth is awesome, the flavours tracking the bouquet until the rancio and acidity of the finish take over, and last for minutes. Cork. 23.7% alc.
Rating 100 **To** 2011 $299

✪ **Rare Rutherglen Tokay NV** Full mahogany, olive rim; an intensely fragrant and equally complex bouquet; the flavours are more intense and piercing than those of the Muscat, rancio now a cornerstone, but the wine is not heavier or more luscious, simply marking the difference between tokay and muscat; 375 ml. Cork. 17% alc. **Rating** 97 **To** 2011 $59

✪ **Paramount Tokay 500 ml NV** Even more olive and viscous than the Paramount Muscat; an extraordinary wine of great age, yet not the least stale; mouthfilling cake, toffee and tea; perfect finish and aftertaste. The solera started with the great 1922 vintage, with numerous subsequent vintages included. Cork. 17.3% alc. **Rating** 97 **To** 2011 $249

✪ **Rare Rutherglen Muscat NV** Deep mahogany-brown, grading to olive on the rim; explosively rich on the palate; raisins, singed toffee, plum pudding, almond and multi-spices race along the vibrant, wonderfully complex palate; rancio and associated acidity keeps the wine lithe and lively; 375 ml. Cork. 17% alc. **Rating** 97 **To** 2011 $69

✪ **Rare Tawny DP90 NV** Full-on tawny colour; the bouquet immediately proclaims the age and the class of the wine; the palate is electric in its intensity and vibrancy, the rancio penetrating and lingering; the aftertaste goes on and on, and it is here that the glorious breed and quality of the wine is most apparent. Cork. 20.5% alc. **Rating** 96 **To** 2011 $69

✪ **Paramount Tawny 500 ml NV** True tawny colour; loaded with flavour, Christmas cake, biscuit and honey, the sweetness continuing through its length, the obvious rancio preventing the wine from cloying; the concentration and complexity reflects the inclusion of a small percentage of every vintage of the 100 Year Old Para since 1878. Cork. 20.5% alc. **Rating** 96 **To** 2011 $349

✪ **Grand Rutherglen Tokay NV** Bright mahogany, with a rim of olive; in another tokay category altogether, its piercing complexity coupled with elegance, a vivid line of rancio running through the butterscotch, tea leaf and honey flavours; has great length and balance. Serve chilled; 500 ml. Screwcap. 16.5% alc. **Rating** 96 **To** 2011 $32

✪ **Paramount Muscat 500 ml NV** Brown, rimmed by olive; the penetrating bouquet introduces the extremely rich, incredibly luscious raisin fruit of the palate; great balance, rancio part of the game, but doesn't cut too hard. The base of the solera dates back to the mid-1960s, with parcels from the subsequent finest (Rare) vintages blended in. Cork. 17.6% alc. **Rating** 96 **To** 2011 $249

Selma Melitta Rare Luscious NV Bright mahogany brown, a blush of olive on the rim; into another realm of richness and sweetness, yet always with the counter punch of rancio; flavours of slightly burnt toffee and raisined sultanas; the finish has great balance; 500 ml. Screwcap. 18.5% alc. **Rating** 95 **To** 2011 $40

Flora Fino DP117 NV Pale straw-green; a great bouquet, highly aromatic, tangy and fresh; the palate follows precisely in the footsteps of the bouquet, with a mix of nutty/green apple characters on the mid-palate, then a gloriously fresh, dry and breezy finish. This has more character than Manzanilla; 500 ml. Screwcap. 16.1% alc. **Rating** 95 **To** 2010 $22

XO Paramount Oloroso 500 ml NV A slight touch of orange to the golden colour; a wonderfully rich wine, sweet honeyed fruit on the mid-palate, then drying out on the long finish thanks to the rancio. The solera from which it is drawn dates back to the mid-20th century. Cork. 22.5% alc. **Rating** 95 **To** 2011 $150

✪ **Grand Rutherglen Muscat NV** Brown-gold; another step up in richness and lusciousness, an unctuous, essency palate with spicy plum pudding and caramel overtaking outright raisin flavours; the finish is sleek and lingering; 10-15 years' barrel age. Serve chilled; 500 ml. Screwcap. 17% alc. **Rating** 95 **To** 2011 $32

✪ **XO Paramount Amontillado 500 ml NV** Pale golden brown; very complex biscuity and dried fruit aromas; the palate is long, dry and with a lingering biscuity/rancio aftertaste that is seemingly endless. Cork. 25.2% alc. **Rating** 94 **To** 2011 $149

⦿   **Para 1988** Bright tawny; wonderfully tangy and spicy, with dried mandarin peel and hazelnut biscuit aromas and flavours on the extremely long palate; rancio is in play, but not dominant. Screwcap. 20.5% alc. **Rating** 94 **To** 2011 $75

🍷🍷🍷🍷🍸 Grand Para NV Rating 93 To 2011 $32
Glenpara Gert's Blend Sparkling Shiraz NV Rating 91 To 2015 $25
Glenpara Lost Garden Clare Valley Rose 2008 Rating 90 To 2011 $18

🍷🍷🍷🍷 Ruby Lightly Fortified Grenache Rose NV Rating 87 To 2011 $20

Serafino Wines ★★★★☆

McLarens on the Lake, Kangarilla Road, McLaren Vale, SA 5171 **Region** McLaren Vale
T (08) 8323 0157 **F** (08) 8323 0158 **Open** Mon–Fri 10–4.30, w'ends & public hols 10–4.30
Winemaker Charles Whish **Est.** 2000 **Cases** 20 000 **Vyds** 98 ha
In the wake of the sale of Maglieri Wines to Beringer Blass in 1998, Maglieri founder Steve Maglieri acquired the McLarens on the Lake complex originally established by Andrew Garrett. The accommodation has been upgraded and a larger winery was commissioned in 2002. The operation draws upon 40 ha each of shiraz and cabernet sauvignon, 7 ha of chardonnay, 2 ha each of merlot, semillon, barbera, nebbiolo and sangiovese, and 1 ha of grenache. Part of the grape production is sold. Exports to the UK, the US and other major markets.

🍷🍷🍷🍷🍷 **McLaren Vale Shiraz 2008** Dense, dark red; a quintessential McLaren Vale shiraz
⦿   that, while full-bodied, dodged the heatwave bullet of '08; opulent, luscious black fruits married with lashings of dark chocolate and plum, tannins and oak in second place. Screwcap. 14.5% alc. **Rating** 94 **To** 2016 $26

🍷🍷🍷🍷🍸 **Reserve McLaren Vale Chardonnay 2008** Remarkable achievement for
⦿   McLaren Vale, surely picked before the heatwave. Although 100% French oak barrel-fermented with lees stirring, it is primarily driven by citrus zest flavours, the finish crisp, fresh and balanced. Screwcap. 13.5% alc. **Rating** 91 **To** 2014 $15

🍷🍷🍷🍷 Bellissimo Pinot Grigio 2009 Rating 89 To 2011 $18
Bellissimo Vermentino 2009 Rating 89 To 2011 $18
McLaren Vale Cabernet Sauvignon 2008 Rating 89 To 2016 $26

Seraph's Crossing ★★★★

PO Box 5753, Clare, SA 5453 **Region** Clare Valley
T 0412 132 549 **Open** Not
Winemaker Harry Dickinson **Est.** 2006 **Cases** 400 **Vyds** 5 ha
In a moment of enlightened madness, Harry Dickinson gave up his career as a lawyer in a major London law firm to work in the wine business. He helped run the International Wine Challenge for three years, followed by stints with various wine retailers, and some PR work for the German Wine Information Service. He worked his first vintage in Australia at Hardys Tintara winery in 1997 with Stephen Pannell and Larry Cherubino; their work with open fermenters, basket presses and winemaking philosophy made a huge impression. Following a period as a wine retailer in North Adelaide, he returned to winery work in 1999, in various wineries in the Clare Valley. During this time he and wife Chan bought a 75-ha property. They restored the 1880s house on the property, and the vineyards have been extended from the original 1 ha to now comprise shiraz (2 ha), grenache, mourvedre and zinfandel (1 ha each). The shiraz is hand-picked, de-stemmed, fermented with wild yeast, and, at the end of fermentation, is pressed directly to barrel where it remains for 28 months (with no racking) prior to blending and bottling with no fining or filtration. Exports to the UK and the US.

🍷🍷🍷🍷🍸 **Clare Valley Shiraz 2008** Intense inky crimson-purple; a determined effort to make sure every last ounce of flavour from the grapes has succeeded; a lighter touch and earlier picking might have been equally successful. Leave it alone for a decade. Screwcap. 15.5% alc. **Rating** 93 **To** 2030 $35

Serrat   ★★★★★

PO Box 478, Yarra Glen, Vic 3775 **Region** Yarra Valley
T (03) 9730 1439 **F** (03) 9730 1579 **www.serrat.com.au Open** Not
Winemaker Tom Carson **Est.** 2001 **Cases** 25 **Vyds** 2.04 ha
Serrat is the family business of Tom Carson (after a 12-year reign at Yering Station, now running Yabby Lake and Heathcote Estate for the Kirby family) and partner Nadege Suné. They have close-planted (at 8800 vines per ha) 0.8 ha each of pinot noir and chardonnay, 0.42 ha of shiraz, and a sprinkling of viognier. The vineyard was significantly damaged by the Black Saturday bushfires of 7 February 2009, but has been replanted where necessary.

ΨΨΨΨΨ Yarra Valley Pinot Noir 2008 Light bright colour; the complex bouquet has
✪   spice, small red fruits and violets (often written about but seldom encountered),
         the palate offering the full range of similar flavours; however it is the outstanding
         drive and length in the mouth that makes the wine as great as it is. Screwcap.
         13.5% alc. **Rating** 97 **To** 2017 $30

✪   **Yarra Valley Shiraz Viognier 2008** Typical vibrant crimson colour; a fragrant
         bouquet of berries and spice leads into a silky palate with very good balance
         and great length; the oak has been judged to perfection. Screwcap. 13.5% alc.
         Rating 96 **To** 2020 $30

Setanta Wines   ★★★★★

RSD 43 Williamstown Road, Forreston, SA 5233 (postal) **Region** Adelaide Hills
T (08) 8380 5516 **F** (08) 8380 5516 **www.setantawines.com.au Open** Tues–Sun 11–4
Winemaker Rod Chapman, Rebecca Wilson **Est.** 1997 **Cases** 6000
Setanta is a family-owned operation involving Sheilagh Sullivan, her husband Tony, and brother Bernard; the latter is the viticulturist, while Tony and Sheilagh manage marketing, administration and so forth. Of Irish parentage (they are first-generation Australians), they chose Setanta, Ireland's most famous mythological hero, as the brand name. The beautiful and striking labels tell the individual stories that give rise to the names of the wines. Exports to Ireland, of course; also to the UK, Dubai, Singapore, Hong Kong and Japan.

ΨΨΨΨΨ Black Sanglain Adelaide Hills Cabernet Sauvignon 2008 Exceptional
✪   crimson-purple hue; a bounce back to top form; near-perfect varietal fruit
         expression, with blackcurrant, plum and cassis fruit in a fine web of ripe tannins, oak
         precisely judged; immaculate length. Screwcap. 14.5% alc. **Rating** 96 **To** 2023 $29

✪   **Speckled House Eden Valley Riesling 2009** Has a highly complex and
         aromatic bouquet, with floral and spice notes, then a lime juice–infused palate with
         good intensity, length and purity. Screwcap. 11.5% alc. **Rating** 94 **To** 2017 $22

✪   **Emer Adelaide Hills Chardonnay 2008** An exercise in restraint from start
         to finish, with stone fruit, citrus, fig and cashew subtly underpinned by oak and
         crisp acidity; food style is not an implied criticism, just fact. Screwcap. 13.3% alc.
         Rating 94 **To** 2016 $24

✪   **Cuchulain Adelaide Hills Shiraz 2008** Has the fragrant bouquet with echoes
         of spice and pepper so typical of cool-grown shiraz – and the addition of a small
         amount of viognier; the medium-bodied palate is supple, bright and fresh, with an
         array of red and black fruits. Screwcap. 14.1% alc. **Rating** 94 **To** 2021 $29

✪   **Cuchulain Adelaide Hills Shiraz 2007** Bright colour; a fragrant, perfumed
         bouquet leads into a medium-bodied palate with fine red fruits liberally dusted
         with spices; good acidity underlines the length of the palate. Understated style
         with considerable elegance. Screwcap. 13.5% alc. **Rating** 94 **To** 2017 $29

ΨΨΨΨΨ Speckled House Adelaide Hills Riesling 2007 Rating 92 **To** 2017 $22
         Diahmid Adelaide Hills Sauvignon Blanc 2009 Rating 90 **To** 2011 $22
✪   **Talunga Ridge Adelaide Hills Cabernet Merlot 2008** Deep red-purple;
         a bold, full-bodied wine with strong blackcurrant and red fruit flavours, then a
         strong, slightly hot, finish. Red meat called for. Screwcap. 15% alc. **Rating** 90
         To 2015 $20

ΨΨΨΨ Talunga Ridge Adelaide Hills Pinot Noir 2008 Rating 89 **To** 2014 $20

Sevenhill Cellars ★★★★☆

College Road, Sevenhill, SA 5453 **Region** Clare Valley
T (08) 8843 4222 **F** (08) 8843 4382 **www.**sevenhill.com.au **Open** Mon–Fri 9–5,
w'ends & public hols 10–5
Winemaker Liz Heidenreich, Brother John May, Neville Rowe **Est.** 1851 **Cases** 22 000
Vyds 74.46 ha
One of the historical treasures of Australia; the oft-photographed stone wine cellars are the
oldest in the Clare Valley, and winemaking is still carried out under the direction of the
Jesuitical Manresa Society. Value for money is excellent, particularly that of the powerful Shiraz
and Riesling; all the wines reflect the estate-grown grapes from old vines. Exports to the UK,
the US, Switzerland, Indonesia, Korea and Japan.

ȲȲȲȲȲ **Inigo Shiraz 2008** Good colour; vivid purple hue; deep, dark and inky bouquet,
✪   with blackberry and liqueur cherry on offer; the palate is dense and chewy, with
      tarry tannins offsetting the generous fruit; a big wine, made very well, and given
      the dimensions of the wine and the 100-year-old vines, amazing value. Screwcap.
      15% alc. **Rating** 94 **To** 2025 $19 BE

ȲȲȲȲȲ **Inigo Merlot 2008** Good concentration of dark fruits, with a distinct savoury
✪   edge, reminiscent of sage and olive; medium-bodied, there is plenty of stuffing
      on the palate (often a problem for the variety), and the structure is offset by
      a generous mouthful of sweet dark fruit; long and quite satisfying. Screwcap.
      14.5% alc. **Rating** 93 **To** 2016 $19 BE

✪   **Inigo Semillon 2009** Meyer lemon, quince and a mere suggestion of straw; the
      palate is squeaky clean and quite precise, leaving a tangy and fresh impression of
      mandarin; should age with grace. Screwcap. 12.5% alc. **Rating** 92 **To** 2018 $19 BE

✪   **Inigo Verdelho 2009** Good concentration with a generous dollop of honeydew
      melon and a touch of straw and spice; the palate is quite rich, yet maintains
      lightness through vibrant acidity, and finishes with a distinct mandarin quality that
      is quite appealing. Screwcap. 14% alc. **Rating** 91 **To** 2014 $19 BE

Seville Estate ★★★★★

65 Linwood Road, Seville, Vic 3139 **Region** Yarra Valley
T (03) 5964 2622 **F** (03) 5964 2633 **www.**sevilleestate.com.au **Open** 7 days 10–5
Winemaker Dylan McMahon **Est.** 1970 **Cases** 4000 **Vyds** 8.08 ha
Dr Peter McMahon and wife Margaret commenced planting Seville Estate in 1972, part of
the resurgence of the Yarra Valley. Peter and Margaret retired in 1997, selling to Brokenwood.
Graham and Margaret Van Der Meulen acquired the property in '05, bringing it back into
family ownership. Graham and Margaret are hands-on in the vineyard and winery, working
closely with winemaker Dylan McMahon, who is the grandson of Peter and Margaret. The
philosophy is to capture the fruit expression of the vineyard in styles that reflect the cool
climate. Exports to Korea, Hong Kong and Singapore.

ȲȲȲȲȲ **Reserve Yarra Valley Chardonnay 2008** A rich and heady combination of
      pear, nectarines, grilled nuts and a touch of spice from the carefully chosen oak;
      the palate delivers what the bouquet promises, with layers of intense white fruits,
      rapier-like acidity and a finish that holds on for a seriously long time; this will age
      beautifully. Screwcap. 13.5% alc. **Rating** 96 **To** 2020 $45 BE

      Old Vine Reserve Yarra Valley Cabernet Sauvignon 2008 Another
      beautiful wine; highly perfumed, incredibly pure and precise, with aromas redolent
      of cassis and violets in abundance; the palate is medium-bodied, racy and silky, and
      provides a cerebral roller coaster from start to finish; fine oak enhances the fruit's
      natural concentration and the length is outstanding. Screwcap. 14% alc. **Rating** 96
      To 2040 $55 BE

✪   **Yarra Valley Chardonnay 2008** An aromatic bouquet of pear, melon and
      white peach, with a light touch of oak; the palate is complex and long, fruit, oak
      and acidity in a seamless stream. Gold medal Sydney Wine Show '10. Screwcap.
      13.5% alc. **Rating** 94 **To** 2016 $30

The Barber Yarra Valley Shiraz 2008 Bright colour; a live-wire, cool-climate
✪   shiraz, with spice, pepper and licorice dancing around the juicy black cherry fruit,
         acidity darting across the palate. Screwcap. 13.5% alc. **Rating** 93 **To** 2018 $19
         Old Vine Reserve Yarra Valley Shiraz 2007 Rating 92 **To** 2015 $60 BE
✪   **The Barber Yarra Valley Chardonnay 2008** Immediately proclaims its Yarra
         Valley origin with its length and persistence of flavour, with little or no oak
         impact; the flavours range through green apple, grapefruit and citrus rind, with
         balanced acidity; will grow in bottle. Screwcap. 13% alc. **Rating** 91 **To** 2016 $19
✪   **The Barber Yarra Valley Chardonnay 2009** A tightly wound expression of
         chardonnay, with pear and lemon coming to the fore; the palate is tight and linear,
         with acidity providing line and a steely backbone to the fruit; made in a Chablis
         style. Screwcap. 12% alc. **Rating** 90 **To** 2015 $20 BE
✪   **Yarra Valley Shiraz 2007** Bright colour; vibrant red fruit bouquet with a
         touch of tar adding complexity; medium-bodied and quite juicy on entry, with
         ample tannins and a little oak evident on the finish. Screwcap. 14% alc. **Rating** 90
         To 2014 $27 BE

♟♟♟♟ **The Barber Yarra Valley Riesling 2009 Rating** 87 **To** 2014 $23 BE
       Yarra Valley Pinot Noir 2008 Rating 87 **To** 2012 $30 BE

Shadowfax ★★★★★

K Road, Werribee, Vic 3030 **Region** Geelong
T (03) 9731 4420 **F** (03) 9731 4421 **www**.shadowfax.com.au **Open** 7 days 11–5
Winemaker Matt Harrop **Est.** 2000 **Cases** 15 000
Shadowfax is part of an awesome development at Werribee Park, a mere 20 mins from
Melbourne. The truly striking winery, designed by Wood Marsh Architects, built in 2000, is
adjacent to the extraordinary private home built in the 1880s by the Chirnside family and
known as The Mansion. It was then the centrepiece of a 40 000-ha pastoral empire, and the
appropriately magnificent gardens were part of the reason why the property was acquired by
Parks Victoria in the early 1970s. The Mansion is now The Mansion Hotel, with 92 rooms
and suites. Exports to the UK, Japan, NZ and Singapore.

♟♟♟♟♟ **Gippsland Chardonnay 2008** Glorious green colour; a vibrant single-vineyard
        (at Tambo) wine, with citrus, nectarine and white peach fruit; barrel fermentation
        and maturation in used French oak has not impacted on the flavour. Screwcap.
        13.5% alc. **Rating** 96 **To** 2015 $45
        Macedon Ranges Chardonnay 2008 Bright pale green-straw; a crisp and very
        fine wine, with a strong mineral structure to the palate, length and balance in no
        way impaired by the low alcohol. Screwcap. 12.8% alc. **Rating** 95 **To** 2016 $45
✪   **Chardonnay 2008** A small winery taking tricks from the likes of Foster's and
        Constellation with this blend from the Macedon Ranges/Geelong/Yarra Valley/
        Gippsland/Mornington Peninsula; the net result is an elegant and fine chardonnay
        with fruit in the white peach and grapefruit spectrum; lees maturation has
        substituted for oak. Screwcap. 13% alc. **Rating** 94 **To** 2013 $30
        Pink Cliffs Heathcote Shiraz 2006 Light but bright hue; a fragrant bouquet
        and an almost juicy palate, with red cherry flavours balanced by more earthy,
        albeit fine, tannins. An elegant medium-bodied wine away from the mainstream
        Heathcote style, but none the worse for that. Screwcap. 12.9% alc. **Rating** 94
        To 2019 $65
        One Eye Heathcote Shiraz 2006 Good hue; a spotlessly clean and fresh
        medium-bodied wine, with notes of spice, licorice and blackberry all in perfect
        harmony; fine, silky tannins are a high point. Screwcap. 13.5% alc. **Rating** 94
        To 2018 $45

♟♟♟♟♟ **Pinot Gris 2009 Rating** 93 **To** 2012 $22
✪   **Sauvignon Blanc 2009** Bright, light straw-green; a very focused and intense
        wine from the Adelaide Hills, with real depth to the palate, the gently tropical
        flavours in an embrace of minerally notes and balanced acidity. Screwcap. 12% alc.
        Rating 92 **To** 2012 $18

Werribee Shiraz 2006 Rating 92 To 2016 $29
Pinot Noir 2006 Rating 90 To 2013 $25

❂   **Shiraz 2008** Light, bright red-purple; a light- to medium-bodied Werribee/
Goulburn Valley/Heathcote blend, made in a bright and breezy fashion for
relatively early consumption, the flavours more in the red than black fruit
spectrum, the tannins' support good. Screwcap. 14% alc. **Rating** 90 To 2014 $18

♈♈♈♈   **Riesling 2009** Rating 89 To 2016 $18

Shantell ★★★★

1974 Melba Highway, Dixons Creek, Vic 3775 **Region** Yarra Valley
T (03) 5965 2155 **F** (03) 5965 2331 **www**.shantellvineyard.com.au
Open Thurs–Mon 10.30–5, or by appt
Winemaker Shan and Turid Shanmugam **Est.** 1980 **Cases** 1200 **Vyds** 10 ha
The fully mature Shantell vineyards provide the winery with a high-quality fruit source; part
is sold to other Yarra Valley makers, the remainder vinified at Shantell. Chardonnay, Semillon
and Cabernet Sauvignon are its benchmark wines, sturdily reliable, sometimes outstanding.
Exports to the UK and Singapore.

♈♈♈♈♉   **Yarra Valley Chardonnay 2008** Bright green-yellow; an attractive bouquet and
mouthfilling nectarine and grapefruit flavours; barrel ferment oak undoubtedly
used, but contributing as much to texture as flavour. Screwcap. 13.5% alc.
Rating 93 To 2015 $28
Yarra Valley Cabernet Sauvignon 2005 Holding hue well; has started to
develop some secondary complexity to its core of ripe blackcurrant fruit, and
has the typical Yarra Valley length; oak plays only a minor role. Cork. 13% alc.
Rating 91 To 2018 $28
Yarra Valley Shiraz 2005 Hue still predominantly purple; licorice, spice, leather
and black fruit aromas, then a very ripe, full-bodied palate; a slightly congested
finish with an illusion of sweetness. ProCork. 13% alc. **Rating** 90 To 2020 $28

Sharmans ★★★

Glenbothy, 175 Glenwood Road, Relbia, Tas 7258 **Region** Northern Tasmania
T (03) 6343 0773 **F** (03) 6343 0773 **www**.sharmanswines.com **Open** W'ends 10–5
Winemaker Josef Chromy Wines (Jeremy Dineen), Bass Fine Wines (Guy Wagner)
Est. 1987 **Cases** 1000 **Vyds** 4.25 ha
Mike Sharman pioneered one of the more interesting wine regions of Tasmania, not far south
of Launceston but with a distinctly warmer climate than (say) Pipers Brook. Ideal north-facing
slopes are home to the vineyard (planted to pinot choir, chardonnay, riesling, sauvignon blanc,
cabernet sauvignon and malbec). This additional warmth gives the red wines greater body
than most Tasmanian counterparts.

♈♈♈♈   **Riesling 2009** Pleasant lime and tropical fruit aromas flow into a palate with
good balance, length and acidity. Screwcap. 12.5% alc. **Rating** 89 To 2015 $20
Noble Late Harvest 2008 Not riesling, possibly sauvignon blanc; a complex
and textured palate, but lacks the purity of the rieslings. Screwcap. 11.6% alc.
Rating 89 To 2013 $20
Shaman 2006 Bright straw-green; fine mousse; still very firm and still building
complexity. Cork. 12% alc. **Rating** 88 To 2012 $25

Shaw & Smith ★★★★★

Lot 4 Jones Road, Balhannah, SA 5242 **Region** Adelaide Hills
T (08) 8398 0500 **F** (08) 8398 0600 **www**.shawandsmith.com **Open** Sat–Mon &
public hols (Mon) 11–4
Winemaker Martin Shaw, Darryl Catlin **Est.** 1989 **Cases** NFP **Vyds** 52.6 ha
Cousins Martin Shaw and Michael Hill Smith MW already had unbeatable experience when
they founded Shaw & Smith as a virtual winery in 1989. The brand was firmly established as a
leading producer of sauvignon blanc by the time they acquired a 42-ha property at Woodside,

known as the M3 Vineyard (27.8 ha planted), as it is owned by Michael and Matthew Hill Smith and Martin Shaw. It produces the grapes for the M3 Chardonnay, and the most important part of the Sauvignon Blanc. In 1999 Martin and Michael purchased the 36-ha Balhannah property (24.8 ha planted), building the superbly designed winery in 2000 and planting more sauvignon blanc, shiraz, pinot noir and riesling. It is here that visitors can taste the wines in appropriately beautiful surroundings. Exports to all major markets.

ŸŸŸŸŸ **Adelaide Hills Sauvignon Blanc 2009** Grass, herb and citrus aromas lead
✪   into a tightly focused and vibrant palate, where citrus fruit flavours and minerally acidity are Siamese twins, joined from head to toe. Screwcap. 13% alc. **Rating** 96 To 2011 $25

✪   **Adelaide Hills Riesling 2009** Pale green-straw; a flowery bouquet leads into a delicate palate with citrus and green apple flavours, the palate drawn out by lingering, fresh acidity. The last of the line, the vines now removed. Screwcap. 13% alc. **Rating** 94 To 2015 $24

Adelaide Hills Shiraz 2008 Vivid crimson hue; loaded with dark plum, mulberry, smoked meat and attractive warm spices; the palate delivers layers of ripe red and black fruit, hints of oak and ample fine-grained tannins; firm, savoury and thoroughly appealing to conclude. Screwcap. 14% alc. **Rating** 94 To 2018 $38 BE

ŸŸŸŸŸ **Adelaide Hills Pinot Noir 2008 Rating** 93 To 2015 $45 BE

Shaw Vineyard Estate ★★★★★

34 Isabel Drive, Murrumbateman, NSW 2582 **Region** Canberra District
T (02) 6227 5827 **F** (02) 6227 5865 **www**.shawvineyards.com.au **Open** Wed–Sun & public hols 10–5
Winemaker Bryan Currie, Graeme Shaw **Est.** 1999 **Cases** 14 000 **Vyds** 33 ha
Graeme and Ann Shaw established their vineyard (cabernet sauvignon, merlot, shiraz, semillon and riesling) in 1998 on a 280-ha fine wool–producing property established in the mid-1800s known as Olleyville. It is one of the largest privately owned vineyard holdings in the Canberra area, and one of the few to produce 100% estate-grown wines. Their children are fully employed in the family business, Michael as viticulturist and Tanya as cellar door manager. The cellar door offers a wide range of local produce, and also handmade ceramics from Deruta in Italy. Fifty dollars from each case sale from the Laughter Series range is donated to Camp Quality. Exports to The Netherlands, Vietnam, China and Singapore.

ŸŸŸŸŸ **Isabella Reserve Canberra District Riesling 2009** Utterly delicious wine,
✪   flooded with lime juice fruit that lingers on the finish and aftertaste. Will live for as long as your patience allows, but a strong case for drinking it now, or tomorrow, or whenever. Isabella Anderson, born 1919, 'retired' from sheep growing in 2007 on property owned by family since 1850s. Screwcap. 11% alc. **Rating** 95 To 2024 $28

Premium Canberra Riesling 2009 Has lime, green apple and a touch of slate on the bouquet; there is a hint of ginger on the palate, highlighting the attractive citrus elements, and the acidity is fresh, direct and long; a very good expression of Canberra riesling. Screwcap. 12% alc. **Rating** 94 To 2020 $22 BE

ŸŸŸŸŸ **Laughter Series Canberra Semillon Sauvignon Blanc 2008** Something for
✪   everyone in this wine, which is fresh and lively, with lemon sherbet on the long palate. The $50 donation to Camp Quality for every case is remarkable. Screwcap. 13% alc. **Rating** 90 To 2011 $10.75

Premium Canberrra Cabernet Merlot 2008 Rating 90 To 2015 $22 BE

ŸŸŸŸ **Laughter Series Canberra Riesling 2009** Clean, crisp and fully expressive of
✪   the variety; dry minerally characters run through the palate. Screwcap. 12% alc. **Rating** 89 To 2017 $15

Premium Canberra Semillon Sauvignon Blanc 2009 Rating 89 To 2012 $22 BE

✪   **Laughter Series Canberra Cabernet Sauvignon 2008** Inky colour; an ultra-powerful, black-fruited palate, with strong tannins making it an ideal BBQ red. Screwcap. 14.5% alc. **Rating** 87 To 2016 $10.75

She-Oak Hill Vineyard ★★★★☆

82 Hope Street, South Yarra, Vic 3141 (postal) **Region** Heathcote
T (03) 9866 7890 **www**.sheoakhill.com.au **Open** Not
Winemaker Sanguine Estate (Mark Hunter) **Est.** 1995 **Cases** 400 **Vyds** 5 ha

This is the venture of Judith Firkin, Gordon Leckie and Julian Leckie, who between 1975 and '95 planted shiraz (4.25 ha) and chardonnay (0.75 ha). The vineyard is located on the southern and eastern slopes of She Oak Hill, 6 km north of Heathcote. It lies between Jasper Hill, Emily's Paddock and Mt Ida vineyards, and thus has the same type of porous, deep red Cambrian soil. The decision to opt for dry-grown vines has meant low yields. Lower than usual alcohol level is a feature of the wines, which have won a number of wine show medals.

🍷🍷🍷🍷🍷 **Reserve Heathcote Shiraz 2007** Here the savoury tannins are present from start to finish, but the greater density of the blackberry, spice and licorice fruit is sufficient to carry those tannins. Screwcap. 14.8% alc. **Rating** 94 **To** 2027 $40

🍷🍷🍷🍷½ ✪ **Estate Heathcote Shiraz 2008** Good depth of colour; a medium- to full-bodied shiraz with attractive plum and blackberry fruit; the handling of tannins and oak is very good, providing length and balance. From 15- and 35-year-old estate vines. Screwcap. 14.8% alc. **Rating** 93 **To** 2023 $25
Reserve Heathcote Shiraz 2008 **Rating** 91 **To** 2023 $40
Estate Heathcote Shiraz 2007 **Rating** 90 **To** 2020 $25

🍷🍷🍷🍷 ✪ **Heathcote Chardonnay 2008** A lot of viticulture and winemaking in a wine at this price; barrel ferment and 50% mlf in a ripe stone fruit spectrum; ready to drink now or later. Screwcap. 13% alc. **Rating** 89 **To** 2014 $20

Shelmerdine Vineyards ★★★★★

Merindoc Vineyard, Lancefield Road, Tooborac, Vic 3522 **Region** Heathcote
T (03) 5433 5188 **F** (03) 5433 5118 **www**.shelmerdine.com.au **Open** 7 days 10–5
Winemaker De Bortoli (Yarra Valley) **Est.** 1989 **Cases** 7000 **Vyds** 62 ha

Stephen Shelmerdine has been a major figure in the wine industry for well over 20 years, like his family (who founded Mitchelton Winery) before him, and has been honoured for his many services to the industry. The venture has vineyards spread over three sites: Lusatia Park in the Yarra Valley, and Merindoc Vineyard and Willoughby Bridge in the Heathcote region. Substantial quantities of the grapes produced are sold to others; a small amount of high-quality wine is contract-made. Exports to the UK, Singapore and Hong Kong.

🍷🍷🍷🍷🍷 ✪ **Yarra Valley Sauvignon Blanc 2009** Has more than a passing nod to France, the wild yeast and fermentation in old oak adding an extra layer of texture and complexity, without stifling the herbaceous lemon and gooseberry flavours. Screwcap. 12.5% alc. **Rating** 95 **To** 2012 $24

Yarra Valley Chardonnay 2008 Vibrantly juicy and compelling, with citrus of various types at the core of the wine, oak barely relevant; has purity and length, braced by natural acidity. Screwcap. 12.5% alc. **Rating** 94 **To** 2018 $30

✪ **Heathcote Shiraz 2008** Bright and focused bouquet of blue and red fruits, gently spicy and showing a mere suggestion of bay leaf; the palate is medium-bodied, focused, bright and incredibly fresh on the finish, with attractive gravelly tannins providing an appropriate framework for the polished fruit. Screwcap. 14.5% alc. **Rating** 94 $32 BE

🍷🍷🍷🍷½ **Merindoc Vineyard Heathcote Shiraz 2008** **Rating** 92 $65 BE
Heathcote Viognier 2009 **Rating** 91 **To** 2013 $29

✪ **Yarra Valley Rose 2009** Light pink; whole bunch-pressed, estate-grown, pinot noir is fermented in older oak barrels to produce a delicate rose with Old World savoury characters and good length. No expense spared. Screwcap. 13% alc. **Rating** 91 **To** 2011 $20

Heathcote Cabernet Sauvignon 2008 **Rating** 90 $32 BE

🍷🍷🍷🍷 **Heathcote Riesling 2009** **Rating** 89 **To** 2015 $24
Yarra Valley Pinot Noir 2008 **Rating** 89 **To** 2012 $34

Shenton Ridge ★★★

PO Box 37, Margaret River, WA 6285 **Region** Margaret River
T (08) 9726 1284 **F** (08) 9726 1575 **www**.shentonridge.com.au **Open** Not
Winemaker Dave Johnson **Est.** 2002 **Cases** 3500 **Vyds** 6.5 ha
The Catalano family purchased the Shenton Ridge property in the Jindong area of Margaret River in 2002. The choice lay between extracting the gravel-rich soils or planting a vineyard; the coin came down on the side of a vineyard, and vines (predominantly shiraz, chardonnay and merlot) were planted. Andrea Catalano is now the sole owner and manager of the vineyard.

ŸŸŸŸ **Margaret River Semillon Sauvignon Blanc 2009** A touch of CO_2 on pouring is part of a light but lively wine; lime/lemon with a distinct touch of fruit sweetness (not sugar sweetness). Needs a touch more drive. Screwcap. 13.5% alc. **Rating** 89 **To** 2012 $23.50
Margaret River Shiraz Merlot 2007 The somewhat eclectic blend works quite well, with juicy red fruit aromas and flavours supported by dusty tannins. Screwcap. 13.8% alc. **Rating** 89 **To** 2014 $23.50
Reserve Margaret River Shiraz 2007 Is light- to medium-bodied, the tannins on the back-palate somewhat taking away from the fresh red fruits of the mid-palate; garrulous back label doesn't add much. Screwcap. 14% alc. **Rating** 87 **To** 2013 $30

Shepherd's Hut ★★★★☆

PO Box 194, Darlington, WA 6070 **Region** Porongurup
T (08) 9299 6700 **F** (08) 9299 6703 **www**.shepherdshutwines.com **Open** Not
Winemaker Rob Diletti **Est.** 1996 **Cases** 1500 **Vyds** 18 ha
The shepherd's hut that appears on the wine label was one of four stone huts used in the 1850s to house shepherds tending large flocks of sheep. When WA pathologist Dr Michael Wishart (and family) purchased the property in 1996, the hut was in a state of extreme disrepair. It has since been restored, still featuring the honey-coloured Mount Barker stone. Riesling, chardonnay, sauvignon blanc, shiraz and cabernet sauvignon have been established. The business is now owned by son Philip and wife Cathy, who also run a large farm of mainly cattle. Most of the grapes are sold to other makers in the region.

ŸŸŸŸŸ
✪ **Porongurup Shiraz 2007** Strong crimson-purple; an immediately appealing wine both for its mouthfeel and flavour; spicy black fruits, fine but ripe tannins, and oak all come into play simultaneously. Follows surely in the footsteps of the gold medal-winning '05, demonstrating the instinctive skills of winemaker Rob Diletti. Screwcap. 14% alc. **Rating** 95 **To** 2020 $22

ŸŸŸŸ♀
✪ **Porongurup Sauvignon Blanc 2009** A vibrant and juicy style ranging through grass, citrus, gooseberry and tropical aromas and flavours, the length and balance good. Screwcap. 13.5% alc. **Rating** 91 **To** 2012 $21

Shingleback ★★★★☆

Cnr Main Road/Stump Hill Road, McLaren Vale, SA 5171 **Region** McLaren Vale
T (08) 8323 7388 **F** (08) 8323 7336 **www**.shingleback.com.au **Open** 7 days 10–5
Winemaker John Davey, Dan Hills **Est.** 1995 **Cases** 100 000 **Vyds** 90 ha
Shingleback has substantial vineyards in McLaren Vale, all of which are vinified for their own labels. Originally a specialist export business, now the wines are also available in Australia. Quality has risen greatly, as has total production. Which is the chicken, which is the egg? It doesn't really matter, is the best answer. As one might expect, the 2006 Jimmy Watson Trophy for its '05 D Block Cabernet Sauvignon was a major boost for sales. The rating reflects the '07 vintage on the one hand, the track record of Shingleback on the other. Exports to the US, Canada, The Netherlands, Germany, China and NZ.

ΨΨΨΨΨ **McLaren Vale Cabernet Sauvignon 2007** Retains bright colour; a complex wine with black fruits, tannins and quality oak seamlessly fused; notes of cedar and a hint of dark chocolate add to the flavour spectrum; especially praiseworthy are the ripe, soft tannins. Screwcap. 14% alc. **Rating** 93 **To** 2020 $24.95

✪ **Red Knot McLaren Vale Shiraz 2008** Good colour; neatly side-stepped the heatwave bullet; it is hard to say whether this is more regional than varietal, or vice versa. It probably doesn't matter; blackberry fruit and dark chocolate are supported by ripe tannins and a waft of oak. Screwcap. 14% alc. **Rating** 90 **To** 2016 $14.95
McLaren Vale Shiraz 2007 Bright hue; the expressive bouquet offers black fruits, mocha and dark chocolate, the medium- to full-bodied palate adding some cherry notes; does shorten slightly on the finish despite the tannins. Screwcap. 14.5% alc. **Rating** 90 **To** 2016 $24.95

ΨΨΨΨ **Haycutters McLaren Vale Shiraz Viognier 2007** While the bouquet is more
✪ regional than varietal, the viognier contribution can be seen on the palate; even here, however, the wine is as much about texture and structure as it is about fruit flavours. Screwcap. 14.5% alc. **Rating** 89 **To** 2013 $16.95
Black Bubbles McLaren Vale Sparkling Shiraz NV **Rating** 88 **To** 2013 $22.95

Shottesbrooke   ★★★★☆

Bagshaws Road, McLaren Flat, SA 5171 **Region** McLaren Vale
T (08) 8383 0002 **F** (08) 8383 0222 www.shottesbrooke.com.au
Open Mon–Fri 10–4.30, w'ends & public hols 11–5
Winemaker Nick Holmes, Hamish Maguire **Est.** 1984 **Cases** 12 000 **Vyds** 24 ha
For many years the full-time business of former Ryecroft winemaker Nick Holmes (now with stepson Hamish Maguire), drawing primarily on estate-grown grapes (cabernet sauvignon, shiraz, chardonnay and merlot) and sauvignon blanc purchased from the Adelaide Hills. The style of the wines has oscillated somewhat over recent years, some wines more elegant, others more complex and full-bodied. Exports to the UK, the US and other major markets.

ΨΨΨΨΨ **Eliza Reserve McLaren Vale Shiraz 2007** A monumental wine, with more of everything; chock full of dark fruit, bitter chocolate and lashes of new oak; the palate is rich, thick and unctuous, but pulls back from being heavy at the last; hedonistic pleasure for those with a penchant for big flavour. Screwcap. 14.5% alc. **Rating** 94 $37.95 BE

ΨΨΨΨ **McLaren Vale Merlot 2008** **Rating** 89 $19.95 BE

Sidewood Estate   ★★★★

2 Hunt Road, Hahndorf, SA 5245 (postal) **Region** Adelaide Hills
T (08) 8388 7084 **F** (08) 8388 1752 www.sidewood.com.au **Open** Not
Winemaker Natasha Mooney **Est.** 2000 **Cases** 8000 **Vyds** 49.76 ha
The establishment date of Sidewood Estate in fact marks the year when 32 ha of vineyard were planted by the Lloyd family of Coriole. Owen and Cassandra Inglis purchased the property in 2004, not only because of the vines, but also with an eye on the horse stables and horse training facilities. Owen has owned, ridden and raced horses since his early childhood, and both he and Cassandra were committed wine drinkers, which sealed the deal. They have since planted more sauvignon blanc, pinot gris, chardonnay (Dijon clone) and shiraz. Much care and attention has been given to the vineyard, and in 2008 Owen sold his Hong Kong business (he lived in Hong Kong and China for many years). It is not surprising that the principal export market is Asia. Exports to the UK, the US, Canada, Malaysia, Hong Kong, Singapore and Thailand.

ΨΨΨΨΨ **Adelaide Hills Shiraz 2007** Good hue; fine example of cool-grown shiraz;
✪ nuances of spice, pepper and licorice are woven through the well-textured black cherry fruit of the medium-bodied palate, silky tannins supporting the finish. Screwcap. 13.5% alc. **Rating** 93 **To** 2020 $22.50

Adelaide Hills Chardonnay 2009 An aromatic bouquet leads into an energetic palate, with flavours of white peach and grapefruit sustained by crisp acidity on the long finish. Prime unoaked style. Screwcap. 13% alc. **Rating** 91 **To** 2013 $21

Adelaide Hills Pinot Gris 2009 The wine has a touch of grainy minerality and sharper texture than most, suggesting barrel or lees work when there is in fact none; it adds appeal to the pear and apple fruit base. Screwcap. 14% alc. **Rating** 91 **To** 2011 $21

Adelaide Hills Sauvignon Blanc 2009 Pale crystal green; the bouquet is highly focused, with light passionfruit and lychee aromas, the crisp, minerally palate finishing with a touch of citrus. Screwcap. 13.5% alc. **Rating** 90 **To** 2011 $21

Sieber Road Wines   ★★★☆

Sieber Road, Tanunda, SA 5352 **Region** Barossa Valley
T (08) 8562 8038 **F** (08) 8562 8681 **www**.sieberwines.com **Open** 7 days 11–4
Winemaker Tony Carapetis **Est.** 1999 **Cases** 4000 **Vyds** 18 ha
Richard and Val Sieber are the third generation to run Redlands, the family property, traditionally a cropping/grazing farm. They have diversified into viticulture with shiraz (14 ha) the lion's share, the remainder viognier, grenache and mourvedre. Son Ben Sieber is a viticulturist. Exports to Canada.

♀♀♀♀♀ **Ernest Barossa Valley Shiraz 2008** Deep, opaque, crimson-purple; an extremely dense and deep palate, with ripe tannins and oak woven through the opulent fruit; needs more drive and life on the finish for higher points, but will repay cellaring. Screwcap. 15.2% alc. **Rating** 90 **To** 2020 $20

♀♀♀♀ **Barossa Valley Shiraz Viognier 2008 Rating** 89 **To** 2023 $18

Silk Hill   ★★★★☆

33 Deviot Road, Robigana, Tas 7275 **Region** Northern Tasmania
T (03) 6394 3383 **F** (03) 6394 3383 **Open** By appt
Winemaker Gavin Scott **Est.** 1989 **Cases** 250 **Vyds** 1.5 ha
Pharmacist Gavin Scott has been a weekend and holiday viticulturist for many years, having established the Glengarry Vineyard, which he sold, and then establishing the 1.5-ha Silk Hill (formerly Silkwood Vineyard) in 1989, planted exclusively to pinot noir.

♀♀♀♀♀ **Pinot Noir 2008** Deep colour; fragrant dark fruit aromas; the palate has very complex texture and structure, with sophisticated use of oak; impressive drive and length. Screwcap. 14% alc. **Rating** 94 **To** 2015 $27

♀♀♀♀ **The Supply Pinot Noir 2006 Rating** 89 **To** 2015 $40

Silkwood Wines   ★★★

5204/9649 Channybearup Road, Pemberton, WA 6260 **Region** Pemberton
T (08) 9776 1584 **F** (08) 9776 1540 **www**.silkwoodwines.com.au **Open** Fri–Mon 10–4
Winemaker Blair Meiklejohn **Est.** 1998 **Cases** 8000 **Vyds** 23.5 ha
Third-generation farmers Pam and John Allen returned from a short break running small businesses in Adelaide and Perth to purchase Silkwood in 1998. The vineyard is patrolled by a large flock of guinea fowl, eliminating most insect pests and reducing the use of chemicals. Under new ownership (2004), a modern winery was built in time for the '06 vintage, and in '05 Phillips Estate was purchased, lifting estate vineyard holdings to 23.5 ha. Plantings include shiraz (5.4 ha), cabernet sauvignon (4.3 ha), merlot (3.5 ha), sauvignon blanc (2.8 ha), chardonnay (2.5 ha), pinot noir, riesling (2 ha each) and zinfandel (1 ha). The new cellar door overlooks a large lake on the property.

♀♀♀♀ **Pemberton Sauvignon Blanc 2009** Exceedingly pale colour; a strong lychee aroma dominates the bouquet, the crisp palate adding some lemon/citrus; unusual wine. Screwcap. 12.5% alc. **Rating** 89 **To** 2011 $26

Pemberton Chardonnay 2008 Pale straw-green; distinctly light-bodied, but does have fresh nectarine fruit and good length; minimal oak influence. Screwcap. 14% alc. **Rating** 88 **To** 2013 $24

Pemberton Cabernet Merlot 2007 Bright red-purple; offers more ripe fruit characters than the other Silkwood reds, although they are unmistakably cool-grown, with some leafy/minty notes. Screwcap. 14% alc. **Rating** 87 **To** 2013 $24

Silver Wings Winemaking ★★★

28 Munster Terrace, North Melbourne, Vic 3051 **Region** Central Victoria Zone
T (03) 9329 8161 **F** (03) 9329 6879 **www**.silverwingswines.com **Open** By appt
Winemaker Keith Brien **Est.** 2003 **Cases** 1000 **Vyds** 4 ha
This is the venture of Keith Brien, formerly of Cleveland. After several hermit crab moves, he has (he hopes) made his final move to Mt Monument Winery, Romsey. As well as making wine at Mt Monument, he will be consultant winemaker for that label. He offers contract winemaking and export consulting, as well as making the Silver Wings wines from contract-grown grapes (3 ha of mourvedre and 1 ha of shiraz) coming from 50-year-old vines. The cellar door, which also runs wine education programs and social events, has now moved to North Melbourne. Exports to the US.

♥♥♥♥ **Vincenzo Old Vines Mourvedre Shiraz 2006** Stained Diam is a worry, although the colour is bright; this 60/40 blend comes from a single vineyard in the Shepparton area; while barely medium-bodied, it does have elegance and length to its black fruit flavours. 14% alc. **Rating** 89 **To** 2014 $27

Silverstream Wines ★★★☆

2365 Scotsdale Road, Denmark, WA 6333 **Region** Great Southern
T (08) 9840 9119 **F** (08) 9384 5657 **www**.silverstreamwines.com **Open** By appt
Winemaker Harewood Estate (James Kellie), Mt Shadforth Crush (Michael Garfund)
Est. 1999 **Cases** 2000 **Vyds** 8.95 ha
Tony and Felicity Ruse have almost 9 ha of chardonnay, merlot, cabernet franc, pinot noir, riesling and viognier in their vineyard 23 km from Denmark. The wines are contract-made, and after some hesitation, the Ruses decided their very pretty garden and orchard more than justified their recently opened cellar door, a decision supported by the quality on offer at very reasonable prices.

♥♥♥♥♥ **Cane Cut Denmark Chardonnay 2009** The period after the canes were cut
✪ and the grapes start to desiccate is critical; here, the timing was right, investing the wine with peachy sweetness and enough acidity for balance. Screwcap. 10.5% alc. **Rating** 90 **To** 2012 $15

♥♥♥♥ **Denmark Unwooded Chardonnay 2009** **Rating** 88 **To** 2012 $18
Four Vines White 2009 **Rating** 87 **To** 2012 $17

Silverwood Wines ★★★★☆

66 Bittern-Dromana Road, Balnarring, Vic 3926 **Region** Mornington Peninsula
T 0419 890 317 **F** (03) 8317 6642 **www**.silverwoodwines.com.au **Open** Not
Winemaker Paul Dennis, Phillip Kittle, Andrew Thomson **Est.** 1997 **Cases** 900 **Vyds** 3.2 ha
Paul and Denise Dennis were inspired to establish Silverwood after living in France for a year. They, with members of their family, did much of the establishment work on the vineyard (pinot noir, chardonnay and sauvignon blanc), which is meticulously maintained. All of the grapes are now used for Silverwood (in earlier years some were sold), reflecting the quality of the wines. Exports to Hong Kong and Singapore.

♥♥♥♥♥ **Estate Mornington Peninsula Pinot Noir 2008** Bright colour; an attractive array of red fruits and exotic spices are evident on the bouquet; the palate is fine, quite pure, and exhibits lovely focus and lively character; long, supple and even, there is a backbone of structure that belies the fleshy and generous fruit. Screwcap. 13.8% alc. **Rating** 94 **To** 2015 $36.50 BE

♥♥♥♥ **The Reserve Pinot Noir 2007** **Rating** 88 **To** 2011 $55 BE

🍇 Simon Whitlam & Co ★★★☆

PO Box 1108, Woollahra, NSW 1350 **Region** Hunter Valley Zone
T (02) 9007 5331 **F** (02) 9328 0499 **Open** Not
Winemaker Graeme Scott (Contract) **Est.** 1979 **Cases** 2000
My association with the owners of Simon Whitlam, Andrew and Hady Simon, Nicholas and
Judy Whitlam, and Grant Breen, dates back to the late 1970s, at which time I was a consultant
to the Simons' leading wine retail shop in Sydney, Camperdown Cellars. The association
continued for a time after I moved to Melbourne in '83, but ceased altogether in '87 when
Camperdown Cellars was sold, thereafter being merged with Arrowfield Wines. Simon
Whitlam was part of the deal, and it passed through a number of corporate owners until 20
years later, when the original partners regained control of the business. It is a virtual winery,
the grapes purchased and the wine contract-made. This reflects the combined marketing and
financial expertise of the partners. Exports to New Caledonia.

🍷🍷🍷🍷 **Hunter Valley Chardonnay 2008** The best in the current Simon Whitlam
✪ range, with bright colour, good varietal fruit expression (mainly stone fruit) on
both bouquet and palate, and subtle French oak all in balance. Screwcap. 12.5% alc.
Rating 90 **To** 2012 $20

🍷🍷🍷🍷 **Hunter Valley Sauvignon Blanc 2009** Rating 89 To 2011 $20
Hunter Valley Merlot 2008 Rating 89 To 2014 $20

Sinapius Vineyard ★★★★

4232 Bridport Road, Pipers Brook, Tas 7254 **Region** Northern Tasmania
T 0417 341 764 **www.**sinapius.com.au **Open** By appt
Winemaker Vaughn Dell, Linda Morice **Est.** 2005 **Cases** 600 **Vyds** 1.2 ha
When Vaughn Dell and Linda Morice purchased the former Golders Vineyard from Richard
Crabtree in 2005, they were only 24. Both were originally from Tasmania, but between '01
and '05 lived in various parts of Australia; Linda completed a university degree in occupational
therapy and Vaughn worked at wineries in the Hunter Valley, Yarra Valley (at Wedgetail Estate)
and Margaret River (Barwick Estates) before returning to Tasmania to undertake vintage
at Tamar Ridge in '05. The vineyard had 1 ha of mature pinot noir and 0.2 ha of mature
chardonnay. They have now also leased the Bellingham Vineyard, which has 1.2 ha of riesling
and 0.8 ha of chardonnay. Vaughn made the 2007 Pinot Noir and Chardonnay at Holm Oak
under the guidance of Rebecca Wilson; a small winery and cellar door opened in 2010.

🍷🍷🍷🍷 **Pipers Brook Pinot Noir 2007** Very light colour, but fresh crimson hue; a
fragrant and elegant wine that tells you (once again) never to judge a pinot on
the depth of its colour, for this is a delicious, if light-bodied, pinot with lovely
red cherry and strawberry fruit flavours and a long finish. Screwcap. 13.5% alc.
Rating 91 **To** 2014 $28

🍷🍷🍷🍷 **Bellingham Vineyard Riesling 2009** Rating 89 To 2017 $22
Pipers Brook Chardonnay 2008 Rating 89 $28

Sinclair of Scotsburn ★★★★

256 Wiggins Road, Scotsburn, Vic 3352 **Region** Ballarat
T 0419 885 717 **F** (03) 8699 7550 **www.**sinclairofscotsburn.com.au **Open** By appt
Winemaker Scott Ireland **Est.** 1997 **Cases** 260 **Vyds** 2 ha
David and Barbara Sinclair purchased their property in 2001. At that time 1.2 ha of
chardonnay and 0.8 ha of pinot noir had been planted, but had struggled, the pinot noir
yielding less than 0.25 tonnes in '02. With the aid of limited drip irrigation, cane pruning,
low crop levels and bird netting, limited quantities of high-quality chardonnay and pinot have
since been produced. Half the annual production is sold to Tomboy Hill, the other half made
for the Sinclair of Scotsburn label.

🍷🍷🍷🍷 **Wallijak Chardonnay 2007** Vivid green-gold; delicious mouthfilling white
peach, nectarine and a touch of grapefruit has an almost honeyed overtone, oak
merely a bit player. Screwcap. 13.5% alc. **Rating** 93 **To** 2014 $21

✪ **Manor House Pinot Noir 2007** Very bright and clear red-purple; well made; red berry and forest play tag with each other on bouquet and palate alike; the mouthfeel is good, the notably long palate with a foresty, spicy background to the small red fruits. Screwcap. 13.5% alc. **Rating** 92 **To** 2013 $21

Sinclair Wines ★★★★

1667 Graphite Road, Glenoran, WA 6258 **Region** South West Australia
T 0418 531 656 **F** (08) 9433 5489 **www.**sinclairwines.com.au **Open** By appt
Winemaker Darelle Sinclair, Simon Ding (Contract) **Est.** 1994 **Cases** 2800 **Vyds** 5 ha
Sinclair Wines is the child of Darelle Sinclair, a science teacher, wine educator and graduate viticulturist from CSU, and John Healy, a lawyer, traditional jazz musician and graduate wine marketing student of Adelaide University, Roseworthy campus. The estate plantings (cabernet sauvignon, sauvignon blanc, chardonnay, merlot, cabernet franc and shiraz) underpin high-quality wines at mouthwatering prices. Exports to Canada, The Netherlands and Japan.

▼▼▼▼♀ **Jezebel Cabernet Merlot 2009** Bright crimson; an immediately appealing
✪ wine, its blackcurrant, cassis and plum bouquet precisely replayed on the medium-bodied palate; here the texture and structure are an added feature, the tannins ripe, the French oak integrated. Screwcap. 14.5% alc. **Rating** 93 **To** 2024 $20

✪ **Giovanni Cabernet Sauvignon 2009** Bright, youthful hue; when tasted, not long in bottle and still coming together, curious given that Jezebel has already done so; the bright fruit and cedary oak will drive the wine on in the years ahead. Screwcap. 14.5% alc. **Rating** 90 **To** 2020 $20

▼▼▼▼ **Swallow Hill Sauvignon Blanc 2009** **Rating** 88 **To** 2011 $16

Sinclair's Gully ★★★★

Lot 3 Colonial Drive, Norton Summit, SA 5136 **Region** Adelaide Hills
T (08) 8390 1995 **www.**sinclairsgully.com **Open** W'ends & public hols 12–4 (Aug–June), Fri 5–9 (Nov–Mar), or by appt
Winemaker Contract **Est.** 1998 **Cases** 1000 **Vyds** 1 ha
Sue and Sean Delaney purchased their 10.5 ha property at Norton Summit in 1997. The property had a significant stand of remnant native vegetation, with a State Conservation Rating, and since acquiring the property much energy has been spent in restoring 8 ha of pristine bushland, home to 130 species of native plants and 66 species of native birds, some recorded as threatened or rare. It has been a DIY venture for the Delaneys (supported by family and friends) with Sue hand pruning the 0.4 ha each of chardonnay and sauvignon blanc planted in 1998. The adoption of biodynamic viticulture has coincided with numerous awards for the protection of the natural environment, and most recently, including eco-tourism; they operate the only eco-certified cellar door in the Adelaide Hills, and have won innumerable eco and general tourism awards. Sparkling wine disgorgement demonstrations are a particular attraction.

▼▼▼▼♀ **Late Disgorged Rubida 2006** Distinct partridge eye-pale bronze-pink; some aged chardonnay used as Reserve wine; strawberry and spice speak as loudly as chardonnay; very good mouthfeel; a 50/50 blend of Pinot Noir/Chardonnay. Diam. 13.5% alc. **Rating** 93 **To** 2015 $40

Singlefile Estate

PO Box 487, West Perth, WA 6872 **Region** Denmark
T 1300 885 807 **F** 1300 884 087 **www.**singlefileestate.com **Open** From Oct 2010 7 days 10–5 (summer), Mon–Fri 10–5
Winemaker Larry Cherubino, Brenden Smith, Coby Ladwig (contract) **Est.** 2007
Cases 3000 **Vyds** 5 ha
Reading the background to Singlefile Estate, and its marketing and mission statements, might lead one to think that this is a 50 000-case venture, not a 3000-case business, based on 2.5 ha of 24-year-old estate chardonnay and 1.25 ha each of merlot and shiraz (supplemented

by purchases of semillon, sauvignon blanc and cabernet sauvignon). Owners Phil and Viv Snowden took a circuitous path to the Denmark subregion, exiting Zimbabwe to join academia in South Africa (with a mining focus) before migrating to Australia in the late 1980s to start an Australian mining consultancy. When they sold the business in 2004 for just under $15 million, it had 200 employees and was one of the leaders in its field in WA. This is downsizing on a grand scale, although a cellar door is planned to open in October 2010. Exports to Japan.

ΨΨΨΨΨ Reserve Chardonnay 2009 At the opposite end of the spectrum to the standard, barrel fermentation and lees contact (plus mlf) immediately obvious on the bouquet; the fruit makes a major comeback on the long palate, with the intensity needed to provide balance. For release in 2011. Screwcap. 14% alc. **Rating** 94 **To** 2016 $45

ΨΨΨΨΨ Merlot 2008 Light, clear red-purple; a fragrant and spicy bouquet leads into
✪ a light-bodied palate that has wonderful zest and energy to the flavours, and a particularly long finish. Drink any time. Screwcap. 13% alc. **Rating** 93 **To** 2015 $22
Semillon Sauvignon Blanc 2009 Rating 91 **To** 2012 $24
Shiraz 2008 Rating 90 **To** 2015 $33

ΨΨΨΨ Chardonnay 2009 Rating 88 **To** 2012 $22

Sir Paz Estate   ★★★☆

384 George Street, Fitzroy, Vic 3065 (postal) **Region** Yarra Valley
T (03) 9417 3121 **F** (03) 9417 3981 **www**.sirpaz.com **Open** Not
Winemaker Gary Mills, John Zapris **Est.** 1997 **Cases** 4500 **Vyds** 22 ha
The Zapris family established Sir Paz Estate in 1997, planting just under 6 ha of shiraz; the first release of '01 scored an emphatic gold medal at the Victorian Wines Show '03 as the highest scored entry. The success led to the planting of additional merlot, chardonnay and sauvignon blanc. It is not hard to see the anagrammatic derivation of the name. Exports to the UK, Germany, Sri Lanka, Dubai and China.

ΨΨΨΨΨ Yarra Valley Shiraz 2008 Amazing, impenetrable purple-black colour; the bouquet and palate continue in the same vein, all the more remarkable given that the wine comes from the red soils of the southern Yarra Valley; picked late April, and it may be that reverse osmosis was used to reduce the alcohol to a manageable level. Intriguing. Diam. 14.5% alc. **Rating** 90 **To** 2018 $35

ΨΨΨΨ Yarra Valley Merlot 2008 Rating 87 **To** 2015 $32

Sirromet Wines   ★★★★☆

850–938 Mount Cotton Road, Mount Cotton, Qld 4165 **Region** Queensland Coastal
T (07) 3206 2999 **F** (07) 3206 0900 **www**.sirromet.com **Open** 7 days 10–4.30
Winemaker Adam Chapman, Velten Tiemann **Est.** 1998 **Cases** 50 000 **Vyds** 145.9 ha
This was an unambiguously ambitious venture, which has succeeded in its aim of creating Qld's premier winery. The founding Morris family retained a leading architect to design the striking state-of-the-art winery; the state's foremost viticultural consultant to plant three major vineyards (in the Granite Belt), which total almost 150 ha; and the most skilled winemaker practising in Qld, Adam Chapman, to make the wine. It has a 200-seat restaurant, a wine club offering all sorts of benefits to its members, and is firmly aimed at the domestic and international tourist market, taking advantage of its situation, halfway between Brisbane and the Gold Coast. Alas, the repercussions of the GFC have led to a decision to mothball its Granite Belt vineyards; the restaurant will remain open, and has ample stocks of wines. Exports to South Korea, Papua New Guinea, Hong Kong, China and Japan.

ΨΨΨΨΨ St Jude's Road Grand Reserve Cabernet Sauvignon 2007 Good but not exceptional colour; a fragrant cedar/cigar box/spice/cassis bouquet, then a very rich palate flooded with sweet cassis, blackcurrant and dark chocolate; tannins soft, the oak integrated; some confection characters, but they work well. Numbered bottles, impressive price. Screwcap. 13.5% alc. **Rating** 95 **To** 2020 $300

🍷🍷🍷🍷🍷 Night Sky Premium Reserve Granite Belt Shiraz Viognier 2007 Rating 93
To 2017 $50
Seven Scenes Granite Belt Merlot 2007 Rating 90 To 2015 $27

🍷🍷🍷🍷 820 Above Verdelho 2008 Rating 88 To 2011 $17

Sittella Wines ★★★★
100 Barrett Street, Herne Hill, WA 6056 **Region** Swan Valley
T (08) 9296 2600 **F** (08) 9296 0237 **www.**sittella.com.au **Open** Tues–Sun &
public hols 11–5
Winemaker Matthew Bowness **Est.** 1998 **Cases** 10 000 **Vyds** 9 ha
Perth couple Simon and Maaike Berns acquired a 7-ha block (with 5 ha of vines) at Herne
Hill, making the first wine in 1998 and opening a most attractive cellar door facility later in
the year. They also own the Wildberry Springs Estate vineyard in the Margaret River region.
Consistent and significant wine show success has brought well-deserved recognition for
the wines.

🍷🍷🍷🍷🍷 Reserve Frankland River Shiraz 2007 Strong red-purple; the aromatic
bouquet has attractive plum and blackberry fruit augmented by French oak, the
medium-bodied palate with juicy berry fruits and more French oak, a little more
than ideal. Screwcap. 14.5% alc. **Rating** 90 **To** 2016 $19.95
Show Reserve Liqueur Verdelho NV Orange-brown; has some cask-
developed complexity, with abundant all-up flavour; honey and biscuits in a
smooth, seductive package. Diam. 18.5% alc. **Rating** 90 **To** 2011 $45

Six Gates ★★★☆
Lot 294 Barossa Valley Highway, Lyndoch, SA 5351 (postal) **Region** Barossa Valley
T 0422 030 303 **F** (08) 8333 3103 **www.**6gates.com.au **Open** Not
Winemaker Peter Gajewski (Contract) **Est.** 1998 **Cases** 900 **Vyds** 12 ha
The name Six Gates originates from the six entries to the ancient city of Shiraz, and it is thus
appropriate that this organically managed vineyard should be predominantly planted to that
variety (8 ha; 4 ha of cabernet sauvignon make up the balance). While there is a long history
of viticulture on the property, the present plantings were established in 1998 on highly suitable
soil, with 25 cm of loam on 60 cm of red clay over well-decayed limestone, thus providing
both good drainage and water holding capacity. Every one of the 18 000 vines is pruned by
the vineyard manager, Bruce Wutke, who has spent a long time as a grapegrower. Exports
to China.

🍷🍷🍷🍷🍷 The Majnun Barossa Valley Shiraz 2006 Has a pronounced, lifted bouquet,
with plenty of sweet fruit and fruitcake aromas on offer; the palate is quite
juicy, and the tannins ample, with a little black olive savoury edge to the finish.
Screwcap. 15.8% alc. **Rating** 90 **To** 2016 $23 BE

🍷🍷🍷🍷 The Majnun Barossa Valley Shiraz 2008 Rating 89 To 2018 $27

Skillogalee ★★★★★
Trevarrick Road, Sevenhill via Clare, SA 5453 **Region** Clare Valley
T (08) 8843 4311 **F** (08) 8843 4343 **www.**skillogalee.com.au **Open** 7 days 10–5
Winemaker Dan Palmer **Est.** 1970 **Cases** 15 000 **Vyds** 50.3 ha
David and Diana Palmer purchased the small hillside stone winery from the George family
at the end of the 1980s and have fully capitalised on the exceptional fruit quality of the
Skillogalee vineyards. All the wines are generous and full-flavoured, particularly the reds. In
2002 the Palmers purchased next-door neighbour Waninga Vineyards, with 30 ha of 30-year-
old vines, allowing an increase in production without any change in quality or style. Exports
to the UK, Canada, Switzerland, Hong Kong, Malaysia, Singapore and NZ.

🍷🍷🍷🍷🍷
❂
Basket Pressed Clare Valley Shiraz 2006 First signs of colour development; two years in oak has softened the wine without in any way diminishing its length, nor the persistence of its earthy, black fruit flavours; excellent finish and aftertaste. Screwcap. 14.5% alc. **Rating** 95 **To** 2021 $25.50

❂
Clare Valley Gewurztraminer 2009 There are distinct overtones of Alsace here, the bouquet with strong lychee and pear aromas, the palate texture luscious and rich; a very long finish, first quite fruit sweet, then dry on the aftertaste. Screwcap. 14% alc. **Rating** 94 **To** 2013 $22.50

🍷🍷🍷🍷🍸
❂
Single Vineyard Clare Valley Riesling 2009 Green-straw; citrus blossom aromas lead into a lively, fresh palate with lime/lemon juice flavours, backed by good acidity. Medium-term development. Screwcap. 13% alc. **Rating** 93 **To** 2015 $20

🍷🍷🍷🍷
Take Two Clare Valley Shiraz Cabernet 2006 Rating 87 **To** 2014 $22.50 BE

Skimstone
★★★★☆

1307 Castlereagh Highway, Apple Tree Flat, Mudgee, NSW 2850 **Region** Mudgee
T (02) 6373 1220 **F** (02) 6373 1321 **www**.skimstone.com.au **Open** Thurs–Mon 10–4
Winemaker Joshua Clementson **Est.** 2009 **Cases** 455 **Vyds** 15 ha
This is a joint venture between Josh and Kate Clementson and Michael and Anne-Marie Horton; the Clementsons live on and run the estate and cellar door. Josh had previously worked for Orlando (one year), then Peter Logan (five years), and has been vineyard manager at Huntington Estate for the past three vintages. The partners were thus able to assess the potential of the rundown Apple Tree Flat vineyard in 2007, and have since worked hard to bring the vineyard back to full health. They have particular faith in sangiovese and barbera (5 ha) as varieties for the future. All the fruit is sold under contract, but they keep small amounts of grapes to make the Skimstone wines.

🍷🍷🍷🍷🍷
Mudgee Sangiovese 2009 Clear, light crimson; an elegant and lively wine, exuding cherry/sour cherry aromas and flavours with no hint of green tannins; simply delicious, and even better, I suspect, with Italian food. Top vintage in Mudgee. Screwcap. 12.5% alc. **Rating** 94 **To** 2013 $28

🍷🍷🍷🍸
Mudgee Sangiovese Rose 2009 Rating 90 **To** 2011 $22

🍷🍷🍷🍷
Mudgee Chardonnay 2009 Rating 89 **To** 2012 $22
Mudgee Barbera 2009 Rating 88 **To** 2014 $28

Smallfry Wines
★★★★★

13 Murray Street, Angaston, SA 5353 **Region** Barossa Valley
T (08) 8564 2182 **F** (08) 8564 2182 **www**.smallfrywines.com.au
Open By appt (tel 0412 153 243)
Winemaker Wayne Ahrens, Colin Forbes **Est.** 2005 **Cases** 1800 **Vyds** 27 ha
The engagingly named Smallfry Wines is the venture of Wayne Ahrens and partner Suzi Hilder. Wayne comes from a fifth-generation Barossa family; Suzi is the daughter of well-known Upper Hunter viticulturist Richard Hilder and wife Del, partners in Pyramid Hill Wines. Both have degrees from CSU, and both have extensive experience – Suzi as a senior viticulturist for Foster's, and Wayne's track record includes seven vintages as a cellar hand at Orlando Wyndham and other smaller Barossa wineries. They have a 10-ha vineyard in the Eden Valley (led by cabernet sauvignon and riesling), and a long-established 17-ha vineyard in the Vine Vale subregion of the Barossa Valley has no less than 16 varieties, led by shiraz, grenache, semillon, mourvedre, cabernet sauvignon and riesling. Most of the grapes are sold to other Barossa wineries, enough retained from each vineyard to meet Smallfry Wines' needs.

🍷🍷🍷🍷🍷
❂
Eden Valley Riesling 2009 Vibrant, lively and juicy lime flavour drives through the long and intensely focused palate, mineral and citrus coming together on the bracing but balanced acidity of the finish. Screwcap. 11.5% alc. **Rating** 95 **To** 2019 $18

✪ **Barossa Riesling 2009** A delicately fashioned riesling, with deliberately retained sweetness filling the mouth with lovely lime juice fruit flavours. One of a rapidly growing band; 110 cases made. Screwcap. 11% alc. **Rating** 94 **To** 2013 $18

♟♟♟♟♀ **Barossa Semillon Sauvignon Blanc 2009** Pale straw; a bright and zesty
✪ bouquet, then a crunchy, crisp palate with grass and citrus flavours. An unimaginable style for the Barossa even five years ago, let alone 10. Screwcap. 10.5% alc. **Rating** 93 **To** 2012 $15

✪ **Barossa Semillon 2009** Pale straw; fragrant lemon blossom aromas, then a crisp and lively palate with a mix of lemon and grass notes; modern style of Barossa Valley semillon that works very well. Screwcap. 11.5% alc. **Rating** 92 **To** 2016 $18
Barossa Valley Red Blend 2009 **Rating** 92 **To** 2015 $28

✪ **Eden Valley Cabernet Grenache Rose 2009** Bright pink; fresh and crisp, bordering firm, with redcurrant and a touch of Turkish delight flavours; dry finish; 120 cases made. Screwcap. 11.8% alc. **Rating** 91 **To** 2010 $18
Barossa Valley Grenache 2009 **Rating** 90 **To** 2014 $28

✪ **Barossa Late Harvest Riesling 2008** Cordon-cut before the heatwave, and hurriedly picked during its zenith, successfully avoiding excess desiccation. Flavoursome, but a little hard on the finish. Screwcap. 12.5% alc. **Rating** 90 **To** 2011 $15

♟♟♟♟ **Barossa Shiraz 2008** **Rating** 89 **To** 2017 $28
Tempranillo Garnacha Joven 2009 **Rating** 89 **To** 2012 $20

Smidge Wines   ★★★★☆

62 Austral Terrace, Malvern, SA 5061 (postal) **Region** South Eastern Australia
T (08) 8272 0369 **F** (08) 8272 8491 **www.**smidgewines.com **Open** Not
Winemaker Matt Wenk **Est.** 2004 **Cases** 1000
Matt Wenk and Trish Callaghan have many things in common: joint ownership of Smidge Wines, marriage, and their real day jobs. Matt has a distinguished record as a Flying Winemaker and, in Australia, working with Tim Knappstein and then Peter Leske at Nepenthe Wines. These days he is the winemaker for Two Hands Wines (and Sandow's End). Trish holds a senior position in one of the world's largest IT services companies, and was a finalist in the Australian Young Business Woman of the Year '03. The elegantly labelled wines are Le Grenouille (The Frog) Adelaide Hills Merlot, from a small vineyard in Verdun, and The Tardy Langhorne Creek Zinfandel, which (and I quote) 'is named The Tardy in honour of Matt's reputation for timekeeping (or lack thereof)'. Exports to the UK and the US.

♟♟♟♟♟ **S Smitch Barossa Valley Shiraz 2007** Deeper colour and slightly more purple hue than Adamo; here the wine is full-bodied, awash with layers of dark berry and licorice flavours; the cork presumably signifies the requirements of export markets. 15.5% alc. **Rating** 94 **To** 2020 $65

♟♟♟♟♀ **Houdini Adelaide Hills Sauvignon Blanc 2009** Bright straw-green; a
✪ complex, indeed compelling, Adelaide Hills sauvignon blanc, the textural play coming as much from edgy, yet tropical fruit flavours as more normal origins. Screwcap. 13.5% alc. **Rating** 93 **To** 2011 $16
Adamo Barossa Valley Shiraz 2007 **Rating** 90 **To** 2017 $26

Smith & Hooper   ★★★★

Caves Edward Road, Naracoorte, SA 5271 **Region** Wrattonbully
T (08) 8762 0622 **F** (08) 8762 0514 **www.**smithandhooper.com **Open** By appt
Winemaker Peter Gambetta **Est.** 1994 **Cases** 13 000 **Vyds** 82 ha
On one view of the matter, Smith & Hooper is simply one of many brands within various of the Hill Smith family financial/corporate structures. However, it is estate-based, with cabernet sauvignon (21 ha) and merlot (13 ha) planted on the Hooper Vineyard in 1994, and cabernet sauvignon (15 ha) and merlot (9 ha) planted on the Smith Vineyard in '98. Spread across both vineyards are 15 ha of shiraz and 9 ha of trial varieties. Exports to all major markets.

ŢŢŢŢŢ **Wrattonbully Cabernet Sauvignon Merlot 2008** Deep colour; the blend
✪   is synergistic, although this is no lollipop wine; rather blackcurrant and earth
          are sheathed by fine tannins and neatly judged oak. Cork. 14% alc. **Rating** 92
          To 2015 $17.95
✪   **Wrattonbully Merlot 2008** A strongly savoury, strongly varietal wine with no
          attempt whatsoever to sweeten it with oak; some years have been outstanding, this
          not quite so, although good. The perverse adherence to cork suggests the US is a
          major market. Cork. 13.5% alc. **Rating** 90 To 2014 $17.95

Smiths Vineyard   ★★★★★

27 Croom Lane, Beechworth, Vic 3747 **Region** Beechworth
T 0412 475 328 **F** (03) 5728 1603 **www**.smithsvineyard.com.au **Open** W'ends &
public hols 10–5, or by appt
Winemaker Will Flamsteed **Est.** 1978 **Cases** 1000 **Vyds** 3.3 ha
Pete and Di Smith established the first vineyard in Beechworth in 1978, with the encouragement of John Brown Jr of Brown Brothers. In 2003 the winery and vineyard were taken over
by their daughter Sarah and husband Will Flamsteed. At 550 m, the vineyard is predominantly
chardonnay (1.8 ha), with some cabernet sauvignon (1 ha) and merlot (0.5 ha), which make
the estate wines. Will and Sarah made their first Beechworth Shiraz in 2006. The Heathcote
Shiraz was a response to the smoke taint and frost damage in 2007.

ŢŢŢŢŢ **Beechworth Chardonnay 2008** Pale straw-green; a tight mineral backbone
          runs through the wine, which is as much about texture as fruit flavour, not
          unlike that of Giaconda; some citrus elements to the subtle stone fruit is the fruit
          signature. Screwcap. 13.9% alc. **Rating** 94 To 2015 $40
          310 Beechworth Shiraz 2008 Light red-purple; a light- to medium-bodied
          shiraz highlighted by its multi-spice overtones to the core of black cherry and plum
          fruit; over 18 months in oak has softened the tannins but not imperilled the fruit
          on the long palate; has great finesse. Screwcap. 14.2% alc. **Rating** 94 To 2016 $40
✪   **Beechworth Merlot Cabernet 2008** Well-made wine, the blend synergistic;
          plum, red berry and spice flavours from the merlot are given structural support
          from the darker flavours of the cabernet; a smooth and supple medium-bodied
          palate is the result. Screwcap. 14.4% alc. **Rating** 94 To 2018 $25

Snobs Creek Wines   ★★★★☆

486 Goulburn Valley Highway, via Alexandra, Vic 3714 **Region** Upper Goulburn
T (03) 9596 3043 **F** (03) 9596 3043 **www**.snobscreekvineyard.com.au **Open** W'ends 11–5
Winemaker Marcus Gillon **Est.** 1996 **Cases** 4000 **Vyds** 16 ha
The vineyard is situated where Snobs Creek joins the Goulburn River, 5 km below the Lake
Eildon wall. Originally planted in 1996, the vineyard has recently been increased to 16 ha. The
varieties grown are pinot gris, pinot noir, shiraz, viognier, chardonnay, merlot and dolcetto;
all manage to produce no more then 7.4 tonnes per hectare. Is described as a cool-climate
vineyard in a landscaped environment. Exports to Europe, Antartica (any other contenders in
this market?) and Vietnam.

ŢŢŢŢŢ **Reserve Shiraz 2006** Slightly denser, more purple hue than the varietal; the
          fragrant bouquet adds cigar box to the cedar and spicy black fruits, the palate still
          medium-bodied, but more intense and precise. A very impressive duo. Screwcap.
          13% alc. **Rating** 95 To 2021 $40

ŢŢŢŢŢ **Shiraz 2006** Good hue; a potent array of spice, black fruits and cedary oak on the
✪   bouquet, then a lively, spicy medium-bodied palate with good line, balance and
          length. Screwcap. 13% alc. **Rating** 92 To 2016 $20
          Reserve Pinot Noir 2005 Rating 90 To 2014 $35

ŢŢŢŢ   **Lightly Wooded Chardonnay 2008 Rating** 89 To 2013 $18

✪   RV Classic Dry White 2008 A blend of Roussanne (70%)/Viognier (30%),
     hinted at more by the RV than Classic Dry White. Chalky/lemony crispness of
     the roussanne is the driver, fleshed out a little by the viognier. Screwcap. 14.4% alc.
     Rating 89 To 2013 $16
     Reserve Chardonnay 2005 Rating 88 To 2010 $30
     Dolcetto Syrah 2008 Rating 88 To 2015 $18

Somerled   ★★★★☆

7 Heath Road, Crafers, SA 5152 (postal) **Region** McLaren Vale
T (08) 8339 2617 **F** (08) 8339 2617 **www.**somerled.com.au **Open** Not
Winemaker Rob Moody **Est.** 2001 **Cases** 1800
This is the venture of Robin and Heather Moody, and daughters Emma and Lucinda. The
quietly spoken Robin (with a degree in oenology) joined Penfolds in 1969, and remained
with Penfolds/Southcorp until 2001. This is a classic negociant business: it started with
McLaren Vale Shiraz, but now includes Steeplechase Chardonnay, Steeplechase Sauvignon
Blanc, Picnic Races Red and Somerled Sparkling Pinot Noir. The wines are selected by
Robin from parcels of young wine, during or after fermentation and are blended and matured
at Boar's Rock Winery at McLaren Vale. The name comes from the bay gelding that Robin's
grandfather raced to victory in the amateur steeplechase at the Oakbank Picnic Races in
1908, and which took its name from the Scottish king who defeated the Vikings in 1156.
The other names, obviously enough, follow in the footsteps of Somerled. Exports to Hong
Kong and China.

🍷🍷🍷🍷🍷 Steeplechase Adelaide Hills Sauvignon Blanc 2009 Bright straw-green; the
✪   strikingly fragrant bouquet has citrus, passionfruit and gooseberry all on display,
           the lively palate providing a replay with a piercing and crisp finish. Screwcap.
           12.5% alc. **Rating** 94 **To** 2011 $18

🍷🍷🍷🍷🍷 Steeplechase Adelaide Hills Chardonnay 2009 The impact of very early
✪   picking has been offset by mlf to soften the acidity, and partial barrel fermentation
           likewise. A good example of the new direction of regional chardonnays. Screwcap.
           12.5% alc. **Rating** 91 **To** 2015 $18

Somerset Hill Wines   ★★★☆

540 McLeod Road, Denmark, WA 6333 **Region** Denmark
T (08) 9840 9388 **F** (08) 9840 9394 **www.**somersethillwines.com.au
Open 7 days 11–5 summer, 11–4 winter
Winemaker Contract **Est.** 1995 **Cases** 2000 **Vyds** 10.25 ha
Graham Upson commenced planting pinot noir, chardonnay, semillon, merlot, pinot meunier
and sauvignon blanc in 1995 on one of the coolest and latest-ripening sites in WA. The
limestone cellar door area has sweeping views out over the ocean and to the Stirling Ranges,
and also sells Belgian chocolates. Graham makes the red wines, James Kellie (Harewood Estate)
the whites. Exports to the UK, Denmark, Russia, Poland and Canada.

🍷🍷🍷🍷🍷 Reserve Semillon 2000 Bright green-gold; toasty/lemony/honey aromas and
           flavours are backed by good acidity, but the wine does shorten a little on the finish.
           Impressive nine-year-old wine. Cork. 12% alc. **Rating** 91 **To** 2014 $21

Songlines Estates   ★★★★☆

PO Box 221, Cessnock, NSW 2325 **Region** Hunter Valley
T (02) 4932 0054 **F** (02) 4998 7058 **www.**songlinesestates.com **Open** By appt
Winemaker David Fatches, John Duval **Est.** 2002 **Cases** 7000 **Vyds** 29 ha
This is another of the multinational, multi-talented boutique wine operations springing up
like mushrooms after autumn rain. The English end is represented by Martin Krajewski (who
also owns Chateau de Sours in Bordeaux) and the Australian by David Fatches and John Duval
as winemakers. While the red wines are made from McLaren Vale grapes, Songlines is from
110-year-old vines, and the wines are in fact made in the Hunter Valley winery, which takes

advantage of 3 ha each of chardonnay and semillon to produce estate-based varietal releases. Songlines heads the three-tiered range of wines, followed by Bylines and then Leylines. Exports to the UK, Canada, France and Hong Kong.

ŸŸŸŸŸ Bylines Hunter Valley Semillon 2009 Pale colour; tightly wound lemon sherbet with a mere suggestion of straw; the palate is linear, focused and completely unevolved; will cellar gracefully over time. Screwcap. 11% alc. **Rating** 94 **To** 2025 $35 BE

ŸŸŸŸŸ Bylines Hunter Valley Chardonnay 2009 Rating 91 **To** 2015 $35 BE

Sons & Brothers Vineyard ★★★★

PO Box 978, Orange, NSW 2800 **Region** Orange
T (02) 6366 5117 **www.**sonsandbrothers.com.au **Open** Not
Winemaker Chris Bourke **Est.** 1978 **Cases** 250 **Vyds** 2 ha
Chris and Kathryn Bourke do not pull their punches when they say, 'Our vineyard has had a checkered history because in 1978 we were trying to establish ourselves in a non-existent wine region with no local knowledge and limited personal knowledge of grapegrowing and winemaking. It took us about 15 years of hit and miss before we started producing regular supplies of appropriate grape varieties at appropriate ripeness levels for sales to other NSW wineries.' In 2001 their vineyard produced their first commercial vintage of Cabernet Shiraz (a 70%/30% blend). They mature the wine for a number of years before release, and use a unique closure involving a stainless-steel crown cap, an oxygen barrier foil and a small plastic bidule, a variant of champagne closures used during tirage.

ŸŸŸŸŸ Cabernet Shiraz 2007 Very attractive spice and black pepper notes help build
✪ the varietal components on the long, lingering palate, with no false notes on the finish and aftertaste. Cabernet Sauvignon (85%)/Shiraz (10%)/Savagnin (5%). Crown seal. 13.5% alc. **Rating** 93 **To** 2017 $25

Sons of Eden ★★★★★

Penrice Road, Angaston, SA 5353 **Region** Barossa Valley
T (08) 8564 2363 **F** (08) 8564 3823 **www.**sonsofeden.com **Open** By appt
Winemaker Corey Ryan, Simon Cowham **Est.** 2000 **Cases** 5000 **Vyds** 52 ha
Sons of Eden is the venture of winemaker Corey Ryan and viticulturist Simon Cowham, who both learnt and refined their skills in the vineyards and cellars of Eden Valley. Corey is a trained oenologist with over 20 vintages under his belt, having cut his teeth as a winemaker at Henschke. Thereafter he worked for Rouge Homme and Penfolds in Coonawarra, backed up with winemaking stints in the Rhône Valley, and in 2002 took the opportunity to work in NZ, heading up the winemaking team for Villa Maria Estates (he remains a consultant to Villa Maria). In 2007 he won the Institute of Masters of Wine scholarship, awarded to the student with the highest marks across the theory and practical sections of wine assessment. Simon has a similarly international career covering such diverse organisations as Oddbins, UK and the Winemakers' Federation of Australia. Switching from the business side to grapegrowing when he qualified as a viticulturist, he worked for Yalumba as technical manager of the Heggies and Pewsey Vale vineyards. With this background, it comes as no surprise to find the estate-grown wines are of outstanding quality. Exports to the US, Hong Kong, Singapore, Malaysia and Philippines.

ŸŸŸŸŸ Remus Old Vine Eden Valley Shiraz 2006 Deep purple-crimson; a great example of an ultra-powerful, full-bodied shiraz that manages to retain some elegance; spicy black fruits with a cedary backdrop from 22 months in French oak provide a coherent play from the bouquet right through to the long finish. Cork. 14.5% alc. **Rating** 96 **To** 2026 $52

✪ **Kennedy Barossa Valley Grenache Shiraz Mourvedre 2007** Good hue; it is far from usual for a Barossa Valley blend of these varieties to yield a wine with as much stature as this, nor for the flavours to veer as much into black fruits as red; a case of having one's cake and eating it, for it has the glossy, supple texture expected of the blend. Screwcap. 14.5% alc. **Rating** 96 **To** 2017 $22

Romulus Old Vine Barossa Valley Shiraz 2006 Similar colour to Remus; once again, no-holds-barred, full-bodied shiraz; here 20 months in American oak and grapes from the Barossa result in a robust, fleshy, vanilla-accented wine; good texture, structure and balance. Cork. 14.5% alc. **Rating** 95 **To** 2026 $52

❂ **Freya Eden Valley Riesling 2009** The purity of the wine reflects hand-picked, whole bunch-pressed grapes from a single vineyard, then cool fermented; comes into full focus on the soaring finish and lingering aftertaste. Screwcap. 12% alc. **Rating** 94 **To** 2020 $22

♟♟♟♟♙ **Zephyrus Barossa Valley Shiraz Viognier 2006 Rating** 93 **To** 2020 $32
Zephyrus Barossa Valley Shiraz Viognier 2007 Rating 92 **To** 2014 $32

Sorby Adams Wines ★★★★☆

Lot 18, Gawler Park Road, Angaston, SA 5353 **Region** Eden Valley
T (08) 8564 2741 **F** (08) 8564 2437 **www.**sorbyadamswines.com **Open** At Taste Eden Valley, Angaston
Winemaker Simon Adams **Est.** 2004 **Cases** 15 000 **Vyds** 11.5 ha
Simon Adams and wife Helen purchased a 3.2-ha vineyard in 1996, which had been planted by Pastor Franz Julius Lehmann (none other than Peter Lehmann's father) in 1932. Peter Lehmann always referred to it as 'Dad's Block'. They have added 0.25 ha of viognier, which, as one might expect, is used in a shiraz viognier blend. Most recent plantings are of shiraz (2.5 ha), riesling (1.7 ha), cabernet sauvignon (0.7 ha) and traminer (1.5 ha). Nonetheless, the top wines, The Family Shiraz and The Thing Shiraz, need no assistance from viognier. Only six barrels of The Thing are made each year, using the best grapes from Dad's Block. The name Sorby Adams has overtones of a chameleon: it comes from a female ancestor of long-serving Yalumba winemaker Simon Adams, whose full name is Simon David Sorby Adams. A recent development has seen Simon venturing to WA and NZ to take advantage of surpluses. Exports to Hong Kong, China and NZ.

♟♟♟♟♟ **The Thing Eden Valley Shiraz 2005** Good colour; blackberry and plum aromas, along with a touch of oak, lead into a palate with great drive and focus; perfectly ripened fruit flavours from vines more than 70 years old; extract and oak impeccable. Screwcap. 14% alc. **Rating** 95 **To** 2025 $55

♟♟♟♟♙ **The Family Margaret River Barossa Cabernet Shiraz 2008** Crimson-
❂ purple; another intriguing blend that works very well; for those who are on the ball, grape and wine surpluses provide exciting opportunities, as this delicious, vibrant, fresh red and black berry wine demonstrates. Screwcap. 14% alc. **Rating** 92 **To** 2016 $22

❂ **The Family Pemberton Marlborough Semillon Sauvignon Blanc 2009** Presumably the semillon is from Pemberton; the complicated blend is seamless, fresh and elegant, justifying the lateral thinking. Screwcap. 12% alc. **Rating** 91 **To** 2011 $18

♟♟♟♟ **Morticia Sparkling Shiraz NV Rating** 89 **To** 2011 $22
The Canon Barossa Shiraz 2006 Rating 88 **To** 2014 $22

Sorrenberg ★★★★★

Alma Road, Beechworth, Vic 3747 **Region** Beechworth
T (03) 5728 2278 **F** (03) 5728 2278 **www.**sorrenberg.com **Open** By appt
Winemaker Barry and Jan Morey **Est.** 1986 **Cases** 1600 **Vyds** 4.8 ha
Barry and Jan Morey keep a low profile, but the wines from their vineyard at Beechworth have a cult following not far removed from that of Giaconda; chardonnay, sauvignon blanc, semillon, pinot noir, merlot, cabernet franc, cabernet sauvignon and gamay are the principal varieties planted on the north-facing, granitic slopes. Gamay and Chardonnay are the winery specialities. Exports to Japan.

ŸŸŸŸŸ Sauvignon Blanc Semillon 2009 Vibrant mid–gold hue; a rich, complex bouquet of ripe grapefruit, guava and seasoned with cinnamon thanks to the fine oak; the palate shows plenty of weight and depth of personality, with the refreshing acidity providing contrast to the overall power of the wine; a unique style on the Australian wine landscape. Cork. 13.6% alc. **Rating** 94 **To** 2014 $38 BE

Chardonnay 2008 Quite deep, yet bright colour; the winemaker has left nothing on the table with this wine, as it is rich, complex, over the top and still maintains interest and balance; straw, fig, yellow peach, grilled nuts and cinnamon are evident on the bouquet and palate; the finish is unctuous, long, luscious and full of nutty complexity; a rich style, handled well. Cork. 13.8% alc. **Rating** 94 **To** 2014 $52 BE

Soul Growers   ★★★★☆

PO Box 805, Tanunda, SA 5352 (postal) **Region** Barossa Valley
T 0439 026 727 **F** (08) 8563 0582 **www**.soulgrowers.com **Open** By appt
Winemaker James Lindner, Paul Lindner, David Cruickshank, Paul Heinicke **Est.** 1998
Cases 700 **Vyds** 6.8 ha
Soul Growers is owned by its four winemaker partners headed by James Lindner. Its estate vineyards are mainly situated on hillside country in the Seppeltsfield region, with shiraz, cabernet sauvignon, grenache and chardonnay the most important, with lesser plantings of mataro and black muscat; there are then pocket handkerchief blocks of shiraz at Tanunda, mataro at Nuriootpa and a 1.2-ha planting of grenache at Krondorf. Exports to the US, Canada, Singapore and Hong Kong.

ŸŸŸŸŸ Barossa Valley Shiraz 2007 Very good colour; improbably, perhaps, better than the '06, despite the lesser vintage and higher alcohol, the latter carried remarkably well by the complex black fruits and oak of the palate. Hard to imagine a more perfect cork. 15.5% alc. **Rating** 94 **To** 2022 $50

ŸŸŸŸŸ Barossa Valley Cabernet Sauvignon 2007 **Rating** 91 **To** 2020 $50
Barossa Valley Shiraz Grenache Mourvedre 2007 **Rating** 90 **To** 2015 $25

Southern Dreams   ★★★

10293 Deeside Coast Road, Northcliffe, WA 6262 **Region** Pemberton
T (08) 9775 1027 **F** (08) 9387 3222 **Open** By appt
Winemaker Mark Aitken **Est.** 1997 **Cases** 250 **Vyds** 32.4 ha
John Akehurst and family have planted sauvignon blanc, semillon, pinot noir, chardonnay and cabernet merlot. Giant Karri, Marri and Jarrah trees surround the property, which has the Shannon National Park on one side. The adjacent 10-ha dam is home to a family of black swans, ducks and visiting pelicans.

ŸŸŸŸ Pemberton Sauvignon Blanc Semillon 2009 An ever-so-easy to enjoy mix
❂ of citrus and tropical fruit in a delicate, low-alcohol framework. Screwcap. 11% alc. **Rating** 89 **To** 2011 $15

Southern Highland Wines   ★★★★

Oldbury Road, Sutton Forest, NSW 2577 **Region** Southern Highlands
T (02) 4868 2300 **F** (02) 4868 1808 **www**.southernhighlandwines.com **Open** 7 days 10–5
Winemaker Eddy Rossi, Dominic Bosch **Est.** 2002 **Cases** 20 000 **Vyds** 40 ha
Southern Highland Wines is owned by Eddy Rossi (general manager, winemaker and export director), Frank Colloridi (production director) and Darren Corradi (viticulture and sales director). Both Darren and Eddy have had lengthy careers in various Griffith wineries. The venture has increased significantly since its foundation, the vineyard area doubling, and sales increasing from 6000 cases to their present level, with wines coming from other regions, notably the Altitude 676 range. Exports to China and NZ.

ΨΨΨΨΨ Cool Climate Pinot Noir 2008 Bright clear red-purple; has a bell-clear
◑ bouquet and palate, the red berry fruits neatly offset by some forest floor nuances;
has very good line, length and balance. Screwcap. 13% alc. **Rating** 92 **To** 2014 $24
Oldbury Reserve Cool Climate Pinot Noir 2008 The hue is fractionally
more developed than the standard pinot, possibly due to an extra four months
(16 in total) in oak; has more power and complexity, but less finesse; eliminating
the American oak might help. Screwcap. 13% alc. **Rating** 91 **To** 2014 $32

ΨΨΨΨ Cool Climate Shiraz 2008 **Rating** 89 **To** 2014 $24
Oldbury Reserve Cool Climate Sauvignon Blanc 2009 **Rating** 88
To 2011 $28

Spence   ★★★★☆
760 Burnside Road, Murgheboluc, Vic 3221 **Region** Geelong
T (03) 5265 1181 **F** (03) 5265 1181 www.spencewines.com.au **Open** 1st Sun each month
Winemaker Peter Spence **Est.** 1997 **Cases** 500 **Vyds** 3.2 ha
Peter and Anne Spence were sufficiently inspired by an extended European holiday, which
included living on a family vineyard in Provence, to purchase a small property specifically for
the purpose of establishing a vineyard and winery. It remains a part-time occupation; Peter is
an engineering manager at the Ford product development plant at Geelong, Anne a teacher,
but presently full-time mother looking after two young children. They have planted 3.2 ha on
a north-facing slope in a valley 7 km south of Bannockburn; the lion's share to three clones
of shiraz (1.83 ha), the remainder to chardonnay, pinot noir and fast-diminishing cabernet
sauvignon (which is being grafted over to viognier for use in the Shiraz). The vineyard attained
full organic status prior to the '08 vintage, and is moving to biodynamic, with certification to
come in the future. The well-priced wines have been made with the sure hand of the fast-
learning Peter.

ΨΨΨΨΨ Oakbough Chardonnay 2008 A fresh, lively chardonnay with good focus and
◑ intensity on both bouquet and palate, its tangy citrus and stone fruit flavours gently
buttressed by barrel ferment oak. Screwcap. 13.3% alc. **Rating** 94 **To** 2015 $25

ΨΨΨΨΨ Oakbough Pinot Noir 2008 Bright, clear red-purple; a highly fragrant red fruit
◑ bouquet, the palate with cherry and plum fruit, superfine tannins running through
its length. Impressive wine. Screwcap. 13.5% alc. **Rating** 93 **To** 2014 $25
◑ **Oakbough Shiraz 2007** Bright purple-crimson; has a particularly complex and
fragrant bouquet (the shiraz was co-fermented with 5% viognier), offering spice,
leather, licorice and abundant black fruits; the medium-bodied palate is tangy
and supple, finishing with gently savoury tannins. Screwcap. 13.6% alc. **Rating** 93
To 2017 $25

Spinifex   ★★★★★
PO Box 511, Nuriootpa, SA 5355 **Region** Barossa Valley
T (08) 8564 2059 **F** (08) 8564 2079 www.spinifexwines.com.au **Open** By appt
Winemaker Peter Schell **Est.** 2001 **Cases** 4000
Peter Schell and Magali Gely are a husband and wife team from NZ who came to Australia
in the early 1990s to study oenology and marketing, respectively, at Roseworthy College.
Together they have spent four vintages making wine in France, mainly in the south, where
Magali's family were vignerons for generations near Montpellier. The focus at Spinifex is
the red varieties that dominate in the south of France: mataro (more correctly mourvedre),
grenache, shiraz and cinsaut. The wine is made in open fermenters, basket-pressed, partial wild
(indigenous) fermentations, and relatively long post-ferment maceration. This is at once a very
old approach, but nowadays à la mode. The wines are made at Spinifex's winery in Vine Vale,
where Peter also makes wines for a number of clients to whom he consults. So far as I am
concerned Spinifex out-Torbrecks Torbreck. Exports to the UK, the US, Canada, Belgium,
Taiwan, Singapore, Hong Kong and NZ.

ŸŸŸŸŸ   **Luxe 2009** Has greater purity, intensity, line and focus than its lesser (Rose)
✪   brother; the length of the floral garden of red fruits is exceptional. Screwcap.
         13.5% alc. **Rating** 96 **To** 2012 $26
         Indigene 2008 Much deeper colour than Esprit; a profound wine in every way,
         obviously made from older, lower-yielding vines; here black fruits and licorice take
         centre state, with a velvety texture and very long finish. Shiraz/Mataro/Grenache.
         Screwcap. 14.5% alc. **Rating** 96 **To** 2028 $48
✪   **Barossa Rose 2009** In inimitable Spinifex style, a bridge between Australia and
         the South of France (or even northern Spain); gentle red fruits are within a web
         of gossamer tannins and spice; very good balance and length. Screwcap. 13.5% alc.
         Rating 94 **To** 2012 $19
         Bete Noir 2008 Bright purple-crimson; a particularly expressive and fragrant
         bouquet with spicy black fruits, the medium- to full-bodied palate with licorice
         and more warm spice notes; we are not told why shiraz should be Pete Schell's
         enemy. Screwcap. 14.5% alc. **Rating** 94 **To** 2023 $36
         La Maline 2008 Good purple-red, although not particularly vibrant; a very rich
         and complex wine, texture and structure excellent; the bouquet is aromatic and
         the full-bodied palate has abundant fruit, but this blend (Shiraz/Viognier) best
         delivers vibrancy in cool climates. Screwcap. 14.5% alc. **Rating** 94 **To** 2023 $48
✪   **Cigale Barossa Valley Grenache Mourvedre Shiraz 2007** Brilliantly clear
         red hue; an elegant and supple wine with highly expressive spicy red fruit flavours
         lengthened by excellent acidity. 63/21/16% blend. Screwcap. 14.5% alc. **Rating** 94
         To 2013 $19
✪   **Taureau 2008** Good bright colour; a fragrant bouquet with the Spinifex stamp
         all over it, the texture silky and fine, the fruit flavours in a seamless whole ranging
         from light red to dark black, tannins playing a wholly positive role. Tempranillo/
         Graciano/Carignan/Cabernet Sauvignon. Screwcap. 14.5% alc. **Rating** 94
         To 2015 $24

ŸŸŸŸŸ   **Lola 2009** Bright, lively green-straw; this is not a wine about fruit aromatics,
✪   rather an exploration of texture, structure and length. There is enough positive
         flavour to suit any need, but the wine is content to back off on the fresh, dry and
         lively finish. Semillon/Viognier/Ugni Blanc/Vermentino. Screwcap. 12.7% alc.
         Rating 93 **To** 2014 $19
         Esprit 2008 Rating 93 **To** 2018 $28
         Pablo VP 2007 Rating 93 **To** 2022 $28
         Papillon 2009 Rating 90 **To** 2013 $22.50

Spring Vale Vineyards   ★★★★☆

130 Spring Vale Road, Cranbrook, Tas 7190 **Region** East Coast Tasmania
T (03) 6257 8208 **F** (03) 6257 8598 **www**.springvalewines.com **Open** 7 days 10–4
Winemaker Kristen and David Cush **Est.** 1986 **Cases** 8500 **Vyds** 12.1 ha
Rodney Lyne has progressively established pinot noir (6.5 ha), chardonnay (2 ha), gewurztraminer (1.6 ha), pinot gris and sauvignon blanc (1 ha each). In 2007 Spring Vale purchased
the Melrose Vineyard from Bishops Rock (not the Bishops Rock brand or stock), planted to
pinot noir (3 ha), sauvignon blanc, riesling (1 ha each) and chardonnay (0.5 ha). Exports to
the US, Canada, Taiwan and Hong Kong.

ŸŸŸŸŸ   **Reserve Chardonnay 2008** Has an array of flavours on the citrus side of the
         rainbow, with grapefruit to the fore; oak has been used to good effect, providing
         as much structure as flavour; all in all, has great energy and length. Screwcap.
         13.7% alc. **Rating** 94 **To** 2016 $30

ŸŸŸŸŸ   **Gewurztraminer 2009 Rating** 93 **To** 2015 $28
         Cellar Release Pinot Noir 2005 Rating 92 **To** 2017 $80
         Pinot Noir 2007 Rating 91 **To** 2015 $40
         Sauvignon Blanc 2009 Rating 90 **To** 2011 $24
         Chardonnay 2009 Rating 90 **To** 2014 $22

ŸŸŸŸ   **Pinot Gris 2009 Rating** 89 **To** 2010 $28

Springs Hill Vineyard ★★★★

Schuller Road, Blewitt Springs, SA 5171 **Region** McLaren Vale
T (08) 8383 7001 **F** (08) 8383 7001 **www**.springshill.com.au **Open** Sun & public hols
Winemaker Anthony and Gary Whaite **Est.** 1998 **Cases** 1000 **Vyds** 17.1 ha
Anthony and Gary Whaite began the planting of their vineyard in 1975 with cabernet sauvignon and shiraz and have slowly expanded it over the following years with merlot, mourvedre and grenache. The vines are dry-grown, and the whole operation from vine to wine is carried out by the pair. They use traditional small batch winemaking techniques of open fermenters, which are hand-plunged, basket-pressed, etc.

ŶŶŶŶŶ **Blewitt Springs Merlot 2008** Good colour; in typical McLaren Vale style; rich
✪   and full of plum and blackcurrant fruit, with the savoury dark olive tannins of the
          variety. Screwcap. 14.5% alc. **Rating** 93 **To** 2018 $29
✪   **Blewitt Springs Shiraz 2008** Good crimson; a mix of spice, licorice and dark
          chocolate aromas lead into a spicy medium-bodied palate that has juicy fruit
          flavours and a long finish. Screwcap. 14.5% alc. **Rating** 92 **To** 2023 $29

Springs Road Vineyard ★★★★

76 Dauncey Street, Kingscote, Kangaroo Island, SA 5223 **Region** Kangaroo Island
T 0409 673 640 **F** (08) 8553 0325 **www**.springsroadvineyard.com.au **Open** 7 days 9–5
Winemaker Briony Hoare **Est.** 1994 **Cases** 1000 **Vyds** 11 ha
Roger Williams (who has lived on Kangaroo Island all his life) and wife Kate planted the first vines on their property in 1995, and after some trial and error, have now settled on shiraz, cabernet sauvignon and chardonnay. They personally do all the work in the vineyard, including pruning, spraying and – of course – picking. They also have an al fresco café/restaurant in Kingscote (Roger's Cafe), which seats 60 and is the cellar door sales outlet for the wines. The quality of the wines is impressive.

ŶŶŶŶŶ **Single Vineyard Kangaroo Island Shiraz 2007** A fragrant, medium-bodied
          wine with spice, blackberry and plum flavours on the palate, supported by fine,
          ripe and gently savoury tannins; oak handling precise. Screwcap. 13.9% alc.
          Rating 93 **To** 2017 $18
          Single Vineyard Kangaroo Island Cabernet Sauvignon 2006 Strong
          colour; a wine that exudes power from every pore, albeit in a dark savoury mode,
          with overtones of earth and dark chocolate; two years in older oak has paid
          dividends. Screwcap. 14.4% alc. **Rating** 92 **To** 2020 $18

Springton Hills Wines ★★★★★

41 Burnbank Grove, Athelstone, SA 5076 (postal) **Region** Eden Valley
T (08) 8337 7905 **F** (08) 8365 5303 **www**.springtonhillswines.com.au **Open** Not
Winemaker John and Remo Ciccocioppo **Est.** 2001 **Cases** 700 **Vyds** 6 ha
The Ciccocioppo family migrated from central Italy in the 1950s; as is so often the case, wine was in their veins. In 2001 second generation John Ciccocioppo and wife Connie purchased a grazing property at Springton, and began the planting of shiraz and riesling. Each year they increased the shiraz and riesling blocks, but also added smaller amounts of cabernet sauvignon, grenache and a smaller amount still of montepulciano. As the plantings got underway John, and brother Remo, undertook a winemaking course at Regency Park TAFE, a year later undertaking a chemical analysis course. Prior to the 2005 vintage, a small winery was erected onsite, and it is here that the Shiraz, Riesling and Cabernet Grenache Montepulciano are made. The '06 Eden Valley Shiraz won a double gold medal at the Sydney International Wine Show '09. The wines are available for tasting at the Barossa Small Winemakers Centre at Chateau Tanunda. Good label design and packaging.

ŶŶŶŶŶ **Eden Valley Riesling 2007** Glowing yellow-green; has developed impressively,
          with supple lemon and lime fruit backed by crisp, minerally acidity; very good
          length. Screwcap. 11.3% alc. **Rating** 94 **To** 2017 $18

Eden Valley Cabernet Grenache Montepulciano Blend 2008 A very interesting wine; grenache should by rights be the unwanted child, but the cabernet and montepulciano do sufficient talking to carry the grenache, with their lifted cassis and black cherry fruits running through the long palate and savoury finish. Screwcap. 14.3% alc. **Rating** 94 **To** 2018 $28

ŶŶŶŶŶ **Eden Valley Shiraz 2006** Rating 92 To 2021 $30
Eden Valley Shiraz 2007 Rating 90 To 2019 $37

Squitchy Lane Vineyard   ★★★★☆

PO Box 208, Coldstream, Vic 3770 **Region** Yarra Valley
T (03) 5964 9114 **F** (03) 5964 9017 **www**.squitchylane.com.au **Open** Not
Winemaker Robert Paul (Consultant) **Est.** 1982 **Cases** 1000 **Vyds** 5.75 ha
Owner Mike Fitzpatrick acquired his taste for fine wine while a Rhodes scholar at Oxford University in the 1970s. Returning to Australia he guided Carlton Football Club to two premierships as captain, then established Melbourne-based finance company Squitchy Lane Holdings. The wines of Mount Mary inspired him to look for his own vineyard, and in 1996 he found a vineyard of sauvignon blanc, chardonnay, pinot noir, merlot, cabernet franc and cabernet sauvignon planted in '82 just around the corner from Coldstream Hills and Yarra Yering. Between then and 2003 the grapes were sold to well-known local wineries, but in '04 he began to put in place a team to take the venture through to the next stage, with wines under the Squitchy Lane label, commencing with the '05 vintage, launched in '07. In 2009 and '10 the wines were made at Sticks.

ŶŶŶŶŶ **Yarra Valley Cabernet Sauvignon 2008** Crimson-purple; a fragrant bouquet, then a deliciously juicy palate flooded with cassis and blackcurrant, tannins and oak playing pure support roles. Screwcap. 13% alc. **Rating** 94 **To** 2018 $32

ŶŶŶŶŶ **Yarra Valley Chardonnay 2008** Rating 91 To 2014 $28

ŶŶŶŶ **SQL Yarra Valley Merlot 2008** Rating 89 To 2014 $22
SQL Yarra Valley Sauvignon Blanc 2009 Rating 87 To 2011 $19
Yarra Valley Pinot Noir 2008 Rating 87 To 2013 $30
SQL Yarra Valley Red Square 2008 Rating 87 To 2012 $22

Staindl Wines   ★★★★

63 Shoreham Road, Red Hill South, Vic 3937 (postal) **Region** Mornington Peninsula
T (03) 9813 1111 **www**.staindlwines.com.au **Open** By appt
Winemaker Rollo Crittenden (Contract) **Est.** 1982 **Cases** 800 **Vyds** 3.1 ha
As often happens, the establishment date for a wine producer can mean many things. In this instance it harks back to the planting of the vineyard by the Ayton family, and the establishment of what was thereafter called St Neots. Juliet and Paul Staindl acquired the property in 2002, and, with the guidance of Phillip Jones, have extended the plantings to 2.5 ha of pinot noir, 0.4 ha of chardonnay and 0.2 ha of riesling. The vineyard is run on a low chemical regime, heading towards biodynamic viticulture. Paul says, 'It's all good fun and lots of learning.' I would add it's also more than slightly demanding.

ŶŶŶŶŶ **Mornington Peninsula Chardonnay 2008** Straw-green; attractive nectarine and white peach fruit on the bouquet and palate; barrel fermentation has imparted a touch of grilled cashew, balanced by citrussy acidity on the finish. Good length. Screwcap. 13% alc. **Rating** 93 **To** 2015 $35
Mornington Peninsula Riesling 2008 Fragrant, with an intriguing peppery hint on the bouquet akin to that of gruner veltliner; the palate is dry, the alcohol reflecting super-early picking, as does the high acidity. Has biodynamic growing played a (negative) role? Screwcap. 11% alc. **Rating** 90 **To** 2017 $25

Stanley Lambert Wines ★★★

Barossa Valley Way, Tanunda, SA 5352 **Region** Barossa Valley
T (08) 8563 3375 **F** (08) 8563 3758 **www**.stanleylambert.com.au **Open** Mon–Fri 10–5,
w'ends & public hols 11–5
Winemaker Lindsay Stanley **Est.** 1994 **Cases** 12 000 **Vyds** 16.4 ha
Former Anglesey winemaker and industry veteran Lindsay Stanley established his own
business in the Barossa Valley when he purchased (and renamed) the former Kroemer Estate
in late 1994. As one would expect, the wines are competently made, although often light-
bodied. The estate plantings have provided virtually all the grapes for the business (shiraz,
riesling, chardonnay, cabernet sauvignon, zinfandel, tempranillo, grenache, mourvedre, merlot
and viognier). Exports to the UK, the US and other major markets.

♀♀♀♀   **The Family Tree Barossa Valley Shiraz 2006** Quite developed, but showing
gently fleshy fruit, with a dominant fruitcake aroma and flavour; quite oaky on the
finish. Diam. 14.5% alc. **Rating** 87 **To** 2014 $65 BE

Stanton & Killeen Wines ★★★★★

Jacks Road, Murray Valley Highway, Rutherglen, Vic 3685 **Region** Rutherglen
T (02) 6032 9457 **F** (02) 6032 8018 **www**.stantonandkilleenwines.com.au **Open** Mon–
Sat 9–5, Sun 10–5
Winemaker Brendan Heath **Est.** 1875 **Cases** 20 000 **Vyds** 35.41 ha
The tragic and premature death of Chris Killeen was much mourned by his numerous
admirers, myself included. However, son Simon is already studying wine science, and Chris's
right-hand-man for 15 years, Michael Oxlee, is now CEO. Brendan Heath, who has likewise
worked at the winery for some years, has been promoted to winemaker. Exports to the UK
and Denmark.

♀♀♀♀♀   **Rare Rutherglen Muscat NV** All hints of red have gone, leaving a brown
✪   centre grading to hints of olive on the rim; this is the final step up the ladder of
lusciousness, incredibly rich, the rancio sufficient to do its job of balancing the
wine, but no more; there is a cornucopia of flavours and spices. Wherever your
imagination takes you, it will be in the glass. 375 ml. Cork. 18.5% alc. **Rating** 97
To 2011 $100

✪   **Grand Rutherglen Muscat NV** With 25 years' average age, the rim of the
colour has touches of olive-brown; the bouquet is very complex and powerful, the
palate with multiple layers of flavour and glorious texture; the art here has been to
keep the wine fresh despite its great age. Cork. 18.5% alc. **Rating** 96 **To** 2011 $80

✪   **Classic Rutherglen Tokay NV** Golden brown; strong tea leaf, toffee and malt
varietal aromas and flavours are indeed classic; the wine has an average age of 12
years, substantial for a Classic style. 500 ml. Cork. 18% alc. **Rating** 95 **To** 2011 $30

✪   **Classic Rutherglen Muscat NV** Reddish-brown, correct for its average age of
12 years; wonderfully luscious, raisin and Christmas pudding flavours, cut by just
the right amount of rancio. 500 ml. Cork. 18% alc. **Rating** 95 **To** 2011 $30

✪   **Rutherglen Shiraz Durif 2007** Expected strong colour; both bouquet and
palate have a persuasive mix of black fruits, licorice and dark chocolate, with spicy
tannins adding support to a wine with a real sense of place – and also balance.
Diam. 14.5% alc. **Rating** 94 **To** 2015 $20

✪   **Rutherglen Durif 2007** This is a variety that can sustain high alcohol levels, for
this wine shows no heat or sweetness; instead it is spicy/savoury, with appealing
notes of leather and spice to its dark fruits; very good texture and structure. Diam.
15% alc. **Rating** 94 **To** 2017 $32

✪   **Rutherglen Vintage Fortified 2005** A multifaceted bouquet with aromas of
numerous spices and fruit cadences; a very rich and complex palate with black
fruits, a dash of chocolate, clean spirit and a wonderfully sweet finish. Shiraz/
Durif/Tinta Cao/Tinta Roriz/Touriga Nacional. Cork. 18.2% alc. **Rating** 94
To 2025 $29

♀♀♀♀♀   **The Prince Reserva 2008 Rating** 93 **To** 2016 $45

Starvedog Lane   ★★★★★

Reynell Road, Reynella, SA 5161 (postal) **Region** Adelaide Hills
T (08) 8392 2300 **F** (08) 8392 2301 **www.**starvedoglane.com.au **Open** Not
Winemaker Glenn Barry **Est.** 1999 **Cases** NFP
Starvedog Lane came into existence as part of a joint venture with John and Helen Edwards
of Ravenswood Lane, who had established 28 ha of vineyards in 1993. Part of that production
was sold to the joint venture for the Starvedog Lane brand, part reserved for release under
the Ravenswood Lane brand, which morphed into The Lane (see separate entry). Confusing,
but the situation is now much simpler, as the Edwards and Hardys (technically, Constellation
Wines Australia) have severed all commercial ties. The Starvedog Lane brand is wholly owned
by CWA and relies on contract-grown grapes from growers in the Adelaide Hills.

ΨΨΨΨΨ   Adelaide Hills Shiraz Viognier 2008 Deep, bright crimson-purple; a very
✪   good example of the style, the vibrant black fruits lifted by the viognier on the
         bouquet and supple, medium-bodied palate alike; fruit, oak and tannins all in
         balance. Screwcap. 13.5% alc. **Rating** 94 **To** 2018 $25.50
✪   Adelaide Hills Shiraz Viognier 2007 The three gold medals attest to the
         success of the blend and the sheer charm of this medium-bodied wine, with red
         fruits and spices, the tannins silky. Screwcap. 13.5% alc. **Rating** 94 **To** 2015 $26
✪   Adelaide Hills Chardonnay Pinot Noir Pinot Meunier 2004 A wine
         with considerable character and power; white peach and lemon zest come
         rushing through on the palate, picking up some nutty characters on the finish
         and aftertaste. Gold medal Sydney Wine Show '10. Cork. 12.5% alc. **Rating** 94
         To 2015 $28.50

ΨΨΨΨΨ   Adelaide Hills Chardonnay 2008 **Rating** 93 **To** 2015 $29
✪   Adelaide Hills Cabernet Merlot 2007 Bright purple-red; a potent wine, with
         the full suite of black and red berry aromas and flavours thrusting through to the
         long, gently savoury finish. Screwcap. 13.3% alc. **Rating** 93 **To** 2016 $25.50
         Adelaide Hills Pinot Grigio 2009 **Rating** 92 **To** 2011 $25.50
         Adelaide Hills Pinot Noir Chardonnay 2003 **Rating** 90 **To** 2012 $29

Station Creek   ★★★

Edi Road, Cheshunt, Vic 3678 **Region** King Valley
T (03) 5729 8265 **F** (03) 5729 8056 **Open** 7 days
Winemaker David Steer, Warren Proft (Consultant) **Est.** 1999 **Cases** 900 **Vyds** 4.5 ha
David and Sharon Steer have established their vineyard at Cheshunt, planted to sauvignon
blanc, merlot, shiraz and cabernet sauvignon. The cellar door offers light meals, crafts, a gallery
and local produce.

ΨΨΨΨ   King Valley Cabernet Sauvignon 2004 The aromas and flavours are riper and
        more juicy than the alcohol would suggest, with pronounced cassis characters,
        although the wine is medium-bodied at best. Screwcap. 13.5% alc. **Rating** 88
        To 2013 $25
        King Valley Shiraz 2004 Has retained bright hue, fresh aromas and a lively
        light-bodied palate with a mix of red fruits and spices, and enough tannins to give
        structure. Screwcap. 13.5% alc. **Rating** 87 **To** 2015 $15

Stefani Estate   ★★★★★

389 Heathcote-Rochester Road, Heathcote, Vic 3523 **Region** Heathcote
T (03) 9570 8750 **F** (03) 9579 1532 **www.**stefaniestatewines.com.au **Open** By appt
Winemaker Mario Marson **Est.** 2002 **Cases** 3000 **Vyds** 27.6 ha
Stefano Stefani came to Australia in 1985. Business success has allowed Stefano and wife Rina
to follow in the footsteps of Stefano's grandfather, who had a vineyard and was an avid wine
collector. The first property they acquired was at Long Gully Road in the Yarra Valley, planted
with pinot grigio, cabernet sauvignon, chardonnay and pinot noir. The next was in Heathcote,
where he acquired a property adjoining that of Mario Marson, built a winery and established

14.4 ha of vineyards, planted to shiraz, cabernet sauvignon, merlot, cabernet franc, malbec and petit verdot. In 2003 a second Yarra Valley property named The View, reflecting its high altitude, was acquired and Dijon clones of chardonnay and pinot noir were planted. In addition, 1.6 ha of sangiovese, mammolo bianco, malvasia, aleatico, trebbiano and crepolino bianco have been established, using scion material from the original Stefani vineyard in Tuscany. Mario Marson (ex Mount Mary) oversees the operation of all the vineyards and is also the winemaker. He is also able to use the winery to make his own brand wines, completing the business link. Exports to Italy and China.

ŸŸŸŸŸ The View Yarra Valley Chardonnay 2007 Gleaming green-straw; a notably complex wine with barrel ferment inputs to intense stone fruit and some citrus flavours; has compelling length. Diam. 13.5% alc. **Rating** 94 **To** 2014 $45
The View Yarra Valley Pinot Noir 2007 Exceptional crimson hue for a three-year-old pinot; has a complex and rich bouquet of plum and black cherry fruit, characters than in turn drive the long, textured palate and lingering aftertaste. Diam. 13.5% alc. **Rating** 94 **To** 2015 $50

ŸŸŸŸŸ The Gate Yarra Valley Cabernet Sauvignon Merlot 2007 Rating 91 To 2014 $45
Heathcote Vineyard Shiraz 2007 Rating 90 To 2014 $50 BE
Vino Rosso Shiraz Cabernet Sauvignon 2007 Rating 90 To 2014 $25 BE

ŸŸŸŸ The View Yarra Valley Pinot Gris 2008 Rating 89 To 2012 $35

Stefano de Pieri ★★★★
27 Deakin Avenue, Mildura, Vic 3502 **Region** Murray Darling
T (03) 5021 3627 **F** (03) 5021 0842 **www.**stefano.com.au **Open** Mon–Fri 8–6, w'ends 8–2
Winemaker Sally Blackwell, Stefano de Pieri **Est.** 2005 **Cases** 24 000
Stefano de Pieri decided to have his own range of wines that reflect his Italian spirit and the region he lives in. Mostly hand-picked, the fruit comes from a variety of Mildura vineyards including the highly respected Chalmers Nursery vineyard. They are intended to be fresh and zesty, deliberately aiming at lower alcohol to retain as much natural acidity as possible. They are designed to go with food, and are inexpensive and easy to enjoy, reflecting Stefano's philosophy of generosity and warmth. The emphasis is on the Italian varieties from arneis to aglianico, including a frizzante pinot grigio and the innovative blend of moscato gialla, garganega and greco, while retaining some of the local workhorses like cabernet and chardonnay.

ŸŸŸŸŸ Sangiovese Rose 2009 Fuchsia-pink; a fragrant bouquet, the palate flooded with bright cherry fruit coupled with a slight twist of citrus on the finish. Screwcap. 10.5% alc. **Rating** 90 **To** 2011 $20.50
Aglianico 2009 Bright crimson-magenta of rose depth; in fact, has a lot of supple, fresh red fruit flavour; as good as a light-bodied red can be. Screwcap. 12% alc. **Rating** 90 **To** 2011 $20.50

ŸŸŸŸ Arneis 2009 Rating 88 To 2011 $20.50

Stefano Lubiana ★★★★★
60 Rowbottoms Road, Granton, Tas 7030 **Region** Southern Tasmania
T (03) 6263 7457 **F** (03) 6263 7430 **www.**slw.com.au **Open** Sun–Thurs 11–3
(closed some public hols)
Winemaker Steve Lubiana **Est.** 1990 **Cases** NFP **Vyds** 18 ha
When Stefano (Steve) Lubiana moved from the Riverland to Tasmania, he set up a substantial contract sparkling winemaking facility to help cover the costs of the move and the establishment of his new business. Over the years, he has steadily decreased the amount of contract winemaking, now focusing on his estate biodynamically grown wines from beautifully located vineyards sloping down to the Derwent River, surrounded by water on three sides. Exports to the UK, Sweden, Korea, Singapore, Japan, Hong Kong and Indonesia.

ΨΨΨΨΨ **Estate Pinot Noir 2008** Strong, clear purple; the bouquet is complex, with dark
berry fruits and some spice, the imperious palate with intense black cherry and
dark plum fruit sustained and complexed by superb tannins; built for the long haul.
Screwcap. 14% alc. **Rating** 96 **To** 2018 $55
Riesling 2009 A wine that doesn't creep up on you so much as ambush you with
its explosive flavour and aftertaste; pure Tasmanian riesling, pure Tasmanian acidity.
Will flourish in bottle for decades. Screwcap. 13.5% alc. **Rating** 95 **To** 2030 $28
Estate Pinot Noir 2007 Bright, clear red-purple; a fragrant bouquet of red fruits
and rose petals is followed by a palate with thrust and drive and slightly darker
fruit and forest flavours, the tannin structure once again admirable. Screwcap.
13.5% alc. **Rating** 95 **To** 2015 $50
Sauvignon Blanc 2009 Yet another wine demonstrating that Tasmanian
sauvignon blanc has come of age; the almost glossy, slippery acidity carries waves
of gooseberry, apple and stone fruit flavours through to the long finish. Screwcap.
12.5% alc. **Rating** 94 **To** 2012 $28
Tasmania Chardonnay 2006 Almost no colour change from the '09 Primavera;
you have to wonder then this wine will ever throw off the shackles of youth, so
strict is the acidity underlying the fruit; this out-Chablis's Chablis; the points are
given in hope. Screwcap. 14% alc. **Rating** 94 **To** 2026 $50
Primavera Pinot Noir 2008 Vivid purple hue; an extremely powerful, highly
charged pinot, its dark fruits clasped by spicy acidity and fine but firm tannins.
Cries out for time. Screwcap. 14% alc. **Rating** 94 **To** 2023 $33

ΨΨΨΨΨ **Primavera Chardonnay 2009 Rating** 93 **To** 2019 $28
NV Brut NV Rating 92 **To** 2013 $35
Merlot 2007 Rating 91 **To** 2017 $33
Alfresco Riesling 2009 Rating 90 **To** 2013 $28

Steinborner Family Vineyards ★★★★

91 Siegersdorf Road, Tanunda, SA 5352 **Region** Barossa Valley
T 0414 474 708 **F** (08) 8522 4898 **www.**sfvineyards.com.au **Open** By appt
Winemaker David Reynolds, Neil Doddridge, Sally Blackwell **Est.** 2003 **Cases** 3000
Vyds 9 ha
This is a partnership between David and Rebecca Reynolds, and Rebecca's parents, Michael
and Heather Steinborner. They say, 'David, hailing from UK/Irish heritage and with a chance
meeting in Tokyo (with Rebecca), brings some fresh blood to the Steinborner clan. He
oversees (or does himself wherever possible) much of both the vineyard and wine production.'
The oldest vines include some 80+ and 40+-year-old shiraz, and all varieties (including
semillon, viognier, durif and marsanne) are planted on the typical sand-over-clay profile of
Vine Vale, one of the noted subregions of the Barossa Valley. Exports to Switzerland, Indonesia,
Hong Kong, China and Japan.

ΨΨΨΨΨ **Barossa Deutsche Shiraz 2006** Retains excellent purple-red hue; laden with
juicy blackberry and plum fruit, mocha/vanilla and ripe tannins; warms slightly on
the finish. Cork. 14.5% alc. **Rating** 91 **To** 2016 $25
Barossa Ancestry Shiraz Viognier 2007 The five-generation family tree is
shown on the front label, dating back to the arrival of the family in 1865. The
wine, with 3% co-fermented viognier, is 21st century in style; somehow, the
viognier overcomes the alcohol. Cork. 15% alc. **Rating** 90 **To** 2017 $25

ΨΨΨΨ ✪ **Caroliene Barossa Valley Semillon 2009** Successfully follows the Peter
Lehmann path of earlier picking, exclusion of oak and early bottling; bright
and fresh, citrus notes click in on the finish. Screwcap. 11.5% alc. **Rating** 89
To 2016 $15

Stella Bella Wines ★★★★★

PO Box 536, Margaret River, WA 6285 **Region** Margaret River
T (08) 9757 6377 **F** (08) 9757 6022 **www.**stellabella.com.au **Open** Not
Winemaker Janice McDonald, Stuart Pym **Est.** 1997 **Cases** 50 000 **Vyds** 40 ha
This enormously successful, privately owned winemaking business produces wines of true
regional expression, with fruit sourced from the central and southern parts of Margaret River.
Owns or controls more than 80 ha of vineyards, recently acquired a 3000-tonne (potential)
winemaking facility at Karridale, and a cellar door is in the pipeline, just minutes from the
township at the original Isca Vineyard. It's hard to imagine the wines getting better, but we
shall see. Exports of Stella Bella, Suckfizzle and Skuttlebutt labels to the UK, the US, Canada,
China, Hong Kong and Singapore.

🍷🍷🍷🍷🍷 **Suckfizzle Margaret River Sauvignon Blanc Semillon 2007** Bright straw-
green; as always, combines elegance with flavour in a seamless stream of ripe citrus
and stone fruit flavours, oak embedded in the structure. Built to age. Screwcap.
13% alc. **Rating** 96 **To** 2014 $45

✪ **Margaret River Chardonnay 2008** Vivid green-gold; a masterful exercise
in winemaking, with intense citrus and stone fruit flavours driving through the
length of the palate, oak made largely redundant, the finish as fresh as a spring day.
Screwcap. 13% alc. **Rating** 96 **To** 2018 $30

✪ **Margaret River Cabernet Sauvignon Merlot 2007** Fragrant and pure
black and redcurrant aromas lead into a precise, beautifully structured medium-
to full-bodied palate, with emery board tannins drawing out the finish, as does
cedary oak; very good line, length and balance. Screwcap. 14% alc. **Rating** 96
To 2027 $32

✪ **Margaret River Sauvignon Blanc 2009** Bright, fresh and breezy, the wine has
a crisp array of aromas and flavours spanning citrus, gooseberry and passionfruit,
with no hint of being blown off course. Trophy Sydney Wine Show '10. Screwcap.
13% alc. **Rating** 94 **To** 2011 $24

🍷🍷🍷🍷♀ **Margaret River Pink Muscat 2009 Rating** 92 **To** 2010 $19
Suckfizzle Margaret River Cabernet Sauvignon 2007 Rating 90
To 2017 $55

🍷🍷🍷🍷 **Skuttlebutt Margaret River Shiraz Cabernet Merlot 2007 Rating** 89
To 2015 $18

Stephen John Wines ★★★★

Sollys Hill Road, Watervale, SA 5452 **Region** Clare Valley
T (08) 8843 0105 **F** (08) 8843 0105 **www.**stephenjohnwines.com **Open** 7 days 11–5
Winemaker Stephen John **Est.** 1994 **Cases** 10 000 **Vyds** 5 ha
The John family is one of the best known in the Barossa Valley, with branches running
Australia's best cooperage (AP John & Sons) and providing the former chief winemaker
of Lindemans (Philip John) and the former chief winemaker of Quelltaler (Stephen John).
Stephen and Rita John have now formed their own family business in the Clare Valley, based
on a vineyard (riesling, shiraz, cabernet sauvignon) overlooking Watervale, and supplemented
by grapes from a few local growers. The cellar door is a renovated 80-year-old stable full of
rustic charm. Exports to Canada, Malaysia, Thailand, Maldives and Singapore.

🍷🍷🍷🍷♀ **Dry Grown Clare Valley Shiraz 2008** Dense purple-crimson; from the dark
side of the moon, with impenetrable black fruit aromas and flavours; despite this,
the wine is not jammy or unduly extractive; just needs time. Screwcap. 15% alc.
Rating 90 **To** 2023 $25

✪ **The Loquat Tree MGS 2008** Deep colour; has greater depth of flavour than
most such blends (Mourvedre/Grenache/Shiraz) from the Clare Valley, with black
fruits, licorice and even a touch of tar; a sturdy wine with good cellaring prospects.
Screwcap. 14.5% alc. **Rating** 90 **To** 2018 $20

🍷🍷🍷🍷 **Watervale Riesling 2009 Rating** 88 **To** 2017 $25

Sticks ★★★★☆

179 Glenview Road, Yarra Glen, Vic 3775 **Region** Yarra Valley
T (03) 9730 1022 **F** (03) 9730 1131 **www.sticks.com.au Open** 7 days 10–5
Winemaker Travis Bush **Est.** 2000 **Cases** 60 000
In 2005 the former Yarra Ridge winery, with a 3000-tonne capacity and 25 ha of vineyards planted mainly in 1983, was acquired by a partnership headed by Rob 'Sticks' Dolan. The estate production is significantly supplemented by contract-grown grapes sourced elsewhere in the Yarra Valley and surrounding regions. Sticks also provides substantial contract-making facilities for wineries throughout the Yarra Valley. While remaining a shareholder, Rob has ceased to have any management or winemaking role at Sticks. Exports to the UK, the US, Hong Kong and China.

ŸŸŸŸŸ **No. 29 Strathbogie Ranges Shiraz 2008** Bright colour, vivid hue; lifted red and purple fruits dominate the bouquet, with a light sprinkling of cinnamon and clove; medium-bodied, with ample fine-grained tannins, black pepper and juicy acidity drawing out the finish harmoniously. Screwcap. 14.5% alc. **Rating** 94 To 2020 $40 BE

ŸŸŸŸŸ **No 29. Yea Valley Cabernet Shiraz 2007 Rating** 93 To 2020 $35
✪ **Yarra Valley Chardonnay 2008** A slightly funky bouquet is probably deliberate as part of an early-picked style, with tight fruit flavours (citrus/apple/melon); good acidity lengthens the palate and finish. Screwcap. 13% alc. **Rating** 90 To 2015 $20

ŸŸŸŸ **Yarra Valley Cabernet Sauvignon 2008 Rating** 88 To 2014 $20
Yarra Valley Botrytis Semillon 2008 Rating 88 To 2013 $25 BE

🍇 Stockman's Ridge Wines ★★★☆

GPO Box 155, Sydney, NSW 2001 **Region** Orange
T (02) 9972 3440 **F** (02) 9972 3443 **www.stockmansridge.com.au Open** Not
Winemaker Jonathan Hambrook **Est.** 2004 **Cases** 2800 **Vyds** 3 ha
Jonathan Hambrook purchased what he aptly named Stockman's Ridge in 2002. Situated 20 km north of Bathurst at 900 m above sea level, it has spectacular views to the south. Since it was acquired, barely a month has gone by without activities involving the Hambrook family. A cherry orchard was established, cattle grazing commenced, a 1 million litre dam completed, and sequential planting throughout 2004 and '05 with shiraz, pinot gris, pinot noir and savagnin the varieties chosen. Over and above this, Jonathan has leased two vineyards in Orange planted to merlot, shiraz, pinot gris and sauvignon blanc. While he has no formal winemaking qualifications, he is able to draw on advice from David Lowe (Lowe Family Wines), Mark Renzaglia (Winburndale Wines) and Phil Kerney (Ross Hill).

ŸŸŸŸŸ **Shiraz 2008** Good crimson hue, although not entirely bright; typical cool-climate shiraz with bright fruit, spice and pepper notes; well-handled oak and tannin inputs. Screwcap. 14.5% alc. **Rating** 90 To 2016 $25

ŸŸŸŸ **Sauvignon Blanc 2009 Rating** 87 To 2010 $21

Stomp Wine ★★★

891 Milbrodale Road, Broke, NSW 2330 (postal) **Region** Hunter Valley
T (02) 6579 1400 **F** (02) 6579 1400 **www.stompwine.com.au Open** Not
Winemaker Michael McManus **Est.** 2004 **Cases** 500
After a lifetime in the food and beverage industry, Michael and Meredith McManus have finally made a decisive move to full-time occupation in all aspects of winemaking. They have set up Stomp Winemaking, a contract winemaker designed to keep small and larger parcels of grapes separate through the fermentation and maturation process, thus meeting the needs of boutique wine producers in the Hunter Valley. The addition of their own label, Stomp, is a small but important part of their business, the Chardonnay, Verdelho and Shiraz made from purchased grapes.

ŶŶŶŶ   **Hunter Valley Verdelho 2009** Has the classic fruit salad mix of the variety, enhanced by the lemony acidity of the year. Screwcap. 13.5% alc. **Rating** 88 To 2011 $17
Hunter Valley Rose 2009 Bright crimson-purple; plenty of overall flavour, red fruits plus a touch of sweetness, but not the finesse of the best. Screwcap. 12.5% alc. **Rating** 87 **To** 2010 $15

Stone Bridge Wines   ★★★★☆

Section 113 Gillentown Road, Clare, SA 5453 **Region** Clare Valley
T (08) 8843 4143 **F** (08) 8843 4143 **Open** Thurs–Mon 10–4
Winemaker Craig Thomson **Est.** 2005 **Cases** 2500 **Vyds** 0.5 ha
Stone Bridge Wines started out as a hobby but has turned into a commercial enterprise for its owners, Craig and Lisa Thomson. They say that Craig's 16 years as a baker has assisted in the art of winemaking: 'It's all about the mix.' Their small patch of shiraz provides only a small part of the annual crush; riesling, pinot gris, cabernet sauvignon and malbec are purchased from local growers. The cellar door is a rammed-earth and iron building with picturesque surrounds, where on Sundays Sept–May (weather permitting), visitors can relax and enjoy a gourmet wood oven pizza.

ŶŶŶŶŶ   **Clare Valley Riesling 2009** Bright green-straw; a precocious but delicious
❂   wine already displaying an array of citrus-based aromas and flavours, but has an undoubted future. Gold medal Clare Valley Wine Show '09. Screwcap. 12.2% alc. **Rating** 94 **To** 2019 $18

ŶŶŶŶŶ   **Clare Valley Shiraz 2007** Convincing purple-red; an aromatic dark berry
❂   bouquet leads into a supple, medium-bodied palate with blackberry, plum and vanilla flavours backed by fine tannins. Screwcap. 14.5% alc. **Rating** 93 **To** 2020 $20

Stonehurst Cedar Creek   ★★★★

Wollombi Road, Cedar Creek, NSW 2325 **Region** Hunter Valley
T (02) 4998 1576 **F** (02) 4998 0008 **www**.cedarcreekcottages.com.au **Open** 7 days 10–5
Winemaker Monarch Winemaking Services **Est.** 1995 **Cases** 4000 **Vyds** 6.5 ha
Stonehurst Cedar Creek has been established by Daryl and Phillipa Heslop on a historic 220-ha property in the Wollombi Valley, underneath the Pokolbin Range. The vineyards (chambourcin, semillon, chardonnay and shiraz) are organically grown. A substantial part of the business, however, is the six self-contained cottages on the property. Skilled contract winemaking has produced great results. Exports to all major markets.

ŶŶŶŶŶ   **Hunter Valley Golden Dessert Semillon 2003** Deep orange-gold; has kept a delicious skein of acidity to counterbalance the voluptuous butterscotch and cumquat fruit. Cork. 9.7% alc. **Rating** 92 **To** 2012 $25
Methode Champenoise Chardonnay Semillon 2006 Good mousse; pale straw-green; fresh and lively with good length, although still to build complexity. Will benefit from further time on cork. Trophy Hunter Valley Boutique Winemakers Show '09. 11.5% alc. **Rating** 90 **To** 2012 $29.50

ŶŶŶŶ   **Reserve Hunter Valley Chardonnay 2007** **Rating** 88 **To** 2012 $25

Stoney Rise   ★★★★★

Hendersons Lane, Gravelly Beach, Tas 7276 **Region** Northern Tasmania
T (03) 6394 3678 **F** (03) 6394 3684 **www**.stoneyrise.com **Open** Thurs–Mon 11–5
Winemaker Joe Holyman **Est.** 2000 **Cases** 1500
This is the venture of Joe and Lou Holyman. The Holyman family has been involved in vineyards in Tasmania for 20 years, but Joe's career in the wine industry, first as a sales rep, as a wine buyer, and more recently working in wineries in NZ, Portugal, France, Mount Benson and Coonawarra, gave him an exceptionally broad-based understanding of wine. In 2004 Joe

and Lou purchased the former Rotherhythe vineyard, which had been established in '86 but was in a somewhat rundown state, and set about restoring the vineyard to its former glory, with 3 ha of pinot noir and 1 ha of chardonnay. There are two ranges: the Stoney Rise wines focusing on fruit and early drinkability, the Holyman wines with more structure, more new oak and the best grapes, here the focus on length and potential longevity. The 2006 Pinots had spectacular success at the Tas Wine Show '07. Exports to the UK.

ŦŦŦŦŦ **Holyman Pinot Noir 2008** The bouquet is very pure and fragrant, the fruit in a plum and black cherry mode. There is indeed greater texture, structure and depth than the varietal, the fruit carrying the oak with aplomb. Screwcap. 14% alc. **Rating** 96 **To** 2017 $45

Holyman Chardonnay 2008 A fragrant bouquet in the grapefruit and white peach spectrum of cool-grown chardonnay, and has abundant thrust and energy on the palate; the oak is well integrated, the overall line and length all you could ask for. Screwcap. 14% alc. **Rating** 94 **To** 2014 $45

✪ **Pinot Noir 2008** Deep crimson-purple; has the richness of depth that only Tasmania can produce without losing varietal character; black cherry and plum fruit drive the wine, cleansing acidity on the long finish. Screwcap. 14% alc. **Rating** 94 **To** 2018 $29

ŦŦŦŦŢ **Riesling 2008** Pale bright green, quite striking; the vibrancy and freshness of
✪ the citrussy fruit is built around typical Tasmanian acidity not duplicated on the mainland; has excellent length to its flinty finish. Screwcap. 12.5% alc. **Rating** 92 **To** 2018 $25

Chardonnay 2008 Rating 90 **To** 2014 $29

Stonier Wines   ★★★★★
Cnr Thompson's Lane/Frankston-Flinders Road, Merricks, Vic 3916
Region Mornington Peninsula
T (03) 5989 8300 **F** (03) 5989 8709 **www**.stoniers.com.au **Open** 7 days 11–5
Winemaker Michael Symons **Est.** 1978 **Cases** 25 000 **Vyds** 6.25 ha
One of the most senior wineries on the Mornington Peninsula, now part of the Petaluma group, which is in turn owned by Lion Nathan of NZ. Wine quality is assured, as is the elegant, restrained style of the Chardonnay and Pinot Noir. In 2008 long-serving winemaker Geraldine McFaul left to take up another position, and it remains to be seen whether the style will change. Replacement winemaker Mike Symons has a track record of nearly 20 years with the Petaluma group, both before and after its acquisition by Lion Nathan. Exports to Europe, Canada, Malaysia, Vietnam and China.

ŦŦŦŦŦ **Reserve Mornington Peninsula Pinot Noir 2008** An elegant red-fruited bouquet, framed by sappy spice and a gentle seasoning of oak; the palate is restrained, and takes time to let the bright cherry fruits unravel to a complex array of spices; silky in structure, with ample fine-grained tannins, and refreshing acidity draws out the even finish. Screwcap. 13.5% alc. **Rating** 95 **To** 2016 $50 BE

Windmill Vineyard Mornington Peninsula Pinot Noir 2007 Bright cherry fruit is augmented by an unusual and interesting bouquet of sappy, slightly herbaceous tones from the use of stems; the palate reveals a firm structure, with cherry again coming to the fore; whole bunch Asian spice and green sappy notes combine well, and the acidity provides a clean and linear conclusion. Screwcap. 13.5% alc. **Rating** 95 **To** 2016 $60 BE

✪ **Mornington Peninsula Pinot Noir 2008** Light colour, but hue good; fragrant spicy red fruits on the bouquet, the warm spicy notes even more apparent on the palate, which also has delicious red fruits and a long finish. Screwcap. 13.5% alc. **Rating** 94 **To** 2015 $28

ŦŦŦŦŢ **KBS Vineyard Mornington Peninsula Pinot Noir 2007 Rating** 93 **To** 2015 $60 BE

Reserve Mornington Peninsula Chardonnay 2008 Rating 92 **To** 2015 $42 BE

KBS Vineyard Mornington Peninsula Chardonnay 2007 Rating 91
To 2015 $55 BE

ҮҮҮҮ   Mornington Peninsula Chardonnay 2008 Rating 88 To 2013 $24 BE

Streicker   ★★★★★

412 Abbeys Farm Road, Yallingup, WA 6282 (postal) **Region** Margaret River
T (08) 9755 2108 **F** (08) 9755 2139 **www**.streickerwines.com.au **Open** Not
Winemaker Naturaliste Vintners (Bruce Dukes) **Est.** 2002 **Cases** 1850 **Vyds** 146.09 ha
This is a multifaceted business owned by New York resident John Streicker. It began in 2002
when he purchased the Yallingup Protea Farm and Vineyards, followed by the purchase of the
Ironstone Vineyard in '03, and finally the Bridgeland Vineyard, which has one of the largest
dams in the region, 1 km long and covering 18 ha. The Ironstone Vineyard is one of the
oldest vineyards in the Wilyabrup subregion, and required significant rehabilitation after its
acquisition, notably the removal of a pine tree plantation that had made large inroads into the
water table, as well as providing protection from marauding kangaroos. Virtually all the grapes
from the three vineyards are sold, and the proteas (from 12 ha) are exported to the US. The
Ironstone Block Old Vine Chardonnay has received numerous awards. Exports to the US and
Hong Kong.

ҮҮҮҮҮ   Ironstone Block Old Vine Margaret River Chardonnay 2008 This wine
and two prior vintages are style triplets, the elegant and harmonious fusion of
stone fruit with subtle French oak is common to all, as is excellent length. It
may be just youth, but this has the most character. Screwcap. 14% alc. **Rating** 95
To 2015 $32.50
Ironstone Block Old Vine Margaret River Chardonnay 2007 Very similar
in style to the '06, equally bright in colour and youthful in flavour; here a touch
of citrus enters the equation which, by rights, should have been in the '06; again,
harmonious and long. Screwcap. 14% alc. **Rating** 95 To 2014 $32.50
Ironstone Block Old Vine Margaret River Chardonnay 2006 Still
unevolved colour, green-straw; a thoroughly elegant wine, with white peach and
nectarine fruit backed by subtle French oak; very good balance to a harmonious
wine. Screwcap. 14% alc. **Rating** 95 To 2013 $32.50

ҮҮҮҮҮ   Ironstone Block Old Vine Margaret River Cabernet Sauvignon 2007
Rating 91 To 2020 $38.50

Stringy Brae of Sevenhill   ★★★★

Sawmill Road, Sevenhill, SA 5453 **Region** Clare Valley
T (08) 8843 4313 **F** (08) 8843 4319 **www**.stringybrae.com.au **Open** By appt
Winemaker O'Leary Walker **Est.** 1991 **Cases** 2200 **Vyds** 5 ha
Donald and Sally Willson began planting their vineyard in 1991, having purchased the
property in '83. In 2004 daughter Hannah Rantanen took over day-to-day management.
Subsequently, the estate vineyard has been trimmed to 5 ha of cabernet sauvignon, and wine
production reduced. On the other side of the equation, shiraz and malbec are purchased from
Clare Valley growers. Exports to Canada, Denmark and Indonesia.

ҮҮҮҮҮ   Clare Valley Shiraz 2006 From a good vintage, to be sure, but this medium-
❂   bodied wine has more juicy and lively fruit flavour than is common in the Clare
Valley; the tannins, too, are fine. Screwcap. 14.5% alc. **Rating** 93 To 2016 $24
Clare Valley Riesling 2009 Bright colour; still very firm and tight, needing
time to open up and display the fruit presently locked up in a minerally finish.
Screwcap. 12% alc. **Rating** 90 To 2024 $24

ҮҮҮҮ   Clare Valley Cabernet Shiraz Malbec 2006 Rating 89 To 2018 $22

Stuart Wines ★★★★★

105 Killara Road, Gruyere, Vic 3770 (postal) **Region** Yarra Valley
T (03) 5964 9312 **F** (03) 5964 9313 www.stuartwinesco.com.au **Open** Not
Winemaker Peter Wilson **Est.** 1999 **Cases** 95 000 **Vyds** 131.4 ha
Hendra Widjaja came to Australia from Indonesia to establish a vineyard and winery, and
he initially chose the Yarra Valley for the first vineyard, thereafter establishing a larger one in
Heathcote. The Yarra Valley vineyard is 61.9 ha (pinot noir, shiraz, cabernet sauvignon, merlot,
chardonnay, sangiovese, pinot gris, mataro, petit verdot and viognier), the Heathcote vineyard
75.5 ha (shiraz, nebbiolo, tempranillo, merlot, viognier and cabernet sauvignon). The wines
are made at the Heathcote winery. While the major part of the production is exported, there
are also direct sales in Australia. Wines are released under the Cahillton, White Box and Huma
labels. Exports to Germany, The Netherlands, Indonesia, Malaysia, Macau, Taiwan, Hong
Kong, China and NZ.

ȲȲȲȲȲ **Whitebox Cellar Release Heathcote Shiraz 2005** A supple and lively
❂   medium-bodied shiraz with appealing plum and spicy fruitcake characters; has
      particularly good length and fine mouthfeel through to the finish. Screwcap.
      14.8% alc. **Rating** 95 **To** 2015 $24.95
❂   **Cahillton Heathcote Shiraz 2007** Bright purple-crimson; an unusually elegant
      expression of Heathcote, and also a complex one, fruit and oak making more or
      less equal contributions, the flavours running from plum to mocha. Screwcap.
      14.5% alc. **Rating** 94 **To** 2022 $22.50
❂   **Cahillton Deja Vu Yarra Valley Cabernet Merlot 2006** Has retained
      excellent colour; a classy medium-bodied wine that reflects the synergy between
      the blend as such and also its region; blackcurrant, cassis and quality cedary
      oak are coupled with fine-grained tannins. Screwcap. 14.5% alc. **Rating** 94
      To 2021 $22.50

ȲȲȲȲȲ **Cahillton Deja Vu Yarra Valley Pinot Noir 2008** Bright, clear red-purple; the
❂   fragrant bouquet has red cherry and plum, the palate totally seductive satin and silk
      texture; good length. Screwcap. 14.5% alc. **Rating** 93 **To** 2014 $22.50
❂   **Whitebox Heathcote Shiraz 2007** Vivid colour; in near total style contrast
      to Cahillton, with greater density and extract of black fruits, dark chocolate,
      tannins and oak; will richly repay cellaring. Screwcap. 14.5% alc. **Rating** 93
      To 2025 $19.50
      Cahillton Reserve Yarra Valley Pinot Gris 2008 Rating 91 **To** 2015 $19.95
❂   **Whitebox Yarra Valley Pinot Noir 2008** Strong, clear colour; in a very
      different style to Deja Vu; both the bouquet and palate are notably complex, with
      spice, forest, leaf and game; the texture lacks the silk of the Deja Vu. Screwcap.
      14% alc. **Rating** 90 **To** 2015 $19.50
❂   **Huma Reserve Heathcote Shiraz 2006** Fresh colour; red and black fruits
      on the palate lead into a medium-bodied palate with similar fresh fruits and
      fractionally disconnected tannins on the finish. Screwcap. 14.5% alc. **Rating** 90
      To 2015 $14.95

ȲȲȲȲ **Huma Yarra Valley Shiraz 2006** Bright red-crimson; despite its alcohol, is only
❂   light- to medium-bodied at best; the flavours are fresh and correct in a red cherry/
      plum spectrum, and no confection. The tannins are barely present, French oak
      integrated. A bewildering price for a wine ready right now. Screwcap. 14% alc.
      Rating 89 **To** 2013 $10
❂   **Huma Yarra Valley Cabernet Merlot 2006** The elegant label design (and
      the mythological bird of paradise theme – the Huma) are at odds with the price,
      although here there are a few slightly syrupy notes among the blackcurrant fruit.
      Screwcap. 14% alc. **Rating** 88 **To** 2013 $10
❂   **Huma Yarra Valley Pinot Noir 2008** Bright, clear colour; the otherwise
      inexplicable price is explained by some sarsparilla/confection fruit flavours, but
      served chilled with Chinese roast duck, all would be forgiven. Screwcap. 14.5% alc.
      Rating 87 **To** 2012 $10

Studley Park Vineyard   ★★★

5 Garden Terrace, Kew, Vic 3101 (postal) **Region** Port Phillip Zone
T (03) 9254 2777 **F** (03) 9853 4901 **www**.studleypark.com **Open** Not
Winemaker Llew Knight (Contract) **Est.** 1994 **Cases** 250 **Vyds** 0.5 ha
Geoff Pryor's Studley Park Vineyard is one of Melbourne's best-kept secrets. It is on a bend
of the Yarra River barely 4 km from the Melbourne CBD, on a 0.5-ha block once planted to
vines, but for a century used for market gardening, then replanted with cabernet sauvignon. A
spectacular aerial photograph shows that immediately across the river, and looking directly to
the CBD, is the epicentre of Melbourne's light industrial development, while on the northern
and eastern boundaries are suburban residential blocks.

ŸŸŸŸ   **Cabernet 2006** The colour is quite good, even though the wine spent three and
a half years in oak; the wine has a slightly dusty bouquet (not uncommon with
cabernet) contrasting with the almost liqueur sweetness of the palate. Still, a real
curio. Screwcap. 14.5% alc. **Rating** 89 **To** 2015 $25

Stumpy Gully   ★★★★☆

1247 Stumpy Gully Road, Moorooduc, Vic 3933 **Region** Mornington Peninsula
T (03) 5978 8429 **F** (03) 5978 8419 **www**.stumpygully.com.au **Open** W'ends 11–5
Winemaker Wendy, Frank and Michael Zantvoort **Est.** 1988 **Cases** 8600 **Vyds** 33 ha
Frank and Wendy Zantvoort began planting their first vineyard in 1988; Wendy, having
enrolled in the oenology course at CSU, subsequently graduated with B. App.Sc (Oenology).
Together with son Michael, the Zantvoorts look after all aspects of grapegrowing and
winemaking. In addition to the original vineyard, they have deliberately gone against
prevailing thinking with their Moorooduc vineyard, planting it solely to red varieties,
predominantly cabernet sauvignon, merlot and shiraz. They believe they have one of the
warmest sites on the Peninsula, and that ripening will present no problems. In all they now
have 10 varieties planted, producing two ranges (Peninsula Panorama is their second label).
Exports to all major markets.

ŸŸŸŸŸ   **Mornington Peninsula Cabernet Sauvignon 2007** Retains good depth
✪   and hue; a very good example of cool-climate cabernet, with intense black fruits
and fully ripe, but balanced tannins in support on the long, full-bodied palate.
Screwcap. 14% alc. **Rating** 94 **To** 2022 $25

ŸŸŸŸŸ   **Mornington Peninsula Marsanne 2008** Very interesting to see marsanne
✪   performing so well in such a cool climate; has excellent mouthfeel, and all of the
honeysuckle – and indeed, honey – expected of the variety. Theoretically, should
benefit from cellaring. Screwcap. 14% alc. **Rating** 92 **To** 2013 $25
Magic Black Zantvoort Reserve Pinot Noir 2007 Rating 91 **To** 2017 $48
✪   **Mornington Peninsula Merlot 2008** Strong red-purple; a powerful evocation
of the variety on bouquet and palate alike, with plum and cassis fruit supported by
positive tannins and French oak. Screwcap. 14% alc. **Rating** 91 **To** 2016 $25
✪   **Mornington Peninsula Sangiovese 2008** Bright red-purple; a fragrant
bouquet and a light, but supple and smooth sour cherry palate and a clean finish.
Little to be gained by cellaring it. Screwcap. 13.5% alc. **Rating** 90 **To** 2011 $22

ŸŸŸŸ   **Mornington Peninsula Sauvignon Blanc 2009 Rating** 89 **To** 2010 $20
Mornington Peninsula Chardonnay 2008 Rating 89 **To** 2013 $22
Mornington Peninsula Pinot Grigio 2009 Rating 89 **To** 2010 $22
✪   **Peninsula Panorama Pinot Noir 2009** Light, brilliantly clear magenta; red
cherry and strawberry aromas and flavours on a perfect light-bodied, drink-now
style at an enticing price. Screwcap. 13.4% alc. **Rating** 89 **To** 2012 $15
✪   **Peninsula Panorama Shiraz 2008** Purple-crimson; specifically made for
early consumption, but this is not a namby pamby wine: the fruit flavours are
generous and sweet, the tannins all but invisible. Screwcap. 13.3% alc. **Rating** 89
To 2012 $15

Sugarloaf Ridge ★★★★

336 Sugarloaf Road, Carlton River, Tas 7173 **Region** Southern Tasmania
T (03) 6265 7175 **F** (03) 6266 7275 **www**.sugarloafridge.com **Open** Fri–Mon 10–5 Oct–May
Winemaker Winemaking Tasmania (Julian Alcorso) **Est.** 1999 **Cases** 300
Dr Simon Stanley and wife Isobel are both microbiologists, but with thoroughly unlikely
specialities: he in low-temperature microbiology, taking him to the Antarctic, and she in
a worldwide environmental geosciences company. Sugarloaf Ridge is an extended family
business, with daughter Kristen and husband Julian Colville partners. Multiple clones of pinot
noir, sauvignon blanc, pinot gris, viognier and lagrein have been planted, and 1580 native trees,
210 olive trees and 270 cherry trees have also helped transform the property.

🍷🍷🍷🍷🍷 **Sauvignon Blanc 2009** A very pure and precise proportioned and balanced
sauvignon; while the flavours are numerous, they are seamlessly moulded into
a tangy profile that is neither tropical nor grassy, just somewhere in between.
Screwcap. 12.8% alc. **Rating** 92 **To** 2011 $25
Pinot Noir 2007 Youthful red-purple; offers a mix of dark cherry, plum and spice
on bouquet and palate alike; good intensity and length. Time to go. Screwcap.
13.4% alc. **Rating** 90 **To** 2014 $33

🍷🍷🍷🍷 **Chardonnay 2007 Rating** 89 **To** 2014 $27

Summerfield ★★★★★

5967 Stawell-Avoca Road, Moonambel, Vic 3478 **Region** Pyrenees
T (03) 5467 2264 **F** (03) 5467 2380 **www**.summerfieldwines.com **Open** 7 days 9–5
Winemaker Mark Summerfield **Est.** 1979 **Cases** 8000 **Vyds** 13.49 ha
Founder Ian Summerfield has now handed over the winemaking reins to son Mark,
who produces consistently outstanding and awesomely concentrated Shiraz and Cabernet
Sauvignon, both in varietal and Reserve forms. The red wines are built for the long haul, and
richly repay cellaring. Exports to the US, Canada, Hong Kong and China.

🍷🍷🍷🍷🍷 **Reserve Shiraz 2008** Healthy red-purple; a thoroughly attractive wine, its
flavours achieved at modest alcohol; the bouquet has plum and mocha aromas,
joined by touches of spice and chocolate on the medium-bodied palate; the
texture of the tannins is very good, as is the oak balance. Screwcap. 14% alc.
Rating 95 **To** 2025 $50
Jo Cabernet 2008 Has the brightest colour of the three Summerfield
Cabernets; this is an altogether finer wine, with far more precision to the varietal
fruit expression and more thrust to the palate; there is no easy ride here, nor
should there be; the palate is long, bright, blackcurrant and cassis to the fore, the
tannins firm but not aggressive, the oak less overt and less vanillan. Screwcap. 14%
alc. **Rating** 95 **To** 2028 $80
Saieh 2008 Similar colour to the Reserve; an opulent shiraz exclusively available
through the Summerfield Members Club; has all the richness that lies at the heart
of the Summerfield style. Screwcap. 14.8% alc. **Rating** 94 **To** 2020 $35
✪ **Shiraz 2008** Curiously, the colour is the brightest of the three '08 Shirazs; the
bouquet is full of dark plum and blackberry fruit, the multiple layers of flavour on
the medium- to full-bodied palate encompass blackberry fruit, vanillan oak and
plum cake. Screwcap. 14.5% alc. **Rating** 94 **To** 2023 $27
Reserve Cabernet 2008 Strong red-purple; the bouquet has abundant
blackcurrant, cassis and cedary oak, the latter not too obvious; the palate is very
supple, with built-in tannins woven through ripe (but not overripe) black fruits.
Screwcap. 14.8% alc. **Rating** 94 **To** 2023 $50

🍷🍷🍷🍷🍷 **Tradition 2008 Rating** 93 **To** 2020 $27
Cabernet 2008 Rating 92 **To** 2016 $27

🍷🍷🍷🍷 **Merlot 2008 Rating** 88 **To** 2014 $27

Summit Estate ★★★★★

291 Granite Belt Drive, Thulimbah, Qld 4377 **Region** Granite Belt
T (07) 4683 2011 **F** (07) 4683 2600 **www.**summitestate.com.au **Open** 7 days 9–5
Winemaker Paola Cabezas Rhymer **Est.** 1997 **Cases** 2500
Summit Estate is the public face of the Stanthorpe Wine Co, owned by a syndicate of 10
professionals who work in Brisbane, and share a love of wine. They operate the Stanthorpe
Wine Centre, which offers wine education as well as selling wines from other makers in the
region (and, of course, from Summit Estate). The 17-ha vineyard is planted to chardonnay,
marsanne, pinot noir, shiraz, merlot, tempranillo, petit verdot and cabernet sauvignon, and they
have set up a small, specialised contract winemaking facility. The wines have improved out of
all recognition under the direction of Paola Cabezas Rhymer. Exports to the UK.

ΨΨΨΨΨ **The QC Queensland Cabernets Cabernet Sauvignon Merlot Petit**
✪   **Verdot Malbec 2008** Excellent colour; a convincing example of the blend, the
        flavours a basket of black fruits, the silky tannins ripe and running through the
        length of the palate. Screwcap. 14% alc. **Rating** 94 **To** 2018 $30
✪   **Alto Spanish Collection Monastrell Garnacha Shyra Tempranillo**
        Cabernet Tannat 2008 Good colour; shyra is an Austrian synonym for shiraz,
        and the apparently ambitious blend works very well; there is deceptive power in
        the seemingly medium-bodied palate, the texture fusing tannins and juicy yet
        sultry fruit flavours. Screwcap. 14.2% alc. **Rating** 94 **To** 2020 $30

ΨΨΨΨΨ **The Finest Acre Reserve Shiraz 2008 Rating** 93 **To** 2020 $25
        Barrel Ferment Chardonnay 2009 Rating 92 **To** 2015 $25
        Alto Spanish Collection Tempranillo 2008 Rating 92 **To** 2015 $30
        The Pinnacle Premium White 2007 Rating 90 **To** 2012 $19

ΨΨΨΨ   **The Pinnacle Premium Red 2007 Rating** 89 **To** 2017 $19

Sunset Winery ★★★

Main Penneshaw-Kingscote Road, Penneshaw, SA 5222 **Region** Kangaroo Island
T (08) 8553 1378 **F** (08) 8553 1379 **www.**sunset-wines.com.au **Open** 7 days 11–5
Winemaker Colin Hopkins **Est.** 2003 **Cases** 2500
This boutique winery is owned and run by friends and business partners Colin Hopkins and
Athalie and David Martin. Construction of the winery and cellar door, with elevated sea views
overlooking Eastern Cove and beyond, was completed in 2003. It is otherwise surrounded by
14 ha of native bushland, with a profusion of wildlife. Sunset Winery was the first dedicated
cellar door on Kangaroo Island, and offers a range of products to accompany the Chardonnay,
Cabernet Sauvignon, Shiraz and Sparkling Shiraz sourced from local growers.

ΨΨΨΨ   **Summertime Kangaroo Island Chardonnay 2008** Pale straw-quartz; entirely
        fruit-driven on both bouquet and palate, with white and yellow peach fruit; gentle
        acidity and good length. Screwcap. 13.5% alc. **Rating** 89 **To** 2012 $18
        Kangaroo Island Shiraz 2006 Good colour; has the depth of aroma and flavour
        missing from some of the Sunset wines; there are spicy overtones to the dark
        cherry fruit of the medium-bodied palate; good tannin and oak management.
        Screwcap. 14.3% alc. **Rating** 89 **To** 2016 $18
        Kangaroo Island Sauvignon Blanc 2009 Pale quartz-green; a light-bodied
        sauvignon blanc neatly balanced between the grassy and tropical styles; delicate
        snow pea in the former, lychee in the latter. Screwcap. 12.3% alc. **Rating** 87
        To 2011 $19

Surveyor's Hill Winery ★★★★☆

215 Brooklands Road, Wallaroo, NSW 2618 **Region** Canberra District
T (02) 6230 2046 **www.**survhill.com.au **Open** W'ends & public hols, or by appt
Winemaker Brindabella Hills Winery (Dr Roger Harris) **Est.** 1986 **Cases** 1000 **Vyds** 10 ha
The Surveyor's Hill vineyard is on the slopes of the eponymous hill, at 550–680 m above
sea level. It is an ancient volcano, producing granite-derived, coarse-structured (and hence

well-drained) sandy soils of low fertility. This has to be the ultimate patchwork-quilt winery, with 1 ha each of chardonnay, shiraz and viognier; 0.5 ha each of roussanne, marsanne, aglianico, nero d'alpha, mourvedre, grenache, muscadelle, moscato giallo, cabernet franc and riesling; and lesser amounts of semillon, sauvignon blanc, touriga nacional and cabernet sauvignon.

Hills of Hall Shiraz Cabernet 2008 Good colour; the 50/50 blend is totally synergistic, the abundant black and red berry fruits backed by ripe, smooth tannins underlining more spicy savoury notes of the fruit. Screwcap. 13.9% alc. **Rating** 94 To 2020 $25

Hills of Hall Riesling 2008 Bright straw-green; a powerful, tightly knit riesling, citrus and mineral wrapped around each other; good natural acidity will sustain long-term development. Screwcap. 11.5% alc. **Rating** 91 **To** 2020 $18

Hills of Hall Cabernet Franc Rose 2008 Pale pink; has the distinctive perfume (violet to the fore) of the variety; the palate opens up with red fruits before moving on to a dry finish. Good rose, even if the alcohol is relatively high. Screwcap. 14% alc. **Rating** 90 **To** 2011 $16

Hills of Hall Autumn Gold 2004 Glowing green-gold; has not become flabby and overblown as some of these wines can do with age, rather it has dried out a touch, emphasising its structure and minerality. Same points as when tasted three years ago. Cork. 8% alc. **Rating** 90 **To** 2012 $15

Hills of Hall Sweet Touriga NV A wine of some merit, mainly because of the low baume that takes it towards Portuguese styles; dark spicy fruit runs through the palate, the spirit relatively neutral. Anything could emerge with age. Screwcap. 19% alc. **Rating** 90 **To** 2020 $15

Hills of Hall Sauvignon Blanc Semillon 2009 Rating 88 To 2012 $18

Sutton Grange Winery ★★★☆

Carnochans Road, Sutton Grange, Vic 3448 **Region** Bendigo
T (03) 5474 8277 **F** (03) 5474 8294 **www**.suttongrangewines.com **Open** Mon–Fri 9–4, w'ends 11–5
Winemaker Gilles Lapalus **Est.** 1998 **Cases** 4000 **Vyds** 12.5 ha
The 400-ha Sutton Grange property is a horse training facility acquired in 1996 by Peter Sidwell, a Melbourne businessman with horse racing and breeding interests. A lunch visit to the property by long-term friends Alec Epis and Stuart Anderson led to the decision to plant syrah, merlot, cabernet sauvignon, viognier and sangiovese, and to the recruitment of French winemaker Gilles Lapalus, who just happens to be the partner of Stuart's daughter. The winery, built from WA limestone, was completed in 2001. Exports to the UK, Canada, Switzerland and Malaysia.

Fairbank Viognier 2009 Brilliant straw-green; skilled winemaking avoids phenolics, but leaves varietal character on display; whole bunch-pressed and wild yeast-fermented results in a complex wine. Screwcap. 14% alc. **Rating** 91 To 2012 $30

Fairbank Rose 2009 Rating 88 To 2012 $22

Swinging Bridge ★★★★☆

'Belubula', Fish Fossil Drive, Canowindra, NSW 2804 **Region** Central Ranges Zone
T 0409 246 609 **F** (02) 6344 3232 **www**.swingingbridge.com.au **Open** By appt
Winemaker Tom Ward, Chris Derrez (Contract) **Est.** 1995 **Cases** 2000 **Vyds** 77 ha
This is the venture of the Ward family, headed by Mark, who immigrated to Australia in 1965 from the UK with an honours degree in agricultural science from Cambridge University. The vineyard is part of a farming property, Gayton, 10 km from Canowindra. The name comes from a suspension walking bridge that crosses the Belubula River at the foot of the vineyard. Since the first wines were made in 1997, Swinging Bridge has had considerable success in wine shows.

♟♟♟♟♟ Canowindra Shiraz 2008 Good hue; has attractive black cherry and blackberry on the bouquet and medium-bodied palate alike; good balance and length. Gold medal Sydney Wine Show '10. Screwcap. 14.1% alc. **Rating** 94 **To** 2018 $19.95

♟♟♟♟♀ Canowindra Chardonnay 2008 **Rating** 90 **To** 2012 $19

♟♟♟♟ Orange Sauvignon Blanc 2009 **Rating** 89 **To** 2012 $19

Swings & Roundabouts ★★★★☆

2807 Caves Road, Yallingup, WA 6232 **Region** Margaret River
T (08) 9756 6640 **F** (08) 9756 6736 **www**.swings.com.au **Open** 7 days 10–5
Winemaker Brian Fletcher **Est.** 2004 **Cases** 25 000
The Swings & Roundabouts name comes from the expression used to encapsulate the eternal balancing act between the various aspects of grape and wine production. Swings aims to balance the serious side with a touch of fun. There are now four ranges: Kiss Chasey, Life of Riley, Swings & Roundabouts and the top-shelf Laneway. Exports to the UK, the US, Canada, Singapore and China.

♟♟♟♟♟ Premium Margaret River Chardonnay 2009 Bright green-straw; barrel-fermented and lees-contacted, but retains a core of vibrant fresh fruit, the oak framing that fruit and providing layered structure. Screwcap. 13.5% alc. **Rating** 94 **To** 2017 $29

♟♟♟♟♀ Margaret River Sauvignon Blanc Semillon 2009 All about drinkability;
✪ modest alcohol helps the freshness, but in no way detracts from the basket of fruit flavours running through citrus to white peach, perhaps reflecting the touch of chardonnay (a salute to Pierro). Screwcap. 12.5% alc. **Rating** 91 **To** 2012 $19
✪ Kiss Chasey Premium Red 2008 Light, bright crimson; a delicious fresh, flavoursome blend with at least some cabernet and merlot; significantly better than the price might suggest. Screwcap. 13.5% alc. **Rating** 91 **To** 2013 $15

♟♟♟♟ Margaret River Chardonnay 2009 **Rating** 89 **To** 2014 $19
✪ Kiss Chasey Rose 2009 Bright fuchsia; has an intensity of flavour well above many unwooded white wines, especially pinot gris and most verdelhos, its crunchy small red fruits (strawberry to the fore) needing no sweetness. Screwcap. 12.5% alc. **Rating** 89 **To** 2011 $15
Margaret River Shiraz 2008 **Rating** 89 **To** 2017 $19
Margaret River Cabernet Merlot 2008 **Rating** 89 **To** 2014 $19

🍇 Swish Wine ★★★★☆

247 Wilderness Road, Lovedale, NSW 2320 **Region** Hunter Valley
T (02) 8088 4222 **F** (02) 8088 1066 **www**.swishwine.com **Open** Thurs–Mon 10–5
Winemaker Sarah Crowe **Est.** 2008 **Cases** 9000 **Vyds** 20.3 ha
Katrina and Russell Leslie moved to the Hunter Valley in 2007 when they purchased Gartelmann Estate. Since then they have added Warraroong Estate, and employed former Brokenwood winemaker Sarah Crowe as chief winemaker, who presides over the new winery and cellar door on Wilderness Road. Tin Soldier wines were another impressive branch of the business at its inception. The Warraroong Vineyard was planted in 1978, the name an Aboriginal word for 'hillside', reflecting the southwesterly aspect of the property, which looks back toward the Brokenback Range and Watagan Mountains. The May 2010 acquisition of Wandin Valley Estate significantly increases the size and reach of the Swish Wine portfolio. Gartemann Estate is being retained as a separate entity.

♟♟♟♟♟ Saltire Hunter Valley Semillon 2009 Pale, bright colour; has capitalised on
✪ the perfect weather of the '09 vintage; grass and citrus aromas and flavours are the markers of a very elegant and restrained Lovedale subregion style. Screwcap. 10.8% alc. **Rating** 94 **To** 2020 $25

ΨΨΨΨ♀ Warraroong Estate Hunter Valley Semillon 2009 Rating 93 To 2020 $30
✪ Tin Soldier Hunter Valley Canberra District Semillon Sauvignon Blanc 2009 A fragrant, delicate wine, the two components combining synergistically, the semillon with freshness, the sauvignon blanc with passionfruit; very good balance and length. Screwcap. 12% alc. Rating 93 To 2012 $16
Saltire Hunter Valley Semillon 2009 Rating 92 To 2018 $17
✪ Tin Soldier Hunter Valley Merlot 2009 Bright colour; a fragrant and lively wine with a mix of black cherry and blackberry fruits, the tannins ripe and fine, oak in a pure support role. The Hunter Valley on a major roll. Screwcap. 13.5% alc. Rating 91 To 2016 $20
Warraroong Estate Claremont Chardonnay Methode Champenoise 2004 Rating 91 To 2013 $50
✪ Tin Soldier Hunter Valley Chardonnay 2009 Bright straw-green; bright, fresh and crisp in 'new' Hunter Valley style, with aromas and flavours of citrus and nectarine, finishing with crisp acidity, oak buried somewhere in the package. Screwcap. 13.1% alc. Rating 90 To 2015 $16
Warraroong Estate Hunter Valley Verdelho 2009 Rating 90 To 2013 $25

ΨΨΨΨ Tin Soldier Hunter Valley Semillon 2009 Rating 89 To 2015 $16
Warraroong Estate Long Lunch White 2009 Rating 87 To 2012 $22
Tin Soldier Hunter Valley Rose 2009 Rating 87 To 2011 $16

Swooping Magpie   ★★★☆

860 Commonage Road, Yallingup, WA 6282 **Region** Margaret River
T 0417 921 003 **F** (08) 9756 6227 **www.**swoopingmagpie.com.au **Open** 7 days 11–5
Winemaker Mark Standish (Contract) **Est.** 1998 **Cases** 2000 **Vyds** 4 ha
Neil and Leann Tuffield have established their vineyard in the hills behind the coastal town of Yallingup. The name, 'was inspired by a family of magpies who consider the property part of their territory'. Four hectares of vineyard (semillon, chenin blanc, sauvignon blanc, verdelho, cabernet franc, cabernet sauvignon, shiraz, merlot and muscat a petit grains) are supplemented by purchased sauvignon blanc, chenin blanc, shiraz, cabernet sauvignon and merlot.

ΨΨΨΨ♀ Le Commonage Margaret River Semillon 2009 Pale quartz-green; Margaret
✪ River semillon is very different from that of the Hunter Valley, in particular with its affinity for (controlled) French oak; this is a perfect example, the wine with purity and finesse, citrus/grass fruit the farewell on the palate, not oak. Screwcap. 13.5% alc. Rating 93 To 2016 $23

ΨΨΨΨ Margaret River Semillon Sauvignon Blanc 2009 Rating 89 To 2012 $18
Margaret River Shiraz 2006 Rating 89 To 2014 $18
Le Commonage Margaret River Cabernet Sauvignon 2007 Rating 87 To 2013 $25
Le Commonage Margaret River Cabernet Franc 2006 Rating 87 To 2013 $23

Symphonia Wines   ★★★★

1019 Snow Road, Oxley, Vic 3678 **Region** King Valley
T (03) 5727 3888 **F** (03) 5727 3853 **www.**sammiranda.com.au
Open At Sam Miranda (see separate entry)
Winemaker Sam Miranda **Est.** 1998 **Cases** 3000 **Vyds** 15 ha
Peter Read and his family were veterans of the King Valley, commencing the development of their vineyard in 1981 to supply Brown Brothers. As a result of extensive trips to both Western and Eastern Europe, Peter embarked on an ambitious project to trial a series of grape varieties little known in this country. The process of evaluation and experimentation produced a number of wines of great interest and no less merit. In 2005 Rachel Miranda (wife of Sam Miranda), with parents Peter and Suzanne Evans, purchased the business, and keeps its identity intact and separate from the Sam Miranda brand. Exports to China.

🍷🍷🍷🍷🍷 **Quintus King Valley Saperavi Tempranillo Tannat Merlot Cabernet**
2006 Has an element of Bill Clinton's 'because I could', but the outcome is far more successful, with a velvety mix of black fruits, licorice, plum, prune and spice. Screwcap. 14.5% alc. **Rating** 92 **To** 2015 $40

Symphony Hill Wines ★★★★☆

2017 Eukey Road, Ballandean, Qld 4382 **Region** Granite Belt
T (07) 4684 1388 **F** (07) 4684 1399 **www.**symphonyhill.com.au **Open** 7 days 10–4
Winemaker Mike Hayes **Est.** 1999 **Cases** 6000 **Vyds** 14 ha
Ewen and Elissa Macpherson purchased what was then an old table grape and orchard property in 1996. In partnership with Ewen's parents, Bob and Jill Macpherson, they developed 4 ha of vineyards, while Ewen completed his Bachelor of Applied Science in viticulture (2003). The vineyard (now much expanded) has been established using state-of-the-art technology; vineyard manager and winemaker Mike Hayes has a degree in viticulture and is a third-generation viticulturist in the Granite Belt region. It is planted to verdelho, viognier, pinot noir, shiraz, cabernet sauvignon, chardonnay, sauvignon blanc and pinot gris. Symphony Hill has firmly established its reputation as one of the Granite Belt's foremost wineries. Exports to Singapore and China.

🍷🍷🍷🍷🍷 **The Bolivian Reserve Shiraz 2008** Deep purple-red; the bouquet ranges between red and black fruits, spice a constant; the medium- to full-bodied palate combines juicy dark berry fruits with balanced tannins. A good result for a difficult vintage. Screwcap. 14.5% alc. **Rating** 93 **To** 2010 $65
Reserve Cabernet Sauvignon 2008 Deeper colour than the standard; has particularly good overall texture, structure and balance; the flavours are complex, with black fruits to the fore, and dark chocolate, vanilla and spice in the wings. Screwcap. 14.8% alc. **Rating** 93 **To** 2018 $45
Pinot Gris 2009 Very pale bronze; the ecstatic back label description is at least half justified; the wine has correct pear, apple and spice aromas and flavours, but it is the racy delivery of the palate that lifts it from the ruck. Screwcap. 12.9% alc. **Rating** 92 **To** 2012 $30
✪ **Granite Belt Cabernet Sauvignon 2008** Good colour; a fresh light- to medium-bodied cabernet that dismisses its alcohol with a flick of its wrist; black and redcurrant fruit is balanced by fine, supple tannins and subtle oak. Screwcap. 15% alc. **Rating** 91 **To** 2015 $25
Reserve Petit Verdot 2008 Good hue, although not the depth others achieve; an unusually perfumed red fruit profile, with an utterly unexpected touch of mint thrown in for good measure; a long way away from textbook petit verdot. Screwcap. 15% alc. **Rating** 91 **To** 2018 $45
✪ **Viognier 2009** Succeeds where others fail; the wine has positive varietal fruit in an apricot/peach/dried peach spectrum and has texture that is neither phenolic nor oily. Screwcap. 13% alc. **Rating** 90 **To** 2012 $20
🍷🍷🍷🍷 **Wild Child Viognier 2009 Rating** 89 **To** 2012 $30
Danying Cabernet Sauvignon Shiraz 2008 Rating 89 **To** 2015 $25
Reserve Granite Belt Verdelho 2009 Rating 88 **To** 2012 $25

Syrahmi ★★★★☆

PO Box 438, Heathcote, Vic 3523 **Region** Heathcote
T 0407 057 471 **www.**syrahmi.com.au **Open** Not
Winemaker Adam Foster **Est.** 2004 **Cases** 750
Adam Foster worked as a chef in Vic and London before moving to the front of house and becoming increasingly interested in wine. He then worked as a cellar hand with a who's who of Australia and France, including Torbreck, Chapoutier, Mitchelton, Domaine Ogier, Heathcote Winery, Jasper Hill and Domaine Pierre Gaillard. He became convinced that the Cambrian soils of Heathcote could produce the best possible shiraz, and since 2004 has purchased grapes from the region, using the full bag of open ferment techniques, with 30% whole bunches,

extended cold soak, wild yeast and mlf and hand plunging, then 13 months in French oak, bottled unfined and unfiltered. Exports to the US.

ŶŶŶŶŶ Maelstrom Heathcote Shiraz 2008 Some colour development; potent warm spice aromas are a component of an intense and complex palate, with smoky bacon oak and an array of fine, savoury flavours; there is a nagging question about the lack of voice from the fruit. Screwcap. 13.8% alc. **Rating** 92 **To** 2018

T'Gallant ★★★★

1385 Mornington-Flinders Road, Main Ridge, Vic 3928 **Region** Mornington Peninsula
T (03) 5989 6565 **F** (03) 5989 6577 **www**.tgallant.com.au **Open** 7 days 10–5
Winemaker Kevin McCarthy **Est.** 1990 **Cases** NFP
Husband-and-wife consultant winemakers Kevin McCarthy and Kathleen Quealy carved out such an important niche market for the T'Gallant label that in 2003, after protracted negotiations, it was acquired by Beringer Blass. The acquisition of a 15-ha property, and the planting of 10 ha of pinot gris gives the business a firm geographic base, as well as providing increased resources for its signature wine. La Baracca Trattoria is open 7 days for lunch and for specially booked evening events.

ŶŶŶŶŶ Cyrano Pinot Noir 2008 Bright, clear colour; a complex wine, with plentiful dark cherry fruit and underlying savoury forest floor flavours; good texture and length. Screwcap. 14% alc. **Rating** 93 **To** 2015 $28
Tribute Pinot Noir 2008 A note of sage and thyme frames the bright dark berry fruit; acidity drives the fruit, with a citrus/mandarin note providing contrast; showing depth of personality and firm structure, there is an element of perfume and power to this wine. Screwcap. 14% alc. **Rating** 91 **To** 2016 $40 BE

Taemas Wines ★★★★

121 Magennis Drive, Murrumbateman, NSW 2582 **Region** Canberra District
T (02) 6227 0346 **F** (02) 6227 0346 **www**.taemaswines.com.au **Open** By appt
Winemaker Alex McKay **Est.** 1997 **Cases** 350 **Vyds** 4 ha
Taemas is situated 15 km southwest of Murrumbateman and roughly 10 km north of the ACT, in a topographical area of the same name bestowed by Hume and Hovell when they passed through the district in the early 1820s; it is believed to be an old variation of the word Thames. Owners Peter McPherson and Peter Wheeler began planting the vineyard in 1997, and over eight years established 1 ha each of shiraz and cabernet sauvignon, adding 0.6 ha each of merlot, pinot noir (clone MV6) and shiraz in '99 and 2000, finishing with 0.1 ha each of viognier and pinot noir (clone 777), the last planted in '05. Interestingly, the 150 vines of viognier were sourced from Yarra Yering, a different clone from that of Yalumba. No Shiraz or Pinot were made in 2010 because of untimely rain, but Cabernet Sauvignon, Merlot and Malbec were unaffected.

ŶŶŶŶŶ Canberra District Shiraz Viognier 2008 Good crimson colour; a fragrant bouquet of dark cherry and spice, courtesy of the co-fermented viognier, then a medium-bodied palate with a pronounced lift to its structure, the flavours approaching raspberry. Screwcap. 14% alc. **Rating** 90 **To** 2018 $40
Canberra District Merlot 2008 Developed red; while relatively light-bodied, has a potent black olive varietal core to its red berry fruits; good length. Screwcap. 13.9% alc. **Rating** 90 **To** 2016 $35

ŶŶŶŶ Canberra District Pinot Noir 2008 Rating 87 **To** 2012 $40

Tahbilk ★★★★★

Goulburn Valley Highway, Tabilk, Vic 3608 **Region** Nagambie Lakes
T (03) 5794 2555 **F** (03) 5794 2360 **www**.tahbilk.com.au **Open** Mon–Sat 9–5, Sun 11–5
Winemaker Alister Purbrick, Neil Larson, Alan George **Est.** 1860 **Cases** 120 000
Vyds 222 ha

A winery steeped in tradition (with National Trust classification), which should be visited at least once by every wine-conscious Australian, and which makes wines – particularly red wines – utterly in keeping with that tradition. The essence of that heritage comes in the form of the tiny quantities of Shiraz made entirely from vines planted in 1860. In 2005 Tahbilk opened its wetlands project, with a series of walks connected (if you wish) by short journeys on a small punt. Serendipitous, perhaps, but the current release wines are absolutely outstanding, coinciding with the winery's 150th birthday (and concomitant celebrations). Exports to all major markets.

ŢŢŢŢŢ **1860 Vines Shiraz 2004** The wine has gloriously supple texture and structure
✪   directed to presenting pure red and black fruit shiraz flavours in the best possible
            light; has extreme length, and was a clear first preference among the 23 vintages
            of this wine made to date at the Tahbilk 150th birthday vertical tastings of all its
            wines. Cork. 14.3% alc. **Rating** 97 **To** 2024 $160
            Eric Stevens Purbrick Shiraz 2004 Showed superbly at the 150th tastings.
            Great balance and structure, supple and fine dark berry fruits; good oak. Rated top
            wine between 1960 and 2007. Cork. 13.8% alc. **Rating** 96 **To** 2024 $69.95
            Eric Stevens Purbrick Cabernet Sauvignon 2004 Some colour development;
            a complex medium-bodied wine, both bouquet and palate with a mix of
            blackcurrant, cedar and earth characters; the tannins are truly excellent, giving
            great mouthfeel. Ranked first of the 33 vintages (back to '56) at the 150th tastings.
            Cork. 14.1% alc. **Rating** 96 **To** 2030 $69.95
✪   **Cabernet Sauvignon 2006** Still crimson-purple; classic Tahbilk, built to last,
            the blackcurrant fruit interwoven through firm but balanced tannins, oak in the
            background; the finish is the strong point of a complete cabernet. Screwcap.
            14.5% alc. **Rating** 95 **To** 2026 $21.50
✪   **Shiraz 2006** Bright hue; in mainstream Tahbilk style, but with an extra edge from
            the vintage (excellent) and French oak; it is medium-bodied, the tannins are fine,
            the length and balance spot-on. Screwcap. 14% alc. **Rating** 94 **To** 2021 $21.50

ŢŢŢŢŢ **1927 Vines Marsanne 2000** **Rating** 92 **To** 2020 $45.50
✪   **Marsanne 2009** Pronounced honeysuckle aromas, the flavour and structure
            offering more than is usual so young. Could be special with a few more years
            bottle age. Screwcap. 13.5% alc. **Rating** 91 **To** 2015 $15.65
            Viognier 2009 **Rating** 90 **To** 2013 $21.50

ŢŢŢŢ   **Riesling 2009** **Rating** 89 **To** 2014 $16.45
            Chardonnay 2008 **Rating** 88 **To** 2012 $16.45

Tait   ★★★

Yaldara Drive, Lyndoch, SA 5351 **Region** Barossa Valley
T (08) 8524 5000 **F** (08) 8524 5220 **www.taitwines.com.au** **Open** By appt
Winemaker Bruno Tait **Est.** 1994 **Cases** 11 000 **Vyds** 5 ha
The Tait family has been involved in the wine industry in the Barossa for over 100 years, making not wine but barrels. Their more recent venture into winemaking was immediately successful. Their estate vineyards (3 ha of shiraz and 2 ha of 80-year-old cabernet sauvignon) is supplemented by contract-grown grapes. Winemaker Bruno Tait works with wife Michelle and brother Michael looking after various facets of the business. Exports to the US, Canada, Israel and Singapore.

ŢŢŢŢ   **The Ball Buster 2008** A blend of Shiraz/Merlot/Cabernet Sauvignon clearly
            destined for the US market with its pure corn, gushing back label. The colour is
            good, and the wine also meets all the requirements of the US with its voluminous,
            high-alcohol, black flavours. Screwcap. 16% alc. **Rating** 88 **To** 2014 $20

Tallavera Grove Vineyard & Winery   ★★★★☆

749 Mount View Road, Mount View, NSW 2325 **Region** Hunter Valley
T (02) 4990 7535 **F** (02) 4990 5232 **www.tallaveragrove.com.au** **Open** Thurs–Mon 10–5
Winemaker Luke Watson **Est.** 2000 **Cases** 2000 **Vyds** 40 ha

Tallavera Grove is one of the many wine interests of John Davis and family. The family is a 50% owner of Briar Ridge, a 12-ha vineyard in Coonawarra, a 100-ha vineyard at Wrattonbully (Stonefields Vineyard) and a 36-ha vineyard at Orange (Jokers Peak). The 40-ha Hunter Valley vineyards are planted to chardonnay, shiraz, semillon, verdelho, cabernet sauvignon and viognier. The Mount View winery will eventually be equipped to handle 200–300 tonnes of fruit. The Davis family are looking for a cellar door location in the Orange region to expand and localise the Jokers Peak label.

ΥΥΥΥΥ Jokers Peak The Volcanics Single Vineyard Orange Cabernet Sauvignon
2008 A thoroughly impressive cabernet; strong cassis and blackcurrant aromas lead in an unusually supple palate, the flavours rolling along the tongue, the finish perfectly in tune with what has gone before; not a simple fruit bomb, it has all the tannin structure and oak needed by the fruit. Screwcap. 14.5% alc. **Rating** 96 To 2020 $40

ΥΥΥΥΥ Hunter Valley Verdelho 2009 It was hard to make a poor white wine in the
❂ Hunter Valley in '09, and this verdelho is a very good one, with a citrussy intensity built into the more normal cornucopia of fruit salad flavours. Screwcap. 13% alc. **Rating** 93 To 2013 $20
Stonefields Vineyard Arbitrage Wrattonbully Cabernet Sauvignon 2008 **Rating** 93 To 2028 $40
Jokers Peak The Crystals Single Vineyard Orange Chardonnay 2009 **Rating** 92 To 2016 $28

❂ Jokers Peak Orange Cabernet Merlot 2008 Bright purple-red; a well-composed wine, ripe blackcurrant, plum and cassis the mainstay, oak and soft tannins on the side. Trophy Best Bordeaux Blend NSW Small Winemakers Show '09. Screwcap. 14% alc. **Rating** 91 To 2014 $22

ΥΥΥΥ Jokers Peak Orange Sauvignon Blanc 2009 **Rating** 88 To 2011 $20
Hunter Valley Chardonnay 2009 **Rating** 88 To 2013 $22

Tallis Wine   ★★★★☆

PO Box 10, Dookie, Vic 3646 **Region** Central Victoria Zone
T (03) 5823 5383 **F** (03) 5828 6532 **www.**talliswine.com.au **Open** Not
Winemaker Richard Tallis, Gary Baldwin (Consultant) **Est.** 2000 **Cases** 2000 **Vyds** 24 ha
Richard and Alice Tallis have 16 ha of shiraz, 5.4 ha of cabernet sauvignon, 2 ha of viognier and a small planting of sangiovese and merlot. While most of the grapes are sold, they have embarked on winemaking with the aid of Gary Baldwin, and have had considerable success. The philosophy of their winemaking and viticulture is minimal intervention to create a low-input and sustainable system; use of environmentally harmful sprays is minimised. The searing heat in January 2009 resulted in the destruction of 80% of the crop, and the hand-picking and selection of the remainder. It was a scenario repeated in various parts of South Eastern Australia, as far south as the Yarra Valley.

ΥΥΥΥΥ The Silent Showman Shiraz Viognier 2006 Developed red, although no
❂ brick hue yet; a supple wine that (appropriately) has many of the characters of the '07, although it is surprising there is only 12 months' difference; a percentage of co-fermented viognier works well, and the more the wine is tasted, the more the length of the palate manifests itself. Screwcap. 14% alc. **Rating** 94 To 2026 $25

ΥΥΥΥΥ The Silent Showman Shiraz 2007 **Rating** 92 To 2027 $25

ΥΥΥΥ Dookie Hills Viognier 2008 **Rating** 88 To 2012 $18

Taltarni   ★★★★☆

339 Taltarni Road, Moonambel, Vic 3478 **Region** Pyrenees
T (03) 5459 7900 **F** (03) 5467 2306 **www.**taltarni.com.au **Open** 7 days 10–5
Winemaker Loïc Le Calvez **Est.** 1972 **Cases** 80 000 **Vyds** 97 ha

In 2009 American owner and founder of Clos du Val (Napa Valley), Taltarni, and Clover Hill (see separate entry) brought the management of these three businesses, together the Lalla Gully vineyard purchased later, and Domaine de Nizas (Languedoc) under the one management roof. The group is known as Goelet Wine Estates. Taltarni is the largest of the Australian ventures, its estate vineyards of great value and underpinning the substantial annual production. There is no question it makes good red wines, but given its region, the climate/terroir of its very large estate vineyards and the age of the vines, one has the constantly nagging feeling it ought to do better. Exports to all major markets.

ΨΨΨΨΨ **Heathcote Shiraz 2006** Bright colour; backward and unevolved black fruit bouquet, with a strong savoury mineral streak at its core; full-bodied, dark, dense and brooding palate, with precise red and black fruits and fine tannins to conclude. Screwcap. 14.5% alc. **Rating** 94 **To** 2018 $35 BE

ΨΨΨΨΨ **Reserve Shiraz Cabernet Sauvignon 2005** **Rating** 92 **To** 2016 $65 BE

ΨΨΨΨ **T Series Sauvignon Blanc Semillon 2009** **Rating** 88 **To** 2012 $15 BE

Tamar Ridge   ★★★★★
Auburn Road, Kayena, Tas 7270 **Region** Northern Tasmania
T (03) 6394 1111 **F** (03) 6394 1126 **www**.tamarridge.com.au **Open** 7 days 10–5
Winemaker Andrew Pirie, Tom Ravech, Matt Lowe **Est.** 1994 **Cases** 75 000 **Vyds** 134.6 ha
Gunns Limited, of pulp mill fame, purchased Tamar Ridge in 2003. With the retention of Dr Richard Smart as viticultural advisor, the largest expansion of Tasmanian plantings is now underway, with several vineyards in the vicinity of the winery. Richard Smart has constructed a micro-vinification winery, with $1.9 million (including a federal grant of $900 000) as funding to employ a number of PhD students. Their subjects are varied, ranging from clonal trials to canopy trials. A further development at Coombend, on the east coast, is also underway. Dr Andrew Pirie is CEO and chief winemaker, adding further lustre to the brand. Exports to the UK, the US and other major markets.

ΨΨΨΨΨ **Kayena Reserve Limited Release Pinot Noir 2007** Attractive vibrant hue; incredibly youthful bouquet, unevolved and thoroughly beguiling; layered and sophisticated, with red fruits coming to the fore, but only to be trumped by intriguing aromas of subtle spices and a touch of the forest floor; the palate delivers a lovely velvet-like experience that is truly expansive and the oak merely supports the array of flavours; the finish is surprisingly long. Screwcap. 14% alc. **Rating** 96 **To** 2015 $50 BE
Kayena Vineyard Limited Release Botrytis Riesling 2007 Deep gold-green; extraordinary lusciousness venturing into tokay territory; candied citrus peel, cumquat and banana. 375 ml. Screwcap. 9% alc. **Rating** 95 **To** 2017 $25.60

ΨΨΨΨΨ **Kayena Vineyard Riesling 2009** **Rating** 93 **To** 2020 $23 BE
Kayena Vineyard Pinot Noir 2008 **Rating** 92 **To** 2014 $30 BE
Kayena Vineyard Gewurztraminer 2008 **Rating** 91 **To** 2013 $23 BE
Kayena Vineyard Sauvignon Blanc 2009 **Rating** 91 **To** 2013 $23 BE
Kayena Vineyard Pinot Gris 2008 **Rating** 91 **To** 2012 $25
Research Series 81-2 Savagnin 2009 **Rating** 91 **To** 2010 $25
Kayena Vineyard Riesling 2008 **Rating** 90 **To** 2017 $23
✪   **Devil's Corner Pinot Grigio 2009** Tight and crisp, with considerable length to its fresh citrus, green apple and pear-accented palate; modest alcohol helps. Screwcap. 12.5% alc. **Rating** 90 **To** 2011 $19

ΨΨΨΨ **Kayena Vineyard Chardonnay 2008** **Rating** 89 **To** 2013 $25
Devil's Corner Pinot Noir 2009 **Rating** 89 **To** 2013 $18 BE
Devil's Corner Non Vintage Cuvee NV **Rating** 89 **To** 2012 $20 BE
Devil's Corner Sauvignon Blanc 2009 **Rating** 87 **To** 2012 $18 BE

Tamburlaine

★★★★★

358 McDonalds Road, Pokolbin, NSW 2321 **Region** Hunter Valley
T (02) 4998 7570 **F** (02) 4998 7763 **www.**mywinery.com **Open** 7 days 9.30–5
Winemaker Mark Davidson, Simon McMillan, Patrick Moore **Est.** 1966 **Cases** 100 000
A thriving business that sells over 90% of its wine through the cellar door and by mailing
list (with an active tasting club members' cellar program offering wines held and matured at
Tamburlaine). The maturing of the estate-owned Orange vineyard has led to a dramatic rise
in quality across the range. Both the Hunter Valley and Orange vineyards are now certified
organic. Exports to the UK, the US and other major markets.

🍷🍷🍷🍷🍷   **Wine Lovers Petite Fleur Orange Rose 2008** Made from Grenache/
✪   Chambourcin from certified organic estate vineyards in Orange/Hunter Valley.
          Bright pink; a very attractive outcome, with a burst of strawberry and cherry fruit
          on the mid-palate, the low alcohol adding to the freshness. Screwcap. 10.9% alc.
          Rating 92 **To** 2011 $20
          Reserve Hunter Valley Syrah 2008 Attractive red fruits, leather and clove meld
          together seamlessly on the bouquet; medium-bodied, with vibrant acidity, the
          red fruits persisting on a fresh, focused and pure conclusion. Screwcap. 13.4% alc.
          Rating 92 **To** 2016 $32 BE
          Reserve Noble Chardonnay 2008 While unusual to see this variety used this
          way, the level of botrytis is impressive; orange marmalade, quince and spice, with
          unctuous levels of sugar, and reasonable acidity; very sweet indeed, but very well
          made. Screwcap. 8.4% alc. **Rating** 91 **To** 2012 $28 BE
          Wine Lovers Orange Sauvignon Blanc 2008 The colour is still very pale, but
          the wine has generous lychee, gooseberry and tropical fruit on offer, with balanced
          acidity. Screwcap. 13.1% alc. **Rating** 90 **To** 2011 $20
          Reserve Hunter Valley Chardonnay 2009 Melon and lemon sherbet bouquet;
          lean and racy, with vibrant acidity, plenty of drive and a fairly long conclusion.
          Screwcap. 12.8% alc. **Rating** 90 **To** 2016 $28 BE
          Reserve Orange Syrah 2008 Deeply fruited with blackberry and redcurrant
          prominent, framed by a suggestion of orange rind; the palate is medium-bodied,
          soft, fleshy and quite forward, with the finish being drawn out by nervy acidity.
          Screwcap. 14.8% alc. **Rating** 90 **To** 2014 $40 BE

🍷🍷🍷🍷   **Wine Lovers Orange Chardonnay 2007 Rating** 89 **To** 2012 $20
          Reserve Hunter Valley Chambourcin 2008 Rating 88 **To** 2012 $32 BE
          Reserve Orange Riesling 2009 Rating 87 **To** 2014 $28 BE

Taminick Cellars

★★★★★

339 Booth Road, Taminick via Glenrowan, Vic 3675 **Region** Glenrowan
T (03) 5766 2282 **F** (03) 5766 2151 **www.**taminickcellars.com.au **Open** Mon–Sat 9–5,
Sun 10–5
Winemaker James Booth **Est.** 1904 **Cases** 3000 **Vyds** 19.7 ha
Peter Booth is a third-generation member of the Booth family, who have owned this winery
since Esca Booth purchased the property in 1904. James Booth, fourth-generation and current
winemaker, completed his wine science degree at CSU in 2008. The red wines are massively
flavoured and very long lived, notably from the 9 ha of shiraz planted in 1919. Trebbiano and
alicante bouschet were also planted in 1919, with much newer arrivals including nero d'Avola.
The wines are sold through the cellar door, mail order and a selection of independent retailers
in Melbourne and Sydney. Exports to Hong Kong.

🍷🍷🍷🍷🍷   **1919 Series Alicante Rose 2009** Vivid light crimson; early hand-picking of
✪   this teinturier (red-fleshed) variety produces a wine with bright cherry and
          raspberry fruit balanced by crisp acidity on the long finish. Vines 90 years old.
          Screwcap. 11% alc. **Rating** 94 **To** 2011 $15
          Generations IV Shiraz 2008 Interesting wine; while relatively light in colour
          and body for vines approaching 90 years of age, it has considerable finesse,
          reflecting hand-plunging of open fermenters and 100% French oak maturation.
          Impressive winemaking. Screwcap. 14% alc. **Rating** 94 **To** 2018 $24

♀♀♀♀♀
☯ Chardonnay 2008 A surprising wine, although chardonnay is a very accommodating variety and James Booth is a very talented winemaker; most surprising is the price, for this is a fresh, lively wine with stone fruit, citrus and barrel ferment oak all coalescing on the well-balanced and long palate. Screwcap. 14.2% alc. **Rating** 91 **To** 2013 $12

☯ Ianus 2008 Light, clear colour; shiraz co-fermented with a small amount of trebbiano, both from the 1919 estate plantings; the trebbiano seems to underline the sweet fruit flavours, making the wine seem higher in alcohol than it in fact is. Two-faced indeed (Ianus is an alternative spelling of Janus). Screwcap. 14% alc. **Rating** 91 **To** 2014 $18

♀♀♀♀
☯ 1919 Series Shiraz 2007 A generous, full-bodied and rich wine; marked style contrast to the '08, more traditional Rutherglen, perhaps; has some warmth to the finish; good-quality cork, property inserted. Cork. 14.5% alc. **Rating** 89 **To** 2014 $16

☯ Durif 2007 Remarkably youthful colour, especially compared to Stanton & Killeen Durif of the same vintage; the flavour and structure is also youthful, and the question is whether the wine has been over-acidified. Cork. 14.5% alc. **Rating** 89 **To** 2013 $15

☯ Liqueur Muscat NV The brown colour attests to the 15–18 years average age of this unctuously rich and strongly raisiny muscat. It may not have the finesse of the best, but is remarkably cheap. Screwcap. 18.2% alc. **Rating** 89 **To** 2011 $16

☯ Taminick Gold NV The solera dates back to 1972, when the first fortified trebbiano was put into barrel. The back label says 'the wine can be cellared over the next 10 years to develop further aged complex characters'. If it does, it will be unique, for these wines cease developing once they lose contact with air, and are more likely to simply lose their edge in bottle. Screwcap. 18.2% alc. **Rating** 89 **To** 2011 $15

The Associates Cabernet Merlot 2008 **Rating** 88 **To** 2014 $18

Tapanappa ★★★★★

PO Box 174, Crafers, SA 5152 **Region** South Australia
T 0419 843 751 **F** (08) 8370 8374 **www**.tapanappawines.com.au **Open** Not
Winemaker Brian Croser **Est.** 2002 **Cases** 4170 **Vyds** 20.7 ha
The Tapanappa partners are Brian Croser (formerly of Petaluma), Jean-Michel Cazes of Chateau Lynch-Bages in Pauillac and Société Jacques Bollinger, the parent company of Champagne Bollinger. The partnership has four vineyard sites in Australia: the Whalebone Vineyard at Wrattonbully (planted to cabernet sauvignon, shiraz and merlot 30 years ago); the Daosa Vineyard, also in Wrattonbully (cabernet sauvignon); the Tiers Vineyard (chardonnay) at Piccadilly in the Adelaide Hills (the remainder of the Tiers Vineyard chardonnay continues to be sold to Petaluma); and the Foggy Hill Vineyard on the southern tip of the Fleurieu Peninsula (pinot noir). Exports to all major markets.

♀♀♀♀♀ Tiers Vineyard Piccadilly Valley Chardonnay 2008 Let's hope the chateau-length quality cork does justice to the wine through its life time, for this has marvellous varietal fruit flavour and intensity; immaculate oak handling adds the finishing touch; swells on the mid-palate, but is held by impressive acidity, the flavour lingering long in the mouth. 13.5% alc. **Rating** 96 **To** 2014 $80

Foggy Hill Vineyard Fleurieu Peninsula Pinot Noir 2008 Good hue; a very intense pinot, with red and black fruits, the latter predominant, interlaced with fine but markedly savoury tannins. Needs at least three years. Cork. 14% alc. **Rating** 94 **To** 2015 $50

Whalebone Vineyard Wrattonbully Merlot 2006 Excellent crimson hue; potent merlot red fruits and hints of savoury herb on the way through the palate meeting firm, slightly dry tannins on the back-palate and finish. Needs patience. Cork. 13.5% alc. **Rating** 94 **To** 2020 $71.50

Whalebone Vineyard Wrattonbully Cabernet Shiraz 2006 Good hue; a 60/30/10 blend of Cabernet Sauvignon/Shiraz/Merlot with a very obvious infusion of French oak on bouquet and palate; has excellent texture and structure, and none of the tannin challenges of the Merlot. Cork. 14% alc. **Rating** 94 To 2016 $71.50

Tar & Roses/Trust ★★★★☆

61 Vickers Lane, Nagambie, Vic 3608 (postal) **Region** Central Victoria Zone
T (03) 5794 1811 **F** (03) 5794 1833 **www**.trustwines.com.au **Open** Not
Winemaker Don Lewis, Narelle King **Est.** 2004 **Cases** 15 000 **Vyds** 5 ha

Tar & Roses is one of the more interesting new arrivals on the Australian winemaking scene, even though the partners, Don Lewis and Narelle King, have been making wine together for many years at Mitchelton and – for the past three years – Priorat, Spain. Don came from a grapegrowing family in Red Cliffs, near Mildura, and in his youth was press-ganged into working in the vineyard. When he left home he swore never to be involved in vineyards again, but in 1973 found himself accepting the position of assistant winemaker to Colin Preece at Mitchelton, where he remained until his retirement 32 years later. Narelle, having qualified as a chartered accountant, set off to discover the world, and while travelling in South America met a young Australian winemaker who had just completed vintage in Argentina, and who lived in France. The lifestyle appealed greatly, so on her return to Australia she obtained her winemaking degree from CSU and was offered work by Mitchelton as a bookkeeper and cellar hand. Together they are making wines that are a mosaic of Australia, Italy and Spain in their inspiration.

 TTTTY **Tar & Roses Heathcote Shiraz 2008** Clear and bright colour, less dense than
✪ the '07; a very lively, spicy light- to medium-bodied shiraz, the red and black cherry fruit with a twist of licorice; fine tannins to close. Screwcap. 14.5% alc. **Rating** 93 To 2018 $18.50
Tar & Roses Heathcote Alpine Valleys Tempranillo 2008 Some colour development; an attractive bouquet, with hints of spice with the red fruits; a supple, fresh palate with spicy fruits and a long finish. Screwcap. 14% alc. **Rating** 93 To 2014 $25
Trust Shiraz 2007 Sourced from four vineyards in Central Victoria; no more than medium-bodied at best, it has a bright and lively palate with some juicy aspects to the red cherry and plum fruit; good length. Screwcap. 14.2% alc. **Rating** 92 To 2017 $35

TTTT **Tar & Roses Pinot Grigio 2009** Rating 88 To 2012 $18.50
Tar & Roses Heathcote Nebbiolo 2007 Rating 87 To 2015 $45

Tarrawarra Estate ★★★★★

311 Healesville-Yarra Glen Road, Yarra Glen, Vic 3775 **Region** Yarra Valley
T (03) 5962 3311 **F** (03) 5962 3887 **www**.tarrawarra.com.au **Open** 7 days 11–5
Winemaker Clare Halloran **Est.** 1983 **Cases** 18 000 **Vyds** 29 ha

Clare Halloran has lightened the Tarrawarra style, investing it with more grace and finesse, but without losing complexity or longevity. The opening of the large art gallery (and its attendant café/restaurant) in early 2004 added another dimension to the tourism tapestry of the Yarra Valley. The gallery, as the *Michelin Guide* says, it is definitely worth a detour. The deluxe MDB label made its way (very quietly, because of the tiny production) in '09. The release of the new Reserve range introduced a second tier, followed by the Tarrawarra varietal releases alongside the Tin Cows range, which is not 100% estate grown nor necessarily limited to the Yarra Valley. Exports to the UK, the US and other major markets.

TTTTT **Reserve Yarra Valley Chardonnay 2008** Some depth starting to develop to the colour; a subtle, sophisticated wine, stone fruit, melon, citrus and French oak all seamlessly joined, the balance and length all one could ask for. Screwcap. 13% alc. **Rating** 94 To 2016 $50

Reserve Yarra Valley Pinot Noir 2008 Bright, clear crimson-red; while light-bodied, has above-average complexity and length; bright, supple red and black fruits are balanced by a nice foresty twist on the aromatic bouquet and silky palate. Screwcap. 13.5% alc. **Rating** 94 **To** 2016 $50

Yarra Valley Pinot Noir 2006 Light red, no browning; a complex bouquet with many of the foresty notes that come through on the equally complex palate, with plum and black cherry fruit supported by chalky tannins. Screwcap. 14% alc. **Rating** 94 **To** 2014 $50

K-Block Yarra Valley Merlot 2008 Convincing colour; a distinguished medium- to full-bodied merlot, with greater fruit flavour and structure than most; has strong blackcurrant fruit interwoven with forest/black olive notes; ripe, persistent tannins on the back-palate and finish. Screwcap. 13.5% alc. **Rating** 94 **To** 2016 $30

♀♀♀♀♀ **MRV 2009 Rating** 92 **To** 2015 $30

Yarra Valley Tumbarumba Pinot Noir 2009 Rating 92 **To** 2014 $22

Tassell Park Wines ★★★★

Treeton Road, Cowaramup, WA 6284 **Region** Margaret River
T (08) 9755 5440 **F** (08) 9755 5442 **www.tassellparkwines.com Open** 7 days 10.30–5
Winemaker Peter Stanlake (Consultant) **Est.** 2001 **Cases** 4500 **Vyds** 6.85 ha
Ian and Tricia Tassell have neatly covered all the bases with their estate plantings of sauvignon blanc, chenin blanc, chardonnay, semillon, shiraz, cabernet sauvignon, petit verdot and merlot, and have had consistent success with their wines in wine show, magazine and book medals and awards. What was intended to be a retirement hobby has become anything but, as they assiduously enter or submit their wines to all and sundry. While Sauvignon Blanc has been their forte, they received gold medals for both the '07 Cabernet Sauvignon and the '07 Private Bin Cabernet Sauvignon at the Sydney Wine Show '09, one of the toughest forums. In the local category of the WA Wine Industry Awards in Nov '09, Tassell Park won the Best Estate Grown White and Best Estate Grown Red awards. Here the winning wines were '08 Chardonnay (their first chardonnay) and '07 Private Bin Shiraz.

♀♀♀♀♀ **Private Bin Margaret River Chardonnay 2009** Pale colour; straw, grapefruit and plenty of toasty oak evident on the bouquet; zesty grapefruit palate, showing vibrant acidity, with the charry oak prominent on the finish. Screwcap. 13.5% alc. **Rating** 90 $32 BE

Private Bin Margaret River Shiraz 2008 Bright colour; toasty oak prominent on the bouquet, with red fruit evident; the palate is oaky, quite rich and certainly at the firm end of the spectrum; plenty of flavour in the wine. Screwcap. 14.5% alc. **Rating** 90 $38 BE

Margaret River Cabernet Merlot 2008 Bright colour; prominent leafy notes sit neatly alongside cassis and a touch of oak; the palate shows a little green prickle, but there is certainly generosity and freshness to conclude. Screwcap. 13.5% alc. **Rating** 90 $23 BE

Margaret River Petit Merlot 2007 Bright red fruits with a distinct floral lift to the bouquet; medium-bodied and full of juicy red fruit, and supple tannins to finish. Petit Verdot/Merlot. Screwcap. 14.5% alc. **Rating** 90 $24 BE

♀♀♀♀ **Margaret River Sauvignon Blanc Semillon 2009 Rating** 89 $23 BE

Tatachilla ★★★★☆

151 Main Road, McLaren Vale, SA 5171 **Region** McLaren Vale
T (08) 8323 8656 **F** (08) 8323 9096 **www.tatachillawines.com.au Open** Not
Winemaker Fanchon Ferrandi **Est.** 1903 **Cases** 50 000 **Vyds** 12.4 ha
Tatachilla was reborn in 1995 but has had an at-times tumultuous history going back to 1903. Between 1903 and '61 the winery was owned by Penfolds; it was closed in 1961 and reopened in '65 as the Southern Vales Co-operative. In the late 1980s it was purchased and renamed The Vales but did not flourish; in '93 it was purchased by local grower Vic Zerella

and former Kaiser Stuhl chief executive Keith Smith. After extensive renovations, the winery was officially reopened in 1995 and won a number of tourist awards and accolades. It became part of Banksia Wines in 2001, in turn acquired by Lion Nathan in '02. Exports to all major markets.

🍷🍷🍷🍷🍷 Foundation McLaren Vale Shiraz 2005 A long, but wine-stained cork had no adverse impact on the purple-red colour, nor the intense regional manifestation of the black fruits and bitter chocolate aromas and flavours; has very good length and intensity, French oak judged to perfection. With a screwcap, this wine would live for 40-plus years. 14.5% alc. Rating 95 To 2025 $50

🍷🍷🍷🍷 ✪ Growers Sauvignon Blanc Semillon 2009 Clean and fresh, with citrus and lemon flavours running through to a crisp, clean and dry finish. Screwcap. 11% alc. Rating 87 To 2010 $12

✪ Partners Cabernet Shiraz 2008 Bright crimson; juicy red and black fruits on the light- to medium-bodied palate make an attractive red for immediate drinking. Screwcap. 14.5% alc. Rating 87 To 2010 $12

Tatler Wines   ★★★★☆

477 Lovedale Road, Lovedale, NSW 2321 **Region** Hunter Valley
T (02) 4930 9139 **F** (02) 4930 9145 **www**.tatlerwines.com **Open** 7 days 9.30–5.30
Winemaker First Creek Winemaking **Est.** 1998 **Cases** 6500 **Vyds** 11 ha

Tatler Wines is a family-owned company headed by Sydney hoteliers Theo and Spiro Isak (Isakidis). The name comes from the Tatler Hotel on George Street, Sydney, which was purchased by James (Dimitri) Isak from the late Archie Brown, whose son Tony is general manager of the wine business. Together with wife Deborah, Tony runs the vineyard, cellar door, café and accommodation. The 40-ha property has 11 ha of chardonnay, shiraz and semillon. In 2008 Tatler acquired and renovated the Allanmere winery, where 75% of Tatler wines are now made. Exports to the US.

🍷🍷🍷🍷🍷 ✪ Over the Ditch Hunter Valley Marlborough Semillon Sauvignon Blanc 2009 Tatler directors Spiro and Theo Isakidis were born not in Greece but NZ, and this, they say, inspired the blend; this is the best yet, with great drive to its citrus and passionfruit flavours. Screwcap. 12% alc. Rating 94 To 2013 $26

🍷🍷🍷🍷½ Dimitri's Paddock Hunter Valley Chardonnay 2009 Rating 92 To 2014 $25

🍷🍷🍷🍷 The Nonpariel Hunter Valley Shiraz 2007 Rating 88 To 2014 $45

Taylor Ferguson   ★★★★☆

Level 1, 62 Albert Street, Preston, Vic 3072 (postal) **Region** South Eastern Australia
T (03) 9487 2599 **F** (03) 9487 2588 **www**.alepat.com.au **Open** Not
Winemaker Norman Lever **Est.** 1996 **Cases** 50 000

Taylor Ferguson is the much-altered descendant of a business of that name established in Melbourne in 1898. A connecting web joins it with Alexander & Paterson (1892) and the much more recent distribution business of Alepat Taylor. The development of the Taylor Ferguson wine label under the direction of winemaker Norman Lever, using grapes and wines purchased in Coonawarra, Langhorne Creek and the Riverina, is yet another strand, leading to a significant increase in the size of the negociant business, with multiple labels. Exports to Germany, Iraq, Singapore, Malaysia, Taiwan, Vietnam and China.

🍷🍷🍷🍷🍷 Fernando The First Cabernet Sauvignon 2006 Excellent hue and depth; a complex, full-bodied wine exuding varietal blackcurrant fruit from every pore, supported by powdery tannins and cedary oak. An impressive blend of Wrattonbully/Coonawarra/Barossa. High-quality cork. 13.8% alc. Rating 95 To 2020 $40

🍷🍷🍷🍷½ ✪ Premium Selection Marlborough Sauvignon Blanc 2009 If you can't beat them, joint them; a mix of stone fruit, passionfruit and citrus is a good expression of the region. Screwcap. 13% alc. Rating 90 To 2010 $14

Fernando The First Shiraz 2006 Rating 90 To 2016 $40

✪ Willbriggie Estate Durif 2006 Typical dense colour; dense black fruits, dark chocolate and licorice supported by soft tannins. Surely the most malleable and accommodating red variety. Screwcap. 14% alc. Rating 90 To 2013 $12

🍷🍷🍷🍷 Premium Selection Langhorne Creek Shiraz 2007 Rating 89 To 2017 $16.60

✪ Coonawarra Cabernet Sauvignon 2006 Is relatively light-bodied, but does have clear-cut cabernet varietal fruit flavours in a blackcurrant and cedar spectrum; has enough structure. Screwcap. 14% alc. Rating 89 To 2014 $12

Premium Selection Langhorne Creek Cabernet Sauvignon 2007 Rating 87 To 2013 $16.60

Taylors   ★★★★★

Taylors Road, Auburn, SA 5451 **Region** Clare Valley

T (08) 8849 1111 **F** (08) 8849 1199 **www**.taylorswines.com.au **Open** Mon–Fri 9–5, Sat & public hols 10–5, Sun 10–4

Winemaker Adam Eggins, Helen McCarthy **Est.** 1969 **Cases** 400 000 **Vyds** 340 ha

The family-founded and owned Taylors continues to flourish and expand – its vineyards now total over 300 ha, by far the largest holding in Clare Valley. There have also been changes both in terms of the winemaking team and in terms of the wine style and quality, particularly through the outstanding St Andrews range. With each passing vintage, Taylors is managing to do the same for the Clare Valley as Peter Lehmann is doing for the Barossa Valley. Exports (under the Wakefield brand due to trademark reasons) to all major markets.

🍷🍷🍷🍷🍷 St Andrews Clare Valley Riesling 2007 A highly fragrant array of apple, spice and lemon zest aromas leads into a super-intense and extremely long palate, the finish lingering for minutes. Screwcap. 13% alc. Rating 96 To 2027 $37.95

St Andrews Clare Valley Shiraz 2004 Clear, deep colour; a distinguished full-bodied shiraz from a distinguished vintage; blackberry fruit is woven through ripe tannins and quality oak, all three components in great balance. Screwcap. 14% alc. Rating 95 To 2024 $60

40th Anniversary Cabernet Sauvignon 2006 Good colour; a very well made and balanced wine that has clear-cut varietal expression on both bouquet and the medium-bodied palate, blackcurrant, cassis and cedar intermingling, the tannins fine and oak balanced and integrated. Screwcap. 14.7% alc. Rating 95 To 2026 $100

✪ Jaraman Clare Valley Eden Valley Riesling 2009 Vivid green hue; lime and talc bouquet, and showing just a little steel in the background; lemon comes to the fore on entry, with vibrant acidity and surprisingly generous texture from start to finish; will age well, but early consumption will be rewarded. Screwcap. 12.5% alc. Rating 94 To 2020 $24.50 BE

St Andrews Clare Valley Chardonnay 2007 Exceptional green colour; has equally exceptional varietal aromas and flavours for a region that seldom allows chardonnay to express itself with the intensity and flair of this impeccably balanced wine. Screwcap. 13.5% alc. Rating 94 To 2013 $30

St Andrews Clare Valley Cabernet Sauvignon 2005 Strong colour; a powerful, medium- to full-bodied cabernet with the savoury earthy notes typical of Clare, and enough blackcurrant fruit and cedary French oak to fill out the long palate. Screwcap. 14.5% alc. Rating 94 To 2020 $59.95

🍷🍷🍷🍷🍷 Jaraman Adelaide Hills Yarra Valley Pinot Noir 2008 Rating 91 To 2015 $30

🍷🍷🍷🍷 Jaraman Clare Valley Adelaide Hills Chardonnay 2008 Rating 89 To 2013 $24.95

✪ Promised Land Shiraz 2008 Bright hue; a very well made, juicy shiraz with red and black fruits jostling for a position on the first row of the grid, tannins and oak somewhere in the pit lane. Great value. Screwcap. 13.5% alc. Rating 89 To 2016 $13.95

Jaraman Clare Valley McLaren Vale Shiraz 2007 Rating 89 To 2014 $29.95

Clare Valley Shiraz 2008 Rating 88 To 2016 $19

✪ Eighty Acres Clare Valley Shiraz Viognier 2007 Bright colour; while relatively light-bodied, has a distinctive juicy character to the fruit flavours, and just enough tannins to provide structure. Screwcap. 14% alc. Rating 88 To 2012 $13.95

✪ Promised Land Shiraz Cabernet 2007 Bright colour; clean, well-made, light- to medium-bodied wine with sweet fruit elements and soft tannins; fair length. Gold medals San Francisco International Wine Competition '09, and Mondiales des Vins Canada '09. Screwcap. 14.5% alc. Rating 88 To 2012 $13.95

Clare Valley Adelaide Hills Chardonnay 2008 Rating 87 To 2011 $18.95

Adelaide Hills Clare Valley Pinot Gris 2009 Rating 87 To 2011 $18.95

Adelaide Hills Pinot Noir 2009 Rating 87 To 2015 $18.95

✪ Eighty Acres Clare Valley Cabernet Shiraz Merlot 2007 A well-constructed commercial wine, the accent on fruit rather than structure. Fulfils its purpose admirably. Screwcap. 14% alc. Rating 87 To 2011 $13.95

TeAro Estate   ★★★★

18 Queen Street, Williamstown, SA 5351 **Region** Barossa Valley
T (08) 8524 6860 **F** (08) 8524 6863 **www**.tearoestate.com **Open** Fri–Mon 10–6, or by appt
Winemaker Ryan Fromm, Todd Rowett **Est.** 2001 **Cases** 2500 **Vyds** 58 ha
TeAro Estate is a family-owned and operated wine business located in Williamstown in the southern Barossa Valley. In 1919 great-grandfather Charlie Fromm married Minnie Kappler, who named their home block TeAro. They planted shiraz and semillon, their only equipment a single crowbar (and their bare hands). Under the guidance of second- and third-generation family members Ron and Trevor, the vineyard has grown to 58 ha. Until 2001 the grapes were sold, but in that year Trevor decided to have a tonne of shiraz made for the local football club. It has been the fourth generation, including vigneron Ryan Fromm and brother-in-law Todd Rowett, that has been responsible for the proliferation of varieties. The vineyards are planted (in descending size) to shiraz, cabernet sauvignon, semillon, chardonnay, pinot noir, riesling, viognier, sauvignon blanc, pinot gris, tempranillo, merlot, mourvedre and grenache. Exports to China and Hong Kong.

🍷🍷🍷🍷🍷 The Charred Door Barossa Valley Shiraz 2008 Good colour; fragrant blackberry and dark chocolate aromas are replayed on the lively medium-bodied palate along with fine tannin support. Carry a magnifying glass to read the tantalising text on the bottom of the front label. Screwcap. 14.5% alc. Rating 93 To 2020 $28

The Charging Bull Barossa Valley Tempranillo 2008 Bright purple-red; medium-bodied, with a delicious array of redcurrant, cherry and raspberry fruit, the palate smooth and supple; in theory needs a cooler climate, but not true here. Screwcap. 14.5% alc. Rating 92 To 2015 $30

✪ Jokers Grin 2008 Good hue; sometimes a blend such as this (Shiraz/Cabernet Sauvignon/Merlot) results in each component getting in the way of the other two; here, each adds its voice to a harmonious chorus of predominantly black fruits; ready right now. Screwcap. 14.5% alc. Rating 90 To 2014 $18

The Pump Jack Barossa Valley Cabernet Sauvignon 2008 Solid colour; ripe blackcurrant/cassis aromas lead on to a lusciously fruity mid-palate, then touches of mint and earth towards the finish. Screwcap. 14.5% alc. Rating 90 To 2014 $28

🍷🍷🍷🍷 The Charred Door Barossa Valley Shiraz 2007 Rating 88 To 2014 $22

🍂 Tellurian   ★★★★☆

PO Box 748, Heathcote, Vic 3523 **Region** Heathcote
T 0438 429 151 **www**.tellurianwines.com.au **Open** Not
Winemaker Tobias Ansted **Est.** 2008 **Cases** 800 **Vyds** 9.2 ha

This is a single-variety vineyard, with 5.6 ha of shiraz planted in 2003, and 3.6 ha in '06. The vineyard is situated on the western side of Mt Camel at Toolleen on the red Cambrian soil that has made Heathcote one of the foremost regions in Australia for the production of shiraz (Tellurian means 'of the earth'). Planning is underway for the construction of a winery on the Toolleen vineyard site, and viticultural consultant Tim Brown not only supervises the Tellurian estate plantings, but also works closely with the growers of grapes purchased under contract for Tellurian. Further plantings of Rhône red and white varieties on the Tellurian property will follow in 2011.

ŶŶŶŶŶ Heathcote Shiraz 2008 Crimson-purple; picked 23 Feb, two weeks before the heatwave; a very complex medium- to full-bodied shiraz, with black fruits, spice, pepper and a touch of licorice held in a basket of persistent, savoury tannins that are ripe and ultimately in balance. Has eaten the 50% new oak in which it was matured. Screwcap. 14.5% alc. Rating 94 To 2023 $35

ŶŶŶŶŶ Heathcote Viognier 2009 Rating 90 To 2012 $25

Tempus Two Wines   ★★★★☆
Broke Road, Pokolbin, NSW 2321 Region Hunter Valley
T (02) 4993 3999 F (02) 4993 3988 www.tempustwo.com.au Open 7 days 9–5
Winemaker Scott Comyns Est. 1997 Cases 100 000
Tempus Two is the name for what was once Hermitage Road Wines. It is a mix of Latin (Tempus means time) and English; the change was forced on the winery by the EU Wine Agreement and the prohibition of the use of the word 'hermitage' on Australian wine labels. It has been a major success story, production growing from 6000 cases in 1997 to 100 000 cases today. Its cellar door, restaurant complex (including the Oishii Japanese restaurant), and small convention facilities are situated in a striking building. The design polarises opinion; I like it. Exports to all major markets.

ŶŶŶŶŶ Pewter Coonawarra Cabernet 2008 Medium red-purple; savoury, earthy nuances surround the blackcurrant fruit of the bouquet and medium-bodied palate; French oak, too, plays a role. Unusual cork, granular version of Diam. 14.5% alc. Rating 92 To 2018 $30
Copper Wilde Chardonnay 2008 Charry oak dominates the palate, with some struck match sulphide and nectarine fruit to support; the palate is purer and fresher than expected, with vibrant acidity driving the fruit through the toastiness of the oak. Screwcap. 13% alc. Rating 91 To 2016 $20 BE
Pewter Vine Vale Shiraz 2008 While the pewter medallion label may not appeal to everyone, the wine in the glass should present no problems; the blackberry fruit of the palate has a tweak on the finish that is very appealing. Diam. 14.5% alc. Rating 91 To 2016 $30
Pewter Pinot Gris 2009 As in '08, a pinot gris with above-average character and quality, the flavours ranging from brown pear to citrus/orange; brisk acidity prevents the wine from blowing out; no indication of regional source. Diam. 12% alc. Rating 90 To 2012 $30
✪ Copper Grenache Shiraz Mourvedre 2007 Has the usual light colour of this blend, but more than usual bright red fruit aromas and flavours, particularly in the context of '07; quite juicy, the tannins gentle. Screwcap. 13.5% alc. Rating 90 To 2014 $20

ŶŶŶŶ Copper Moscato 2009 Rating 89 To 2011 $20 BE
Copper Zenith Semillon 2009 Rating 88 To 2013 $25

Ten Men   ★★★★☆
870 Maroondah Highway, Coldstream, Vic 3770 (postal) Region Yarra Valley
T 0409 767 838 F (03) 5962 4938 www.dominiqueportet.com Open Not
Winemaker Ben Portet Est. 2009 Cases 250

Owner Ben Portet is the 10th-generation winemaker in the Portet family, father Dominique (for many years in charge of Taltarni) and uncle Bernard (long-serving winemaker at Clos Duval in the Napa Valley) members of the ninth generation. Ben has a winemaking background second to none, building on his degree in oenology from Adelaide University with four vintages at Petaluma (while completing his university studies), thereafter Bordeaux (Chateau Beychevelle), Champagne (Louis Roederer), the Rhône Valley (M Chapoutier), Stellenbosch (Warwick Estate), and the Napa Valley (Vineyard 29). His 'day job' is assisting his father at Dominique Portet (see separate entry).

♀♀♀♀♀ **Yarra Valley Shiraz 2008** Good purple-hue; a spicy black cherry bouquet is a promising start, but it is the structure of the palate, and specifically the tannins, that gives this shiraz its special quality. Screwcap. 14.5% alc. **Rating** 94 **To** 2018 $38

♀♀♀♀♀ **Yarra Valley Sauvignon Blanc 2009 Rating** 90 **To** 2010 $28

Ten Miles East   ★★★☆

8 Debneys Road, Norton Summit, SA 5136 **Region** Adelaide Hills
T (08) 8390 1723 **F** (08) 8390 1723 **www**.tenmileseast.com **Open** Sun 11–4
Winemaker John Greenshields, Taiita and James Champniss **Est.** 2003 **Cases** 600
Vyds 2.1 ha
Ten Miles East takes its name from the fact that it is that distance and direction from the Adelaide GPO. It is the venture of industry veteran John Greenshields, and Robin and Judith Smallacombe and is, to put it mildly, an interesting one. Its home vineyard in the Adelaide Hills is planted principally to riesling and sauvignon blanc, with smaller plantings of pinot noir, shiraz, carmenere and saperavi, a Joseph's coat if ever there was one. Next, there is a joint-venture vineyard on the Yorke Peninsula planted to shiraz (3000 vines) and carmenere (1000 vines). Finally, Ten Miles East purchases 2–4 tonnes of shiraz per year from Wrattonbully (where, many years ago, John founded Koppamurra, now Tapanappa). The winery is in what was the Auldwood Cider Factory, built in 1962, and also houses the cellar door that opened in 2009.

♀♀♀♀♀ **Adelaide Hills Sauvignon Blanc 2009** Light straw-green; an appealing balance of tropical/passionfruit and snow pea/citrus aromas and flavours. By some distance, the best of the Ten Miles East wines. Screwcap. 11.7% alc. **Rating** 90 **To** 2011 $15

Ten Minutes by Tractor   ★★★★★

1333 Mornington-Flinders Road, Main Ridge, Vic 3928 **Region** Mornington Peninsula
T (03) 5989 6455 **F** (03) 5989 6433 **www**.tenminutesbytractor.com.au **Open** 7 days 11–5
Winemaker Richard McIntyre, Martin Spedding **Est.** 1999 **Cases** 7000 **Vyds** 17.2 ha
The energy, drive and vision of Martin Spedding has transformed Ten Minutes by Tractor since he acquired the business in early 2004. He has entered into long-term leases of the three original vineyards, thus having complete management control over grape production courtesy of vineyard manager Alan Murray, who has been involved with those vineyards since 1999. A fourth vineyard has been added on the site of the new cellar door and restaurant; its first vintage was 2008, and it has been managed organically since day one. It is being used to trial various organic viticultural practices, which will ultimately be employed across all of the plantings. Martin is completing a wine science degree at CSU, and has taken over active winemaking alongside Richard McIntyre (the latter as an all-important mentor). The restaurant has one of the best wine lists to be found at any winery. Exports to the UK, Canada, Hong Kong and Singapore.

♀♀♀♀♀ **Wallis Vineyard Mornington Peninsula Chardonnay 2008** Similar colour to the standard wine; the bouquet is fresh and focused, but the palate takes the wine to another level, with its energy and penetrating shaft of minerally acidity carrying the stone fruit and grapefruit along in its wake, and long, lingering finish. Screwcap. 13.8% alc. **Rating** 96 **To** 2020 $55

McCutcheon Vineyard Mornington Peninsula Chardonnay 2008 Bright colour; the most complex of the chardonnays, due to the greater generosity of the white peach and nectarine fruit plus a touch of creamy cashew; however, doesn't have the same energy as Wallis. Screwcap. 13.8% alc. **Rating** 95 **To** 2017 $55

Wallis Vineyard Mornington Peninsula Pinot Noir 2008 Bright and clear colour; the bouquet has a little more spice than the other two single-vineyard pinots, the palate particularly elegant and long, with a silky mouthfeel to its lively red fruits. Screwcap. 13.8% alc. **Rating** 95 **To** 2015 $70

10X Mornington Peninsula Chardonnay 2008 Bright straw-green; a delicious, vibrant chardonnay with nectarine and citrus aromas repeated on the long, even palate that accelerates through to the finish. Screwcap. 13.8% alc. **Rating** 94 **To** 2017 $30

10X Mornington Peninsula Pinot Noir 2008 Has all the precision, focus and brightness that marks well-made Mornington Peninsula pinots, the flavours of plum and black cherry, the tannins firm but fine. Screwcap. 13.5% alc. **Rating** 94 **To** 2015 $36

Judd Vineyard Mornington Peninsula Pinot Noir 2008 All three single-vineyard Pinots share a light but brilliantly clear colour, this with marginally more purple; a graceful and fluid palate of ripe plum fruit and a lingering finish and aftertaste. Screwcap. 13.8% alc. **Rating** 94 **To** 2015 $70

McCutcheon Vineyard Mornington Peninsula Pinot Noir 2008 Has a fragrant bouquet, then a light-bodied but intense and long palate achieved with apparent ease, here with a slightly more savoury, foresty cast redeemed by the slippery, red-fruited finish. Screwcap. 13.8% alc. **Rating** 94 **To** 2014 $70

10X Barrel Fermented Mornington Peninsula Sauvignon Blanc 2009 **Rating** 90 $26 BE

10X Mornington Peninsula Pinot Gris 2009 **Rating** 90 $28 BE

Tenafeate Creek Wines ★★★★★

Lot 2 Gawler-One Tree Hill Road, One Tree Hill, SA 5114 **Region** Adelaide Zone
T (08) 8280 7715 **F** (08) 8280 7790 **www.**tenafeatecreekwines.com **Open** Fri–Sun 11–5
Winemaker Larry Costa **Est.** 2002 **Cases** 3000 **Vyds** 1 ha
Long-term friends Larry Costa, a former hairdresser, and Dominic Rinaldi, an accountant, embarked on winemaking as a hobby in 2002. The property, with its 1 ha of shiraz, cabernet sauvignon and merlot, is situated on the rolling countryside of the One Tree Hill in the Mount Lofty Ranges. From a small beginning, the business has grown rapidly, with grenache, nebbiolo, sangiovese, petit verdot, chardonnay, semillon and sauvignon blanc purchased to supplement the estate-grown grapes. Despite Larry's eye illness (macular degeneration), which forced his retirement from hairdressing, he is the hands-on winemaker at Tenafeate Creek. Both Larry and Dominic have Italian family winemaking traditions, and Larry learnt much from his late father. The red wines have won many medals over the years, none more impressive than the trophy for the 2004 Shiraz at the Great Australian Shiraz Challenge '09, for Best Wine Under $25. As at December '09 four vintages of shiraz ('03 to '06) and two vintages of cabernet sauvignon ('04 and '06) were among the 21 wines available ex cellar door, all at modest prices.

Shiraz Cabernet Sauvignon 2005 Excellent hue; a lively, flavoursome 70/30 blend; has black and red fruits set against a spicy backdrop, the tannins fine, the finish long. Remarkably youthful for a nearly five-year-old wine. Screwcap. 14.5% alc. **Rating** 94 **To** 2015 $20

Cabernet Sauvignon 2006 Deep, dense colour; while only medium- to full-bodied, has great richness and texture to the black fruits; the tannins and oak are well balanced and integrated. Screwcap. 14.5% alc. **Rating** 94 **To** 2021 $25

Basket Press Shiraz 2004 Excellent colour; more concentrated and powerful black fruits meshed with substantial tannins; a long road ahead. Screwcap. 14.5% alc. **Rating** 91 **To** 2016 $20

○   **Basket Press Grenache 2005** Bright hue, especially for age; sweet fruitcake cherry flavours complexed by just the right amount of tannins. Screwcap. 14.5% alc. **Rating** 91 **To** 2013 $20

○   **Basket Press Petit Verdot 2005** Strong colour; has the earthy, chocolatey, savoury black fruit flavours of the variety without the heavy tannins so easy to extract. Screwcap. 14.5% alc. **Rating** 90 **To** 2015 $20

♀♀♀♀   **Sangiovese Rose 2009** Rating 89 To 2010 $18
Shiraz 2006 Rating 89 To 2014 $20
VP Fortified Shiraz Cabernet Grenache 2004 Rating 89 To 2013 $15
Blush Sparkling Sangiovese NV Rating 87 To 2010 $19

Terra Felix   ★★★★

PO Box 2029, Wattletree Road, Malvern East, Vic 3134 **Region** Upper Goulburn
T (03) 9807 9778 **F** (03) 9923 6167 **www.**terrafelix.com.au **Open** Not
Winemaker Terry Barnett **Est.** 2001 **Cases** 14 600
Terra Felix was for many years a brand of Tallarook Wines, jointly owned by the Riebl family and by Peter Simon, Stan Olszewski and John Nicholson. In 2005 it was decided to separate the businesses, with Luis Riebl now solely concerned with the production of the Tallarook wines. Peter and Stan had run the Stanley Wine Company in Clare over 20 years ago, leaving it in the early 1980s, but always harbouring a desire to be involved in the industry as owners. Grapes continue to be sourced from Tallarook, and supplemented by other local growers. They have worked hard to establish export markets as well as on-premise distribution in Australia, with one-third of the production exported to the US, China and Hong Kong.

♀♀♀♀♀   **La Vie En Rose 2009** Vivid magenta; unusually, made from mourvedre, but
○   to full effect, with lively red and dark fruit flavours on the long and perfectly poised palate, with just a twang of citrus acidity. Screwcap. 12.9% alc. **Rating** 94 To 2011 $17.50

♀♀♀♀   **Shiraz Viognier 2008** Rating 89 To 2015 $17
Moscato Gold 2009 Rating 88 $17.50
Central Victoria Viognier 2009 Rating 87 To 2011 $17
E'Vette's Block Mourvedre 2008 Rating 87 To 2012 $17

🍇 Terre à Terre   ★★★★★

PO Box 3128, Unley, SA 5061 **Region** Wrattonbully
T 0400 700 447 **F** (08) 8272 5734 **www.**terroir-selections.com.au **Open** Not
Winemaker Xavier Bizot **Est.** 2008 **Cases** 1000 **Vyds** 4 ha
It would be hard to imagine two better credentialled owners than Xavier Bizot (son of the late Christian Bizot of Bollinger fame) and wife Lucy Croser (daughter of Brian and Ann Croser). They have close-planted sauvignon blanc and cabernet sauvignon on a limestone ridge, adjacent to Tapanappa's Whalebone Vineyard. Terre à Terre, incidentally, is a French expression meaning down-to-earth. Somehow I missed the first vintage of Sauvignon Blanc, the '09 a wine of extraordinary quality and character. The wines are available through independent retailers and leading restaurants, but also direct from the winery.

♀♀♀♀♀   **Wrattonbully Sauvignon Blanc 2009** A fascinating wine from a close-planted
○   (1.5 m x 15 m) French clone vineyard, hand-picked, crushed and cold-settled before fermentation in two French 600-litre barrels (one new, one second use) and 11 older French barriques, then matured in barrel for nine months, lees stirred every two weeks; the sheer intensity of the wine is almost shocking, its minerally structure tightly folded around grassy/citrussy fruit, the oak simply a background whisper. Wow. Screwcap. 12.7% alc. **Rating** 96 To 2014 $24

Tertini Wines   ★★★★☆

Kells Creek Road, Mittagong, NSW 2575 **Region** Southern Highlands
T (02) 4878 5213 **F** (02) 4878 5540 **www**.tertiniwines.com.au **Open** Thurs–Mon 10–5,
or by appt
Winemaker High Range Vintners **Est.** 2000 **Cases** 3000 **Vyds** 7.9 ha
When Julian Tertini began the development of Tertini Wines in 2000, he followed in the
footsteps of Joseph Vogt 145 years earlier. History does not relate the degree of success that
Joseph had, but the site he chose then was, as it is now, a good one. Tertini has pinot noir and
riesling (1.8 ha each), cabernet sauvignon and chardonnay (1 ha each), arneis (0.9 ha), pinot
gris (0.8 ha), merlot (0.4 ha) and lagrein (0.2 ha). Early indications that riesling and arneis
would be particularly well suited have been brought to fruition. Exports to Asia.

♟♟♟♟♟ **Reserve Southern Highlands Arneis 2009** Light straw-green; has a positively
perfumed bouquet of spiced pear and apple, the palate bringing some grainy citrus
flavours into play, verging on herbal. Screwcap. 13% alc. **Rating** 93 **To** 2012 $35
Reserve Barrel Fermented Southern Highlands Arneis 2009 Fermentation
in large French oak barrels (probably puncheons) has added to the textural
complexity, but – so far – diminished the exotic fruit of the Reserve. Screwcap.
13.5% alc. **Rating** 90 **To** 2013 $40

♟♟♟♟ **Reserve Southern Highlands Pinot Noir 2006 Rating** 88 **To** 2013 $45
Reserve Southern Highlands Noble Riesling 2008 Rating 88 **To** 2013 $25

Teusner   ★★★★★

29 Jane Place, Tanunda, SA 5352 (postal) **Region** Barossa Valley
T (08) 8252 4147 **F** (08) 8252 4147 **www**.teusner.com.au **Open** By appt (tel 0409 351 166)
Winemaker Kym Teusner, Michael Page **Est.** 2001 **Cases** 15 000
Teusner is a partnership between former Torbreck winemaker Kym Teusner and brother-
in-law Michael Page, and is typical of the new wave of winemakers determined to protect
very old, low-yielding, dry-grown Barossa vines. Kym was crowned *Gourmet Traveller* Young
Winemaker of the Year in 2007. The winery approach is based on lees ageing, little racking, no
fining or filtration, and no new American oak. The reasonably priced wines are made either
from 100% shiraz or from Southern Rhône blends. Exports to the UK, the US, Canada, The
Netherlands and Hong Kong.

♟♟♟♟♟ **Albert 2008** Dark chocolate and savoury smoked meat nuances sit pleasantly
atop rich black fruit; the palate follows the theme with impressive concentration,
turned earth, tar, blackberry and chewy tannins in abundance; rich and ripe,
but not overdone, the finish is long, fleshy and harmonious. Shiraz. Screwcap.
14.5% alc. **Rating** 95 **To** 2020 $48 BE

✪ **Joshua 2009** Super bright and vibrant, with crunchy, clearly defined blackberry
fruit framed by attractive mocha notes; the palate is fruitful on entry, and then
moves to great depths of minerals and licorice; long, satisfying and eminently
slurpable, no need to wait for this wine to come around. Grenache/Shiraz/Mataro.
Screwcap. **Rating** 94 **To** 2014 $28 BE

✪ **The Dog Strangler 2008** The name belies the accessibility of this usually difficult
variety (mataro); dark, inky and full of pitch and tar, with a juicy core of pure black
fruit; the palate reveals opulent fruit, tannins and chewy savoury elements that all
work brilliantly together; the crisp acid crunch on the finish brings you back for
more. Mataro. Screwcap. 14.5% alc. **Rating** 94 **To** 2020 $25 BE

♟♟♟♟♟ **Woodside Adelaide Hills Sauvignon Blanc 2009** An interesting take on the
✪ variety, building in a little struck match complexity to complement the tropical
fruit and cut grass aromas; the palate is generous yet light and fine to conclude;
excellently put together, and proof of success with style variations of sauvignon.
Screwcap. 13.5% alc. **Rating** 93 **To** 2013 $17 BE
The Mahlo Shiraz 2008 Rating 93 **To** 2018 $48 BE

✪   **The Independent Shiraz Mataro 2008** Essency aromas of blackberry and
fresh pitch are evident on the bouquet; the palate is warm, unctuous and fleshy,
and finishes with an ironstone minerality, thanks in no small part to the work of
the mataro; chewy and lipsmacking to conclude. Screwcap. 14.5% alc. **Rating** 93
To 2018 $22 BE
Joshua 2008 Rating 90 To 2015 $28

♀♀♀♀   **Barossa Valley Salsa 2009 Rating** 89 To 2012 $17 BE

The Colonial Estate   ★★★★★
Lot 264, Kalimna Road, Light Pass, SA 5355 **Region** Barossa Valley
T (08) 8562 1244 **F** (08) 8562 1288 **www.**maltus.com **Open** By appt
Winemaker Jonathan Maltus, Neil Whyte **Est.** 2002 **Cases** 25 000 **Vyds** 39.85 ha
The brand names of The Colonial Estate wines tell part of the story: Exile, Emigre, Exodus,
Explorateur, Etranger, Envoy, Expatrie, Evangeliste and Enchanteur. It will come as no surprise,
then, to find that this is a French-managed business with an extensive export program to many
parts of the world including France and other European countries. Thoroughly European
winemaking methods are used, most obviously being two sorting tables, one for the bunches
before they pass through the de-stemmer, and another for individual berries after the de-
stemming process. The company runs an active membership program for direct sales. Offered
for sale by receivers at the time of going to press.

♀♀♀♀♀   **Exile 2006** Good colour; a very complex shiraz, with black fruits, chocolate,
vanilla and notably soft tannins woven in a velvety shroud. While it will live
for many years, it is in fact ready to drink right now. Cork. 15% alc. **Rating** 95
To 2020 $220
**John Speke Single Vineyard Barossa Valley Grenache Shiraz Mourvedre
2008** Deeper colour and more purple in the hue than Alexander Laing; the vines
range from 60–100 years old from the single vineyard near Nuriootpa; while fully
labelled, does not show the alcohol, but there is no reason to suppose it is less than
15.5%; it matters not, for this sumptuous wine is packed with luscious black fruits
and ripe tannins. Another immaculate cork, hand-sorted. **Rating** 95 To 2028 $79
Mungo Park Single Vineyard Barossa Valley Shiraz 2008 Strong, deep
colour; waves of blackberry essence, plum and licorice emanate from the bouquet
and carry through unchanged to the full-bodied palate; there is sufficient activity
to carry the alcohol; 80–100-year-old vines. The cork is of good quality, but the
sides are stained. 15.5% alc. **Rating** 94 To 2018 $110
Richard Lander Single Vineyard Barossa Valley Shiraz 2008 Dense, dark
crimson-red; a massively built full-bodied wine, flooded with black fruits, dark
chocolate and licorice; very chewy, although ripe tannins and new French oak
add their contributions. Low-yielding 100-year-old vines, stained but good-quality
cork. 15.5% alc. **Rating** 94 To 2023 $85
Emigre 2006 Signs of colour change obvious; the bouquet has the gamut of
aromas reflecting the blend (Grenache/Shiraz/Mourvedre), with ripe confit fruit,
warm spices and a touch of chocolate; the velvety palate has a welcome savoury
twist on the finish. Cork. 14.5% alc. **Rating** 94 To 2016 $110

♀♀♀♀♀   **Eclaireur Old Vine Barossa Valley Grenache 2008 Rating** 93 To 2020 $79
Expatrie Single Vineyard Reserve Semillon 2007 Rating 91 To 2013 $35
Expatrie Single Vineyard Reserve Semillon 2008 Rating 90 To 2012 $35

♀♀♀♀   **Exile 2008 Rating** 87 To 2018 $220 BE

The Cups Estate   ★★★★☆
269 Browns Road, Fingal, Vic 3939 **Region** Mornington Peninsula
T 1300 131 741 **F** (03) 9886 1254 **www.**thecupsestate.com **Open** 7 days 10–5
Winemaker Moorooduc Estate, Pfeiffer, Kilchurn Wines **Est.** 1999 **Cases** 2500
Vyds 6.67 ha

Joe Fisicaro has returned to his roots after a career as a financial executive, establishing The Cups Estate near Rye. The name comes from the rolling dune region of the Peninsula known as 'the cups country'; the soils are light, with relatively low fertility, but drainage is excellent. Wind and frost have been problems, and the composition of the vineyard has been somewhat modified by a grafting program placing more emphasis on early ripening varieties (pinot noir, shiraz, pinot gris, chardonnay, merlot and moscato).

ŸŸŸŸŸ **Mornington Peninsula Chardonnay 2008** In the same impressive style as the '09, but has benefited from the additional 12 months in bottle, which seems to have given it more power and depth without becoming soft or blowsy. Screwcap. 13.5% alc. **Rating** 94 **To** 2015 $30

ŸŸŸŸŸ **Mornington Peninsula Chardonnay 2009 Rating** 93 To 2015 $30

ŸŸŸŸ **Peninsula Rose 2009 Rating** 89 To 2011 $25
Mornington Peninsula Blanc de Noir 2007 Rating 88 To 2011 $35

The Grapes of Ross ★★★★

PO Box 14, Lyndoch, SA 5351 **Region** Barossa Valley
T (08) 8524 4214 **F** (08) 8524 4214 **www**.grapesofross.com.au **Open** Not
Winemaker Ross Virgara **Est.** 2006 **Cases** 1500
Ross Virgara spent much of his life in the broader food and wine industry, finally taking the plunge into commercial winemaking in 2006. The grapes come from a fourth-generation family property in the Lyndoch Valley, and the aim is to make fruit-driven styles of quality wine. His fondness for frontignac led to the first release of Moscato, followed in due course by Rose, Merlot Cabernet and Old Bush Vine Grenache. Exports to China.

ŸŸŸŸŸ **Black Rose Single Vineyard Barossa Valley Shiraz 2007** A very traditional style, with high levels of toasty oak leading the way to the rich black fruit, licorice and dark chocolate; the palate is fleshy and lively, with the oak receding while the fruit comes to the fore. Screwcap. 14.9% alc. **Rating** 91 **To** 2018 $30 BE

✪ **Ruby Tuesday Barossa Valley Rose 2009** Deep colour, and loaded with vibrant light red fruits, strawberry and cherry; a big style with plenty of flavour and power, and even a little grip to conclude; Gold medal Barossa Wine Show '09. Screwcap. 12.5% alc. **Rating** 90 **To** 2012 $19 BE

 # The Hairy Arm ★★★☆

18 Plant Street, Northcote, Vic 3070 (postal) **Region** Sunbury
T (03) 9486 5396 **www**.hairyarm.com **Open** Not
Winemaker Steven Worley **Est.** 2004 **Cases** 300
The Hairy Arm is a name and label not easy to forget, so marketing experts will surely applaud. Steven and Natalie Worley's business may be small, but it certainly meets a marketing mantra. Steven graduated as an exploration geologist with a Master of Geology degree, followed by a postgraduate Diploma in Oenology and Viticulture. Until December 2009 he was general manager of Galli Estate Winery, The Hairy Arm Wine Company having started as a university project in '04. It has grown from a labour of love to a semi-commercial undertaking, focusing exclusively on shiraz grown variously in the Upper Goulburn Valley, Yarra Valley and Sunbury regions. The hairy arm, incidentally, is Steven's.

ŸŸŸŸŸ **Sunbury Shiraz 2007** Retains good purple hue; a strongly spicy, savoury bouquet and palate, with blackberry and licorice also in play; has length, the tannins firm but balanced. Screwcap. 14% alc. **Rating** 91 **To** 2017 $30

ŸŸŸŸ **Sunbury Shiraz 2008 Rating** 89 To 2016 $30
Yarra Valley Shiraz 2005 Rating 89 To 2014 $30

The Islander Estate Vineyards ★★★★★

PO Box 96, Parndana, SA 5220 **Region** Kangaroo Island
T (08) 8553 9008 **F** (08) 8553 9228 **www**.iev.com.au **Open** By appt
Winemaker Jacques Lurton **Est.** 2000 **Cases** 5000 **Vyds** 11 ha

Established by one of the most famous Flying Winemakers in the world, Bordeaux-born, trained and part-time Australian resident Jacques Lurton. He has established a close-planted vineyard; the principal varieties are cabernet franc, shiraz and sangiovese, with lesser amounts of grenache, malbec, semillon and viognier. The wines are made and bottled at the onsite winery, in true estate style. The flagship wine (Yakka Jack) is an esoteric blend of Sangiovese/Cabernet Franc. Exports to the US, Canada, France, Denmark, Holland, Finland, United Arab Emirates, Hong Kong and China.

ΨΨΨΨΨ Old Rowley Grenache Shiraz Viognier 2006 An elegant, light- to medium-bodied wine, the slightly improbable blend working very well, with quite intense spicy nuances, and red fruits, rather than confection, dominant; very good length and aftertaste. Screwcap. 13.5% alc. **Rating** 95 **To** 2016 $37.50

ΨΨΨΨΨ Kangaroo Island Chardonnay 2009 **Rating** 90 **To** 2012 $16 BE
Wally White Kangaroo Island Semillon Viognier 2008 **Rating** 90
To 2013 $40 BE

ΨΨΨΨ Kangaroo Island Shiraz 2008 **Rating** 88 **To** 2014 $16

The Lake House Denmark ★★★★
106 Turner Road, Denmark, WA 6333 **Region** Denmark
T (08) 9848 2444 **F** (08) 9848 3444 **www.lakehousedenmark.com.au Open** 7 days 11–5
Winemaker Harewood Estate (James Kellie) **Est.** 1995 **Cases** 6000 **Vyds** 5.2 ha
When Gary Capelli and partner Leanne Rogers purchased the vineyard (formerly known as Jindi Creek) in 2005, it had vines planted 10 years earlier to mainstream varieties: chardonnay (2 ha), sauvignon blanc (1 ha) and pinot noir and merlot (0.8 ha each). They have since moved to incorporate biodynamic principles into the vineyard, which also has small plantings of semillon and marsanne.

ΨΨΨΨΨ Premium Reserve Frankland Shiraz 2007 Fleshy and forward with dark fruit, struck match and chewy tannins all playing a role; the acidity provides life and energy on the finish. Screwcap. 14.5% alc. **Rating** 90 **To** 2015 $45 BE

❂ He Said She Said Classic Red 2008 Bright colour; light red fruit bouquet, with spice playing a pivotal role; the palate is vibrant, lively and medium-bodied, with early drinking a must for overall enjoyment. Merlot/Shiraz/Cabernet Sauvignon. Screwcap. 14% alc. **Rating** 90 **To** 2014 $17 BE

ΨΨΨΨ Premium Reserve Pinot Noir 2008 **Rating** 89 **To** 2014 $45 BE
He Said She Said Classic White 2009 **Rating** 88 **To** 2012 $17 BE

The Lane Vineyard ★★★★☆
Ravenswood Lane, Hahndorf, SA 5245 **Region** Adelaide Hills
T (08) 8388 1250 **F** (08) 8388 7233 **www.thelane.com.au Open** 7 days 10–4.30
Winemaker Michael Schreurs, Hugh Guthrie **Est.** 1993 **Cases** 30 000 **Vyds** 56.55 ha
After 15 years at The Lane Vineyard, Helen and John Edwards, and sons Marty and Ben, took an important step in realising their long-held dream – to grow, make and sell estate-based wines that have a true sense of place. In 2005, at the end of the Starvedog Lane joint venture with Hardys, they commissioned a state-of-the-art 500-tonne winery, bistro and cellar door overlooking the family's vineyards on picturesque Ravenswood Lane. Exports to all the UK, the US, Ireland, Belgium and China.

ΨΨΨΨΨ Single Vineyard John Crighton Adelaide Hills Shiraz Cabernet Sauvignon 2007 Good crimson hue; the bouquet has a typical cool-grown melange of black cherry, blackberry and licorice, the medium- to full-bodied palate simply building on that foundation, tannins exactly weighted, oak likewise. Screwcap. 14% alc. **Rating** 95 **To** 2030 $100

ΨΨΨΨΨ Beginning Adelaide Hills Chardonnay 2008 **Rating** 93 **To** 2015 $39
Single Vineyard Adelaide Hills Shiraz Viognier 2008 **Rating** 91
To 2018 $25

Block 10 Single Vineyard Adelaide Hills Sauvignon Blanc 2009 Rating 90
To 2011 $25
Block 2 Single Vineyard Adelaide Hills Pinot Gris 2009 Rating 90
To 2011 $30
Single Vineyard Adelaide Hills Viognier 2008 Rating 90 To 2010 $39

ΨΨΨΨ   Reunion Adelaide Hills Shiraz 2007 Rating 88 To 2017 $65

The Little Wine Company   ★★★★

Small Winemakers Centre, 426 McDonalds Road, Pokolbin, NSW 2320
Region Hunter Valley
T (02) 6579 1111 **F** (02) 6579 1440 **www.thelittlewinecompany.com.au Open** 7 days 10–5
Winemaker Ian and Suzanne Little **Est.** 2000 **Cases** 12 000
Having sold their previous winery, Ian and Suzanne Little moved in stages to their new
winery at Broke. The Little Wine Company is part-owner of the 20-ha Lochleven Vineyard
in Pokolbin, and contracts three vineyards in the Broke–Fordwich area (where the winery
is situated). It also has access to the Talga Vineyard in the Gundaroo Valley near Canberra.
Exports to Hong Kong, Taiwan, China and Japan.

ΨΨΨΨΨ   Semillon 2009 Very typical of the great vintage, with that extra layer of almost
✪   juicy fruit, lemon and lime flavours to the fore; correct acidity holds it all together.
           Screwcap. 10.5% alc. **Rating** 94 **To** 2019 $20.95

ΨΨΨΨ   Olivine Shiraz Viognier 2005 Rating 87 To 2011 $24.95

The Old Faithful Estate   ★★★★★

c/- PO Box 235 (Kangarilla Road), McLaren Vale, SA 5171 **Region** McLaren Vale
T 0419 383 907 **F** (08) 8323 9747 **www.haselgrovevignerons.com Open** By appt
Winemaker Nick Haselgrove, Warren Randall **Est.** 2005 **Cases** 2500
This is a 50/50 joint venture between American John Larchet (with one-half) and a quartet
of Nick Haselgrove, Warren Randall, Warren Ward and Andrew Fletcher. Larchet has long
had a leading role as a specialist importer of Australian wines into the US, and guarantees
the business whatever sales it needs there. The shiraz, grenache and mourvedre come from
selected blocks within Tinlins wine resources, with which the quartet has a close association.
It's a winning formula. Exports to the US and China.

ΨΨΨΨΨ   Top of the Hill McLaren Vale Shiraz 2007 Retains good, bright colour; the
           bouquet is pure McLaren Vale, dark berry fruits and dark chocolate; the palate
           flavours follow on in similar fashion, but it is the texture that is so compelling
           particularly in a tough vintage such as '07. Cork. 15% alc. **Rating** 94 **To** 2027 $75

The Old Orchard Winery   ★★★★☆

254 Scoresby Road, Boronia, Vic 3155 **Region** Yarra Valley
T (03) 9801 2183 **www.theoldorchardwinery.com.au Open** Fri–Sun 11–5
Winemaker Tony Pelosi, Jeff Wright **Est.** 1981 **Cases** 388 **Vyds** 2.45 ha
The establishment date of 1981 is the year during which 2.45 ha of chardonnay, cabernet
sauvignon, shiraz, cabernet franc and malbec were planted under a 'work for the dole' scheme
sponsored by Knox City Council on 8 ha of Crown land in Boronia. Care of the vineyard
changed hands several times until 2005 when the Council requested expressions of interest
in operating the vineyard. English-born couple Pat and David Smith (who had married in
Germany) had moved to Australia in '82, and settled down to separate business lives, David
starting a software development business in '83, Pat becoming a long-term member of the
Myer company until retiring in '04. During his time in Germany, David was responsible for
buying French and German wines for a British retail chain that serviced British members
of NATO, and part of his computer business was the installation of Dan Murphy's first
electronic point of sale system in the Prahran in '84. This somewhat tenuous connection with
grapegrowing and winemaking was sufficient for them to acquire a long-term lease of the

vineyard, and employ contract winemakers who have produced a series of wines since '08, collecting the trophy for Best Shiraz at the Victorian Wines Show '09, one silver and three bronze medals at the same show.

ҬҬҬҬҬ Shiraz 2008 Deep crimson-purple; classic cool-grown shiraz aromas and flavours
✪ with an array of blackberry, blueberry, spice and earth on its finely textured medium-bodied palate. Trophy Victorian Wines Show '09. Screwcap. 12.5% alc. Rating 95 To 2020 $25

ҬҬҬҬҬ Unwooded Chardonnay 2008 Rating 90 To 2013 $17.50

ҬҬҬҬ Lightly Oaked Chardonnay 2008 Rating 88 To 2013 $17.50
Cabernet Sauvignon 2008 Rating 87 To 2015 $17.50
Special Reserve Cabernet Sauvignon 2008 Rating 87 To 2018 $25
Cabernet Franc 2008 Rating 87 To 2014 $17.50

The Pawn   ★★★★☆
PO Box 139, Langhorne Creek, SA 5255 **Region** Langhorne Creek
T 0438 373 247 **F** (08) 8537 3109 **www**.thepawn.com.au **Open** Not
Winemaker Tom Keelan, Rebecca Willson **Est.** 2004 **Cases** 2500 **Vyds** 50 ha
This is a partnership between Tom and Rebecca Keelan and David and Vanessa Blows. Tom was for some time manager of Longview Vineyards at Macclesfield in the Adelaide Hills, and consulted to the neighbouring vineyard owned by David and Vanessa. In 2004 Tom and David decided to make some small batches of petit verdot and tempranillo at the Bremerton winery, where Tom is now vineyard manager. The wines now come either from Bremerton's Langhorne Creek vineyards or the Adelaide Hills vineyards owned by the Blows. The remainder of the grapes from the Adelaide Hills property supplies brands such as Starvedog Lane, Nepenthe and Orlando.

ҬҬҬҬҬ Jeu de Fin Reserve Release Adelaide Hills Sauvignon Blanc 2008 Has benefited considerably from an extra year in bottle and partial barrel fermentation; the bouquet is powerful, with zesty citrus and tropical notes, the palate following on persuasively. Screwcap. 13.9% alc. Rating 94 To 2011 $24

ҬҬҬҬҬ Jeu de Fin Reserve Release Adelaide Hills Shiraz 2007 Rating 93 To 2020 $33
✪ En Passant Adelaide Hills Tempranillo 2007 Attractive light- to medium-bodied wine, with an array of red fruits ranging from cherry to raspberry, the tannins very fine indeed. Screwcap. 13.7% alc. Rating 90 To 2014 $24

ҬҬҬҬ The Gambit Adelaide Hills Sangiovese 2007 Distinctly light colour; shows
✪ sangiovese for what it is when the vines are relatively young; red cherry fruits, spice and an earthy/minerally finish. Screwcap. 13.7% alc. Rating 89 To 2014 $18
Caissa Adelaide Hills Pinot Grigio 2008 Rating 87 To 2010 $18

The Poplars Winery   ★★★☆
Riddoch Highway, Coonawarra, SA 5263 **Region** Coonawarra
T (08) 8736 3130 **F** (08) 8736 3163 **www**.thepoplarswinery.com **Open** 7 days 9–6
Winemaker Grant Semmens **Est.** 2006 **Cases** NA **Vyds** 22.6 ha
It all looked too good to be true, and so it proved for this new name in Coonawarra. It is part of Coonawarra Developments Pty Ltd, which is in turn the owner of Chardonnay Lodge, the only large-scale (and ever-growing) accommodation complex in the heart of Coonawarra. Founded by the Yates family 22 years ago, now offering 38 large suites and a deservedly popular restaurant. Most recently, and in a way most significantly, Coonawarra Developments also purchased the former Jamiesons Run Winery from Foster's. The vineyard opposite the winery, and adjacent to Chardonnay Lodge, underpins one of the most diverse tourism developments in SA. But the turbulence of the global financial crisis and the Australian wine surplus led to major financial problems in 2009, the final outcome some time away. Exports to the US and China.

ŢŢŢŢŢ **Reserve Coonawarra Cabernet Sauvignon 2007** Slightly diffuse colour; attractive medium-bodied cabernet, with the freshness and purity of varietal expression that comes easily in Coonawarra; well-handled cedary French oak another plus. Screwcap. 13.1% alc. **Rating** 92 **To** 2022 $29

ŢŢŢŢ **Coonawarra Pinot Noir 2008 Rating** 89 **To** 2014 $26

The Roy Kidman Wine Co ★★★☆

Comaum School Road, Coonawarra, SA 5263 **Region** Coonawarra
T 0417 878 933 **F** (08) 8331 7960 **www.**roykidman.com.au **Open** Not
Winemaker Peter Douglas (Contract) **Est.** 2003 **Cases** 4000 **Vyds** 55.9 ha
Branches of the Kidman family have been part of Coonawarra viticulture since 1970, and long before that one of the great names in the Australian cattle industry. Tim, Philip and Mardi Kidman (brothers and sister) run a separate business from that of cousin Sid Kidman, with 40.2 ha of cabernet sauvignon and 15.7 ha of shiraz, planting the first 2 ha of shiraz in 1970, and moving into wine production in 2003, albeit still selling the major part of the grape production. The first wine (Cabernet Sauvignon) was made in 2004, labelled Roy the Cattleman, a tribute to their paternal grandfather, who worked as a stockman for his uncle Sir Sidney Kidman. Exports to Hong Kong and China.

ŢŢŢŢŢ **Bar Over Box Limestone Coast Sauvignon Blanc 2009** Light straw-green;
✪ an interesting wine with the firm texture and structure of young semillon, and a similarly crisp finish; the aromas and flavours are all in the herbal citrus end of the spectrum. Screwcap. 11.9% alc. **Rating** 90 **To** 2012 $15

ŢŢŢŢ **Roy The Cattleman Coonawarra Shiraz 2008 Rating** 89 **To** 2018 $27.50

The Story Wines ★★★★★

3/88 Grosvenor Street, Balaclava, Vic 3183 (postal) **Region** Grampians
T 0411 697 912 **F** (03) 9534 8881 **www.**thestory.com.au **Open** Not
Winemaker Rory Lane **Est.** 2004 **Cases** 1000
Over the years I have come across winemakers with degrees in atomic science, innumerable doctors with specialities spanning every human condition, town planners, sculptors and painters, the list going on and on, and Rory Lane adds yet another: a degree in ancient Greek literature. He says that after completing his degree, and 'desperately wanting to delay an entry into the real world, I stumbled across and enrolled in a postgraduate wine technology and marketing course at Monash University, where I soon became hooked on … the wondrous connection between land, human and liquid'. Vintages in Australia and Oregon germinated the seed, and he zeroed in on the Grampians, where he purchases small parcels of high-quality grapes for his Shirazs, making the wines in a small factory shell where he has assembled a basket press, a few open fermenters, a mono pump and some decent French oak. Exports to Singapore.

ŢŢŢŢŢ **Westgate Vineyard Grampians Shiraz 2008** Bright crimson-purple foretells
✪ a vibrant wine, with as much red berry as black berry fruit, and particularly good line and length; good acidity completes the story. The difference is style, not quality. Screwcap. 13.5% alc. **Rating** 96 **To** 2025 $40
✪ **Rice's Vineyard Grampians Shiraz 2008** Strong crimson; the aromatic bouquet promises the spicy black fruits that duly appear in a tapestry of flavours and textures on the medium-bodied palate, which has remarkable finesse. Screwcap. 14.5% alc. **Rating** 96 **To** 2028 $40
✪ **Grampians Shiraz 2008** Bright crimson hue; a fragrant, welcoming bouquet that, like the medium-bodied palate, has a spicy mix of red and black fruits in a cherry plum spectrum; the tannins and oak are judged to perfection. Screwcap. 13.5% alc. **Rating** 94 **To** 2023 $22

The Trades ★★★

13/30 Peel Road, O'Connor, WA 6163 (postal) **Region** Various
T (08) 9331 2188 **F** (08) 9331 2199 **Open** Not
Winemaker Geoff Johnston (Contract) **Est.** 2006 **Cases** 1200
Thierry Ruault and Rachel Taylor have run a wholesale wine business in Perth since 1993, representing a group of top-end Australian and imported producers. By definition, the wines they offered to their clientele were well above $20 per bottle, and they decided to fill the gap with a contract-made Shiraz from the Adelaide Hills, and a Sauvignon Blanc from Margaret River, selling at $17.50. This is, without question, a virtual winery.

ⵣⵣⵣⵣⵣ **Grasscutter's Margaret River Sauvignon Blanc 2009** A fragrant bouquet of grass, herb and pink grapefruit leads into a bright, crisp palate, with good varietal expression and length. Screwcap. 13.2% alc. **Rating** 90 **To** 2011 $17.50

The Wanderer ★★★★★

2850 Launching Place Road, Gembrook, Vic 3783 **Region** Yarra Valley
T 0415 529 639 **F** (03) 5968 1699 **www**.wandererwines.com **Open** By appt
Winemaker Andrew Marks **Est.** 2005 **Cases** 500
Andrew Marks is the son of Ian and June Marks, owners of Gembrook Hill, and after graduating from Adelaide University with a degree in oenology he joined Southcorp, working for six years at Penfolds (Barossa Valley) and Seppelt (Great Western), as well as undertaking vintages in Coonawarra and France. He has since worked in the Hunter Valley, Great Southern, Sonoma County in the US and Costa Brava in Spain – hence the name of his business.

ⵣⵣⵣⵣⵣ **Upper Yarra Valley Pinot Noir 2008** Light but bright colour; a complex bouquet, with plum and black cherry aromas, then an intense and juicy palate adding red fruit notes; sophisticated wine. Mega bottle and wax seal, god and mammon. Diam. 13.5% alc. **Rating** 95 **To** 2016 $50
Yarra Valley Pinot Noir 2008 Lighter colour than the Upper Yarra; a fragrant, savoury red fruit bouquet and light-bodied palate run in unison; has deceptive length thanks to superfine tannins. Screwcap. 13% alc. **Rating** 94 **To** 2015 $35
Yarra Valley Shiraz 2008 Bright crimson hue; fragrant black and red cherry fruit with a strong sprinkle of spice and black pepper; the medium-bodied palate has juicy fruit coupled with good line and length. Screwcap. 13.8% alc. **Rating** 94 **To** 2020 $35

The Willows Vineyard ★★★☆

Light Pass Road, Light Pass, Barossa Valley, SA 5355 **Region** Barossa Valley
T (08) 8562 1080 **F** (08) 8562 3447 **www**.thewillowsvineyard.com.au
Open Wed–Mon 10.30–4.30, Tues by appt
Winemaker Peter and Michael Scholz **Est.** 1989 **Cases** 6500 **Vyds** 42.74 ha
The Scholz family have been grapegrowers for generations and have over 40 ha of vineyards, selling part and retaining the remainder of the crop. Current generation winemakers Peter and Michael Scholz make smooth, well-balanced and flavoursome wines under their own label, all marketed with some bottle age. Exports to the UK, the US, Canada, Singapore, Thailand and NZ.

ⵣⵣⵣⵣⵣ **Barossa Valley Riesling 2009** Bright straw-green; an aromatic display of citrus
✪ and apple on the bouquet and palate, with an appealing juicy character to the fruit flavours; good balance. Will develop well over the next five years. Screwcap. 11% alc. **Rating** 90 **To** 2015 $14

ⵣⵣⵣⵣ **Seven 2009** Fresh, bright colour; made by the seventh generation of the Scholz
✪ family from grapes planted by the fifth generation; has juicy flavours needing little or no oak. Grenache/Shiraz. Screwcap. 15% alc. **Rating** 89 **To** 2016 $20
The Doctor Sparkling Red NV Rating 89 **To** 2012 $30

Third Child ★★★★
134 Mt Rumney Road, Mt Rumney, Tas 7170 (postal) **Region** Southern Tasmania
T 0419 132 184 **F** (03) 6223 8042 **www**.thirdchildvineyard.com.au **Open** Not
Winemaker John Skinner, Rob Drew **Est.** 2000 **Cases** 250 **Vyds** 3 ha
John and Marcia Skinner planted 2.5 ha of pinot noir and 0.5 ha of riesling in 2000. It is very
much a hands-on operation, the only concession being the enlistment of Rob Drew (from
an adjoining property) to help John with the winemaking. When the first vintage (2004) was
reaching the stage of being bottled and labelled, the Skinners could not come up with a name
and asked their daughter Claire. 'Easy,' she said. 'You've got two kids already; considering the
care taken and time spent at the farm, it's your third child.'

♛♛♛♛♛ **Riesling 2009** An off-dry riesling that comes as a surprise, there being no warning
✪ on the label; gentle lime and apple flavours with a clean, lingering finish. Could
have carried a little more acidity. Screwcap. 10.5% alc. **Rating** 90 **To** 2016 $15
Benjamin Daniel Pinot Noir 2008 Light, bright red; a fragrant bouquet of red
berries and a touch of spice, the light- to medium-bodied palate adding a touch
of plum; a multi-clone blend with good length and purity. Screwcap. 13.5% alc.
Rating 90 **To** 2014 $25

♛♛♛♛ **Thomas Nicholas Pinot Noir 2008** Rating 89 To 2013 $25

Thistle Hill ★★★★☆
74 McDonalds Road, Mudgee, NSW 2850 **Region** Mudgee
T (02) 6373 3546 **F** (02) 6373 3540 **www**.thistlehill.com.au **Open** Mon–Sat 9.30–4.30,
Sun & public hols 9.30–4
Winemaker Michael Slater **Est.** 1976 **Cases** 3500 **Vyds** 33 ha
In 2009 Rob and Mary Loughan, owners of the adjoining Erudgere since '04, acquired
Thistle Hill from Lesley Robertson (who is staying on in a marketing capacity). Thistle
Hill was already certified organic (by the National Association for Sustainable Agriculture
Australia (NASAA), which means no weedicides, insecticides or synthetic fertilisers), and
Erudgere became certified organic in July 2010. From the 2011 vintage, all of the Erudgere
and Thistle Hill wines will be sold under the Thistle Hill label. The appointment of Michael
Slater as winemaker paid immediate dividends, the 2009 Riesling winning multiple trophies.
It is fascinating that, at a time of global warming, Thistle Hill and Robert Stein should be
producing Rieslings of the highest quality. Exports to the UK, the US, Canada and Japan.

♛♛♛♛♛ **Riesling 2009** Pale straw-green; a pure and refined wine on both bouquet and
✪ palate; citrus flavours and an underlying minerality build progressively through
the palate. Trophies Best Organic Wine, NSW Wine Awards '09 and Australia/NZ
Organic Wine Show '09. Screwcap. 11% alc. **Rating** 94 **To** 2020 $30

♛♛♛♛♛ **Erudgere Hill End Road Premium Mudgee Shiraz Cabernet 2008**
Rating 92 To 2017 $25
Erudgere Premium Mudgee Riesling 2009 Rating 90 To 2017 $20
Mudgee Chardonnay 2009 Rating 90 To 2013 $22
✪ **Erudgere Hill End Road Premium Mudgee Chardonnay 2008** Well-
timed picking has kept the structure tight and the flavours fresh; nectarine and
citrus fruit is neatly balanced by gentle French oak. Screwcap. 13% alc. **Rating** 90
To 2012 $20
Erudgere Premium Mudgee Rose 2009 Rating 90 To 2011 $18

♛♛♛♛ **Erudgere Hill End Road Premium Mudgee Shiraz 2008** Rating 87
To 2014 $20
Erudgere Hill End Road Premium Mudgee Cabernet Sauvignon 2005
Rating 87 To 2014 $20

Thomas Vineyard Estate ★★★★☆

PO Box 490, McLaren Vale, SA 5171 **Region** McLaren Vale
T (08) 8557 8583 **F** (08) 8557 8583 **www**.thomasvineyard.com.au **Open** Not
Winemaker Trevor Tucker **Est.** 1998 **Cases** 500 **Vyds** 5.26 ha
Merv and Dawne Thomas thought long and hard before purchasing the property on which
they have established their vineyard. It is 3 km from the coast of the Gulf of St Vincent on the
Fleurieu Peninsula, with a clay over limestone soil known locally as 'Bay of Biscay'. They had
a dream start to the business when the 2004 Shiraz won the trophy for Best Single Vineyard
Wine (red or white) at the McLaren Vale Wine Show '05, the Reserve Shiraz also winning a
gold medal. Exports to the US.

♀♀♀♀♀ **McLaren Vale Shiraz 2007** Bright crimson; typical McLaren Vale, blackberry
✪   fruits intermingling with dark chocolate on the bouquet and palate alike; has good
          texture and structure, with none of the toughness commonly found in '07 wines.
          Diam. 14% alc. **Rating** 93 **To** 2020 $20

Thomas Wines ★★★★★

c/- The Small Winemakers Centre, McDonalds Road, Pokolbin, NSW 2321
Region Hunter Valley
T (02) 6574 7371 **F** (02) 6574 7392 **www**.thomaswines.com.au **Open** 7 days 10–5
Winemaker Andrew Thomas, Phil Le Messurier **Est.** 1997 **Cases** 5000 **Vyds** 14 ha
Andrew Thomas came to the Hunter Valley from McLaren Vale to join the winemaking team
at Tyrrell's. After 13 years with Tyrrell's, he left to undertake contract work and to continue
the development of his own label, a family affair run by himself and his wife Jo. He makes
individual vineyard wines, simply to underline the subtle differences between the various
subregions of the Hunter. Plans for the construction of an estate winery have been delayed and
for the time being he has leased the James Estate winery on Hermitage Road through to Dec
2010; all being well, the '11 vintage will be in his new winery. It hasn't prevented him being
voted Winemaker of the Year '08 by his Hunter Valley winemaking peers, nor continuing to
win an avalanche of trophies and gold medals for his Semillons (in particular) and Shirazs. Is
one of the top four makers of semillon. Exports to Canada and Singapore.

♀♀♀♀♀ **Braemore Individual Vineyard Hunter Valley Semillon 2005** Aged Release.
✪   Bright, glowing green-yellow; still very youthful, yet packed with juicy lemon
          flavours; has outstanding length, and flawless balance; a great semillon with another
          10 years' minimum under its belt. Due for re-release Dec '10. Screwcap. 10.2% alc.
          Rating 96 **To** 2020 $45
✪   **Braemore Individual Vineyard Hunter Valley Semillon 2004** Aged Release.
          Even greener colour than the '05; the higher alcohol invests the wine with a
          slightly softer, rounder texture/mouthfeel, the lemon moving a little to lime;
          glorious mouthfeel. Screwcap. 11% alc. **Rating** 96 **To** 2018 $45
          Braemore Individual Vineyard Hunter Valley Semillon 2009 The bouquet
          is multifaceted, with more fruit than normal in a young semillon; the palate
          verged on the astonishing when six months old, with a panoply of citrus fruit,
          and the supple mouthfeel of a more mature wine. Screwcap. 11.5% alc. **Rating** 95
          To 2018 $27
✪   **Six Degrees Vineyard Selection Hunter Valley Semillon 2009** The
          inspiration of Mosel Kabinett wine is as clear with this vintage as it was with prior
          releases. It is quite astonishing that early picking and the retention of residual sugar
          can so convincingly capture the essence of the Mosel style. Doubtless, has to be
          hand-sold if it is not going to frighten the horses. It will be fascinating to watch
          the development of this wine in bottle. Screwcap. 9% alc. **Rating** 94 **To** 2016 $22
✪   **DJV Individual Vineyard Hunter Valley Shiraz 2007** Deep purple; a rich
          bouquet of sweet leather and confit plums, then a succulent palate redolent
          of black, gently savoury fruits, rounded tannins and quality oak; revels in its
          moderate alcohol and finishes with good acidity. Screwcap. 13.5% alc. **Rating** 94
          To 2020 $30

🍷🍷🍷🍷 **The O.C. Individual Vineyard Hunter Valley Semillon 2009** Rating 89
To 2012 $24

Thompson Estate ★★★★★

299 Harmans Road South, Wilyabrup, WA 6284 **Region** Margaret River
T (08) 9386 1751 **F** (08) 9755 6406 **www**.thompsonestate.com **Open** 7 days 10–5
Winemaker Bob Cartwright **Est.** 1994 **Cases** 8000 **Vyds** 28 ha
Cardiologist Peter Thompson planted the first vines at Thompson Estate in 1997, inspired by
his and his family's shareholdings in the Pierro and Fire Gully vineyards, and by visits to many
of the world's premium wine regions. The vineyard is planted to cabernet sauvignon, cabernet
franc, merlot, chardonnay, sauvignon blanc, semillon and pinot noir. Thompson Estate wines
have been made solely by Bob Cartwright (former Leeuwin Estate winemaker) since 2006,
with its new state-of-the-art winery coming onstream in '09. Exports to the UK, the US and
other major markets.

🍷🍷🍷🍷🍷 **Margaret River Chardonnay 2008** Bright green-straw; has all the layered
depth that is the hallmark of Margaret River chardonnay, with nectarine, melon
and fig swathed in fine oak and lengthened by citrussy acidity. Screwcap. 13.5% alc.
Rating 94 To 2015 $38
Andrea Reserve Margaret River Cabernet Merlot 2007 Good hue;
cedary, savoury, spicy aromas flow into the redcurrant and blackcurrant fruit of
the medium-bodied palate; it has good texture and structure, French oak well
integrated. Screwcap. 14.2% alc. Rating 94 To 2020 $38
Margaret River Cabernet Sauvignon 2007 Bright crimson; ticks all the
boxes for Margaret River cabernet; the bouquet is fragrant, promising the cedar
and blackcurrant fruit that the medium-bodied palate duly delivers; the fruit, oak
and tannins are totally in balance, and the finish is long and satisfying. Screwcap.
14.4% alc. Rating 94 To 2022 $38

🍷🍷🍷🍷🍷 **Locum Margaret River Sauvignon Blanc Semillon 2009** Light straw-green;
✪ with a bit of teasing, some zesty lemon and passionfruit aromas emerge, and build
further on the well-balanced and long palate. Screwcap. 12.5% alc. Rating 93
To 2012 $22
Margaret River Chardonnay Pinot Noir 2006 Rating 91 To 2014 $38

Thorn-Clarke Wines ★★★★★

Milton Park, Gawler Park Road, Angaston, SA 5353 **Region** Barossa Valley
T (08) 8564 3036 **F** (08) 8564 3255 **www**.thornclarkewines.com.au **Open** Mon–Fri 9–5,
w'ends 12–4
Winemaker Derek Fitzgerald **Est.** 1987 **Cases** 80 000 **Vyds** 267.88 ha
Established by David and Cheryl Clarke (née Thorn), and son Sam, Thorn-Clarke is one of
the largest family-owned, estate-based businesses in the greater Barossa region. Their winery
is close to the border between the Barossa and Eden valleys, and they are often regarded as
a Barossa Valley winery. In fact three of their four vineyards are in the Eden Valley, the Mt
Crawford Vineyard is at the southern end of the Eden Valley, while the Milton Park and
Sandpiper vineyards are further north in the Eden Valley. The fourth vineyard is at St Kitts in
the northern end of the Barossa Ranges, established when no other vignerons had ventured
onto what was hitherto considered unsuitable soil. In all four vineyards careful soil mapping
has resulted in matching of variety and site, with all of the major varieties represented. The
quality of grapes retained for the Thorn-Clarke label has resulted in a succession of trophy and
gold medal-winning wines at very competitive prices. Exports to all major markets.

🍷🍷🍷🍷🍷 **Sandpiper Eden Valley Riesling 2009** An aromatic lime-infused bouquet, then
✪ a totally delicious palate, with bright lime juice flavours and a crisp finish built
around well-balanced acidity. Screwcap. 12.5% alc. Rating 94 To 2019 $16.95
✪ **Shotfire Barossa Shiraz 2008** Slightly less dense colour than Sandpiper; lifted
plum, dark chocolate and blackberry fruit aromas are followed by an energetic
palate that gains velocity on the finish and aftertaste. A conundrum, given the
benefit of doubt. Screwcap. 14.5% alc. Rating 94 To 2020 $22.95

ΥΥΥΥ **Sandpiper Barossa Shiraz 2008** Dense purple-crimson sets the scene for a
✪ densely packed bouquet and medium- to full-bodied palate. Strong plum and
blackberry fruit flavours drive the wine, which avoids dead fruit characters and
carries its alcohol very well. Screwcap. 15% alc. **Rating** 93 **To** 2016 $16.95

ΥΥΥΥ **Sandpiper Barossa Cabernet Sauvignon 2008** Good colour, with
✪ blackcurrant flavours in abundance; the palate is rich and complex, with clean
and clearly defined black fruit to conclude. One of the rare cabernets ex '08 with
controlled alcohol. Screwcap. 13.5% alc. **Rating** 89 **To** 2014 $16 BE
Sandpiper Barossa Merlot 2008 Rating 88 **To** 2012 $16 BE

3 Drops   ★★★★★
PO Box 1828, Applecross, WA 6953 **Region** Mount Barker
T (08) 9315 4721 **F** (08) 9315 4724 **www.3drops.com Open** Not
Winemaker Robert Diletti (Contract) **Est.** 1998 **Cases** 4500 **Vyds** 21.5 ha
The 3 Drops are not the three owners (John Bradbury, Joanne Bradbury and Nicola Wallich),
but wine, olive oil and water, all of which come from the substantial property at Mount Barker.
The plantings are riesling, sauvignon blanc, semillon, chardonnay, cabernet sauvignon, merlot,
shiraz and cabernet franc, like the olive trees, irrigated by a large wetland on the property. The
business expanded significantly in 2007 with the purchase of the 14.7-ha Patterson's Vineyard.
Exports to the UK, Canada and Hong Kong.

ΥΥΥΥΥ **Mount Barker Riesling 2009** A highly perfumed and flowery bouquet; lime
✪ and apple blossom foretell the flavours on the palate; a beautifully cadenced wine,
finishing with crisp lemony acidity. Screwcap. 12.5% alc. **Rating** 95 **To** 2020 $22
✪ **Mount Barker Chardonnay 2008** Straw-green; has a vibrant array of stone
fruits and grapefruit on the bouquet, the intense drive of the palate focusing on
nectarine and grapefruit; a high-quality chardonnay in every respect. Screwcap.
13.5% alc. **Rating** 95 **To** 2016 $24

ΥΥΥΥ **Mount Barker Sauvignon Blanc 2009 Rating** 89 **To** 2011 $22

Three Wishes Vineyard   ★★★★
604 Batman Highway, Hillwood, Tas 7252 **Region** Northern Tasmania
T (03) 6331 2009 **F** (03) 6331 0043 **www.threewishesvineyard.com.au**
Open 7 days 11–5 Boxing Day to Easter, or by appt
Winemaker Holm Oak (Rebecca Wilson) **Est.** 1998 **Cases** 1000 **Vyds** 3 ha
Peter and Natalie Whish-Wilson began the establishment of their vineyard in 1998 while
they were working in Hong Kong, delegating the management tasks to parents Rosemary
and Tony until 2003. Peter and Natalie took a year's sabbatical to do the first vintage, with
their children aged six and four also involved in tending the vines. The seachange became
permanent, Peter completing his winegrowing degree from CSU in 1996. The original
vineyard has been extended, and now comprises 1 ha each of pinot noir, chardonnay and
riesling. Exports to Sweden.

ΥΥΥΥΥ **Riesling 2008** Bright straw-green; intense citrus and lime fruit; full of flavour
✪ through to a long finish. Screwcap. 13.1% alc. **Rating** 92 **To** 2016 $20
✪ **Chardonnay 2007** Light straw-green; interesting wine; supple, round and
smooth, its mouthfeel is less brisk and sharp than many Tasmanian chardonnays,
the stone fruit flavours joined by a hint of passionfruit; good oak handling.
Screwcap. 13.5% alc. **Rating** 91 **To** 2013 $25
Pinot Noir 2007 Bright, light crimson-purple; a fragrant bouquet with spicy red
fruit aromas, then a lively, juicy red fruit palate; has developed very well over the
past 12 months. Screwcap. 13.5% alc. **Rating** 90 **To** 2015 $35
Botrytis Riesling 2008 The cool climate is ideally suited to these wines; this is
very elegant, with only a mild botrytis infection, but has very good length and
balance to its lime fruit, the flavour not altered by botrytis. Screwcap. 9% alc.
Rating 90 **To** 2015 $30

Tibooburra Vineyard ★★★★☆

Stringybark Lane, Yellingbo, Vic 3139 (postal) **Region** Yarra Valley
T 0418 367 319 **F** (03) 5964 8577 **www**.tibooburra.com **Open** Not
Winemaker Timo Mayer (Contract) **Est.** 1996 **Cases** 1500 **Vyds** 34 ha
The Kerr family has done much with Tibooburra since they began assembling their 1000-ha property in 1967. They have established a champion Angus herd, planted a vineyard in '96 on elevated northern and northwest slopes, established a truffiere in 2001 to supply Japanese and northern hemisphere restaurants with black truffles, and launched the Tibooburra Wines label in '02. Four generations have been, or are, involved in the business. Most of the grapes are sold. Plantings (in descending order) are chardonnay, sauvignon blanc, pinot noir shiraz and merlot, and the quality of the early releases is all one could possibly ask for.

♀♀♀♀♀ **Solitude Yarra Valley Chardonnay 2008** Light, clear green-straw; a highly fragrant bouquet of white peach and grapefruit, the palate delicate but long, with excellent energy and balance. Screwcap. 12.5% alc. **Rating** 94 **To** 2016 $40

Tidswell Wines ★★★★☆

PO Box 94, Kensington Park, SA 5068 **Region** Limestone Coast Zone
T (08) 8363 5800 **F** (08) 8363 1980 **www**.tidswellwines.com.au **Open** Not
Winemaker Ben Tidswell, Wine Wise Consultancy **Est.** 1997 **Cases** 7000 **Vyds** 119 ha
The Tidswell family (now in the shape of Andrea and Ben Tidswell) has two large vineyards in the Limestone Coast Zone near Bool Lagoon; the lion's share is planted to cabernet sauvignon and shiraz, with smaller plantings of merlot, sauvignon blanc, chardonnay, petit verdot and vermentino. Fifty per cent of the vineyards are organically certified, and more will be converted in due course. Wines are released under the Jennifer, Heathfield Ridge and Caves Road labels. Exports to Canada, Denmark, Germany, Singapore and Japan.

♀♀♀♀♀ **Jennifer Cabernet Sauvignon 2006** Very good hue and depth to the colour; the blackberry and cassis aromas are pure cabernet, the full-bodied palate likewise; the tannins need to soften, but the wine is in balance, so will do so. Deserves a better quality cork (or a screwcap). 14% alc. **Rating** 94 **To** 2016 $45

♀♀♀♀♀ **Heathfield Ridge Shiraz 2005** **Rating** 90 **To** 2016 $22.50
Heathfield Ridge Cabernet Sauvignon 2006 **Rating** 90 **To** 2016 $22.50

Tiger Ranch Wines ★★★★

116 Allisons Road, Lower Barrington, Tas 7306 (postal) **Region** Northern Tasmania
T (03) 6492 3339 **F** (03) 6492 3356 **www**.tigerranch.com.au **Open** Not
Winemaker Neil Colbeck **Est.** 2000 **Cases** 300 **Vyds** 2 ha
Neil Colbeck developed a fascination with fine wine during his time as sommelier at Hayman Island between 1987 and '90. At that time the Island was at its zenith, with a cellar of over 38 000 bottles worth $750 000. All good things have to come to an end, and when he returned to Tasmania in '90, he planted his first vineyard. In 2000 Tiger Ranch was relocated to Lower Barrington and a new vineyard is being progressively planted. In the meantime grapes are coming from Lake Barrington Vineyard and a second vineyard at Eugenana. Ultimately production will focus on pinot noir (two-thirds), chardonnay (one-third) and a small amount of gewurztraminer.

♀♀♀♀♀ **Chardonnay 2007** Has flourished since January '08. The palate has tightened up rather than broadened out, with fine peach and nectarine fruit; a long and supple finish. Screwcap. 13% alc. **Rating** 93 **To** 2017 $22
Chardonnay 2008 Light green-straw; a very powerful wine, in an Indian arm wrestle between fruit and oak; piercing palate acidity adds its piece. Screwcap. 13% alc. **Rating** 92 **To** 2016 $22

Tilbrook Estate   ★★★★☆

17/1 Adelaide Lobethal Road, Lobethal, SA 5241 **Region** Adelaide Hills
T (08) 8389 5318 **F** (08) 8389 5315 **www.**marketsatheart.com/tilbrookestate
Open Fri–Sun 11–5 & public hols, or by appt
Winemaker James Tilbrook **Est.** 2001 **Cases** 2000 **Vyds** 5.2 ha

James and Annabelle Tilbrook have 4.4 ha of multi-clone chardonnay and pinot noir, and 0.8 ha of sauvignon blanc at Lenswood. The winery and cellar door are in the old Onkaparinga Woollen Mills building in Lobethal; this not only provides an atmospheric home, but also helps meet the very strict environmental requirements of the Adelaide Hills in dealing with winery waste water. English-born James came to Australia in 1986, aged 22, but a car accident led to his return to England. Working for Oddbins and passing the WSET diploma set his future course. He returned to Australia, met wife Annabelle, purchased the vineyard and began planting the vineyard in 1999. Plantings are continuing for the Tilbrook label, and for the moment the major part of the plantings (chardonnay and pinot noir) is sold to d'Arenberg.

♀♀♀♀♀ **Adelaide Hills Sauvignon Blanc 2009** Has considerable richness and depth to the gooseberry, passionfruit and stone fruit of both bouquet and palate, so much so it loses energy on the slightly congested finish. A gentler hand needed at some point. Screwcap. 13% alc. **Rating** 91 **To** 2011 $22
Adelaide Hills Pinot Gris 2008 Quite deep colour, but fresh and lively bouquet, not unlike the wines of Alsace; there is some work evident on the wine here, with plenty of texture, spice and just a hint of bitterness on the finish, providing contrast in the wine. Screwcap. 13.5% alc. **Rating** 90 **To** 2012 $22 BE

Tim Adams   ★★★★

Warenda Road, Clare, SA 5453 **Region** Clare Valley
T (08) 8842 2429 **F** (08) 8842 3550 **www.**timadamswines.com.au **Open** Mon–Fri
10.30–5, w'ends 11–5
Winemaker Tim Adams **Est.** 1986 **Cases** 50 000 **Vyds** 145 ha

After almost 20 years slowly and carefully building the business, based on the classic Clare Valley varieties of riesling, semillon, grenache, shiraz and cabernet sauvignon, Tim and Pam Goldsack decided to increase their production from 35 000 to 50 000 cases. Like their move to a total reliance on screwcaps, there is nothing unexpected in that. However, the makeup of the new plantings is anything but usual: they will give Tim Adams more than 10 ha of tempranillo and pinot gris, and about 3.5 ha of viognier, in each case with a very clear idea about the style of wine to be produced. In 2009 the business took a giant step forward with the acquisition of the 75-ha Leasingham vineyards from Constellation for a reported price of $850 000. Exports to all major markets.

♀♀♀♀♀ **Clare Valley Riesling 2009** Sophisticated winemaking (starting with early
✪   harvesting) has resulted in a superbly pure and focused wine, with the structure to blossom with age, built on a foundation of minerally acidity. Screwcap. 11% alc. **Rating** 95 **To** 2020 $22
Reserve Clare Valley Riesling 2008 A riesling at the very start of what will undoubtedly be a very long life; the lemon and lime fruit and minerally acidity in lockstep balance. Leave for at least five years, and then have patience. Screwcap. 10% alc. **Rating** 95 **To** 2030 $40
✪   **Clare Valley Semillon 2008** The works: 12 hours' skin contact, 100% new French oak, barrel fermentation and five months' maturation. The knot that ties the wine together is good acidity; given the cost of its making, remarkable value. Screwcap. 13% alc. **Rating** 94 **To** 2023 $23

♀♀♀♀♀ **Clare Valley Pinot Gris 2009 Rating** 91 **To** 2011 $23
Clare Valley Cabernet 2005 Rating 91 **To** 2020 $28.50

Tim Gramp ★★★★

Mintaro/Leasingham Road, Watervale, SA 5452 **Region** Clare Valley
T (08) 8344 4079 **F** (08) 8342 1379 **www**.timgrampwines.com.au **Open** W'ends &
hols 11–4
Winemaker Tim Gramp **Est.** 1990 **Cases** 6000 **Vyds** 16 ha
Tim Gramp has quietly built up a very successful business and by keeping overheads to a
minimum provides good wines at modest prices. Over the years the estate vineyards (shiraz,
riesling, cabernet sauvignon and grenache) have been expanded significantly. Exports to the
UK, Taiwan, Malaysia and NZ.

ꟼꟼꟼꟼꟼ **Mt Lofty Ranges Shiraz 2005** Attractive wine starting to show some secondary
✪ characters, with a mix of spicy, chocolatey savoury flavours and fine tannins.
Screwcap. 14.5% alc. **Rating** 91 **To** 2015 $21.50
Watervale Riesling 2009 Green-quartz; a powerful riesling, with citrus and
apple aromas and flavours to a rock-solid palate; good short-term development.
Screwcap. 12% alc. **Rating** 90 **To** 2014 $19.90

ꟼꟼꟼꟼ **McLaren Vale Grenache 2008 Rating** 89 **To** 2015 $18.20

Tim McNeil Wines ★★★

PO Box 1088, Clare, SA 5453 **Region** Clare Valley
T (08) 8843 4348 **F** (08) 8843 4272 **www**.timmcneilwines.com.au **Open** Not
Winemaker Tim McNeil **Est.** 2004 **Cases** 500 **Vyds** 3 ha
When Tim and Cass McNeil established Tim McNeil Wines, Tim had long since given up
his teaching career, graduating with a degree in oenology from Adelaide University in 1999.
During his university years he worked at Yalumba, then moved with Cass to the Clare Valley
in 2001, spending four years as a winemaker at Jim Barry Wines before moving to Kilikanoon
in '05, where he currently works as a winemaker alongside Kevin Mitchell. The McNeils'
16-ha property at Watervale includes mature, dry-grown riesling, and they intend to plant
shiraz, currently purchasing that variety from the Barossa Valley. A cellar door facility is under
construction, scheduled to open in mid-2010.

ꟼꟼꟼꟼ **Clare Valley Riesling 2009** Fresh squeezed lime and bath talc bouquet; zesty,
clean focused and finishing with a lively acid kick. Screwcap. 12.5% alc. **Rating** 88
To 2016 $20 BE

Tim Smith Wines ★★★★

PO Box 446, Tanunda, SA 5352 **Region** Barossa Valley
T (08) 8563 0939 **F** (08) 8563 0939 **Open** Not
Winemaker Tim Smith **Est.** 2001 **Cases** 1000
Tim Smith aspires (and succeeds) to make wines in the mould of the great producers of
Côte Rôtie and Chateauneuf du Pape, but using a New World approach. It is a business in its
early stages, with only four wines: a Shiraz, Botrytis Semillon, Viognier and Grenache/Shiraz/
Mourvedre. Exports to the UK and the US.

ꟼꟼꟼꟼꟼ **Barossa Mataro Grenache Shiraz 2008** Strong colour; a luscious array of
✪ dusky black fruits that glide across the tongue, leading to a fresh finish; very good,
though atypical. Screwcap. 14.5% alc. **Rating** 93 **To** 2017 $28

Tinderbox Vineyard ★★★★☆

Tinderbox, Tas 7054 **Region** Southern Tasmania
T (03) 6229 2994 **Open** By appt
Winemaker Contract **Est.** 1994 **Cases** 220 **Vyds** 2 ha
Liz McGown may have retired from specialist nursing (some years ago), but is busier than
ever, having taken on the running of the 400-ha Tinderbox fat lamb and fine merino wool
property after a lease (which had run for 22 years) terminated. Liz describes Tinderbox as a
vineyard between the sun and the sea, and looking out over the vineyard towards Bruny Island

in the distance, it is not hard to see why. The attractive label was designed by Barry Tucker, who was so charmed by Liz's request that he waived his usual (substantial) fee.

♥♥♥♥♡ Pinot Noir 2008 Clear red-purple; a complex bouquet of dark plum and cherry fruit; the substantial palate is deeply fruited, with tannins to sustain it for some years to come. Screwcap. 13.7% alc. **Rating** 92 **To** 2015 $35

Tinklers Vineyard   ★★★★

Pokolbin Mountains Road, Pokolbin, NSW 2320 **Region** Hunter Valley
T (02) 4998 7435 **F** (02) 4998 7469 **www**.tinklers.com.au **Open** 7 days 10–5
Winemaker Usher John Tinkler **Est.** 1997 **Cases** 1500 **Vyds** 41 ha
Three generations of the Tinkler family have been involved with the property since 1942. Originally a beef and dairy farm, vines have been both pulled out and replanted at various stages, and part of the adjoining 80-year-old Ben Ean Vineyard acquired. Plantings include semillon (14 ha), shiraz (11.5 ha), chardonnay (6.5 ha) and smaller plantings of merlot, muscat and viognier. In 2008 a new winery, adjoining the cellar door, was completed; all Tinklers wines are now vinified here, distinguished by a gold strip at the bottom of the label. The majority of the grape production continues to be sold to McWilliam's.

♥♥♥♥♡ U & I Reserve Shiraz 2007 The bouquet has abundant plum and blackberry fruit, replicated in the flavours of the almost glossy, very smooth and supple palate. A fruit-driven wine from start to finish. Screwcap. 14.5% alc. **Rating** 93 **To** 2020 $32

Tintara   ★★★★★

202 Main Road, McLaren Vale, SA 5171 **Region** McLaren Vale
T (08) 8329 4124 **F** (08) 8329 4155 **www**.tintara.com.au **Open** 7 days 10–4.30
Winemaker Paul Carpenter **Est.** 1863 **Cases** NFP
Tintara was the third of the three substantial winery and vineyard enterprises in the early days of McLaren Vale. It was established by Dr Alexander Kelly, who purchased 280 ha of land in 1861 and planted the first vines in 1863. It grew rapidly – indeed, too rapidly, because it ran into financial difficulties and was acquired by Thomas Hardy in 1876. He in turn recovered his purchase price by wine sales over the following year. It has been a proud label for almost 150 years, but gained additional vigour with the 2008 release of the Single Vineyard wines, which in the years prior to their release collected a swag of trophies and accolades.

♥♥♥♥♥ Single Vineyard Clarendon Shiraz 2005 An aromatic bouquet, with spicy black berry fruit framed by opulent oak; a very powerful full-bodied palate, yet manages to retain a certain cool, spicy elegance reflecting the cooler climate and 60-year-old vines. Cork. 14% alc. **Rating** 95 **To** 2025 $80 BE
Single Vineyard Upper Tintara Shiraz 2005 Still exceptionally youthful, the bouquet rich, the full-bodied palate super-intense, with powerful but balanced tannins running through to the long finish. Gold medal Sydney Wine Show '10. Cork. 14% alc. **Rating** 94 **To** 2025 $80

♥♥♥♥♡ McLaren Vale Shiraz 2007 Rating 92 To 2022 $27

♥♥♥♥ McLaren Vale Cabernet Sauvignon 2007 Rating 89 To 2020 $27 BE

Tintilla Wines   ★★★★★

725 Hermitage Road, Pokolbin, NSW 2320 **Region** Hunter Valley
T (02) 6574 7093 **F** (02) 9767 6894 **www**.tintilla.com.au **Open** 7 days 10.30–6
Winemaker James and Robert Lusby **Est.** 1993 **Cases** 4000 **Vyds** 7 ha
The Lusby family has established shiraz (2.2 ha), sauvignon blanc (1.6 ha), merlot, semillon (1.5 ha each), sangiovese (1.6 ha) and cabernet sauvignon (0.2 ha) on a northeast-facing slope with red clay and limestone soil. Tintilla was the first winery to plant sangiovese in the Hunter Valley (1995). The family has also planted an olive grove producing four different types of olives, which are cured and sold from the estate.

🍷🍷🍷🍷🍷 **Patriarch Hunter Valley Syrah 2007** Clear crimson-purple; a fragrant bouquet leads into a supremely elegant and supple palate with an array of red and black fruits, the oak well-balanced and integrated; while eminently drinkable now, this has a multi-decade future. Screwcap. 13.6% alc. **Rating** 96 **To** 2040 $60

Angus Hunter Semillon 2009 Bright straw-green; a faint background of spice, or even pepper, comes through on the bouquet; the same spicy echo runs through the long palate, here with a contrasting note verging on white flesh peach. Thoroughly interesting wine. Screwcap. 10.5% alc. **Rating** 94 **To** 2017 $26

✪ **Reserve Hunter Semillon 2004** Light, bright green-straw; a very good wine in its youth, and even better now; still vibrantly fresh, but with the first hints of honey and toast starting to appear. Screwcap. 10.2% alc. **Rating** 94 **To** 2020 $30

Pebbles Brief Hunter Valley Chardonnay 2009 Light, bright colour; a very fine and tightly structured chardonnay, the impact of barrel fermentation barely touching the melon and citrus fruit; bright acidity contributes more to the structure and texture than oak. Screwcap. 14% alc. **Rating** 94 **To** 2017 $26

🍷🍷🍷🍷🍷 **Saphira Hunter Valley Sangiovese 2007** **Rating** 90 **To** 2015 $26

Tobin Wines ★★★★

34 Ricca Road, Ballandean, Qld 4382 **Region** Granite Belt
T (07) 4684 1235 **F** (07) 4684 1235 **www**.tobinwines.com.au **Open** 7 days 10–5
Winemaker Adrian Tobin, David Gianini **Est.** 1964 **Cases** 1350 **Vyds** 5.3 ha

In the early 1960s the Ricca family planted table grapes, followed by shiraz and semillon in 1964–66, which are said to be the oldest vinifera vines in the Granite Belt region. The Tobin family (headed by Adrian and Frances) purchased the vineyard in 2000 and has increased plantings, which now consist of shiraz, cabernet sauvignon, merlot, tempranillo, semillon, verdelho, chardonnay, muscat sauvignon blanc, with some remaining rows of table grapes. The emphasis has changed towards quality bottled wines, with some success.

🍷🍷🍷🍷🍷 **Max Granite Belt Shiraz 2008** Good crimson-purple; a complex bouquet and palate featuring spice, pepper, licorice and black cherry fruit that is not overripe; nice savoury twist on the finish. Scarred and stained ProCork. 14.7% alc. **Rating** 92 **To** 2018 $35

Elliott Granite Belt Merlot 2008 Good colour, bright red-purple; while only light- to medium-bodied, this fragrant red-fruited merlot has a supple and very well balanced palate, again focusing on red fruits, finishing particularly well. Numbered bottle (neck tag) 144 of 1900. ProCork. 13.5% alc. **Rating** 92 **To** 2016 $35

Luella Plum Granite Belt Cabernet Sauvignon 2008 Yet another impressive release, the colour excellent, the bouquet aromas and palate flavours right in the heartland of red and blackcurrant fruit; slightly better oak choice could have produced a spectacular wine. ProCork. 14% alc. **Rating** 92 **To** 2016 $35

Lily Granite Belt Chardonnay 2009 Bright straw-green; lively and fresh grapefruit and nectarine aromas and flavours do the talking, the touch of French oak barely apparent. The numbered neck ties are a unique marketing tool; this bottle 423 of 1700. Screwcap. 13% alc. **Rating** 90 **To** 2014 $28

🍷🍷🍷🍷 **Kate Granite Belt Sauvignon Blanc 2009** **Rating** 89 **To** 2010 $28

Tokar Estate ★★★☆

6 Maddens Lane, Coldstream, Vic 3770 **Region** Yarra Valley
T (03) 5964 9585 **F** (03) 5964 9587 **www**.tokarestate.com.au **Open** 7 days 10.30–5
Winemaker Paul Evans **Est.** 1996 **Cases** 5000 **Vyds** 14 ha

Leon Tokar established 14 ha of now mature chardonnay, pinot noir, shiraz, cabernet sauvignon and tempranillo at Tokar Estate, one of many vineyards on Maddens Lane. All the wines are from the estate, badged Single Vineyard (which they are), and have performed well in regional shows, with early success for the Tempranillo.

ŦŦŦŦŦ **Cabernet Sauvignon 2006** Spent almost three years in barrel and tank, bottled in Feb '09, the cedar/mocha notes that are part of the makeup of this wine doubtless stem from that; all up, a very pleasant medium-bodied cabernet that doesn't need cellaring to produce its best. Screwcap. 14% alc. **Rating** 90 To 2014 $30

ŦŦŦŦ **Yarra Valley Tempra Rosa 2009 Rating** 89 To 2012 $19
Le'ori Yarra Valley Unwooded Chardonnay 2009 Rating 87 To 2011 $22
Shiraz 2007 Rating 87 To 2013 $28

Tollana ★★★★★

GPO Box 753, Melbourne, Vic 3001 **Region** South Australia
T 1300 651 650 **Open** Not
Winemaker Angus Ridley, Joanna Marsh **Est.** 1888 **Cases** 10 000
Tollana survived a near-death experience during the turbulent days of the Rosemount management of Southcorp; where it will ultimately fit in the Foster's scheme of things remains to be seen, but in the meantime, Tollana is back in business.

ŦŦŦŦŦ **Brian and Julie Hurse Vineyard Bin TR568 Bendigo Shiraz 2008** An unusually elegant and vibrant Bendigo shiraz; with the aid of a magnifying glass you learn a touch of riesling was co-fermented, part of the wine finished its ferment in French oak, wild yeast was in play, and it spent 19 months in 50% new French oak; the wine has excellent length, line and balance. (Made by Joanna Marsh.) Screwcap. 14% alc. **Rating** 96 To 2020 $40

ŦŦŦŦŦ **Robinson Family Bin TR474 Pinot Noir 2009 Rating** 93 To 2016 $20

Tomboy Hill ★★★★★

204 Sim Street, Ballarat, Vic 3350 (postal) **Region** Ballarat
T (03) 5331 3785 **Open** Not
Winemaker Scott Ireland (Contract) **Est.** 1984 **Cases** 1300 **Vyds** 3.6 ha
Former schoolteacher Ian Watson seems to be following the same path as Lindsay McCall of Paringa Estate (also a former schoolteacher) in extracting greater quality and style than any other winemaker in his region, in this case Ballarat. Since 1984 Watson has slowly and patiently built up a patchwork quilt of small plantings of chardonnay and pinot noir. In the better years, the single-vineyard wines of Chardonnay and/or Pinot Noir are released; Rebellion Chardonnay and Pinot Noir are multi-vineyard blends, but all 100% Ballarat. I have a particular fondness for the style, not necessarily shared by others.

ŦŦŦŦŦ **Garibaldi Farm Ballarat Goldfields Chardonnay 2008** Pale colour, bright; tight lemon fruit bouquet, with grilled nuts on show; the palate is restrained on entry with lemons again coming to the fore, but it quickly deepens and fleshes out with rich nutty flavours, focused acidity providing line to the finish. Screwcap. 12.7% alc. **Rating** 94 To 2016 $35 BE
Ava's Picking Ballarat Goldfields Pinot Noir 2008 Vibrant colour; charry oak dominates the bouquet, with dark fruits, bay leaf and thyme playing a supporting role; the palate is quite rich and attractively textured, with plenty of stuffing and power, while retaining varietal integrity; a strong wine with vibrant acidity providing length to the depth of fruit. Previously labelled 'The Tomboy'. Screwcap. 13.3% alc. **Rating** 94 To 2016 $75 BE

ŦŦŦŦŦ **Smythes Creek Ballarat Goldfields Pinot Noir 2008 Rating** 92 To 2015 $50 BE

ŦŦŦŦ **Ava's Picking Ballarat Goldfields Chardonnay 2008 Rating** 89 To 2014 $45 BE
Rebellion Ballarat Goldfields Pinot Noir 2008 Rating 89 To 2014 $35 BE
Rebellion Ballarat Goldfields Chardonnay 2008 Rating 88 To 2013 $25 BE

Tomich Wines ★★★★

87 King William Road, Unley, SA 5061 **Region** Adelaide Hills
T (08) 8272 9388 **F** (08) 8373 7229 **www**.tomich.com **Open** Mon–Fri 10–4
Winemaker John Tomich, Peter Leske (Contract) **Est.** 2002 **Cases** 10 000 **Vyds** 80 ha
There is an element of irony in this family venture. Patriarch John Tomich was born on
a vineyard near Mildura, where he learnt first-hand the skills and knowledge required for
premium grapegrowing. He went on to become a well-known Adelaide ear, nose and throat
specialist. Taking the wheel full circle, he completed postgraduate studies in winemaking at
the University of Adelaide in 2002, and is now venturing on to the Master of Wine revision
course from the Institute of Masters of Wine. His son Randal is a cutting from the old vine
(metaphorically speaking), having invented new equipment and techniques for tending the
family's 80-ha vineyard in the Adelaide Hills near Woodside, resulting in a 60% saving in time
and fuel costs. Most of the grapes are sold, but the amount of wine made under the Tomich
Hill brand is far from a hobby. Exports to China and Hong Kong.

ΨΨΨΨΨ **Adelaide Hills Sauvignon Blanc 2009** Light straw-green; a fragrant but
✪   delicate wine, with hints of nettle at one end, tropical/guava at the other; has good
       length, but isn't quite intense enough for top points, just value. Screwcap. 13% alc.
       Rating 93 **To** 2011 $20
       Reserve Adelaide Hills Chardonnay 2008 Brilliant green-quartz; poles apart
       from the unwooded, toasty/nutty barrel ferment oak characters to open up with,
       then deep white flesh stone fruit and rock melon to support and balance that oak;
       half a degree less of alcohol would have made a giant killer. Screwcap. 14.5% alc.
       Rating 93 **To** 2016 $45
✪   **Adelaide Hills Unwooded Chardonnay 2009** Has an unusually fragrant,
       almost flowery, bouquet and a high-flavoured palate to match, with nectarine and
       white peach in abundance. Screwcap. 14% alc. **Rating** 92 **To** 2016 $16
       Reserve Adelaide Hills Vin Gris 2009 Pale salmon-pink; barrel-fermented
       pinot noir with a spicy rose petal bouquet, and a long, well-balanced palate; dry
       finish. Ambitious price, but it's a good wine. Screwcap. 14.5% alc. **Rating** 92
       To 2012 $35
       Adelaide Hills Pinot Noir 2008 Good colour; a powerful pinot, with red and
       black cherry aromas and a palate crammed full of pinot fruit; a little short on
       finesse, but the balance and length suggest it will smooth out the wrinkles in a
       year or two. Screwcap. 14.5% alc. **Rating** 91 **To** 2015 $30
       Adelaide Hills Riesling 2009 Light straw-green; a floral bouquet of lime and
       apple blossom runs into a well-balanced, relatively soft but quite juicy palate.
       Screwcap. 13% alc. **Rating** 90 **To** 2016 $20
       Adelaide Hills Pinot Gris 2009 Where the grigio wanders, this wine focuses,
       its pear and red apple fruit typical of the variety, along with a touch of spice.
       Screwcap. 13.5% alc. **Rating** 90 **To** 2011 $30
       Adelaide Hills Syrah 2008 Bright colour; a fresh and vibrant bouquet and
       palate, with red cherry, spice and raspberry fruit untroubled by tannins (fine)
       and oak (subtle). An open invitation to drink generously. Screwcap. 14.5% alc.
       Rating 90 **To** 2016 $30

ΨΨΨΨ **Reserve Adelaide Hills Pinot Chardonnay NV Rating** 89 **To** 2013 $25
       Reserve Adelaide Hills Gewurzt 2009 Rating 88 **To** 2013 $45

Toms Waterhole Wines ★★★☆

'Felton', Longs Corner Road, Canowindra, NSW 2804 **Region** Cowra
T (02) 6344 1819 **F** (02) 6344 2172 **www**.tomswaterhole.com.au **Open** 7 days 10–4
Winemaker Graham Kerr **Est.** 1997 **Cases** 1200
Graham and Jan Kerr began the development of Tom's Waterhole Wines in 1997, progressively
establishing 6 ha of shiraz, cabernet sauvignon, semillon and merlot, completing the planting
program in 2001. They have decided to bypass the use of irrigation, so the yields will always
be low, and the vineyards are certified organic. The Kerrs also run balloon joy flights from
the winery base.

ŢŢŢŢ Semillon 2008 Classic young semillon in colour, aroma and flavour, picked at
✪   the right moment and very well made; grass, lemon and mineral notes are folded
    together by the crisp acidity that will underwrite the long future of this wine.
    Screwcap. 10.5% alc. **Rating** 91 **To** 2020 $13

ŢŢŢŢ The Waterhole Blend Semillon Chardonnay NV No frills whatsoever, but
✪   this is a remarkably good wine at the price and its non-vintage antecedents; fresh
    and lively, with grass, citrus and mineral flavours. Screwcap. 11.5% alc. **Rating** 87
    To 2011 $12

✪   Grenache Rose NV Pale blush pink; fragrant and juicy small red fruits; the palate
    is very well balanced, the light touch of sweetness balanced by acidity. Screwcap.
    11.5% alc. **Rating** 87 **To** 2010 $13
    Cabernet Sauvignon 2008 **Rating** 87 **To** 2013 $17

Toolangi Vineyards ★★★★★
PO Box 9431, South Yarra, Vic 3141 **Region** Yarra Valley
T (03) 9827 9977 **F** (03) 9827 6626 **www**.toolangi.com **Open** Not
Winemaker Various contract **Est.** 1995 **Cases** 10 000 **Vyds** 13 ha
Garry and Julie Hounsell acquired their property in the Dixons Creek subregion of the
Yarra Valley, adjoining the Toolangi State Forest, in 1995. The primary accent is on pinot
noir and chardonnay, accounting for all but 2.8 ha, which is predominantly shiraz and a little
viognier. Winemaking is by Yering Station, Giaconda and Shadowfax, as impressive a trio of
winemakers as one could wish for.

ŢŢŢŢŢ Reserve Yarra Valley Shiraz 2008 Classic cool-climate shiraz, with a complex
    spider's web of black cherry, spice and pepper aromas and flavours; the tannins
    on the mid-palate are perfect, master-minding the long finish. Screwcap. 14% alc.
    Rating 96 **To** 2028 $60
    Estate Yarra Valley Pinot Noir 2006 Red-purple, showing little sign of
    development; a rich and powerful bouquet of dark berry fruit is replayed on the
    palate; will be very long lived. Screwcap. 14% alc. **Rating** 95 **To** 2016 $38
✪   Yarra Valley Chardonnay 2008 Part estate-grown, part from Yarra Glen
    contract-grown fruit, part made at Shadowfax, part at Yering Station (where the
    wine was blended and bottled). Complex, certainly, but more focused than one
    might expect, with white peach, nectarine and grilled nut flavours through to a
    long finish. Screwcap. 13% alc. **Rating** 94 **To** 2016 $25

ŢŢŢŢŢ Yarra Valley Pinot Noir 2008 **Rating** 93 **To** 2014 $25

Toorak Winery ★★★
Vineyard 279 Toorak Road, Leeton, NSW 2705 **Region** Riverina
T (02) 6953 2333 **F** (02) 6953 4454 **www**.toorakwines.com.au **Open** Mon–Fri 10–5,
Sat by appt
Winemaker Robert Bruno **Est.** 1965 **Cases** 300 000 **Vyds** 150 ha
A traditional, long-established Riverina producer with a strong Italian-based clientele around
Australia. Production has been increasing significantly, utilising substantial estate plantings and
grapes purchased from other growers, both in the Riverina and elsewhere. Wines are released
under the Toorak Estate, Willandra Estate and Amesbury Estate labels. While, in absolute terms,
the quality is not great, the low-priced wines in fact over-deliver in many instances. Exports
to the US, India, Singapore and China.

ŢŢŢŢ Willandra Estate Premium Tumbarumba Chardonnay 2005 Quite fresh
    for the age, and showing a little of the high-altitude sweet/sour fruit; quite nutty
    and evolved on the palate, the flavour is quite long, and not devoid of interest.
    Screwcap. 13.5% alc. **Rating** 87 **To** 2013 $18 BE
    Willandra Estate Leeton Selection Shiraz 2008 Vibrant and primary, with
    blackberries and redcurrants combining with ease; medium-bodied, easy-drinking
    style, best consumed in the full flush of youth. Screwcap. 14.5% alc. **Rating** 87
    To 2013 $14 BE

Topper's Mountain Vineyard   ★★★★

5 km Guyra Road, Tingha, NSW 2369 **Region** New England
T (02) 6723 3506 **F** (02) 6723 3222 **www.**toppers.com.au **Open** By appt
Winemaker Symphony Hill (Mike Hayes) **Est.** 2000 **Cases** 1000 **Vyds** 9.8 ha
Following a partnership dissolution, Topper's is now solely owned by Mark Kirkby. Planting began in the spring of 2000, with the ultimate fruit salad trial of 15 rows each of innumerable varieties and clones. The total area planted was made up of 28 separate plantings, many of these with only 200 vines in a block. As varieties proved unsuited, they were grafted to those that hold the most promise. Thus far, Gewurztraminer and Sauvignon Blanc hold most promise among the white wines, the Mediterranean reds doing better than their French cousins.

ΨΨΨΨΨ **New England Nebbiolo 2008** Good hue and depth, bright red; an aromatic
✪   bouquet is followed by a delicious and unusually approachable palate, with red
         berry fruits and fine, unexpectedly soft tannins. Screwcap. 12.5% alc. **Rating** 94
         To 2015 $30

ΨΨΨΨ **New England Gewurztraminer 2009** Rating 88 To 2011 $20

Torbreck Vintners   ★★★★★

Roennfeldt Road, Marananga, SA 5352 **Region** Barossa Valley
T (08) 8562 4155 **F** (08) 8562 4195 **www.**torbreck.com **Open** 7 days 10–6
Winemaker David Powell **Est.** 1994 **Cases** 50 000 **Vyds** 70.95 ha
Of all the Barossa Valley wineries to grab the headlines in the US, with demand pulling prices up to undreamt levels, Torbreck stands supreme. David Powell has not let success go to his head, or subvert the individuality and sheer quality of his wines, all created around very old, dry-grown, bush-pruned vineyards. The top trio are led by The RunRig (Shiraz/Viognier); then The Factor (Shiraz) and The Descendant (Shiraz/Viognier); next The Struie (Shiraz) and The Steading (Grenache/Mataro/Shiraz). Notwithstanding the depth and richness of the wines, they have a remarkable degree of finesse. In 2008 the ownership was restructured, Californian vintner Peter Kight (of Quivira Vineyards) acquired the shares held by the investors, who had been introduced earlier in the decade. The best wines were not submitted for this edition; the winery rating has been retained. Exports to all major markets.

ΨΨΨΨΨ **Barossa Valley Saignee 2009** Light pink with a faint touch of salmon; juice
         drawn from freshly crushed mourvedre, barrel-fermented and aged for six months
         in used French barriques. Serious rose? Yes, it is, with good texture and complex
         spicy aromas and flavours before a long, dry finish. Screwcap. 14% alc. **Rating** 94
         To 2012 $23.50

ΨΨΨΨℐ **The Gask 2007** Rating 93 To 2017 $75
         Barossa Valley Roussanne Marsanne Viognier 2009 Rating 92
         To 2016 $37.50
✪   **Woodcutter's Barossa Valley Shiraz 2008** Deep colour; a succulent, ripe and
         rich wine awash with black fruits and dark chocolate flavours; oak is incidental, as
         are tannins. Screwcap. 14.5% alc. **Rating** 90 To 2015 $19.50

Torzi Matthews Vintners   ★★★★☆

Cnr Eden Valley Road/Sugarloaf Hill Road, Mount McKenzie, SA 5353 **Region** Eden Valley
T (08) 8565 3393 **F** (08) 8565 3393 **www.**torzimatthews.com.au **Open** By appt
Winemaker Domenic Torzi **Est.** 1996 **Cases** 2500 **Vyds** 13 ha
Domenic Torzi and Tracy Matthews, former Adelaide Plains residents, searched for a number of years before finding a block at Mt McKenzie in the Eden Valley. The block they chose is in a hollow and the soil is meagre, and they were in no way deterred by the knowledge that it would be frost-prone. The result is predictably low yields, concentrated further by drying the grapes on racks and reducing the weight by around 30% (the Appassimento method is used in Italy to produce Amarone-style wines). Four wines are made: Riesling and Shiraz under both the Frost Dodger and Schist Rock labels, the Shiraz wild yeast-fermented and neither fined

nor filtered. Newer plantings of sangiovese and negroamaro, and an extension of the original plantings of shiraz and riesling, is likely to see the wine range increase in the future. Exports to the UK, the US, Denmark and Singapore.

ŶŶŶŶŶ **Frost Dodger Eden Valley Shiraz 2008** Solid red-purple; has the Torzi Frost
✪ Dodger DNA written large on the bouquet and palate, with its interwoven black fruits, spice, leather and licorice characters rising to a crescendo on the finish. Diam. 14.5% alc. **Rating** 94 **To** 2018 $30

ŶŶŶŶŶ **Schist Rock Eden Valley Shiraz 2008** Good colour; has that edge of
✪ refinement and elegance typical of good Eden Valley shiraz, the spicy edge to the black fruits no less typical; a medium-bodied wine driven by terroir. Diam. 14% alc. **Rating** 92 **To** 2017 $17
Frost Dodger Eden Valley Shiraz 2007 Rating 90 **To** 2015 $30
✪ **Vigna Cantina Barossa Valley Sangiovese 2008** Very interesting wine; has far more colour, weight and depth than most sangioveses, but is not particularly varietal; plum rather than cherry, sour or otherwise, flavours rule the roost. Difficult to point. Diam. 14% alc. **Rating** 90 **To** 2016 $18

Totino Estate   ★★★★

982 Port Road, Albert Park, SA 5014 (postal) **Region** Adelaide Hills
T (08) 8268 8066 **F** (08) 8268 3597 www.totinowines.com.au **Open** Not
Winemaker Charles Wish **Est.** 1992 **Cases** 12 700 **Vyds** 29 ha
Don Totino migrated from Italy in 1968, and at the age of 18 became the youngest barber in Australia. He soon moved on, into general food and importing and distribution. Festival City, as the business is known, has been highly successful, recognised by a recent significant award from the Italian government. In 1998 he purchased a run-down vineyard at Paracombe in the Adelaide Hills, since extending the plantings to 29 ha of chardonnay, pinot grigio, sauvignon blanc, sangiovese and shiraz. Various family members, including daughter Linda, are involved in the business. Exports to Italy, Germany and China.

ŶŶŶŶŶ **Adelaide Hills Shiraz 2007** Has retained good hue; an elegant light- to
✪ medium-bodied shiraz with spice and pepper notes to its core of red and black cherry fruit; gold medal Adelaide Wine Show '09. Screwcap. 14% alc. **Rating** 93 **To** 2017 $17.95
✪ **Adelaide Hills Sangiovese Rose 2008** Light, bright pink; for once, the back label warns of a sweetness; paradoxically, that sweetness is less than many cellar door honey traps, nor is late picking obvious. Screwcap. 11.5% alc. **Rating** 90 **To** 2011 $13.95
✪ **Adelaide Hills Cabernet Sauvignon 2008** Light, bright red-purple; fresh cassis blackcurrant fruit aromas and flavours mix with cedary/spicy characters; has the freshness and integrity missing from most Barossa Valley cabernets in '08. Screwcap. 14.5% alc. **Rating** 90 **To** 2017 $17.95

ŶŶŶŶ **Adelaide Hills Sauvignon Blanc 2009 Rating** 87 **To** 2010 $14.95

Tower Estate   ★★★★★

Cnr Broke Road/Hall Road, Pokolbin, NSW 2320 **Region** Hunter Valley
T (02) 4998 7989 **F** (02) 4998 7919 www.towerestatewines.com.au **Open** 7 days 10–5
Winemaker Samantha Connew **Est.** 1999 **Cases** 10 000 **Vyds** 4.9 ha
Tower Estate was founded by the late Len Evans, with the award-winning 5-star Tower Lodge accommodation and convention centre a part of the development. It is anticipated there will be little day-to-day change in either part of the business since Len's passing. Tower Estate will continue to draw upon varieties and regions that have a particular synergy, the aim being to make the best possible wines in the top sector of the wine market. The appointment of Samantha (Sam) Connew as winemaker in December 2009, with a long career as chief winemaker at Wirra Wirra, adds icing to the cake. Exports to the UK, Hong Kong, Japan and Canada.

ŸŸŸŸŸ Museum Release Hunter Valley Semillon 2003 A victory for the cork in this bottle, for the wine is as fresh as a daisy, although it has unquestionably introduced a quasi-oak nuance to the wine; has great line and length, with grass and citrus flavours and a truly excellent finish. 12% alc. **Rating** 95 **To** 2018 $45

Clare Valley Riesling 2009 A complex bouquet and palate, with ripe fruit flavours supported by grainy acidity that provide both texture and length. Gold medal Sydney Wine Show '10. Screwcap. 13% alc. **Rating** 94 **To** 2019 $28

Adelaide Hills Sauvignon Blanc 2009 A fragrant herb and citrus bouquet leads into an elegantly structured, fine-boned palate that is crisp, fresh and zesty. Earlier picking has paid off handsomely. Screwcap. 13% alc. **Rating** 94 **To** 2011 $28

Adelaide Hills Pinot Gris 2009 Blush colour, then a wine that makes no apology, with vibrant pear and quince aromas and flavours; the finish has amazing energy and thrust, with citrussy acidity. Screwcap. 13.5% alc. **Rating** 94 **To** 2013 $28

ŸŸŸŸŸ Hunter Valley Semillon 2009 **Rating** 92 **To** 2019 $28
Tasmania Pinot Noir 2008 **Rating** 91 **To** 2014 $58

Train Trak   ★★★
957 Healesville-Yarra Glen Road, Yarra Glen, Vic 3775 **Region** Yarra Valley
T (03) 9730 1314 **F** (03) 9427 1510 **www**.traintrak.com.au **Open** Wed–Sun
Winemaker Contract **Est.** 1995 **Cases** 7000 **Vyds** 16 ha
The unusual name comes from the Yarra Glen to Healesville railway, which was built in 1889 and abandoned in 1980 – part of it passes by the Train Trak vineyard. The vineyard is planted (in descending order) to pinot noir, cabernet sauvignon, chardonnay and shiraz. The restaurant makes exceptional pizzas in a wood-fired oven. Train Trak has had a hard time of it in recent years, the 2007 crop destroyed by frost, the '09 by fire and smoke taint. It was not surprising to find that it was listed for sale in May 2010. Exports to Canada, Pacific Islands, China and Japan.

Trappers Gully   ★★★★☆
130 Boyup Road, Mount Barker, WA 6324 **Region** Mount Barker
T (08) 9851 2565 **F** (08) 9851 2565 **www**.trappersgullywines.com **Open** W'ends 10–4
Winemaker Clea Candy, James Kellie (Consultant) **Est.** 1998 **Cases** 1000 **Vyds** 4 ha
The Lester family began the development of Trappers Gully in 1998, bringing varied backgrounds with them. Clea Candy has the most directly relevant CV, as a qualified viticulturist and practised winemaker, and, according to the official history, 'mother, daughter and wife, and pretty much the instigator of all heated discussions'. The families have progressively planted 1 ha each of chenin blanc, sauvignon blanc, cabernet sauvignon and shiraz. An onsite winery was built prior to the '04 vintage.

ŸŸŸŸŸ Mount Barker Cabernet Sauvignon 2004 Holding its purple hue
✪   exceptionally well; typical cool-grown cabernet characters, with briary savoury notes running alongside blackcurrant and mulberry fruit; good tannins. Screwcap. 13.8% alc. **Rating** 91 **To** 2014 $18

ŸŸŸŸ Mount Barker Chenin Blanc 2008 **Rating** 88 **To** 2013 $16
Mount Barker Sauvignon Blanc 2008 **Rating** 87 **To** 2011 $16

Treeton Estate   ★★★
163 North Treeton Road, Cowaramup, WA 6284 **Region** Margaret River
T (08) 9755 5481 **F** (08) 9755 5051 **www**.treetonestate.com.au **Open** 7 days 10–6
Winemaker David McGowan **Est.** 1982 **Cases** 3500 **Vyds** 7.5 ha
In 1982 David McGowan and wife Corinne purchased the 30-ha property upon which Treeton Estate is established, planting the vineyard two years later (shiraz, sauvignon blanc, chenin blanc, cabernet sauvignon and chardonnay). David has tried his hand at a lot of

different things in his life, and in the early years was working in Perth, which led to various setbacks for the vineyard. The wines are light and fresh, sometimes rather too much so. Exports to Southeast Asia and China.

ΨΨΨΨ **Margaret River Shiraz 2007** Good colour; offers a mix of spice, leaf and berry on the bouquet, savoury, spicy characters dominating on the medium-bodied palate; good tannin support. Twin top. 14.8% alc. **Rating** 89 **To** 2015 $20
Margaret River Sauvignon Blanc Semillon 2009 Pale straw-green; gentle passionfruit and grassy aromas lead into a light-bodied palate as much juicy as it is slightly sweet (sweetness mercifully disclosed on the back label). Screwcap. 13.9% alc. **Rating** 87 **To** 2010 $18
Margaret River Unwooded Chardonnay 2009 Pale colour; this is a real conundrum: a chardonnay with 14.3% alcohol tasting as if it has 12% or less, its light body and grassy edge to its stone fruit making it an appropriate unwooded style. Screwcap. 14.3% alc. **Rating** 87 **To** 2010 $18
Margaret River Chenin Blanc 2009 Sensible hands-off winemaking has allowed the ripe tropical fruits of the bouquet and palate to have free rein. Screwcap. 14.9% alc. **Rating** 87 **To** 2011 $18

Trentham Estate   ★★★★☆

Sturt Highway, Trentham Cliffs, NSW 2738 **Region** Murray Darling
T (03) 5024 8888 **F** (03) 5024 8800 **www.**trenthamestate.com.au **Open** 7 days 9.30–5
Winemaker Anthony Murphy, Shane Kerr **Est.** 1988 **Cases** 65 000 **Vyds** 48.57 ha
Remarkably consistent tasting notes across all wine styles from all vintages attest to the expertise of ex-Mildara winemaker Tony Murphy, a well-known and highly regarded producer, with estate vineyards on the Murray Darling. With an eye to the future, but also to broaden the range of the wines on offer, Trentham Estate is selectively buying grapes from other regions with a track record for the chosen varieties. The value for money is unfailingly excellent. Exports to the UK and other major markets.

ΨΨΨΨΨ **Yarra Valley Chardonnay 2008** Very well made, with markedly juicy stone fruit/tropical flavours given focus and structure by good acidity, which draws out the length; the oak is subtle. Screwcap. 13% alc. **Rating** 94 **To** 2014 $30

ΨΨΨΨ♀ **Mornington Peninsula Pinot Noir 2006 Rating** 92 **To** 2013 $30
✪   **Shiraz 2007** Healthy, bright purple-red; another winemaking tour de force from Tony Murphy; the wine has the sort of flavour and texture complexity one expects from cool-grown dryland vineyards, with spicy black cherry and plum aromas and flavours. Screwcap. 14% alc. **Rating** 91 **To** 2017 $14
✪   **Estate Chardonnay 2009** Light straw-green; how this intensity and type of flavour is acquired at this alcohol and in this region is beyond me; it has tight citrus and white peach flavours, French oak a salad dressing for the long, fresh palate. Screwcap. 13.5% alc. **Rating** 90 **To** 2013 $16
✪   **Viognier 2009** An impressive varietal example at this price, full of varietal character on both bouquet and palate; flavours of apricot, pear and a touch of ginger are fresh and crisp. Screwcap. 12.5% alc. **Rating** 90 **To** 2012 $16

ΨΨΨΨ **Pinot Noir 2009** As best I understand the back label, this comes from the Big
✪   Rivers Zone; that being so, it is an extraordinary achievement by Tony Murphy, for it has the texture, plum and forest flavours and length of cool-grown pinot – and no 'dry red' characters whatsoever. Screwcap. 13.5% alc. **Rating** 89 **To** 2013 $14
✪   **Estate Merlot 2007** Light red-purple; a controlled mix of plum and red berry fruit on the one hand, and lesser savoury/olive characters on the other; best is its light- to medium-bodied structure and texture, entirely appropriate for merlot. Screwcap. 13% alc. **Rating** 89 **To** 2013 $16
✪   **Noble Taminga 2006** Glowing gold; very sweet and soft, with apricot and honey flavours that don't stand a chance in comparison with good botrytis riesling. Screwcap. 11% alc. **Rating** 89 **To** 2014 $16
La Famiglia Vermentino 2009 Rating 88 **To** 2012 $16

○ **La Famiglia Sangiovese Rose 2009** Pale, bright puce; light floral cherry and spice aromas; the palate is clean and dry, not intense, but quite long. Screwcap. 11.5% alc. **Rating** 88 **To** 2011 $14

Trevelen Farm ★★★★
506 Weir Road, Cranbrook, WA 6321 **Region** Great Southern
T (08) 9826 1052 **F** (08) 9826 1209 **www.**trevelenfarm.com.au **Open** Fri–Mon 10.30–4.30, or by appt
Winemaker Harewood Estate (James Kellie, Luke Hipper) **Est.** 1993 **Cases** 3600 **Vyds** 6.5 ha
In 2008 John and Katie Sprigg decided to pass ownership of their 1300-ha wool, meat and grain-producing farm to son Ben and wife Louise. However, they have kept control of the 6.5 ha of sauvignon blanc, riesling, chardonnay, cabernet sauvignon and merlot planted in 1993. Henceforth, each wine will be made as a 100% varietal, and if demand requires, they will increase production by purchasing grapes from growers in the Frankland River region. Riesling will remain the centrepiece of the range. Exports to China, Macau, Japan, Malaysia and Hong Kong.

ΨΨΨΨΨ **Aged Release Riesling 2004** Glorious green-gold; an extremely rich and complex wine; it does show similar characters to the '09, with ripe lime and a touch of toast on the palate that in riesling terms can only be described as full-bodied. Screwcap. 12.5% alc. **Rating** 93 **To** 2014 $30
Frankland Reserve Shiraz 2007 Good hue, although not especially deep; an attractive spicy overtone to the red and black fruits of the bouquet tells of the cool climate medium-bodied palate that follows, the flavours similar and supported by fine, ripe tannins. Screwcap. 14.5% alc. **Rating** 91 **To** 2017 $25
Riesling 2009 Bright green-straw; the bouquet is full of personality, with lime and passionfruit aromas that flow through to the palate; here the story changes, for the finish becomes somewhat grippy. Screwcap. 12.5% alc. **Rating** 90 **To** 2016 $20
○ **Sauvignon Blanc 2009** In the full-flavoured Trevelen Farm style, full of rich sauvignon blanc fruit with elements of tropical fruit, stone fruit and ripe citrus; everything to be gained from drinking it sooner rather than later. Screwcap. 14% alc. **Rating** 90 **To** 2010 $16

ΨΨΨΨ **Chardonnay 2008** Rating 89 To 2013 $20
The Tunney Cabernet Sauvignon 2008 Rating 89 To 2020 $20

Trevor Jones/Kellermeister ★★★★★
Barossa Valley Highway, Lyndoch, SA 5351 **Region** Barossa Valley
T (08) 8524 4303 **F** (08) 8524 4880 **www.**kellermeister.com.au **Open** 7 days 9.30–5.30
Winemaker Trevor Jones, Paula Thomas **Est.** 1976 **Cases** 40 000 **Vyds** 2 ha
Trevor Jones is an industry veteran, with vast experience in handling fruit from the Barossa Valley, Eden Valley and the Adelaide Hills. His business operates on two levels: Kellermeister was founded in 1976 with the emphasis on low-cost traditional Barossa wine styles. In '96 he expanded the scope by introducing the ultra-premium Trevor Jones range, with a strong export focus. Exports to the US, Switzerland, Denmark, Macau, Singapore, Hong Kong and Japan.

ΨΨΨΨΨ **Trevor Jones Reserve Riesling 2008** Bright straw-green; a finely structured wine, still in its infancy, with a fragrant mix of lime and apple on the long, well-balanced palate. Its best years are still in front of it. Screwcap. 12.5% alc. **Rating** 94 **To** 2020 $25

ΨΨΨΨΨ **Kellermeister Black Sash Barossa Valley Shiraz 2008** Rating 93 To 2020 $30
Trevor Jones AA160 Shiraz Tawny NV Rating 93 To 2011 $40
Trevor Jones Mana Shiraz 2006 Rating 92 To 2026 $125 RWJ

Trevor Jones Methode Champenoise Sparkling Shiraz NV Rating 90
To 2014 $25

ϼϼϼϼ Trevor Jones Boots Eden Valley Riesling 2009 Rating 88 To 2014 $16
Kellermeister Adelaide Hills Barossa Valley Tempranillo 2008 Rating 88
To 2015 $19.50

Truffle Hill Wines ★★★★★

Seven Day Road, Manjimup, WA 6248 **Region** Pemberton
T (08) 9777 2474 **F** (08) 9387 7489 **www**.wineandtruffle.com.au **Open** 7 days 10–4.30
Winemaker Mark Aitken **Est.** 1997 **Cases** 8500 **Vyds** 11 ha
Owned by a group of investors from various parts of Australia who have successfully achieved their vision of producing fine wines and black truffles. The winemaking side is under the care of Mark Aitken, who, having graduated as dux of his class in applied science at Curtin University in 2000, joined Chestnut Grove as winemaker in 2002. The truffle side of the business is run under the direction of Harry Eslick, with 13 000 truffle-inoculated hazelnut and oak trees on the property, which have now produced truffles, some of prodigious size. A new cellar door sells the wines and (subject to seasonal availability) truffles. Exports to Japan.

ϼϼϼϼϼ Reserve Series Pemberton Riesling 2009 Pale straw-green; a delicate but
fragrant bouquet sets the scene, with its lime blossom aromas backed by a hint
of passionfruit; a long, clean palate fulfils the promise of the bouquet. Screwcap.
12% alc. **Rating** 94 **To** 2020 $24

✪ Pemberton Merlot 2008 Bright crimson-purple; the debate continues on the
best varieties for Pemberton; this wine mounts a compelling case for merlot: it has
the medium-bodied weight, silky tannins and utterly seductive red berry and plum
aromas and flavours of top merlot. Screwcap. 14.3% alc. **Rating** 94 **To** 2018 $20

ϼϼϼϼϼ Pemberton Sauvignon Blanc 2009 A fresh, juicy and vibrant wine, the delicate
✪ aromas taking shape on the delicious palate, with a mix of passionfruit, citrus and
grass before a cleansing finish. Screwcap. 12% alc. **Rating** 92 **To** 2011 $20
Pemberton Sauvignon Blanc 2008 **Rating** 92 **To** 2010 $20
Reserve Series Pemberton Cane-cut Riesling 2008 **Rating** 92 **To** 2013 $24
✪ Pemberton Sauvignon Blanc Semillon 2009 Light straw-green; bright and
zesty, the wine is basically in a citrus/herbal spectrum, but there is some of the
lychee fruit that crops up from time to time in sauvignon blanc; very good length.
Screwcap. 12% alc. **Rating** 91 **To** 2012 $17
Manjimup Pinot Noir Brut NV **Rating** 90 **To** 2012 $30

ϼϼϼϼ Reserve Series Pemberton Chardonnay 2008 **Rating** 89 **To** 2013 $26
Pemberton Chardonnay 2008 **Rating** 88 **To** 2013 $20
Pemberton Shiraz 2008 **Rating** 88 **To** 2016 $20
Pemberton Shiraz Cabernet Merlot 2008 **Rating** 88 **To** 2015 $17

Tuart Ridge ★★★

344 Stakehill Road, Baldivis, WA 6171 **Region** Peel
T (08) 9524 3333 **F** (08) 9524 2168 **www**.tuartridgewines.com **Open** W'ends 10–4
Winemaker Phil Franzone **Est.** 1996 **Cases** 2000 **Vyds** 5 ha
Phil Franzone has established chardonnay, verdelho, shiraz, cabernet sauvignon, grenache and merlot on the coastal Tuart soils. Phil also acts as contract winemaker for several of the ventures springing up in the Peel region.

ϼϼϼϼ Peel Semillon Sauvignon Blanc 2009 Light straw-green; crisp, fresh and lively,
the varieties speaking with a single voice; citrus, herb and mineral, with bracing
acidity; long finish. Screwcap. 12.8% alc. **Rating** 89 **To** 2012 $16
Peel Merlot 2003 Amazing clear and bright red; doesn't have much depth, but
is reminiscent of cabernet franc from the Loire Valley; a rose substitute if you are
looking for savoury flavours. Screwcap. 12.6% alc. **Rating** 88 **To** 2013 $14

Tuck's Ridge ★★★★★

37 Shoreham Road, Red Hill South, Vic 3937 **Region** Mornington Peninsula
T (03) 5989 8660 **F** (03) 5989 8579 **www.**tucksridge.com.au **Open** 7 days 11–5
Winemaker Peninsula Winemakers **Est.** 1985 **Cases** 4500 **Vyds** 3.04 ha
Tuck's Ridge has changed focus significantly since selling its large Red Hill vineyard. It retained the Buckle Vineyards of chardonnay and pinot noir that consistently provide outstanding grapes (and wine). The major part of the production is purchased from the Turramurra Vineyard. Exports to the US, Germany, the Netherlands and Hong Kong.

♈♈♈♈ **Buckle Pinot Noir 2008** Excellent colour; a rich and fragrant bouquet of perfectly ripened plummy fruit sets the scene for the deeply flavoured and very long palate; great mouthfeel and length. This is a great vineyard, producing top-class wines year in, year out. Screwcap. 13.7% alc. **Rating** 97 **To** 2018 $100

Buckle Chardonnay 2008 Light green-straw; an extremely fragrant bouquet of white peach leads into an intense and very long palate that is nonetheless delicate, so pure is the fruit, the oak seamless, the finish with juicy acidity. Screwcap. 13.3% alc. **Rating** 96 **To** 2023 $60

✪ **Mornington Peninsula Chardonnay 2009** Bright light straw-green; a super-fragrant and complex bouquet, intense fruit and oak both in play, the palate with tremendous energy and drive, finishing with grapefruit-flavoured acidity. Screwcap. 13.8% alc. **Rating** 95 **To** 2018 $29

✪ **Mornington Peninsula Shiraz 2008** Crimson colour; a lively and vibrant cool-grown shiraz, spice and black pepper accompanying the black cherry and plum fruit, perfectly ripened tannins giving texture and structure to the medium-bodied palate. Screwcap. 14.5% alc. **Rating** 95 **To** 2020 $29

Turramurra Vineyard Chardonnay 2008 Here the clone is the commonly encountered I10VI clone; the wine is almost serene compare to Buckle, so perfect is the integration of oak (30% new French) into the nectarine, citrus and white peach flavours. Screwcap. 13.7% alc. **Rating** 94 **To** 2016 $50

Mornington Peninsula Pinot Noir 2008 Light but very bright and clear crimson; delicious plum and cherry aromas, joined on the long palate by some savoury, spicy tannins. Screwcap. 13.7% alc. **Rating** 94 **To** 2015 $42

Tulloch ★★★★★

'Glen Elgin', 638 De Beyers Road, Pokolbin, NSW 2321 **Region** Hunter Valley
T (02) 4998 7580 **F** (02) 4998 7226 **www.**tulloch.com.au **Open** 7 days 10–5
Winemaker Jay Tulloch, First Creek Winemaking Services (Liz Jackson) **Est.** 1895
Cases 40 000 **Vyds** 80 ha
The Tulloch brand continues to build success on success. Its primary grape source is estate vines owned by part shareholder Inglewood Vineyard in the Upper Hunter Valley. It also owns the JYT Vineyard established by Jay Tulloch in the mid-1980s at the foot of the Brokenback Range in the heart of Pokolbin. The third source is contract-grown fruit from other growers in the Hunter Valley and further afield. Skilled winemaking by First Creek Winemaking Services has put the icing on the winemaking cake, and Julie Tulloch is a live-wire marketer. Exports to Belgium, Canada, Philippines, Singapore, Hong Kong, Malaysia, Japan and China.

♈♈♈♈♈ **Hector of Glen Elgin Limited Release Shiraz 2006** An elegant, medium-bodied wine that proclaims its regional origins in the best way, nuances of spice, earth and leather underneath the panoply of black and red fruits; sourced from vineyards more than 100 years old. Screwcap. 14% alc. **Rating** 95 **To** 2030 $60

Limited Release Julia Semillon 2009 A bright bouquet of lemon and talc, then a marvellously juicy palate, citrussy fruit and acidity Siamese twins joined from head to toe. Drink now or in 15 years. Screwcap. 11.5% alc. **Rating** 94 **To** 2024 $28

✪ **Semillon Sauvignon Blanc 2009** Sauvignon blanc from WA introduces some passionfruit, the drive and energy provided by the semillon, with lemony acidity on the finish, the mark of a top vintage. Screwcap. 12.5% alc. **Rating** 94 **To** 2012 $16

ŸŸŸŸŸ Hunter Valley Semillon 2009 More restrained than many '09s, the aromas
⊙   and flavours less exuberant; that said, the drive through the length of the palate is
       excellent, and lemon-grassy notes swell on the back-palate. Screwcap. 10.5% alc.
       Rating 93 To 2019 $16
       JYT Selection 2007 Rating 91 To 2022 $50
       Cellar Door Release Beechworth Sangiovese 2008 Rating 91 To 2014 $22
       EM Limited Release Chardonnay 2008 Rating 90 To 2013 $28
⊙   **Cellar Door Release Hunter Valley Marsanne 2009** The history of
       marsanne elsewhere in Australia suggests this wine will cellar well, gaining honey/
       toast/honeysuckle characters as it does so. Well worth a try. Screwcap. 13.5% alc.
       Rating 90 To 2015 $20
⊙   **Cellar Door Release Hunter Valley Viognier 2009** Very well made; there are
       some stone fruit (including apricot) aromas and flavours, but no oily phenolics; a
       little barrel ferment has seemingly worked magic. Screwcap. 12.3% alc. **Rating** 90
       To 2012 $20
       Cellar Door Release Hunter Valley Tempranillo 2008 Rating 90
       To 2014 $22

ŸŸŸŸ **Cellar Door Release Orange Pinot Gris 2009 Rating** 89 To 2010 $20
       Vineyard Selection Hunter Valley Verdelho 2009 Rating 89 To 2012 $20
       Pokolbin Dry Red Shiraz 2007 Rating 89 To 2013 $25
       Cabernet Sauvignon 2008 Rating 88 To 2014 $16
       Cellar Door Release Hunter Valley Tannat Shiraz 2008 Rating 88
       To 2013 $22
       Hunter Valley Verdelho 2009 Rating 87 To 2011 $16
       Cellar Door Release Hunter Valley Verscato 2008 Rating 87 To 2010 $16

Turkey Flat   ★★★★★

Bethany Road, Tanunda, SA 5352 **Region** Barossa Valley
T (08) 8563 2851 **F** (08) 8563 3610 **www.**turkeyflat.com.au **Open** 7 days 11–5
Winemaker Julie Campbell **Est.** 1990 **Cases** 20 000 **Vyds** 46.6 ha
The establishment date of Turkey Flat is given as 1990 but it might equally well have been
1870 (or thereabouts), when the Schulz family purchased the Turkey Flat vineyard, or 1847,
when the vineyard was first planted to the very old shiraz that still grows there today alongside
8 ha of equally old grenache. Plantings have since expanded significantly, now comprising
shiraz (24 ha), grenache (10.5 ha), cabernet sauvignon (6.7 ha), mourvedre (3.7 ha), viognier
and marsanne (0.6 ha each) and dolcetto (0.5 ha). In late 2009 a long-term goal was realised
with the installation of a new bottling line replacing the use of outside contractors and/or a
mobile bottling plant. The '08 red wines were thus bottled onsite. Exports to the UK, the US
and other major markets.

ŸŸŸŸŸ **Barossa Valley Rose 2009** Bright fuchsia; the bouquet has fragrant small red
⊙   fruits plus a touch of spice; the palate with structure and length way above average,
       the finish deliciously dry, spice coming again on the aftertaste. Screwcap. 12.5% alc.
       Rating 96 To 2010 $23
⊙   **Barossa Valley Shiraz 2008** Excellent crimson–purple; a bouquet that has the
       same allure as a great pinot, drawing you back again repeatedly before you taste
       the wine; Turkey Flat nailed the '08 vintage, capturing all of its luscious black fruits
       without a scintilla of jam or confection; the texture of the ripe tannins is perfect, as
       is the oak balance. Screwcap. 14.5% alc. **Rating** 96 To 2033 $45
⊙   **Barossa Valley Mourvedre 2008** Light but bright colour; a highly perfumed
       bouquet leads into a palate with more drive and intensity than I can recollect from
       any previous vintage; no confection here, just silky power. Screwcap. 14.5% alc.
       Rating 96 To 2020 $35
⊙   **Butchers Block Shiraz Grenache Mourvedre 2008** The aromas and flavours
       are those of a harlequin, dancing from red fruits and Turkish delight to warm
       spices and fruit, then to black fruit, good tannins providing just the right amount
       of structure. Screwcap. 14.5% alc. **Rating** 94 To 2018 $27

✪   **Barossa Valley Grenache 2008** Typical light, bright colour of Barossa Valley grenache, notwithstanding 90-year-old estate bush-pruned vines; the bouquet is ultra-fragrant, and while the palate has the red fruit and Turkish delight varietal flavour, it has great drive and zest. Screwcap. 15% alc. **Rating** 94 **To** 2016 $28
Barossa Valley Sparkling Shiraz NV Blend No. 5 disgorged Nov '09. Deep colour; typically rich and textured, with layers of black fruits sustained by perfect dosage; will develop and age with grace if given the chance. Crown seal. 13% alc. **Rating** 94 **To** 2016 $45

♟♟♟♟♟   **Butchers Block Barossa Valley Marsanne Viognier Roussanne 2009** **Rating** 93 **To** 2015 $27
Barossa Valley Grenache 2007 **Rating** 93 **To** 2015 $28
Pedro Ximenez (375 ml) NV **Rating** 90 **To** 2011 $32

Turner's Crossing Vineyard ★★★★★

PO Box 103, Epsom, Vic 3551 **Region** Bendigo
T (03) 5448 8464 **F** (03) 5448 7150 **www**.turnerscrossing.com **Open** W'ends (tel (03) 5944 4599)
Winemaker Sergio Carlei **Est.** 2002 **Cases** 8000 **Vyds** 41 ha
The name of this outstanding vineyard comes from local farmers crossing the Loddon River in the mid- to late-1800s on their way to the nearest town. The vineyard was planted in 1999 by former corporate executive and lecturer in the business school at La Trobe University, Paul Jenkins. However, Jenkins' experience as a self-taught viticulturist dates back to 1985, when he established his first vineyard at Prospect Hill, planting all the vines himself. The grapes from both vineyards have gone to a who's who of winemakers in Central Victoria, but an increasing amount is being made under the Turner's Crossing label, not surprising given the exceptional quality of the wines. Phil Bennett and winemaker Sergio Carlei have joined Paul as co-owners of the vineyard, with Sergio putting his money where his winemaking mouth is. Exports to the UK, the US, Canada, China and Taiwan.

♟♟♟♟♟   **The Cut Shiraz 2007** Deep purple-crimson; a complete wine with a virtuoso display of aromas and flavours attesting to site and climate; black fruits, licorice and multi-spices, including star anise, have a web of fine tannins to hold them together on the long palate. Diam. 14.9% alc. **Rating** 96 **To** 2022 $90

✪   **Bendigo Shiraz Viognier 2008** Deep purple-crimson; a very complex bouquet of blackberry, plum, leather and licorice; the highly structured palate confidently captures all of those aromas, finishing with a balanced display of tannins and oak. Screwcap. 14.5% alc. **Rating** 95 **To** 2023 $25

♟♟♟♟♟   **Bendigo Viognier 2009 Rating** 90 **To** 2012 $39

Twelve Acres ★★★

Nagambie-Rushworth Road, Bailieston, Vic 3608 **Region** Goulburn Valley
T (03) 5794 2020 **F** (03) 5794 2020 **Open** Thurs–Mon 10.30–5.30
Winemaker Peter and Jana Prygodicz **Est.** 1994 **Cases** 300
The property name comes from the fact that the original subdivision created a tiny 12-acre block in the midst of 1000-acre properties, giving rise to the local nickname of 'Bastard Block', less suited for a winery brand. When purchased in 1987, it was completely overgrown, and Peter and Jana Prygodicz have done all the work themselves, doing it the tough way without any mains power, relying on a generator and solar panels. This is their house, winery and cellar door block; the grapes for the wines come from local grapegrowers.

♟♟♟♟   **Shiraz 2003** Produced from grapes grown at Shepparton; good colour; blackberry and plum fruit with good tannin structure; a touch of vanillan/ American oak works well. ProCork. 13.7% alc. **Rating** 88 **To** 2014 $18

24 Karat Wines   ★★★★

PO Box 165, Mosman Park, WA 6912 **Region** Margaret River
T (08) 9383 4242 **F** (08) 9383 4502 **www**.24karat.com.au **Open** Not
Winemaker Claudia Lloyd, Bruce Dukes (Contract) **Est.** 1998 **Cases** 1000 **Vyds** 46.3 ha
In 1979 Dr Graham Lloyd, a qualified metallurgist with particular expertise in gold mining,
established his now world-leading metallurgical services company Ammtec. By 1997 he was
ready for a new challenge, and as he and his family had a long association with the Augusta
area, the idea of a vineyard was natural. He found an 82-ha property in Karridale, and
acquired it in 1997. He then did what many fail to do: in 1998 he signed a 15-year contract
with Brookland Valley for sale of the grapes, but included the right to retain 10% for his own
label. The vineyard has the major varieties of the region, importantly including 8.7 ha of six
clones (including the outstanding French Dijon clones) of chardonnay all planted in individual
blocks. It is managed with biodynamic principles, and the driving force is to procure quality-
based bonus grape payments from Brookland Valley. Graham and Penny's younger daughter
Claudia is a winemaker with both Australian and overseas experience, and the expectation is
that she will have a long-term involvement with the business.

♛♛♛♛♛ **Chardonnay 2008** Bright green-straw; the impact of 100% barrel ferment is
obvious, adding toasty/nutty characters to the peachy fruit aromas and flavours.
An altogether generous wine for early consumption. Screwcap. 13.3% alc.
Rating 91 **To** 2014 $29

🍇 Twisted Gum Wines   NR

2271 Eukey Road, Ballandean, Qld 4382 (postal) **Region** Granite Belt
T (07) 4684 1282 **www**.twistedgum.com.au **Open** Not
Winemaker Jim Barnes (Contract) **Est.** 2007 **Cases** 600 **Vyds** 3.2 ha
Tim and Michelle Coelli bring diverse and interesting backgrounds to this venture. During
his university days in the early 1980s Tim began reading weekly wine columns of a certain
journalist and bought recommended red wines from Wynns and Peter Lehmann, liked the
wines, and with wife Michelle 'bought cases and cases …' Tim became a research economist,
and during periods of living and working in Europe, he and Michelle became well acquainted
with the wines of France, Spain and Italy. She has a degree in agricultural science which, she
says, 'has not been well utilised because four children came along (currently aged 5 to 16)'.
When they found a beautiful 40-ha bush property on a ridge near Ballandean (at an altitude
of 900 m) with a little over 3 ha of vines already planted, they did not hesitate. The vineyard
was in need of TLC, and this has been provided in various ways, including the spreading of
mulch under the vines to retain moisture, suppress weeds and improve soil structure. There is
no cellar door, but there is weekend accommodation in the newly renovated Twisted Gum
Vineyard Cottage. Sales are through the website.

🍇 Two Bud Spur   ★★★★☆

21 De Wit Street, Battery Point, Tas 7004 (postal) **Region** Southern Tasmania
T (03) 6234 4252 **www**.twobudspur.com.au **Open** Not
Winemaker Winstead (Neil Snare) **Est.** 1996 **Cases** 200 **Vyds** 2.2 ha
Marine scientists Craig Mundy and Karen Miller purchased the Two Bud Spur vineyard in
2006 as a stress release from their day jobs (they still work full-time, managing the vineyard
in their spare time). Their viticultural expertise came from voracious reading of whatever
books and scientific literature they could lay their hands on, and the management of a
nearby 0.5 pinot vineyard in the lead-up to the '06 vintage, an experience that led directly to
their purchase of Two Bud Spur. This vineyard has had a chequered history, with its present
name between '96 and '03, then Grandview Vineyard '04 to '06, and '07 onwards back to
its original name. The vineyard had been run organically, but with disastrous results: disease,
weeds, nutrients, canopy management and pruning issues all required attention, as did the
boundary fences and not-quite-complete trellis. They were emboldened by the fact that, as
they say, 'it couldn't get much worse, so there was not much risk of ruining anything'. The
partners depict a two-bud spur on their label, which is in fact the base architecture for all
spur-pruned vineyards.

♈♈♈♈♈ Pinot Noir 2008 Excellent colour; very complex aromatics; a similarly complex
✪   and very impressive palate, with depth and length to its dark fruits and spice.
            Screwcap. 13.5% alc. **Rating** 94 **To** 2016 $25

♈♈♈♈♀ Pinot Noir 2007 **Rating** 92 **To** 2015 $25

♈♈♈♈ Nouveau 2009 **Rating** 88 **To** 2011 $20

Two Dorks Estate   ★★★★

PO Box 19204, Southbank, Vic 3006 **Region** Heathcote
T 0409 134 332 **Open** Not
Winemaker Mark Bladon **Est.** 2001 **Cases** 44 **Vyds** 2 ha
Owners Mark Bladon and Nektaria Achimastos (described by Mark as 'Vineyard Goddess')
have an exceptionally keen sense of humour. Having chosen a site in the southern end of
Heathcote off the Cambrian soil ('In truth the land in the area is not the best,' Mark admits)
they planted 2 ha of dry-grown vines in 2001. The ensuing seven years of drought meant that
development of the vines has been painstakingly slow, and simultaneously demanding much
TLC and that sense of humour. The vineyard is predominantly shiraz, with a patch of viognier
and 0.5 ha of cabernet sauvignon and merlot. The frost, drought, fire and brimstone of 2009
meant no estate-grown wine from that year, and all replacement vines in the future will be
shiraz. Mark has given the Vineyard Goddess a yellow card, but acknowledges 'to be fair, even
Jesus – an acknowledged miracle worker, wine-wise – needed water to make the stuff!'

♈♈♈♈♀ Heathcote Shiraz Cabernet Merlot 2008 Good crimson hue; a light- to
            medium-bodied wine that is fresh and lively, and has no green/unripe notes; red
            cherry, cassis and some plum fruit supported by fine tannins; an 80/11/6 blend, the
            missing 3% including malbec. Screwcap. 12.8% alc. **Rating** 90 **To** 2016 $22

Two Hands Wines   ★★★★★

Neldner Road, Marananga, SA 5355 **Region** Barossa Valley
T (08) 8562 4566 **F** (08) 8562 4744 **www.twohandswines.com Open** 7 days 10–5
Winemaker Matthew Wenk **Est.** 2000 **Cases** 40 000 **Vyds** 15 ha
The 'hands' in question are those of SA businessmen Michael Twelftree and Richard Mintz,
Michael in particular having extensive experience in marketing Australian wine in the US
(for other producers). On the principle that if big is good, bigger is better, and biggest is best,
the style of the wines has been aimed fairly and squarely at the palate of Robert Parker Jr
and *Wine Spectator*'s Harvey Steiman. Grapes are sourced from the Barossa Valley (where the
business has 15 ha of shiraz), McLaren Vale, Clare Valley, Langhorne Creek and Padthaway. The
retention of cork closures, the emphasis on sweet fruit, and the soft tannin structure all signify
the precise marketing strategy of what is a very successful business. Exports to the UK, the
US and other major markets.

♈♈♈♈♈ Bella's Garden Barossa Valley Shiraz 2008 Dense, impenetrable colour;
            a massive wine in every respect, '08 magnifying the Two Hands chosen style;
            luscious black fruits, oak and alcohol chase each other around the glass. A
            deliberate policy to give all but Sophie's Garden the same points: while characters
            differ, the quality is very similar. Cork. 15.8% alc. **Rating** 94 **To** 2028 $60
            Lily's Garden McLaren Vale Shiraz 2008 Dense crimson-purple; a very
            different bouquet to Bella's Garden; spice, dark chocolate and licorice aromas and
            flavours, McLaren Vale showing its special ability to carry high alcohol better than
            most other regions. Cork. 15.8% alc. **Rating** 94 **To** 2028 $60
            Max's Garden Heathcote Shiraz 2008 The cork (as with the others, no doubt
            for the US market) caused the neck of the bottle to fracture, with shards of glass
            scattering (trusty hand-held Screwpull not to blame). Here the alcohol is less
            intrusive than that of Lily's Garden; juicy black fruits, supple tannins and good oak
            take the wine through to its long finish. Cork. 15.3% alc. **Rating** 94 **To** 2028 $60

Samantha's Garden Clare Valley Shiraz 2008 Paradoxically, the highest alcohol delivers the most savoury wine, albeit still of massive proportions; blackberry, some prune and spice, and supple tannins fill the palates; while the region of each wine speaks loudly, there is a shared suppleness that comes from the skilled application of a winemaking philosophy. 16.2% alc. **Rating** 94 **To** 2028 $60

𝟗𝟗𝟗𝟗𝟗 **Angels Share McLaren Vale Shiraz 2008** Fractionally hazy colour; an archetypal McLaren Vale shiraz, the plum and blackberry fruit wrapped in dark chocolate; the tannins are soft, the oak restrained. Screwcap. 14.8% alc. **Rating** 93 **To** 2020 $27

Gnarly Dudes Barossa Valley Shiraz 2008 The colour has a slightly brighter hue than Angel's Share, the aromas and flavours more focused on sweet plum and blackberry fruit, although ultimately restrained by gently savoury tannins. Screwcap. 14.9% alc. **Rating** 92 **To** 2018 $27

The Bull and the Bear Barossa Valley Shiraz Cabernet Sauvignon 2007 Rating 92 **To** 2020 $45

Sophie's Garden Padthaway Shiraz 2008 Rating 90 **To** 2023 $60

Brave Faces Barossa Valley Grenache Shiraz Mataro 2008 Rating 90 **To** 2014 $27

Brilliant Disguise Barossa Valley Moscato 2009 Rating 90 **To** 2010 $18

201   NR

PO Box 731, Caringbah, NSW 1495 **Region** Hunter Valley
T 0420 905 608 **F** (02) 9332 6143 **www**.201.com.au **Open** Not
Winemaker Scott Stephens **Est.** 1998 **Cases** 750 **Vyds** 4 ha
Yet another winery with a numeric name giving book indexers and sommeliers nightmares, but better than the unpronounceable GPS co-ordinates used by another winery. Owners and partners Barbara Smith and Geoff Schippers purchased the 4-ha former Rothbury Ridge vineyard in 2006. At that stage it had a quixotic planting of 1.6 ha of durif and 1.8 ha of chambourcin dating back to the early 1990s, when both varieties were uncommon, and the new owners sensibly decided to plant an additional 0.6 ha of semillon. It is a weekend retreat for Barbara and Geoff, who have busy lives in Sydney.

2 Mates   ★★★★

PO Box 131, McLaren Vale, SA 5171 **Region** McLaren Vale
T 0411 111 198 **F** (08) 8295 7589 **www**.2mates.com.au **Open** Not
Winemaker Matt Rechner **Est.** 2003 **Cases** 500
The two mates are Mark Venable and David Minear, who say, 'Over a big drink in a small bar in Italy a few years back, we talked about making "our perfect Australian Shiraz". When we got back, we decided to have a go.' The wine (2005) was duly made, and went on to win a silver medal at the *Decanter* Magazine World Wine Awards in London, along with some exalted company. The '06 was better still, the '07 good but unable to entirely escape the clutches of that difficult year.

𝟗𝟗𝟗𝟗𝟗 **McLaren Vale Shiraz 2007** Quintessential McLaren Vale, with swirls of dark and milk chocolate running through the black fruit background of the bouquet and palate alike the alcohol is obvious, but does add a touch of softness to the fruit flavours. Screwcap. 15.3% alc. **Rating** 90 **To** 2017 $30

Two Rivers   ★★★★★

2 Yarrawa Road, Denman, NSW 2328 (postal) **Region** Upper Hunter Valley
T (02) 6547 2556 **F** (02) 6547 2546 **www**.tworiverswines.com.au **Open** 7 days 11–4
Winemaker First Creek Winemaking Services **Est.** 1988 **Cases** 10 000 **Vyds** 75.62 ha
A significant part of the viticultural scene in the Upper Hunter Valley, with over 75 ha of vineyards, involving a total investment of around $7 million. Part of the fruit is sold under long-term contracts, and part is made for the expanding winemaking and marketing operations

of Two Rivers, the chief brand of Inglewood Vineyards. The emphasis is on Chardonnay and Semillon, and the wines have been medal winners at the Hunter Valley Wine Show. It is also a partner in the Tulloch business, together with the Tulloch and Angove families, and supplies much of the grapes for the Tulloch label. A contemporary cellar door has recently opened, adding significantly to the appeal of the Upper Hunter Valley as a wine-tourist destination.

ΨΨΨΨΨ **Reserve Hunter Valley Chardonnay 2008** Bright pale green; a model of
✪ restraint and finesse, the citrus and white stone fruit flavours having as much cool
climate as warm; the new French oak used in fermentation and maturation has
simply added a light touch of cashew. Gold medal Hunter Valley Wine Show '09
and Sydney Wine Show '10. Screwcap. 12.3% alc. **Rating** 94 **To** 2013 $20

✪ **Hidden Hive Hunter Valley Verdelho 2009** What a vintage '09 was: glorious
fruit flavours and intensity across all white varieties, and this is no exception –
really long, vibrant, fruit-filled finish. Verdelho doesn't come much better. Screwcap.
13.5% alc. **Rating** 94 **To** 2013 $14

ΨΨΨΨΩ **Stone's Throw Hunter Valley Semillon 2009** May not have the ultimate
✪ intensity of the best semillons of '09, but certainly has the hallmark of the vintage;
the citrus and grass-tinged palate has great length. NSW Top 40. Screwcap.
10.9% alc. **Rating** 92 **To** 2019 $14

✪ **Reserve Hunter Valley Chardonnay 2009** Fresh and clean, the emphasis
firmly on the lively citrus and nectarine fruit, barrel ferment oak simply providing
a backdrop to the long palate. Screwcap. 13.1% alc. **Rating** 92 **To** 2014 $20
Reserve Hunter Valley Semillon 2007 **Rating** 91 **To** 2017 $20
Reserve Hunter Valley Shiraz 2007 **Rating** 91 **To** 2017 $24

✪ **Hunter Valley Semillon Sauvignon Blanc 2009** Decidedly odd labelling,
semillon in small print, sauvignon blanc in bold; the back label shows the
sauvignon blanc comes from Canberra, not mentioned on the front label, just
Hunter Valley. The wine itself? There is a seamless union between the varieties, ripe
citrus and the barest touch of tropical fruit on a long palate. Screwcap. 12.5% alc.
Rating 90 **To** 2012 $14

Tyrone Estate   ★★★

PO Box 2187, Berri, SA 5343 **Region** Riverland
T (08)b8584 1120 **F** (08) 8584 1388 **www.**tyroneestate.com.au **Open** Not
Winemaker Melanie Kargas **Est.** 2008 **Cases** 20 000
While this is the venture of Bob and Sylvia Franchitto, it has been set up for the benefit of
their son Tyrone. When Bob began his various horticultural and farming activities, he applied a
holistic view, preferring the use of selected cover crops and mulching instead of chemicals for
weed control and soil conditioning. Care for the environment also extends to the winemaking
process: the winery is fully undercover, eliminating storm water run off and allowing the
collection of rain water for further use. The water used in winery wash-down procedures is
processed before being recycled for supplementary irrigation of the vineyards. All the marc
and grape skins are taken offsite and distilled to recover alcohol and tartaric acid before being
combined with other ingredients for organic fertilisers. This is a sister winery to that of Salena
Estate. Exports to Singapore, Taiwan, Korea and China.

ΨΨΨΨ **Sandy Creek Block A-22 Barossa Shiraz 2005** Bright colour; juicy red fruits,
and quite unevolved for the age, the wine offers accessible drinking with a little
bottle age; quite surprising. Screwcap. 13.5% alc. **Rating** 89 **To** 2015 $15 BE
Home Block Cabernet Sauvignon 2007 Bright cassis fruit bouquet, with a
touch of black olive; fleshy, with a firm backbone of tannins; juicy on the finish.
Screwcap. 13.5% alc. **Rating** 88 $15 BE
Home Block Shiraz 2007 Ripe fruit bouquet of spiced mulberry and a little
toast from the oak; charry palate, with good concentration; travels along a single
plane. Screwcap. 13.5% alc. **Rating** 87 $15 BE
Three Generations Cabernet Sauvignon 2008 Vibrant colour; good
concentration and a pleasant level of fruit sweetness; not overly varietal, but clean
and well made. Screwcap. 13.5% alc. **Rating** 87 **To** 2013 $12 BE

Tyrrell's   ★★★★★

Broke Road, Pokolbin, NSW 2321 **Region** Hunter Valley
T (02) 4993 7000 **F** (02) 4998 7723 **www.**tyrrells.com.au **Open** Mon–Sat 8.30–5, Sun 10–4
Winemaker Andrew Spinaze, Mark Richardson **Est.** 1858 **Cases** 500 000 **Vyds** 288.34 ha
One of the most successful family wineries, a humble operation for the first 110 years of its
life that has grown out of all recognition over the past 40 years. In 2003 it cleared the decks by
selling its Long Flat range of wines for an eight-figure sum, allowing it to focus on its premium,
super-premium and ultra-premium wines: Vat 1 Semillon is one of the most dominant wines
in the Australian show system, and Vat 47 Chardonnay is one of the pacesetters for this variety.
It has an awesome portfolio of single-vineyard Semillons released when 5–6 years old. Its
estate plantings comprise 212 ha in the Hunter Valley, 34 ha in McLaren Vale, 26 ha in the
Limestone Coast and 26 ha in Heathcote. Exports to all major markets.

ＹＹＹＹＹ **Johnno's Hand Pressed Semillon 2009** What next from Tyrrell's? One
hundred-year-old (planted 1908) on sandy flats (Johnno's Block), hand-picked,
then basket-pressed (the press last used 30 years ago) and bottled in the riesling
bottle used until 1989; absolutely bursting with citrus-tinged flavour, and of great
length; a 'softer style' says Tyrrell's, and is certainly an each-way drink-now-or-
cellar proposition. Screwcap. 11.5% alc. **Rating** 96 **To** 2024 $45

✪ **Belford Reserve Semillon 2005** Vivid green hue; completely unevolved,
pristine and as fresh as a daisy; lemon, slate and a touch of straw are evident; the
full tale is told on the palate, with rapier-like acidity, drawing out the tightly
wound fruit to a staggeringly long conclusion; a wonderful single-vineyard
experience. Screwcap. 11.4% alc. **Rating** 96 **To** 2030 $30 BE

✪ **Single Vineyard Stevens Hunter Shiraz 2007** Bright colour; the bouquet
has black and red cherry fruit and French oak; the supple texture of the medium-
bodied palate is outstanding, allowing the vibrant and fresh fruit full play; great
balance and length. Screwcap. 13.5% alc. **Rating** 96 **To** 2027 $35

✪ **Single Vineyard HVD Hunter Semillon 2005** A little more open knit than
the Belford, showing riper lemon fruit and a little more straw; the palate shows
more weight and generosity at this stage of its evolution; almost juicy on entry, the
palate seems to wind up and tighten and leaves the impression of lemon sherbet to
conclude. Screwcap. 11.6% alc. **Rating** 95 **To** 2028 $30 BE

✪ **Single Vineyard Stevens Hunter Semillon 2006** The colour is still pale,
although bright; the wine is in transition between youth and maturity, but has
the best of both worlds, its lemon/citrus fruit still vibrant, the acidity still fresh,
yet is just starting to build weight before the first signs of honey and toast appear.
Screwcap. 10.5% alc. **Rating** 94 **To** 2021 $30 BE

Single Vineyard HVD Hunter Chardonnay 2009 Pale gold, vivid green hue;
poised and precise bouquet showing plenty of lemon fruit, with a suggestion of
fig; the palate is quite steely, with fine acidity the centrepiece, and layers of flavour
cascading across the palate; certainly an elegant Hunter Chardonnay. Screwcap.
13% alc. **Rating** 94 **To** 2016 $30 BE

✪ **Brokenback Hunter Valley Shiraz 2007** Bright red and black fruits on a
medium-bodied palate are the first impression, then the unexpected intensity and
length, underpinned by fine, savoury tannins, oak nowhere in the picture and not
needed. Surprise packet. Screwcap. 13.5% alc. **Rating** 94 **To** 2015 $20

Vat 8 Hunter Shiraz 2007 Good purple hue; the bouquet is starting to show
the first signs of Hunter earth and leather; although the intense palate is still full
of plum and blackberry fruit; has very good texture and balance, and is built for
the long haul. Only the second time since '89 that Vat 8 has been 100% shiraz.
Screwcap. 13.5% alc. **Rating** 94 **To** 2027 $45

Lunatiq Heathcote Shiraz 2006 Rich and luscious red and black fruits, spice,
licorice and a hint of dark chocolate are enriched by positive oak and supported
by ripe, soft but persistent tannins. Overall, no more than medium-bodied. Diam.
14.5% alc. **Rating** 94 **To** 2018 $30

ŸŸŸŸ♀ **Belford Single Vineyard Hunter Chardonnay 2008** Rating 92 To 2016
$35 BE

✪ **Rufus Stone McLaren Vale Shiraz 2008** Bright colour; immaculately
clean and precise aromas of black cherries, dark plums and bitter chocolate; the
American oak merely frames the voluminous fruit on offer, with all aspects
combining effortlessly to conclude; long and luscious. Screwcap. 14.5% alc.
Rating 92 To 2020 $20 BE

✪ **Old Winery Shiraz 2008** Bright crimson; aromas of spice and dark chocolate
speak of the regions involved (Heathcote/McLaren Vale); a well-balanced medium-
bodied palate with plenty of black and red fruits; good finish. Screwcap. 14.5% alc.
Rating 90 To 2015 $14

ŸŸŸŸ **Lost Block Semillon 2009** Lost Block is now simply a brand sourced from a
✪ number of Hunter Valley vineyards, not the block that escaped picking until late
in the season many years ago. Fresh and lively, it has bright citrus lemon fruit; no
particular need of cellaring, but will gain complexity in bottle. Screwcap. 11% alc.
Rating 89 To 2015 $16

✪ **Old Winery Verdelho 2009** Attractive example; some depth to the tropical
fruit salad flavours without the detriment of phenolics; good balance and length.
Screwcap. 13% alc. Rating 89 To 2011 $13

✪ **Old Winery Semillon 2009** Only Tyrrell's could produce a semillon of this
quality and character at this price, although the vintage obviously played its part;
soft citrus and grass fruit on a balanced palate, the wine ready now. Screwcap.
11.5% alc. Rating 88 To 2013 $13

✪ **Old Winery Cabernet Merlot 2008** As the label indicates, a SA/WA blend;
for those with the ability to sell wine (particularly at this price) opportunities to
buy in bulk abound; this has good black and red berry fruit flavours, and enough
structure to satisfy. Screwcap. 14% alc. Rating 88 To 2012 $13

Ulithorne   ★★★★
The Mill at Middleton, 29 Mill Terrace, Middleton, SA 5213 **Region** McLaren Vale
T 0419 040 670 **F** (08) 8554 2433 **www**.ulithorne.com.au **Open** W'ends 10–4
Winemaker Rose Kentish, Brian Light, Natasha Mooney (Contract) **Est.** 1971 **Cases** 1800
Sam Harrison and partner Rose Kentish have sold the Ulithorne vineyard (but with the right
to select and buy part of the production each vintage) and have purchased the Middleton
Mill on the south coast of the Fleurieu Peninsula. It is now their home, and Sam has resumed
full-time painting while Rose is running a wine bar in the Middelton Mill, with Ulithorne
and other local wines, beers and platters of regional food on offer. In 2008 Rose was made
McLaren Vale's Bushing Queen, the title going to the maker of the best wine at the McLaren
Vale Wine Show. Exports to the UK, the US, Canada, The Netherlands, Malaysia and Korea.

ŸŸŸŸ♀ **Chi McLaren Vale Shiraz Grenache 2007** Good colour; a positive bouquet
and an even more emphatic palate, with black fruits and tannins ex the shiraz,
the grenache filling in any cracks on the mid-palate; 40-year-old vines; unfiltered.
Screwcap. 14.5% alc. Rating 92 To 2020 $40

Paternus McLaren Vale Cabernet Shiraz 2008 Modest red-purple; a 68/32
blend that is more elegant and savoury than the majority of '08 reds from the
region; black fruits, dark chocolate, fine tannins and integrated oak run through
the medium- to full-bodied palate. Screwcap. 14.5% alc. Rating 92 To 2023 $40

Frux Frugis McLaren Vale Shiraz 2008 Strong red-purple; a left-field
combination of dark fruits on the one hand, and a spicy/savoury bitter chocolate
twist on the other; certainly complex and long, but difficult to read. Screwcap.
15% alc. Rating 91 To 2023 $50

Umamu Estate ★★★★☆

PO Box 1269, Margaret River, WA 6285 **Region** Margaret River
T (08) 9757 5058 **F** (08) 9757 5058 **www**.umamuestate.com **Open** Not
Winemaker Bruce Dukes (Contract) **Est.** 2005 **Cases** 7000 **Vyds** 20.8 ha
Chief executive Charmaine Saw explains, 'My life has been a journey towards Umamu. An upbringing in both eastern and western cultures, graduating in natural science, training as a chef, combined with a passion for the arts, and experience as a management consultant have all contributed to my building the business creatively yet professionally.' The palindrome Umamu, says Charmaine, is inspired by balance and contentment. In practical terms this means an organic approach to viticulture and a deep respect for the terroir. In 2004 Charmaine purchased the property and its plantings, dating back to '78, of cabernet sauvignon (6.9 ha), shiraz (4.1 ha), chardonnay (3.5 ha), merlot (2 ha), semillon and sauvignon blanc (1.5 ha each) and cabernet franc (0.7 ha); the maiden vintage under the Umamu label followed in '05. Exports to the UK, the US, Hong Kong, Malaysia and Singapore.

🍷🍷🍷🍷🍷 **Margaret River Cabernet Merlot 2007** Strong purple notes retained in the
✪ colour; the pure and fragrant cassis and blackcurrant aromas of the bouquet are replayed on the medium- to full-bodied palate, with tannins providing precisely the right amount of texture and structure. Screwcap. 13.5% alc. **Rating** 95 To 2022 $28

🍷🍷🍷🍷🍷 **Margaret River Shiraz 2007** Rating 92 To 2017 $28

Undercliff ★★★★

Yango Creek Road, Wollombi, NSW 2325 **Region** Hunter Valley
T (02) 4998 3322 **F** (02) 4998 3322 **www**.undercliff.com.au **Open** 7 days 10–5, or by appt
Winemaker David Carrick, Peter Hamshere **Est.** 1990 **Cases** 1200 **Vyds** 4.7 ha
Peter and Jane Hamshere are the new owners of Undercliff, but it continues to function as both winery cellar door and art gallery. The wines, produced from estate plantings of shiraz, semillon, chambourcin and muscat, have won a number of awards in recent years at the Hunter Valley Wine Show and the Hunter Valley Small Winemakers Show. Exports to Japan.

🍷🍷🍷🍷🍷 **Semillon 2003** The crumbling cork notwithstanding, it's not hard to see why
✪ the wine won a gold medal at the Hunter Valley Boutique Wine Show '09; crisp grassy/lemony flavours drive the bouquet and palate. The drinking span reflects cork concerns. 11.2% alc. **Rating** 93 To 2013 $20

Uplands ★★★

174 Richmond Road, Cambridge, Tas 7170 **Region** Southern Tasmania
T (03) 6248 5460 **Open** By appt
Winemaker Frogmore Creek (Alain Rousseau) **Est.** 1998 **Cases** 240 **Vyds** 0.5 ha
Michael and Debbie Ryan bought the historic Uplands House (1823) in 1998 and decided to plant the front paddock with chardonnay, joining the grapegrowing trend in the Coal River Valley of southern Tasmania. The vineyard is planted with the two most suitable clones for the area, 8127 for sparkling and the Penfold clone for their lightly wooded Chardonnay. They have developed a partnership with another small vineyard in the valley to produce a Pinot Noir Chardonnay that will spend at least four years on lees prior to disgorgement. The 2007 Chardonnay is a quite beautiful wine.

Upper Reach ★★★☆

77 Memorial Avenue, Baskerville, WA 6056 **Region** Swan Valley
T (08) 9296 0078 **F** (08) 9296 0278 **www**.upperreach.com.au **Open** 7 days 11–5
Winemaker Derek Pearse **Est.** 1996 **Cases** 5000 **Vyds** 7.24 ha
This 10-ha property on the banks of the upper reaches of the Swan River was purchased by Laura Rowe and Derek Pearse in 1996. The original 4-ha vineyard has been expanded, and plantings now include chardonnay, shiraz, cabernet sauvignon, verdelho, semillon, merlot,

petit verdot and muscat. All wines are estate-grown. The fish on the label, incidentally, is black bream, which can be found in the pools of the Swan River during the summer months. Exports to the UK.

ŢŢŢŢŢ **Reserve Swan Valley Chardonnay 2009** Spicy melon and nectarine bouquet, with a strong presence of cinnamon from the toasty oak; rich, ripe and warm, with a grilled nut savoury finish. Screwcap. 13.5% alc. **Rating** 90 **To** 2014 $28 BE

ŢŢŢŢ **Tempranillo 2009 Rating** 89 **To** 2013 $22 BE

Vale Creek Wines ★★★★

438 Cow Flat Road, Cow Flat, NSW 2795 **Region** Central Ranges Zone
T (02) 6337 2011 **F** (02) 6337 2012 www.valecreek.com.au **Open** By appt
Winemaker Tony Hatch, David Lowe (Consultant) **Est.** 2001 **Cases** NFP **Vyds** 4.5 ha
In 1994 retired airline pilot Tony Hatch and former accountant partner Liz McFarland purchased their 120-ha property near Bathurst. Over the following years Tony acquired an advanced diploma in farm management from the University of Sydney, with electives in viticulture, and both Tony and Liz have completed winemaking courses at TAFE, attended numerous AWRI workshops, and worked in vineyards and wineries in Bathurst, Mudgee and Orange. The turning point was a 2002 visit by Tony to leading oenologist Dr Alberto Antonini in Tuscany, who designed the vineyard layout and trellis system. The sangiovese clone selected by Dr Antonini was propagated by Chalmers Nursery, and became available at the end of '04; arneis had also been procured. A 100-tonne winery was completed in mid-2005, and the first experimental vintage (with purchased grapes) made in '06. In '06 Tony worked the vintage at Castello di Bossi in Chianti, gaining firsthand experience with sangiovese and vermentino. The estate plantings of sangiovese, barbera, dolcetto, pinot grigio and arneis are supplemented by limited purchases of other varieties, notably vermentino.

ŢŢŢŢŢ **La Cadenza Sangiovese Riserva 2008** Positive varietal character, with plenty of sour cherry fruit on an unusually full-bodied palate; very promising, and good use of French oak. Screwcap. 14% alc. **Rating** 91 **To** 2014 $35
Barbera 2008 Crimson hue; attractive cherry fruit with some savoury notes; medium-bodied, with supple mouthfeel and good length. Screwcap. 13.6% alc. **Rating** 90 **To** 2014 $25

ŢŢŢŢ **Vermentino 2008 Rating** 88 **To** 2011 $17
Sangiovese 2008 Rating 88 **To** 2014 $25
Dolcetto 2008 Rating 87 **To** 2013 $22

Vale Wines ★★★☆

2914 Frankston-Flinders Road, Balnarring, Vic 3926 **Region** Mornington Peninsula
T (03) 5983 1521 **F** (03) 5983 1942 www.valewines.com.au **Open** 7 days 11–5
Winemaker John Vale, Caroline Vale **Est.** 1991 **Cases** 400 **Vyds** 1.7 ha
After a lifetime in the retail liquor industry, John and Susan Vale took a busman's retirement by purchasing a grazing property at Balnarring in 1991. After some trial and error the estate plantings are now riesling, gewurztraminer, tempranillo and durif, the intake supplemented by the purchase of chardonnay and pinot gris from local growers. The onsite winery was built in 1997 from stone and mudbrick, and incorporates the cellar door. The Vales have a continuing business, Winemaking Supplies & Services Pty Ltd, a winery supply wholesaler. In Dec '09, daughter Caroline formally opened a contract sparkling wine production facility in the winery utilising clients' estate-grown grapes, or estate-grown base wines, or base wines sourced from other growers in the region. Caroline, with a science degree from Melbourne University and a winemaking degree from CSU, has had a varied international and Australian winemaking career, which piqued her interest in sparkling wine, her venture known as Mousse and Bead. The ultimate extension is into sparkling ciders, cherry-based wines and liqueurs, all made from Mornington grapes.

ΥΥΥΥ♀   **Gewurztraminer 2008** Bright straw-green; has distinctive spice rose petal
✪   aromas, and a palate that continues the varietal theme, with its slightly fuller
          mouthfeel than that of riesling. ProCork. 12% alc. **Rating** 91 **To** 2014 $18

ΥΥΥΥ   **Caroline V Reserve Cuvee 2006 Rating** 89 **To** 2012 $29

Valhalla Wines   ★★★☆

163 All Saints Road, Wahgunyah, Vic 3687 **Region** Rutherglen
T (02) 6033 1438 **F** (02) 6033 1728 **www**.valhallawines.com.au **Open** 7 days 10–4
Winemaker Anton Therkildsen **Est.** 2001 **Cases** 1400 **Vyds** 2.5 ha
This is the venture of Anton Therkildsen and wife Antoinette Del Popolo. They acquired the
property in 2001, and in '02 began the planting of shiraz (1.6 ha) and durif (0.9 ha). They
intend to expand the vineyard with marsanne, viognier, grenache, mourvedre and riesling,
reflecting their primary interest in the wines of the Rhône Valley. For the time being, they
are relying on contract-grown grapes to develop these wine styles. The straw bale winery was
built in 2007, underlining their desire for sustainable viticulture and biodiversity, with minimal
use of sprays and annual planting of cover crops between the rows. A worm farm and the
composting of grape skins and stalks completes the picture.

ΥΥΥΥ♀   **Rutherglen Durif 2007** Deep, vibrant purple-crimson; a very good example of
          this unique variety; plum, blackberry, prune and dark chocolate are all to be found
          in its velvety texture; dismisses its alcohol with contemptuous ease. Screwcap.
          15.4% alc. **Rating** 93 **To** 2017 $28

ΥΥΥΥ   **Riesling 2009 Rating** 89 **To** 2016 $18
          Rutherglen Viognier 2009 Rating 89 **To** 2013 $20
          Rutherglen Shiraz 2008 Rating 89 **To** 2017 $25
          Rutherglen Grenache Shiraz Mourvedre 2008 Rating 89 **To** 2014 $20
          Marsanne 2008 Rating 88 **To** 2013 $24
          Rutherglen Shiraz Viognier 2008 Rating 88 **To** 2017 $28
          Rutherglen Bella Rosa 2009 Rating 87 **To** 2011 $16
          The Ranga 2007 Rating 87 **To** 2013 $16

Vardon Lane/Kanta   ★★★★

22–26 Vardon Lane, Adelaide, SA 5000 (postal) **Region** Adelaide Hills
T (08) 8232 5300 **F** (08) 8232 2055 **Open** Not
Winemaker Egon Muller, Stephen Pannell **Est.** 2005 **Cases** 1400
This is the ultimate virtual winery, a joint venture between famed Mosel-Saar-Ruwer
winemaker (and proprietor) Egon Muller, Michael Andrewartha from Adelaide's East End
Cellars, and Armenian-born vigneron and owner of La Corte from Italy's Puglia region, Vahe
Keushguerian. A three-year search for the perfect riesling site ended almost where the journey
began, at the Shaw & Smith Adelaide Hills vineyard. Muller arrived on the day of picking to
oversee the whole production, carried out at Shaw & Smith with input from Steve Pannell
and Shaw & Smith's winemaker, Daryl Catlin. The grapes were crushed and cold-soaked
for up to 16 hours, the juice settled without enzyme and kept at 12°C until spontaneous
fermentation began. Small wonder that the wine is so different from other Australian rieslings,
and even more different from the gloriously fine wines that Muller makes at home. Exports
to the UK, the US and Germany.

ΥΥΥΥ♀   **Kanta Egon Muller Adelaide Hills Riesling 2008** As with prior vintages,
          a wine that primarily turns on its almost thick texture; strikingly different
          from conventional Australian rieslings, this is a square peg in a round hole.
          Bottle development could change the picture. Screwcap. 13.6% alc. **Rating** 90
          To 2018 $30

 Vasarelli Wines   ★★★★

164 Main Road, McLaren Vale, SA 5171 **Region** McLaren Vale
T (08) 8323 7980 **F** (08) 8323 8439 **Open** 7 days 8–5
Winemaker Hamish Seabrook (Contract) **Est.** 1995 **Cases** 25 000 **Vyds** 33 ha
Pasquale (Pat) and Vittoria (Vicky) Vasarelli moved with their parents from Melbourne to McLaren Vale in 1976. They began the establishment of their vineyard, and over the succeeding years increased the area under vine to its present size, planted to semillon, sauvignon blanc, chardonnay, pinot gris, vermentino, shiraz, cabernet sauvignon and merlot. Until '95 the grapes were sold to other producers, but in that year they joined Cellarmaster Wines and the Vasarelli label was born. In a reverse play to the usual pattern, they opened a cellar door (for the first time) in '09 on a small property they had purchased in '92.

♀♀♀♀♀ **Pallino McLaren Vale Cabernet Sauvignon Shiraz Malbec 2006** Why inflict a cork on this wine is beyond comprehension; it is certainly full-bodied, with dark berry fruits running through the length of the palate, so may withstand cork's frailties for some years, but is that all there is to it? 14.5% alc. **Rating** 92 To 2016 $50
Family Reserve McLaren Vale Cabernet Sauvignon 2008 Strong crimson-purple; the bouquet offers a potent mix of blackcurrant and dark chocolate; the palate follows suit, the flavours good, with just a slight echo of alcohol on the finish. Screwcap. 14.5% alc. **Rating** 90 To 2023 $23

♀♀♀♀ **Family Reserve McLaren Vale Shiraz 2008 Rating** 89 To 2018 $23
McLaren Vale Chardonnay 2008 Rating 87 To 2012 $20

Vasse Felix   ★★★★★

Cnr Caves Road/Harmans Road South, Cowaramup, WA 6284 **Region** Margaret River
T (08) 9756 5000 **F** (08) 9755 5425 **www**.vassefelix.com.au **Open** 7 days 10–5
Winemaker Virginia Willcock **Est.** 1967 **Cases** 150 000 **Vyds** 195.45 ha
Vasse Felix was the first winery to be built in the Margaret River. Owned and operated by the Holmes à Court family since 1987, Vasse Felix has undergone extensive changes and expansion. Its two flagship wines are Heytesbury Chardonnay and Heytesbury (cabernet sauvignon-based) supported by 10 varietal wines, Classic Dry Red and Dry White and budget-priced Theatre White and Theatre Shiraz. Exports to all major markets.

♀♀♀♀♀ **Heytesbury Margaret River Chardonnay 2008** Oak plays a key role in the bouquet of this wine, but the quality of the fruit beneath is superb; grapefruit and nectarine, seductive spices and beguiling toastiness frames the fruit; the palate is deep and compelling, with vibrant fruit and acidity that provide a staggeringly long finish. Screwcap. 13% alc. **Rating** 96 To 2018 $45 BE
Heytesbury 2007 The bouquet reveals an electric array of black fruits, cedar, olive, violets and dried leaf; its complexity and completeness is revealed on the full-bodied palate, as the layers of fruit give way to fine-grained tannins and precise acidity; the finish is long, succulent and thoroughly mesmerising. Cabernet/Malbec/Petit Verdot. Screwcap. 14.5% alc. **Rating** 96 To 2025 $75 BE
✪ **Margaret River Semillon 2009** Light green-straw; a fragrant bouquet with grass and citrus to the fore, the partial barrel fermentation in French oak a backdrop; the palate provides a replay of what is a perfectly made, delicious wine. Screwcap. 12.5% alc. **Rating** 95 To 2019 $25
✪ **Margaret River Sauvignon Blanc Semillon 2009** Bright light green-straw; a beautifully focused and balanced blend, with tropical fruit offset by intense citrus acidity; the small proportion of barrel ferment in French oak is almost invisible. Gold medal Sydney Wine Show '10. Screwcap. 12.5% alc. **Rating** 95 To 2012 $25
Margaret River Cabernet Sauvignon 2008 Essency regional bouquet relying on fruit purity rather than oak to provide an alluring array of aromas; red fruit and cedar are gracefully supported by fine, almost silky tannins; elegant, long and harmonious to conclude. Screwcap. 14.5% alc. **Rating** 95 $38 BE

Margaret River Cabernet Sauvignon 2007 Strong colour; ripe cassis and blackcurrant bouquet with some oak in background; medium- to full-bodied palate with identical flavours supported by ripe tannins and quality French oak. Trophy Sydney Wine Show '10. Screwcap. 14.5% alc. **Rating** 95 **To** 2027 $38

✪ **Margaret River Chardonnay 2008** Lively and fresh stone fruit and grapefruit aromas and flavours are given emphasis by the low alcohol, oak largely incidental. Very much in the modern style; gold medal WA Wine Show '09. Screwcap. 12.5% alc. **Rating** 94 **To** 2016 $25

✪ **Margaret River Cabernet Merlot 2008** Gently leafy with a lovely dollop of cassis and cedar on the bouquet; the palate delivers a plush medium-bodied mouthful of flavour, with ripe tannins and generous levels of fruit to conclude; complex with a friendly hand. Screwcap. 14.5% alc. **Rating** 94 $25 BE

♟♟♟♟♟ **Margaret River Classic Dry White 2009** **Rating** 91 **To** 2010 $19

♟♟♟♟ **Classic Dry Red Margaret River Shiraz Cabernet 2008** **Rating** 89 **To** 2014 $20

Velo Wines   ★★★★☆

755 West Tamar Highway, Legana, Tas 7277 **Region** Northern Tasmania
T (03) 6330 3677 **F** (03) 6330 3098 **Open** 7 days 10–5
Winemaker Micheal Wilson, Winemaking Tasmania (Julian Alcorso) **Est.** 1966 **Cases** 1800
The story behind Velo Wines is fascinating, wheels within wheels. The 0.9 ha of cabernet sauvignon and 0.5 ha of pinot noir of the Legana Vineyard were planted in 1966 by Graham Wiltshire, legitimately described as one of the three great pioneers of the Tasmanian wine industry. Fifteen years ago Micheal and Mary Wilson returned to Tasmania after living in Italy and France for a decade. Micheal had been an Olympic cyclist and joined the professional ranks, racing in all of the major European events. Imbued with a love of wine and food, they spent 'seven long hard years in the restaurant game'. Somehow, Micheal found time to become a qualified viticulturist, and was vineyard manager for Moorilla Estate based at St Matthias, and Mary spent five years working in wine wholesaling for leading distributors. In 2001 they purchased the Legana Vineyard, planted so long ago, and have painstakingly rehabilitated the 40-year-old vines. They have built a small winery where Micheal makes the red wines, and Julian Alcorso makes the white wines, sourced in part from 0.6 ha of estate riesling and from grapes grown on the East Coast.

♟♟♟♟♟ **Wooded Chardonnay 2008** Light straw-green; long, intense grapefruit and white peach flavours with seamless oak; Chablis-esque, thanks in part to Tasmanian acidity. Gold medal Tas Wine Show '10. Screwcap. 13.5% alc. **Rating** 96 **To** 2016 $30

♟♟♟♟♟ **Late Harvest Riesling 2009** **Rating** 90 **To** 2015 $20

♟♟♟♟ **Willo's Reserve Shiraz 2007** **Rating** 89 **To** 2016 $42
Riesling 2009 **Rating** 88 **To** 2014 $25

🍇 Verdun Park Wines   ★★★★☆

PO Box 41, Verdun, SA 5245 **Region** Adelaide Hills
T (08) 8388 7358 **F** (08) 8388 7357 **www.verdunparkwines.com.au** **Open** Not
Winemaker Michael Sykes **Est.** 2009 **Cases** 700 **Vyds** 2 ha
Verdun Park is owned by Sandy and Bob Voumard (with backgrounds in education and accountancy) and run with the assistance of their daughter Danielle and son-in-law Shaun (viticulturist). The initial release of 2009 Lyla Sauvignon Blanc was made from specifically selected contract-grown grapes, and went on to win a gold medal at the fiercely contested (for sauvignon blanc) Adelaide Hills Wine Show '09. A Shiraz will be released in 2011.

♟♟♟♟♟ **Lyla Adelaide Hills Sauvignon Blanc 2009** It is easy to see why this wine should have won a gold medal at the Adelaide Hills Wine Show '09; the bouquet and palate alike have intense and pure varietal expression, with ripe citrus and gooseberry fruit in abundance, the finish long and balanced. Screwcap. 12% alc. **Rating** 94 **To** 2012 $18

Veronique ★★★

PO Box 599, Angaston, SA 5353 **Region** Barossa Valley
T (08) 8565 3214 **www.**veroniquewines.com.au **Open** Not
Winemaker Domenic Torzi, Peter Manning **Est.** 2004 **Cases** 1400
Peter Manning, general manager of Angas Park Fruits, and wife Vicki moved to Mt McKenzie
in the 1990s. His wine consumption soon focused on Barossa shiraz, and he quickly became
a close drinking partner with Domenic Torzi of all things shiraz. By 2004 the Mannings
decided it was high time to produce a Barossa shiraz of their own, and, with the help of Torzi,
sourced grapes from three outstanding blocks. The vineyards also include mataro and grenache
(thoroughly excusable in the context) and sauvignon blanc.

♈♈♈♈ **Regions Barossa Shiraz 2007** Light colour; a light-bodied regional blend of
Greenock/Lyndoch/Eden Valley grapes that offers a mix of mocha, vanilla and
sweet berry fruit. Ready now. Screwcap. 14.5% alc. **Rating** 88 **To** 2012 $19

Victory Point Wines ★★★★☆

4 Holben Road, Cowaramup, WA 6284 **Region** Margaret River
T 0417 954 6555 **F** (08) 9388 2449 **www.**victorypointwines.com **Open** By appt
Winemaker Ian Bell (red), Mark Messenger (white) (Contract) **Est.** 1997 **Cases** 2500
Vyds 14.8 ha
Judith and Gary Berson (the latter a partner in the Perth office of a national law firm) have
set their aims high. With viticultural advice from Keith and Clare Mugford of Moss Wood,
they have established their vineyard without irrigation, emulating those of the Margaret River
pioneers (including Moss Wood). The plantings comprise 4.5 ha chardonnay, the remainder
the Bordeaux varieties, with cabernet sauvignon (6 ha), merlot (2 ha), cabernet franc (1 ha),
malbec (0.6 ha) and petit verdot (0.5 ha). In some vintages, a Petit Verdot and Malbec
Cabernet Franc are made in limited quantities.

♈♈♈♈♈ **The Mallee Root Margaret River 2007** A wine that is as much about its
✪ delicious finish and aftertaste as those things that provide the foundation for what
follows. It has slinky and supple fruit flavours, the 18% malbec making a major
contribution. Cabernet Sauvignon/Malbec/Merlot. Screwcap. 14% alc. **Rating** 94
To 2015 $26

♈♈♈♈♈ **Margaret River Cabernet Sauvignon 2007** **Rating** 92 **To** 2022 $30
Margaret River Petit Verdot 2007 **Rating** 92 **To** 2027 $40
Margaret River Rose 2009 **Rating** 90 **To** 2011 $23

Vinden Estate ★★★★

17 Gillards Road, Pokolbin, NSW 2320 **Region** Hunter Valley
T (02) 4998 7410 **F** (02) 4998 7175 **www.**vindenestate.com.au **Open** 7 days 10–5
Winemaker Guy Vinden, John Baruzzi (Consultant) **Est.** 1998 **Cases** 3500 **Vyds** 6.5 ha
Sandra and Guy Vinden have a beautiful home and cellar door, landscaped gardens and a
vineyard that includes shiraz (2.5 ha), merlot and alicante bouschet (2 ha each), with the
Brokenback mountain range in the distance. The winemaking is done onsite, using estate-
grown red grapes; semillon and chardonnay are purchased from other growers. The reds are
open-fermented, hand-plunged and basket-pressed.

♈♈♈♈♈ **Hunter Valley Semillon 2008** Lively, fresh and crisp, with nuances of citrus
✪ woven through more grassy/minerally characters. Screwcap. 10.5% alc. **Rating** 90
To 2016 $20
Estate Reserve Hunter Valley Verdelho 2009 Has all the extra fruit power
of the vintage, taking it into medium-bodied territory; the fruit salad is rich and
ripe, and a touch more acidity would have been welcome. Screwcap. 13.5% alc.
Rating 90 **To** 2012 $23

♈♈♈♈ **Hunter Valley Merlot 2006** **Rating** 88 **To** 2014 $28

Vinrock   ★★★★☆

23 George Street, Thebarton, SA 5031 (postal) **Region** McLaren Vale
T (08) 8408 8900 **F** (08) 8408 8966 www.vinrock.com **Open** Not
Winemaker Contract **Est.** 2004 **Cases** 6000 **Vyds** 30 ha
Owners Don Luca, Marco Iannetti and Anthony De Pizzol all have backgrounds in the wine
industry, none more than Don, a former board member of Tatachilla. He also planted the
Luca Vineyard in 1999 (20 ha of shiraz, 5 ha each of grenache and cabernet sauvignon). The
majority of the grapes are sold, but since 2004 limited quantities of wine have been made from
the best blocks in the vineyard. Exports to Malaysia, Singapore and China.

♀♀♀♀♀ **McLaren Vale Grenache 2008** Light but clear crimson hue; the fragrant
✪   bouquet leads into bright red fruits on the palate, savoury/spicy notes coming
        through on the back-palate and finish. Trophy McLaren Vale Wine Show '09.
        Screwcap. 15% alc. **Rating** 94 **To** 2015 $18.95

♀♀♀♀♀ **McLaren Vale Shiraz 2008** Dense, inky purple; full-bodied shiraz, with layers of
✪   black fruits plus the expected touch of bitter chocolate; has good texture, and no
        hint of dead fruit. Screwcap. 14.7% alc. **Rating** 93 **To** 2020 $19.95

Vintners Ridge Estate   ★★★

Lot 18 Veraison Place, Yallingup, Margaret River, WA 6285 **Region** Margaret River
T (08) 9447 2086 **F** (08) 9448 0018 www.vintnersridge.com.au **Open** By appt
Winemaker Vasse River Wines (Sharna Kowalczuk) **Est.** 2001 **Cases** 700 **Vyds** 2.1 ha
When Maree and Robin Adair purchased the Vintners Ridge vineyard in 2006, it had already
produced three crops, having been planted in Nov '01 (which is a perfectly permissible
establishment date). Small acorns, great oaks. The vineyard (cabernet sauvignon) overlooks the
picturesque Geographe Bay.

♀♀♀♀   **Margaret River Cabernet Sauvignon 2008** A perfectly generous helping
        of oak and soft tannins dominates the bouquet (oak) and palate (both); there is
        some nice blackcurrant fruit in the background. Screwcap. 14.5% alc. **Rating** 87
        To 2014 $30

Voyager Estate   ★★★★★

Lot 1 Stevens Road, Margaret River, WA 6285 **Region** Margaret River
T (08) 9757 6354 **F** (08) 9757 6494 www.voyagerestate.com.au **Open** 7 days 10–5
Winemaker Steve James, Travis Lemm **Est.** 1978 **Cases** 35 000 **Vyds** 118 ha
Voyager Estate has come a long way since it was acquired by Michael Wright (of the mining
family) in 1991. It now has a substantial high-quality vineyard, which means it can select the
best parcels of fruit for its own label, and supply surplus (but high-quality) wine to others. The
Cape Dutch–style tasting room and vast rose garden are a major tourist attraction. Exports to
the UK, the US and other major markets.

♀♀♀♀♀ **Margaret River Cabernet Sauvignon Merlot 2005** Set in the context of
        the six preceding vintages, this wine has developed an extra degree of polish
        and finesse, red fruit nuances emerging alongside the black fruit flavours of its
        youth; the line, length and balance are impeccable. Screwcap. 14% alc. **Rating** 96
        To 2025 $60
        Margaret River Shiraz 2008 A dark and savoury bouquet, showing highly
        polished black fruits and well-integrated oak; the abundant fruit gives way to firm,
        slightly gravelly tannins, but the fruit returns on the finish, leaving the impression
        of generosity and harmony. Screwcap. 14% alc. **Rating** 94 $32 BE

♀♀♀♀♀ **Margaret River Sauvignon Blanc Semillon 2009** A seamless blend of
✪   Sauvignon Blanc (60%)/Semillon (38%) plus the Pierro little touch of chardonnay;
        flows easily across the tongue, no one fruit character predominant, and has a gentle
        finish. Screwcap. 13.2% alc. **Rating** 93 **To** 2011 $24

Margaret River Chardonnay 2008 **Rating** 93 $42 BE
Girt by Sea Margaret River Cabernet Merlot 2008 **Rating** 92 $24

🍷🍷🍷🍷 Margaret River Chenin Blanc 2009 **Rating** 89 **To** 2013 $20

Wallington Wines ★★★

Eugowra Road, Canowindra, NSW 2904 **Region** Cowra
T (02) 6344 7153 **F** (02) 6344 7105 **www**.wallingtonwines.com.au **Open** By appt
Winemaker Murray Smith (Consultant), Margaret Wallington **Est.** 1992 **Cases** 1500
Vyds 17 ha

Margaret and the late Anthony Wallington began their Nyrang Creek Vineyard in 1994. Today the plantings include chardonnay (8 ha), shiraz (2 ha), cabernet sauvignon and grenache (1.5 ha each), and lesser amounts of petit verdot, mourvedre, tempranillo, cabernet franc, semillon and viognier. Most of the grape production is sold. Exports to the US.

🍷🍷🍷🍷 Canowindra Petit Verdot 2004 Has retained exceptional crimson-purple; the bouquet is promising, but you have to wonder whether the tannins will ever soften sufficiently to come back into balance. Screwcap. 14.7% alc. **Rating** 88 **To** 2017 $20

Walter Clappis Wine Co ★★★★

Rifle Range Road, McLaren Vale, SA 5171 **Region** McLaren Vale
T (08) 8323 8818 **F** (08) 8323 8610 **www**.hedonistwines.com.au **Open** Not
Winemaker Walter and Kimberly Clappis **Est.** 1982 **Cases** 10 000 **Vyds** 38 ha

Walter Clappis (once known as Bill) has been a stalwart of the McLaren Vale wine scene for decades. The estate plantings of shiraz (15 ha), cabernet sauvignon (12 ha), merlot (8 ha) and tempranillo (3 ha) are the cornerstone of his new business, which also provides the home for the separately owned Amicus business (see separate entry).

Wandin Valley Estate ★★★★★

Wilderness Road, Lovedale, NSW 2320 **Region** Hunter Valley
T (02) 4930 7317 **F** (02) 4930 7814 **www**.wandinvalley.com.au **Open** 7 days 10–5
Winemaker Matthew Burton **Est.** 1973 **Cases** 7000 **Vyds** 8.1 ha

At the time of going to press, the on-again, off-again sale of Wandin Valley Estate finally materialised, with Swish Wine adding another substantial business to its portfolio.

🍷🍷🍷🍷🍷 ✪ Reserve Hunter Valley Semillon 2009 Reserved indeed, but intense and fine; the two Wandin Valley Estate Semillons are closer to a normal style, with lemon, grass and mineral notes. A question of style, not quality. Screwcap. 10.5% alc. **Rating** 94 **To** 2024 $25

Reserve Hunter Valley Chardonnay 2008 Light but bright green; a very elegant wine, with surprising cool-grown characteristics; white peach and citrus intertwine with subtle, well-balanced French oak; good length. Screwcap. 14% alc. **Rating** 94 **To** 2013 $30

Bridie's Reserve Hunter Valley Shiraz 2007 Crimson hue; a fragrant bouquet of red and black fruit leads into an elegant, medium-bodied palate with supple texture and very good balance; nice tension between sweet fruit notes and savoury, earthy, regional inputs. Diam. 13.5% alc. **Rating** 94 **To** 2022 $40

🍷🍷🍷🍷½ Reserve Hunter Valley Chardonnay 2009 **Rating** 93 **To** 2016 $30

✪ Single Vineyard Hunter Valley Semillon 2009 Classic powder puff bouquet hinting at the mineral core of the palate, which is fine, elegant and pure; lemon, lemon zest and mineral. Screwcap. 11% alc. **Rating** 92 **To** 2019 $20

Single Vineyard Hunter Valley Viognier 2009 **Rating** 90 **To** 2012 $25

🍷🍷🍷🍷 Pavilion Hunter Valley Rose 2009 **Rating** 89 **To** 2012 $20

Wangolina Station ★★★★

Cnr Southern Ports Highway/Limestone Coast Road, Kingston SE, SA 5275
Region Mount Benson
T (08) 8768 6187 **F** (08) 8768 6149 **www**.wangolina.com.au **Open** 7 days 10–5
Winemaker Anita Goode **Est.** 2001 **Cases** 4500 **Vyds** 13 ha
Four generations of the Goode family have been graziers at Wangolina Station, but now Anita Goode has broken with tradition by becoming a vigneron. She has planted sauvignon blanc (5 ha), shiraz (3 ha), cabernet sauvignon and semillon (2 ha each), and pinot gris (1 ha).

♥♥♥♥♡ **Section 67 Limestone Coast Cabernet Sauvignon 2008** Good colour; is flooded with an abundance of ripe (not overripe) cassis and blackcurrant fruit on bouquet and palate alike; the tannins are soft, the balance and length good. Screwcap. 14.5% alc. **Rating** 90 **To** 2018 $24
Mount Benson Cabernet Sauvignon Shiraz 2008 Deep, purple-crimson; while full-flavoured, is only medium-bodied thanks to soft tannins in support of the luscious array of red and blackcurrant fruits; the oak subtle. Screwcap. 14% alc. **Rating** 90 **To** 2016 $18

♥♥♥♥ **Section 67 Limestone Coast Shiraz 2008 Rating** 89 **To** 2015 $22
Mount Benson Sauvignon Blanc 2009 Rating 88 **To** 2010 $18

Wanted Man ★★★★☆

School House Lane, Heathcote, Vic 3523 **Region** Heathcote
T (03) 9654 4664 **F** (03) 9639 2038 **www**.wantedman.com.au **Open** Not
Winemaker Andrew Clarke, Peter Bartholomew, Matt Harrop **Est.** 1996 **Cases** 1500
Vyds 10.3 ha
The Wanted Man vineyard was planted in 1996, and has been managed by Andrew Clarke since 2000, producing Jinks Creek's Heathcote Shiraz. That wine was sufficiently impressive to lead Andrew and partner Peter Bartholomew (a Melbourne restaurateur) to purchase the vineyard in 2006, and give it its own identity. The vineyard has shiraz (5 ha), marsanne (2 ha), viognier (1.5 ha), roussanne (1 ha) and dolcetto (0.8 ha). The quirky Ned Kelly label is the work of Mark Knight, cartoonist for the *Herald Sun*. Exports to the UK, Canada, Denmark, France and Hong Kong.

♥♥♥♥♥ **Single Vineyard Heathcote Marsanne Viognier 2009** Bright straw-green; while both varieties come from the northern Rhône Valley, the blend doesn't always work well. Here it succeeds brilliantly, the marsanne providing structure, the viognier fruit flavour in abundance without phenolics. Screwcap. 13% alc. **Rating** 94 **To** 2015 $34

♥♥♥♥ **Pink Ned 2009 Rating** 89 **To** 2011 $19.50

Wantirna Estate ★★★★★

Bushy Park Lane, Wantirna South, Vic 3152 **Region** Yarra Valley
T (03) 9801 2367 **F** (03) 9887 0225 **www**.wantirnaestate.com.au **Open** Not
Winemaker Maryann and Reg Egan **Est.** 1963 **Cases** 900 **Vyds** 4.2 ha
Reg and Tina Egan were among the early movers in the rebirth of the Yarra Valley. The vineyard surrounds the house in which they live, which also incorporates the winery, which explains how in the early years Reg (with help from Tina) was able to combine his career as full-time solicitor and then barrister with that of grapegrower and winemaker. Daughter Maryann Egan is now one of the owners, and has assumed the role of winemaker, having filled that role at Domaine Chandon in the early years of its development. Exports to Hong Kong, Singapore and Japan.

♥♥♥♥♥ **Isabella Chardonnay 2008** Full straw-green; has a complex array of fig, cashew and oak aromas, the nectarine and citrus fruit coming through strongly on the palate, which, while generous, has the hallmark Yarra Valley length. Diam. 14.2% alc. **Rating** 94 **To** 2013 $60

Lily Pinot Noir 2008 Light, clear crimson-red; an expressive bouquet with a mix of red fruits and spices, the palate following suit, the tannins adding some forest floor notes. Diam. 14.2% alc. **Rating** 94 To 2015 $65

Lily Pinot Noir 2007 Light but bright and clear colour; a very elegant and precisely defined pinot, reminiscent of Mount Mary style, and will have the same unexpected ability to age. Diam. 13.5% alc. **Rating** 94 To 2015 $65

Amelia Yarra Valley Cabernet Sauvignon 2007 Good colour; is what can only be described as a suave wine, with a complex web of blackcurrant, spice and cedary oak on the bouquet and the medium-bodied, finely textured, palate. Diam. 13% alc. **Rating** 94 To 2020 $65

ȚȚȚȚȚ Isabella Chardonnay 2007 Rating 92 To 2013 $60
Amelia Yarra Valley Cabernet Sauvignon Merlot 2006 Rating 90
To 2015 $65

Warrabilla ★★★★★

6152 Murray Valley Highway, Rutherglen, Vic 3685 **Region** Rutherglen
T (02) 6035 7242 **F** (02) 6035 7298 **www**.warrabillawines.com.au **Open** 7 days 10–5
Winemaker Andrew Sutherland Smith **Est.** 1990 **Cases** 10 000 **Vyds** 20 ha
Andrew Sutherland Smith and wife Carol have built a formidable reputation for their wines, headed by the Reserve trio of Durif, Cabernet Sauvignon and Shiraz, quintessential examples of Rutherglen red wine at its best. Their vineyard has been extended with the planting of some riesling and zinfandel. Andrew spent 15 years with All Saints, McWilliam's, Yellowglen, Fairfield and Chambers before setting up Warrabilla, and his accumulated experience shines through in the wines.

ȚȚȚȚȚ Reserve Shiraz 2009 Deep, intense crimson-purple; the red wines of Warrabilla
✪ defy logic: why would you even contemplate 17% alcohol in the first place, but how do you end up with a shiraz that has no alcohol warmth, let alone heat, and not be extractive? And be drinkable now? While it is not a style I particularly enjoy, it is hard to deny its place. Diam. **Rating** 94 To 2017 $24

✪ Reserve Durif 2009 Similar colour to Parola's; strange how you can regard a wine with 16.5% alcohol as luscious and palate-friendly – but not so strange when it was tasted after one at 18% alcohol; there is warmth here, but not the heat of Parola's, and the tannins provide texture. Diam. 16.5% alc. **Rating** 94 To 2020 $24

ȚȚȚȚȚ Reserve Durif 2008 Rating 92 To 2014 $24
✪ Reserve Vintage Port 2006 It hardly needs be said, has very deep colour; deliberately made in Herculean style, the luscious fruit absorbing the alcohol and tannins. Will live for decades if that is what you wish. Diam. 19.5% alc. **Rating** 92 To 2036 $22
Parola's Limited Release Shiraz 2008 Rating 91 To 2015 $32
Reserve Shiraz 2008 Rating 90 To 2015 $24
Parola's Limited Release Durif 2009 Rating 90 To 2029 $32
✪ Reserve Zinfandel 2009 The colour is suggestive of relatively high pH, the red and black spicy fruits ranging from cherry to raspberry; does have balance and length. Diam. 15% alc. **Rating** 90 To 2015 $18

ȚȚȚȚ Reserve Cabernet Sauvignon 2009 Rating 89 To 2019 $24

Warramate ★★★★★

27 Maddens Lane, Gruyere, Vic 3770 **Region** Yarra Valley
T (03) 5964 9219 **F** (03) 5964 9572 **www**.warramatewines.com.au **Open** 7 days 10–6
Winemaker David Church **Est.** 1970 **Cases** 2000 **Vyds** 6.6 ha
A long-established and perfectly situated winery reaping the full benefits of its 40-year-old vines; recent plantings have increased production. All the wines are well made, the Shiraz providing further proof (if such be needed) of the suitability of the variety to the region; has moved to another level since son David Church took the full mantle of winemaker.

🍷🍷🍷🍷🍷 White Label Yarra Valley Shiraz 2008 Similar bright red-crimson to the Black Label, but with significantly greater aroma and flavour intensity from vines planted in 1970; that intensity is achieved effortlessly, the fruit still in a red spectrum, the tannins and French oak in immaculate balance. Screwcap. 13.5% alc. **Rating** 95 To 2023 $50

White Label Yarra Valley Cabernet Merlot 2007 Excellent colour, deep crimson-purple; a luscious wine with waves of blackcurrant fruit supported by fine tannins and good acidity. Screwcap. 13.5% alc. **Rating** 94 **To** 2020 $35

✪ Black Label Yarra Valley Cabernet Sauvignon 2008 Good colour; impressively concentrated blackcurrant fruit on the bouquet flows directly through to the medium- to full-bodied, juicy palate, supported by French oak; this is a delicious cabernet. Screwcap. 13.5% alc. **Rating** 94 **To** 2025 $23

🍷🍷🍷🍷🍷 White Label Yarra Valley Pinot Noir 2008 Clear crimson; fragrant red and
✪ black cherry aromas are sustained on the supple, well-balanced palate, which has considerable length and very good mouthfeel. Screwcap. 13.5% alc. **Rating** 93 To 2015 $25

✪ Black Label Yarra Valley Shiraz 2008 Bright and spicy red berry fruits on the bouquet and light- to medium-bodied palate; good length and balance, French oak hovering in the background. From vines planted in 2000 as part of the vineyard extension. Screwcap. 13.5% alc. **Rating** 93 **To** 2018 $23

Warrego Wines   ★★★☆

9 Seminary Road, Marburg, Qld 4306 **Region** Queensland Coastal
T (07) 5464 4400 **F** (07) 5464 4800 **www**.warregowines.com.au **Open** 7 days 10–5
Winemaker Kevin Watson, Jason Hannay, Taka Akizawa **Est.** 2000 **Cases** 3000 **Vyds** 0.2 ha
Kevin Watson completed his wine science degree at CSU, and the primary purpose of his business is custom winemaking for the many small growers in the region, including all the clients of Peter Scudamore-Smith MW. In 2001, the Marburg Custom Crush company developed a state-of-the-art winery (as the cliché goes), cellar door and restaurant. $500 000 in government funding, local business investment and significant investment from China provided the funds, and the complex opened in 2002. Since then, the business has expanded further with a public share raising. The own-brand Warrego wines come from grapes purchased in various regions, and a tiny amount of estate-grown viognier (0.2 ha). Part proceeds from each bottle sold goes to the Australian Koala Foundation. Warrego is Qld's only certified organic winery. Exports to Canada.

🍷🍷🍷🍷🍷 Very Own Viognier 2009 Now this is something different for viognier, quite
✪ aromatic, with a citrussy tang to its flavour and no phenolics whatsoever. Whether it is particularly varietal is another question. ProCork. 12.5% alc. **Rating** 90 To 2013 $19.50

🍷🍷🍷🍷 Reserve Shiraz 2007 **Rating** 89 **To** 2017 $35.50
Seminary Shiraz 2008 **Rating** 87 **To** 2015 $22.50

Warrenmang Vineyard & Resort   ★★★★☆

Mountain Creek Road, Moonambel, Vic 3478 **Region** Pyrenees
T (03) 5467 2233 **F** (03) 5467 2309 **www**.warrenmang.com.au **Open** 7 days 10–5
Winemaker Sean Schwager **Est.** 1974 **Cases** 8000 **Vyds** 32.1 ha
Luigi and Athelie Bazzani continue to watch over Warrenmang; a new, partially underground barrel room with earthen walls has been completed, wine quality remains high, and the accommodation and restaurant underpin the business. But if a fair offer were made, it would be accepted. Exports to Denmark, Poland, Taiwan and Singapore.

🍷🍷🍷🍷🍷 Black Puma Shiraz 2007 Deep colour, some development; a very powerful shiraz, with multiple layers of flavour in a dark berry spectrum plus a goodly amount of spice and licorice; small batch-fermented, basket-pressed and 18 months in French oak. Stained cork. 15% alc. **Rating** 94 **To** 2020 $80

♀♀♀♀ Pyrenees Sauvignon Blanc 2009 Rating 89 To 2011 $20
✪ Bazzani Pyrenees Shiraz Cabernet 2006 A nice medium-bodied wine, easier
to approach than bigger Pyrenees reds; has spice and mocha overtones to its red
and black fruits, the tannins supple. Screwcap. 14.5% alc. **Rating** 88 **To** 2014 $13

Water Wheel ★★★☆

Bridgewater-on-Loddon, Bridgewater, Vic 3516 **Region** Bendigo
T (03) 5437 3060 **F** (03) 5437 3082 **www.**waterwheelwine.com **Open** Mon–Fri 9–5,
w'ends & public hols 12–4
Winemaker Peter Cumming, Bill Trevaskis **Est.** 1972 **Cases** 35 000 **Vyds** 134 ha
Peter Cumming, with more than two decades of winemaking under his belt, has quietly built
on the reputation of Water Wheel year by year. The winery is owned by the Cumming family,
which has farmed in the Bendigo region for 50+ years, with horticulture and viticulture
special areas of interest. Over half the vineyard area is planted to shiraz (75 ha), followed by
chardonnay, sauvignon blanc (15 ha each), cabernet sauvignon, malbec (10 ha each), petit
verdot, semillon and roussanne (3 ha each). The wines are of remarkably consistent quality and
modest prices. Exports to the UK, the US and other major markets.

♀♀♀♀♀ Memsie Homestead Shiraz Cabernet Sauvignon Malbec 2008 The front
✪ label should read Shiraz Malbec Cabernet, but that is a pedantic quibble about a
full-flavoured wine, with blackberry and blackcurrant fruit from the minor partners.
Great value, and will cellar well. Screwcap. 14% alc. **Rating** 90 **To** 2017 $14

♀♀♀♀ Memsie Chardonnay Sauvignon Blanc Semillon Roussanne 2008 A
✪ strange blend that actually works very well, because the chardonnay is transformed
by the zest that the other varieties bring to the table. Screwcap. 13% alc. **Rating** 89
To 2011 $14
Bendigo Shiraz 2008 Rating 89 To 2018 $20
Bendigo Cabernet Sauvignon 2007 Rating 89 To 2017 $19
Bendigo Petit Verdot 2008 Rating 88 To 2013 $19

Watershed Wines ★★★★★

Cnr Bussell Highway/Darch Road, Margaret River, WA 6285 **Region** Margaret River
T (08) 9758 8633 **F** (08) 9757 3999 **www.**watershedwines.com.au **Open** 7 days 10–5
Winemaker Severine Logan **Est.** 2002 **Cases** 105 000 **Vyds** 187 ha
Watershed Wines has been established by a syndicate of investors, and no expense has been
spared in establishing the substantial vineyard and building a striking cellar door, and a 200-
seat café and restaurant. Situated towards the southern end of the Margaret River region, its
neighbours include Voyager Estate and Leeuwin Estate. Exports to the UK, the US and other
major markets.

♀♀♀♀♀ Awakening Margaret River Sauvignon Blanc 2008 Pale bright colour; the
✪ complex bouquet reveals 50% barrel fermentation in French oak, but also bright
citrus and grass aromas; the palate is tight, intense and long, the subtle oak infusion
adding as much to the texture as flavour, the finish crisp and clean. Gold medal
Sydney Wine Show '09. Screwcap. 12.5% alc. **Rating** 94 **To** 2011 $24.95
Awakening Single Vineyard Margaret River Chardonnay 2009 Bright
colour; pure grapefruit and grilled almond bouquet, showing a little spice from
fine French oak; the palate is tightly wound and full of life, with zesty grapefruit
again providing the backbone of flavour; fresh vanilla provides seasoning, and the
finish is long and lively. Screwcap. 14% alc. **Rating** 94 **To** 2020 $44.95 BE
Awakening Margaret River Cabernet Sauvignon 2008 Bright colour;
crushed red fruits and a fragrant violet note to the bouquet; full-bodied with the
oak coming to the fore on the palate; firmly structured and tightly wound, the
concentration of fruit is unquestionable; a little time is needed to settle things
down. Screwcap. 13.5% alc. **Rating** 94 **To** 2018 $54.95 BE

♀♀♀♀♀ **Shades Margaret River Sauvignon Blanc Semillon 2009** A lively and
✪ fragrant bouquet leads into a palate that gains pace and intensity from the
midpoint to the finish and aftertaste, with an array of citrus, passionfruit and grass
notes, the aftertaste lingering. Screwcap. 12% alc. **Rating** 93 **To** 2011 $16.95

✪ **Shades Margaret River Unoaked Chardonnay 2008** Classy unoaked style,
with the combination of white peach and grapefruit expected from Margaret
River, sustained and lengthened by good acidity. Unoaked chardonnay of high
quality. Screwcap. 13.5% alc. **Rating** 93 **To** 2012 $16.95

✪ **Shades Margaret River Rose 2009** Vivid pink hue; savoury bouquet, with
a little struck match framing the red fruits; quite dry, with plenty of flavour and
interest, continuing with surprising length and complexity for the style. Screwcap.
13.5% alc. **Rating** 91 **To** 2012 $16.95 BE
Senses Margaret River Shiraz 2008 **Rating** 90 **To** 2018 $24.95 BE

♀♀♀♀ **Senses Margaret River Sauvignon Blanc 2009** **Rating** 89 **To** 2012 $24.95 BE

Waterton Vineyards   ★★★☆

PO Box 125, Beaconsfield, Tas 7270 **Region** Northern Tasmania
T (03) 6394 7214 **F** (03) 6394 7614 **www**.watertonhall.com.au **Open** Not
Winemaker Winemaking Tasmania (Julian Alcorso) **Est.** 2006 **Cases** 300 **Vyds** 2 ha
Jennifer Baird and Peter Cameron purchased this remarkable property in 2002. Waterton
Hall was built in the 1850s and modified extensively by well-known neo-gothic architect
Alexander North in 1910. The property was owned by the Catholic church from 1949–96,
variously used as a school, a boys' home and retreat. Following its sale the new owners
planted 1 ha of riesling at the end of the 1990s, and then Jennifer and Peter extended the
vineyard with 1 ha of shiraz, electing to sell the riesling until 2006, when part was made
under the Waterton label. The plans are to use the existing buildings to provide a restaurant,
accommodation and function facilities.

♀♀♀♀♀ **Late Picked Riesling 2008** Crisp, clean, firm; at low end of sweetness, but will
age very well. Screwcap. 10.6% alc. **Rating** 90 **To** 2015 $23.50

♀♀♀♀ **Riesling 2009** **Rating** 89 **To** 2015 $23.50
Shiraz 2008 **Rating** 89 **To** 2017 $34.50

Watson Wine Group   ★★★★☆

PO Box 167, Fullarton, SA 5063 **Region** Coonawarra
T (08) 8338 3200 **F** (08) 8338 3244 **www**.rexwatsonwines.com **Open** Not
Winemaker Michelle Heagney, Greg Tilbrook **Est.** 1997 **Cases** 240 000 **Vyds** 347 ha
Rex Watson started in the Australian wine industry in 1991 and began growing wine grapes
in Coonawarra in '97. In 1999 he began planting the most significant modern vineyard
development in Coonawarra. In less than five years this was built into a venture that now
controls and manages almost 350 ha over three vineyards, all close to the historic township of
Coonawarra and well within the Coonawarra GI. Production under the Watson Wine Group
(200 000 cases made by Michelle Heagney) and Coonawarra Premium Vineyards (40 000 cases
made by Greg Tilbrook) has soared from the previous total of 80 000 cases. Exports to the US,
Canada, Sweden, Russia, Singapore, Malaysia, India, Sri Lanka, Taiwan, China and NZ.

♀♀♀♀♀ **Rex Watson Coonawarra Sauvignon Blanc 2009** Light straw-green; a major
✪ surprise, with delicious varietal expression on the fragrant bouquet and palate
alike, the flavours ranging through kiwi fruit, passionfruit and grapefruit; achieves
elegance and intensity in the same breath or sip. Screwcap. 12.5% alc. **Rating** 94
To 2012 $16.95

♀♀♀♀♀ **Coonawarra Premium Vineyards Cabernet Sauvignon 2008** Strong
✪ colour; potent blackcurrant and cassis permeates both bouquet and palate,
largely drowning out the tannin and oak inputs. Screwcap. 14% alc. **Rating** 92
To 2030 $24.95

Coonawarra Premium Vineyards Reserve Cabernet Sauvignon 2008
Rating 92 To 2018 $24.95
Coonawarra Premium Vineyards Sauvignon Blanc 2008 Rating 90
To 2010 $24.95
Coonawarra Premium Vineyards Shiraz 2008 Rating 90 To 2020 $24.95

ΨΨΨΨ   Rex Watson Coonawarra Shiraz 2008 Rating 87 To 2014 $16.95 BE

Wattle Ridge Vineyard ★★★

Loc 11950 Boyup-Greenbushes Road, Greenbushes, WA 6254 **Region** Blackwood Valley
T (08) 9764 3594 **F** (08) 9764 3594 **www**.wattleridgewines.com.au **Open** Thurs–Mon 11–5
Winemaker Contract **Est.** 1997 **Cases** 1500 **Vyds** 6.4 ha
James (Jim) and Vicky Henderson's Nelson Vineyard is planted to cabernet sauvignon (4.2 ha),
merlot, verdelho (0.8 ha each) and sauvignon blanc (0.6 ha). The wines are sold by mail order
and through the cellar door, which also offers light meals, crafts and local produce. Exports to
the UK, Singapore and Japan.

ΨΨΨΨ   Two Tinsmiths Old Bishop Cabernet Sauvignon 2008 Purple-red; savoury
        black fruits on the bouquet and palate are accompanied by ample oak (75%
        French/25% America); as with the '07, there is an unexpected break in the line on
        the back-palate. Screwcap. 13% alc. **Rating** 88 To 2017 $16

Wayawu Estate ★★★★

1070 Bellarine Highway, Wallington, Vic 3221 **Region** Geelong
T (03) 5250 4457 **F** (03) 5250 4459 **www**.wayawawinerybb.com.au **Open** Tues–Sun 10–5
Winemaker John and Stephanie Henry **Est.** 2004 **Cases** 100 **Vyds** 0.5 ha
In 2004 John and Stephanie Henry planted 0.5 ha of shiraz, with four different clones, and
the results so far have been impressive. The name comes from northeast Arnhem Land, and
means 'where the land touches the Milky Way'. The Henrys have been given permission by
Arnhem Land artist, Nami Maymuru-White, to reproduce one of her paintings of the Milky
Way on their label.

ΨΨΨΨΨ   Harry's Shiraz 2008 A striking label; bright crimson; the wine has an intense
✪   bouquet and a full-bodied palate of plum, crushed raspberries and cherries; needs a
        little more structure for top points. Diam. 14% alc. **Rating** 92 To 2023 $20

Wedgetail Estate ★★★★★

40 Hildebrand Road, Cottles Bridge, Vic 3099 **Region** Yarra Valley
T (03) 9714 8661 **F** (03) 9714 8676 **www**.wedgetailestate.com.au **Open** W'ends &
public hols 12–5, or by appt, closed from 25 Dec–reopens Australia Day w'end
Winemaker Guy Lamothe **Est.** 1994 **Cases** 1500 **Vyds** 5.5 ha
Canadian-born photographer Guy Lamothe and partner Dena Ashbolt started making wine
in the basement of their Carlton home in the 1980s. The idea of their own vineyard started
to take hold, and the search for a property began. Then, in their words, 'one Sunday, when we
were "just out for a drive", we drove past our current home. The slopes are amazing, true goat
terrain, and it is on these steep slopes that in 1994 we planted our first block of pinot noir.'
While the vines were growing Lamothe enrolled in the winegrowing course at CSU, having
already gained practical experience working in the Yarra Valley (Tarrawarra), the Mornington
Peninsula and Meursault (Burgundy). 2008 marked the 10th vintage for Wedgetail Estate
which, like many others in the Yarra Valley, suffered significant damage from frost and smoke in
'07, smoke and fire in '09. Exports to the UK, Canada, Singapore, Hong Kong and China.

ΨΨΨΨΨ   Single Vineyard Yarra Valley Shiraz 2008 Bright colour; stacked with intense
        cool-grown shiraz aromas and flavours ranging through blood plum to black
        cherry, licorice, spice and pepper, with a seductive generosity on the mid-palate,
        but no hint of overripe fruit. Screwcap. 14.5% alc. **Rating** 95 To 2020 $40

The North Face 2008 Impressive depth of colour; almost luscious blackcurrant and cassis fruit with great generosity on the palate is amplified by quality cedary oak; the tannins are invisible. Cabernet Sauvignon/Merlot. Screwcap. 14% alc. Rating 95 To 2020 $42

Single Vineyard Yarra Valley Chardonnay 2008 Bright pale green-straw; fine and elegant, with nectarine, white peach, citrus and mineral elements all intermingling, oak a junior partner. Screwcap. 13% alc. Rating 94 To 2015 $35

Reserve Pinot Noir 2008 Bright and clear colour; a lively and elegant wine, the bouquet fragrant, the palate delivering finely tuned texture and spicy structure to the black cherry fruit and spicy tannins. Diam. 13.5% alc. Rating 94 To 2015 $65

ΨΨΨΨΨ **Single Vineyard Yarra Valley Pinot Noir 2008** Rating 90 To 2014 $42

Wehl's Mount Benson Vineyards   ★★★★

Wrights Bay Road, Mount Benson, SA 5275 **Region** Mount Benson
T (08) 8768 6251 **F** (08) 8678 6251 **www**.wehlsmtbensonvineyards.com.au
Open 7 days 10–4
Winemaker Contract **Est.** 1989 **Cases** 2000 **Vyds** 20 ha

Peter and Leah Wehl were the first to plant vines in the Mount Benson area, beginning the establishment of their vineyard, planted to shiraz, cabernet sauvignon and merlot, in 1989. While primarily grapegrowers, they have moved into winemaking via contract makers, and have increased the range of wines available.

ΨΨΨΨΨ **Shiraz 2007** Deep red-purple; rich plum, blackberry and mocha aromas lead into a medium- to full-bodied palate, with a bed of ripe tannins providing plenty of structure for the opulent fruit. Screwcap. 14.5% alc. Rating 90 To 2020 $24

✪ **Cabernet Sauvignon Merlot 2007** It's a tough school when a wine such as this is tasted in a throng of very good Margaret River cabernet merlots; the more you focus on the blackcurrant fruit, the more the tannins impose themselves; nonetheless the wine does have potential with a few more years in bottle. Screwcap. 14.5% alc. Rating 90 To 2017 $19

Cabernet Sauvignon 2007 Healthy purple-red; very much in the Wehl style, with strong varietal fruit and strong savoury tannins providing the base for the medium- to full-bodied palate; needs time in bottle or a charcoal-grilled rump steak (or both) to bring out the best still locked in the wine. Screwcap. 14.5% alc. Rating 90 To 2020 $24

Wendouree   ★★★★★

Wendouree Road, Clare, SA 5453 **Region** Clare Valley
T (08) 8842 2896 **Open** Not
Winemaker Tony Brady **Est.** 1895 **Cases** 2000 **Vyds** 12 ha

An iron fist in a velvet glove best describes these extraordinary wines. They are fashioned with passion and precision from the very old vineyard (shiraz, cabernet sauvignon, malbec, mataro and muscat of alexandria), with its unique terroir, by Tony and Lita Brady, who rightly see themselves as custodians of a priceless treasure. The 100-year-old stone winery is virtually unchanged from the day it was built; this is in every sense a treasure beyond price. I should explain, I buy three wines from Wendouree every year, always including the Shiraz. This is the only way I am able to provide tasting notes, and it's almost inevitably a last-minute exercise as I suddenly realise there are no notes in place. Moreover, Wendouree has never made any comment about its wines, and I realise that the change in style away from full-bodied to medium-bodied seems a permanent fixture of the landscape, not a one-off result of a given vintage. The best news of all is that I may actually get to drink some of the Wendourees I have bought over the past 10 years before I die, and not have to rely on my few remaining bottles from the 1970s (and rather more from the '80s and '90s). The Lord moves in mysterious ways.

ŶŶŶŶŶ Shiraz Malbec 2006 More purple than the Shiraz Mataro; consistently with the colour, has more drive and focus; the mouthfeel and length of the medium- to full-bodied palate are excellent, with almost juicy fruit sparking off the fine-grained tannins. Great now, great in another 15 years. Cork. 13.2% alc. **Rating** 96 To 2026 $48

Shiraz Mataro 2006 Full red-purple; rich and luscious dark berry fruits and some meaty characters run through the full-bodied palate, the tannins ripe and plentiful. A robust wine needing at least five years before you touch it. Cork. 14% alc. **Rating** 94 To 2031 $45

Were Estate ★★★★★
Cnr Wildberry Road/Johnson Road, Wilyabrup, WA 6280 **Region** Margaret River
T (08) 9755 6273 **F** (08) 9755 6195 **www**.wereestate.com.au **Open** W'ends, public & school hols 10.30–5
Winemaker Clive Otto (Contract) **Est.** 1998 **Cases** 4000 **Vyds** 9.72 ha
Owners Diane and Gordon Davies say, 'We are different. We're original, we're bold, we're innovative.' This is all reflected in the design of the unusual back labels (incorporating pictures of the innumerable pairs of braces that real estate agent Gordon wears at work in Perth), in the early move to screwcaps for both white and red wines, and, for that matter, in the underground trickle irrigation system (plus a move towards to organic methods) in their Margaret River vineyard, which can be controlled from Perth. Exports to Hong Kong, China and Singapore.

ŶŶŶŶŶ ✪ Single Vineyard Reserve Margaret River Chardonnay 2008 A fragrant and multifaceted array of stone fruit and citrus on the bouquet is followed by an exemplary palate, with intense and juicy fruit backed by citrussy acidity; sensitive oak handling a plus. Screwcap. 14% alc. **Rating** 95 To 2014 $30

✪ Margaret River Shiraz 2007 Bright colour; a fragrant bouquet with red and black fruits plus a touch of spice, then a penetrating and potent palate with intense plum, spice and blackberry fruit. Delicious. Screwcap. 14.5% alc. **Rating** 94 To 2016 $22

ŶŶŶŶŶ ✪ Margaret River Sauvignon Blanc 2009 An attractive wine that marries ripe tropical fruit (particularly passionfruit) with a subtle touch of oak; falters ever so slightly on the finish. Screwcap. 14% alc. **Rating** 92 To 2011 $22

✪ Margaret River Cabernet Sauvignon 2007 A fragrant bouquet of cassis and red fruits leads into an elegant, expressive medium-bodied palate with particularly good length. Screwcap. 13.5% alc. **Rating** 92 To 2022 $22

Margaret River Semillon Sauvignon Blanc 2009 Rating 90 To 2012 $19

ŶŶŶŶ Margaret River Shiraz Cabernet 2007 Rating 88 To 2013 $19

West Cape Howe Wines ★★★★★
Lot 14923 Muir Highway, Mount Barker, WA 6324 **Region** Mount Barker
T (08) 99892 1444 **F** (08) 9848 2903 **www**.westcapehowewines.com.au **Open** 7 days 10–5
Winemaker Gavin Berry, Dave Cleary, Andrew Siddell **Est.** 1997 **Cases** 75 000 **Vyds** 105 ha
After a highly successful seven years, West Cape Howe founders Brenden and Kylie Smith moved on, selling the business to a partnership including Gavin Berry (until 2004, senior winemaker at Plantagenet) and viticulturist Rob Quenby. As well as existing fruit sources, West Cape Howe now has the 80-ha Lansdale Vineyard, planted in 1989, as its primary fruit source. In March '09 it purchased the 7700-tonne capacity Goundrey winery and 237-ha Goundrey estate vineyards from CWA; the grapes from these plantings will be purchased by CWA for years to come. The move vastly increases West Cape Howe's business base, and facilitates contract-winemaking to generate cash flow. Exports to the UK, the US, Denmark, Germany, Singapore and Hong Kong.

ΥΥΥΥΥ Book Ends Great Southern Cabernet Sauvignon 2007 Very good colour;
✪   a rich cabernet with abundant varietal flavour thanks to picking at the right
       moment and skilled blending; achieves maximum expression while only medium-
       bodied, for the savoury tannins will underpin long-term development. Screwcap.
       14% alc. **Rating** 95 **To** 2020 $25

✪   Great Southern Riesling 2009 A classically austere style that reveals more
       and more on retasting; it has immaculate balance, structure and length, with a
       continuing interplay between lime and mineral; deserves five years to fully open
       up. Screwcap. 12% alc. **Rating** 94 **To** 2019 $19

✪   Sauvignon Blanc 2009 Juicy, crisp and lively, with an appealing mix of citrus,
       grass and gooseberry fruit; excellent acidity gives the wine a long and clean finish.
       Screwcap. 12.5% alc. **Rating** 94 **To** 2011 $19

ΥΥΥΥΥ Semillon Sauvignon Blanc 2009 **Rating** 93 **To** 2012 $16
✪   Unwooded Chardonnay 2009 A wine style to seduce the most ardent
       sauvignon blanc lover, with crisp and vibrant grapefruit and nectarine flavours
       running through to the long, clean finish. Screwcap. 13% alc. **Rating** 93
       To 2012 $16

✪   Tempranillo 2008 Obviously grown in a climate (cool) that suits it; red cherry
       and raspberry fruit has a nice cut, making the wine fresh and lively, but not green.
       Screwcap. 14% alc. **Rating** 90 **To** 2013 $19

ΥΥΥΥ Rose 2009 **Rating** 89 **To** 2010 $16

Westend Estate Wines   ★★★★☆

1283 Brayne Road, Griffith, NSW 2680 **Region** Riverina
T (02) 6969 0800 **F** (02) 6962 1673 **www**.westendestate.com **Open** Mon–Fri 8.30–5,
w'ends 10–4
Winemaker William Calabria, Bryan Currie, Sally Whittaker **Est.** 1945 **Cases** 300 000
Vyds 52 ha
Along with a number of Riverina producers, Westend Estate has made a successful move to
lift both the quality and the packaging of its wines. Its leading 3 Bridges range, which has an
impressive array of gold medals to its credit since being first released in 1997, is anchored in
part on estate vineyards. Bill Calabria has been involved in the Australian wine industry for
more than 40 years, and is understandably proud of the achievements both of Westend and
the Riverina wine industry as a whole. It is moving with the times, increasing its plantings
of durif, and introducing aglianico, nero d'avola, and st macaire (a problematic variety not
recognised by the ultimate authority of such matters, Jancis Robinson, who says it is a small
town in the Bordeaux region). These new plantings have paralleled an increase in Westend's
wine production. Equally importantly, it is casting its net over Hilltops and the Canberra
District, premium regions not too far from home. Exports to the UK, the US and other
major markets.

ΥΥΥΥΥ 3 Bridges Reserve Botrytis 2007 Deeper gold; more complex and better
       balanced than the Golden Mist by acidity, cumquat marmalade and some toffee;
       long finish. Cork. 12.5% alc. **Rating** 94 **To** 2012 $24.95

ΥΥΥΥΥ 3 Bridges Museum Release Botrytis Semillon 2000 **Rating** 93 **To** 2011 $25
✪   3 Bridges Golden Mist Botrytis 2008 Already deep gold; intensely luscious
       and sweet yellow peach, cumquat and vanilla; not quite enough acidity. Screwcap.
       11% alc. **Rating** 92 **To** 2011 $19.95

✪   Cool Climate Series Canberra District Riesling 2009 Some colour
       deepening, although the hue is good; utterly correct lime/citrus/mineral varietal
       fruit on bouquet and palate alike; a sturdy, well-balanced wine, for consumption
       over the next few years. Screwcap. 12% alc. **Rating** 90 **To** 2013 $14.95

✪   Cool Climate Series Canberra District King Valley Semillon Sauvignon
       Blanc 2009 Pale, bright straw-green; a wine with above-average aromas and
       flavours, citrus, grass, stone fruit and tropical notes all to be found at some
       point along the journey from the bouquet to the aftertaste. Screwcap. 13% alc.
       Rating 90 **To** 2012 $14.95

✪ **Cool Climate Series Tumbarumba Pinot Noir 2008** Strong crimson-purple; a very powerful wine, with dark plum and black cherry aromas and flavours; a forest/herb nuance on the finish. Will develop well over the next few years. Screwcap. 14% alc. **Rating** 90 **To** 2015 $14.95

✪ **Cool Climate Series Hilltops Shiraz 2009** Vivid purple hue; fragrant blackberry and mulberry spiced bouquet; medium-bodied, with smoked meats, tar and chewy tannins to conclude. Screwcap. 14.5% alc. **Rating** 90 **To** 2016 $14.95 BE

✪ **Riverina Cabernet Shiraz 2008** An example of Riverina cabernet with controlled yields and skilled winemaking; the wine is only medium-bodied at best, and there is a slight question over its tannins, but it is good value. Trophy Best Young Red Blend NSW Wine Awards '09. Diam. 14.5% alc. **Rating** 90 **To** 2015 $15
3 Bridges Durif 2008 Rating 90 **To** 2014 $22.95 BE

�♺ **Richland Sauvignon Blanc 2009** Effusive tropical fruit aromas tighten up on
✪ the crisp palate, which is long and clean with a crisp finish. Screwcap. 12.5% alc. **Rating** 89 **To** 2011 $11
3 Bridges Winemakers Selection Chardonnay 2008 Rating 89 **To** 2012 $17.95

Westlake Vineyards   ★★★★★

Diagonal Road, Koonunga, SA 5355 **Region** Barossa Valley
T (08) 8565 6249 **F** (08) 8565 6208 **www.**westlakevineyards.com.au **Open** By appt
Winemaker Darren Westlake **Est.** 1999 **Cases** 200 **Vyds** 36.2 ha
Darren and Suzanne Westlake tend 22 ha of shiraz, 6.5 ha of cabernet sauvignon, 2 ha of viognier, and smaller plantings of petit verdot, durif, mataro, grenache and graciano planted on two properties in the Koonunga area of the Barossa Valley. The soil is red-brown earth over tight, heavy red clay, with scatterings of ironstone and quartz, and the vines normally yield between 2.5 and a maximum of 7.5 tonnes per ha. They, and they alone (other than with some help in the pruning season), work in the vineyards, and have a long list of high-profile winemakers queued up to buy the grapes, leaving only a small amount for production under the Westlake label. Suzanne is a sixth-generation descendant of Johann George, who came to SA from Prussia in 1838, while the 717 Convicts label draws on the history of Darren's ancestor Edward Westlake, who was transported to Australia in 1788.

♴♴♴♴♴ **Albert's Block Barossa Valley Shiraz 2007** Dense, dark purple-crimson; opulent black fruits drive the bouquet and palate alike; this is a particularly distinguished '07 wine, with a textured palate where fleshy fruit is held in the embrace of fine, ripe tannins. Cork. 14.5% alc. **Rating** 94 **To** 2017 $28
717 Convicts The Warden Barossa Valley Shiraz 2006 Intense crimson-purple; as the colour foretells, an extremely rich and luscious full-bodied shiraz in vinous black hole style; there is so much happening the alcohol doesn't take a lethal hold on the wine, rather an array of blackberry, prune, dark chocolate and balanced oak and tannins take the limelight. Cork. 15.5% alc. **Rating** 94 **To** 2021 $45

WH Sweetland   **NR**

146 Parker Road, Bannockburn, Vic 3331 (postal) **Region** Geelong
T (03) 5281 1651 **Open** Not
Winemaker Lethbridge Wines (Ray Nadeson) **Est.** 2001 **Cases** NFP **Vyds** 2.5 ha
Bill Sweetland's family crest depicts ears of wheat and bunches of grapes, and the family first settled in the Hunter Valley in the 1820s. Thus Bill says it was inevitable he should start a vineyard, and has done so with pinot noir, with the infinitely experienced Gary Farr as consultant.

Whicher Ridge ★★★★

PO Box 328, Cowaramup, WA 6284 **Region** Geographe
T (08) 9753 1394 **F** (08) 9753 1394 **www**.whicherridge.com.au **Open** Not
Winemaker Cathy Howard **Est.** 2004 **Cases** 750 **Vyds** 5 ha
Whicher Ridge may be a recent arrival on the wine scene, but it is hard to imagine a
husband and wife team with such an ideal blend of viticultural and winemaking experience
accumulated over a collective 40-plus years. Cathy Howard (nee Spratt) was a winemaker for
16 years at Orlando and St Hallett in the Barossa Valley, and at Watershed Wines in Margaret
River. She now has her own winemaking consulting business covering the southwest region
of WA, as well as making the Whicher Ridge wines. Neil Howard's career as a viticulturist
spans more than 25 years, beginning in the Pyrenees region with Taltarni Vineyards and Blue
Pyrenees Estate, before moving to Mount Avoca as vineyard manager for 12 years. When he
moved to the west, he managed the Sandalford Wines vineyard in Margaret River for several
years, then developed and managed a number of smaller vineyards throughout the region.
Whicher Ridge's Odyssey Creek Vineyard at Chapman Hill has 2.5 ha of sauvignon blanc,
1.8 ha of cabernet sauvignon and 0.7 ha of viognier. They have chosen the Frankland River
subregion of the Great Southern to supply shiraz and riesling, and also intend to buy grapes
from Margaret River.

▼▼▼▼▼ **Frankland River Riesling 2009** The bouquet is still to build fragrance, but the
palate has a strong base of lime and lemon fruit running through to the finish and
aftertaste, supported by good acidity. Screwcap. 12.5% alc. **Rating** 92 **To** 2019 $28
Geographe Viognier 2009 Has the fuller mouthfeel that should be a first
requirement for viognier, and also the dried peach and apricot flavours; all
achieved without any oily phenolic characters. Screwcap. 14.5% alc. **Rating** 90
To 2012 $28

Whinstone Estate ★★★

295 Dunns Creek Road, Red Hill, Vic 3937 **Region** Mornington Peninsula
T (03) 5989 7487 **F** (03) 5989 7641 **www**.whinstone.com.au **Open** W'ends & public
hols 11–5, 7 days Jan
Winemaker Phaedrus Estate **Est.** 1994 **Cases** 500 **Vyds** 2.88 ha
Ken and Leon Wood began the development of their vineyard in 1994, planting 1.01 ha of
chardonnay, 0.81 ha of pinot gris, 0.6 ha of pinot noir, 0.4 ha of sauvignon blanc and a few
rows of melon (a grape of Muscadet, France). Initially the grapes were sold to other makers
in the region, with a small amount made under the Whinstone label for friends and family.
Demand has grown and, with it, production.

▼▼▼▼ **Mornington Peninsula Pinot Noir 2008** Bright, light crimson-red; a very
correct and precise pinot in a light-bodied mode; needs more emphasis and
conviction for higher points, possibly through thinning the crop. Screwcap.
13.9% alc. **Rating** 88 **To** 2013 $25

Whiskey Gully Wines ★★★

25 Turner Road, Severnlea, Qld 4352 **Region** Granite Belt
T (07) 4683 5100 **F** (07) 4683 5155 **www**.whiskeygullywines.com.au **Open** 7 days 9–5
Winemaker Rod MacPherson (Contract) **Est.** 1997 **Cases** NA
Close inspection of the winery letterhead discloses that The Media Mill Pty Ltd trades as
Whiskey Gully Wines. It is no surprise, then, to find proprietor John Arlidge saying, 'Wine
and politics are a heady mix; I have already registered the 2000 Republic Red as a voter in
26 marginal electorates and we are considering nominating it for Liberal Party preselection
in Bennelong.' John decided to sell Whiskey Gully in 2010 and move to Paris (a sea/cultural
change of awesome proportions), but the brand has not been run down, and business is
continuing as usual with the same winemaking team.

ΨΨΨΨ   **Leap'n Liz Colombard 2009** The acid retention qualities of colombard may draw it back on centre stage if temperatures rise permanently; this is a crisp, lemony wine with a long and fresh finish. Screwcap. 12.5% alc. **Rating** 89 To 2011 $22

Black Rod Shiraz 2006 Yet another wine to underline the increasing quality of the Granite Belt offerings; it is well made, the texture built around fine tannins, flavours combining American oak, plum and blackberry. Screwcap. 14% alc. **Rating** 89 To 2014 $26

EB Sparkling Chardonnay Brut Reserve 2006 Full straw-green; a complex wine with full flavours of peach and toast; not overly fine, but honest. Diam. 12% alc. **Rating** 89 To 2010 $34

Rep Red 2006 Very deep colour; a full, dense bouquet, then a powerful, albeit rather extractive, palate; tonnes of personality, but some weight loss would have improved the result. Cabernet Sauvignon/Shiraz. Screwcap. 14% alc. **Rating** 88 To 2015 $18

Whispering Brook ★★★☆
Hill Street, Broke, NSW 2330 **Region** Hunter Valley
T (02) 9818 4126 **F** (02) 9818 4156 **www**.whispering-brook.com **Open** W'ends 11–5, Fri by appt
Winemaker Nick Patterson, Susan Frazier **Est.** 2000 **Cases** 1000 **Vyds** 3 ha
Susan Frazier and Adam Bell say the choice of Whispering Brook was the result of a five-year search to find the ideal viticultural site (while studying for wine science degrees at CSU). Some may wonder whether the Broke–Fordwich subregion of the Hunter Valley needed such persistent effort to locate, but the property does in fact have a combination of terra rossa loam soils on which the reds are planted, and sandy flats for the white grapes. The partners have also established an olive grove and accommodation for 6–14 guests in the large house set in the vineyard. Exports to the UK, Japan, Thailand and Cambodia.

ΨΨΨΨΨ   **Hunter Valley Semillon 2006** The very nature of cork means the outcome of each bottle is different; here the cork has done its job well, for the wine is still fresh and grassy, the crisp acidity unchanged from its youth. 10.5% alc. **Rating** 90 To 2012 $19

ΨΨΨΨ   **Hunter Valley Semillon 2009 Rating** 89 To 2016 $19
Hunter Valley Shiraz 2006 Rating 88 To 2013 $24

Whispering Hills ★★★★
580 Warburton Highway, Seville, Vic 3139 **Region** Yarra Valley
T (03) 5964 2822 **F** (03) 5964 2064 **www**.whisperinghills.com.au **Open** 7 days 10–6
Winemaker Murray Lyons **Est.** 1985 **Cases** 1500
Whispering Hills is owned and operated by the Lyons family (Murray, Marie and Audrey). Murray (with a degree in viticulture and oenology from CSU) concentrates on the vineyard and winemaking, Marie (with a background in sales and marketing) and Audrey take care of the cellar door and distribution of the wines. The 3.5-ha vineyard was established in 1985 (riesling, chardonnay and cabernet sauvignon), with further plantings in '96 and some grafting in '03. Exports to Japan.

ΨΨΨΨΨ   **Appassimento 2005** Fortune favours the bold; the bunches of cabernet were partially dried on the vine and on racks in the winery, then foot-stamped in open fermenters, all-in Italian Amarone style; amazingly, it has produced a very attractive, elegant wine. ProCork. 14.5% alc. **Rating** 95 To 2020 $40

ΨΨΨΨ   **Yarra Valley Riesling 2009 Rating** 88 To 2013 $18
Yarra Valley Chardonnay 2008 Rating 88 To 2012 $25
Yarra Valley Cabernet Shiraz 2007 Rating 87 To 2013 $25

Whistler Wines ★★★★

Seppeltsfield Road, Marananga, SA 5355 **Region** Barossa Valley
T (08) 8562 4942 **F** (08) 8562 4943 **www**.whistlerwines.com **Open** 7 days 10.30–5
Winemaker Troy Kalleske, Christa Deans **Est.** 1999 **Cases** 7400 **Vyds** 14 ha
Brothers Martin and Chris Pfeiffer and their families have created one of the Barossa's hidden secrets: both the vines and the cellar door are tucked away from the view of those travelling along Seppeltsfield Road. Martin has over 25 years' viticultural experience with Southcorp, and Chris brings marketing skills from many years as a publisher. The wines are estate-grown from shiraz (6 ha), merlot (2 ha), cabernet sauvignon, riesling (1.3 ha each), mourvedre, grenache (1.2 ha each) and semillon (1 ha). Exports to Canada, Denmark, Taiwan, Hong Kong and China.

ŶŶŶŶ**Barossa Riesling 2009** Deep colour; ripe Meyer lemon bouquet, with an interesting touch of spice; there is a touch of bitterness on the palate, but it is matched with abundant sweet fruit; best enjoyed in its youth. Screwcap. 12.5% alc. **Rating** 90 **To** 2014 $21 BE
The Reserve Barossa Shiraz 2008 Impenetrable colour; dark and brooding bouquet, with blackberry, tar and licorice coming to the fore; the lavish oak comes through on the thick, unctuous palate, and the finish has a strong mocha toasty note to conclude. Screwcap. 16.5% alc. **Rating** 90 **To** 2016 $60 BE
Barossa Shiraz 2007 Well-made medium-bodied shiraz from a difficult vintage; while the blackberry and plum fruit is far from juicy, there is no toughness or roughness, just a twitch of heat on the finish. Screwcap. 15% alc. **Rating** 90 **To** 2016 $29

ŶŶŶŶ**The Black Piper GSM 2008 Rating** 89 **To** 2016 $25

White Rock Vineyard ★★★★

1171 Railton Road, Kimberley, Tas 7304 (postal) **Region** Northern Tasmania
T (03) 6497 2156 **F** (03) 6497 2156 **Open** At Lake Barrington Estate
Winemaker Winemaking Tasmania (Julian Alcorso), Phil Dolan **Est.** 1992 **Cases** 150
Phil and Robin Dolan have established White Rock Vineyard in the northwest region of Tasmania, which, while having 13 wineries and vineyards, is one of the least known parts of the island. Kimberley is 25 km south of Devonport in the sheltered valley of the Mersey River. The Dolans have planted 2.4 ha of pinot noir, chardonnay, riesling and pinot gris, the lion's share going to the first two varieties. It has been a low-profile operation not only because of its location, but because most of the grapes are sold, with only Riesling, Pinot Noir and Chardonnay being made and sold through local restaurants and the cellar door at Lake Barrington Estate.

ŶŶŶŶ**Riesling 2009** Still youthful and slightly raw, with mineral and acid notes very evident, but has the length to suggest better things are in store down the track. Screwcap. 11.3% alc. **Rating** 89 **To** 2019 $22

Whitfield Estate ★★★☆

198 McIntyre Road, Scotsdale, Denmark, WA 6333 **Region** Great Southern
T (08) 9840 9016 **F** (08) 9840 9016 **www**.whitfieldestate.com.au **Open** Thurs–Mon 10–5, 7 days during school hols
Winemaker Dave Cleary **Est.** 1994 **Cases** 1200 **Vyds** 4 ha
Graham and Kelly Howard acquired the Whitfield Estate vineyard (planted in 1994) in 2005. The estate plantings are of chardonnay and shiraz, the majority of which is sold to West Cape Howe, who contract-make the remaining production for Whitfield Estate. Other varieties are also purchased from growers in the region. Estate plantings have decreased by 0.8 ha, simply to provide room for future plantings of new varieties. A café, called Picnic in the Paddock, was opened in 2008.

ΨΨΨΨΨ **Catriona's Chardonnay 2009** Light straw-green; an extremely juicy wine with citrus/grapefruit characters foremost, but sufficient stone fruit (and a touch of oak) bringing up the rear to establish a clear varietal identity. Screwcap. 12.1% alc. **Rating** 90 **To** 2014 $22.50

ΨΨΨΨ **Semillon Sauvignon Blanc 2009** Grass and herb aromas of the semillon are set
✪   against the citrus and lemon of the sauvignon blanc on both bouquet and palate; a breezy, long and crisp wine for summer seafood. Screwcap. 12.3% alc. **Rating** 89 **To** 2012 $16

        Cabernet Merlot 2007 Rating 89 **To** 2017 $19
✪   **Picnic Red Shiraz 2008** Fractionally hazy colour; a light- to medium-bodied shiraz, with spicy/foresty overtones to its red fruits, texture its strong point. A surprising silver medal at the WA Wine Show '09, but undoubted value. Screwcap. 14% alc. **Rating** 88 **To** 2014 $13.50
✪   **Picnic Pink Rose 2009** Vivid magenta; has considerable red fruit flavour, the sweetness for the cellar door market. Silver medal Australian Small Winemakers Show '09. Screwcap. 12.5% alc. **Rating** 87 **To** 2011 $13.50

Wicks Estate Wines   ★★★★☆

21 Franklin Street, Adelaide, SA 5000 (postal) **Region** Adelaide Hills
T (08) 8212 0004 **F** (08) 8212 0007 **www**.wicksestate.com.au **Open** Not
Winemaker Tim Knappstein, Leigh Ratzmer **Est.** 2000 **Cases** 10 000 **Vyds** 38.8 ha
Tim and Simon Wicks had a long-term involvement with orchard and nursery operations at Highbury in the Adelaide Hills prior to purchasing the 54-ha property at Woodside in 1999. They promptly planted fractionally less than 40 ha of chardonnay, riesling, sauvignon blanc, shiraz, merlot and cabernet sauvignon, following this with the construction of a state-of-the-art winery in early 2004. Exports to the UK, the US, China and Malaysia.

ΨΨΨΨΨ **Eminence Adelaide Hills Shiraz Cabernet 2007** An imposing blend of Shiraz (75%)/Cabernet (25%), with a cedar and spice background to the intense black fruits of the bouquet and long, medium- to full-bodied palate; despite this power, it is remarkably elegant. Screwcap. 14.5% alc. **Rating** 94 **To** 2027 $60

ΨΨΨΨΨ **Adelaide Hills Shiraz 2007** Excellent crimson colour, not common in this
✪   vintage in SA; while only light- to medium-bodied, the wine has great verve and freshness to its spiced plum and blackberry fruit, tannins and oak incidental. Screwcap. 14.5% alc. **Rating** 93 **To** 2015 $20
✪   **Adelaide Hills Chardonnay 2008** Bright colour; has good freshness and intensity from relatively early picking, the accent on varietal fruit, partial barrel ferment giving a gentle touch of nutty oak. Screwcap. 13% alc. **Rating** 90 **To** 2014 $18
✪   **Adelaide Hills Shiraz 2008** Purple-crimson; an aromatic bouquet with spice, black cherry and blackberry fruit and a slash of licorice; there is a juicy element to the medium-bodied palate that also has good texture and length. Screwcap. 14.5% alc. **Rating** 90 **To** 2016 $19

ΨΨΨΨ **Adelaide Hills Sauvignon Blanc 2009 Rating** 89 **To** 2010 $18
        Adelaide Hills Cabernet Sauvignon 2007 Rating 88 **To** 2012 $18
        Adelaide Hills Chardonnay 2009 Rating 87 **To** 2012 $17
        Adelaide Hills Chardonnay Pinot Noir 2008 Rating 87 **To** 2011 $25

wightwick   ★★★★☆

323 Slatey Creek Road North, Invermay, Vic 3352 **Region** Ballarat
T (03) 5332 4443 **F** (03) 5332 8944 **www**.wightwick.com.au **Open** By appt
Winemaker Simon Wightwick **Est.** 1996 **Cases** 130 **Vyds** 3 ha
wightwick might best be described as an angel on a pinhead exercise. Keith and Ann Wightwick planted the tiny estate vineyard to 0.12 ha of chardonnay and 0.29 ha of pinot noir in 1996. In 2003 they purchased a 20-year-old vineyard at Cottlesbridge (1.5 ha chardonnay,

0.5 ha cabernet sauvignon and 0.1 ha each of riesling and sauvignon blanc); most of the grapes from this vineyard are sold to other producers, a small amount of cabernet sauvignon being retained for the wightwick label. Son Simon works as a viticulturist and winemaker in the Yarra Valley, and looks after the vineyards on weekends (using organic principles) and the micro-winemaking during vintage. The Pinot Noir is hand-plunged and basket-pressed, with racking via gravity and minimal fining.

ΨΨΨΨΨ **Ballarat Chardonnay 2008** Bright quartz-green; another wine pointing to the progressive emergence of Ballarat as a significant region; has ripe citrus/grapefruit and white peach on its fragrant bouquet, the palate following suit; there are also some riper melon notes to add complexity and fruit depth. Screwcap. 13.3% alc. **Rating** 93 **To** 2015 $28
Ballarat Pinot Noir 2007 Light purple-crimson; a fragrant bouquet of spice and red fruits, red cherry and strawberry flavours following on the palate; while light-bodied, has impressive length and persistence. Screwcap. 13.6% alc. **Rating** 93 **To** 2015 $32

Wignalls Wines   ★★★★☆
448 Chester Pass Road (Highway 1), Albany, WA 6330 **Region** Albany
T (08) 9841 2848 **F** (08) 9842 9003 **www.**wignallswines.com.au **Open** 7 days 11–4
Winemaker Rob Wignall, Michael Perkins **Est.** 1982 **Cases** 10 000 **Vyds** 18.5 ha
While the estate vineyards have a diverse range of sauvignon blanc, semillon, chardonnay, pinot noir, merlot, shiraz, cabernet franc and cabernet sauvignon, founder Bill Wignall was one of the early movers with pinot noir, producing wines that, by the standards of their time, were well in front of anything else coming out of WA (and up with the then limited amounts being made in Vic and Tasmania). The star dimmed, problems in the vineyard and with contract winemaking, both playing a role. The establishment of an onsite winery in 1998, and the assumption of the winemaking role by son Rob led to a significant increase in both the style and range of the wines made. Exports to the US, Denmark, Japan, Taiwan and China.

ΨΨΨΨΨ **Albany Chardonnay 2009** Bright quartz-green; a fragrant bouquet promises much, and the palate duly delivers, indeed over-delivers, with its intense but fine array of grapefruit and white peach flavours spearing through to the finish, French oak ex barrel ferment and lees contact merely a spectator. Gold medal Sydney Wine Show '10. Screwcap. 14.5% alc. **Rating** 96 **To** 2020 $35

ΨΨΨΨΨ **Albany Sauvignon Blanc 2009** Pale quartz-green; the bouquet is not intense,
✪   but does hint at the attractive flavours of the palate, ranging from grass and snow pea through to citrus and passionfruit; very elegant. Screwcap. 13.5% alc. **Rating** 93 **To** 2011 $19
✪   **Great Southern Unwooded Chardonnay 2009** A fragrant bouquet and lively palate are perfectly judged for the unwooded style, with grapefruit, nectarine and white peach fruit; I haven't the faintest idea how this was achieved at 14.5% alcohol. Screwcap. 14.5% alc. **Rating** 91 **To** 2011 $17
Albany Pinot Noir 2009 Rating 90 **To** 2015 $32
Albany Pinot Noir 2006 Rating 90 **To** 2013 $32

ΨΨΨΨ **Albany Shiraz 2008 Rating** 89 **To** 2015 $21

Wild Dog Winery   ★★★★☆
Warragul-Korrumburra Road, Warragul, Vic 3820 **Region** Gippsland
T (03) 5623 1117 **F** (03) 5623 6402 **www.**wilddogwinery.com **Open** 7 days 10–5
Winemaker Folkert Janssen **Est.** 1982 **Cases** 5000 **Vyds** 13.5 ha
An aptly named winery that produces somewhat rustic wines from the estate vineyards; even the Farringtons (the founders) say that the 'Shiraz comes with a bite', but they also point out that there is minimal handling, fining and filtration. Following the acquisition of Wild Dog by Gary and Judy Surman, upgrading of the vineyard has resulted in new plantings, and the grafting over of vines, the estate plantings now mainly devoted to shiraz (4 ha), chardonnay

(3.5 ha), pinot noir (2 ha), riesling (1.5 ha), cabernet sauvignon (1.5 ha) with smaller blocks of cabernet franc, merlot, semillon, sauvignon blanc, viognier and pinot gris. The payback came at the Gippsland Wine Show '08 when Wild Dog Winery won four trophies (and attendant gold medals). As the tasting notes indicate, there is much to be confident about. Exports to China and Japan.

ＹＹＹＹＹ Gippsland Shiraz 2008 Good hue and clarity; savoury, spicy aromas drive
✪ the bouquet but yield to supple black fruits on the palate, which have excellent intensity and length. Screwcap. 14% alc. Rating 94 To 2023 $23

ＹＹＹＹＹ Gippsland Chardonnay 2008 Brilliant straw-green; a generous wine, with
✪ layers of nectarine, peach and fig fruit woven through creamy/nutty barrel ferment and lees contact notes. Screwcap. 13% alc. Rating 93 To 2015 $23
Reserve Gippsland Shiraz 2007 Rating 92 To 2017 $35
Gippsland Riesling 2009 Rating 91 To 2016 $21
✪ **Gippsland Cabernet Sauvignon 2008** Some pleasantly earthy spicy nuances on the bouquet and palate give interest to the core of blackcurrant and blackberry fruits; tannin extract well handled. Screwcap. 13% alc. Rating 91 To 2018 $23
Gippsland Sauvignon Blanc 2009 Rating 90 To 2010 $21
Gippsland Wild Rose 2009 Rating 90 To 2010 $21
Gippsland Pinot Noir 2008 Rating 90 To 2013 $23
Gippsland Cabernet Franc 2008 Rating 90 To 2015 $23
Gippsland Sparkling 2006 Rating 90 To 2012 $28

Wildcroft Estate ★★★★

98 Stanleys Road, Red Hill South, Vic 3937 **Region** Mornington Peninsula
T (03) 5989 2646 **F** (03) 9783 9469 **www.**wildcroft.com.au **Open** 7 days 10–5
Winemaker Bass Phillip **Est.** 1988 **Cases** NA
Wildcroft Estate is the brainchild of Devendra Singh, best known as the owner of one of Vic's oldest Indian restaurants. In 1988 he purchased the land upon which 4 ha of pinot noir, chardonnay, shiraz and cabernet sauvignon have been established, with the management and much of the physical work carried out by Devendra's wife Shashi Singh, who undertook a viticulture course. The vineyard is one of the few unirrigated vineyards on the Peninsula. The mudbrick cellar door also has a restaurant — Café 98 — allowing Devendra to explore the matching of Indian food with wine. The café serves modern cuisine with Indian and Middle Eastern influences, using local produce wherever possible.

ＹＹＹＹＹ Wild One Shiraz 2006 Retains good hue; while only light- to medium-bodied (partly due, perhaps, to the low alcohol) has juicy fruit and a plethora of cool-climate spices; needs more depth for higher points. Diam. 12.3% alc. Rating 91 To 2016 $62

Wildwood ★★★★

St John's Lane, Oaklands Junction, Vic 3063 **Region** Sunbury
T (03) 9307 1118 **F** (03) 9331 1590 **www.**wildwoodvineyards.com.au **Open** 7 days 10–5
Winemaker Dr Wayne Stott **Est.** 1983 **Cases** 1800 **Vyds** 10.75 ha
Wildwood is just 4 km past Melbourne airport, at an altitude of 130 m in the Oaklands Valley, which provides unexpected views back to Port Phillip Bay and the Melbourne skyline. Plastic surgeon Dr Wayne Stott has taken what is very much a part-time activity rather more seriously than most by completing the wine science degree at CSU.

ＹＹＹＹＹ Shiraz 2008 Solid red-purple colour; blackberry, licorice and spice aromas lead into a medium- to full-bodied palate that has an array of near-identical flavours supported by ripe tannins and a twist of oak. Screwcap. 13.8% alc. Rating 91 To 2023 $34.95

Will Taylor Wines   ★★★★☆

1B Victoria Avenue, Unley Park, SA 5061 **Region** South Eastern Australia
T (08) 8271 6122 **F** (08) 8271 6122 **Open** By appt
Winemaker Various contract **Est.** 1997 **Cases** 1500
Will Taylor is a partner in the leading Adelaide law firm Finlaysons, and specialises in wine law. He and Suzanne Taylor have established a classic negociant wine business, having wines contract-made to their specifications. Moreover, they choose what they consider the best regions for each variety; thus Clare Valley Riesling, Adelaide Hills Sauvignon Blanc, Hunter Valley Semillon and Yarra Valley Pinot Noir. Exports to Canada, Hong Kong, China and Singapore.

🍷🍷🍷🍷🍸 **Clare Valley Riesling 2004** Aged Release. Vibrant green hue; a good example of aged riesling with toast and lemon curd on display; the palate is very fresh and lively, with the minerality of age, combining forces with the fresh citrus flavours elegantly; long and toasty to conclude. Screwcap. 13% alc. **Rating** 93 **To** 2016 $22.50 BE
Hunter Valley Semillon 2003 Aged Release. Quite a staggeringly toasty bouquet, with straw and ripe lemons the centrepiece; there is plenty of richness, and strong toasty flavours that really continue on for a very long time; not a style for everyone, but for those who like aged complexity combined with freshness, this may be for you. Screwcap. 11.6% alc. **Rating** 92 **To** 2016 $25.50 BE

Willespie   ★★★★

555 Harmans Mill Road, Wilyabrup via Cowaramup, WA 6284 **Region** Margaret River
T (08) 9755 6248 **F** (08) 9755 6210 **www**.willespie.com.au **Open** 7 days 10.30–5
Winemaker Nathan Schultz **Est.** 1976 **Cases** 7000 **Vyds** 22 ha
Willespie has produced many attractive white wines over the years, typically in brisk, herbaceous Margaret River style; all are fruit- rather than oak-driven. The wines have had such success that the Squance family (which founded and owns Willespie) has increased winery capacity, drawing upon estate vineyards. Exports to the UK, Japan and Singapore.

🍷🍷🍷🍷🍸 **Old School Barrel Fermented Margaret River Semillon 2008** The pungent green nettle character of Margaret River semillon dominates the bouquet, with the barrel fermentation nowhere to be seen; the palate clarifies with a good deal of generous fruit counterbalancing the overt pea pod fruit; an extreme style, well made. Diam. 12.5% alc. **Rating** 91 **To** 2016 $28 BE
✪ **Margaret River Sauvignon Blanc 2009** True to Willespie style, with fresh pea pod aromas supported by a mere suggestion of riper tropical fruit; the palate is fresh and zesty, with a generous mid-palate core of sweet fruit; a very good alternative for those who like sauvignon from across the Tasman. Screwcap. 12.5% alc. **Rating** 91 **To** 2012 $19.50 BE

William Downie   ★★★★★

121 Yarragon South Road, Yarragon, Vic 3823 (postal) **Region** Yarra Valley
T 03 5634 2216 **F** (03) 5634 2216 **www**.williamdownie.com.au **Open** Not
Winemaker William Downie **Est.** 2003 **Cases** 500
William (Bill) Downie spends six months each year making wine in Burgundy, the other six based in the Yarra Valley with De Bortoli. He uses purchased grapes from older vines to make the wines, avoiding the use of pumps, filtration and fining. The striking label, designed by artist Reg Mombassa, has helped obtain listings at The Prince Wine Store and elsewhere. In the 2006 *Gourmet Traveller* Winemaker of the Year Awards, Bill was awarded the Kemeny's Medal for the Best Young Winemaker. His boss at De Bortoli, Stephen Webber, goes a little further when he says, 'Downie is the best winemaker in Australia.'

🍷🍷🍷🍷🍷 **Mornington Peninsula Pinot Noir 2008** Good colour; a lively and supple wine from start to finish, yet with tangy elements in the fruit flavour spectrum; silky mouthfeel and finish. Diam. 13.5% alc. **Rating** 94 **To** 2016 $55

Yarra Valley Pinot Noir 2008 The most developed colour of the three William Downie pinots; a mix of red fruits and spice on the bouquet leads into a distinctly savoury/foresty palate courtesy of fine tannins; has excellent length. Diam. 13.5% alc. Rating 94 To 2016 $55

�♀ Gippsland Pinot Noir 2008 Rating 93 To 2018 $55

Willow Bridge Estate   ★★★★☆

Gardin Court Drive, Dardanup, WA 6236 **Region** Geographe
T (08) 9728 0055 **F** (08) 9728 0066 **www**.willowbridge.com.au **Open** 7 days 11–5
Winemaker Simon Burnell **Est.** 1997 **Cases** 40 000 **Vyds** 59 ha
The Dewar family has followed a fast track in developing Willow Bridge Estate since acquiring the spectacular 180-ha hillside property in the Ferguson Valley: chardonnay, semillon, sauvignon blanc, shiraz and cabernet sauvignon were planted, with tempranillo added in 2000. The winery is capable of handling the 1200–1500 tonnes from the estate plantings. Not too many wineries in Australia better the price/value ratio of the mid-range wines of Willow Bridge. Exports to the UK, the US and other major markets.

♀♀♀♀♀ Gravel Pit Shiraz Viognier 2008 Bright colour; a fragrantly spicy and lifted bouquet is followed by a lively medium-bodied palate, licorice and black fruits lifted by viognier's special spicy quality; very good balance and finish. Screwcap. 14.5% alc. Rating 94 To 2018 $30

♀♀♀♀♀ Dragonfly Sauvignon Blanc Semillon 2009 The passionfruit and kiwi fruit
❂   aromas and flavours are there right from the word go, flowing evenly through the well-balanced and long palate. No need to sweat over a wine like this. Screwcap. 12.5% alc. Rating 91 To 2010 $16.50

❂   Dragonfly Unwooded Chardonnay 2009 Aromas of white flowers and grapefruit, then a tangy palate moving more to white peach; very good length. Screwcap. 13% alc. Rating 90 To 2011 $16.50

❂   Dragonfly Shiraz 2008 A brightly coloured, light- to medium-bodied shiraz with a fresh display of red fruits and spice, oak and tannins neatly folded in the background. Screwcap. 14% alc. Rating 90 To 2016 $16.50

♀♀♀♀ Dragonfly Cabernet Merlot 2008 Rating 89 To 2014 $16.50
Solana Geographe Tempranillo 2008 Rating 89 To 2012 $22

Willow Creek Vineyard   ★★★★★

166 Balnarring Road, Merricks North, Vic 3926 **Region** Mornington Peninsula
T (03) 5989 7448 **F** (03) 5989 7584 **www**.willow-creek.com.au **Open** 7 days 10–5
Winemaker Geraldine McFaul **Est.** 1989 **Cases** 5000 **Vyds** 11.15 ha
Willow Creek Vineyard is a significant presence in the Mornington Peninsula, with the large vineyard planted to pinot noir, chardonnay, cabernet sauvignon, sauvignon blanc and pinot gris. The grape intake is supplemented by purchasing small, quality parcels from local growers. The Willow Creek wines rank with the best from the Peninsula, the arrival of Geraldine McFaul as winemaker promising a continuation in (if not bettering) the quality of the wines. Exports to Japan.

♀♀♀♀♀ Tulum Mornington Peninsula Pinot Noir 2008 Gloriously fragrant and
❂   effusive; the palate is long and refined, with a vibrant array of red and black cherry, plum and spice; French oak is totally integrated. Screwcap. 14% alc. Rating 96 To 2015 $40

Tulum Mornington Peninsula Sauvignon Blanc 2009 Bright green-straw; aromas of spice and nettle lead into a long and intensely focused palate, reflecting 100% barrel ferment and maturation in seasoned French oak; very much in Loire Valley style. Screwcap. 13% alc. Rating 95 To 2012 $35

Tulum Mornington Peninsula Chardonnay 2008 Bright straw-green; while the bouquet is somewhat restrained, the palate is not, with grapefruit, nougat and almond flavours held in a glaze of acidity; great length. Screwcap. 13.5% alc. Rating 95 To 2016 $35

○ Tulum Mornington Peninsula Pinot Noir 2007 Clear, bright red; fragrant red cherry and plum on the bouquet; the flavours start in the same register, but are then strengthened by gently foresty tannins. Screwcap. 14.5% alc. Rating 95 To 2014 $35

Tulum Mornington Peninsula Pinot Gris 2009 A thoroughly impressive pinot gris, whole bunch-pressed and 100% barrel ferment in old oak barrels; the wine is intense, the oak providing texture but not impacting on flavour, the line of the pear and citrus palate long and clear. Screwcap. 14% alc. Rating 94 To 2011 $35

ΨΨΨΨΨ Tulum Mornington Peninsula Rose 2009 Rating 92 To 2011 $25

Wills Domain ★★★★★

Cnr Brash Road/Abbey Farm Road, Yallingup, WA 6281 **Region** Margaret River
T (08) 9755 2327 **F** (08) 9756 6072 **www**.willsdomain.com.au **Open** 7 days 10–5
Winemaker Naturaliste Vintners (Bruce Dukes) **Est.** 1985 **Cases** 7500 **Vyds** 20.8 ha
When Michelle and Darren Haunold purchased the original Wills Domain vineyard in 2000, they were adding another chapter to a family history of winemaking stretching back to 1383 in what is now Austria. Remarkable though that may be, more remarkable is that 32-year-old Darren, who lost the use of his legs in an accident in 1989, runs the estate (including part of the pruning) from his wheelchair. Prior to the Haunolds' purchase of the property, the grapes were all sold to local winemakers, but since '01 they have been made for the Wills Domain label, and the vineyard holdings (shiraz, semillon, cabernet sauvignon, sauvignon blanc, chardonnay, merlot, petit verdot, malbec, cabernet franc and viognier) have been expanded. Exports to the UK, the US, Singapore, Malaysia, Indonesia and Hong Kong.

ΨΨΨΨΨ Margaret River Chardonnay 2008 Glowing yellow-green; a coherent and expressive wine, with elegant nectarine and grapefruit flavours held in a fine web of acidity, the finish and aftertaste bright and fresh. Screwcap. 13.5% alc. Rating 95 To 2018 $45

Aged Release Margaret River Semillon 2003 Exceptionally youthful and bright straw-green; marries intensity, finesse and complexity; the flavours are in the vineyard style, with grass, nettle and herb plus a touch of citrus, the finish long and lingering. Screwcap. 13% alc. Rating 94 To 2018 $40

○ Margaret River Semillon Sauvignon Blanc 2009 Has a very aromatic and expressive bouquet of passionfruit, grapefruit and a touch of herb, the palate providing more of the same, with energy and drive. Screwcap. 13% alc. Rating 94 To 2011 $19.50

Margaret River Shiraz 2008 Vivid, deep purple-crimson; stylish, cool-grown shiraz, spice and bramble running through the dark fruits of the bouquet and palate; the tannins are full, a touch of sweet oak just what the doctor ordered. Screwcap. 14% alc. Rating 94 To 2020 $28

Margaret River Cabernet Merlot 2008 Crimson-purple; a full-bodied wine, with strong blackcurrant, cassis and plum fruit swathed in equally strong tannins; a vin de garde that will flourish in bottle thanks to its balance. Screwcap. 13.5% alc. Rating 94 To 2028 $28

Reserve Margaret River Cabernet Sauvignon 2008 Good hue, although not particularly deep; a classically restrained and elegant cabernet, with blackcurrant fruit accompanied by a touch of dried herb, cedar and gently earthy tannins; no more than medium-bodied, but long. Screwcap. 13.5% alc. Rating 94 To 2013 $40

ΨΨΨΨΨ Margaret River Semillon 2007 Rating 93 To 2020 $25

ΨΨΨΨ Margaret River Rose 2009 Rating 89 To 2011 $21.50

Willunga 100 Wines   ★★★★☆

Office 2, Rear 227-235 Unley Road, Unley, SA 5061 **Region** McLaren Vale
T 0427 271 280 **F** (08) 8323 7622 **www.**willunga100.com **Open** By appt
Winemaker Steve Pannell, Kate Day **Est.** 2005 **Cases** 20 000
This is a joint venture between Blackbilly and Liberty Wines UK, the latter a well-known
importer of quality wines from Australia, and UK industry veteran John Ratcliffe. It is a grape-
to-retail venture, the foundation being grapes supplied by 400 ha of McLaren Vale vineyards,
with a particular emphasis on viognier, shiraz, grenache and cabernet sauvignon. Most of the
wine is exported to the UK, Europe and Asia, however distribution has begun in Australia,
with wines also available by mail order; has hit the scene running, with outstanding value
for money.

�♀ **McLaren Vale Cabernet Shiraz 2008** Dark deep colour; unequivocally full-
bodied, with blackberry, blackcurrant, dark chocolate and licorice fruit matched
by persistent savoury tannins that give texture and balance. Screwcap. 14.5% alc.
Rating 93 **To** 2020 $22

✪ **McLaren Vale Shiraz Viognier 2006** The colour is not as brilliant as the blend
normally gives, but the bouquet certainly has the fragrance; the palate is rich and
juicy, with plush plum and blackberry fruit, the tannins soft and round. Screwcap.
14.5% alc. **Rating** 92 **To** 2010 $20

✪ **McLaren Vale Grenache 2007** Slightly idiosyncratic, but attractive raspberry,
spice and fern aromas slide into the medium-bodied, long and evenly balanced
palate, with no cosmetic characters whatsoever. Screwcap. 14.5% alc. **Rating** 92
To 2015 $22

Adelaide Hills Pinot Gris 2009 Light straw and a glimmer of pink; has the
correct pear and apple varietal fruit, pleasingly grainy acidity on the back-palate,
and no less pleasingly dry finish. Screwcap. 13.5% alc. **Rating** 90 **To** 2011 $22

McLaren Vale Adelaide Hills Viognier 2009 Praise be; unoaked dry and fresh,
with sufficient crisp apricot and peach nuances to establish its identity without
shaking its fist in your face. Screwcap. 14% alc. **Rating** 90 **To** 2012 $22

Wilson Vineyard   ★★★★★

Polish Hill River, Sevenhill via Clare, SA 5453 **Region** Clare Valley
T (08) 8843 4310 **www.**wilsonvineyard.com.au **Open** W'ends 10–4
Winemaker Dr John and Daniel Wilson **Est.** 1974 **Cases** 4000
In 2009 founder Dr John Wilson passed the business on to son Daniel under the banner head
'70% of family businesses do not survive their first succession ...' Daniel is determined to be
in the 30% that survive this big step. I'm willing to wager he will, because he has been solely
responsible for winemaking since 2003. For his part, John intends to continue pruning the
vines wearing his 1970s green vinyl jacket when it rains.

♀♀♀♀♀ **Polish Hill River Riesling 2009** A delicious wine, the fragrant bouquet and
✪   lively palate with a mix of lemon and lime fruit; the low pH and (relatively) high
acidity guarantee a long life, but it does not need cellaring for any particular time.
Screwcap. 12.5% alc. **Rating** 95 **To** 2024 $22.95

Hand Plunge Clare Valley Shiraz 2006 Dense colour as powerful, dense and
rich as the colour suggests, but shows no sign of dead fruit; indeed, there is an edge
of freshness around the black fruits and dark chocolate flavours; oak and tannins fill
in the background. Screwcap. 15% alc. **Rating** 95 **To** 2026 $35

✪ **Stonecraft Clare Valley Cabernet Sauvignon 2006** Good retention of hue;
the bouquet has an aromatic array of blackcurrant, mulberry and spice aromas, the
finely tempered palate carrying the flavours through to a long finish. Screwcap.
14.5% alc. **Rating** 94 **To** 2021 $22.95

♀♀♀♀♀ **DJW Clare Valley Riesling 2009** Only 300 dozen bottles made, much less
✪   than usual; has a reserved bouquet and tight palate, with chalky/minerally acidity
throughout providing structure for the lime-accented fruit. Screwcap. 12.5% alc.
Rating 93 **To** 2020 $19.95

☉   **RX Blend Shiraz Cabernet 2006** Excellent hue; a thoroughly synergistic blend of Shiraz (65%)/Cabernet (35%) there is an unexpected burst of spice, along with bitter chocolate and blackberry fruit on the medium-bodied, long palate. Screwcap. 14.5% alc. **Rating** 93 To 2016 $19
Pepperstone Clare Valley Shiraz 2006 Rating 92 To 2016 $22.95
Clare Valley Merlot 2006 Rating 90 To 2016 $24

♀♀♀♀   **Pink Poppy Clare Valley Rose 2009 Rating** 87 To 2010 $19.95

Wily Trout   ★★★

Marakei-Nanima Road, via Hall, NSW 2618 **Region** Canberra District
T (02) 6230 2487 **F** (02) 6230 2211 **www**.wilytrout.com.au **Open** 7 days 10–5
Winemaker Dr Roger Harris, Nick Spencer (Contract) **Est.** 1998 **Cases** 8000 **Vyds** 20 ha
The Wily Trout vineyard, owned by Robert and Susan Bruce, shares its home with the Poachers Pantry, a renowned gourmet smokehouse. The quality of the wines is very good, and a testament to the skills of the contract winemakers. The northeast-facing slopes, at an elevation of 720 m, provide some air drainage and hence protection against spring frosts. The production increase (from 3000 cases) speaks for itself.

♀♀♀♀   **Canberra District Shiraz 2008** Red-purple; a light- to medium-bodied wine with attractive spicy peppery notes to its fresh, dark fruits; the oak and tannins are well balanced and integrated. Screwcap. 14% alc. **Rating** 89 To 2018 $34
Canberra District Shiraz 2006 Good colour for age; in the mainstream of Wily Trout style, elegant and light- to medium-bodied; offers a mix of spicy/peppery/savoury elements against the black fruit background. Screwcap. 13.6% alc. **Rating** 89 To 2016 $34
Canberra District Chardonnay 2006 The very cool Wily Trout vineyard gives all its wines a restrained fruit profile; here the grapefruit/lemon flavours are prominent, and 50% barrel ferment has not resulted in any softening of that profile. Screwcap. 12.5% alc. **Rating** 88 To 2013 $28
Premium Late Disgorged Methode Champenoise 2006 Pale straw-yellow; has developed complexity from extended lees contact, and the dosage was probably a little more than needed. Crown seal. 13.3% alc. **Rating** 88 To 2010 $34

☉   **Fingerlings Semillon Sauvignon Blanc 2008** Bright straw-green; a zesty wine with no shortage of tropical fruit ex the sauvignon blanc, and structure from the semillon. Screwcap. 12.5% alc. **Rating** 87 To 2011 $18

☉   **Fingerlings Chardonnay 2008** Pale straw; fragrant citrus and stone fruit aromas, then a juicy palate with similar flavours. Screwcap. 12.5% alc. **Rating** 87 To 2012 $18
Canberra District Pinot Noir 2006 Light clear developed colour; light-bodied but has good varietal expression on the bouquet and palate, with spicy red fruits; green stemmy characters are the downside. Screwcap. 12.8% alc. **Rating** 87 To 2014 $34

Wimbaliri Wines   ★★★☆

3180 Barton Highway, Murrumbateman, NSW 2582 **Region** Canberra District
T (02) 6227 5921 **Open** By appt
Winemaker John Andersen **Est.** 1988 **Cases** 600 **Vyds** 2.2 ha
John and Margaret Andersen moved to the Canberra District in 1987 and began establishing their vineyard at Murrumbateman in '88; the property borders highly regarded Canberra producers Doonkuna and Clonakilla. The vineyard is close-planted with chardonnay, pinot noir, shiraz, cabernet sauvignon and merlot (plus a few vines of cabernet franc). After the failure of crops in 2007 and '08, the Andersons have sold Wimbaliri to a yet-to-be-named purchaser.

ҬҬҬҬҬ Merlot Cabernet Sauvignon 2005 Very good colour for age; has developed
✪   well over five years; juicy plum, blackcurrant and blackberry flavours on a
            medium-bodied palate have good oak and soft tannins support. Diam. 14.5% alc.
            Rating 90 **To** 2015 $20

ҬҬҬҬ Gravel Block Shiraz 2006 **Rating** 88 **To** 2015 $20

Wimmera Hills   NR

606 Glenpatrick Road, Glenpatrick, Vic 3469 **Region** Pyrenees
T (03) 5354 8484 **F** (03) 5354 8483 **www**.wimmerahills.com.au **Open** By appt
Winemaker Benjamin Baker **Est.** 2001 **Cases** 500 **Vyds** 1.7 ha
Jane and Benjamin Baker are both science graduates from Melbourne University; following
his retirement from full-time IT consulting Benjamin took a short winemaking course at
Dookie, and Jane studied winemaking at NMIT in Ararat, Vic. They have planted shiraz, and
three generations of the Baker family work at the vineyard and winery. They say, 'Our remote
valley is a natural haven for echidnas, platypus, wedgetail eagles, poets, environmentalists, frogs
and kangaroos.' It will thus come as no surprise to find that they endeavour to use sustainable
practices in the vineyard, and up to the point of bottling the wine (unfiltered), they calculate
the operation to be carbon neutral. The currently available 2007 Fire Engine Red Pyrenees
Shiraz sells for $14 a bottle, $9 of which is donated to the Elmhurst Fire Brigade.

Winbirra Vineyard   ★★★★

173 Point Leo Road, Red Hill South, Vic 3937 **Region** Mornington Peninsula
T (03) 5989 2109 **F** (03) 5989 2109 **www**.winbirra.com.au **Open** 1st w'end of month
(every w'end Jan) & public hols 11–5, or by appt
Winemaker Sandro Mosele (Contract) **Est.** 1990 **Cases** 1500 **Vyds** 4.1 ha
Winbirra is a small, family-owned and run vineyard that has been producing grapes since
1990, between then and '97 selling the grapes to local winemakers. Since 1997 the wine has
been made and sold under the Winbirra label. The close-planted vineyard includes pinot noir
(2 ha), pinot gris (1.37 ha), viognier (0.69 ha) and 700 shiraz vines.

ҬҬҬҬҬ Mingary Vineyard Mornington Peninsula Viognier 2009 Has above-average
            intensity and length; although the flavours stray somewhat from the usual core,
            citrus in particular playing a role along with green pear. Screwcap. 13.5% alc.
            Rating 90 **To** 2012 $35
            The Brigadier Mornington Peninsula Pinot Noir 2008 Very light colour;
            a perfumed bouquet is attractive, but the very long cold soak (10 days) and
            thrice daily plunging for the next 14 days seems to have accentuated the savoury
            characteristics and somewhat diminished the fruit on the palate. Diam. 14% alc.
            Rating 90 **To** 2014 $35

Winburndale   ★★★★

116 Saint Anthony's Creek Road, Bathurst, NSW 2795 **Region** Central Ranges Zone
T (02) 6337 3134 **F** (02) 6337 3106 **www**.winburndalewines.com.au
Open Mon–Fri 10–4, w'ends 11–4
Winemaker Mark Renzaglia, David Lowe (Consultant) **Est.** 1998 **Cases** 3500 **Vyds** 10.4 ha
Michael and Helen Burleigh acquired the 200-ha Winburndale property in 1998: 160 ha is
forest, to be kept as a nature reserve; three separate vineyards have been planted under the
direction of viticulturist Mark Renzaglia. The winery paddock has shiraz facing due west at
an altitude of 800–820 m; the south paddock, with north and northwest aspects, varying from
790–810 m, has chardonnay, shiraz and cabernet sauvignon. The home paddock is the most
level, with a slight north aspect, and has merlot. The name derives from Lachlan Macquarie's
exploration of the Blue Mountains in 1815. Exports to the US and Denmark.

ҬҬҬҬҬ Alluvial Chardonnay 2009 Shiraz may be Winburndale's flagship wine, but this
✪   is better; barrel fermentation in new and one-year-old French barriques has done
            no more than support the very attractive cool-grown white peach and nectarine
            fruit; very good length and balance. Screwcap. 13% alc. **Rating** 93 **To** 2015 $25

Solitary Shiraz 2007 Good hue, moderately deep; a spicy, light- to medium-bodied shiraz that proclaims its cool-climate origins; the use of 50% new American and French barriques has been well handled, giving the wine a touch of flavour warmth; good balance and length. Screwcap. 14% alc. **Rating** 90 **To** 2015 $30

♥♥♥♥ **Alluvial Chardonnay 2008 Rating** 89 **To** 2014 $25

Windance Wines   ★★★★

2764 Caves Road, Yallingup, WA 6282 **Region** Margaret River
T (08) 9755 2293 **F** (08) 9755 2293 **www**.windance.com.au **Open** 7 days 10–5
Winemaker Damon Eastaugh, Simon Ding **Est.** 1998 **Cases** 4000 **Vyds** 7.5 ha
Drew and Rosemary Brent-White own this family business, situated 5 km south of Yallingup. Cabernet sauvignon, shiraz, sauvignon blanc, semillon and merlot have been established, incorporating sustainable land management and organic farming practices where possible. The wines are exclusively estate-grown.

♥♥♥♥♀ **Reserve Margaret River Chardonnay 2007** An unusually fine and elegant Margaret River chardonnay, the alcohol seeming even lower than it in fact is; sensibly, the oak input has been restrained, allowing the melon and nectarine fruit to express itself. Almost into Chablis territory. Screwcap. 13.2% alc. **Rating** 93 **To** 2013 $32
Reserve Margaret River Cabernet Sauvignon 2008 An elegant, medium-bodied cabernet with a mix of cedary oak, redcurrant and blackcurrant fruit; the tannins are fine and persistent, likewise the oak. Screwcap. 14.9% alc. **Rating** 93 **To** 2018 $50
Reserve Margaret River Shiraz 2008 American oak comes through strongly on the bouquet and palate; while the balance, mouthfeel and overall flavour are good, the oak seems to cloud regional expression. Strange business. Screwcap. 14.5% alc. **Rating** 91 **To** 2020 $40
✪ **Margaret River Chardonnay 2009** A fragrant and fresh unoaked style, with zesty grapefruit and white peach fruit; good acidity and length. Screwcap. 13.2% alc. **Rating** 90 **To** 2012 $20

♥♥♥♥ **Margaret River Sauvignon Blanc Semillon 2009 Rating** 89 **To** 2011 $20

Windowrie Estate   ★★★★

Windowrie Road, Canowindra, NSW 2804 **Region** Cowra
T (02) 6344 3234 **F** (02) 6344 3227 **www**.windowrie.com.au **Open** At the Mill, Vaux Street, Cowra
Winemaker Anthony D'Onise **Est.** 1988 **Cases** 15 000 **Vyds** 73 ha
Windowrie Estate was established by the O'Dea family in 1988 on a substantial grazing property at Canowindra, 30 km north of Cowra and in the same viticultural region. A portion of the grapes from the substantial vineyard is sold to other makers, but increasing quantities are being made for the Windowrie Estate and The Mill labels; the Chardonnays have enjoyed show success. The cellar door is in a flour mill built in 1861 from local granite. It ceased operations in 1905 and lay unoccupied for 91 years until restored by the O'Dea family. Exports to the UK, Ireland, Canada, Denmark, Holland, Japan and China.

♥♥♥♥♀ **Pig in the House Shiraz 2008** Good hue and clarity; plum, spice and vanilla aromas and flavours are built on a base of attractive silky tannins. Screwcap. 15% alc. **Rating** 91 **To** 2018 $25
Family Reserve Shiraz 2007 Yet another red from Cowra to challenge (and change) the perception that it is only suited to chardonnay. Has a supple and sweet leading edge to the plum fruit and vanillan oak; good length. Cork. 14% alc. **Rating** 90 **To** 2014 $25

♥♥♥♥ **Family Reserve Chardonnay 2007 Rating** 89 **To** 2012 $25

❂   The Mill Central Ranges Sangiovese 2007 Light but clear red, no signs
of brick; attractive light- to medium-bodied wine that is developing nicely, the
savoury cherry fruit and tannins in good balance. Diam. 13.5% alc. **Rating** 89
To 2015 $17

Windows Estate   ★★★★

4 Quininup Road, Yallingup, WA 6282 **Region** Margaret River
T (08) 9755 2719 **F** (08) 9755 2719 **www**.windowsestate.com **Open** 7 days 10–5
Winemaker Chris Davies, Navneet Singh, Mick Scott (Consultant) **Est.** 1996
Cases 7000 **Vyds** 6.14 ha
Len and Barbara Davies progressively established their vineyard (cabernet sauvignon, shiraz,
chenin blanc, chardonnay, semillon, sauvignon blanc and merlot), initially selling the grapes. In
2006 the decision was taken to move to winemaking. Son Chris makes the red wines, Navneet
Singh the whites, with Mick Scott filling an overall consulting role. It has been rewarded with
considerable show success for its consistently good, enticingly priced wines. Exports to the
US, Canada, Cyprus, Malaysia, Singapore and Hong Kong.

♟♟♟♟♟   Cabernet Sauvignon Merlot 2008 Bright crimson-red; fresh red fruit aromas
accurately point to the lively light- to medium-bodied palate, with its juicy red
fruit flavours neatly balanced by fine tannins on the finish. Screwcap. 13.8% alc.
Rating 93 **To** 2016 $22
Chardonnay 2008 Bright, light green; a fragrant, floral and very pure bouquet
is replayed on the lively, elegant palate; citrus, white peach and fig all make an
appearance; falters fractionally on the finish. Screwcap. 13.2% alc. **Rating** 92
To 2014 $28

WindshakeR Ridge   ★★★☆

PO Box 106, Karrinyup, WA 6921 **Region** Swan District
T (08) 6241 4100 **F** (08) 9240 6220 **www**.windshaker.com.au **Open** Not
Winemaker Ryan Sudano **Est.** 2003 **Cases** 5000 **Vyds** 20 ha
The Moltoni family has owned a 2000-ha farming property for three generations. Robert
Moltoni is the driving force, establishing WindshakeR Ridge in 2003. The vineyard (5 ha
each of carnelian, semillon, shiraz and verdelho) is 9 km north of Gingin, and looks out over
the hills to the sea. Moltoni is an accomplished poet, and I cannot help but quote one of
his poems: 'Easterlies whistle through the gums/Crashing over silent ridges/Bathing vines
in Namatjira Crimson/WindshakeR, WindshakeR, WindshakeR/The ghost winds whisper
down/Off the red plains to the sea.' Exports to the US and China.

♟♟♟♟♟   Reserve Shiraz 2008 Has plenty of varietal presence throughout, with spicy/
❂   savoury nuances to the blackberry and plum fruit, the palate with fine but
persistent tannins providing texture and underpinning the length. Screwcap.
15% alc. **Rating** 90 **To** 2015 $19.50

♟♟♟♟   Verdelho 2009 Interesting wine; the aromas and flavours include some pinot
❂   gris-like characters of pear and apple; overall, the wine has pleasing lightness of
foot. Screwcap. 14% alc. **Rating** 89 **To** 2012 $14
Semillon Verdelho 2009 **Rating** 88 **To** 2013 $14
Semillon 2009 **Rating** 87 **To** 2012 $14

wine by brad   ★★★★

PO Box 475, Margaret River, WA 6285 **Region** Margaret River
T 0409 572 957 **F** (08) 9757 1897 **www**.winebybrad.com.au **Open** Not
Winemaker Brad Wehr **Est.** 2003 **Cases** 7000
Brad Wehr says that wine by brad 'is the result of a couple of influential winemakers and
shadowy ruffians deciding there was something to be gained by putting together some pretty
neat parcels of wine from the region, creating their own label, and releasing it with minimal
fuss'. In 2007 a premium range was introduced under the Mantra label, from separately
sourced grapes. Exports to Ireland, Canada and South Korea.

ŢŢŢŢ♀ **Mantra Invocation Margaret River Chardonnay 2009** Vibrant hue; a
✪ restrained bouquet of cashew and grapefruit highlighted by toasty oak; the palate
is quite linear, with the acidity providing drive and nerve; an elegant and restrained
style. Screwcap. 13.5% alc. **Rating** 91 **To** 2016 $20 BE

✪ **Margaret River Rose 2009** Has its roots in the Houghton Cabernet Rose style
of years gone by; savoury notes combine with almost citrussy acidity to give plenty
of punch to a dry rose. Screwcap. 13.2% alc. **Rating** 90 **To** 2010 $17

Mantra Journey Margaret River Shiraz 2008 Bright colour; tar and licorice
dominate the savoury bouquet, mulberry lurking beneath; spicy pepper and red
fruits emerge on the palate, gravelly tannins providing the framework for the
medium-bodied fruit. Screwcap. 13.6% alc. **Rating** 90 **To** 2015 $25 BE

ŢŢŢŢ **Margaret River Cabernet Merlot 2008** Redcurrant, tobacco and toasty oak
✪ combine to give a medium-bodied style; easy-going in keeping with the label, will
be enjoyed most in its youth. Screwcap. 13.8% alc. **Rating** 89 **To** 2015 $18 BE
Mantra Abundance Margaret River Cabernet Sauvignon 2008 Rating 89
To 2016 $25 BE

Winetrust Estates ★★★☆
PO Box 541, Balgowlah, NSW 2093 **Region** South Eastern Australia
T (02) 9949 9250 **F** (02) 9907 8179 **www.**winetrustestates.com **Open** Not
Winemaker Andrew Peace, Rob Moody **Est.** 1999 **Cases** 37 000 **Vyds** 88.9 ha
Mark Arnold is the man behind Winetrust Estates, drawing on a lifetime of experience in
wine marketing. It is a virtual winery operation, drawing grapes from three states and five
regions using contract winemakers according to the origin of the grapes (either contract-
grown or produced under a joint venture). The top-of-the-range Picarus red wines come
from the Limestone Coast; the other ranges are Ocean Grove and Firebox, covering all
the major varietal wines plus a few newcomers. Exports to the US, Canada, China, Japan,
Singapore, Hong Kong and Thailand.

ŢŢŢŢ♀ **Picarus Wrattonbully Shiraz 2007** Bright crimson; well-made wine from
quality grapes; plum and black cherry fruit, a hint of spice, ripe but fine tannins
and vanillan oak all combine. Screwcap. 13.5% alc. **Rating** 91 **To** 2017 $22.95

ŢŢŢŢ **Picarus Wrattonbully Cabernet Sauvignon 2007 Rating** 89 **To** 2016 $22.95
Firebox Vineyard Selection Clare Valley Tempranillo 2007 Rating 89
To 2014 $17.95
Firebox Victoria Sauvignon Blanc 2009 Rating 88 **To** 2010 $14.95
Ocean Grove Merlot 2007 Rating 88 **To** 2012 $13.95
Ocean Grove Chardonnay 2008 Rating 87 **To** 2012 $13.95
Ocean Grove Shiraz 2008 Rating 87 **To** 2013 $13.95

Winstead ★★★★☆
75 Winstead Road, Bagdad, Tas 7030 **Region** Southern Tasmania
T (03) 6268 6417 **Open** By appt
Winemaker Neil Snare **Est.** 1989 **Cases** 350
The good news about Winstead is the outstanding quality of its extremely generous and rich
Pinot Noirs, rivalling those of Freycinet for the abundance of their fruit flavour without
any sacrifice of varietal character. The bad news is that production is so limited, with only
0.8 ha of pinot noir and 0.4 ha riesling being tended by fly-fishing devotee Neil Snare and
wife Julieanne.

ŢŢŢŢŢ **Ensnared Sparkling Pinot Noir 2004** Pink-bronze; very good fine mousse;
very attractive rose style; full-flavoured but not heavy; balance and length very
good; aromatic. Silver medal Tas Wine Show '10. **Rating** 94 **To** 2013 $39

ŢŢŢŢ♀ **Reserve Pinot Noir 2006 Rating** 91 **To** 2015

ŸŸŸŸ   Riesling 2008 Rating 89 To 2017
Pinot Noir 2008 Rating 89 To 2014
Riesling GR 2008 Rating 87 To 2016

Winter Creek Wine   ★★★★

Barossa Junction, Barossa Valley Way, Tanunda, SA 5352 **Region** Barossa Valley
T (08) 8524 6382 **F** (08) 8524 6384 **www**.wintercreekwine.com.au **Open** 7 days 10–5
Winemaker David Cross **Est.** 2000 **Cases** 2500 **Vyds** 6 ha
David and Pam Cross acquired their small vineyard at Williamstown in the cooler foothills
of the southern Barossa Valley in 2000, in time for their first vintage that year. There are 4 ha
of shiraz, and a 2 ha vineyard of 70-year-old grenache acquired in 2001. More recently they
have added a Sauvignon Blanc and a Pinot Gris to the range, the grapes purchased from the
Adelaide Hills.

ŸŸŸŸŸ   **Adelaide Hills Sauvignon Blanc 2009** Light straw-green; a crisp, clean
✪   bouquet leads into a tangy palate, with citrus and herb characters interspersed with
tropical/passionfruit nuances, the former the more powerful and driving the long
palate. Screwcap. 12.5% alc. **Rating** 91 To 2012 $18
✪   **The Old Barossa Blend Grenache Shiraz 2008** Bright red-purple; the juicy
red cherry fruit of grenache is foremost, but avoids confection partly due to the
shiraz, the latter also providing tannins on the medium-bodied palate; a very
successful blend in this instance. Screwcap, 14% alc. **Rating** 90 To 2015 $25
The Sommelier Tawny NV A solid tawny style with rancio and oak character
working together seamlessly; the nutty tones from the oxidation exit right on
the edge, but manage to come back with fresh raisins and toffee to conclude;
warm, complex and worthy of the 25 years of average material. Cork. 19.5% alc.
Rating 90 To 2011 $60 BE
✪   **Barossa Valley Fortified Vintage Shiraz 2004** Spice, licorice, black fruits; very
good spirit and balance; particularly not too sweet; on the march as long as the
cork holds. 20% alc. **Rating** 90 To 2017 $22

ŸŸŸŸ   **Second Eleven Barossa Valley Shiraz Grenache 2007** Rating 87
To 2012 $18

Wirra Wirra   ★★★★★

McMurtrie Road, McLaren Vale, SA 5171 **Region** McLaren Vale
T (08) 8323 8414 **F** (08) 8323 8596 **www**.wirrawirra.com **Open** Mon–Sat 10–5,
Sun & public hols 11–5
Winemaker Paul Smith, Paul Carpenter **Est.** 1969 **Cases** 180 000 **Vyds** 57.6 ha
Long respected for the consistency of its white wines, Wirra Wirra has now established an
equally formidable reputation for its reds. Right across the board, the wines are of exemplary
character, quality and style, The Angelus Cabernet Sauvignon and RSW Shiraz battling with
each other for supremacy. Long may the battle continue under the direction of new managing
director Andrew Kay following the retirement of highly respected Tim James, particularly in
the wake of the death of the universally loved co-founder/owner Greg Trott in early 2005.
In Dec '07 Wirra Wirra purchased the 20-ha Rayner Vineyard (with blocks dating back to
the 1950s), which had hitherto supplied Brokenwood with the grapes for its eponymous icon
Shiraz. There has been a smooth transition since long-serving winemaker Samantha Connew
decided to take a break to complete her masters degree and run in the New York Marathon.
Exports to all major markets.

ŸŸŸŸŸ   **RSW McLaren Vale Shiraz 2008** Strong, deep purple; one of the most
✪   powerful RSWs made to date, redolent of black fruits, licorice and a touch of dark
chocolate; has deep-set tannins that balance the richness of the fruit; a long life
ahead. Screwcap. 14.5% alc. **Rating** 96 To 2033 $65

✪ **The Lost Watch Adelaide Hills Riesling 2009** In 1947 Wirra Wirra founder Greg Trott lost the only watch he ever had (a gift from his father) and never bothered to replace it, time being unimportant. Here, a fragrant bouquet leads into an intense palate, with lime juice, apple and mineral singing in unison, reaching a crescendo on the finish. Screwcap. 12.5% alc. **Rating** 95 **To** 2020 $18

✪ **Hiding Champion Adelaide Hills Sauvignon Blanc 2009** Has wonderful energy and thrust from start to finish, aromas and flavours principally revolving around citrus and gooseberry, but with lesser intrusions here and there in Trott fashion; the vibrant finish and crystal-clear aftertaste are the best parts of a delicious, food-friendly wine. Screwcap. 13% alc. **Rating** 95 **To** 2011 $22

RSW McLaren Vale Shiraz 2007 An extremely well made, medium-bodied wine, both bouquet and palate suffused with black fruits, dark chocolate, fruitcake and mocha/vanilla, the tannins soft and ripe. The only thing amiss was the vintage. Screwcap. 14.5% alc. **Rating** 95 **To** 2022 $60

The Angelus McLaren Vale Cabernet Sauvignon 2007 Good depth to colour; a fragrant cedary bouquet leads into a palate with extremely good texture and structure encasing spicy black fruits; the back-palate and finish have excellent savoury tannins. A triumph for the vintage. Screwcap. 13.5% alc. **Rating** 95 **To** 2030 $60

✪ **The 12th Man Adelaide Hills Chardonnay 2008** Glowing yellow-green, it has very attractive juicy notes to the white peach and nectarine fruit, plus creamy/nutty wild yeast barrel ferment inputs. Screwcap. 13.5% alc. **Rating** 94 **To** 2015 $28.50

✪ **Mrs Wigley McLaren Vale Grenache Rose 2009** Bright colour; a highly perfumed bouquet is followed by a wonderfully lively palate of raspberry and redcurrant, the finish bright and clear. Screwcap. 13% alc. **Rating** 94 **To** 2010 $18.50

♉♉♉♉♉ **Original Blend McLaren Vale Grenache Shiraz 2008** Light, bright and clear;
✪ a deliciously juicy and vibrant wine, with a cornucopia of red fruit flavours on the light- to medium-bodied palate; great summer drinking while it retains its freshness over the next few years. Screwcap. 14.5% alc. **Rating** 93 **To** 2014 $22

Woodhenge McLaren Vale Shiraz 2008 Rating 90 **To** 2018 $30
Church Block McLaren Vale Cabernet Sauvignon Shiraz Merlot 2008 **Rating** 90 **To** 2016 $20

♉♉♉♉ **Scrubby Rise Sauvignon Blanc Semillon Viognier 2009** A cunningly
✪ made wine, the sauvignon blanc tempered by a little semillon and viognier plus 10% barrel ferment in new French oak; it has enough flavour to satisfy but not enough to distract from the more important jobs of talking and eating. Screwcap. 12.5% alc. **Rating** 89 **To** 2010 $16.50

✪ **Scrubby Rise Shiraz Cabernet Sauvignon Petit Verdot 2008** A lively light- to medium-bodied wine with juicy black cherry, plum and blackberry fruit doing the talking, fine tannins and oak supporting the finish. Screwcap. 14.5% alc. **Rating** 89 **To** 2013 $15

Scrubby Rise Unwooded Chardonnay 2009 Rating 88 **To** 2010 $16.50
Mrs Wigley Moscato 2009 Rating 88 **To** 2011 $18.50

Wise Wine   ★★★★★

Lot 4 Eagle Bay Road, Eagle Bay, WA 6281 **Region** Margaret River
T (08) 9756 8627 **F** (08) 9756 8770 **www**.wisewine.com.au **Open** 7 days 10–5
Winemaker Jake Bacchus, Imogen Casely, Larry Cherubino (Consultant) **Est.** 1986
Cases 15 000 **Vyds** 16.6 ha
Wise Wine, headed by Perth entrepreneur Ron Wise, has been a remarkably consistent producer of high-quality wine. The vineyard adjacent to the winery in the Margaret River is supplemented by contract-grown grapes form Pemberton, Manjimup and Frankland. The estate plantings are (in descending order of size) shiraz, cabernet sauvignon, chardonnay, sauvignon blanc, merlot, verdelho, cabernet franc and zinfandel. Exports to the UK, the US, Vietnam, Malaysia, Hong Kong and Singapore.

♥♥♥♥♥ Eagle Bay Pemberton Chardonnay 2008 Light green-gold; the fragrant
bouquet has grapefruit and nectarine aromas that come through on the expressive
palate, with a surge of flavour on the finish, oak under control. Screwcap.
13.9% alc. **Rating** 95 **To** 2018 $45

Eagle Bay Margaret River Cabernet Sauvignon 2008 Vibrant deep garnet-
purple; the bouquet exhibits a concentrated array of aromas, including oak; cassis
and cedar are also there in abundance; the palate is powerful and full-bodied,
with black olive complexity lingering beneath the pure cassis and ample tannins;
built for a long haul, this will need at least 3 years to come together. Screwcap.
14.5% alc. **Rating** 95 **To** 2025 $50 BE

♥♥♥♥♀ Frankland River Riesling 2008 Pale straw-green; a tightly wound wine on
both bouquet and palate, but with the requisite balance to develop with grace, and
reveal more of its secrets. Screwcap. 12.5% alc. **Rating** 93 **To** 2018 $19

Eagle Bay Margaret River Shiraz 2007 **Rating** 93 **To** 2020 $30

Eagle Bay Pemberton Chardonnay 2009 **Rating** 92 **To** 2016 $35 BE

✪ **Reserve Pemberton Chardonnay 2008** Straw and yellow peach are
overshadowed by a fairly generous lashing of toasty new oak; good concentration
and depth of fruit, with a huge sweet spot on the mid-palate, toasty oak
dominating the finish; the quality of the fruit is undeniable. Screwcap. 13.9% alc.
Rating 92 **To** 2016 $28 BE

Lot 80 Margaret River Cabernet Sauvignon 2008 **Rating** 91 **To** 2018
$28 BE

✪ **Sauvignon Blanc Semillon 2009** A very pretty wine, with a mix of passionfruit
and citrus on the long palate leaving the mouth as fresh as a daisy. Screwcap.
13% alc. **Rating** 90 **To** 2010 $19

Eagle Bay Margaret River Shiraz 2008 **Rating** 90 **To** 2016 $35 BE

✪ **The Coat Door Classic Red 2009** Vibrant colour; incredibly juicy spiced plum
and dark cherry fruit bouquet; juicy on the palate, with a little savoury bitumen
to add depth; excellent early drinking style. Shiraz/Grenache. Screwcap. 13.5% alc.
Rating 90 **To** 2014 $14 BE

♥♥♥♥ The Coat Door Wine Company Classic White 2009 **Rating** 87 **To** 2012
$14 BE

Witchcliffe Estate   ★★★★☆

Wickham Road, Witchcliffe, WA 6285 **Region** Margaret River
T (08) 9757 6279 **F** (08) 9757 6279 **www**.witchcliffe-estate.com.au
Open 7 days (summer), Wed–Sun (winter) 11–5
Winemaker Peter Stanlake **Est.** 2003 **Cases** 2000 **Vyds** 20 ha
While the establishment date of Witchcliffe Estate is shown as 2003, 8 ha of semillon,
sauvignon blanc, chardonnay and shiraz plantings date back to the early 1990s. Tony and
Maureen Cosby acquired the 69-ha property in 2000, at which time it was best known as the
Margaret River Marron Farm. The Cosbys still farm marron on a small scale, selling them at
the farm gate and through the cellar door. It has been a very impressive start.

♥♥♥♥♥ Margaret River Shiraz 2007 Strong purple; another shiraz to emphatically
✪ underline the synergy between the region and the variety; very fresh red and black
fruits have energy and thrust on the medium- to full-bodied and long palate,
tannins and oak in balanced support. Screwcap. 14.9% alc. **Rating** 94 **To** 2019 $25

♥♥♥♥♀ Margaret River Semillon Sauvignon Blanc 2009 Early picking has given
✪ the wine extreme freshness and brightness without sacrificing the array of
herb, grapefruit and apple flavours and a long, zesty finish. Screwcap. 11.7% alc.
Rating 93 **To** 2014 $19

Margaret River Chardonnay 2007 **Rating** 90 **To** 2014 $28.50

♥♥♥♥ Milis Mire NV **Rating** 89 **To** 2011 $25

Witches Falls Winery   ★★★★

79 Main Western Road, North Tamborine, Qld 4272 **Region** Granite Belt
T (07) 5545 2609 **F** (07) 5545 0189 www.witchesfalls.com.au **Open** 7 days 10–4
Winemaker Jon Heslop **Est.** 2004 **Cases** 6500 **Vyds** 0.4 ha
Witches Falls is the venture of Jon and Kim Heslop. Jon has a deep interest in experimenting
with progressive vinification methods in order to achieve exceptional and interesting results.
He has a degree in applied science (oenology) from CSU, and experience working in the
Barossa and Hunter Valleys as well as Domaine Chantel Lescure, Burgundy. Witches Falls has
a small estate planting of durif, with the majority of wines being made from contract-grown
grapes sourced predominantly from the Granite Belt.

ΨΨΨΨΨ **Granite Belt Syrah 2007** Vibrant cherry red; bright red fruit bouquet, showing
✪   some savoury complexity with a suggestion of Provençal herbs; the palate is lively
        and truly medium-bodied with fine tannins, crisp acid and a quite long and even
        conclusion. Screwcap. 13% alc. **Rating** 93 **To** 2016 $24 BE
✪   **Granite Belt Grenache 2008** Clearly defined varietal raspberry fruit, exhibiting
        flashes of Provençal herbs adding complexity; light to medium-bodied, with a fine
        structure and elegant fruit to conclude; a very good example of grenache with
        structure. Screwcap. 15% alc. **Rating** 92 **To** 2014 $28 BE

ΨΨΨΨ   **Prophecy Wild Ferment Granite Belt Chardonnay 2008** Rating 89
        To 2014 $28 BE
        Granite Belt Cabernet Sauvignon 2007 Rating 89 **To** 2015 $24 BE
        Co-Inoculated Granite Belt Verdelho 2009 Rating 88 **To** 2012 $20 BE

Witchmount Estate   ★★★★

557 Leakes Road, Plumpton, Vic 3335 **Region** Sunbury
T (03) 9747 1055 **F** (03) 9747 1066 www.witchmount.com.au **Open** Mon–Wed 10–4,
Thurs–Sun 10–5
Winemaker Steve Goodwin **Est.** 1991 **Cases** 10 000 **Vyds** 31 ha
Gaye and Matt Ramunno operate Witchmount Estate in conjunction with its Italian restaurant
and function rooms. The vineyard is planted (in descending order) to shiraz (13.5 ha), cabernet
sauvignon (7 ha), pinot gris (3 ha) and chardonnay (2 ha), with lesser amounts of sauvignon
blanc, merlot, tempranillo and barbera. The quality of the wines has been consistently
excellent, the prices very modest. Exports to Canada, Denmark and Singapore.

ΨΨΨΨΨ **Shiraz 2008** Some colour development obvious; a complex bouquet of licorice,
        multi-spice and black fruits sets the scene for the medium-bodied palate; here
        the texture and structure are commendable. Screwcap. 14.5% alc. **Rating** 91
        To 2020 $33
✪   **Lowen Park Sauvignon Blanc 2009** Has an unusually potent bouquet of
        cut grass and citrus zest, the flavours of the palate adding green capsicum and
        asparagus to the citrus. Striking wine, although not for the faint hearted. Screwcap.
        13.5% alc. **Rating** 90 **To** 2011 $18

ΨΨΨΨ   **Pinot Gris 2009** Rating 89 **To** 2012 $26
        Merlot 2007 Rating 88 **To** 2014 $29

Wolf Blass   ★★★★★

Bilyara Vineyards, 97 Sturt Highway, Nuriootpa, SA 5355 **Region** Barossa Valley
T (08) 8568 7300 **F** (08) 8568 7380 www.wolfblass.com.au **Open** Mon–Fri 9.15–5,
w'ends & public hols 10–5
Winemaker Chris Hatcher (Chief), Matt O'Leary, Marie Clay **Est.** 1966 **Cases** NFP
Although merged with Mildara and now under the giant umbrella of Foster's, the brands (as
expected) have been left largely intact. The wines are made at all price points, ranging through
Red Label, Yellow Label, Gold Label, Brown Label, Grey Label, Black Label and Platinum
Label, at one price point or another covering every one of the main varietals. The pre-eminent

quality of the red wines has reasserted itself over the white wines, but without in any way diminishing the attraction the latter have. All of this has occurred under the leadership of Chris Hatcher, who has harnessed the talents of the winemaking team and encouraged the changes in style. Exports to all major markets.

ŸŸŸŸŸ **Black Label Cabernet Sauvignon Shiraz Malbec 2006** As ever, a complex blend; Cabernet Sauvignon (51%) from Barossa Valley/Langhorne Creek/ Shiraz (44%)/Malbec (9%) from Langhorne Creek; has retained superb purple-crimson hue, and all the intensity and power of the '06 vintage; while there is the obligatory coat of French and American oak, the cascade of black and red fruits more than copes, as do the ripe tannins in a full-bodied red that somehow retains elegance. Screwcap. 15% alc. **Rating** 96 **To** 2030 $130

Grey Label McLaren Vale Shiraz 2008 Deep purple-crimson; right in the heartland of Blass red wine style; lush black fruits, chocolate, mocha and vanilla flavours, oak threaded through the wine from start to finish, the tannins ripe and smooth. What you see is what you get. Screwcap. 15% alc. **Rating** 95 **To** 2023 $41

✪ **Gold Label Eden Valley Clare Valley Riesling 2009** Bright green-straw; a scented, flowery bouquet, almost into lavender, leads into a palate bursting with an array of citrus flavours; good length and balance, the acidity spot on. Screwcap. 12.5% alc. **Rating** 94 **To** 2020 $25

✪ **Gold Label Barossa Shiraz 2007** A super-generous, multi-layered shiraz that nonetheless avoids going over the top. Replete with supple black fruits, it has a long and well-balanced palate, oak and tannins just where they should be. Screwcap. 14.5% alc. **Rating** 94 **To** 2020 $26

Platinum Label Barossa Shiraz 2007 Purple-crimson; a super-rich and fragrant bouquet ranges across blackberries, spice, mocha and (unexpectedly) fresh ground coffee, the opulent full-bodied palate echoing the aromas plus the usual integrated tannins from barrel fermentation of the last part of the fermentation; the alcohol is evident, but is the price to pay for such opulent fruit. Screwcap. 15.5% alc. **Rating** 94 **To** 2027 $165

Grey Label Langhorne Creek Cabernet Sauvignon 2008 If you wondered why Wolf Blass (the man) pinned his future on Langhorne Creek and on finishing red wine fermentation in lots of new American oak (latterly adding French), simply taste this wine, with all of its generous, soft but explicit varietal fruit, tannins a small, although important, part of the picture. Screwcap. 14.5% alc. **Rating** 94 **To** 2020 $41

ŸŸŸŸŸ **Gold Label Mount Gambier Sauvignon Blanc 2009 Rating** 91 **To** 2011 $25

Gold Label Adelaide Hills Chardonnay 2009 Rating 90 **To** 2014 $25

✪ **Yellow Label Cabernet Sauvignon 2008** Bright purple-red; a light- to medium-bodied cabernet that focuses on blackcurrant and cassis fruit rather than tannins or earthy notes that are also part of varietal expression if you pursue them. This wine is bone dry and not oaky, carping English journalists take note. Screwcap. 13.5% alc. **Rating** 90 **To** 2015 $17

Grey Label Langhorne Creek Cabernet Sauvignon 2007 Rating 90 **To** 2016 $41

Gold Label Coonawarra Cabernet Sauvignon 2007 Rating 90 **To** 2020 $26

Gold Label Adelaide Hills Pinot Noir Chardonnay 2007 Rating 90 **To** 2012 $25

✪ **Gold Label Adelaide Hills Pinot Noir Chardonnay 2006** Surprisingly good mousse; has abundant flavour, with white peach, nectarine and strawberry notes all to be found; clean, balanced finish. Cork. 12% alc. **Rating** 90 **To** 2014 $26

Wombat Lodge   ★★★☆

PO Box 460 Cowaramup, WA 6284 **Region** Margaret River
T 0418 948 125 **F** (08) 9755 6070 **www**.wombatlodgewines.com.au **Open** Not
Winemaker Ian McIntosh, Ian Bell **Est.** 1997 **Cases** 650 **Vyds** 4 ha

It pays to have a keenly developed sense of humour if you are a small winemaker committed to producing the very best possible wine regardless of cost and market constraints. The short version (and I quote) is: 'Warick (sic) Gerrard, owner/consumer; Jan McIntosh, winemaker and life partner; Danny Edwards, viticulture and adopted son; 60 ha of central Wilyabrup land, two houses and 60 cows; 4 ha of spoilt vines and 600 cases of red wine.' There is a much longer version, underlining Danny's freedom to organically grow the vines with limited irrigation limiting yield and maximising quality, and Jan's freedom to buy as much French oak as she wishes. The outcome is four clones of cabernet sauvignon, merlot, cabernet franc, malbec and petit verdot in the 650-case make up, selling for the ludicrously low price of $120 per case plus postage. No wine was produced in 2008; the '09 wines will not be released prior to going to press.

ΨΨΨΨΨ **Margaret River Cabernet Sauvignon Merlot Petit Verdot Malbec**
✪ **Cabernet Franc 2007** Bright purple-red; while medium-bodied at best, has very good balance and length to the array of red and black fruits, framed by fine, savoury tannins. Absolute bargain. Screwcap. 13.5% alc. **Rating** 90 **To** 2015 $10

ΨΨΨΨ **South Point Margaret River Cabernet Sauvignon Merlot Shiraz 2007**
✪ Good colour; has more weight to the palate and its flavours than the cabernet blend, but slightly less complexity and finesse; nice wine and excellent value nonetheless. Screwcap. 13.5% alc. **Rating** 88 **To** 2014 $10

Wonga Estate   ★★★★
204 Jumping Creek Road, Wonga Park, Vic 3115 **Region** Yarra Valley
T 0417 346 953 **F** (03) 9722 1715 **www**.wongaestate.com.au **Open** By appt (7 days 10–5)
Winemaker Greg Roberts **Est.** 1997 **Cases** 1000 **Vyds** 2.5 ha
Greg and Jady Roberts developed their vineyard (equally split between chardonnay and pinot noir) in 1997, with a minor expansion in 2002. Greg makes the wines at the onsite micro-winery, set among the pretty bushland surroundings of Wonga Park. Limited production has not stopped the listing of the wines at an impressive array of Melbourne, Yarra Valley and Brisbane restaurants. Exports to China.

ΨΨΨΨΨ **Heathcote Shiraz 2007** Dense purple-red; in the typical robust, very full-bodied style of Wonga Park; thickly layered and textured blackberry, fruitcake and a generous helping of warm spices all coming together, ripe tannins also in the mix. Diam. 15.5% alc. **Rating** 93 **To** 2027 $60

ΨΨΨΨ **Yarra Valley Pinot Noir Rose 2009** Rating 88 **To** 2011 $20

🍃 Wood Block Wines   ★★★☆
PO Box 318, Coonawarra, SA 5263 **Region** Coonawarra
T 0417 878 933 **www**.woodblockwines.com.au **Open** At Terra Rossa Wine Club, Penola, 7 days 10–6
Winemaker Peter Douglas (Contract) **Est.** 2009 **Cases** 400 **Vyds** 34.7 ha
This is the property of Tim and Sarah Kidman, a family name that resonates in Coonawarra and in the minds of those who know the history of the eponymous cattle-grazing family. Tim was only three years old when his maternal grandfather, Grant Wood, first planted shiraz on the terra rossa soil. He and Sarah are now the third generation to care for the vineyard, which now comprises cabernet sauvignon, shiraz and viognier. Only a small part of the production is vinified under the Wood Block Wines label by the infinitely experienced Peter Douglas.

ΨΨΨΨΨ **Scribblestick Coonawarra Cabernet Sauvignon 2005** Excellent hue for age; abundant black fruits on the bouquet, then an intense palate bringing blackcurrant, mulberry and licorice all into play. Screwcap. 14.7% alc. **Rating** 90 **To** 2020 $30

ΨΨΨΨ **Scribblestick Coonawarra Shiraz 2008** Rating 88 **To** 2015 $30

Wood Park ★★★★☆

263 Kneebones Gap Road, Markwood, Vic 3678 **Region** King Valley
T (03) 5727 3367 **F** (03) 5727 3682 **www**.woodparkwines.com.au **Open** At Milawa
Cheese Factory 7 days 10–5
Winemaker John Stokes **Est.** 1989 **Cases** 10 000
John Stokes planted the first vines at Wood Park in 1989 as part of a diversification program
for his property at Bobinawarrah, in the hills of the Lower King Valley, east of Milawa. The
vineyard is managed with minimal chemical use, winemaking a mix of modern and traditional
techniques. In an unusual twist, Stokes acquires his chardonnay from cousin John Leviny, one
of the King Valley pioneers, who has his vineyard at Meadow Creek. The quality of the wines
made in 2004 and subsequent vintages is very impressive. Exports to China and NZ.

ŸŸŸŸŸ **Home Block King Valley Viognier 2008** This is a particularly good viognier,
✪ managing to combine richness of stone fruit flavour with fine structure and a
clean, bright finish. Screwcap. 13.5% alc. **Rating** 94 **To** 2012 $25

ŸŸŸŸŸ **Whitlands Pinot Noir 2008** Bright, clear crimson; without question, the best
✪ pinot from Wood Park to date, with a silky cherry palate complexed by delicate
savoury/darker notes on the finish. Screwcap. 13.5% alc. **Rating** 92 **To** 2015 $25
Reserve King Valley Cabernet 2006 Rating 91 **To** 2026 $40

ŸŸŸŸ **Whitlands Pinot Gris 2009** Rating 89 **To** 2011 $20
✪ **Forgotten Patch King Valley Sangiovese 2008** A super-fragrant bouquet
of spicy cherries, the palate juicy to the point of citrus, the tannins not the least
overbearing. Screwcap. 13.5% alc. **Rating** 89 **To** 2016 $20
✪ **Wild's Gully King Valley Sauvignon Blanc Semillon 2009** Gentle tropical
fruit and ripe citrus aromas and flavours combine well to provide both length and
depth. Screwcap. 13% alc. **Rating** 88 **To** 2011 $15
Meadow Creek King Valley Chardonnay 2008 Rating 88 **To** 2012 $25

 # Woodgate Wines ★★★★

PO Box 71, Manjimup, WA 6258 **Region** Manjimup
T (08) 9772 4288 **F** (08) 9772 4222 **www**.woodgatewines.com.au **Open** Not
Winemaker Mark Aitken **Est.** 2006 **Cases** 1250 **Vyds** 5 ha
This is a family-owned business of Mark and wife Tracey Aitken, Tracey's mother Jeannette
Smith, and her brother Robert and his wife Linda Hatton. Mark became a mature-age
student at Curtin University, obtaining his oenology degree in 2001 as Dux, earning a trip
to Bordeaux to undertake vintage, returning to work at Manjimup's Chestnut Grove winery
from '02. In '05 he and Tracey began their own contract-winemaking business, as well as
making wine for their Woodgate brand. Most of the grapes come from the estate plantings
of cabernet sauvignon, chardonnay, sauvignon blanc, pinot noir and merlot, supplemented by
some purchases. A cellar door opened in '10, along with B&B accommodation. The name
of the sparkling wine, Bojangles, reflects the family's musical heritage, which stretches back
three generations and includes vocalists, guitarists, pianists, a trumpeter, a saxophonist, two
drummers and a double bass player.

ŸŸŸŸŸ **Reserve Chardonnay 2008** Bright straw-green; has above-average intensity to
the grapefruit and white peach fruit on the bouquet and palate alike; the finish
is long and well-balanced, oak playing a support role throughout. Screwcap.
13.4% alc. **Rating** 92 **To** 2015 $28
✪ **Cabernet Sauvignon Rose 2009** Bright pink; fragrant red berry aromas lead
into a delicious palate with lively raspberry and cherry fruits, the finish long and
balanced. Deserved silver medal Sheraton Wine Awards '09. Screwcap. 12.8% alc.
Rating 91 **To** 2010 $16
✪ **Merlot 2008** Bright colour; a fragrant bouquet with spice, mulberry and cedar
aromas is followed by a medium-bodied palate, with a soft texture and good
length. The blending in of Shiraz (6%)/Cabernet (4%) works well. Screwcap.
14% alc. **Rating** 91 **To** 2016 $16

ŸŸŸŸ **Shiraz Cabernet Merlot 2008** The illustration on the label of what looks
✪ like an upside-down vine certainly catches the eye; the medium-bodied palate
is complex, with alternating black and red fruit flavours, oak also playing a role.
Plenty happening here. Screwcap. 14% alc. **Rating** 89 **To** 2015 $16
Pinot Noir 2008 Rating 88 **To** 2012 $22
Reserve Cabernet Sauvignon 2007 Rating 87 **To** 2015 $28

Woodlands   ★★★★★
3948 Caves Road, Wilyabrup, WA 6284 **Region** Margaret River
T (08) 9755 6226 **F** (08) 9755 6236 **www**.woodlandswines.com **Open** 7 days 10.30–5
Winemaker Stuart and Andrew Watson **Est.** 1973 **Cases** 8500 **Vyds** 18.87 ha
Founder David Watson had spectacular success with the Cabernets he made in 1979 and the
early '80s. Commuting from Perth on weekends and holidays, and raising a family, became
all too much, and for some years the grapes from Woodlands were sold to other Margaret
River producers. With the advent of sons Stuart and Andrew (Stuart primarily responsible for
winemaking), the estate has bounced back to pre-eminence. The wines come in four price
bands, the bulk of the production under the Chardonnay and Cabernet Merlot varietals, then a
series of Reserve and Special Reserves, then Reserve de la Cave, and finally Robert Cabernet
Sauvignon. The top-end wines primarily come from the original Woodlands Vineyard, where
the vines are over 35 years old. Exports to the UK and other major markets.

ŸŸŸŸŸ **Chloe Reserve Margaret River Chardonnay 2008** Bright straw-green; a
chardonnay that combines finesse with power, elegance and length; the flavours
are in a grapefruit spectrum, the acidity part and parcel of a high-quality wine that
will have a long life. Screwcap. 13.5% alc. **Rating** 96 **To** 2017 $60
✪ **Margaret River Chardonnay 2009** Pale straw-green; a highly fragrant bouquet
of peach blossom, grapefruit and some barrel ferment oak leads into a fine but
intense palate, with fruit, oak and acid seamlessly flowing through to the long
finish and aftertaste. Screwcap. 13.5% alc. **Rating** 95 **To** 2019 $23
✪ **Margaret 2008** Bright crimson; a fragrant blend of Cabernet Sauvignon/
Merlot/Malbec with the aromas primarily in the red fruit zone; the long palate
is elegant and fine, yet intense and very well balanced, tannins dancing around,
but not impeding, the bright fruit flavours Screwcap. 13.5% alc. **Rating** 95
To 2023 $39.50
Emily Special Reserve 2008 Vivid crimson-purple; a luscious red fruit display
on the bouquet and the effortlessly long palate, the tannins fine but savoury, the
oak subtle. Screwcap. 13.5% alc. **Rating** 95 **To** 2028 $39.50
Reserve de la Cave Margaret River Cabernet Franc 2008 Bottle 9989 of
160 doesn't compute, even if 160 means 160 dozen, but never mind. The relatively
light but bright colour heralds a bouquet with violets and red berries typical
of (good) cabernet franc; the light- to medium-bodied palate is juicy, fresh and
particularly well balanced. Screwcap. 13.5% alc. **Rating** 94 **To** 2016 $65

ŸŸŸŸ͡ **Margaret River Cabernet Merlot 2008** Good crimson colour; an elegant
✪ medium-bodied wine with an interplay between finely drawn fruit flavours and
a background flourish of cedary oak; the finish is long and savoury. Screwcap.
13.5% alc. **Rating** 93 **To** 2020 $23
Margaret River Cabernet Sauvignon 2007 Rating 93 **To** 2022 $105
Reserve de la Cave Margaret River Malbec 2008 Rating 90 **To** 2015 $65

Woodside Valley Estate   ★★★★★
PO Box 332, Greenwood, WA 6924 **Region** Margaret River
T (08) 9345 4065 **F** (08) 9345 4541 **www**.woodsidevalleyestate.com.au **Open** Not
Winemaker Kevin McKay **Est.** 1998 **Cases** 1500 **Vyds** 19.4 ha
Woodside Valley Estate has been developed by a small syndicate of investors headed by Peter
Woods. In 1998 they acquired 67 ha of land at Yallingup, and have now established chardonnay,
sauvignon blanc, cabernet sauvignon, shiraz, malbec and merlot. The experienced Albert

Haak is consultant viticulturist, and together with Peter, took the unusual step of planting south-facing in preference to north-facing slopes. In doing so they indirectly followed in the footsteps of the French explorer Thomas Nicholas Baudin, who mounted a major scientific expedition to Australia on his ship *The Geographe*, and defied established views and tradition of the time in (correctly) asserting that the best passage for sailing ships travelling between Cape Leeuwin and Bass Strait was from west to east. Exports to the UK, the US, Singapore, China and Japan.

ＹＹＹＹＹ **Le Bas Margaret River Chardonnay 2008** Gloriously intense and focused, the aromas and flavours spanning grapefruit through to nectarine; you know French oak is there, but it has been utterly absorbed by the fruit; tremendous length. Diam. 13% alc. **Rating** 96 **To** 2015 $48
Bonnefoy Margaret River Shiraz 2007 Good hue; has a fragrant bouquet of spiced plum and black cherry fruit, the medium-bodied palate with good focus, intensity and length; the tannins are silky and long lasting. Diam. 14% alc. **Rating** 94 **To** 2022 $55
Baudin Margaret River Cabernet Sauvignon 2007 Good hue, although not deep; blackcurrant and cedar aromas set the scene for the long palate, with notes of each as well as forest joining the blackcurrant and cedary tannins. Diam. 14% alc. **Rating** 94 **To** 2022 $58

ＹＹＹＹ **Bissy Margaret River Merlot 2007 Rating** 89 **To** 2015 $50

Woodstock ★★★★☆

Douglas Gully Road, McLaren Flat, SA 5171 **Region** McLaren Vale
T (08) 8383 0156 **F** (08) 8383 0437 **www**.woodstockwine.com.au **Open** 7 days 10–5
Winemaker Scott Collett, Ben Glaetzer **Est.** 1973 **Cases** 25 000 **Vyds** 16 ha
One of the stalwarts of McLaren Vale, owned by Scott Collett, who produces archetypal and invariably reliable full-bodied red wines, spectacular botrytis sweet whites and high-quality (24-year-old) Tawny Port. Also offers a totally charming reception-cum-restaurant, which does a roaring trade with wedding receptions. Exports to Northern Ireland, Switzerland, Malaysia, Philippines, Hong Kong, Japan, Singapore, Cambodia, Vietnam and Taiwan.

ＹＹＹＹＹ **The Stocks Single Vineyard McLaren Vale Shiraz 2007** This is a selection of the best barrels of shiraz from the century-old vines near the winery; the colour is good, the wine with a great array of spice, dark chocolate, black cherry and blackberry fruit; while only medium-bodied, it has outstanding length bolstered by fine, savoury tannins. Screwcap. 14.5% alc. **Rating** 96 **To** 2027 $60

ＹＹＹＹＹ **McLaren Vale Shiraz 2007** A wine that captures all that is good about McLaren
✪ Vale regional characters, black fruits wrapped in a coat of dark chocolate and ripe, savoury tannins; clever use of oak also helps. Screwcap. 14.5% alc. **Rating** 93 **To** 2017 $22
✪ **McLaren Vale Botrytis Semillon 2006** Woodstock was one of the early players with these botrytis wines, using chenin blanc and other varieties. The switch to semillon has paid dividends, this wine still remarkably fresh and lively, the colour still green. Screwcap. 10.5% alc. **Rating** 93 **To** 2013 $20
McLaren Vale Very Old Fortified NV Rating 93 **To** 2014 $45
✪ **McLaren Vale Semillon Sauvignon Blanc 2009** A very interesting wine, assuming its low alcohol came from early picking rather than alcohol reduction via reverse osmosis. It was a good vintage for semillon, and the vibrant flavours seem spot on the money, sauvignon blanc merely a handmaiden. Screwcap. 10.5% alc. **Rating** 92 **To** 2012 $18
McLaren Vale Cabernet Sauvignon 2007 Rating 90 **To** 2017 $22

ＹＹＹＹ **McLaren Vale Riesling 2009 Rating** 89 **To** 2013 $20
McLaren Vale Shiraz Cabernet Sauvignon 2006 Rating 89 **To** 2014 $18

Woody Nook ★★★★
506 Metricup Road, Wilyabrup, WA 6280 **Region** Margaret River
T (08) 9755 7547 **F** (08) 9755 7007 **www**.woodynook.com.au **Open** 7 days 10–4.30
Winemaker Neil Gallagher, Michael Brophy **Est.** 1982 **Cases** 5000 **Vyds** 14.23 ha
Woody Nook, with a backdrop of 18 ha of majestic marri and jarrah forest, does not have the
high profile of the biggest names in Margaret River, but has had major success in wine shows
over the years. It was purchased by Peter and Jane Bailey in 2000, and major renovations and
expansions in '02 and '04 have transformed Woody Nook. There is a new winery, a gallery
tasting room for larger groups, two new kitchens and an alfresco dining area by the pond,
all reached by a long drive through an avenue of prunus trees. The continuing link with the
past is Neil Gallagher's continuing role as winemaker, viticulturist and minority shareholder.
Exports to the UK, the US, Canada, Bermuda, Singapore and Hong Kong.

ΨΨΨΨΨ **Margaret River Shiraz 2007** Dense crimson-purple; dark fruits, spice and
vanilla run through bouquet and palate alike; the fruit has been able to soak up
two years' maturation in American oak, although its contribution is obvious. Diam.
14.5% alc. **Rating** 93 **To** 2017 $34.95
Gallagher's Choice Margaret River Cabernet Sauvignon 2007 Great
crimson-purple colour; a full-bodied, potent cabernet flush with blackcurrant
and dark plum fruit backed by an abundance of ripe tannins; all this before the
alcohol heat catches up with you on the finish. Diam. 15.5% alc. **Rating** 91
To 2022 $50.95

Word of Mouth Wines ★★★★☆
Campbell's Corner, 790 Pinnacle Road, Orange, NSW 2800 **Region** Orange
T (02) 6362 3509 **F** (02) 6365 3517 **www**.wordofmouthwines.com.au **Open** Fri–Sat
11–5, Sun 11–3.30 or by appt (tel 0429 653 316)
Winemaker David Lowe (Contract) **Est.** 1991 **Cases** 2000 **Vyds** 9 ha
The 1991 plantings (made by the former Donnington Vineyard) have changed over the years,
and, in particular, since the business was acquired by Word of Mouth Wines in 2003. Pinot gris,
viognier, riesling, chardonnay, sauvignon blanc, merlot, pinot noir and cabernet sauvignon are
all in bearing, and were joined by plantings of petit manseng in the winter of '08.

ΨΨΨΨΨ **Orange Riesling 2009** Bright pale green; a highly floral bouquet with
❂ passionfruit and lime, then a gloriously juicy sunburst of lime flavours on the long
palate, the touch of sweetness in perfect balance. Screwcap. 12% alc. **Rating** 96
To 2020 $23

ΨΨΨΨΨ **Orange Sauvignon Blanc 2009 Rating** 93 **To** 2011 $25
Pinnacle Orange Pinot Gris 2009 Rating 92 **To** 2011 $25
❂ **Sweet Milli 2009** A good example of early intervention of fermentation, giving
an intense, supple lime juice palate with good balance. Drink as an aperitif or
with fresh fruit at the end of the meal. Riesling. Screwcap. 6.6% alc. **Rating** 92
To 2010 $15
Orange Viognier 2008 Rating 90 **To** 2012 $23
Orange Pinot Noir 2007 Rating 90 **To** 2013 $25

Wyndham Estate ★★★★☆
700 Dalwood Road, Dalwood, NSW 2335 **Region** Hunter Valley
T (02) 4938 3444 **F** (02) 4938 3555 **www**.wyndhamestate.com **Open** 7 days 9.30–4.30
except public hols
Winemaker Nigel Dolan **Est.** 1828 **Cases** 800 000 **Vyds** 55 ha
This historic property is now merely a shop front for the Wyndham Estate label. The Bin
wines often surprise with their quality, representing excellent value; the Show Reserve wines,
likewise, can be very good. The wines come from various parts of South Eastern Australia,
sometimes specified, sometimes not. The wines are all made in the Barossa Valley, from 2009
under the vastly experienced Nigel Dolan, long-term winemaker at Saltram and thereafter

Group Red Winemaker with Foster's, before moving to Wyndham Estate. It's easy to dismiss these wines with faint praise, which does no justice whatsoever to their quality and their value for money. Exports to Canada, Europe and Asia.

ŸŸŸŸŸ **George Wyndham Founder's Reserve Shiraz Grenache 2007** Has a
✪ fragrant and spicy bouquet, then a medium-bodied palate with very good length and balance; gold medals from Queensland Wine Show '08 and Sydney Wine Show '10. McLaren Vale/Barossa Valley. Screwcap. 15% alc. **Rating** 94 **To** 2015 $21

ŸŸŸŸŸ **George Wyndham Founder's Reserve Langhorne Creek Shiraz 2006**
✪ Vibrant colour; a great deal of wine for $20 or so, with a rich display of blackberry and mulberry fruit with a touch of chocolate into the bargain. Great value. Screwcap. 14.5% alc. **Rating** 93 **To** 2016 $21

✪ **Bin 555 Shiraz 2008** Bright hue; fruit and mocha oak on the bouquet come through well on the medium-bodied palate, which has surprising structure, length, fruit, oak and tannins very well balanced. Screwcap. 14% alc. **Rating** 91 **To** 2018 $16

Black Cluster Hunter Valley Shiraz 2006 Rating 91 **To** 2020 $67
✪ **George Wyndham Founder's Reserve Shiraz Tempranillo 2007** A blend of Adelaide Hills Shiraz/Barossa Valley Tempranillo, it is an elegant, light- to medium-bodied wine with bright and spicy red fruit flavours that earned it a Blue-Gold at the Sydney International Wine Competition '09. Screwcap. 13.5% alc. **Rating** 91 **To** 2014 $21.60

Regional Selection Hunter Valley Shiraz 2006 Rating 90 **To** 2017 $21.60
Regional Selection McLaren Vale Shiraz 2006 Rating 90 **To** 2019 $21.60
George Wyndham Founder's Reserve Cabernet Merlot 2004 Rating 90 **To** 2016 $21.60

ŸŸŸŸ **Bin 525 Shiraz Grenache 2008** Light red-purple; the promise of the fragrant
✪ bouquet is fulfilled on the lively and fresh red-fruited palate; ready for immediate enjoyment. Screwcap. 14.5% alc. **Rating** 89 **To** 2012 $16

George Wyndham Founder's Reserve Shiraz Grenache 2008 Rating 89 **To** 2013 $21.60
✪ **Bin 444 Cabernet Sauvignon 2006** Savoury/earthy nuances run through both the bouquet and palate of a wine with good structure and varietal character, the touch of austerity adding rather than detracting. Screwcap. 14% alc. **Rating** 89 **To** 2016 $15.49

Regional Selection Coonawarra Shiraz 2006 Rating 87 **To** 2014 $21.60

Wynns Coonawarra Estate ★★★★★

Memorial Drive, Coonawarra, SA 5263 **Region** Coonawarra
T (08) 8736 2225 **F** (08) 8736 2228 **www.**wynns.com.au **Open** 7 days 10–5
Winemaker Sue Hodder, Sarah Pidgeon **Est.** 1897 **Cases** NFP
Large-scale production has not prevented Wynns from producing excellent wines covering the full price spectrum, from the bargain basement Riesling and Shiraz through to the deluxe John Riddoch Cabernet Sauvignon and Michael Shiraz. Even with steady price increases, Wynns offers extraordinary value for money. The large investments since 2000 in rejuvenating and replanting key blocks under the direction of Allen Jenkins, and skilled winemaking by Sue Hodder, has resulted in wines of far greater finesse and elegance than most of their predecessors. Exports to the UK, the US and Canada.

ŸŸŸŸŸ **Cabernet Sauvignon 2007** Excellent crimson-purple, it has richly scented cassis
✪ and blackcurrant fruit with cedar notes on the bouquet, then a medium- to full-bodied palate with remarkable power and energy. Screwcap. 14% alc. **Rating** 96 **To** 2032 $32

✪ **John Riddoch Cabernet Sauvignon 2006** A wine with a proud history and proven development for 20 years or more; it has a deep, rich and full-bodied well of blackcurrant, blackberry and black olive flavours encased in a web of perfectly formed tannins. Screwcap. 14% alc. **Rating** 96 **To** 2026 $76

Glengyle Single Vineyard Cabernet Sauvignon 2007 Good colour; an estate vineyard that was hit by the frosts in the spring of '06, ultimately yielding 2 tonnes per hectare of very concentrated fruit that comes through strongly on the fruit-laden palate, which also has wonderful texture, structure and length. Screwcap. 14% alc. **Rating** 95 **To** 2022 $39

Alex 88 Single Vineyard Cabernet Sauvignon 2006 Normal colour development; an unabashed full-bodied cabernet made from vines replanted in 1988, full of dark, savoury black fruits embraced by perfect tannins giving structure and quality oak to conclude. As winemaker Sue Hodder accurately says, can be cellared for 5–20 years depending on personal taste. Screwcap. 14% alc. **Rating** 95 **To** 2026 $39

✪ **Shiraz 2008** Deep colour; a fragrant burst of cherry, plum and spice on the bouquet leads into a palate that moves into more powerful black fruits and licorice, the tannins round and soft. Screwcap. 14% alc. **Rating** 94 **To** 2028 $20

✪ **Cabernet Shiraz Merlot 2008** Solid colour; has an abundance of blackberry and blackcurrant fruit softened by a dash of plum and spice; the tannin structure is excellent, oak in its due place; one of the best for some years. Screwcap. 14% alc. **Rating** 94 **To** 2020 $20

🍷🍷🍷🍷🍷
✪ **Riesling 2009** Pale straw-green; a typical flowery bouquet, with citrus and apple blossom, the palate picking up precisely where the bouquet leaves off; easy to overwork when young, this will come into full flower over the next five years. Screwcap. 12% alc. **Rating** 93 **To** 2020 $20

Chardonnay 2009 Rating 91 **To** 2015 $20

Xabregas   ★★★★☆

Cnr Spencer Road/Hay River Road, Narrikup, WA 6326 **Region** Great Southern
T (08) 9321 2366 **F** (08) 9327 9393 **www.**xabregas.com.au **Open** Not
Winemaker The Vintage Wineworx (Martin Cooper) **Est.** 1996 **Cases** 18 000 **Vyds** 118 ha
Owners of Xabregas, the Hogan family, have five generations of WA history and family interests in sheep grazing and forestry in the Great Southern dating back to the 1860s. Terry Hogan, founding chairman, felt the Mount Barker region was 'far too good dirt to waste on blue gums' and vines were planted in 1996, the first wines released in 2002. The Hogan family has begun to evolve and shape the future of Xabregas by concentrating on the region's strengths – shiraz and riesling. Exports to the US, China and NZ.

🍷🍷🍷🍷🍷
✪ **Riesling 2009** Pale quartz; yet another of the skilfully made rieslings balancing modest residual sugar with acidity, which operate in tandem to highlight the lime juice lurking behind apple and mineral notes. Screwcap. 9.8% alc. **Rating** 94 **To** 2014 $17

🍷🍷🍷🍷🍷
✪ **Show Reserve Great Southern Dry Riesling 2009 Rating** 93 **To** 2019 $25

Great Southern Shiraz 2008 Strong red-purple; at once opulent yet restrained, the cool-grown fruit doing most of the hard yards, the unique Ganimede fermenters the rest. Every manner of black fruits and spices are woven together on the powerful, long palate. Screwcap. 14% alc. **Rating** 93 **To** 2023 $17

✪ **Cabernet Sauvignon 2008** Strong purple-crimson; the bouquet has rich, pure blackcurrant varietal fruit, the palate equally generous and equally pure; this is a ridiculous price for such a lovely cabernet, its cellaring future a bonus. Screwcap. 14% alc. **Rating** 93 **To** 2018 $17

Xanadu Wines   ★★★★★

Boodjidup Road, Margaret River, WA 6285 **Region** Margaret River
T (08) 9758 9500 **F** (08) 9757 3389 **www.**xanaduwines.com **Open** 7 days 10–5
Winemaker Glenn Goodall **Est.** 1977 **Cases** 70 000 **Vyds** 109.5 ha
Xanadu fell prey to over-ambitious expansion and to the increasingly tight trading conditions in 2005 as wine surpluses hit hard. The assets were acquired by the Rathbone Group, completing the Yering Station/Mount Langi Ghiran/Parker Coonawarra Estate/Xanadu group. The prime

assets were (and are) the 110 ha of vineyards and winery. The increasing production is matched by a major lift in quality and exports to most major markets.

ŢŢŢŢŢ **Reserve Margaret River Chardonnay 2008** The floral, fragrant citrus blossom aromas are intense, a harbinger of the almost surreal purity of the wine in the mouth. Where the 100% barrel ferment and the alcohol went I have no idea, but this wine has a near-indefinite life. Screwcap. 14% alc. **Rating** 96 **To** 2023 $70

✪ **Margaret River Semillon 2009** Pale quartz-green; a lithe and intense semillon with many facets to its make-up; the wild herb and lemon citrus bouquet has a feather-light touch of oak; the palate is incredibly long and fine; has all manner of complexities to evolve with time. Screwcap. 12% alc. **Rating** 95 **To** 2025 $26

Margaret River Sauvignon Blanc Semillon 2009 Has more structural complexity than most, and complementary flavour complexity, with herbs, grass, strong citrus and an envelope of more tropical fruit; good acidity to close. Screwcap. 13% alc. **Rating** 94 **To** 2012 $25

✪ **Margaret River Shiraz 2008** Bright red fruit and mulled spice present an attractive offering on the bouquet; this is followed through on the palate with fleshy red fruits, silky tannins and alluring spices combining seamlessly for a fresh and lively conclusion. Screwcap. 14.5% alc. **Rating** 94 **To** 2020 $26 BE

ŢŢŢŢŢ **Margaret River Mourvedre 2008** **Rating** 93 **To** 2020 $28 BE

✪ **Next of Kin Margaret River Sauvignon Blanc Semillon 2009** The bouquet is fragrant and lively, as is the delicious palate, with its mix of passionfruit and guava, the finish bright and juicy. Screwcap. 12.5% alc. **Rating** 92 **To** 2012 $18

✪ **Next of Kin Margaret River Shiraz 2008** Very good crimson hue; has a fragrant bouquet of blackberry and dark cherry, then an unexpectedly full-bodied palate with spice and licorice added to the fruit of the bouquet; the texture is good, as is the length. Screwcap. 14% alc. **Rating** 92 **To** 2023 $18

ŢŢŢŢ **Next of Kin Margaret River Cabernet Sauvignon 2008** **Rating** 89 **To** 2016 $18

Margaret River Viognier 2009 **Rating** 88 **To** 2011 $26

Next of Kin Margaret River Rose 2009 **Rating** 88 **To** 2010 $18

Cane Cut Margaret River Semillon Sauvignon Blanc 2009 **Rating** 88 **To** 2014 $26

Yabby Lake Vineyard ★★★★★

Level 1, 500 Chapel Street, South Yarra, Vic 3141 (postal) **Region** Mornington Peninsula
T (03) 9667 6541 **F** (03) 9827 3970 **www**.yabbylake.com **Open** Not
Winemaker Tom Carson, Larry McKenna (Consultant) **Est.** 1998 **Cases** 3350
Vyds 50.8 ha

This high-profile wine business was established by Robert and Mem Kirby (of Village Roadshow) who had been landowners in the Mornington Peninsula for decades. In 1998 they established Yabby Lake Vineyard, under the direction of vineyard manager Keith Harris; the vineyard is on a north-facing slope, capturing maximum sunshine while also receiving sea breezes. The main focus is the 25.4 ha of pinot noir, 14 ha of chardonnay and 7.7 ha of pinot gris; shiraz, merlot and sauvignon blanc take a back seat. The arrival of the hugely talented Tom Carson as Group Winemaker has added lustre to the winery and its wines. The initiative of opening cellar doors in five cities in China is without parallel, facilitated by the involvement of a Chinese partner. The Yabby Lake, Heathcote Estate, Cooralook and Red Claw wines are all part of this arrangement. On the home front, after 10 years of planning, Robert and Mem handed control of the family's vineyards and brands to their children Nina and Clark in 2008.

ŢŢŢŢŢ **Block 5 Pinot Noir 2008** Brighter colour than Block 2; if anything, even more
✪ fragrant than Block 2, with wonderful red fruit aromas, a silky palate continuing the red berry fruit theme. Less powerful, perhaps, but has greater finesse. Gold medal Sydney Wine Show '10. Screwcap. 14.2% alc. **Rating** 97 **To** 2018 $75

Block 6 Chardonnay 2008 Pale straw-green; a prime example of the ultra-fine, precise and pure style Tom Carson seeks to make. You know the oak is there, but it is the intense white peach and grapefruit flavours that drive the wine, underpinned by firm, natural acidity. Screwcap. 12.9% alc. **Rating** 96 **To** 2018 $75

✪ **Mornington Peninsula Chardonnay 2008** Brilliant pale straw-green; fractionally less tightly wound than Block 6, and slightly more white peach and nectarine components, but still flawless in its purity, line and length. Screwcap. 13% alc. **Rating** 96 **To** 2016 $42

Block 2 Pinot Noir 2008 Light colour, although good hue; a super-fragrant bouquet, with pure varietal expression courtesy of red and black cherry and plum fruit, the palate adding some savoury nuances as it drives through to an emphatic finish. Screwcap. 14.2% alc. **Rating** 96 **To** 2016 $75

✪ **Mornington Peninsula Pinot Noir 2007** Bright clear crimson-red; a fragrant bouquet of gently spicy berries leads into a beautifully balanced and proportioned palate, the dark berry fruits in a silky web of tannins. Screwcap. 13.5% alc. **Rating** 96 **To** 2017 $58

✪ **Red Claw Mornington Peninsula Sauvignon Blanc 2009** Very pale straw-green; the bouquet is positively varietal, but the intensity, length and balance of the palate lifts the wine into a higher echelon altogether, and a top-line outcome for the vintage. Screwcap. 12% alc. **Rating** 95 **To** 2011 $22.50

Mornington Peninsula Chardonnay 2007 Green-gold; fragrant and fine, fruit and oak seamlessly interwoven on the bouquet; the palate is particularly elegant, with nectarine and white peach on an almost feathery finish. Screwcap. 13.5% alc. **Rating** 95 **To** 2016 $42

Mornington Peninsula Pinot Noir 2008 Bright and clear colour, good hue; a complex bouquet, with red and black berries backed by spicy notes, then a savoury palate with black fruits woven through textured mouthfeel. Has a long life ahead. Screwcap. 14% alc. **Rating** 95 **To** 2018 $58

🍷🍷🍷🍷🍷 **Red Claw Mornington Peninsula Chardonnay 2008** Bright straw-green;
✪ the bouquet and palate are chock-full of peach and nectarine fruit, tied up with a band of citrussy acidity, the finish long and balanced, oak well in the background. Screwcap. 14.5% alc. **Rating** 93 **To** 2012 $25

✪ **Red Claw Mornington Peninsula Chardonnay 2009** A restrained wine chasing savoury complexity and succeeding; lemon, white nectarine and wet flint on the bouquet; lemony acidity plays a pivotal role on the palate providing line and drive, and giving way to nutty complexity introduced by the hand of the winemaker. Screwcap. 12.5% alc. **Rating** 92 **To** 2017 $22.50 BE

Red Claw Mornington Peninsula Pinot Noir 2008 Rating 92 **To** 2013 $28
Red Claw Mornington Peninsula Pinot Gris 2009 Rating 91 **To** 2013 $22.50 BE
Red Claw Mornington Peninsula Pinot Noir 2009 Rating 91 **To** 2014 $25 BE

Yalumba   ★★★★★

Eden Valley Road, Angaston, SA 5353 **Region** Eden Valley
T (08) 8561 3200 **F** (08) 8561 3393 **www.**yalumba.com **Open** 7 days 10–5
Winemaker Louisa Rose (chief), Brian Walsh, Peter Gambetta, Kevin Glastonbury, Andrew Lanauze **Est.** 1849 **Cases** 950 000 **Vyds** 107 ha
Family-owned and run by Robert Hill Smith, Yalumba has long had a commitment to quality and has shown great vision in its selection of vineyard sites, new varieties and brands. It has always been a serious player at the top end of full-bodied (and full-blooded) Australian reds, and was the pioneer in the use of screwcaps. While its estate vineyards are largely planted to mainstream varieties, it has taken marketing ownership of viognier. However, these days its own brands revolve around the Y Series and a number of stand-alone brands across the length and breadth of SA. Yalumba has been very successful in building its export base. Exports to all major markets.

ŢŢŢŢŢ The Virgilius Eden Valley Viognier 2008 Hand-picked grapes are whole
✪ bunch-pressed direct to barrel (used) and lees stirred for 11 months. The most
remarkable feature is its depth of white peach and apricot flavour, achieved
without the phenolics that can so easily destroy the finish of this variety. Screwcap.
13.5% alc. **Rating** 96 **To** 2011 $49.95

✪ FDW[7c] Adelaide Hills Chardonnay 2008 This wine has already achieved
cult status among the cognoscenti; the Burgundian (Dijon) clones 76 and 95 have
performed magnificently in cool Australian regions, giving the wines made from
them exceptional focus and felicity, the beautiful fruit gliding across the tongue.
Screwcap. 13.5% alc. **Rating** 95 **To** 2018 $24.95

✪ Eden Valley Viognier 2008 Bright green-straw; an aromatic bouquet leads into
a wine that has opulent stone fruit on the one hand, and zesty citrussy acidity on
the other; tremendous length. Screwcap. 14% alc. **Rating** 95 **To** 2015 $22.95

✪ The Scribbler Cabernet Sauvignon Shiraz 2008 A compellingly luscious
wine that offers an array of blackcurrant, blackberry and plum fruit on both
bouquet and palate, with enough savoury tannins on the finish to tighten the
structure to the degree needed; balanced oak. Screwcap. 14% alc. **Rating** 94
To 2023 $19.95

ŢŢŢŢ♀ Running With Bulls Barossa Tempranillo 2008 One of the more
✪ controversial trophy winners at the Adelaide Wine Show '09, but it does have
entrancing texture and impeccable balance. Great drink-now style. Screwcap.
13.5% alc. **Rating** 92 **To** 2014 $18.95

ŢŢŢŢ Langhorne Creek Vermentino 2009 **Rating** 89 **To** 2010 $14.95

Yalumba The Menzies (Coonawarra)   ★★★★

Riddoch Highway, Coonawarra, SA 5263 **Region** Coonawarra
T (08) 8737 3603 **F** (08) 8737 3604 **www**.yalumba.com **Open** 7 days 10–4.30
Winemaker Peter Gambetta **Est.** 2002 **Cases** 5000 **Vyds** 29 ha
The Hill Smith family had been buying grapes from Coonawarra and elsewhere in the
Limestone Coast Zone long before it became a landowner there. In 1993 it purchased the
20-ha vineyard that had provided the grapes previously purchased, and a year later added a
nearby 16-ha block. Together, these vineyards now have 22 ha of cabernet sauvignon and 3.5
ha each of merlot and shiraz. The next step was the establishment of the 35-ha Mawson's
Vineyard in the Wrattonbully region. The third step was to build The Menzies Wine Room
on the first property acquired – named Menzies Vineyard – and to offer the full range of
Limestone Coast wines through this striking rammed-earth tasting and function centre.
Exports to all major markets.

ŢŢŢŢ♀ The Cigar 2006 The cigar is not that of RG Menzies, but the cigar-shaped
terra rossa strip in Coonawarra; has clear-cut varietal character, with a medium-
bodied mix of blackcurrant, earth and strongly savoury tannins. Cork. 14.5% alc.
Rating 93 **To** 2020 $24.95

✪ Mawson's Hill Block 3 Wrattonbully Cabernet Sauvignon 2006 Excellent
colour; has very pure cabernet aroma and flavour, the balance and line also
very good; the Achilles heel is a lack of depth to the fruit, a limitation from the
vineyard, not the winery. Screwcap. 14% alc. **Rating** 90 **To** 2015 $15.95

Yangarra Estate   ★★★★

Kangarilla Road, McLaren Vale, SA 5171 **Region** McLaren Vale
T (08) 8383 7459 **F** (08) 8383 7518 **www**.yangarra.com **Open** 7 days 11–5
Winemaker Peter Fraser, Shelley Thompson **Est.** 2000 **Cases** 15 000 **Vyds** 89.3 ha
This is the Australian operation of Kendall-Jackson, one of the leading premium wine
producers in California. In 2000 Kendall-Jackson acquired the 172-ha Eringa Park vineyard
from Normans Wines (the oldest vines dating back to 1923). The renamed Yangarra Estate is
the estate base for the operation, which has, so it would seem, remained much smaller than
originally envisaged by Jess Jackson. Exports to the UK, the US and other major markets.

♥♥♥♥♀ **McLaren Vale Shiraz 2008** Fresh and cooked blackberry bouquet, with mocha and fruitcake spice aplenty; rich, warm and showing generosity and depth of fruit to conclude. Screwcap. 14.5% alc. **Rating** 92 **To** 2016 $30 BE
Iron Heart Shiraz 2007 Very good colour for the vintage; a very complex, full-bodied wine, with blackberry, plum, licorice and the mandatory regional dark chocolate all in abundance, the tannins ripe, the oak balanced. Most will presumably head to the US, where the alcohol (and attendant warmth) will please. Screwcap. 15.5% alc. **Rating** 92 **To** 2027 $80

♥♥♥♥ **High Sands McLaren Vale Grenache 2007 Rating** 89 **To** 2016 $80 BE

Yarra Burn   ★★★★★

21-23 Delaneys Road, Warrandyte South, Vic 3134 **Region** Yarra Valley
T 1800 088 711 **F** (08) 8392 2202 **www**.yarraburn.com.au **Open** Not
Winemaker Mark O'Callaghan **Est.** 1975 **Cases** NFP **Vyds** 88 ha
The headquarters of Constellation's Yarra Valley operations centring on the large production from its Hoddles Creek vineyards. The new brand direction has taken shape; all the white and sparkling wines are sourced from the Yarra Valley, as is the Pinot Noir; the Shiraz Viognier is a blend of Yarra and Pyrenees grapes. Exports to the UK and the US.

♥♥♥♥♥ **Bastard Hill Chardonnay 2008** Deeply toasty, with a strong savoury bent to the
✪   nectarine and yellow pear fruit; rich, powerful, structured and very long, the oak is a powerful driver to the focused fruit on display; the fruit manages to swallow the oak, despite its delicacy over the length of the finish. Screwcap. 13% alc. **Rating** 95 **To** 2018 $57 BE
Pinot Noir 2009 Deep, clear purple-red; a very rich and powerful pinot with dark plum flavours; good control of extract provides texture and structure. Screwcap. 13.5% alc. **Rating** 94 **To** 2015 $65
✪   **Cellar Release Pyrenees Shiraz 2008** Dense purple-crimson; manages to combine power and intensity with elegance, with layers of black fruits and fine, savoury tannins; positive oak. Screwcap. 13.5% alc. **Rating** 94 **To** 2030 $32
Blanc de Blancs 2005 Bright pale straw-green still very tight after four years 'maturation', the time on lees not revealed; very tangy flavours, and a long finish on a distinguished wine, 100% from Upper Yarra estate-grown grapes. Trophy Sydney Wine Show '10. Cork. 12.5% alc. **Rating** 94 **To** 2013 $45
✪   **Blanc de Blancs 2004** Very fine, elegant and long; obvious citrus and lemon; fine nutty notes. Cork. 12.4% alc. **Rating** 94 **To** 2014 $45

♥♥♥♥♀ **Chardonnay 2008 Rating** 92 **To** 2014 $26 BE
✪   **Premium Cuvee Brut NV** Plenty of impact on the bouquet, with punchy pinot fruit coming to the fore; the palate is fresh, crisp and lively, with a bit of grip on the finish, providing punch and persistence. Cork. 12.5% alc. **Rating** 92 **To** 2012 $20 BE
Pinot Noir Chardonnay Pinot Meunier 2007 Rating 91 **To** 2014 $27.50
Pinot Noir Chardonnay Rose 2006 Rating 90 **To** 2014 $27.50
✪   **Premium Cuvee Rose NV** A light and accessible rose style, with sweet red fruits in abundance; the palate is soft and supple, and while not overly complex, is completely balanced. Cork. 12.5% alc. **Rating** 90 **To** 2012 $20 BE

Yarra Park Vineyard   ★★★★☆

4 Benson Drive, Yering, Vic 3770 **Region** Yarra Valley
T (03) 9739 1960 **F** (03) 9841 7522 **www**.yarrapark.com.au **Open** By appt
Winemaker Mac Forbes (Contract) **Est.** 1996 **Cases** 750 **Vyds** 2.5 ha
Stephen and Rosalind Atkinson established 1 ha each of chardonnay and cabernet sauvignon, and 0.5 ha of sauvignon blanc, between 1996 and '97. The vineyard is run on organic principles, with heavy mulching and what is technically termed 'integrated pest management'. Yields are deliberately kept low. Until 2006 the wines were made by Phil Kerney at Willow Creek in the Mornington Peninsula, but since '07 have been made by Mac Forbes. The vineyard is situated in what the Atkinsons call 'the golden mile', 1 km to the north of Mount Mary.

ϘϘϘϘϘ Chardonnay 2008 An understated, finely textured and structured chardonnay, with taut citrus and stone fruit, and an improbable touch of ginger peaking through the acidity on the finish. Screwcap. 13.5% alc. **Rating** 94 **To** 2015 $30

ϘϘϘϘϘ Cabernet Sauvignon 2006 **Rating** 90 **To** 2014 $35

Yarra Yarra   ★★★★★

239 Hunts Lane, Steels Creek, Vic 3775 **Region** Yarra Valley
T (03) 5965 2380 **F** (03) 5965 2086 **www**.yarrayarravineyard.com.au **Open** By appt
Winemaker Ian Maclean **Est.** 1979 **Cases** NFP **Vyds** 9.3 ha
Despite its small production, the wines of Yarra Yarra found their way into a veritable who's who of Melbourne's best restaurants, encouraging Ian Maclean to increase the estate plantings from 2 ha to over 7 ha in 1996 and '97. Demand for the beautifully crafted wines continued to exceed supply, so the Macleans planted yet more vines and increased winery capacity. All this seemed to go up in flames as the terrible 2009 Black Saturday bushfires consumed the winery, irreplaceable museum stock from '83 to 2000, the then yet-to-be-bottled '08 Syrah and '06 and '08 Sauvignon Blanc Semillon (the '07 vintage having been destroyed by frost), and scorched or burnt 50% of the estate vineyards. Friends rallied to the cause, and Ian has embarked on the long job of repairing/replacing the vineyard trellis system, and methodically replanting the half of the vineyard destroyed by fire and introducing the use of organic/biodynamic sprays. The new winery was finished end April '10, too late for the vintage, which was made in one of the farm buildings not destroyed. When friends asked why he should do all this having turned 65, his answer was simple: 'My greatest wines have yet to be made.' Exports to Singapore, Malaysia and Hong Kong.

ϘϘϘϘϘ Sauvignon Blanc Semillon 2005 Bright colour; is fully developed; a very complex wine, with layers of flavour framed by texture and structure from barrel ferment through to bottle age; great length. Diam. 13% alc. **Rating** 94 **To** 2013 $40

Syrah Viognier 2006 Elegant wine, with strongly spicy/peppery overtones to the bright red berry fruit flavours; cedary oak and fine, savoury tannins complete the picture. Diam. 13.5% alc. **Rating** 94 **To** 2016 $50

The Yarra Yarra 2005 A wine that is all about texture and structure rather than fruit flavour; it is very complex, with savoury, tarry black fruits and persistent tannin support. Blink and you're in Bordeaux. Diam. 13.5% alc. **Rating** 94 **To** 2020 $75

Cabernets 2005 A powerful multifaceted bouquet and multi-layered plate; a certain imperious austerity to the wine, reinforced by the uncompromising tannins. Demands a minimum of a decade, twice that if possible. Diam. 13% alc. **Rating** 94 **To** 2025 $50

Yarra Yering   ★★★★★

Briarty Road, Coldstream, Vic 3770 **Region** Yarra Valley
T (03) 5964 9267 **F** (03) 5964 9239 **www**.yarrayering.com **Open** Sat 10–5,
Sun 2–5 while stocks last
Winemaker Paul Bridgeman **Est.** 1969 **Cases** 4000 **Vyds** 26.37 ha
In September 2008, founder Bailey Carrodus died, and in April '09 Yarra Yering was on the market. It was Bailey Carrodus' clear wish and expectation that any purchaser would continue to manage the vineyard and winery, and hence the wine style, in much the same way as he had done for the previous 40 years. Its acquisition in June 2009 by a partnership headed by Swiss-born, Singapore-based Edward (Ed) Peters seems certain to fulfil that wish. The low-yielding, unirrigated vineyards have always produced wines of extraordinary depth and intensity, and there is every reason to suppose there will be no change in the years ahead. Dry Red No. 1 is a cabernet blend; Dry Red No. 2 a shiraz blend; Dry Red No. 3 is a blend of touriga, tinta cao, tinta amarela, roriz and sousao; Pinot Noir and Chardonnay are not hidden behind delphic numbers; Underhill Shiraz is from an adjacent vineyard purchased by Yarra Yering over a decade ago; and Potsorts is an extraordinary vintage style made from the same varieties as Dry Red No. 3. Exports to the UK, the US and other major markets.

ŢŢŢŢŢ **Carrodus Cabernet Merlot 2007** As should be the case, has distinctly greater intensity than Agincourt; has perfectly ripened cassis, blackcurrant and plum fruit, the tannins ripe and fine, the 100% new French oak enveloped by the wine. Cork. 12.2% alc. **Rating** 96 **To** 2020 $150

Pinot Noir 2007 Excellent hue and depth; aromas of plum and black cherry lead into a finely boned and structured palate, the fruit and tannins in perfect unison right through to the very long finish. Cork. 13.5% alc. **Rating** 95 **To** 2014 $90

Dry Red No. 2 2007 Relatively bright but light colour; a super-elegant, supple palate and spotless bouquet; natural acidity gives the wine its special brightness and length; new French oak and tannins play a pure support role to a classy wine that has tremendous length. Cork. 13.5% alc. **Rating** 95 **To** 2017 $90

Potsorts Vintage Fortified 2007 Is in the heartland of Potsorts, intense and spicy blackcurrant fruits, with great texture provided by the fine, spicy/savoury tannins; intense fruit, not sweetness. Cork. 23% alc. **Rating** 95 **To** 2022 $75

Carrodus Viognier 2007 Glowing yellow-green; a viognier that resolves the dilemma about varietal flavour and phenolics, achieving the former and avoiding the latter; has soaked up the oak in which it was fermented and matured; good length and balance. Cork. 14% alc. **Rating** 94 **To** 2012 $150

Underhill Shiraz 2007 Better hue than Gruyere, although no deeper; an elegant, spicy, medium-bodied palate with impressive energy and drive, the mix of red and black fruits with a sprinkling of spice and pepper, the length almost taken for granted. High-quality cork. 13.5% alc. **Rating** 94 **To** 2022 $75

Carrodus Merlot 2007 Good bright hue; a vibrant and juicy merlot, with cassis and blackcurrant fruit, the texture very good and the finish long; there is, it must be said, a hint of mint. Cork. 12.6% alc. **Rating** 94 **To** 2017 $150

Dry Red No. 1 2007 Bright but light crimson; tangy juicy wine, all about finesse and elegance, but not at the expense of length or drive, and does have very attractive red fruits despite very low alcohol. Cabernet Sauvignon/Merlot/Malbec/Petit Verdot. Cork. 12.3% alc. **Rating** 94 **To** 2017 $90

ŢŢŢŢŢ **Agincourt Cabernet Merlot 2007 Rating** 92 **To** 2017 $75
Gruyere Shiraz 2007 Rating 91 **To** 2014 $35

Yarrabank   ★★★★★

38 Melba Highway, Yarra Glen, Vic 3775 **Region** Yarra Valley
T (03) 9730 0100 **F** (03) 9739 0135 **www**.yering.com **Open** 7 days 10–5
Winemaker Michel Parisot, Willy Lunn, Darren Rathbone **Est.** 1993 **Cases** 5000 **Vyds** 4 ha
Yarrabank is a highly successful joint venture between the French Champagne house Devaux and Yering Station, established in 1993. Until 1997 the Yarrabank Cuvee Brut was made under Claude Thibaut's direction at Domaine Chandon, but thereafter the entire operation has been conducted at Yarrabank. There are 4 ha of dedicated 'estate' vineyards at Yering Station; the balance of the intake comes from other growers in the Yarra Valley and southern Vic. Wine quality has consistently been outstanding, frequently with an unmatched finesse and delicacy. Exports to all major markets.

ŢŢŢŢŢ **Cuvee 2005** Very pale straw-green, with fine and persistent mousse; a blend of Pinot Noir/Chardonnay that does not undergo mlf and has four years on lees; there is a strong case for another period on lees, and I look forward to a late disgorged version in due course. Cork. 13% alc. **Rating** 95 **To** 2013 $38

Late Disgorged 2001 Some colour development, its mousse is fine and persistent; the palate has extreme length, with fruit notes and brioche intermingling on an impressive finish. Cork. 12.5% alc. **Rating** 95 **To** 2010 $45

YarraLoch   ★★★★★

58 Stead Street, South Melbourne, Vic 3205 (postal) **Region** Yarra Valley
T (03) 9696 1604 **F** (03) 9696 8387 **www**.yarraloch.com.au **Open** By appt
Winemaker David Bicknell, Ray Nadeson **Est.** 1998 **Cases** 4500 **Vyds** 12 ha

This is the ambitious project of successful investment banker Stephen Wood. He has taken the best possible advice, and has not hesitated to provide appropriate financial resources to a venture that has no exact parallel in the Yarra Valley or anywhere else in Australia. Twelve ha of vineyards may not seem so unusual, but in fact he has assembled three entirely different sites, 70 km apart, each matched to the needs of the variety/varieties planted on that site. Pinot noir (4.4 ha) is planted on the Steep Hill Vineyard, with a northeast orientation, and a shaley rock and ironstone soil. Cabernet sauvignon (4 ha) has been planted at Kangaroo Ground, with a dry, steep northwest-facing site and abundant sun exposure in the warmest part of the day, ensuring full ripeness. Just over 3.5 ha of merlot, shiraz, chardonnay and viognier are planted at the Upper Plenty vineyard, 50 km from Kangaroo Ground. This has an average temperature 2°C cooler and a ripening period two–three weeks later than the warmest parts of the Yarra Valley. Add skilled winemaking and some sophisticated (and beautiful) packaging, and you have a 5-star recipe for success.

ŶŶŶŶŶ **Stephanie's Dream Chardonnay 2008** The same Swiss-watch precision is
✪   evident here as in the standard wine, but with a deliberate fretwork of complexity, particularly on the bouquet; the oak influence is restrained, but an integral part of the wine; the freshness of the finish is remarkable. Screwcap. 13% alc. **Rating** 96 To 2020 $45

✪   **The Collection Heathcote Shiraz 2006** Strong red-purple; a wine still with the exuberance of youth, yet beautifully balanced and textured; the full array of black fruits have spice and oak lurking in the background; great drive and length. Diam. 14% alc. **Rating** 96 To 2025 $40

✪   **Chardonnay 2008** Light straw-green, near-identical to Stephanie's Dream; a super-elegant and super-refined wine, every note carefully calibrated as you move through from the bouquet, to the palate, to the finish and aftertaste; the flavours are first and foremost of white fleshed stone fruit, polished by perfect acidity. Screwcap. 12.5% alc. **Rating** 95 To 2018 $32

     Stephanie's Dream Pinot Noir 2008 While sharing many of the flavours and aromas of the standard wine, this has significantly greater focus, intensity and length; the flavours drive through the palate and aftertaste with rare elan. Screwcap. 13.5% alc. **Rating** 95 To 2016 $45

✪   **Merlot 2008** Clear, red-crimson; has the medium-bodied weight, texture and structure needed for good merlot; the flavours, too, are spot on, with plum, redcurrant and black olive/bay leaf interwoven with fine tannins; exemplary length. Screwcap. 14% alc. **Rating** 94 To 2016 $30

     Stephanie's Dream Merlot 2006 Purple-crimson hue; significantly more complex than the standard merlot, and greater structure; the question is whether the tannins will soften before the fruit; the answer is very likely yes, but I doubt it's an issue for most tasters anyway. Diam. 14% alc. **Rating** 94 To 2021 $40

     Stephanie's Dream Cabernet Sauvignon 2006 A somewhat savoury/austere, albeit correct, expression of cabernet, blackcurrant fruit impregnated with powdery tannins along the length of the palate; a good wine, although not in the normal polished style of YarraLoch. Diam. 14% alc. **Rating** 94 To 2021 $40

ŶŶŶŶŶ **Pinot Noir 2008 Rating** 90 To 2014 $30

Yarrambat Estate   ★★★☆

45 Laurie Street, Yarrambat, Vic 3091 (postal) **Region** Yarra Valley
T (03) 9717 3710 **F** (03) 9717 3712 **www.**yarrambatestate.com.au **Open** By appt
Winemaker John Ellis (Contract) **Est.** 1995 **Cases** 1500 **Vyds** 2.6 ha
Ivan McQuilkin has chardonnay, pinot noir, cabernet sauvignon and merlot in his vineyard in the northwestern corner of the Yarra Valley, not far from the Plenty River. It is very much an alternative occupation for Ivan, whose principal activity is as an international taxation consultant to expatriate employees. While the decision to make wine was at least in part triggered by falling grape prices, hindsight proves it to have been a good one, because some of the wines have impressed. Exports to Singapore.

ŸŸŸŸ♀ **Shiraz 2006** Bright colour; a savoury bouquet of red fruits, Asian spices and a touch of liqueur cherry; medium-bodied, with fine tannins, crisp acidity and reasonable persistence; a charming wine. Gold medal Strathbogie Ranges Wine Show '08. Screwcap. 14.6% alc. **Rating** 91 **To** 2016 $19.50 BE

ŸŸŸŸ **Cabernet Merlot 2008 Rating** 87 **To** 2014 $17.50 BE

🍇 Yarran Wines   ★★★★

178 Myall Park Road, Yenda, NSW 2681 **Region** Riverina
T (02) 6968 1125 **F** (02) 6968 1017 **www**.yarranwines.com.au **Open** 7 days 10–5
Winemaker Sam Brewer **Est.** 2000 **Cases** 4000 **Vyds** 30 ha
John and Lorraine Brewer have been grapegrowers for over 30 years, but when son Sam went to CSU to complete a degree in wine science, they celebrated his graduation by crushing 1 tonne of shiraz, fermenting the grapes in a milk vat. The majority of the grapes from the estate plantings are sold, but each year a little more was made under the Yarran banner, and along the way a winery with a crush capacity of 150 tonnes was built. Sam worked for Southcorp and De Bortoli in Australia, and overseas (in the US and China), but after 10 years decided to take the plunge in 2009 and concentrate on the family winery, together with his parents. The majority of the grapes come from the family vineyard, but some parcels are sourced from growers including Lake Cooper Estate in the Heathcote region. In future years it is intended that the portfolio of different regions will be gradually increased; making silk purses out of sow's ears is not easily done.

ŸŸŸŸ♀ ✪ **Leopardwood Reserve Petit Verdot 2008** Typical deep colour; a full-bodied wine whose lush black fruits have completely absorbed 12 months' maturation in new French and American oak barriques; open-fermented and basket-pressed, techniques nearly always resulting in the soft tannins exhibited in this wine. Screwcap. 13.5% alc. **Rating** 91 **To** 2018 $14

✪ **Leopardwood Reserve Shiraz 2008** Has assembled an unusual array of medals, with a gold medal from NSW Small Makers Wine Show '09 the most significant; skilled winemaking has produced an elegant, fragrant red-fruited wine, its texture and length particularly impressive. Screwcap. 13.5% alc. **Rating** 90 **To** 2016 $14

ŸŸŸŸ ✪ **Chardonnay 2009** A manifestation of the surplus of chardonnay (even though it's estate-grown), for it has some truly attractive stone fruit and citrus flavours; the mention of French oak on the back label is interesting, for it's not obvious in the wine. Screwcap. 13% alc. **Rating** 87 **To** 2012 $9

Yarrawood Estate   ★★★☆

1275 Melba Highway, Yarra Glen, Vic 3775 **Region** Yarra Valley
T (03) 9730 2003 **F** (03) 9730 1144 **www**.yarrawood.com.au **Open** 7 days 10–5
Winemaker Contract **Est.** 1997 **Cases** 28 000 **Vyds** 40.6 ha
Yarrawood Estate has pinot noir (10.6 ha), cabernet sauvignon (7.9 ha), chardonnay (7.2 ha), merlot (5.3 ha), shiraz (4.5 ha) and lesser amounts of sauvignon blanc, riesling and verdelho. The major part of the production is sold, and the Yarrawood Tall Tales wines are contract-made. It does, however, have a café and cellar door on the Melba Highway, 3 km north of Yarra Glen. Exports to the US, Japan, Singapore and China.

ŸŸŸŸ♀ **Tall Tales Shiraz 2008** Bright crimson hue; has certainly been picked ripe, and has a lot of extract, but works well in a full-bodied frame, plum and black fruits supported by persistent, although ripe, tannins. Screwcap. 15% alc. **Rating** 91 **To** 2020 $20.50

ŸŸŸŸ **Tall Tales Rose 2008 Rating** 89 **To** 2011 $16.50
Tall Tales Verdelho 2009 Rating 88 **To** 2012 $17

Yarrh Wines ★★★

380 Greenwood Road, Murrumbateman, NSW 2582 **Region** Canberra District
T (02) 6227 1474 **F** (02) 6227 1584 **www.**yarrhwines.com.au **Open** Aug–June w'ends &
public hols 11–5
Winemaker Fiona Wholohan **Est.** 1997 **Cases** 3000 **Vyds** 6 ha
It is probably best to quickly say that Yarrh is Aboriginal for 'running water', and is neither
onomatopoeic nor letters taken from the partners names, the partners being Fiona Wholohan,
Neil McGregor and Peta and Christopher Mackenzie Davey. The vineyard was planted in
three stages between 1997 and 2000, and there are now cabernet sauvignon, shiraz, sauvignon
blanc, riesling, pinot noir and sangiovese (in descending order), and all of the wines are estate-
grown, and competently made by Fiona. Exports to Norway, Vietnam and China.

♀♀♀♀ **Canberra District Riesling 2009** A strict bouquet of freshly squeezed lemon
and candied lime; the acidity dominates the palate, driving the tangy citrus fruit to
its conclusion. Screwcap. 11.7% alc. **Rating** 87 **To** 2015 $18 BE
Canberra District Sangiovese 2008 Bright cherry fruit bouquet with a
brambly savoury character in tow; the palate is savoury and shows plenty of acid
and nerve. Screwcap. 14% alc. **Rating** 87 **To** 2012 $25 BE

Yass Valley Wines ★★★☆

5 Crisps Lane, Murrumbateman, NSW 2582 **Region** Canberra District
T (02) 6227 5592 **www.**yassvalleywines.com.au **Open** Wed–Sun & public hols 10–5,
or by appt
Winemaker Michael Withers **Est.** 1978 **Cases** 400 **Vyds** 2.87 ha
Michael (Mick) Withers and Anne Hillier purchased Yass Valley Wines in 1991 and have
subsequently rehabilitated the existing run-down vineyards and extended the plantings
(merlot, shiraz, barbera, chardonnay, verdelho, gewurztraminer and semillon). Mick is a
chemist by profession and has completed a wine science degree at CSU; Anne is a registered
psychologist and has completed a viticulture diploma at CSU.

♀♀♀♀♀ **Riesling 2009** A rich bouquet with ripe citrus aromas in abundance; the palate
✪ has similar ripe citrus flavours, but is fine and focused thanks to the low alcohol
and fresh acidity. Trophy NSW Wine Awards '09. Screwcap. 11.6% alc. **Rating** 94
To 2017 $25

♀♀♀♀ **Barbera 2008 Rating** 87 **To** 2013 $20

Yelland & Papps ★★★★★

PO Box 256, Greenock, SA 5360 **Region** Barossa Valley
T 0408 250 005 **www.**yellandandpapps.com **Open** By appt
Winemaker Michael Papps **Est.** 2005 **Cases** 1200
Michael and Susan Papps (née Yelland) set up this venture after their marriage in 2005. Susan
decided she did not want to give up her surname entirely, and thus has been able to keep
her family name in the business. Michael has the technical background, having lived in the
Barossa Valley for more than 20 years, working at local wineries, bottling facilities and wine
technology businesses. Susan, who grew up on the Yorke Peninsula, headed to New York for a
year, working and studying at the Windows of the World Wine School. The quantity of wine
made is limited by the scarcity of the high-quality grapes they have managed to secure from
the Greenock area for their wines.

♀♀♀♀♀ **Delight Barossa Valley Grenache Rose 2009** Light bright crimson-fuchsia;
✪ 36-hours' skin contact then a cold, 3-week fermentation has produced a rose with
notable length and structure underneath the vibrant red fruit flavours. Screwcap.
13% alc. **Rating** 94 **To** 2011 $17
✪ **Devote Greenock Barossa Valley Shiraz 2008** Deeply coloured; a rich and
generous shiraz with complex blackberry and fruitcake aromas and flavours allied
with a dash of chocolate; the supple and even texture prevents the wine going
over the top. Screwcap. 14.5% alc. **Rating** 94 **To** 2020 $30

✪ **Devote Barossa Valley Cabernet Sauvignon 2008** A gentle, fragrant, cassis-accented bouquet then a luscious medium- to full-bodied palate following, the cassis introduction adding blackcurrant to the palate; the tannins and 20 months' French oak maturation add more to the wine. Screwcap. 14.5% alc. **Rating** 94 **To** 2023 $30

🍷🍷🍷🍷 ✪ **Delight Barossa Valley Grenache Shiraz 2008** Grenache (71%) from 40-year-old vines and 20-year-old shiraz, both from small vineyards in the Greenock area, were separately fermented and matured before final barrel selection and bottling, the shiraz adding black fruits to the red of the grenache; very rich and luscious. Screwcap. 14.5% alc. **Rating** 92 **To** 2013 $19.95

Devote Old Vine Barossa Valley Grenache 2008 Rating 90 **To** 2016 $30

Yellowglen ★★★☆

77 Southbank Boulevard, Southbank, Vic 3006 **Region** South Eastern Australia
T 1300 651 650 **F** (03) 9633 2002 **www**.yellowglen.com.au **Open** Not
Winemaker Charles Hargrave **Est.** 1975 **Cases** NFP

It may come as a surprise to some (it certainly did to me) that Yellowglen is the clear leader in the value share of the sparkling wine category in Australia, with 22.9%, and growing at 4.3% per annum, way in front of Jacob's Creek at 7.6%, and with zero growth. It is this dominant position (and a spread of RRP prices from $13.99 for Yellow up to $29 for Vintage Perle) that underpins its separate listing. Exports to the UK, the US and NZ.

🍷🍷🍷🍷 ✪ **Limited Release Perle Rose NV** Pale salmon; quite aromatic and complex, the red fruits obvious, with biscuit spice from the pinot meunier on both bouquet and palate; good length and balance. Cork. 12% alc. **Rating** 93 **To** 2012 $29

Yering Station ★★★★★

38 Melba Highway, Yarra Glen, Vic 3775 **Region** Yarra Valley
T (03) 9730 0100 **F** (03) 9739 0135 **www**.yering.com **Open** 7 days 10–5
Winemaker Willy Lunn, Darren Rathbone **Est.** 1988 **Cases** 60 000 **Vyds** 112 ha

The historic Yering Station (or at least the portion of the property on which the cellar door sales and vineyard are established) was purchased by the Rathbone family in 1996 and is also the site of the Yarrabank joint venture with French Champagne house Devaux (see separate entry). A spectacular and very large winery has been erected, handling the Yarrabank sparkling wines and the Yering Station and Yarra Edge table wines. It immediately became one of the focal points of the Yarra Valley, particularly as the historic Chateau Yering, where luxury accommodation and fine dining are available, is next door. Yering Station's own restaurant is open every day for lunch, providing the best cuisine in the Valley. In July 2008, winemaker Tom Carson moved to take up the position of Group Winemaker/General Manager of Heathcote Estate and Yabby Lake Vineyard, with overall responsibility for winemaking at those two properties. His replacement is William (Willy) Lunn, a graduate of Adelaide University with more than 24 years' cool-climate winemaking experience around the world, including Petaluma, Shaw & Smith and Argyle Winery (Oregon). Exports to all major markets.

🍷🍷🍷🍷🍷 **Single Vineyard Coombe Farm Vineyard Yarra Valley Chardonnay 2007** Bright straw-green; has a racy cut and drive, with connotations of Chablis in its minerality; the flavours, too, are towards grapefruit, although with white peach also present; oak a given, acidity more important. Screwcap. 13.5% alc. **Rating** 96 **To** 2020 $55

✪ **Single Vineyard Smedley Lane Vineyard Yarra Valley Shiraz Viognier 2006** Great colour; an outstanding bouquet with strong nuances of Côte Rôtie, spice and black fruits in abundance, the palate rich and complex, with potent fruit, ripe tannins and good oak. Screwcap. 14.5% alc. **Rating** 96 **To** 2026 $55

✪ **Yarra Valley Chardonnay 2008** Light straw-green; an immaculately balanced chardonnay, fragrant and pure; white peach fruit, a hint of mineral and subtle barrel ferment French oak combine seamlessly, giving the wine both elegance and length. Screwcap. 13% alc. **Rating** 95 **To** 2016 $28

Carr C Block Vineyard Yarra Valley Shiraz Viognier 2006 Colour still strong and holding hue; distinctly richer and deeper than the normal Yering Station style, the exotic bouquet with black fruits, spice and licorice, the palate very long and sustained by fine but persistent tannins. Screwcap. 15% alc. **Rating** 95 **To** 2018 $60
Single Vineyard Yarra Edge Vineyard Yarra Valley Cabernet Sauvignon 2006 Deep colour; a sumptuous cabernet attesting to its very low 1.2-tonne per acre background; cassis, blackcurrant and pronounced cedary oak (23 months, 100% new French) together with ripe tannins make for a complete wine. Screwcap. 14.5% alc. **Rating** 95 **To** 2036 $55
Single Vineyard Willow Lake Old Vine Yarra Valley Chardonnay 2007 Still very pale; a challenging wine, mineral, slate and acid tightly wrapped around the green apple and citrus fruit; this is not a wannabe sauvignon blanc, simply a light-bodied wine of amazing length. Screwcap. 10.8% alc. **Rating** 94 **To** 2020 $55
✪ **Yarra Valley Pinot Noir 2008** Light, bright red; lifted red cherry/berry fruit aromas, then a light-bodied palate with fresh red fruit flavours and silky tannins. Elegant light style. Screwcap. 13.5% alc. **Rating** 94 **To** 2015 $26
✪ **Yarra Valley Cabernet Sauvignon 2008** Strong purple-crimson; a complex bouquet of cassis, red fruits, cedar and spice then a medium- to full-bodied palate with good length and some savoury tannins to add to the overall complexity of cool-grown cabernet. Screwcap. 14.5% alc. **Rating** 94 **To** 2020 $28

♀♀♀♀♀ **Yarra Valley Fume Blanc 2009 Rating** 93 **To** 2012 $28
✪ **MVR Yarra Valley Marsanne Viognier Roussanne 2008** Has as much to do with structure and texture as varietal fruit flavour; taking a line through the Yeringberg Marsanne Roussanne, could really distinguish itself with a few years' bottle age. Screwcap. 14% alc. **Rating** 91 **To** 2014 $26
✪ **Little Yering Chardonnay 2008** Striking label, Yering in bold type, the name recalling the 19th-century heydays of the Yarra Valley; as yet, the wine is wrapped up in swaddling clothes, barely able to make itself heard. All lies in the future. Screwcap. 13% alc. **Rating** 90 **To** 2015 $20
Little Yering Pinot Noir 2008 Rating 90 **To** 2013 $21

Yeringberg   ★★★★★

Maroondah Highway, Coldstream, Vic 3770 **Region** Yarra Valley
T (03) 9739 1453 **F** (03) 9739 0048 **www.**yeringberg.com **Open** By appt
Winemaker Guill and Sandra de Pury **Est.** 1863 **Cases** 1200 **Vyds** 2.9 ha
Makes wines for the new millennium from the low-yielding vines re-established in the heart of what was one of the most famous (and infinitely larger) vineyards of the 19th century. In the riper years, the red wines have a velvety generosity of flavour rarely encountered, yet never lose varietal character, while the long-lived Marsanne Roussanne takes students of history back to Yeringberg's fame in the 19th century. Exports to the UK, the US, Switzerland, Singapore, Japan and Hong Kong.

♀♀♀♀♀ **Yarra Valley Chardonnay 2008** An immaculately made wine from vines over
✪ 30 years old; has white peach, nectarine and fig, and light nutty barrel ferment oak in the background. Delicious now or in a decade. Diam. 13.5% alc. **Rating** 95 **To** 2018 $40
✪ **Yarra Valley Viognier 2008** The first release from the estate plantings in 2001, and a thoroughly impressive one at that. There is no doubt this is viognier, its ripe stone fruit (including apricot) flavours plain to see, its mouthfeel rich and supple. Diam. 14.5% alc. **Rating** 94 **To** 2014 $30
✪ **Yarra Valley Marsanne Roussanne 2008** Bright green-gold; by far the most distinguished of these Rhône-style blends in Australia, grown at Yeringberg over 100 years ago, and now with well over 30-year-old marsanne. Powerful, it is a minerally framework for honeysuckle to climb on, honey and toast to come in the years ahead. Diam. 13.5% alc. **Rating** 94 **To** 2014 $40

Yilgarnia ★★★★
1847 Redmond West Road, Redmond, WA 6327 **Region** Denmark
T (08) 9845 3031 **F** (08) 9845 3031 **www**.yilgarnia.com.au **Open** Fri–Mon, school &
public hols 11–5 (Summer 11–9), closed May–Aug
Winemaker Harewood Estate (James Kellie) **Est**. 1997 **Cases** 3000 **Vyds** 12.5 ha
Melbourne-educated Peter Buxton travelled across the Nullarbor and settled on a bush block
of 405 acres on the Hay River, 6 km north of Wilson Inlet over 40 years ago. For the first
10 years Peter worked for the WA Department of Agriculture in Albany, surveying several of
the early vineyards in WA, and recognised the potential of his family's property. The vineyard
(chardonnay, sauvignon blanc, shiraz, cabernet sauvignon, shiraz and semillon) is planted on
north-facing blocks, the geological history of which stretches back 2 billion years. A new cellar
door opened Easter 2009.

ŸŸŸŸŸ **Denmark Shiraz 2007** Relatively light but bright colour; has a very fragrant
✪   bouquet of red cherry and spice, then a lively, supple palate with juicy cherry
          and blackberry flavours, the spices ranging through baker's to butcher's. Screwcap.
          14.5% alc. **Rating** 93 **To** 2020 $20.95
✪   **Denmark Merlot 2007** Youthful crimson; an attractive and strongly regional
          bouquet offers spiced plum fruitcake aromas, the smooth and supple medium-
          bodied palate simply adopting the bouquet as its message. Screwcap. 14% alc.
          Rating 92 **To** 2014 $20.95
          Denmark Sparkling Shiraz NV Dark colour; the base wine is a blend of four
          vintages assembled and then bottle-fermented; a very good result for a complex,
          spicy wine, the dosage appropriately restrained. Cork. 14.5% alc. **Rating** 92
          To 2013 $33.95
✪   **Denmark Sauvignon Blanc 2009** Light straw-green; fragrant aromas of
          passionfruit and guava, adding a touch of citrus on the palate; good acidity drives
          the clean finish. Screwcap. 12.5% alc. **Rating** 90 **To** 2011 $15.95

ŸŸŸŸ **Denmark Chardonnay 2009 Rating** 87 **To** 2011 $15.95
      Remembrance Methode Champenoise 2006 Rating 87 **To** 2012 $33.95

Z Wine ★★★★
PO Box 135, Lyndoch, SA 5351 **Region** Barossa Valley
T 0411 447 986 **F** (08) 8524 6987 **www**.zwine.com.au **Open** At Barossa Small
Winemakers Centre, Chateau Tanunda
Winemaker Janelle Zerk **Est**. 1999 **Cases** 400 **Vyds** 60 ha
Z Wine is the venture of vigneron Robert Zerk, a fifth-generation family owner of the
old Zerk Vineyard at Lyndoch, and daughters Kristen, who has a degree in wine marketing
from Adelaide University, and oenology graduate (with 11 vintages under her belt) Janelle.
It is a minor part of the partners' lives, with only a tiny part of the production from the
family-owned vineyard being used; the remainder is sold to wineries in the area. Janelle has a
'real' winemaker's job elsewhere, the Z Wines being made in borrowed space.

ŸŸŸŸŸ **Barossa Valley Shiraz 2008** Strong colour, lifted red fruits and licorice are the
          central theme of the bouquet; medium-bodied with accentuated acidity driving
          the red fruits from start to finish. Screwcap. 14% alc. **Rating** 90 **To** 2016 $45 BE

Zarephath Wines ★★★★☆
424 Moorialup Road, East Porongurup, WA 6324 **Region** Porongurup
T (08) 9853 1152 **F** (08) 9853 1151 **www**.zarephathwines.com **Open** Mon–Sat 10–5,
Sun 12–4
Winemaker Robert Diletti **Est**. 1994 **Cases** 1500 **Vyds** 9 ha
The Zarephath vineyard is owned and operated by Brothers and Sisters of The Christ Circle,
a Benedictine community. They say the most outstanding feature of the location is the feeling
of peace and tranquility that permeates the site, something I can well believe on the basis of

numerous visits to the Porongurups. Plantings include chardonnay, cabernet sauvignon, pinot noir, shiraz, riesling and merlot. Exports to the UK, the US and NZ.

Cabernet Sauvignon 2005 All the components of blackcurrant, cedar and tannins come together gracefully on a supple medium-bodied palate that has very good length. Ageing impressively slowly. Screwcap. 14% alc. **Rating** 94 To 2021 $29.95

Riesling 2008 Developing slowly, promising much for the future; citrus elements drive the bouquet and palate, which is encased in a shield of mineral/slate; the innate power of the wine clicks in on the back-palate and long finish. Screwcap. 12.3% alc. **Rating** 93 To 2018 $23.95
Chardonnay 2008 Rating 91 To 2014 $29.95

Pinot Noir 2008 Rating 89 To 2013 $30
Shiraz 2004 Rating 88 To 2013 $29.95

Zema Estate ★★★★★

Riddoch Highway, Coonawarra, SA 5263 **Region** Coonawarra
T (08) 8736 3219 **F** (08) 8736 3280 **www.**zema.com.au **Open** 7 days 9–5
Winemaker Greg Clayfield **Est.** 1982 **Cases** 20 000 **Vyds** 61 ha
Zema is one of the last outposts of hand-pruning in Coonawarra, with members of the Zema family tending a 61-ha vineyard progressively planted since 1982 in the heart of Coonawarra's terra rossa soil. Winemaking practices are straightforward; if ever there was an example of great wines being made in the vineyard, this is it. The extremely popular and equally talented former Lindemans winemaker Greg Clayfield has joined the team, replacing long-term winemaker Tom Simons. Exports to the UK, the US and other major markets.

Family Selection Coonawarra Shiraz 2006 Deeper colour, and altogether more concentrated than the varietal; while luscious, carries its alcohol with ease, the flavours ranging through plum, black cherry and bramble; has absorbed 24 months in oak. Screwcap. 15% alc. **Rating** 95 To 2021 $45
Saluti Coonawarra Cabernet Shiraz 2006 Strong colour; an extremely rich 55/45 blend, the fruit luscious and supple, the flavours of ripe black fruits, the tannins ripe and the oak positive. Has a storehouse of flavour for a long life ahead. Screwcap. 15% alc. **Rating** 95 To 2030 $75

Coonawarra Shiraz 2007 There is plenty happening on the bouquet, with blackberry and plum fruit, toasty/spicy oak and allied aromas then a solid, medium-bodied palate that will develop for decades. Screwcap. 15.5% alc. **Rating** 93 To 2030 $25.95
Coonawarra Cabernet Sauvignon 2007 The wine has clear regional characters, some earthy notes just starting to appear and adding complexity to the blackcurrant and mulberry fruit; good oak and tannins. Screwcap. 14.5% alc. **Rating** 93 To 2022 $25.95
Family Selection Coonawarra Cabernet Sauvignon 2006 Rating 93 To 2026 $45
Cluny Coonawarra Cabernet Merlot 2006 Fragrant red and black fruits with some earthy nuances on the bouquet; the medium-bodied palate provides more of the same before thinning out fractionally on the finish. Screwcap. 14% alc. **Rating** 90 To 2014 $25

Z4 Wines ★★★★

PO Box 57, Campbell, ACT 2612 **Region** Canberra District
T (02) 6248 6445 **F** (02) 6249 8482 **www.**Z4wines.com.au **Open** Not
Winemaker Canberra Winemakers **Est.** 2007 **Cases** 1200
Z4 Wines is the venture of the very energetic Bill Mason and wife Maria. The name derives from the Mason's four children, each having a Christian name starting with 'Z'. Bill has been

distributing wine in Canberra since 2004, with a small but distinguished list of wineries, which he represents with considerable marketing flair. The Z4 wines are listed on many Canberra restaurant wine lists, and are stocked by leading independent wine retailers. Exports to China.

ΨΨΨΨΩ **Zoe Canberra District Riesling 2009** Light straw-green; a fragrant and delicate
✪ wine, with cunningly counterpoised sweetness and acidity encircling the citrus
fruit, even a touch of passionfruit. Screwcap. 12.2% alc. **Rating** 90 **To** 2017 $16

✪ **Zachary Canberra District Cabernet Merlot 2008** Purple-red; a fresh and
fragrant medium-bodied wine with some juicy red and blackcurrant fruit, the
tannins fine, the oak integrated but a little too vanillan; 51/49. Screwcap. 13.8% alc.
Rating 90 **To** 2014 $25

ΨΨΨΨ **Zane Canberra District Shiraz 2008 Rating** 87 **To** 2012 $19

Zilzie Wines ★★★★

Lot 66 Kulkyne Way, Karadoc via Red Cliffs, Vic 3496 **Region** Murray Darling
T (03) 5025 8100 **F** (03) 5025 8116 **www.**zilziewines.com **Open** Not
Winemaker Mark Zeppel **Est.** 1999 **Cases** 110 000 **Vyds** 572 ha
The Forbes family has been farming Zilzie Estate since the early 1990s; it is currently run by Ian and Ros Forbes, and sons Steven and Andrew. A diverse range of farming activities now includes grapegrowing from substantial vineyards. Having established a position as a dominant supplier of grapes to Southcorp, Zilzie formed a wine company in 1999 and built a winery in 2000, expanding it in '06 to its current capacity of 35 000 tonnes. The business includes contract processing, winemaking and storage. The recent expansion may face problems given the state of the Murray Darling Basin. Exports to the UK, the US, Canada and Hong Kong.

ΨΨΨΨΩ **Regional Collection Barossa Shiraz 2008** Deep crimson-purple; a generous
✪ medium- to full-bodied shiraz with an abundance of plummy black fruits, and
avoids any dead fruit characters. Top value. Screwcap. 14.5% alc. **Rating** 92
To 2014 $16

✪ **Regional Collection Victoria Chardonnay 2008** Evidently sourced from 'the
coolest to the warmest' regions of Victoria, with the cooler components (happily)
dominating, providing length to the nectarine and citrus flavours. Value plus.
Screwcap. 12.5% alc. **Rating** 90 **To** 2013 $16

✪ **Regional Collection Adelaide Hills Pinot Gris 2009** Very faint touch of pink;
a lively and fresh wine, with more character than many, zesty lemon, pear and
apple flavours at work. Screwcap. 12% alc. **Rating** 90 **To** 2011 $16

ΨΨΨΨ **Selection 23 Chardonnay 2009** Hard to ask for more at this price point, with
✪ gentle peach and melon flavours, and the barest hint of vanillan oak. Screwcap.
13.5% alc. **Rating** 88 **To** 2010 $10

Regional Collection Wrattonbully Merlot 2008 Rating 88 **To** 2012 $15
✪ **Selection 23 Merlot 2008** Light, bright colour; a good example of a warm-
grown merlot, with medium-bodied black fruits and a black olive/forest
component. Screwcap. 14.5% alc. **Rating** 88 **To** 2012 $11

Regional Collection Coonawarra Cabernet Sauvignon 2008 Rating 88
To 2013 $16
Selection 23 Sauvignon Blanc 2009 Rating 87 **To** 2010 $11
✪ **Selection 23 Rose 2009** Bright puce; fresh and flavoursome, with lively red
fruits and balanced acidity; not complex, and not meant to be. Screwcap. 13.5% alc.
Rating 87 **To** 2010 $11

Zitta Wines ★★★★

3 Union Street, Dulwich, SA 5065 (postal) **Region** Barossa Valley
T 0419 819 414 **F** (08) 8331 1147 **www.**zitta.com.au **Open** Not
Winemaker Angelo De Fazio **Est.** 2004 **Cases** 1000 **Vyds** 26.3 ha

Owner Angelo De Fazio says that all he knows about viticulture and winemaking came from his father (and generations before him). It is partly this influence that has shaped the label and brand name: Zitta is Italian for 'quiet' and the seeming reflection of the letters of the name Zitta is in fact nothing of the kind; turn the bottle upside down, and you will see it is the word Quiet. The Zitta vineyard is on a property dating back to 1864, with a few vines remaining from that time, and a block planted with cuttings taken from those vines. Shiraz dominates the plantings (22 ha), the balance made up of chardonnay, grenache and a few mourvedre vines (only a small amount of the production is retained for the Zitta Wines label). The property has two branches of the Greenock Creek running through it, and the soils reflect the ancient geological history of the site, in part with a subsoil of river pebbles reflecting the course of a long-gone river. Tradition there may be, but there is also some highly sophisticated writing and marketing in the background material and the website.

♟♟♟♟♟ **Greenock Single Vineyard Barossa Valley Shiraz 2007** Has retained good colour; from an estate-owned vineyard, this full-bodied wine has very good richness after spending two years in American and French oak; somehow, doesn't trip over its alcohol. Screwcap. 15.5% alc. **Rating** 90 **To** 2027 $40

Zonte's Footstep   ★★★★☆

Main Road, McLaren Vale, SA 5171 **Region** McLaren Vale
T (08) 8556 2457 **F** (08) 8556 4462 **www**.zontesfootstep.com.au **Open** 7 days 10–5
Winemaker Ben Riggs **Est.** 1997 **Cases** 50 000 **Vyds** 214.72 ha
Zonte's Footstep has been very successful since a group of long-standing friends, collectively with deep knowledge of every aspect of the wine business, decided it was time to do something together. Along the way since, there has been some shuffling of the deck chairs, all achieved without any ill feelings by those who moved sideways or backwards. The major change has been a broadening of the regions (Langhorne Creek, McLaren Vale, the Barossa Valley and elsewhere) from which the grapes are sourced. Even here, however, most of the vineyards supplying grapes are owned by members of the Zonte's Footsep partnership. The wine quality is as good as the prices are modest. Exports to all major markets.

♟♟♟♟♟ **Scarlet Ladybird Single Site Fleurieu Peninsula Rose 2009** Zar Brooks
✪ has not forgotten how to write a book and put it on the back label. Bright, light crimson; the gently spiced red fruit bouquet is followed by a palate packed with flavours in the same spectrum while keeping the wine focused and dry. This is a rose for all occasions, especially with food. Screwcap. 13% alc. **Rating** 94 **To** 2012 $17.50

♟♟♟♟♟ **Lady of the Lake Single Site Langhorne Creek Viognier 2009** Has
✪ altogether unexpected varietal character, with vibrant peach, ginger and (perhaps) apricot; no excess phenolics and a long finish. Screwcap. 13.5% alc. **Rating** 91 **To** 2012 $17.50

✪ **The Love Symbol Single Site Langhorne Creek Savignin Blanc 2009** You say savignin, I say savagnin; Zar Brooks is too busy composing back labels to worry about proofreading the front, it seems. Whatever, this wine actually does have echoes of gewurztraminer, surprising given the region. Worth a second look. Screwcap. 11% alc. **Rating** 90 **To** 2011 $17.50

♟♟♟♟ **Sea Mist Single Site Langhorne Creek Verdelho 2009** Rating 88 **To** 2012 $17.50
Doctoressa di Largo Single Site Langhorne Creek Pinot Grigio 2009 **Rating** 87 **To** 2011 $17.50

Index

♀	**Cellar door sales**
¶¶	**Food:** lunch platters to à la carte restaurants
⊨	**Accommodation:** B&B cottages to luxury vineyard apartments
◔	**Music events:** monthly jazz in the vineyard to spectacular yearly concerts

Various/South Eastern Australia

The following wineries appear on www.winecompanion.com.au:

Abbey Rock ♀
Abercorn ♀
Acacia Ridge ♀
Acreage Vineyard & Winery ♀
Across the Lake ♀
Adelina Wines
Adinfern Estate ♀ ⊨
Affleck ♀
Ainsworth & Snelson
Ainsworth Estate ♀ ¶ ⊨
Albert River Wines ♀ ¶
Alderley Creek Wines ♀
Aldgate Ridge ♀ ⊨
Aldinga Bay Winery ♀
Alexandra Bridge Wines
Allison Valley Wines
Allusion Wines ♀
Allyn River Wines ♀ ⊨
Amarok Estate
Ambar Hill
Ambrook Wines ♀
Amicus
Ammitzboll Wines
Amulet Vineyard ♀
Anakie Ridge Vineyard ♀ ¶
Andraos Bros ♀ ¶
Andrew Garrett
Andrew Harris Vineyards ♀
Andrew Peace Wines ♀ ¶
Andrew Seppelt Wines ♀
Antcliff's Chase ♀
Apsley Gorge Vineyard ♀
Apthorpe Estate ♀
Archer Falls Vineyard ♀
Arimia Margaret River ♀
Armstrong Vineyards
Arranmore Vineyard ♀
Arrivo
Artamus
Arthurs Creek Estate

Ashley Estate ♀
Ashley Wines ♀
Aussie Vineyards ♀
Australian Domaine Wines ♀
Australian Old Vine Wine ♀
Avalon Vineyard ♀
Avalon Wines ♀
Aventine Wines ♀
Avenue Wines
Avonbrook Wines ♀
Avonmore Estate ♀
B'darra Estate ♀
Baarrooka Vineyard ♀
Bacchanalia Estate ♀
Bago Vineyards ♀
Baie Wines ♀
Bainton Family Wines
Bald Mountain ♀
Bald Rock Vineyard
Ballanclea
Ballinaclash Wines ♀
Bamajura ♀
Banca Ridge ♀
Banderra Estate ♀
Banks Thargo Wines ♀
Baptista ♀
Barak Estate ♀ ¶ ⊨
Baratto's ♀
Bare Rooted
Barfold Estate ♀
Barley Stacks Wines ♀
Barmah Park Wines ♀ ¶
Barossa Cottage Wines ♀
Barossa Settlers ♀
Barrecas ♀
Barretts Wines ♀
Barrymore Estate
Bartagunyah Estate ♀
Barwite Vineyards
Barwon Plains ♀
Barwon Ridge Wines ♀
Basket Range Wines ♀